CATALOGUE OF THE CONSTABLE COLLECTION

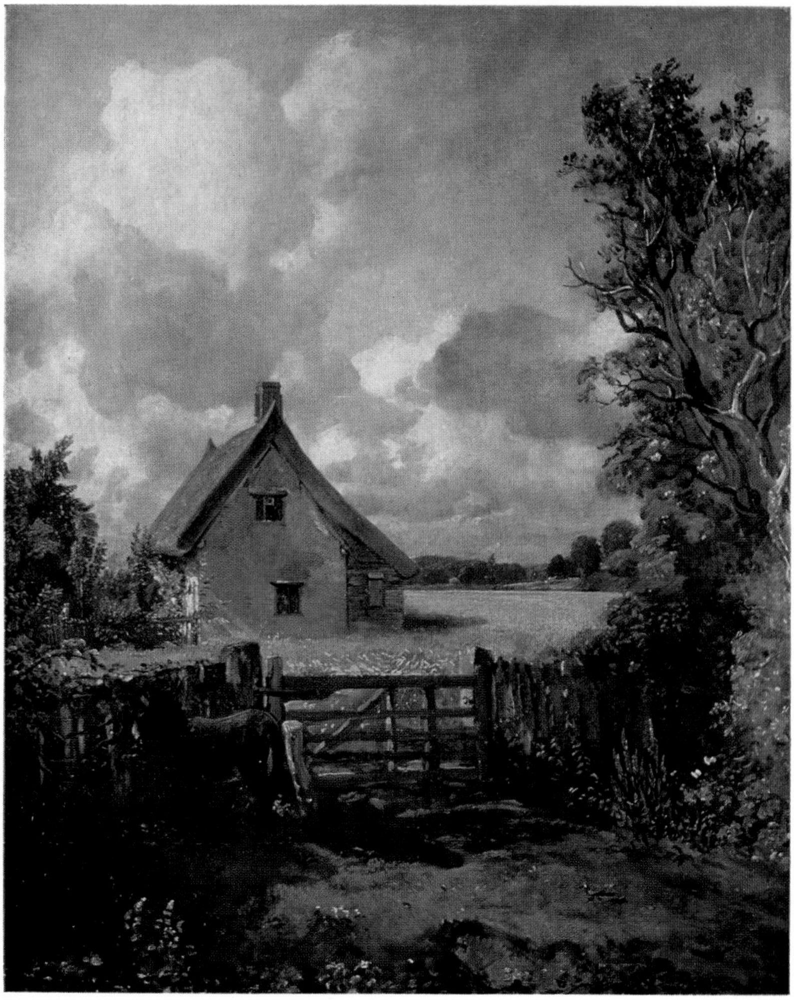

352. The Cottage in a Cornfield.

VICTORIA AND ALBERT MUSEUM

CATALOGUE OF THE CONSTABLE COLLECTION

By GRAHAM REYNOLDS

LONDON
HER MAJESTY'S STATIONERY OFFICE
1973

First published 1960
Second edition 1973

SBN 11 290112 3*

CONTENTS

FOREWORD TO THE FIRST EDITION

THE Victoria and Albert Museum possesses the finest and most comprehensive collection of works by John Constable in existence, thanks to the generosity of John Sheepshanks, Miss Isabel Constable and Henry Vaughan. In it some of his most important paintings, such as 'Salisbury Cathedral from the Bishop's Grounds', 'Dedham Mill', and 'The Cottage in a Cornfield', together with the masterly full-scale sketches for 'The Hay Wain' and 'The Leaping Horse', are to be seen alongside an unrivalled group of oil sketches, drawings and sketch-books.

Constable occupies a unique position among our artists by virtue of the vivid directness with which he recorded the English countryside and the degree to which he combined truth of representation with romantic feeling. His affection for the small area of the "Constable country" (the Stour Valley near Flatford, Dedham, and East Bergholt), the hesitating but determined steps by which he attained greatness, and the raw materials out of which he built his most ambitious pictures, may be studied more fully in this collection than anywhere else.

The present Catalogue Raisonné, in which for the first time everything in the Constable Collection is fully discussed in relation to the artist's life and to other collections, is the work of Mr. Graham Reynolds, Keeper of the Department of Paintings. Many of his debts to other scholars are acknowledged in the body of the book; here he wishes to record his especial indebtedness to his colleagues in the Department: Mr. Jonathan Mayne, who has constantly given help on many matters, and Miss M. M. Glass, who has taken unstinting care in preparing the text for the press. Mr. Martin Davies of the National Gallery has generously made much valuable information available to him. For the extracts from unpublished portions of Farington's *Diary* he has been privileged to use the full edition made by the Royal Library, Windsor Castle.

TRENCHARD COX
Director
1960

AUTHOR'S FOREWORD TO THE SECOND EDITION

In revising this Catalogue for its second edition, I have taken account of the advances which have been made in our knowledge of Constable's work during the last ten years. The bulk of the text remains unaltered, but the additions recently made to the collection (Nos. 16A, 16B, 16C) have been included. A number of topographical identifications have been made since the publication of the first edition. The sources of these have been acknowledged in the relevant entries, but I should add a special note of gratitude to Lt.-Col. C. A. Brooks, who has freely put his knowledge of the Constable country at my disposal, and given many convincing demonstrations of the artist's accuracy in delineating his homeland. In a few cases I have revised the proposed dating of individual works, but here again there is little variation from the original scheme.

GRAHAM REYNOLDS
Keeper of the Department of Prints & Drawings and Paintings
January 1971

The Scope and Arrangement of the Catalogue

THIS volume comprises a catalogue of all the paintings, oil sketches, watercolours and drawings by John Constable in the Victoria and Albert Museum. The arrangement is, so far as practicable, chronological; the way in which this principle has been applied is explained in more detail on pp. 7–9, and other notes on the methods adopted in the Catalogue are on pp. 10–11 of the introduction. With the exceptions of inscriptions on the backs of oil sketches and drawings, insignificant scribbles, and one or two unimportant drawings, everything described in the Catalogue is reproduced among the plates. Including the few oil sketches on the reverse of visible ones, the *verso* sides of drawings and the individual pages of the three intact sketch-books Nos. 121, 132 and 382, the total number of items described slightly exceeds 600; of these 600 are reproduced. The arrangement of the plates follows in the main that of the catalogue entries, but the strict numerical order has sometimes been departed from, so that oil paintings or drawings may be grouped together and the detached pages of sketch-books brought into closer conjunction.

HISTORY OF THE COLLECTION

The first works by Constable received in the Museum were the six oil paintings given by John Sheepshanks, Nos. 137, 184, 254, 301, 321, 323. These were included in the collection of 233 paintings, of which 231 were by modern British artists, which Sheepshanks gave to the South Kensington Museum* in 1857, with the intention of founding a National Gallery of British Art "in an open and airy situation, possessing the quiet necessary to the study and enjoyment of works of Art, and free from the inconveniences and dirt of the main thoroughfares of the metropolis" and attached to the schools of art at South Kensington. His pictures formed the nucleus of a collection which was called the National Gallery of British Art until the establishment of the Tate Gallery, when the Victoria and Albert Museum virtually ceased to acquire oil paintings by contemporary British artists.

John Sheepshanks had met Constable at least as early as 1829, the year in which he lent the artist an etching by Swanevelt from which he made the copy now in

* The Victoria and Albert Museum was known as the South Kensington Museum until 1899.

the British Museum (No. L.B. 2). Although Sheepshanks is known to have owned at least two works by Constable by 1835, only one of those in his gift to the nation (No. 301) can be identified as a picture he acquired while the artist was still alive. Certainly four of the six in his gift, and probably also the fifth, were bought by him at the Executors' sale of the contents of Constable's studio in 1838. All these paintings had been exhibited by the artist at the Royal Academy, or had been finished by him to the extent he considered necessary for their exhibition or sale. For a time the Vernon collection of paintings by modern British artists hung at South Kensington, and during this period 'The Valley Farm' (now in the Tate Gallery) was to be seen near the paintings by Constable in the Sheepshanks Gift.

From the outset the Museum has been a repository for important loans, and during the 1860's and 1870's in particular there were to be seen in it many famous collections of Old Masters and other paintings of a kind which no longer falls within its scope. Mr. Henry Vaughan lent his two full-scale sketches for 'The Hay Wain' and 'The Leaping Horse' in 1862. As recounted in the catalogue entry to No. 209, he allowed them to remain in the Museum with short intermissions until his death in 1900, when it was found that he had bequeathed to the collection of works by Constable its two largest, most valuable and most remarkable features.

The next works by Constable to be received in the permanent collections were the four studies of the male nude given by the Rev. R. C. Lathom Browne in 1873 (Nos. 17–20), and the sepia drawing of Stoke-by-Nayland bought in 1876 (No. 331). It is remarkable that the last-named drawing, together with 'Elm trees in Old Hall Park' (No. 162) bought in 1891, the small portrait study of a seated lady (No. 64) added in 1942, and the three early water-colours acquired in 1970 (Nos. 16A, 16B and 16C) are the only purchases made out of Museum funds for this rich collection.

A temporary but important addition to the representation of Constable's work was made in 1880, when Mrs. A. M. Constable, the widow of John Constable's son, Captain Charles Constable, offered the loan of her late husband's collection. This consisted of six large oil paintings (including the sketch for 'The Valley Farm' which is now in the possession of Lord Forteviot), forty-four oil sketches or small oil paintings, twenty-six water-colours and fifty-seven pencil drawings. It was at first intended that this collection should remain on loan until Capt. Constable's children attained their majority. A dispute, into the details of which it is not necessary to enter, arose with Mrs. Constable about the conditions of exhibition, and the loan was transferred to the Museum of Science and Art, Edinburgh, in 1883. The greater part of the collection lent to the Museum from 1880 to 1883 was sold at Messrs. Christie's on 11 July 1887. The remainder, which was the personal property of Mrs. A. M. Constable, was sold in the same rooms on 23 June 1890.

Meanwhile the remaining contents of the artist's studio had mostly become the property of Miss Isabel Constable, his last surviving daughter. Although her sister-in-law's loan had come to an abrupt end it may have played its part in suggesting to her that she should give a substantial portion of her collection of works by Constable to the Museum. This decision, which at once raised the Museum's collection of Constable to its present commanding position, was communicated in the following letter, written less than eight months before Miss Constable's death:

64 Hamilton Terrace N.W.
Dec 29th 1887

Dear Mr. Thompson

I should like to present to the Kensington Museum some Landscape Sketches by J. Constable R.A. If this should meet with the approval of the Directors & they are accepted they can be put in a box quite ready for removal. I am sorry they are not in frames as they would look so much better, but I should like to give the frames to make them complete. I shall be very glad to hear about them.

I remain
Yours very truly
Isabel Constable.

R. Thompson Esq

R. A. Thompson, to whom this letter was written, was one of the two Assistant Directors of the South Kensington Museum. He is described as an intimate friend of Miss Constable's and the gift may well have been at his prompting. When completed (it was received in more than one portion) it accounted for 390 of the 418 entries in this Catalogue.

Miss Isabel Constable's gift also contained some material which is outside the scope of this Catalogue: that is, a tempera portrait of John Constable painted in 1796 by Daniel Gardner; a copy of Watts's *Songs, Divine and Moral*, 1832, with one water-colour sketch and six cuts coloured by Constable*; two letters written by Constable to his wife (one in 1816 when she was still Miss Bicknell); two letters to his children Charles and Emily, written in 1833, relating to the coloured copy of Watts's *Songs*; two etchings by Constable; eight engravings after his paintings and drawings, including a touched proof of Lucas's mezzotint of 'Salisbury Cathedral from the Meadows', and a copy of the 1833 edition of *English Landscape Scenery*. The *Songs, Divine and Moral*, were a birthday present to Emily

* Discussed by J. Irene Whalley in the article 'Illustrations for Isaac Watts's Divine and Moral Songs', *Victoria and Albert Museum Bulletin*, Vol. IV, No. 4, October 1968, pp. 149–57 (the half-title and title reproduced on pp. 152–3).

Constable in 1833; Capt. A. L. Fletcher, R.N., has a similarly coloured copy which Constable give to Harriet Jane, the daughter of C. R. Leslie, R. A. The Museum's copy of this book, and the autograph letters, are kept in the Art Library, which contains a further collection of thirty-three letters written by Constable to C. R. Leslie, J. Carpenter and Archdeacon John Fisher between 1822 and 1836, and other letters received by him from a variety of correspondents. In 1968 the Library acquired a school-book which belonged to Constable when he was thirteen. This is the *Juvenile Introduction to History; or, Historical Beauties for Youth, Selected from Various Authors. With an Appendix of Historical Tales from Scripture*, published in London in 1790. The fly leaf is inscribed *John Constable 1790*, and contains 2 crude pencil sketches, which are in all probability by him. One shows the silhouettes of two windmills on the brow of a hill; the other of shipping and with three figures in a boat appears to be a reminiscence of part of the engraved frontispiece, representing 'Fraternal Affection'. The engravings described above are kept in the Department of Prints and Drawings, which has a third etching by Constable, other sets of *English Landscape Scenery* in various editions, and other engravings after the artist. The portrait by Gardner is exhibited with Constable's paintings and oil sketches.

Miss Constable's munificence toward the Museum had not been exhausted by this remarkable gift. When she died on 13 August 1888 in her sixty-sixth year the Museum was informed of her bequest of the three oil paintings 'Trees at Hampstead' (No. 223), 'The Cottage in a Cornfield' (No. 352) and 'A Watermill at Gillingham, Dorset' (No. 288), and the two great water-colours 'Old Sarum' (No. 359) and 'Stonehenge' (No. 395). She expressed in her will her desire that these five pictures should be described as a gift from Maria Louisa Constable, Isabel Constable and Lionel Bicknell Constable, that is from herself and her elder sister and younger brother, both of whom had predeceased her.

The Constable Collection was then virtually in the form in which it now exists. Mr. Vaughan's two oil sketches were, as has been explained, already on loan to the Museum: his bequest of them became effective on his death in 1900. In 1908 Mr. Lindo S. Myers gave the four large drawings used by Constable to illustrate his lectures (Nos. 397–400). The addition of the drawing 'Elm trees in Old Hall Park' (No. 162), the small drawing bought in 1942 (No. 64), a single drawing from the Harrod Bequest (No. 95) and the purchase of the three early water-colours in 1970 (Nos. 16A, 16B and 16C) complete the history of the formation of the collection catalogued in this book.

In spite of the vast size of Miss Isabel Constable's gift to the South Kensington Museum, it by no means disposed of her entire collection, still less of the work left by the artist at his death. Taking Miss Isabel Constable's collection first, we find that in 1888, the year of her gift to South Kensington, she gave forty-five drawings to the British Museum, fifteen oil sketches to the Diploma Gallery of the Royal Academy, and gave or bequeathed jointly with Maria and Lionel eleven paintings and oil sketches to the National Gallery (six of the latter are now in the Tate Gallery). The principle on which drawings were divided between the British Museum and the Victoria and Albert Museum was on the whole that the more finished sketch-book pages, those with much water-colour in them, went to the former. To this extent the impression given by the collections in the Victoria and Albert Museum, that Constable hardly used water-colour in his sketch-books until the 1830's, is a misleading one, and must be corrected by study of the British Museum's collection.

It is commonly believed that many intact sketch-books by Constable were broken up after they had been received in the Museum, but a study of the evidence shows that this was not so. Many sketch-book pages were already mounted in the family's collection, and the existence in the British Museum of pages given by Miss Isabel Constable from the books represented also in the Victoria and Albert Museum shows that they had been split up before her gifts took effect. As the note on Nos. 147–154 shows, this dismemberment was at least in some instances probably undertaken by the artist himself.

To revert to the size of Miss Constable's collection: there was sufficient of it left after all her gifts for some 360 pictures, drawings and sketches in oil to be sold from it at Messrs. Christie's in May 1891 and June 1892. If to these we add the number of works included in the sales of Capt. Charles Constable, his widow, and the artist's grandchildren Eustace and Clifford Constable; the works bought by Messrs. Leggatt's from the artist's family in 1899; and those still in the family's possession, we find that the contents of Constable's studio at his death (excluding the works now in the Victoria and Albert Museum) amounted to at least some 800 drawings and 400 paintings and oil sketches.* Miss Constable's gift and bequest to the Museum of 95 paintings, 297 drawings and 3 sketch-books therefore accounts for a substantial proportion of the works which are recorded as having passed to the artist's family on his death.

That the Constable Collection in the Victoria and Albert Museum is a representative one is suggested by these figures, and this is confirmed by an examination of the collection itself. With the exception of some aspects of his early work, and of his latest manner on a large scale, every phase, almost every year, of his artistic career is represented, and there is hardly anything which does not merit

* These figures of course refer to works of widely varying degrees of importance. One lot in Eustace Constable's sale of 16 April 1896 consisted of 90 items. For drawings sold privately by Eustace Constable and not included in the above totals, see the note following No. 400 in the Catalogue.

its place through its quality or for its interest in illuminating a particular facet of the artist's style.

PREVIOUS CATALOGUES

The earliest catalogue of Miss Constable's gift is provided by the Museum's *Inventory of Art Objects 1888*. This publication was an annual printed list of the art objects of all kinds received by the Museum during the year; the order of the Constable material in the list was largely haphazard, though oil paintings and drawings are mainly separated in the groups which represent dates of acquisition within the year 1888. This early inventory is of little value now, but it does provide some topographical identifications which may represent an authentic tradition received orally from Miss Isabel Constable.

The oil paintings and sketches of the Constable gift, together with those of the Sheepshanks gift, were then listed in the *Catalogue of the National Gallery of British Art, Part I, Oil Paintings* of which there are editions of 1888, 1893, 1907 and (abridged) 1908. The method adopted in these lists was to segregate the more important finished oil paintings at the beginning of the section devoted to Constable and to list the remaining oil sketches topographically under counties. A similar system was adopted for the drawings, culminating in the list given in the *Catalogue of Water-Colour Paintings*, 1927, in which a more systematic record of the inscriptions and dates on drawings was introduced. Useful though the topographical method was, it necessarily left a large reserve of drawings which could not be assigned to any particular locality, and there can be no doubt that a chronological scheme is preferable. Indeed some topographical queries have been cleared up by attending to the dates of sketches and drawings, and much valuable assistance from those with a special knowledge of particular areas has been gratefully acknowledged in the text of the Catalogue.

In the catalogues up to that of 1907 are included five oil paintings attributed to Constable but not by him. These are:

'Stacking Hay'. No. 1417–1869. Townshend Bequest.
'Farm-house with Water-wheel'. No. 516–1870. Parsons Bequest.
'A Water Mill'. No. 1910–1900. Ashbee Bequest.
'Landscape'. No. 1913–1900. Ashbee Bequest.
'An Old Suffolk Mill'. No. C.A.I.77. Ionides Bequest.

The catalogues of drawings up to that of 1927 include three works attributed to Constable but not by him. These are:

'Study of Trees'. No. 9187.
'Dutch River Boat'. D. 151–1890.

'Hampstead Heath'. (With a landscape sketch on the back.) No. 102–1894. Given by J. E. Taylor, Esq.

These apocryphal works are not noticed further in the present Catalogue.

METHOD OF ARRANGEMENT

The statement that the arrangement of items in the Catalogue is chronological does not imply that every item in the collection can be exactly dated, but Constable's methods of work have made it possible to carry the application of this principle further than might be expected. For one thing, he was in the habit of dating a substantial proportion of his oil sketches and pencil drawings, and these form a series on which the dating of other, uninscribed works can be based. But the most useful single consideration which assists in the arrangement of his drawings into a chronological sequence is the identification of pages from sketch-books. There are in the collection pages from over two dozen dismembered sketch-books: in particular, an almost continuous series from 1814 till 1835 (a list is given on pp. 250–1). As has already been explained, the division of the sketch-books into isolated sheets was not made by the Museum, but was undertaken by the artist or his family. In many cases it is evident that the sheet on which a drawing has been made has come from a sketch-book: the punctures in the paper caused by the sewing, and the bending up of the leaf at its inner edge, are both apparent. In these instances the exact measurement will correspond with that of other sheets from the same book. If one of the sheets so grouped together is dated and if there is not more than one sketch-book of identical size in question, an undated sheet can usually be assigned approximately to the year thus established. There is some ambiguity: for instance Constable used sketch-books with leaves measuring 115 × 186 mm. in 1817, 1820 and 1828, and perhaps also in 1812; but sometimes these doubtful cases can be resolved by stylistic or other factors.

Some pages which have been in a sketch-book have had the hinge marks trimmed away, but may remain close to their original measurements, and bear such other outward signs of having been in a book as frayed or discoloured outer edges. More difficult to place are the drawings which have been trimmed on at least two sides, very often as a preparation to being laid down on card. As has been stated, it is probable that this was frequently done by the Constable family, for many framed drawings were included in the sales of their collections and some drawings were received framed by the South Kensington Museum. All the drawings from the Isabel Constable gift in the British Museum have been trimmed and laid down. Where, in spite of both measurements falling short of that of the standard sketch-book page, a particular drawing is assigned to a specific book, the reason is discussed in the entry for that drawing. It is necessary to stress the need for exactness in measurement to avoid vagueness in applying this criterion, and for the purposes of this Catalogue all the drawings have been measured to the nearest millimetre: their measurements in inches (expressed to the nearest $\frac{1}{8}$th of an inch) have been derived from those in millimetres. There is some lack of uniformity even in the untrimmed pages of the sketch-books; for instance, though the average height of pages from the sketch-book of 1801 is given in the Catalogue as 175 mm., two of them (Nos. 22, 23) measure more nearly 176 mm. in this direction. There are greater variations in the width of pages, according to their position in the sketch-book and the method used in detaching them.

The assignment of a drawing to a particular sketch-book does not necessarily fix it exactly to a year, since at times Constable used the same sketch-book in two or three consecutive years. It gives at least an approximate date; and often an incompleted date or a place-name on the drawing enables us to improve upon the approximation. Only in one case does the grouping together of pages from a particular sketch-book lead to no definite year of dating: the ten drawings Nos. 385–394 each come from a sketch-book with leaves of *c.*130 × 211 mm. but not one is dated. It appeared also that none was inscribed until more careful inspection revealed an almost illegible pencil inscription, apparently *Findon Wood*, on No. 385. This, if correctly read, shows that the sketch-book may be assigned to 1834 or 1835, when Constable paid visits to Sussex, and this result is consistent with the style of the drawings, which is that of Constable's latest period.

Dated drawings and oil sketches, together with drawings which may be dated approximately on the principles assigned, account for the greater part of the material in the Catalogue. But there remain a number of works otherwise unassigned and these have been arranged in accordance with the following principles:

> Sketches and drawings connected with an exhibited work have been placed under the date of exhibition unless there is reason to the contrary, such as clear evidence of their existence at an earlier date.
>
> Works with close affinity in style and subject-matter to dated works have been grouped with them.
>
> The paintings and drawings not accounted for by any of these means have been assigned on grounds of style to one or other of a number of approximate groups. These groups are:

*c.*1796–1799	Nos. 14–16
*c.*1800–1805	Nos. 57–61, 63–64
*c.*1806–1809	Nos. 96–98

*c.*1810–1815 Nos. 109–113
*c.*1820–1830 Nos. 323–327
*c.*1830–1836 Nos. 402–415

These principles have not always been followed when the balance of advantage seemed to lie with grouping similar studies at a particular point of the Catalogue. For instance the undated studies at Brighton, most of which were made between 1824 and 1828, have been generally grouped together after those which bear the date 1824. Departures of this nature are indicated in the text. The degree of assurance attaching to the dating of any item is shown by the form of the entry in the outer margins, which may be as precise, in the case of dated drawings, as the year, month and day; or within a wide range as, for instance, [*c.*1820–30?]. As is customary the use of square brackets here and elsewhere indicates editorial suggestions. Works exhibited by the artist at the Royal Academy have been placed first under the year of exhibition, followed by sketches for them when these are not more exactly dated. In a few such cases no marginal date is given.

Dating on grounds of style has only been resorted to when all other evidence is lacking. Holmes, who in his *Constable and his Influence on Landscape Painting* has made the only sustained attempt so far to suggest a chronological dating for Constable's work, relied more largely upon the criterion of style. He did so with magnificent success, based on a very thorough knowledge and a strong intuition for the dating of particular works. Yet, as Holmes himself was fully aware, no artist is more difficult to date on grounds of technique alone than Constable. An example is afforded by No. 243, which is dated *c.*1806 by Holmes but comes from a sketch-book used in 1821. While errors of this magnitude are possible to the most instructed critic, it has seemed best not to attempt to pinpoint undated sketches to a specific year without other compelling reasons. Holmes's list has inadvertently become a source for ostensibly exact datings, and has sometimes been followed somewhat uncritically by later writers. In many instances, however, his datings have been accepted in the ensuing Catalogue as sufficiently probable or worthy of respect to provide the best ground for ordering a particular sketch or drawing. An important case in point is the series of dazzling oil sketches made at East Bergholt in which Constable first fully showed his originality and mastery: 'Flatford Mill from a lock on the Stour' and 'Barges on the Stour' (Nos. 103 and 104 in the Catalogue). It is tantalising that these crucial pieces should be undated. For the reasons given in the text of the Catalogue, Holmes's dating of 1811 for the former has been accepted as giving the best available basis for the place of both these works in a chronological sequence of Constable's work. It is, however, quite possible that this approximate date may need revision in the light of further information.

The short notes given in the yearly headings of the Catalogue are not intended to supply a complete biography and list of related works, but are given merely as a guide to Constable's more important activities and those which were relevant to works in the Museum's collections. Other versions of pictures in the Museum and drawings from the sketch-books represented here have, when known, been mentioned in the appropriate place; but there has been no attempt to make this part of the work even approximate to completeness.

The books to which reference is most frequently made are cited in the text by abbreviations, and a key to these is given on pp. 248–9; such references have been reduced as far as is consistent with giving due credit for original contributions to the subject under discussion. In particular, it has not seemed necessary to quote Holmes's and Shirley's standard works when they merely record the date on a clearly inscribed drawing. One feature commonly found in such a catalogue as this is lacking: that is, a list of exhibitions to which individual items have been sent. After their entry into the Museum, many of the important paintings, sketches and drawings have been drawn on for representative exhibitions of British Art or of the works of John Constable; but since this is in no way relevant to the history of the work before it entered the Museum, and since the catalogue entries for such exhibitions have rarely added to our knowledge of the works, the text has not been burdened with these references. Those who wish to pursue this aspect of the matter will find contributions from the Victoria and Albert Museum listed, *inter alia*, in the catalogues of the following exhibitions:

1934 Royal Academy: Exhibition of British Art.
1937 Tate Gallery: John Constable Centenary Exhibition (to which all the works in oil were lent).
1938 Musée du Louvre: Exhibition of British Painting.
1946 Art Institute of Chicago: Masterpieces of English Painting—Hogarth, Constable, Turner.
1951 Royal Academy: The First Hundred Years of the Royal Academy.
1956 Manchester City Art Gallery: John Constable.

Since the first edition of this catalogue was published, the late R. B. Beckett concluded the publication of his edition of the letters of John Constable and his friends, in six volumes, under the title *John Constable's Correspondence*, with a seventh volume *John Constable's Discourses*. This exhaustive work has added greatly to our knowledge of the artist's life, has provided much additional illustrative material, and has helped to solve some otherwise puzzling problems; the student of Constable will find that it makes an absorbing contribution to his knowledge of the artist's mind and milieu. The text of quotations has in the present Catalogue mainly been given in the form printed in Shirley's edition of

Leslie's *Memoirs of the Life of John Constable, R.A.*, 1937, but Mr. Beckett's text has been quoted where it reveals any important changes.

Unless described otherwise the drawings are on white wove paper; the measurments given throughout are those of the sheets on which they are drawn. Where a sheet is irregular, the greatest height or width is given. Watermarks are recorded as they appear, with an upright stroke to show where they are cut by the edges of the sheet of paper. In the descriptions of technique the term indian ink has been avoided and the more general one, grey wash, used instead. Inscriptions written by the artist are recorded as such; unless otherwise stated they are in the same medium as the drawing. In many instances copies or elaborations of these inscriptions have been made on the backs of drawings and sketches; these copies are usually by one or other of the artist's children, notably Maria and Isabel, but it has not been thought necessary for the present purpose to assign them to a specific individual. Constable's spelling and punctuation were unorthodox and unsystematic (he was especially prone to put a dash for a comma or full stop) and his hand-writing is notoriously difficult to read; but the idiosyncrasies of his inscriptions have been transcribed as accurately as possible.

The entries are arranged chronologically without separating oil paintings from drawings in different lists.

Throughout this introduction and in the cross-references in the main text the serial numbers of the present Catalogue are used. The number in the right-hand side of each entry is that of the Museum's registration: e.g. No. 120–1888 (No. 271 in the Catalogue) was the 120th acquisition made by the Museum as a whole in the year 1888. A concordance between the two series of numbers is given on pp. 244–47. Either set may be used in correspondence concerning the Museum's collection, for instance, in ordering photographs.

The Characteristics and Development of Constable's Art

as illustrated by the Museum's Collection

As his lectures show, Constable had an unusually detailed knowledge of the history of landscape painting and could make a trenchant analysis of those masters in this branch of art who were familiar to him and his contemporaries. Long before he came to systematise his opinions towards them in his discourses, he had decided on his attitude to the help he might derive in his own practice from earlier painters. He intended to portray Nature with the same heightened sensitivity as was to be found in his forerunners, but determined that he would not allow his paintings to appear as though they were actually the work of other men. He kept to this resolution, characteristic both in its clear-headed self-knowledge and the implicit criticism of his contemporaries, with unfaltering determination. This does not mean that he failed to learn from the example of the Old Masters both in the construction of his paintings and the handling of their details. The naturalism of Ruysdael, the atmospheric ideal landscape of Claude, the wide-ranging colour and exuberance of Rubens, and the idyllic romanticism of his fellow-countrymen Wilson and Gainsborough, all had their effect in the formation of his mature and individual style. A chronological study of Constable's development such as the Museum's collection makes possible is fascinating in revealing the tenacity, almost the obstinacy, with which, working on these foundations, he sought and achieved originality.

The characteristics of his art, as seen in his works as a whole, and its interrelationships with that of earlier masters has been discussed in a number of books: for instance, by C. J. Holmes in *Constable and his Influence on Landscape Painting*, 1902, by J. Meier-Graefe in *Modern Art* (English translation, 1908), by the Hon. A. Shirley in the introduction to his edition of Leslie's *Memoirs of the Life of Constable*, 1937, by S. J. Key in *John Constable. His Life and Work*, 1948 and in the present author's *Constable the Natural Painter*, 1965. A specialised study of his relationship to Rubens is to be found in J. G. Böhler's *Constable und Rubens*, 1955. It is not intended to cover the same field of enquiry here, where the aim is to discuss the drawings and paintings in the Museum's collection in so far as they illustrate the progress of Constable's art, and to relate them to works of greater importance or cognate interest in other collections.

Constable's reputation quite properly derives from his oil painting; but he based that painting on a conscientious study of drawing, and became a sensitive and varied draughtsman. If his drawings have remained much less well known than his oil paintings, it is because it is less easy to study them systematically: the Museum's collection, in which drawings preponderate numerically, is the most convenient source for assessing the relationship between his drawing and his painting.

The earliest drawings in the collection, excluding the two in the school book described on p. 4, were made in 1796 (Nos. 1–13). These are only remarkable in showing how far Constable, at the age of twenty, had to go before he could acquire the competence to translate his intentions into works of art. They combine a fresh naiveté of vision with a technique rather sketchily derived from the works of J. T. Smith and the etchers in whom Constable was then interested. The impress of Smith's example is seen particularly in the choice of picturesque cottages for subject-matter, and this interest, once awakened, was a lasting one. In 'The Hay Wain' and 'The Valley Farm' Willy Lott's house is seen with the same eye for the picturesque, and one of the last sketch-books used by Constable at East Bergholt shows him drawing—with a very different skill—similar scenes in 1832 (Nos. 339, 346, 348, 349). The reality of his affection for Nature, despite his inability to express it, is better seen in the pure landscapes of the early sketch-book, Nos. 2 and 9. These drawings are in pen outline only, with no attempt at the chiaroscuro which was to become Constable's main preoccupation. They render entirely credible his claim about the scenery of the Stour valley, "These scenes made me a painter and I am grateful—that is, I had often thought of pictures of them before I touched a pencil".

Constable summed up his early ambitions, and the influences to which he had so far been subject, in the water-colours he made as a wedding-present for his friend Lucy Hurlock (Nos. 16A, 16B and 16C). Into these carefully elaborated drawings he put the utmost concentration of which he was capable, and he filled them with minute observation of the local scene which was so familiar to him and to the recipient. After he settled in London there is the sense of a new direction: we see him attempting to come to grips with professional standards of accomplishment, as in the painstakingly feeble academic nudes, Nos. 17–20. In landscape it is mainly the influences of Sir George Beaumont, Girtin and Gainsborough which now contend for mastery in his style. It is singular that although he had formulated his dislike of a derivative manner in painting by 1802, and was already striking out on an original line of his own in his oils in that year, his drawings and water-colours do not become truly individual till much later.

The water-colour drawings of East Bergholt Church which he made in June 1806 (Nos. 66, 67) are possibly the first in this collection in which his individual note is fully apparent, and yet these were almost immediately succeeded by the series of Lake District drawings in which the stimulus of Girtin's spaciousness of planning and narrowness of colour range is to be found. However, in this exceptional instance Constable probably felt himself forced to pay close attention to an established model, since he was rendering scenery alien to his true sympathies.

In spite of some uncertainty of direction and the rapid alternation of influences, there is much that is pleasing in this early florescence of Constable's talent. The drawings Constable made in Derbyshire in 1801 (Nos. 21–32) are a false start, for he soon afterwards abandoned the contemporary practice of visiting picturesque places, such as the Peak District, for grand and appealing scenery. Yet, if Leslie had had in mind Nos. 21, 23, 28 and 29 when he wrote of the sketch-book from which they were extracted he might have modified his opinion that the drawings in it showed no force of chiaroscuro.

The complete story of these early years of Constable's professional career is not to be gleaned from the Museum's collection alone. The black chalk drawings in which the influence of Gainsborough is most to be seen, transmitted through his friendship with Frost, are represented only by two examples (Nos. 38 and 57). The portrait studies of which he made so many at a time when he was trying to succeed as a portrait painter are as sparsely shown (No. 64). A larger number of drawings of the former type are described and reproduced from a private collection by Holmes in *Constable, Gainsborough, and Lucas*, 1921; Constable's portrait drawings are well represented in the British Museum and the Louvre.* Examples of his drawings from the antique, which were made at the same time as his early studies from the nude, are also to be seen in the British Museum.

In these formative years Constable discovered by a process of trial and error the path along which he was going to advance with dogged determination. He found that he had no desire to become a professional portrait-painter and no bent for constructing altarpieces for churches. He travelled once only to the Peak District and to the Lake District and he realised that these were not the scenes he wished to depict. He did not follow the example of almost all the landscape painters of the period by visiting Wales. Nor did he attempt to foster his imagin-

* Mr. R. B. Beckett gives a useful account of works in other collections in his article 'Constable's Early Drawings' in the *Art Quarterly*, Detroit, Vol. XVII, 1954. But it should be noted that of the two drawings singled out as early copies of etchings one (No. 169 in this Catalogue) is dated 1818; and the other (British Museum, L.B. 2) is dated 1829. More recently Charles Rhyne has discussed other aspects of Constable's early drawing style in 'Fresh Light on John Constable', *Apollo*, Vol. LXXXVII, 1968, pp. 227–30, and John Hayes has illustrated the influence of George Frost on Constable in *Master Drawings*, Vol. 4, No. 2, 1966, pp. 163–8.

ative power by joining one of the Sketching Societies working in the first decade of the nineteenth century, as Girtin and Cotman had done. His aspiration to paint sea-pieces like Van de Velde did not go further than his studies on board the East Indiaman *Coutts* and the large, gloomy water-colour of 'Trafalgar' (No. 65). During this period he grew into an understanding of his exclusive devotion to Dedham Vale, which was only to be widened when friendship and personal association led him to know and feel at home in other places. Some drawings he made of Dedham Vale in this period—such as Nos. 56 and 60—show as clearly as the oils of the same decade that devotion developing from the enthusiasm already apparent in the drawings he had made in 1800 for Lucy Hurlock (Nos. 16A, 16B, 16C). It was a self-imposed limitation which made for concentration of effort, without which his later achievement would not have been possible.

The drawings made in 1806 in the Lake District (Nos. 72–94) are not characteristic of Constable either in subject-matter or treatment, and they may be undervalued on that account. Yet they form an impressive series in their own right, and there is in fact little else in English art which does better justice to the romantic splendour of the Lakeland scenery. In this series Constable was able to indulge fully for the first time his interest in transient atmospheric effects—the shafts of sunlight in No. 76, the lowering mists of No. 85. On these drawings we meet also for the first time with Constable's practice of recording the effect of sky and the time of day—a practice more generally familiar in his tree and sky studies of 1821 and 1822. On the back of No. 74, for instance, he comments "... tone very mellow like the mildest of Gaspar Poussin and Sir G[eorge] B[eaumont] & on the whole deeper toned than this drawing", and on No. 80 the artist has written "Dark autumnal day at noon,—tone more blooming than this—the effect exceeding terrific ..." One or two pencil drawings on the backs of the water-colours (Nos. 79a, 81a) show a freedom of draughtsmanship not apparent before.

After his visit to the Lake District Constable took serious counsel with himself as he had done in 1802, and this new effort of concentration led to the sudden liberation of his style. Yet there is little in oil and nothing in pencil or water-colour in the Museum's collection which can certainly be assigned to these decisive years of his development, and hardly more is known elsewhere. Where next we encounter his black and white drawings—in the studies made at Salisbury in 1811 (Nos. 105–108)—there is a dryness about them which is unexpected when they are compared with the oil sketches made at the same time. The chief emphasis is on the accurate and careful delineation of architecture, and in this regard Constable was sufficiently successful to be able to use one of the most painstaking studies of Salisbury Cathedral (No. 105) as the basis of the painting of 1823 for Bishop Fisher (No. 254). Though the trees are carefully particularised in drawings of this year the rendering of their foliage in diagonal hatching has an aridity similar to that seen in the handling of the architecture.

Not until he spent a long summer at East Bergholt in 1813 did Constable show in his drawings the freedom and novelty now apparent in his oil paintings. On seventy-two leaves of a pocket sketch-book (No. 121), which measures only $3\frac{1}{2} \times 4\frac{3}{4}$ ins., he has crammed the observation suggested by half a lifetime's love of his native fields, and drawn the whole range of subjects natural to that countryside in a wide variety of graphic styles. The draughtsmanship varies from the freely scribbled sketches of 'Flatford Old Bridge' (p. 29) and 'Stoke-by-Nayland Church' (p. 17) to broad landscapes realised in every shadow of tree and cloud, such as 'Dedham from Langham' (p. 39). Some are ready for translation into oil paintings, such as 'The Sky Lark' (p. 36); others actually were so translated, as the 'Dedham from Langham' already mentioned, and the scribbles on pp. 31 and 70 which twenty-two years later made their contribution to 'The Valley Farm'. In such a drawing as that of a path through a cornfield (p. 21) Constable expresses with complete and unaffected simplicity the depth of his feeling for the scenery near his birthplace.

Few artist's sketch-books are more intimate and moving than this and its companion of 1814 (No. 132), in which Constable recorded such a succession of vividly seen images of the countryside and its life, the fruit of an intense communion with Nature at the period when he was separated from Maria Bicknell and could see no prospect of a successful outcome of the love he had long felt for her. These books were used at a time when he was writing to her "I believe we can do nothing worse than indulge in an useless sensibility—but I can hardly tell you what I feel at the sight from the window where I am now writing of the fields in which we have so often walked". In the drawings he made then Constable mirrored the Stour valley with a power of minute observation as intense as that conveyed in the letters of William Cowper which formed his favourite reading.

The main sketch-book of 1814 (No. 132, with No. 133 as a detached leaf) is in some ways of a different character from No. 121. In the drawings in this book Constable has given more attention to broad massing of light and shade, and less to careful drawing of detail. With this in mind he drew some scenes (pp. 62, 81) at early hours of the day, when the sun threw long sloping shadows across the ground and emphasised the silhouettes of the trees. There are more full-page drawings, and more drawings devoted to working out the details of a single composition. For instance, no less than nine leaves have drawings connected with the 'Stour Valley and Dedham Village' in the Museum of Fine Arts, Boston; and in this book also is the working out of the plan and *staffage* of 'Boat-building near Flatford Mill' (pp. 55–7). While making these drawings Constable was reaching toward a more studied pictorial composition; he deliberately chose viewpoints in which a foreground tree dominated the right- or left-hand side (pp. 25, 27); or he introduced a tree for this purpose (p. 65). So successfully did he solve these problems that he could use the drawings in the book for some of the large-scale paintings of the Stour which first made his wider reputation. The germ of the 'View on the Stour near Dedham' is on p. 52, possibly with hints from pp. 27 and 59; a section of 'Flatford Mill' is derived from the drawing on p. 61, and the middle part of the composition of 'The White Horse' from that on p. 66.

Constable emerged from his summers of seclusion at East Bergholt fully certain in his own mind of the way to compose into large-scale paintings the unemphatic features of the Suffolk countryside. More than this, he was at last a complete master of drawing, and from now onward his black and white sketches are serene and assured. He took sketch-books of a larger size on his journeys and filled them with rapid or detailed drawings as the mood might take him. A drawing such as No. 157, probably made during Constable's first visit to East Bergholt after his marriage, is an expression of his art no less complete in that colour has been abstracted from it and that it is diminutive in scale.

To the same year, 1817, belong the first dated drawings in the Museum of trees sufficiently particularised to be regarded as portrait studies of their subjects (Nos. 161, 162). These show the extent of Constable's departure from the art theories of the eighteenth century. Whereas Sir Joshua Reynolds would abstract the ideal tree from a variety of individual instances, Constable concentrated on the form of a particular tree which was known to him almost as a personal thing. The trees in No. 161 are to be recognised—before the foremost one had been lopped—in the sketch-books of 1813 and 1814 no less than in the foreground of the painting 'Flatford Mill' in the Tate Gallery. Such drawings are an embodiment of that emotion which Leslie records: "I have seen him admire a fine tree with an ecstasy of delight like that with which he would catch up a beautiful child in his arms".

Just as he never travelled expressly for subjects, so Constable did not draw expressly as a preliminary to paintings, though he might at any later time turn back to neglected pages of his sketch-books for subjects, as he did with 'Hadleigh Castle', painted in 1829 from a sketch of 1814 (No. 127), and with 'Stonehenge', the water-colour of which was made in 1836 from a sketch of 1820 (Nos. 395, 186). His sketch-books were a pictorial diary, the more vivid counterpart of the letters he wrote when he was away from his wife and family; and, like all good diaries, have a power of fascinating far beyond the intimate circle for whom they were intended. He was endowed with a less retentive visual memory and a less inventive imagination than Turner, who could compose in the greatest detail from an unintelligible shorthand note made years before; and it was always his instinct to carry his drawings, whether more or less bold or detailed, to a pictorially complete and effective conclusion. Leslie, with his usual perception of the essential features of his friend's art, has written: "An extremely interesting portion of Constable's work is known only to his intimate friends,—I mean the contents of his numerous sketch-books. In these are many complete landscapes in miniature, often coloured, and when not tinted the chiaroscuro is generally given in lead pencil, sometimes with greater depth of effect and always with exquisite taste. The name of nearly every spot sketched is added, and in looking through these books one thing is striking, which may be equally noticed of his pictures, that the subjects of his works form a history of his affections.—Bergholt and its neighbourhood—Salisbury—Osmington—Hampstead—Gillingham—Brighton—Folkestone (where his boys were at school)—and scenes in Berkshire visited by him with Mr. Fisher". The drawings in the Museum illustrate every phase of this inventory of Leslie's.

Even in a review confined to the more striking features in the last twenty years of Constable's life, the Berkshire sketch-book of 1821 mentioned by Leslie in this passage deserves special attention (Nos. 210–219). In it Constable had made a number of drawings on a fairly large scale, making three or four studies in one day of places near to one another, as he had done in the Lake District. While some of the pages of the book bear detailed pencil drawings (Nos. 217, 218) others are more lightly drawn and then washed over with grey tint or light colour (No. 210). The extent to which Constable used water-colour in this book is not apparent from the pages in this Museum alone, since (as noted on p. 5) Miss Constable gave the more fully coloured ones to the British Museum. No. 242 probably came from the book and with No. 241 (reworked by the artist ten years later) represents this type of water-colour, shown in the British Museum by Nos. L.B. 26*a*, *b*.

From now on Constable used neutral and water-colour washes more frequently, as for instance in the drawings he made in the grove at Coleorton in 1823. His visits to Brighton in 1824 and the following years were marked by a further variation in his graphic style. In making a large series of studies of scenes on the beach, boats and shipping, Constable resorted to a somewhat rough-and-ready method (Nos. 273–284). These are predominantly wash drawings, and some of the outlines which have the appearance of being drawn with a pen are more probably drawn with the point of the brush. The crudity of some of these drawings, for example No. 283, misled Holmes into thinking them early works contemporary with Nos. 14–16; if there is any substance in the suggestion that a selection from them was to be engraved their comparative casualness may be explained. Certainly, whatever the reason, the more agreeable record by Constable of the coast at Brighton is found in his oil sketches, but from the many drawings he made at the same time he was able to choose a composition and foreground details for 'The Marine Parade and Chain Pier, Brighton' (Nos. 289, 275).

The sketch-book he took on his autumn holiday in Flatford in 1827 was one of the largest he ever used and contains the most attractive of his later pencil drawings, recapitulating his favourite Suffolk subjects: a lock on the Stour, cottages in the country lanes, barges on the canal, the bridge and cottage at Flatford and gnarled willow stumps similar to those he had introduced into 'The Leaping Horse' (Nos. 290–300).

Some of the drawings he made at Brighton in the spring of the following year presage the storminess and agitation of his late drawings in sepia and wash (Nos. 305–307). On his last two visits to Salisbury in 1829 he made many free drawings of the cathedral. The larger sketch-book he used on these visits was broken up and its contents much dispersed. Miss Constable gave three pages from it to the British Museum, including one dated 19 November 1829, in pencil and full water-colour, which is finer than any of the pages catalogued here (L.B. 33). At the same time Constable was developing in a small sketch-book a rather dry combination of pen outline and water-colour washes (Nos. 313, 316); he made a much more agreeable use of these methods on his visit to East Bergholt in 1832 (Nos. 348–352).

Although Salisbury was to figure no more among his sketches, Constable was still capable of forming an attachment to new localities to which he might be attracted by bonds of personal interest. His sketches at Folkestone, where he visited his schoolboy sons around 1833, are more adequately represented in the British Museum; only one of his water-colour sketches, 'Folkestone Harbour', is found in this collection (No. 357). His distant prospects of London from Hampstead (No. 358), subjects painted from his own doorstep, are also more plentifully shown in the British Museum. But his visits to Arundel in 1834 and 1835 and to Petworth in 1834 are represented by a great number of drawings, including the intact sketch-book No. 382 of which twenty-five pages are drawn upon, the eleven drawings Nos. 362–372, and almost certainly also the dismembered and undated sketch-book Nos. 385–394.

So enthusiastic did he become about the Sussex countryside which he now saw for the first time that Constable felt momentarily disloyal to the subjects which had sustained him all his life: "I have too much preferred the picturesque to the beautifull" he wrote to Leslie, and again to George Constable "I have never seen such scenery as your county affords; I prefer it to any other for my pictures". He lived to embody this enthusiasm in one important composition only—the 'Arundel Mill and Castle' which he left not quite finished at his death—but the wide range of sketches he made shows the thoroughness of his newly-aroused interest. By preference he now made finished water-colour drawings in his sketch-books, combining the washes sometimes with pen outline (No. 364), sometimes with a fairly heavy under-drawing of pencil, as in the water-colour of Cowdray (No. 369). The well-known 'Fittleworth Mill' (No. 370) is far lighter and freer in its use of water-colour. In pencil drawing Constable was equally broad in method, ranging from the massive light and shade of 'The ruins of the Maison Dieu, Arundel' (No. 378) to the slight and remarkable shorthand of 'Fittleworth Mill and Bridge, on the Rother' (No. 371).

Prolonged ill health was the reason why Constable was only able to send water-colours and drawings to the Royal Academy exhibition of 1834: one of them, 'Old Sarum' (No. 359), was by far the most ambitious essay he had yet made in this medium. Its success encouraged him to the larger 'Stonehenge' shown in 1836 (No. 395); into this he introduced the rainbow which had fascinated him for over twenty years as a symbol and embodiment of colour.

In these years also he made a few book illustrations; some of his preparations for plates for Gray's *Elegy* and for the *Seven Ages of Shakespeare* are seen in this collection in Nos. 354, 355 and 407. The development of his interests in yet another direction is represented by the copies of engravings of early works of art made—presumably with the help of assistants—for the lectures on the history of landscape painting which he gave between 1833 and 1836 (Nos. 397–400), but these make no pretence at being more than diagrams, with the exception of that related to Titian's 'St. Peter Martyr'. The two large drawings of ash-trees (Nos. 375, 376), which may have been used to illustrate a lecture, as well as serving in the former case as a study for 'The Valley Farm', rank, however, amongst his finest renderings of these, his favourite trees.

The most remarkable drawings he made in this last decade of his life are the sepia sketches of Suffolk scenes (Nos. 410, 411). A few other late monochrome drawings (Nos. 412–414) may be grouped with them, as may the equally unrestrained and masterly 'Landscape study' in full water-colour (No. 415): otherwise these stand isolated and without precedent in his work. In spite of his unflattering reference to Payne Knight's purchase of 273 drawings by Claude, now in the British Museum—"They looked just like papers used and otherwise mauled, & purloined from a Water Closet—but they were certainly old, & much rent, & dissolved, &c. but their meer charm was their age"—Constable may have had the drawings of Claude in mind when he made these two sketches on the torn halves of a piece of thin paper. Evidence has come to light since the first edition of this book which suggests that they are both paraphrases of existing compositions. To that extent they resemble the 'blots' which he sometimes added to his letters to give Fisher or Leslie an idea of one of the paintings he was working on. Possibly his prolonged experience with Lucas in translating his paintings into mezzotint for the *English Landscape Scenery* suggested to him these sudden and dramatic statements in black and white. Whatever the cause it is fitting that they should come at the end of his career. Light seen as brightness in pure contrast with shade, transient atmospheric effects in the sky and on the water, compositions framed by a tall foreground tree, the familiar forms of Dedham Church and barges on the Stour; all the essential elements of Constable's art are concentrated into these magnificent and summary affirmations. Nearly forty years before he had first attempted to express his love for his native soil; now he was able to sum it up conclusively in these masterly drawings, which combine breadth of execution with fullness of realisation and intensity of feeling.

THE WORKS IN OIL

In former Museum catalogues a distinction has been drawn between, on the one hand, important completed oil paintings, of the kind painted for exhibition or sale, and, on the other, the oil sketches mostly made in the open air as preliminaries for more finished works. The paintings classified under the first of these headings comprised all those in the Sheepshanks Gift: that is, 'Boat-building near Flatford Mill' (No. 137), 'Dedham Mill' (No. 184), the 'Hampstead Heath' of 1828 (No. 301) and the earlier view of the Heath (No. 323), 'Water-meadows near Salisbury' (No. 321) and 'Salisbury Cathedral from the Bishop's Grounds' (No. 254). Of these the 'Boat-building' (1815), 'Salisbury Cathedral' (1823) and the 'Hampstead Heath' (1828) alone are known to have been exhibited at the Royal Academy; the 'Water-meadows' was rejected in the circumstances described in the catalogue note on it. The three oils bequeathed by Miss Isabel Constable in her name and that of her brother and sister were also included under the first head: of these 'A Water-mill at Gillingham, Dorset' (No. 288) was probably shown at the Royal Academy in 1827 and 'The Cottage in a Cornfield' (No. 352) was shown in 1833. 'Trees at Hampstead' (No. 223) may have been shown in 1822, but this is not certain. The two large oil sketches for 'The Hay Wain' (No. 209) and' The Leaping Horse' (No. 286) bequeathed by Mr. Henry Vaughan have always been grouped with these exhibited works.

The remaining ninety-two works are all in the gift of Miss Isabel Constable, and have been classified as oil sketches, though in a few cases (such as the early works Nos. 36, 37) the artist may have regarded them as finished pictures, and others were painted specifically as studies for engravings in *English Landscape Scenery*.

The earliest dated oil sketches in the Museum are of 1802. By this time Constable had not only put behind him the style of such juvenilia as 'The Chymist' and 'The Alcymist 'of 1797 (in the collection of Lt.-Col. C. A. Brooks); he had renounced mannerism in a famous pronouncement which is quoted in the Catalogue (note following No. 40), and he had revealed the beginnings of his mature naturalism on an impressive scale in 'Old Hall, East Bergholt' (formerly in the collection of the Misses M. and K. Gore).

These early oils (Nos. 36, 37, 39 and 40) justify West's encouragement of the young man: "You must have loved Nature very much before you could have painted this", and they contain in germ many of the leading features of his later style. Throughout his life he was to be a painter of light, and when these fresh open-air sketches are compared with typical examples of eighteenth-century English landscape painting the rendering of light is seen to be already the most original feature in them. The subject-matter is taken from the immediate neighbourhood of his birthplace; and he has now begun to pay close attention to the details of natural form. The trees in these scenes from the countryside endeared to him from its associations with his childhood are not forced into the mould of ideal form, mixed in species and improved upon in structure, but recognisably portrayed as they existed; the advance upon the parsley-like foliage to be seen in his drawings of the previous year is profound and striking.

The details of handling also presage to some extent his later style, although he uses a coarse canvas, and allows its texture to be more of an element in the surface than he normally did later on, when the smooth millboard or paper supplied all the key he required for his sketches. But he has already adopted a reddish-brown grounding which he allows to appear as part of the general effect. In the daylight scenes small areas of bright light reflected from the leaves or the dewy ground attract his eye, thus marking the start of roughness and that appearance of being unfinished which his contemporaries were to regard as the leading characteristic of his style. The influence of Wilson and Girtin is more apparent in the evening scene (No. 36); yet in this sketch also there are broad sweeps of the brush, where the light of the setting sun catches the slopes, which foreshadow the fluency of brushwork of his maturity. In it the painting of the violet tones on the slopes of Dedham Vale has much in common with the similar background of 'Old Hall, East Bergholt'.

The main types of oil painting in which Constable was engaged in the succeeding six or seven years are barely represented in the collections of the Museum. Much of his activity at this period was to prove a false line of development, in retrospect uncharacteristic of his career. It was a time when he tried to meet his family's wishes by establishing himself as a portrait-painter, then the only sure way of making a living as an artist, but this side of his art is seen here only in the pencil drawing No. 64 and the oil sketch which probably represents Mary Constable (No. 97). The technical accomplishment of the portrait of his sister lifts it above the general level of his early portraits, and shows that it was painted after he had been making his copies of Reynolds and Hoppner for the Dysarts; it shows also that, as in landscape, he painted his best portraits when his affections were deeply engaged. Of his religious paintings—altarpieces in the style of West for the churches at Brantham and Nayland—there is no echo; nor are there to be found here any of the oil sketches or finished oil paintings which he derived from the journey to the Lakes so abundantly illustrated by the water-colours Nos. 72–94. The latter is the only deficiency in the Museum's representation of Constable's early work in oils which is much to be regretted. So far as can be deduced from the one or two Lake District scenes which have been seen recently in England, they indicate that his style was developing rapidly towards full mastery. Although he forced the colour in them as he never did when painting the scenery of Dedham and East Bergholt, the oil sketches of the Lake District appear to show in 1806 and 1807 much of the sweep and vigour usually assigned to the years after 1810. Though these six or seven years were relatively unproductive, at their close Constable was within reach of his real aims; he had mastered drawing, his colour was suddenly to become rich and natural and he had learned to limit his subject-matter to his native countryside.

His entrance into the full possession of his powers as a painter in oils is first displayed, so far as dated works in the Museum are concerned, by 'A cart on a country road' of May 1811 (No. 100), together with 'A village fair, probably at East Bergholt' (No. 101) of July in the same year. These are in fact the only dated examples in the Museum of this crucial series of sketches, though there is reason to believe that the dating of 'Flatford Mill from a lock on the Stour' (No. 103) to the year 1811 may be well founded. The 'View of Dedham from a road leading to East Bergholt' (No. 109) is another keypoint in the development of Constable's style, of which it would be desirable to have more than an approximate dating, since it may be earlier than the three works just discussed.*

The earliest known appearance in dated sketches of breadth combined with assurance and natural colour combined with richness are in the Tate Gallery's 'View at Epsom' which is dated June 1809† and in the 'Lane near East Bergholt with a resting man', formerly in the Gregory Collection, which is dated 13 October 1809. These show that as soon as he had exhausted the material provided by the Lake District—material alien to his true sympathies—Constable set himself to paint the countryside he knew best, and that between 1809 and about 1815 he overcame all the difficulties in the way of a personal rendering of it, at

* For an examination of this period see the article 'John Constable, 1810–1816: a chronological study' by Michael Kitson, *Journal of the Warburg and Courtauld Institutes*, Vol. XX, Nos. 3–4, 1957 and the article by Charles Rhyne referred to in the footnote on p. 14.

† M. Chamot, 'The Constable Room at the Tate Gallery', *Connoisseur*, Vol. CXXXVII, 1956, p. 260.

least when painting for his private eye alone. His command of effects of light ranges from the brilliantly colourful buildings and trees of 'Flatford Mill' seen under a bright cloudy summer sky to the subtle misty tones of storm in 'Barges on the Stour' (No. 104). The immediacy of his apprehension of all the features of the landscape, their relevance to and subordination in the general effect, is conveyed by the dashing slashes of his fully charged brush, which encompass detail without losing breadth.

In 1811 Constable excelled all he had previously sent for exhibition at the Royal Academy with the 'Dedham Vale' now in the collection of Sir Richard Proby. This painting, which was warmly praised by Leslie, gives so clear and detailed a panorama of the heart of Constable's country that it has often been referred to in the pages of the ensuing Catalogue for the identification of topographical features and landmarks beloved by the artist.

The paintings dated 1812 (Nos. 115–117, 119) are an interlude in this remarkable development. More drawn with the brush than painted, they recall in their linear technique the later work of Gainsborough; Böhler has associated them with a renewed interest which Constable was then taking in the work of Rubens. Their subjects comprise two evening scenes of the fields of Dedham Vale (Nos. 115, 116), a remarkable study of the silent heat before a summer storm (No. 119) and, on a strangely patched up combination of paper and canvas (No. 117), the earliest known appearance in Constable's work of the rainbow which was later to become a symbol—almost an obsession—with him. As a study of rain-soaked foliage swept by the wind and seen under a stormy sky, the last-named work is a forerunner of the studies he made at Hampstead in the 1820's.

Constable had now perfected an ability for making complete pictures, of which the composition need not necessarily be changed when painted on a larger scale, of the oil sketches he made in the open air. At the same time he made studies in oil, just as he would have done in pencil or wash, for the individual details of a larger picture. The studies of flowers probably made in 1814 (Nos. 129, 130) are an approach towards this sytem: his two studies of a cart and horses (Nos. 134, 135), and that of a plough (No. 136), also made in 1814, are unusual in that identical pencil sketches, doubtless made at the same time, are found in his pocket sketch-book (No. 132).

The period which he spent largely in seclusion and which was marked latterly by that concentration on drawing already discussed in connexion with the sketch-books of 1813 and 1814 (pp. 15, 16), was a decisive time in which Constable acquired a mastery of all aspects of his art and formed a stock of images on which he was to draw for many years. The first oil sketch of his often repeated composition 'Dedham Mill' (No. 113), the germ of 'The Glebe Farm' (No. 111) and two sketches of 'Willy Lott's House' later used for 'The Hay Wain' (Nos. 110, 110a) all date from this period, as does the sketch for the engraving 'Spring. East Bergholt Common' (No. 122). The engraved compositions 'A Summerland' (No. 121, pp. 12, 43) and 'Summer Morning: Dedham from Langham' (No. 121, pp. 39, 51, 52), for which there are pencil drawings, were also conceived in this most creative passage of Constable's life.

'Boat-building near Flatford Mill' (No. 137) is the first fully typical exhibited picture by Constable to be found in the collection. (The sombre water-colour 'H.M.S. *Victory* in the battle of Trafalgar' (No. 65) shown in 1806 is in fact the earliest exhibited picture here, but cannot be called typical.) In a sense the 'Boat-building' owes its particular qualities to family pressure and to advice from Farington, as a result of which Constable made a renewed study of the paintings of Claude before going into the country with the resolve that he would paint a picture entirely in the open air and more highly finished than was his custom. Three pages of the sketch-book of 1814 are devoted to a full-page study for this composition, and to studies of the figures and the tools used in barge-building, with a thoroughness almost as great as that he adopted in the same sketch-book for the details in the painting 'Stour Valley and Dedham Village' now at Boston. The cool colour of the 'Boat-building', which Leslie noted as eminently expressive of the heat of a summer day, is also evidence that Constable had studied Claude to good effect. Compared with the dash and freedom of his oil sketches there is an atmosphere of constraint about some of the detail and the management of the composition; but he was able to introduce more breadth in a few details, such as the boy's back and the high-lights on the tools. There is an unassuming naturalism about the work consistent with its having been painted in the open air, but the greater pains bestowed upon the composing of the work have deprived it of some of the spontaneity seen in Sir Richard Proby's 'Dedham Vale' of 1811.

The next five years—from 1816 to 1821—are marked by a change in Constable's habits of work. After his marriage he set himself to paint pictures which should embody much more ambitiously than anything he had yet produced his sentiment for the valley of the Stour. He had laid the foundations and had a variety of sketches to draw on: he soon settled down to concentrate in earnest into welding them into large compositions to be painted not in the open air but, without loss of natural colour and feeling, in his studio. 'Flatford Mill', now in the Tate Gallery, was the forerunner of this group of paintings, on which he counted for his future fame. With the completion, exhibition and sale of 'The White Horse' in 1819 he first succeeded in this aim: and the canal and river scenes which followed it—' Stratford Mill', 'The Hay Wain', 'View on the Stour near Dedham', 'The Lock' and 'The Leaping Horse'—were variations upon the same basic theme.

This long and sustained effort left him at first little leisure for oil sketching, though he did make a number of oil studies during his honeymoon. Of these, only 'Weymouth Bay' (No. 155) has found its way to the Museum, a bold rendering of a stormy November coast which is in essence as much a diary entry as are his pencil sketches. From this sketch he made two oil paintings, one of which was the source of the engraving in *English Landscape Scenery*.

There is a gap, so far as dated work in oils in the Museum is concerned, between this study made late in 1816 and the 'Branch Hill Pond, Hampstead' (No. 171) made just three years later. This bold and dramatically lighted study is Constable's earliest known painting of a locality with which he was to have associations for the rest of his life, and was regarded by him with such favour that it became one of his stock subjects, repeated at least five times, as well as being the foundation of another engraving in *English Landscape Scenery*. The oil sketch of 'Waterloo Bridge, from Whitehall Stairs' (No. 174) may be contemporary with it: if this is in fact the study he showed to Farington in the same year it is the earliest version in colour of a theme which was to occupy his attention on and off for thirteen years.

From this time onwards when he received private commissions he was willing to repeat one of a number of standard compositions—witness the variants of 'Branch Hill Pond, Hampstead' and of 'Dedham Mill' recorded under Nos. 171 and 184—and when he painted for exhibition he returned year after year to the basic theme of a Suffolk canal scene. At the same time he continued to multiply his oil sketches. In 1820 he made studies, both in pencil and in oil, at Salisbury; those of the cathedral (Nos. 196, 197 in this collection: no doubt there were others) were of use when he came to complete the Bishop's picture for the exhibition of 1823. 1820 also marks the modest beginning (Nos. 207, 208) of the series of studies of sky and trees on which he worked mainly in 1821. He found the rising ground at Hampstead admirably adapted for the seizing of transient appearances in the sky. From where he sat—often no doubt in the garden of his house—the ground fell away from his feet and he could see the sky over and through bushes, trees and the chimney pots of neighbouring cottages. He observed the foliage catching the sunlight in small patches of light, and recorded the direction and force of the wind which was causing the rapid change of the clouds. There is a much greater sense of changing light and the catching of passing effects in the studies of this type than in the pure cloud studies, which belong mainly to the following year, 1822 (No. 249).

Constable was not an impulsive artist given to unpremeditated acts of creation. From the moment he grew conscious of his powers he worked to a carefully planned strategy: "I imagine myself driving a nail. I have driven it some way —by persevering with this nail I may drive it home" he wrote to Fisher. So he undertook these studies of skies and trees, not as ends in themselves, but for the deliberate purposes which he set out lucidly in a letter to Fisher quoted in the note following No. 235: one particular natural effect of illumination on the earth could only be consistent with one aspect of the sky. Constable was to apply this theory increasingly in the works of his later years; for instance, in each of his repetitions of Hampstead Heath the sky is varied, and with it the lighting of the ground. The cold tone, the shadowed foreground and bleak watery reflections of the original sketch, seen under the slanting rays of a cold November sky (No. 171), contrast forcibly with the warmer foreground and clearer distance of the version he exhibited in 1828 (No. 301), in which a summer storm is passing off. Sometimes there may seem an element of contrivance in the juxtaposition of earth and sky when Constable was aiming at highly dramatic effects in the later versions, but there can be no doubt of the sense of immediacy about the cloud and tree studies on which the skies of his larger paintings were based. He could not have painted those studies without both his acute powers of observation and rapid notation, and the ability to conceive the theory of their use. It is probable that in the formulation of this theory Luke Howard's book *The Climate of London* played its part, conceivably not by suggesting considerations which had not previously occurred to him, but rather by crystallizing his ideas.*

The years immediately following his election as A.R.A. in 1819 were among the most productive of his life. Besides his studies of skies and trees he made a number of sketches of buildings and landscapes near his Hampstead lodgings, especially in the neighbourhood of the Branch Hill pond. In some of these he set out to represent effects of light which he did not normally reproduce in his work—the yellow-green of the October light (No. 227) and the austere misty light of a stormy summer evening (No. 247). At the same time he was continuing his series of large-scale scenes from the Suffolk landscape for exhibition at the Royal Academy, usually preluding the painting of the exhibited work with a full-scale sketch.

The sketch for 'The Hay Wain' (No. 209: 1820–1) has hung so long in the Museum as a companion piece to that for 'The Leaping Horse' (No. 288: 1824–5) that there might seem to be a unique relationship between the two works for which they are studies. The compositions are in fact separated by an interval of four years and are two of the series of five horizontal canal and river scenes: 'The White Horse' (1819); 'Stratford Mill' (1820); 'The Hay Wain' (1821); 'View on the Stour near Dedham' (1822); 'The Leaping Horse' (1825). The vertical composition of 'The Lock' (1824) was of a similar nature, apart from format: this was repeated in the horizontal composition of 1827 on a slightly smaller scale, which Constable presented to the Royal Academy as his Diploma work, and

* Kurt Badt, *John Constable's Clouds*, London, 1950.

which virtually ends this succinct group, among which are his most famous paintings. The full-scale sketch for 'The White Horse' is in the National Gallery of Art, Washington, the finished version being in the Frick Collection, New York; the full-scale sketch for 'The View of the Stour near Dedham' is at Royal Holloway College, Egham, the finished version being in the Henry E. Huntington Library and Art Gallery, San Marino, California.

The study for 'The Hay Wain' is by any standard a sketch. Its masses are broadly blocked in; the general effect of lighting is established by it, but the prevailing colour scheme is that of the golden toned canvas on which it is painted and does not vie with the naturalism of the sketches of 'Willy Lott's House' from which it is partly derived (Nos. 110, 110a) nor with that of the finished work. The study for 'The Leaping Horse', on the other hand, is carried so far that we may well believe, as is hinted by Leslie in the first edition of his life of Constable, that it was at first intended to be the finished picture, but afterwards turned into a sketch. Here the effect of overwhelming power and of demoniac energy is primarily conveyed by the summary treatment. Its solemnity is aided by the remarkable unity of light, and the multitude of small accents do not disturb it by a distracting glitter, for they are all subordinate to, and justified by, the main effect. This is perhaps the only composition by Constable in which the action of the figures gives the key to the feeling of the whole; the energy of the horse's leap has transmitted itself to the landscape, the sky and the painter's method. The painting is not so much the exhaustion of a rich stream of ideas as its conclusive summing up.

The 'Salisbury Cathedral from the Bishop's Grounds' exhibited in 1823 (No. 254) was an interruption to this series of canal scenes, undertaken rather grudgingly as a commission for Bishop Fisher. Constable has left a vivid account of his struggles with this picture, in which he had to meet his patron's desire for an exact portrayal of the cathedral, and to combine this with his own conception of a pictorial or picturesque treatment. The latter required the animated sky with its black cloud behind the cathedral spire, which never satisfied the Bishop and which, after remaining a bone of mild contention for two years, was the occasion of Constable's painting another version without it. After he had painted the last of the many versions Constable regarded the work as one of his standard pictures from which he could not part. Constable always had difficulty in reconciling the two opposed elements of the pictorial and the topographical when he was asked to paint houses: he felt it as early as his paintings of 'Old Hall, East Bergholt', and as late as that of 'Englefield House' (see note following No. 344). He never overcame the difficulties more successfully than in the picture of the cathedral; for here he was able to make the most of its setting and show it through an arch of trees, as well as introducing the dramatic sky.

Although he found nothing to commend in the countryside round Brighton and thought that sea-shore scenes were too hackneyed to make fit subjects for exhibition, the oil sketches which Constable made there form one of the most distinct and accomplished groups in his work. The seaside skies were generally clear, and less cloud-ridden than those he usually painted; their luminosity, and that of the sea, is pleasantly diversified by the shipping and the figures on the beaches. The Museum has a large proportion of these vibrant sketches, which are painted on rough paper and, like the Hampstead sky studies, often have notes about the climatic conditions written on their backs. Among them is certainly one, and in all probability there are more, of the sketches which Constable sent to Fisher so that Mrs. Fisher might be cheered by a sight of the sea in an illness (No. 266, and note following No. 272). As with the drawings of Brighton, the undated oil sketches have been arranged in the Catalogue after those dated 1824, though some were no doubt painted during the subsequent four years. One at least which is later is the study of the sun setting through a coastal haze (No. 303).

Apart from any Brighton studies he may have made in these years, the Museum's collections suggest that there was a falling off in his activity as an outdoor sketcher in oils in the years 1825 to 1828. Even the charming study of a donkey and her foal for 'The Cornfield' may have been a study copied from an earlier work (No. 287). 'A Water-mill at Gillingham, Dorset' (No. 288), probably exhibited at the Royal Academy in 1827, is a painting in vertical format of a subject which Constable twice treated in a landscape shape. An interesting record of a contemporary's appreciation of this picture is contained in the letter from E. Leader Williams, quoted in the Catalogue.

Constable's last visit to Salisbury, in 1829, is marked by three oil sketches, and the small oil painting 'Water-meadows near Salisbury' which is to all intents and purposes an out-of-doors sketch (Nos. 311, 312, 320 and 321). There is an ease and calmness about them which shows that the stormy mood of 'Hadleigh Castle' (which he exhibited in this, the year after his wife's death), and of the oil sketch for 'Old Sarum' (No. 322) (which was the basis for one of the earliest and most characteristic of Lucas's mezzotints), was not the sole, even if it was the dominant affection of his mind. So strikingly is the impression of serenity in these sketches that Holmes was led by it to assign the two undated ones to a much earlier part of Constable's career.

Of the works in oil which have not been precisely dated, but here assigned to the period 1820 to 1830, the most considerable is the view of Hampstead Heath near the Vale of Health pond (No. 323), one of the simplest and most masterly of his Hampstead scenes, probably painted soon after he had first begun to live there.

From 1829 until 1833 Constable was occupied with and harassed by the preparations for David Lucas's mezzotints after his paintings in *English Landscape Scenery*. In some cases he brought out early works for Lucas to engrave: the paintings 'Shipping on the Orwell, near Ipswich' (No. 96), 'Summer Evening' (No. 98) and 'Autumnal Sunset' (No. 120) in this collection are cases in point. For other plates he painted studio replicas or made versions from earlier studies: the studies for 'Willy Lott's House' (No. 329a), 'Stoke-by-Nayland' (No. 330) and 'Summer Morning: Dedham from Langham' (No. 332) are here assigned to this category. The direct comparison which can be made between the sketch for the mezzotint of 'Willy Lott's House' and the two studies of the subject from nature (Nos. 110, 110a) shows in the former the variations in drawing which might be expected of a copy, and a brown unnatural tone to which Constable would not have had recourse had he been painting in the open air. Similar characteristics are noticeable in the sketches for 'Summer Morning: Dedham from Langham' and 'Stoke-by-Nayland', which also were probably made at the time when the engravings were contemplated, and not at that earlier period (1813, 1814) when Constable was making his original pencil sketches (Nos. 121, p. 39 etc., No. 132, p. 21 etc.) of the scenes. There is a comparable divergence between the sketch made in 1811 of 'A cart on a country road' (No. 100) and the larger version (No. 329), which has on the other side the sketch for the engraved version of 'Willy Lott's House'. No. 329, then, may have been intended for an engraving, but rejected before a plate was started.

For most of the major oil paintings on which Constable worked in the last ten years of his life the relevant material in the Museum is earlier and often consists of a small pencil drawing. Thus for 'Hadleigh Castle' the germ is the pencil sketch of 1814 (No. 127); for 'The Glebe Farm' (on which he was working *c.*1827) there is the undated oil sketch which was probably painted before 1820 (No. 111); for 'Waterloo Bridge, from Whitehall Stairs', there are drawings (Nos. 173, 175) and an oil sketch (No. 174) which may antedate the exhibited pictures by eight or twelve years. 'The Valley Farm' of 1835 owes something to a faint sketch in the notebook of 1813; and 'The Cenotaph' of 1836 originates from the drawing Constable made at Coleorton in 1823 (No. 259). The only two considerable oils of this time to owe their origin to the travels and studies he made in the 1830's are the 'Englefield House' (exhibited in 1833; sketched in 1832) and the 'Arundel Mill and Castle' (exhibited posthumously in 1837) based on the drawing of 1835 (No. 379). Although he was enthusiastic about the new scenery he saw in these later years he was not sufficiently familiar with it to make it the subject of many paintings.

Among the exhibited pictures of these years 'The Cottage in a Cornfield' (No. 352) occupies an anomalous position. So fully does it possess the marks of Constable's early maturity and lack the mannerisms and over-elaborated surfaces of his last years that it had been long accepted as the painting of this title shown in 1817. But the evidence summarised in the Catalogue shows conclusively that it was not that work, and was certainly the painting of the same title shown in 1833. The dilemma can only be resolved by supposing either that Constable—being short of material for the exhibition—sent in a work of much earlier origin or that he was able when copying an earlier picture to imitate most of the qualities of his manner of nearly twenty years before.

With Constable's increasing use of water-colour for outdoor sketching in the 1830's went a corresponding decline in his use of oil for the same purpose. The three studies in the Museum's collection which are believed to have been painted after 1830 (Nos. 404–406) are not dated; but the plausibility of the dating suggested for them by Holmes is confirmed by their sharing the wild expressionism of the later water-colours made at Arundel and by their consistency with the studies for 'The Valley Farm'. At first sight the careless wind-tossed lights of the foliage may seem to have much in common with those in the Hampstead sky studies: but these are more summary still. Constable's sense of colour is changing too; he no longer matches the greens of trees and blues of skies but modifies them to a less natural but more expressive gamut. The subjects are familiar—a lock on the Stour, a cottage buried in trees—but in the end the real subject is, more than ever before, the infinitely complicated momentary effects of a cloudy sky swept by the wind, and the light on the earth, water and trees under it. They are perhaps the last studies we know in which Constable sought to express the evanescent aspects of the visible world which had for so long obsessed him, and in them he conveyed with a final perfection his sense of the energy of Nature manifested in its most changeable elements.

CATALOGUE

Notes on the arrangement of the Catalogue and method of compiling the entries will be found on pp. 7–11 of the Introduction

1776–1799

John Constable was born in East Bergholt, Suffolk, on 11 June 1776, the second son of Golding Constable, a well-to-do mill-owner, and Ann Watts. His fondness for painting, without any marked precocity, had already declared itself by the time he was 16 or 17: and he was encouraged in this taste by his friendship with John Dunthorne, a plumber and glazier of East Bergholt, who was an amateur painter.

Excluding copies after engravings, Nos. 1–13 are the earliest dated drawings by Constable of which the whereabouts are now known. In 1796, when they were made, it had not been settled that he should become a professional artist, and in 1797 he was following his father's business in Suffolk. In 1799 he went to London to pursue his career in the arts, and on Farington's recommendation he was admitted as a probationer to the Academy Schools in March of that year.

1 *A Gothic building with a square tower.* 1796

Pencil. $7\frac{1}{8} \times 11\frac{3}{4}$ ins. (180×299 mm.) (No Museum number)
Front page of a sketch-book with two faint pencil drawings showing different sides of the same building.
Inscribed in pencil by the artist above the top drawing *S.E.* and above the lower one *N.W.* An inscription in ink at the top in another hand reads *Very early drawings by J.C. Cottages—.*
(Not reproduced amongst the plates)
(See note following No. 13)

2 *Landscape with a stream at Wenham.* 1796

Plate 2

Pen and ink. $7\frac{1}{8} \times 11\frac{3}{4}$ ins. (180×299 mm.) No. 358*h*–1888
Inscribed at top in ink by the artist [with deletion as shown] *W~~K~~enham Suffolk.*
(See note following No. 13)

1796 **3** *Cottage at Brantham, with a view of Mistley Hall.*

Plate 2

Pen and ink. $7\frac{1}{8} \times 11\frac{3}{4}$ ins. (180 × 299 mm.) No. 358*j*–1888
Inscribed at top in ink by the artist *A Fisherman's Cottage in Brantham Suffolk with a view of Mistly Hall lately the Seat of Lord Viscount Galway.*
(See note following No. 13)
Lt.-Col. C. A. Brooks considers that this drawing represents a cottage at Marsh Farm, Brantham, which was demolished in 1958.

1796 **4** *Cottage at East Bergholt, with a well.*

Plate 3

Pen and ink. $7\frac{1}{8} \times 11\frac{3}{4}$ ins. (180 × 299 mm.) No. 358*b*–1888
Inscribed at top in ink by the artist *E Bergholt Suffolk.*
(See note following No. 13)

1796 **5** *Cottage at Capel, Suffolk.*

Plate 3

Pen and ink. $7\frac{1}{8} \times 11\frac{3}{4}$ ins. (180 × 299 mm.) No. 358*c*–1888
Inscribed at top in ink by the artist *Caple Suffolk.*
(See note following No. 13)

1796 **6** *An inscription in a cartouche.*

Pencil. $7\frac{1}{8} \times 11\frac{3}{4}$ ins. (180 × 299 mm.) (No Museum number)
The inscription reads *Cecy fait a laide de Diev lan de grace 1569.*
(Not reproduced among the plates)
(See note following No. 13)
This inscription still exists on a stone above the doorway at Little Wenham Hall (information from Major T. Binney, the present owner of the house). It is referred to in Constable's letter of 27 October 1796 to J. T. Smith: "I would thank you or some of your learned Friends to make out the inclos'd inscription I took from over a door of an old building near us, which has been the residence of some Catholic family" (Beckett II, p. 5 and footnote 1).

1796 **7** *Cottage at East Bergholt, with a cottager.*

Plate 1

Pen and ink. Drawn surface $5\frac{5}{8} \times 7$ ins. (143 × 179 mm.) No. 358*e*–1888
Inscribed at top in ink by the artist *E Bergholt Suffolk.*
This drawing is on the same page as No. 8.
(See note following No. 13)

1796 **8** *Cottage at East Bergholt.*

Plate 1

Pen and ink. Drawn surface 6 × 7 ins. (154 × 179 mm.) No. 358*f*–1888

Inscribed at top in ink by the artist *E Bergholt Suffolk*.
This drawing is on the same page as No. 7.
(See note following No. 13)

9 *Landscape: a stream running between trees.* 1796
Plate 4

Pen and ink. $7\frac{1}{8} \times 11\frac{3}{4}$ ins. (180×299 mm.) No. 358*g*–1888
(See note following No. 13)

10 *Cottage at Holton.* 1796
Plate 4

Pen and ink. $7\frac{1}{8} \times 11\frac{3}{4}$ ins. (180×299 mm.) No. 358*d*–1888
Signed and dated in the gable above the window in ink *J.C. 1796*. Inscribed at top in ink by the artist *Holton Suffolk with the Church in the Back Ground.*
(See note following No. 13)

11 *Cottage at East Bergholt.* 1796
Plate 5

Pen and ink. $7\frac{1}{8} \times 11\frac{3}{4}$ ins. (180×299 mm.) No. 358*i*–1888
Inscribed at top in ink by the artist *E Bergholt Suffolk.*
(See note following No. 13)

12 *Cottage at East Bergholt.* 1796
Plate 5

Pen and ink. $7\frac{1}{8} \times 11\frac{3}{4}$ ins. (180×299 mm.) No. 358–1888
Inscribed at top in ink by the artist *East Bergholt Suffolk.*
(See note following No. 13)

13 *A ruined cottage at Capel, Suffolk.* 1796
Plate 6

Pen and ink. $7\frac{1}{8} \times 11\frac{3}{4}$ ins. (180 × 299 mm.) No. 358*a*–1888
Inscribed at top in ink by the artist [with deletion as shown] *Caple Suffolk. a Curious circumstance happened in this Cottage a few years since of a poor Woman being burnt ~~to death~~ intirely to ashes* . . . [the rest erased].

A visitor to the Museum from the neighbourhood of Capel St. Mary said (*c*.1920–30) that the tradition about the old woman being burnt still persisted although the cottage had disappeared. The peculiar circumstance was that nothing in the cottage except the old woman was burnt; apparently witchcraft was suspected.

NOTE ON NOS. 1–13

These drawings are on leaves detached from a sketch-book of 14 pages. The sketch-book, which consists of three sheets folded but not sewn and one half-sheet, all of coarse laid paper, was used in Suffolk and the date 1796 on No. 10 may be assumed to be that of the other drawings of the book.

Constable had met J. T. ('Antiquity') Smith in Edmonton in August 1796 (Beckett, II, p. 3) at a time when the latter was collecting material for his *Remarks on Rural Scenery; With twenty etchings of Cottages, from Nature; and some observations and precepts relative to the pictoresque*, published in June 1797. In a letter of 27 October 1796 he wrote to Smith from East Bergholt (L. ed. S., p. 8): "I have in my walks pick'd up several Cottages and peradventure I may have been fortunate enough to hit upon one or two that might please. If you think it is likely that I have, let me know and I'll send you my sketch-book and make a drawing of any you like if there should not be enough to work from". On 16 January 1797 (*ibid.*, p. 10) he wrote: "You flatter me highly respecting my 'Cottages', and I am glad you have found one or two amongst them worthy of your needle". Shortly afterwards he again wrote from East Bergholt (*ibid.*, p. 9 but not dated 2 December 1796 as there stated): "A favourable oppertunity occuring of sending the Cottages, which I mentioned to you some time back, I would not let it pass, but I doubt they will not be worth the trouble of your looking over. If I should be so fortunate as to have found any that should suit you I should be glad". These passages show that Constable was sending to Smith sketches of Suffolk cottages, and perhaps this identical sketch-book; but none of these sketches (1–13) was used in the published edition of *Remarks on Rural Scenery* and no plates in that book after Constable have been identified. The published plates are all lettered *Drawn and etch'd* (or *engraved*) *by J. T. Smith* and represent cottages in or near London and the Home Counties; in particular, some are from Edmonton and its vicinity.

*c.*1796–9
Plate 6

14 *East Bergholt Street, East Bergholt.*

Pen and water-colour. $7\frac{5}{8} \times 12\frac{5}{8}$ ins. (195 × 321 mm.) No. 625–1888

On laid paper watermarked: GR surmounted by a crown.

Inscribed on the back in pencil *L.C. house East Bergholt* and *L.C.*

The inscriptions on the back of the drawing were presumably written by Lionel Bicknell Constable, the artist's youngest son. According to information communicated by Mr. D. Charman, Archivist to the East Suffolk County Council, L. B. Constable owned two properties in East Bergholt Street, which he had inherited from John Constable: a house and garden, and a cottage and garden. These were purchased by John Constable from Robert Grimes in 1802. Lionel Bicknell Constable was admitted to his father's property in 1837, according to the custom of the manor, since John Constable had died intestate. The present-day East Bergholt Post Office occupies the space between the two cottages in the centre of this view, and the gable end of the taller building on the left is virtually unchanged. Stylistically the drawing belongs to the time when Constable was under the influence of J. T. Smith; compare, for instance, the copy made by Constable after a drawing by Smith (reproduced by Key, p. 15). Holmes, p. 238, dates 1797.

15 *East Bergholt Church: the exterior from the S.W.* *c.*1796–9 Plate 7

Pen and water-colour, squared for enlargement in pencil.
$10\frac{1}{8} \times 15\frac{5}{8}$ ins. (258 × 397 mm.) No. 201–1888
On laid paper watermarked: PORTAL & CO 1794.

The drawing is of the same type as No. 14. Holmes, p. 238, dates 1798, and says that it is probably a study for the oil 'East Bergholt Church', No. 55 in the exhibition held at Messrs. Leggatt's in 1899, with which it is nearly identical. However, Constable wrote to Smith on 9 November 1796, to say that he would soon be sending off a drawing of East Bergholt Church, which he was thinking of painting in oil, and this might be the drawing in question (Beckett, II, p. 6), in which case an earlier date might be assigned to the oil painting. In the fabric as shown here the ruined tower of the church is on the left, and the porch with the sundial on the right; the view is taken from the entrance of the lane to Flatford.

16 *A river scene with vessel at sunset.* *c.*1796–9 Plate 7

Pen and grey wash. $7\frac{7}{8} \times 10$ ins. (201 × 252 mm.) No. 607–1888
On laid paper watermarked: 1796.
Inscribed at top in pencil by the artist *about 10 minutes before Sunset, all the foreground in shadow*, over a church tower on the other side of the river *very warm & glowing*, and under the boat *sun tipt waves.*

The tentative handling, especially of the foreground, and the unusually neat writing attest that this is an early drawing. Though the line is firmer, the use of the pen and ink outline, with wash, recalls the drawings done under the influence of J. T. Smith (Nos. 14, 15), and this perhaps justifies a dating before 1800.

1800

Constable had come to London in February 1799, with a letter of introduction from Mrs. Priscilla Wakefield, the Quaker philanthropist, to Joseph Farington. (The date 1798 which has previously been accepted for this journey was derived from entries published under that year in the printed edition of Farington's *Diary* (Greig, Vol. 1, p. 229); but they are dated 1799 in the original MS.) He entered the Academy Schools as a probationer in March 1799, and was enrolled as a student on 19 February 1800. In the summer of 1800 he stayed by himself sketching in Helmingham Park, the grounds of a seat of the Earl of Dysart.

1800 **16A** *The valley of the Stour, with Langham Church in the distance.*

Plate 6a

Pen and water-colour. $13\frac{5}{8} \times 21$ ins. (346×533 mm.) No. P. 25–1970

Langham Church is to be seen on the crest of the ridge, left. A man, in the right foreground, is walking towards it along the Gun Hill road. The tower of Higham Church is just visible below the windmill, at the extreme right edge. For the history and provenance of this drawing and for further details of the topography see the note following No. 16C.

1800 **16B** *The valley of the Stour, with Stratford St. Mary in the distance.*

Plate 6a

Pen and water-colour. $13\frac{1}{2} \times 20\frac{1}{2}$ ins. (342×520 mm.) No. P. 26–1970

The view shows the coach road to Stratford St. Mary at the point where it crosses the Stour, with the Talbooth on the left. Stratford St. Mary Church is seen on the right hand side of the drawing. Gun Hill road runs down to the tollgate from the left.

For the history and provenance of this drawing and for further details of the topography see the note following No. 16C.

1800 **16C** *The valley of the Stour, looking towards East Bergholt.*

Plate 6b

Pen and water-colour. $13\frac{3}{8} \times 20\frac{5}{8}$ ins. (338×523 mm.) No. P. 27–1970

East Bergholt is seen on the ridge over the river. The three most prominent buildings, from left to right, are West Lodge (now called Stour), East Bergholt Church, and Old Hall.

NOTE ON NOS. 16A, 16B AND 16C

These are three of a set of four elaborate water-colour drawings which Constable made as a wedding present for his friend Lucy Hurlock when she married Thomas Blackburne at Dedham Church on 22 November 1800. Lucy Hurlock was the daughter of the Rev. Brooke Hurlock, rector of Lamarsh and curate of Langham, (Beckett, II, pp. 18–21). The four drawings descended in the family, and appear first to have been recorded by Martin Davies when they were the property of Miss Eva Ducat (letter of 27 November 1933 to B. S. Long in the Departmental archives). The set was sold by Miss Ducat at Messrs. Christie's on 6 July 1934 (Lot 4) dubiously attributed to Constable, and purchased by Walker's Galleries for 3 guineas. When placed on exhibition in Walker's Galleries in the 31st Annual Exhibition of Early English Watercolours, 1935 (Nos. 74–76) they were unattributed. The fourth drawing in the series, a view of the estuary at Harwich with the tower of Dedham Church prominent in the distance, was later acquired by the Whitworth Art Gallery, Manchester, in 1943 as the work of the Swiss artist Michel Vincent Brandoin (1733–1790) (reproduced in Reynolds, *Constable the Natural Painter*, 1965, Pl. I). Nos. 16A, 16B and 16C became the property of R. B. Beckett, from whom they were purchased by the Museum in 1970. (See also 'A Wedding Present from John Constable' by R. B. Beckett, *Connoisseur*, June 1955, pp. 16–9.) Lt.-Col. C. A. Brooks has supplied identifications of all the scenes, which are executed with exceptional attention to detail and accuracy. He has also shown that the three drawings in the Museum in the order 16A, 16B, 16C and the fourth, at Manchester, complete a panorama of the Stour Valley from west to east, and stretching from Langham Church to the estuary. Three of the scenes, Nos. 16A, 16B and the drawing in the Whitworth Institute, Manchester, are taken from the same view point on the hill immediately south of the Stratford St. Mary bridge. The fourth, No. 16C, is taken from a point slightly to the east and lower down, from a lane opposite the present Dedham Vale Hotel. The aim was evidently to provide Lucy Hurlock with a clear and comprehensive survey of the landscape familiar to her throughout her childhood. Lt.-Col. Brooks has pointed out that Constable again achieved a study of meticulous accuracy when he painted a later picture as a wedding present—the 'Stour Valley and Dedham Village' (Museum of Fine Arts, Boston, Mass.), made for Miss Philadelphia Godfrey in 1814. The quotation given in the entry for No. 279a shows that he later had second thoughts about a panoramic survey of "a valley filled with imagery".

17 *Study of a nude male figure, seated, with his left arm outstretched and resting his head on his right arm.* *c.*1800 Plate 8

Black and white chalk on brown paper. $21\frac{3}{4} \times 17\frac{1}{4}$ ins. (555 × 438 mm.)
No. 42–1873

Given by the Rev. R. C. Lathom Browne.
Inscribed on the back in ink *Drawn by my Father John Constable R.A. C. G. Constable.*
Shirley, *Connoisseur*, Vol. XCI, 1933, p. 218, No. 33, dates *c.*1820, but the drawing is clearly contemporary with Nos. 18–20.
(See note following No. 20)

18 *Study of a nude male figure, standing with his back bent and his left arm shading his eyes.* *c.*1800 Plate 8

Black and white chalk on grey paper. $22\frac{5}{8} \times 12\frac{7}{8}$ ins. (576 × 328 mm.)
No. 43–1873 (E.5768–1910)

Given by the Rev. R. C. Lathom Browne.

Inscribed on the back in pencil *Drawn by my Father John Constable R.A. C. G. Constable.*
Shirley, *Connoisseur*, Vol. XCI, p. 215, No. 3 (as *c.*1800).
(See note following No. 20)

*c.*1800 Plate 9

19 *Study of a recumbent nude male figure.*

Black and white chalk on brown paper. $16\frac{5}{8} \times 19\frac{1}{2}$ ins. (424 × 495 mm.)
No. 44–1873

Given by the Rev. R. C. Lathom Browne.
Inscribed on the back in pencil *Drawn by my Father John Constable R.A. C. G. Constable* and again *Drawn by my Father John Constable R.A.*
Shirley, *Connoisseur*, Vol. XCI, p. 215, No. 2 (as *c.*1800) and reproduced fig. V.
Holmes, p. 239, dates 1800; he does not list Nos. 17, 18 or 20.
(See note following No. 20)

*c.*1800 Plate 9

20 *Study of a nude male figure, seated, with his right foot on a round block and his head thrown back.*

Charcoal and black and white chalk on grey paper.
$20\frac{3}{8} \times 14\frac{1}{8}$ ins. (518 × 360 mm.) No. 45–1873 (E. 3005–1911)
Given by the Rev. R. C. Lathom Browne.
Inscribed on the back in ink *Drawn by my Father John Constable R.A. C. G. Constable.*
Shirley, *Connoisseur*, Vol. XCI, p. 215, No. 1 (as *c.*1800).

NOTE ON NOS. 17–20

On admission to the Academy Schools Constable worked hard at the customary academic discipline of drawing from the antique and from the life. Leslie (L. ed. S., p. 13) says "I have seen no studies made by Constable at the Academy from the antique, but many chalk drawings and oil paintings from the living model, all of which have great breadth of light and shade, though they are sometimes defective in outline".
Shirley, in the article cited in Nos. 17–20, entitled 'John Constable and The Nude', points out that Constable drew from the life throughout his career, and he sets out to classify the known drawings and paintings of the nude by Constable in groups by date. He gives reasons for assigning three of those in the Museum to the earliest group, from the first period of Constable's career as an art student, *c.*1800; the fourth is clearly contemporary with them. More than any of the groups assigned to later dates they conform to Leslie's characterisation—breadth of light and shade and weakness of outline.
The inscriptions on the back were all written by the artist's second son, Charles Golding Constable (1821–79).

1801

In 1801 Constable painted for Mr. John Reade a view of 'Old Hall, East Bergholt' (see note following No. 32, and No. 42a). Nos. 21–32 are pages from the sketch-book he used on his visit to Derbyshire in the same year.

21 *Matlock High Tor.* 1801, August 4 Plate 10

Pencil and sepia wash. $6\frac{7}{8} \times 10\frac{3}{8}$ ins. (175×264 mm.) No. 247*a*–1888
Page from a sketch-book.
Inscribed in top right corner in pencil by the artist with an almost illegible inscription which appears to read *Matlock Tor . . . 4 1801*. Inscribed on the back in ink in another hand *Aug 4th 1801*.

Mr. A. L. Thorpe, Curator of the Derby Museum and Art Gallery, confirms that the view is of Matlock High Tor from the south, taken from the centre of what is now Matlock Bath village; compare No. 29.
(See note following No. 32)

22 *A lead mine at the foot of Mam Tor.* 1801, August 12 Plate 10

Pencil and sepia wash. $7 \times 10\frac{3}{8}$ ins. (176×264 mm.) No. 247*e*–1888
Page from a sketch-book.
Inscribed in top right corner in pencil by the artist *Augst 12. Lead Mine at the foot of Mam Tor*; also with the serial number *11*. On the back is a copy of the inscription in ink in another hand (with *Man* for *Mam*).
(See note following No. 32)

23 *On the Dove near Buxton.* 1801, August 12 Plate 11

Pencil and sepia wash. $7 \times 10\frac{1}{4}$ ins. (176×262 mm.) No. 247*b*–1888
Page from a sketch-book.
Inscribed in top left corner in pencil by the artist *Augst 12 on the Dove near Buxton*; also with the serial number *13*. On the back is a copy of the inscription in ink in another hand.
(See note following No. 32)

24 *Chatsworth Park.* 1801, August 17 Plate 11

Pencil and sepia wash. $6\frac{3}{4} \times 10\frac{1}{8}$ ins. (171×257 mm.) No. 602–1888
Page from a sketch-book.

Inscribed at top right in pencil by the artist *Chatsworth Park Augst 17*; also at top left with a truncated serial number, perhaps *2*. Inscribed on the back in ink in another hand *Augst 17th* and in pencil *M.L.C.* [Maria Louisa Constable].
(See note following No. 32)

1801, August 17
Plate 12

25 *Bridge with trees and buildings, at Haddon.*

Pencil and sepia wash. $6\frac{3}{4} \times 10\frac{1}{4}$ ins. (171×259 mm.) No. 610–1888
Page from a sketch-book.
Inscribed at top right in pencil by the artist *Haddon 17 Aug* [the 7 appears to be written over an *8* or *6*]; also with the serial number *15*. On the back are three or four sketchy pencil drawings of figures (not reproduced). Inscribed on the back in ink in another hand *Haddon Aug 17*—and in pencil *M.L.C.* [Maria Louisa Constable].
(See note following No. 32)

1801, August 17
Plate 12

26 *Haddon Hall.*

Pencil and sepia wash. $6\frac{3}{4} \times 10\frac{1}{8}$ ins. (171×258 mm.) No. 805–1888
Page from a sketch-book.
Inscribed in top right corner in pencil by the artist *Haddon Augst 17*; also with the serial number *18*. Inscribed on the back in ink in another hand *17th Aug*—and in pencil *M.L.C.* [Maria Louisa Constable].
(See note following No. 32)

1801, August 18
Plate 13

27 *The entrance to the village of Edensor.*

Pencil and sepia wash. $6\frac{7}{8} \times 10\frac{3}{8}$ ins. (175×264 mm.) No. 247*c*–1888
Page from a sketch-book.
Inscribed in top right corner in pencil by the artist *Edensor Augst 18*; also with the serial number *21*, and in lower left corner in pencil *Edensor 18 Augst 1801*. On the back is an inscription in ink in another hand to the same effect.
No. 28 is drawn from almost exactly the same viewpoint.
(See note following No. 32)

[1801, August]
Plate 13

28 *The entrance to the village of Edensor.*

Pencil and sepia wash. $6\frac{5}{8} \times 10\frac{1}{8}$ ins. (170×257 mm.) No. 601–1888
Page from a sketch-book.
Inscribed in top right corner in pencil with the serial number *20*.
This view is taken from almost exactly the same point as No. 27, but it is somewhat more elaborately treated.

28a On the back is a rough pencil drawing of a wooded landscape. Plate 27
Drawn surface $4\frac{1}{8} \times 6\frac{5}{8}$ ins. (106×170 mm.)
(See note following No. 32)

29 *Matlock High Tor.* [1801, August] Plate 14

Pencil and sepia wash. $6\frac{7}{8} \times 10\frac{3}{8}$ ins. (175×264 mm.) No. 247–1888
Page from a sketch-book.
Inscribed in top right corner in pencil with the serial number *6*.
Mr. A. L. Thorpe has identified the view as Matlock High Tor from the south; compare No. 21.
(See note following No. 32)

30 *A view in Derbyshire.* [1801, August] Plate 14

Pencil and sepia wash. $6\frac{7}{8} \times 10\frac{3}{8}$ ins. (175×265 mm.) No. 247*d*–1888
Page from a sketch-book.
Inscribed at top in pencil with the serial number *28*.
Mr. A. L. Thorpe considers that the view may be of the River Wye above Monsal Dale, but that it may be of the upper reaches of the River Dove.
(See note following No. 32)

31 *A quarry for mill-stones in Derbyshire.* [1801, August] Plate 15

Pencil and sepia wash. $6\frac{7}{8} \times 10\frac{3}{8}$ ins. (175×263 mm.) No. 247*f*–1888
Page from a sketch-book on paper with truncated watermark: I| J WH| .
(See note following No. 32)

32 *A quarry for mill-stones in Derbyshire.* [1801, August] Plate 15

Pencil and sepia wash. $6\frac{7}{8} \times 10\frac{3}{8}$ ins. (175×264 mm.) No. 247*g*–1888
On paper with truncated watermark: I| J WH| .

32a On the back is a pencil sketch of the quarry seen from above. Plate 27

NOTE ON NOS. 21–32

The twelve leaves of Whatman paper Nos. 21–32 come from the same sketch-book. Leslie (L. ed. S., p. 16) gives the following description of its contents: "In the year 1801, it appears by one of his sketch books, he visited Derbyshire. The sketches he made there, like those at Helmingham, are slight and general. They are washed in one tint only, and with no attempt at the beautiful finish or force of chiaroscuro seen

in his later studies". The hinge marks are not always apparent, having in some cases been trimmed away, but the general coincidence of style, medium, subject-matter and size justifies the linking of the undated drawings (Nos. 28–32) with the visit to the Peak District and Derbyshire. The height of the untrimmed pages of the sketch-book tapers from about 175 mm. (hinge side) to 170 mm.
The dated drawings give the following itinerary: 4 Aug. Matlock; 12 Aug. Mam Tor and the Dove near Buxton; 17 Aug. Chatsworth Park and Haddon Hall; 18 Aug. Edensor. The entry in Farington's *Diary* for 19 August 1801 (Greig, Vol. I, p. 312) shows that Constable was still in Dovedale on that day: "At 9 o'clock we entered *Dovedale, I made a sketch of the first appearance of the entrance*, and while I was so employed *Mr Constable* came up to me, He having come a 2d time to make studies here. He was accompanied by a Mr Whaley who lives near Newcastle in Staffordshire". (Mr. Whalley was a member of the family into which Constable's sister Martha had married.)
Two sketches in the collection of Dr. H. A. C. Gregory (sold at Messrs. Sotheby's, 20 July 1949), which appear from their measurements to have come from the same sketch-book, are thus described in the sale catalogue (entries slightly abbreviated): "Lot 63. A view of Derwent Dale, inscribed *Derwent Dale Aug 8*; pen and sepia wash, $6\frac{1}{2} \times 10$ in."
"Lot 64. A view near Derwent Dale; sepia wash, $6\frac{1}{2} \times 10\frac{1}{16}$ ins."
A drawing made on the same tour, but not from the sketch-book, was Lot 65 at the same sale: "A view of Baslow, inscribed *Baslow Augt. 14 1801*; pencil heightened with white on blue paper, $10\frac{3}{8} \times 13\frac{5}{8}$ ins."
Mr. Iolo Williams has pointed out the strong resemblance between the style of these drawings and those of Sir George Beaumont (*The Times*, 1 May 1953). Farington's *Diary* for 1800 and 1801 records, largely in unpublished extracts, many visits paid by Constable to Sir George Beaumont to study his collections, to copy pictures, and for encouragement. Farington's entry for 13 July 1801 describing the painting 'Old Hall, East Bergholt' shows that he was aware of the resemblance in style at this stage: "Constable called on me & I on him to see a picture, a view of Mr. Reads house near Dedham. It is painted on a coloured ground which He has preserved through the blue of his sky as well as the clouds.—His manner of painting the trees is so like Sir George Beaumont's that they might be taken for his" (Greig, Vol. I, p. 309).

1802

Constable exhibited for the first time at the Royal Academy in 1802, his entry being called 'A Landscape'; this painting has not yet been identified. He visited Windsor in May (see Nos. 33–35), and was at East Bergholt in the summer and autumn.

33 *Windsor Castle from the river.* 1802, May 17 Plate 16

Pencil and red chalk and water-colour. $10\frac{1}{4} \times 14\frac{3}{8}$ ins. (259×365 mm.) No. 804–1888

Inscribed in lower left corner in pencil by the artist *May 17. 1802. 7—morning.* (See note following No. 35)

34 *Windsor Castle from the river.* 1802, May Plate 16

Pencil and red chalk and water-colour. $10\frac{1}{4} \times 14\frac{5}{8}$ ins. (259×370 mm.) No. 803–1888

Not dated, but clearly made on the same occasion as No. 33 from a viewpoint further to the right.
(See note following No. 35)

35 *The Thames, with Eton College and Chapel.* [1802, May] Plate 17

Pencil and water-colour. $7\frac{1}{8} \times 14\frac{1}{4}$ ins. (181×361 mm.) No. 239–1888
This early drawing is carried out in a fuller range of colour than Nos. 33 and 34. Since Constable is not recorded to have made another visit to Windsor or its neighbourhood until 1816, it may reasonably be assigned to the visit of May 1802.

NOTE ON NOS. 33–35

An unpublished extract in Farington's *Diary* for 12 May 1802 records that Constable called on him to say that he was going to Windsor with Dr. Fisher (the future Bishop of Salisbury) to be introduced to General Harcourt, who wanted someone to teach drawing at a military School. Constable called on Dr. Fisher later, on 20 May, having paid the visit and being very much exercised in mind as to whether he should take the offered position. Leslie (L. ed. S., p. 20) records that Benjamin West strongly dissuaded him from accepting it, and undertook to approach Dr. Fisher and to decline it on Constable's behalf without giving offence. In his letter of 29 May 1802 to Dunthorne, from which another excerpt is given below (see note following No. 40), Constable says, referring to his visit to Windsor: "I have had much ado to keep my mind together enough to write to be understood owing to a reumatick pain in one side of my head particularly in my teeth and lower jaw which has caused one cheek to swell very much. I beleive I got cold at Windsor as I was there in the late severe weather" (L. ed. S., p. 21). Nos. 33, 34 and probably 35 were made during this visit.

36 *Dedham Vale: evening.* 1802, July Plate 18

Oil on canvas. $12\frac{1}{2} \times 17$ ins. (318×432 mm.) No. 587–1888
The canvas was relined in 1893. The stretcher is inscribed in pencil *July 1802* and *Towards Evening painted by J Constable RA 1802.* These are presumably

based upon inscriptions on the original canvas. The *Inventory of Art Objects 1888* notes that the painting was dated at the back *July 1802.*
Lt.-Col. C. A. Brooks identifies this as a scene from the fields near Vale Farm, East Bergholt, looking up the valley towards Stoke-by-Nayland. No. 98 is from a similar view point.
(See note following No. 40)

1802, September
Plate 21

37 *Dedham Vale.*

Oil on canvas. $17\frac{1}{8} \times 13\frac{1}{2}$ ins. (435 × 344 mm.) No. 124–1888
The canvas has been relined. A T-shaped tear to the right of the lower fork in the large tree (right foreground) has been repaired, and also a line of small holes on the right. The stretcher is inscribed in pencil *Sep 1802 John . . . . . Isabel Constable.* The gap indicated by the dots is occupied by a label recording that three small damaged areas were coloured over by the restorers in 1893.
The date on the stretcher is presumably based upon some inscription visible on the back of the canvas before it was relined at an unrecorded date. The picture is painted over a brown ground which is visible in places.

The painting has long been recognised as the source from which Constable composed his large oil painting 'Dedham Vale', exhibited at the Royal Academy in 1828 (Holmes, p. 239). Shirley (L. ed. S., p. 22) points out that the composition is based upon Claude's 'Hagar and the Angel' (now in the National Gallery, No. 61). Leslie (L. ed. S., p. 5) records that Constable first saw the picture, which was then in the collection of Sir George Beaumont, at the house of the Dowager Lady Beaumont in Dedham, and that he regarded this event as an important epoch in his life. An unpublished entry in Farington's *Diary* (for 29 May 1800) says that Constable was then copying Sir George Beaumont's "small upright Claude"; and a letter to Dunthorne printed by Leslie without date (L. ed. S., p. 14) refers to his copying the 'Hagar'. A copy by Constable of the same work was Lot 48 on the first day of the Executors' sale of 1838, and fetched £53. 11s. 0 (Holmes, p. 230).
(See note following No. 40)

1802, October 3
Plate 17

38 *A mill on the banks of the River Stour.*

Black chalk, charcoal and traces of red chalk. $9\frac{1}{2} \times 11\frac{3}{4}$ ins. (240 × 298 mm.)
No. 841–1888
Inscribed on the back in pencil by the artist *3 Octr. Noon 1802.* This inscription is repeated in ink in another hand. The last figure in Constable's inscription might be read as *3*, but the ink copy is clear.
Mr. Harold Day has presented to the collections a hitherto unrecorded engraving of this composition, which he acquired at the sale of the contents of Kentwell

Hall, Long Melford, 8 September 1970 (E. 1029–1970). It is lettered: *A Mill on the Banks of the River Stour. J. Constable pinxt. J. Ogborne Fecit. Published by Thos. Thane 1810.* There are slight variations from No. 38: a boat with figures has been added on the right, and the line of posts omitted at the bottom right hand edge. The use of the word *pinxt* in the inscription might suggest that Constable made an oil painting or water-colour from the drawing.
John Hayes, in 'The Drawings of George Frost', *Master Drawings*, Vol. 4, No. 2, 1966, p. 167 and n. 34 refers to this drawing as being specially close to Frost in style.

39 *Valley scene, with trees.* 1802, October 16

Plate 20

Oil on canvas. $14\frac{1}{8} \times 12\frac{7}{8}$ ins. (359×326 mm.) No. 142–1888

The canvas, which has not been relined, is inscribed on the back in red by the artist *Oct 16. 1802* (the year is virtually unreadable by ordinary light but is clear under ultra-violet radiation). Holmes, p. 239, who did not know of the date on the canvas, which was not recorded in the *Inventory of Art Objects 1888*, assigns the painting to the year 1804 on grounds of style.
(See note following No. 40)

40 *A wood.* *c.*1802

Plate 19

Oil on canvas. $13\frac{1}{2} \times 17$ ins. (343×432 mm.) No. 586–1888

The canvas was relined in 1893. The stretcher is inscribed in pencil *A Wood. Painted by J. Constable R.A. early beautiful.* This appears to have been written in the reliner's workshop but there is nothing to show whether or not it was based upon an earlier inscription on the original canvas.

Holmes, p. 239, dates the sketch *c.*1804, the year to which he assigned No. 39 at a time when the date on it had not been read. Shirley (L. ed. S., p. 34) dates *c.*1803. Holmes is probably right in thinking that there are no stylistic grounds for separating this picture from No. 39 in date, and No. 40 may accordingly be dated *c.*1802.

NOTE ON NOS. 36, 37, 39 AND 40

In the letter of 29 May 1802 to Dunthorne which contains the first systematic formulation of his artistic faith, Constable says (L. ed. S., p. 21) "For these two past years I have been running after pictures and seeking the truth at secondhand. I have . . . endeavoured to make my performances look as if really *executed* by other men . . . I shall shortly return to Bergholt where I shall make some laborious studies from nature—and I shall endeavour to get a pure and unaffected representation of the scenes that may employ me with respect to Colour particularly and anything else—drawing I am prety well master of.—There is little or nothing in the [Royal

Academy] exhibition worth looking up to. *There is room enough for a natural painture*★." Nos. 36, 37 and 39 which bear dates in July, September and October 1802, and perhaps also No. 40, are among the fruits of this resolve. They are recognised as the paintings in which Constable's true bent first expresses itself, and the first auguries of his forthcoming excellence in the realistic interpretation of Nature. In the following year four works by Constable were accepted for the Royal Academy exhibition, his greatest official success in this decade. Two of them were listed as 'A Study from Nature', and two as 'A Landscape'. Although their late numbers in the Academy catalogue indicate that two or three may have been drawings, there is a possibility that one or more of Nos. 36, 37, 39 and 40 may have been among those exhibited in 1803. In any event these sketches may have been among those which Constable showed Farington on 23 March 1803: "Constable called & brought several small studies which He painted from nature in the neighbourhood of Dedham" (Greig, Vol. II, p. 88). A painting of similar type, 'The Vale of Dedham', is reproduced in the *Connoisseur*, Vol. CII, 1938, p. 323.

1803

In 1803 Constable exhibited four works at the Royal Academy (see note following No. 40). In April he made the trip from London to Deal in the East Indiaman *Coutts* (see Nos. 41–50). He took leave of Farington before going into Essex on 20 June (Greig, Vol. II, p. 111).

1803, April 24
Plate 24

41 *A ship under sail.*

Pencil and grey wash. $8\frac{1}{8} \times 10$ ins. (205×255 mm.) No. 809–1888
On laid paper watermarked: H & W below a horn in a cartouche.
Inscribed along lower edge in pencil (in part illegible) by the artist . . . *ton 24 Apl. 1803.*
(See note following No. 50)

[1803, April]
Plate 22

42 *View from the shore over the Thames or the Medway.*

Pencil and grey wash. $9\frac{1}{2} \times 13\frac{1}{4}$ ins. (240×338 mm.) No. 806–1888
On laid paper with slightly truncated watermark: J WHATMAN.
(See note following No. 50.)

★ Some commentators have interpreted this as a nonce-word for "style of painting"; but in the same letter, as transcribed by Shirley, Constable refers to "a good painture" and "the french painture" where he can only mean "painter" by the noun.

42a *Old Hall, East Bergholt.* Plate 26

Pencil; with additional rough ink scribbles on the sheet.

The house shown in the drawing on the *verso* is identifiable as the manor house of East Bergholt by comparison with the oil painting 'Old Hall, East Bergholt', painted by Constable in 1801 for Mr. John Reade and until recently in the possession of Miss Muriel and Miss Kathleen Gore, descendants of Mr. Peter Godfrey, who succeeded Mr. John Reade as owner of Old Hall in 1804 and as lord of the manor in 1811 (*Country Life*, Vol. CXX, 1956, pp. 998–9, with reproduction p. 998; sold at Messrs. Sotheby's, 2 July 1958, Lot 135).

43 *Shipping under a cloudy sky in the Thames.* [1803, April] Plate 22

Pencil and grey wash. $7\frac{3}{4} \times 12\frac{3}{4}$ ins. (197×323 mm.) No. 807–1888
On laid paper watermarked: Britannia in a cartouche, surmounted by a crown.
(See note following No. 50)

44 *Shipping in the Thames.* [1803, April] Plate 23

Pencil and grey wash and water-colour. $7\frac{1}{2} \times 12\frac{3}{8}$ ins. (193×316 mm.) No. 808–1888
On laid paper watermarked: T WICKWAR 1801.
(See note following No. 50)

45 *Shipping in the Thames.* [1803, April] Plate 24

Pencil. 8×10 ins. (205×255 mm.) No. 831–1888
On laid paper watermarked: M below a horn in a cartouche.
(See note following No. 50)

46 *A ship at anchor and other shipping in the Thames.* [1803, April] Plate 25

Pencil. $7\frac{7}{8} \times 13\frac{3}{8}$ ins. (200×341 mm.) No. 830–1888
On laid paper watermarked: T WICKWAR 1801.
(See note following No. 50)

47 *A man-of-war.* [1803, April] Plate 24

Pencil. $8\frac{1}{8} \times 10\frac{1}{8}$ ins. (207×257 mm.) No. 829–1888
On laid paper watermarked: M below a horn in a cartouche.

47a On the back is a pencil sketch of men-of-war in the Medway. Plate 24
(See note following No. 50)

[1803, April] Plate 25

48 *A brig at anchor and other shipping in the Thames.*

Pencil. $7\frac{7}{8} \times 10$ ins. (199×253 mm.) No. 612–1888
On laid paper watermarked: an ornamental cartouche surmounted by a crown.
(See note following No. 50)

[1803, April] Plate 23

49 *Shipping in a breeze in the Thames or Medway.*

Pencil and grey wash. $4 \times 6\frac{5}{8}$ ins. (100×169 mm.) No. 810–1888
On laid paper with truncated watermark: Britannia in a cartouche.

Plate 27

49a On the back is a slight pencil sketch of a ship under sail.
(See note following No. 50)

[1803, April] Plate 26

50 *Off the North Foreland, Kent.*

Pencil, pen and ink and water-colour. $4\frac{1}{8} \times 12\frac{5}{8}$ ins. (108×321 mm.)
No. 180–1888
On laid paper with slightly truncated watermark: GR surmounted by a crown.
On the back (not reproduced amongst the plates) is a slight sketch of the top of a mast.

NOTE ON NOS. 41–50

Constable describes his trip in April from London to Deal in the East Indiaman *Coutts* in his letter of 23 May 1803 to Dunthorne (L. ed. S., pp. 23–5). He left the ship at Gravesend to walk to Rochester and Chatham: from Chatham he hired a boat to see the men-of-war in the Medway and sketch H.M.S. *Victory* in three views. Then he rejoined the ship at Gravesend. She lay under the North Foreland three days because the weather was stormy and, in the confusion of leaving the ship when Deal was finally reached, he left his drawings behind. As he had been nearly a month on board and had been "much employed in making drawings of ships in all situations" this was a serious loss to him. However, Leslie records that he recovered his sketches, which were about 130 in number. Subsequently he made use of some of the sketches for the drawing 'His Majesty's Ship *Victory*, Capt. H. Harvey, in the memorable Battle of Trafalgar, between two French ships of the line' (No. 65 in this Catalogue).
The ten drawings Nos. 41, 42 *recto* and 43–50 are all assigned to this voyage down the Thames and the Medway. No. 41 was certainly made then, since it is dated 24 April 1803, and the others are clearly homogeneous in style and subject-matter. A drawing from the same series in the collection of Lady Harrington shows the East Indiaman *Coutts* and another named ship, the *Woodford*. It is on a sheet of paper measuring $7\frac{5}{8} \times 12\frac{7}{8}$ ins, and watermarked: T WICKWAR 1801. A drawing of the same series was No. 49 in an exhibition at Colchester in 1950 of drawings from Lt.-Col. J. H. Constable's collection; it measured 8×10 inches, and was reproduced in the

catalogue of that exhibition. Other drawings of the series were in the collections of the late Sir Bruce Ingram and the late Mr. A. P. Oppé. Four others were sold as Lots 1–4 at Messrs. Christie's, 26 July 1957; Lot 3 showed Tilbury Fort and Gravesend Church and Lot 4, of Chalk Church near Gravesend, was dated on the back 18 April 1803.
The influence of Van de Velde has been seen in these drawings (Key, p. 22) and it is interesting to note that in an unpublished entry of Farington's *Diary* (21 May 1803) Constable is recorded as saying that he did not think Turner's pictures were "true to nature and a fine selection like the works of Vandevelde, Backhuysen etc. . . ."

51 *Landscape with cows and trees.* 1803, June 28 Plate 28

Pencil and water-colour. $7\frac{1}{2}\times9\frac{1}{8}$ ins. (189×233 mm.) No. 627–1888
Inscribed on the back in pencil (not in the artist's usual hand; perhaps rewritten by another hand from an erased inscription) *Tuesday Noon 28 June 1803* and *J. Constable R.A.*
On laid paper watermarked: an ornamental cartouche surmounted by a crown.

Holmes, p. 239, comments "Apparently an imitation of Gainsborough". The drawing is certainly in the style of Gainsborough's landscape compositions, yet the inscription shows that it was not a studio work but made from nature in the open air. Constable was in Suffolk or Essex at the time this drawing was made.

52 *Warehouses and shipping on the Orwell at Ipswich.* 1803, October 5 Plate 29

Pencil and water-colour. $9\frac{5}{8}\times13$ ins. (245×331 mm.) No. 626–1888
Inscribed on the back in pencil by the artist *5 Oct—1803 Ipswich.*
Lt.-Col. C. A. Brooks has shown that the building on the right is an old malting next to Stoke Bridge, now used as a seed granary.

1804

In 1804 Constable did not exhibit; according to Farington he spent much of his time at East Bergholt painting portraits of the local farmers and their wives. He first saw 'The Château de Steen' by Rubens in Sir George Beaumont's collection in this year (Greig, Vol. II, p. 189). His visit to Hampshire is established by the inscription on No. 53.

1804
Plate 29

53 *A view at Hursley, Hampshire.*

Black chalk and water-colour. $4\frac{3}{8} \times 14\frac{3}{4}$ ins. (112 × 374 mm.) No. 796–1888
On a sheet of laid paper which had at one time been folded in the middle, with truncated watermark: W S| 17|.
Inscribed on the back in ink by the artist *Hursley Hants 1804.*

Hursley House was at this time the property of Sir William Heathcote, 3rd Bart. He was a cousin of Sir Gilbert Heathcote, 4th Bart., of Normanton Hall, whose wife Katherine Sophia Manners was later a patroness of Constable. She was connected with the Dysart family, with which Constable had relations from an early stage of his career (see note to No. 54). It is therefore possible that he was staying at Hursley House as the guest of Sir William Heathcote when he made this drawing, but nothing else is recorded of the visit.
Lot 33 in the sale of the property of Eustace Constable held at Messrs. Christie's, 16 April 1896 (described in the catalogue as "Thursley [*sic*], Hants, 1804") was evidently made on the same visit and Lot 198 in the sale at Messrs. Christie's, 17 June 1892, of the property of Miss Isabel Constable (also described as "Thursley, Hants") may also have been made then.

1805

In 1805 Constable exhibited 'A Landscape: Moonlight' at the Royal Academy. According to an unpublished entry in the *Diary*, he called on Farington on 1 June to say that he had been engaged to paint an altarpiece for a country church. This picture was probably the altarpiece for Brantham Church which Leslie assigns to the previous year (Beckett, I, pp. 18–9).

1805, November 3
Plate 30

54 *Study of trees in a park, perhaps Helmingham Park.*

Pencil and water-colour. $6\frac{3}{4} \times 5\frac{3}{8}$ ins. (173 × 137 mm.) No. 598–1888
Inscribed on the back in ink, apparently over a pencil inscription by the artist, and with an ink copy in another hand of this inscription *3 Novr. 1805—Noon—the Park.*

Shirley identifies the scene (L. ed. S., p. 35 and Pl. 28) as Helmingham. Helmingham Park, Suffolk, was a seat of the Earl of Dysart, for whom Constable was to copy portraits in 1807. As early as 1800 Constable had written to Dunthorne "Here I am quite alone among the oaks and solitudes of Helmingham Park . . . There are abundance of fine trees of all sorts, and the park on the whole affords good objects rather than fine scenery" (L. ed. S., p. 16). It remained a favourite sketching ground for Constable.

55 *Landscape with trees and a distant mansion.* c.1805 Plate 30

Pencil and water-colour. 7×7 ins. (177×178 mm.) No. 213–1888
Close in technique to No. 54 and like it with autumn tints; therefore ascribed to the same year and season. The composition recalls that of No. 37, which in its turn has been associated with Claude's 'Hagar and the Angel'.

56 *Dedham Vale.* c.1805 Plate 33

Pencil and water-colour. $6\frac{3}{4}\times 10\frac{5}{8}$ ins. (171×271 mm.) No. 599–1888
Close in technique to No. 54 and therefore ascribed to the same year; the autumn tints suggest the same conclusion. Holmes, p. 240, identifies as a view of Dedham from East Bergholt, and dates 1806. He may well be justified in this dating by the similarity between No. 56 and L.B.20*a* in the British Museum, which is dated June 1806.

57 *Study of ash and other trees.* c.1800–5 Plate 31

Black and white chalk on blue laid paper. $19\frac{5}{8}\times 14$ ins. (497×355 mm.) No. 843–1888
This undated drawing, with its similarity to those produced by Constable's sketching companion George Frost under the influence of Gainsborough, may be compared with the black chalk drawings reproduced in Holmes, *Constable, Gainsborough and Lucas* (privately printed, 1921), and in particular with Nos. 2, 4 and 14 in that volume, which Holmes assigns respectively to 1801, 1802 and 1799. Holmes, p. 239, assigns the Museum's drawing to 1804; Shirley (L. ed. S., p. 35) to 1806. For a discussion of the influence of Frost on Constable, with a number of comparative illustrations, see 'The Drawings of George Frost, 1745–1821' by John Hayes, *Master Drawings*, Vol. 4, No. 2, 1966, esp. pp. 166–8. Hayes considers that the results of Constable's imitation of Frost are to be seen most clearly in 1802, e.g. in No. 38.

58 *Landscape with buildings in the distance.* c.1800–5 Plate 32

Pencil and water-colour. $7\frac{3}{8}\times 11$ ins. (186×280 mm.) No. 214–1888
(See note following No. 60)

59 *A bridge over the Stour.* c.1800–5 Plate 32

Pencil and water-colour. $6\frac{3}{4}\times 8\frac{3}{4}$ ins. (171×221 mm.) No. 593–1888
On laid paper.
Lt.-Col. C. A. Brooks has identified this structure as the New Fen Bridge over the Stour: it no longer exists. The same bridge is to be seen in the left hand edge

of No. 109. The tower of Dedham Church is seen in the distance in this drawing. (See following No. 60.)

c.1800–5
Plate 33

60 *Dedham Vale, from East Bergholt: sunset.*

Pencil and water-colour. 4×8 ins. (101×202 mm.) No. 592–1888
On laid paper.
Inscribed on the back in pencil by the artist *E. Bergholt* and with monogram *JC*. That the scene is Dedham Vale is established by the presence in the foreground of the trees seen in the middle distance of Sir Richard Proby's painting 'Dedham Vale' of 1811, with the ridge beyond seen from much the same angle.

NOTE ON NOS. 58–60

These drawings may be grouped together as all being executed with a firm under-drawing in pencil or black chalk washed with water-colour in greyish tones of green and blue, perhaps suggested by the example of Girtin. They appear to be more confident in handling than the Derbyshire sketches (Nos. 21–32) of 1801, but less free than the Lake District sketches (Nos. 72–94) of 1806, which represent the furthest advance made by Constable in this particular manner. The dated drawings nearest in style are No. 35, assignable to 1802, and L.B.20*a* in the British Museum, of June 1806. Holmes, p. 240, lists Nos. 58–60 together with No. 56, under the year 1806.

c.1800–5
Plate 28

61 *Cattle near the edge of a wood.*

Pencil and water-colour. 8×9¾ ins. (203×249 mm.) No. 595–1888
On laid paper watermarked: Britannia in a cartouche, surmounted by a crown.

Holmes, p. 240, says "Apparently an imitation of Gainsborough" and dates *c.* 1805. Comparison with No. 51, which is dated 1803, suggests that it may have been painted slightly earlier; indeed, in that year. See also Mary Woodall, *Gainsborough's Landscape Drawings*, London, 1939, p. 87.

c.1792–3?
Plate 34

62 *Ruins of a church.*

Pencil. 6×9 ins. (152×230 mm.) No. 280–1888
On coarse laid paper, much foxed.
Since the first edition of this catalogue was published a drawing of the High Street, Dedham has come to light, which had formerly been in the collections of Isabel Constable and Alfred Tidey. This was executed in the same technique and was said to be of *c.*1792–3; the costume of the figures appeared to be consistent with this dating. No. 62 may therefore well be the earliest drawing by Constable in the collection, apart from the sketches of 1790 in the *Juvenile Introduction to History* described on p. 4.

63 *The valley of the Stour, with Dedham in the distance.* c.1800–5 Plate 35

Oil on paper laid on canvas. 19⅝×23¾ ins. (498×600 mm.)

No. 321–1888

The sketch has been relined at an unknown date, and has been treated for damp and discoloration of the whites while in the Museum.

The scene is a panoramic view over the Stour valley looking south towards the estuary; in the foreground is Stratford St. Mary bridge, which divides Suffolk from Essex. The building on the right is the Talbooth.

The back of the stretcher is stencilled with Messrs. Christie's reference number *138 F* and inscribed in chalk *Feb. 17/77*. The lot number, which is partially obscured by the paper backing-up of the picture, is *195*. Lots 171–197 of the sale at Messrs. Christie's on 17 February 1877 comprised "Sketches by J. Constable R.A., the property of the Artist's Family". Lot 195 'Valley of the Stour' was bought in for £49. 7s. Holmes, p. 242, says that No. 63 is possibly the sketch which Constable is said to have made from the top of Langham Church tower but Lt.-Col. C. A. Brooks states that this is not so. He identifies the viewpoint as a cleft slightly to the west of Gun Hill about 600 yards to the east of Langham Church and close to that of No. 37. The view was a favourite one with Constable. Davies, p. 33, in his note on N.G. No. 1822 links that sketch with No. 63 and lists other variants of the view. Of these, the work he records from the J. P. Heseltine collection now belongs to Lt.-Col. C. A. Brooks; it was exhibited at Messrs. Leggatt's Summer Exhibition, 1956 (No. 43, and reproduction on p. 12 of the catalogue).

Holmes dates No. 63 *c.*1810. In view of the tentative nature of the drawing and technique this seems certainly too late. The dated oils of 1802 (Nos. 36, 37 and 39) lay emphasis on the structure of the trees, a feature which is not apparent here. A dating nearer 1800 than 1805 is suggested by these considerations. The other versions discussed in this entry do not appear to be contemporary with No. 63. In 1964 the painting was lightly cleaned and revarnished. During this process certain darkened areas of old retouching were removed. These had been applied to cover small areas of paint loss where the red ground was exposed; these losses had apparently been caused by some form of impurity in the support, ground or adhesive used in laying the paper on canvas. The more disturbing areas of damage were retouched, and the painting now has a far more serene and homogeneous appearance, but this does not appear to call for a revision of the views expressed above about its date.

64 *A lady seated.* c.1805 Plate 34

Pencil and water-colour. 4¼×4¾ ins. (106×121 mm.) No. P.44–1942

On laid paper.

Inscribed on the back in pencil with an illegible scribble, perhaps *11 4* or *Mrs.*

The drawing was bought by the Museum from Messrs. Agnew, November 1942.

The costume is characterised by the strange fashion of a woman's wearing a man's high cravat. This feature is also to be seen in a drawing reproduced from the collection of Mr. L. G. Duke as 'Mr. Hobson of Markfield and Family' in L. ed. S., Pl. 14. It appears from sketch-books and sketches in the Louvre (R.F.1870: 08700, 06078, 06085) that Constable was drawing the Hobson family in 1806. If, as the owner believed, the drawing represents John Harden and his family, this would equally point to a date of 1806 (see note following No. 94). No. 64 in any case belongs to the period when Constable was very active in portraiture, from 1803 onwards, and is probably to be dated not far from the middle of the decade.
There are many portrait sketches of a similar type in the British Museum.

1806

Constable's only exhibit at the Royal Academy in 1806 was No. 65. In June he was at East Bergholt, as is attested by Nos. 66 and 67. In the autumn he paid a visit of some two months to the Lake District and made many drawings, among them Nos. 72–94.

1806 **65** *His Majesty's ship* Victory, *Capt. E. Harvey, in the memorable battle of*
Plate 36 *Trafalgar, between two French ships of the line.*

Water-colour. $20\frac{3}{8} \times 28\frac{7}{8}$ ins. (516×735 mm.) No. 169–1888
On paper laid down on a second sheet watermarked: J WHATMAN | 1804.

The drawing was exhibited with this title as No. 787 in the Royal Academy, 1806. Leslie (L. ed. S., p. 25) says "This subject was suggested to him by hearing an account of the battle from a Suffolk man, who had been on Nelson's ship". Farington (Greig, Vol. III, p. 181) noted on 10 April 1806 "Constable called. He had sent a picture of Ld. Nelson's engagement to the Exhibition". In making the drawing Constable made use of the group of sketches of men-of-war etc. he had made in the Medway in 1803, of which Nos. 41–50 form part. A broadside view of H.M.S. *Victory* dated 18 April 1803, and from the collection of Capt. C. Constable is reproduced in Laird Clowes's *The Royal Navy, a history*, Vol. V. p. 25. It is one of the series of drawings described in the note on Nos. 41–50. That No. 65 is much faded is evident from a band of darker pigment, at the top and right; but it is probable that it was always low in tone and reflected the influence of Girtin, as do the Lake District sketches of this year.

This was the last attempt Constable made to paint a sea-battle. On 2 July 1824, he noted in his diary "There comes a letter from the Gallery [the British Institution], to offer prizes for the best sketches and pictures of the Battles of the Nile and Trafalgar; it does not concern me much" (L. ed. S., p. 168).

66 *East Bergholt Church: south archway of the ruined tower.* — 1806, June 9; Plate 38

Pencil and water-colour. $6\frac{1}{4} \times 4\frac{3}{8}$ ins. (158 × 112 mm.) No. 224–1888
Inscribed on the back in pencil by the artist *E. Bergholt June 9 1806*. The inscription is repeated in ink in another hand.
(See note following No. 71)

67 *East Bergholt Church: view from the east.* — 1806, June; Plate 38

Pencil and water-colour. $5\frac{1}{8} \times 7$ ins. (130 × 179 mm.) No. 346–1888
Inscribed on the back in pencil by the artist *June 1806*; the inscription repeated with brush and water-colour. Also on the back in ink is the serial number *13*.

The drawing does not appear to come from a sketch-book.
(See note following No. 71)

68 *East Bergholt Church: north archway of the ruined tower.* — *c.*1805–11; Plate 37

Pencil and water-colour. $9\frac{7}{8} \times 7\frac{7}{8}$ ins. (250 × 199 mm.) No. 343–1888
On paper watermarked: 1794 J WHATMAN.
Inscribed on the back in pencil *Drawing of East Bergholt Church by J. Constable* and again *East Bergholt Church.*
This drawing is listed at this point of the Catalogue because of its affinities in subject-matter and style with Nos. 66 and 67. Holmes, p. 240, implies that the drawing is dated June 1806, but this is not the case.
(See note following No. 71)

69 *Part of the exterior of East Bergholt Church: the north side.* — *c.*1805–11; Plate 37

Pencil and water-colour. $9\frac{7}{8} \times 7\frac{7}{8}$ ins. (251 × 200 mm.) No. 344–1888
Inscribed on the back in pencil *J. Constable R.A. EB. Church*; also in ink with serial number *20*.
Although Nos. 68 and 69 are of the same size and in similar technique, neither appears to have come from a sketch-book; they are, however, probably contemporary. Holmes, p. 240, implies that No. 69 is dated June 1806, but this is not the case.
(See note following No. 71)

*c.*1805–11
Plate 39

70 *East Bergholt Church: exterior view from the east.*

Pencil and water-colour. $15\frac{3}{8} \times 13\frac{7}{8}$ ins. (389 × 351 mm.) No. 200–1888
There is an old horizontal fold across the centre of the drawing; a tear at the right of it has been repaired.

This large finished water-colour drawing shows the church from a viewpoint near to that of No. 66 and is of similar style. It is also close in style to the drawing 'East Bergholt Church from the south-east', No. 324 in the Lady Lever Art Gallery (Pl. 83 of the catalogue of that Gallery by R. R. Tatlock, 1928, and reproduced in colour in the *Connoisseur*, Vol. XC, 1932, p. 105). The latter drawing, which is signed and dated February 1811, was a copy made at the suggestion of Constable's mother of a drawing her son had given her previously. It was presented to Dr. Rhudde in an attempt to weaken his opposition to Constable's courtship of his grand-daughter Maria Bicknell (Beckett, I, pp. 56–9, correcting Leslie's account of the incident).
(See note following No. 71)

*c.*1805–11
Plate 38

71 *Porch and transept of a church.*

Indian ink and grey and sepia wash. $13\frac{1}{4} \times 17$ ins. (336 × 432 mm.)
No. 608–1888

On the back (not reproduced amongst the plates) is a slight pencil sketch, apparently of the porch of a church, and the pencil inscription *J. Constable R.A.* No. 71 is comparable in style and subject-matter with Nos. 66–70.

NOTE ON NOS. 66–71

These drawings are carried out in a manner which Constable preserved for a number of years when making water-colours of East Bergholt Church, the consistency of which makes the precise dating of uninscribed examples, such as Nos. 68–70, impracticable. An early instance is found in the water-colour 'East Bergholt Church' in the National Gallery of Canada, Ottawa, which is signed and dated 1805, and is virtually identical with No. 70 apart from being two inches more in height. A later example is the drawing of 1811 recorded in the note on No. 70.

1806, September 21
Plate 40

72 *Saddleback and part of Skiddaw.*

Pencil and water-colour. $3 \times 11\frac{5}{8}$ ins. (76 × 295 mm.) No. 794–1888
The drawing was laid on a card inscribed (copying the artist's inscription on the back of the drawing) *Saddle back and part of Skeddaw Sep 21—1806 Stormy Day —Noon.* The inscription is transcribed to this effect in the *Inventory of Art Objects 1888.* On removal of the card it was found that the drawing had been trimmed at the top, cutting off the first half of the artist's inscription in pencil, which runs

obliquely to the present top edge. All that can now be seen of it is *21 Sep. 1806 Stormy Day—noon.* Holmes, p. 240, identifies the viewpoint as Lonscale Fell. (See note following No. 94)

73 *Helvellyn.* 1806, September 21 Plate 40

Pencil and water-colour. $6\frac{1}{4} \times 14\frac{3}{8}$ ins. (158 × 366 mm.) No. 348–1888
Inscribed on the back in pencil by the artist, with deletions as shown ~~*Hellvel*~~ *Helvellin 21st Sepr. 1806—~~rain~~ evening—stormy with slight rain.*
On rough-surfaced laid paper.
Holmes, p. 240, identifies as Helvellyn and the Vale of St. John. A drawing by Constable made on the same day (Boston, Museum of Fine Arts, No. 92.2632, *Catalogue of Paintings . . . in Water Color*, p. 57 and reproduced on p. 225) is inscribed *21 Sepr 1806 St. John's Dale.*
(See note following No. 94)

74 *View in Borrowdale.* 1806, September 25 Plate 42

Pencil and water-colour. $9\frac{1}{2} \times 13\frac{5}{8}$ ins. (243 × 346 mm.) No. 192–1888
On paper watermarked: E & P 1801.
A strip of grey at the top of the sky indicates fading. Inscribed on the back in pencil by the artist *25 Sepr. 1806—Borrowdale—fine clouday day tone very mellow like—the mildest of Gaspar Poussin and Sir G*[*eorge*] *B*[*eaumont*] *& on the whole deeper toned than this drawing—.*
Capt. S. H. Badrock has identified the scene as looking towards Glaramara in the same direction as No. 90, but closer to Glaramara. No. 85 is also taken from a viewpoint near this (see also Nos. 84 and 88).
(See note following No. 94.)

75 *Taylor Ghyll, Sty Head, Borrowdale.* 1806, September 26 Plate 52

Pencil, with grey and pink wash. $19 \times 13\frac{1}{2}$ ins. (484 × 343 mm.)
No. 812–1888
Inscribed on the back in pencil by the artist *26 Sepr. 1806—Sty Head fall—or the Taylor's Ghill—Head of Borrowdale.*
(See note following No. 94)

76 *View in Borrowdale.* 1806, Sept. 2 [. . .] or October 2 Plate 41

Pencil and water-colour. $7\frac{1}{8} \times 18\frac{7}{8}$ ins. (181 × 480 mm.) No. 170–1888
On paper watermarked: E & P 1801.
A strip of blue at the top indicates fading. The drawing is mounted on thin card, which is inscribed on the back in pencil *Borrowdale 2nd Sepr. 1806 morning previous*

to a fine day. This is a copy of the original inscription which was visible before the drawing was mounted on card, and is still discernible when it is held to the light, though Constable wrote *2 Sept.*

The date, though it appears to be correctly transcribed (with the exception of the inserted *nd*), cannot be accepted, since Constable was staying near Kendal in the early part of the month and dated a drawing of Whitbarrow Scar, between Kendal and Windermere, on 2 September (Holmes, p. 240). Constable presumably miswrote 2 September for 2 . . . September or 2 October. He was certainly in Borrowdale from 25 September to 6 October.
(See note following No. 94)

1806, October 2 **77** *View from the top of Honister Crag.*

Plate 41

Pencil and water-colour. $5\frac{5}{8} \times 19\frac{1}{4}$ ins. (144×489 mm.) No. 185–1888
A strip of bluish grey at the top indicates fading. Inscribed on the back in pencil by the artist *from the top of Onister Craig—Oct. 2. 1806—noon.* The word *Onister* is transcribed as *Thiston*(?) in the *Catalogue of Water-Colour Paintings*, 1927, p. 106.
(See note following No. 94.)

1806, October 2 **78** *A bridge, Borrowdale.*

Plate 47

Pencil and water-colour. $7\frac{1}{2} \times 10\frac{5}{8}$ ins. (189×271 mm.) No. 188–1888
On paper watermarked: J RUSE 1800.
There is a small repair at the top left corner. A strip at the top indicates fading. Inscribed on the back in pencil by the artist *Borrowdale Oct. 2. 1806—twylight after a very fine day.*
Holmes, p. 240, identifies as 'Bridge at Grange'.
(See note following No. 94)

1806, October 4 **79** *View in Borrowdale.*

Plate 44

Pencil and water-colour. $5\frac{1}{2} \times 14\frac{7}{8}$ ins. (139×375 mm.) No. 184–1888
A strip at the top indicates fading.

Plate 44 **79a** On the back is a rough pencil sketch of mountains and the inscription by the artist *Borrowdale 4 Octr. 1806 Noon Clouds breaking away after Rain.* Also inscribed in another hand *Constable.*
(See note following No. 94)

1806, October 4 **80** *View in Borrowdale*

Plate 43

Pencil and water-colour. $7\frac{1}{2} \times 10\frac{3}{4}$ ins. (191×274 mm.) No. 187–1888

A strip at the top indicates fading. The back has a rough grey wash over the greater part of it and is inscribed in pencil by the artist, with deletions as shown

Borrowdale 4 Oct 1806—Dark Autumnal day at noon—tone more blooming ~~that~~ [? ~~than~~] this . . . the effect exceeding ~~terrific~~ terrific—and much like the beautiful Gaspar I saw in Margaret St. and in another hand *J. Constable RA.*

Capt. S. H. Badrock has identified the scene as looking towards Gate Crag with Castle Crag to the left. The old Keswick road is seen on the shoulder of the hill on the right. Holmes, p. 240, confuses Nos. 80 and 88, and states that No. 88 is dated 4 October.
(See note following No. 94)

81 *Lodore.* 1806, October 6

Pencil and water-colour. $7\frac{3}{8}\times 10\frac{3}{4}$ ins. (187×273 mm.) No. 178–1888 Plate 45
A strip on the right indicates fading.

81a On the back is a pencil drawing of the same scene from an almost identical view-point, inscribed below in pencil by the artist *Lodore 6 Octr. 1806 noon.* Plate 45

Holmes, p. 240, correctly identifies No. 81 *recto* as Lodore: the inscription had been read (*Inventory of Art Objects 1888*) as *Keswick*, and the drawing had been laid down on card with the inscription inaccurately transcribed *Keswick Oct 5 Morning*. (See note following No. 94)

82 *Derwentwater: stormy evening.* 1806, October 6

Pencil and water-colour. $4\frac{1}{8}\times 9\frac{3}{8}$ ins. (104×239 mm.) No. 179–1888 Plate 46
Inscribed on the back in pencil by the artist *Derwent Lake—Sunday 6 Oct. 1806 —Stormy Evening*. There is possibly another word under *Derwent*. Also on the back, some pencil scribbles, a patch of water-colour and the faint inscription in pencil *24 Sepr—1806*.
Holmes, p. 240, identifies the waterfall on the left as Lodore.
(See note following No. 94)

83 *Sty Head Tarn, Borrowdale.* 1806, October 12

Pencil and water-colour. $4\frac{3}{4}\times 10\frac{5}{8}$ ins. (121×269 mm.) No. 177–1888 Plate 46
On paper watermarked: E & P 1802.
Holmes, p. 240, tentatively identifies as Watendlath Tarn.
On the back (not reproduced amongst the plates) is a rough pencil sketch of the same scenery and the inscription in pencil by the artist *Sty Head Tearn—Borrowdale—Sunday Octr. 12 1806—Noon Great End—Scorfell—Longmell—*.
(See note following No. 94)

1806, October 13
Plate 47

84 *View in Borrowdale.*

Pencil and water-colour. $7\frac{1}{8} \times 15$ ins. (181×382 mm.) No. 193–1888
A strip of blue at the top indicates fading. Inscribed below on left in pencil by the artist *Borrowdale 13th Oct 1806—afternoon.* Inscribed in pencil on the back *Borrowdale—1806 afternoon* and beside a few pencil outlines of hills (not reproduced amongst the plates) *Rostwaite Cum.*

Capt. S. H. Badrock has identified the scene on the *recto* as looking towards Chapel Fell or Rosthwaite Fell and Glaramara. The same fells as in No. 74 are seen in the background. Holmes, p. 240, describes as 'Bridge at Grange'.
(See note following No. 94)

1806, October 13
Plate 48

85 *View in Borrowdale.*

Pencil and water-colour. $5\frac{1}{4} \times 14\frac{7}{8}$ ins. (135×378 mm.) No. 183–1888
A strip of blue and greyish blue along the top indicates fading in the sky, and a band of grey along the right edge indicates that the mountain mass was darker in tone. Inscribed on the back in pencil by the artist *Borrowdale 13 Oct—1806. Evng*—and in another hand *J. Constable.*
Capt. S. H. Badrock has identified this as a scene looking up to the Sty Head Pass, with Glaramara on the left (see Nos. 74, 84, 88 and 90).
(See note following No. 94)

1806, October 19
Plate 48

86 *View in Langdale.*

Pencil and grey wash. $13\frac{1}{2} \times 19\frac{1}{8}$ ins. (344×486 mm.) No. 1256–1888
On paper watermarked: E & P 1801.
Inscribed on the back in pencil by the artist *19 Oct 1806 Langdale* and in another hand *J. Constable.*
(See note following No. 94)

[1806]
Plate 51

87 *Gate Crag, Borrowdale.*

Pencil and water-colour. $17\frac{1}{2} \times 13\frac{1}{2}$ ins. (444×344 mm.) No. 596–1888
On paper watermarked: E & P 1801.
Inscribed in pencil on the back, not in the artist's hand *Cumberland.*
Capt. S. H. Badrock has identified this as a view of Gate Crag, Borrowdale.
(See note following No. 94)

[1806]
Plate 50

88 *Borrowdale: view towards Glaramara.*

Pencil and water-colour. $13\frac{1}{2} \times 17\frac{1}{2}$ ins. (342×441 mm.) No. 181–1888
On paper watermarked: E & P 1801.

Strips of stronger pigment at the top left and right indicate fading. There are some small holes in the paper in the centre of the sky.

Capt. S. H. Badrock has identified the view as a scene from the Watendlath path looking towards Glaramara (see No. 74), the summit of Glaramara being partly obscured by mist (see also Nos. 84, 85 and 90). Holmes, p. 240, confuses Nos. 80 and 88, and states that No. 88 is dated 4 October.
(See note following No. 94)

89 *View in Borrowdale.* [1806] Plate 49

Pencil and water-colour. $7\frac{1}{2} \times 10\frac{3}{4}$ ins. (191 × 274 mm.) No. 182–1888
On paper watermarked: E & P 1802.
Strips at the top to right and left indicate fading.
The title derives only from the entry for this drawing in the *Inventory of Art Objects 1888*.

89a On the back is a pencil sketch of a seated female figure; also a water-colour sketch of a mountain valley. Plate 54
(See note following No. 94)

90 *Borrowdale, looking towards Glaramara.* [1806] Plate 49

Pencil and grey wash. $13\frac{5}{8} \times 19\frac{1}{8}$ ins. (347 × 486 mm.) No. 1257–1888
Inscribed in pencil on the back, not in the artist's hand *J. Constable.*
The scene was formerly described as Langdale but Capt. S. H. Badrock has identified it as a scene linked with Nos. 74, 84, 85 and 88, looking towards Glaramara, perhaps from the Watendlath path.
(See note following No. 94)

91 *A waterfall in the Lake District.* [1806] Plate 52

Pencil, grey and pinkish wash. $15\frac{1}{4} \times 9\frac{5}{8}$ ins. (386 × 245 mm.) No. 811–1888
Inscribed in pencil on the back, not in the artist's hand *Cumberland.*
Capt. S. H. Badrock has suggested that this drawing might represent Lodore Falls. Holmes, p. 240, identifies as Lodore.
(See note following No. 94)

92 *View in the Lake District.* [1806] Plate 53

Pencil and water-colour. $6\frac{3}{4} \times 9\frac{5}{8}$ ins. (173 × 246 mm.) No. 349–1888

Plate 55 **92a** On the back is a pencil and water-colour sketch of a country girl in a shawl; also the inscription in pencil, not in the artist's hand *J. Constable RA.*
(See note following No. 94)

[1806]
Plate 53
93 *View in the Lake District.*

Pencil and water-colour. $11 \times 15\frac{3}{8}$ ins. (279×390 mm.) No. 186–1888
On rough-surfaced laid paper.
A strip of blue at the top indicates fading.
Holmes, p. 240, tentatively identifies as Wetherlam.
(See note following No. 94)

[1806]
Plate 54
94 *Leathes Water (Thirlmere).*

Pencil and grey wash. $5\frac{1}{8} \times 15\frac{1}{4}$ ins. (129×387 mm.) No. 194–1888
On the back (not reproduced amongst the plates) is a slight pencil sketch of mountain scenery.

No. 94 was engraved in mezzotint by Henry Dawe, and published in 1815. The example in the Museum (No. 1253–1888) is lettered: *Drawn by John Constable . . . Engraved by Henry Dawe Leathes Water, or Wythburn Lake, Cumberland. This view is taken from the elevated part of the valley, on the road leading from Grassmere to Keswick, near Dunmail Raise. To the North in the extreme distance, rises Saddleback, and on the right is Helvellyn. London, Published by Mr. Constable, 63, Charlotte Street, Fitzroy Square, May 1, 1815.*

NOTE ON NOS. 72–94

Nos. 72–94 are drawings made by Constable during his only visit to the English Lake District, which occupied him for about two months in the autumn of 1806. An account of this expedition is given by Beryl and Noel Clay in their article 'Constable's visit to the Lakes' (*Country Life*, Vol. LXXXIII, 1938, pp. 393–5), which quotes relevant extracts from the diary of Mrs. Harden of Brathay Hall, with whom Constable stayed for part of the time; the following résumé is based upon that article. Constable undertook the journey on the suggestion of his uncle, David Pike Watts, and at his expense. He travelled with one Gardner (perhaps George, son of the artist Daniel Gardner, a native of Kendal in Westmorland), and they were to stay at the outset of the tour with Worgan, a tenant of a house on Windermere which belonged to Watts. It is not known when Constable arrived in the Lake District, and the earliest date is that on a water-colour drawing in Mr. Gilbert Davis's collection inscribed at the back *Sepr. 1st, 1806, Kendall castle.* On 8 September Constable and Worgan were staying at Brathay Hall, the Hardens' house on Windermere. Constable seems to have left Brathay Hall on or soon after 16 September for a tour of Borrowdale, and he returned there on 16 October. The latest recorded date of the visit is that of 19 October on No. 86. Mrs. Harden comments in her diary on Constable's assiduity in sketching and, besides the twenty-three drawings in the Museum's collections, many others made on this visit are known. Drawings in other ownership which help to fill in the itinerary given by the dated drawings in the Museum's collections are the following:

2 September Whitbarrow Scar. (Holmes, p. 240, when in the possession of H. P. Horne; now in the Ashmolean Museum)

30 September Borrowdale. (Gregory sale, 20 July 1949, Lot 70, *verso*)

1 October Borrowdale. (In extra-illustrated edition of Leslie's *Life of Constable*, formerly belonging to Lord Lee of Fareham)

12 October Ashcourse [Esk Hause?]. (Holmes, p. 240, formerly in the collection of Sir T. Gibson Carmichael, Bart.)

Mrs. Harden's diary also records that Constable painted a portrait of her in oils, apparently beginning it on 14 September (when it rained all day) and finishing it in nine hours. Sketches by John Harden of the house-party, including Constable, and of Constable painting Mrs. Harden, are reproduced in Beryl and Noel Clay's article, as is Constable's drawing of the party. Although Constable told Leslie in later life that "the solitude of mountains oppressed his spirits" (L. ed. S., p. 25), he exhibited three Lake District scenes at the Royal Academy in 1807, and another three there in 1808; he also sent some of these on to the British Institution's exhibition in 1808 and another three to their exhibition of 1809. His inscriptions made at the time on the backs of the drawings are often enthusiastic; besides those on the Museum's drawings Nos. 74 and 80 may be noted that quoted by Holmes from Sir T. Gibson Carmichael's drawing of 12 October "The finest Scenery that ever was".

Most of the drawings in the Museum were made in the period between the two visits to Brathay Hall. Nos. 72–85 are of places in Borrowdale or easily reached from Keswick, and the identifications suggested for the undated drawings Nos. 87–91 would put them within the same locality and section of the visit. Mrs. Harden noted in her diary on 30 September "Gardner left his friend Constable in Borrowdale drawing away at no allowance, but he got tired of looking on, so came off here". The drawing of Langdale (No. 86) was no doubt, as pointed out by Beryl and Noel Clay in the article cited above, drawn during the artist's second stay at Brathay Hall. Among the oil paintings made by Constable of Lake District scenes may be noted 'Keswick Lake' in the National Gallery of Victoria, Melbourne (L. ed. M., Pl. 5) and 'Keswick Lake' in the collection of Mr. and Mrs. Paul Mellon (L.ed.S., Pl. 32). Holmes, pp. 240–1, lists others.

95 *Epsom Church.* 1806

Plate 55

Pencil. $4\frac{1}{8} \times 7$ ins. (103 × 179 mm.) No. E. 191–1948

Bequeathed by H. H. Harrod.

On paper with truncated watermark: |E

Inscribed on the back in pencil by the artist *Epsom book 1806.*

The word after *Epsom* was read, uncertainly, as *Novr* in the first edition of this Catalogue, and the drawing dated accordingly. Professor Charles Rhyne has pointed out, however, that the words *Epsom book 1806* occur on the back of a drawing (59.55.263) in the Huntington Library and Art Gallery, San Marino, and that the doubtful word here should also be read as *book*. See also *John Constable Drawings & Sketches*, the catalogue by R. R. Wark of an exhibition at the Henry E. Huntington Library and Art Gallery, 1961, No. 10. Constable is known to have visited Epsom, where his aunt Mrs. Gubbins lived, this year; a water-colour drawing by him of Epsom Common dated 4 August 1806 is in an extra-illustrated volume of Leslie's *Life of Constable* which at one time belonged to Lord Lee of Fareham, and a view of Epsom dated 6 August 1806 was formerly in the collection of Sir Michael Sadler. The building represented in No. 95 is presumably the old church at Epsom which was rebuilt, except for the tower, in 1824.

1807–1809

There are no paintings or drawings in the Museum's collections known certainly to have been made during the years 1807–1809. In 1807, 1808, and to some extent in 1809, Constable was painting Lake District subjects for exhibition; and in 1807 he was copying portraits of the Dysart family by Reynolds and Hoppner. Some of these copies by Constable are at Ham House.

*c.*1806–09 **96** *Shipping in the Orwell, near Ipswich.*
Plate 56 Oil on millboard. 8×9¼ ins. (202×235 mm.) No. 160–1888

Plate 56 **96a** On the back is a group of five cows in a landscape. Inscribed on the back in ink, not in the artist's hand, *Engraved in Englh. Land* [. . .] and with monogram *JC.* Mr. Colin Thompson has drawn attention to a sketch of a bridge on the Stour in the National Gallery of Scotland (millboard, 8×9¼ ins. Isabel Constable sale 28 May 1891, Lot 217; George Salting; Lady Binning gift, 1918) which bears on the *verso* a study of cows which is a companion piece to No. 96a. No. 96 *recto* is the original sketch for the mezzotint by David Lucas published with the title 'View on the Orwell. Near Ipswich' (S. 24). Although intended for the original edition of *English Landscape Scenery* it was not published till Moon's edition of 1838. In his correspondence with Lucas about the plate Constable sometimes referred to this subject by such titles as "Ships aground". The following references are of especial interest:
*c.*February 1831 "I have found a little drawg which will help me on greatly with the Ips river" (S. : L., p. 41).

27 September 1831 "The ships I now feer, are too common plaice & vulgar—& will never unite with the general feeling of the book. Though I want variety I dont want a 'Hotch potch'—we must not have any one '*uncongenial*' subject. if we have, it cannot fail of tinging the whole book—& imparting a discordant feeling" (S. : L., p. 59). Shirley (S. : L., p. 185) states that the mezzotint was probably begun by December 1830; certainly by February 1831.
The dating of the sketch is difficult, because there is nothing of precisely similar type among the dated works in the collection. The low tone of colouring and slightly haphazard brushwork suggest a fairly early date, and Holmes's suggestion, p. 241, of *c.*1809 has been adopted here as the best guide available. An origin in the decade 1800 to 1810 might be supported by the style of the sketch of cows on the back, always supposing that both sketches were made around the same time. Key, p. 46, however, assigns this sketch together with Nos. 122 and 235 to 1815. He seems from the context to be partly influenced by the subject-matter. The phrase "fresh natural colour keyed high in tone" which he uses to characterise all three works is hardly appropriate either to the *recto* or the *verso* of No. 96. Another, though remote, possibility is that the sketch was made *ad hoc*, *c.*1831, as Nos. 329, 329a, 330 and 332 are believed to have been, for the mezzotint. Holmes, p. 241, records a replica of No. 96 in the collection of Alexander Young of Blackheath, in 1902.

97 *Head of a girl, probably a portrait of Mary Constable.* *c.*1806–09

Plate 57

Oil on canvas. 12¼×12 ins. (312×305 mm.) No. 1255–1888
The original canvas, which is somewhat irregularly cut, has been relined at an unknown date. The measurements refer to the pigmented surface.

Beckett, I, p. 7, identifies this as a portrait of Mary Constable, the artist's younger sister, who is portrayed on the right of the double portrait of his sisters in the collection of Lt.-Col. J. H. Constable (L. ed. M., Pl. II). The identification is plausible and is supported by the two pencil sketches which were made by Constable of his sister Mary in April 1812, one of which is in the Witt Collection, Courtauld Institute, London. The latter drawing is reproduced from the collection of the late Mr. R. B. Beckett in the *Art Quarterly*, Detroit, Vol. XVII, 1954, p. 383, fig. 10.
The style of the coiffure in No. 97 would be consistent with a date of *c.*1806 onwards. Constable was making his copies of the portraits by Reynolds and Hoppner of the Dysart family in 1807 (L. ed. S., pp. 28 and lxxvi, lxxix) and the effect of this practice on his technique is perhaps to be seen in this portrait.
Holmes, p. 242, dates *c.*1810. The *Inventory of Art Objects 1888*, followed by other authorities, dates No. 97 *c.*1830, but this is ruled out as being too late on the grounds of costume alone.

*c.*1806–09 Plate 58 **98** *Summer Evening: view near East Bergholt showing Langham Church, Stratford Church and Stoke-by-Nayland Church.*

Oil on canvas. $12\frac{1}{2} \times 19\frac{1}{2}$ ins. (317×495 mm.) No. 585–1888
The canvas has been relined at an unknown date. A label on the stretcher is inscribed, not in the artist's hand and probably copying an inscription on the original canvas: "*A summer Evening*" *John Constable R.A. Taken from the fields near E. Bergholt In the distance on the left is Langham Church, in the middle of the picture is Stratford Church and on the higher land in the distance under the tree in the middle is Stoke Church (by Nayland).*
The stretcher is also inscribed on the top in ink *Varnished with Fields lack varnish by C. R. Leslie R.A. in 1840.*

This painting was mezzotinted by David Lucas and published in *English Landscape Scenery* under the title 'Summer Evening' (S. 6). In some lists of contents the title of the plate is given as 'Summer Evening. Cattle reposing. East Bergholt' (S. : L., pp. 230–1). Shirley (S. : L., p. 163) says that the plate was begun by September 1829 and published in the third part of *English Landscape Scenery* in September 1831.
The moon, at the top left, has been moved an inch to the right and slightly lowered, as a *pentimento* shows.
The style is fairly close to that of No. 99 in its dark rich tonality and dragged brush-strokes. Holmes, p. 241, dates *c.*1809. For the scene depicted and the viewpoint, see note to No. 36 above.

1810

Constable exhibited two pictures, entitled 'A Landscape' and 'A Churchyard', at the Royal Academy in 1810. The latter is believed to be No. 1245 in the Tate Gallery (see No. 99 in this Catalogue).

*c.*1810 Plate 59 **99** *Porch of East Bergholt Church.*

Oil on canvas. $9\frac{5}{8} \times 11\frac{7}{8}$ ins. (244×301 mm.) No. 138–1888
The canvas has been relined at an unknown date. The new stretcher is inscribed in ink, perhaps copying an inscription on the original canvas, *Church Porch evening J. Constable RA.*

The moon is rising, or the sun is setting, behind the porch. Three figures are on the path leading to the porch.

A view of the same section of the church, from a viewpoint slightly further to the left, is No. 1245, now in the Tate Gallery, which is believed to have been the picture 'A Churchyard' exhibited at the Royal Academy in 1810, and is almost certainly the picture 'A Church porch' exhibited at the British Institution in 1811 (Davies, pp. 26–7). The latter showed "the stillness of a summer afternoon", and the view held by Davies that No. 99 is "vaguely connected" with his No. 1245 is to be preferred to that of Shirley (L. ed. S., p. 37) that it is a study for the latter. Either consideration leads more or less decisively to a dating of *c.*1810, which is also arrived at by Holmes, p. 242.

1811

In the year 1811 Constable's exhibits at the Royal Academy comprised 'Twilight', and 'Dedham Vale: morning' (now in the collection of Sir Richard Proby). He visited Suffolk in the spring and paid his first visit to Salisbury in the autumn: this was probably the occasion of his first meeting with John Fisher, who was to become his closest friend. His attachment to Maria Bicknell became known during this year, and he received her father's permission to write to her in October.

100 *A cart on a lane at Flatford.* 1811, May 17

Plate 60

Oil on paper laid on canvas. 6 × 8½ ins. (152 × 216 mm.) No. 326–1888

A label on the stretcher is inscribed in ink *17 May, 1811 L.B.C.* This is presumably based on an inscription on the back of the paper on which the sketch is painted. The initials are those of Lionel Bicknell Constable, the artist's youngest son.

No. 45 in the exhibition held at Messrs. Leggatt's in 1899 was an oil sketch called 'At East Bergholt' and dated 16 May 1811: this sketch was made on the following day. Lt.-Col. C. A. Brooks identifies the scene as the lane leading to Flatford from the present coach park. The rising smoke marks the position of Flatford Mill or a near-by building, and the trees on the further ridge are on the Lawford Hall estate. For another version by Constable of the same scene see No. 329 *recto*, which is here regarded as a much later reworking by the artist in his studio of this study from nature.

(See note following No. 104)

101 *A village fair at East Bergholt.* 1811, July

Plate 60

Oil on canvas. 6¾ × 14 ins. (172 × 355 mm.) No. 128–1888

The canvas has been relined at an unknown date. A label on the stretcher is inscribed in ink *Painted in 1811*; this is presumably based on an inscription on the original canvas.

Drawings by Constable of the village fête at East Bergholt in July 1813 are on pp. 85 and 87 of the sketch-book No. 121, and of a village Jubilee fête of 1814 on p. 13 of the sketch-book No. 132. Baskett (*Constable Oil Sketches*, 1966, p. 20 and Pl. I) conclusively identifies the scene as East Bergholt. The house on the left is West Lodge (now called Stour), East Bergholt. He suggests that the view is taken from an upper window of Golding Constable's house. Another view of the same house (once erroneously called Wooling Hall) is in the collection of Mr. and Mrs. Paul Mellon. According to William White's *History, Gazetteer, and Directory of Suffolk* (2nd edn. 1855, p. 214) a fair for toys etc. took place in East Bergholt on the last Wednesday in July. The rule earlier seems to have been to hold the fair during the last week in July (see *East Bergholt in Suffolk*, by T. F. Paterson, 1923, p. 105).
A small oil sketch showing West Lodge, the red brick house on the left of this composition, was Lot 117 in the Gregory Sale at Messrs. Sotheby's 20 July 1949; the sale catalogue wrongly described the house as that of Golding Constable, which is shown in Nos. 102, 133 etc.
(See note following No. 104)

*c.*1811 **102** *Mr. Golding Constable's house, East Bergholt, the birthplace of the painter.*
Plate 61

Oil on millboard laid on panel. $7\frac{1}{8} \times 19\frac{7}{8}$ ins. (181 × 505 mm.) No. 583–1888
On the back was a label in ink, now preserved in the Museum's records, which reads *The House in which John Constable R.A. was born Painted by John Constable RA.*

This painting is a long panoramic view, apparently from the garden of the house, with East Bergholt Church seen towards the left-hand side. The left-hand portion of the painting is in a worse state of preservation, and appears to have been folded behind or detached from the right at one time: only the right half is reproduced by Holmes, p. 58.
Holmes, p. 241, dates No. 102 *c.*1809; it is very similar in treatment to No. 101 and is accordingly listed here next to that sketch of 1811.
(See note following No. 104)

*c.*1811? **103** *Flatford Mill from a lock on the Stour.*
Plate 62

Oil on canvas. $9\frac{3}{4} \times 11\frac{3}{4}$ ins. (248 × 298 mm.) No. 135–1888
The canvas has been relined at an unknown date. The stretcher is inscribed in ink *Minna* [Maria Louisa Constable] *Decr 27th 47* and has incised in it the trade label "BROWN 163 HIGH HOLBORN".

The scene is the mill at Flatford which was owned by Constable's father and is shown in the sketch-book No. 121, p. 10 and in the painting 'Flatford Mill' now in the Tate Gallery, No. 1273 (see also Nos. 104 and 300, and sketch-book No. 132, p. 63). The same scene from a very similar viewpoint, but with the foregound less finished, is No. 65 in the Diploma Gallery, Burlington House, the gift of Miss Isabel Constable in 1888 (L. ed. S., Pl. 9).
No. 103 is the sketch for the painting measuring 26 × 36½ ins., which was lent to the International Exhibition, 1862 (No. 126) by R. Newsham, and was in the sale of the collection of Senator W. A. Clark by the American Art Association, Inc., New York, 12 January 1926, Lot 99 (reproduced in the sale catalogue). In his letter to Maria Bicknell of 12 November 1811 Constable says "You ask me what I have been doing this summer. I fear I can give but a poor account of myself. I have tried flatford Mill again, from the lock (whence you once made a drawing) and some smaller things. One of them (a view of Mrs. Roberts's Lawn—by the summer's evening) has been quite a pet with me" (L. ed. S., p. 47); the continuation of the letter is quoted in the note to No. 108. Other references in the Constable family's correspondence, while no more necessarily connected with No. 103 than is that quoted above, show that the subject was one on which he had been concentrating at this period. Constable's mother writes to him on 8 January 1811: "Your Uncle D. P. W. [David Pike Watts] . . . was so much taken with one of your sketches of Flatford Mills, House &c. that he has requested you to finish it for him" (Beckett, I, p. 55). And again, the same correspondent, writing on 26 October 1811, says: "Your Father . . . rode down to Flatford on Friday. Your pretty view from there is so forward, that you can sit by the fireside and finish it, as highly as you please" (*ibid.*, p. 67). In 1812 he exhibited a painting of Flatford Mill at the Royal Academy, the composition of which has not yet been identified; it may be the work mentioned above, from the Clark Sale.
Holmes, p. 242, dates No. 103 *c.*1811. The style indicates a date *c.*1810–15, and Holmes's dating would be fully justified if the painting in the Clark Sale could be shown to be that exhibited at the Royal Academy in 1812.
(See note following No. 104)

104 *Barges on the Stour, with Dedham Church in the distance.* *c.*1811? Plate 63

Oil on paper laid on canvas. 10¼ × 12¼ ins. (260 × 311 mm.) No. 325–1888
Mr. Douglas Thomson states that the lock gates shown here are those near Flatford Mill: they appear on the right in No. 103 (see the sketch-book, No. 132, p. 63).
Holmes, p. 242, dates this sketch *c.*1810. It is sufficiently close in style and subject to No. 103 to warrant its being listed here in conjunction with that work.

NOTE ON NOS. 100–104

Nos. 100 and 101 are the earliest dated oil sketches in the Museum's collections to show the full originality of Constable's mature style, its vivid naturalism of colouring and boldness of handling. The earliest dated sketch in which these characteristics are applied to Suffolk scenery is probably the 'Country road near East Bergholt' inscribed *October 13th 1809 E[ast] B[ergholt]*. This was Lot 116 *recto* (on the *verso* is a sketch of a country house) in the Gregory sale at Messrs. Sotheby's, 20 July 1949. This sketch was reproduced in monochrome in the sale catalogue and in colour as the frontispiece to the Arts Council's catalogue *An Exhibition of Sketches & Drawings by John Constable from the collection of Dr. H. A. C. Gregory, M.C.*, 1949. In 'Fresh Light on John Constable' (*Apollo*, Vol. LXXXVII, 1968, pp. 227–30) Charles Rhyne draws attention to oil sketches dated 27 September 1810 and 30 September 1810 in the John G. Johnson collection, Philadelphia, and a landscape with houses dated 8 October 1810 in the collection of Mrs. Woodman. The style may be seen in embryo in some of the oil sketches Constable made of Lake District scenery in 1806: for instance in 'Keswick Lake' formerly in the possession of Sir Michael Sadler (L. ed. S., Pl. 32). The reasons for grouping Nos. 102, 103 and 104 with these two dated oil sketches have been explained; they do not amount to a conclusive dating. Sketching in oils from nature was in fact prominent in Constable's practice in 1811, for he called on Farington on 4 June to say he had been three weeks in the country painting from nature, and on 17 December Farington called on Constable to see the painted studies of landscapes from nature which he had made during the autumn (Greig, Vol. VI, p. 279; VII, p. 70). Another set of studies conveniently, though more loosely, grouped here with the appearance of Constable's completely matured naturalism is to be found in Nos. 109–113.

1811, Sept. 11 & 12
Plate 73

105 *Salisbury Cathedral: exterior from the south-west.*

Black and white chalk on grey paper. $7\frac{5}{8} \times 11\frac{3}{4}$ ins. (195 × 299 mm.)

No. 292–1888

Inscribed on the back in pencil by the artist *Salisbury Cathedral Sepr. 11 & 12—1811—S.W.view—.*

Although the relation of this drawing to the preliminary stages of the oil painting 'Salisbury Cathedral from the Bishop's Grounds' (No. 254) had naturally led to its being dated *c.*1820–3, for example by John Steegman in the *Art Quarterly*, Detroit, Vol. XIV, 1951, pp. 195–205, its recent removal from the card on which it had been laid down has revealed that it was, together with Nos. 106–108, a product of Constable's first visit to Salisbury. Nevertheless it was to this drawing that Constable turned when Bishop Fisher gave him the commission to make the large oil painting of the Cathedral which was exhibited in 1823 (No. 254).
(See note following No. 108)

106 *Salisbury Cathedral: exterior from the south-east.* 1811, September 30
Plate 74

Pencil. $5\frac{1}{4} \times 3\frac{1}{2}$ ins. (133×89 mm.) No. 825–1888
On laid paper.
Inscribed vertically below on left by the artist *.1811* (the inscription may have been truncated) and on the back in pencil in the artist's hand *Sep 30 1811*. This date has been copied on to the card on which the drawing was mounted.
The turrets of the west end of the cathedral are seen beyond the chapter house.
(See note following No. 108)

107 *Salisbury Cathedral: the west front.* [1811, September]
Plate 74

Pencil. $5\frac{7}{8} \times 3\frac{1}{2}$ ins. (150×89 mm.) No. 832–1888
On laid paper with truncated watermark: |05.
Holmes, p. 242, assigns to 1811.
(See note following No. 108)

108 *Salisbury Cathedral: exterior view of the east end.* [1811, September]
Plate 74

Pencil. $5\frac{7}{8} \times 3\frac{1}{2}$ ins. (149×89 mm.) No. 614–1888
On laid paper.

NOTE ON NOS. 105–108

Nos. 105 and 106 were made during Constable's first visit to Salisbury, and Nos. 107 and 108 are so similar in technique, size and subject-matter that they were almost certainly drawn at the same time. The zig-zag diagonal scribble which represents foliage is characteristic of Constable's pencil drawings at this period (see No. 114). On this visit Constable was the guest of his early mentor and patron, Dr. John Fisher, Bishop of Salisbury. He told Farington (Greig, Vol. VII, p. 70) that he stayed three weeks. It was probably at this time that he first met the Bishop's nephew, John Fisher, recently ordained deacon at Salisbury (Beckett, VI, pp. 11–14).
In his letter of 12 November 1811 to Miss Bicknell, Constable says, after the extract quoted in the note to No. 103, "Salisbury has afforded some sketches. Mr. Stothard admired them and one in particular (a general view of Sarum) he recommends me to paint, and of a respectable size" (L. ed. S., pp. 47 and 48). This in due course became one of Constable's exhibits at the Royal Academy in 1812, 'Salisbury: Morning'. Other drawings made by the artist on the same visit are known, for example 'Old Sarum', dated 14 September 1811, in the Oldham Art Gallery and 'St. Anne's Gate, Salisbury', dated 17 September 1811, shown at Messrs. Spink's, 1947. A drawing of the west end of Salisbury Cathedral in the Beckett collection, of the same type as Nos. 106–108, and measuring $5\frac{7}{8} \times 3\frac{1}{4}$ ins., was No. 101 in the exhibition of the work of Constable in the Manchester City Art Gallery, 1956. A

drawing of the gardens of Sir Richard Colt Hoare at Stourhead, dated 2 October 1811, now in the Fogg Art Museum, Cambridge, U.S.A., is reproduced from the collection of Sir Robert Witt in L. ed. S., Pl. 35.

*c.*1810–15
Plate 64

109 *View of Dedham from the lane leading from East Bergholt Church to Flatford.*

Oil on paper laid on canvas. $9\frac{3}{8} \times 11\frac{7}{8}$ ins. (239 × 302 mm.) No. 134–1888
The stretcher is inscribed in ink *Painted on Paper* and a label on it reads *Kensington Museum.*

Holmes, p. 242, dates *c.*1810. Considering only the dated oil sketches in the Museum, the style of this is closest to that of No. 100 of 1811. While the sketch may well have been painted around that year, it may be dated less rigidly *c.*1810–15.
(See note following No. 113)

*c.*1810–15?
Plate 65

110 *Willy Lott's House, near Flatford Mill.*

Plate 65

110a On the back is another view of Willy Lott's House.
Oil on paper. Each $9\frac{1}{2} \times 7\frac{1}{8}$ ins. (241 × 181 mm.) No. 166–1888
As numbered here the view on the *recto* is taken nearer the house, and shows a black-and-white dog running along the footpath by the side of the stream; No. 110a is taken from slightly further away, and the footpath curves off the picture at the left. The cottage is seen from a slightly different angle in the latter, and a horse grazing in the foreground is seen from behind.

No. 329a is regarded in this Catalogue as a later replica of No. 110a with suggestions from No. 110. Lucas's mezzotint (S. 33) of Willy Lott's house and its relation to Nos. 110, 110a and 329a are discussed in the note on the latter. The relationship of these two sketches to other paintings by Constable of the same subject, and the extent to which this makes it possible to form an estimate of their date, is discussed in the notes made by Davies, pp. 23–6 on 'The Hay-Wain' (N.G. 1207). He gives reasons for believing that the 'Mill Stream' in the Ipswich Museum was being painted in 1814. It may be the work exhibited as 'Landscape: the Ferry' at the Royal Academy that year. The version of the same composition at the Tate Gallery (No. 1816) (reproduced in L. ed. S., Pl. 43), which indeed appears to be a sketch for the Ipswich picture, is dated by Holmes, p. 242, *c.*1811. Nos. 110 and 110a seem likely from their manner of treatment and viewpoint to have been painted at about the same time as the Tate Gallery's sketch and probably not later than the Ipswich picture which was at that time Constable's most careful treatment of the theme of Willy Lott's house. This would suggest a date of *c.*1811–14 for Nos. 110 and 110a, if Holmes's estimate for the Tate

Gallery's picture No. 1816 is accepted. This result is in accordance with the agreement in style between the two sketches and No. 109 above, here dated *c.*1810–15. A small sketch of Willy Lott's house also at Ipswich Museum, which is comparable in style with Nos. 110 and 110a, is, however, dated on the back 23 July 1816; it was No. 28 in the exhibition of the works of Constable at Manchester City Art Gallery, 1956. Davies (*loc. cit.*) suggests that Constable may have used Nos. 110 and 110a for 'The Hay-Wain' though the sketches may well have been made "long before". He points out that the feature of a browsing horse in No. 110a was used, with a boy on it, for the finished picture, but was painted out. Both the black-and-white dog of No. 110 and the horse of 110a are used in the full-scale sketch for 'The Hay-Wain' (No. 209 below). These considerations alone would show that the dating of *c.*1824 given by Holmes, p. 247, for No. 110 is too late, since 'The Hay-Wain' is of 1821.
(See note following No. 113)

111 *A cottage and lane at Langham: sketch for 'The Glebe Farm'.* *c.*1810–15? Plate 66

Oil on canvas. $7\frac{3}{4} \times 11$ ins. (197×280 mm.) No. 161–1888
Inscribed on the back in ink with the monogram *JC*.

This is a preliminary study, presumably from nature, for the cottage and lane seen in the composition known as 'The Glebe Farm', of which there are two versions in the Tate Gallery (Nos. 1823 and 1274), and another version, the authenticity of which is open to question, in the Barber Institute (see the *Catalogue of Paintings . . . in the Barber Institute*, Cambridge, 1952, pp. 18–19; and for the two pictures in the Tate Gallery see M. Chamot, 'The Constable Room at the Tate Gallery', *Connoisseur*, Vol. CXXXVII, 1956, pp. 260–1). Constable used also to call the composition 'The Green Lane'. That Langham Church does not figure in No. 111 is accounted for by the fact that 'The Glebe Farm' shows a composite view; Shirley (L. ed. S., pp. 215–16) says that the composition of the two pictures in the Tate Gallery seems to combine two viewpoints and that the church cannot be seen from the path at the bottom of the hill shown in No. 111. Leslie (L. ed. S., p. 372) remarks that he visited Langham in 1840 "where all is so much changed excepting the church, that we could scarcely recognise it as the scene of the 'Glebe Farm' ". Shirley reproduces the two paintings in the Tate Gallery on Pl. 102 and Pl. 103a.
Shirley (S.: L., pp. 181–2) says that No. 111 is apparently the original sketch from which Lucas began his first plate of 'The Glebe Farm', which was subsequently changed into a composition called 'Castle Acre Priory' (S. 22). This plate, however, seems to have had the church in it from the beginning, and the basis of the engraving may have been a version resembling the Tate Gallery's painting No. 1823. A farmhouse similar to that shown here, but placed by the water's edge, is seen in the large sketch 'On the Stour' in the Kennedy Memorial

Gallery, Los Angeles, but this composition is more nearly related to our No. 403 and is discussed in the note on that sketch. Shirley (L. ed. S., p. 223) dates No. 111 *c.*1826, basing his opinion upon the year when the finished version of 'The Glebe Farm' was exhibited, in 1827, but this must be held on grounds of style to be far too late. Badt (*John Constable's Clouds*, 1950) reproduces No. 111 on Pl. 6 with the Tate Gallery's 'Mill Stream' (No. 1816) and implies in his text, p. 52, that he regards them as having been made at the same time, in 1811, that being the year assigned by Holmes to Tate Gallery No. 1816. Whether or not Constable's methods changed after 1820 as a result of the publication of Luke Howard's *The Climate of London*, the stylistic deduction is perfectly valid. The clouds here are rather angular in form and painted with conspicuous bristle marks. Both these features are to be seen in No. 103, here assigned tentatively to *c.*1811. As with No. 110 then, the analogy with Tate Gallery No. 1816 may be held to justify a dating of *c.*1810–15.
(See note following No. 113)

*c.*1810–15? Plate 67

112 *East Bergholt Church: the ruined tower at the west end.*

Oil on canvas. $9\frac{3}{4} \times 13\frac{3}{8}$ ins. (248 × 340 mm.) No. 130–1888
The canvas has been relined at an unknown date.

Holmes, p. 244, dates *c.*1819, and compares this sketch with the pencil drawing of the same subject, No. 179, which it is suggested in this Catalogue may have been drawn in 1817. The drawing is from almost exactly the same viewpoint: but evidently both it and No. 112 are taken from nature and there is no reason to assume in the case of a subject frequently sketched by Constable that they were necessarily made at the same time. The oil sketch, with the angular clouds, conspicuous bristle marks and inky blue sky may be compared with No. 111, and the same reasons would hold for assigning this to a date *c.*1810–15.
(See note following No. 113)

*c.*1810–15 Plate 68

113 *Dedham Mill.*

Oil on paper. $7\frac{1}{8} \times 9\frac{3}{4}$ ins. (181 × 248 mm.) No. 145–1888

This is a sketch for No. 184, of 1820. Holmes, p. 242, dates No. 113 *c.*1812, and he is probably correct in thinking that it is some years earlier than the finished picture. It may be compared with the sketch for the 'Mill Stream' (Tate Gallery No. 1816) discussed in the note to No. 110, a comparison which helps to support a dating of *c.*1810–15 for this sketch.
Mr. Gilbert Davis has a pencil drawing of the subject seen from an almost identical viewpoint, but showing the water-wheel. Beckett (*Burlington Magazine*, Vol. XCVII, 1955, pp. 52–5) suggests that it may have been made in 1817.

Probably the drawing and No. 113 are independent studies from nature of the same scene.
For further notes on the finished composition, variants and replicas, see note to No. 184.

NOTE ON NOS. 109–113

Nos. 109–113 form a miscellaneous and somewhat unhomogeneous group. Most of them have either been assigned to a date near 1811 or may be compared with another oil sketch assigned to that date. Accordingly, though their general character hardly warrants a dating more exact than *c.*1810–15 or within even wider limits, they are grouped together here. Their relationship to Nos. 100 and 101, the earliest oil sketches in the Museum to show the full effect of the revolution in Constable's style, helps to justify this grouping.

1812

In 1812 Constable's exhibits at the Royal Academy were 'Salisbury: Morning', 'A Watermill' (Flatford Mill) (see No. 103) and two small landscapes. Apart from a possible brief visit to Salisbury (see No. 118) he spent most of the summer in Suffolk.

114 *East Bergholt Church: part of the west end seen beyond a group of elms.* 1812, June 29
Plate 72

Black and white chalk on grey paper. $12\frac{1}{4} \times 7\frac{3}{4}$ ins. (310 × 197 mm.)
No. 842–1888

Inscribed in top left corner in pencil by the artist *29 June 1812—E. Bergholt.* The inscription is repeated on the back in ink in another hand.
The ruined tower is just visible on the left, and the south porch, with the sun-dial, on the right.

115 *A hayfield near East Bergholt at sunset.* 1812, July 4
Plate 70

Oil on paper. $6\frac{1}{4} \times 12\frac{1}{2}$ ins. (160 × 318 mm.) No. 121–1888
The paper has been laid down on canvas at a later date.
Inscribed in lower right corner in oil by the artist *July 4 1812.*
The scene is near East Bergholt: the sun is setting amid red clouds in undulating country, illuminating stooks of hay in a field in the foreground.

Writing to Maria Bicknell on 10 July Constable said "For more than this week past I have been wholly engaged on a portrait of Mr. William Godfrey [of Old Hall, East Bergholt] which was just compleated in time" (Beckett, II, pp. 79 and 80). In the same letter Constable goes on to comment on sketches such as Nos. 115 and 116 and incidentally to explain why they are of evening scenes: "I am however perverse enough to be vain of some studies of landscapes which I have done . . . I am sure you will laugh when I tell you I have found another very promising subject at *Flatford Mill.* I do not study much abroad in the middle of these very hot bright days. I am become quite *carefull of myself,* last year I almost put my eyes out by that pastime".
(See note following No. 120)

1812, July 7 **116** *A landscape near East Bergholt: evening.*
Plate 70

Oil on canvas. $6\frac{1}{2} \times 13\frac{1}{4}$ ins. (165×337 mm.) No. 146–1888
Painted on a larger piece of canvas which has been cut down: a strip about an inch wide (25 mm.) at the right and on the top had been tacked round the edge of a stretcher.
Inscribed in lower left corner in oil by the artist *7 July 1812.* Inscribed on the back in ink *M.L.* [Maria Louisa Constable).
The sun is setting in red clouds; in the foreground, rolling park land with trees. (For the locality and circumstances of painting see note on No. 115; see also note following No. 120)

1812, July 28 **117** *Landscape and double rainbow.*
Plate 69

Oil on paper laid on canvas. $13\frac{1}{4} \times 15\frac{1}{8}$ ins. (337×384 mm.) No. 328–1888
This painting is on an irregularly torn piece of paper laid on canvas and the canvas itself is laid on a linen backing; the pigmented surface covers both the paper and the canvas: an area of the lower right corner, triangular in shape and approximately 5 inches long by 12 high (127×305 mm.) appears to be painted direct on the canvas. Baskett (*Constable Oil Sketches*, 1966, p. 26 and Pl. 4) suggests that the repairs and the windmill on the right are later additions to an earlier, damaged oil sketch which the artist had retrieved and laid down on canvas. Plausible as the suggestion is, it must be noted that the date is on the extending canvas, and that the style of painting seen in the bushes and the foreground is consistent with other oil sketches made in 1812.
Inscribed in top left corner in oil by the artist *28 July 1812.* On the back is the date *28 July 1812* repeated twice in ink, once on the linen, once on the stretcher; and on the stretcher is written in pencil *Isey or Min* [Isabel or Minna (Maria) Constable, the artist's daughters]. Also on the back is chalked the lot mark *48/3*: this indicates that the sketch formed part of Lot 48 at the Executors' sale,

16 May 1838, the catalogue entry for which reads: "Three—Moonlight; Landscape, and a ditto, with a Rainbow". The three works were bought in for the family by Leslie for £5 5s.
(See note following No. 120)

118 *Pond and cottage at Salisbury(?).* 1812 (?), August 2
Plate 75

Pencil. $4\frac{1}{2} \times 7\frac{3}{8}$ ins. (115 × 186 mm.) No. 263–1888
Page from a sketch-book.
Inscribed by the artist in pencil in lower left corner *2d Aug 1812 Salisbury*[?].
There seems to be a word after that read as *Salisbury*, which may be *Avon*.

The inscription has been so read from the time the drawing entered the Museum (for example in the *Inventory of Art Objects 1888*) and the reading seems to be correct, but it raises difficulties since there is no other indication that Constable visited Salisbury in 1812. On 27 May he had written to Miss Bicknell "My friend John Fisher is half angry with me because I will not pass a little time with him at Salisbury: but I am determined not to friter away the summer, if I can help it" (L. ed. S., p. 51). In his letter of 9 August 1812 to Maria Bicknell, Constable says nothing of such a visit and only mentions news of East Bergholt (Beckett, III, p. 83). Since he was apt to miswrite dates it seems probable that Constable meant to put *1821* or *1820*. The style of drawing would be consistent with one or other of the sketch-books used in 1820; as may be seen from Nos. 190, 191, Constable was near Salisbury on 2 August 1820.

119 *Landscape, with trees and cottages under a lowering sky.* 1812, August 6
Plate 71

Oil on canvas laid on millboard. $3\frac{5}{8} \times 9\frac{1}{2}$ (92 × 241 mm.) No. 324–1888
An unpigmented strip of canvas at the bottom is about $\frac{3}{4}$ in. wide (19 mm.).
Inscribed in top right corner in oil by the artist *Augt 6. 1812*. The last figure of the date is not absolutely clear; it has been read as *8* in the *Inventory of Art Objects 1888*; as *o* by Holmes, p. 241; and as *2*. This last reading is almost certainly correct, and is supported by considerations of style. Constable was in the habit of dating the oil sketches of this year (see Nos. 115 and 116).
(See note following No. 120)

120 *Autumnal Sunset.* *c.*1812
Plate 71

Oil on paper and canvas. $6\frac{3}{4} \times 13\frac{1}{4}$ ins. (171 × 336 mm.) No. 127–1888
The sketch appears to be mainly on a piece of paper laid down by the artist on canvas so that he could extend the pigmented surface at the bottom and on the right. It has been relined at an unknown date.
A label on the stretcher inscribed *Autumnal Sun Set engraved for the 'English Landscape'* possibly records an inscription on the back of the original canvas.

No. 120 is a sketch for the mezzotint engraving by Lucas entitled 'Autumnal Sunset' (S. 14) which was first proposed as a subject by Constable in September 1829, and was published in *English Landscape Scenery* in June 1832. There are a number of variations from this sketch in the plate, of which the most conspicuous are the addition of a small tree on the right and stooks of corn in the foremost field. These were touched in on the progress proofs at various stages by Constable; Shirley (S.: L., p. 173) gives details. Writing to Lucas on 2 June 1832, Constable said "The Evng ['Autumnal Sunset']—is spoild owing to your having fooled with the Rooks—they were the chief feature—which caused me to adopt the subject—nobody knew what they are—but took them only for blemishes on the plate—" (S.: L., p. 86). In the letter to Lucas of 15 September 1829 in which he first mentioned the subject, Constable calls it "Evg, with a flight of Rookes" (L. ed. S., p. 245). Leslie in his note on the letter records that this scene is sketched in the fields near East Bergholt. The tower of Stoke Church is on the right and Langham Hill and Church on the left. These details, however, were added on the plate and are not discernible on the sketch. Lt.-Col. C. A. Brooks takes the view to be from the end of Cemetery Lane (Vale Farm), looking towards Langham Church.

Holmes, p. 242, dates No. 120 *c.*1812. The similarity in style and subject to Nos. 115, 116, 117 and 119 fully justifies this dating. In the lists of contents of the complete sets of *English Landscape Scenery* this plate is known as 'Sunset. Peasants returning homeward' (S.: L., p. 230).

E. E. Leggatt (*Complete Works of David Lucas*, 1903, pp. 33–4) says of the plate, presumably from notes left by Lucas: "It may almost be said that Constable knew every tree in that neighbourhood by name; the large one on the left, and in the middle distance, Dunthorne and he called the 'wig tree', from its shape"

NOTE ON NOS. 115, 116, 117, 119 AND 120

Another oil sketch of the same type, 'Dedham Vale' in the Ashmolean Museum, is dated 13 July 1812; and an oil sketch dated 12 July 1812 was in the Staats Forbes Collection. J. G. Böhler, *Constable und Rubens*, pp. 36 ff. discusses Nos. 115, 116, 117 and 120, and suggests that the influence of Rubens to be found in them may have been mediated through Lord Radnor's 'Escurial'. Constable is known to have seen this painting at some time between May and November, 1812.

1813

In 1813 Constable exhibited at the Royal Academy 'Landscape: Boys Fishing' and a second landscape. He spent most of the summer and autumn in Suffolk.

121 *Bound sketch-book of 90 pages, together with one intercalated leaf (pp. 91–2) from a sketch-book of 1815.* 1813, July–October

Pencil. $3\frac{1}{2} \times 4\frac{3}{4}$ ins. (89 × 120 mm.); the intercalated leaf $3\frac{1}{8} \times 4$ ins. (78 × 101 mm.) No. 317–1888
The sketch-book half-bound in black leather, gold-tooled, marbled boards.
The paper watermarked: J WHATMAN 1810. The intercalated leaf on laid paper of light green tinge with a truncated watermark in a cartouche.
This sketch-book was used in Essex and Suffolk between July and October 1813. The inserted leaf is from a sketch-book of the year 1815, of which Nos. 140, 143 and 145 also formed a part.
There are drawings on 72 pages of the original book, and on each side of the inserted leaf, making 74 in all. Pages bearing inscriptions or scribbles without drawings are not reproduced amongst the plates. Unless otherwise recorded, the inscriptions are evidently by the artist.

121 Inside front cover inscribed beneath an illegible top line *Essex From 1st. July 1813.*

p. 1 Faint scribble.

p. 2 Inscribed *6 feet 2 inches—by—7 feet 6 inches the extreme size of the compartment projecting over the fireplace—above the dado—in the Chapel.*

p. 3 The tomb of Viscountess Falkland in the churchyard at Widford, near Chelmsford, Essex. Plate 76
Inscribed on the left vertically *Vist. Falkland Irish died 76 1762* [or *Ae. 62*].
This is a rough record of the inscription on the tomb which although now partly obliterated records that the Viscountess Falkland died on 27 May 1776, aged 62.

p. 4 Blank.

p. 5 St. Mary-ad-Murum Church, Colchester, seen from the garden of a house. Plate 76

p. 6 Inscribed *Colchester*, in reference to p. 5: the inscription probably not written by the artist.

p. 7 Three drawings on one page. A donkey standing, facing the spectator, by a fence. A donkey standing sideways to the spectator, facing left up a hill: behind him is a short hedge. A much rubbed indistinct drawing of a barge (with sail arm visible) in a pool with a cottage on the right, and vague indications of trees in the left background. Plate 76

p. 8 A pool on a river (presumably the Stour) by moonlight; to the right the full moon shining over a squarish church tower is reflected in the water of the pool; to the left is a gable-ended cottage with a chimney in the centre of the roof. Plate 76

p. 9 Two drawings on one page. The tower of Stratford St. Mary church seen over a group of gable-ended buildings amid trees; inscribed Plate 77 below *Stratford Hall Suffolk, a house formerly inhabited by one of Oliver Cromwell's Generals*. Mr. Norman Scarfe has communicated the information that Sergeant-Major-General Skippon bought Stratford Hall in 1657. A group of two cows, the foremost one standing to the left, the other lying half-hidden, head to the right.

Plate 77 **121** p. 10 Flatford Mill seen over the Stour between trees, and on the left the end of Flatford Old Bridge.
The two trees on the right are those which occur in the right foreground of the oil painting 'Flatford Mill' (Tate Gallery No. 1273), and are also seen in the sketch-book No. 132, p. 61 and in the drawing No. 161. The mill buildings are seen at the same angle here as in the oil painting, which also shows the edge of the wooden bridge.

Plate 77 p. 11 Two sketches on one page of men or boys propelling barges. One shows a boy propelling a barge with a pole, and the other, which is slighter, shows a man and a boy each with poles. The former probably served as the sketch for the detail of the boy and the foremost barge in the 'View on the Stour near Dedham' in the Huntington Library and Art Gallery, San Marino.

Plate 77 p. 12 Two drawings on one page. A view over Dedham Vale; inscribed below on left *25 July—noon—Suffolk*. This has been identified by Oppé (*Old Master Drawings*, Vol. XI, 1936–7, p. 55), as being connected with the sketch for the mezzotint 'A Summerland' (S. 10). The drawing contains the left-hand two-thirds of the mezzotinted design. The mezzotint is subtitled 'A view near East Bergholt' in Bohn's edition of *English Landscape Scenery*, 1855. The Glebe Farm, Langham, is above the poplar: the church tower of Stoke-by-Nayland beyond. Also a slight sketch of a farm labourer seen from behind.

Plate 78 p. 13 Stoke-by-Nayland Church seen over cottages and trees; inscribed at top left *Stoke—by Neyland. Suffolk.* (See also pp. 15 and 17)

Plate 78 p. 14 A mill or barn seen over water with trees on the right on near bank: inscribed below on left *July 10. 1813*.

Plate 78 p. 15 Stoke-by-Nayland Church seen over cottages and trees from a slightly different viewpoint from that in p. 13. (See also p. 17)

Plate 78 p. 16 Two drawings on one page. The east end of East Bergholt Church. A view over rising ground to cottages on a ridge.

Plate 79 p. 17 Stoke-by-Nayland Church tower seen above trees, with a cottage on the left. (See also pp. 13 and 15)

Plate 79 p. 18 East Bergholt: a street with trees and cottages on the left, and on the right the ruined tower of the church seen from the south.

Plate 79 p. 19 East Bergholt Church: the ruined tower seen from the north and, partially obscured, a cottage with two chimneys; indistinctly inscribed below *July 20* [?]. If correctly read, the date is the same as that on p. 24, when Constable made another drawing of East Bergholt Church.

121 p. 20 Blank.

p. 21 An extensive landscape, with a path through standing corn and a large tree on the left; inscribed in the top left corner *13 July. 1813.* The inscription on p. 22 doubtless refers to this drawing, identifying the scene as East Bergholt, in which case the trees and slopes in the distance are those of Dedham Vale. The group silhouetted against the sky, right, closely resembles that in the middle distance of 'Autumnal Sunset' (No. 120). Plate 79

p. 22 Inscribed on the left, presumably with reference to p. 21 *13. July. 1813. Bergholt J.C.*

p. 23 Sketches of cows: three cows lying and one standing in a field; below, slight sketches of other cows. Plate 80

p. 24 The ruined tower of East Bergholt Church from the north, with a cottage on the right; inscribed below on right *20 July.* Plate 80

p. 25 Three sketches on one page. A thatched gable-ended cottage. An artist wearing a tall hat seated on a folding stool and drawing in a sketch-book. The porch of East Bergholt Church seen in profile from the west. Plate 80

p. 26 Part of the north side of East Bergholt Church seen in a gap in trees: on the left a rainbow in a stormy sky; inscribed below *22. July—1813—E Bergholt—.* Plate 80

p. 27 A barge passing under Flatford old bridge: on the left a gable-ended cottage with a thatched roof [Bridge Cottage] and on the right, beyond, another cottage. The cottage and bridge are also to be seen on pp. 29 and 53 of this sketch-book, on p. 52 of the sketch-book No. 132, and in Nos. 297, 298 and 324. Plate 81

p. 28 A woman seated at a table writing, while a girl seen in profile stands watching her; inscribed in lower left corner *19. July. 1813.* The same date occurs on p. 34 on a drawing of Golding Constable's house. Plate 81

p. 29 A barge passing under Flatford old bridge, beyond which is Bridge Cottage. (See also pp. 27 and 53 of this sketch-book, p. 52 of the sketch-book No. 132, and Nos. 297, 298 and 324) Plate 81

p. 30 Three sketches on one page. Looking up sloping and undulating country towards a ridge with trees and a long low building (probably, from its resemblance to pp. 34 and 37, Golding Constable's house at East Bergholt). A slight sketch of trees in front of a ridge. An indefinite scribble, somewhat geometrical and partly resembling a face. Plate 81

p. 31 Two sketches on one page. Willy Lott's house seen from the river Stour. Constable used this in composing 'The Valley Farm' (L. ed. M., p. 420) (see note following No. 374); the sketch on p. 70 appears to be related to the composition. To the left of this, and slightly overlapping it, is a more elaborated but small sketch of undulating ground, Plate 82 with a gate-post prominent in the foreground and a single tree beyond by the bend of a river.

Plate 82 **121** p. 32 Three sketches on one page. A wide view over a valley under a cloudy sky, with two figures in the foreground; inscribed below *24th July. 1813.* A sketch of a cottage or house, on the left of which is a dark shadowy group of trees. A small sketch of a donkey craning upwards to eat from a hedge (see also the oil sketch No. 287 and the note on it).

Plate 82 p. 33 View over a wide landscape: a solitary figure in the left foreground and a square church tower in the middle distance. The scene is probably Dedham Vale taken from a viewpoint nearer the three poplar trees in Sir Richard Proby's oil painting 'Dedham Vale'.

Plate 82 p. 34 Two drawings on one page. A lane at East Bergholt with Golding Constable's house on the right: the house is marked with a cross and the drawing inscribed below *19 July 1813 House in which I was born*× (see also pp. 30 and 37). A landscape, with a figure in the foreground, looking toward a long, low house, probably also Golding Constable's house; inscribed below *21* [altered from *19* and written twice] *July 1813.*

p. 35 Blank.

Plate 83 p. 36 A landscape with Dedham Church in the distance, right, and a bird soaring in a cloudy sky; inscribed below *Dedham The Sky Lark.*

Plate 83 p. 37 East Bergholt: a lane, with Golding Constable's house and other houses and cottages on the left, seen from a similar viewpoint to that in p. 34; inscribed at top left *23* [? *23rd*].

p. 38 Blank.

Plate 83 p. 39 Dedham Vale, with the tower of the church in the distance; inscribed below on left *Dedham from Langham.*

For the relation of this drawing, and those on pp. 51 and 52, to the mezzotint 'Summer Morning: Dedham from Langham' see the note on the oil sketch No. 332.

p. 40 Blank.

Plate 83 p. 41 Three sketches on one page. View up a slope on which is a flock of cattle or sheep; inscribed below on right *27 July—1813 Eving*—(the same date as that on p. 26, which was drawn upon at East Bergholt).

A small sketch of a man with a horse and cart. A very faint sketch of a river winding between wooded banks.

Plate 84 p. 42 The seashore, with boats moored near low cliffs; inscribed above *Mistley near Harwich* and below on left *30 July.* Wrabness Point is visible to the right of the masts.

Plate 84 p. 43 Two sketches on one page. A wide view over Dedham Vale; inscribed *28 July. 1813. E*[*ast*] *B*[*ergholt*]. Oppé (*Old Master Drawings*, Vol. XI, 1936–7, p. 55) says this is a repetition of p. 12 and is also related to the mezzotint 'A Summerland': he gives the date as 28 August; the drawing appears, however, to give a different view of Dedham Vale. A very slight and indistinct sketch, possibly of a church tower amid trees.

121 p. 44 Two sketches on one page. A gable-ended cottage at East Bergholt, to the left of a wood, behind a clearing, with the sun setting above the trees; inscribed below *Augst 12. E[ast] B[ergholt] Twylight.* A clump of trees, seen in a similar light. Plate 84

p. 45 East Bergholt Church: the ruined tower and west end of the church on the right, seen from the village street, with trees on the left and a gable-ended cottage beyond; inscribed below on left *E Bergholt Church.* Plate 84

p. 46 Four sketches on one page. A view over a wide landscape with cows under the shade of a tree in the left foreground, and a squarish church tower in the distance. A road, leading towards a gable-ended cottage and trees, with a figure walking along it. A man carrying a scythe, seen from behind. A similar figure is seen in the middle distance, right, of 'Flatford Mill' (Tate Gallery). A sketch of two men in tall hats. Plate 85

p. 47 Three sketches on one page. A close-up view of a rope amid stones and rocks on a seashore. A seashore or estuary scene: three boats on a shelving beach, and on the right a fisherman with a net going down to the water; inscribed below on right *30 July*— (the same date as that on p. 42, when Constable was at Mistley, near Harwich). An indistinct small landscape with a windmill. Plate 85

p. 48 Three sketches on one page. Open rolling landscape with a windmill in the distance. A wide landscape with the ground sloping toward a clump of trees on the right. A smaller sketch of a landscape with a group of trees on the right. Plate 85

p. 49 Three sketches on one page. A view over two fields: two cows are in the nearer, which is closed by a five-barred gate at either end. A clump of trees with part of a cottage to the left, a man leaning on a fence in the foreground, and a crescent moon in the sky. A smaller sketch of a cottage amid trees. Plate 85

p. 50 Two sketches on one page. A road bending to the right past trees to some cottages on a lower level. A road running past East Bergholt Church, seen on the left; inscribed vertically on left *7 Augst 1813.* Plate 86

p. 51 Five sketches on one page. A small landscape under an overcast sky, with a squarish church tower silhouetted in the distance. A larger slight sketch of Dedham Vale from Langham, with the tower of the church in the distance (see also pp. 39, 52 and No. 332). The outline of the distance is faintly repeated above this sketch. Two slight sketches of a dog. Plate 86

p. 52 Four sketches on one page. Dedham from Langham (see also pp. 39, 51 and No. 332). Three slight sketches of a man and horse ploughing (see also the drawings on pp. 71 and 72 connected with 'A Summerland'). Plate 86

Plate 86 **121** p. 53 A slight sketch, apparently of Bridge Cottage seen from Flatford old bridge (see also pp. 27 and 29 of this sketch-book, p. 52 of the sketch-book No. 132, and Nos. 297, 298 and 324).

Plate 87 p. 54 Two drawings on one page. A scene on the Stour: a horse on the towpath drawing a barge through meadows; inscribed (in the sky of the second sketch) *Augst 11 1813*. A view over water towards barges by the lock at Flatford, with Bridge Cottage and trees beyond; inscribed below *Augt 12 1813* and *Lock*.

The latter drawing was made on the same day as that of East Bergholt on p. 44.

Plate 87 p. 55 Two drawings on one page. A bank with two trees in the left foreground and a ploughed field beyond. A close-up view of water-lilies and reeds. Similar groups of water-lilies and reeds occur in the foregrounds of 'The White Horse' (Frick Collection, New York), 'Stratford Mill' (collection of Sir Reginald Macdonald-Buchanan) and 'View on the Stour near Dedham' (Huntington Library and Art Gallery, San Marino).

Plate 87 p. 56 Eight studies on one page. Seven studies (some very faint) of cows, seen singly or in pairs; one is inscribed *22d Augt*. A woman and a man with a stave, seen from behind.

Plate 87 p. 57 Two sketches on one page. View over meadows: in the foreground a woman is crossing a small footbridge over a ditch; inscribed below on left *14 Augst. 1813*. A horse, cart and driver seen from behind: inscribed below *29th Sp.*[?]; if correctly read this drawing bears the same date as pp. 68, 69 and 83 which were made at Colchester.

Plate 88 p. 58 Blank.

p. 59 Two sketches on one page. A gable-ended thatched cottage, on the right of a lane with trees behind; inscribed below on left *25 Augst—1813*. The ruined tower of East Bergholt Church, seen from the north-west with the crocketed turret beyond; inscribed below on left *E*[*ast*] *B*[*ergholt*] or *26*[?].

Plate 88 p. 60 Blank.

p. 61 Three sketches on one page. A view over a wide landscape, with a barn or cottage in the middle distance to left; inscribed above the sketch below, but probably in reference to this sketch *31. Augst. 1813*. A horse and cart, with a man standing beside the cart, and beyond on the left a man with a horse and foal. A flock of sheep lying in the shade of a tree of which only the trunk and lower foliage are seen.

p. 62 Blank.

Plate 88 p. 63 Two sketches on one page. A view over a field to a group of cottages with a screen of trees behind them; inscribed below on right *Sepr. 1 1813*. A view over a valley from rising ground: in the foreground a flock of sheep, with trees beyond and in the middle distance a church

(? Dedham) with a squarish tower; inscribed below on right *Monday Evng. Sepr. 5. 1813.* (In the year 1813, however, September 5th fell on a Sunday.)

121 p. 64 Blank.

p. 65 Dedham Church, seen over a fence and a clump of trees; inscribed below on left *26 Sepr. 1813. Dedham* beneath some faintly legible writing, apparently to the same effect. Plate 88

p. 66 Colchester Castle, with trees and a cottage on the left and figures on a path in the foreground; inscribed below on left *Colchester Castle.* Plate 89

p. 67 Two drawings on one page. A cottage seen to the left of a path beside a tree and hedgerow, with indistinct figures. A view over water and rising ground to a tall mansion with a pitched roof, standing on a ridge. Plate 89

p. 68 St. Mary-ad-Murum Church, Colchester, seen across a street in which figures are standing, and behind and to the right of a group of cottages; inscribed below on the left *St. Mary's on the Walls Colchester 29 Sepr. 1813.* Plate 89

p. 69 Two drawings on one page. Four horses working a threshing pit in a farmyard with a man with a whip controlling them; inscribed at top *Threshing* and below *28 Sepr. 1813* (the scene has been identified by Mr. Rudsdale of Scarborough Museum as a threshing pit between East Bergholt and Colchester). St. Mary-ad-Murum, Colchester, seen over buildings as in p. 5; inscribed below *29 Sepr. 1813. Colchester.* Plate 89

p. 70 Two sketches on one page. St. Mary-ad-Murum Church, Colchester, seen to the right of trees (the scene identified by Mr. Rudsdale of Scarborough Museum). A slight sketch of buildings (? Willy Lott's house) among trees. As far as can be seen, this is of the same type as the drawing on p. 31 and related to 'The Valley Farm' (see note following No. 374). Plate 90

p. 71 A man ploughing with two horses. This may be compared with the very similar sketches on pp. 52 and 72. This drawing was used as the sketch for the figures in the mezzotint 'A Summerland' (S. 10); the fuller title given to the mezzotint was 'Summerland. Rainy Day. The Ploughman' (S.: L., p. 230). Plate 90

p. 72 Five sketches on one page. The sun shining behind a large cloud formation seen above open country. A long narrow landscape with two horses, one standing and one lying, in a field to left, and to the right a windmill and cottages. Three sketches of a man ploughing, in two with horses and in one, alone. (See also the sketches on pp. 52 and 71 connected with 'A Summerland'.) Plate 90

p. 73 Blank.

p. 74 Blank.

p. 75 A cottage seen amid trees. Plate 90

Plate 91 **121** p. 76 A post made of three pieces of timber, on the bank of a stream (see also p. 77).

Plate 91 p. 77 Two sketches on one page. A post similar to that on p. 76, but made of four pieces of timber. This was used as a sketch for the construction seen in the right foreground of 'Stratford Mill' (collection of Sir Reginald Macdonald-Buchanan). A mill seen across a pool; inscribed below *22 Ocr. 1813 friday The Martin Cats—Shot—by G.C.* The building seen in profile resembles Flatford Mill, but it is not clear that all the details (such as the fenestration and the outbuildings) support the identification. The event referred to in the inscription is connected with the painting 'Martin Cats' which Constable exhibited as No. 216 at the British Institution in 1814. Of this he wrote to Maria Bicknell on 19 February 1814 "When I told you I had sent nothing to the British Gallery I meant nothing new—I did not recollect the Cats which I painted just before I left Suffolk to please Golding who brought it(*sic*) from the woods at the back of the village" (Beckett, II, p. 118). Golding Constable, the artist's elder brother, was a notable shot.

Plate 91 p. 78 View of St. Mary's, Church Street, Colchester, with the tower of St. Mary-ad-Murum Church beyond. St. Mary's was the residence of Constable's cousin, William Mason; it still stands, though the facade has been somewhat altered (information from Mr. E. O'R. Dickey and Mrs. Fell; see also Beckett, I, p. 277–8).

p. 79 Blank.

Plate 91 p. 80 Scene in Colchester: in the foreground part of the old Roman wall (now destroyed) and, beyond, the church of St. James's. Inscribed below *19. Octr. East Hill. Colchester* and above the church *St. James's.*

Plate 92 p. 81 Two sketches on one page. The gateway of St. John's Abbey, Colchester, seen at the end of a path; inscribed below *St. John Abbey gate Colchester.* A church tower on a ridge, seen across fields; inscribed *Octr. 18 1813. St. Mary's Colchester.*

Plate 92 p. 82 Two sketches on one page. Colchester Castle with trees on the left and a church tower beyond; inscribed below on left *Ocr. 1. 1813. Colchester.* A slight sketch of a ridge on which are silhouetted a clump of trees, a church tower and a house; inscribed at top left *18 Octr. 1813.*

Plate 92 p. 83 A view of Colchester seen from the river Colne; inscribed below *29 Sepr. 1813* and *Colchester Castle from North Bridge.*

p. 84 Blank.

Plate 92 p. 85 The village fair at East Bergholt: the village street with booths on either side and houses in the background; inscribed below on left *E.B. fair July 1813* (see also the oil sketch No. 101 of 1811, p. 87 of this sketch-book and No. 132, p. 13). For the reasons given in the note on No. 101, the sketch was made towards the end of July.

121 p. 86 Blank.

p. 87 A crowd of people watching a performance on a stage at a village fair: probably a scene at the East Bergholt July Fair (see also p. 85 of this sketch-book). Plate 93

p. 88 Two sketches on one page. An indistinct thumbnail sketch, perhaps of one or two barges passing trees or buildings. A man wearing a hat and bending forward. The page is inscribed vertically *Dec 1809 12 st 2 lbs.*, and with an illegible line above. Plate 93

p. 89 The tower of St. Mary-ad-Murum Church seen beyond buildings; inscribed below *St. Mary ad Murum—Colchester.* Plate 93

p. 90 A faint sketch of a landscape: in the foreground a figure crossing a bridge over a stream; on the left, on the other bank of the stream, two or three trees and, beyond, a ridge rising to the right. Plate 93

p. 91 (Intercalated leaf.) Two sketches on one page. The tower of Stratford St. Mary Church, seen on the left of a tree. Two figures playing musical instruments: in front, a seated man playing a pipe and, behind, a violoncellist. Plate 118

p. 92 (Intercalated leaf.) A wide landscape: in the foreground a man ploughing with two horses down a sloping field, with indistinct figures on the right; inscribed at top left *19. Sepr. 1815.* Plate 118

pp. 91 and 92 are drawn on a leaf from a sketch-book of pages measuring $3\frac{1}{8} \times 4$ ins. (78×101 mm.) of 1815, of which other detached leaves are Nos. 140, 143 and 145.

NOTE ON THE SKETCH-BOOK NO. 121

This book represents the work of a long summer spent in sketching at East Bergholt. In a letter which Beckett (II, p. 120) dates in March 1814 Constable wrote to Maria Bicknell, doubtless referring to this sketch-book, "You once talked to me about a journal. I have a little one that I made last summer that might amuse you could you see it—you will then see how I amused my leisure walks, picking up little scraps of trees, plants, ferns, distances &c &c." Most of the named or identifiable scenes are within easy reach of East Bergholt, though there are excursions to Chelmsford, Colchester and Mistley. It is probable that all the scenes in the book of a canalised river with barges are on the Stour (such as p. 54 top), and that many of the wide vistas of landscape are of Dedham Vale and its immediate vicinity. The sketch-book contains studies on pp. 12, 52, 71 and 72 connected with the design mezzotinted as 'A Summerland' (S. 10) and on pp. 39, 51 and 52 variant views of the composition known as 'Summer Morning: Dedham from Langham' (S. 26). It also contains sketches connected with 'The Valley Farm' (pp. 31 and 70), 'Flatford Mill' (pp. 10, 46), 'The White Horse' (p. 55), 'Stratford Mill' (pp. 55, 77) and 'View on the Stour near Dedham' (p. 55).

The dated pages in the sketch-book, with place-names where known, or with brief descriptions of subject, are:

July 10	p. 14	A mill or barn.
July 13	p. 21	East Bergholt.
July 19	pp. 28, 34	East Bergholt.
July 20	p. 24	East Bergholt.
July 20[?]	p. 19	East Bergholt.
July 21	p. 34	East Bergholt.
July 24	p. 32	A valley scene.
July 25	p. 12	Dedham Vale?
July 27	p. 26	East Bergholt.
July 27	p. 41	A landscape with cattle.
July 28	p. 43	Dedham Vale.
July 30	pp. 42, 47	Mistley.
End of July	pp. 85, 87	The fair at East Bergholt.
August 7	p. 50	East Bergholt.
August 11	p. 54	A scene on the Stour.
August 12	pp. 44, 54	East Bergholt; Flatford.
August 14	p. 57	A view over meadows.
August 22	p. 56	Studies of cows.
August 25	p. 59	A thatched cottage.
August 31	p. 61	A landscape with a cottage.
September 1	p. 63	A field with cottages beyond.
September 5 or 6	p. 63	Dedham?
September 26	p. 65	Dedham.
September 28	p. 69	Between East Bergholt and Colchester.
September 29	pp. 68, 69, 83	Colchester.
September 29[?]	p. 57	A horse and cart.
October 1	p. 82	Colchester.
October 18	pp. 81, 82	Colchester.
October 19	p. 80	Colchester.
October 22	p. 77	A mill.

1814

In 1814 Constable exhibited at the Royal Academy 'Landscape: Ploughing scene in Suffolk' (see note on No. 122); also 'Landscape: the ferry', probably the painting 'Mill Stream' now in the Ipswich Museum. He visited the Revd. Mr. Driffield at Feering in June (see Nos. 124–128) and spent much of the rest of the year in Suffolk.

122 *Spring. East Bergholt Common.* *c.*1809–16? Plate 94

Oil on panel. $7\frac{1}{2} \times 14\frac{1}{4}$ ins. (190×362 mm.) No. 144–1888

122a The *verso* is thinly painted with a now much discoloured sketch of a row of houses in a village street. (No. 122a is on the original front of the panel; No. 122 is painted on the rough unprepared underside, which has bevelled edges. Plate 96

The sketch No. 122 was engraved by David Lucas for *English Landscape Scenery* (S. 7). A row of notches at intervals of approximately 1 inch along the top and a corresponding row along the bottom are evidently traces of the engraver's squaring. Shirley (S.: L., pp. 164–5) says that the plate was probably begun by September 1829; it was published in the first number of *English Landscape Scenery*, June 1830. In different lists of plates the mezzotint appears under the titles 'Spring. East Bergholt Common' (1830 edition) and 'Spring. A Mill on a Common. Hail Squalls' (1832 edition). Leslie (L. ed. S., p. 4) remarks that the windmill in the engraving 'Spring' is one of those in which Constable worked as a young man, and that "its outline, with the name of 'John Constable, 1792', very accurately and neatly carved by him with a penknife, still remains on one of its timbers". Lucas also made a smaller mezzotint of the same subject (S. 52), which was published as an illustration in the second edition of Leslie's *Memoirs of the Life of John Constable*, 1845, facing p. 5. Constable subsequently composed a long text for publication with the engraving, with quotations from his favourite poets. Shirley (S.: L., pp. 249–55) gives seven different drafts of it, and Leslie (L. ed. S., p. 5) gives a somewhat abbreviated extract. The text makes it clear that this sketch embodied Constable's feeling for the spring. He expatiates upon the variety of colours to be seen in the early part of the year, making a point of controverting the theory that the autumn only is the painter's season. He also dwells upon what he calls the "natural history of the skies"; and his remark that a certain type are called by "wind-millers and sailors 'Messengers' " helps to reinforce the view that it was his early training as a miller which focused his attention upon cloud forms.

In style and subject matter No. 122 belongs to the period *c.* 1809–16. Holmes (p. 243) suggested that it was a sketch for the landscape which Constable exhibited at the Royal Academy in 1814 with the title 'Landscape: Ploughing scene in Suffolk'. The hypothesis advanced in the first edition of this catalogue that the exhibit of 1814 was in fact the composition mezzotinted by David Lucas as 'A Summerland' (S. 10) has been substantiated by the discovery of a version of that work, now in the collection of Mr. and Mrs. Paul Mellon. This comes from the collection of John Allnutt, and is reproduced, with a discussion of the two versions which Allnutt acquired from Constable, in *Constable Oil Sketches* by John Baskett, 1966, Plate 13 and p. 44. In his article 'A Runover Dungle and a Possible Date for "Spring" ' (*Burlington Magazine*, Vol. CXIV, 1972, pp. 386–93) Ian Fleming-Williams gives reasons for adopting the date 1816 for No. 122.

The version of No. 122 in the Louvre (No. 1810a) is a copy from Lucas's mezzotint: it faithfully reproduces the rooks which were added by Constable during the proof stages of the engraving (see P. M. Turner's article in the *Burlington Magazine*, Vol. X, 1906–7, p. 342). A pen-and-ink sketch of a windmill formerly in the collection of Major P. W. Leggatt (Windsor, reproduced facing p. 16) is connected with the engraving of the subject. Lucas (Windsor, p. 6) records "This blot of the Windmill has reference to the engraving of 'Spring' or 'The Mill on East Bergholt Common'. It was done to explain the altered shapes of the vanes in their different positions . . .". The sketch however was made purely as a demonstration, and it bears only a rough resemblance to the windmill as engraved.

[1814, February] Plate 75

123 *A windmill at Stoke, near Ipswich.*

Pen and water-colour. $4\frac{3}{4} \times 6\frac{5}{8}$ ins. (121 × 170 mm.) No. 342–1888

This is the drawing made for the engraving by John Landseer which appears facing p. 92 in the poem *The Social Day* by Peter Coxe, published in 1823. The drawing was commissioned for engraving in 1814, when it was at first intended that the book should appear. In the British Museum Library (*Catalogue of Printed Books*, Vol. 44, 1949, col. 452) is a prospectus for the book in which it is originally promised for 1814: this date is altered in manuscript to 1822. The proofs of the engravings illustrating the poem were published by James Carpenter in 1822, the year before he produced the complete book.

In his letter of 17 February 1814 to Maria Bicknell, Constable wrote: "I have lately made(?) a little picture for Mr. Peter Cox, to help to illustrate his poem (the Social Day), which is forthcoming. I think it will be a pretty book and he has a very noble subscription for it, in which I see the names of the Bishop of Salisbury & Mr Watts" (revised text communicated by Mr. Ian Fleming-Williams). He wrote to John Dunthorne, senior on 22 February 1814: "Tell Abram [Constable] that Mr Cox intends having my 'Windmill' engraved and has put it into Mr Landseer's hands for that purpose, who is a very superior landscape engraver. This I am glad of, for it is a pretty subject—it is one of the Stoke mills I was at with you & Mr Frost when I did it many years ago" (Beckett, I, p. 101). In his article "Constable as an illustrator" (*Connoisseur*, Vol. CXXXIV, 1954, pp. 79–80), Beckett points out that the connection with George Frost of Ipswich helps to identify this Stoke as the place near that town, and not Stoke-by-Nayland. For a drawing of the same subject by George Frost see, 'The Drawings of George Frost 1745–1821' by John Hayes, *Master Drawings*, Vol. 4, No. 2, 1966, p. 167 and n. 31. The drawing by Constable in the British Museum No. 1936–3–14–1 is a monochrome version with variations of No. 123. It is inscribed in ink *Drawn by J. Constable 1815 & given to his friend J. T. Smith Esq. 1823*. Beckett's suggestion (*loc. cit.*) that this is the original sketch from nature, based on his reading of the first date as 1805, is unlikely; the drawing appears rather to have been made at the time the engraving was in question. In the inscription written in 1823 Constable was probably relying on memory for the date 1815 (see also No. 162 for an error made in the date in similar circumstances). No. 342a–1888 in the Victoria and Albert Museum is a proof of the engraving by J. Landseer from No. 123.

124 *Southend.* 1814, June 23
Plate 100

Pencil and water-colour. $3\frac{1}{4} \times 4\frac{1}{4}$ ins. (81 × 107 mm.) No. D.228–1888
Page from a sketch-book.
Inscribed at top in pencil by the artist *Southend—eveng—23d June 1814*, and below *South End Jun 23 1814*. The back is inscribed in pencil by the artist, referring to an adjacent sheet of the sketch-book, now in the Christchurch Mansion Museum, Ipswich, *Prittlewell Church near Southend.*

In the letter of 3 July from which other extracts are quoted in the note which follows No. 128, Constable writes to Miss Bicknell "While Mr. D.—[Driffield] was engaged at his parish I walked upon the beach at South End. I was always delighted with the melancholy grandeur of a sea shore".

125 *The porch of Feering Church.* 1814, June 28
Plate 101

Pencil. $4\frac{1}{4} \times 3\frac{1}{4}$ ins. (107 × 81 mm.) No. D.230–1888
Page from a sketch-book, trimmed.
Inscribed below by the artist *28 June 1814. Porch—Feering Church.*

125a On the back is a slighter pencil sketch of the same porch viewed from the front and inscribed vertically by the artist *Porch (Red Brick) of Feering Church time of Hnry. 8 or Elizabeth.* Plate 101
(See note following No. 128)

126 *Two sketches on one sheet: Sheerness, and a coast scene near Southend.* 1814
Plate 100

Pencil. $3\frac{1}{4} \times 4\frac{1}{4}$ ins. (81 × 109 mm.) No. D.229–1888
Page from a sketch-book.

Inscribed on the back at top by the artist *Sheerness*, and below *Southend Hadleigh Castle*. Also inscribed in another hand *M. C.* [Maria Constable].
The lower sketch on this sheet was formerly called 'Southend, Hadleigh Castle' but Oppé pointed out in *Old Master Drawings*, Vol. XI, 1936–7, p. 56, that the lower inscription on the back must refer to the following page of the sketch-book, probably No. 127.
(See note following No. 128)

1814 **127** *Hadleigh Castle near Southend.*
Plate 100

Pencil. $3\frac{1}{4} \times 4\frac{3}{8}$ ins. (81 × 111 mm.) No. D.234–1888
Page from a sketch-book.

This drawing is the basis of the painting 'Hadleigh Castle' exhibited at the Royal Academy in 1829 (Oppé, *Old Master Drawings*, Vol. XI, 1936–7, p. 56; Davies, pp. 39 and 40). The Tate Gallery has the full-scale oil sketch for the exhibited picture, which is in the collection of Mr. and Mrs. Paul Mellon.
In his letter to Miss Bicknell cited in the note on Nos. 124–128 below, Constable says "At Hadleigh there is a ruin of a castle which from its situation is really a fine place—it commands a view of the Kent hills the nore and the north foreland & looking many miles to sea".
A pen drawing based on our No. 127, extending the composition to the right as in the Tate Gallery's full-scale sketch, is in the collection of Mrs. A. M. Austin, having been given to her father, Dr. G. D. D'Arcy Adams, by Miss Isabel Constable. It measures $4 \times 6\frac{5}{8}$ ins. (102 × 167 mm.) and may have been of about the same date as the oil painting.
(See note following No. 128)

1814 **128** *Feering Church.*
Plate 100

Pencil. $3\frac{1}{4} \times 4\frac{3}{8}$ ins. (81 × 110 mm.) No. D.231–1888
Page from a sketch-book.
Inscribed on the back by the artist *Feering Church—dedicated to All Saints—This church was given, with the manor, to Westminster Abbey—ordained a vicarage in Henry 3ds. reign*—and below *Twilight.* Also inscribed on the back in ink in another hand *I. Constable.*

NOTE ON NOS. 124–128

Nos. 124–128 are leaves from a sketch-book used by Constable while on a visit to the Rev. Mr. Driffield, vicar of Feering, Essex. Constable describes the visit in a letter of 3 July 1814 to Miss Bicknell, the original of which is in the Library of the Victoria and Albert Museum, No. D.236–1888. In addition to the passages quoted above (Nos. 124, 127) the following are relevant to the sketch-book "I have been absent from this place [East Bergholt] for near a fortnight, on a visit to the Rev. Mr. Driffield at Feering near Kelvedon . . . Some time ago, I promised him a drawing of his house and church at Feering; and, during my visit, he had occasion to visit his living of Southchurch, and I was happy to embrace his offer of accompanying him; by which I saw much more of the county of Essex than I ever had before, and the most beautiful part of it; as I was at Malden, Rochford, South End, Hadleigh, Dansbury, etc. etc. . . . I have filled as usual a little book of hasty memorandums of the places which I saw, which you will see". The water-colour 'Feering Church and Parsonage'

in the Whitworth Art Gallery, Manchester, was a result of this visit. The Minories, Colchester has acquired a page from the same sketch-book, washed with a blue tone; it is inscribed by the artist *18 June feering Bury mill.*
With the drawings Nos. 124–128 is another page from the same sketch-book, with no drawing on it and no Museum number but bearing on one side a copy with variations, in ink, not in the artist's hand, of the inscription of No. 128, and inscribed in pencil on the other *M.C.* [Maria Constable].

129 *Study of flowers in a hyacinth glass.* 1814(?), July 26
Plate 97

Oil on millboard, laid on panel. $19\frac{1}{2} \times 13$ ins. (495×330 mm.)

No. 582–1888

Inscribed below on left in oil by the artist *July 26. 18*[*14*].
A large cockle has developed in the millboard in the lower left corner and the surface of the painting is traversed by nine or ten vertical marks, where the paint has perished. A similar deterioration is noticeable near the flower to right of top centre. Each of the corners of the millboard shows signs of old damage.
On the back of the panel is a label inscribed *South Kensington Museum Flowers painted by John Constable R.A.*

The two figures following *18* in the date are now virtually illegible. They are transcribed as *04* in the *Inventory of Art Objects 1888.* Holmes, p. 242, reads the year as 1814, and this is more plausible on grounds of style.
Constable called on Farington on 23 July 1814 (Greig, Vol. VII, p. 272) and, according to an unpublished extract, also on 30 July, the day he was leaving London for the season: he was therefore in town on 26 July 1814.

130 *Study of flowers in a glass vase.* *c.*1814?
Plate 98

Oil on millboard, laid on panel. $19\frac{7}{8} \times 13$ ins. (505×330 mm.)

No. 581–1888

On the back of the panel is a label inscribed *South Kensington Museum Flowers painted by John Constable R.A.*
Holmes, p. 243, dates *c.*1814, comparing it with No. 129, with which it is likely to be contemporary.

131 *Study of flowers in a glass vase.* Plate 97

Oil on canvas. $8\frac{1}{2} \times 7\frac{1}{2}$ ins. (216×190 mm.) No. 331–1888

The canvas on which the study is painted is irregularly cut from a larger piece, and the left half at the bottom is about $\frac{1}{2}$ in. higher than the right half.
Holmes, p. 242, dates *c.*1812. The painting is perhaps slightly less free than that of Nos. 129 and 130, but there is little to differentiate No. 131 from them, and it is placed here in order to group it with these other flower studies.
For a flower study assigned to a later date, see No. 351.

1814, July–October **132** *Bound sketch-book of* 84 *pages.*

Pencil (p. 15 pencil and wash). $3\frac{1}{8} \times 4\frac{1}{4}$ ins. (80 × 108 mm.) No. 1259–1888
The sketch-book full-bound in brown leather, with (broken) metal clasp. The binding has recently been partly renewed. For a leaf which was possibly detached from the sketch-book before it entered the Museum see No. 133. Another, missing between the present pp. 24 and 25, was also removed before the book was received in the Museum, and its present whereabouts is not known. The sketch-book was used in Essex and Suffolk between July and October 1814. There are drawings on 58 pages of the sketch-book. Pages bearing inscriptions or scribbles without drawings, are not reproduced amongst the plates. Unless otherwise recorded the inscriptions are evidently by the artist.

132 Inside front cover. Scribble.

p. 1 Scribble.

p. 2 Blank.

Plate 102 p. 3 Two sketches on one page. A man seated on a bank with a stick in his right hand, looking down. A group of three figures, perhaps two children watching a third who is fishing; inscribed below *Augt. 1. 1814.*

p. 4 Blank.

p. 5 Faint scribble.

Plate 102 p. 6 A distant view of Dedham: the church tower seen in the middle distance from a lane running downhill beside a steep bank with a tree growing on top; inscribed below on left *Augst. 9. 1814.*

Plate 102 p. 7 A church seen across fields under a cloudy sky; inscribed below on left *Augst. 9. 1814* (the same date as that on p. 6, which shows a distant view of Dedham, and probably also that on p. 19, which shows Stratford Church).

p. 8 Blank.

Plate 102 p. 9 Close-up study of dock leaves.

p. 10 Blank.

Plate 103 p. 11 East Bergholt Church, seen from the north-east; inscribed below *23d Octr. 1814 Saturday morning. 9. o'clock.* The reading *Saturday* seems clear, but 23 October fell on a Sunday in the year 1814 (see note on p. 79 of this sketch-book).

p. 12 Inscribed, probably not by the artist, *East Bergholt Church;* this inscription evidently refers back to p. 11.

Plate 103 p. 13 The village fair at East Bergholt. A line of booths, with flags flying at either end and crowds of people, with trees and houses seen behind. (See also the oil sketch No. 101 and the sketch-book No. 121, pp. 85 and 87, for the fair at East Bergholt, which will have begun at the end of July.)

p. 14 Inscribed, probably not by the artist (in reference to p. 13) *I think this is the Jubilee fête 1814.*

132 p. 15 Landscape: a scene over a wide valley, probably Dedham Vale; inscribed below on left *Augst. 1st. 1814.* Plate 103
Faint wash over pencil.

p. 16 Blank.

p. 17 Faint scribble.

p. 18 Blank.

p. 19 The east end of Stratford Church, seen over the churchyard wall, with trees on the left; inscribed below on left *Augt 9*[?] *1814 Stratford.* If correctly read the date is the same as that on pp. 6 and 7, on the first of which is a distant view of Dedham. Plate 103

p. 20 Blank.

p. 21 Stoke-by-Nayland: the church tower seen above houses to the left of the village street; inscribed above with an almost illegible line ending ... *N.W.* (the view of the church is in fact from the north-west). (See also pp. 23, 24, 39, 40, 41 and 43) Plate 104

p. 22 Inscribed, probably not by the artist, in reference to pp. 21 and 23 *Stoke by Nayland.*

p. 23 Two drawings on one page. Stoke-by-Nayland Church seen in a gap between trees and a cottage. Another sketch of the tower of Stoke-by-Nayland Church, seen closer at hand. (See also pp. 21, 24, 39, 40, 41 and 43) Plate 104

p. 24 Stoke-by-Nayland Church: inscribed below on right *10 Augt 1814. eving.* A similar view to that described first on p. 23. (See also pp. 21, 39, 40, 41 and 43) Plate 104
Between pp. 24 and 25 a leaf was removed before the book came into the possession of the Museum.

p. 25 View, probably on the Stour, looking across a waterway with a barge, to fields with distant trees: a tree is seen on the nearer bank on the right and a man on horseback on the further bank. (See also pp. 48 and 51 for similar compositions) Plate 104

p. 26 Blank.

p. 27 View over a winding waterway towards a squarish church tower: two trees are seen on the left and a bank with cows in the right foreground. Probably a view on the Stour, perhaps looking towards Dedham. (See also p. 59 for a similar composition) Plate 105

p. 28 Scribble.

p. 29 Inscribed at top *Tattingstone 28*[?]*th Augst. 1814*—(see note on p. 33 of this sketch-book). A scribble below.

p. 30 Blank.

p. 31 A woman holding a child, seated facing right, seen from behind. Plate 105

p. 32 Blank.

p. 33 The tower of Tattingstone Church, seen amidst dense trees, enclosed by a fence; inscribed below on left *Tattingstone 23d. Augst. 1814.* Plate 105

Constable says in his letter of 28 August 1814 to Maria Bicknell that he had been staying for several days at Tattingstone Hall painting a new uniform for his portrait of Admiral Western (Beckett, II, pp. 130–1).

132 p. 34 Blank.

Plate 105 p. 35 Three sketches on one page. A view over Dedham Vale with sheep in a field in the foreground. The two poplar trees and the bushier trees in the foreground identify the scene as Dedham Vale, seen from a viewpoint nearer than that in Sir Richard Proby's painting 'Dedham Vale'. A flock of sheep huddled together; inscribed below *Augst 28. 1814—E*[*ast*] *B*[*ergholt*]*—Morning—*. Tree stems and hurdles on sloping ground.

Plate 106 p. 36 Three sketches on one page. A windmill, and on the left a repetition of the sails; inscribed below *23d. Sepr.* Two sketches of men digging; probably drawn at the dunghill seen in the 'Stour Valley and Dedham Village' in the Museum of Fine Arts, Boston (see note on p. 81 of this sketch-book).

Plate 106 p. 37 A gable-ended house or mill on the left beside water and on the right and in the distance trees reflected in the water; inscribed below after an erased number [perhaps *29*] *29th. Augst—1814*, and illegibly inscribed in top left corner.

Plate 106 p. 38 View over fields with a windmill prominent in the middle distance; inscribed below on left *22d. Sepr. 1814*. This is the middle distance of the scene from an upper window in Golding Constable's house (cf. No. 176).

Plate 106 p. 39 Stoke-by-Nayland: the top of the church tower seen above trees, with the east end of the nave visible above and to the right of a gable-ended cottage; inscribed in top right corner *Augt. 30 1814*. The later water-colour in the British Museum No. L.B. 34 appears to be based upon this sketch, though the tower of the church is shown at a slightly different angle. (See also pp. 21, 23, 24, 40, 41 and 43 of this sketch-book and the note on No. 330)

Plate 107 p. 40 Stoke-by-Nayland Church, seen from the south; inscribed faintly below *Stoke*. (See also pp. 21, 23, 24, 39, 41 and 43)

Plate 107 p. 41 Stoke-by-Nayland Church, seen from sloping ground and partly obscured by trees; inscribed below on left *Stoke Augst. 30. 1814*. (See also pp. 21, 23, 24, 39, 40 and 43)

Plate 107 p. 42 Two drawings on one page. A small landscape with a windmill in the centre. A sketch of a carved escutcheon.

Plate 107 p. 43 The tower of Stoke-by-Nayland Church, seen above trees. (See also pp. 21, 23, 24, 39, 40 and 41)

p. 44 Scribble.

p. 45 Scribble.

Plate 108 p. 46 A workman kneeling on his left knee, seen from behind.

132 p. 47 A winding river with a boat in the right foreground and a windmill in the middle distance, seen against a cloudy sky; inscribed at top right *Sepr. 3d 1814 Saturday noon* [or *morng*]. Plate 108

p. 48 A slight sketch of water-meadows, with a tree or trees on the right; probably a view of the Stour. (See also pp. 25 and 51 for similar compositions) Plate 108

p. 49 A water-wheel. Plate 108

p. 50 A water-wheel with a hanging chain behind it and the water trough in front right; inscribed at top right *11 Octr*—and vertically on the left *Gs—lift* [? or *left*]—*E*[*ast*] *B*[*ergholt*]—*12th—Octr—1814*. Plate 109

p. 51 Trees by water, with a faint indication of barges and of a man on horseback on the left. This sketch is a variant of the composition on p. 25 and comparable with that on p. 48; these drawings were probably made on the Stour. Plate 109

p. 52 View on the Stour, taken from the bank below Bridge Cottage and Flatford old bridge. Probably used as a sketch for the oil painting 'View on the Stour near Dedham' (now in the Huntington Library and Art Gallery, San Marino). (See also the sketch-book No. 121, pp. 27, 29 and 53 and Nos. 297, 298 and 324) Plate 109

p. 53 A post with studs and indications of water flowing past it; probably a detail of a lock. Plate 109

p. 54 Five sketches on one page. Two men loading a cart which has a horse in the shafts. An identical cart seen from the same angle, but with two horses, is to be found in the oil sketch No. 134, dated 24 October 1814. To the right of them is a smaller repetition of a similar horse and cart. A sketch of a labourer standing with a spade is superimposed on the horse and cart first described. An indistinct sketch of clothes, spades etc. lying on a bank. A slight sketch of a cart and horses. Plate 110

All these sketches were drawn at the dunghill seen in the 'Stour Valley and Dedham Village' in the Museum of Fine Arts, Boston (see note on p. 81 of this sketch-book).

p. 55 A number of slight sketches of figures. Probably *en suite* with pp. 56 and 57, in which case the top sketch at least is of men engaged on boat-building. Plate 110

p. 56 A number of slight sketches of men engaged on boat-building; that of the seated boy, below on right, was used by Constable in 'Boat-building near Flatford Mill' (No. 137) and those of the cauldrons and the ladle, below on left, resemble those in the painting and on p. 57 of this sketch-book. Plate 110

p. 57 Study for the oil painting 'Boat-building near Flatford Mill' (No. 137); inscribed at top left *Sepr. 7. 1814. Wednesday*. The arrangement of the figures differs in the completed oil-painting, into which the seated Plate 110 boy from p. 56 of this sketch-book is introduced. (See also p. 55 of this sketch-book and the note on No. 137)

132 p. 58 Faintly inscribed, probably not by the artist, in relation to p. 57 *boat building*.

Plate 111 p. 59 View of a winding river with barges in the right foreground, trees on the left, and a squarish church tower in the distance. Probably the river Stour, looking towards Dedham. (See also p. 27 for a very similar composition)

Plate 111 p. 60 Two sketches on one page. Two men digging in a dunghill. This is a sketch of the scene in the left foreground of 'The Vale of Dedham' in the City Art Gallery, Leeds (L. ed. S., Pl. 51), which is dated 5 September 1814. The painting at Leeds is itself connected with the 'Stour Valley and Dedham Village' in the Museum of Fine Arts, Boston (see note on p. 81 of this sketch-book). Above, a thumbnail sketch of a windmill.

Plate 111 p. 61 View along the towpath of the Stour looking towards Flatford Mill; inscribed below on left *14 Augst 1814*. This sketch is related to the central section of the oil painting 'Flatford Mill' (Tate Gallery, No. 1273) (L. ed. M., p. 410). In the sketch-book No. 121, p. 10 is a drawing of the foreground trees from a different viewpoint (see also No. 161).

Plate 111 p. 62 View over Dedham Vale, with the church tower in the middle distance and trees throwing long shadows in the foreground; inscribed vertically on the right *26 Sepr morning* $\frac{1}{2}$ *8 o'cl*[?]. The drawing shows the valley from a viewpoint near to that in 'The Vale of Dedham' in the City Art Gallery, Leeds (see note on p. 81 of this sketch-book).

Plate 112 p. 63 View on the Stour: probably the lock at Flatford Mill seen from the weir below the confluence of waters, with part of the mill buildings visible on the left. The scene may be compared with the oil sketch No. 103 and the oil painting 'Flatford Mill' (Tate Gallery No. 1273) (see also Nos. 104 and 300).

Plate 112 p. 64 Water escaping from a sluice: a detail of that shown in the foreground on p. 63.

Plate 112 p. 65 View over Dedham Vale. The angle of vision is similar to that on p. 81, and may be compared with that on p. 62. On the left Constable has started to block in a tree as an inserted element of the composition, which is connected with that of the 'Stour Valley and Dedham Village' in the Museum of Fine Arts, Boston (see note on p. 81 of this sketch-book).

Plate 112 p. 66 A house and thatched boat-shelter at a confluence of the Stour. A sketch for the leftward and central section of 'The White Horse' (Frick Collection, New York). Mayne (L. ed. M., p. 410) records an oil study which follows this sketch fairly closely. (See also pp. 69 and 70 for studies apparently of the same scene from different viewpoints)

132 p. 67 A thatched cottage on the right, with trees beyond it to the left over which a crescent moon is rising; inscribed vertically on the right *Sunday. eveng. Sepr. 18th. 8 o'clock.* The moon and its halo are touched in with white. Plate 113

p. 68 Four drawings on one page. A plough. A distant sketch of a team of horses. A wide valley landscape. A close view of two horses harnessed to a cart, with trees in the background; inscribed below on left *Octr. 1. 1814.* Plate 113

The plough in the first sketch is also to be seen on p. 69 of this sketch-book and in the oil sketch No. 136, which is dated 2 November 1814. The sketch of the horse and cart is one of the series discussed in the note on p. 81 of this sketch-book.

p. 69 Three sketches on one page. A plough superimposed on a fainter, whole page drawing of a landscape, with a house on the further bank of a river with trees to left and right of it. A faint sketch in the vertical sense, at top left, perhaps of a horse and cart. Plate 113

The details of the whole page landscape are not clear, but the house in the centre of the composition may be that seen on pp. 66 and 70 of this sketch-book, and the composition itself may be connected with the series discussed in the note on No. 403. The plough is the same as that seen on p. 68 of this sketch-book, and the oil sketch No. 136 of 2 November 1814 represents it from an identical viewpoint.

p. 70 A scene on the Stour: figures on the nearer bank, a barge in the river and a group of buildings on the further bank which may be compared with those seen on p. 66 (drawn from a different position) and on p. 69. Plate 113

p. 71 Inscribed *28 Sepr. ½ past 8 o'clock James* [. . .] [the surname illegible] (see also the inscription on p. 72).

p. 72 Moonlight scene: a figure walking along a road flanked by the ruined tower of East Bergholt Church on the left, and a cottage and trees on the right; inscribed below *28 Sepr. ½* [. . .] *8 o'clock* (see also the inscription on p. 71). Plate 114

p. 73 Three sketches on one page. A man loading a cart, to which two horses are harnessed, seen from the rear. A dog lying down. A bird's-eye view of a bend on a river, with a barge rounding it. Plate 114

The sketch of the horse and cart is one of the series discussed in the note on p. 81 of this sketch-book.

p. 74 Four sketches on one page. Men loading a cart with a horse in the shafts seen from behind. Above, a slight sketch, probably also of a horse and cart in profile. Stratford St. Mary Church; inscribed above *Stratford 5 Oct eveng.* Superimposed on this, a girl wearing a bonnet and seen from the side. Plate 114

The horse and cart in the larger sketch on this page is seen at the same angle in the oil sketch No. 135. For the relation with the painting 'Stour Valley and Dedham Village' in the Museum of Fine Arts, Boston, see the note on p. 81 of this sketch-book.

Plate 114 **132** p. 75 View of a field, with a road in the foreground winding past a clump of bushes and trees on the left, and a windmill in the distance; inscribed below on right *6. Oct. 1814.*

p. 76 Blank.

Plate 115 p. 77 Tattingstone Church seen from the south-east; inscribed at top right *Tatingstone. S.E. 19. Octr. 1814—.*

Plate 115 87 Tattingstone Church: a closer view of the porch and tower seen from the same angle as in the sketch on p. 77; inscribed below on right *19. Octr. 1814.*

Plate 11 p. 79 Two drawings on one page. A view at Stoke-by-Nayland over a wooded valley towards a distant ridge on which the church tower is seen; inscribed below on left with deletion as shown *Stoke Oct. 23d. 1814. Saturday ~~morning~~ noon.* A nearer view of the same ridge.

Writing to Maria Bicknell on 25 October, Constable said that he had intended writing to her on the Sunday "when the beauty of the day (which perhaps might be the last this autumn) tempted me to take a walk to Neyland to pass the day with my poor Aunt, who is now a great invalid. My way was cheifly through woods and nothing could exceed the beauty of the foliage" (Beckett, II, p. 134). The reading *Saturday* seems clear, but October 23, in fact, fell on a Sunday in 1814 (see also p. 11 of this sketch-book).

p. 80 Blank.

Plate 115 p. 81 View of Dedham Vale; inscribed below on right *9th Octr—.* This drawing is a sketch, made under conditions of pronounced light and shade, for the oil painting 'Stour Valley and Dedham Village' in the Museum of Fine Arts, Boston. Beckett (*Burlington Magazine*, Vol. XCVIII, 1956, p. 18 and reproduction) has identified the painting at Boston as the work commissioned from Constable in 1814 as a wedding present for Miss Philadelphia Godfrey, and has established the connection of the sketches Nos. 134 and 135 and of the painting 'The Vale of Dedham' in Leeds Art Gallery with the Boston picture. A letter from the author of this Catalogue in the *Burlington Magazine*, Vol. XCVIII, 1956, p. 132, also drew attention to the connection of drawings on pp. 36, 54, 60, 62, 65, 68, 73, 74 and 81 of this sketch-book, either with the finished painting, with the oil sketch at Leeds or with the preliminary sketching which Constable carried out near the dunghill which is seen in the foreground of the composition. Of all this preliminary material, p. 81 is nearest to the picture at Boston, since it shows the dunghill and the valley from almost the same viewpoint, has a tree in the left foreground and a horse and cart (though seen in profile). The heap in the foreground, described as a gravel-pit in the first edition of this Catalogue, has been identified by Mr. Ian Fleming-Williams as a dunghill (*Burlington Magazine*, Vol. CXIV, 1972, pp. 386–93).

The Leeds oil sketch is dated 5 September 1814 and No. 134 below is dated 24 October; accordingly Constable was working on the details of the painting over a period of at least seven weeks.

132 p. 82 The porch of East Bergholt Church, showing the sundial and a tree and a cottage beyond; inscribed at top *Saturday 17th Sepr. 1814. E*[*ast*] *B*[*ergholt*]. Plate 116

p. 83 A small sketch of a woman carrying a child. Also on the page are figures relating to standard sizes of canvases: Plate 116

Half length {*40 by 50 Inches—*
4 by 5—

Three quarters {*25 by 30 Inches*
25 by 31¼—

{*20 by 24—*
20 25—

p. 84 A long inscription on this page has been erased.

Inside back cover. Inscribed *Colchester Ju*[. . .] *1814*

{*5 feet 2—Inches*
4 do by 4 do

Mr. [. . .] (the name almost illegible, perhaps *Mason*; see note on the sketch-book No. 121, p. 78).

NOTE ON THE SKETCH-BOOK NO. 132

The drawings in this sketch-book were made by Constable during his summer and autumn visit to East Bergholt, during which he stayed at his parent's house from 30 July until 4 November. The progress of his engagement with Maria Bicknell was particularly discouraging at the time, and Constable admitted to a tendency to become a recluse. His subjects, to judge from those which are identifiable in the sketch-book, were drawn mainly from the neighbourhood of his home. Besides the extensive material connected with the 'Stour Valley and Dedham Village' enumerated in the note on p. 81, this book contains the full-page composition sketch for 'Boat-building near Flatford Mill' of 1815 (No. 137 below) and figure studies made in connection with that composition (pp. 55, 56, and 57); a drawing (p. 61) related to 'Flatford Mill' (Tate Gallery); a drawing used for 'The White Horse' of 1819 (Frick Collection, New York) and another connected with it (pp. 66 and 70); and the original sketch (p. 52) for 'View on the Stour near Dedham' of 1822 (Huntington Library and Art Gallery, San Marino). Three river scenes with tall trees in the foreground, right, are on pp. 28, 48 and 51; two with tall trees in the foreground, left, on pp. 27 and 59. The latter may have contributed to the formation of the final composition of the 'View on the Stour', and the faint full-page sketch on p. 69 was possibly used in building up the Stour scene discussed in the note on No. 403 of this Catalogue. The many sketches of Stoke-by-Nayland Church (pp. 21, 23, 24, 39, 40, 41 and 43) may have been referred to by Constable when he was varying the composition of his mezzotint 'Stoke-by-Nayland' (S. 9); and that on p. 39 was used by him as a sketch for the later water-colour 'View at Stoke-by-Nayland' in the British Museum (No. L.B. 34).

The dated pages in the sketch-book, with place-names where known, or with brief descriptions of subject, are:

End of July	p. 13	The fair at East Bergholt.
August 1	p. 15	Dedham.
August 1	p. 3	A group of three figures.
August 9	pp. 6, 7	Dedham.
August 9[?]	p. 19	Stratford.
August 10	p. 24	Stoke-by-Nayland.
August 14	p. 61	Flatford.
August 23	p. 33	Tattingstone.
August 28	p. 35	East Bergholt.
August 28[?]	p. 29	Tattingstone (inscription only).
August 29	p. 37	A house or mill.
August 30	pp. 39, 41	Stoke-by-Nayland.
September 3	p. 47	A river scene.
September 7	p. 57	Flatford.
September 17	p. 82	East Bergholt.
September 18	p. 67	A cottage by moonlight.
September 22	p. 38	A valley with a windmill.
September 23	p. 36	A windmill.
September 26	p. 62	Dedham Vale.
September 28	p. 72	East Bergholt; p. 71 (inscription only).
October 1	p. 68	East Bergholt.
October 2, 3		East Bergholt (No. 133, detached leaf from this sketch-book).
October 5	p. 74	Stratford.
October 6	p. 75	A landscape with a distant windmill.
October 9	p. 81	Dedham Vale, from East Bergholt.
October 11	p. 50	East Bergholt.
October 12	p. 49	East Bergholt.
October 19	pp. 77, 78	Tattingstone.
October 23	p. 11	East Bergholt.
October 23	p. 79	Stoke-by-Nayland.

133 *The house of Mr. Golding Constable at East Bergholt (the artist's birthplace).* 1814, October 2, 3
Plate 116

Pencil. $4\frac{1}{4} \times 3\frac{1}{4}$ ins. (108 × 81 mm.) No. 437–1888

Two sketches on one page. The house by moonlight; inscribed below by the artist in pencil *Oct 2d. 1814*. The house in sunlight; inscribed below on left by the artist in pencil *3d Oct.*

Page from a sketch-book, mounted with an envelope in which it appears to have been kept by Miss Isabel Constable. This page possibly comes from the sketch book No. 132, since the measurements and dates correspond. If so, it was detached before it was received into the Museum's collections.

The house is seen from the drive, that is, from the opposite side to that shown in No. 102. The back is inscribed in pencil *The House in which J.C. was born.* A larger pencil drawing of the house, corresponding to the lower of these two drawings, was Lot 84 in the Gregory Sale, 20 July 1949. It was inscribed *Oct 5. 1814 ½ past 8 i morning* and the measurements were $7\frac{1}{2} \times 11\frac{7}{8}$ ins.

134 *Study of a cart with two horses.* 1814, October 24
Plate 99

Oil on paper with a brown ground. $6\frac{1}{4} \times 10\frac{3}{8}$ ins. (159 × 264 mm.)
No. 333–1888

Inscribed below on left in oil by the artist *24 Octr. 1814.*

This is one of the sketches made at the dunghill at East Bergholt by Constable when he was engaged upon the painting 'Stour Valley and Dedham Village' now in the Museum of Fine Arts, Boston. For other material in the Museum related to the same painting, see the note on p. 81 of the sketch-book No. 132.

135 *Study of a cart and horses, with a carter and dog.* [1814, October]
Plate 99

Oil on paper with a brown ground. $6\frac{1}{2} \times 9\frac{3}{8}$ ins. (165 × 238 mm.)
No. 332–1888

Inscribed on the back in ink with the monogram *JC.*

No. 135 has been identified by Beckett (*Burlington Magazine*, Vol. XCVIII, 1956, p. 18) as a sketch used for the cart and horses at the dunghill introduced into the oil painting 'Stour Valley and Dedham Village' in the Museum of Fine Arts, Boston. In the finished picture the man standing by the cart is replaced by the two figures seen at the left of it in the sketch on p. 74 of the sketch-book No. 132. The dog, horses and cart occur as in No. 125.

For the other material in the Museum related to the painting at Boston, see note on p. 81 of the sketch-book No. 132.

136 *Studies of two ploughs.* 1814, November 2
Plate 96

Oil on paper with a brown ground. $6\frac{3}{4} \times 10\frac{1}{4}$ ins. (172 × 260 mm.)
No. 789–1888

The front of the oil sketch is inscribed in ink *2d Novr. 1814*. The purple back of the thick paper on which the sketch is painted is inscribed in ink in another hand with the same date. Also on the back are chalk scribbles, probably a child's drawing.

This sketch was made shortly before Constable left Suffolk; as noted by Farington (Greig, Vol. VII, p. 286), he arrived in London on 4 November.

Pencil studies of the lower plough seen from the same angle, and therefore perhaps made on the same occasion, are on pp. 68 and 69 of the sketch-book No. 132. Constable appears to have made use of No. 136 as a sketch for the plough seen in 'The Cornfield' (National Gallery) and for that in 'Stoke-by-Nayland' (Art Institute of Chicago).

1815

In 1815 Constable exhibited five paintings and three drawings at the Royal Academy, including 'Boat-building' (No. 137). His mother died early this year and he was in Suffolk in May. He left London again for Suffolk on 6 July and remained there most of the year, being detained during December by his father's serious illness.

1815 **137** *Boat-building near Flatford Mill.*

Plate 95

Oil on canvas. Size of painted surface 20 × 24¼ ins. (508 × 616 mm.) No. F.A. 37. Sheepshanks Gift.

The painting was relined on a larger canvas and provided with a new stretcher in 1893. There are wide bituminous cracks in the brown shadows.

The painting was exhibited at the Royal Academy in 1815 (No. 215) with the title 'Boat-building'. Holmes, p. 243, plausibly identifies it with No. 59 in the Executors' sale, 16 May 1838, 'View at Flatford, with barge building', bought by Smith of Lyall St. for £51 9s. Whether it passed straight into the hands of Mr. Sheepshanks is not recorded; it was in his possession when the handlist *The Collection of Pictures formed by John Sheepshanks, Esq.* was drawn up *c.*1850, and it came to the Museum with his Gift in 1857.

On p. 57 of sketch-book No. 132 there is a full-page pencil sketch dated 7 September 1814 for the composition, but with different *staffage*; p. 56 of the same book has a sketch used for the figure of the boy in the foreground, and pp. 55 and 56 bear other sketches of figures apparently engaged in the operations of barge-building.

Leslie (L. ed. S., pp. 74 and 75) quotes from Constable's letter of 18 September 1814, addressed from East Bergholt to Miss Bicknell: "This charming season, as you will guess, occupies me entirely in the feilds; and I believe I have made some landscapes that are better than is usual with me, at least that is the opinon of all here". Leslie comments "Among the landscapes mentioned in this letter was one which I have heard him say he painted entirely in the open air. It was exhibited the following year at the Academy, with the title of 'Boat-building'. In the midst of a meadow at Flatford, a barge is seen on the stocks, while just beyond it the river Stour glitters in the still sunshine of a hot summer's day. This picture is a proof, that in landscape, what painters call warm colours are not necessary to produce a warm effect. It has indeed no positive colour, and there is much of grey and green in it; but such is its atmospheric truth, that the tremulous vibration of the heated air near the ground seems visible. This perfect work remained in his possession to the end of his life."

The entry made by Farington for 23 July 1814 helps to explain why Constable painted the picture in the open air and throws light on certain of its features: "Constable called upon me.—We talked abt. filling the vacancies of Associates in November next. I told him the objection made to His pictures was their being unfinished; that Thomson [Henry Thomson, R.A.] gave him great credit for the taste of His design in His larger picture last exhibited, & for the indication shown in the colouring, but He had not carried His finishing far enough.—I recommended to Him to look at some of the pictures of *Claude* before He returns to His country studies, and to attend to the admirable manner in which all the parts of His pictures are completed.—He thanked me much for the conversation we had, from which he sd. He shd. derive benefit" (Greig, Vol. VII, p. 272). The unpublished extract for 30 July 1814 shows that Constable took Farington's advice: "Constable called being this day to leave London for the season. He was, by my advice, at Mr. Angerstein's on Wednesday last to study the pictures by Claude, particularly the *finishing* before he commenced his studies from nature in the country". Farington recorded on 10 November that he had been told by Constable that his uncle, Mr. D. P. Watts, had seen his painted studies; he had noticed their being more finished than his other works, and bespoke one of them (Greig, Vol. VII, p. 287). The five Angerstein Claudes were among the thirty-eight works purchased from him to found the National Gallery in 1824: they are Nos. 2, 5, 12, 14 and 30 in that Gallery's catalogues.

No. 137 is notable among Constable's work as much for the Claude-like quality of its colouring as for the truth to atmospheric effect noted by Leslie: and the extract from Farington's diary given above shows that this was the result of a conscious intention on Constable's part. Although doubtless painted entirely in the open air, its close dependence on the drawings in the sketch-book No. 132 shows that Constable took the same pains with it as with a picture painted in his studio, and it is, to that extent, different from his usual open-air oil sketches. Lucas says that Constable told him that when working on this picture "he was always informed of the time to leave off by the pillar of smoke ascending from a chimney in the distance that the fire was lighted for the preparation of supper on the labourers' return for the night" (Beckett, I, p. 107).

1815, July 3 **138** *Wimbledon Park.*
Plate 101

Pencil. $1\frac{1}{2} \times 3$ ins. (38×76 mm.) No. 305–1888
Drawn on the back of a visiting card, on which is engraved *Mr. I. CONSTABLE. 63, Charlotte Street, Fitzroy Square.* The engraved side is inscribed in pencil by the artist *Wimbledon Park July 3d 1815.*
Maria Bicknell was staying this summer in a cottage taken by her father at Putney. Constable wrote proposing a meeting on Putney Bridge on Monday 3 July, and Beckett (II, pp. 141, 145) points out that he must have made this drawing on that visit.

1815, August 5 **139** *Shipping, near Ipswich.*
Plate 119

Pencil. $4\frac{1}{2} \times 7$ ins. (115×179 mm.) No. 308–1888
Page from a sketch-book on paper with truncated watermark: |TMAN |13.
Inscribed below on right by the artist *5 Augt 1815 Ipswich.*
This page comes from the same sketch-book as Nos. 141 and 144.
The drawing was made when Constable was returning from a visit to the Rev. F. H. Barnwell at Brightwell (Beckett, I, p. 128).

1815, August 15 **140** *Wheatsheaves at East Bergholt.*
Plate 118

Pencil. $3\frac{1}{8} \times 4$ ins. (78×101 mm.) No. 827–1888
Page from a sketch-book on laid paper of light green tinge with a truncated watermark: W.
Inscribed below by the artist *15 Augst 1815. East Bergholt.*
This page comes from the same sketch-book as Nos. 143 and 145, and pp. 91 and 92 intercalated in the sketch-book No. 121.

1815, August 20 **141** *Overbury Hall.*
Plate 119

Pencil. $4\frac{1}{2} \times 7\frac{1}{8}$ ins. (115×181 mm.) No. 300–1888
Page from a sketch-book, trimmed.
Inscribed in lower left corner by the artist *Overberry* [or *Overbury*] *Hall. Augst 20. 1815.*

The inscription had been taken to apply to Overbury Court, Tewkesbury, Worcestershire, but in 1936 Mr. Robert Holland-Martin informed the Museum that it was not of that house, of which he was owner. It is of Overbury Hall, at Layham, near Hadleigh, Suffolk (L. ed. S., p. 88).
This page comes from the same sketch-book as Nos. 139 and 144.

1815(?), August 22 **142** *Harwich: the seashore and lighthouse.*
Plate 120

Pencil. $4\frac{1}{2} \times 7\frac{3}{8}$ ins. (115×187 mm.) No. 302–1888

Inscribed below on right by the artist *Harwich 22d Augst 181*[5?]. The last figure of the date is now illegible, but was read as 5 when the drawing was received by the Museum (*Inventory of Art Objects 1888*).

This drawing was the sketch for the oil painting 'Harwich: Sea and Lighthouse' (Tate Gallery, No. 1276) which was perhaps exhibited at the Royal Academy as No. 148 in 1820 (Holmes, pp. 243 and 245); another version belongs to Mrs. I. Ashcroft.

Although this is also a page from a sketch-book, in spite of the similar measurements it is doubtful whether it comes from the same sketch-book as Nos. 139, 141 and 144 of 1815. The outer (right-hand) edge of the page in No. 142 measures 115 mm.; in the three cited the measurement is only 114 mm. (The measurements given above are of the greater, left-hand, side.) Possibly the year should have been read as 1817, one of the years in which Constable was using a sketch-book of 115 × 187 mm. (see note following No. 160).

143 *A lawn at East Bergholt.* 1815, August 24 Plate 117

Pencil. 4 × 3⅛ ins. (100 × 78 mm.) No. D.232–1888

Page from a sketch-book on laid paper of a light green tinge. Inscribed below by the artist: *24 Augt 1815—Lawn—EB—.*

This page comes from the same sketch-book as Nos. 140 and 145, and pp. 91 and 92 intercalated in the sketch-book No. 121.

144 *The breakwater at Harwich, with ships on the beach.* 1815, September 1 Plate 120

Pencil. 4½ × 7⅛ ins. (115 × 181 mm.) No. 306–1888

On paper with truncated watermark: J WHA| 18| .

Inscribed at top right by the artist *Harwich Sepr 1st* [there is a tear here] *1815*.

There is no hinge mark but from the discoloured top, bottom and right edges the sheet appears to be a page from a sketch-book, presumably the same as the source of Nos. 139 and 141, with the dimensions of which it accords. The sheet has been mounted, probably before it was received into the Museum's collections, on a larger sheet of paper, which is inscribed below on the left in pencil *The Breakwater Harwich.* Mr. Frank Hussey has pointed out that on the right may be seen the *Orwell*, the first steamer to come to Harwich; she began service a few days before the visit on which Constable made the drawing. There is a rough drawing of the steamer in Col. J. H. Constable's collection, and an etching of it attributed to Constable in the National Maritime Museum.

A pencil drawing also made at Harwich on 1 September 1815, and measuring 4½ × 7 ins., was in the collection of Sir Bruce Ingram.

145 *The Cottage in a Cornfield, East Bergholt.* *c.*1815 Plate 117

Pencil. 4 × 3⅛ ins. (102 × 78 mm.) No. 828–1888

Page from a sketch-book on laid paper of light green tinge. Inscribed by the artist at top with an inscription of which *E[ast] B[ergholt]* is alone now legible. Inscribed in pencil on the back, probably not by the artist, *The Cottage in the Cornfield.*

Although undated this is evidently from the same sketch-book as Nos. 140 and 143, and pp. 91 and 92 intercalated in the sketch-book No. 121; this justifies the dating of *c.*1815 suggested by Holmes, p. 244. The drawing is a sketch for Constable's oil painting 'The Cottage in a Cornfield', No. 352, another version of which he appears to have exhibited in 1817.

1816

In 1816 Constable exhibited 'The Wheatfield' and 'A Wood: Autumn' at the Royal Academy. His father died on 14 May. He spent some of the summer in Suffolk and paid two visits to Wivenhoe. He was married by his friend John Fisher to Miss Bicknell on 2 October at St. Martin's-in-the-Fields, and they spent part of the honeymoon staying with Fisher at his vicarage at Osmington, Dorsetshire.

1816, July 27
Plate 118

146 *Fishing with a net on the lake in Wivenhoe Park.*

Pencil and grey wash. $3\frac{1}{2} \times 4\frac{5}{8}$ ins. (88×116 mm.) No. D.233–1888
Page from a sketch-book, trimmed.
Inscribed in top right corner in pencil by the artist *Wivenhoe Park July 27 1816.*
Also inscribed on the back in ink *J.C.* and in pencil *M.C.* [Maria Constable].
This page is from the same sketch-book as No. 147.

The first recorded visit by Constable to Wivenhoe Park, near Colchester, the seat of Major-General Rebow, was made in September 1812 (L. ed. S., p. 55). Writing to Maria Bicknell on 21 August 1816, on his return from another visit to General Rebow, Constable said "The general and Mrs. Rebow are determined to be of some service to me. I am going there again, and shall stay a week, in all probability [this he did at the end of August] . . . I am to paint two small landscapes for the general; one in the park, of the house, and a beautiful wood and piece of water; and another a wood, with a little fishing house, where the young lady (who is the heroine of all these scenes) goes occasionally to angle. . . . They are both well acquainted with our history, and hope to see us there together" (L. ed. S., p. 93).

The former of these paintings, representing Wivenhoe Park, and exhibited at the Royal Academy in 1817, is now in the National Gallery of Art, Washington: Widener Collection (reproduced in L. ed. M., Pl. 14). In this painting, two men are seen fishing from a boat, but neither the composition nor that detail is taken from this drawing. The latter painting, which represents The Quarters House, Alresford Hall, is now the property of the National Gallery of Victoria, Melbourne.

147 *Netley Abbey: the east window.* 1816, October 11 Plate 117

Pencil. $4\frac{3}{8} \times 3\frac{1}{2}$ ins. (112 × 88 mm.) No. 823–1888
Page from a sketch-book, trimmed.
Inscribed below by the artist *11 Oct 1816—Netley*. Inscribed on the back in pencil, apparently by the artist, but possibly written over by another hand *East Window—Netley Abbey 11 Octr. 1816*. Also inscribed on the back in pencil with the monogram *JC* and at top *J* or 7[?].
This page is from the same sketch-book as No. 146. Two drawings from the same sketch-book as Nos. 146 and 147 belong to Uppingham School. The earlier, showing an octagonal house amidst trees, is inscribed in pencil by the artist *Putney Heath. Augst 6 1816*; the later, showing the interior of a small church, is dated in pencil by the artist *17 Oct 1816*.
(See note following No. 154)

148 *Netley Abbey: the exterior seen amid trees.* [1816, October] Plate 121

Pencil. $4\frac{1}{2} \times 7\frac{1}{8}$ ins. (115 × 181 mm.) No. 268–1888
Page from a sketch-book, trimmed.

On the back is a sketch-map, traced with a stilus and partly pencilled, of the roads from Ringwood, Hampshire to Osmington, Dorset. One route passes through Poole, Lytchett Minster, Wareham, Wool, Winfrith and the other pursues a more northerly course; the directions of Christchurch and Sarum are indicated. This map was no doubt used by Constable and his wife on their journey to spend their honeymoon with John Fisher at Osmington. The drawing is the original sketch for Constable's etching of Netley Abbey. Holmes, p. 243, points this out and states that Constable made a study in oil from this drawing late in life, which was No. 9 in the exhibition at Messrs. Leggatt's, 1899. This or a similar oil painting is reproduced by Beckett in his article 'Constable's Honeymoon' (*Connoisseur*, Vol. CXXIX, 1952, p. 4 and fig. II); compare also the late water-colour 'Netley Abbey by Moonlight', formerly in the Beckett collection, and exhibited at Manchester 1956 (No. 129).
This is a page from the same sketch-book as Nos. 149, 151, 152, 153 and 154.
(See note following No. 154)

149 *Netley Abbey: the interior.* [1816, October] Plate 122

Pencil and sepia wash. $7\frac{1}{8} \times 4\frac{5}{8}$ ins. (180 × 116 mm.) No. 606–1888
Page from a sketch-book, trimmed.

This page has been mounted (see also Nos. 151–154) apparently by the artist, on a larger page from a sketch-book measuring $9\frac{1}{2} \times 7\frac{1}{8}$ ins. (240 × 180 mm.) watermarked J WHATMAN 1813. The larger page is inscribed in pencil, probably by the artist, *Netley Abbey*. *Netley* is repeated below on the right in another hand. This is a page from the same sketch-book as Nos. 148, 151, 152, 153 and 154. (See note following No. 154)

[1816, October] Plate 12

150 *Netley Abbey, with Southampton Water in the background.*

Pencil. $4\frac{1}{2} \times 7$ ins. (113 × 178 mm.) No. 613–1888

There is no evidence to show that this drawing came from a sketch-book, but it was in all probability made at the same time as Nos. 147–149. Beckett points out (*Connoisseur. loc. cit.*, p. 4, note) that a drawing sold at Messrs. Sotheby's on 4 May 1949 was said to be of Netley Abbey and dated 20 May 1823: but there is no likelihood that Constable revisited this part of the country at that period. (See note following No. 154)

1816, November 7 Plate 123

151 *Osmington Bay, with Portland Island in the distance.*

Pencil. $4\frac{1}{2} \times 7\frac{1}{8}$ ins. (115 × 181 mm.) No. 311–1888
Page from a sketch-book, trimmed.
Inscribed below on left by the artist *Novr. 7. 1816—Osmington Bay.*

Plate 123

151a On the back is a pencil drawing showing a figure in the foreground, seen from behind, seated on the downs and looking to the sea and coast beyond. Presumably this represents Weymouth Bay.
There are signs, including a portion of paper adhering to the back, that the drawing was once laid down on a larger sheet, as were Nos. 149, 152–154.
This is a page from the same sketch-book as Nos. 148, 149, 152, 153 and 154. (See note following No. 154)

1816, November 20 Plate 124

152 *Portland Island from Chesil Bank.*

Pencil and water-colour. $4\frac{1}{2} \times 7\frac{1}{8}$ ins. (115 × 181 mm.) No. 628–1888
Probably a page from a sketch-book, trimmed.
Inscribed in top left corner in pencil by the artist *Portland Island Novr. 20. 1816.* The date has been inked over.
With the drawing is a piece of paper measuring $3\frac{1}{2} \times 9\frac{1}{4}$ ins. (90 × 235 mm.) on which it was apparently at one time mounted (see also Nos. 149, 151, 153 and 154). This detached sheet bears in pencil the monogram *JC* and the inscription written by the artist *Island Portland.*

152a On the back of No. 152 is a pencil drawing of a beach scene with figures and boats in the foreground. The composition resembles in its foreground No. 151 *recto*; the drawing may be from the same part of the coast. Plate 124

Shirley (L. ed. S., p. 96) says of the drawing No. 152 *recto* "The colour is so dead that it may have been touched on by the Archdeacon or his sister, both of whom were privileged in this way". The drawing hardly bears out this hypothesis; the colouring seems delicate and consistent, bearing in mind the time of the year at which it was made.
This is a page from the same sketch-book as Nos. 148, 149, 151, 153 and 154. (See note following No. 154)

153 *Preston Church near Weymouth.* 1816, November 21
Plate 125

Pencil. $4\frac{1}{2} \times 7\frac{1}{8}$ ins. (115×181 mm.) No. 303–1888
Probably a page from a sketch-book, trimmed.
Inscribed in lower left corner in pencil by the artist *21st. Novr. 1816. Preston.*
The drawing is mounted on a larger sheet of paper, measuring $6\frac{1}{8} \times 9\frac{1}{8}$ ins. (154×231 mm.) (see also Nos. 149, 151, 152 and 154) which is inscribed below in pencil by the artist *Preston—near Weymouth.*

153a On the back of No. 153 is a pencil drawing showing the interior of the church, with the clergyman in the pulpit. Inscribed vertically in pencil by the artist *Preston Church Sunday Decr. 1st. 1816.* 1816, December 1
Plate 122
The Rev. E. V. Tanner, who has examined the Church Registers, states that the clergyman is almost certainly John Fisher, who undertook most of the work at this church during a period, from March 1816 till December 1817, in which there was no vicar of Preston.
This is a page from the same sketch-book as Nos. 148, 149, 151, 152 and 154. (See note following No. 154)

154 *Coast scene near Osmington, with Portland Island in the distance.* [1816]
Plate 125

Pencil and water-colour. $4\frac{1}{2} \times 7\frac{1}{8}$ ins. (115×181 mm.) No. 791–1888
Page from a sketch-book.
This page has been mounted on a page from a larger sketch-book measuring $7\frac{1}{8} \times 9\frac{1}{2}$ ins. (180×242 mm.) (see also Nos. 149, 151, 152 and 153), the back of which is inscribed in pencil by the artist *Portland.*
The scene has formerly been described as 'Coast scene near Portland Island' but the island is no nearer than in No. 151. Mr. Harold Day has pointed out that the boat in the foreground of 'Weymouth Bay' (Musée du Louvre) closely resembles the one in No. 154, in reverse.

Plate 126 **154a** On the back of No. 154 is another drawing in pencil of a coast scene with Portland Island in the distance.

This is a page from the same sketch-book as Nos. 148, 149, 151–153.

NOTE ON NOS. 147–154

Nos. 147–154 were all drawn by Constable on his honeymoon. He was married by John Fisher at St. Martin's-in-the-Fields on 2 October, and Fisher had invited the newly-married couple to stay at his vicarage at Osmington on the coast near Weymouth, in Dorsetshire. The visit to Netley Abbey on 11 October, when Nos. 147 to 149 and probably also No. 150 were made, was probably undertaken from Southampton on the way down. As Beckett suggests (*Connoisseur, loc. cit.*) the map on the back of No. 148 would be of use in journeying from Southampton to Osmington, and may also suggest a break of journey at Ringwood. The latest recorded date for a drawing made at Osmington is that on the back of our drawing No. 153 of 1 December. No. 147 is drawn in the smaller sketch-book which Constable had used earlier in the year, from which No. 146 also comes.

Although the hinge marks and the other obvious signs have been trimmed off Nos. 148, 149, and Nos. 151–154, there can be little doubt that these six sheets once formed part of the same sketch-book. The trimming and cutting up of the sketch-book seems in this instance to have been carried out by the artist himself, since the inscriptions on the larger sketch-book pages on to which some of them are mounted (Nos. 149, 153 and 154) are almost certainly in his hand. Among other drawings which may come from the same sketch-book are: 'View of Osmington and the Downs with the figure of George III on horseback at Sutton Poyntz' ($4\frac{5}{16} \times 7$ ins.) which was Lot 93 in the Gregory sale, 20 July 1949; 'Portland Roads' ($4\frac{7}{8} \times 7$ ins.), then in the collection of R. B. Beckett (*Connoisseur, loc. cit.*, fig. VII). In the article cited Beckett discusses other drawings and oil sketches made at the time. See also Beckett, VI, pp. 30–1 and Plate 5. An oil sketch of the coast with Portland Island in the distance, similar to the pencil drawings Nos. 151, 152, 154 and 154a, is in the City Art Museum, St. Louis (reproduced in the Bulletin of that Museum, Vol. XIV, 1929, p. 8).

[1816] Plate 127 **155** *Weymouth Bay.*

Oil on millboard. $8 \times 9\frac{3}{4}$ ins. (203×247 mm.) No. 330–1888

Inscribed on the back in ink with the monogram *JC*.

Differing opinions have been expressed about the order in which Constable's three known versions of this subject may have been painted: the other two are at the National Gallery (No. 2652) and at the Louvre (No. 1808). Holmes (*Burlington Magazine*, Vol. XVII, 1910, p. 85) regards the picture in the National Gallery as the earliest, and as having been painted during Constable's honeymoon. He identifies the Louvre picture as that exhibited at the British Institution in 1819, and dates No. 155 rather later than the National Gallery picture, suggesting that it is a sketch for the picture exhibited at the British Institution. He therefore dates in *c.*1819 (see also Holmes, p. 244). Davies (pp. 33 and 34) records the literature up to 1946, with reference to the National Gallery version. Beckett (*Connoisseur*, Vol. CXXIX, 1952, pp. 6–8) considers that No. 155 is the original version, accepts the Louvre picture as that shown at the British Institution, and suggests that No. N.G. 2652 may be later.

As far as the date of No. 155 is concerned, it is almost certainly the open-air sketch from nature made by Constable on his honeymoon. The other paintings would then be later versions based upon it. This view, which is supported by the similarity in size to other oil sketches made by Constable on his honeymoon (Beckett, *loc. cit.*, p. 7), is virtually established by a point of detail. In the National Gallery's picture and in the mezzotint of the subject by David Lucas a man is to be seen in the middle distance driving a flock of sheep along the sands. This part of the composition in No. 155 is a line of white pigment, not differentiated into the form of a man and a flock of sheep, and perhaps representing distant water, mist or smoke. It is probable that this shows what Constable had in front of him when he made the sketch on the beach, and that the decision to change it into the shepherd with his sheep was an afterthought, suggested by the rough, indefinite forms in the sketch.

No. 155 has long been considered as the work from which Lucas engraved the mezzotint 'Weymouth Bay, Dorsetshire' (S. 13) (*Inventory of Art Objects 1888*, "Engraved with variations in *English Landscape Scenery*"; see also S.: L., p. 172). However, as Davies, p. 34, points out, the pedigree of the Louvre picture shows that it is the one from which Lucas made the mezzotint, and No. 155 only enters into the matter as the source from which the Louvre picture as well as the other versions were painted (see also Beckett, *loc. cit.*, p. 7).

1817

In 1817 Constable exhibited four works at the Royal Academy: 'Scene on a navigable river' ('Flatford Mill on the River Stour') (Tate Gallery No. 1273); 'A Cottage' (see No. 352); 'Wivenhoe Park, Essex, the seat of Major-General Rebow' (National Gallery of Art, Washington: Widener Collection); and a portrait of John Fisher, still in the Fisher family collection. He spent ten weeks of the summer at East Bergholt. His first child, John Charles, was born on 4 December.

156 *Approach to a lane, near East Bergholt.* 1817, July 25

Plate 128

Pencil. $4\frac{1}{2} \times 7\frac{3}{8}$ ins. (115×186 mm.) No. 298–1888
Page from a sketch-book.

Inscribed below on left by the artist *25 July 1817*, and on the back in ink in a careful script:

"*Hic locus ætatis nostræ primordia novit*
"*Annos felices, lætitiæque dies.*
"*Hic locus ingenuis pueriles imbuit annos*
"*Artibus, et nostræ laudis origo fuit*".

These lines were inscribed under the engraving of Constable's birthplace which forms the frontispiece to *English Landscape Scenery* (S. 27). Leslie (L. ed. S., p. 371) says that the following translation by John Fisher is in one of Constable's sketch-books:

This spot saw the day-spring of my life,
Hours of Joy and years of Happiness;
This place first tinged my boyish fancy with a love of the Art,
This place was the origin of my Fame.

No source has been suggested for the Latin verses: they are probably modern. In a letter to Lucas of 13 October 1831, Constable proposes changing 'Hic locus' to 'Haec Domus' in the first line; this seems not to have been done.
Lt.-Col. C. A. Brooks has identified the scene as the lane leading to New Fen Bridge at its junction with the road from East Bergholt Church to Flatford. (See note following No. 160)

1817?, August 3
Plate 128

157 *A cottage and road at East Bergholt.*

Pencil. Slight traces of squaring for enlargement. $4\frac{1}{2} \times 7\frac{3}{8}$ ins. (115 × 186 mm.)
No. 278–1888

Page from a sketch-book.
Inscribed below on right by the artist *E*[*ast*] *B*[*ergholt*] *3d. August* [. . .] (here there is a repair where the rest of the date has been torn off the edge). Inscribed on the back in pencil with the monogram *JC*.

That part of the inscription before *3d. August* has been read *Wed* (*Catalogue of Water-Colour Paintings*, 1927, p. 123) but seems certainly to be *E.B.* The sketch is placed here since it is more likely to have come from the sketch-book Constable was using in 1817 than from those of the same size used in other years. (See note following No. 160)

1817, August 27
Plate 126

158 *Ship on the stocks at Ipswich.*

Pencil. $4\frac{1}{2} \times 7\frac{3}{8}$ ins. (116 × 187 mm.) No. 819–1888
Page from a sketch-book with truncated watermark: JOHN DICK| 18| .

Inscribed below *Ipswich 27 Augst 1817* and on the back with the serial number *12* and *Ipswich M.L.C.* [Maria Louisa Constable].
(See note following No. 160)

159 *Wivenhoe Park.* 1817, August 29 Plate 129

Pencil. $4\frac{1}{2}\times7\frac{3}{8}$ ins. (115×187 mm.) No. 822–1888
Page from a sketch-book with truncated watermark: JOHN DICK| 18| .
Inscribed below on left by the artist *Wivenhoe Park Augst. 29. 1817* and on the back with the serial number *37*, *Wivenhoe Park* and *M.L.C.* [Maria Louisa Constable].
(See note following No. 160)

160 *Churn Wood and Greenstead Church.* 1817, August 29 Plate 129

Pencil. $4\frac{1}{2}\times7\frac{3}{8}$ ins. (116×187 mm.) No. 611–1888
Page from a sketch-book with truncated watermark: JOHN DICK| 18| .
Inscribed in lower left corner by the artist *29 Augst. 1817. Wivenhoe Park. Churn Wood.*
Mr. E. M. O'R. Dickey and Mr. P. E. Goldsmith have identified the scene as a view looking north to Churn Wood, with Greenstead Church on the left.

NOTE ON NOS. 156–160

Nos. 156, 158, 159 and 160 are evidently from the same sketch-book, used in the summer of 1817, and measuring about $4\frac{1}{2}\times7\frac{3}{8}$ ins. (115×186 mm.). Nos. 179–182 may also come from this book. No. 157 is provisionally placed here as it agrees in style and measurement with the 1817 sketch-book. The inscription on No. 156 indicates that he had arrived by 25 July.
For a drawing of St. Mary-ad-Murum, Colchester, which comes from a sketch-book of size $4\frac{1}{2}\times7\frac{3}{8}$ ins. (115×186 mm.) and may be dated 9 August 1817, see No. 180. For a drawing of East Bergholt Church, possibly also from the sketch-book of 1817, see No. 179. For a drawing of Harwich which may have been made on 22 August 1817, see No. 142.

161 *Trees at East Bergholt.* 1817, October 17 Plate 130

Pencil. $21\frac{3}{4}\times15\frac{1}{8}$ ins. (552×385 mm.) No. 256–1888
On paper indistinctly watermarked: E & O [?]| 180 [7?].
Inscribed below on left by the artist *Octr. 17th. 1817. E. Bergholt.* On the back (not reproduced amongst the plates), a few scribbles resembling foliage.

This is a study of the two trees which are seen in the right foreground of the oil painting 'Flatford Mill' (exhibited at the Royal Academy, 1817; now in the

Tate Gallery, No. 1273); but, as Davies, p. 29, points out, it cannot have been used as a study for that picture since it bears a date after the completion and exhibition of the oil painting. The same two trees at an earlier state of growth (before the right-hand limb had been cut from the foremost) are seen in the sketch-books No. 121, p. 10 and No. 132, p. 61. (See Holmes, p. 244; L. ed. M., p. 410.) They are seen again in relation to Bridge Cottage in No. 324.

1817, October 22
Plate 131

162 *Elm trees in Old Hall Park, East Bergholt.*

Pencil, with slight grey and white washes. $23\frac{1}{4} \times 19\frac{1}{2}$ ins. (592 × 494 mm.)
No. 320–1891 (E.3237–1911)

Inscribed in lower left corner in pencil by the artist *Octr. 22d 1817 East Bergholt* and *John Constable 1817*. Inscribed on the back in pencil by the artist *This noble Elm—stood in the Park of Peter Godfrey Esq—called "Old Hall" Park at East Bergholt—Suffolk it was blown down April 1835. it broke even with ground—it measured when standing upright*[?] *10 × d having*[?] *formerly*[?] *lost the large arm on the Right J.C. This drawing was made 1816. in the Autumn.* Inscribed in another hand in pencil *The above is the Handwriting of John Constable R.A.* (*who made the Drawing*)*—Purchased at the sale of his Pictures and Drawings, at Fosters in—Pall Mall. 16 May 1838—A. James.*

Holmes (p. 244) plausibly identifies this with the drawing 'Elms' exhibited by Constable at the Royal Academy in 1818; it was on this basis included in the exhibition 'The First Hundred Years of the Royal Academy' 1951–2, No. 443. Holmes's further statement that the drawing was bought in at the Executors' sale, 16 May 1838, is disproved by the inscription on the back, identifying it with Lot 63 (sold for 7 gns. to White junr.). The drawing was Lot 168 at Miss James's sale at Messrs. Christie's, 22 June 1891, whence it was bought for the Museum. The year 1817, written on the front at the time when the drawing was made, is doubtless right; 1816 was added on the back by the artist from memory some eighteen years later.

The symbol *10 ×* in the inscription perhaps implies that the elm measured about ten times the height of a man, or ten diameters; the tree in Constable's drawing is in fact about twelve times the height of the man standing under it. A label inscribed in ink *Miss James No. 8* (the figure *8* in pencil) from the back of the frame is preserved in the archives of the Department of Paintings.

For Old Hall see the note to No. 42a.

Plate 132

163 *Study of ash trees.*

Pencil. $13 \times 9\frac{3}{8}$ ins. (328 × 238 mm.) No. 252–1888

On paper watermarked: J WHATMAN. The paper has been laid down on thin card; as far as can be seen by transmitted light, there is no inscription on the back.

The foremost tree in this study from nature is the same as that in the right foreground of 'The Valley Farm' (Tate Gallery No. 327), recognisable from the dead branch hanging vertically downwards on the left, a little more than half way up the tree. See note to No. 375 for a fuller discussion of the relationship between the foremost tree in this study from nature and 'The Valley Farm'.
The drawing is placed in this position in the catalogue because it has close affinities with Constable's other detailed drawings of trees in the collection; compare, for instance, the undetailed treatment of the background with that in No. 161. But, for the reason given in the note to No. 376, there is a slight possibility that No. 375 as well as No. 376 may have been drawn from a tree at Hampstead. If that were so, No. 163 would probably not have been drawn before 1819, when Constable first stayed at Hampstead.

1818

In 1818 Constable exhibited at the Royal Academy four landscapes and two drawings, one of the latter being entitled 'Elms' (probably No. 162 in this Catalogue).

164 *St. Mary's Church, Hendon: the churchyard.* 1818, June 28 Plate 134

Pencil. $4 \times 5\frac{1}{4}$ ins. (100 × 133 mm.) No. 267–1888
Page from a sketch-book.
Inscribed below on left by the artist *Hendon 28 June 1818.*
The inscription had been read as *Findon* (Sussex) until Key, p. 54, pointed out that the scene represented is the churchyard of St. Mary's, Hendon.
(See note following No. 170)

165 *Houses at Putney Heath.* 1818, August 13 Plate 133

Pen and water-colour. $4\frac{3}{4} \times 10\frac{5}{8}$ ins. (121 × 270 mm.) No. 172–1888
The drawing is laid down on an old mount.
Inscribed below on left in ink, in sloping script, by the artist *Putney Heath Augst. 13th. 1818.*

Beckett (II, p. 237) identifies the scene as a terrace which possibly contains "Louisa Cottage" where Mrs. Constable was staying this summer with her sister Louisa Bicknell. He records a pencil sketch, probably the original for this and other replicas, in the Fitzwilliam Museum, on two sketch-book pages, dated 13 August [1818]. Other water-colour replicas are in the Whitworth Art

Gallery, Manchester, and formerly with Mr. H. A. Sutch. One of these replicas is recorded by Holmes, p. 244, when on exhibition at Messrs. Leggatt's in 1899 (No. 109).

1818, September 9 **166** *Richmond Bridge with barges in the Thames.*

Plate 134

Pencil. 4×5¼ ins. (100×134 mm.) No. 264–1888
Page from sketch-book.
Inscribed below on left by the artist *Richmond Sep 9. 1818.* Inscribed on the back in pencil with the monogram *JC.*
(See note following No. 170)

1818 **167** *St. George's Chapel, Windsor.*

Plate 134

Pencil. 5¼×4 ins. (134×100 mm.) No. 276–1888
Page from a sketch-book.
Inscribed on the back in pencil by the artist *1818.* The back also bears a long erased inscription.
Holmes, p. 251, who did not know of the date on the back, dates *c.*1834.
(See note following No. 170)

[1818] **168** *St. George's Chapel, Windsor: the west end.*

Plate 134

Pencil. 5¼×4 ins. (135×100 mm.) No. 275–1888
Page from a sketch-book.
Beckett (VI, p. 38) suggests that Constable may have been accompanying Archdeacon Fisher on a visitation of Berkshire when he made the two drawings Nos. 167 and 168. Holmes, p. 251, dates *c.*1834.
(See note following No. 170)

1818 **169** *The Wheatfield. After Jacob Ruysdael.*

Plate 135

Pen and sepia ink. 4×6 ins. (103×152 mm.) No. 258–1888
On laid paper, impressed with an imitation plate mark.
The drawing is inscribed in the top right-hand corner in ink, in imitation of the etcher's signature *Ruysdael. fe:.* It is inscribed on the back in ink by the artist *J.C. fe: 1818.* and in pencil, perhaps in another hand, *JC. 1818.*

This is a copy of Jacob Ruysdael's etching (Bartsch 5) of which an example is reproduced in the *Print Collector's Quarterly*, Vol. VII, 1917, p. 157. A pen and ink copy by Constable, dated from Hampstead 17 May 1829, and made from an etching by Swanevelt lent to him by John Sheepshanks, is in the British Museum (L.B. 2).

170 *Cows and herdboy. After Aelbert Cuyp.* *c.*1818 Plate 135

Pencil. 4×5 ins. (100×128 mm.) No. 307–1888

Page from a sketch-book.

Inscribed on the back in pencil *Copy from Cuype by J. Constable.* This inscription is possibly in the artist's hand as far as *J.C* but the name *Constable* appears to have been completed by another hand.

Allowing for the trimming which has evidently taken place on the left, the measurements agree with those of the sketch-book used in 1818, and the style with its heavy angular shading accords with that seen in No. 164, so this may well come from the same book.

NOTE ON NOS. 164, 166, 167, 168 AND 170

Nos. 164, 166, 167 and 168 evidently come from the same sketch-book, measuring 4×5¼ ins. (100×134 mm.) and used in 1818. No. 170 may, for the reasons given above, come from the same source.

1819

In 1819 Constable exhibited at the Royal Academy 'A Scene on the River Stour' ('The White Horse'), bought by John Fisher, and now in the Frick Collection, New York (see the sketch-book No. 132, pp. 66 and 70). His second child Maria Louisa (Minna) was born on 19 July. He took a house at Hampstead for the first time at the end of the summer. He was elected A.R.A. on 1 November.

171 *Branch Hill Pond, Hampstead.* 1819, October Plate 136

Oil on canvas. 10×11⅞ ins. (254×300 mm.) No. 122–1888

The canvas has not been relined, and is on the original stretcher.

The top bar of the stretcher is inscribed in ink *End of Octr. 1819* and in pencil at top left *Isey* [Isabel Constable]. The date, presumably written by the artist or from indications left by him, has not previously been recorded. Holmes, p. 246, had dated the sketch on stylistic grounds *c.*1823.

Constable first moved to Hampstead in the summer of 1819: he rented Albion Cottage, Upper Heath, towards the end of August (Beckett, II, p. 253). On 2 November 1819 Farington noted in his diary "He [Constable] brought two pictures, Studies on Hampstead Heath, which he had painted" (Greig, Vol. VIII, p. 234). No. 171 is possibly one of the studies shown to Farington on this occasion.

Constable used No. 171 as the sketch for many paintings of Hampstead Heath at Branch Hill Pond. Among them are:

i No. 301 in this Catalogue. $23\frac{1}{2} \times 30\frac{1}{2}$ ins. Exhibited at the Royal Academy in 1828.

ii Tate Gallery No. 1275. 20×30 ins. Painted for W. G. Jennings in 1836. Bequeathed by Miss Isabel Constable.
This version has a rainbow and a windmill added to the scene. (L. ed. S., Pl. XII, in colour)

iii Tate Gallery No. 1813. $13 \times 19\frac{1}{2}$ ins. Painted for Jack Bannister. Bequeathed by Henry Vaughan. (L. ed. S., Pl. 84)

iv A painting sold as Lot 126 at the Henry Hebbert sale held at Messrs. Christie's, 21 April 1894. $24\frac{1}{2} \times 31\frac{1}{4}$ ins.

In his catalogue entry for Tate Gallery No. 1275 (which was then in the National Gallery), Davies (p. 29) lists iii as a related design; he also gives the evidence for identifying the scene as Branch Hill Pond. Constable may also have used this sketch in preparing those paintings by him of the Branch Hill Pond which have different compositions; for example, the cow drinking from the water on the left recurs in the design engraved by Lucas as 'Hampstead Heath' (S. 51). (See also No. 251)

1819, October
Plate 135

172 *A baby, perhaps Maria Louisa Constable.*

Pencil. $2\frac{1}{4} \times 4\frac{1}{8}$ ins. (59×105 mm.) No. D.235–1888
On laid paper of light green tinge.
Inscribed on the back by the artist [. . .]*mpstead* [. . .]. *Octr 1819* (the inscription has been truncated when the drawing was at some time laid down on thin card).

Constable's second child and first daughter, Maria Louisa, was born on 19 July 1819. Constable's family was at Hampstead in the autumn of this year (see also No. 171), so the drawing may represent her.

*c.*1819?
Plate 139

173 *Waterloo Bridge from the west.*

Pencil. $12 \times 16\frac{1}{8}$ ins. (306×410 mm.) No. 290–1888
On paper watermarked: J WHATMAN 1811.
The sketch has been laid down on thin card. By transmitted light a pencil inscription *21 × 16* can be read; this has been copied on to the back of the card.

This drawing is connected with the painting 'Waterloo Bridge, from Whitehall Stairs, June 18th, 1817' which Constable exhibited at the Royal Academy in 1832. For the early stages of this design and bibliographical references see the note to No. 174, and see the drawing No. 175. No. 173 belongs to a group of studies made from nature for the subject in which the ceremonial is not shown: these are listed by Sutton (*Connoisseur*, Vol. CXXXVI, 1955, pp. 249 and 250).

He points out that No. 173 is probably drawn from the upper windows of a house on the river. The gardens in the foreground appear to be those of Fife House, but may be nearer to the bridge (Sutton, *loc. cit.*, p. 250). No. 173 has usually been regarded as having been made about 1817, the year of the opening of the Bridge (see the *Inventory of Art Objects 1888*, p. 26; Holmes, p. 243; L. ed. S., p. 284; L. ed. M., p. 417). There is, however, no evidence that Constable thought of painting the subject before 1819. The style of the drawing would suggest that it was made at an early stage of the composition, but the possibility cannot be excluded that it may have been made as late as 1826 when Constable visited Pembroke House to sketch the terrace and add to his canvas.

174 *Waterloo Bridge from Whitehall Stairs.* *c.*1819?

Oil on millboard. 11½×19 ins. (292×483 mm.) No. 322–1888 Plate 138

174a A woodland scene. Plate 137

No. 174 *recto* is a study for the painting 'Waterloo Bridge, from Whitehall Stairs, June 18th, 1817' exhibited by Constable at the Royal Academy in 1832, and once in the collection of Mr. Harry Ferguson; the composition had engaged Constable intermittently from 1819. A full discussion of the relationship of the many sketches and alternative compositions is given together with 14 illustrations by Sutton (*loc. cit.*) pp. 248–55: he gives full references to earlier literature and quotes hitherto unpublished material. Meanwhile an oil sketch for the mezzotint by David Lucas has been rediscovered (collection of Mr. and Mrs. Paul Mellon). G. R. Rennie's Waterloo Bridge was opened by the Prince Regent on 18 June 1817: it is presumed that Constable saw the ceremony, since he was in London. The first known reference to his having conceived the idea of painting the opening ceremony is found in his letter of 17 July 1819 to John Fisher "I have made a sketch of my scene on the Thames—which is very promising" (Beckett, VI, p. 45). It is not entirely clear to which phase in the long history of the work No. 174 belongs, and the woodland sketch on the *verso*, which is an early work, does not provide any relevant information. Holmes identifies No. 174 tentatively with the picture referred to by Constable in his letter to Fisher of 22 January 1824: "I have done the little *Waterloo*, a small balloon to let off as a forerunner of the large one" (L. ed. S., p. 162). This view has been widely accepted, but the phrase surely refers to a somewhat larger and much more finished version, of the type Constable was likely to exhibit. It is more possible that No. 174 is the sketch of 1819 of which Constable wrote to Fisher, and which he showed to Farington on 11 August 1819. The entry in Farington's *Diary* (Greig, Vol. VIII, p. 225) reads: "Constable called, and brought a painted sketch of his view of Waterloo bridge &c and the river as it appeared on the day of the *opening the Bridge*. I objected to his having made it so much a 'Birds eye view' and thereby lessening magnificence of the bridge & buildings.—He sd. he would reconsider his sketch". In favour of the identification of No. 174 with this sketch of 1819, it may be noted that it does in fact give a bird's eye view of the bridge and buildings—as do all the versions with the exception of the type represented by that belonging to Viscountess Camrose. The style of No. 174 is hardly more advanced than that of No. 171, which is known to have been painted in 1819. No. 174 certainly represents a stage of the composition before 1826, when Constable added two feet to his canvas after visiting and sketching the terrace of Lord Pembroke's house: the house and terrace form the left foreground of the exhibited picture (see L. ed. S., p. 214, Constable's letter of 7 July [1826] to Fisher, and Leslie's footnote on it). (See also No. 175)

The oil sketch No. 174a bears some resemblance to those made by Constable in Helmingham Dell, but these provide no basis for a definite identification.

*c.*1819? Plate 139

175 *The Thames with Waterloo Bridge.*

Pen and bistre, with alterations in pencil and repairs in Indian ink. $6\frac{1}{2} \times 10\frac{3}{4}$ ins. (165×273 mm.) No. 604–1888

The drawing is on thin paper which has been laid on card. The surface of the drawing is damaged in places and the repairs are carried out on the card and extended over to the original drawing; this suggests that the mounting and repair were the work of the artist. It has not been considered practicable to remove the drawing from the card to examine the back.

The main lines of the composition in bistre are the same as those in the oil sketch No. 174 and the drawing may therefore have been made at approximately the same time. It differs in details, such as the height of the terrace on the left, the terrace architecture and the absence of the large barge in the foreground. Possibly it was the sketch from which No. 174 was made; but there are indications that the drawing was copied by the artist from the oil sketch in order to try out the effect of the pencil alterations in the left foreground. The main result of these is to give the principal tree a higher crown and more elongated appearance. This effect does not occur in No. 174 nor in the large oil study in the collection of Lord Fairhaven, but something similar is to be found in the exhibited picture of 1832. Sutton (*loc cit.*, p. 251) inclines to the same view.

*c.*1812–16 Plate 140

176 *View at East Bergholt over the kitchen garden oj Golding Constable's house.*

Pencil. $11\frac{7}{8} \times 17\frac{3}{4}$ ins. (302×449 mm.) No. 623–1888

On paper watermarked: J WHATMAN 1811, which has been laid down by the artist on a mount formed of two sheets of paper each watermarked: J RUSE 1804. On the inside of one of these two sheets is the inscription in ink *Mr. Constable.* The back of the mount is inscribed in pencil *From the Garden*; this appears to be written over an inscription by the artist *The Garden belonging to G Constable Esq.*

The second inscription, which would seem to have been the original one, suggests, if correctly transcribed, that the drawing was made before the death of Constable's father, which occurred in 1816. The drawing may therefore be dated, bearing the watermark in mind, *c*.1812 to 1816. The house was sold by November 1818 (Beckett, I, p. 172), which provides an extreme date. Holmes, p. 242, compares this drawing with No. 133, the small page from a sketch-book showing two views of Golding Constable's house, but the resemblance is one of subject matter rather than style. Two oil paintings in the Ipswich Museum (given by the National Art-Collections Fund in 1955 from the E. E. Cook collection) were described in the sale of paintings formerly the property of Captain Charles Constable held at Messrs. Christie's, 11 July 1887, as:

Lot 85 The Kitchen Garden of the House of Golding Constable, father of John Constable, with the mill, at which the latter worked, in the distance.

Lot 86 The Flower Garden of the House of Golding Constable.

Charles Rhyne has pointed out that the two paintings at Ipswich form a panorama; that the scene in No. 176 overlaps them both, and that the sketchbook page No. 132, p. 38 shows the middle distance of the view seen here. He takes them all to be scenes from an upper window of Golding Constable's house.

177 *East Bergholt Church: south archway of the ruined tower.* — *c*.1812–16? Plate 141

Pencil. $10\frac{5}{8} \times 8\frac{1}{8}$ ins. (269 × 207 mm.) No. 291–1888

The drawing has been laid down on an old mount—perhaps by the artist, in view of the similarity to the mounting of No. 176. The drawing itself resembles No. 176 in style, and may be assigned to roughly the same period.

178 *An oak tree in a hayfield.* — [1810–19?], July 22 Plate 142

Pencil. $4\frac{3}{4} \times 6\frac{3}{4}$ ins. (120 × 172 mm.) No. 357–1888

The paper is indistinctly watermarked, apparently: E & P. The paper is badly foxed on both front and back. A green mark, perhaps of water-colour, is to be seen in the top of the tree to right.

Inscribed on the back *22 July Afternoon* and with the serial number *36*.

The emphasis on the long shadows cast by the stooks of hay recalls the oil sketch No. 115 of 1812, but there is little on which to assign a definite dating for this sketch, and it may be earlier than 1810.

179 *East Bergholt Church: ruined tower from the north.* — *c*.1817? Plate 142

Pencil. $4\frac{1}{2} \times 7\frac{3}{8}$ ins. (115 × 186 mm.) No. 265–1888

Page from a sketch-book.

Inscribed on the back, not in the artist's hand, *E Bergholt J. Constable RA*; also with the monogram *JC*.

The measurements agree with sketch-books in use in 1812 (No. 118), 1815? (No. 142), 1817 (Nos. 156–160), and also with the two Salisbury sketch-books of 1820 (see note following No. 205). Should it come from any of these, that of 1817 is the most likely source. Holmes, p. 244, compares the drawing with the oil sketch No. 112, which he lists under the year 1819, but he may only be comparing the subject matter.

[–], August 9
Plate 143

180 *St. Mary-ad-Murum Church, Colchester.*

Pencil and chinese white. $4\frac{1}{2} \times 7\frac{3}{8}$ ins. (115 × 186 mm.) No. 301–1888
Page from a sketch-book.
The slight wash of chinese white has been added to suggest a rainbow over the cottage.
Inscribed below on left in pencil by the artist *Aug 9* followed by some marks which may be fortuitous or may represent a year: in the latter event it might be possible to read the date as *1811* or *1817*. Inscribed on back in pencil *Colchester. St Mary's* and with the monogram *JC*.

The measurements agree with sketch-books in use in 1812, 1815?, 1817 and 1820 (see note to No. 179). On 9 August 1820, Constable was in Salisbury (see No. 193). Of the other dates 1817 seems most plausible, in view of the resemblance of the style of drawing of the architecture to that in No. 148 of 1816. (See also note following No. 160)

*c.*1817?
Plate 143

181 *River scene at Mistley, Essex.*

Pencil. $4\frac{5}{8} \times 7\frac{3}{8}$ ins. (116 × 186 mm.) No. 620–1888
Page from a sketch-book.
The drawing is inscribed in the lower right corner by the artist *20*, followed by an indistinct word, perhaps *Aug*.
Lt.-Col. C. A. Brooks has identified the scene as the waterfront at Mistley, with the twin towers of Mistley Church, built by Robert Adam, in the distance, right. Beckett has pointed out that a drawing sold as Lot 20 in the Capt. C. Constable sale, Christies 11 July 1887, was of Mistley and dated 20 August 1817. It is probable that No. 181 was made on the same visit.

*c.*1810–19?
Plate 144

182 *A countryman walking, and two teams harrowing.*

Pencil. $4\frac{5}{8} \times 7\frac{3}{8}$ ins. (116 × 187 mm.) No. 295–1888
Page from a sketch-book.
There are two separate drawings on the page together with detailed studies of the packet of provisions and keg of liquor suspended from the countryman's pole.

The measurements agree with sketch-books in use in 1812, 1815?, 1817 and 1820 (see note to No. 179). The detail of the accessories of costume accords with those in the small sketch-books of 1813 and 1814; but too much stress cannot be laid on this analogy.

183 *River scene with houses.* c.1810–19? Plate 144

Pencil. $3\frac{7}{8} \times 5\frac{1}{8}$ ins. (97 × 129 mm.) No. 826–1888
Inscribed below in left corner by the artist *8 Sepr.*
Beckett states that the scene is probably at Shepperton.

183a On the back, in water-colour, is a sketch of a rainbow above fields and trees. Plate 144

The drawing on the *recto* is placed here because it has some affinities with No. 166: but it may be later than 1820.

1820

In 1820 Constable exhibited at the Royal Academy 'Stratford Mill' (now in the collection of Sir Reginald Macdonald-Buchanan) and 'A View of Harwich Lighthouse' (see No. 142 above).
He stayed with Fisher at Salisbury in July and August, settled his wife and children at Hampstead by 1 September, and paid a brief visit to Malvern Hall.

184 *Dedham Lock and Mill.* 1820 Plate 145

Oil on canvas. $21\frac{1}{8} \times 30$ ins. (537 × 762 mm.)
Sheepshanks Gift. No. F.A. 34
The canvas has been relined at an unknown date.
Signed and dated below on right *John Constable. ARA. pinxt. 1820.*

Dedham Mill belonged to Golding Constable, and the artist worked in it as a boy. No. 113 is an oil sketch from nature for the painting, and a related pencil sketch is mentioned under the entry on that sketch. The following versions by or attributed to Constable are recorded:

i A sketch on panel, sold as Lot 46 at Messrs. Sotheby's, 15 April 1953. $11 \times 14\frac{1}{2}$ ins. This came from the collection of G. Hilditch, and is said to be the work sold as Lot 39 of the Executors' sale, 16 May 1838, 'Sketch of a Mill on the Stour', bought by Hilditch, £7 17s. 6d.

ii Tate Gallery No. 2661. $21 \times 30\frac{1}{4}$ ins. This is a full-scale oil sketch with no boat in the left foreground, and no tow-horse in the right foreground. (L. ed. S., Pl. 61a)

iii A picture in the Currier Gallery of Art, Manchester, New Hampshire, U.S.A. $21\frac{1}{2} \times 30\frac{1}{2}$ ins. Signed below on right *John Constable. London.* Formerly in the collection of the Spedding family, members of which were friends of Constable's. A letter of 19 January 1841 from C. R. Leslie to Maria Constable refers to the acquisition of it by Miss Spedding, and states that this version too was painted in 1820. This is similar to No. 184, but the rope from the boat is attached to the bollard, and not to the harness of the tow-horse. (*Burlington Magazine*, Vol. XCVII, 1955, p. 54, fig. 25)

iv A picture from the T. Horrocks Miller and T. Pitt Miller collections sold as Lot 17 at Messrs. Christie's, 26 April 1946. 28×35 ins. This picture may have been acquired by Mr. Thomas Miller, who was forming his collection of British paintings around the year 1850 (W. P. Frith, *My Autobiography and Reminiscences*, I, 1887, p. 261). For Holmes's discussion of this version, see below.

v A picture in a private collection. Inscribed on the back *J. Constable F. London 1827.* In this version the mill has gothic windows. It is reproduced (fig. 26) and discussed in relation to Nos. 113 and 184, the pencil sketch in the Gilbert Davis collection, and ii and iii above, by Beckett in the *Burlington Magazine*, Vol. XCVII, 1955, pp. 52–55.

Constable exhibited 'A Mill' at the British Institution in 1819 (No. 78, framed measurement 39×47 ins.). Holmes, p. 244, identifies this exhibit either with No. 184 or iv above. The identification of one of the versions of 'Dedham Mill' with the picture exhibited in 1819 is plausible on grounds of style, title and the date of the sketches, and is not inconsistent with the framed measurements given in the British Institution catalogue. But it could not be No. 184, since that is dated in the following year.

Holmes also identifies either No. 184 or iv with Lot 80 in the Executors' sale, 16 May 1838, 'Dedham Mill and Church', bought by Brown for £45 3s. No certain conclusion can be reached in the absence of Mr. Sheepshanks' records, but he was actively buying works by Constable at this sale, and Brown may have been acting for him. As the note on iv shows, Mr. Thomas Miller belonged to a slightly later generation of collectors.

For a repetition of the central section of the composition see the sepia drawing No. 410.

1820, July 13
Plate 146

185 *Farm buildings and a bridge, near Salisbury.*

Pencil. $4\frac{1}{2} \times 7\frac{1}{8}$ ins. (115×180 mm.) No. 296–1888
Page from a sketch-book.

Inscribed in lower right corner by the artist *13 July 1820*. On the back, a small pencil scribble, possibly a carry-over from an adjacent sheet.
Constable was staying with John Fisher at Salisbury when this was drawn, so the buildings are in that neighbourhood.
(See note following No. 205)

186 *Stonehenge.* 1820, July 15 Plate 146

Pencil. $4\frac{1}{2} \times 7\frac{3}{8}$ ins. (115 × 187 mm.) No. 309–1888
Page from a sketch-book.
Inscribed below on left by the artist *15 July 1820* (not *18 July*, as transcribed in the *Catalogue of Water-Colour Paintings*, 1927, p. 118). Inscribed on the back in pencil *Stone Henge*. Water-colour has been dropped on the lower right-hand corner of the drawing.

This is the original study from nature (of which No. 396 is a later elaboration) for the water-colour (No. 395) which Constable exhibited at the Royal Academy in 1836.
(See note following No. 205)

187 *Salisbury Cathedral, from the south-west.* 1820, July 20 Plate 147

Pencil. $4\frac{1}{2} \times 7\frac{1}{4}$ ins. (115 × 184 mm.) No. 619–1888
Page from a sketch-book on paper with truncated watermark: J WH| TURKE| I| .
Inscribed below on left by the artist *20 July 1820*. Inscribed on the back in ink with the serial number *42* and in pencil *M.L.C.* [Maria Louisa Constable].
(See note following No. 205)

188 *View near Salisbury, showing the Cathedral.* 1820, July Plate 147

Pencil. $4\frac{1}{2} \times 7\frac{1}{4}$ ins. (115 × 185 mm.) No. 824—1888
Page from a sketch-book.
Inscribed in lower left corner by the artist with an almost illegible date . . . *4*[?] *July 1820*. Inscribed on the back in pencil with the serial number *43* and *M.L.C.* [Maria Louisa Constable].
(See note following No. 205)

189 *Entrance into Gillingham, with the church in the background.* 1820, July 30 Plate 148

Pencil. $4\frac{1}{2} \times 7\frac{1}{4}$ ins. (115 × 185 mm.) No. 820–1888
Inscribed in lower left corner by the artist *Sunday* [?] *30 July Gillingham*. Inscribed on the back in pencil in another hand *Gillingham*.

The day of the week is difficult to read, as it is written over some strokes of the drawing, but it appears to be *Sunday*, and this agrees with the calendar for 1820.

In 1823, the only other year in which he visited Gillingham, Dorset, Constable did not arrive there till after 20 August (Beckett, VI, p. 129), so the drawing must have been made in 1820. John Fisher had become Vicar of Gillingham in 1819. (See note following No. 205)

1820, July 31 Plate 148

190 *A cart at Gillingham.*

Pencil. $4\frac{1}{2} \times 7\frac{1}{4}$ ins. (115 × 185 mm.) No. 293–1888
Page from a sketch-book on paper with truncated watermark: J WHA| TURKE| 18| .
Inscribed in top left corner by the artist *Gillingham Dorset July 31st 1820.*
(See note following No. 205)

1820, August 4 Plate 153

191 *Cottages and trees in the New Forest.*

Pencil. $6\frac{3}{8} \times 9\frac{3}{8}$ ins. (161 × 237 mm.) No. 297–1888
Page from a sketch-book on paper with truncated watermark: J WH| 18| .
Inscribed below on left by the artist *New Forest Augt. 4. 1820.* Inscribed on the back in pencil *New Forest* and with the monogram *JC.*

The drawing of Downton, Wiltshire, in the British Museum (No. 1910–2–12–227) ($4\frac{3}{8} \times 7$ ins.; 112 × 177 mm.) was made on the same day, probably in one of the smaller sketch-books in use during this year.
(See note following No. 200)

[1820] Plate 153

192 *A bridge and cart at Gillingham.*

Pencil and grey wash. $6\frac{3}{8} \times 9\frac{3}{8}$ ins. (161 × 237 mm.) No. 257–1888
Page from a sketch-book.
Inscribed on the back in ink with serial number *32*, and in pencil *M.L.C.* [Maria Louisa Constable].
A drawing of the same scene from a viewpoint slightly to the right, in the British Museum (No. 1910–2–12–229) ($6\frac{1}{8} \times 9$ ins.; 156 × 229 mm.), is inscribed *Gillingham Dorset 29 July, 1820.* Though No. 192 is undated it was doubtless made during the same visit as the drawing No. 190 and that in the British Museum.
(See note following No. 200)

1820, August 9 Plate 149

193 *A road leading into Salisbury.*

Pencil. $4\frac{1}{2} \times 7\frac{1}{4}$ ins. (115 × 185 mm.) No. 262–1888
Page from a sketch-book on paper with truncated watermark: |TMAN |Y MILLS |17.

Inscribed in lower right corner by the artist *Salisbury Augst. 9. 1820.* and on the back in pencil, also by the artist *22d Augt. 1820 West doors of Salisbury.* The latter inscription evidently refers to No. 195, and shows that it was drawn on the following page of the sketch-book.
(See note following No. 205)

194 *Scene on a river, with a punt, near Salisbury.* 1820, August 20 Plate 149

Pencil. $4\frac{1}{2} \times 7\frac{1}{4}$ ins. (115 × 185 mm.) No. 261–1888
Page from a sketch-book.
Inscribed at top left by the artist *Salisbury Sunday 20. 1820 Augst.* Inscribed on the back in pencil with an undeciphered inscription [. . .] *23d Aug*[?] and with the monogram *JC*. Also a sum *3 . 2* [. . .] (an undeciphered word)
3 . 2
6 . 4 [. . .] (an undeciphered word)
(See note following No. 205)

195 *Salisbury Cathedral: the west door.* 1820, August 22 Plate 150

Pencil. $4\frac{1}{2} \times 7\frac{1}{4}$ ins. (115 × 185 mm.) No. 279–1888
Page from a sketch-book.
Inscribed on the back *22 Aug 1820 West doors of Salisbury* (see also the inscription on the back of No. 193) and with the monogram *IC*.
(See note following No. 205)

196 *Salisbury Cathedral and the Close.* 1820, August Plate 156

Oil on canvas. $9\frac{7}{8} \times 11\frac{7}{8}$ ins. (251 × 302 mm.) No. 318–1888
The canvas has been relined at an unknown date. The top of the stretcher is inscribed in pencil *Close Salisbury Augst. 1820.*

197 *Salisbury Cathedral from the south-west.* [1820] Plate 157

Oil on canvas. $9\frac{7}{8} \times 11\frac{7}{8}$ ins. (251 × 302 mm.) No. 319–1888
The canvas has been relined at an unknown date.
This sketch is of identical size with No. 196 and in closely similar style. It was therefore probably made at about the same time, during Constable's visit to Salisbury of July and August, 1820.
Holmes, p. 245, dates the sketch 1820.

198 *Trees and wattle hurdles at Hampstead.* 1820, September 7 Plate 150

Pencil. $4\frac{1}{2} \times 7\frac{1}{4}$ ins. (115 × 185 mm.) No. 310–1888
Page from a sketch-book in paper with truncated watermark: JOHN DIC| 18| .

Inscribed in lower left corner by the artist *7 Sepr. 1820. Hampstead. Day of the Eclipse.*
The eclipse referred to in the inscription was of the sun. It was visible from London, the period of greatest obscuration being just before 2 p.m.
(See note following No. 205)

1820, September 13
Plate 151

199 *Knowle Hall.*

Pencil. $4\frac{1}{2} \times 7\frac{1}{4}$ ins. (115 × 184 mm.) No. 617–1888
Page from a sketch-book.
Inscribed in top left corner by the artist *Knowle Hall Warwickshire Sepr. 13th. 1820.* Inscribed on the back in ink in another hand *Residence of Lord Brooke who was killed at the seige of Litchfield.—Knowle Hall*, and in lighter ink at top right *Hinge.*
For the visit to Malvern Hall during which this drawing was made see L. ed. S., p. 111; Davies, p. 35.
(See note following No. 205)

[1820, September]
Plate 154

200 *Corbels in Solihull Church.*

Pencil. $6\frac{1}{4} \times 9\frac{1}{8}$ ins. (158 × 233 mm.) No. 622–1888
Four drawings of different corbels on one sheet; each squared in pencil.
Inscribed by the artist under the top line of three drawings *Corbels—branch*[?] *long stands to hold figures* and along the lower edge *Gothick Brackets in Church of Solihull Warwickshire.*

Since Malvern Hall, Warwickshire, is just outside Solihull, this drawing must have been made on one of Constable's visits to the Hall; the visit of 1820 is more probable on grounds of style than the one he appears to have paid in 1809 (L. ed. S., p. 111; Davies, p. 35). A drawing dated 11 September 1820 of Whitley, near Solihull, was in Captain Charles Constable's collection.
This drawing bears no signs of having been in sketch-book; it was, however, mounted on card, and may have been trimmed.

NOTE ON NOS. 191, 192, 200, 203, 204, 206, 220, 238 AND 239

Nos. 191, 192, 220 and 239 are untrimmed leaves from a sketch-book, of which the pages measure $6\frac{3}{8} \times 9\frac{3}{4}$ ins. (161 × 237 mm.) and some bear the Whatman watermark of 1818. The dimensions of Nos. 200, 203, 204, 206 and 238, all of which have been mounted on card and probably trimmed, show that they almost certainly come from the same sketch-book. The dated leaves show that Constable used this sketch-book in 1820 (Nos. 191, 203 and 206) and in 1821 (Nos. 220 and 238).

201 *A church and graveyard.* c.1820 Plate 151

Pencil. $4\frac{1}{2} \times 7\frac{3}{8}$ ins. (115 × 186 mm.) No. 299–1888
Page from a sketch-book on paper with truncated watermark: |ATMAN |Y MILLS |17.
Inscribed on the back in pencil with the monogram *JC*. Also on the back in pencil, not reproduced amongst the plates, is a slight sketch of a tree, carried over from the next page of the sketch-book.

The church has not been identified. The size of page and the watermark show that the drawing comes from one of the sketch-books in use in 1820, and the scene may therefore be in the Salisbury area.
(See note following No. 205)

202 *Landscape with elm trees and a house.* c.1820 Plate 152

Pencil. $4\frac{1}{2} \times 7\frac{3}{8}$ ins. (115 × 187 mm.) No. 621–1888
Page from a sketch-book on paper with truncated watermark: JOHN DICK| 18| .
The size of page and the watermark show that the drawing comes from the same sketch-book as No. 198.
(See note following No. 205)

203 *Fir trees at Hampstead.* 1820, October 2 Plate 155

Pencil. $9\frac{1}{8} \times 6\frac{1}{4}$ ins. (233 × 160 mm.) No. 251–1888
On paper with truncated watermark: |ATMAN |18.
Inscribed vertically in top right corner by the artist *Wedding day. Hampstead Octr. 2. 1820*. Inscribed on the back in pencil *M.L.C.* [Maria Louisa Constable].

The close similarity of size, the position of the inscription, and the possibility that the watermark could be the truncated portion of that on No. 191, all suggest that this may have been a drawing from the sketch-book discussed in the note following No. 200. It had been mounted on card, and this might account for the absence of clearer evidence on the point.
Constable was married on 2 October 1816.
Possibly this is the drawing which is the subject of C. R. Leslie's anecdote about William Blake (L. ed. S., p. 367): "The amiable but eccentric Blake, looking through one of Constable's sketch books, said of a beautiful drawing of an avenue of fir trees on Hampstead Heath, 'Why, this is not drawing, but *inspiration*'; and he replied, 'I never knew it before; I meant it for drawing'."
(See note following No. 200)

204 *Elm trees.* c.1820? Plate 155

Pencil. $9\frac{1}{4} \times 6\frac{1}{4}$ ins. (234 × 160 mm.) No. 351–1888
This drawing has been placed here to be in series with the tree drawings No. 203

and 205, and because its measurements coincide with those of No. 203. For a discussion of the possibility that it comes from a sketch-book used in 1820 and 1821, see the note following No. 200.

Plate 152 **205** *Trees at Hampstead.*

Pencil. $4\frac{5}{8} \times 7\frac{1}{4}$ ins. (116 × 185 mm.) No. 821–1888
Page from a sketch-book.
Inscribed below on left by the artist . . . *nine evening*— [the beginning torn away]. The back is inscribed in another hand in ink with the serial number *35*, and in pencil *Hampstead nine evening*—. This inscription doubtless preserves the missing word from the front of the drawing.

The sketch has been placed here to be in series with the tree drawings Nos. 203 and 204, and because its measurements agree with those of the smaller sketch-books used in 1820. However, it should be noted that the drawing No. LB.13*a* in the British Museum, which measures $10\frac{1}{8} \times 6\frac{5}{8}$ ins. (259 × 170 mm.), though larger, closely resembles No. 205 in style and subject, and is inscribed *Hampstead June 21 1823 Wednesday 9 o clock Eveng Ash*. No. 205 may then have been made at the same time, although there is no other evidence for the use by Constable of a sketch-book of the size $4\frac{5}{8} \times 7\frac{1}{4}$ ins. (116 × 185 mm.) in 1823.

NOTE ON NOS. 185–190, 193–195, 198, 199, 201, 202, AND 205

In 1820 Constable used two sketch-books each measuring 115 × 186 mm., one with the Whatman watermark of 1817, the other with the watermark of Dickinson (unless, of course, he had a single book made up of these different papers). Nos. 187, 190, 193 and 201 come from the Whatman book, Nos. 198 and 202 from the Dickinson book. Nos. 185, 186, 188, 189, 194, 195, 199 and perhaps also No. 205, come from one or other of the books, but bear no watermarks. Constable used sketch-books of the size 115 × 186 mm. in 1812? (No. 118), unless, as seems more probable, he has misdated a page of one of the 1820 sketch-books, in this instance, 1815? (No. 142), 1817, and again later in 1828 (Nos. 302, 304–309), whilst books measuring 115 × 181 mm. were in use in 1815 and 1816. (See also Nos. 179–182 for other sketch-book pages of this size)

1820, October 8 **206** *Bridge at Hendon.*
Plate 154

Pencil. $6\frac{1}{4} \times 9\frac{1}{4}$ ins. (160 × 235 mm.) No. 271–1888
Inscribed in lower left corner by the artist *Hendon 8 Oct. 1820*.
The drawing is nearly the same size as Nos. 203 and 204, and may come from the same sketch-book as No. 191. The drawing has been mounted on card, and may have been trimmed.
(See note following No. 200)

207 *Sketch at Hampstead: stormy sunset.* 1820, October 17

Plate 158

Oil on paper or card. 5×6¾ ins. (127×171 mm.) No. 147–1888
Inscribed on the back in ink, not in the artist's hand, *Hampd. 17th Octr 1820 Stormy Sunset. Wind. W.*
The source of the inscription is not clear; possibly the sketch has been re-backed.

208 *Sketch at Hampstead: evening.* [1820], October 28

Plate 158

Oil on card. 6¼×8 ins. (159×203 mm.) No. 159–1888
The thin card on which the sketch was painted was probably originally intended as a mount for a water-colour, since it has washes and lines on the back (see also No. 322).
Inscribed on the back in pencil by the artist *28th Octr. fine Evening Wind Gentle at S.W.* The same inscription is repeated in ink, together with the monogram *JC*. Also on the back are brush scribbles, mainly in green, and a comic face.

The shrubs in the foreground are the same as, or nearly identical with, those in No. 207 and the treatment is so similar as to leave little doubt that the two sketches were made at about the same time. The missing year of the inscription may therefore be supplied as 1820, and the scene taken to be Hampstead. Holmes, p. 246, dates *c.*1822 and suggests Hampstead for the locality.

1821

The chief of Constable's four exhibits in 1821 was 'Landscape: Noon' ('The Hay Wain') (National Gallery No. 1207; for the full-scale sketch see No. 209 in this Catalogue). His third child, Charles Golding Constable, was born on 29 March. He accompanied Archdeacon John Fisher on his visitation of Berkshire in June, took No. 2 Lower Terrace, Hampstead, for his family during the summer and autumn and paid a visit to Fisher at Salisbury in November.

209 *Full-scale study for 'The Hay Wain'.* *c.*1821

Plate 159

Oil on canvas. 54×74 ins. (1370×1880 mm.) No. 987–1900
Bequeathed by Mr. Henry Vaughan.

This is the full-scale study for the painting exhibited by Constable at the Royal Academy in 1821 (No. 339 'Landscape: Noon') and now in the National

Gallery, No. 1207. For a full account of the finished painting, its history, and other sketches for it, see Davies, pp. 23–6. See also Sir K. Clark, *The Haywain in the National Gallery* (*The Gallery Books*, No. 5, 1944), in which he discusses the relation between the sketch and the finished picture, and reproduces details.

No. 209 is broadly blocked in to establish the general balance of the values and the masses. In many areas the brown ground is left uncovered: for example in the foliage of the trees and in the water. The central chimney of Willy Lott's house, in the extreme left of the canvas, is not expressed. The exhibited version is painted with far greater elaboration of detail and range of colour: the only substantial variation from the sketch is in the omission of the figure on horseback in the foreground—this was originally included but subsequently painted out. Among the sketches from nature used by Constable in the planning of the composition are Nos. 110 and 110a in this Catalogue; No. 329a is independently related to these earlier sketches of Willy Lott's house.

The history of No. 209 and No. 286 (the sketch for 'The Leaping Horse') has probably been the same, but the information available to us about their ownership before 1853 is not complete. In view of his predilection for keeping his studies ("He used to say . . . that he had no objection to part with the corn, but not with the field that grew it", R. and S. Redgrave, *A Century of Painters*, Vol. II, 1866, p. 396), it is likely that Constable would have retained them both until his death. Lot 38 in the Executors' sale, 16 May 1838, is listed as "Two—Sketches of Landscapes, *the pictures now in France*". Holmes, p. 232, has a note saying that these "are said to have been the two large studies for 'The Hay Wain' and 'The Leaping Horse' ". This identification, if correct, shows that the sale catalogue is partly in error, for it was not 'The Leaping Horse' but the 'View on the Stour near Dedham' which went to France as a companion piece to 'The Hay Wain'; H. Isherwood Kay in pointing this out (*Burlington Magazine*, Vol. LXII, 1933, p. 286) shows that the catalogue is also at fault elsewhere.

Lot 38 was bought for £14 10s. by Purton, who was apparently buying it in on behalf of the family. In that event, both these sketches may have been bought in and remained for a time as the property of the artist's family. The next information about the two works comes from the manuscript volume of notes on 'The Hay Wain' kept by Mr. Henry Vaughan, and bequeathed by him to the National Gallery. Mr. Vaughan owned the exhibited version of 'The Hay Wain', and gave it to the National Gallery in 1886. After quoting some passages about the sketches extracted from Redgrave's *A Century of Painters*, Vol. II, pp. 383–96, Mr. Vaughan writes "The two studies above alluded to by Mr. Redgrave have now (1886) been exhibited at the Kensington Museum for many years. They are the 'Leaping Horse' and the 'Hay Wain'. They were first seen by me (H.V.) at the house of Mr. C. R. Leslie, R.A. who admired them greatly. Eventually they came into my possession, by purchase of Mr. D. T. White. I was told by Mr. White that Troyon came frequently to see these studies and desired much to become the owner of them had circumstances permitted. The two studies are at this time (1886) in the Edinburgh International Exhibition. On the occasion of my visit to Mr. Leslie to see the sketches or studies I noticed a small copy by Mr. Leslie of the 'Hay Wain' sketch which shews some variation in the figures in the foreground from those in the finished picture of the 'Hay Wain' in the National Gallery".

Leslie was storing the paintings "for want of room elsewhere". He cleaned the surfaces with the help of his son R. C. Leslie, and the latter made small copies of each (R. C. Leslie's edition of C. R. Leslie's *Life*, 1896, p. xiii; his copy of the sketch for 'The Leaping Horse' is reproduced facing p. 175 of this edition). Mr. D. T. White was a dealer active in the eighteen-fifties, and the occasion of Troyon's admiration will have been his first visit to London in 1853 or his second visit in 1857. The first visit is perhaps more likely as Troyon had undertaken it to get into touch with London dealers, and a sketch-book attributed to this visit contains notes by him about Constable and the importance of the sky in his paintings. (The sketch-book is described by L. C. Watelin "Un Voyage de Constant Troyon en Angleterre", in *L'Art et les Artistes*, n.s. I, 1920, pp. 305–307.) Mr. Vaughan lent the sketches to the Museum in or before 1862. The earliest reference to them in the Museum's records is contained in a list of pictures on loan at 24 October 1862. Redgrave, in the extract on which Vaughan wrote the comments quoted above, mentions that at the time of the International Exhibition, London, 1862, it was possible to compare the sketches with the completed 'Hay Wain', since the sketches were hung in the Sheepshanks Galleries, and the other in an adjacent gallery. The sketches seem to have remained permanently on loan in the Museum except when they were withdrawn for the International Exhibition, London, 1874, and the Edinburgh International Exhibition, 1886. When Mr. Vaughan died in 1900, his bequest of the two works to the Museum became effective.

In brief: Nos. 209 and 286 appear to have formed Lot 38 in the Executors' sale, 16 May 1838; they were bought in, were stored for the artist's family by Leslie; were subsequently acquired by the dealer D. T. White, who had them in about 1853, when Troyon saw them; Mr. Henry Vaughan bought them from White, lent them to the Museum in or before 1862, and eventually bequeathed them to the Museum.

210 *Banks of the canal near Newbury, Berks.* 1821, June 4
Plate 160

Pencil, and grey wash. $6\frac{3}{4} \times 10\frac{1}{4}$ ins. (173 × 260 mm.) No. 284–1888

Page from a sketch-book on paper with truncated watermark: TURKE| J WHA| 18| .

Inscribed in top left corner in ink by the artist *Banks of the Canal, near Newbury Berks, June 4th. 1821.*

(See note following No. 219)

1821, June 4 Plate 160 **211** *A water-mill at Newbury, Berks.*

Pencil and grey wash. $6\frac{3}{4} \times 10\frac{1}{4}$ ins. (173 × 260 mm.) No. 285–1888
Page from a sketch-book on paper with truncated watermark: TURKE| J WHA| 18| .
Inscribed in top left corner in ink by the artist *Newbury Berks June 4, 1821.*
(See note following No. 219)

1821, June 5 Plate 161 **212** *A view of the canal, Newbury, Berks.*

Pencil and grey wash. $6\frac{3}{4} \times 10\frac{1}{4}$ ins. (173 × 261 mm.) No. 283–1888
Page from a sketch-book.
Inscribed in lower left corner in ink by the artist *Newbury Berks June 5. 1821.*
(See note following No. 219)

1821, June 5 Plate 161 **213** *A view of Newbury, with the tower of St. Nicholas's Church.*

Pencil and grey wash. $6\frac{3}{4} \times 10\frac{1}{4}$ ins. (173 × 260 mm.) No. 246–1888
Page from a sketch-book.
Inscribed in top left corner in ink by the artist *Newbury Berks June 5. 1821.*
(See note following No. 219)

1821, June 6 Plate 162 **214** *The Abbey Gate, Reading.*

Pencil. $6\frac{3}{4} \times 10\frac{1}{4}$ ins. (173 × 260 mm.) No. 286–1888
Page from a sketch-book.
Inscribed in top left corner in ink by the artist *Abbey Gate Reading June 6. 1821.* The date has been read as *5* (*Catalogue of Water-Colour Paintings*, 1927, p. 104), but is more probably a *5* changed into a *6*, especially as Constable had already made two drawings at Newbury on 5 June (Nos. 212 and 213) and the other drawing of Reading in this collection (No. 215) is of 6 June.
(See note following No. 219)

1821, June 6 Plate 162 **215** *A view of Reading from the river.*

Pencil. $6\frac{3}{4} \times 10\frac{1}{4}$ ins. (173 × 260 mm.) No. 287–1888
Page from a sketch-book on paper with truncated watermark: |Y MILLS |TMAN |19.
Inscribed in lower left corner in ink by the artist *The Abbey at Reading. St. Helens, St. Laurence. June 6 1821.*
(See note following No. 219)

216 *A ruin near Abingdon, Berks.* 1821, June 7 Plate 163

Pencil. $6\frac{3}{4} \times 10\frac{1}{4}$ ins. (173×261 mm.) No. 288–1888
Page from a sketch-book on paper with truncated watermark: |Y MILLS |TMAN |19.
Inscribed in top left corner in ink by the artist *Ruin near Abingdon. June 7th. 1821.*
(See note following No. 219)

217 *The old bridge at Abingdon, Berks.* 1821, June 7 Plate 163

Pencil. $6\frac{3}{4} \times 10\frac{1}{4}$ ins. (173×261 mm.) No. 282–1888
Page from a sketch-book.
Inscribed in top left corner in ink by the artist *Old Bridge. Abingdon June 7. 1821.*
On the back (not reproduced amongst the plates) are a few scribbles in pencil, including one which appears to represent a weather vane.
(See note following No. 219)

218 *A view of Abingdon from the river.* 1821, June 7 Plate 164

Pencil. $6\frac{3}{4} \times 10\frac{1}{4}$ ins. (173×261 mm.) No. 618–1888
Page from a sketch-book.
Inscribed in top left corner in ink by the artist *Abingdon June 7. 1821.*
(See note following No. 219)

219 *Blenheim Palace and Park, Woodstock.* 1821, June 8 Plate 164

Pencil. $6\frac{3}{4} \times 10\frac{1}{4}$ ins. (173×261 mm.) No. 355–1888
Page from a sketch-book on paper with truncated watermark: |Y MILLS |TMAN |19.
Inscribed in top left corner in pencil by the artist *Blenheim. June 1821.* Inscribed on the back in ink with the serial number *30* and in pencil *M.L.C.* [Maria Louisa Constable].

NOTE ON NOS. 210–219 AND NOS. 240–242

Leslie says (L. ed. S., pp. 113, 114) "In June [1821], Constable accompanied his friend Fisher during his visitation in Berkshire, and made some beautiful pencil and washed drawings of the scenery in the neighbourhood of Reading, Newbury and Abingdon. He also visited Oxford with Fisher, and made an exquisite drawing of Blenheim, from the Park". Fisher's Archdeaconry consisted of four rural deaneries, Newbury, Reading, Wallingford and Abingdon, and the itinerary established by the dated drawings accounts for all these places except Wallingford.
Nos. 210–219 are evidently, from their subject and date, pages from the sketch-book

Constable used on this occasion, and No. 219 may be the drawing of Blenheim described by Leslie. The sketch-book measures 173 × 261 mm. ($6\frac{3}{4} \times 10\frac{1}{4}$ ins.) and is made up of paper watermarked J WHATMAN TURKEY MILLS 1819. No. 240 comes from the same book, but is not connected with the Berkshire visitation. Two drawings in the British Museum which are seen from their subject, date and size, to be on leaves from the same sketch-book are:

L.B. 26*b* Cottage near Reading, dated 6 June 1821.

L.B. 17 High Street, Oxford, dated 9 June 1821.

Two pages exhibited at Messrs. Wildenstein's, 1937, appear to come from the same source: No. 136 inscribed *Newbury Berks June 4 1821* ($6\frac{3}{4} \times 9\frac{3}{4}$ ins.) (lent by G. Lawrence) and No. 137 inscribed *A Lock near Newbury June 5, 1821* ($6\frac{3}{4} \times 10$ ins.) (from the collection of Capt. Charles Constable).

There is some uncertainty about the dating of uninscribed drawings not connected with Berkshire but of approximately the same size, since there are in the British Museum four drawings the measurements of which are almost identical with Nos. 210–219, but which bear dates in 1823.

These are:

L.B. 9 Bentley, Suffolk. 168 × 254 mm. Inscribed *Bentley 21 April 1823.* (Reproduced, M. S. Henderson, *Constable*, 1905, facing p. 67)

L.B. 11*a* View on the Stour. 169 × 254 mm. Inscribed *E.B. June 20 1823.*

L.B. 13*a* Study of an ash tree. 259 × 170 mm. (For inscription see note on No. 205 above)

L.B. 20*b* View at Hampstead. 169 × 253 mm. Inscribed *Hampd. 26 June 1823.*

These pages indicate either that Constable was again using the Berkshire sketch-book in 1823, or, more probably, that in that year he used another of about the same size. Nos. 241 and 242 come from one or other of the books, and may therefore be assigned either to 1821 or to 1823. Among the undated drawings in the British Museum L.B. 26*a*, a canal scene, may be assigned from its subject matter to the sketch-book of 1821; L.B. 11*b*, a scene at Hampstead, was probably made in 1823, and L.B. 22*b* and 28*b* are not to be dated more closely than to one or other of these years.

In his letters of 5 January 1825, 8 April 1825 and 1 February 1826 (Beckett, VI, pp. 189, 198, 214) Constable asks for the return of a sketch-book which he has lent to Fisher with a drawing of the bridge at Oxford on the front page. Since he describes it as small in comparison with another of "good size" it seems that he can hardly be referring to the source of Nos. 210–219, but to a smaller book used on the same excursion.

1821, August 21
Plate 165

220 *A cart and horses.*

Pencil. $6\frac{3}{8} \times 9\frac{3}{8}$ ins. (161 × 237 mm.) No. 353–1888

Page from a sketch-book on paper with truncated watermark: |ATMAN |818. Inscribed in lower left corner in pencil by the artist *Augst 21st. 1821.* On the back a few pencil scribbles, including a cartouche.

Possibly drawn at Hampstead, since Constable wrote thence to Fisher on 4 August and 20 September 1821 and does not mention any other excursions in the meantime.
The size and watermark show that this comes from the sketch-book discussed in the note following No. 200.

221 *Study of sky and trees.* [1821], September 3
Plate 166

Oil on paper. $9\frac{1}{2} \times 11\frac{3}{4}$ ins. (241×298 mm.) No. 151–1888
Inscribed on the back in ink by the artist *September 3d. Noon. very sultry. with large drops of Rain falling on my palate light air from S.W.*

The year is not given in the inscription but was supplied in the Museum's catalogues from 1893 onwards as 1823 (?). This conjecture was apparently based upon the date of No. 258, which bears the next Museum serial number. Holmes, p. 245, dates 1821, and no doubt this is correct, for the sketch is evidently in series with Nos. 222, 226, etc., and forms one of the sky studies discussed in the note following No. 235. The topographical features of the scene would in any case render 1823 unlikely since Constable was staying with Fisher at Gillingham on 3 September of that year.
(See note following No. 235)

222 *Study of sky and trees, with a red house, at Hampstead.* 1821, September 12
Plate 167

Oil on paper. $9\frac{1}{2} \times 11\frac{3}{4}$ ins. (241×298 mm.) No. 156–1888
Inscribed in ink on the back by the artist *Sepr. 12. 1821. Noon. Wind fresh at West* . . . [3 or 4 words are erased here] *Sun very Hot. looking southward exceedingly bright vivid & Glowing, very heavy showers in the Afternoon but a fine evening. High wind in the night.* Above this inscription is the following, also written in ink by the artist, but deleted *Sepr. 10 1821 Eleven o'clock Sultry with warm gentle rain*[?] *falling large heavy clouds* . . . [a word here is illegible] *a heavy downpour and thunder.* Also inscribed below on left in ink *M.L.* [Maria Louisa Constable].

An oil sketch entitled 'Harrow, from Hampstead. Sunset September 12th, 1821' was No. 262 at the Grosvenor Gallery Winter Exhibition, 1889 (size $9\frac{1}{2} \times 12$ ins.) (lent by the Executors of the late Miss Isabel Constable); the title and date of this sketch confirm that No. 222 was also made at Hampstead.
The existence of two inscriptions relating to different dates suggests that the artist sometimes wrote these on the backs of his oil sketches later, from rough notes made at the time or from memory, and that the first one written here was intended for another sky study of the series (perhaps No. 280 at The Grosvenor Gallery, 1889, which is dated 10 September 1821). See also No. 229 for a sketch with the wall of a red house on the extreme right.
(See note following No. 235)

[1821, September] **223** *Trees at Hampstead: The path to Church.*
Plate 168

Oil on canvas. 36×28½ ins. (914×724 mm.) No. 1630–1888
Isabel Constable Bequest.

This painting is one of five works bequeathed to the Museum in 1888 by Miss Isabel Constable with the request that they should be described as a gift from Maria Louisa Constable, Isabel Constable and Lionel Bicknell Constable. It is described in her will as "the upright and large picture of 'Trees at Hampstead' which is sometimes called 'The path to Church' ".
Hampstead Parish Church is just visible on the extreme left of No. 223. The painting is unfinished in some details, for example at the foot of the fence on the right.
Holmes, p. 245, dates *c.*1821. Shirley (L. ed. S., pp. 116 and 117) tentatively identifies No. 223 with the painting mentioned by Constable in his letter of 20 September 1821 to Fisher: "And independent of my *jobs* I have done some studies, carried further than I have yet done any, particularly a natural (but highly Elegant) group of trees. Ashes, Elms, and Oaks etc which will be of quite as much service to me as if I had bought the feild and Hedge Row, which contains them. and perhaps one time or another will fetch as much for my children. It is rather larger than a kitcat & upright". The kitcat size is 36×28 ins. and No. 223 differs from it only in being ½ in. wider, so the statement about size hardly applies, but in style and subject the identification is plausible. If it be accepted, the further suggestion made by Key, p. 61, that the picture was one of Constable's exhibits at the Royal Academy in 1822, No. 314 'A Study of Trees from Nature', may well be correct. The position of this exhibit indicates that it was an oil.

[1821], Sept. 24 **224** *Study of sky and trees.*
Plate 169

Oil on paper. 9¾×12 ins. (248×305 mm.) No. 167–1888
Inscribed on the back in ink by the artist *Sepr. 24th . . 10 o'clock morning wind S.W. warm & fine till afternoon, when it rained & wind got more to the north.* Also inscribed in ink with the monogram *JC.*
The year is not given but this sketch doubtless belongs to the same series as Nos. 222, 226, etc.: that is, to the group of sky studies made at Hampstead. Holmes, p. 245, dates 1821.
(See note following No. 235)

1821, September 27 **225** *A cart and team.*
Plate 180

Pencil. 3⅜×4⅜ ins. (84×113 mm.) No. 839–1888
Page from a sketch-book, partially laid down on a larger piece of paper (see also Nos. 236, 237, 243, 244 and 245).

Inscribed in right lower corner in pencil by the artist *27 Sepr 1821*. The date has been copied on to the back by another hand in ink.
A cloud study bearing the same date was Lot 88 in the sale of paintings formerly the property of Captain Charles Constable held at Messrs. Christie's, 23 June 1890.
(See note following No. 245)

226 *Study of sky and trees at Hampstead.* 1821, October 2 Plate 170

Oil on paper. 9⅝×11¾ ins. (245×298 mm.) No. 168–1888
Inscribed on the back in ink by the artist *Ocr. 2d. 1821. 8. to 9. very fine still morning. turned out a may day. Rode with Revd. Dr. White. round by Highgate. Muswell Hill. Coney Hatch. Finchley. by Hendon Home.* Also inscribed in ink with the monogram *JC*.
A small white patch in the centre of the bushes in the foreground where pigment had become detached was filled in with water-colour in 1936.
(See note following No. 235)

227 *Buildings on rising ground near Hampstead.* 1821, October 13 Plate 171

Oil on paper. 9¾×11¾ ins. (248×298 mm.) No. 781–1888
Inscribed on the back in pencil by the artist *Octr—13th. 1821.—4 to 5 afternoon—very fine with Gentle Wind at N.E.* The inscription is repeated in ink in another hand.

The topography of the pond and the paths on the rising ground beyond bear a resemblance to those features in the painting 'The Salt Box' (Tate Gallery, No. 1236). This may therefore be a sketch from nature of the Branch Hill Pond and the house known as The Salt Box (Davies, pp. 26, 29 and 37–9).

228 *A sandbank at Hampstead Heath.* 1821, November 2 Plate 172

Oil on paper. 9¾×11¾ ins. (248×298 mm.) No. 164–1888
Inscribed on the back in ink by the artist *Novr. 2d 1821. Hampstead Heath windy afternoon.* Also inscribed in ink with the monogram *JC*.
(See note following No. 235)

229 *Study of sky and trees.* *c.*1821 Plate 173

Oil on paper. 10×11¾ ins. (254×298 mm.) No. 157–1888
Inscribed on the back in ink *M.L.* [Maria Louisa Constable], and in the top left corner *4d*. Inscribed on the back in pencil *J.C.*

Holmes, p. 245, dates 1821. This is certainly justified, since the sketch is in series with the sky and tree studies made at Hampstead in that year, and No. 222 presents a similar view closed in on the right with the side of a red house. (See note following No. 235)

*c.*1821
Plate 174

230 *Study of sky and trees.*

Oil on paper. $9\frac{3}{4} \times 11\frac{3}{4}$ ins. (248×298 mm.) No. 162–1888
Inscribed on the back in pencil *Charles Constable.*
Holmes, p. 245, states wrongly that this sketch is dated 12 September 1821 but it is clearly in series with No. 222 which is so dated, and can be associated with the group of sky and tree studies which Constable made at Hampstead in that year. (See note following No. 235)

*c.*1821?
Plate 175

231 *View in a garden, with a shed on the left.*

Oil on paper laid on canvas. $11\frac{7}{8} \times 9\frac{3}{8}$ ins. (302×238 mm.) No. 133–1888
The stretcher is inscribed in ink. *On paper J. Constable R.A. Peel Feb 18 48. 5.*

Holmes, p. 251, regards this as an example of Constable's latest manner, and dates it *c.*1834. While there is something in favour of regarding No. 231 as a late work (for example there is much use of the palette knife, though this also occurs in No. 171), it seems more consistent to consider the sketch as one of the series of sky studies made by Constable at Hampstead *c.*1821. The manifest freedom of treatment can be paralleled in some of the sketches dated for this year, and the intention of the sketch is evidently to portray a dark stormy effect of sky. It might even be conjectured that the wooden building on the left is the coal cellar in the garden of No. 2 Lower Terrace which Constable cleared out for use as a studio. "At this little place I have [sundry] small works going on—for which purpose I have cleared a small shed in the garden, which held sand, coals, mops & brooms & that is literally a coal hole, and have made it a workshop, & a place of refuge—when I am down from the house" (Beckett, VI, p. 71: letter of 4 August 1821 to Fisher). The sketch has hitherto been known as 'Part of a rustic building'. The inscription on the stretcher has not been identified with any recorded sale. It seems probable that it is a stock mark, possibly made by the firm of John Peel, 17 and 18 Golden Square, listed in London directories of the 1830's and 1840's as 'picture liner and restorer'. A similar inscription has been seen on an oil sketch which was in the art trade in 1961.
(See note following No. 235)

*c.*1821?
Plate 176

232 *View in a garden with a red house beyond.*

Oil on canvas. 14×12 ins. (355×305 mm.) No. 136–1888
The canvas has been relined at an unknown date.

Holmes, p. 244, dates this sketch *c.*1817, and comments "This date is only tentative: the style of the sketch affords no definite clue to the time at which it was done". The painting of the foliage however may be compared with that in Nos. 221, 222, etc., and this together with the emphasis on the sky serves to link it with the studies of sky and trees made at Hampstead in and around 1821. The presence of washing in the garden perhaps indicates that the sketch was made in the garden of a house the artist was then occupying. John Baskett suggests, in *Constable Oil Sketches*, 1966, that it may be a study from the upper windows of No. 2 Lower Terrace.
(See note following No. 235)

233 *Branch Hill Pond, Hampstead* (?) *c.*1821–2

Plate 177

Oil on canvas. $9\frac{5}{8} \times 15\frac{1}{2}$ ins. (245 × 394 mm.) No. 125–1888
The canvas has been relined. The artist has enlarged the painting area of the canvas by the extent of the turn-over round the original stretcher, that is, about $\frac{3}{4}$ in. at either side and 1 in. at the bottom.

Holmes, p. 248, dates *c.*1827. This sketch is, however, close in style to 'Harrow from Hampstead Heath: sunset' in the Manchester City Art Gallery, 10 × 12 ins. (reproduced in the Gallery's publication *English Paintings, 1800–1870*, Pl. 7), which is dated August 1821, and to Nos. 247 and 248 of 1822. No. 233 may therefore have been painted in 1821 or 1822.
Comparison with No. 171 and with the Tate Gallery paintings Nos. 1236 and 4237, shows that the scene is probably Branch Hill Pond. The solitary tree in the centre of the sketch is a conspicuous landmark, and appears to be the same as that seen in the other pictures cited.

234 *Study of tree trunks.* *c.*1821?

Plate 178

Oil on paper. $9\frac{3}{4} \times 11\frac{1}{2}$ ins. (248 × 292 mm.) No. 323–1888
On the purplish back of the paper (not reproduced amongst the plates) is a child's drawing in white chalk of a face.

Holmes, p. 249, dates *c.*1830. While the sketch has many affinities with Constable's later work, it seems possible that this may have been produced nearer to the time when he was making his systematic studies of skies and trees. The freedom of brushwork in the drawing of the foliage can be paralleled in Nos. 226 and 228, and the colour is more naturalistic than is always the case in Constable's last manner; nor is there any trace of the use of the palette knife. The sketch is accordingly grouped here with the works of 1821.
(See note following No. 235)

c.1821? **235** *Study of the trunk of an elm tree.*
Plate 179

Oil on paper. $12 \times 9\frac{3}{4}$ ins. (306×248 mm.) No. 786–1888
Inscribed on the back in ink with the monogram *JC*.

Holmes, p. 243, dates *c.*1815, and this view has been generally accepted (for example by Shirley, p. 97 and by Key, p. 46). But though the first impression given by the sketch is of uncompromising and 'photographic' naturalism, the treatment, particularly of the foliage in the background, lays more emphasis on linear brushwork than is usual in the sketches made around that date. The treatment of the foliage and the glimpse of the house beyond recall similar features in Nos. 222 and 226, and the sketch is accordingly listed here under the year 1821.

NOTE ON NOS. 221, 222, 224, 226, 228–232, 234 AND 235

Nos. 222, 226 and 228 are fully dated and inscribed examples of the studies of sky and trees which Constable was making in 1821. Although the year is not given in the inscriptions to Nos. 221 and 224, there can hardly be any doubt that they were made at the same time as the fully dated ones. On grounds of similarity of style, Nos. 229 and 230 can be assigned to the same group. It may be noted that chimneys, or roofs and chimneys, occur low down in Nos. 221, 224, 229 and 230, as they do in the fully dated sketch No. 226. The four sketches in question were therefore almost certainly made in the same parts of Hampstead as Nos. 222, 226 and 228. The assignment of Nos. 231 and 232 to the same group is more conjectural, and Nos. 234 and 235 are only tentatively placed with them to draw attention to a specific feature of the way in which they were painted.

Constable gives in some detail, in his correspondence with Fisher, the motives which induced him to undertake this series of sky and tree studies. In his letter of 20 September 1821 (Beckett, VI, pp. 73–4) he says (following the reference to 'Trees at Hampstead' quoted in the note to No. 223): "I have likewise made many *skies* and effects—for I wish it could be said of me as Fuselli says of Rembrandt, 'he followed nature in her calmest abodes and could pluck a flower on every hedge—yet he was born to cast a stedfast eye on the bolder phenomena of nature'. We have had noble clouds & effects of light & dark & color—as is always the case in such seasons as the present".

In a letter of 23 October 1821 from Hampstead to Fisher, Constable gives an extended analysis of the place of skies in his paintings: "I have done a good deal of skying—I am determined to conquer all difficulties and that most arduous one among the rest. and now talking of skies—

It is quite amusing and interesting to us to see how admirably you fight their battles you certainly take the best possible ground for getting your friend out of a scrape—'(the examples of the great masters)'—that Landscape painter who does not make his skies a very material part of his composition—neglects to avail himself of one of his greatest aids. Sir Joshua Reynolds speaking of the 'Landscape' of Titian & Salvator

& Claude—says '*Even their skies seem to sympathise with the Subject*'—I have often been advised to consider my *Sky*—as a '*White Sheet drawn behind the Objects*'—Certainly if the Sky is *obtrusive*—(as mine are) it is bad—but if they are *evaded* (as mine are not) it is worse. they must and always shall with me make an effectual part of the composition. it will be difficult to name a class of Landscape—in which the sky is not the '*key note*'—*the standard of* '*Scale*'—and the chief '*Organ of sentiment*'—You may conceive then what a '*white sheet*' would do for me. impressed as I am with these notions. and they cannot be Erroneous. the sky is the '*source of light*' in nature—and governs every thing—Even our common observations on the weather of every day—are suggested by them but it does not occur to us—Their difficulty in painting both as to composition and Execution is very great. because with all their brilliancy and consequence—they ought not to come forward or be hardly thought about in a picture—any more than extreme distances are—
But these remarks do not apply to *phenomenon*—or what the painters call *accidental Effects of Sky*—because they always attract particularly.
I hope you will not think I am turned critic instead of painter. I say all this *to you* though you do not want to be told—that I know very well what I am about . & that my skies have not been neglected though they often failed in execution—and often no doubt from over anxiety about them—which alone will destroy that Easy appearance which nature always has—in all her movements."
(Text corrected from the original letter, given by Lord Clark to the Minories, Colchester, in 1962).The sketches of 1821 in the Museum are as much studies of foliage in motion under sun and wind as analytical paintings of the clouds. The earliest dated pure cloud studies by Constable are of 1822 (see note following No. 251).
Among other dated sketches of this year are the following, in the gift made by Miss Isabel Constable to the Diploma Gallery of the Royal Academy in 1888; all were exhibited at the Constable Exhibition held in Manchester in 1956 and the numbers quoted in brackets refer to the catalogue of that Exhibition.

'Hampstead Heath, looking West' (10 × 12 ins.) 14 July 1821. (No. 39)
'Study of Clouds and Trees' ($9\frac{1}{2}$ × 12 ins.) 11 September 1821. (No. 48)
'Hampstead Heath, looking over to Harrow' ($9\frac{1}{2}$ × $11\frac{1}{2}$ ins.) 27 September 1821. (No. 43)
'Cloud Study with Trees below' (10 × $11\frac{1}{2}$ ins.) 27 September. (No. 51).
(Although no year appears in the date, this study was doubtless made on the same day as the immediately preceding sketch.)

For a study of the possible influence of *The Climate of London*, 1818–1820, by Luke Howard, upon Constable's sky studies, see *John Constable's Clouds* by Kurt Badt.

236 *Salisbury Cathedral with trees.* 1821, November 9

Plate 180

Pencil and water-colour. $2\frac{5}{8}$ × $3\frac{3}{8}$ ins. (68 × 84 mm.) No. 797–1888
Possibly a page from a sketch-book. The top has been trimmed, and it is

conceivable that this may have been cut from a sheet of the book measuring $3\frac{3}{8} \times 4\frac{1}{2}$ ins. (84 × 113 mm.) discussed in the note following No. 245.
Inscribed in top left corner in pencil by the artist *Novr 9. 1821*. The date has been copied erroneously in ink as *Nov. 2. 1821.* on to the small paper mount on which the drawing is placed (see also Nos. 225, 237, 243, 244 and 245). Constable did not arrive at Salisbury for his autumn visit in this year until 8 November: he says in his letter of 3 November to Fisher "I now really believe that before 9 oclock on Novr. the 8th. I shall be enjoying my tea with you & Mrs. Fisher laughing at all the anxieties I have left" (Beckett, VI, p. 79).

[1821, November]
Plate 180

237 *Winchester Cathedral: entrance to the Deanery from the south.*

Pencil and water-colour. $3\frac{3}{8} \times 4\frac{3}{8}$ ins. (84 × 112 mm.) No. 792–1888
Page from a sketch-book, trimmed.
On the back (not reproduced amongst the plates) are a few pencil scribbles. The drawing has been mounted on a small piece of paper (see also Nos. 225, 236, 243, 244 and 245).

This drawing, formerly described as 'Church and other buildings' was identified by Mr. G. H. Palmer and Mr. Mansford in 1937. The identification makes it almost certain that the drawing was made during Constable's visit to Fisher of November 1821. Fisher had proposed a visit to Winchester in his letter of 24 October 1821, and Constable replied in his letter of 3 November "I open my letter again to say how much I shall like to see Winchester—should that still be your plan" (Beckett, VI, p. 81). The coincidence of size with that of the sketch-book known to have been used in 1821 (No. 225), the similarity of style to No. 236, and the autumnal tints, are all corroborative features which link the drawing to an excursion made at this time. Moreover, No. 238 is dated on the back November 1821 (referring to No. 239) and also represents Winchester Cathedral. For discussion of the sketch-book from which the page comes, see note following No. 245.

1821, November
Plate 182

238 *Winchester Cathedral: west front.*

Pencil and grey wash. $6\frac{1}{4} \times 9\frac{1}{4}$ ins. (159 × 234 mm.) No. 609–1888
Page from a sketch-book trimmed, on paper with truncated watermark: J WH| I|. Inscribed on the back in pencil by the artist (referring to No. 239) *very ancient Cope in the Cathedral—Salisbury Nov. 1821 portrait of the Revd. E. Benson* (the last word is written over another, erased). Also inscribed on the back in pencil *M.L.C.* [Maria Louisa Constable]

Plate 183

238a A water-colour drawing on the back of No. 238, of the top of a head, completes the drawing on No. 239.

For Constable's visit of November 1821 to Winchester, see note to No. 237. The drawing had been laid down on card, and the inscription and drawing on the back remained unrecorded until the back was examined during the preparation of this Catalogue. If, as appears likely, the note on the back of No. 239 referring to the loss of the sketch completing the head was written by one of the artist's children, the drawing had presumably been laid down before it entered the Museum.
No. 238 evidently comes from the same sketch-book as No. 239; that is to say, from the sketch-book measuring in full $6\frac{3}{8} \times 9\frac{3}{8}$ ins. (161 × 237 mm.) which was first in use in 1820.
(See note following No. 200)

239 *Portrait of the Rev. Edmund Benson wearing a medieval chasuble, Salisbury.* 1821, November
Pencil and water-colour. $9\frac{3}{8} \times 6\frac{3}{8}$ ins. (237 × 161 mm.) No. 799–1888 Plate 183
Page from a sketch-book on paper with truncated watermark: J WH| 1| .
Inscribed on the back in pencil *Study of a Chasuble Salisbury—The other leaf of sketch-book finishing head is lost.* The last line is written on top of the faint pencil inscription *M.L.C.* [Maria Louisa Constable]. Also inscribed on the back in ink with the serial number *15*.

Despite the inscription on the back, the other leaf of the sketch-book, finishing the head and identifying the clergyman wearing the chasuble, was revealed when No. 238 was removed from the card on which it had been mounted. The Rev. Edmund Benson was priest-vicar of Salisbury Cathedral (Beckett, VI, p. 15, footnote). There are some references to him in Fisher's correspondence with Constable, but none mentions the occasion of this drawing. As the chasuble, which is of late fifteenth century design, is reversed to display the back orphrey, it is presumably not being worn for liturgical purposes.
It is difficult to establish the authorship of the inscription on the back of the drawing. It was probably there when the drawing came to the Museum, since it is partially transcribed in the *Inventory of Art Objects 1888* (p. 71), but is unlikely to have been written by Maria Louisa Constable. Her initials, over which the inscription on No. 239 is written, also appear on the back of No. 238, and it may be presumed that with both sheets in her possession she would have remembered that the page completing the head was not lost. The most likely explanation is that the inscription was written by Isabel Constable, after the drawing No. 238 had been laid down on card. The inscription implies some familiarity with the circumstances, such as might be expected in the family circle.
The size and watermark indicate that the sheet, with No. 238, comes from the sketch-book discussed in the note following No. 200, which was first in use in 1820.

240 *Old houses on Harnham Bridge, Salisbury.* 1821, November 14 (retouched 9 Sept. 1831)
Pencil and water-colour. $6\frac{3}{4} \times 10\frac{1}{4}$ ins. (173 × 262 mm.) No. 218–1888 Plate 184
Page from a sketch-book.

Inscribed below on left with the brush by the artist *14 Nov 182*[1]. Inscribed on the back in pencil by the artist *Old Houses on Harnham Bridge. Salisbury Novr. 14 1821*, and *retuouch* [? *retouched*] *at Hampstd. the day after the Coronation. of Wm. 4th, at which I was present—being* ~~11~~ [deleted] *eleven hours in the Abbey*.

The Coronation of William IV and Queen Adelaide took place on 8 September 1831 and Constable describes the scene in his letter of 9 September to Leslie (P. Leslie, pp. 37–8).
This sheet comes from the sketch-book used earlier in 1821 in Berkshire (see note following No. 219). As noted by Holmes, p. 245, there is a drawing of the same bridge from a near-by viewpoint in the British Museum (L.B. 29). This is dated 23 November 1829, and comes from the sketch-book measuring $9\frac{1}{4} \times 13\frac{1}{4}$ ins. (234 × 337 mm.) which Constable used in that year (see note following No. 319). Possibly Constable made use of the latter drawing when retouching No. 240 on 9 September 1831.

c.1821–3 **241** *A group of trees on broken ground.*
Plate 165

Pencil and grey wash. $6\frac{3}{4} \times 10\frac{1}{4}$ ins. (173 × 260 mm.) No. 616–1888
Page from a sketch-book.
The measurements of the sheet show that it comes from one or other of the sketch-books of 1821 or 1823, discussed in the note following No. 219.

c.1821–3 **242** *Trees, sky and a red house.*
Plate 182

Pencil and water-colour. $6\frac{3}{4} \times 10$ ins. (173 × 255 mm.) No. 594–1888
Page from a sketch-book.

Plate 183 **242a** On the back is a full-page drawing of a wooden pump, carried out in pencil and water-colour washes.

The measurements of this sheet show that it comes from one or other of the sketch-books of 1821 or 1823, discussed in the note following No. 219.
L.B. 28*b* in the British Museum 'Study of Clouds and Trees' $6\frac{5}{8} \times 10$ ins. (170 × 254 mm.) resembles the drawing on the *recto* of No. 242 in style and subject and was doubtless made at much the same time. The scene is probably at Hampstead.

c.1821 **243** *A sandbank with trees beyond.*
Plate 181

Pencil and water-colour. $3\frac{3}{8} \times 4\frac{1}{2}$ ins. (84 × 113 mm.) No. 798–1888
Page from a sketch-book, trimmed.

Plate 181 **243a** On the back is a pencil drawing of a cart and horses. The cart is being loaded, and the labourers are watched by an onlooker.

The measurements agree with those of Nos. 225 and 237, and the use of pencil and water-colour accords with that in Nos. 236 and 237. In addition the drawing is mounted on a small sheet of old paper in the same fashion as Nos. 225, 236, 237, 244 and 245. This sheet may therefore be dated *c.*1821. Holmes, p. 240, dates No. 243 *c.*1806.
(See note following No. 245)

244 *Scene in a wood: a shepherd lying under the trees.* *c.*1821 Plate 180

Pencil and grey wash with touches of water-colour. $3\frac{3}{8} \times 4\frac{3}{8}$ ins. (84 × 112 mm.)
No. 840–1888

Page from a sketch-book, trimmed.

The measurements agree with those of No. 225 and 237, and the sheet is mounted in the same fashion on old paper (see also Nos. 225, 236, 237, 243 and 245). It may therefore be dated *c.*1821.
(See note following No. 245)

245 *Two sketches on one sheet: a countryman walking, and a group of people beside two donkeys.* *c.*1821 Plate 181

Pencil and water-colour. $3\frac{3}{8} \times 4\frac{3}{8}$ ins. (84 × 112 mm.) No. 793–1888
Page from a sketch-book, trimmed.

245a On the back is a scene in a wood or park. Plate 181
Pencil and grey wash.

The measurements accord with those of Nos. 225, 237, 243 and 244 and the drawing is mounted in the same fashion on old paper. The scene on the *verso* (as now mounted) is close in style to that on No. 244 and this sheet may be dated *c.*1821.

NOTE ON NOS. 225, 236, 237, 243, 244 AND 245

Nos. 225, 237, 243, 244 and 245 all appear to come from the same sketch-book, with leaves measuring about 84 × 113 mm., which, as the date on No. 225 shows, was used in 1821. For the reasons given in the note on that drawing No. 236 may be on a trimmed leaf from the same book. The mounting to which reference is made was probably done before the drawings entered the Museum, and may be due to the artist or his family.

In 1822 Constable's exhibits at the Royal Academy included: 'View on the Stour near Dedham' (now in the Huntington Library and Art Gallery, San Marino) (see sketch-book No. 132, p. 52), 'View from the Terrace, Hampstead' (see No. 252) and 'A Study of Trees from Nature' (see No. 223). Constable's fourth child Isabel, the donor of the greater part of the collection catalogued here, was born at No. 2 Lower Terrace, Hampstead, on 23 August.

1822, July 30
Plate 185

246 *A view at Hampstead with trees and figures.*

Oil on paper. $9\frac{1}{2} \times 11\frac{3}{4}$ ins. (242×298 mm.) No. 165–1888
Inscribed on the back in ink by the artist *July, 30th 1822. Noon under the Sun.* Also inscribed in ink *M.L.* [Maria Louisa Constable]. The back of the paper is blue.

The inscription on No. 247 shows that the artist was at Hampstead on the next day, and it may therefore be assumed that he painted this sketch on Hampstead Heath. The sketch 'Hampstead Heath' reproduced by Shirley (L. ed. S., Pl. 114) (now in the collection of Sir Edward and Lady Hulton) is of a similar character. The 'Study of Trees and Sky, with a Building' ($11\frac{1}{2} \times 9\frac{1}{2}$ ins.) included in Miss Isabel Constable's gift to the Diploma Gallery of the Royal Academy is dated 29 July 1822 (Manchester, Constable Exhibition, 1956, No. 52).

1822, July 31
Plate 186

247 *A view at Hampstead: evening.*

Oil on paper. $6\frac{1}{2} \times 11\frac{3}{4}$ ins. (165×298 mm.) No. 337–1888
Inscribed on the back in ink by the artist *Evening, 31st July, 1822 Shower Approaching* and in pencil, also by the artist *Schroth.* Below this is inscribed the figure *9* and below on the left *3d.* The back is also inscribed in ink, not by the artist, *Evening July 1822 J Constable R A Hampstead.*

Schroth, the French art dealer, called on Constable on 22 May 1824 and bespoke three paintings, two of which were views of Hampstead (L. ed. S., pp. 165–6). Davies, pp. 38–9, has identified these two views as those engraved by Lucas with the titles 'Hampstead Heath, Harrow in the distance' and 'Hampstead Heath' (*English Landscape Scenery*, Bohn's edition, 1855, Nos. 10 and 13; S. 47 and S. 51). The latter is in the collection of Herr Oskar Reinhart of Winterthur (Beckett, IV, p. 194). No. 247 has no obvious connection with either of these paintings. If then the inscription on the back could be interpreted to mean that Schroth had ordered a picture to be made for him from his sketch, it would help to establish the composition of one of the other works Constable made for him. Schroth ordered at least six pictures from Constable at various times (L. ed. S., pp. 187 and 206).

248 *Hampstead: stormy sunset.* 1822, July 31 Plate 187

Oil on paper. $6\frac{3}{8} \times 12$ ins. (162×305 mm.) No. 336–1888
Inscribed on the back in ink by the artist *July 31. 1822 Stormy sunset.*
The inscription on No. 247 shows that Constable was at Hampstead on the day this sketch was painted, and the scene is therefore of the environs of the Heath. Harrow is to be seen in the distance, left.

249 *Study of clouds.* 1822, September 5 Plate 188

Oil on paper. $11\frac{3}{4} \times 19$ ins. (298×483 mm.) No. 590–1888
Inscribed on the back in ink by the artist *Sepr. 5. 1822. looking S.E. noon. Wind very brisk. & effect bright & fresh. Clouds. moving very fast. with occasional very bright openings to the blue.*
Also on the back is a child's pencil drawing of a house, inscribed in ink by the artist *Drawn by John. Augst—1822.* This evidently refers to John Charles, the artist's eldest son, who was born in December 1817, and was accordingly four years old when he made the drawing.
For the cloud studies of this year, see note following No. 251.

250 *Study of cirrus clouds.* c.1822 Plate 189

Oil on paper. $4\frac{1}{2} \times 7$ ins. (114×178 mm.) No. 784–1888
Inscribed on the back in ink *Painted by John Constable R.A.* This inscription is written over an earlier inscription in ink (rendering it nearly illegible), which appears to have been written by the artist and perhaps reads *cirrus.*

Holmes, p. 245, who dates *c.*1821, lists the sketch as of cirrus clouds. If the inscription was in fact written by the artist and is correctly read as *cirrus* it confirms that Constable was familiar with the classification of cloud forms introduced by Luke Howard (Badt, pp. 50 and 51).
(See note following No. 251)

251 *Branch Hill Pond: evening.* c.1822 Plate 190

Oil on paper. $9 \times 7\frac{1}{2}$ ins. (229×190 mm.) No. 339–1888

251a On the back is an oil study of clouds. Plate 189
The view on the *recto* shows Branch Hill Pond from much the same viewpoint as in No. 171.

Holmes, p. 248, dates *c.*1827. Mayne (L. ed. M., p. 413) dates *c.*1822. The cloud study No. 251a justifies a dating *c.*1822, and the style of the sketch on the *recto* is consistent with the views of Hampstead made in 1821 and 1822.

NOTE ON NOS. 249, 250 AND 251A

In his letter of 7 October 1822 to Fisher, Constable says (L. ed. S., p. 131) "I have made about fifty carefull studies of *skies*, tolerably large to be carefull". In his comment on this letter Leslie remarks: "Twenty of Constable's studies of skies made during this season are in my possession, and there is but one among them in which a vestige of landscape is introduced. They are painted in oil, on large sheets of thick paper, and all dated, with the time of day, the direction of the wind, and other memoranda on their backs. On one, for instance, is written '5th of September, 1822. 10 o'clock, morning, looking south-east, brisk wind at west. Very bright and fresh grey clouds running over a yellow bed, about half way in the sky. Very appropriate to the "coast at Osmington" ' ". The sketch thus described by Leslie is now in the National Gallery of Victoria, Melbourne, having been purchased from the collection of Sir Michael Sadler by the Felton Bequest in 1938; it measures 18 × 12 ins.

No. 249 is the only dated oil sketch in the Museum from the series described by Leslie, but Nos. 250 and 251a, although smaller, may perhaps be assigned to the same period. The absence of landscape mentioned by Leslie serves to differentiate the pure cloud studies of 1822 from the sky and tree studies of 1821 (see note following No. 235). Cloud studies dated 28 July, 31 August, 6 September and 21 September 1822 were in the collection of the late Sir Farquhar Buzzard. The last-named of these was sold at Messrs. Sotheby's, 26 July 1961 (Lot 160). It measured $11\frac{1}{4} \times 19$ ins. and was inscribed on the back *Sept. 21. 1822. ½ past one o'clock Looking South. Wind very fresh at East, but warm.* Another, dated 1 August 1822, is in the collection of Gilbert Davis (reproduced by Badt, Pl. 5). Nos. 313 and 238 at the Grosvenor Gallery Winter Exhibition, 1889, were cloud studies, dated 6 September and 28 September 1822 respectively; the latter measured 9 × 11 ins. and had a description of the weather on the back. Both these sketches were lent by the executors of Miss Isabel Constable.

c.1822? **252** *View of Lower Terrace, Hampstead.*

Plate 193

Oil on canvas. $9\frac{3}{4} \times 13\frac{7}{8}$ ins. (248 × 352 mm.) No. 584–1888

The canvas has been relined. A strip about 2 inches wide on the left is unfinished and was at one time doubled under the body of the sketch.

This has been known, while in the Museum, as 'Red Brick House on Hilly Road' (*Inventory of Art Objects 1888*, and subsequent catalogues). Holmes, p. 243, dates *c.*1815 and describes as 'Houses and Trees, Hampstead?'. The Borough Librarian of Hampstead, however, confirms that the scene represented is at the Lower Terrace, Hampstead. The corner house shown in the painting is No. 4 Lower Terrace, and it has since been remodelled or rebuilt as Fountains House. A portion of the next door house, No. 3, is also to be seen on the left-hand side of the picture. Constable lodged at No. 2 Lower Terrace in 1821 and 1822.

In a letter received in the Museum on 24 April 1888, Miss Isabel Constable wrote to Mr. R. Thompson (see p. 3 of the Introduction): "The House in the old fashioned garden is at Hampstead though it is not the Well Walk House, I am not quite sure but I think that it was called The Terrace—Hampstead". This sentence refers to a painting or drawing—hitherto unidentified—in Miss Isabel Constable's gift to the Museum. Despite the implication that the house depicted was one lived in by Constable, No. 252 does not show in fact No. 2 Lower Terrace, but its next door neighbours Nos. 3 and 4; but clearly Miss Constable had this sketch in mind when she wrote. Although born in No. 2 Lower Terrace, she had not lived there subsequently.

Among Constable's exhibits at the Royal Academy in 1822 was a work described in the Royal Academy Catalogue, No. 295, as 'View from the Terrace, Hampstead' and by Leslie (L. ed. S., p. 130) as 'A View of the Terrace, Hampstead'. If Leslie's correction is justified, it is possible that No. 252 in this Catalogue may have been this painting or a sketch for it. The criticism of the exhibited work in the periodical *Museum* as 'cold and raw' suggests, however, a more considerable and a different picture (Whitley, *Art in England, 1821–1837*, p. 29). No. 252 was in any event probably painted when Constable was living in the Terrace, that is in 1821 or 1822, and is placed here accordingly.

For a view taken from the window of No. 2 Lower Terrace see No. 402.

253 *Fishing boats at anchor.* 1822, November 9

Plate 194

Pen and bistre wash. $7\frac{1}{4} \times 8\frac{7}{8}$ ins. (185 × 224 mm.) No. 814–1888

On laid paper.

Inscribed in lower left corner in bistre ink by the artist *Novr. 9. 1822.* Inscribed on the back in pencil *J Constable.*

On the back (not reproduced amongst the plates) are five slight pencil sketches of ropes and pulleys.

The extant correspondence contains no specific record of an excursion by Constable to the coast in November of this year. It can hardly have been a long one, since his letters to Fisher at the time show that he was busy in London moving into his new house in Charlotte Street, and completing his unfinished work. In his letter of 6 December to Fisher (Beckett, VI, p. 106) he mentions the altar-piece commissioned from him for the church at Manningtree and it is possible that he may have drawn No. 253 on a quick visit connected with that business.

1823

In 1823 Constable's chief exhibit at the Royal Academy was 'Salisbury Cathedral from the Bishop's Grounds' (No. 254 in this Catalogue). He visited Fisher in August (see Nos. 256 and 257), and stayed with Sir George Beaumont at Coleorton from the last week of October until the end of November (see Nos. 259–262).

1823 **254** *Salisbury Cathedral from the Bishop's Grounds.*

Plate 192

Oil on canvas. $34\frac{1}{2} \times 44$ ins. (876×1118 mm.) No. F.A.33
Sheepshanks Gift.

The painting is executed on a thin linen laid on a coarser canvas; it has not been relined and is on the original stretcher.

The painting is signed and inscribed, below on left. This inscription is rubbed and no longer fully legible. In the Museum's manuscript inventory of the Sheepshanks Collection it is transcribed as *John Constable A.R.A. London 1823.* More recent attempts to read it have resulted in the suggestions *John Constable A R A pinxt* or *pt 1823* or *pnx 23* possibly followed by *London* on a separate line. A label on the stretcher is inscribed in ink by the artist *Salisbury Cathedral—from the Bishop's Grounds, John Constable. 35 Upper Charlotte Street Fitzroy Square.* This was doubtless the label for the exhibition at the Royal Academy in 1823 (see also those on Nos. 301 and 352). The stretcher is also inscribed in chalk —*Sheepshanks Esqr. Bottom of Buckingham St. Strand.* This direction doubtless followed the purchase at the Executors' sale in 1838.

The figures in the foreground are Dr. Fisher, Bishop of Salisbury, and his wife (Beckett, VI, pp. 119–20).

Constable made two other commissioned versions of No. 254, and there are in existence five other versions with claims to be regarded either as sketches for the picture or as replicas of it. The history of the main variants is a complicated one. Mr. J. Steegman, in the *Art Quarterly*, Detroit, Vol. XIV, 1951, pp. 195–205, has performed a useful service in listing the variants and tracing their recent history. But the confusion of the earlier records has betrayed him into some errors, and the fuller publication of Constable's correspondence with Fisher has made certain aspects of the transactions plainer. It is accordingly desirable to go over the history of the painting in detail.*

No. 254 was commissioned by Constable's old friend, John Fisher, Bishop of Salisbury, the uncle of Archdeacon John Fisher. The commission was initiated by the sketches referred to in Constable's letter to Fisher of 1 September 1820: "My Salisbury sketches are much liked—that in the palace grounds—the bridges—& your house from the meadows—the moat—&c." (Beckett, VI, p. 56). That the approval of the sketches was on the part of the Bishop and his family, and that an oil sketch of the composition of No. 254 was among them, may be deduced from Miss Dolly Fisher's letter of 8 October 1820 to Constable: "Papa desires me to say, he hopes you will finish for the Exhibition the view you

* Beckett reviewed the problem in the *Art Quarterly*, Detroit, Vol. XX, 1957, pp. 140–51, and reached much the same results.

took from our Garden of the Cathedral by the water side, as well as Waterloo Bridge" (Beckett, VI, p. 58). But in settling the lines of the oil sketch, and painting the exhibited version from it, he used the drawing he had made in 1811 (No. 105). In his letter to Constable of 3 January 1821, Archdeacon Fisher says "The Bishop likes your picture 'all but the clouds' he says. He likes 'a clear blue sky' " (Beckett, VI, p. 60). Since the Bishop's objection to the clouds in No. 254 is a recurring theme, this is probably a reference to the same sketch for the 'Salisbury Cathedral from the Bishop's Grounds'. It was some time before Constable resumed work on it. Mrs. Constable, writing to her husband on 11 May 1822 about a visit paid by the Bishop to the artist's studio the day before says "He rummaged out the Salisbury & wanted to know what you had done" (Beckett, VI, pp. 93–4). The next reference to the commission is found in the Bishop's letter of 4 November 1822 (Beckett, VI, pp. 101, 102) ". . . I was in hopes you would have taken another *peep* or *two* at the view of our Cathedral from my Garden near the Canal. But perhaps you retain enough of it in your memory to finish the Picture which I shall hope will be ready to grace my Drawing Room in London". On 10 November the Bishop wrote again, in reply to a missing letter from Constable: "I am glad to find that you are about your View of Sarum for me" (Beckett, VI, p. 102). In the same letter he asks Constable to employ Smith of Kensington to make the frame for the picture, thereby enabling him to work off a debt.

Leslie records that the Bishop wrote again on 12 November enclosing an advance payment for the picture, tactfully described as a retaining fee. On the same day Fisher also wrote to Constable: "But I would not press you to leave London now: as time is as you say money, & you want it just at present. I recommend you to get on with the Bishops picture. He is quite eager about it. He asked me last night whether I thought he should affront you by sending you part of your price. I replied that I was of opinion he would *not* offend you: as Sir T. Lawrence himself took earnest money" (Beckett, VI, p. 103). On 6 December 1822 Constable wrote to Fisher "The Cathedral is advancing—& Smith has the frame in hand" (Beckett, VI, p. 106). After Christmas Constable and his family were ill, and his work was held up.

On 1 February 1823 he wrote to Fisher: "It is not the least of my anxiety that the Good Bishop's picture is not fit to be seen. Pray my dear Fisher prepare his Lordship for this—it has been no fault of my own. Add to it that I can make nothing of the wretched Smith's, to whom I gave the order for the frame more than 2 months ago—I think—I know not if it is even in hand—as they have never noticed one of my notes" (Beckett, VI, p. 109).

On 21 February he wrote to Fisher that he hoped to have the Bishop's picture ready for the Royal Academy exhibition, and again complaining of the dilatoriness of the frame-maker Smith; he adds later on in the letter "I have not yet called on the Bishop—and I wrote to him before to say, that he could not see his picture" (Beckett, VI, p. 112). In the event, No. 254 was ready for exhibition at the Academy, and formed Constable's chief exhibit there, since he did not have time to finish a larger upright landscape (believed to be 'The Lock') (*ibid.*).

After the Exhibition had opened Constable wrote to Fisher on 9 May saying "My Cathedral looks very well. Indeed I got through that job uncommonly well considering how much I dreaded it. It is much approved by the Academy and moreover in Seymour St. [that is, by the Bishop and his family] though I was at one time fearfull it would not be a favourite there owing to a *dark cloud*—but we got over the difficulty, and I think you will say when you see it I have fought a better battle with the Church than old Hume, Brogham and their coadjutors have done. It was the most difficult subject in landscape I ever had upon my easil. I have not flinched at the work, of the windows, buttresses, &c, &c, but I have as usual made my escape in the evanescence of the chiaro-scuro. I think you will like it but you could have done me much good" (Beckett, VI, p. 115).

The Exhibition closed on 12 July 1823. Constable was now called upon to paint a smaller version (25 × 30 ins.; the 'wedding present' version), and later on also a full-scale replica, which he signed and dated 1826. This train of events begins with a letter from the Bishop of 3 August 1823. Leslie, whose reading has hitherto been accepted in the absence of the original, dates the letter 1822, but it is evident that Constable's letter of 18 August 1823 refers directly to it, and also that the extracts from his correspondence given above show that he was in 1822 only at work on one version, and was hard pressed to finish that in time for the exhibition.

The Bishop's letter, which is therefore to be dated 3 August 1823, reads: "My daughter Elizabeth is about to change her situation, and try whether she cannot perform the duties of a wife as well as she has done those of a daughter. She wishes to have in her house in London a recollection of Salisbury; I mean, therefore, to give her a picture, and I must beg of you either to finish the first sketch of my picture, or to make a copy of the small size. I wish to have a more serene sky. . ." (L. ed. S., p. 131). On 18 August Constable wrote to Fisher: "I have had some troublesome letters from the Bishop—one of which walked me off from Hampstead to Kensington—after the wretched Smiths. The Bishops frame for the Salisbury remains in the same state it was in at X'mas—wood much injured at the Exhibition. The Bishop wants another Salisbury, for Elizabeth who is going to be married—to whom? I wish they would take my frame & let my copy be the same size as that & so use the Bishop's frame" (Beckett, VI, p. 128).

The Bishop's letter shows that Constable did not, as had been suggested to him by Miss Dolly Fisher in 1820, complete his compositional sketch, but transferred the design to a new canvas before painting the work he sent to the Royal Academy in 1823. The existence of an oil sketch (listed as (a) in the table near the end of this note), following the drawing No. 105 more closely than any other of the known versions, and its virtual coincidence in measurements with the picture actually painted for the Bishop's daughter indicates that Constable did not adopt the suggestion now repeated that he should finish the first sketch for this purpose. Nor, it appears, did the Bishop agree to Constable's painting another the same size as the original to use up the other frame. The sketch in question is that in the collection of Mr. A. W. Bacon, and measures 24 × 29 ins. (L. ed. S., Pl. 81). On 30 September 1823 Constable wrote to Fisher: "I have just received a letter from the Bishop to forward my small picture of the Church, that it may be ready to 'greet and *surprize* the Bride' on her arrival in Seymour St. I had fortunately got it very forward. When must it be ready?" (Beckett, VI, p. 133). In his reply Fisher indicates that the Bishop was still concerned about the kind of sky Constable was to introduce "He hopes that you put your *marriage* picture of Salisbury into a little sunshine" (Beckett, VI, p. 135).

Elizabeth Fisher was married to John Mirehouse on 16 October 1823. In the letter communicating this news, Fisher adds: "The Bishop has been fishing up some old drawings of Bucklers against your arrival in Salisbury. With the intent I guess that you should copy & improve them. Retaining so much of Buckler* as shall exclude light & shadow (the Bishops detestation) & improving his rawness with some of your colour & facility.—'[If] Constable would but leave out his black clouds! Clouds are only black when it is going to rain. In fine weather the sky is blue' " (Beckett, VI, p. 138). It will be noted that the wedding present picture was at first also to be hung in the Bishop's house in Seymour Street. Constable wrote on 19 October: "I hung up my '*bridal picture*' with my own hands yesterday in Seymour Street—to 'greet & *surprize*' the Bride on her arrival ... It will be better liked than the large one, because it is not 'too good' ". He adds that he had postponed going to Coleorton for a week to finish the picture (Beckett, VI, p. 139). Fisher comments on 12 December 1823 "Mrs. Mirehouse [the former Elizabeth Fisher] is warm in the praises of your picture of the Cathedral" (Beckett, VI, p. 145). Constable complains of Smith's delays in cutting the frame for Mrs. Mirehouse's picture (Beckett, VI, p. 146–7). On 6 January 1824 the Bishop authorised Elizabeth's servant to return to Constable the picture of Salisbury Cathedral which was at his house in town, presumably her small version. On 17 January 1824 Constable wrote to Fisher "I want to see the picture of the Cathedral belonging to Mr Mirehouse in a frame, in order to [? tone] it. But the Bishop has involved me with that wretch at Kensington and therefore a frame is hopeless. I will not get another on my own acct. I do not think that Mr M. admires it—but speaking to a lawyer about pictures is something like talking to a butcher about humanity" (Beckett, VI, p. 149). In the same letter he says that he has sent the Bishop's picture of the Cathedral to the British Institution. From this it appears that it had been in his studio; presumably it had been sent back to him when he was making the copy for Mrs. Mirehouse, and had not yet been returned to the Bishop. It may be noted in passing that

* John Buckler, F.S.A. (1770–1851) is well known for his drawings and aquatints of English cathedrals.

the framed measurements of the picture are given in the British Institution catalogue as 3 ft. 0 ins. by 4 ft. 9 ins. The width is fairly exact, but the height must be at least 6 inches out. When at the British Institution, No. 254 received an enthusiastic notice in the *Somerset House Gazette*, I, 1824, pp. 311 and 312. Meanwhile, Constable, after some reminders from the Bishop, finished his work on Mrs. Mirehouse's version and sent it to her house in Orchard Street at the beginning of April 1824 (Beckett, VI, pp. 154–55). On 8 May 1824, Constable wrote to Fisher referring to the return of the Bishop's painting from the British Institution: "I have just deposited my picture in its place in the *back drawing room* in Seymour St. and opposite and as a companion to a *landscape of Mrs. MacTaggett.** To what honors are some men born" (Beckett, VI, p. 157).

The event which led to Constable's making a full-scale replica of No. 254 was an interview with the Bishop, recorded on 25 June 1824 in the journal which Constable kept for his wife: "After breakfast called on the bishop by his wish. He had to tell me that he thought of my improving the picture of the Cathedral and mentioned many things.—'He hoped I would not take his observations amiss.' I said, 'Quite the contrary, as his lordship had been my kind monitor for twenty-five years.' I am to have it home to-morrow" (L. ed. S., pp. 167–8). Constable sent John Dunthorne round to fetch the picture a day or so later 'to be varnished' (Beckett, II, p. 345). From the subsequent developments it appears that the Bishop's dislike of the dark cloud behind the Cathedral had at last caused him to instruct the artist either to paint it out or to paint a new version without it. The latter course of action was the one taken by Constable. It seems, though this is not referred to in the extant correspondence, that Constable in consequence decided to offer to Archdeacon Fisher the original full-scale version (No. 254). As Constable is later found at work again on the small wedding present picture belonging to Mrs. Mirehouse, he was presumably prevailed upon to introduce into that version also some of the modifications called for by the Bishop in his version.

On 18 July 1824, Constable wrote to Fisher: "I have got the picture of the Cathedral, from the Bishop's—and Johnny [Dunthorne] has made me a delightfull outline of the same size . . . We must not let the Good Bishop have the bridal in his hand again. He will ruin both our reputations—I mean yours & mine" (Beckett, VI, p. 167). Fisher replied on 24 July: "I congratulate you on the repossession of the Cathedral. Have Buckler or Reinagle to make him a copy of it" (Beckett, VI, p. 170). On 24 January 1825 Constable enquired of Fisher "Tell me if you think a print of the Cathedral (the Bishops picture) would answer enough to pay £20 or £30. I should think it might, it would make a good one, especially that which I am now about. You cannot think how I regret being about this picture to the neglect of my large landscape, for every reason—

* Mrs. A. MacTaggart exhibited five landscapes at the British Institution in 1824. Constable described her as "a laughing ignorant vulgar fat uncouth old woman, but very good natured".

besides I can make no part of art pay now so well as my own landscape. But I will not quarrel with kind friends & kick down the ladder" (Beckett, VI, p. 192). Fisher replied on 27 January: "I do think that an impression of your Cathedral would sell well at Salisbury. But it entirely depends on the brilliancy of the engraving. If it be added at the foot, 'from the original in the possession of the Bishop of Salisbury' it would be as good as giving the Palace, a commission & brokerage, to sell" (Beckett, VI, pp. 193–4).

Bishop Fisher died on 8 May 1825. At this time Constable still had in his studio the original 'Salisbury Cathedral' (No. 254); the new full-size version was not yet completed, and Mrs. Mirehouse's smaller version was eventually to be altered. He refers to these matters in his journal on 1 October 1825: "I must make my mind easy as to my dead horses, namely, *Salisbury Cathedral*, . . . and Mr. Mirhouse's picture to be altered" (L. ed. S., p. 198). Again on 31 October "have secured the new picture of the Cathedral . . . and the little picture of the Cathedral for Mr. Mirhouse" (L. ed. S., p. 199). On 12 November he wrote to Fisher: "I have nearly compleated a second Cathedral which I think you will (perhaps) prefer to the first—but I will send them both to Salisbury for your inspection if you like" (Beckett, VI, pp. 206–7). This may perhaps be taken to confirm the supposition that Fisher was to have the first full-scale version when the other was returned to the Bishop's family. On 25 November Constable noted in his journal: "Painted all day on Mr. Mirehouse's little picture of the *Cathedrum*, making in all, as pretty Minna says, three *Cathedrums*" (L. ed. S., p. 203). The next day he wrote to Fisher: "My new picture of Salisbury is very beautiful and I have repainted entirely that of Mrs. Mirehouse—I am now delighted with it, but when I thus speak of my pictures remember it is to you and only in a comparison with myself" (Beckett, VI, p. 210). The repainting of the small wedding present picture was shortly afterwards completed, as is shown by Constable's letter to Fisher of 1 February 1826: "Mr. Mirehouse sent for the '*Cathedrum*' as your pretty goddaughter calls it—it is wholly a new picture and very pretty" (Beckett, VI, p. 213).

Constable had borrowed Fisher's large landscape 'The White Horse', and it had been exhibited at Lille. Fisher's letter of acknowledgement, written on 1 July 1826, shows that Constable sent it back with one of the two large versions of 'Salisbury Cathedral from the Bishop's Grounds': "The two pictures arrived safe on Friday, & within an hour were up in their places; the white horse looking very placid & not as if just returned from the continent . . . The Cathedral looks splendidly over the chimney peice. The pictures require a room full of light. Its internal splendour comes out in all its power, the spire sails away with the thunder-clouds. The only criticism I pass on it, is, that it does not go *out* well with the day. The light is of an unpleasant shape by dusk. I am aware how severe a remark I have made" (Beckett, VI, pp. 221–2). But on 15 December 1829, Fisher had to write to Constable to ask whether he could turn his "two great pictures" into money for him; or whether he would advance £200 on them (L. ed. S., p. 223). Constable decided to buy the two pictures for £200 (*loc. cit.*; Beckett, VI, p. 255). One of the two pictures in question was evidently 'The White Horse'. This was Lot 77 in the Executors' sale, 16 May 1838, bought in for £157 10s. The other was probably the version of 'Salisbury Cathedral' which Fisher described in his letter of 1 July 1826, quoted above; that is, No. 254. The fact that the original picture painted for the Bishop, and exhibited at the Royal Academy in 1823, also figured in the Executors' sale is most convincingly accounted for by the supposition that it was this version which Archdeacon Fisher had in 1826, and was the second painting that he sold back to Constable in 1829. In that event the Bishop's family will have had the newer version with the outline by Dunthorne. This is entirely consistent with the pedigree of the version of 1826 (Steegman, p. 201; see (b) in the table near the end of this note), which descended directly from Dolly Fisher, daughter of Bishop Fisher and sister of Mrs. Mirehouse. On 17 December 1833, Constable wrote to his friend George Constable: "I have not an idea that I shall be able to part with the *Salisbury*; the price will of necessity be a very large one, for the time expended on it was enormous for its size. I am also unwilling to part with any of my standard pictures: they being all points with me in my practice, and will much regulate my future productions, should I do any more large works" (L. ed. S., p. 308). In a footnote Leslie identifies the picture as "One of his repetitions of the beautiful picture of the 'Cathedral from the Bishop's Grounds'". Steegman thinks that the painting is more possibly the 'Salisbury Cathedral from the Meadows', which was exhibited at the Royal Academy in 1831, but Leslie's identification is probably correct. Constable's description of the work as one of his standard pictures, and reference to the labour expended upon it would fit exactly with the history of No. 254. He exhibited a painting of 'Salisbury Cathedral from the Bishop's Grounds' at Worcester in 1834 (not 1835; see Beckett, *Art Quarterly*, Detroit, Vol. XX, 1957, p. 150). If the suppositions made above are correct, both the version which Constable refused to sell to George Constable and the one exhibited at Worcester may have been No. 254.

It remains to mention the other versions in the sale held after Constable's death and those extant today. In the Executors' sale, 16 May 1838, were the items:

Lot 12. Two—Salisbury Cathedral, *study for the finished picture*, and Helmingham Park. (Bt. Allnutt, £9 9s.)

Lot 30. Salisbury Cathedral, from the Bishop's Garden, *nearly finished*. (Bt. Archbutt, £16 16s.)

Lot 72. Salisbury Cathedral *from the Bishop's Garden. Exhibited* 1823. (Bt. Tiffin, £64 1s.)

Views of Salisbury Cathedral also appear as parts of an item in Lots 13, 23 and 34, but the descriptions give no further details, so it is not possible to say whether any of these were of the same composition. Lot 72 is No. 254, and it may be presumed that Tiffin was acting for Sheepshanks when he bought it.

The following versions are recorded (L. ed. M., p. 412; Steegman, pp. 204–5):

(a) A sketch. 24×29 ins. Now in the collection of Mr. A. W. Bacon. In the Exhibition of British Art at the Royal Academy, 1934, this was No. 385 in the Commemorative Catalogue, reproduced Pl. CX.

(b) Frick Collection, New York. Signed and dated 1826. 34½×43½ ins. Collections: Bishop Fisher's daughter Mrs. Pike-Scrivener (*née* Dolly Fisher); thence to her nieces the Misses Fanny and Emma Mirehouse; S. G. Holland; sold at Messrs. Christie's, 25 June 1908, Lot 12.

(c) Huntington Library and Art Gallery, San Marino. 25×30 ins. Signed and dated 1823. Collections: Mr. and Mrs. John Mirehouse and their descendants. Sold at Messrs. Christie's, 16 May 1952, Lot 49.

(d) Laing Art Gallery, Newcastle. 29×35 ins. (unfinished). Collections: E. L. Raphael; F. J. Nettlefold.

(e) Metropolitan Museum of Art, New York. 34½×44 ins. Collections: Davies, Manchester; Foswell, before 1907; Sir Joseph Beecham; sold at Messrs. Christie's, 3 May 1917, Lot 6; Edward Harkness.

(f) Sao Paolo Museum. 35¼×45 ins. Collections: Sir Arthur Du Cros; J. Mountain.

(g) Montreal, Museum of Fine Arts. 29×37 ins. Collection: Mrs. C. F. Martin. Reproduced in R. M. Hubbard *European Paintings in Canadian Collections. Earlier Schools.* Toronto, 1952, Pl. LXIV.

Of the above, (a) is said to be Lot 30 in the Executors' sale, but is more probably to be identified with Lot 12 in that sale. (b) is the full-scale replica which Constable painted for the Bishop, which is presumed to have been delivered to his widow after the Bishop's death. (c) is the small wedding present picture painted for the Bishop's daughter Elizabeth Mirehouse and subsequently repainted. Unless Constable painted and sold any other unrecorded replicas of the subject in his lifetime, (d), (e), (f) and (g) have to dispute identification with Lot 30, and possibly with Lots 13, 23 and 34 in the Executors' sale.

In his description of the picture No. 254, Leslie says: "In the foreground he introduced a circumstance familiar to all who are in the habit of noticing cattle. With cows there is generally, if not always, one which is called, not very accurately, *the master cow*, and there is scarcely anything the rest of the herd will venture to do until the *master* has taken the lead. On the left of the picture this individual is drinking, and turns with surprise and jealousy to another cow approaching the canal lower down for the same purpose; they are of the Suffolk breed, without horns; and it is a curious mark of Constable's fondness for everything connected with his native county, that scarcely an instance can be found of a cow in any of his pictures, be the scene where it may, with horns" (L. ed. S., p. 134).

The statement that the Bishop rejected the picture, which is made in the Museum's Catalogues from 1859 to 1893, and followed by Holmes, p. 246, is a somewhat misleading one if made without awareness of the full facts of the matter, as set out above. After accepting the painting for his home, where it was hung for some time, the Bishop did indeed ask Constable to make alterations, which in effect obliged the artist to paint a new and somewhat changed version, but this is not tantamount to rejection in the usual sense of the word.

1823, August 6
Plate 191

255 *View at Hampstead, looking due east.*

Oil on paper. $9\frac{3}{4} \times 12$ ins. (248×305 mm.) No. 154–1888
Inscribed on the back in ink, probably by the artist, *Hampstead. Augst 6th 1823 Eveng. looking due East* . . . [a word here, perhaps *ward* or *wind*, is deleted]; also inscribed in pencil by the artist *Eveg—6th Augt 1823* together with a number of scribbles and financial sums. Inscribed on the back in ink with the monogram *JC*.

1823, August 20
Plate 195

256 *Salisbury Cathedral, seen over the river from the south-west.*

Pencil. $7\frac{1}{8} \times 10\frac{1}{8}$ ins. (181×259 mm.) No. 281–1888
Page from a sketch-book, trimmed.
Inscribed at top right in pencil by the artist *Augst. 20. 1823.*

Constable arrived at Salisbury for his summer visit to Fisher on 19 August of this year; subsequently he went to stay at Fisher's new vicarage at Gillingham, from which he visited Sherborne (see No. 257) and Fonthill (Beckett, VI, pp. 128–9). (See note following No. 262)

1823, September 2
Plate 194

257 *The Abbey Church, Sherborne.*

Pencil. $7\frac{1}{8} \times 10\frac{1}{4}$ ins. (181×261 mm.) No. 354-1888
Page from a sketch-book, trimmed, on paper with truncated watermark: J WHA| TURKE| 18| .
Inscribed in lower left corner in pencil by the artist *Sherborne Sep 2. 1823* and on the back in pencil by the artist *Sherborne Collegiate Church Sepr. 2. 1823.* [the year written twice] *went in the autumn to Coleorton Hall* and, in another hand [erroneously] *September 9 1823*. The main inscription at the back was evidently added by the artist some years after the drawing had been made, as was that on No. 262.

No. 257 is unusual in the drawings of Constable's maturity in having no sky. Constable made a pencil drawing of the same subject on 22 August 1823 which was sold by his family as Lot 171 at Messrs. Christie's on 17 February 1877. He refers to the visit on which the drawing No. 257 was made in his letter of 5 September from Gillingham to his wife: "On Monday Fisher took me a magnificent ride to Sherborne, a fine old town with a magnificent church finer than Salisbury Cathedral" (Beckett, II, p. 287). Monday in fact fell on 1 September in 1823. (See note following No. 262)

258 *Study of a house amidst trees: evening.* 1823, October 4

Plate 198

Oil on paper. $9\frac{7}{8} \times 12\frac{1}{8}$ ins. (251 × 307 mm.) No. 152–1888
Inscribed on the back in pencil by the artist *Saturday Evg 4th Oct 1823* and with an inaccurate transcript of this inscription in ink.

Constable wrote to Fisher from Charlotte Street on 30 September 1823, and from Hampstead on 19 October (Beckett, VI, pp. 132–4, 139–40), and does not mention any excursion into the country between those two dates. The scene therefore may be at Hampstead.

259 *Cenotaph to Sir Joshua Reynolds amongst lime trees in the grounds of Coleorton Hall.* 1823, November 28

Plate 196

Pencil and grey wash. $10\frac{1}{4} \times 7\frac{1}{8}$ ins. (260 × 181 mm.) No. 835–1888
Page from a sketch-book on paper with truncated watermark: |TMAN |MILL |21[?].
Inscribed on the back in ink by the artist:

Ye Lime-trees rang'd before this Hallowed Urn
Shoot forth with lively power at Springs return
And be not slow a stately growth to rear
Of Pillars branching off from year to year
Till ye at length have † framed a Darksome Isle*
Like a recess within that sacred Pile
Whare Reynolds—mid our countrey's noblest dead
In the last sanctity of fame is laid
And worthily within those sacred bounds
The excelling Painter sleeps—yet here may I
Unblamed upon my patrimonial Grounds
Raise this frail tribute to his memory
An humble follower of the soothing Art
That he professed—attatched to him in heart
Admiring—loving—and with Grief and Pride
Feeling what England lost when Reynolds died
written by Mr. W. Wordsworth
and engraven on the Urn. in the Garden
Coleorton Hall. Novr. 28. 1823.

Constable took this drawing as the basis of the large oil painting he exhibited at the Royal Academy (No. 9) in 1836, under the title 'Cenotaph to the memory of Sir Joshua Reynolds, erected in the grounds of Coleorton Hall, Leicestershire, by the late Sir George Beaumont, Bart.'. The verses by Wordsworth written

* Corrected in pencil from *it*.

† Corrected in pencil from *has*.

for the monument are quoted in the Royal Academy catalogue, following the text transcribed above from the reverse of the drawing with only minor variations. Leslie (L. ed. S., p. 342) gives a different text, with two more lines.
The exhibited oil painting is now in the National Gallery, No. 1272. Full notes and references are given by Davies, pp. 27, 28. Briefly, the first stone of the memorial to Reynolds, erected by Sir George Beaumont in the grounds of Coleorton, was laid on 30 October 1812. The lines by Wordsworth were composed in November 1811 and first published in 1815. Constable refers to the memorial in his letter of 2 November 1823 to Fisher "In the dark recesses of these gardens, and at the end of one of the walks, I saw an urn—& bust of Sir Joshua Reynolds—& under it some beautifull verses, by Wordsworth" (Beckett, VI, p. 143). Davies, p. 28, suggested that No. 259 may have been drawn in London, but Constable wrote to his wife on 26 November postponing his departure from Coleorton until Friday 28 November, the day this drawing was made.
For another instance of Sir George Beaumont's fondness for erecting altars in his grounds (a predilection mentioned by Allan Cunningham in his *Lives of the most eminent British Painters*, Bohn's edition, 1879, Vol. III, p. 9) see No. 260. Other inscriptions for the grounds of Coleorton are printed in Wordsworth's *Collected Poems*.
(See note following No. 262)

1823, November 28 **260** *A Stone dedicated to Richard Wilson in the Grove of Coleorton Hall.*
Plate 197

Pencil and grey wash. $10\frac{1}{4} \times 7\frac{1}{8}$ ins. (262×181 mm.) No. 815–1888
Page from a sketch-book, irregularly torn from the hinge.
Inscribed on the back in ink by the artist *Stone in the Grove Coleorton Hall. Dedicated to the Memory of Richard Wilson. Novr. 28. 1823.* and in pencil *RW* (one of the forms of signature used by Richard Wilson).
(See note following No. 262)

[1823, November] **261** *A Stone in the Garden of Coleorton Hall.*
Plate 197

Pencil and grey wash. $10 \times 7\frac{1}{8}$ ins. (255×181 mm.) No. 266–1888
Page from a sketch-book, trimmed.
Inscribed on the back in ink by the artist *Stone in the Garden of Coleorton Hall.*
(See note following No. 262)

[1823, October] **262** *Trees in a lane at Staunton Harold, Leicestershire.*
Plate 195

Pencil. $7\frac{1}{8} \times 10\frac{1}{4}$ ins. (181×262 mm.) No. 356–1888
Page from a sketch-book.
Inscribed on the back in pencil by the artist *Leicestershire—the lane leading to*

Ferrars Hall—Ld Ferriers[?] *house I was on horseback with Sir G. B.* [Sir George Beaumont]—*who kindly held my horse when I made this sketch 1823 I think it was the finest ash I ever saw.*

The inscription was evidently added from memory some time after the drawing was made, as was that on the back of No. 257. In a letter in the Department of Paintings the Hon. Andrew Shirley gives reasons for identifying the scene as Staunton Harold. Constable's letter of 27 October 1823 to his wife contains the sentence "I had the opportunity of seeing the ruins at Ashby, the mountain streams and rocks (Such Everdingens) at Griesdieu, and an old convent there, Lord Ferrer's—a grand but melancholy spot" (Beckett, II, p. 292). The Lord Ferrers of the time was living at Ragdale, about 12 miles from Coleorton, where he had built a new house. Staunton Harold had been left incomplete for thirty or forty years and was not much lived in, but being only some 2½ miles from Coleorton it is doubtless the house to which Constable refers.

NOTE ON NOS. 256, 257, 259–262, 273–278

Nos. 256, 257, 259, 260, 261 and 262 all come from the same sketch-book, measuring approximately 181 × 262 mm. (about 7⅛ × 10¼ ins.) and used by Constable both on his summer visit to Salisbury and Gillingham and his autumn visit to Coleorton. The height of the pages tapers from 178 mm. at the outer edge to 181 mm. at the hinge edge. Nos. 273 and 274, and possibly also Nos. 275–278, come from the same sketch-book, and show that he used it at Brighton, probably on his first visit in 1824; for their possible connection with a projected group of engravings, see also the note following No. 284.

1824

In 1824 Constable's sole exhibit at the Royal Academy was 'A Boat passing a Lock' ('The Lock') (now in the collection of Mr. S. Morrison). 'The Hay Wain', the 'View on the Stour near Dedham' and a 'View of Hampstead Heath' were exhibited at the Salon in Paris in this year. He took his wife and family to Brighton for the first time in May, and himself spent some time in London and some with them in Brighton, returning before them at the end of August.

263 *Brighton Beach, with fishing boat and crew.* 1824, June 10

Plate 199

Oil on paper. 9⅝ × 11¾ ins. (244 × 298 mm.) No. 782–1888

There is a ridge in the paper about ½ in. from the right-hand edge and ¼ in. from the top.

Inscribed on the back in pencil by the artist *Brighton June 10 1824*. The inscription is repeated in ink in another hand together with the initials *M.L.* [Maria Louisa Constable].
(See note following No. 272)

1824, June 12 Plate 200 **264** *Brighton Beach.*

Oil on paper. 4¾ × 11⅝ ins. (120 × 297 mm.) No. 783–1888
Inscribed on the back in pencil by the artist *June 12 1824*. This inscription is repeated in pencil and ink in another hand. Also inscribed in ink, with deletions as shown ~~*taking the air*~~ *Squaly day*. This does not seem to be based on a note by the artist.
(See note following No. 272)

1824, July 19 Plate 201 **265** *Brighton Beach.*

Oil on paper. 5⅜ × 11⅞ ins. (136 × 302 mm.) No. 148–1888
Inscribed on the back in pencil by the artist *Beach Brighton July 19. Noon. 1824 my Dear Minna's Birthday*. The inscription is repeated in ink in another hand, together with the initials *M.L.C.* [Maria Louisa Constable, the Minna of the inscription].
(See note following No. 272)

1824, July 19 Plate 202 **266** *Brighton Beach, with colliers.*

Oil on paper. 5⅞ × 9¾ ins. (149 × 248 mm.) No. 591–1888
Inscribed on the back in pencil (probably by the artist, but partly copied in ink, or inked over) *3d tide receeding left the beach wet—Head of the Chain Pier Beach Brighton July 19 Evg., 1824 My dear Maria's Birthday Your Goddaughter—Very lovely Evening—looking Eastward—cliffs & light off a dark grey* [?] *effect—background—very white and golden light*. Inscribed with the monogram *JC*. Also inscribed in ink over an earlier pencil inscription *Colliers on the beach*.

Beckett (Beckett, VI, p. 168) suggests that the inscription is on a mutilated piece of paper on the back of the sketch, possibly part of a contemplated letter to Fisher, but it is on the back of the sketch itself, and in the form customary for the series of sketches Nos. 263–268. As shown in the note following No. 272, the inscription serves to identify the sketch as one of those sent to Fisher by Constable on 5 January 1825. Maria Louisa Constable was Fisher's god-daughter.

1824, July 22 Plate 203 **267** *Brighton Beach.*

Oil on paper. 6½ × 12 ins. (165 × 304 mm.) No. 335–1888
Inscribed on the back in ink by the artist *Beach Brighton 22d July, 1824 Very fine*

Evening. Inscribed on the back in ink in another hand *Painted by J. Constable at Brighton*.
(See note following 272)

268 *A windmill near Brighton.* 1824, August 3 Plate 204

Oil on paper. $6\frac{3}{8} \times 12\frac{1}{8}$ ins. (162 × 308 mm.) No. 149–1888
Inscribed on the back in pencil by the artist *Brighton Augst. 3d 1824 Smock or Tower Mill west end of Brighton the neighbourhood of Brighton—consists of London cow fields—and Hideous masses of unfledged earth called the country*. The inscription is repeated in ink in another hand. Leslie (L. ed. S., p. 172) repeats the last line of the inscription in a footnote to Constable's letter of 29 August 1824 railing at Brighton. No. 272 may show the same mill.
(See note following No. 272)

269 *A windmill near Brighton.* [1824, August 20?] Plate 199

Oil on paper. $6\frac{1}{8} \times 9\frac{5}{8}$ ins. (157 × 244 mm.) No. 158–1888
The top of a church tower is seen in the distance, right.

269a On the back of the sketch, which is on white paper, is a pencil drawing showing a coast scene, probably the beach at Brighton, with houses on the West Cliff in the background. Plate 209
Inscribed at top left in pencil by the artist *Battery* (referring to the guns on the sea wall) and vertically across the sky, right, with an indistinct date, perhaps *Aug 20*. Also inscribed in another hand below on left *M.L.* [Maria Louisa Constable].

According to J. A. Erredge, *History of Brighthelmston*, 1862 (p. 71) the only battery existing at Brighton at this time was on the West Cliff, opposite Artillery Place.
Dr. W. Katz of London had in 1954 a close-up sketch in oil on paper ($5\frac{3}{8} \times 4$ ins.) of the two figures seen gleaning at the left of No. 269. No. 1817 in the Tate Gallery, called 'The Gleaners, Brighton', is dated 20 August 1824 and shows two figures in similar attitudes to those in No. 269 and the sketch mentioned, gleaning in fields near windmills. This, with the conjectural reading of the date on No. 269a, strengthens the possibility that No. 269 was painted on the same day as the work in the Tate Gallery.
(See note following No. 272)

270 *Hove Beach, with fishing boats.* *c.*1824 Plate 206

Oil on paper laid on canvas. $11\frac{3}{4} \times 19\frac{3}{8}$ ins. (298 × 492 mm.) No. 129–1888

The scene has been identified by Mr. G. C. Beresford as a view from Hove

Beach, with Worthing on the extreme left, Highdown Hill nearer the centre, and Cissbury on the right. Holmes, p. 247, dates *c.*1824; the subject and style support this dating.
(See note following No. 272)

c.1824 **271** *Hove beach.*
Plate 207

Oil on paper laid on canvas. $12\frac{1}{2} \times 19\frac{1}{2}$ ins. (317 × 495 mm.) No. 120–1888
The canvas is larger than the paper and the painted area has been extended nearly to the edges of the canvas; it is not clear when or by whom this was done. The sketch was probably painted before being strained on canvas, as there are pin-holes in the corners of the paper. There are numerous *pentimenti* altering the position of the boats on the sky-line.

Mr. G. C. Beresford has identified this as a view, similar to that in No. 270, taken from Hove Beach, with Worthing on the left, Highdown Hill nearer the centre and Cissbury on the right. Holmes, p. 247, dates *c.*1824; the subject and style support this dating.
(See note following No. 272)

c.1824 **272** *A windmill among houses, with a rainbow.*
Plate 205

Oil on paper laid on canvas. $8\frac{1}{4} \times 12$ ins. (210 × 304 mm.) No. 126–1888
The mill seen here with the houses clustering beside it may be the same as that shown in the oil sketch No. 268, dated 3 August 1824. In any event the treatment is sufficiently close to that of No. 268 to justify the assumption that the scene is near Brighton and the date of the sketch *c.*1824. Holmes, p. 247, dates accordingly.

NOTE ON NOS. 263–272

In his letter to Fisher of 29 August 1824 (Beckett, VI, pp. 170–2), Constable gives an unflattering description of Brighton and concludes: "In short there is nothing here for a painter but the breakers—& sky—which have been lovely indeed and always varying. The fishing boats are picturesque, but not so much so as the Hasting boats, which are luggers . . . But these subjects are so hackneyed in the Exhibition, and are in fact so little capable of that beautifull sentiment that landscape is capable of or which rather belongs to landscape, that they have done a great deal of harm to the art—they form a class of art much easier than landscape & have in consequence almost supplanted it . . ." Constable had offered to lend Fisher one of his Brighton sketch-books but was eventually unable to do so because of the suggestion that the sketches should be engraved (see note following No. 284). In place of them he sent a number of oil sketches. He refers to them in his letter of 5 January 1825 (Beckett, VI, p. 189): "I have enclosed in the box a dozen of my Brighton oil sketches—perhaps the sight of

the sea may cheer Mrs F—they were done in the lid of my box on my knees as usual. Will you be so good as to take care of them. I put them in a book on purpose—as I find dirt destroys them a good deal. Will you repack the box as you find it. Return them to me here at your leisure but the sooner the better". In his letter of [6] April 1825 (Beckett, VI, p. 196) Fisher speaks of returning the Brighton sketches, and sending with them two volumes of Paley's sermons: "They are fit companions for your sketches, being exactly like them: full of vigour, & nature, fresh, original, warm from observation of nature, hasty, unpolished, untouched afterwards".
The inscription on the back of No. 266 shows that it was almost certainly one of the Brighton oil sketches in this batch sent by Constable to Fisher. Others among the sketches certainly painted in this year (Nos. 263–265, 267 and 268) may well have been included in the consignment.

273 *Studies of fishing gear on the beach at Brighton.* *c.*1824
Plate 208

Pen, pencil and grey and pink wash. $7\frac{1}{8} \times 10\frac{3}{8}$ ins. (181 × 264 mm.)
No. 605–1888

Page from a sketch-book.

273a On the back are four sketches. Men fishing from a boat with a net. Boats drawn up on the beach. An anchor. A slight pencil sketch of figures and a boat. With the exception of the last, the sketches on this side are in pen, pencil and grey wash. As with many of the Brighton drawings, much of the outline appears to be drawn with the point of the brush. Plate 208

Two of the studies on the *recto*, the anchor in the middle of the top, and the anchor with the net below on left, were used by Constable as sketches for objects on the beach in his large oil painting 'The Marine Parade and Chain Pier, Brighton', which was exhibited at the Royal Academy in 1827, and is now in the Tate Gallery (No. 5957). The drawing was therefore made before 1827, and as the page comes from the sketch-book which Constable was using in 1823 (see note following No. 262) there is every likelihood that the studies were made at Brighton. Although there is no difficulty in supposing that Constable may have reverted to the use of the 1823 sketch-book after a year or two's delay, it is perhaps more probable that this, and Nos. 274 and 275, were drawn in 1824 rather than at a later date.
For a sketch for the composition of 'The Marine Parade and Chain Pier, Brighton' see No. 289.

274 *Scene on the beach at Brighton.* *c.*1824
Plate 210

Pen, pencil and grey wash. $7\frac{1}{8} \times 10\frac{3}{8}$ ins. (181 × 264 mm.) No. 198–1888
Page from a sketch-book.
Inscribed on the back in pencil by the artist *Folignio* [Foligno] *Rapheals Madona*

Head of Old Joseph little Sketches from the Bible—Also on the back (not reproduced amongst the plates) is a sketch of a figure, traced through and outlined in ink from the right-hand figure on the front.

The sheet comes from the sketch-book used in 1823 (see note following No. 262). It is in series with No. 273, and the reasons given in the note on that drawing help to establish the probability that this also was made at Brighton, perhaps on the visit of 1824.

c.1824 **275** *Brighton Beach: fishing boat with net.*
Plate 210

Pen, pencil and water-colour. 7×10¼ ins. (178×260 mm.) No. 171–1888
A thin strip of paper about 136×6 mm. has been pasted to the upper part of the left edge and the drawing carried on to it.

It is possible that this drawing may be a trimmed page from the sketch-book discussed in the note following No. 262, to which Nos. 273 and 274 have been related, though the only corroborative evidence on the sheet itself is the discoloration and dog-eared condition of the right-hand side. The sheet is inscribed in pencil at the back *Brighton Fishing boat with net.* This inscription appears to have been written when the Museum number was put on the back. There is no indication of its origin but no reason to doubt its accuracy, as the top drawing on No. 273a shows a similar scene in a comparable technique, and independent reasons have been given for believing that the latter was drawn at Brighton. The resemblance of No. 275 to No. 273 and the possibility that No. 275 may have come from the same sketch-book justify a dating of *c.*1824.

c.1824 **276** *Brighton Beach, with fishing boats and the Chain Pier.*
Plate 211

Pen, pencil and water-colour. 7×10¼ ins. (178×259 mm.) No. 340–1888
A strip of blue at the top indicates that the sky has almost completely faded. The drawing bears on the back in pencil an inscription by Mr. B. S. Long, formerly Keeper of the Department of Paintings *On the back of modern mount was written in pencil 'Chain Pier Brighton John Constable R.A. 340–1888 Sunshine—' B.S.L. 29/11/1922.* There is no indication of the origin of the inscription copied here, but no doubt it was based on a note made by the artist.
The measurements suggest the possibility that the drawing may be on a trimmed page from the sketch-book discussed in the note following No. 262, to which Nos. 273–275 have been related, though the only corroborative evidence lies in the discoloured condition of the right-hand side. The style is parallel with that of No. 275, and this drawing may therefore also be dated *c.*1824.

c.1824 **277** *A windmill, probably on the Downs near Brighton.*
Plate 211

Grey wash. 7⅛×10¾ ins. (180×274 mm.) No. 245–1888

The sheet of paper on which the drawing is made has two vertical folds at the left-hand side, and a strip of about 15 mm. at this side is not drawn on. Along the left-hand of the two folds is a line of holes which may be sewing marks: these are 262 mm. from the right-hand edge, the same distance as the corresponding marks on No. 273. This and the discoloration of the right-hand side suggest that the sheet may have come from the sketch-book discussed in the note following No. 262, to which Nos. 273–276 have been related. The style of drawing, and the method by which the outlines of the clouds are drawn with the point of the brush, show that the drawing was in any event made at about the same time as Nos. 275 and 276. The subject is therefore likely to be near Brighton.

278 *Beach scene, with boats and fishermen.* *c.*1824

Plate 215

Pen, pencil and grey ink. 7×10⅛ ins. (179×257 mm.) No. 259–1888
The technique (compare the drawing of the clouds in No. 274) and the subject-matter link this drawing with those made at Brighton *c.*1824. The measurements indicate a possibility that the sheet may have come from the sketch-book discussed in the note following No. 262, to which Nos. 273–277 have been related, but as the drawing was trimmed and laid down on card there is no corroborative evidence.

279 *Coast scene, Brighton.* *c.*1824

Plate 212

Pen, sepia and grey wash. 13⅛×16½ ins. (333×420 mm.) No. 191–1888
On rough paper.

279a On the back is a pencil sketch of a wide downland landscape, inscribed below illegibly, identified by Mr. R. B. Beckett as the Devil's Dyke, near the 'Shepherd and Dog' inn; also a slight study of a kneeling figure. Plate 209

That the scene on the *recto* is correctly identified as Brighton is confirmed by a water-colour entitled 'Brighton Beach' by F. L. T. Francia (present whereabouts unknown) which shows the same belfry on the breakwater.
Constable recorded a visit to the Devil's Dyke in a letter to Fisher postmarked 29 [August] 1824 (Beckett, VI, p. 172); the drawing on the *verso* may have been made on this occasion. In the course of his description he comments: "Last Tuesday, the finest day that ever was, we went to the Dyke—which is in fact a Roman remains of an embankment, overlooking—perhaps the most grand & affecting natural landscape in the world—and consequently a scene the most unfit for a picture. It is the business of a painter not to contend with nature & put this scene (a valley filled with imagery 50 miles long) on a canvas of a few inches, but to make something out of nothing, in attempting which he must almost of necessity become poetical."
(See note following No. 284)

*c.*1824 **280** *Coast scene with a capstan, probably near Brighton.*
Plate 212

Pen, sepia and water-colour. $13\frac{1}{8} \times 15$ ins. (332×382 mm.) No. 190–1888
On rough paper.
Its similarity in style and subject-matter to No. 279 indicates that this drawing was made at the same time, and that the coast portrayed is at or near Brighton. (See note following No. 284)

*c.*1824 **281** *Coast scene with shipping, probably near Brighton.*
Plate 213

Pen with grey and blue wash. $10\frac{1}{2} \times 13\frac{1}{4}$ ins. (268×336 mm.) No. 195–1888
On rough paper.
(See note following No. 284)

*c.*1824 **282** *Coast scene, probably near Brighton.*
Plate 213

Pencil, pen and grey wash. $10\frac{5}{8} \times 13\frac{1}{4}$ ins. (269×337 mm.) No. 196–1888
On rough paper.
On the back is a rough brush scribble, resembling a face in an oval.
(See note following No. 284)

*c.*1824 **283** *Coast scene, probably near Brighton.*
Plate 214

Pen and grey wash. $10\frac{1}{2} \times 13\frac{1}{4}$ ins. (268×336 mm.) No. 197–1888
On rough paper.
Holmes, p. 238, dates *c.*1799.
(See note following No. 284)

*c.*1824 **284** *Fishing boats on shore, probably at Brighton.*
Plate 214

Pen and sepia wash. $10\frac{1}{2} \times 13\frac{1}{4}$ ins. (267×336 mm.) No. 817–1888
On rough paper.
On the back (not reproduced amongst the plates) is a slight sketch in pencil of a mother with a child in her lap; also, in ink, the serial number 24.

The child represented on the *verso* appears to be aged about 3 years and to be a boy. If we may assume that the sketch shows Mrs. Constable with one of her children, this could represent Charles Golding Constable (*b.*1821) in 1824. Rather less probable would be Isabella (*b.*1822) in 1824–5 or Emily (*b.*1825) in 1827–8.

NOTE ON NOS. 279–284

Nos. 279–284 may be grouped together because they are executed on the same kind of rough paper, and portray similar scenes in a homogeneous technique. Since

No. 279 may be definitely identified as a scene at Brighton, it follows that the other beach scenes represent places in that neighbourhood and that the drawings were made in 1824 or subsequent years. Similar drawings dated from Brighton on 1 and 13 September 1824, and from Worthing on 22 September 1824, were in the collection of Capt. Charles Constable. Constable tells Fisher in his letter of 17 December 1824 that Arrowsmith the French dealer has engaged him to make twelve drawings to be engraved by S. W. Reynolds in London and published in Paris from one of his sketch-books of Brighton. The plates were to be of the same size as the drawings, about 10 or 12 ins. He describes the sketch-book itself—"This book is larger than my others—and does not contain odds, and ends (I wish it did), but all complete compositions—all of boats, or beach scenes—and there may be about 30 of them" (Beckett, VI, p. 184). This letter might refer to Nos. 273–277 (and perhaps No. 278); alternatively, some of the sketches Nos. 279–284 may be connected with Arrowsmith's scheme. As far as is known the engravings were not made (S.: L., pp. 2, 3).

285 *Coast scene, perhaps near Brighton.* *c.*1824–8
Plate 215

Pen and grey wash. $7\frac{1}{8} \times 10\frac{1}{4}$ ins. (180×261 mm.) No. 833–1888

This is not a page from a sketch-book, even though the measurements approximate to those of the sketch-books discussed in the note following No. 262; it is on different, cream coloured, paper which has been torn roughly at either side. Vertical pencil lines have been ruled at the left- and right-hand edges.

The subject was described when the drawing was received in the Museum as 'Sketch of ships drawn up on the shore of a tidal river: the Orwell(?) near Ipswich' (*Inventory of Art Objects 1888*) and this description has been substantially maintained since. But no opposite shore is visible, and it appears that the boats are drawn up on a beach. The probability is that the sketch is one of those made by Constable while on a visit to Brighton between 1824 and 1828. The way in which the outlines of the clouds are drawn, apparently with the point of the brush, may be compared with Nos. 275–277. Holmes, p. 238, dates *c.*1799. It appears however that the roughness of the drawing is due to carelessness rather than to immaturity.

1825

In 1825 Constable exhibited at the Royal Academy three paintings called 'Landscape'. One was 'The Leaping Horse' (now in the Diploma Gallery, Burlington House; see No. 286); the other two were views of Hampstead Heath (sold to Mr. F. Darby). His fifth child, Emily, was born on 29 March.

c.1825 **286** *Full-scale study for 'The Leaping Horse'.*
216

Oil on canvas. 51×74 ins. (1294×1880 mm.) No. 986–1900
Bequeathed by Mr. Henry Vaughan.
The canvas has been extended at the top and the right-hand side by the amount originally turned round the stretcher.
On the back of the frame is a label recording the loan of the painting to the International Exhibition, London, 1874.

This is the full-scale study for the painting exhibited by Constable at the Royal Academy in 1825 (No. 224 'Landscape'). For its history see note to No. 209. If, as is probable, this study is there correctly identified with part of Lot 38 at the Executors' sale, 16 May 1838, the catalogue of the Exhibition of British Art held at the Royal Academy, 1934, is wrong in identifying it as Lot 35 at the same sale. The latter, bought by Archbutt for £52 10s., was probably the exhibited version; this is now in the Diploma Gallery of the Royal Academy, Burlington House, to which it was given by Mrs. Dawkins in 1889.
The preliminary material for the picture is reproduced and discussed by Charles Johnson in *The Growth of Twelve Masterpieces*, 1947, pp. 83–90 and Pls. 46–50. The British Museum has two drawings for the composition (L.B. 10*a* and 10*b*: black chalk and wash, each 202×300 mm.). An oil sketch on canvas (19×25¼ ins.) was formerly in the possession of Sir Evan Charteris. A pencil study for the willow stump in No. 286, formerly in the collection of the Hon. Ralph Bathurst, was sold as Lot 86 at Messrs. Sotheby's, 24 November 1948 (3½×4½ ins.). Holmes, p. 247, records an oil painting (55½×47 ins.) which repeats the left-hand portion of the composition.
No. 286 follows the British Museum drawing L.B. 10*a* in the position of the leaning willow stump, and L.B. 10*b* in the motif of the leaping horse. The oil sketch formerly belonging to Sir Evan Charteris has an upright willow tree to the left of the leaping horse as well as the leaning stump to the right. It seems that both these small trees were in the exhibited version; that only the left-hand one is now to be seen is explained by the fact that Constable worked on the picture after it had been shown at the Royal Academy. In the diary which he kept for Mrs. Constable he recorded under the date 7 September 1825: "Set to work on my large picture, took out the old willow stump by my horse, which has improved the picture much; almost finished; made one or two other alterations" (L. ed. S., p. 197). Leslie explains in a footnote that this refers to 'The Leaping Horse', which had not found a purchaser. Holmes, p. 247, interprets the alteration described as the transfer of the stunted tree on the right to the left side of the horse; but the reduction from two stumps to one by painting out that on the right and leaving the one on the left seems more probable in view of the composition of the small (Charteris) oil sketch. A confused area of paint in No. 286, where a boy is bending down at the barrier behind the horse, suggests that at one stage this full-scale sketch also contained the left-hand willow stump,

which Constable subsequently removed. The finished picture originally followed No. 286 more closely than it does in its present condition; the barge on the extreme left and the cow watering were painted out, and the contour of the remaining barge in the foreground was altered to present a less head-on appearance. Additions to the exhibited picture include a half-furled sail for the barge, and the tower of Dedham Church in the background, right.

Leslie (L. ed. S., p. 190) explains the title by which the picture is now generally known as follows: "The chief object in its foreground is a horse mounted by a boy, leaping one of the barriers which cross the towing paths along the Stour (for it is that river, and not a canal), to prevent the cattle from quitting their bounds. As these bars are without gates, the horses, which are of a much finer race, and kept in better condition than the wretched animals that tow the barges near London, are all taught to leap; their harness ornamented over the collar with crimson fringe* adds to their picturesque appearance, and Constable, by availing himself of these advantages, and relieving the horse, which is of a dark colour, upon a bright sky, made him a very imposing object". In some early references to the picture it is called 'The Jumping Horse'.

In the first edition of Leslie's *Life of Constable* (1843, p. 51) the following passage about 'The Leaping Horse' is to be found: "So carefully did he study this subject, that he made, in the first place, two large sketches, each on a six-foot canvas. One was, I believe, intended to be the picture, but was afterwards turned into a sketch, not an unusual occurrence with him". This passage was omitted in the second edition of the *Life* (1845) which was in other respects an amplified version. The reason for the omission is not clear, but it suggests that Leslie may have found the statement not to be well founded. No full-scale sketch other than No. 286 figured in the Executors' sale, nor is one recorded elsewhere, but it is possible, if Leslie's original statement was true, that No. 286 may be the work originally intended for exhibition, but turned into a sketch. Stylistically the exhibited version is a sketch with some parts—the horse and boy, the river surface and the sky—more elaborated.

Constable seems to have begun work on 'The Leaping Horse' after his return from Brighton in November 1824. In his letter of 17 November 1824 he says to Fisher: "I am planning a large picture", and in that of 17 December: "I am putting a 6 foot canvas in hand" (Beckett, VI, pp. 181 and 187). On 5 January 1825 he writes: "I am writing this hasty scrawl [in the] dark before a six foot canvas—which I have just launched with all my usual anxieties. It is a canal scene—my next shall contain a scratch with my pen of the subject" (Beckett, VI, p. 190). The scratch did not, apparently, eventuate, but in his next letter, of 23 January 1825, Constable gives a description of the subject: "The large subject now on my easil is most promising and if time allows I shall far excell most of

---

* Lucas in his annotated copy of Leslie's *Life* says that this is a mistake and that Constable introduced the fringe to bring red into the picture (Beckett, II, p. 371).

my other large pictures in it. It is a canal and full of the bustle incident to such a scene where four or five boats are passing with dogs, horses, boys & men & women & children, and best of all old timber-props, water plants, willow stumps, sedges, old nets, &c &c &c." (Beckett, VI, p. 191). On 8 April Constable again wrote: "I have worked very hard—and my large picture went last week to the Academy—but I must say that no one picture ever departed from my easil with more anxiety on my part with it. It is a lovely subject, of the canal kind, lively—& soothing—calm and exhilarating, fresh—& blowing, but it should have been on my easil a few weeks longer" (Beckett, VI, p. 197–8). He gives yet another description of the painting in his letter of 1 August 1825 to Mr. Francis Darby (L. ed. S., p. 192): "Scene in Suffolk, banks of a navigable river, barge horse leaping on an old bridge, under which is a flood gate and an Elibray*, river plants and weeds, a more-hen frightened from her Nest—near by in the meadows is the fine Gothic tower of Dedham". All these references show that Constable planned the work as a continuation of the series of river and canal scenes inaugurated by 'The White Horse' of 1819 and followed by 'Stratford Mill' (1820), 'The Hay Wain' (1821), 'View on the Stour near Dedham' (1822) and 'The Lock' (1824).

For a small copy of No. 286 by R. C. Leslie, see note to No. 209.

1826

In 1826 Constable exhibited at the Royal Academy 'Landscape' ('The Cornfield') (National Gallery, No. 130) and 'A Mill at Gillingham in Dorsetshire' (see No. 288). His sixth child, Alfred Abram, was born on 14 November.

*c.*1826 **287** *A donkey with a foal: study for 'The Cornfield'.*

Plate 218

Oil on paper. $8\frac{1}{2} \times 7\frac{1}{4}$ ins. (216 × 184 mm.) No. 790–1888

Inscribed in ink on the back *L.C.* [Lionel Bicknell Constable]; also *J. Constable RA.*

This is a study for the group of two donkeys in 'The Cornfield' which was exhibited in the Royal Academy in 1826 and is now in the National Gallery (No. 130; Davies pp. 22–3). A donkey cropping the hedge in a similar attitude is to be seen in the 'Dedham Vale' of 1811 (collection of Sir Richard Proby). Holmes, in the *Burlington Magazine*, Vol. XII, 1907–8, p. 76, discussed whether No. 287 could be a sketch of 1811 for the earlier picture, which was then used

* No explanation of this word has been given. Possibly Constable intended "Eel buck".

again for 'The Cornfield'. He concluded that the sketch must be of the later date on grounds of style: this conclusion is fortified by the fact, which Holmes does not seem to have noticed, that the foal of the donkey is to be seen in No. 287, as in the picture 'The Cornfield'. This second donkey, which is head on to the spectator, is difficult to discern, and the subject of the sketch has hitherto been described in the Museum's catalogues as a single donkey browsing. There is a thumbnail sketch of a donkey, in a somewhat similar attitude to that of the mother, in the sketch-book No. 121, p. 32; and at all periods Constable was fond of introducing donkeys into his paintings. In his letter of 3 December 1815 to Maria Bicknell he writes: "Yesterday was so very mild that I went painting in the feild from a donkey that I wanted to introduce in a little picture" (Beckett, II, p. 162). Since the first version of 'The Cottage in a Cornfield' was ready for exhibition in 1817, and the drawing for it (No. 145) was made *c.*1815, this sentence might refer to that composition (see No. 352).

1827

In 1827 Constable exhibited at the Royal Academy 'Chain Pier, Brighton' (Tate Gallery, No. 5957; see No. 289), 'Mill, Gillingham, Dorset' (see No. 288) and 'Hampstead Heath'. To the British Institution he sent a version of 'The Glebe Farm' (see No. 111).

288 *A Water-mill at Gillingham, Dorset.* Perhaps exhibited in 1827

Oil on canvas. $24\frac{3}{4} \times 20\frac{1}{2}$ ins. (630 × 520 mm.) No. 1632–1888 Plate 219

Isabel Constable Bequest.

This painting is one of five works bequeathed to the Museum in 1888 by Miss Isabel Constable with the request that they should be described as a gift from Maria Louisa Constable, Isabel Constable and Lionel Bicknell Constable.

The canvas has been relined at an unknown date.

The following three labels were formerly affixed to the back of the frame:

1. Inscribed, presumably in the artist's hand:
   105 [?] *The Water Mill John Constable R.A.*
2. In another hand:
   An undershot water-mill at Gillingham—worked by a branch of the stream from Stourhead.
3. A printed label showing that the picture was lent by Miss Constable of 64 Hamilton Terrace, N.W., to the Royal Academy Winter Exhibition of Old Masters, 1882. The work was No. 51 in that Exhibition.

Constable exhibited at the Royal Academy in 1826 a painting (No. 122) entitled 'A Mill at Gillingham in Dorsetshire'; also at the Royal Academy in 1827 another painting (No. 48) entitled 'Mill, Gillingham, Dorset'; and at the British Institution in 1827 a painting (No. 321) 'A Mill at Gillingham, Dorset' with framed measurements 2 ft. 6 ins. × 2 ft. 10 ins. The picture exhibited in 1826 is known to be that now in the possession of Mr. and Mrs. Paul Mellon, (L. ed. M., p. 418 and reproduced Pl. 50). An earlier and smaller version of the composition seen in that picture was painted in 1824; this was formerly in the collection of Archdeacon Fisher and is now in the Fitzwilliam Museum, Cambridge. Both these compositions are horizontal, and show the mill from a different angle across the mill-stream. If then No. 288 was painted for exhibition at the Royal Academy it must be the work shown in 1827. It was doubtless the painting of this subject shown by the artist at Worcester in 1835; the description of No. 68 in the exhibition, 'A Water Mill' by Constable, in *Berrow's Worcester Journal*, 23 July 1835, quoted by Windsor, p. 128, mentions the men grinding their scythes, a detail which occurs in No. 288 but in neither of the other versions of the subject mentioned above. The account in the *Worcester Journal* goes on to say that the picture "appears to have been painted some years". Holmes, p. 248, wrongly identifies the painting now belonging to Mr. and Mrs. Paul Mellon (then in the C. A. Barton Collection) as that exhibited at the Royal Academy in 1827. He is doubtless correct in identifying No. 288 as Lot 57, 'Gillingham Mill, Dorsetshire', in the Executors' sale, 16 May 1838. This lot was bought by Leslie—that is to say, bought in—for £37 16s.

No. 288 was engraved by Lucas (S.: L., p. 206; S. 43). The plate is dated 1843, but was not published by Lucas until 1845. The painting was then in the possession of Miss [Maria] Constable, and had evidently remained with the artist's family throughout.

This upright composition may have originated in a commission given by J. P. Tinney, the owner of Constable's 'Stratford Mill', but never fulfilled. Constable had undertaken to paint for him two upright landscapes the size of the 'Cathedral' (L. ed. S., p. 148, Constable's letter of 20 August 1823, to his wife). On the subjects for these projected pictures, Constable wrote to Fisher on 16 December 1823: "I am settled, for the Exhibition. My Waterloo must be done, and one other, perhaps one of Tinney's, Dedham, but more probably my Lock. I must visit Gillingham again for a subject for the other next summer" (Beckett, VI, p. 146). Again, in his letter of 27 May 1824 to Fisher, Constable says: "Tinney . . . is anxious to have his ancestors mill, and a view of Salisbury, which we are [to] look for when I come to you" (Beckett, VI, p. 160). Beckett shows, p. 131, that Tinney, whose full name was John Pern Tinney, probably had a family connection with the mill, which was known as Parham's (or Perne's) Mill. However, at Constable's urgent request, Tinney, in a letter of 4 November 1824, released him from the obligation to paint the two upright pictures for him (Beckett, VI, p. 178). Beckett, p. 230, suggests that No. 288 is actually one of the uprights which Constable had been painting for Tinney before their relations had been broken off. He did not revisit Gillingham to make the sketch for Tinney's picture as he proposed and No. 288 is presumably based on a sketch made in 1823; e.g. that in the collection of the Earl of Haddington. In 1825 the mill was burnt down. Fisher wrote to Constable in September 1825: "The news is, that Mat. Parham's (*alias* Perne's) mill is burnt to the ground, and exists only on your canvas. A huge misshapen, new, bright, brick, modern, improved, patent monster is starting up in its stead" (Beckett, VI, p. 206). When the painting was on loan to Worcester, E. Leader Williams (the honorary secretary of the Worcester Literary and Scientific Institution) wrote to Constable "I have thought so much of that sweet little picture—the gable end of the mill, with the *slimy* mill wheel—that I should be delighted to take a copy of it" (Beckett, V, p. 62). His son, who became known as B. W. Leader, R.A., told Lord Windsor, *c.*1903, that this copy of his father's was sold as the original and that he had seen it hanging at the Grosvenor Galleries as a genuine picture (Windsor, p. 137). It seems however that Mr. Leader was in error and in any case was thinking of the exhibition of No. 288 at the Royal Academy Winter Exhibition in 1882 (Beckett, V, p. 65).

289 *The Marine Parade and Chain Pier, Brighton.* *c.*1826–7
Plate 225

Pencil, with pen additions. $4\frac{3}{8} \times 16\frac{3}{4}$ ins. (111 × 425 mm.) No. 289–1888
The drawing is on a sheet of paper, $14\frac{5}{8}$ ins. (370 mm.) wide, with a fold down the middle, extended by a strip attached on the left, and the larger sheet so formed has also been folded down the middle. The original sheet bears the truncated watermark: |D MILL |24; the continuation sheet bears the remainder of the watermark: BASTE| 18| .
Inscribed by the artist in pencil, over the roofs of the houses, with colour notes: some are illegible, but *Brown* and *Red* can be deciphered.

This is a study used by Constable for his large oil painting 'The Marine Parade and Chain Pier, Brighton', exhibited at the Royal Academy in 1827, and now in the Tate Gallery, No. 5957. Since the Albion Hotel, just built in 1826, is seen in the drawing it is perhaps to be dated to the autumn of that year (information from the Brighton Art Gallery). The sketch was used with minor variations for the middle distance, beginning about a quarter of the way up the canvas and extending to about half way up. The pen alterations introduced, mainly on the continuation sheet, were designed to test the effect of introducing a hut and breakwater at the left of the composition, and Constable carried this addition into the finished picture, placing a fishing boat partially in front of the hut and extending the composition still further to the left. For sketches used for foreground objects in the painting see No. 273. Mayne notes (L. ed. M., pp. 415, 416) two oil studies for the picture in the Philadelphia Museum of Art and a pencil sketch said to be in a private collection in the U.S.A. M. Chamot (*Connoisseur*, Vol. CXXXVII, 1956, p. 262) shows that the composition of the painting in the Tate Gallery has been changed through the cutting down of the canvas, removing a standing figure and a large sail on the extreme left.

1827, October 4
Plate 225

290 *The fore-part of a barge at Flatford.*

Pencil. $8\frac{7}{8} \times 12\frac{7}{8}$ ins. (224×327 mm.) No. 834–1888
Page from a sketch-book.
Inscribed in lower left corner in pencil by the artist *Flatford. Octr. 4. 1827.*
Writing to his wife on the day he made this drawing, Constable says "John & I & Mini went on the river in a barge" (Beckett, II, p. 440).
(See note following No. 300)

1827, October 4
Plate 220

291 *Water Lane, Stratford St. Mary, Suffolk.*

Pencil and grey wash. $13 \times 8\frac{7}{8}$ ins. (330×224 mm.) No. 624–1888
Page from a sketch-book on paper watermarked: J WHATMAN TURKEY MILLS 1824.
Inscribed below on left in pencil by the artist *Stratford Water Lane. Oct 4 1827.*
Lt.-Col. C. A. Brooks has shown that the house seen here still stands, largely unaltered; it is now called 'Raveny's'.
(See note following No. 300)

1827, October 6
Plate 220

292 *An oak in Dedham Meadows.*

Pencil and water-colour. $13 \times 8\frac{3}{4}$ ins. (330×225 mm.) No. 802–1888
Page from a sketch-book.
Inscribed at top in pencil by the artist *Oak. in the Dedham Meadows. Octr. 6 1827.*; also inscribed on the back in ink with the serial number *3*.
(See note following No. 300)

1827, October 11
Plate 222

293 *A lock on the Stour.*

Pencil. $8\frac{7}{8} \times 13\frac{1}{8}$ ins. (224×332 mm.) No. 269–1888
Page from a sketch-book.
Inscribed below on left in pencil by the artist *11 Oct 1827*; also inscribed on the back in ink with the serial number *5*.
(See note following No. 300)

1827, October 13
Plate 221

294 *A willow tree in Flatford Meadows.*

Pencil. $8\frac{7}{8} \times 13$ ins. (224×331 mm.) No. 837–1888
Page from a sketch-book on paper watermarked: J WHATMAN TURKEY MILLS 1824.

Inscribed below on left in pencil by the artist *Flatford Meadows Oct 13 1827.*; inscribed on the back in pencil *2½/* by */1½*, also in ink with the serial number *1*.
(See note following No. 300)

295 *A willow tree in Flatford Meadows.* 1827, October 13
Plate 221

Pencil and slight grey wash. 8⅞ × 13⅛ ins. (224 × 332 mm.) No. 838–1888
Page from a sketch-book on paper watermarked: J WHATMAN TURKEY MILLS 1824.
Inscribed in lower left corner in pencil by the artist *Flatford Meadows Octr 13. 1827.*; also inscribed on the back in ink with the serial number *2*.
A somewhat similar but not identical stump occurs in the preliminary drawings and the oil sketch (No. 286) for 'The Leaping Horse'. This study, and No. 294, were of course made two years after the willow stump in question had been painted out of the exhibited version of 'The Leaping Horse'.
(See note following No. 300)

296 *Water Lane, Stratford St. Mary, Suffolk.* [1827, October]
Plate 223

Pen and grey wash, with touches of pencil and bistre.
8⅞ × 13 ins. (224 × 331 mm.) No. 241–1888
Page from a sketch-book on paper watermarked: J WHATMAN TURKEY MILLS 1824.
Lt.-Col. C. A. Brooks has pointed out that the house seen in this drawing is the same as that shown in No. 291.
(See note following No. 300)

297 *Flatford Old Bridge and Bridge Cottage on the Stour.* [1827, October]
Plate 222

Pencil. 8⅞ × 13 ins. (224 × 331 mm.) No. 313–1888
Page from a sketch-book.
Inscribed on the back in ink with the serial number *6*.

The drawing represents the wooden bridge and the cottage seen in the 'View on the Stour near Dedham' (Huntington Library and Art Gallery, San Marino) (L. ed. S., Pl. 76). Other views of the bridge and cottage described in this Catalogue are in the sketch-book No. 121, pp. 27, 29 and 53; the sketch-book No. 132, p. 52; No. 298; No. 324; No. 346.
Holmes, p. 252, links No. 297 with No. 380 of 1835. However, the leaf comes from the sketch-book used in Suffolk in October 1827 and the drawing was no doubt made at that time.
(See note following No. 300)

[1827, October] **298** *A barge on the Stour.*
Plate 224

Pencil and grey and sepia wash. $8\frac{7}{8} \times 13$ ins. (224×331 mm.) No. 244–1888
Page from a sketch-book on paper watermarked: J WHATMAN TURKEY MILLS 1824.
Inscribed on the back in ink with the serial number *8*.

Lightly washed in for background are the bridge and cottage seen in No. 297. Other views of the bridge and cottage described in this Catalogue are in the sketch-book No. 121, pp. 27, 29 and 53; the sketch-book No. 132, p. 52; No. 324.
(See note following No. 300)

[1827, October] **299** *A village street.*
Plate 223

Pencil. $8\frac{7}{8} \times 13$ ins. (225×331 mm.) No. 274–1888
Page from a sketch-book.
Inscribed on the back in ink with the serial number *10*.
The leaf comes from the sketch-book used in Suffolk in October 1827, and the scene depicted may be in the neighbourhood of Flatford or Dedham.
(See note following No. 300)

[1827, October] **300** *Men loading a barge on the Stour.*
Plate 224

Pencil, pen and grey wash. $8\frac{7}{8} \times 13$ ins. (225×331 mm.) No. 242–1888
Page from a sketch-book.
Inscribed in the left corner of the sky in pencil by the artist *Silvery Clouds Bright* and *Blue*.
The leaf comes from the sketch-book used in Suffolk in October 1827. Lt.-Col. C. A. Brooks has noted that the barrier in the foreground is that seen in the barge-building yard represented in No. 137. Flatford Mill is on the left, and Flatford Lock in the centre, while Dedham Church has been inserted in a fictional position in the right-hand distance. The drawing may therefore be a study for a composition, rather than a sketch from nature.

NOTE ON NOS. 290–300

Nos. 290–300 are all on leaves from the same sketch-book, measuring about 224×331 mm. ($8\frac{7}{8} \times 13$ ins.) used in 1827. Nos. 290, 291, 292, 294 and 295 are inscribed for places in the neighbourhood of Flatford. Nos. 297 and 298 are independently identifiable as scenes in that locality. The drawings were made on a visit of Constable's to Flatford Mill, which lasted nearly a fortnight; he took his two eldest children, John and Maria, and arrived probably on 2 October (Beckett, II, p. 439).

Two sheets from the same sketch-book are in the British Museum:

L.B. 8. The Cottage in the Lane. 221 × 321 mm. (acquired in 1887).

L.B. 15. Lock on the Stour, with Dedham Church in the distance. 222 × 327 mm. On paper watermarked: J WHATMAN TURKEY MILLS 1824. (Gift of Miss Isabel Constable)

The National Gallery of Ireland has a sheet from the sketch-book:—

2057. Flatford Lock, with Flatford Old Bridge and Bridge Cottage. Pencil. 221 × 329 mm. Inscribed by the artist *Flatford Octr. 5 1827.*

Another washed pencil drawing on a leaf from the sketch-book of 1827 is in the possession of Mrs. E. O. Beazley. It represents a large timbered house with a tiled roof, and on the left a haystack with haymaking in progress. It is inscribed by the artist *Flatford 13 Oct 1827.* The sight measurement is 221 × 326 mm. (about $8\frac{3}{4} \times 12\frac{7}{8}$ ins.). At the back is the inscription *This sketch was presented to the late James Beazley by the widow or relative of Constable the artist, out of gratitude for a slight service rendered to her by him. J. H. Beazley.* (Since Mrs. Constable predeceased her husband the gift must have been made by another member of the artist's family.)

1828

In 1828 Constable exhibited at the Royal Academy two paintings called 'Landscape'. One was 'Dedham Vale' (National Gallery of Scotland, No. 2016); the other was 'Hampstead Heath' (No. 301 in this Catalogue). His seventh child, Lionel Bicknell, was born on 2 January. Mrs. Constable died on 23 November.

301 *Hampstead Heath: Branch Hill Pond.* 1828 Plate 217

Oil on canvas. $23\frac{1}{2} \times 30\frac{1}{2}$ ins. (596 × 776 mm.) No. F.A. 35
Sheepshanks Gift.
The canvas was relined in 1893; it was probably at this time that the sides of the canvas were spread out and coloured with a neutral tint.
A label on the stretcher is inscribed in ink by the artist *No. 2 Landscape John Constable 35 Charlotte Street Fitzroy Square.* This is the usual form of label for paintings exhibited by Constable at the Royal Academy (see also Nos. 254 and 352).

No. 171, painted in 1819, is the sketch for this work, and a list of other versions is given in the note on that sketch. No. 301 has hitherto been identified with the painting 'A Heath', exhibited by Constable at the Royal Academy in 1830. This identification goes back before the receipt of the picture in the Museum, to the undated hand-list of *c.*1850 *The Collection of Pictures formed by John Sheepshanks, Esq.*, and therefore evidently represents the belief of Sheepshanks, the purchaser and donor of the painting (see also note to No. 323). To be precise, the hand-list merely records two paintings entitled 'Hampstead Heath', one with 1827 and the other with 1830 as the date of exhibition. As No. 301 was clearly the later in point of style, it was naturally taken to be the one believed to have been exhibited in 1830, and the other, No. 323 in this Catalogue, was taken to be that shown in 1827. It will be seen below that the date assigned to No. 323 was incorrect and that in all probability neither of the dates 1827 nor 1830 applies either to No. 301 or to No. 323.

Mr. R. B. Beckett has communicated two facts which prove that No. 301 was the painting of Hampstead Heath exhibited by Constable as 'Landscape' at the Royal Academy in 1828. The first is that Lucas noted in the margin of his proof copy of Leslie's *Life of Constable* that Sheepshanks had bought for 80 guineas the painting of Hampstead Heath exhibited in 1828 and originally bought by Chantrey. The other is that in the letter from Constable to Lucas of August 1830 outlining his plans for *English Landscape Scenery* (S.: L., p. 32), the phrase doubtfully transliterated as "Chartrup Heath" should be read as "Chantrey's Heath". Since No. 301 is the original of the mezzotint 'A Heath' by Lucas (S. 23) the painting of 1828 purchased by Sheepshanks is thus identified with it. Although Constable regarded the painting as Chantrey's property for a number of years, it appears that Chantrey himself could not decide whether he wanted it or not. The first account of the sale is given in Constable's letter of 11 June 1828 to Fisher: "Painted a large upright landscape (perhaps my best). It is in the Exhibition, noticed (*as a redeemer*) by John Bull, & another, less in size but better in quality, *purchased by Chantrey*" (Beckett, VI, p. 236). The large upright landscape mentioned here is the 'Dedham Vale' now in the National Gallery of Scotland. However, on 4 March 1832 Constable wrote to Leslie: "Mrs. Leslie was so kind as to speak of me (the usual kind way in which you are all so good as to consider me) to Mr Lawley, who called yesterday afternoon—and nothing seemed to me more agreeable than we both were, 'to one another', he admiring my pictures, I admiring him for his so doing—but he has not admired only—he has taken a great fancy to my 'Heath', and to my 'book', which is indeed assuming a very tangible shape—but not so my Heath. That picture is somehow got intangled with Chantrey in a most ridiculous way—who will neither take it nor refuse it. It is plain he must have considered it his by his telling the Watts Russells so—for when he blamed them for not taking my picture of me since, he said—"Well—I have"—this he told me. But when I wrote to him to know his pleasure—and to ask if my 'delay' or 'any seeming lukewarmness on my part',—had 'caused me to forfeit his patronage, of which I should be proud at all times', &c &c—he made me no answer nor did he write any answer to my letter" (Beckett, III, p. 64). Sheepshanks may have bought the painting by June 1835 when two pictures by Constable belonging to him were seen by

Lord Northwick at Tiffin's gallery in the Strand (Beckett, IV, pp. 118–19). One of the two, which Lord Northwick wanted in exchange for a Hobbema, is referred to by Constable as 'The Church' (P. Leslie, p. 135). However, Sheepshanks must have disposed of this painting of a church before he gave his paintings to the nation ('Salisbury Cathedral from the Bishop's Grounds', No. 254, was acquired by him at the Executors' sale in 1838), and therefore it cannot be assumed that he did not also relinquish the second picture which was seen at Tiffin's.
Holmes, p. 249, though he accepted the statement that the picture was exhibited in 1830, suggested that it had been begun two or three years earlier.
The mezzotint by David Lucas, which was much altered by the artist during the proof stages, was published in the third number of *English Landscape Scenery*, September 1831 (S.: L., pp. 183–4). In the early lists of contents it was alternatively entitled 'Hampstead Heath. Stormy noon' and 'Hampstead Heath. Sand Pits. Storm approaching' (S.: L., pp. 230–1).

302 *The Old Parish Church at Hove.* 1828, May 16
Plate 226

Pencil. $4\frac{1}{2}\times7\frac{3}{8}$ ins. (115 × 186 mm.) No. 294–1888
Page from a sketch-book.
Inscribed below on right in pencil by the artist *May 16. 1828.*
Holmes, p. 248, correctly suggests that the building is the same as that shown in No. 309, which is known from the inscription to be Hove Church in its ruined condition, before restoration in 1836. The drawing is on a leaf of a sketch-book shown by its size and the subject to be that which Constable was using in Brighton a little later in the month.
(See note following No. 308)

303 *Coast scene at Brighton: evening.* [1828?], May 22
Plate 228

Oil on paper. $7\frac{7}{8}\times9\frac{3}{4}$ ins. (200 × 248 mm.) No. 155–1888
Inscribed on the back in pencil by the artist *22 May*. The date is repeated in ink in another hand. Also on the back (not reproduced amongst the plates) is a rough scribble in pencil and oil paint of a house with smoking chimneys; also the monogram *JC*.

The identification of the scene as being possibly at Brighton was made when the sketch was received into the Museum (*Inventory of Art Objects 1888*). Holmes, p. 247, who did not know of the inscription on the back, dates *c.*1824. Constable's journal, however, shows that he was in London on 22 May in that year. If the place represented is indeed Brighton the sketch may have been made in 1828, when Constable was at Brighton early in the year. Mr. J. W. Goodison has drawn attention to an oil-sketch painted by Constable on 20 July 1824 and

now in the Fitzwilliam Museum, entitled "Shoreham Bay. The walk to the Chalybeate Wells, Brighton". This appears to show the same section of coast as No. 303, though from a different viewpoint, thus confirming the traditional identification.
(See note following No. 308)

1828, May 30 **304** *Coast scene with vessels at Brighton.*
Plate 226

Pencil and grey wash. $4\frac{1}{2} \times 7\frac{1}{8}$ ins. (115 × 181 mm.) No. 350–1888
Page from a sketch-book on paper with truncated watermark: J WH| TURK| 18| .
Inscribed in top left corner in ink over pencil by the artist *May 30 1828*.
(See note following No. 308)

1828?, May 30? **305** *Coast scene at Brighton.*
Plate 227

Pencil, pen and ink, and grey wash. $4\frac{1}{2} \times 7\frac{3}{8}$ ins. (115 × 186 mm.) No. 199*a*–1888
Page from a sketch-book.
Inscribed, indistinctly, at top left in pencil by the artist *May 30*[?] *1828*[?]. The year is most indistinct; for the possibility that it might be 1825 see the note on No. 309.
Holmes, p. 248, links with Nos. 304 and 307 and dates 1828.
(See note following No. 308)

1828? **306** *Coast scene at Brighton.*
Plate 226

Pencil, pen and grey wash. $4\frac{1}{2} \times 7\frac{3}{8}$ ins. (115 × 187 mm.) No. 199–1888
Page from a sketch-book.
(See note following No. 308)

1828? **307** *Coast scene at Brighton.*
Plate 227

Pencil and grey wash. $4\frac{1}{2} \times 7\frac{3}{8}$ ins. (115 × 186 mm.) No. 199*b*–1888
Page from a sketch-book on paper with truncated watermark: |Y MILL |21.
Holmes, p. 248, links with Nos. 304 and 305 and dates 1828.
(See note following No. 308)

1828? **308** *A boat and an anchor on the beach at Brighton.*
Plate 227

Pencil, pen and grey wash. $4\frac{1}{2} \times 7\frac{1}{4}$ ins. (115 × 185 mm.) No. 199*c*–1888
Page from a sketch-book on paper with truncated watermark: J WH| TURK| 18| .

308a On the back is a pencil drawing of the end of the Brighton Chain Pier. Plate 227

NOTE ON NOS. 302, 304–308 AND 309

Nos. 304–308 appear to come from the same sketch-book, since they are carried out in the same medium and in similar technique on pages of the same size and, where they exist, the watermarks correspond; Nos. 302 and 309 can be referred to the same source. Since the *verso* of No. 308 bears a drawing of the Chain Pier, it may be presumed that the other coast scenes in this series were drawn at or near Brighton. That Constable was there on 16 May 1828 is evidenced by No. 302. There is no published account to show that he was there on May 30 as the identification of the subject of No. 304 requires. He wrote on 11 June to Fisher "My wife is sadly ill at Brighton" (Beckett, VI, p. 237) and these drawings may have been made when he accompanied or visited her there.
For a sketchbook which belonged to Delacroix containing drawings of Brighton by Constable similar in manner to 302, 304–8 and 309, see the article 'Newly discovered drawings by Constable in a Louvre Sketch-Book' by Graham Reynolds, *Burlington Magazine*, Vol. CVIII, 1966, pp. 138–41 and figs. 37–44.

309 *The Old Parish Church at Hove.* [—], November 6

Pencil, pen and water-colour. $4\frac{1}{2} \times 7\frac{3}{8}$ ins. (114 × 186 mm.) No. 207–1888 Plate 226
Page from a sketch-book on paper with truncated watermark: |ATMAN |Y MILL |21.
Inscribed below on left in ink by the artist *Novr. 6th* . . . [a word erased here] *Hove*, and on the back in pencil *Mr. Hudson's* and with the serial number *28*.

This leaf is shown by the size and watermark to come from the same sketch-book as Nos. 302 and 304–308 (on which see the note following No. 308). The earliest dated leaves in that book are of May 1828 (Nos. 302, 304 and 305). It is not easy to determine in which year this drawing was made. Mrs. Constable died on 23 November 1828 at Hampstead, and it is hardly conceivable that Constable should have visited Brighton less than three weeks before that event, since her illness had reached a critical stage. Constable was certainly at Brighton on 6 November 1825; 1826, 1827, 1830 and later years do not seem to be excluded. If the date on No. 305 could be read as 1825 it might be shown that the sketch-book was in use in that year. A drawing of the same church, measuring $4\frac{1}{2} \times 7$ ins. and dated 14 October 1825, was Lot 195 in the sale held at Messrs. Sotheby's, 16 January 1958.
Holmes, p. 248, dates *c.*1834.

310 *A windmill near Brighton.* *c.*1828

Oil on canvas. $5\frac{3}{4} \times 4\frac{1}{2}$ ins. (146 × 114 mm.) No. 588–1888 Plate 233
The pigmented surface does not extend to the edges of the canvas, which has been relined.

This sketch was engraved in mezzotint by David Lucas with the title 'A Mill near Brighton' (S. 4). Shirley (S.: L., p. 161) says that progress proofs are dated 1829. The work on the plate was well advanced in March 1830, but it was not included in the editions of *English Landscape Scenery* published during Constable's lifetime. It first appeared in Moon's edition, 1838. Holmes, p. 248, dates *c.*1828, and Shirley (L. ed. S., p. 230) states categorically that it was painted in that year. The dated progress proofs show that it had been painted by 1829.

1829

Constable was elected R.A. on 10 February 1829. He exhibited 'Hadleigh Castle' (now in the collection of Mr. and Mrs. Paul Mellon; see No. 127 in this Catalogue) and a landscape of a "rich cottage". He paid his last two visits to Fisher at Salisbury, in July and in November. His preparations for *English Landscape Scenery* got under way in this year: the earliest letter on the subject to Lucas printed by Shirley (S.: L., p. 20) is dated 28 August 1829.

1829, July 12
Plate 230

311 *A view at Salisbury, from the library of Archdeacon Fisher's house.*

Oil on paper. $6\frac{3}{8} \times 12$ ins. (162×305 mm.) No. 153–1888
Inscribed on the back in pencil by the artist *Fisher's—Library—Salisbury Sunday July 12. 1829 4 o clock afternoon.* Also on the back is a transcript of this inscription in ink, and in pencil the initials *M.L.C.* [Maria Louisa Constable].
The left-hand group of trees is also to be seen in No. 312, and in the oil sketch 'Water-meadows near Salisbury' in the Ashmolean Museum, Oxford.

1829, July 15
Plate 231

312 *The Close, Salisbury.*

Oil on paper. $10\frac{3}{8} \times 8$ ins. (264×203 mm.) No. 334–1888
Inscribed on the back in pencil by the artist *Close—15 July—1829 11. o clock noon —Wind S.W—very fine.* Also on the back is a copy in ink of the inscription and *J. Constable R.A.*
This sketch is a close-up study, under different light, of the group of trees seen from Fisher's library in the left of No. 311; see also the oil sketch 'Water-meadows near Salisbury' in the Ashmolean Museum, Oxford.

1829, July 22
Plate 234

313 *Archdeacon John Fisher with his dogs, Salisbury.*

Pen and bistre ink and water-colour. $3\frac{5}{8} \times 5$ ins. (93×128 mm.)
No. 206–1888

Page from a sketch-book.
Inscribed on the back in pencil by the artist *22d July 1829—Salisbury Fisher & his dogs*; also in ink with the serial number *14*. Also inscribed in pencil *M.L.C.* [Maria Louisa Constable].
This leaf is from the same sketch-book as Nos. 316 and 318.
(See note following No. 319)

314 *Salisbury Cathedral seen from over the river.* 1829, July 25 Plate 235

Pencil. $9\frac{1}{4} \times 13\frac{1}{4}$ ins. (234×337 mm.) No. 315–1888
Page from a sketch-book.
Inscribed below on left in pencil by the artist *25 July 1829 Eveng.*; also on the back in ink with the serial number *9*.
On the edge of the back a sheet of different paper has been pasted and torn off; it is about 28 mm. wide and has on it a pencil scribble or the edge of a drawing. The pasted sheet can be seen by transmitted light to bear two lines of ink inscription, the upper one of which reads *The Revd Archdeacon Fisher*. The second is cut and cannot be read.
(See note following No. 319)

315 *A cottage and trees near Salisbury.* 1829, July 28 Plate 236

Black chalk and water-colour. $9\frac{1}{4} \times 13\frac{1}{4}$ ins. (234×336 mm.) No. 210–1888
Page from a sketch-book.
Inscribed below on left in pencil by the artist *July 28. 1829 near Salisbury*; also on the back in ink with the serial number *11* and in pencil with the monogram *JC*.
(See note following No. 319)

316 *Cows grazing, Salisbury.* 1829, Nov. 13 & 14 Plate 234

Pen and ink and water-colour washes. $5 \times 3\frac{5}{8}$ ins. (12×793 mm.) No. 253–1888

Page from a sketch-book.
Inscribed on the back in pencil by the artist *13. & 14. of Novr. 1829 done in the Evng—at Salisbury—from the sketch made at the bottom of the Garden.* Also inscribed in pencil with the serial number *51* and *M.L.C.* [Maria Louisa Constable]. This leaf is from the same sketch-book as Nos. 313 and 318. The garden is presumably that of Leydenhall, Archdeacon Fisher's house in Salisbury.
(See note following No. 319)

317 *The demolition or repair of old houses at Salisbury.* 1829, November 20 Plate 237

Pencil, black chalk and light water-colour washes.
$9\frac{1}{4} \times 13\frac{1}{4}$ ins. (234×335 mm.) No. 254–1888

Page from a sketch-book.
Inscribed in lower right corner in pencil by the artist *Sarum 20 Novr 1829*. On the back is a strip, right, about 70 mm. wide, bordered by a vertical line, completing a pencil drawing on the next leaf of the sketch-book.
(See note following No. 319)

[1829] Plate 234

318 *A bridge over a stream, with a cottage beyond.*

Pencil, pen and bistre ink and water-colour. $3\frac{5}{8} \times 4\frac{7}{8}$ ins. (93 × 125 mm.)
No. 205–1888

Page from a sketch-book, trimmed.
This leaf is from the same sketch-book as Nos. 313 and 316; it is homogeneous with the former in style and the drawing may have been made at about the same time.
(See note following No. 319)

[1829] Plate 235

319 *Salisbury Cathedral seen from the north-west, with cottages.*

Pen and bistre ink and water-colour. $9\frac{1}{4} \times 13\frac{1}{4}$ ins. (234 × 337 mm.)
No. 227–1888

Page from a sketch-book.
On the back, on the hinge side, is a strip about 22 mm. wide, completing in black chalk and water-colour the drawing on the next sheet of the sketch-book. The measurements show that this drawing comes from the same sketch-book as Nos. 314, 315 and 317, used at Salisbury in 1829. Since Constable did not visit Salisbury again, this drawing must have been made either in July or November of that year.

NOTE ON NOS. 313–319

Constable used two sketch-books on his visits of 1829 to Salisbury. The smaller one, composed of thin paper, measures about $3\frac{5}{8} \times 5$ ins. (93 × 128 mm.) Nos. 313, 316 and 318 come from this book; the first two drawings were made at Salisbury, and it is possible that the third was made at about the same time. The larger sketch-book measures $9\frac{1}{4} \times 13\frac{1}{4}$ ins. (234 × 337 mm.) Nos. 314, 315, 317 and 319 come from this book. There are in the British Museum three drawings from the latter sketch-book:

- L.B. 16 Landscape Study. (229 × 326 mm.)
- L.B. 29 Harnham Bridge. (229 × 330 mm.) Dated 23 November 1829. (See also No. 240 above)
- L.B. 33 View of Salisbury from the river. (229 × 333 mm.) Dated 19 November 1829.

These three drawings were given by Miss Isabel Constable in February 1888. Other leaves from the same book are the drawing of Old Sarum mentioned in the note to No. 322; the late Mr. L. G. Duke's 'Distant View of Salisbury' (reproduced in L. ed. S., Pl. 121); and Lot 102 in the Gregory sale at Messrs. Sotheby's, 20 July 1949, 'A View of Salisbury Cathedral across meadows', black chalk and pencil, $8\frac{1}{2} \times 13$ ins., dated 23 November 1829.

320 *A view at Salisbury from Archdeacon Fisher's house.* [1829]
Plate 229

Oil on canvas. $7\frac{7}{8} \times 9\frac{7}{8}$ ins. (200 × 251 mm.) No. 320–1888
A label on the stretcher reads *Lionel* [Lionel Bicknell Constable] *1848 Jany.* The stretcher is also inscribed in pencil *borrowed by C. R. Leslie May 20th. 1841.*

Mr. R. B. Beckett has identified the scene as a view from one of the windows in the south wing (now demolished) of Leydenhall, Archdeacon Fisher's house in the close at Salisbury.
The style of the sketch corresponds with that of Nos. 311 and 312, of which the former was also made from a window of Fisher's house. No. 320 may therefore reasonably be linked with them and assigned to Constable's visit of 1829 to Salisbury. Holmes, p. 243, identifies the scene as 'Garden and Paddock, Salisbury (?)' but dates *c.*1815.

321 *Water-meadows near Salisbury.* [1829]
Plate 232

Oil on canvas. $18 \times 21\frac{3}{4}$ ins. (457 × 553 mm.) No. F.A. 38
Sheepshanks Gift.
The canvas has been relined at an unknown date.

This is the painting by Constable which came before the Council of the Academy and was rejected, although it should have been hung without scrutiny, since Constable was then an Academician. Whitley (*Art in England, 1821–1837*, p. 188) assigns the incident, apparently on the authority of Anderdon, to the year 1830. Constable was taking an active part on the Council in that year, as a newly elected Academician, and was one of the three members of the Hanging Committee for the exhibition. The date of 1830 for the incident is consistent with the supposition, which is justified on stylistic grounds, that the painting was made on Constable's last visit to Salisbury in 1829. Holmes, p. 245, dates the picture 1820, but does not notice that Constable could not have been on the committee for selecting the exhibition before his appointment as an Academician in 1829. Whitley quotes Anderdon's version of the incident of the picture's rejection, which he had from Leslie. Richard Redgrave noted a version of the story in his diary entry for 30 April 1866 (printed in *Richard Redgrave, A Memoir by F. M. Redgrave*, 1891, pp. 284–5). Redgrave's informant was F. R. Lee, but he cannot have been present when the episode occurred, as he was not elected an

Academician until 1838. Frith's account is the liveliest and, though it is probably embellished, the fact that its source was Abraham Cooper, who served with Constable on the Hanging Committee in 1830, gives it some authority: "When Constable was a member of the selecting Council, a small landscape was brought to judgment; it was not received with favour. The first judge said, 'That's a poor thing'; the next muttered, 'It's very green'; in short, the picture had to stand the fire of animadversion from everybody but Constable, the last remark being, 'It's devilish bad—cross it'. Constable rose, took a couple of steps in front, turned round, and faced the Council. 'That picture,' said he, 'was painted by me. I have a notion that some of you didn't like my work, and this is a pretty convincing proof. I am very much obliged to you', making a low bow. 'Dear, dear!' said the President [Shee] to the head-carpenter, 'how came that picture amongst the outsiders? Bring it back; it must be admitted, of course.' 'No! it must not!' said Constable; 'out it goes!' and, in spite of apology and entreaty, out it went. This story was told me by Cooper, who witnessed the scene". (W. P. Frith, *My Autobiography and Reminiscences*, Vol. I, 1887, pp. 237–8.)

No. 321 was sold as Lot 50, 'Salisbury Meadows; painted from nature' at the Executors' sale, 16 May 1838, bought on behalf of John Sheepshanks for £35 14s. by Smith of Gower Street. Anderdon wished to buy it and told Leslie "I had been bidding on from ten pounds, hoping to walk off with such a prize, when I heard some one whisper—'Why Sheepshanks is bidding'. I was then the last bidder, but I gave way at once to a competitor with such a long purse". "You would never have got it in any case", replied Leslie. "I have tried in vain to obtain it, and have offered in exchange to paint for Sheepshanks anything he liked. But I can't shake him. He clings to it all the more, because he knows it was thrown out by the Academy Council as 'a nasty green thing' " (Whitley, *loc. cit.*, p. 189). Redgrave confirms Leslie's admiration for the picture: "Of this picture Leslie, who had an intense admiration of Constable's art, once said to me that he would give any work he (Leslie) had painted for it, so warmly did he admire it" (Redgrave, *loc. cit.*, p. 285).

[1829] **322** *Old Sarum.*

Plate 233

Oil on thin card. $5\frac{5}{8} \times 8\frac{1}{4}$ ins. (143 × 210 mm.) No. 163–1888

The back of the card on which the sketch is painted is part of a ruled and washed water-colour mount, as is that of No. 208.

Inscribed on the back in ink *ML* [Maria Louisa Constable].

David Lucas made two mezzotints of approximately the same size from this sketch for Constable's *English Landscape Scenery*. The first (S. 8) was begun in 1829; a progress proof bears that date (S.: L., p. 166, S. 8*d*); it was ready for printing in January 1830, and published in the second number in January 1831

(Shirley, *loc. cit.*). Constable decided to replace it, and had the second plate engraved (S. 32). This was begun by the end of October, 1831, and was published in the second edition of *English Landscape Scenery*, 1833 (S.: L., p. 195). Below the title it bore the inscription: " 'Here we have no continuing city'—St. Paul". In early lists of contents the title is given as 'Mound of the City of Old Sarum. Evening' (S.: L., p. 230).

Leslie says of the plate, and of the reasons which led Constable to call for a new engraving of it: "A city turned into a landscape, independently of the historical associations with Old Sarum, could not but be interesting to Constable; and not satisfied with Mr. Lucas's first engraving of it, in which its mounds and terraces were not marked with sufficient precision, he incurred the expense of a second plate. Sir Thomas Lawrence, who had seen the first, greatly admired the treatment of this subject, and told Constable he ought to dedicate it to the House of Commons" (L. ed. S., pp. 266–7). Old Sarum had been allowed to fall into decay, and was entirely in ruins by the sixteenth century. None the less, as a Rotten Borough, it returned two members to Parliament till the Reform Act of 1832. This last fact may account for Lawrence's comment and for Constable's interest in the subject at the time—he was deeply agitated by the prospect of Reform. Constable subsequently wrote descriptive letterpress for the engraving, in part to give the history of Old Sarum, and in part to express his view that the solemnity of such a subject should be conveyed by the general effect of the light and shade in its pictorial treatment. "We naturally look to the grander phenomena of Nature, as according best with the character of such a scene. Sudden and abrupt appearances of light, thunder clouds, wild autumnal evenings, solemn and shadowy twilights, 'flinging half an image on the straining sight', with variously tinted clouds, dark, cold and gray, or ruddy and bright, with transitory gleams of light; even conflicts of the elements, to heighten, if possible, the sentiment which belongs to a subject so awful and impressive." The text is quoted in full by Shirley (S.: L., pp. 258–9); extracts are given by Leslie (L. ed. S., pp. 267–8). Writing to Lucas on 27 October 1831, Constable said "Keep the new 'Old Sarum' clear, bright, and sharp, but don't lose solemnity" (S.: L., p. 62). For the water-colour of the same subject exhibited by Constable in 1834, see No. 359. No. 322 and the water-colour No. 359 are both based on a pencil drawing dated 20 July 1829, measuring 9×13 ins., which was sold from the collection of Charles Constable, 11 July 1887 (Lot 1).

323 *Hampstead Heath.* *c.*1820–30

Plate 238

Oil on canvas. 21×30½ ins. (533×776 mm.) No. F.A. 36

Sheepshanks Gift.

The canvas was relined in 1893.

The view is taken near the pond at the Vale of Health, looking over to Highgate: East Heath Road near Squire's Mount is on the extreme right.

This painting has hitherto been considered to be the view of Hampstead Heath exhibited by Constable at the Royal Academy in 1827, but there is no corroborative evidence for this identification, though it goes back before the receipt of the picture in the Museum, to the undated hand-list of *c.*1850, *The Collection of Pictures formed by John Sheepshanks Esq.*, and therefore represents the opinion of Sheepshanks, the purchaser and donor (see also note to No. 301). However, Holmes, p. 248, expressed doubts about the supposed date of exhibition and suggested on grounds of style that the picture was probably painted in 1821 or 1822. If the painting is in fact an exhibited work, it may have been the 'Hampstead Heath' shown by Constable at the Royal Academy in 1822; but it has no stronger claim to be identified with that work than some other pictures of the same locality, such as that acquired by the Fitzwilliam Museum from the Eckstein Collection, which is of the same style and size. There is in fact no certainty that the painting was exhibited at all; and it bears no labels of the kind found on Nos. 254, 301 and 352, all of which were exhibited at the Royal Academy. In his letter of 7 October 1822 to Fisher, Constable refers to a painting of 'Green Highgate' (Beckett, VI, p. 98). Nothing is known of its composition, but since Highgate is seen in the middle distance of No. 323 it is conceivable that Constable may have been referring to this work. It is not known when Sheepshanks acquired the painting. Beckett (IV, p. 119) suggests that it may have been one of the two pictures by Constable belonging to Sheepshanks which were seen by Lord Northwick at Tiffin's Gallery in 1835. This identification could only be alternative to the supposition that No. 301 was one of the pictures in question, since the second was 'The Church' (see note to No. 301); another possibility is that No. 323 may have been Lot 53 at the Executors' sale, 16 May 1838—'Hampstead Heath, at the Ponds', bought by Tiffin for £37 5s. 6d. (Tiffin bought 'Salisbury Cathedral from the Bishop's Grounds' (No. 254) for Sheepshanks at the same sale.)

*c.*1820–30
Plate 246

324 *Flatford Old Bridge and Bridge Cottage on the Stour.*

Pencil, pen and bistre ink and grey wash. 7×10$\frac{5}{8}$ ins. (179×269 mm.)
No. 243–1888

On laid paper watermarked: J BUDGEN 1820.

Other views of the bridge and cottage are in the sketch-book No. 121, pp. 27, 29 and 53; the sketch-book No. 132, p. 52; Nos. 297, 298 and 346.
For a more detailed drawing of the trees on the right hand side see No. 161. Since the technique bears affinities to that of No. 300 of 1827 and also to the sketches for 'The Leaping Horse' in the British Museum (L.B. 10a and 10*b*, of *c.*1824), the drawing was perhaps made before 1830. Like them it may be a studio composition (cf. also Nos. 410, 411).

325 *Plants growing near a wall.* c.1820–30 Plate 243

Oil on paper. 12 × 9¾ ins. (305 × 248 mm.) No. 785–1888
On the back of the sketch is a partially erased inscription in ink, perhaps *Minna Ju 27th 47*.
Holmes, p. 243, dates *c.*1815, but there is no evident reason for assigning the sketch to a very different period from that of No. 326, which Holmes dates *c.*1826. Both are here assigned to *c.*1820–30 for the reason given in the note to No. 326.

326 *Study of foliage.* c.1820–30 Plate 243

Oil on paper. 6 × 9½ ins. (152 × 242 mm.) No. 338–1888

The blue paper back of the sketch is inscribed in ink with the monogram *JC*.

Holmes, p. 247, dates *c.*1826. The study has much in common with the foregrounds of Constable's large river and canal scenes but has not been identified as a direct study for any of them. It has particular affinities with the foreground of 'The Lock' (1824), and 'The Leaping Horse' (1825); this circumstance, together with the breadth of style, seems to justify a dating between 1820 and 1830; and No. 325 above may be assigned on grounds of style and subject-matter to the same period. This dating is supported by comparison with the group of eleven oil sketches of foliage, waterfowl, etc., mounted as drawings in the British Museum, one of which (No. 1919–4–15–6) is dated *Brighton July 28 1828*, and another (No. 1919–4–15–4) *July 25 1828*.
W. P. Frith, R.A., in *My Autobiography and Reminiscences*, Vol. III, 1888, pp. 318–19, gives an account of his visit to Constable's studio which is relevant to such studies as these: "There was a piece of the trunk of a tree in the room, some weeds, and some dock-leaves. 'And what line of the art do you intend to follow?' said Constable to me. 'I don't know, Sir', I replied . . . 'Well, whatever it may be,' said the great landscape painter, 'never do anything without nature before you, if it be possible to have it. See those weeds and the dock-leaves? They are to come into the foreground of this picture. I know dock-leaves pretty well, but I should not attempt to introduce them into a picture without having them before me' ".
Frith paid the visit in company with the drawing-master Sass, with whom he was a pupil *c.*1835–7. The episode, if correctly recalled after an interval of fifty years, therefore refers to 'The Valley Farm', 'The Cenotaph' or 'Arundel Mill and Castle'; probably to the latter.

327 *On the edge of a wood.* c.1820–30? Plate 244

Oil on paper. 6½ × 11⅞ ins. (165 × 301 mm.) No. 788–1888
Holmes, p. 249, dates *c.*1829. The implied comparison with the Salisbury

sketches of that year (Nos. 311, 312 and 320) may be taken as the best basis available for the dating of this sketch. Some features however recall the technique of 'The Grove, Hampstead' (Tate Gallery, No. 1246) to which the date of 1832 is assigned (Davies, p. 27).

1830

In 1830 Constable was a member of the Hanging Committee of the Royal Academy (see the note to No. 321 above). He exhibited views of Helmingham Park and Hampstead Heath and another landscape at the Royal Academy. The first number of *English Landscape Scenery* was published in June or July.

1830, September 15
Plate 248

328 *Study of clouds above a wide landscape.*

Pencil and water-colour. $7\frac{1}{2} \times 9$ ins. (190×228 mm.) No. 240–1888
Inscribed on the back in pencil by the artist *about 11—Noon—Sepr 15 1830. Wind— W.* The last figure of the date might be read as *1*, but is probably a blind *o* written with a blunt pencil.
On laid paper watermarked: B & M under a cartouche.

Holmes, p. 249, who gives the date as 5 September 1830, suggests that the drawing was made at Hampstead. This is plausible since the trees and indications of buildings low down in the foreground resemble those in other drawings known to have been made at Hampstead.

*c.*1830
Plate 239

329 *A country road with trees and figures.*

Oil on canvas. $9\frac{1}{2} \times 13$ ins. (242×330 mm.) No. 787–1888

Plate 242

329a *Willy Lott's House.*

Oil on canvas. $10\frac{3}{4} \times 9\frac{1}{2}$ ins. (273×242 mm.)
When the canvas was received in the Museum the sketch of Willy Lott's house was treated as the more important of the two sides in the *Inventory of Art Objects 1888*. The side now framed for exhibition has the appearance of having been folded about $1\frac{1}{2}$ inches from the left-hand side and this roughly corresponds with the top of the sketch on the other side. There is a line of darker colour about 4 inches from the right-hand side.
No. 329 *recto* is a version of the composition seen in No. 100 of 1811. The colder

tonality and sketchier finish suggest that it may have been worked up by Constable in his studio from No. 100, which is the open air sketch, and that this may have been done at the same time as No. 329a, which is here assigned to *c.*1830. Further, it may have been intended, as was No. 329a, to be the sketch for a plate in *English Landscape Scenery*, but no engraving of it is known to have been started. Holmes, p. 249, dates the *recto c.*1830.

No. 329a is painted upon a portion only of the canvas and leaves about $2\frac{1}{4}$ inches unpigmented. The unpigmented part is inscribed in ink *M. L.* [Maria Louisa Constable]. This is the sketch used by Lucas for the mezzotint 'Willy Lott's House' (S. 33). The mezzotint was intended for *English Landscape Scenery* and was in an advanced state by March 1832, but it was not published during the artist's lifetime. Lucas issued it in his supplementary volume to the work in 1845. Shirley (S. : L., p. 196) gives these facts and reproduces as the original sketch for the engraving No. 110 (*recto*); but No. 329a is much closer to the plate than either Nos. 110 or 110a. The main difference between the mezzotint and No. 329a is that the former has a figure on horseback in the right foreground: this was originally a standing figure and was altered by the artist during the proof stages (S. : L., p. 196, No. 33a–e). It is stated in the list of the engravings in Lucas's publication that the figure on horseback is Constable's father, and that the sketch No. 329a then belonged to Miss [Maria] Constable. The deviation from truth of colour and form, the suppression of the middle distance, the simplification of the foreground and the very sketchy quality of the trees, suggest that Constable made this sketch from No. 110a (or from the left-hand side of the study for 'The Hay Wain', No. 209) for the engraver's use. On the other hand, the river appears to be in flood in both No. 329a and the mezzotint, which might imply a further reference to the motif. In either event it may be dated *c.*1830. Davies, p. 24, accepts No. 329a as the basis of the engraving, in preference to Nos. 110 or 110a.

330 *Stoke-by-Nayland, Suffolk.* *c.*1830

Plate 240

Oil on paper. $9\frac{3}{4} \times 13$ ins. (248×330 mm.) No. 150–1888
The sketch has been laid down on card in recent years; there is no record of any inscription on the back.

This sketch was used by David Lucas in the preparation of his mezzotint 'Stoke by Neyland' (S. 9; S. : L., pp. 167 and 168) which was begun in 1829 and published in the second number of *English Landscape Scenery*, December 1830. The plate was much altered during the proof stages, and the published version only partially follows No. 330. It does so in the ramification of the right-hand trees (Holmes, *Burlington Magazine*, Vol. LVIII, 1931, p. 253), and in the figure of the woman carrying the bundle in the right foreground. The latter feature was introduced at the second stage of the proofs (S. 9*b*). The arrangement of the

cottages round the church tower is taken from the drawing No. 331. The oil sketch No. 1819 (now in the Tate Gallery; it was in the National Gallery when the *Catalogue of the British School*, 1946, was prepared) is based upon the same composition, but is not necessarily connected directly with the mezzotint (Davies, pp. 31–2). A large oil-painting based upon this composition is in the Art Institute of Chicago (reproduced in L. ed. S., Pl. 124a).
Holmes, p. 249, dates *c.*1831, under the impression that the plate was published *c.*1832; the history given above shows that the sketch is likely to have been made in 1829 or 1830. Holmes notes that No. 330 does not appear to be a study from nature but a composition from existing studies. This view is fortified by comparison with Nos. 329a and 332, which are here taken to be *ad hoc* productions for the engraver. Constable composed a text for the plate: this is quoted in full (two versions) by Shirley (S. : L., pp. 255–7); an extract is given by Leslie (L. ed. S., pp. 337–8). The thunder-clouds and noon-tide rainbow which form its main theme are atmospheric effects of the finished plate not apparent in No. 330.
Though there are eleven sketches of Stoke-by-Nayland Church in the sketch-books Nos. 121 and 132, none has any close affinity with Nos. 330, 331, or with the mezzotint, but possibly No. 132, p. 39, may have been used for some details.

*c.*1830
Plate 246

331 *Stoke-by-Nayland, Suffolk.*

Sepia. 5×7¼ ins. (127×183 mm.) No. 261–1876
This sketch, together with Nos. 17–20, were the only drawings by Constable in the Museum before the gifts made by Miss Isabel Constable in 1888. It was purchased from Messrs. Hogarth & Sons in May 1876.
On laid paper, mounted on thin card; as the paper is thin and much scraped with the knife by the artist in various *pentimenti*, the drawing has not been removed for the inspection of the back.

No. 331 is closely connected with the oil sketch No. 330 and still more closely with the published state of the mezzotint 'Stoke by Neyland' by David Lucas (S. 9). It has a stylistic affinity with the late sepia and monochrome drawings Nos. 410–414 and is a studio composition rather than a study from nature. The drawing seems to have been used for the arrangement of the cottages round the church tower in the mezzotint, and if it was prepared for that purpose must have been made before December 1830 (S. : L., p. 167). The church tower itself on the other hand does not represent that at Stoke-by-Nayland, being lower, squatter and with different fenestration. The mezzotint is more true to the original in this respect. Shirley (S. : L., p. 168; L. ed. S., p. 339) regards the rainbow effect of the published state as borrowed from No. 331; but though the details are vague the feature in question appears in the drawing to be a rim of light behind a hill, and the impression is given of a moonlit scene with a full moon in the sky. The hill, if it be such, is not topographically exact, and does not appear in any of the stages of the print. This drawing may have been made when there was some intention of generalizing the scene into that of any church in any village. Constable does in fact refer to the plate at an early stage as 'The Church' (S.: L., p. 21; see also Davies, pp. 31–2).

332 *Summer Morning: Dedham from Langham.* *c.*1830

Plate 241

Oil on canvas. 8½×12 ins. (216×305 mm.) No. 132–1888

The canvas has been relined at an unknown date. A paper label on the stretcher is inscribed in ink *John Constable R.A. Summer Morning engraved with alterations for the "English Landscape"*, and the stretcher itself is inscribed in ink *Summer Morning—Engraved.* These inscriptions are not in the artist's hand.

This is the sketch from which Lucas engraved the mezzotint entitled 'Summer Morning' (S. 26). The plate was perhaps begun by December 1830; it was certainly under way by February 1831, and was published in the third number of *English Landscape Scenery* in September 1831 (S. : L., pp. 187–8). The earlier progress proofs followed No. 332 closely; then Constable replaced the figure standing in the foreground by a milkmaid and two cows, introduced a plough into the left foreground, and made other modifications (S. 26*d et seq.*)

The scene is drawn from the same viewpoint in the sketch-book No. 121, pp. 39, 51 and 52; also in the oil sketch formerly in the National Gallery, now in the Tate Gallery, No. 2654 (Davies, p. 36). The former are of 1813: the latter is dated 24 August, without a year. Holmes, p. 243, dates No. 332 as *c.*1815, which is the date he assigns also to the Tate Gallery's painting No. 2654 (*Burlington Magazine*, Vol. XVII, 1910, p. 85; *Constable, Gainsborough, Lucas*, p. 31). It appears, however, that No. 332 was made for the purpose of the engraving and near the date of its execution, and that No. 121, p. 39 and the Tate Gallery's picture were used as sources for its composition. This view is suggested by the resemblance in technique to Nos. 329 and 330, whereas the Tate Gallery's version is, as the date inscribed upon it implies, a sketch from nature.

Oppé, who drew attention to the relationship between the sketch-book pages and the oil sketches, also reproduces a large pencil drawing of the same scene by Constable, which is in the Kobberstiksamling, Copenhagen (*Old Master Drawings*, Vol. XI, 1936–7, p. 55 and Pl. 50). Another oil sketch of the scene from an almost identical viewpoint, dated 13 July 1812, is in the Ashmolean Museum, Oxford (reproduced by Key, p. 39).

Constable wrote a text for the engraving, which is reprinted by Shirley (S. : L., pp. 260–2). In it he observes that the freshness and cheerfulness of the early morning comes from the dewy vegetation, since its shadows are deeper and cooler and its lights more silvery and sparkling than those of the evening. He describes the scene of the sketch: "This view of the beautiful Valley of the Stour ... is taken from Langham an elevated spot to the N.W. of Dedham, where the elegance of the tower of Dedham church is seen to much advantage, being opposed to a branch of the sea at Harwich where this meandering river loses itself". He then goes on to give some account of the history of Dedham. In early contents lists for *English Landscape Scenery* the plate is entitled 'Summer Morning. The Home-field, Dedham' or 'Summer Morning. Harwich Harbour in the Distance' (S. : L., pp. 230–1).

*c.*1820–30
Plate 245

333 *Hampstead Heath, Harrow in the distance.*

Oil on canvas. $7\frac{3}{4} \times 9\frac{7}{8}$ ins. (197 × 251 mm.) No. 123–1888
The canvas was relined in 1893.

This is either a preliminary sketch for the painting formerly in the Bullock Collection which was mezzotinted by David Lucas with the title 'Hampstead Heath, Harrow in the Distance' (S. 47), or a variant for the engraver's use during the production of the mezzotint. In the former case, the sketch will have been made from nature by 1824, when Schroth bespoke the finished version (Davies, pp. 38 and 39). In the latter case, No. 333 may have been painted about 1830, when the mezzotint was apparently first under contemplation, though it was not published until 1845 and Shirley thinks it was not begun till after Constable's death. Holmes, p. 246, who adopts the former and more plausible view, dates *c.*1822. There are some points of style, however, which suggest that it may not be a sketch from nature, and Shirley (S. : L., p. 211) says that No. 333 was used in the touching of the progress proof (S. 47*d*) of the mezzotint, when a cart was eliminated. The mezzotint as published has a cart approaching along the road, cows on the foreground ridge, and a donkey on the right: the only *staffage* in No. 333 is a flock of sheep roughly indicated on the road.
In a letter to Mr. Francis Darby about the replica of the painting in the Bullock collection which he exhibited at the Royal Academy in 1825, Constable gives the topography of the scene: "A scene on Hampstead Heath, called Child's Hill. Harrow with its spire in the distance" (L. ed. S., pp. 191–2).

1831

In 1831 Constable exhibited at the Royal Academy 'Salisbury Cathedral from the Meadows' (now in the collection of Lord Ashton of Hyde) and 'Yarmouth Pier'. He was present in the Abbey at the Coronation of William IV on 8 September (see No. 240), and in the same month he paid a brief visit to Mr. Digby Neave at Epsom.

334 *A dog watching a rat in the water at Dedham.* 1831, August 1 Plate 247

Pencil and water-colour. $7\frac{1}{4}\times8\frac{7}{8}$ ins. (185×226 mm.) No. 235–1888
The drawing is on a piece of writing paper, blind-stamped BATH, on the other side of which the artist has started a letter in ink *My dear Boys* [smudged]. The back also bears a rough pencil sketch (not reproduced amongst the plates), apparently of a dog followed by a man, and is inscribed by the artist in pencil *Dedham August 1st 1831*. It is also inscribed in ink with the serial number *21*, and in pencil '*Rose*' and *M.L.C.* [Maria Louisa Constable].

Constable had taken his daughters to stay with his family in Suffolk, returning to London on 4 July (P. Leslie, p. 30), and it appears that this drawing was made when he went to fetch them back (Beckett, I, p. 264).

335 *The root of a tree, at Hampstead.* 1831, September 22 Plate 247

Pencil. $8\frac{7}{8}\times7\frac{1}{4}$ ins. (227×185 mm.) No. 352–1888
The paper on which the drawing is made is blind-stamped indecipherably in the lower right corner.
Inscribed below in pencil by the artist *22d Sepr. 1831. Well Walk.*

336 *Sketch of a plough, at Epsom.* 1831, September 24 Plate 253

Pencil. $4\frac{1}{2}\times7\frac{1}{2}$ ins. (115×190 mm.) No. 304–1888
Page from a sketch-book.
Inscribed in lower left corner in pencil by the artist *Epsom Sepr 24 1831. Saturday Morng.*, and faintly, in top left corner *Epsom Sep 24*. Inscribed on the back in pencil by the artist *Surrey Plough Double Tom*, and in a less legible hand *Epsom—House in which Ld Littleton saw the Goast—which bikened him—& named the precise hour in which he was to die—& he died at that hour—though they put the clock forward.*

The second part of the inscription on the back relates to the drawing on the next page of the sketch-book, No. 337. Constable again refers to the story of the ghost which announced the hour of Lord Lyttelton's death in his letter of 26 September 1831 to Leslie (L. ed. S., pp. 265, 266, with Leslie's note on p. 265): "I have been passing a day or two with Digby Neave at Epsom. I slept on Friday night in the room in which Lord Lyttelton saw the ghost. But I neither saw nor heard anything of the lady or the bird". In fact, Lord Lyttelton is said to have seen the ghost in his house in Hill Street, Berkeley Square (*Dictionary of National Biography*), but to have died at Pitt Place, Epsom, where Constable was staying when he drew Nos. 336 and 337.
(See note following No. 350).

1831, September
Plate 248

337 *Pitt Place, Epsom, the house of Mr. Digby Neave.*

Pencil, pen and water-colour. $4\frac{1}{2} \times 7\frac{1}{2}$ ins. (115 × 190 mm.) No. 236–1888
Page from a sketch-book on paper with truncated watermark: |TMAN |31.
Inscribed on the back in pencil by the artist *Epsom—Look at back of Plough;* also *Lord Lyttleton.* Inscribed in ink with the serial number *7*.

The inscription on the back refers to the story of the ghost recounted on the back of No. 336. In the letter quoted in the note on that drawing Constable continues: "It is a beautiful and romantic old house; deeply fixed in trees and dells and filled with marble statues, dolphins, cupids, etc.". Leslie comments: "One of Constable's sketch-books contains a beautiful drawing in watercolours of the house, formerly Lord Lyttelton's, now belonging to Digby Neave, Esq. The view is taken from the lawn, which is decorated with statues, urns, etc". Shirley (L. ed. S., p. 266) plausibly identifies No. 337 with the drawing thus described by Leslie: it accords with the description in every detail.
(See note following No. 350)

1832

In 1832 Constable exhibited at the Royal Academy four oil paintings and four drawings. The oil paintings included 'Waterloo Bridge, from Whitehall Stairs, June 18th, 1817' (formerly in the collection of Mr. Harry H. Ferguson; see Nos. 173–175 in this Catalogue); 'A Romantic House, Hampstead' (probably National Gallery No. 1246) and 'Sir Richard Steele's Cottage, Hampstead' (now in the collection of Sir Kenneth Clark). The drawings included one of 'Jaques and the Wounded Stag' (see No. 407 in this Catalogue). Archdeacon John Fisher died on 25 August.

1832, July 31
Plate 249

338 *A barn, trees and a grey horse, near East Bergholt.*

Pen and bistre ink and water-colour. $4\frac{1}{2} \times 7\frac{1}{2}$ ins. (115 × 190 mm.)
No. 221–1888
Page from a sketch-book.
Inscribed below on the left in ink by the artist *July 31. 1832.* Inscribed on the back in ink with the serial number *4*, and in pencil *M.L.C.* [Maria Louisa Constable].

Since No. 339 was made on the same day at East Bergholt, this drawing also was made in that vicinity.
(See note following No. 350)

339 *Cottages at East Bergholt.* 1832, July 31 Plate 249

Pen and ink and water-colour. $4\frac{1}{2} \times 7\frac{1}{2}$ ins. (115 × 190 mm.) No. 232–1888
Page from a sketch-book on paper with truncated watermark: |TMAN |31.
Inscribed below on left in ink by the artist *E.B. July 31. 1832.* Inscribed on the back in ink with the serial number *6*, and in pencil *M.L.C.* [Maria Louisa Constable].
(See note following No. 350)

340 *Englefield House, Berkshire.* 1832, August 24 Plate 252

Pencil, pen and water-colour. $4\frac{1}{2} \times 7\frac{1}{2}$ ins. (115 × 192 mm.) No. 345–1888
Page from a sketch-book.
Inscribed in lower left corner in ink by the artist *24 Augt 1832. 8–9 morg.*, and in ink by the artist on the back *Inglefield House Rd. Benyon de Bouvir Esq. Berkshire. left London. for the above place Augt 22. 1832. with Lane.*
Also on the back (not reproduced amongst the plates) is a slight pencil sketch of a square tower with two pinnacles: and the inscription in ink *For S. Kensington Museum.*
This drawing is a sketch for the painting discussed in the note following No. 344.
(See also the note following No. 350)

341 *Englefield House, Berkshire.* [1832, August] Plate 254

Pencil. $12\frac{5}{8} \times 18\frac{5}{8}$ ins. (322 × 474 mm.) No. 255–1888
The house is seen from the same aspect as in No. 340: a herd of deer is in the foreground. In the sky is a sketch of a man followed by a dog, and to the left the inscription in pencil by the artist *Carter.*
On the back are a few rough pencil scribbles, possibly of tree forms, with a larger one which may be a study of a bracket with scrolling acanthus-leaf ornament.
The drawing is on paper which has been folded across the middle and down the centre, and has been extended by the pasting on of strips at the left, right and top. On the back the added strips bear sections of the proofs of one of the drafts of the introduction to Constable's *English Landscape Scenery*, the form being that printed as No. 4 by Shirley (S. : L., pp. 220–1), which is dated from 35, Charlotte Street, on 28 May 1832.

For a discussion of the painting for which this is a study, see the note following No. 344. The finished picture is more akin to No. 341 than to No. 340 in some details, such as the foliage in the right background. The paling at the extreme right of this drawing was changed to a detached tree with a fence round it in the oil painting; and the man and dog were introduced herding sheep in the finished picture.

[1832, August] **342** *Englefield House, Berkshire.*
Plate 255

Pencil and light grey wash. $10\frac{7}{8} \times 17$ ins. (277 × 434 mm.) No. 1258–1888
Inscribed on the back in pencil *Englefield House Benyon de Beauvoir Esq.*
The drawing is on a sheet of paper which has been folded in four.

The composition has some affinities with the painting of the house by Milbourne, which Constable borrowed while he was working on his picture (L. ed. S., pp. 302–4). In Milbourne's composition the house is seen over ornamental water with some Italianate peasants and cows in the foreground. No. 342 may therefore be a sketch for a different picture which may have been proposed as a pendant to the one Constable completed. There are references to a second picture of the house, which Constable was told not to proceed with, in the letter from Lane, quoted at the citation given above, but it is not clear whether it was to be a repetition of the first or a new composition.
(See note following No. 344)

[1832, August] **343** *Englefield House, Berkshire.*
Plate 253

Pencil. Divided and numbered in pencil for enlargement.
$11\frac{1}{8} \times 8\frac{7}{8}$ ins. (284 × 224 mm.) No. 1258*a*–1888
The drawing is on a sheet of paper which has been folded horizontally above the centre. The top part, with inscription only, not reproduced amongst the plates. Inscribed along the top in pencil by the artist with notes on various individual items: in relation to the left-hand wing *red* and *a little bit of red roof*; in relation to the left-hand tower *a little too wide and too large altogether*; in relation to the entrance bay *Too wide*; in relation to the front of the house *greenish slate roof*; in relation to the right-hand turret *too narrow & too small altogether*; in relation to the left-hand weather vane *gilt*; also *Chimneys all the same size—only trace in the turrets larger.*

The drawing is of the house only and was made for the architectural details. In a letter of early 1832 to Leslie (original in the Victoria and Albert Museum Library), Constable says "My House tires me very much. The windows and window frames & chimneys and chimney pots are endless—but I shall fill the canvas beyond repentance".
(See note following No. 344)

[1832, August] **344** *Englefield House: detail of left-hand turret.*
Plate 253

Pencil. $5\frac{1}{2} \times 8\frac{7}{8}$ ins. (141 × 224 mm.) No. 1258*b*–1888
Inscribed at top left in pencil by the artist *They are all alike.*

Nos. 340, 341, 343 and 344 are all studies for the painting which Constable exhibited at the Royal Academy in 1833, with the title 'Englefield House, Berkshire, the seat of Richard Benyon de Bouvoir, Esq.—morning'. No. 342 was made in connection with the same commission, which was obtained by Constable through the recommendation of Samuel Lane, the deaf-and-dumb painter. The first mention of it is in Constable's journal for 2 June 1824 (Beckett, II, p. 323); as the note on the back of No. 340 shows, he did not start on the picture until he left for Englefield House in the company of his sponsor Lane on 22 August 1832. He took with him the sketch-book which he had used at Epsom in 1831 and again in East Bergholt in this year (see note following No. 350), since it is on a page of this book that No. 340 is drawn. Nos. 343 and 344, being studies of architectural detail, must have been made on the spot: and it is probable that Nos. 341 and 342 were also made there. The man walking with a dog in No. 341 is introduced into the finished picture; and No. 342 shows the house further away and from an angle not found in any of the other drawings, which are the only recorded ones for this work.

On 27 March 1833, Constable wrote to his son Charles (original letter in the Victoria and Albert Museum Library): "I have almost done the large picture of the house, and Mr. Binyon de Bouvoir is much pleased I believe with it. It is called Inglefield House—from a great Battlefield there of the Danes—it is near Reading in Berkshire it looks very bright and cheerful—and all like it who see it". On 3 April 1833, he reported to Leslie that Lady Morley had said of the picture " 'How fresh, how dewy, how exhilarating!' I told her half of this, if I could think I deserved it, was worth all the talk and cant about pictures in the world" (L. ed. S., p. 299). There was a dispute about the hanging of it at the Royal Academy and Constable wrote to Lane "S[hee] told me it was 'only a *picture of a house*, and ought to have been put into the Architectural Room'. I told him it was 'a picture of a summer morning, *including a house*' " (L. ed. S., p. 302). It is interesting to note that this is borne out by Constable's inscription on No. 340. A disagreement with Mr. Benyon de Beauvoir followed, details of which are given in Lane's letter of 21 March 1834 to Constable, printed by Shirley (*loc. cit.*). (See alsoBeckett, IV, pp. 107–17)

The painting now belongs to Mr. H. A. Benyon of Englefield House, and was lent by him to the exhibition 'The First Hundred Years of the Royal Academy', Burlington House, 1951–2 (No. 231). *Pentimenti* in the foreground whereby cows had been painted out and replaced by deer shows that Constable had met his patron's objection that it "looked as if he had his farmyard before his Drawing Room windows".

The painting of Englefield House by Milbourne referred to in the note on No. 342 formerly belonged to the late Mr. Eustace Hoare.

345 *View over a wide landscape, with trees in the foreground.* — 1832, September; Plate 256

Pencil and water-colour. $7\frac{1}{4} \times 8\frac{3}{4}$ ins. (184×223 mm.) — No. 597-1888
On thin paper.

Inscribed by the artist in pencil on the back *12 till 2—looking—East towards the . . . (?) Sepr . . .* [date erased]*—1832.* Also inscribed at top right on the back in ink with the serial number *17*.

When on its way as part of a loan to an exhibition of water-colours at Delft held from March till May 1952, this drawing was involved in a fire at the docks in Rotterdam, and damaged and stained in the sky on the upper right-hand side. The damage has been skilfully repaired by Mr. van Harskamp of the Maritime Museum at Rotterdam, but this has necessitated the laying down of the paper on card, so that the inscriptions on the back can no longer be seen. Holmes, p. 250, plausibly suggests that the scene is at Hampstead; the view into the valley on the right and the red house almost hidden by the trees are certainly features in common with the scenes known to be of Hampstead, such as No. 360. Constable's correspondence with Leslie in this year shows that he spent much of September at Hampstead.

1832, November 12
Plate 250

346 *Bridge Cottage, Flatford.*

Pen and bistre ink and water-colour. $4\frac{1}{2} \times 7\frac{1}{2}$ ins. (115 × 191 mm.)
No. 229-1888

Page from a sketch-book.
Inscribed below on left in ink by the artist *12 Nov 1832.* and at top right in pencil, probably with the same date, though only *1832* is legible. Inscribed on the back in pencil, probably by the artist, *E B—Monday Nov 12 1832*; also in pencil with serial number *25*.
Mr. R. B. Beckett has pointed out that the cottage is that seen in Nos. 297, 298, 324 &c.
(See note following No. 350)

*c.*1832
Plate 250

347 *A barge on the Stour.*

Pencil, pen and bistre ink, and water-colour. $4\frac{1}{2} \times 7\frac{5}{8}$ ins. (115 × 192 mm.)
No. 237–1888

Page from a sketch-book on paper watermarked: |TMAN |31.
Inscribed on the back in ink with the serial number *9*.
The reasons for identifying the river with the Stour are discussed in the note following No. 350. For a repetition of the central section of the composition see No. 411.

*c.*1832
Plate 251

348 *A thatched cottage and two figures.*

Pencil, pen and ink, and water-colour. $4\frac{1}{2} \times 7\frac{1}{2}$ ins. (115 × 191 mm.)
No. 189–1888

Page from a sketch-book.
Inscribed on the back in pencil *M.L.C.* [Maria Louisa Constable].
(See note following No. 350)

349 *A cottage near a cornfield.* c.1832 Plate 251

Pencil, pen and ink and water-colour. $4\frac{1}{2} \times 7\frac{1}{2}$ ins. (115 × 191 mm.)
No. 233–1888

Page from a sketch-book.
Inscribed on the back in ink with the serial number *9*, and in pencil *M.L.C.* [Maria Louisa Constable].
(See note following No. 350)

350 *Houses in Dedham, with the church tower.* c.1832 Plate 252

Pencil and water-colour. $4\frac{1}{2} \times 7\frac{1}{2}$ ins. (115 × 191 mm.) No. 347–1888
Page from a sketch-book on paper with truncated watermark: J WHAT| 18| .
Inscribed on the back in ink with serial number 7 and in pencil *M.L.C.* [Maria Louisa Constable]. There are also rough scribbles on the back and the inscription in ink *For S. Kensington Museum.* Lt.-Col. C. A. Brooks has identified this as a view from Mill House, Dedham, the residence of John Constable's sister, Mrs. Martha Whalley. His daughter Minna spent her holidays with Mrs. Whalley in July 1831 and was there again in July 1832.

NOTE ON NOS. 336–340 AND 346–350

As the measurements and, where they exist, the watermarks show, Nos. 336, 337, 338, 339, 340, 346, 347, 348, 349 and 350 all come from the same sketch-book, which measures approximately 115 × 190 mm. and consists of Whatman paper of 1831. The book was first used by Constable, as far as is known, on his visit to Mr. Digby Neave at Epsom in 1831 (Nos. 336 and 337). He used it again on his summer visit to East Bergholt in July 1832 (Nos. 338 and 339). A drawing in the British Museum (No. L.B. 19*a*, 112 × 188 mm.) is also dated from East Bergholt on 31 July 1832 and comes from the same sketch-book. He then took it to Englefield House (No. 340) and the drawing of Theal, Berkshire, made on 25 August 1832, in the British Museum (No. L.B. 25*a*, 113 × 188 mm.), was made on this visit in the same book. Constable again took it with him to East Bergholt when he attended the funeral there of his friend John Dunthorne on 9 November 1832 (Beckett, I, p. 270) (No. 346). The undated sheets from the book may be assumed to have been drawn whilst he was on one or other of these expeditions, or made near them in date. In particular, No. 347 may be taken to have been drawn on one of the two visits to East Bergholt, since the subject is so exactly in line with Constable's other studies and paintings of barges on the Stour. It may be presumed that Nos. 348 and 349 represent scenes in the same vicinity. No. 350 is exceptional in the group, in being carried out in pencil and water-colour. Three undated drawings in the British Museum which appear from their style, subject matter and measurements to be from the same book are:

L.B. 14 Men with a cart. (111 × 181 mm.)
L.B. 25*b* House among trees. (112 × 188 mm.)
L.B. 28*a* Landscape with trees and cattle. (111 × 187 mm.)

*c.*1832? Plate 300

351 *Study of poppies.*

Oil on paper with a brown ground. $23\frac{7}{8} \times 19\frac{1}{4}$ ins. (605 × 487 mm.)
No. 329–1888

The purple back of the paper bears a rough geometrical diagram in white chalk.

Holmes, p. 243, dates *c.*1815, presumably on grounds of affinity with No. 129, but it may well be considerably later. There is, in a private collection, a similar but unfinished oil study of a poppy on a brown ground, which is indistinctly inscribed in large script: the inscription appears to read *John Constable Aug. 1832.* This sketch could be taken to be a companion piece to No. 351.

1833

In 1833 Constable exhibited four oil paintings and three drawings at the Royal Academy: the former included 'Englefield House, Berkshire . . . morning' (see Nos. 340–344) and 'Cottage in a Cornfield' (No. 352). He gave his first lecture in Hampstead this year.

1833 Frontispiece

352 *The Cottage in a Cornfield.*

Oil on canvas. $24\frac{1}{2} \times 20\frac{1}{4}$ ins. (620 × 515 mm.) No. 1631–1888
Isabel Constable Bequest.
This painting is one of five works bequeathed to the Museum in 1888 by Miss Isabel Constable with the request that they should be described as a gift from Maria Louisa Constable, Isabel Constable and Lionel Bicknell Constable.

A label formerly on the back of the frame but now preserved in the Department of Paintings is inscribed by the artist in ink, apparently touched with oil paint *No 3. Cottage in a Corn field— John Constable 35 Charlotte Street* (another line has been torn off). This label is in the form used by the artist for his exhibits at the Royal Academy (see also those on Nos. 254 and 301). It is written on the back of a part of a proof of the introduction to *English Landscape Scenery*, in the form printed as No. 3 by Shirley (S. : L., pp. 219–20) and dated 28 May 1832. The pencil drawing No. 145 of *c.*1815 is a sketch for No. 352.

There has been confusion over the date of this version of the composition. Constable exhibited two groups of works with similar titles:

Royal Academy 1817, No. 141 A Cottage.
British Institution 1818, No. 129 A Cottage in a Cornfield.
(Framed measurements 1 ft. 7 ins × 1 ft. 5 ins.)
Royal Academy 1833, No. 344 Cottage in a Cornfield.
British Institution 1834, No. 128 A Cottage in a field of corn.
(Framed measurements 2 ft. 10 ins × 2 ft. 6 ins.)

It may be supposed that in each case the works shown at the British Institution were those exhibited in the previous year at the Royal Academy. Taking into account the closer affinity of No. 352 with Constable's earlier manner, and its agreement with Leslie's description quoted below, Holmes identified it with the exhibits of 1817 and 1818. However, the label on the back can only refer to an exhibition after 1832; No. 352 must therefore be identical with 'The Cottage in a Cornfield' shown at the Royal Academy in 1833. That this was so had been conjectured from the measurements given in the British Institution catalogue of 1834, which agree well with No. 352, whereas those for 1818 do not (L. ed. M., pp. 71 and 411; Beckett, III, p. 101). Holmes is probably correct in identifying No. 352 with the painting 'The Cottage in a Corn Field' which was Lot 52 in the Executors' sale, 16 May 1838, bought by Burton (that is to say, bought in) for £27 6s. The presence of No. 352 in the Constable Bequest to the Museum is consistent with its having been bought in at the sale. It was in the possession of Miss [Maria] Constable in 1845, as is shown by the description of the plate in Lucas's supplementary edition of the mezzotints, published in that year (S. 45).

The earlier painting of 'The Cottage in a Cornfield' appears to have been sold from the British Institution in 1818, for Shirley (L. ed. S., p. 101) prints a letter communicating an offer of £20 for it, and in his entry of 3 April 1818 Farington records that Constable had sold two of his landscapes, one for 45 guineas, the other for 20 guineas (Greig, Vol. VIII, p. 173). Describing Constable's exhibits of 1818, Leslie writes (L. ed. S., p. 101) ". . . to the British Gallery he sent, 'A Cottage in a Cornfield', probably exhibited at the Academy the year before. The cottage in this little picture is closely surrounded by the corn, which on the side most shaded from the sun, remains green, while over the rest of the field it has ripened; one of many circumstances that may be discovered in Constable's landscapes, which mark them as the productions of an incessant observer of nature".

From this description it appears that Leslie took No. 352 (which he will have known in the Constable family's collection) as the painting exhibited in 1818. It is also possible that the earlier picture was of the same composition, for Leslie was an established artist and was getting to know Constable at the time of which he is writing. If Shirley is justified in saying (S. : L., p. 209) that Lucas's mezzotint of the subject (S. 45) was contemplated in 1831, there would be reason to believe that No. 352 was in existence before 1833. The reference he gives is confusing. He refers, p. 44, to the draft arrangement No. 44, of 19 February 1831, but does not in the footnotes to that document identify any of the plates with 'The Cottage in the Cornfield'. There are, however, two entries of the 'Woodmans Cottage' in the draft arrangement which in the notes and index Shirley identifies as 'Willy Lott's House'. It seems likely that this is an oversight, and that the intention was to identify the 'Woodmans Cottage' with 'The Cottage in a Cornfield': there would be some plausibility in such an identification. A possible reason for the combination in No. 352 of an early manner of painting with a late date of exhibition is that it may have been painted sometime before 1833, possibly as a larger replica of the exhibit of 1817 and that Constable brought it out when he wanted to increase the number of works he could send in for exhibition in 1833. Thus the meaning of the phrase in his letter of 3 April 1833 to Leslie (L. ed. S., p. 299) "I have brushed up my *Cottage* into a pretty look . . ." may be that he has been retouching an earlier painting for the exhibition. L. C. W. Bonacina in an article 'John Constable's Centenary: His Position as a Painter of Weather' (*Quarterly Journal of the Royal Meteorological Society*, Vol. 63, 1937, No. 272, pp. 483–90, quoted by Badt, p. 47) instances No. 352 as an example of Constable's ability to suggest a succession of changes in the sky: "In the 'Cottage in a Cornfield' (Victoria and Albert Museum) we find a still scene of fierce noonday heat in July or August and get a powerful impression of fast-growing cumulus clouds. That lonely cottage by the ripening corn will hardly escape a crashing storm that afternoon!"

For a reference in Constable's correspondence to a sketch of a donkey which might be related to a version of this composition, see the note to No. 287.

1833, July 5 **353** *Trees in West End Fields, Hampstead.*

Plate 257

Pencil. $9\frac{1}{4} \times 12\frac{7}{8}$ ins. (235 × 327 mm.) No. 270–1888

On paper watermarked: J WHATMAN 1830.

Inscribed in top right corner in pencil by the artist *July 5, 1833 West End feilds.*

354 *Stoke Poges Church, Buckinghamshire. Illustration to Gray's 'Elegy'.* 1833, July Plate 258

Water-colour. $5\frac{1}{4} \times 7\frac{3}{4}$ ins. (133 × 198 mm.) No. 174–1888
Inscribed on the back in pencil by the artist:

Stanza 5th—"The breezy call of incence breathing morn,

. . . .

. . . .

No more shall rouse them from their lowly bed"
John Constable R.A. July 1833.

Beckett (*Connoisseur*, Vol. CXXXIV, 1954, pp. 81–3) has shown that Constable embarked in 1833 upon a series of designs for illustrations to Gray's *Elegy* at the request of John Martin, the bibliographer. Three of them were engraved on wood for the first edition of the book, published in 1834; and a vignette of the exterior of the church was added to the title-page of the second edition of 1839. No. 354 does not correspond with any of the engraved designs, though it bears some resemblance to the vignette added in 1839. The design chosen to illustrate the lines from Stanza V which Constable has copied on to the back of No. 354 was based on a drawing now in the British Museum (L.B. 35*a*); the latter is derived from a similar composition, also in the British Museum (L.B. 35*b*), which appears to have been sketched on the spot.
Constable exhibited at the Royal Academy in 1834 two water-colours illustrating the *Elegy*, one apparently of the exterior of the church, with the churchyard, the other showing the interior in the manner chosen to illustrate Stanza XI: "Can honour's voice provoke the silent dust?" Leslie records that these two drawings were bought by Samuel Rogers (L. ed. S., p. 313). Only one, however, appeared in the sale of Rogers's collection by Messrs. Christie's in April–May 1856, as Lot 1242 "Stoke Church—water-colour", bought by Mr. Matthew Uzielli for 13 guineas. Holmes, p. 251, suggests that Constable visited Stoke Poges to make drawings of the church on his way back from his visit to Englefield House and Theal in 1832 (see Nos. 340–344). Beckett, *loc. cit.*, doubts this, on the ground that the rendering of Stoke Poges Church in No. 352 is not topographically exact. Many details, however, show that Constable was re-arranging the known features of the church when he generalized it for his designs, for example, the *flèche* on the tower, and, in the vignette, the shape of Gray's tomb. Holmes's hypothesis is supported by the circumstance that the drawing of the churchyard at Stoke Poges, L.B. 35*b* in the British Museum, from which the engraved design for Stanza V was derived, appears, as stated above, to have been drawn from nature.

355 *Design for an illustration to Gray's 'Elegy', Stanza III:* c.1833 Plate 258

"Save that from yonder ivy-mantled tower
The moping owl doth to the moon complain."

Charcoal and grey wash. $4 \times 6\frac{3}{8}$ ins. (100×162 mm.) No. 813–1888
On laid paper, irregularly torn at the top left corner, with a truncated watermark, probably of Britannia in a cartouche.

Beckett (*Connoisseur*, Vol. CXXXIV, 1954, p. 82, note 14) identifies this drawing as a preliminary design for Constable's illustration to Stanza III of Gray's *Elegy* (see also No. 354). The wood-engraving by T. Bagg, published in 1834, is reproduced, *loc. cit.*, p. 81, fig. 3. Beckett suggests that Constable derived the design from his oil painting 'Hadleigh Castle'.
The collection of Capt. C. Constable contained two water-colours made "to illustrate swallows twittering in Gray's *Elegy*".

1833, September 26
Plate 256

356 *Study of sky effect.*

Pencil and water-colour. $7\frac{3}{8} \times 9$ ins. (186×229 mm.) No. 202–1888
Inscribed on the back in pencil by the artist *26 Sepr 1833 12 to 1—noon looking North East*; also inscribed in pencil *J. Constable.*

Holmes, p. 251, suggests that the scene is at Hampstead. This is probable both because the drawing is the sort of cloud study which Constable mainly undertook at Hampstead and because Constable's correspondence with Lucas (S.: L., pp. 108–9) implies that he may have been at Hampstead at the time.

1833, October 16
Plate 257

357 *Folkestone Harbour.*

Pencil and water-colour. $5\frac{1}{8} \times 8\frac{1}{4}$ ins. (129×210 mm.) No. 209–1888
Page from a sketch-book.
Inscribed at top right in pencil by the artist *16 Oct 1833*. The last figure of the date is indistinct, and had been read as *1835* (*Inventory of Art Objects 1888*). Holmes pointed out, p. 252, that this could not be correct, as Constable was at Worcester on 14 October 1835. It is in fact 1833.

No. 357 is the only sheet in the Museum's collection from a sketch-book of 129×210 mm. which Constable used in 1833 and 1834. This book is more extensively represented in the British Museum, by drawings in which water-colour preponderates:

L.B. 30*a* Folkestone from the sea. Dated 16 Oct 1833. (127×210 mm.)
L.B. 30*b* Folkestone Harbour. (127×210 mm.)
L.B. 18*b* A sea-port, presumably Folkestone. (127×210 mm.)
No. 1910–2–12–230 Folkestone. (124×205 mm.) (Salting Bequest)

In addition two larger drawings in the British Museum, L.B. 7, of Petworth Park, and No. 1910–2–12–231, of Folkestone, appear to be made up from sheets of the same sketch-book.

Constable spent a fortnight at Folkestone in October 1833 to be with his son John, who was at school there and had hurt himself sleep-walking (S.: L., pp. 109–10; Beckett, I, p. 276).

358 *View at Hampstead, looking towards London.* 1833, December 7 Plate 259

Water-colour. $4\frac{1}{2} \times 7\frac{1}{2}$ ins. (115 × 190 mm.) No. 220–1888
Inscribed on the back in ink, presumably by the artist, *Hampd December 7, 1833 3 oclock—very stormy afternoon—& High Wind*—and in pencil with the serial number *21*.

Although the measurements would tally with those of the series discussed in the note following No. 350, there is no evidence that this drawing came from a sketch-book. The top is torn irregularly as well as the left-hand edge, and the paper appears to be thinner than the sketch-book paper. There are a number of drawings in the British Museum which show a similar view of London from Hampstead, with the dome of St. Paul's in the distance; for example L.B. 21*a*, 21*b*, 31*a*, 31*b*, 32*b*. The last of these is dated 9 June 1831; the others are undated.

1834

In 1834 Constable exhibited at the Royal Academy three water-colour drawings and a pencil drawing: the former included 'The Mound of the City of Old Sarum, from the south' (No. 359) and a view of Stoke Poges Church. He visited George Constable for the first time at Arundel in July and Lord Egremont at Petworth in September.

359 *Old Sarum.* 1834 Plate 265

Water-colour. $11\frac{7}{8} \times 19\frac{1}{8}$ ins. (300 × 487 mm.) No. 1628–1888
Isabel Constable Bequest.
This water-colour is one of five works bequeathed to the Museum in 1888 by Miss Isabel Constable with the request that they should be described as a gift from Maria Louisa Constable, Isabel Constable and Lionel Bicknell Constable. A strip about 37 mm. ($1\frac{1}{2}$ ins.) wide has been added to the right-hand side to enlarge the surface to its present size. The paper is laid on an old mount which is watermarked: J WHATMAN 1830 and has a gilt line round the drawing. No. 395 is mounted in similar fashion, and this was probably the original arrangement.

Although the fact is not recorded in the documents leading to the bequest, there can hardly be any doubt that this drawing is, as noted by Holmes, p. 251, the one exhibited by Constable at the Royal Academy in 1834, under the title 'The Mound of the City of Old Sarum, from the south'. Leslie (L. ed. S., p. 313) records that this exhibit was a water-colour. The size, ambitious scope and detailed handling of No. 359 all go to establish that it was an exhibition drawing, and no variant which might dispute the claim with this one is recorded. No. 395, as has already been noted, is mounted in the same fashion, and is almost certainly the exhibited water-colour of 1836, since it bears on the old mount the quotation with which it was listed in the catalogue.
For an earlier version in oils, the history of the composition, and its significance for Constable, see No. 322.

1834, April 12
Plate 259

360 *Hampstead Heath, from near Well Walk.*

Water-colour. $4\frac{3}{8} \times 7\frac{1}{8}$ ins. (111 × 180 mm.) No. 175–1888
Inscribed on the back in pencil by the artist *Spring Clouds—Hail Squalls—April 12. 1834—Noon Well Walk—.*
The building on the left appears to be Foley House.

1834, April
Plate 258

361 *Study of cows at Hampstead.*

Pencil and water-colour. $2\frac{3}{8} \times 3\frac{1}{2}$ ins. (62 × 90 mm.) No. 219–1888
Painted on a card on which is printed at the back: "Third Application, and last opportunity of applying. To the Trustees and Subscribers of the St. Pancras Female Charity School. Ladies and Gentlemen, The favor of your Vote and Interest is earnestly solicited for Eliza Hall, Aged $10\frac{1}{2}$ years. Her Mother is a Widow, and has lived in the Parish 19 years. Recommended by John Constable. Esq. W. Northage, Esq. G. Paton, Esq. W. Bentham, Esq. J. H. Cansellor, Esq. R. R. Reinagle, Esq. The Election will take place on Monday the 23rd of December next. Sparrow, Printer, 3, Edward Street, Hampstead Road". This side is inscribed in ink . . . *afternoon . . . of April 1834 Hampstead* [a word has become obliterated before *afternoon* and another before the date] and *eveng look S.E 5 oclock wind East.*

Probably the girl referred to in the following note was a sister of Eliza Hall:
"Re *Mrs. Hall.* June 18–35.
E. Sheppard presents his duty to Mr. Constable with thanks for his liberal subscription in favour of the orphan'd children of the late Mrs. Hall of Grafton Street and presumes to solicit his support in behalf of *Caroline Hall* at the ensuing election for the admission of Children into the St. Pancras Female Charity School which will take place on Monday the 22nd June *Inst.*" (Beckett, V, p. 110.)

362 *Bignor Park, Sussex.* 1834, July [10?] Plate 260

Pencil and water-colour. $5\frac{1}{2} \times 9\frac{1}{4}$ ins. (140×235 mm.) No. 217–1888
Page from a sketch-book.
Inscribed on the back in pencil *Mr. Hawkins's house near Petworth.*

This drawing is not dated, but a drawing from the same sketch-book in the British Museum (L.B. 27*a*; 136×230 mm.) is inscribed in pencil by the artist *July 10 1834. Bignor Park looking towards Petworth*, and it is possible that No. 362 was made on the same day. Bignor Park is on the road between Arundel and Petworth, about 5 miles from Arundel and 4 miles from Petworth.
Charlotte Smith (1749–1806), whom Constable quotes at No. 382, p. 10 was at times a visitor to her father's house, Bignor Park. This seventeenth century building was, however, demolished and replaced by the house seen in this drawing in 1823.
(See note following No. 368)

363 *A farmhouse and church at Houghton, Sussex.* 1834, July 12 Plate 260

Pencil and water-colour. $5\frac{1}{2} \times 9\frac{1}{4}$ ins. (140×235 mm.) No. 211–1888
Page from a sketch-book.
Inscribed in top left corner in pencil by the artist *July 12 1834.*
On the back of No. 366 is a strip about 30 mm. ($1\frac{1}{8}$ ins.) wide completing the left-hand side of this drawing, and inscribed vertically in pencil by the artist *Houghton—July 12, 1834.* This inscription evidently refers to No. 363, rather than to No. 366 to which it had previously been taken to apply (*Catalogue of Water-colour Paintings*, 1927, p. 112), both because of its position in relation to the completing strip and because the date tallies with that on No. 363. A drawing in the British Museum (No. L.B. 13*c*) is inscribed by the artist *12 July, 1834, North Stoke, Arundel.* Houghton is near North Stoke, about 3 miles north of Arundel.
(See note following No. 368)

364 *A windmill and cottages.* [1834, July] Plate 261

Pen and bistre ink and water-colour. $5\frac{1}{2} \times 9\frac{1}{4}$ ins. (140×235 mm.). Drawn surface $5\frac{1}{2} \times 4\frac{1}{4}$ ins. (140×135 mm.) No. 204–1888
Page from a sketch-book.
Inscribed at top right in ink with serial number *No. 2/22*, and below on right in pencil *M.L.C.* [Maria Louisa Constable].
The drawing occupies only part of the sheet, on the left-hand side, and the sheet has been folded vertically about 50 mm. (2 ins.) from the right-hand edge.

364a On the *verso*, as at present mounted, is a full-page drawing in pencil of a tree-lined road with a cottage and windmill behind hedges on the left; this drawing is inscribed in pencil by the artist, below on left *15 July 1834.* 1834, July 15 Plate 262

Traces of paper and gum on three of the corners indicate that the sheet was at one time mounted to show the pencil drawing which is at the back in the present arrangement. The initial of Maria Louisa Constable on the same side as the marks of mounting suggest that this may have been done while the sketch was in the possession of the artist's family. The pencil drawing was certainly, and the water-colour drawing probably, made during Constable's stay at Arundel. (See note following No. 368)

1834, July 19
Plate 262

365 *Arundel Castle.*

Pencil. $5\frac{1}{2} \times 9\frac{1}{4}$ ins. (140×235 mm.) No. 277–1888
Page from a sketch-book.
Inscribed in lower left corner in pencil by the artist *19 July 1834 Arundel.*
(See note following No. 368)

[1834, July?]
Plate 263

366 *A cottage and water-mill at Bignor.*

Pencil and water-colour. $5\frac{1}{2} \times 9\frac{1}{4}$ ins. (140×235 mm.) No. 208–1888
Page from a sketch-book.
For the drawing on the back completing the sketch on the next sheet of the sketch-book see No. 363. Also on the back in ink is the serial number *4*.
The inscription on the back (given in the entry for No. 363) had been taken to refer to the subject matter of No. 366, but probably refers to No. 363. Mr. Anthony Bertram has identified the scene as a view in Bignor on the approach from the village of Sutton.

[1834, July?]
Plate 263

367 *Chichester Cathedral.*

Pencil and water-colour. $5\frac{1}{2} \times 9\frac{1}{4}$ ins. (140×235 mm.) No. 223–1888
Page from a sketch-book.
Inscribed on the back in pencil with the serial number *19*.

Since this sheet comes from the sketch-book which Constable used during his summer visit to Arundel, it is probable that this drawing was made at that time. (See note following No. 368)

1834, [August or September]
Plate 261

368 *A woman by an old willow tree at Ham, Surrey.*

Pen and bistre ink. $9\frac{1}{4} \times 5\frac{1}{2}$ ins. (235×140 mm.) No. 818–1888
Page from a sketch-book.
Inscribed below in ink by the artist *Ham. 1834.—*, and in top left corner in pencil with the serial number *49*.

368a On the back is a pencil drawing of the avenue of trees leading from the Petersham road to Ham House. Plate 261

In his letter of 30 August 1834 to Leslie (P. Leslie, p. 121) Constable says "I have been twice at Ham House lately. Lady Dysart is old and rather more infirm, but well . . . We must go there to see the House, it seems as if its inmates of a century and a half back were still in existence & that on opening of the doors some of them would appear". Letters of September 1834 speak of further visits paid by Constable to Ham in that month (P. Leslie, pp. 122 and 127).

NOTE ON NOS. 362–368

These drawings evidently come from the same sketch-book, the leaves of which measure approximately 140×235 mm. (about $5\frac{1}{2}\times9\frac{1}{4}$ ins.). The dates on Nos. 363, 364 *verso* and 365 show that Constable used it on his visit to Mr. George Constable of Arundel in July 1834. No. 362 may be assigned to the same visit on the evidence of the drawing of the same place in the British Museum, referred to in the note to that sketch. It may be presumed that Nos. 364 *recto*, 366 and 367 were also made on this visit. The following leaves in the British Museum appear to come from the same sketch-book: L.B. 27*a* Bignor Park (see note on No. 362); L.B. 27*b* Petworth 14 July 1834 (137×231 mm.); No. 1910–2–12–233 Windmill: man ploughing (137×233 mm.) (Salting Bequest). Holmes notes, p. 251, in Sir J. C. Robinson's sale (21 April 1902) a pencil drawing of Arundel Castle, Sunday morning, 20 July 1834 (5×9 ins.). The date and measurements suggest that this too may have been a page from the sketch-book.

In his letter of 16 July 1834 to Leslie, Constable says of the scenery he encountered on his visit: "The Castle is the cheif ornament of this place—but all here sinks to insignificance in comparison with the woods, and hills. The woods hang from excessive steeps, and precipices, and the trees are beyond everything beautifull: I never saw such beauty in *natural landscape* before. I wish it may influence what I do in future, for I have too much preferred the picturesque to the beautifull—which will I hope account for the *broken ruggedness of my style* . . . The meadows are lovely, so is the delightfull river, and the old houses are rich beyond all things of the sort—but the trees above all" (Beckett, III, pp. 111–12).

369 *The ruins of Cowdray House, Midhurst.* [1834, Sept. 14] Plate 264

Pencil and water-colour. $8\frac{1}{8}\times10\frac{3}{4}$ ins. (207×272 mm.) No. 216–1888
Page from a sketch-book.
Inscribed below on left in pencil by the artist *ruins* [or *view*] *of Cowdray.*

Leslie was himself at Petworth when Constable stayed there, and records: "Lord Egremont . . . ordered one of his carriages to be ready every day, to enable Constable to see as much of the neighbourhood as possible. He passed a day in company with Mr. and Mrs. Phillips and myself, among the beautiful ruins of Cowdry Castle, of which he made several very fine sketches; but he was most delighted with the borders of the Arun, and the picturesque old mills, barns, and farm-houses that abound in the west of Sussex" (L. ed. S., p. 319). The drawing 'Ruins of Cowdray: Interior' in the British Museum (No. L.B. 24) is dated 14 September 1834, and Leslie's narrative implies that No. 369, and the other sketches of Cowdray at the British Museum, were made on the same day. (See note following No. 372)

1834, September 23
Plate 267

370 *Fittleworth Mill, Sussex.*

Pencil and water-colour. $8\frac{1}{8} \times 10\frac{3}{4}$ ins. (206×272 mm.) No. 215–1888
Page from a sketch-book.
Inscribed at top left in pencil by the artist *23 Spr.*

Plate 276

370a On the back are two pencil and water-colour drawings of plants, and the pencil inscription *Fittleworth Mill 1834 23 Sep.*
(See note following No. 372)

1834, September 23
Plate 266

371 *Fittleworth Mill and Bridge, on the Rother, Sussex.*

Pencil. $8\frac{1}{8} \times 10\frac{3}{4}$ ins. (207×272 mm.) No. 273–1888
Page from a sketch-book.
Inscribed below on right in pencil by the artist *23d Sepr 1834.*
On the back (not reproduced amongst the plates) are two small pencil scribbles and the inscription in pencil *Fittleworth Mill.*
(See note following No. 372)

[1834, September]
Plate 266

372 *Petworth House from the Park.*

Pencil and water-colour. $8\frac{1}{8} \times 10\frac{3}{4}$ ins. (207×272 mm.) No. 801–1888
Page from a sketch-book.
On the back (not reproduced amongst the plates) is a pencil drawing of stumps of wood, weeds, etc. The back is inscribed at top left in pencil by the artist *Arundel*; also inscribed below on left in pencil in another hand *Petworth Lord Egremont's.*

Since the other pages of the sketch-book from which this leaf comes are assigned to Constable's stay at Petworth in September 1834, it is probable that this drawing was made at that time rather than on the July visit to Arundel, when he went to Petworth for one day only on 14 July. In a letter of 14 September 1834 to George Constable (L. ed. S., p. 318) Constable says that he will visit him again at Arundel after his stay at Petworth if he has time: this may have some bearing on the inscription *Arundel* on the back of the drawing.

NOTE ON NOS. 369–372

These four drawings are from the same sketch-book, measuring about $8\frac{1}{8} \times 10\frac{3}{4}$ ins. (207×272 mm.). The dates on Nos. 370 and 371 show that Constable used it when he stayed with Lord Egremont at Petworth in September 1834, and No. 369 was made on the same visit. Other drawings from the same sketch-book are in the British Museum:

L.B. 12*a*, 12*b*	Ruins of Cowdray. (Each 203×265 mm.) Each watermarked: J WHATMAN 1828.
L.B. 23*b*	Tillington Church. Dated 17 September 1834. On paper extended from that of the sketch-book page.
L.B. 24	Ruins of Cowdray: Interior: Dated 14 September 1834. On paper extended from that of the sketch-book page.

Leslie (L. ed. S., p. 319) describes the sketch-book as follows: "While at Petworth, where Constable spent a fortnight, he filled a large book with sketches in pencil and watercolours, some of which he finished very highly".

1835

In 1835 Constable's sole exhibit at the Royal Academy was 'The Valley Farm' (see Nos. 373–377). He visited George Constable at Arundel in July. He visited Worcester (where paintings by him had been exhibited in July) to give three lectures, in October.

373 *Sketch for 'The Valley Farm'.* *c.*1835 Plate 268

Oil on canvas. $13\frac{3}{8} \times 11$ ins. (340×280 mm.) No. 143–1888
The canvas has been relined. The stretcher is inscribed in ink *J. Constable. P. Valley Farm*, perhaps copying an earlier inscription on the original canvas or stretcher.
(See note following No. 374)

374 *Sketch for 'The Valley Farm'.* *c.*1835 Plate 269

Oil on canvas. $10 \times 8\frac{1}{4}$ ins. (254×210 mm.) No. 140–1888
The canvas has been relined.

NOTE ON NOS. 373 AND 374

Nos. 373 and 374 are compositional sketches for 'The Valley Farm', the final version of which, measuring $57\frac{1}{2} \times 49$ ins., Constable exhibited at the Royal Academy in

1835; this was bought by R. Vernon, and is now in the Tate Gallery (No. 327). 'The Valley Farm' was the last fully-finished picture which he constructed from the scenery of the banks of the Stour. The farmhouse seen in the sketches and, somewhat elaborated, in the final version is Willy Lott's house.

In 'Fresh Light on John Constable', *Apollo*, Vol. LXXXVII, 1968, pp. 229–30, Charles Rhyne reproduces a drawing of *c.*1800–3 in the Courtauld Institute of Art and records an oil sketch of *c.*1802 in the collection of the Earl of Haddington which show the inception of the composition of 'The Valley Farm'. Its subsequent development is seen in the two small drawings in the sketch-book of 1813 (No. 121, pp. 31, 70). Two other oil paintings of the subject are known. One, the large oil study in the collection of Lord Forteviot, is discussed by M. Chamot in her article "The Constable Room at the Tate Gallery" (*Connoisseur*, Vol. CXXXVII, 1956, p. 263). The other, which measures 24×20 ins., and was formerly in the collections of James Lenox and the New York Public Library, was shown at Messrs. Agnew's in the autumn of 1956; the Tate Gallery's painting follows it closely in such details as the figures on the distant bank of the stream and the bird skimming across the water in the left foreground. Leslie wrote of it to Mr. Lenox that Constable "afterwards painted a larger picture of it, which is in Mr. Vernon's collection". It is therefore possibly the study referred to by him when he writes of 'The Valley Farm' as being based upon an early sketch (L. ed. S., p. 325). However, Lord Forteviot's version, which measures 50×40 ins. and is therefore a nearly full-scale study for the Tate Gallery's picture, is close in style to the 'Mill Stream' of 1814 (Christchurch Mansion Museum, Ipswich) and was probably painted at about the same time as the latter, while the Lenox version can hardly be earlier than the 1820's. On the other hand he may have been referring to either the drawing or the oil-sketch mentioned at the beginning of this paragraph. Nos. 373 and 374 have been considered to antedate the exhibited picture by some years; Holmes, p. 252, says of them "From the style it would seem as if these two sketches had been made at least ten years before the exhibition of the picture". The colouring of these two sketches has, however, that slightly forced and unnatural quality seen in the sketches which Constable made in his studio and which are attributed in this Catalogue to a date *c.*1830 (for example Nos. 329a and 331), and the brushwork has much in common with these sketches for *English Landscape Scenery*. On the other hand there is no affinity between Nos. 373, 374 and the open-air sketches known to be of *c.*1825 in this collection. There seems, then, reason to believe that these two sketches were made at the time Constable was working on the version of the picture which he exhibited and sold to Vernon; one new feature in them both is the boat with a figure in it in the foreground, which occurs in none of the previous versions but is followed in Vernon's picture. No. 373 is nearer to the pencil sketch on p. 31 of the sketch-book No. 121 in the detail of the boat drawn up on dry land by the side of the house. No. 374 is nearer to the sketch on p. 70 of the sketch-book in showing the foreground weeds, and the boat shelter on the left. In the relation between the trees on the right and the house, No. 374 is closer to the composition of Lord Forteviot's sketch and the painting from the Lenox collection; the Tate Gallery's picture, though in it the side of the house concealed by the trees in the two oil sketches is revealed, is also close to No. 374 in general outline; but from No. 373 has been taken the elongated crown of the foreground tree and the figure standing up in the boat punting.

For drawings of trees connected with 'The Valley Farm' see Nos. 163 and 375; also No. 376; and for a drawing of the country-woman sitting in the boat see No. 377.

375 *An ash tree.* *c.*1835 Plate 270

Pencil and water-colour, squared in pencil for enlargement.

39×26¾ ins. (990×680 mm.) No. 1249–1888

On paper watermarked: J WHATMAN 1833, which has been laid down on cartridge paper.

By transmitted light the inscription *Isabel* may be seen on the back in the lower left corner.

The tree is identical with the foremost one in No. 163 and the drawing is therefore presumably enlarged from it.

Shirley (L. ed. S., p. 326) identifies No. 375 as a study for 'The Valley Farm'. The ash tree in the right foreground of the painting is the same as the one depicted in the drawing, which may be clearly identified by the dead branch hanging down vertically. The tree in the drawing is also approximately the same size as that in the oil painting; but Constable added in the painting a branch and another part of the crown springing from a point in the trunk at which there was a break when he made the drawing from nature, No. 163; he has also deviated from No. 375 in details. Constable's letter of 14 February [1835] to John Dunthorne, senior (L. ed. S., p. 324) suggests that this ash was studied from those at East Bergholt: "If you can lend me two or three of poor John's studies of the ashes in the town meadow, and a study of plants that grew in the lane below Mr. Coleman's, near the sprouts which ran into the pond [that is, by John Dunthorne, junior, Constable's boyhood friend and later his assistant, who had died in 1832] I will take great care of them and send them safe back to you soon. I am about an ash or two now". On the other hand the facts given in the note on No. 376 suggest the possibility that he may have made use of studies drawn at Hampstead for both Nos. 375 and 376.

376 *An ash tree.* *c.*1835 Plate 271

Pencil and water-colour, squared in pencil for enlargement.

39×26¾ ins. (990×680 mm.) No. 1248–1888

On paper watermarked: J WHATMAN 1833, which has been laid down on cartridge paper.

By transmitted light the inscription *M.C.* [Maria Constable] may be seen on the back in the lower right corner.

This is a companion piece, in size and handling, to No. 375 and Shirley (L. ed. S., p. 326) suggests that it may be a study for 'The Valley Farm'. This it seems not to be, unless Constable took hints from it in inventing the ramification for the added crown of the tree in the right foreground of the exhibited picture. It is, however, as has been pointed out by Mr. John R. Ovane, similar in all but some details of the lower branches to the tree in the left foreground of 'Salisbury Cathedral from the Meadows'. Since the painting was exhibited in 1831, and the paper on which No. 376 is drawn is watermarked 1833, this drawing was evidently copied from the exhibited oil or a sketch for it, probably for use in his lectures. In the drawing a notice is nailed to the tree, of which the last word can be read as '. . . Law' [possibly 'Against the Law'] and a mother and child are seated below it. It is interesting to compare these features with Leslie's account of Constable's last lecture delivered at Hampstead on 25 July 1836 (L. ed. S., pp. 406 and 407): "Constable then gave some practical rules for drawing from nature, and showed some beautiful studies of trees. One, a tall and elegant ash, of which he said 'many of my Hampstead friends may remember this *young lady* at the entrance to the village. Her fate was distressing, for it is scarcely too much to say that she died of a broken heart. I made this drawing when she was in full health and beauty; on passing some time afterwards, I saw, to my grief, that a wretched board had been nailed to her side, on which was written in large letters, "*All vagrants and beggars will be dealt with according to law*". The tree seemed to have felt the disgrace, for even then some of the top branches had withered. Two long spike nails had been driven far into her side. In another year one half became paralysed, and not long after the other shared the same fate, and this beautiful creature was cut down to a stump, just high enough to hold the board' ". No. 376 clearly falls in with this train of ideas; but it does not exactly tally with Constable's description to his lecture audience, since it shows a tree after a board has been nailed on to it. The general coincidence of particulars strongly suggests that it does represent the tree of which he was speaking, and is therefore based on an ash at Hampstead. Since No. 375 is a companion piece to No. 376, it may in that event also represent a Hampstead tree, but this does not necessarily follow. In any event, No. 375 must have been in existence in 1835 to have been used in the painting of 'The Valley Farm'.

*c.*1835? **377** *A Suffolk Child: sketch for 'The Valley Farm'.*

Plate 272

Pencil and water-colour. $7\frac{1}{4} \times 5\frac{3}{8}$ ins. (185 × 137 mm.) No. 600–1888

The drawing had been mounted upon fairly modern card on which was written in pencil *Suffolk Child.* The back of the drawing itself bears no such inscription, but the outline of the drawing on the front has been traced over on the back in pencil and slightly elaborated. This tracing was made by the artist to facilitate the use of the drawing in painting 'The Valley Farm'; the seated figure of the

countrywoman in the boat in the exhibited version is based upon it (that is, in reverse to the position on the *recto*), but is given older features.
The title on the back, 'Suffolk Child', was perhaps the name by which the drawing was known to Constable's family.

378 *The ruins of the Maison Dieu, Arundel.* 1835, July 8

Plate 277

Pencil. $8\frac{5}{8} \times 11$ ins. (220×281 mm.) No. 272–1888
Inscribed at top right in pencil by the artist *Arundel July 8th. 1835 Maison Dieu.* The drawing has been trimmed and laid down on card, and so has lost any distinguishing marks which it may have had of being a sketch-book page, but the measurements suggest that it came from the sketch-book discussed in the note following No. 384. The drawing 'Stormy Effect, Littlehampton' in the British Museum, L.B. 18*a* (113×185 mm.), bears the same date.

379 *Arundel Mill and Castle.* 1835, July 9

Plate 274

Pencil. $8\frac{5}{8} \times 11$ ins. (219×281 mm.) No. 260–1888
Inscribed at top left in pencil by the artist *Arundel Castle & Mill* and below on right, also by the artist, *Arundel Mill July 9 1835.* The drawing has been trimmed and laid down on card, and has lost any indications it may have had of being a sketch-book page, but the measurements suggest that it came from the sketch-book discussed in the note following No. 384.
This study from nature was used by Constable as the sketch for his last big picture, the 'Arundel Mill and Castle', on which he worked the day he died, and which was exhibited posthumously at the Royal Academy in 1837. The painting is now in the Toledo Museum of Art, Toledo, Ohio (reproduced L. ed. S., Pl. 150; L. ed. M., Pl. 54). See also the sketch-book No. 382, pp, 33, 35.

380 *A windmill at Arundel.* 1835, July 10

Plate 267

Pencil. $8\frac{3}{4} \times 11\frac{1}{4}$ ins. (221×285 mm.) No. 312–1888
Page from a sketch-book.
Inscribed below on left in pencil by the artist *July 10th 1835 Arundel.* Inscribed on the back in ink with the serial number *29.*

Mr. Gerard Young has stated that this windmill, used in the manufacture of cement, stood at the eastern approach to Arundel, between the present-day railway station and the town-bridge.
(See note following No. 384)

381 *Chichester Cathedral: the west end.* 1835, July 18

Plate 273

Pencil. $11\frac{1}{4} \times 8\frac{3}{4}$ ins. (287×221 mm.) No. 615–1888
Page from a sketch-book on paper watermarked: J WHATMAN 1833.

Inscribed in top left corner in pencil by the artist *West End of Chichester Cathedral July 18. 1835 Afternoon* [or *after storm*]. Inscribed on the back in ink with the serial number *26* and in pencil *M.L.C.* [Maria Louisa Constable].
(See note following No. 384)

1835, July 13–27 **382** *Bound sketch-book of 50 pages.*

Pencil, pen and ink, and water-colour. $4\frac{1}{2} \times 7\frac{3}{8}$ ins. (115 × 188 mm.)

No. 316–1888

The sketch-book half-bound in green leather, gold tooled, marbled boards. It bears a label inside the front cover: S. & J. Fuller, Temple of Fancy, 34, Rathbone Place, London. A button with the remains of a green silk ribbon tie is sewn on to the outside of the back cover. The paper watermarked: J WHATMAN 1832. The sketch-book was used mainly in Sussex in July 1835.
Except where otherwise noted, the inscriptions are in pencil; they are all written by the artist.

Inside front cover inscribed with the measurements: *18* $8\frac{1}{4}$ $26\frac{1}{4}$ *by 20. all but* $\frac{1}{8}$—$26\frac{1}{4}$ *by 20*—; also *In* [or *Sn*] and *little Hampton Pier* (referring to p. 1).

Plate 278 p. 1 A view of the sea with wooden jetties in the foreground. Pen and ink. Inscribed at top left *little Hampton Pier.*

p. 2 Blank.

Plate 278 p. 3 A man seen from behind lying on the seashore and looking out to sea, where boats are to be seen. Pencil.

p. 4 Blank.

Plate 279 p. 5 A view of a seaside village: a tree in the foreground, and buildings beyond, with a boat in a creek or basin to the right and the masts of other shipping seen beyond the buildings. Pencil.

p. 6 Blank, but for a slight carry-over (about 7 mm. wide) of the drawing on p. 7.

Plate 279 p. 7 Left, a thatched cottage with a high chimney; right, figures seated on a stile or gate in the road, and trees beyond. Pencil.

p. 8 Inscribed (referring to p. 7 or p. 9) *a Sussex Cottage.*

Plate 280 p. 9 A thatched half-timbered cottage with a high chimney, and trees beyond. Pencil and water-colour.

p. 10 Inscribed at top left (referring to p. 9) *Sussex Cottage* and at top right (referring to p. 11) *Middleton Church Coast of Sussex—in part washed away by the Sea see Charlotte Smith's Sonnet 10 July.*
The leaf comprised by pp. 9 and 10 is stuck behind a small guard strip on which p. 11 is finished. It has cracked, or been cut, along the strip. It is not clear whether a page is missing from the sketch-book at this

point. Charlotte Smith's 'Sonnet written in the Church-Yard of Middleton', which is more specifically illustrated by the drawing on p. 13, reads:

> Press'd by the moon, mute arbitress of tides,
> Whilst the loud equinox its power combines;
> The sea no more its swelling surf confines,
> But o'er the shrinking land sublimely rides!
> The wild blast rising from the western cave
> Drives the huge billows from their heaving bed,
> Tears from their grassy tomb the village dead,
> And breaks the silent sabbath of the grave!
>
> With shells and sea-weed mingled on the shore,
> Lo, their bones whiten in the frequent wave;
> But vain to them the winds and waters rave,
> They hear the warring elements no more:
> Whilst I am doom'd, by life's long storm oppress'd,
> To gaze with envy on their gloomy rest!

382 p. 11 Middleton Church. Pencil and water-colour. Plate 280

p. 12 Inscribed at top left *Look at back of Sussex Cottage* [that is, presumably, at p. 10, where there is a reference to Charlotte Smith's sonnet]. Inscribed at top right *Middleton Churchyard* and *form of a sceleton in the bank of the Churchyard* [Mr. Gerard Young of Flansham, Sussex, supplied the reading *sceleton* and drew attention to the connection with Charlotte Smith's sonnet].

p. 13 A chalk bank in Middleton churchyard, with the form of a skeleton in it. Pencil and water-colour. (See also pp. 10 and 12) Plate 281

p. 14 Middleton Church. Pencil. A drawing from the same aspect as p. 11. The leaf comprised by pp. 13 and 14 is stuck to an irregularly torn guard strip and may be cut from a large sheet of paper and inserted here in place of a torn-out sheet. Plate 281

p. 15 Middleton Church. Pencil. A drawing from the same aspect as that on p. 11. Plate 282

p. 16 Inscribed (referring to p. 17) *Arundul Castle*.

p. 17 View in the grounds of Arundel Castle: in the centre foreground a square tower beside a bridge; on a ridge to right, above trees, another part of the castle. Pencil and water-colour. Plate 282

p. 18 Blank.

p. 19 A woodland scene at Arundel: the sun setting between two trees. Pencil. Inscribed at top left *13th July 1835 Arundul* and below on left *13. July 1835*. Plate 283

p. 20 Blank.

Plate 283 **382** p. 21 Fittleworth: a village street. Pencil. Inscribed at top left *Fittleworth 14 July 1835.*

p. 22 Blank.

Plate 284 p. 23 Fittleworth: the village street with the church on the right. Pencil. Inscribed at top left *Fittleworth Sussex. July. 14 1835.*

p. 24 Blank.

Plate 284 p. 25 A small bridge with a wooden hand-rail over a stream. Pencil and water-colour. Inscribed below on left *Fittleworth 14 July 1835 Sussex.*

p. 26 Inscribed *Sea* [or *seen?*] *over right × shoulder* [?].

Plate 285 p. 27 A lane between steep banks with a tree growing on the right. Pencil. Inscribed below on left *July 16 1835.*
Other drawings made on the same day by Constable (pp. 29 and 31) are inscribed *Fittleworth.*

p. 28 Blank.

Plate 285 p. 29 A tree growing in a hollow. Pencil. Inscribed below on right *Fittleworth 16 July 1835.*

p. 30 Blank.

Plate 286 p. 31 A sunken road, with a cart on it; on the left a high bank with a figure at the top. Pencil. Inscribed below on left *Fittleworth July 16 1835.*

Plate 286 p. 32 Arundel Castle seen above trees. Pencil.

Plate 287 p. 33 Arundel Castle, seen from an aspect similar to that in No. 379 but from a nearer viewpoint and omitting the buildings on the right; compare also p. 35. Pencil. Inscribed below on left *19th. July 1835. Arundel—dear Minna's birthday.*

p. 34 Blank.

Plate 287 p. 35 Arundel Castle seen above trees, from a viewpoint similar to that on p. 33; compare also No. 379. Pencil.

p. 36 A sketch of three cows. Pencil. On the same page is a continuation on a strip about 20 mm. wide of the drawing on p. 37. Inscribed at top right (referring to the drawing on p. 37) *Canbury House my friends the Fishers' Villa.* This was the house at Kingston-on-Thames of Dr. Philip Fisher, Master of Charterhouse and brother of Dr. John Fisher, the late Bishop of Salisbury. Mrs. Philip Fisher had invited Maria Constable to stay with her after her visit to Arundel with her father (Beckett, VI, pp. 270–1). (Not reproduced amongst the plates.)

Plate 288 p. 37 Canbury House, Kingston-on-Thames. An Italianate villa seen from the garden, with a church tower beyond on left. Pencil. Inscribed below on right *July 27 1835.*

pp. 38–45 Blank. Two leaves may have been extracted between pp. 38 and 39.

Plate 288 p. 46 A small parrot perched on a gloved hand, eating. Pencil and water-colour. Inscribed below *done for and at the desire of* [or *in the presence of?*] *Mina July 27th. 1835.*

The dates on pp. 37 and 48 show that Constable was at Canbury House when he made this drawing.

382 p. 47 Blank.

p. 48 Two cows in the shade of a tree in a park. Water-colour. Inscribed below on right *Canbury Villa—July 27. 1835. Noon.* Plate 289

p. 49 Blank.

p. 50 Two sketches on one page. A rough sketch of foliage. Pencil. A peacock on a mound. Pencil and water-colour. Inscribed below on right *fittleworth July 14 1835.* Plate 289

Back cover Inscribed, with deletions and erasures; some words are illegible:

Historian
Mr. Tierney—Catholic Priest
A [or *M*] *Tripp—of Fittleworth*
Douglas. Nenia Britanica
Cartwright/. dead. Old Stoddert [?]*f*[. . .]
wrote Hisy of Sussex.
Wilson. articles recommended by ~~Dalway~~
/Cartwright
of Walberton
Hardy ^ *the Revd. excentric—*
his son the Traveller – / – – –
[. . . . .]—*J* [?]—*Disney.*
[. . . . .] *to Mr. B*

and in ink *Warner Chief*[. . .].

These notes mainly concern writers on the antiquities of Sussex, such as M. A. Tierney, chaplain to the Duke of Norfolk, who published *The History and Antiquities of . . . Arundel* in 1834; and the Rev. Edmund Cartwright who contributed 'The Parochial Topography of the Rape of Bramber, 1830' to James Dallaway's *History of the Western Division of the County of Sussex.* Mr. Gerard Young has pointed out that the Rev. Robert Hardy (1767–1843) was Vicar of Walberton and a friend of William Hayley.

NOTE ON THE SKETCH-BOOK NO. 382

The chronological sequence of dated pages in the sketch-book is: July 13 p. 19 Arundel; July 14 pp. 21, 23, 25 and 50 all of Fittleworth; July 16 pp. (27), 29 and 31 of Fittleworth; July 19 p. 33 Arundel; July 27 pp. 37, 46 and 48 Canbury House, Kingston-on-Thames. All these dates fall within the visit which Constable paid to George Constable at Arundel or his subsequent journeys to accompany Maria to and from the Fishers' house at Kingston. The drawing of Littlehampton in the British Museum (L.B. 18*a*) referred to in the note on No. 378 appears to bear a watermark of 1832 and, though cut on the left, to have come from a sketch-book. If so, it may have been extracted from this book, at the position noted between the present pp. 38 and 39.

1835, October 12
Plate 275

383 *A view of Worcester from the north.*

Pencil. $8\frac{3}{4} \times 11\frac{1}{8}$ ins. (221 × 284 mm.) No. 314–1888
Page from a sketch-book.
Inscribed at top left in pencil by the artist *Worcester 12 Oct 1835. from the North* and in lower right corner also in pencil by the artist *12 Oct 1835 Worcester.*
(See note following No. 384)

1835, October 14
Plate 276

384 *A plough at Bewdley.*

Pencil. $8\frac{1}{8} \times 11\frac{1}{4}$ ins. (207 × 287 mm.) No. 836–1888
Inscribed at top left in pencil by the artist *Worcestershire Plough* and below on left also in pencil by the artist *Bewdley 14 Oct 1835 Worcestershire.*

The top edge of the sheet is curved, showing that it has been cut. It bears traces of having been a sketch-book page, with the hinge marks on the left, and the width suggests that it came from the same book as No. 383, which was drawn on the same visit to Worcester.

NOTE ON NOS. 378–381, 383 AND 384

Nos. 380, 381 and 383 come from the same sketch-book of which the leaves measure 221 × 285 mm. ($8\frac{3}{4} \times 11\frac{1}{4}$ ins.), which was used by the artist on his summer visit to George Constable at Arundel concurrently with the intact sketch-book No. 382, and again when he went to Worcester to lecture in October. For the reasons given in the entries on those drawings, Nos. 378, 379 and 384 are probably from the same book. Holmes, p. 252, notes in the Sir J. C. Robinson sale of 21 April 1902 a drawing 'Landscape with Cottages' dated 15 July 1835 and measuring $8\frac{3}{4} \times 11$ ins. This was made during the visit to Arundel and may have been from the same sketch-book.

1834 or 1835?
Plate 290

385 *A cottage by a wood at Findon, Sussex.*

Pencil, bistre and water-colour. $5\frac{1}{8} \times 8\frac{3}{8}$ ins. (130 × 212 mm.) No. 228–1888
Page from a sketch-book.
Inscribed in top left corner in pencil, apparently *Findon Wood,* followed by a second line which is illegible. Inscribed on the back in ink with the serial number *17*.
Findon is some 6 miles east of Arundel.
(See note following No. 394)

386 *A village seen over a ploughed field.* 1834 or 1835? Plate 290

Pencil and water-colour. $5\frac{1}{8} \times 8\frac{1}{4}$ ins. (130×211 mm.) No. 238–1888
Page from a sketch-book.
Inscribed on the back in ink with the serial number *5*, and in pencil *M.L.C.* [Maria Louisa Constable].

It is suggested in the *Inventory of Art Objects 1888* that the view is at Epsom. Holmes, p. 249, accepts this identification and considers that the scene is a composition worked up from previous sketches. The latter possibility seems to be excluded by the fact that the drawing is on a sketch-book page, and does not differ in style from the other drawings made from nature. The identification with Epsom also is unconvincing, since the form of the church tower and *flèche* is different from that seen in No. 337, which was drawn at Epsom.
(See note following No. 394)

387 *Cottages on high ground.* 1834 or 1835? Plate 291

Pencil and water-colour. $5\frac{1}{8} \times 8\frac{1}{4}$ ins. (130×211 mm.) No. 226–1888
Page from a sketch-book.
Inscribed on the back in ink with the serial number *14*.
If the object faintly indicated in the distance is a church tower, this drawing may represent the same place as that seen in No. 388, from a slightly different view-point.
(See note following No. 394)

388 *Cottages on a high bank.* 1834 or 1835? Plate 291

Pencil and water-colour. $5\frac{1}{8} \times 8\frac{1}{8}$ ins. (130×206 mm.) No. 234–1888
Page from a sketch-book.
Inscribed twice on the back in pencil with the serial number *16*.
(See note following No. 394)

389 *A barn.* 1834 or 1835? Plate 292

Pencil and water-colour. $5\frac{1}{8} \times 8\frac{1}{4}$ ins. (130×211 mm.) No. 231–1888
Page from a sketch-book.
Inscribed on the back in ink with the serial number *11*, and in pencil *M.L.C.* [Maria Louisa Constable].
(See note following No. 394)

390 *A cottage with a red-tiled roof, by a wood.* 1834 or 1835? Plate 292

Pencil and water-colour. $5\frac{1}{8} \times 8\frac{1}{4}$ ins. (130×211 mm.) No. 222–1888
Page from a sketch-book.

On the back (not reproduced amongst the plates) is a slight full-page sketch of cottages and trees; the back is also inscribed in ink with the serial number *12*. (See note following No. 394)

1834 or 1835? Plate 293

391 *A brook with a high bank.*

Pencil and water-colour. $5\frac{1}{8} \times 8\frac{1}{4}$ ins. (130×211 mm.) No. 212–1888
Page from a sketch-book.
Inscribed on the back in ink with the serial number *13*.
(See note following No. 394)

1834 or 1835? Plate 293

392 *A village street with a shed, cottages and windmill.*

Pencil and water-colour. $5\frac{1}{8} \times 8\frac{3}{8}$ ins. (130×213 mm.) No. 230-1888
Page from a sketch-book.
Inscribed on the back in ink with the serial number *15*.
(See note following No. 394)

1834 or 1835? Plate 294

393 *A view of downland country.*

Pencil and water-colour. $5\frac{1}{8} \times 8\frac{1}{4}$ ins. (130×211 mm.) No. 225–1888
Page from a sketch-book on paper with truncated watermark: J WHAT| 182| .
On the back is a slight pencil scribble and the serial number *20*.
(See note following No. 394)

1834 or 1835? Plate 294

394 *A windmill and a flock of sheep.*

Pencil, pen and bistre and water-colour. $5\frac{1}{8} \times 8\frac{3}{8}$ ins. (130×212 mm.)
No. 173–1888
Page from a sketch-book on paper with truncated watermark: J WHAT| 182| .
Inscribed in the sky in pencil by the artist *B*.

NOTE ON NOS. 385–394

The ten drawings evidently come from the same sketch-book, its pages measuring approximately 130×212 mm. (about $5\frac{1}{8} \times 8\frac{3}{8}$ ins.) and the paper bearing the truncated watermark: J WHATMAN 182[. . .]. The only internal clue to the places where the sketch-book was used or to its date is the almost illegible inscription on No. 385. If this is correctly read *Findon Wood*, the book was used by Constable on a visit to George Constable at Arundel, that is, in 1834 or 1835. This supposition is borne out by the style of the drawings, many of which are in the vigorous, unpolished and strong manner which characterises the water-colours of Constable's last years; compare, for instance, No. 390 with p. 9 of No. 382, the intact sketch-book of 1835.

Holmes dates No. 386 (following the identification of the scene as Epsom) *c.*1831; Nos. 385 and 391 he dates *c.*1832, and Nos. 387, 388, 389, 390 and 392 he assigns to *c.*1834. Shirley dates No. 385 *c.*1830.

1836–1837

In 1836 Constable's two exhibits at the Royal Academy were the 'Cenotaph to the memory of Sir Joshua Reynolds' (now in the Tate Gallery, No. 1272) and the water-colour 'Stonehenge' (No. 395). He gave four lectures on 'The History of Landscape Painting' at the Royal Institution in May and June of this year and his last lecture, at Hampstead, on 25 July. Constable died on 31 March 1837. His almost completed painting 'Arundel Mill and Castle' (now in the Toledo Museum of Art, Toledo, Ohio; see No. 379) was exhibited posthumously at the Royal Academy.

395 *Stonehenge.* 1836

Plate 296

Water-colour. $15\frac{1}{4} \times 23\frac{1}{4}$ ins. (387×591 mm.) No. 1629–1888

Isabel Constable Bequest.

This water-colour is one of five works bequeathed to the Museum in 1888 by Miss Isabel Constable with the request that they should be described as a gift from Maria Louisa Constable, Isabel Constable and Lionel Bicknell Constable. The sheet of paper on which most of the water-colour is painted is irregularly torn at the left and top edges, and has been extended by the artist by about 30 mm. ($1\frac{1}{4}$ ins.) in width at the left and 12 mm. ($\frac{1}{2}$ in.) at the top, by being laid on another piece of paper; the drawing is carried over these extensions. The hare in the lower left-hand corner is on a separate piece of paper which has been stuck on to the drawing; the left leg of the hare is flaking off.

No. 395 is the water-colour exhibited by Constable at the Royal Academy (No. 581) in 1836. It is laid down on what may be presumed to be the original mount (see also No. 359), with a gilt line round the drawing. The mount bears the inscription written in ink in a careful script *Stonehenge* "*The mysterious monument of Stonehenge, standing remote on a bare and boundless heath, as much unconnected with the events of past ages as it is with the uses of the present, carries you back beyond all historical records into the obscurity of a totally unknown period*". This quotation was printed with the title of the drawing in the Royal Academy catalogue of 1836. The drawing was finished by 14 September 1835, when Constable wrote to Leslie (L. ed. S., p. 332) "I have made a beautifull drawing of Stonehenge; I venture to use such an expression to you".

For the preliminary sketches see Nos. 186 and 396.

Plate 297 **396** *Stonehenge.*

Pencil and water-colour, lightly squared in pencil for enlargement. 6 × 10 ins. (154 × 253 mm.) No. 800–1888

The drawing has been enlarged to the left by the addition of a strip of about 25 mm. (1 in.).

Both this and L.B. 22*a* in the British Museum are elaborations of the sketch from nature, No. 186, which is dated 15 July 1820; each of the progressive sketches is an experiment in the introduction of the rainbows and a stormy sky. Since the left-hand trilithon was divided in No. 396 in the same way as in No. 186 before the paper was extended, it is possible that this version precedes that in the British Museum, in which the stone is seen whole. Shirley gives (L. ed. S., Pl. 147) a useful conjunction of reproductions, with Nos. 186 and 396 and the British Museum's drawing on the same page.

1836
Plate 298 **397** *The Sacrifice of Noah.*

Sepia and water-colour wash. $39\frac{5}{8} \times 55\frac{3}{4}$ ins. (1006 × 1415 mm.) No. D.1876–1908

Given by Lindo S. Myers.

This drawing was formerly in the collection of Eustace Constable. It is an enlarged and tinted copy of the engraving after the fresco by Paolo Uccello in the Chiostro Verde, S. Maria Novella, Florence, which is Plate XXXIII of W. Y. Ottley's *Early Florentine School*, 1826. In his account of Constable's first lecture on 'The History of Landscape Painting' at the Royal Institution on 26 May 1836, Leslie remarks (L. ed. S., p. 387) "Near the commencement of this lecture, Constable exhibited a drawing from a very grand and simple composition by Paolo Uccello, of Noah and his family kneeling round an altar, while the birds and beasts are leaving the ark, the whole arched by the rainbow. 'Uccello was either the inventor or the perfector of parallel perspective, and this new art is beautifully shown in the flight of the birds. Titian's Cornaro family somewhat resembles this picture'."

(See note following No. 400)

1836
Plate 298 **398** *Study of the fallen figure of the saint in Titian's 'St. Peter Martyr'.*

Bistre and sepia wash. $39\frac{1}{2} \times 69\frac{1}{2}$ ins. (1005 × 1760 mm.) No. D.1877–1908

Given by Lindo S. Myers.

This drawing was formerly in the collection of Eustace Constable. It is a greatly enlarged copy of the figure of the saint in a drawing attributed to Titian; the copy was shown by Constable at his first lecture on 'The History of Landscape Painting' at the Royal Institution on 26 May 1836. The original drawing, which

was in the collection of Sir Thomas Lawrence, is now in the Musée Condé, Chantilly; it is reproduced in the *Jahrbuch der Kunsthistorischen Sammlungen*, Vienna, N.F. X, p. 152, Abb. 130. Leslie (L. ed. S., p. 388) gives an account of Constable's long discussion of Titian's 'St. Peter Martyr' in the lecture, and records: "Constable here showed a copy of an original sketch by Titian (one of the Lawrence Collection), in which the saint has the outlines of three heads drawn one over the other, the first looking down, the others more and more turned up, and said,—'still this made the subject nothing more than a common murder by the roadside, and it wanted the dignity of a martyrdom. The composition was then heightened, the vision of angels introduced, and the head of the saint again altered, so as to look up to the glory that now beamed down on him' ".
(See note following No. 400)

399 *Job and his friends.* c.1836
Plate 299

Grey wash. $39\frac{1}{2} \times 55\frac{3}{4}$ ins. (1005 × 1415 mm.) No. D.1875–1908
Given by Lindo S. Myers.
This drawing was formerly in the collection of Eustace Constable.

The subject is taken from the fresco in the Campo Santo at Pisa. Constable presumably made his copy from the engraving in C. Lasinio's *Pitture a Fresco del Campo Santo di Pisa*, 1828, omitting the left-hand quarter of the composition. In his lecture on landscape painting at the Hampstead Assembly Rooms in June 1833 Constable said "It was fortunate, therefore, for landscape, destined as it was to become so material a feature of the art, that it originated and was in its infancy nursed in the hands of men who were masters of pathos. As early, I believe, as Cimabue, and certainly Giotto, landscape became impressive. I am told that in the Campo Santo at Pisa, the frescoes exhibit wonderful proofs of its use and power" (L. ed. S., p. 377). Constable may have used this drawing at a corresponding stage of his first lecture at the Royal Institution on 26 May 1836.
(See note following No. 400)

400 *The Creation of Eve.* c.1836
Plate 299

Bistre and grey wash. $39\frac{5}{8} \times 52\frac{1}{8}$ ins. (1006 × 1323 mm.) No. D.1874–1908
Given by Lindo S. Myers.
This drawing was formerly in the collection of Eustace Constable.

No. 400 is an enlarged copy of details of an engraving of the early fourteenth century reliefs on the façade of the Duomo at Orvieto, which is Pl. VI of W. Y. Ottley's *Early Florentine School*, 1826. The details are taken from the left- and right-hand sides of the engraving; the reliefs are ascribed by Ottley to

Nicola Pisano. On the back of a letter in the Fitzwilliam Museum begun to Charles Boner and dated 12 March 1836, Constable has noted down some chronological heads for the progress of landscape painting, in which 'Nicola Pisan & Sculptures' stands for the 13th century. In the same list 'Geotto (the Job)' stands for the 14th century (see also No. 399) (Beckett, *Discourses*, p. 86). It may perhaps be assumed that Constable showed this representation of the reliefs then attributed to Nicola Pisano at an early stage of his first lecture at the Royal Institution in 1836 or at the corresponding stage in one of his other courses.

NOTE ON NOS. 397–400

For the reasons given above, Nos. 397 and 398 can be identified with the drawings mentioned by Leslie as having been shown by Constable at his first lecture to the Royal Institution in 1836; and, on the assumption that those lectures (on which Leslie's notes are confessedly incomplete) incorporated all the material in his previous lectures and notes, Nos. 399 and 400 were probably shown at the same lecture. There is no direct evidence that he showed any of the drawings at the earlier lectures, for example, those at Worcester in 1835, though he is known to have shown a diagram of dates and names of the principal painters, and copies of pictures, on that occasion. Nos. 397, 399 and 400 are virtually mechanical enlargements from the engravings, and are probably the work of an assistant. In a letter of April 1836 to Leslie (Beckett, III, p. 137) Constable says: "*Nixon* is helping me with my tables for my lectures". In the case of the Worcester lectures, the tables were literally the lists of painters, but in this context they may well be the copies of engravings which he showed at the Royal Institution. J. M. Nixon was a glass painter and the heavy 'leaded' outline of Nos. 397, 399 and 400 might be due to him. No. 398 is in a freer style, more likely to be Constable's own.

When giving the drawings to the Museum, Mr. Lindo S. Myers wrote on 23 May 1902: "They were purchased by me directly from Mr. Eustace Constable, together with many hundred later drawings and books of sketches by John Constable, and the whole of which (including these two) came from the Court of Chancery where they had been locked up in the will of Miss Isabella Constable". Although the letter only refers to two drawings all four were in fact received from the donor at this time. Mr. Myers was under the impression that they were early works done by Constable as a boy under Dunthorne's instructions: hence his reference to 'later' drawings in the above quotation.

Eustace Constable was the son of Capt. Charles Constable, the artist's second son. A collection of some 70 paintings and 200 drawings by Constable belonging to him was sold at Messrs. Christie's on 16 April 1896.

*c.*1836 **401** *Milford Bridge, with a distant view of Salisbury.*
Plate 306

Pencil, pen and water-colour. $7\frac{1}{8} \times 9\frac{1}{2}$ ins. (182×241 mm.) No. 341–1888

The drawing does not completely cover the surface of a thin piece of gilt-edged card. The edges of the card have been divided into equal distances with the knife, doubtless to assist the engraver.

No. 401 is the original drawing for an engraving by A. R. Freebairn. A copy of the engraving is mounted with the water-colour: its engraved surface measures 65×95 mm. and it is lettered *Constable, R.A. . . . Freebairn*; it follows No. 401 with the exception of the fisherman on the bridge, who is standing upright, with a more visible rod, in the print. The original pencil sketch from nature of the scene, measuring about $4\frac{1}{2} \times 7$ ins., is in the collection of Col. J. H. Constable (L. ed. S., p. 11, exhibited at Colchester, 1950, No. 15). Constable himself made an etching of the scene: an example is in the Department of Prints and Drawings (No. 20142).

The proof of Freebairn's engraving after No. 401 in the British Museum is inscribed in pencil, presumably by the engraver: *Toutched by J. Constable RA 30 April 1836. (first & only time)*. Mr. David Gould and Mr. O'Dwyer have shown that it was published in 1837 in the second volume of *The Book of Gems*, edited by S. C. Hall. It appears on p. 189 as the headpiece to an extract from Thomas Warton's *An Ode to Summer*, and is given the title 'The English Landscape' in the list of plates.

No. 401 was, through being confused with No. 123, described as 'Stoke Mill, Ipswich' in the *Catalogue of Water-colour Paintings*, 1927, p. 113.

402 *The Grove, or Admiral's House Hampstead.* *c.*1821–2

Oil on paper, laid on canvas. $9\frac{5}{8} \times 11\frac{1}{2}$ ins. (245×292 mm.) No. 137–1888 Plate 302

The same house, seen from another angle, is represented in the painting at the Tate Gallery, No. 1246, which is believed to be the picture exhibited by Constable at the Royal Academy in 1832 with the title 'A romantic house at Hampstead'. Davies, p. 27, says that the house was known as 'The Grove' until about 1911; then the main part was renamed 'Admiral's House', and the smaller part, here seen to the right, was called 'Grove Lodge'. Admiral Mathew Barton called the main roof his quarterdeck, and celebrated naval victories by firing two cannons from it in salute. A more finished version of the same view as No. 402, without the rainbow and extended downwards to make a vertical composition, is in the National Galerie, Berlin (reproduced in L. ed. S., Pl. 126). No. 402 may have served as a sketch for the picture at Berlin. Since the publication of the first edition of this catalogue John Baskett has shown in *Constable Oil Sketches*, 1966, that the sketch was painted from an upper window of No. 2 Lower Terrace, and therefore dates from 1821–2, when Constable was living there.

403 *A river scene, with a farmhouse near the water's edge.* *c.*1830–6

Oil on canvas. $10 \times 13\frac{3}{4}$ ins. (254×349 mm.) No. 141–1888 Plate 304

The canvas has not been relined, and is on the original stretcher. It is inscribed in ink, possibly in Isabel Constable's hand, *J. Constable Valley Farm*. This is written over a half-erased ink inscription . . . *Dec. 27 41* [?]. The erased part has been read as *the Farm*.

No. 403 has long been taken to be a sketch for 'The Valley Farm' (see Nos. 373 and 374) and the inscription on the back of the sketch gave this the force of a family tradition. But Shirley (L. ed. S., pp. 325–6) pointed out that this identification was very doubtful. The farmhouse—which is not Willy Lott's house—is seen from an entirely different viewpoint, the main group of trees is in the centre and not on the right, the composition is horizontal, not vertical, and the only point of similarity is in the two figures in the boat in the foreground. In fact, as C. H. Collins Baker has shown in his article 'The Kennedy Memorial Gallery' (*Connoisseur*, Vol. CXXXIV, 1954, pp. 142–4), this is one of a group of four compositions of a different character by Constable, of which the final stage is perhaps seen in the painting 'On the Stour, Willy Lott's House' in the Kennedy Memorial Gallery, Los Angeles (reproduced in colour, Collins Baker, *loc. cit.*). The other versions are:

i The water-colour No. 1888–2–15–33 in the British Museum (reproduced in Sir J. D. Linton, *Constable's Sketches in Oil and Watercolours*, 1905, p. 60).
ii The oil painting 'On the Stour' ($23 \times 30\frac{1}{2}$ ins.) in the Phillips Memorial Gallery, Washington, D.C. (reproduced in Collins Baker, *loc. cit.*).

There is no conclusive external evidence for the dating of this series, but i and ii above, as well as No. 403, are clearly late works. Shirley (*loc. cit.*) suggests that No. 403 may be connected with the picture which Constable was meditating when he wrote to Leslie on 8 September 1834: "I shall put off Worcester—I hope to be better employed for I have almost determined to attack another canal for my large frame" (P. Leslie, p. 129). He dates accordingly *c.*1834. This date is certainly to be preferred on grounds of style to that of *c.*1825 adopted by Collins Baker for the version in the Kennedy Memorial Gallery which he regards as the latest of the series. The method of painting and tonality have much in common with the sketches for 'The Valley Farm', Nos. 373 and 374. It may be that the originating idea for the composition is to be found in the slight full-page sketch in the sketch-book No. 132, p. 69, but the details are too vague for this to be advanced with any assurance.

*c.*1830–6
Plate 301

404 *A sluice, perhaps on the Stour: trees in the background.*

Oil on paper laid on canvas. $8\frac{5}{8} \times 7\frac{3}{8}$ ins. (219×187 mm.) No. 131–1888
There is no firm basis for the identification of the river as the Stour, but it is by no means unlikely.

Holmes, p. 251, dates *c.*1834. The sketch has the rather forced colours seen in such presumably late sketches as Nos. 373 and 374, in particular a greenish-yellow tone, and may reasonably be taken to have been painted in the last period of Constable's working life.

405 *A country road and sandbank.* *c.*1830–6

Plate 303

Oil on paper laid on canvas. $6\frac{1}{2}\times 8$ ins. (165×203 mm.) No. 327–1888

Holmes, p. 252, dates *c.*1835. The subject-matter resembles that in the dismembered sketch-book Nos. 385–394, and the style is consistent with the late date assigned here to those drawings.

406 *A cottage among trees, with a sandbank.* *c.*1830–6

Plate 305

Oil on paper laid on canvas. $7\times 8\frac{5}{8}$ ins. (178×219 mm.) No. 139–1888

Holmes, p. 251, dates *c.*1834. This oil sketch has stylistic affinities with No. 405 and may be given a correspondingly late date.

407 *Jaques and the wounded stag.* *c.*1834–6

Plate 306

Illustration to Shakespeare's *As You Like It*, Act. II, sc. i.

Pen and bistre and water-colour. $5\frac{7}{8}\times 4\frac{1}{4}$ ins. (149×107 mm.) No. 795–1888

No. 407 is one of a series of designs made by Constable for a wood-engraving in *The Seven Ages of Shakespeare*, published by John Van Voorst in 1840. The work was undertaken by Constable at the request of John Martin (see also No. 354), who says in his introduction to the book: "The interest which the first-named took in the trifling affair required of him, is best evinced by the fact that he had made nearly twenty sketches for the 'melancholy Jaques' ". C. R. Leslie chose the design finally used, and drew it on the wood block for the engraver. Beckett (*Connoisseur*, Vol. CXXXIV, 1954, pp. 80–4) discusses, with reproductions, the relationship between Constable's drawings for Van Voorst's publication and the earlier water-colour he had made *c.*1828, based on a painting by Sir George Beaumont which is now in the Tate Gallery (No. 119). It appears that Constable turned his attention to the book illustration about 1834; certainly the style of No. 407 is close to that of No. 368 of 1834.

The notes on Dedham Church on the back of the drawing in the British Museum (L.B. 4), which is closer to the engraved version, suggest a connection with the letterpress Constable was drafting for *English Landscape Scenery*, *c.*1833–5.

The originating idea for the compositions by Beaumont and Constable appears to have been W. Hodges's illustration of the scene, engraved by S. Middiman for Boydell's *Shakespeare*.

408 *Study of a dead French partridge.* *c.*1830–6?

Plate 295

Water-colour. $5\frac{7}{8}\times 12$ ins. (149×305 mm.) No. 1247–1888

On an irregularly cut sheet of paper.

Plate 295 **408a** On the back is a slight full-page cloud study.

The drawing is placed here because Constable's main output of water-colour painting was after 1830, but its dating on grounds of style is a matter of some uncertainty. The cloud study at the back is too slight to form a clear guide, but has some affinities with the somewhat liquid sky drawing in No. 328 of 1833, and with the skies in some of the later water-colours, such as No. 372 of 1834; but it may have been drawn during Constable's earlier phase of 'skying' around 1821.

*c.*1830–6 **409** *View over hilly country, with a stormy sky.*
Plate 297

Water-colour. $4\frac{3}{8} \times 7\frac{3}{8}$ ins. (112 × 186 mm.) No. 176–1888
On thin paper, blind-stamped (illegibly) in top right corner.

This drawing resembles in style, and in the general character of the countryside depicted, some of the late water-colours done at Hampstead, largely as studies of dramatic sky and cloud effects; for instance, No. 358 (of 1833), as well as the drawings at the British Museum listed in the note on No. 358. There is, however, no sign of the dome of St. Paul's in the distance, to confirm that the drawing was made at Hampstead.

*c.*1832–6 **410** *View on the Stour: Dedham Church in the distance.*
Plate 308

Pencil and sepia wash. $8 \times 6\frac{5}{8}$ ins. (203 × 169 mm.) No. 249–1888
On thin laid paper, torn roughly along the right-hand edge, with the truncated watermark: GILLING & (for the completion of the watermark see No. 411).

As Lt.-Col. C. A. Brooks has pointed out, the tower of Dedham Church is seen over the gate of Dedham Lock from a viewpoint close to that in No. 184. This circumstance combined with the similar relationship which appears to exist between No. 411 and No. 347 suggests that both No. 410 and No. 411 are reworkings of earlier ideas rather than sketches after nature. No. 410 is probably a studio composition based upon the central portion of No. 184 "Dedham Lock and Mill" or one of the other versions listed in that entry. For a fuller discussion see "Constable at Work" by Graham Reynolds, *Apollo*, Vol. XCVI, July 1972, pp. 12–19.
(See note following No. 411)

411 *Trees and a stretch of water on the Stour.*

*c.*1832–6
Plate 309 Pencil and sepia wash. $8 \times 6\frac{3}{8}$ ins. (205 × 162 mm.) No. 250–1888
On thin laid paper, roughly torn along the left-hand side, with the truncated watermark: ALLFORD 1829 (the top edge of the name being on the sheet on

which No. 410 is drawn). When No. 410 is turned back to front and top to bottom the irregularly torn edges and the truncated parts of the watermark exactly fit with No. 411, proving that the two sheets of paper were once one. On the back (not reproduced amongst the plates) is a rough pencil scribble, perhaps indicating tree forms. The identification of the scene on the recto as a view on the Stour dates from the time the drawing was received from Miss Isabel Constable (*Inventory of Art Objects 1888*).

A comparison between this drawing and No. 347 shows that it represents a rough reworking of the central section, comprising a barge being towed by a horse on the Stour, with water-meadows and clumps of trees in the distance. It is probably, like No. 410, a studio composition. Since No. 347 comes from a sketch-book used in 1832 both No. 411 and No. 410 are clearly not to be dated earlier than that year. For a fuller discussion see "Constable at Work" by Graham Reynolds, *Apollo*, Vol. XCVI, July 1972, pp. 12–19.

412 *A house, cottage and trees by moonlight.* — *c.*1830–6, Plate 307

Sepia and grey wash, $7\frac{3}{8} \times 9$ ins. (187×228 mm.) — No. 248–1888

The drawing is dated *c.*1830 in the *Inventory of Art Objects 1888*.

(See note following No. 414)

413 *A country cottage amid trees.* — *c.*1830–6, Plate 307

Sepia wash. $3 \times 5\frac{5}{8}$ ins. (77×143 mm.) — No. 816–1888

On laid paper.

(See note following No. 414)

414 *A country road with elm trees.* — *c.*1830–6, Plate 307

Pencil, pen and bistre wash. $3\frac{1}{8} \times 4\frac{3}{8}$ ins. (80×112 mm.) — No. 603–1888

There are a few indefinite pencil scribbles on the back.

NOTE ON NOS. 412–414

Nos. 412, 413 and 414 are monochrome drawings in a style resembling that of No. 331 (here dated *c.*1830), No. 355 (of *c.*1833) and Nos. 410–411 (here dated *c.*1820–6). They are accordingly grouped together as examples of the last phase of Constable's draughtsmanship.

415 *Landscape study* — *c.*1833–6, Plate 310

Pencil and water-colour. $8\frac{3}{8} \times 7\frac{1}{4}$ ins. (213×183 mm.) — No. 203–1888

On paper watermarked: R TASSELL 1833.

This spectacular example of Constable's style in water-colour at its most free has always been recognised as a late work: Shirley (L. ed. S., p. 273) assigns to 1831; the catalogue of the Exhibition of British Art, Royal Academy, 1934, gives a dating of 1832–5. But the watermark which shows that it cannot have been drawn before 1833 has apparently not previously been observed. The composition bears a generic resemblance to that of 'The Cornfield' (N.G. 130) and the scene may be a Suffolk one. If this be so, it could only have been drawn from nature during the visits of 1833 or (more probably) 1835.

Concordance

This table contains, in the left-hand columns, the Museum registered number and, in the right-hand columns, the serial number in the present Catalogue. The latter is used throughout the present work for reference to the items catalogued in it.

Museum No.	*Catalogue No.*	*Museum No.*	*Catalogue No.*	*Museum No.*	*Catalogue No.*
F.A.33	254	134–1888	109	162–1888	230
F.A.34	184	135–1888	103	163–1888	322
F.A.35	301	136–1888	232	164–1888	228
F.A.36	323	137–1888	402	165–1888	246
F.A.37	137	138–1888	99	166–1888	110
F.A.38	321	139–1888	406	167–1888	224
		140–1888	374	168–1888	226
42–1873	17	141–1888	403	169–1888	65
43–1873	18	142–1888	39	170–1888	76
44–1873	19	143–1888	373	171–1888	275
45–1873	20	144–1888	122	172–1888	165
		145–1888	113	173–1888	394
261–1876	331	146–1888	116	174–1888	354
		147–1888	207	175–1888	360
120–1888	271	148–1888	265	176–1888	409
121–1888	115	149–1888	268	177–1888	83
122–1888	171	150–1888	330	178–1888	81
123–1888	333	151–1888	221	179–1888	82
124–1888	37	152–1888	258	180–1888	50
125–1888	233	153–1888	311	181–1888	88
126–1888	272	154–1888	255	182–1888	89
127–1888	120	155–1888	303	183–1888	85
128–1888	101	156–1888	222	184–1888	79
129–1888	270	157–1888	229	185–1888	77
130–1888	112	158–1888	269	186–1888	93
131–1888	404	159–1888	208	187–1888	80
132–1888	332	160–1888	96	188–1888	78
133–1888	231	161–1888	111	189–1888	348

Museum No.	*Catalogue No.*	*Museum No.*	*Catalogue No.*	*Museum No.*	*Catalogue No.*
190–1888	280	226–1888	387	250–1888	411
191–1888	279	227–1888	319	251–1888	203
192–1888	74	228–1888	385	252–1888	163
193–1888	84	D.228–1888	124	253–1888	316
194–1888	94	229–1888	346	254–1888	317
195–1888	281	D.229–1888	126	255–1888	341
196–1888	282	230–1888	392	256–1888	161
197–1888	283	D.230–1888	125	257–1888	192
198–1888	274	231–1888	389	258–1888	169
199–1888	306	D.231–1888	128	259–1888	278
199*a*–1888	305	232–1888	339	260–1888	379
199*b*–1888	307	D.232–1888	143	261–1888	194
199*c*–1888	308	233–1888	349	262–1888	193
200–1888	70	D.233–1888	146	263–1888	118
201–1888	15	234–1888	388	264–1888	166
202–1888	356	D.234–1888	127	265–1888	179
203–1888	415	235–1888	334	266–1888	261
204–1888	364	D.235–1888	172	267–1888	164
205–1888	318	236–1888	337	268–1888	148
206–1888	313	237–1888	347	269–1888	293
207–1888	309	238–1888	386	270–1888	353
208–1888	366	239–1888	35	271–1888	206
209–1888	357	240–1888	328	272–1888	378
210–1888	315	241–1888	296	273–1888	371
211–1888	363	242–1888	300	274–1888	299
212–1888	391	243–1888	324	275–1888	168
213–1888	55	244–1888	298	276–1888	167
214–1888	58	245–1888	277	277–1888	365
215–1888	370	246–1888	213	278–1888	157
216–1888	369	247–1888	29	279–1888	195
217–1888	362	247*a*–1888	21	280–1888	62
218–1888	240	247*b*–1888	23	281–1888	256
219–1888	361	247*c*–1888	27	282–1888	217
220–1888	358	247*d*–1888	30	283–1888	212
221–1888	338	247*e*–1888	22	284–1888	210
222–1888	390	247*f*–1888	31	285–1888	211
223–1888	367	247*g*–1888	32	286–1888	214
224–1888	66	248–1888	412	287–1888	215
225–1888	393	249–1888	410	288–1888	216

Museum No.	*Catalogue No.*	*Museum No.*	*Catalogue No.*	*Museum No.*	*Catalogue No.*
289–1888	289	326–1888	100	358*g*–1888	9
290–1888	173	327–1888	405	358*h*–1888	2
291–1888	177	328–1888	117	358*i*–1888	11
292–1888	105	329–1888	351	358*j*–1888	3
293–1888	190	330–1888	155	437–1888	133
294–1888	302	331–1888	131	581–1888	130
295–1888	182	332–1888	135	582–1888	129
296–1888	185	333–1888	134	583–1888	102
297–1888	191	334–1888	312	584–1888	252
298–1888	156	335–1888	267	585–1888	98
299–1888	201	336–1888	248	586–1888	40
300–1888	141	337–1888	247	587–1888	36
301–1888	180	338–1888	326	588–1888	310
302–1888	142	339–1888	251	590–1888	249
303–1888	153	340–1888	276	591–1888	266
304–1888	336	341–1888	401	592–1888	60
305–1888	138	342–1888	123	593–1888	59
306–1888	144	343–1888	68	594–1888	242
307–1888	170	344–1888	69	595–1888	61
308–1888	139	345–1888	340	596–1888	87
309–1888	186	346–1888	67	597–1888	345
310–1888	198	347–1888	350	598–1888	54
311–1888	151	348–1888	73	599–1888	56
312–1888	380	349–1888	92	600–1888	377
313–1888	297	350–1888	304	601–1888	28
314–1888	383	351–1888	204	602–1888	24
315–1888	314	352–1888	335	603–1888	414
316–1888	382	353–1888	220	604–1888	175
pp. 1–50	pp. 1–50	354–1888	257	605–1888	273
317–1888	121	355–1888	219	606–1888	149
pp. 1–92	pp. 1–92	356–1888	262	607–1888	16
318–1888	196	357–1888	178	608–1888	71
319–1888	197	358–1888	12	609–1888	238
320–1888	320	358*a*–1888	13	610–1888	25
321–1888	63	358*b*–1888	4	611–1888	160
322–1888	174	358*c*–1888	5	612–1888	48
323–1888	234	358*d*–1888	10	613–1888	150
324–1888	119	358*e*–1888	7	614–1888	108
325–1888	104	358*f*–1888	8	615–1888	381

Museum No.	*Catalogue No.*
616–1888	241
617–1888	199
618–1888	218
619–1888	187
620–1888	181
621–1888	202
622–1888	200
623–1888	176
624–1888	291
625–1888	14
626–1888	52
627–1888	51
628–1888	152
781–1888	227
782–1888	263
783–1888	264
784–1888	250
785–1888	325
786–1888	235
787–1888	329
788–1888	327
789–1888	136
790–1888	287
791–1888	154
792–1888	237
793–1888	245
794–1888	72
795–1888	407
796–1888	53
797–1888	236
798–1888	243
799–1888	239
800–1888	396
801–1888	372
802–1888	292
803–1888	34
804–1888	33
805–1888	26
806–1888	42
807–1888	43
808–1888	44

Museum No.	*Catalogue No.*
809–1888	41
810–1888	49
811–1888	91
812–1888	75
813–1888	355
814–1888	253
815–1888	260
816–1888	413
817–1888	284
818–1888	368
819–1888	158
820–1888	189
821–1888	205
822–1888	159
823–1888	147
824–1888	188
825–1888	106
826–1888	183
827–1888	140
828–1888	145
829–1888	47
830–1888	46
831–1888	45
832–1888	107
833–1888	285
834–1888	290
835–1888	259
836–1888	384
837–1888	294
838–1888	295
839–1888	225
840–1888	244
841–1888	38
842–1888	114
843–1888	57
1247–1888	408
1248–1888	376
1249–1888	375
1255–1888	97
1256–1888	86
1257–1888	90

Museum No.	*Catalogue No.*
1258–1888	342
1258*a*–1888	343
1258*b*–1888	344
1259–1888 pp. 1–84	132 pp. 1–84
1628–1888	359
1629–1888	395
1630–1888	223
1631–1888	352
1632–1888	288
320–1891	162
986–1900	286
987–1900	209
D.1874–1908	400
D.1875–1908	399
D.1876–1908	397
D.1877–1908	398
E.5768–1910 (43–1873)	18
E.3005–1911 (45–1873)	20
E.3237–1911 (320–1891)	162
P.44–1942	64
E.191–1948	95
P.25–1970	16A
P.26–1970	16B
P.27–1970	16C
No Museum No.	1
,,	6

List of Books

cited by Abbreviations in the Catalogue

L. ed. S.	C. R. Leslie. *Memoirs of the Life of John Constable, R.A.* The edition edited and enlarged by the Hon. Andrew Shirley, published by The Medici Society, London, 1937.
L. ed. M.	The edition of the above work edited by J. H. Mayne, published by The Phaidon Press, 1951.
Holmes	C. J. Holmes. *Constable and his Influence on Landscape Painting.* Constable and Co., 1902.
S. : L.	Hon. A. Shirley. *Mezzotints by David Lucas after Constable* (with a Catalogue Raisonné). Clarendon Press, Oxford, 1930. Plates are referred to by their Catalogue number: S. 1 etc.
Greig, Vol. I–VIII	*The Farington Diary.* The published edition (not a complete transcript) edited by James Greig in eight volumes. Hutchinson, 1922–8.
Davies	M. Davies. *The National Gallery Catalogues: British School.* 1946. The first edition has been used throughout this Catalogue. A second edition, with additions and corrections, has been published (1959), but, owing to transfers between the National Gallery and Tate Gallery, contains fewer entries for works by Constable. The locations given in this Catalogue, as between the National Gallery and the Tate Gallery, refer to the position in 1970. Further changes may take place.
Key	S. J. Key. *John Constable. His Life and Work.* Phoenix House, Ltd., 1948.
P. Leslie	*The Letters of John Constable, R.A. to C. R. Leslie, R.A., 1826–1837.* Edited by P. Leslie, Constable and Co. Ltd., 1931.
Windsor	Lord Windsor. *John Constable R.A.* The Walter Scott Publishing Co. Ltd., 1903.
Badt	K. Badt. *John Constable's Clouds.* Routledge & Co., 1950.
Beckett I–VI	John Constable's Correspondence. Edited by R. B. Beckett. The Suffolk Records Society 1962–68 (Vol. I published jointly with H.M.S.O.). I The Family at East Bergholt 1807–1837. II Early Friends and Maria Bicknell (Mrs. Constable).

III Correspondence with C. R. Leslie, R.A.
IV Patrons, Dealers and Fellow Artists.
V Various Friends, with Charles Boner and the Artist's Children.
VI The Fishers.

Beckett: *Discourses.*

John Constable's Discourses. Compiled and annotated by R. B. Beckett. The Suffolk Records Society. 1970.

List of Dismembered Sketch-books

This list gives the drawings in the Museum's collections which are assigned in the Catalogue to sketch-books which were broken up before Miss Isabel Constable made her gift. There are in addition the three intact sketch-books Nos. 121, 132 and 382.

Sketch-book used in	*Watermark (if any)*	*Approximate size of page*	*Catalogue numbers*
1796		180 × 299 mm. ($7\frac{1}{8} \times 11\frac{3}{4}$ ins.)	1–13
1801		175 × 264 mm. ($6\frac{7}{8} \times 10\frac{3}{8}$ ins.)	21–32
1812 [?]		115 × 186 mm. ($4\frac{1}{2} \times 7\frac{3}{8}$ ins.)	118 (but possibly from one of the sketch-books used in 1820)
1814		81 × 111 mm. ($3\frac{1}{4} \times 4\frac{3}{8}$ ins.)	124–128
1815	Whatman 1813	115 × 181 mm. ($4\frac{1}{2} \times 7\frac{1}{8}$ ins.)	139, 141, 144
1815	W	78 × 101 mm. ($3\frac{1}{8} \times 4$ ins.)	140, 143, 145 and 121 pp. 91, 92
1815 [?]		115 × 187 mm. ($4\frac{1}{2} \times 7\frac{3}{8}$ ins.)	142
1816		88 × 116 mm. ($3\frac{1}{2} \times 4\frac{5}{8}$ ins.)	146, 147
1816		115 × 181 mm. ($4\frac{1}{2} \times 7\frac{1}{8}$ ins.)	148, 149, 151, 152, 153, 154 (of which 149, 151, 152, 153, 154, were mounted on paper bearing the watermark Whatman, 1813, measuring 240 × 180 mm. ($9\frac{1}{2} \times 7\frac{1}{8}$ ins.))

Sketch-book used in	*Watermark (if any)*	*Approximate size of page*	*Catalogue numbers*
1817	Dickinson 18[..]	115 × 186 mm. ($4\frac{1}{2} \times 7\frac{3}{8}$ ins.)	156, 157, 158, 159, 160 (see also 142, 179–182)
1818		100 × 134 mm. ($4 \times 5\frac{1}{4}$ ins.)	164, 166, 167, 168, 170
1820	Whatman 1817	115 × 186 mm. ($4\frac{1}{2} \times 7\frac{3}{8}$ ins.)	187, 190, 193, 201
1820	Dickinson 18[..]	115 × 186 mm. ($4\frac{1}{2} \times 7\frac{3}{8}$ ins.)	198, 202
1820	(no watermark)	115 × 186 mm. ($4\frac{1}{2} \times 7\frac{3}{8}$ ins.)	185, 186, 188, 189, 194, 195, 199, [205?]
1820	Whatman 1818	161 × 237 mm. ($6\frac{3}{8} \times 9\frac{3}{8}$ ins.)	191, 192, 200, 203, 204, 206, 220, 238, 239
1821	Whatman 1819	173 × 260 mm. ($6\frac{3}{4} \times 10\frac{1}{4}$ ins.)	210–219, 240 (see also 241, 242)
1821		84 × 113 mm. ($3\frac{3}{8} \times 4\frac{3}{8}$ ins.)	225, (236?), 237, 243, 244, 245
1823 and 1824		181 × 262 mm. ($7\frac{1}{8} \times 10\frac{1}{4}$ ins.)	256, 257, 259–262, 273, 274, (275–278?)
1823 [?]		173 × 260 mm. ($6\frac{3}{4} \times 10\frac{1}{4}$ ins.)	241, 242
1827	Whatman 1824	224 × 331 mm. ($8\frac{7}{8} \times 13$ ins.)	290–300
1828	Whatman 1821	115 × 186 mm. ($4\frac{1}{2} \times 7\frac{3}{8}$ ins.)	302, 304–308 (see also 309 for the possibility of this sketch-book having been used earlier)
1829		93 × 128 mm. ($3\frac{5}{8} \times 5$ ins.)	313, 316, 318
1829		234 × 337 mm. ($9\frac{1}{4} \times 13\frac{1}{4}$ ins.)	314, 315, 317, 319
1831 and 1832	Whatman 1831	115 × 190 mm. ($4\frac{1}{2} \times 7\frac{1}{2}$ ins.)	336–340, 346–350
1833		129 × 210 mm. ($5\frac{1}{8} \times 8\frac{1}{4}$ ins.)	357
1834		140 × 235 mm. ($5\frac{1}{2} \times 9\frac{1}{4}$ ins.)	362–368
1834		207 × 272 mm. ($8\frac{1}{8} \times 10\frac{3}{4}$ ins.)	369–372
1835	Whatman 1833	221 × 285 mm. ($8\frac{3}{4} \times 11\frac{1}{4}$ ins.)	378–381, 383, 384
[1834 or 1835]	Whatman 182[—]	130 × 212 mm. ($5\frac{1}{8} \times 8\frac{3}{8}$ ins.)	385–394

THE PLATES

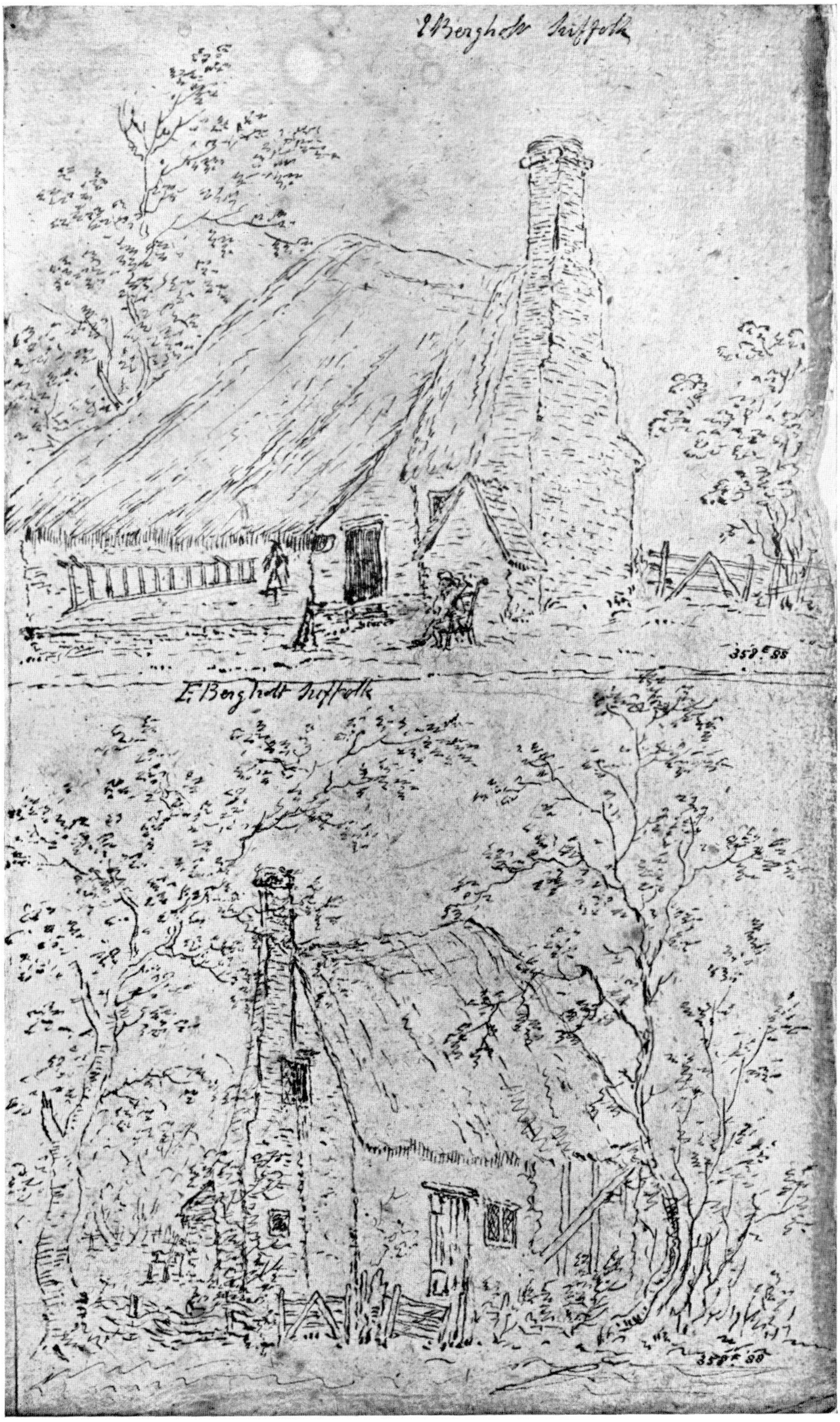

7, 8. Cottages at East Bergholt.

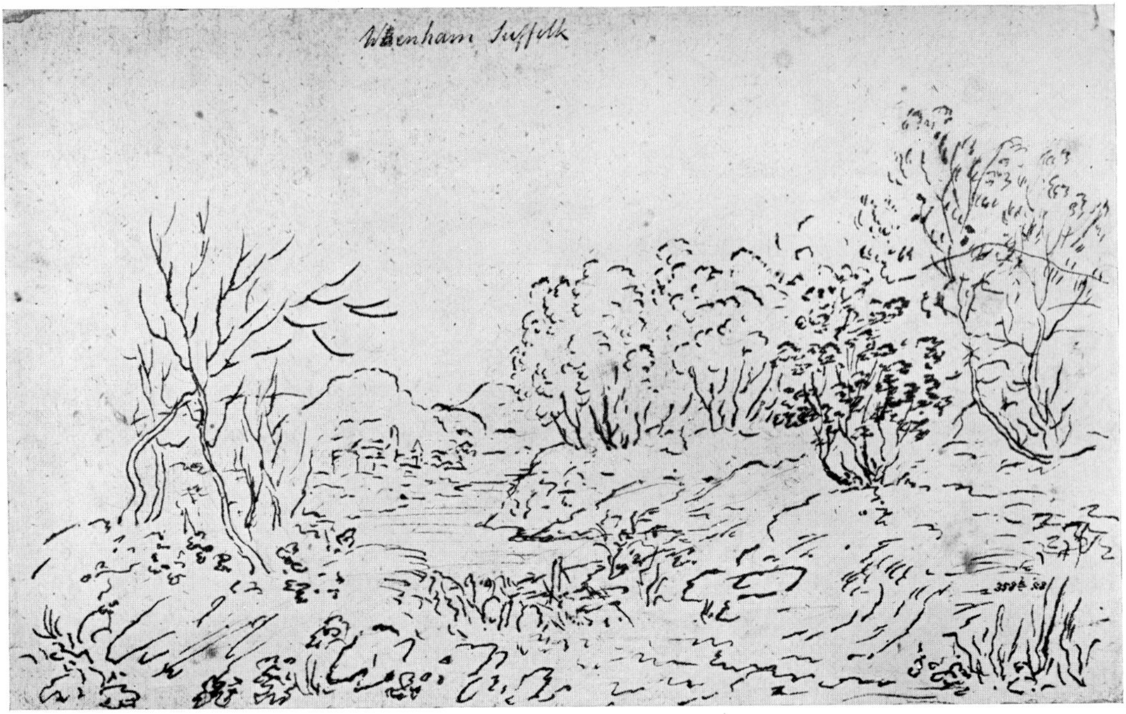

2. Landscape with a stream, Wenham.

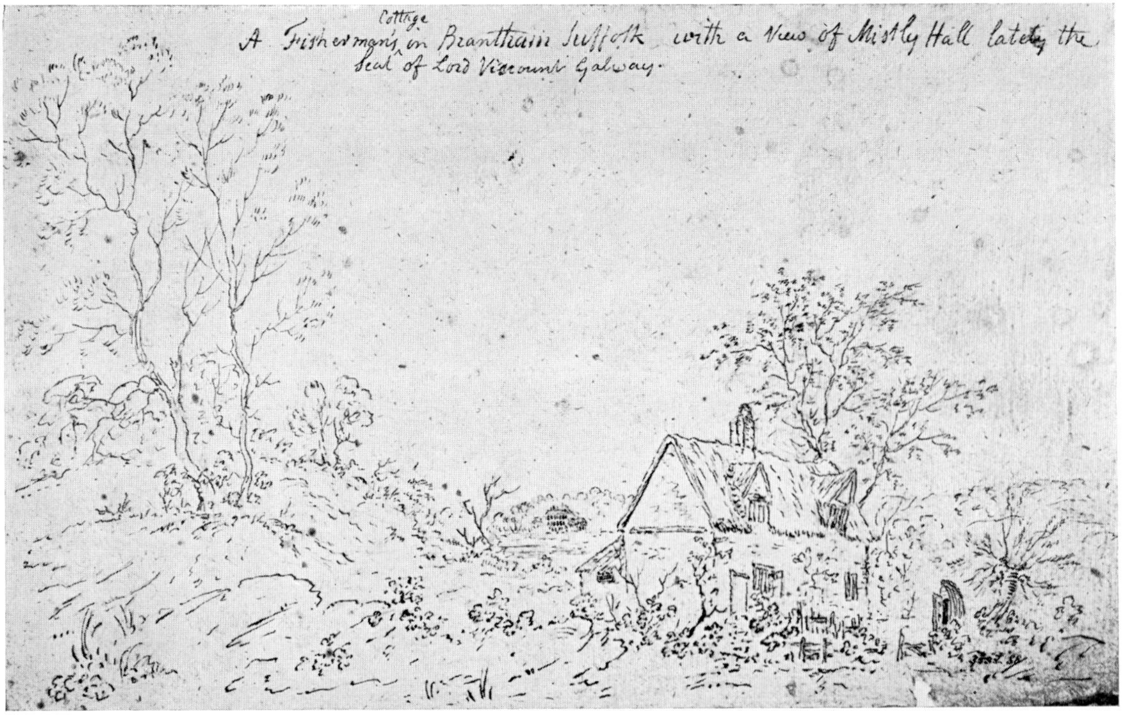

A Fishermans Cottage in Brantham Suffolk with a View of Mistly Hall lately the seat of Lord Viscount Galway.

3. Cottage at Brantham.

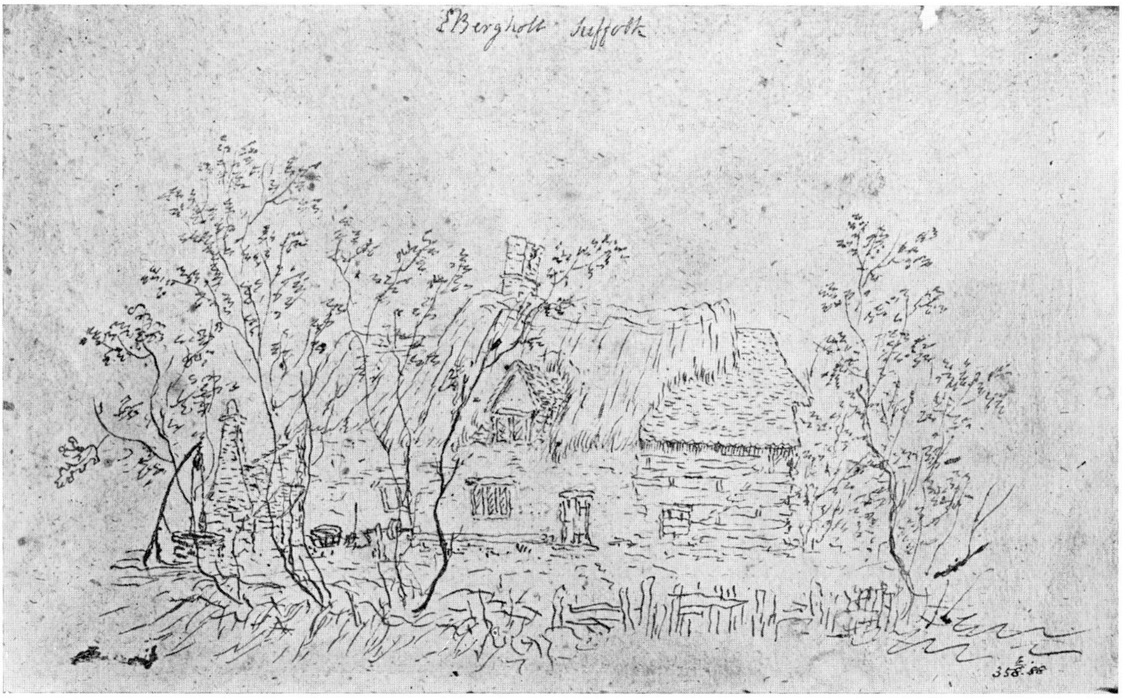

4. Cottage at East Bergholt.

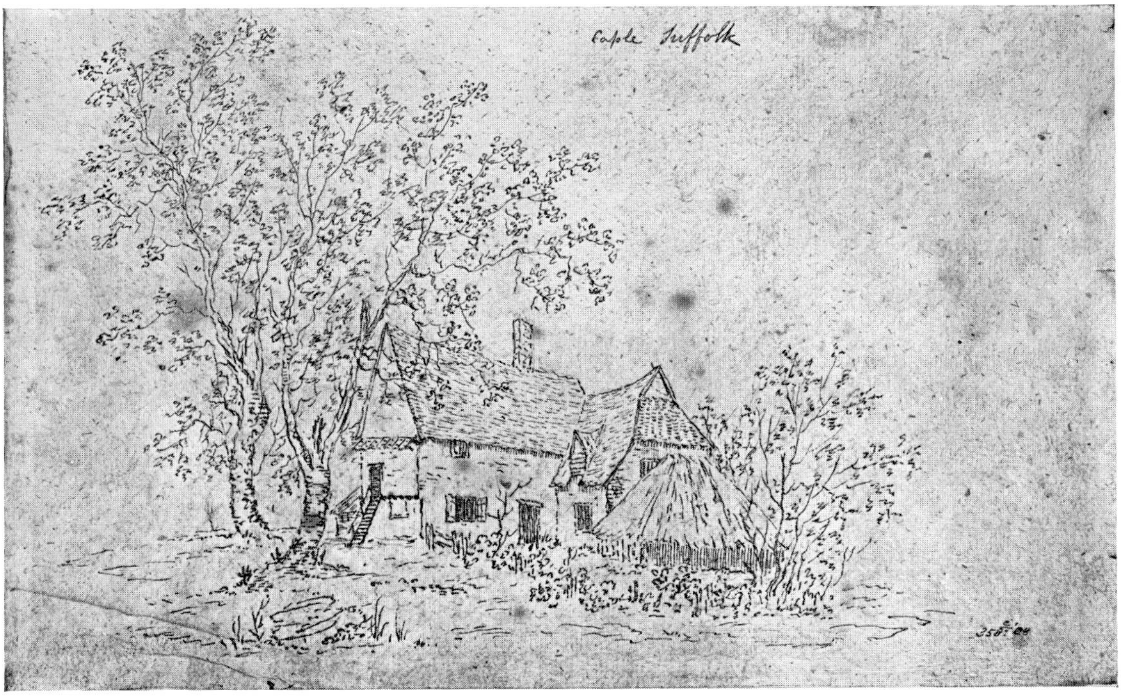

5. Cottage at Capel.

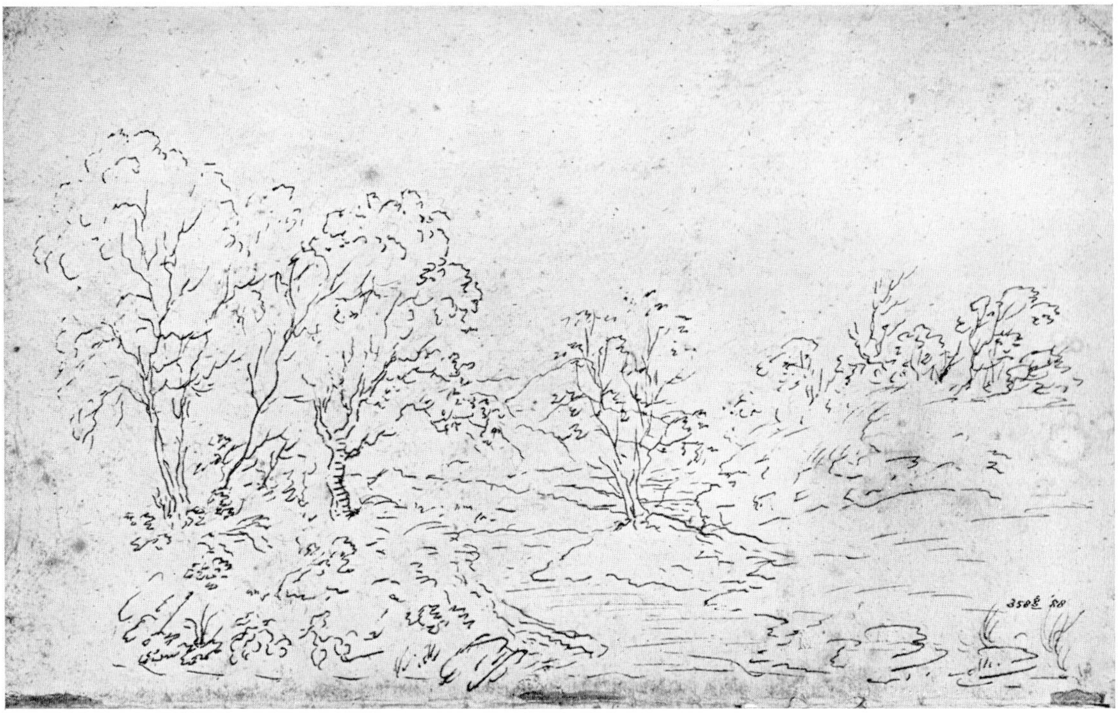

9. Landscape with a stream.

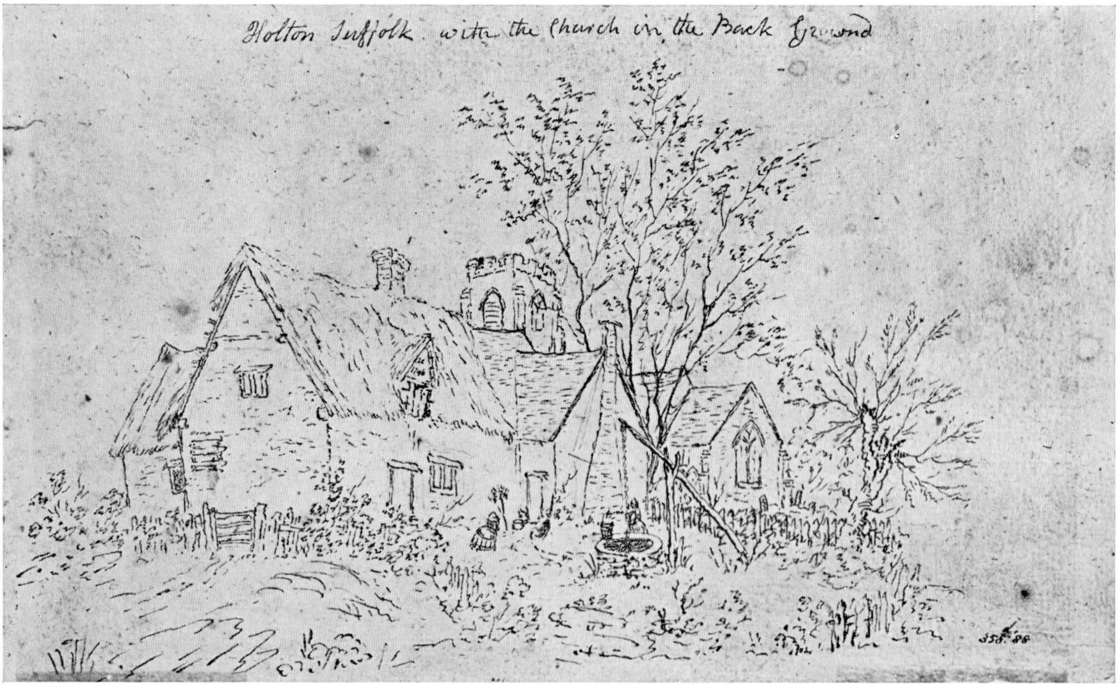

10. Cottage at Holton.

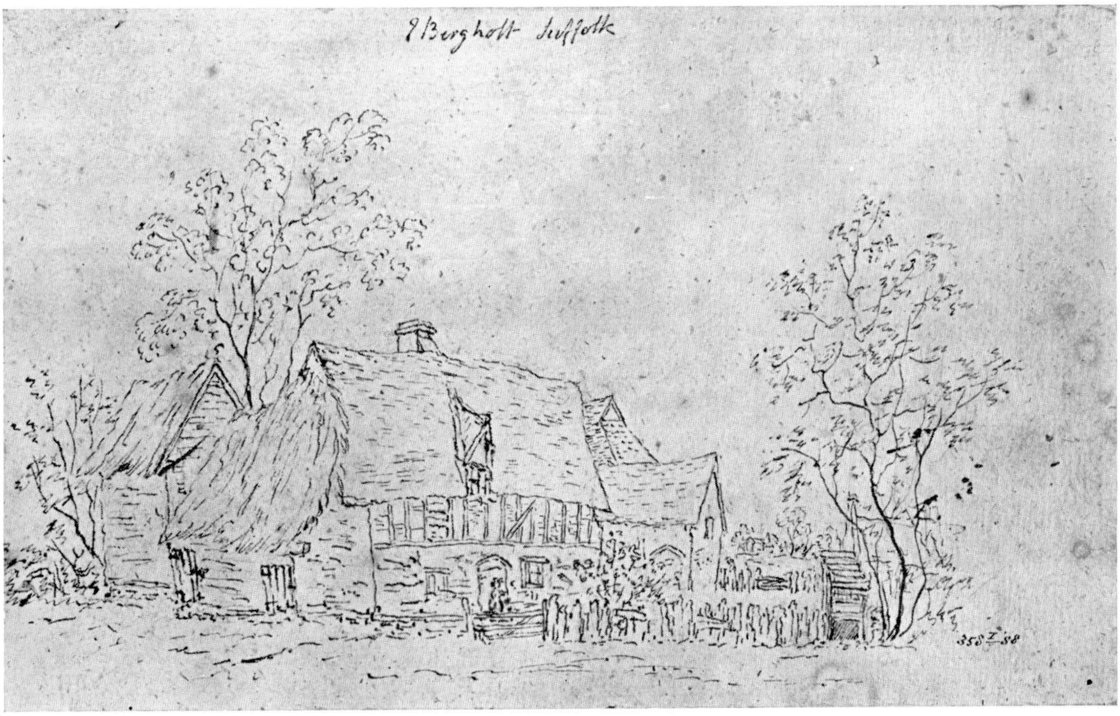

11. Cottage at East Bergholt.

12. Cottage at East Bergholt.

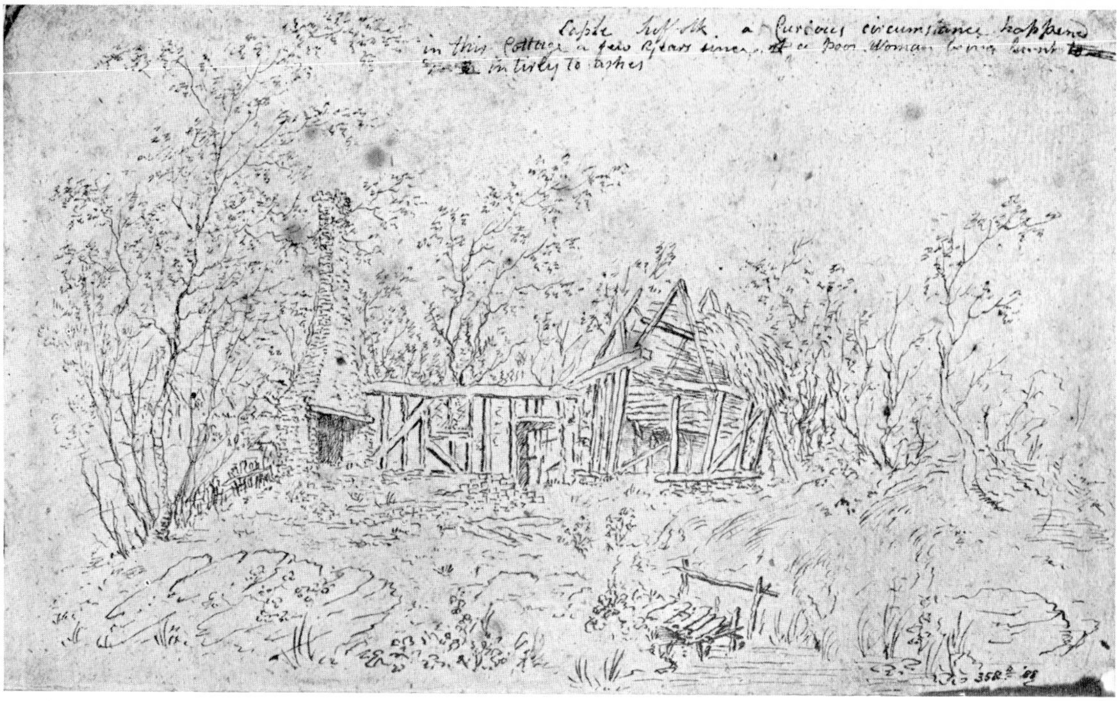

13. A ruined cottage at Capel.

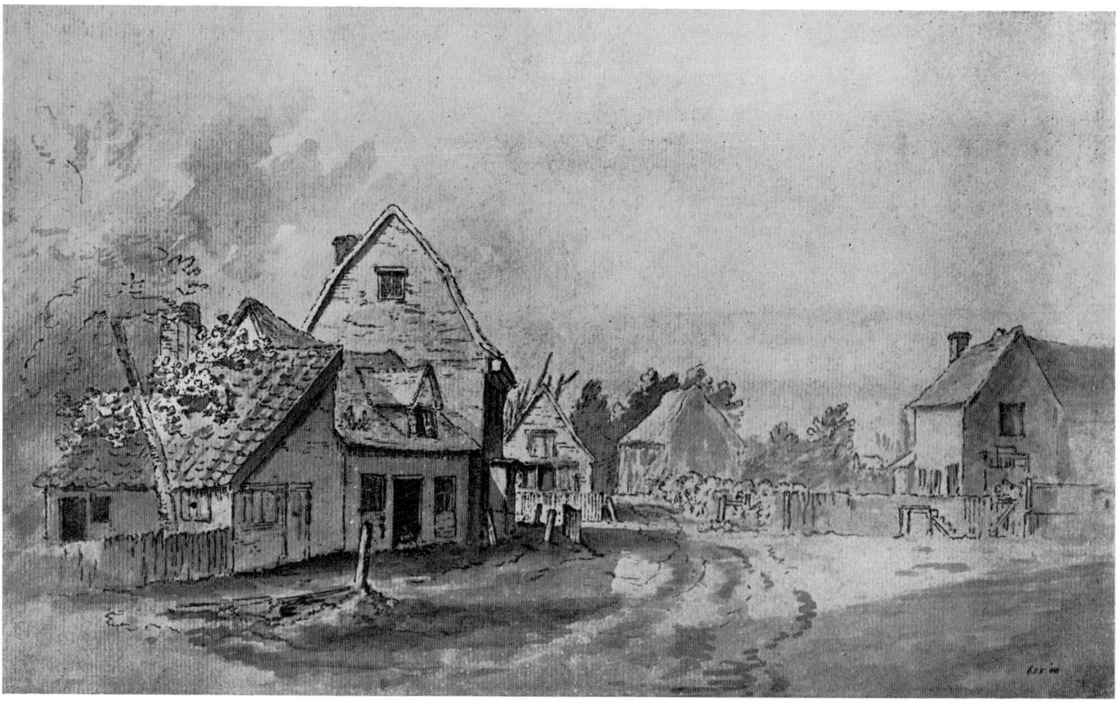

14. East Bergholt Street, East Bergholt.

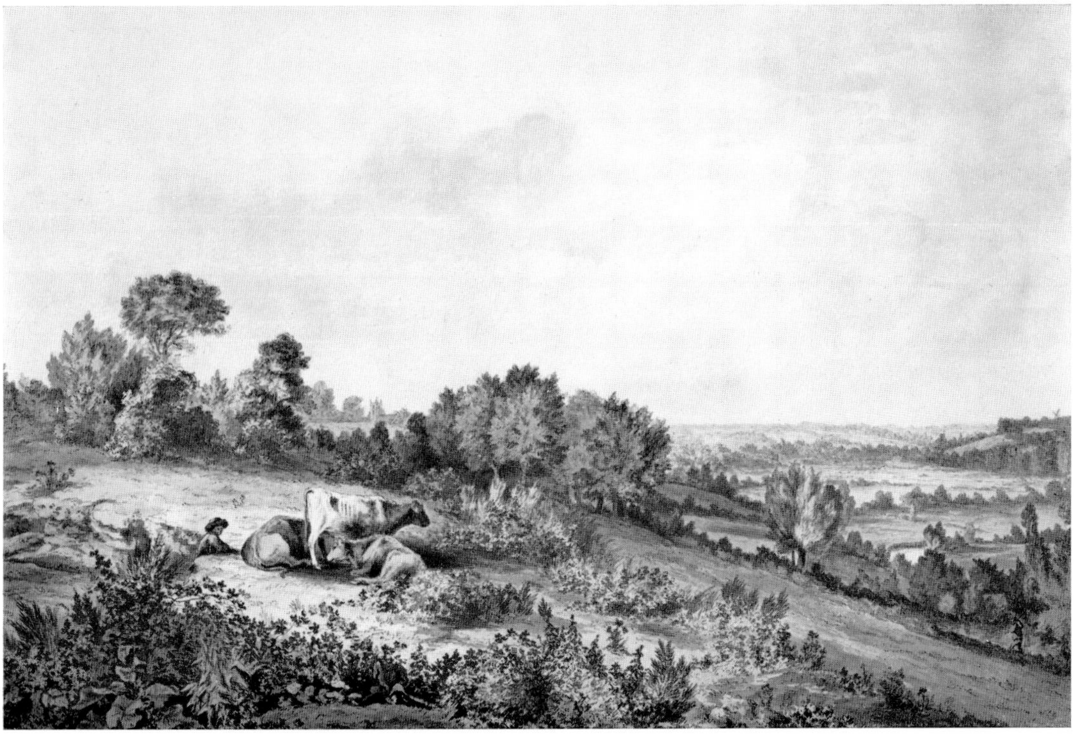

16A. The valley of the Stour, with Langham Church in the distance.

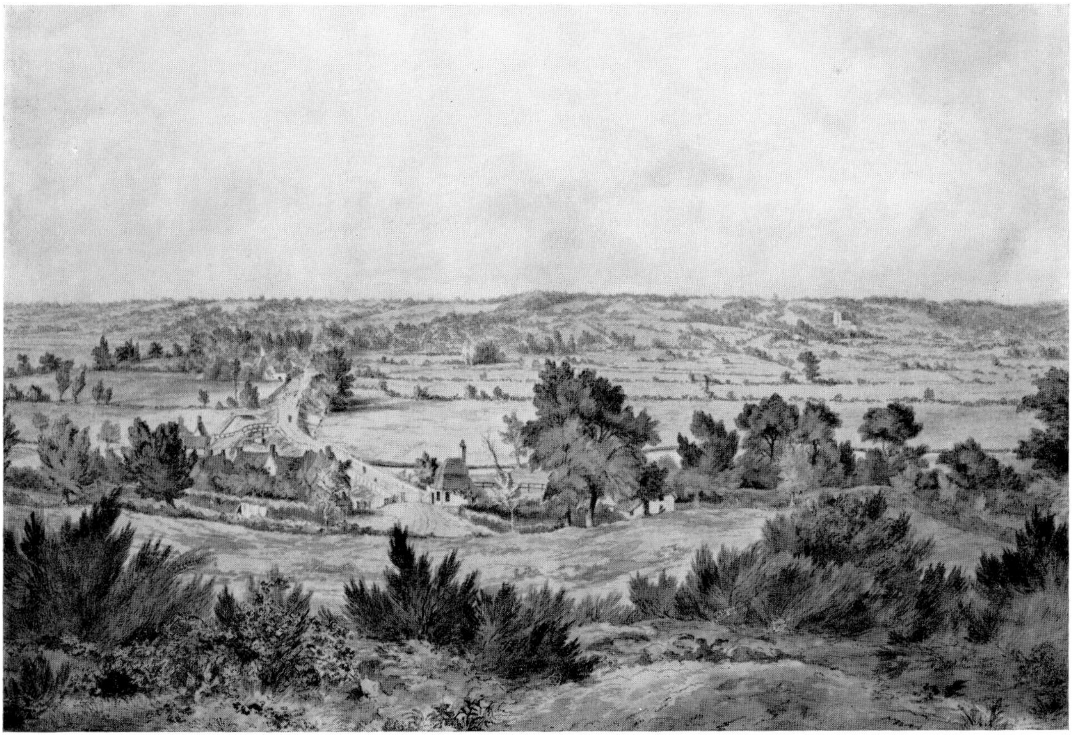

16B. The valley of the Stour, with Stratford St. Mary in the distance.

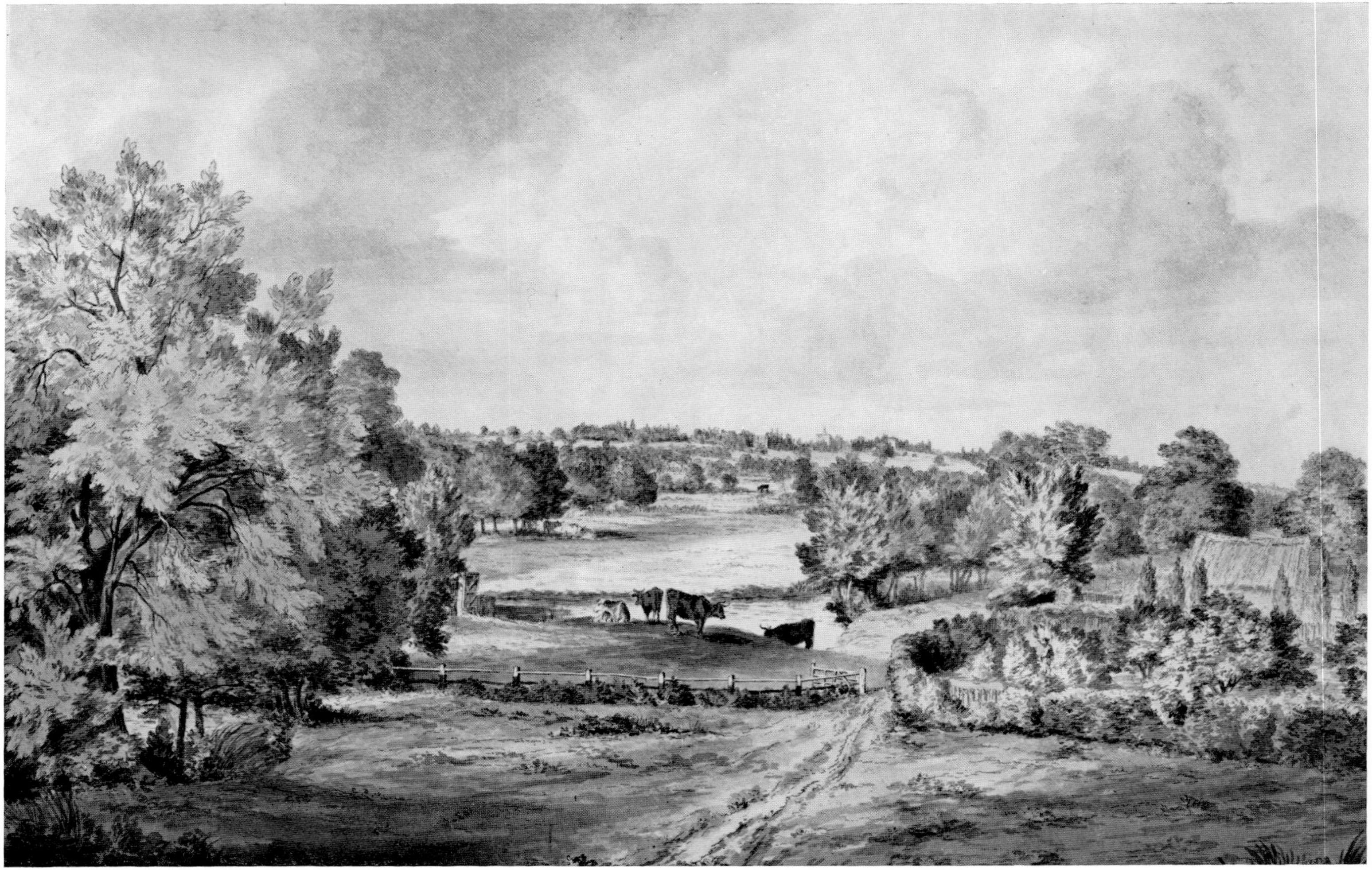

16C. The valley of the Stour, looking towards East Bergholt.

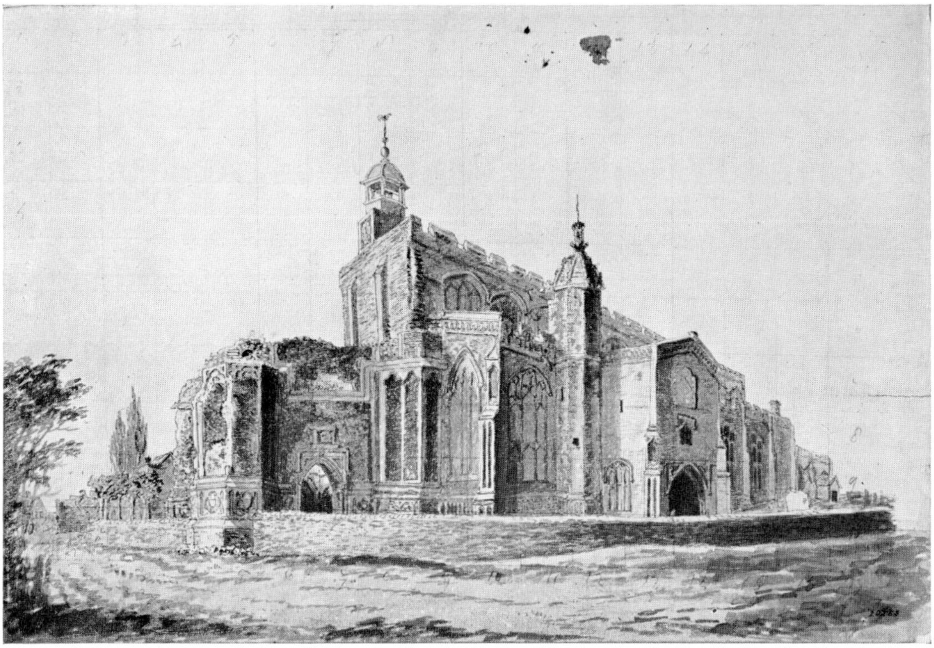

15. East Bergholt Church.

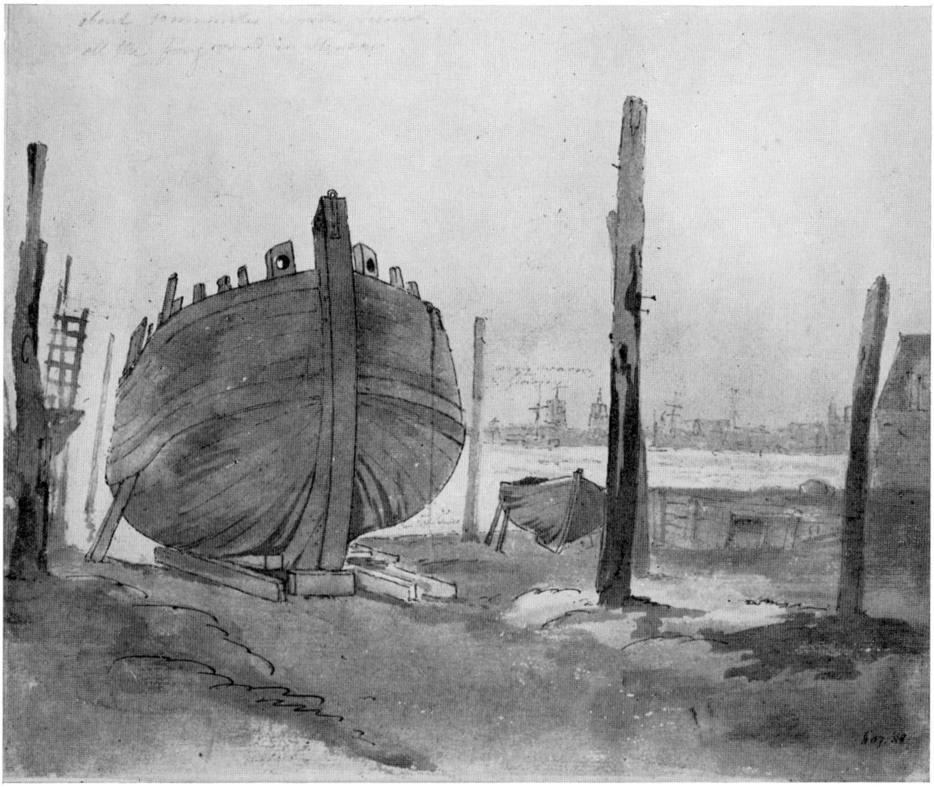

16. A river scene: sunset.

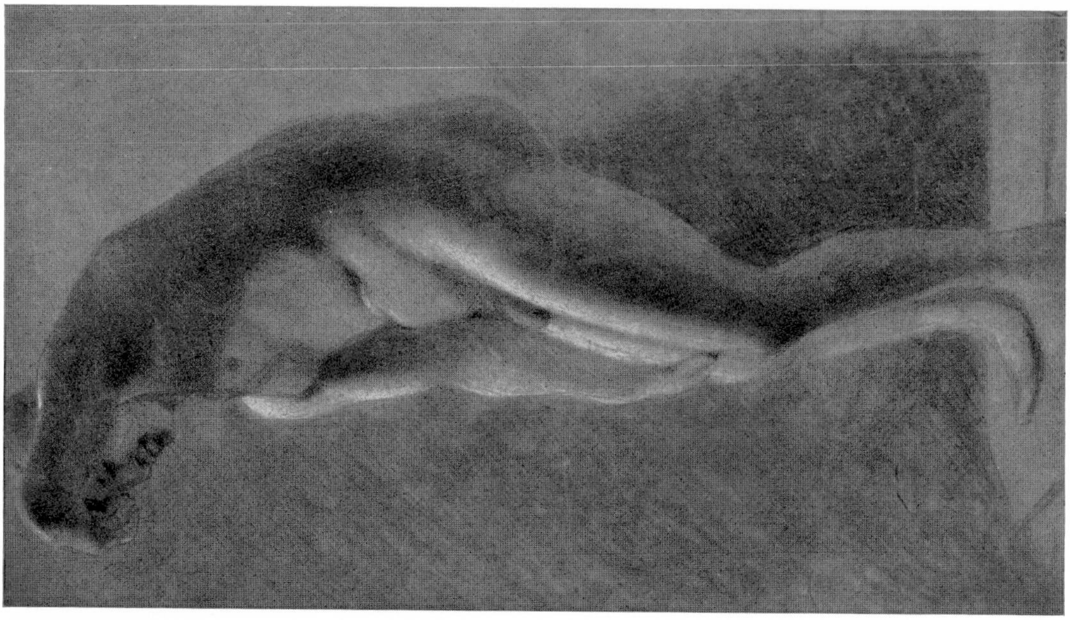

18. Study of male nude.

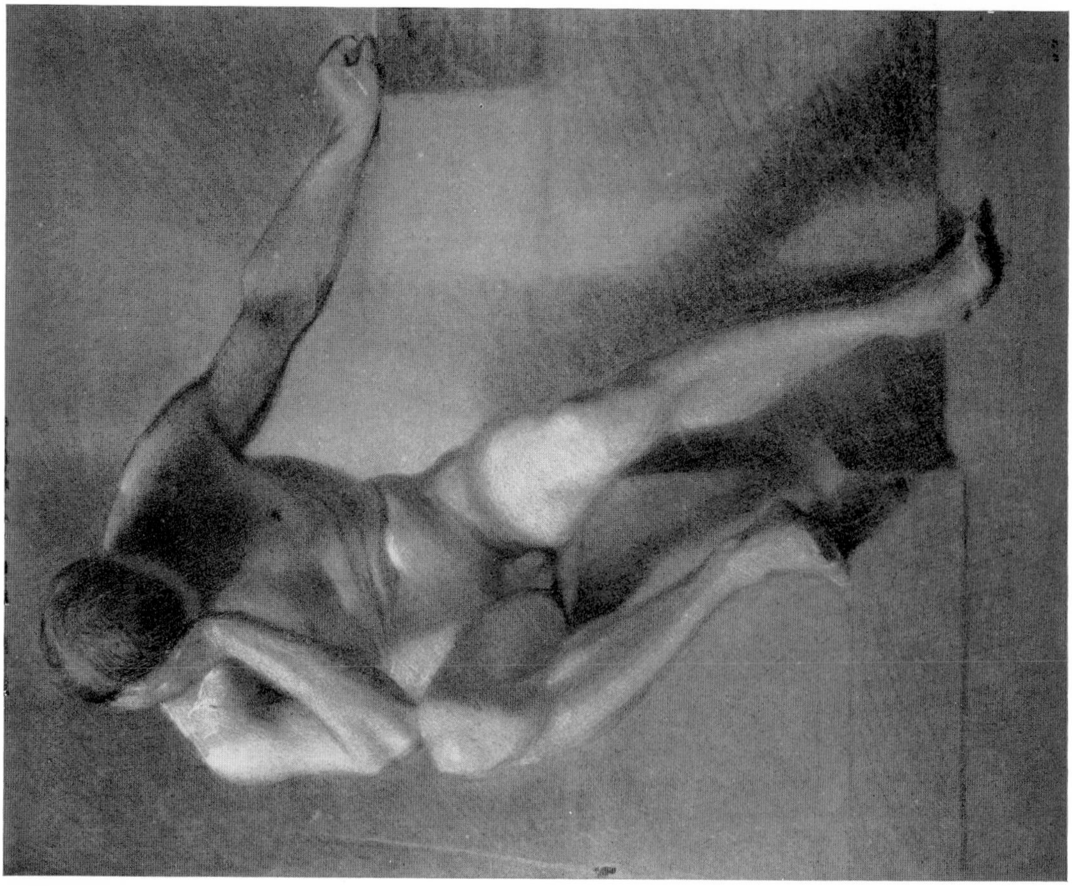

17. Study of male nude.

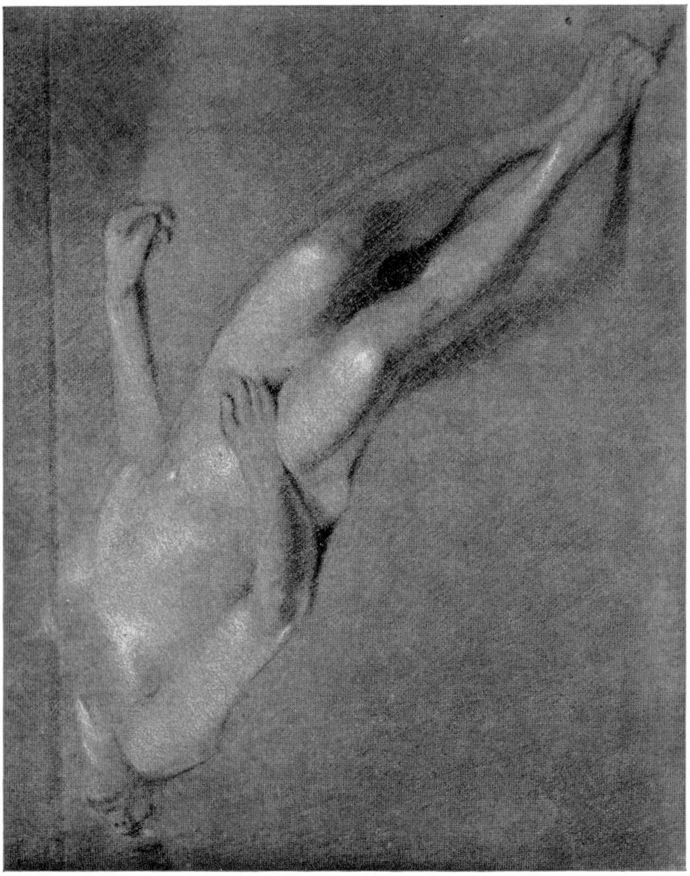

19. Study of male nude.

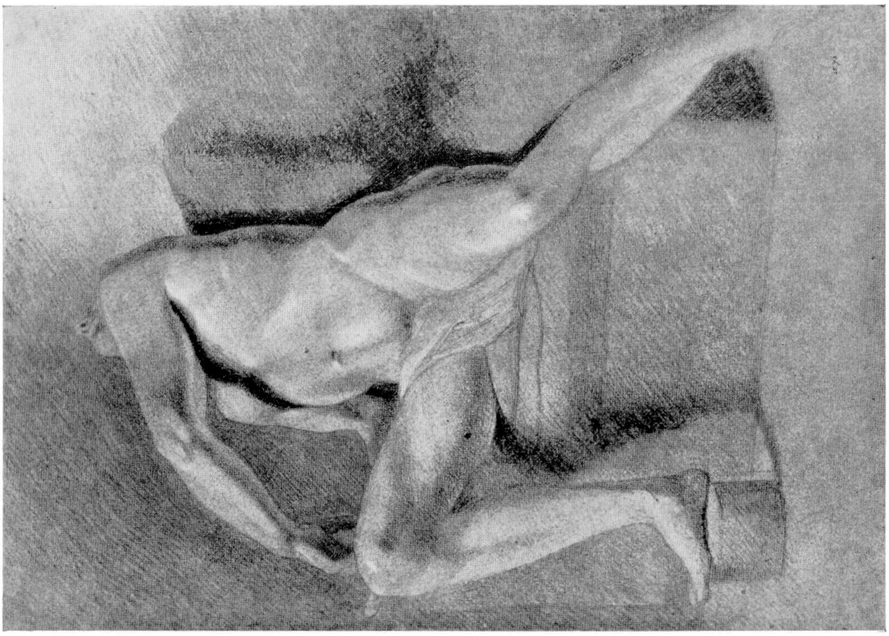

20 Study of male nude.

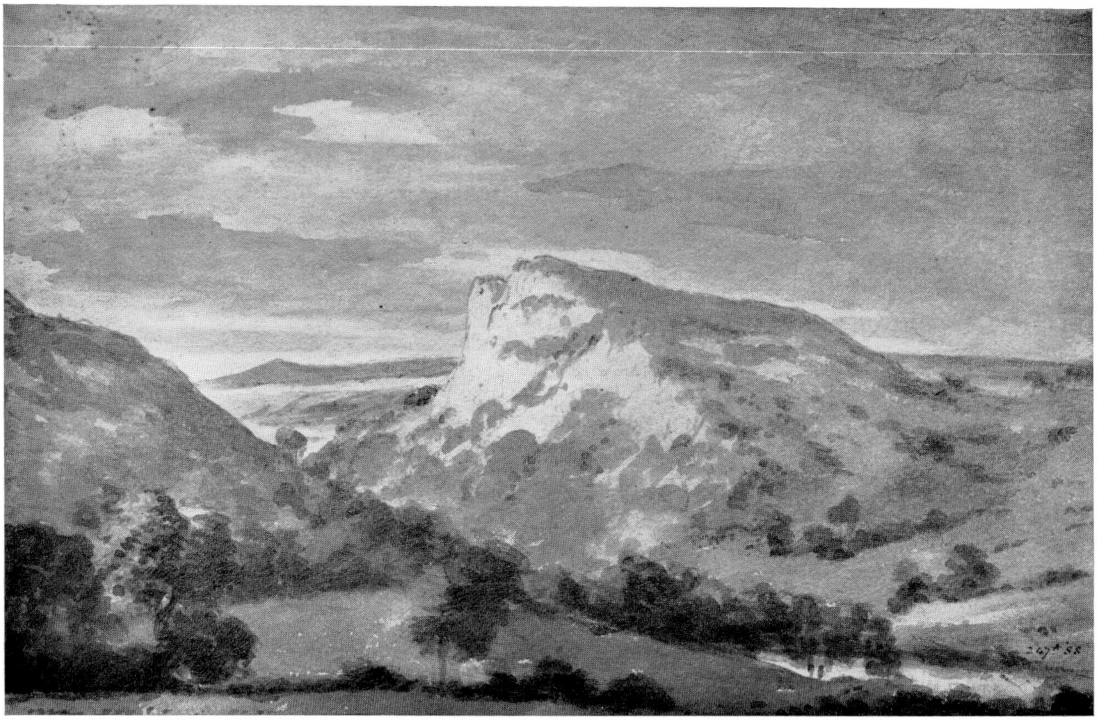

21. Matlock High Tor.

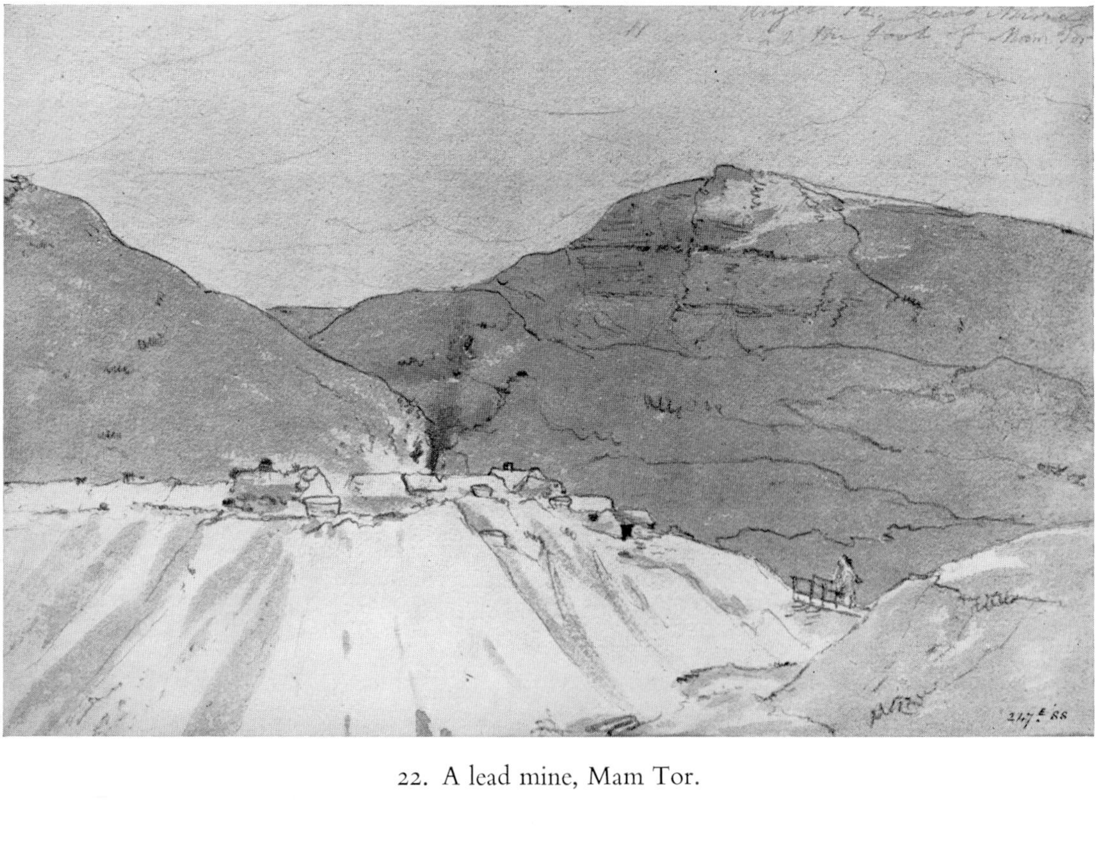

22. A lead mine, Mam Tor.

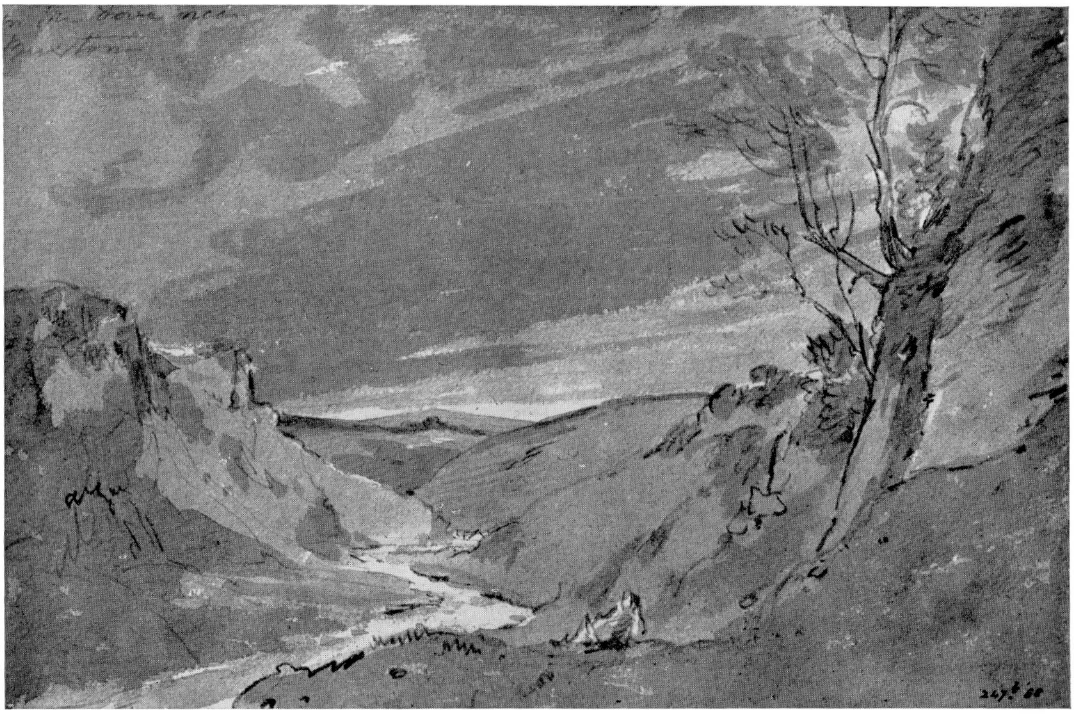

23. On the Dove near Buxton.

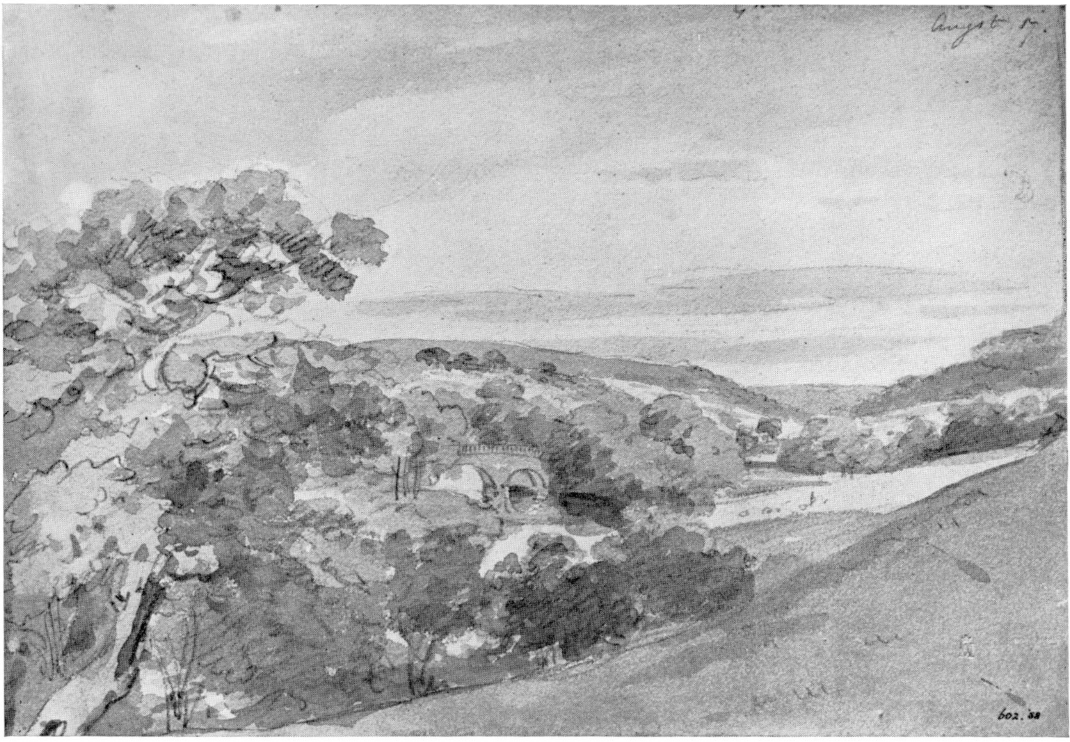

24. Chatsworth Park.

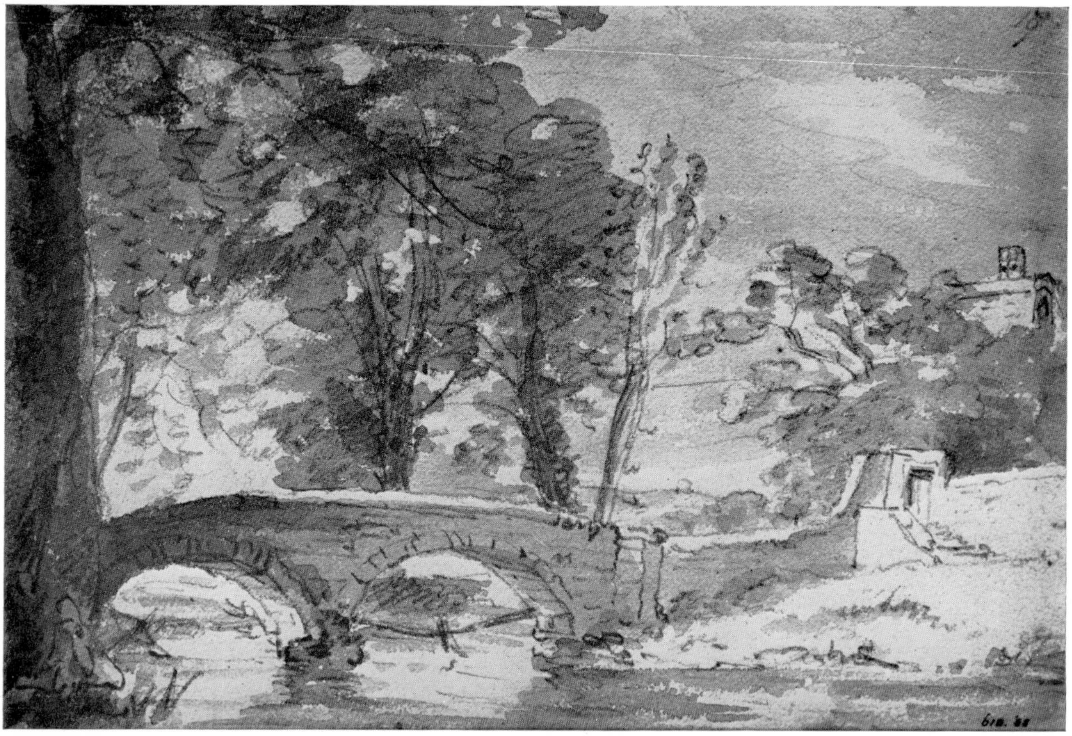

25. Bridge at Haddon.

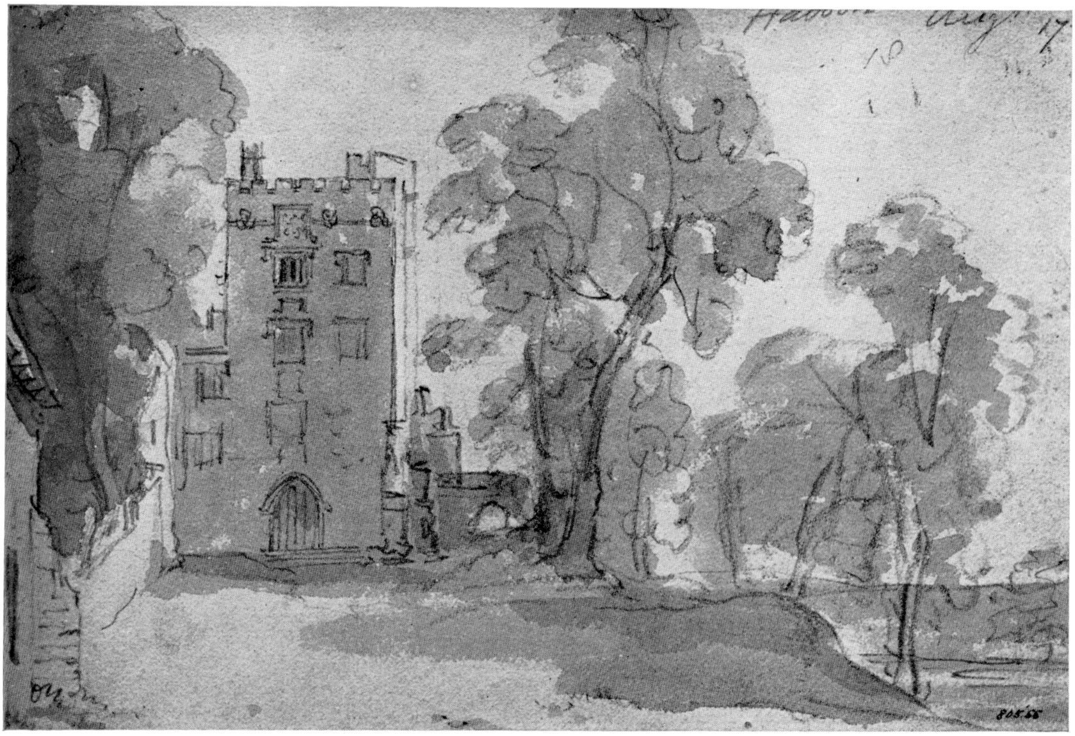

26. Haddon Hall.

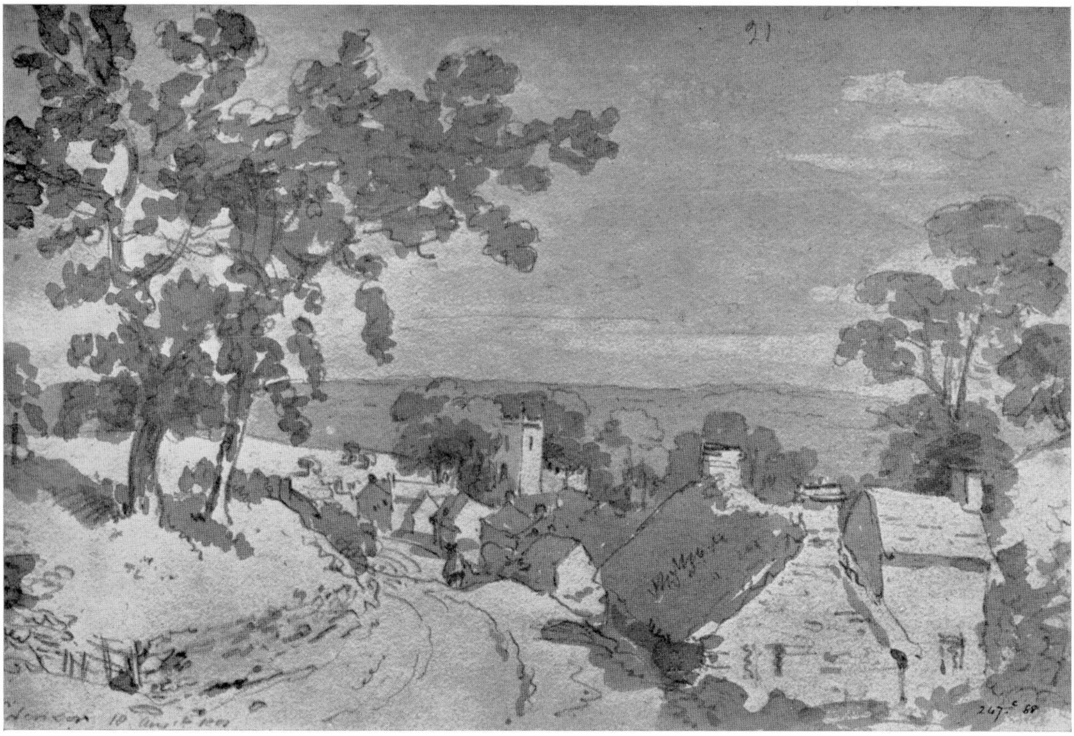

27. Edensor.

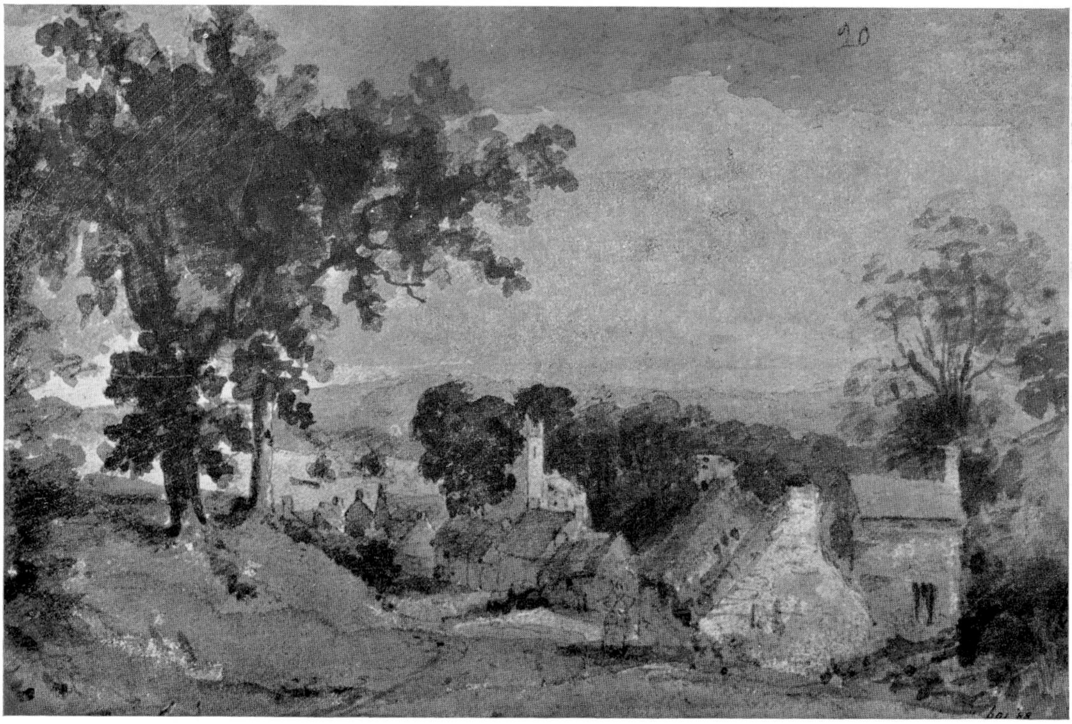

28. Edensor.

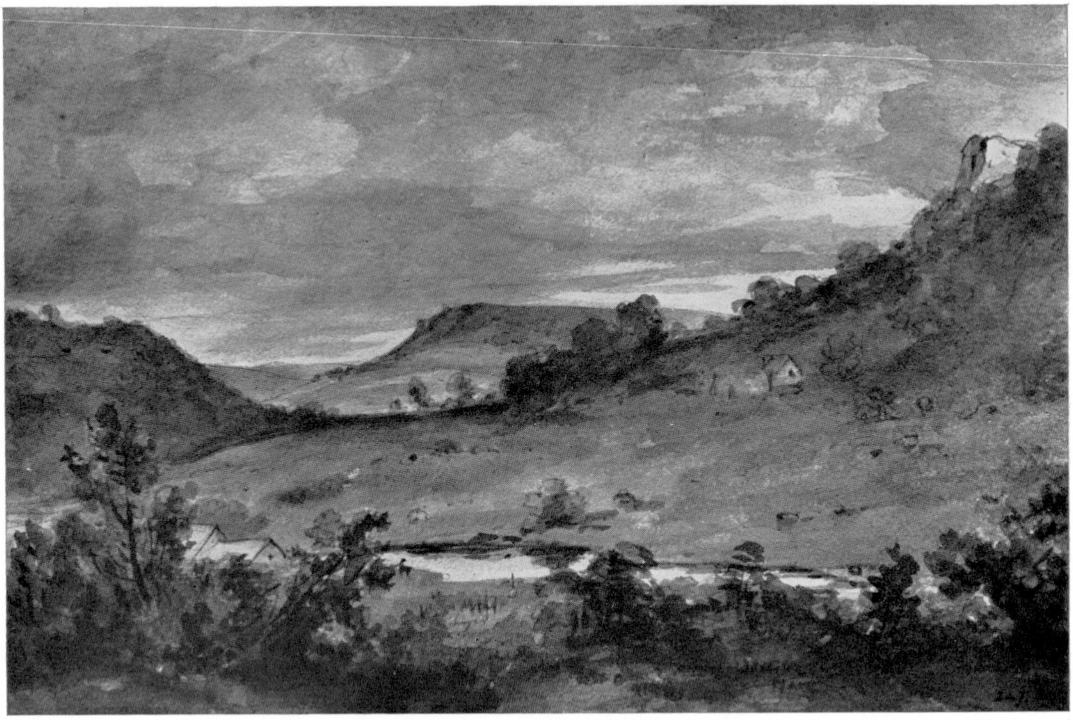

29. Matlock High Tor.

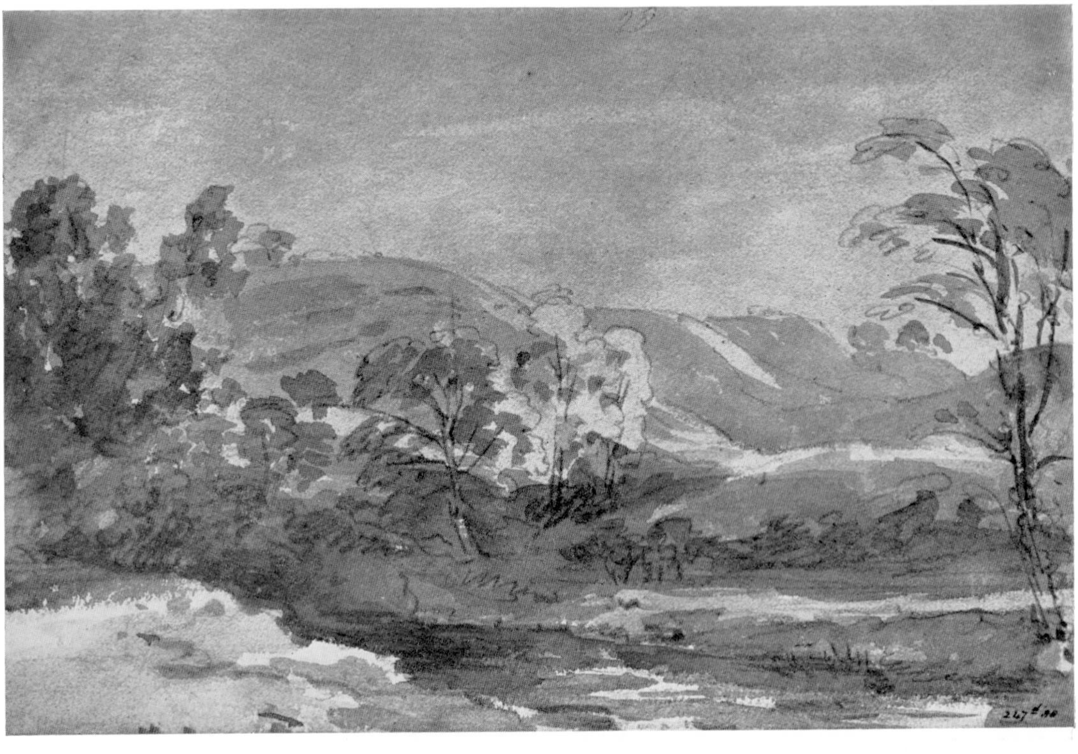

30. View in Derbyshire.

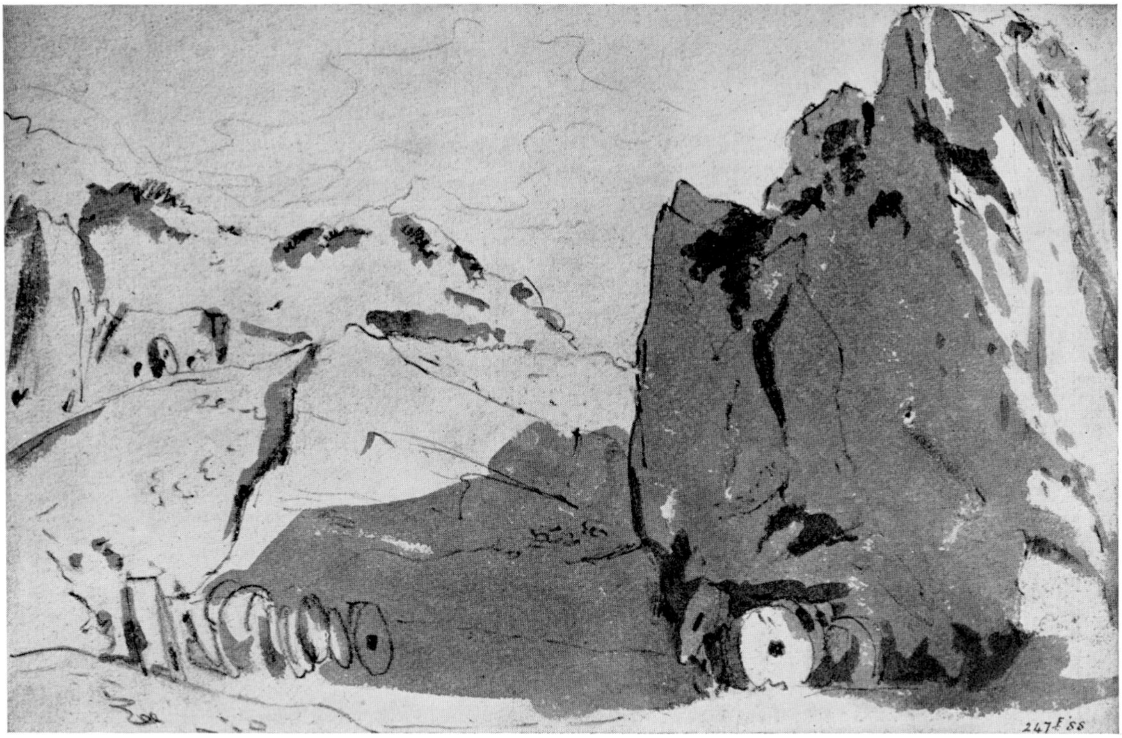

31. A quarry for mill-stones, Derbyshire.

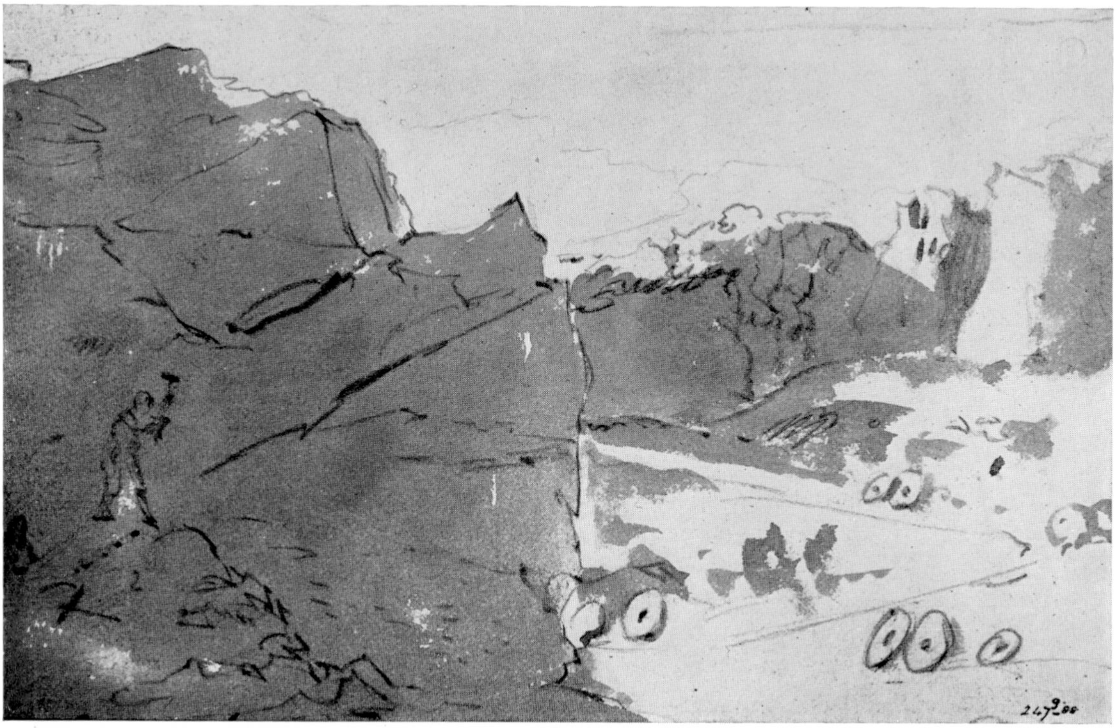

32. A quarry for mill-stones, Derbyshire.

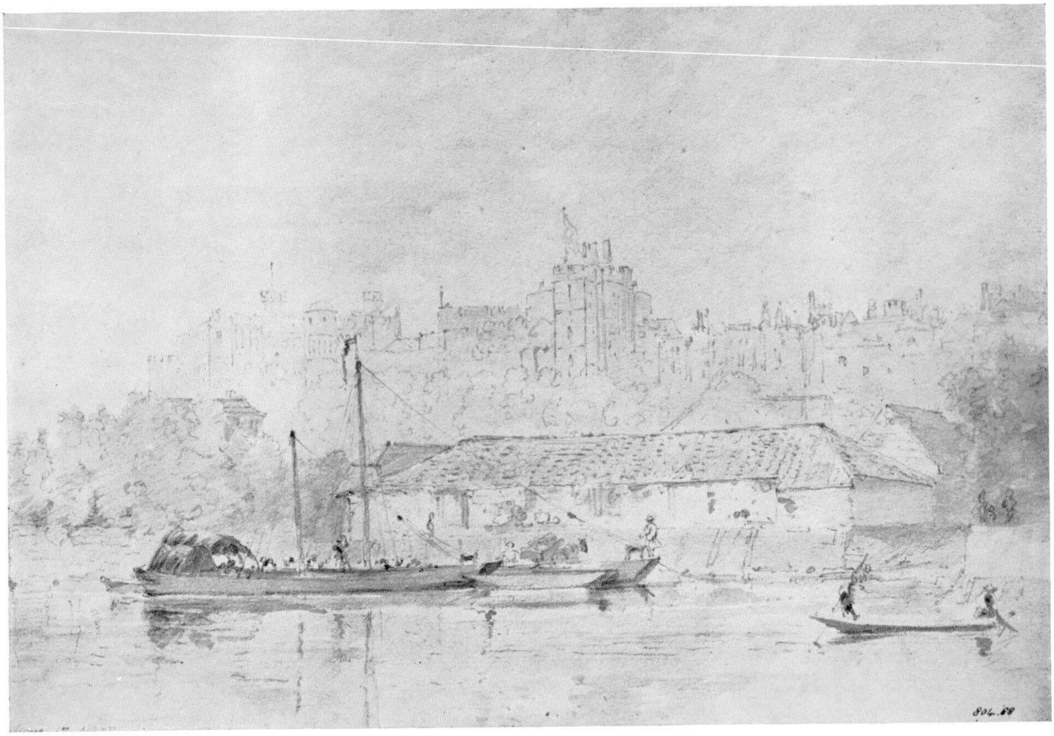

33. Windsor Castle.

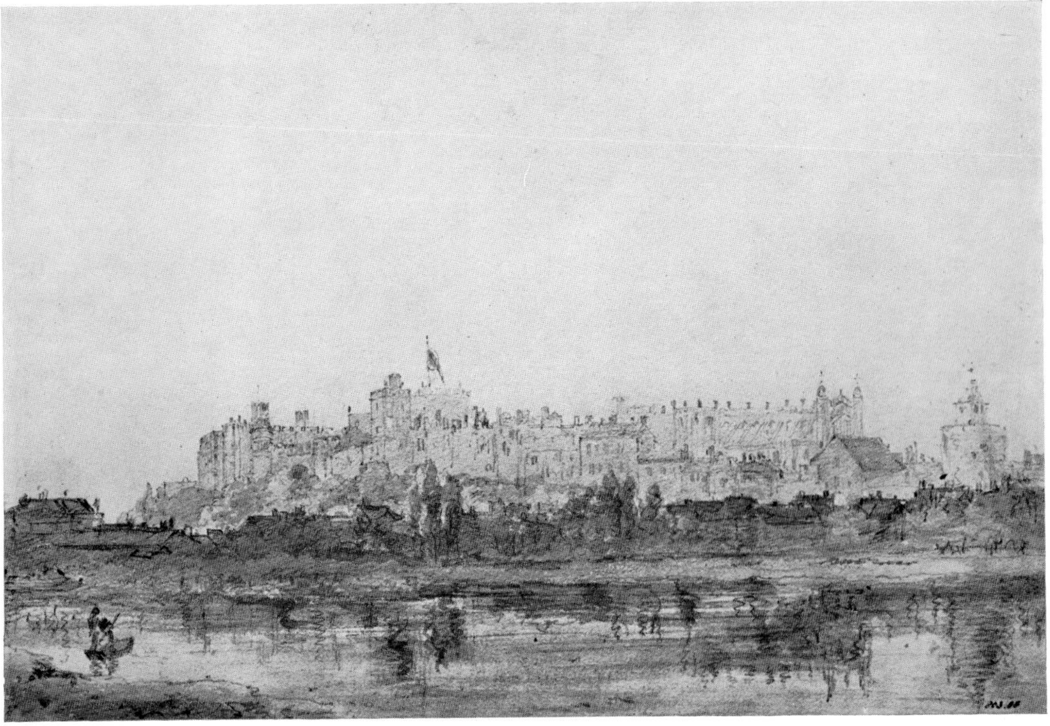

34. Windsor Castle.

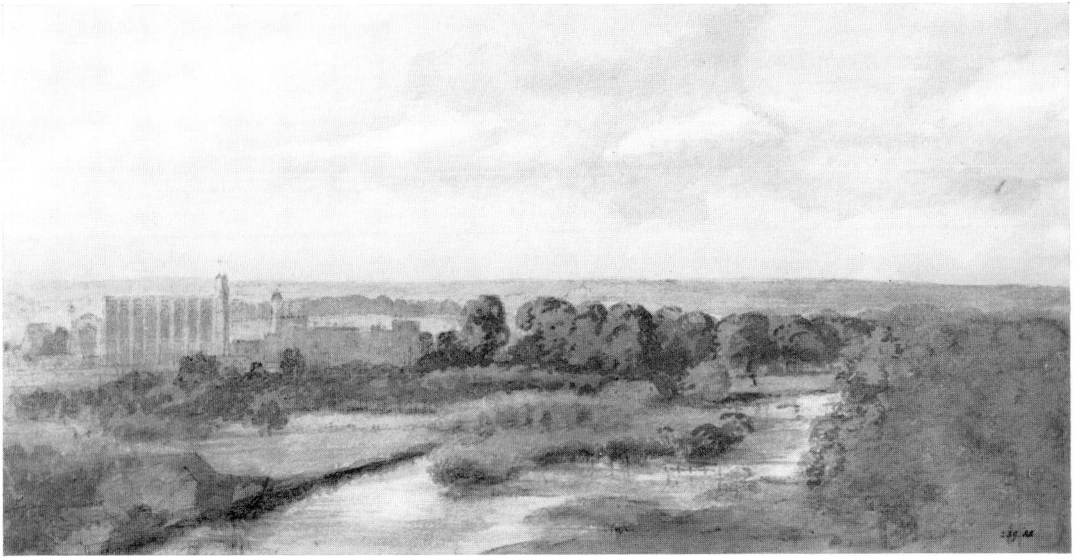

35. The Thames, with Eton College.

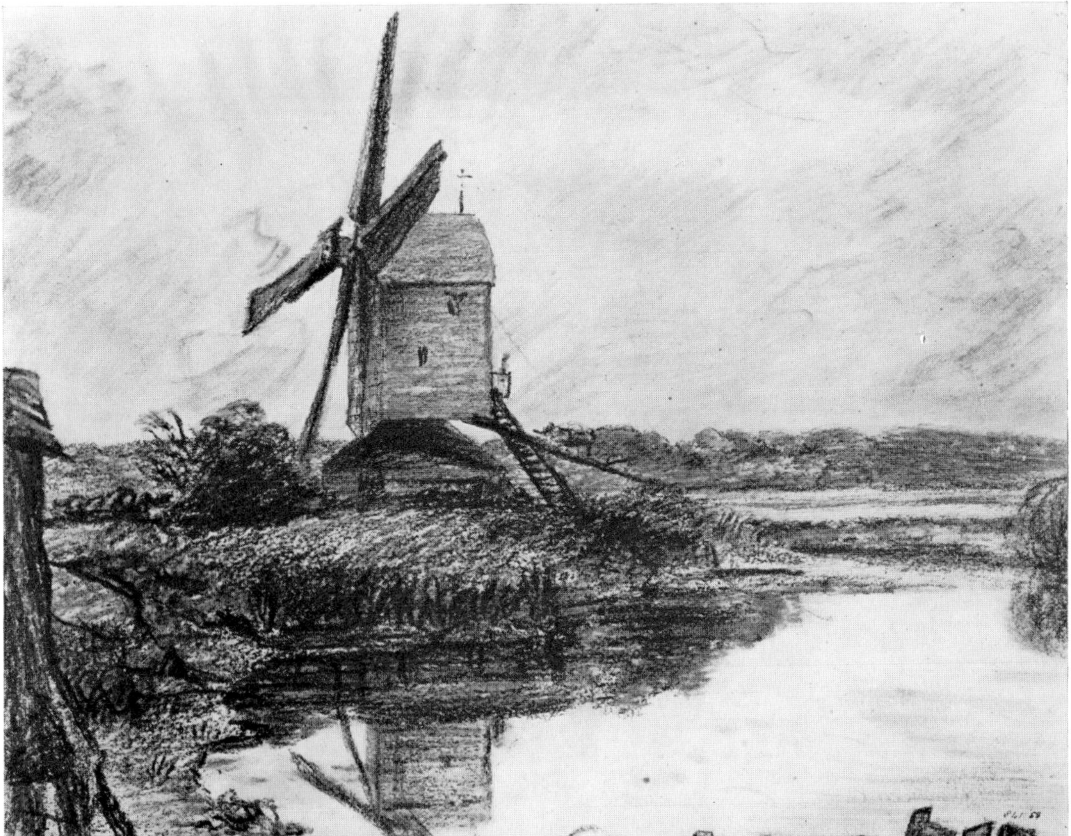

38. A mill on the banks of the River Stour.

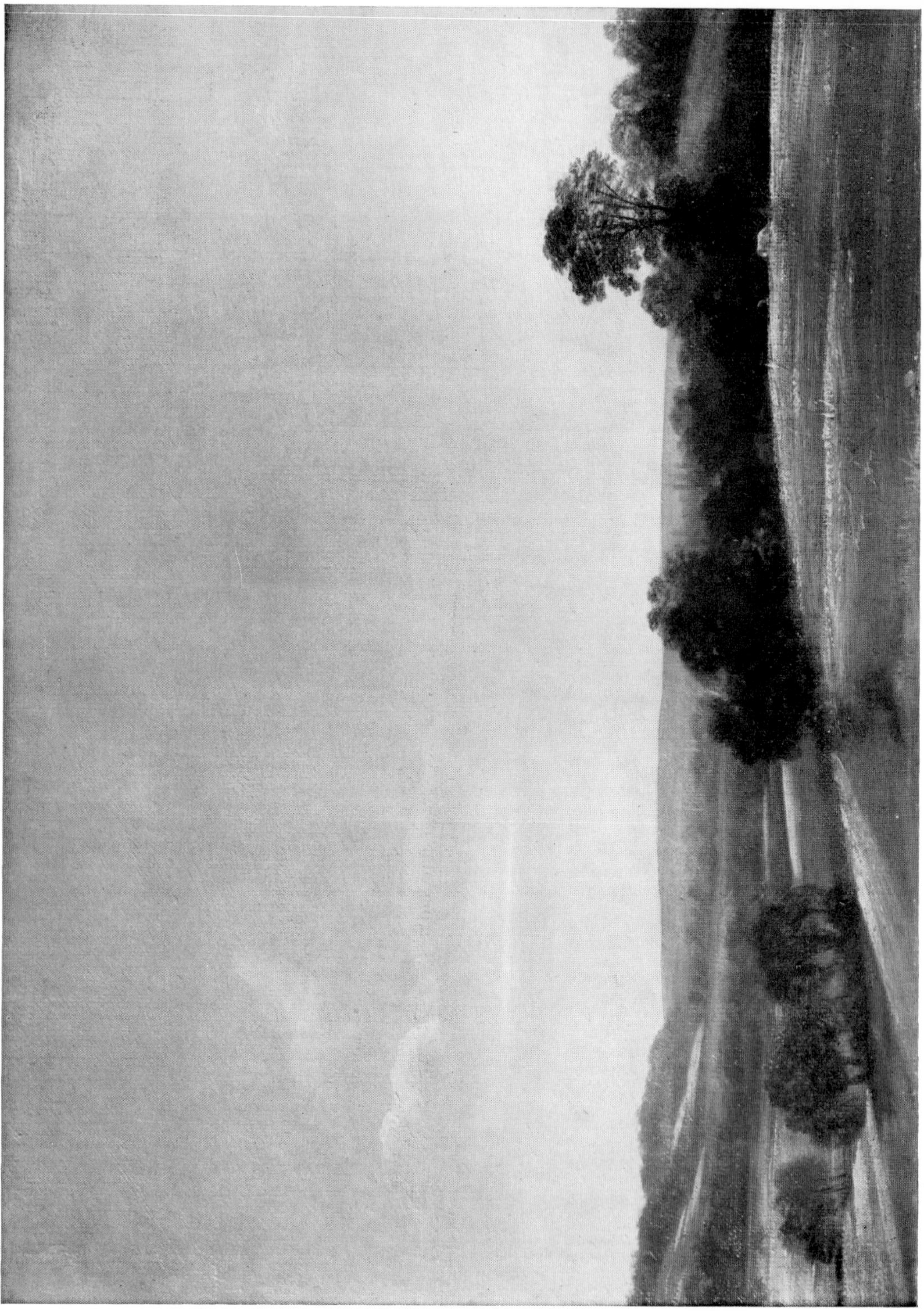

36. Dedham Vale: evening.

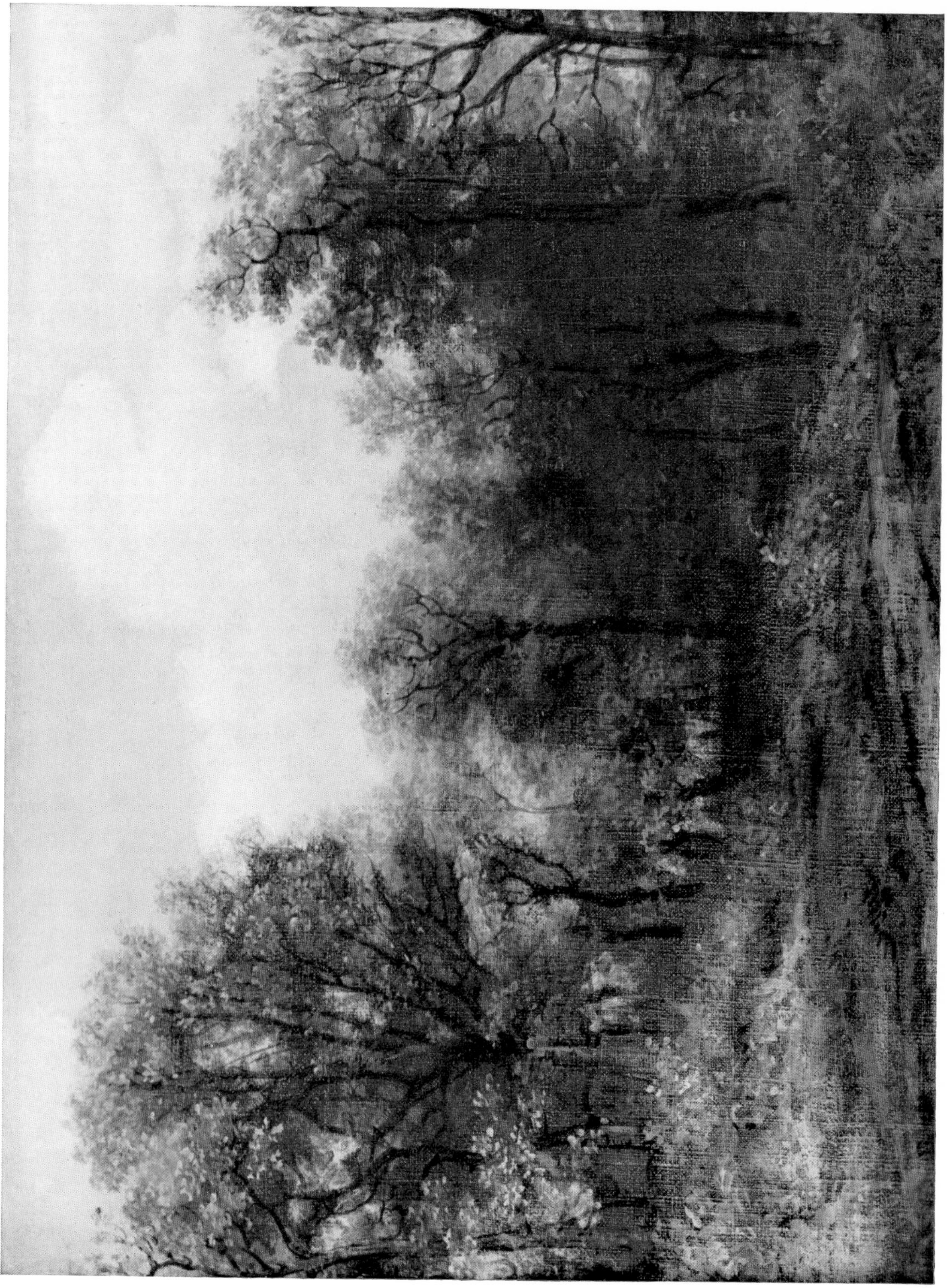

40. A wood.

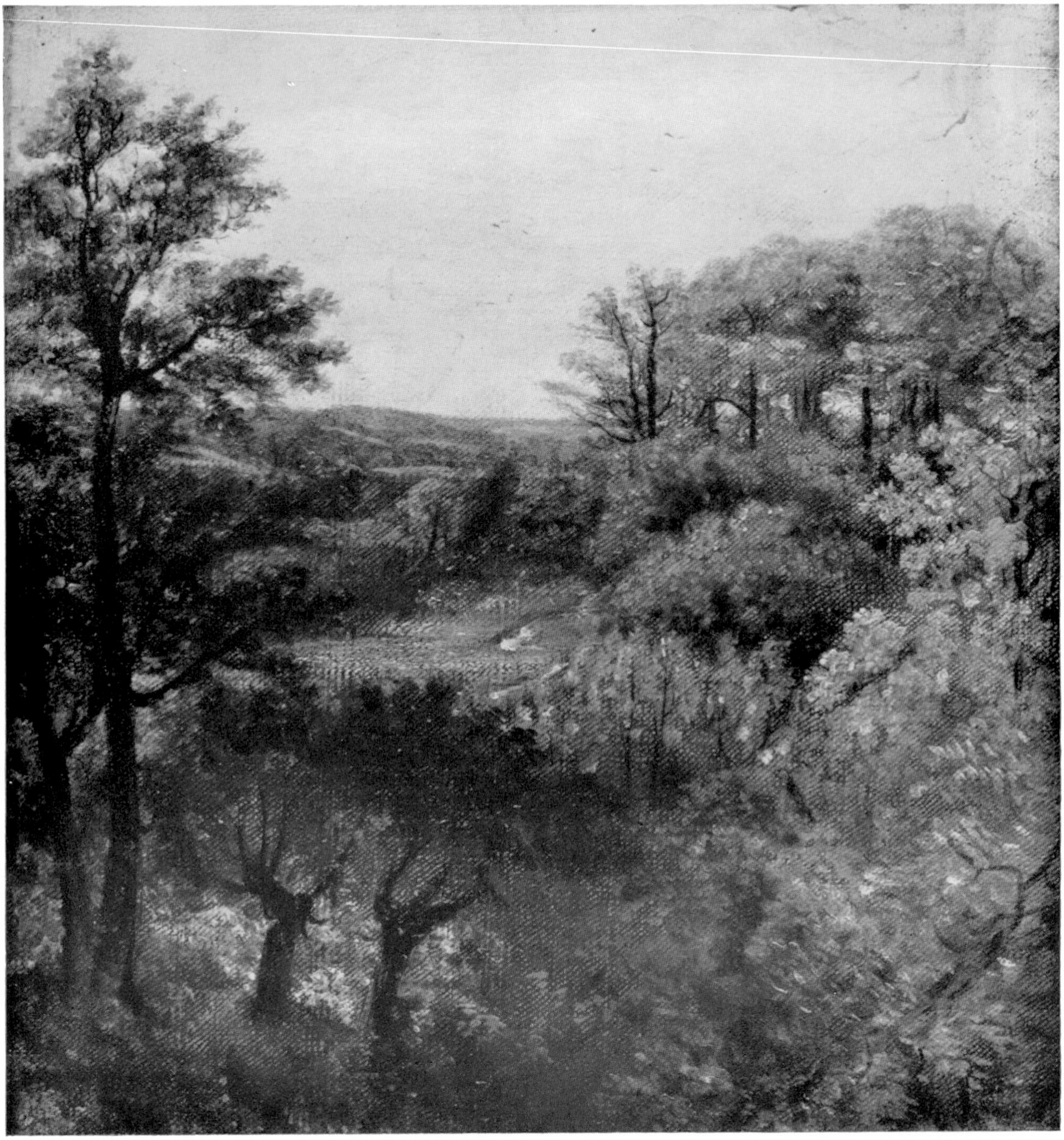

39. Valley scene, with trees.

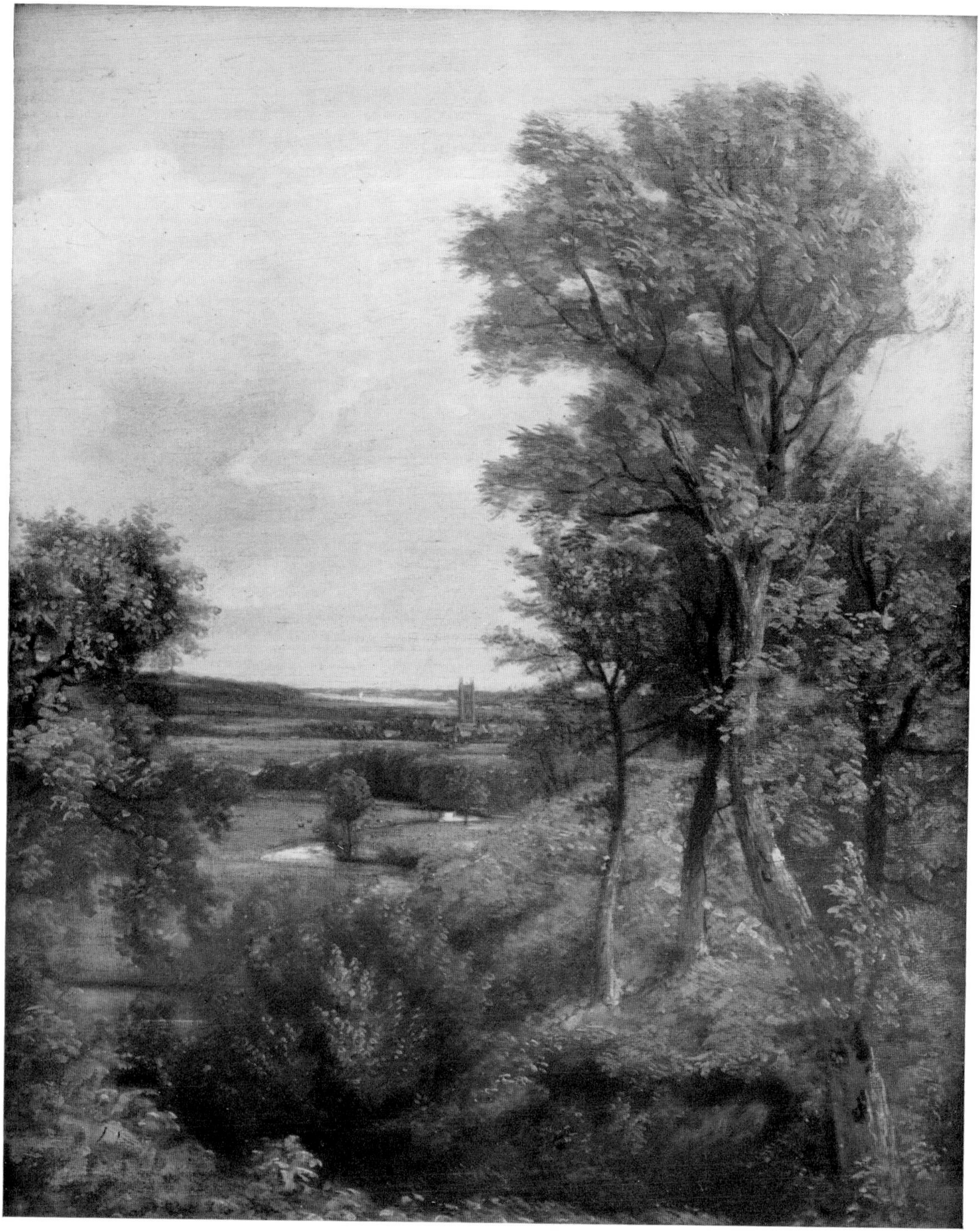

37. Dedham Vale.

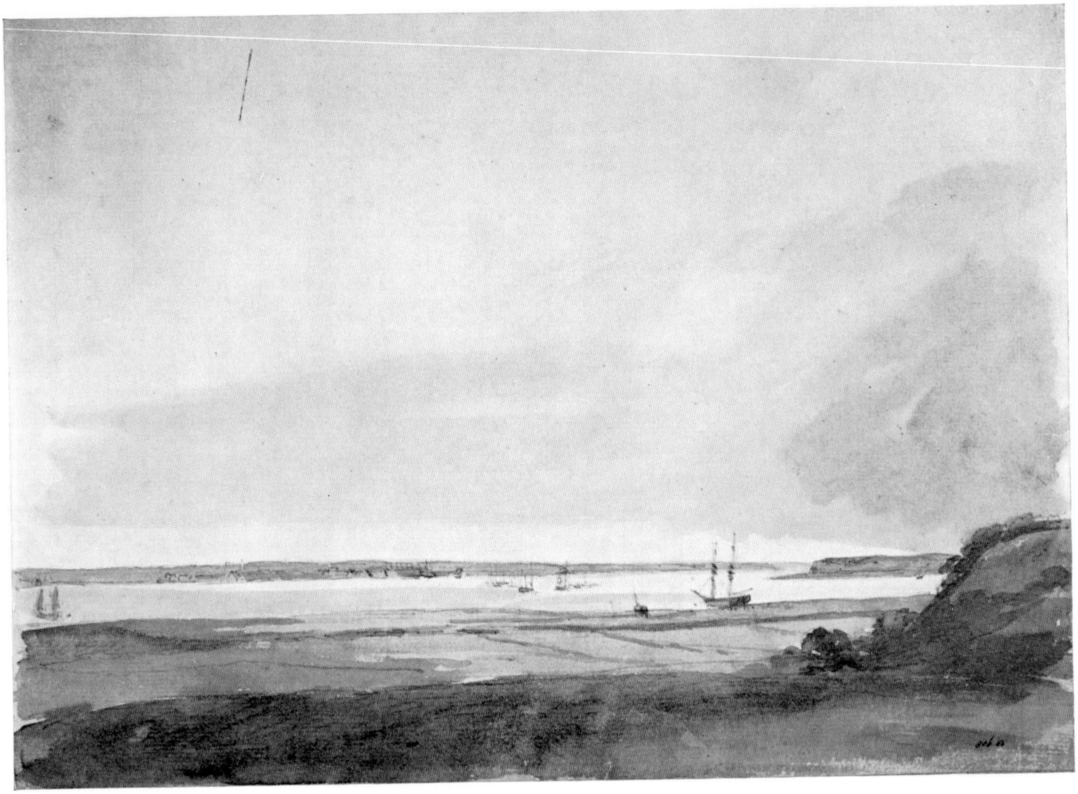

42. View over the Thames or Medway.

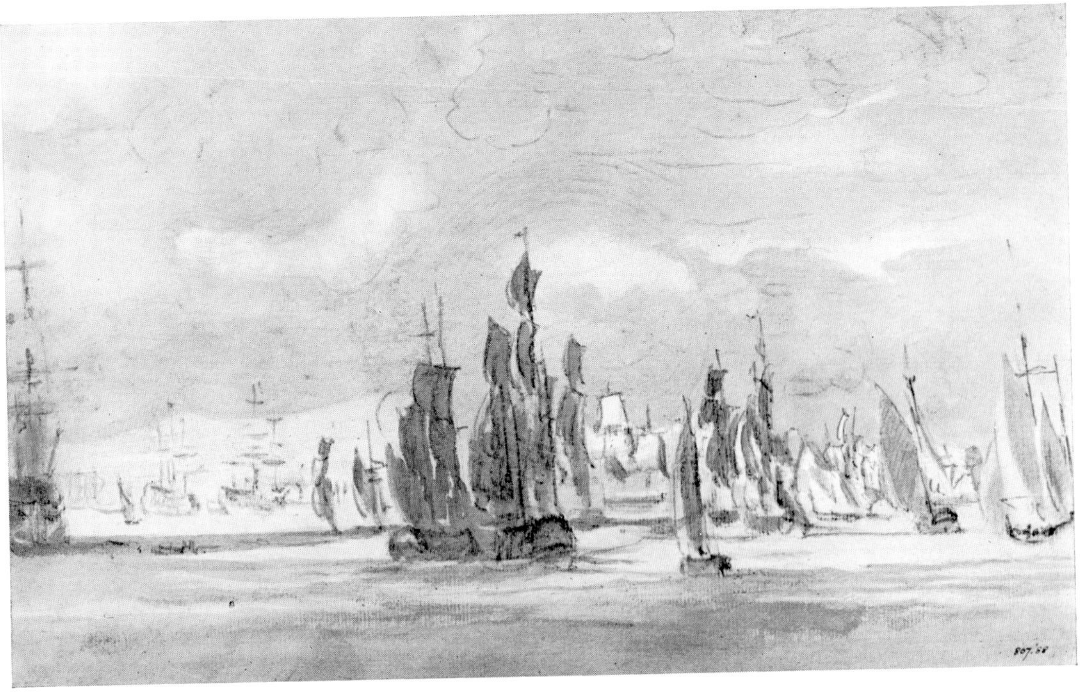

43. Shipping in the Thames.

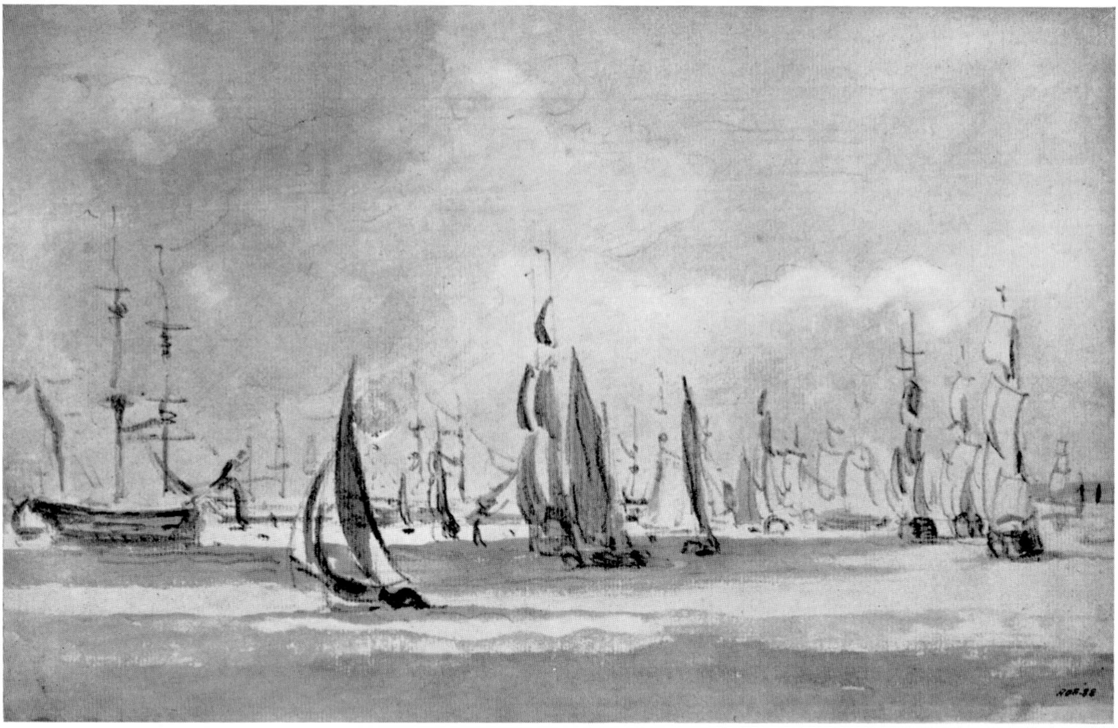

44. Shipping in the Thames.

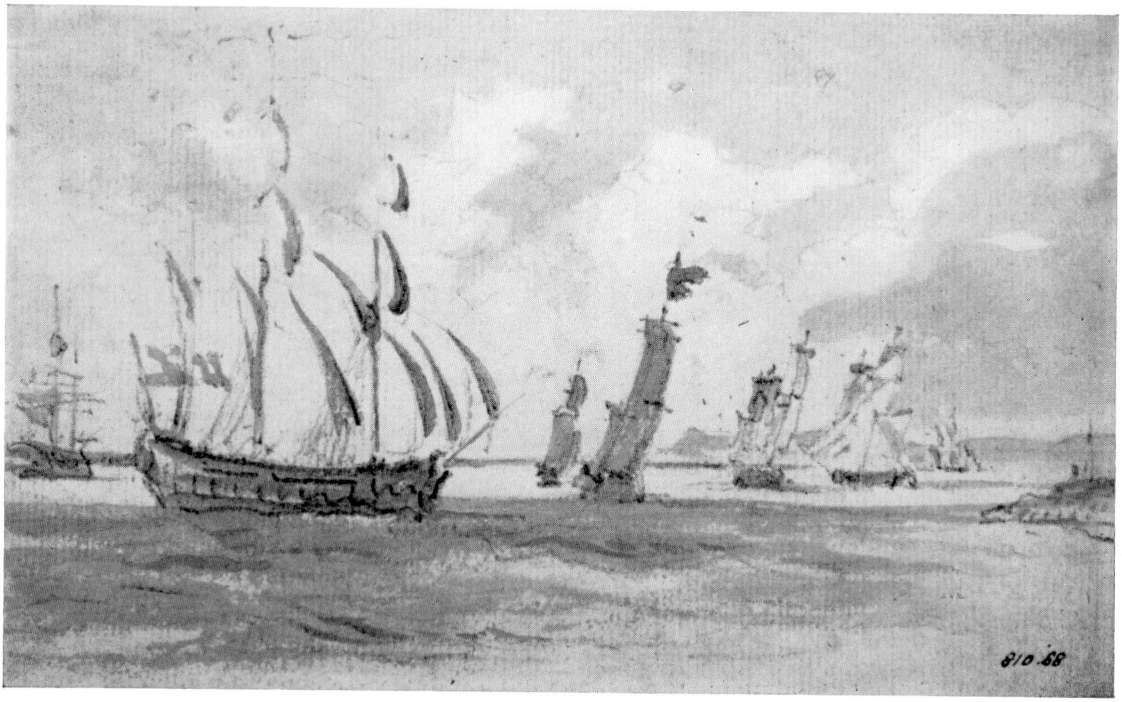

49. Shipping in the Thames or Medway.

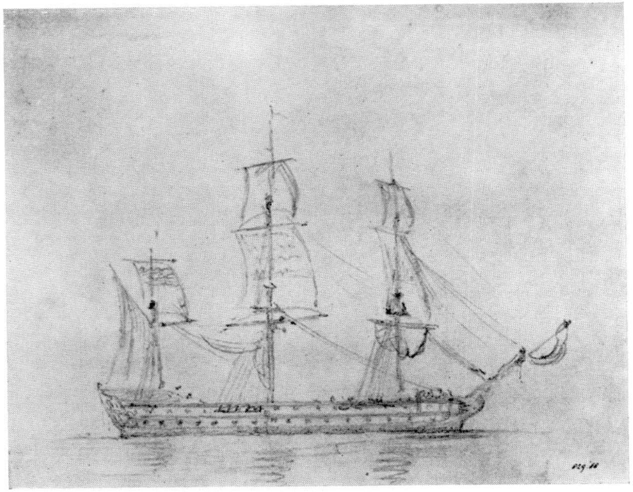

47. A man-of-war.

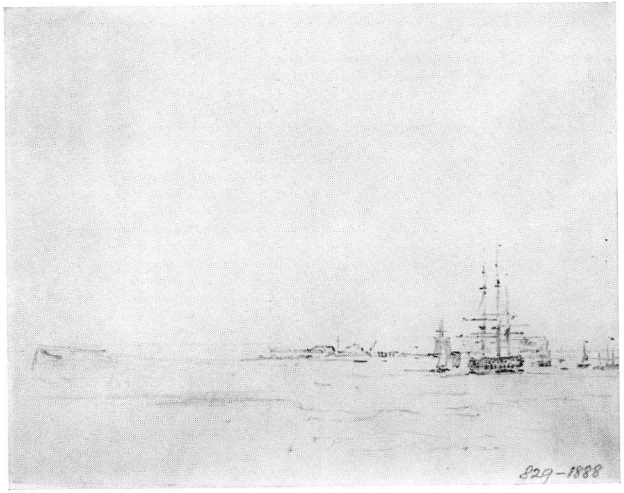

47a. A ship at anchor in the Medway.

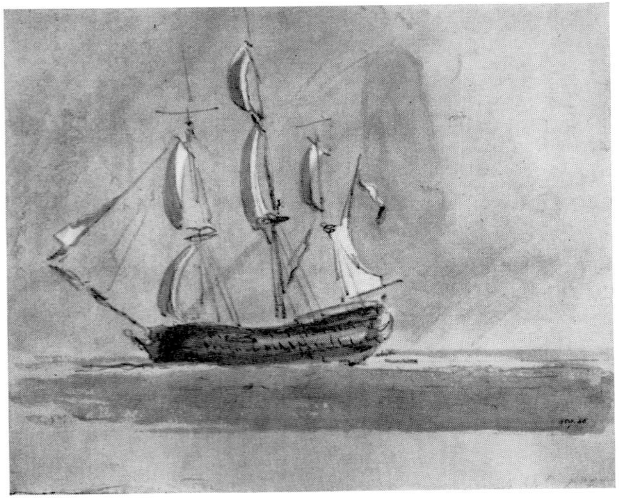

41. A ship under sail.

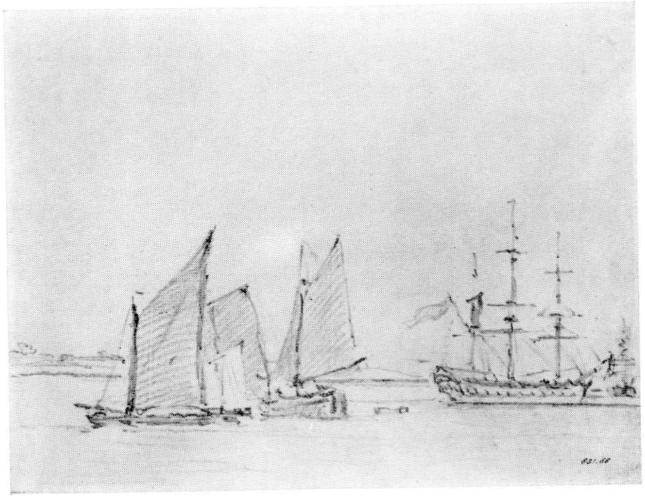

45. Shipping in the Thames.

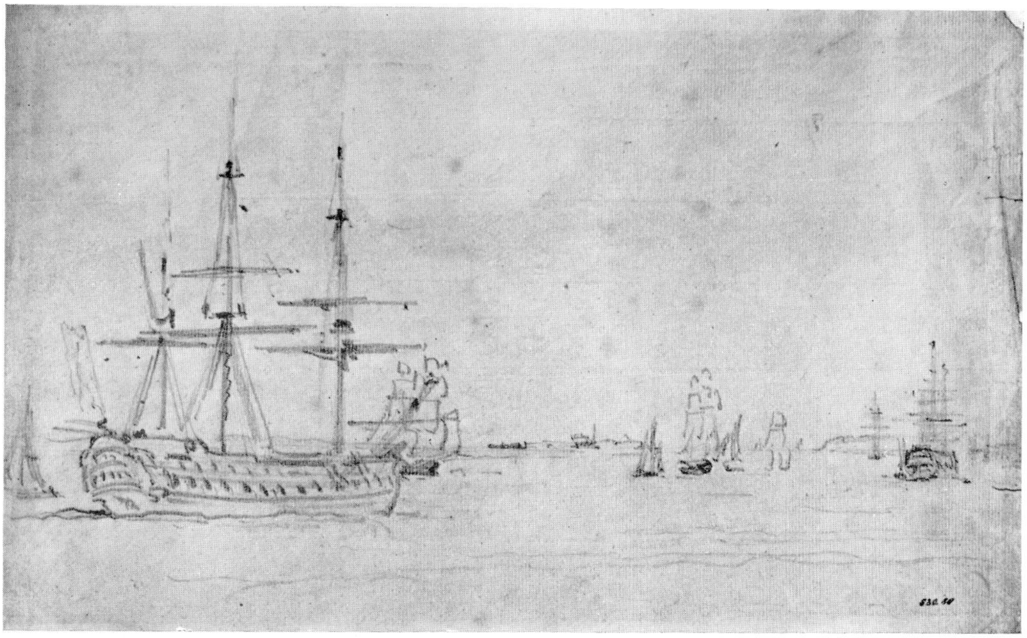

46. A ship at anchor and other shipping in the Thames.

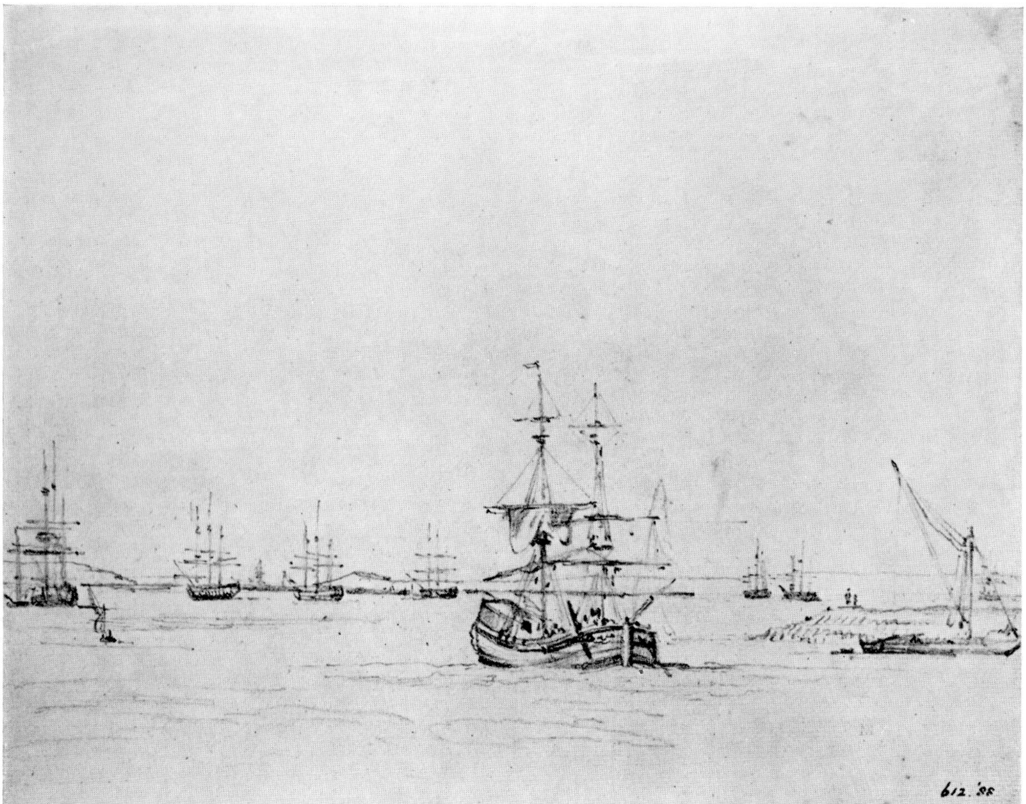

48. A brig at anchor and other shipping in the Thames.

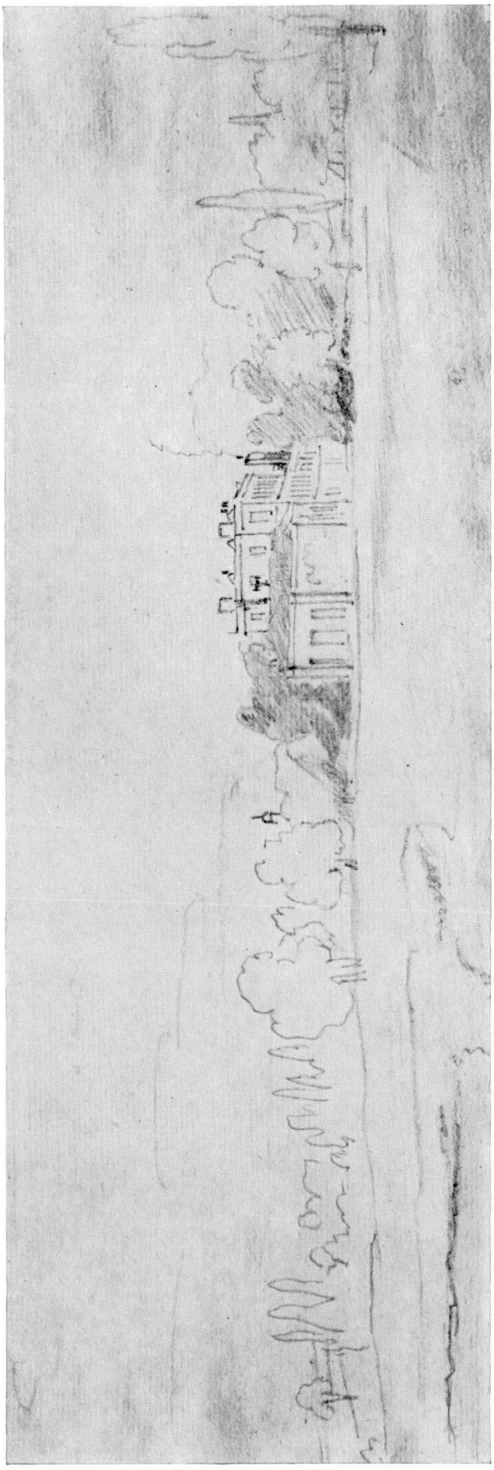

42a. Old Hall, East Bergholt.

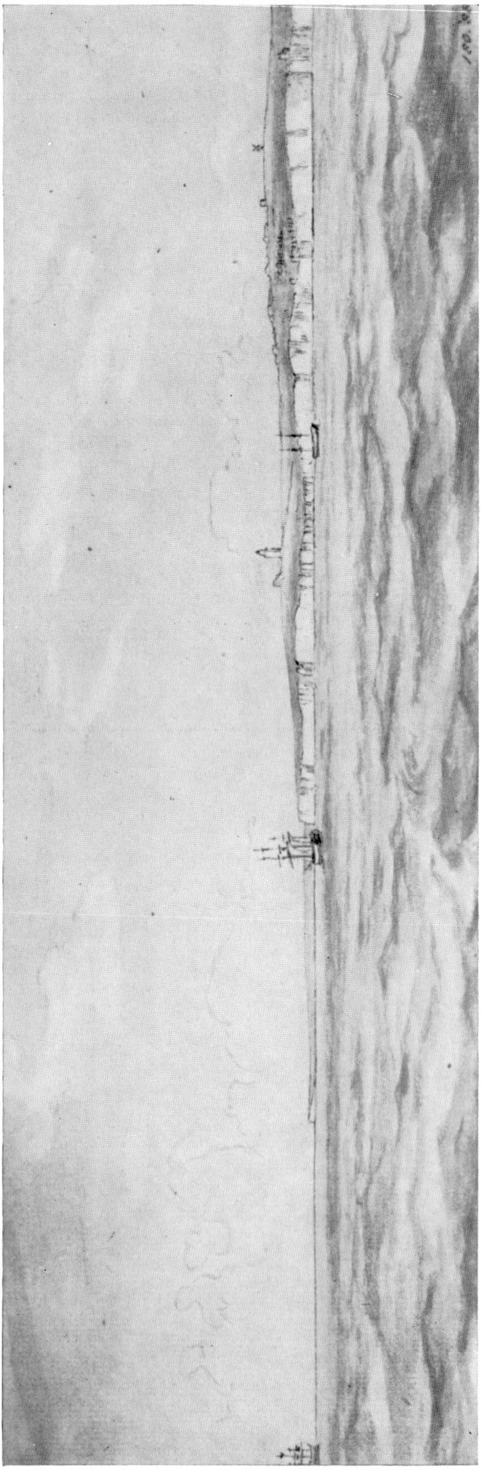

50. Off the North Foreland, Kent.

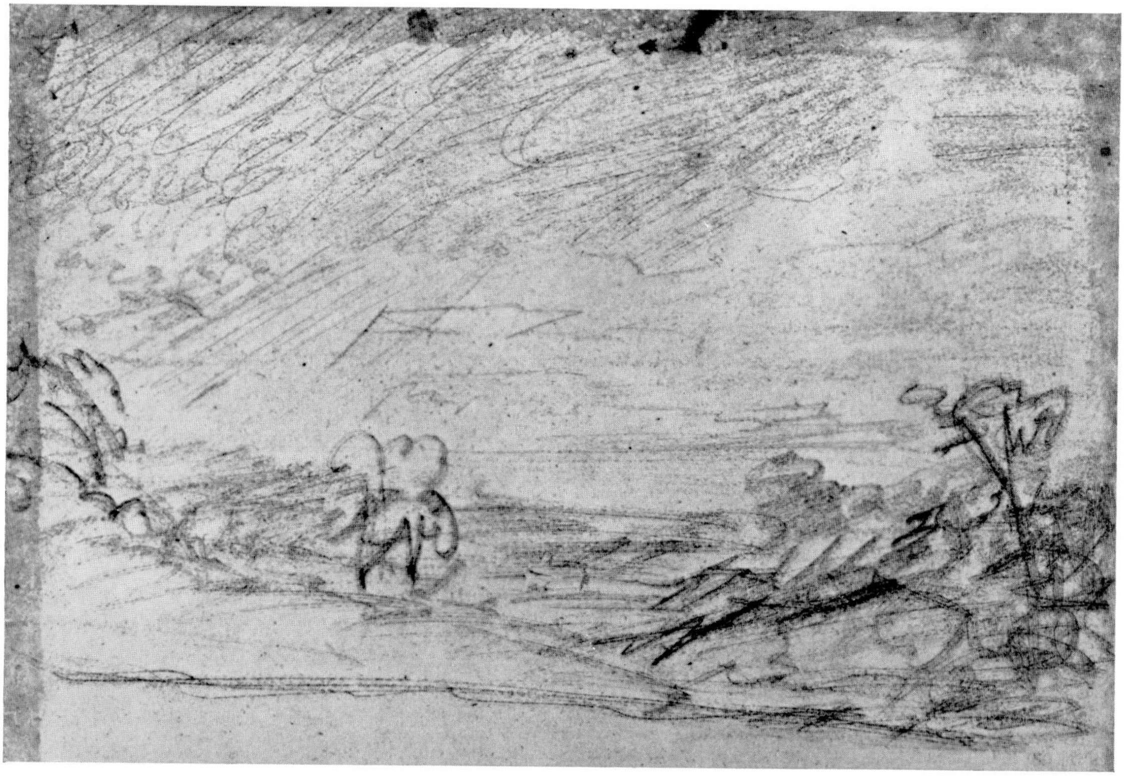

28a. A wooded landscape.

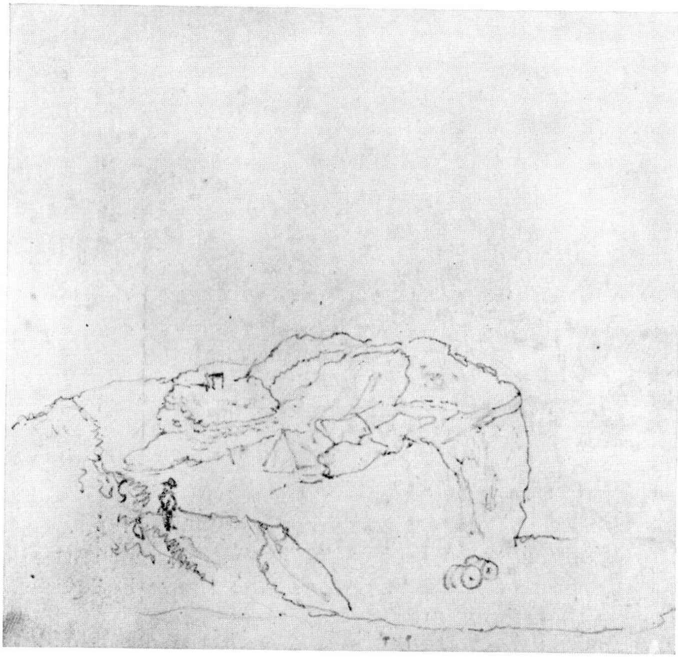

32a. A quarry for mill-stones, Derbyshire.

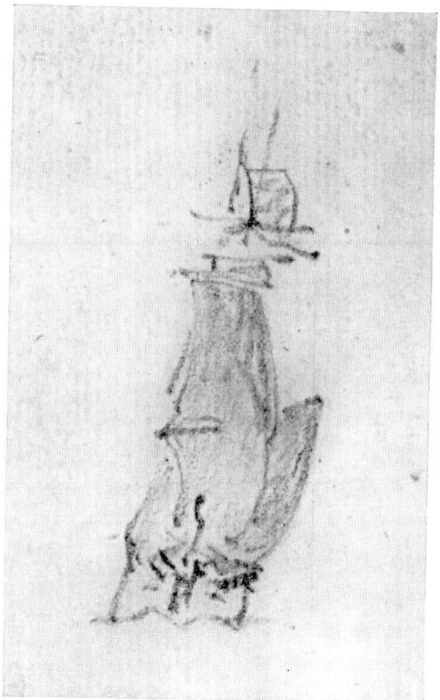

49a. A ship under sail.

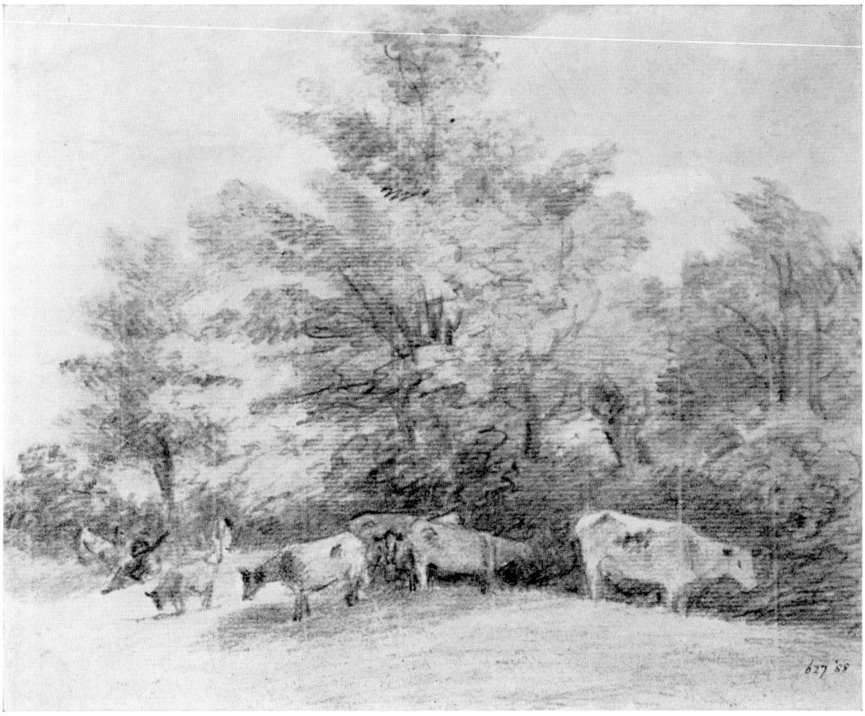

51. Landscape with cows and trees.

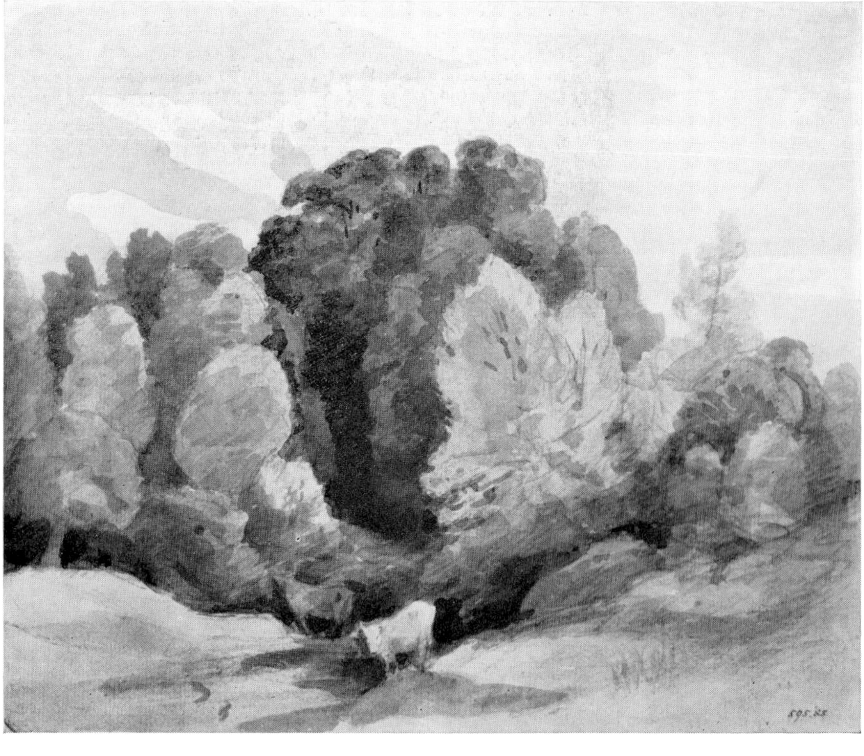

61. Cattle near the edge of a wood.

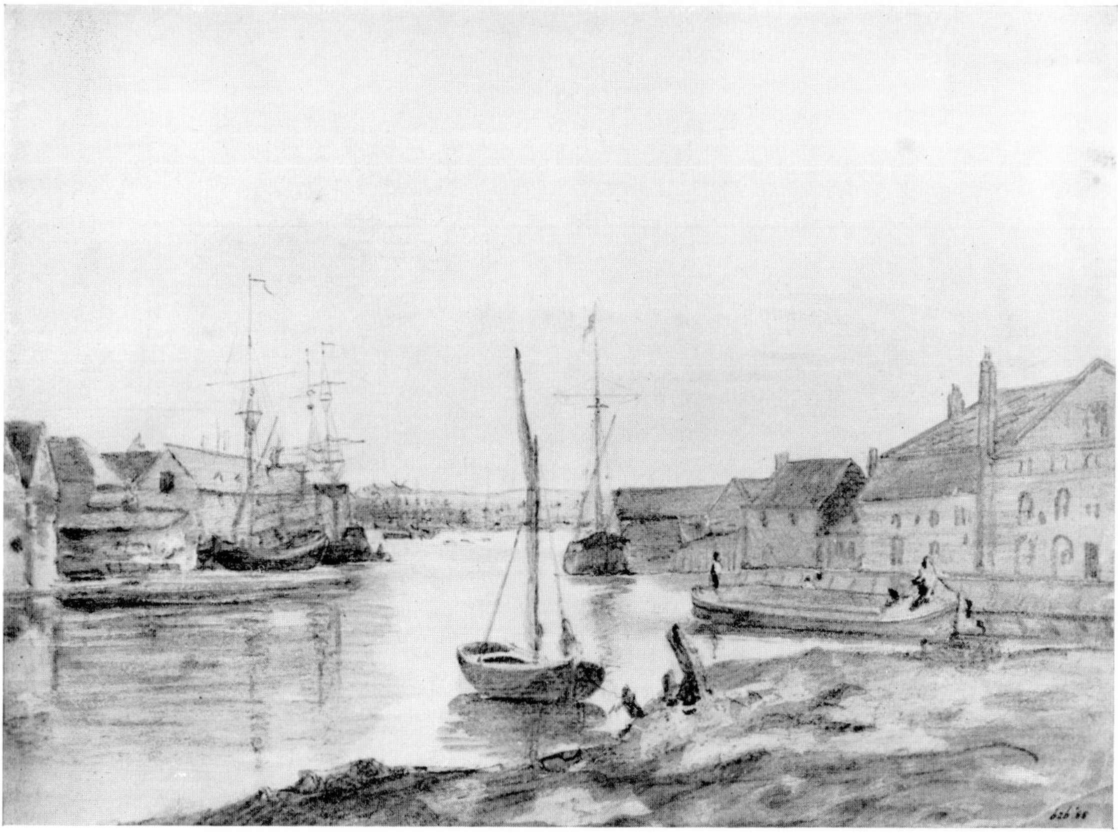

52. Warehouses and shipping on the Orwell at Ipswich.

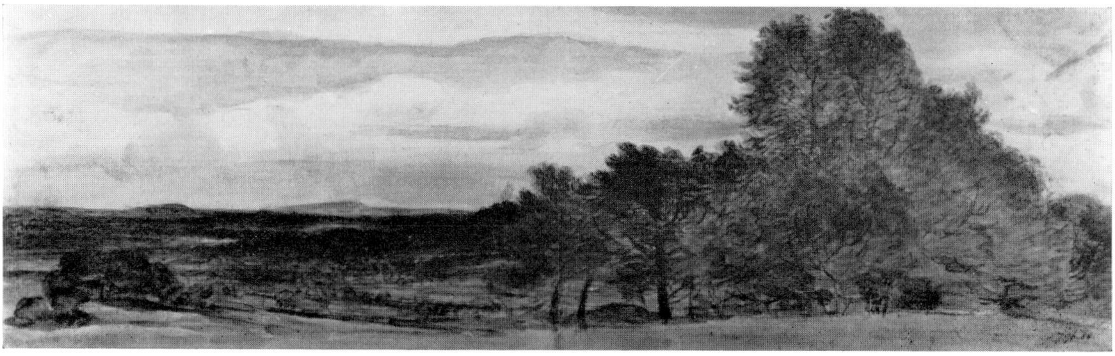

53. View at Hursley.

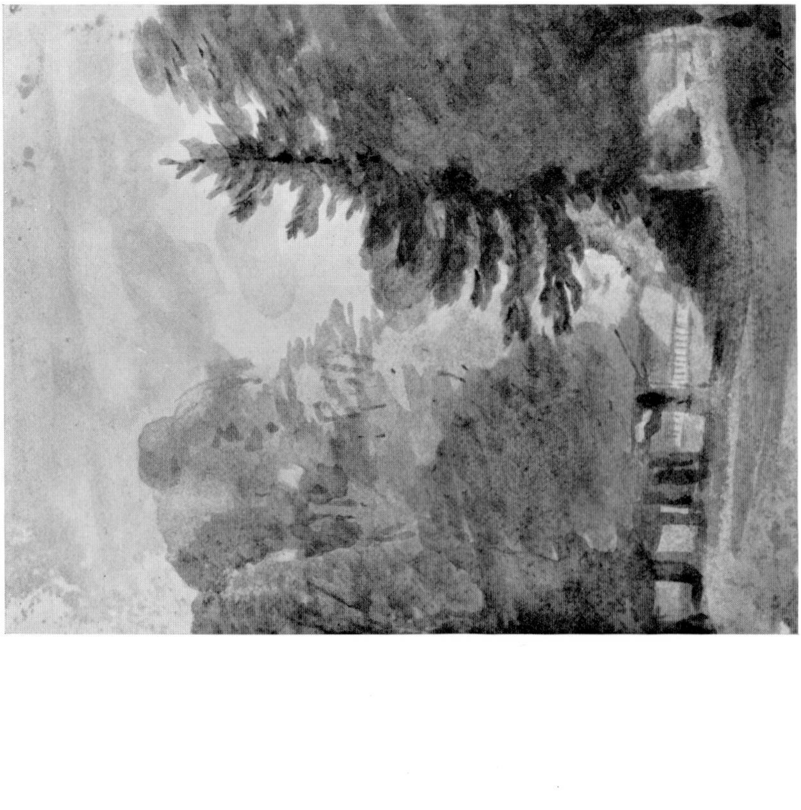

54. Trees, perhaps in Helmingham Park.

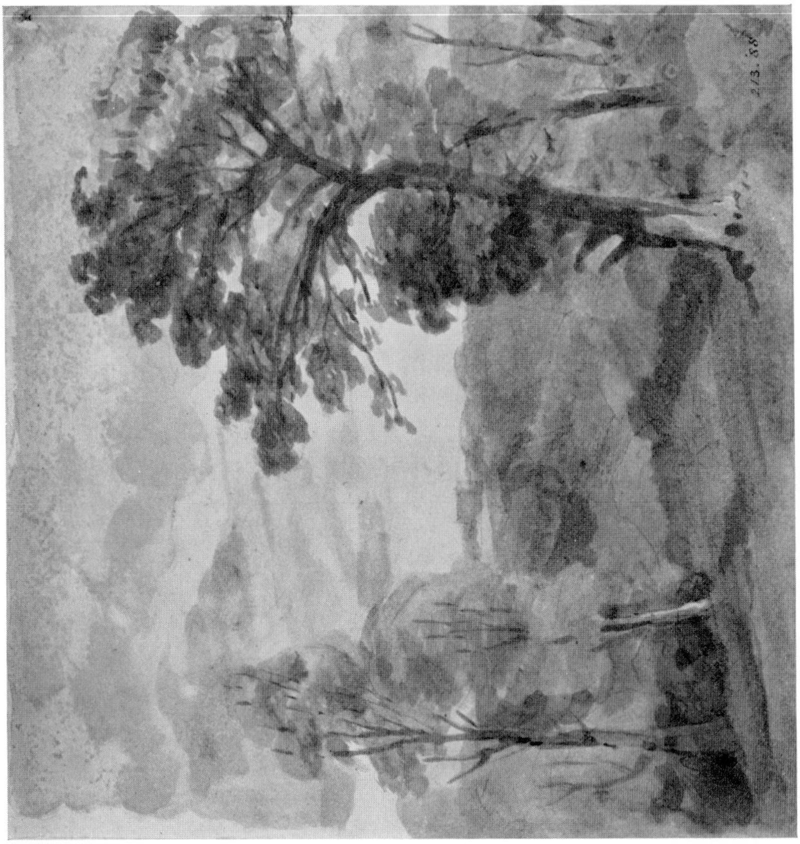

55. Landscape with trees and a distant mansion.

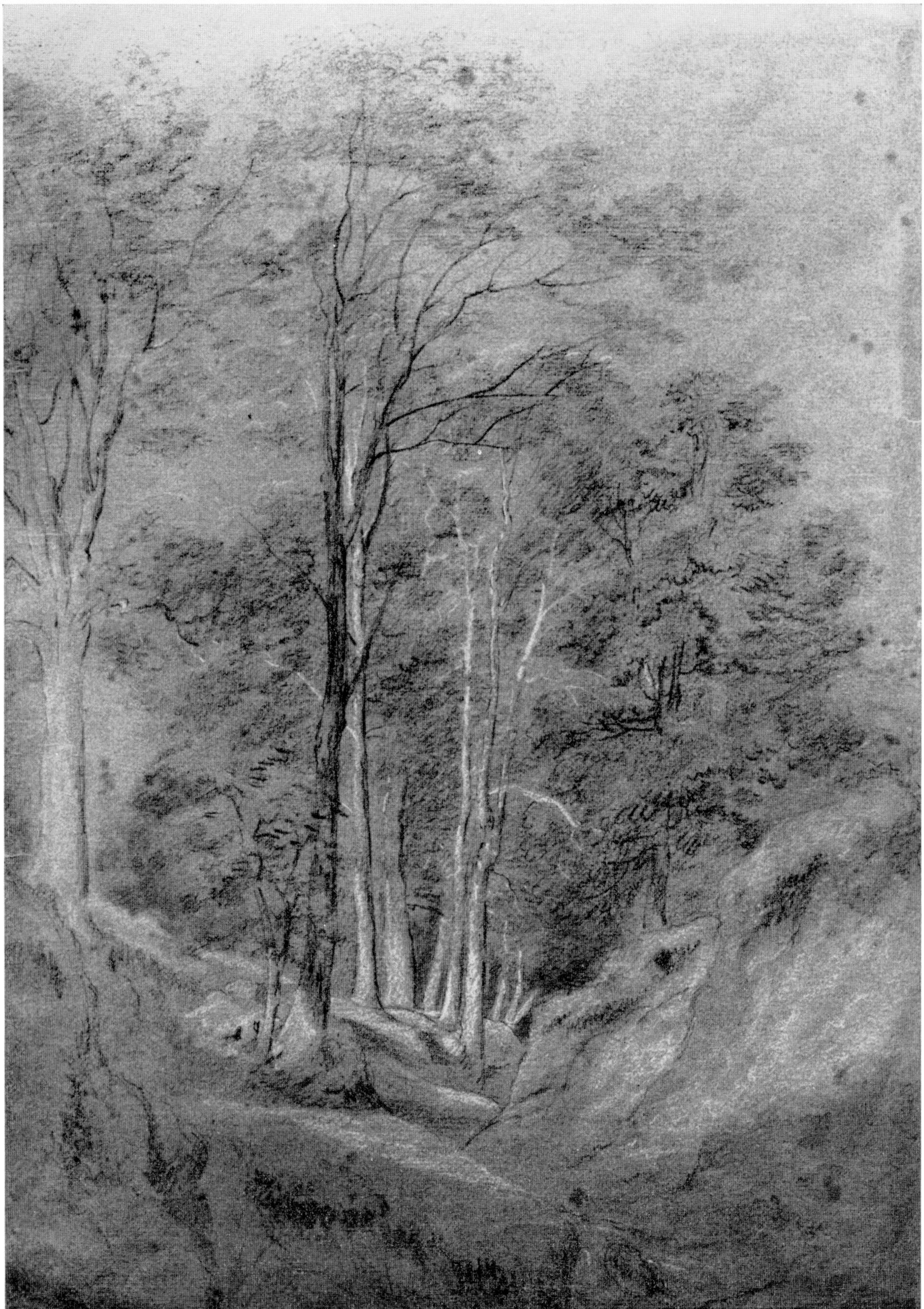

57. Study of ash and other trees.

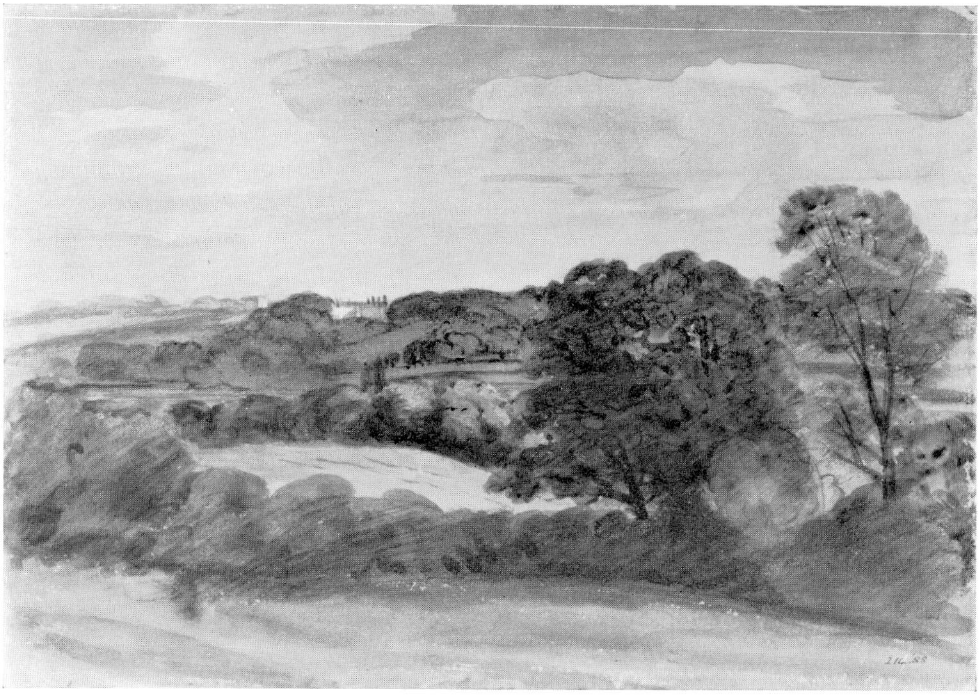

58. Landscape with buildings in the distance.

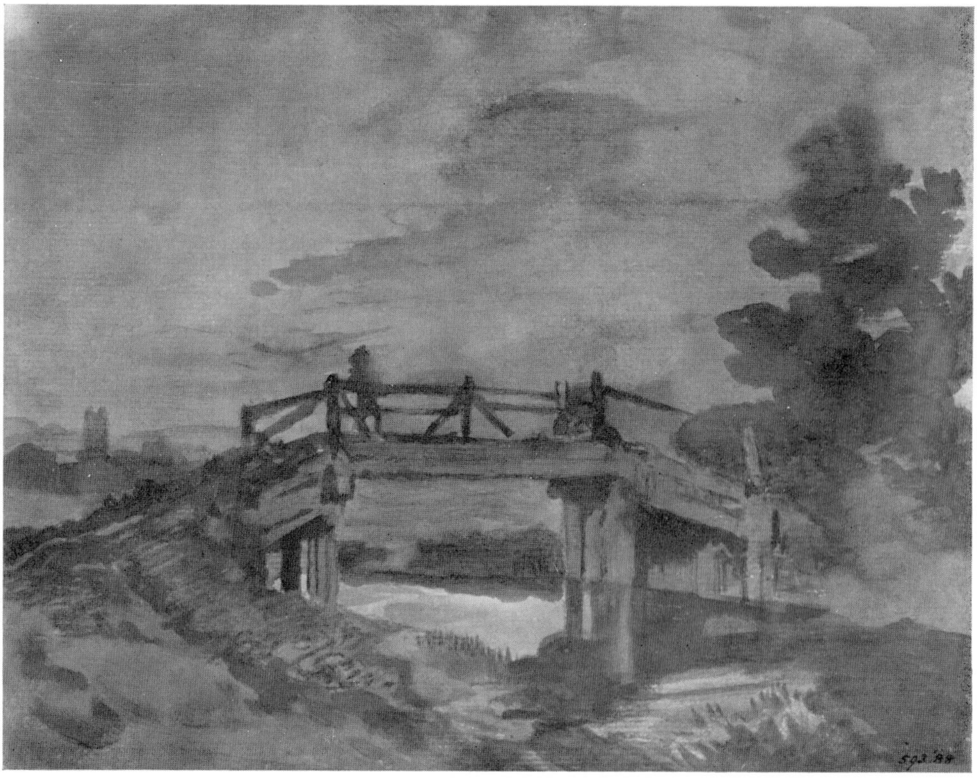

59. The New Fen Bridge over the Stour.

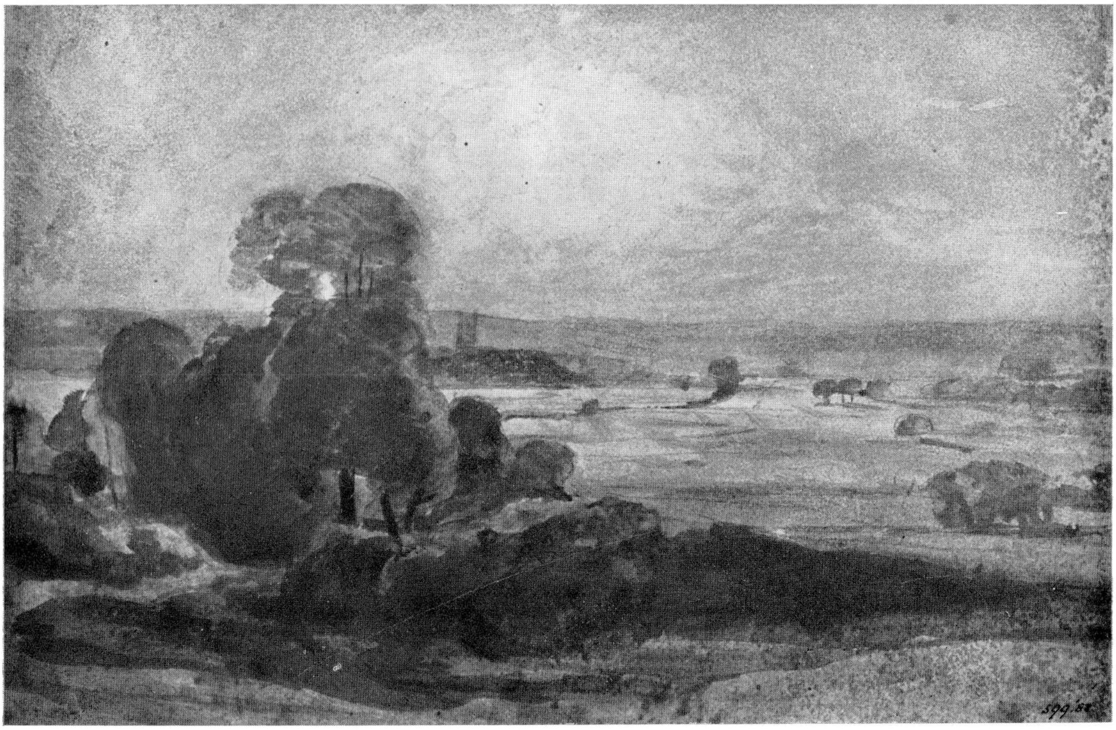

56. Dedham Vale.

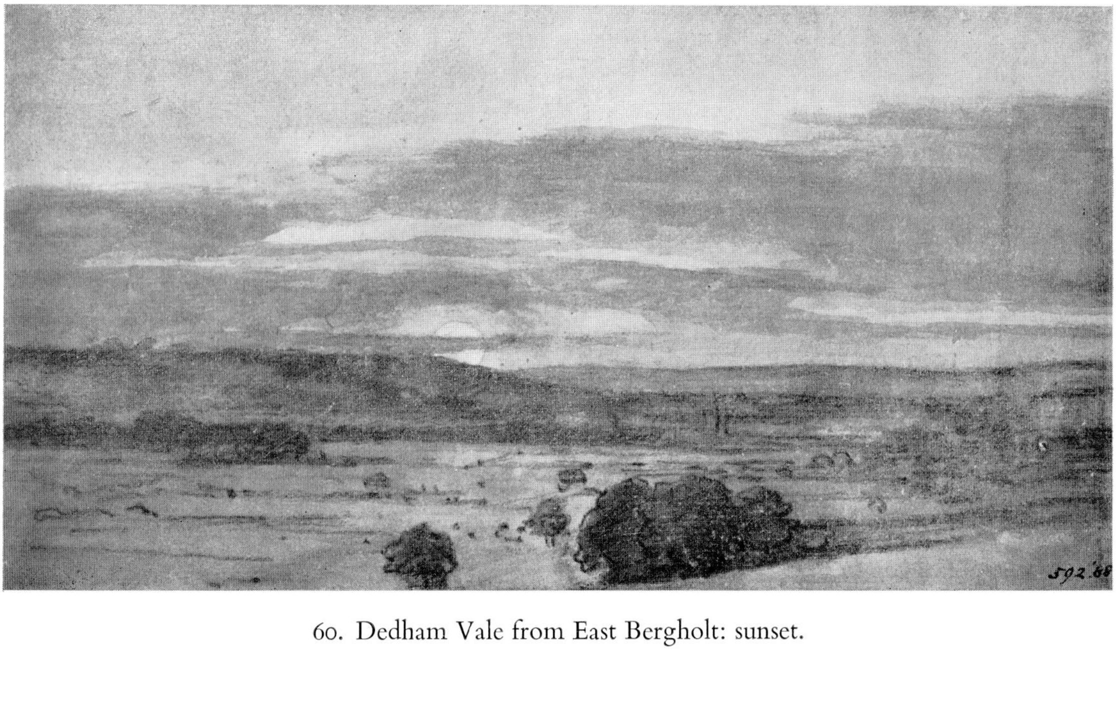

60. Dedham Vale from East Bergholt: sunset.

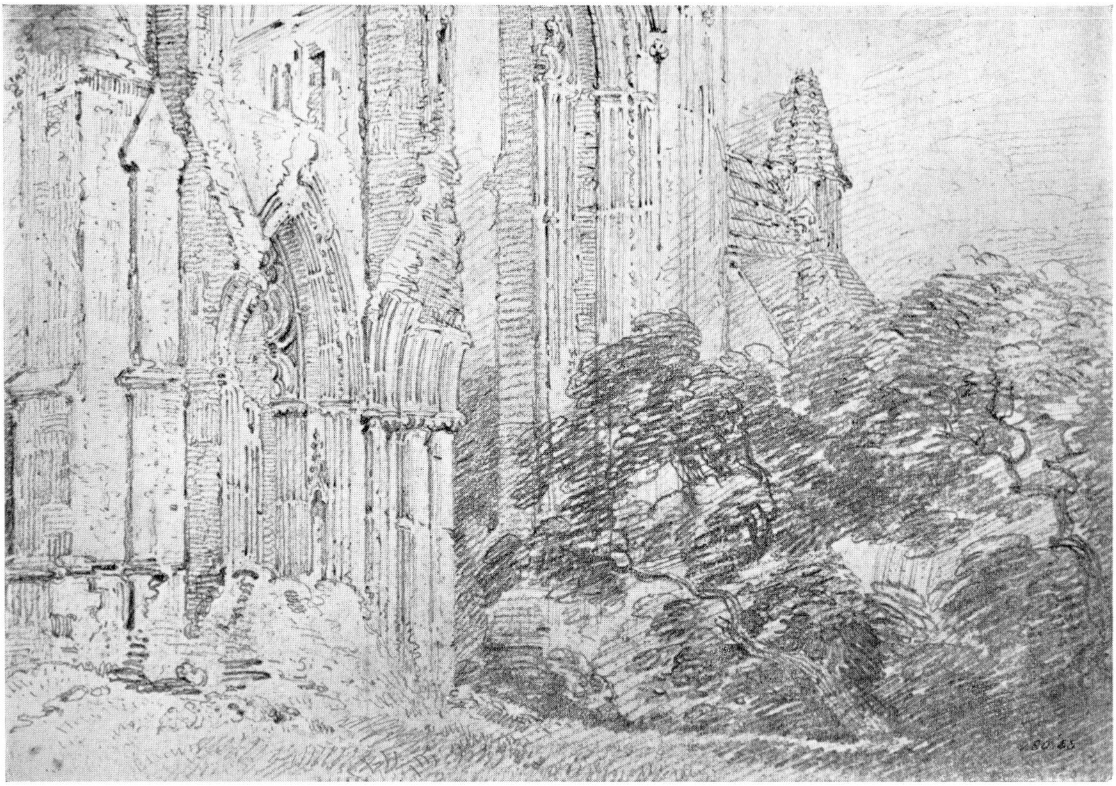

62. Ruins of a church.

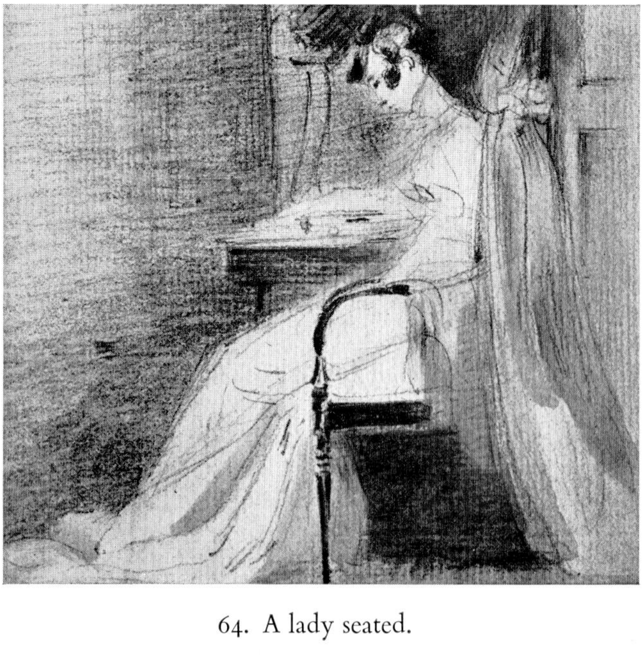

64. A lady seated.

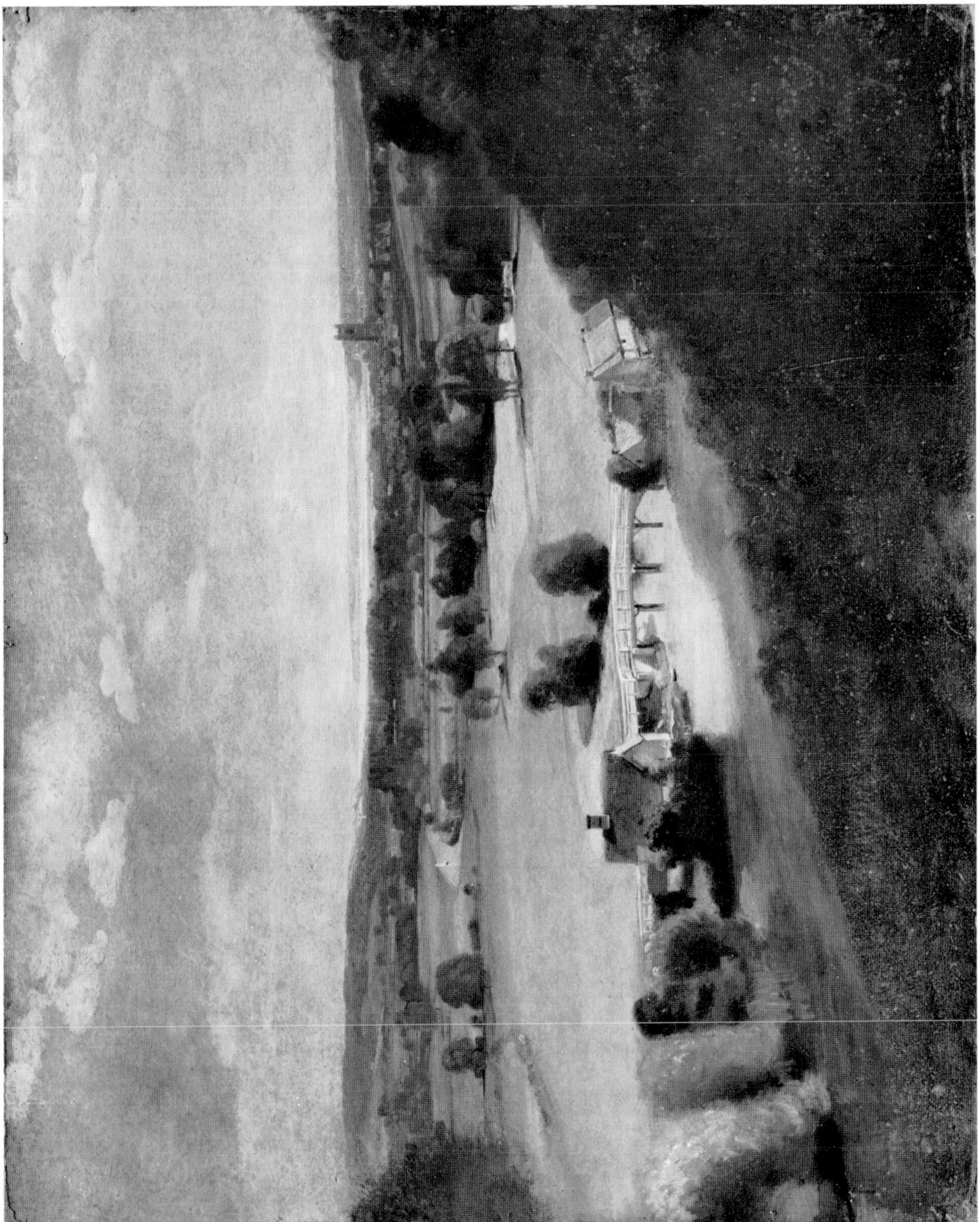

63. The valley of the Stour, with Dedham in the distance.

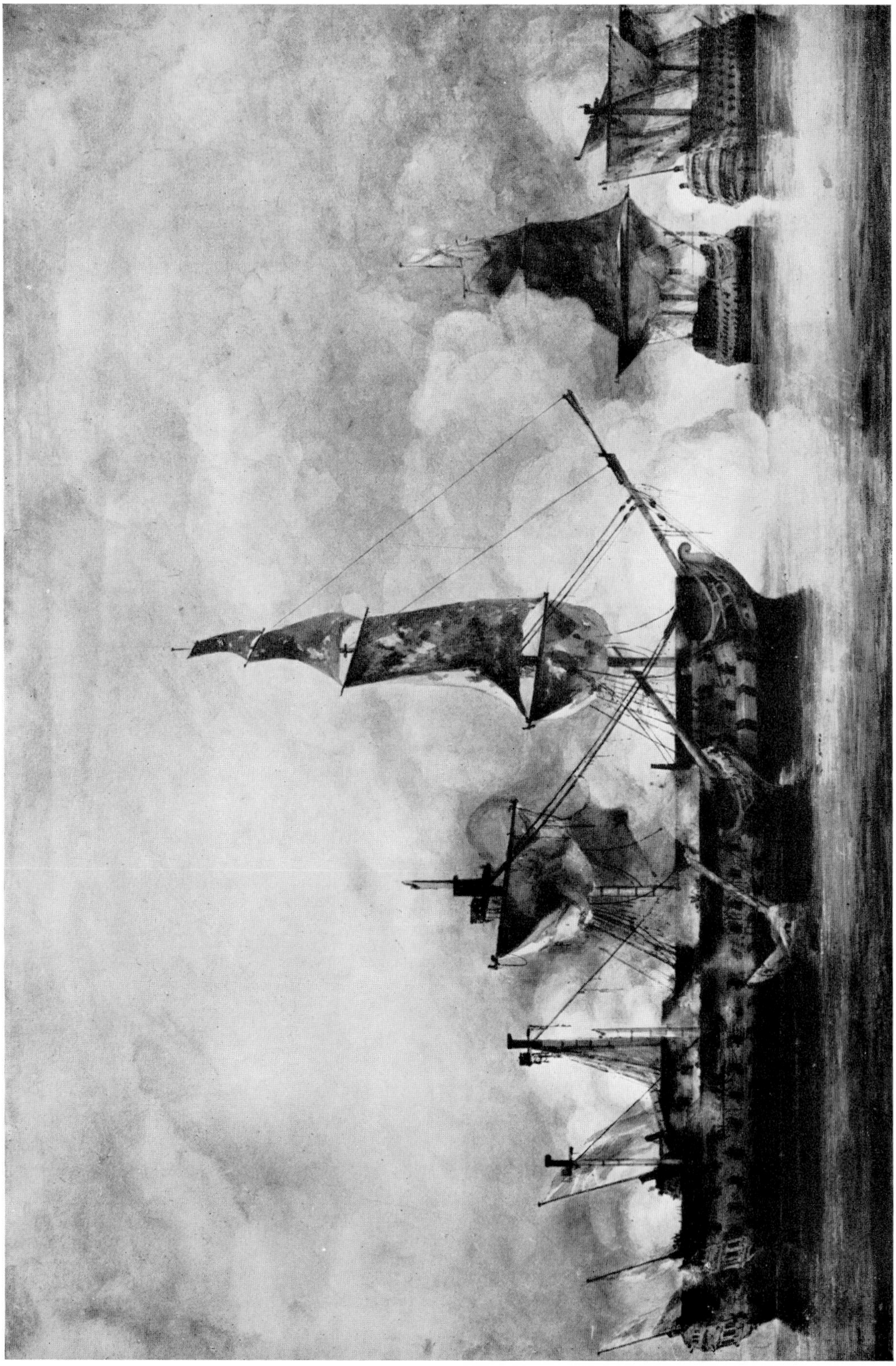

65. H.M.S. *Victory* in the battle of Trafalgar.

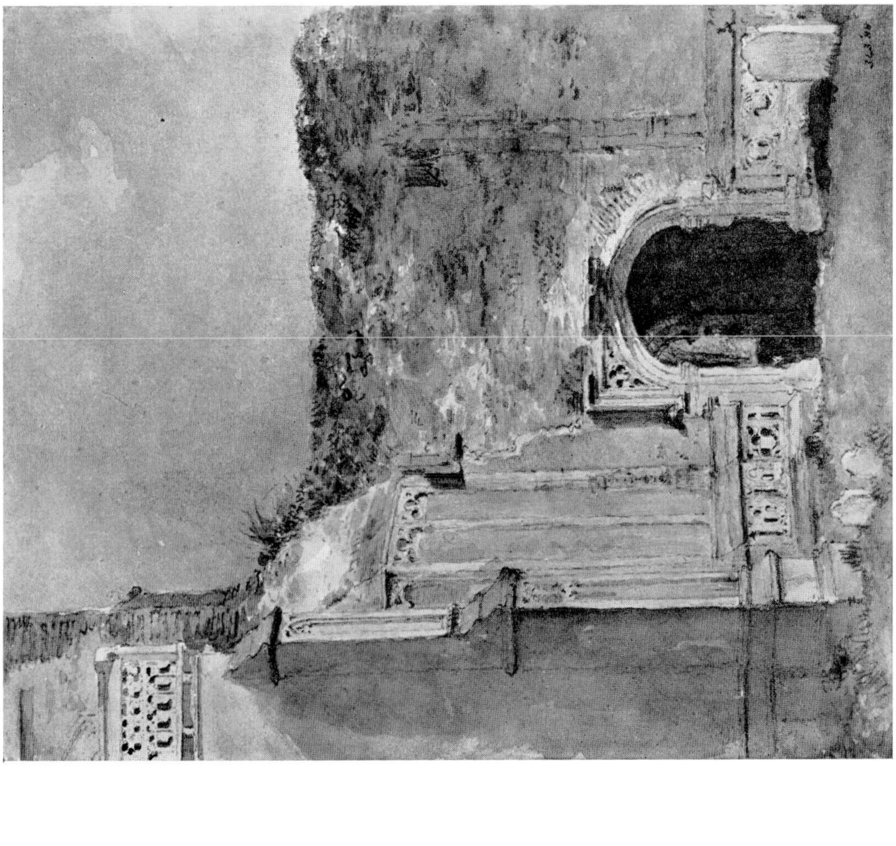

68. East Bergholt Church: ruined tower.

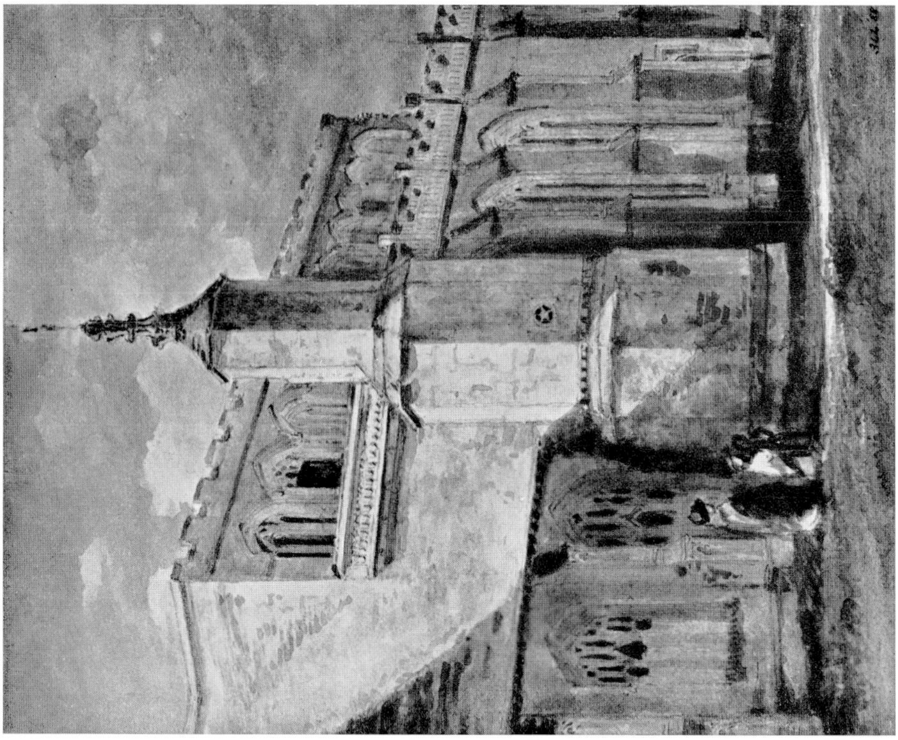

69. East Bergholt Church: N. side.

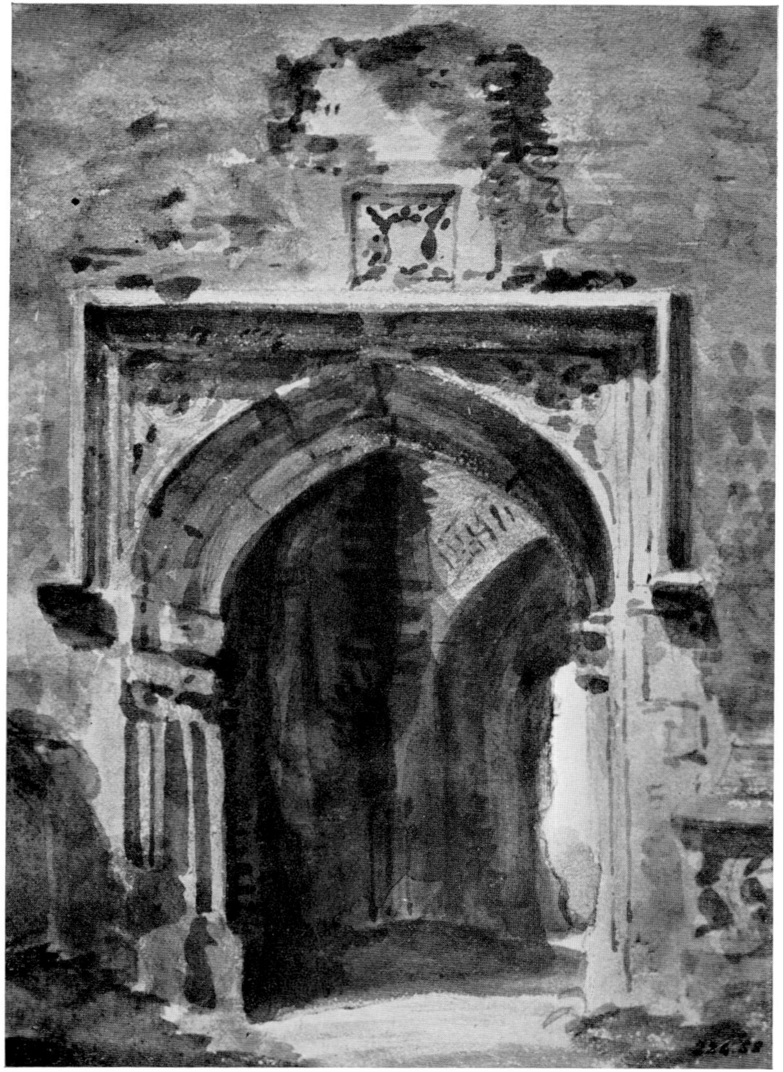

66. East Bergholt Church: S. archway of ruined tower.

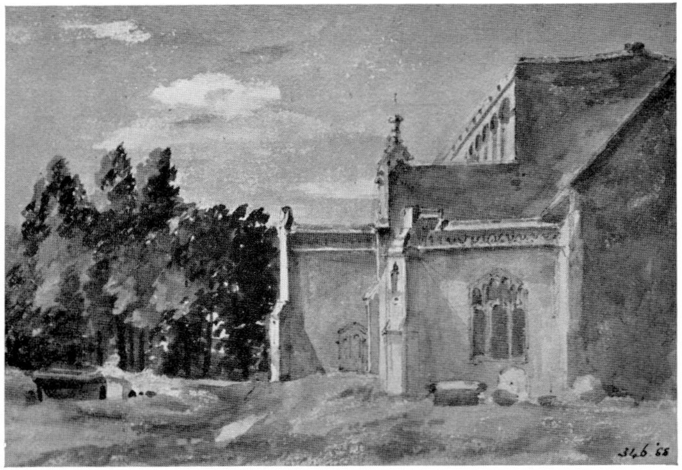

67. East Bergholt Church from the E.

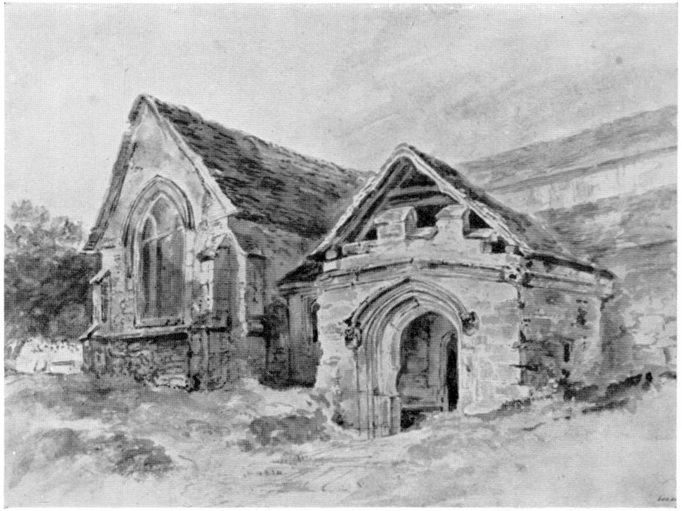

71. Porch and transept of a church.

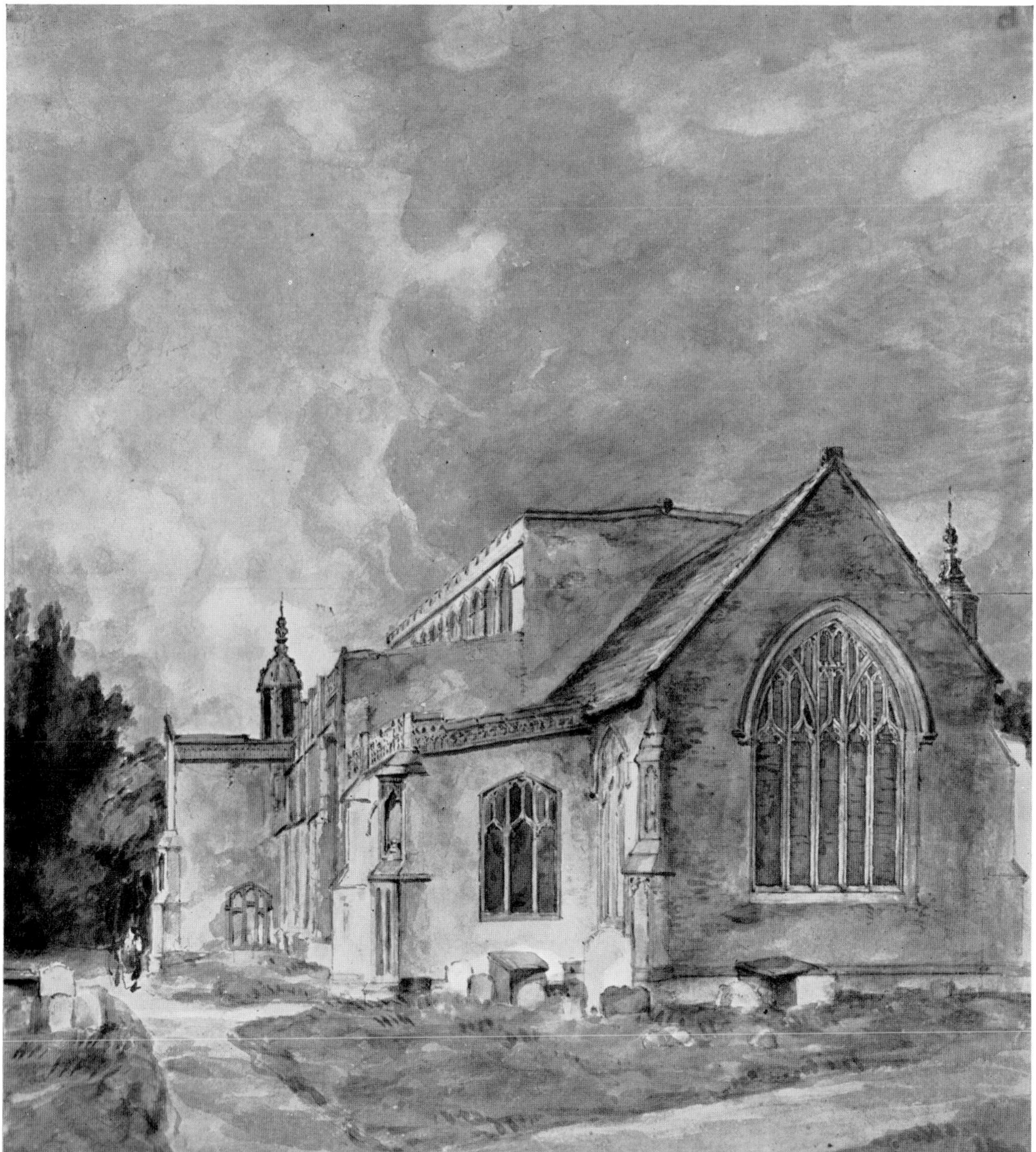

70. East Bergholt Church from the E.

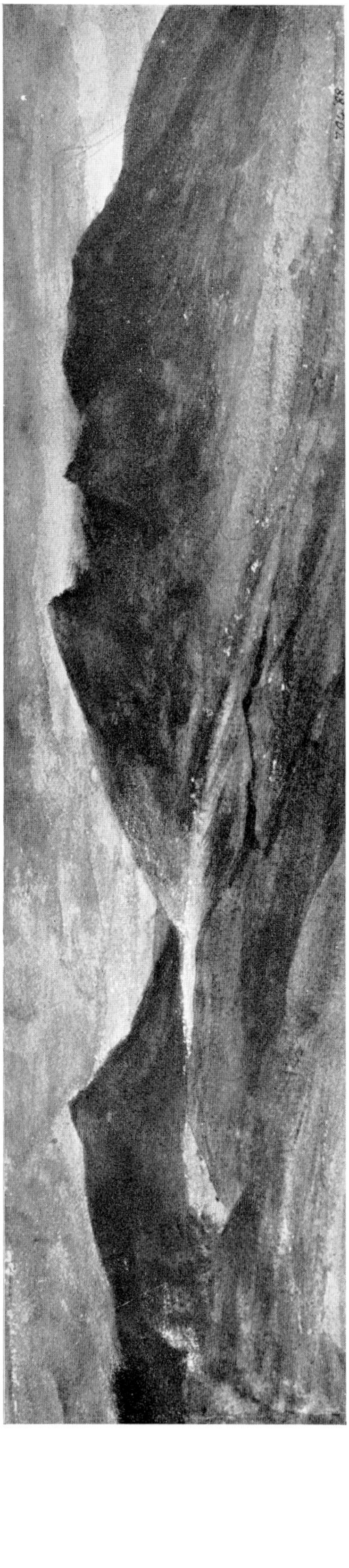

72. Saddleback and part of Skiddaw.

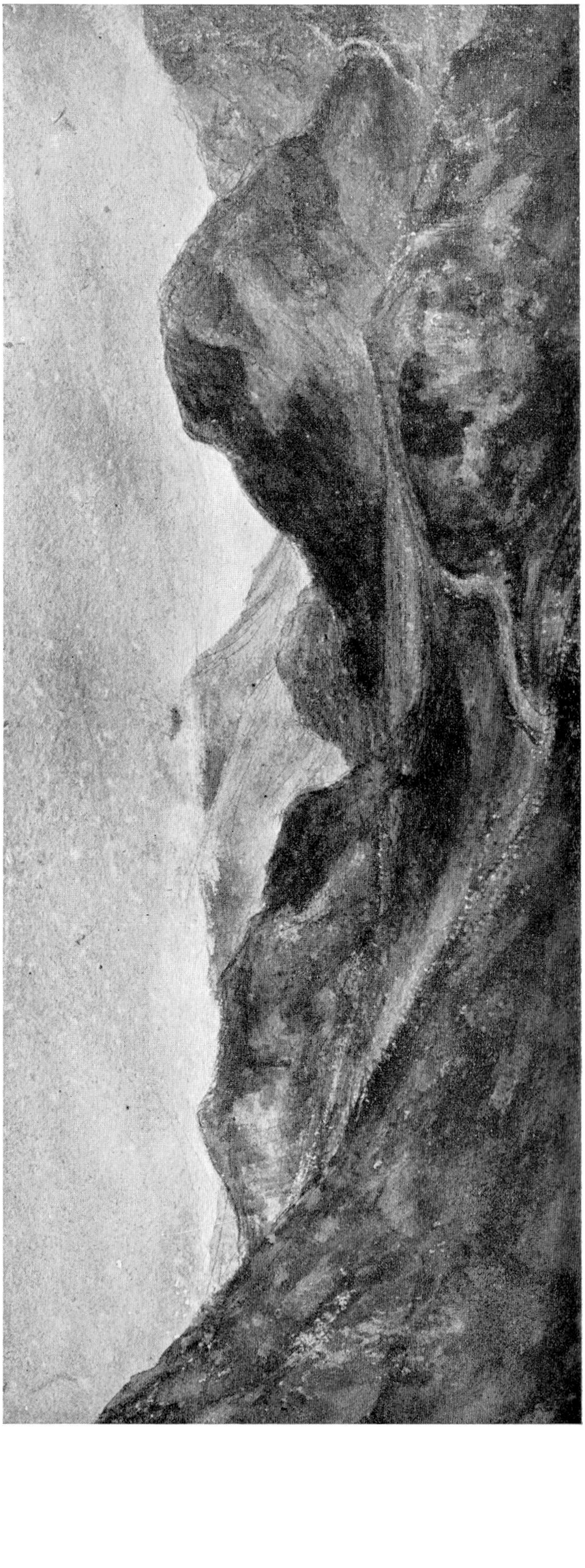

73. Helvellyn.

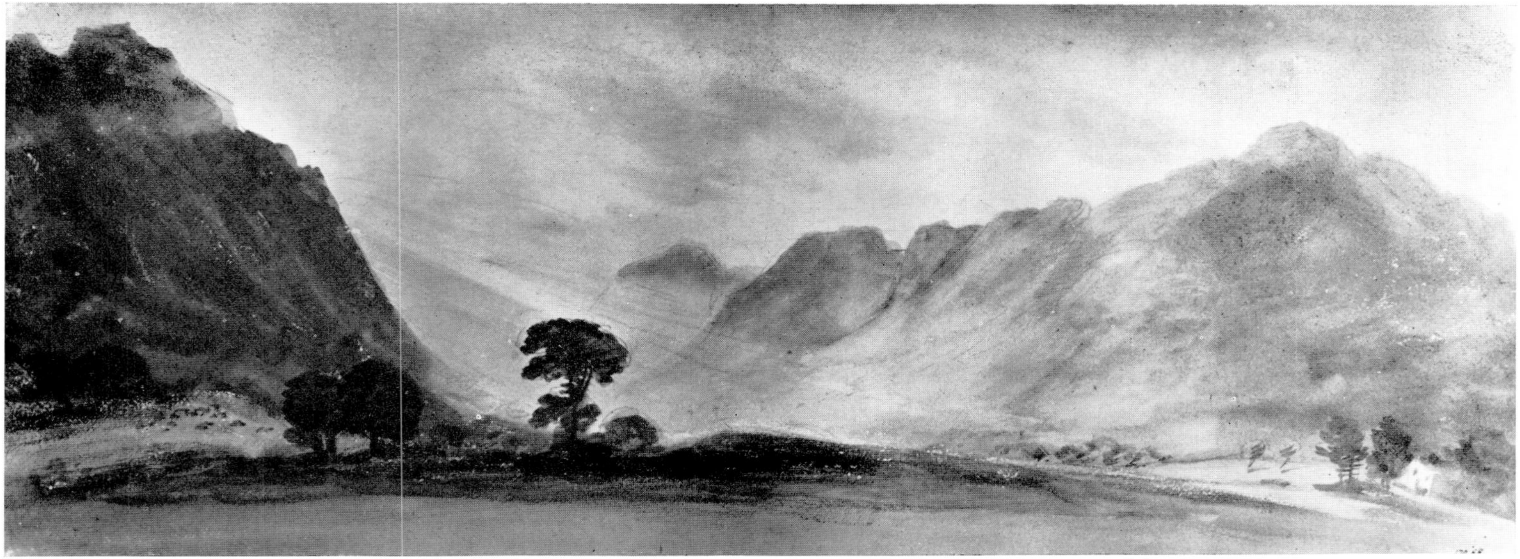

76. View in Borrowdale.

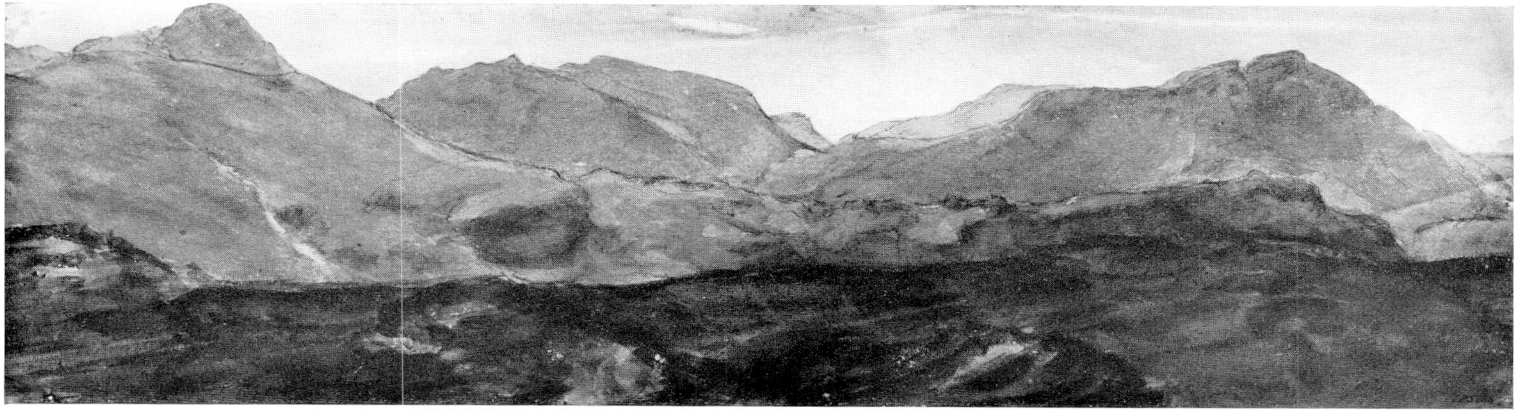

77. View from the top of Honister Crag.

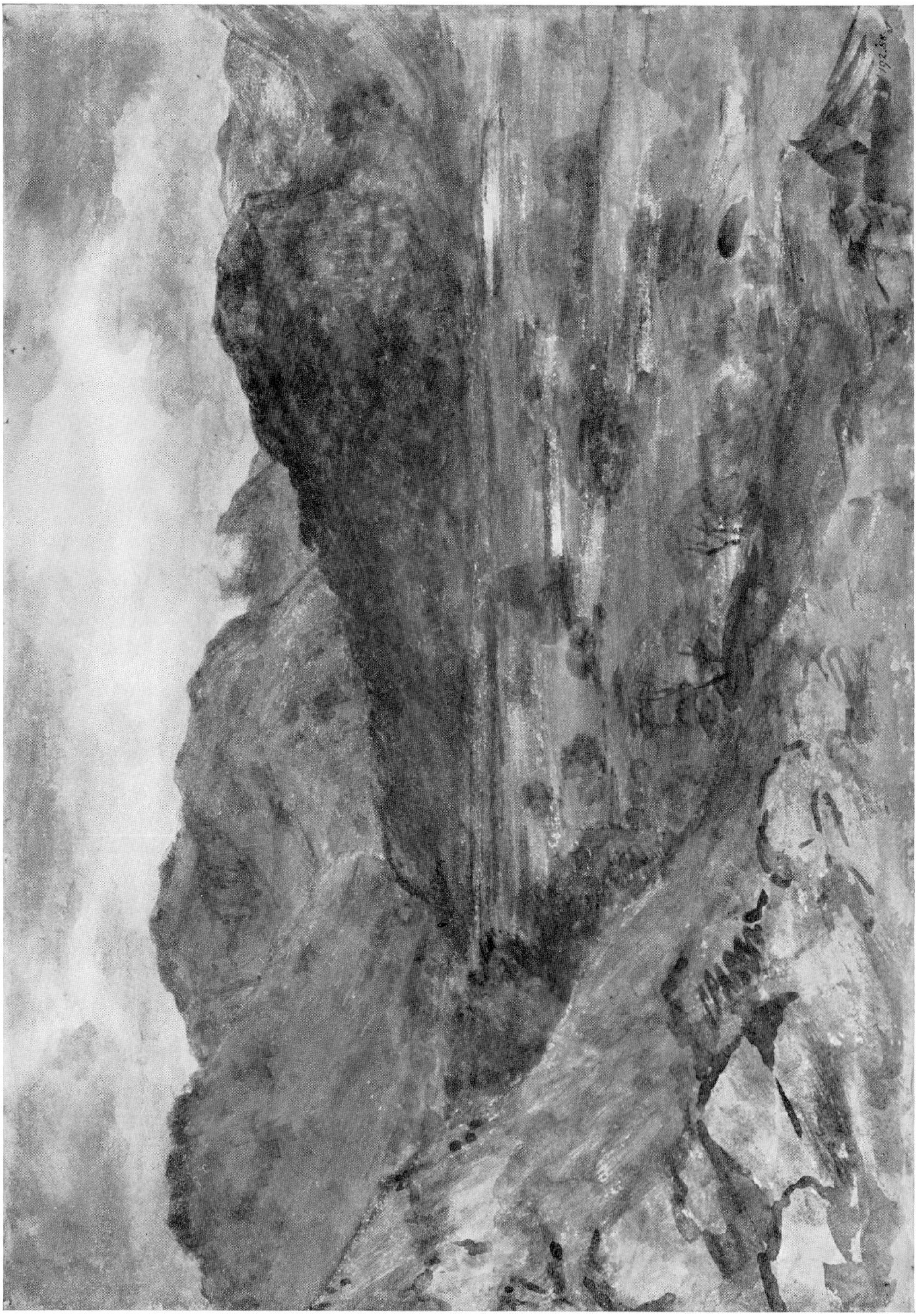

74. View in Borrowdale.

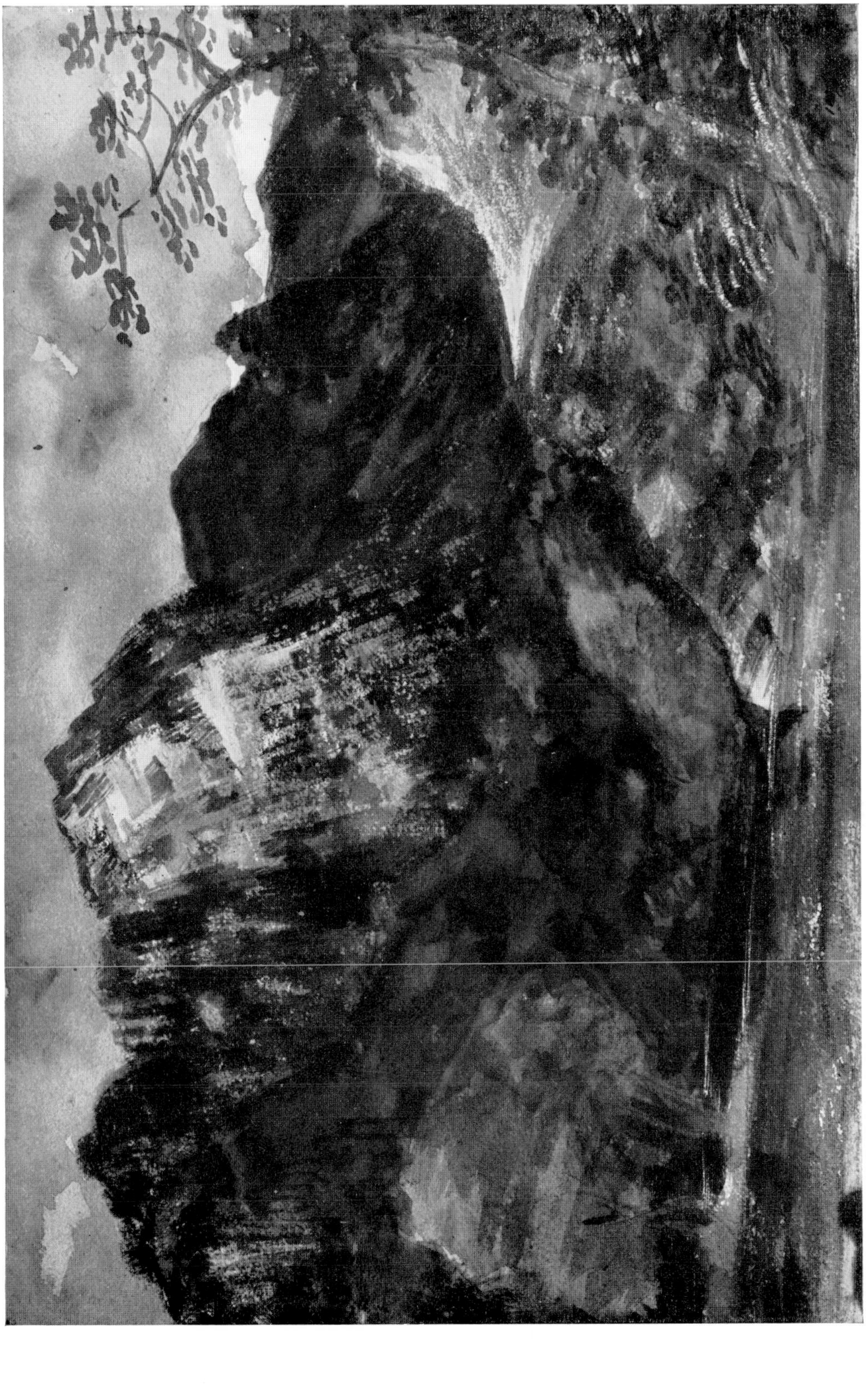

80. View in Borrowdale.

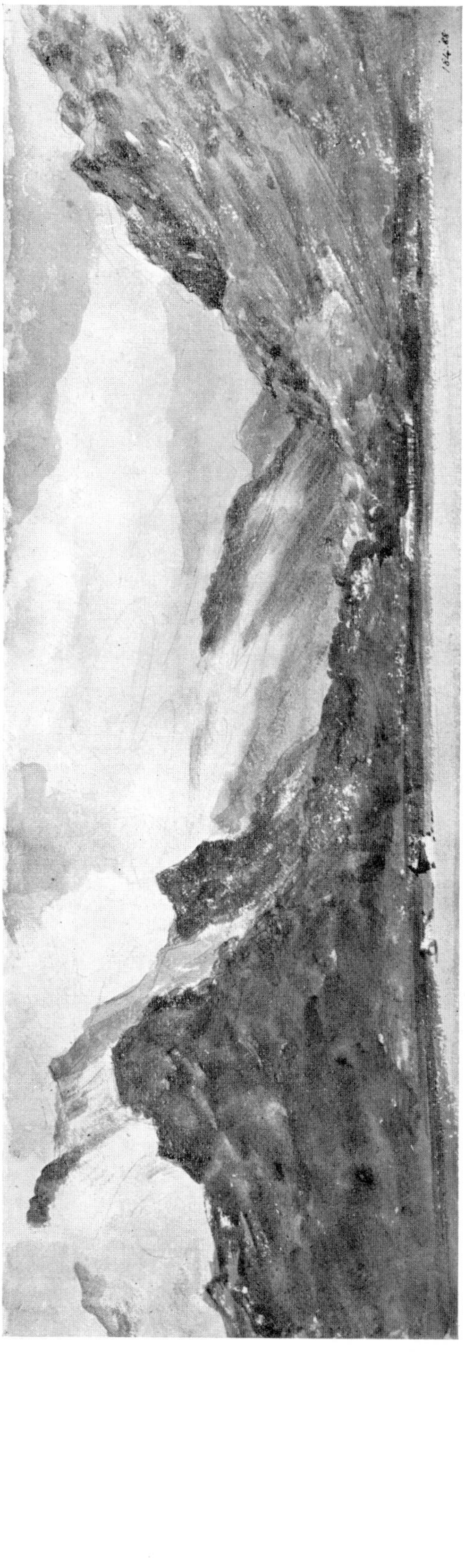

79. View in Borrowdale.

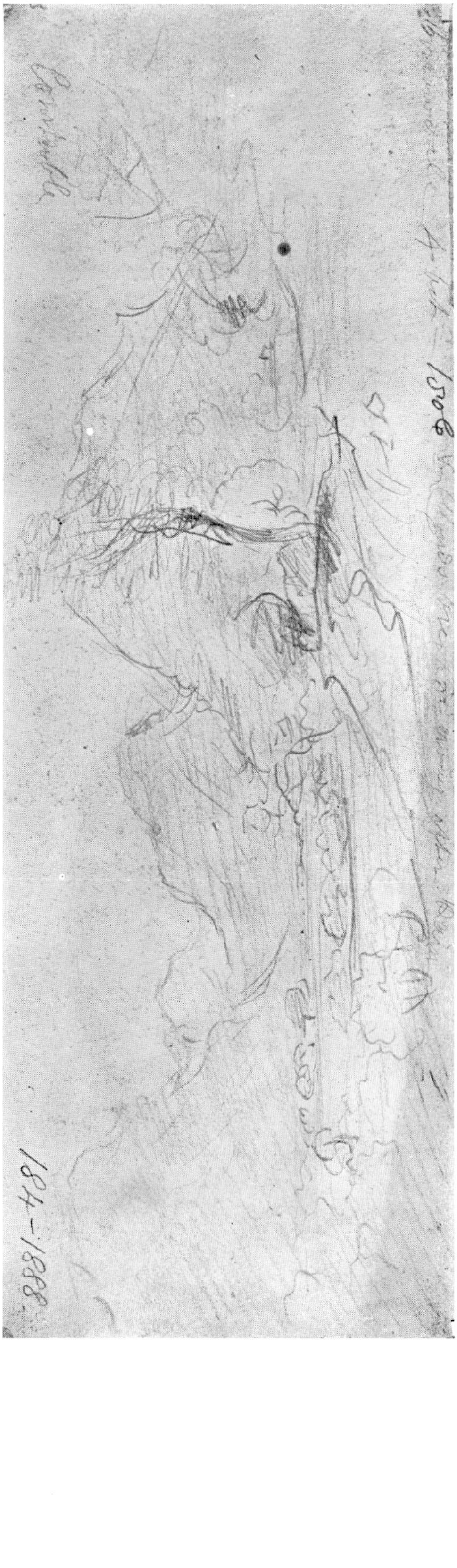

79a. View in Borrowdale.

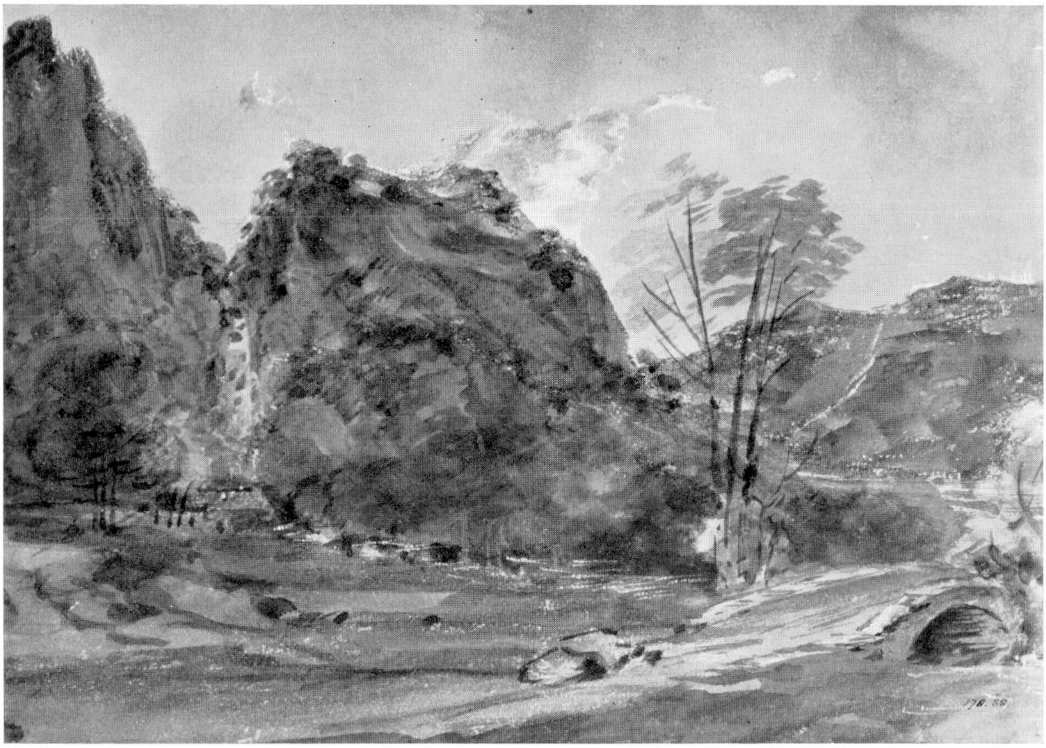

81. Lodore.

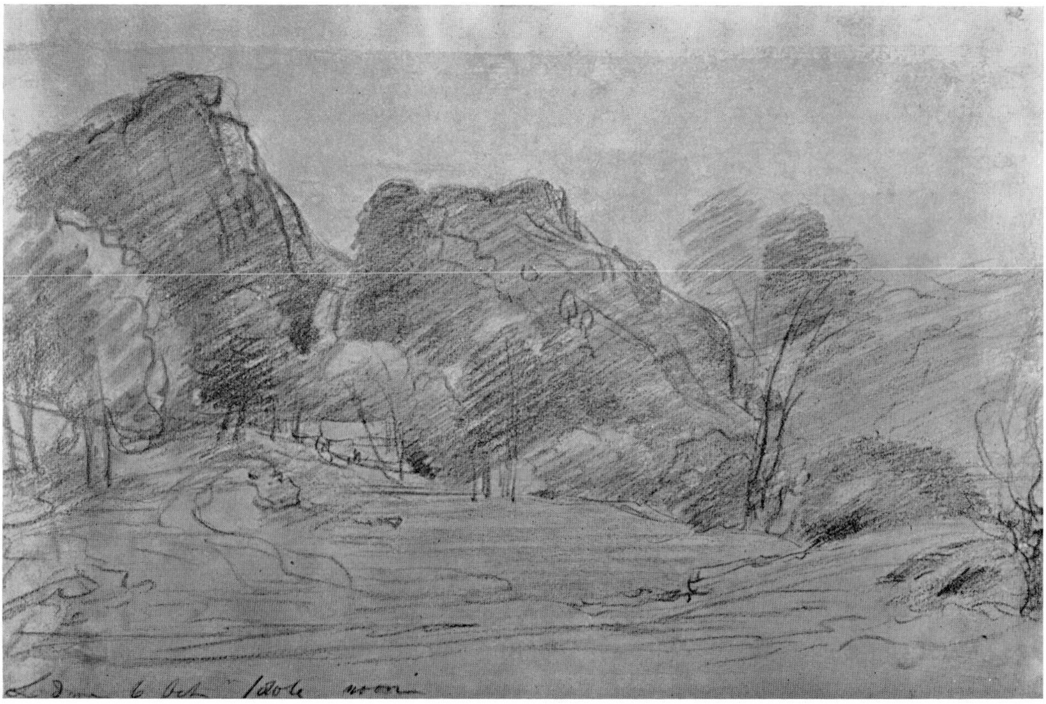

81a. Lodore.

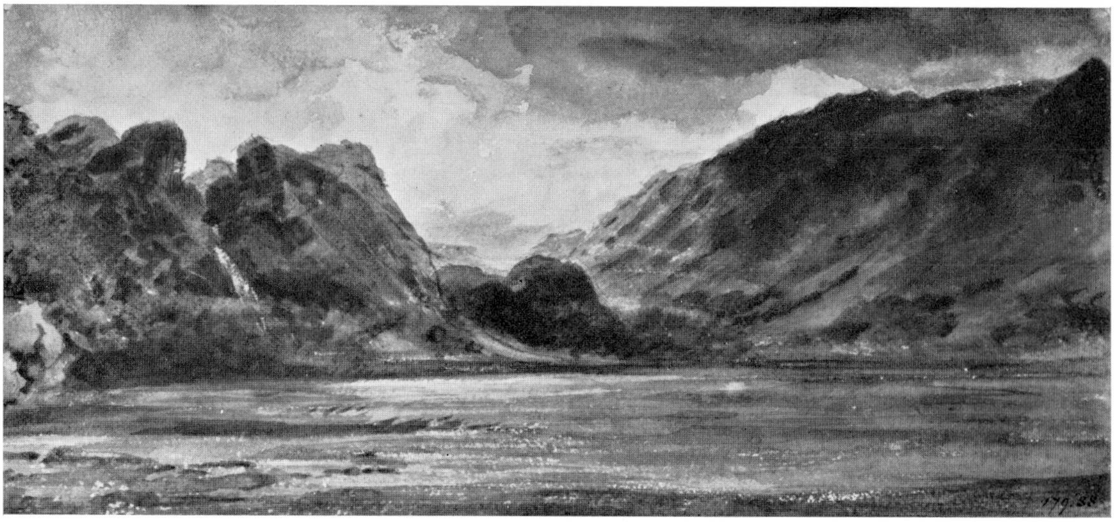

82. Derwentwater: stormy evening.

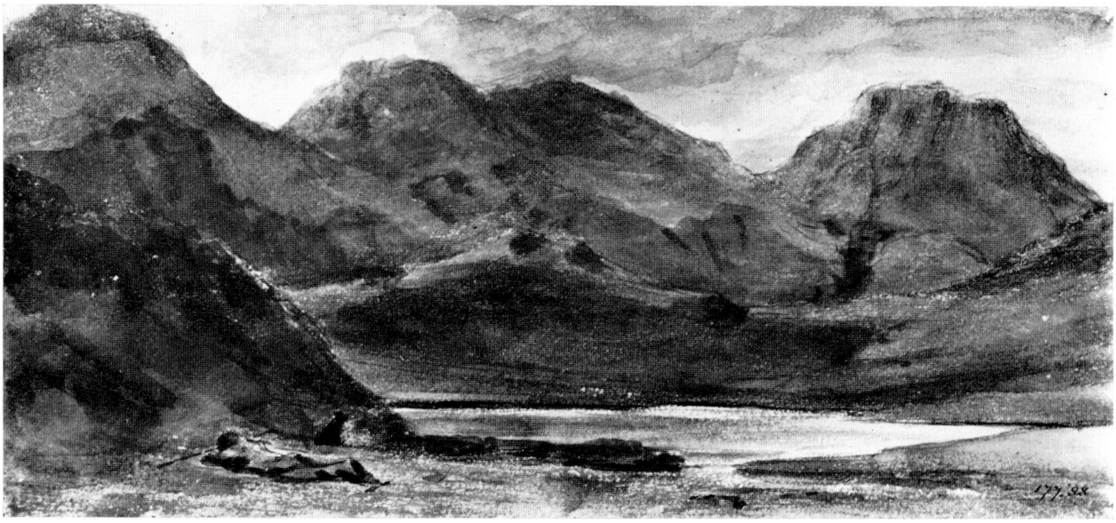

83. Sty Head Tarn, Borrowdale.

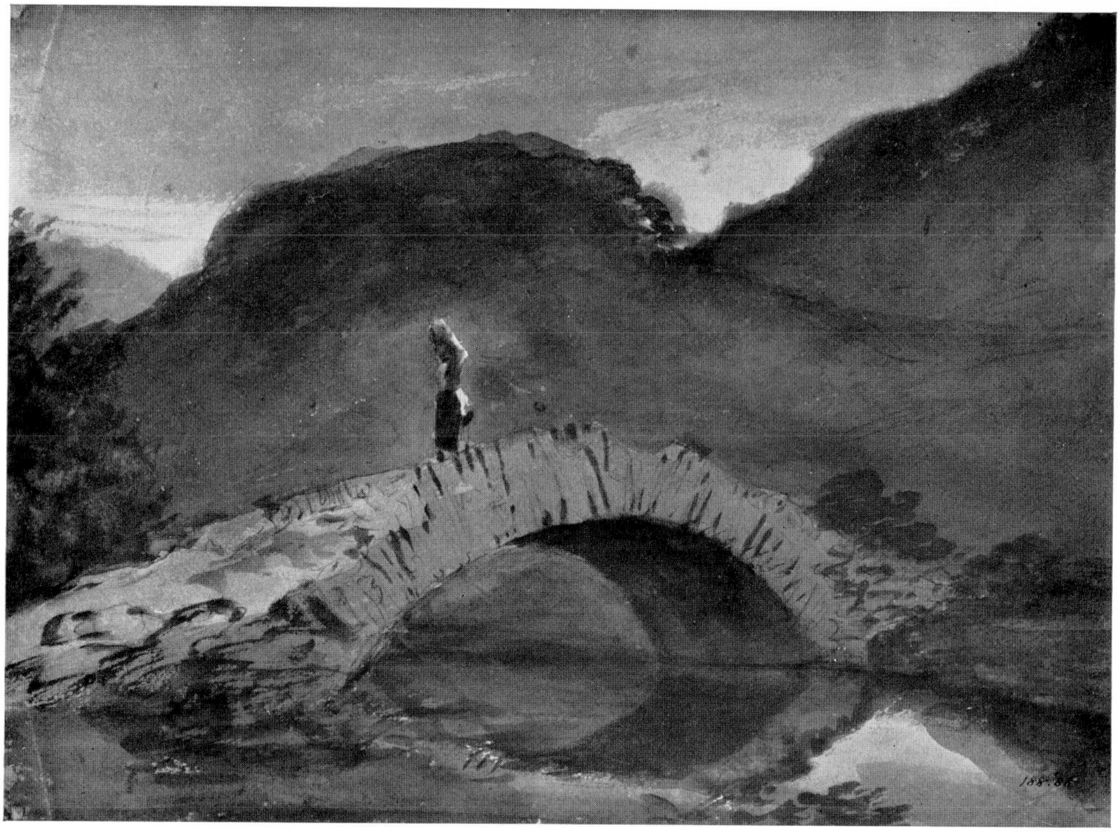

78. A bridge, Borrowdale.

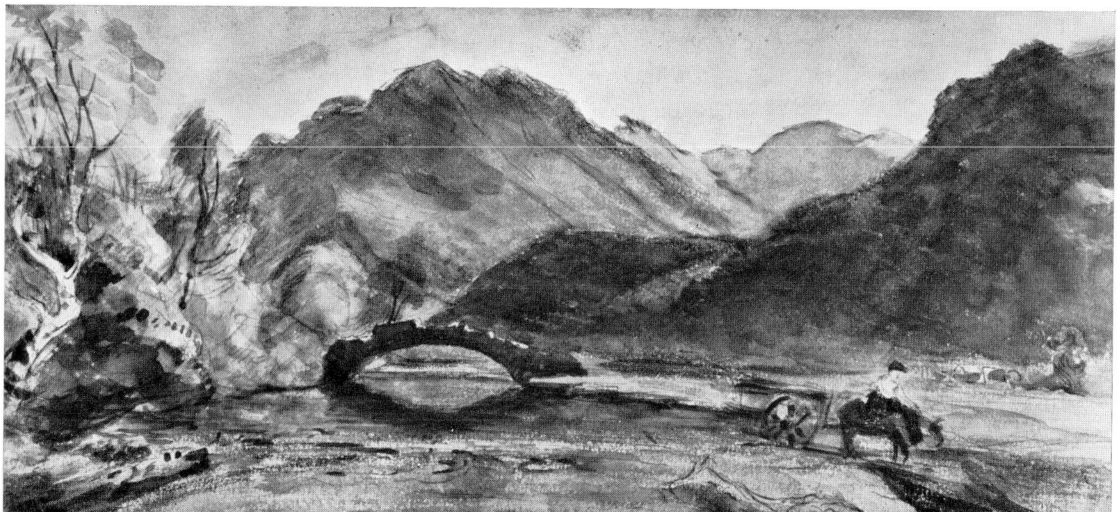

84. View in Borrowdale.

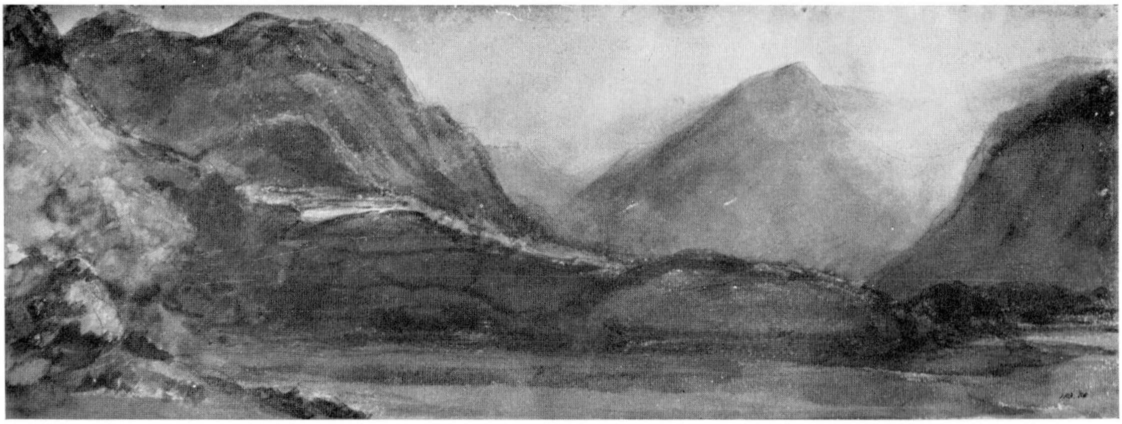

85. View in Borrowdale.

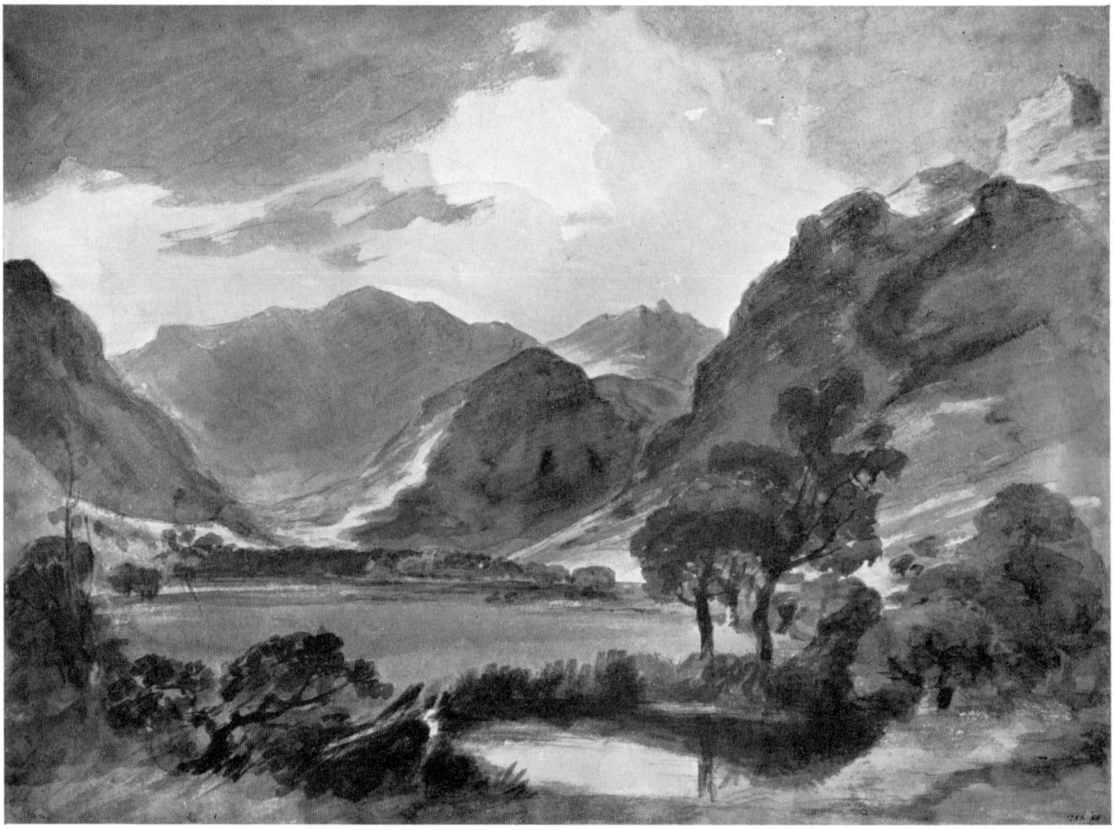

86. View in Langdale.

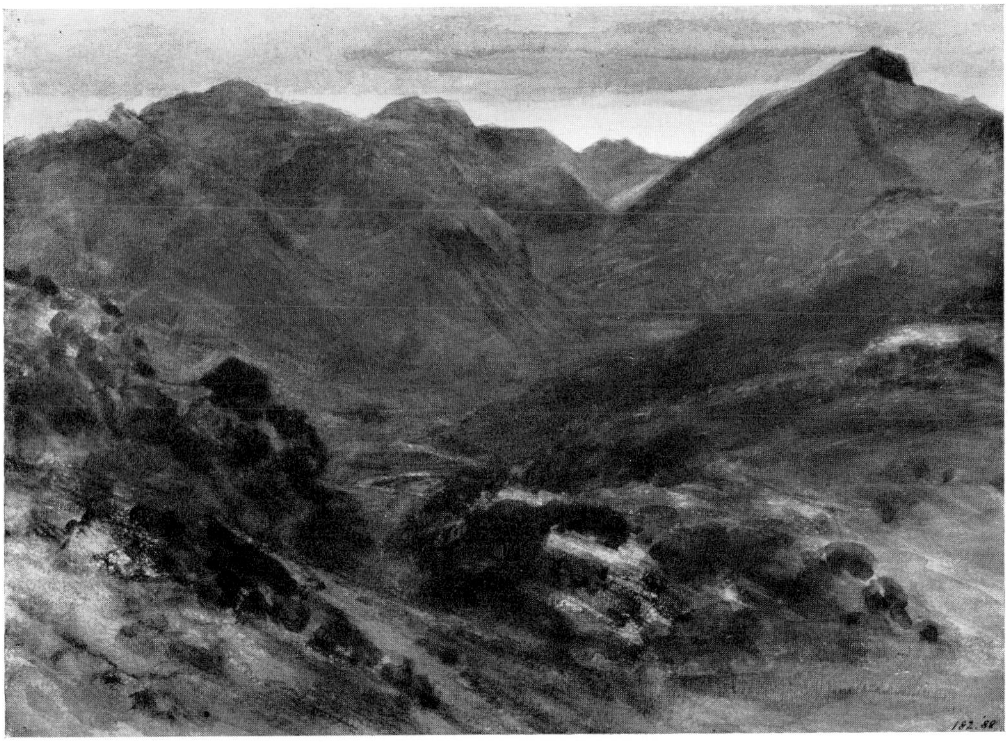

89. View in Borrowdale.

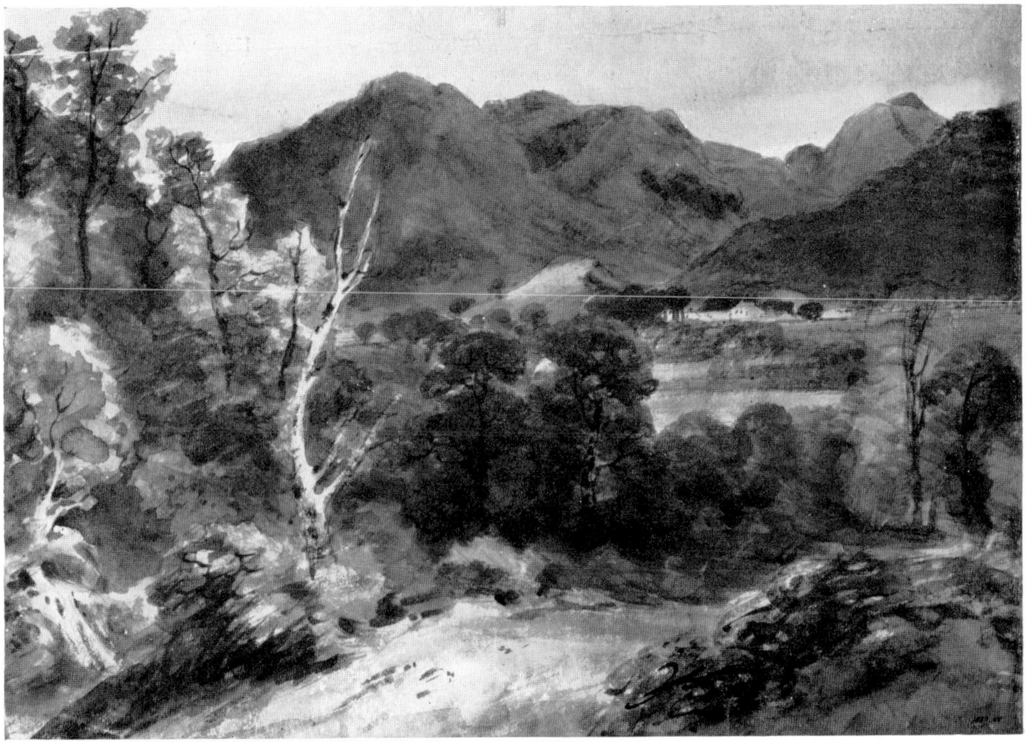

90. Borrowdale, looking towards Glaramara.

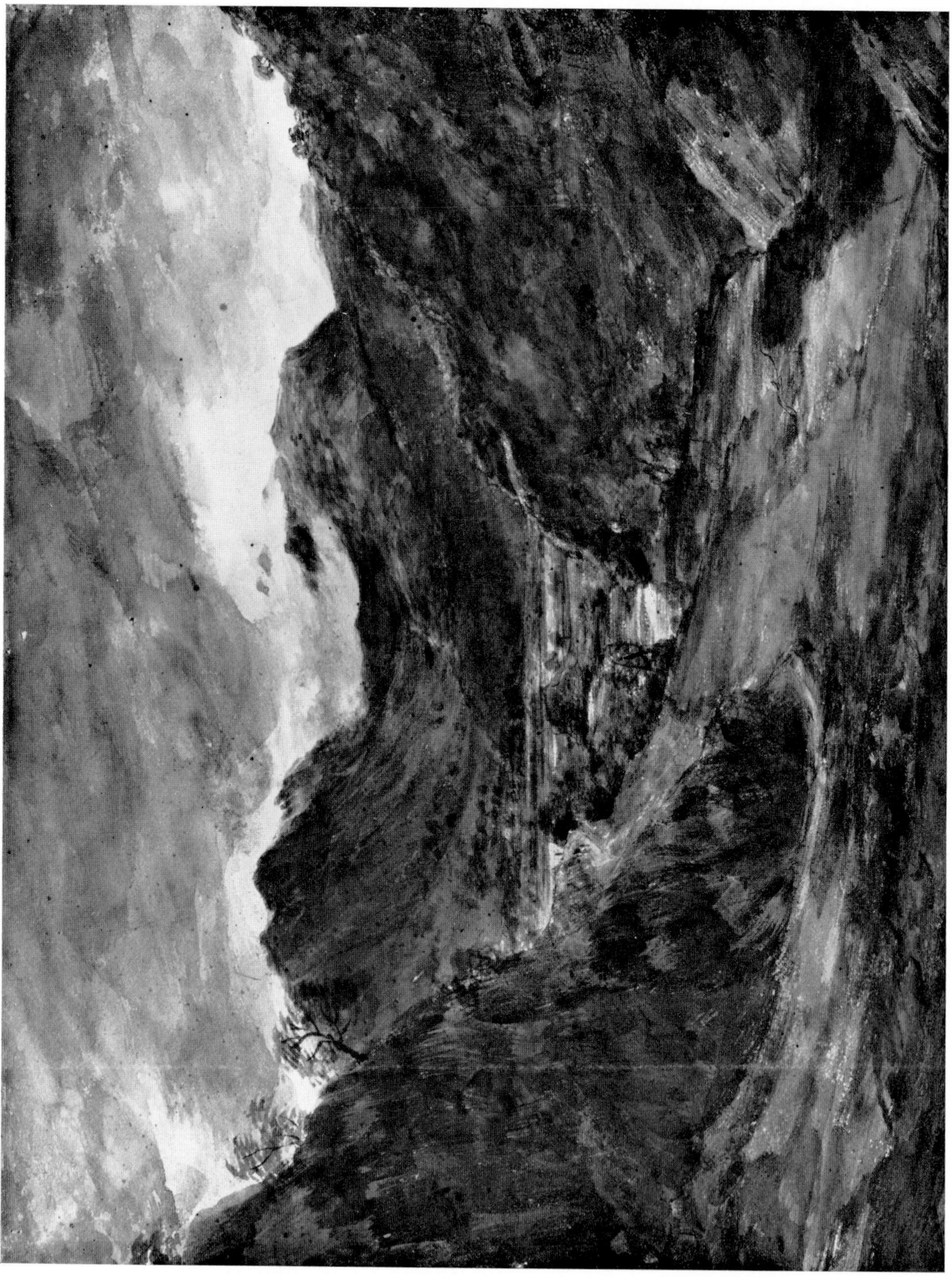

88. Borrowdale: view towards Glaramara.

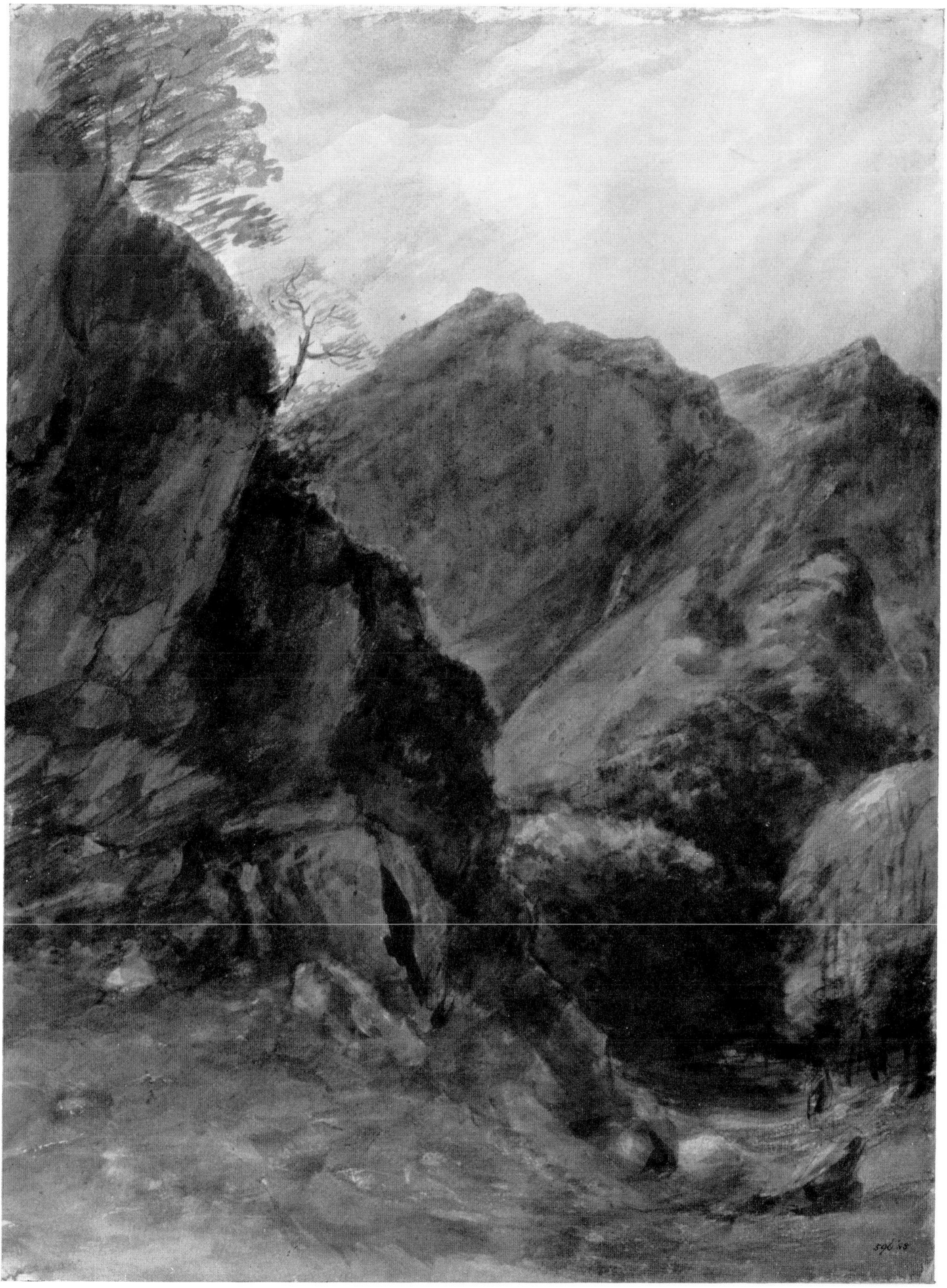

87. Gate Crag, Borrowdale.

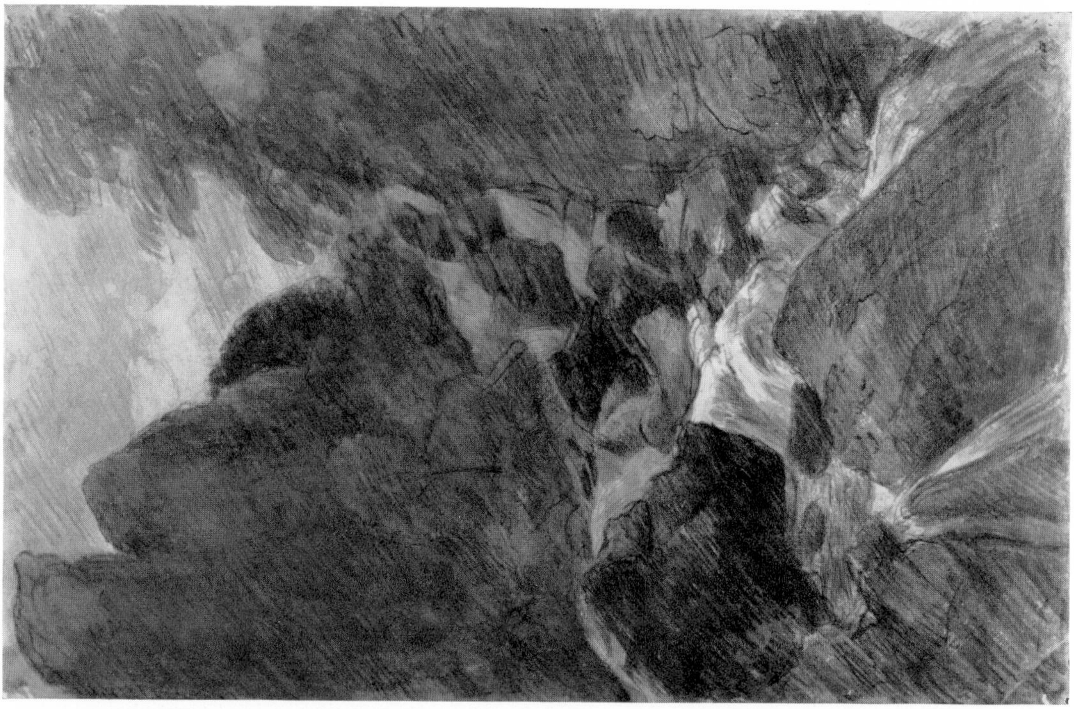

91. A waterfall.

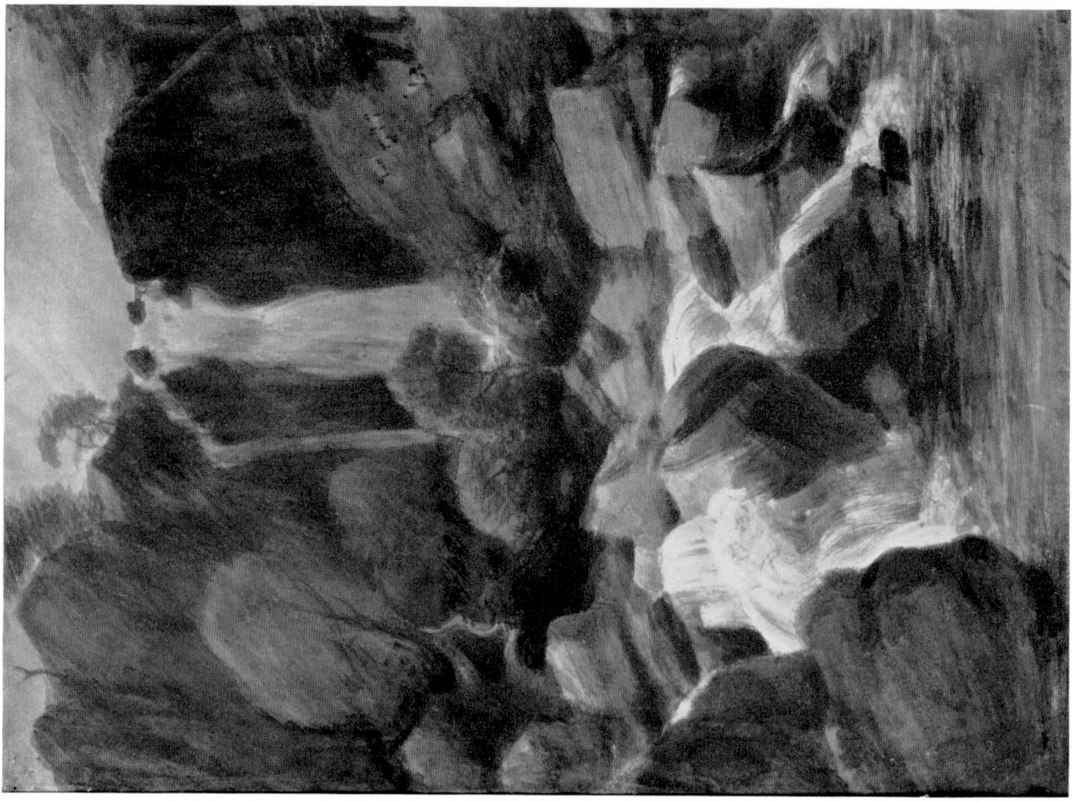

75. Taylor Ghyll, Sty Head.

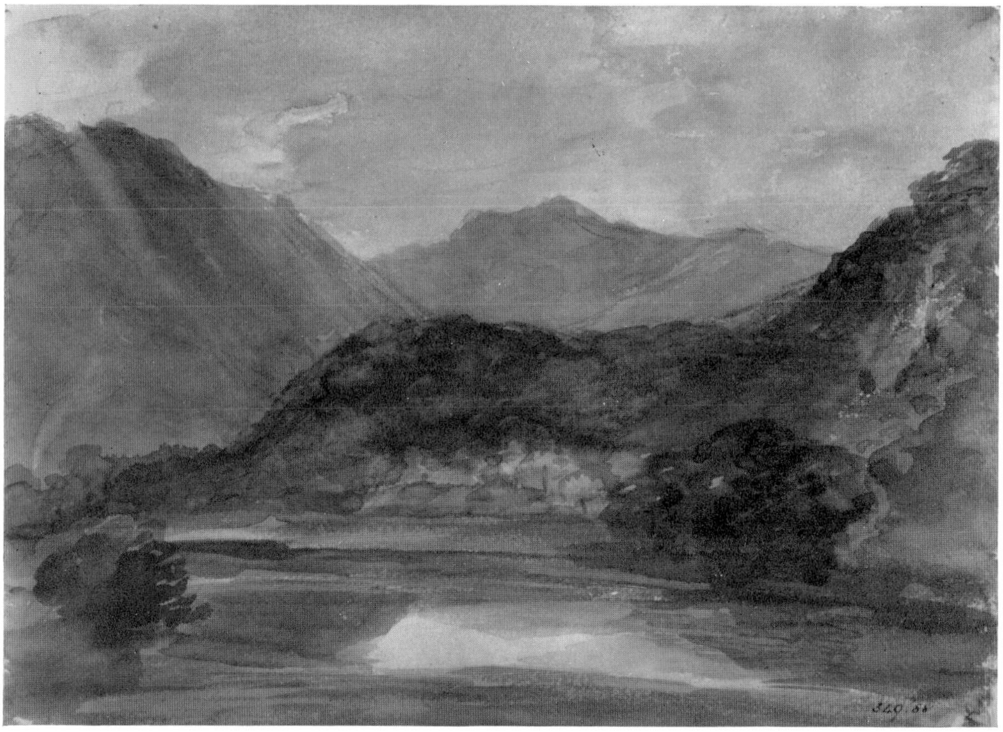

92. View in the Lake District.

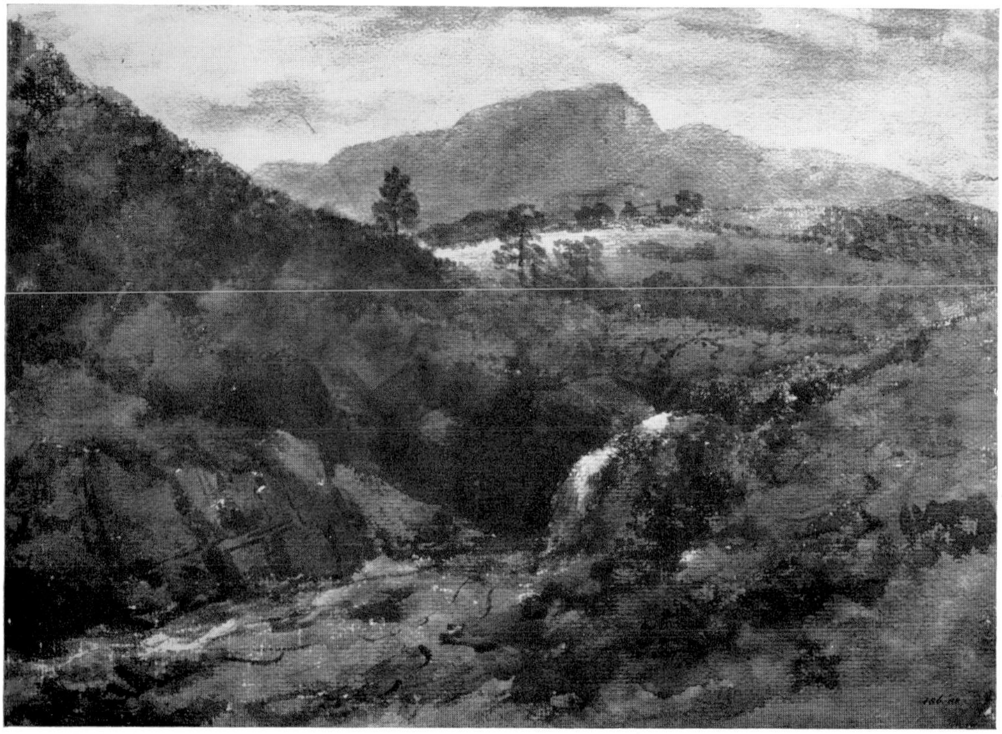

93. View in the Lake District.

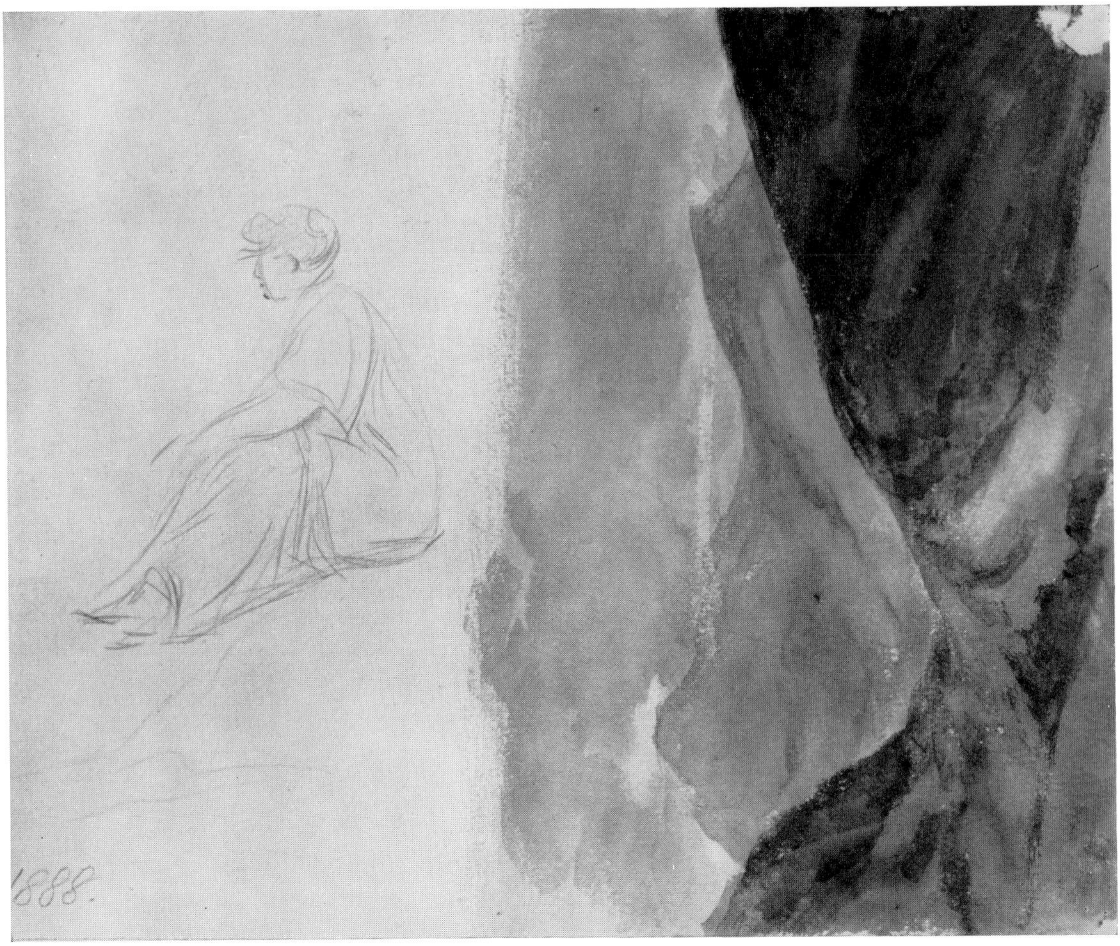

89a. Sketches in the Lake District.

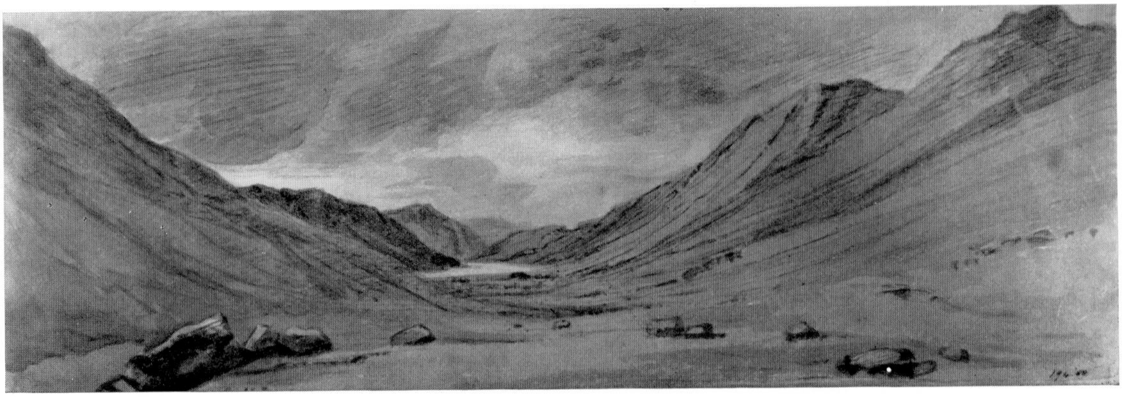

94. Leathes Water (Thirlmere).

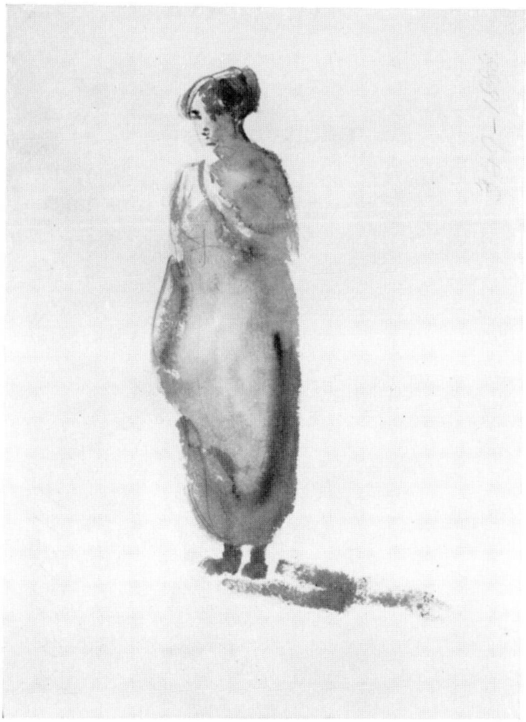

92a. A country girl.

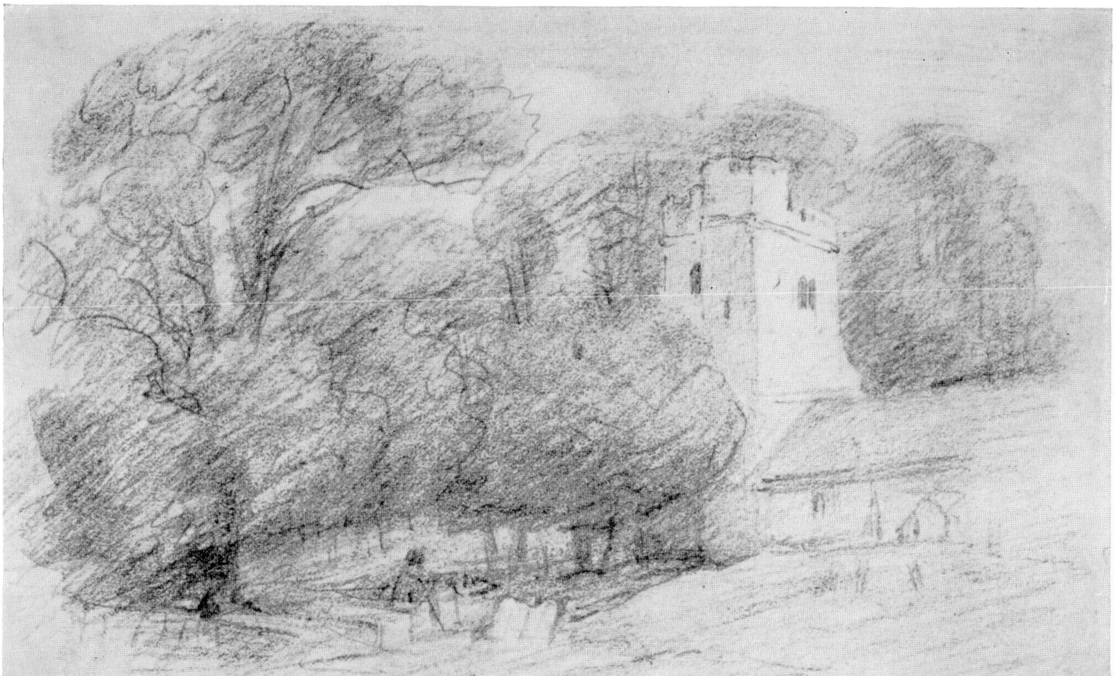

95. Epsom Church.

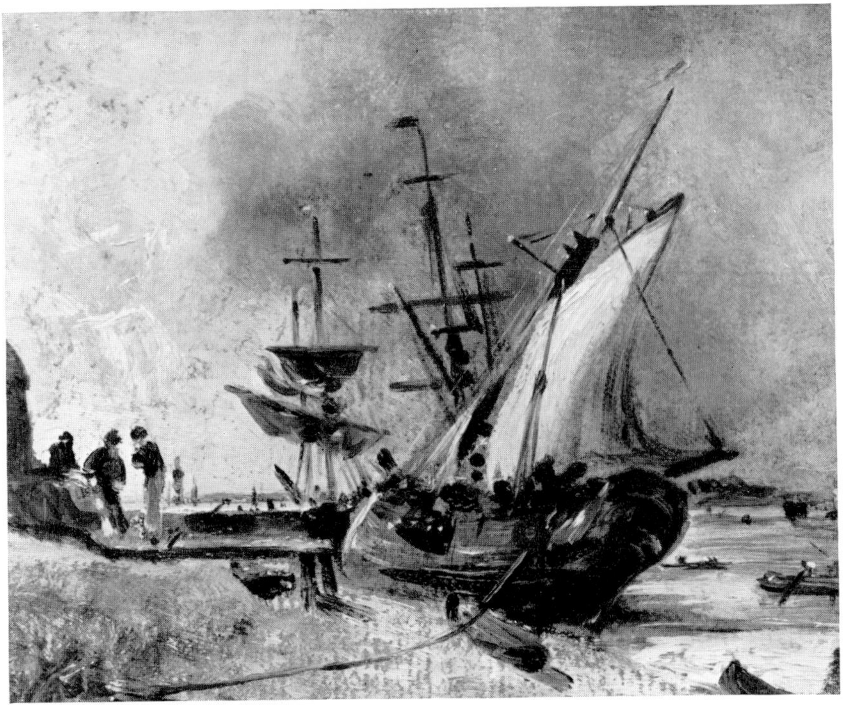

96. Shipping in the Orwell, near Ipswich.

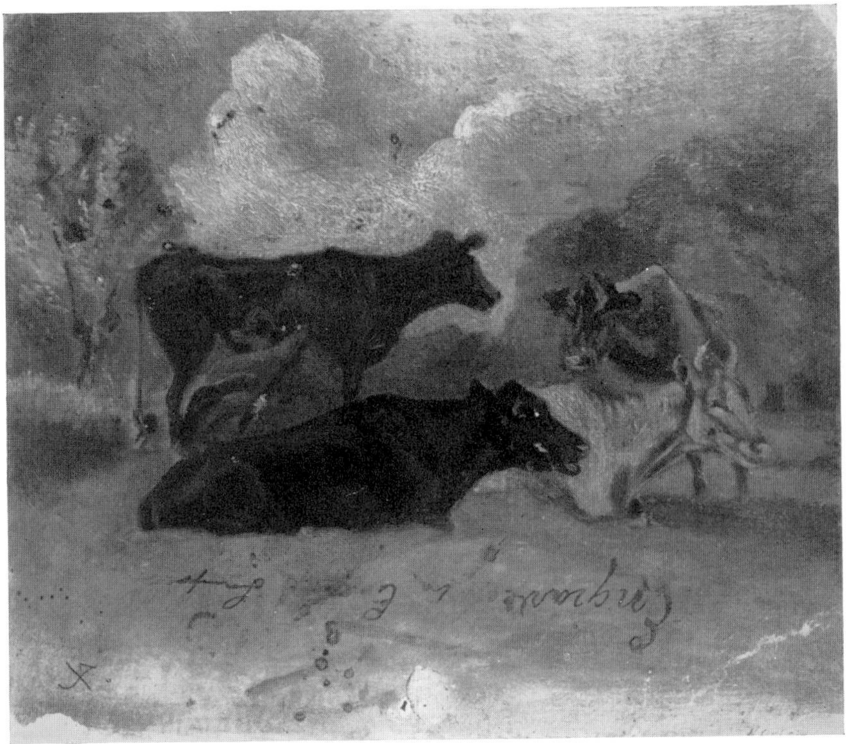

96a. Study of cows.

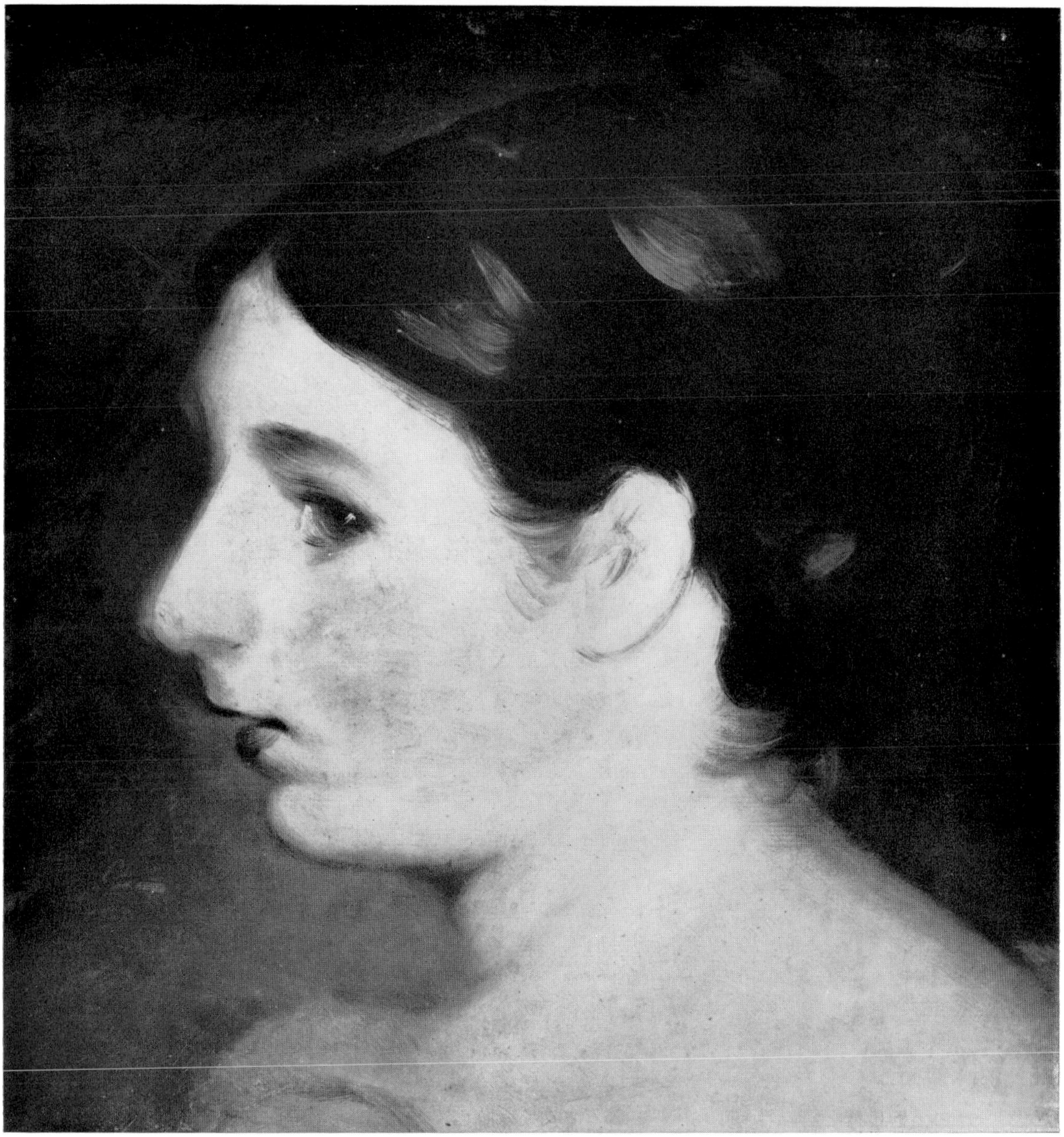

97. Portrait, probably of Mary Constable.

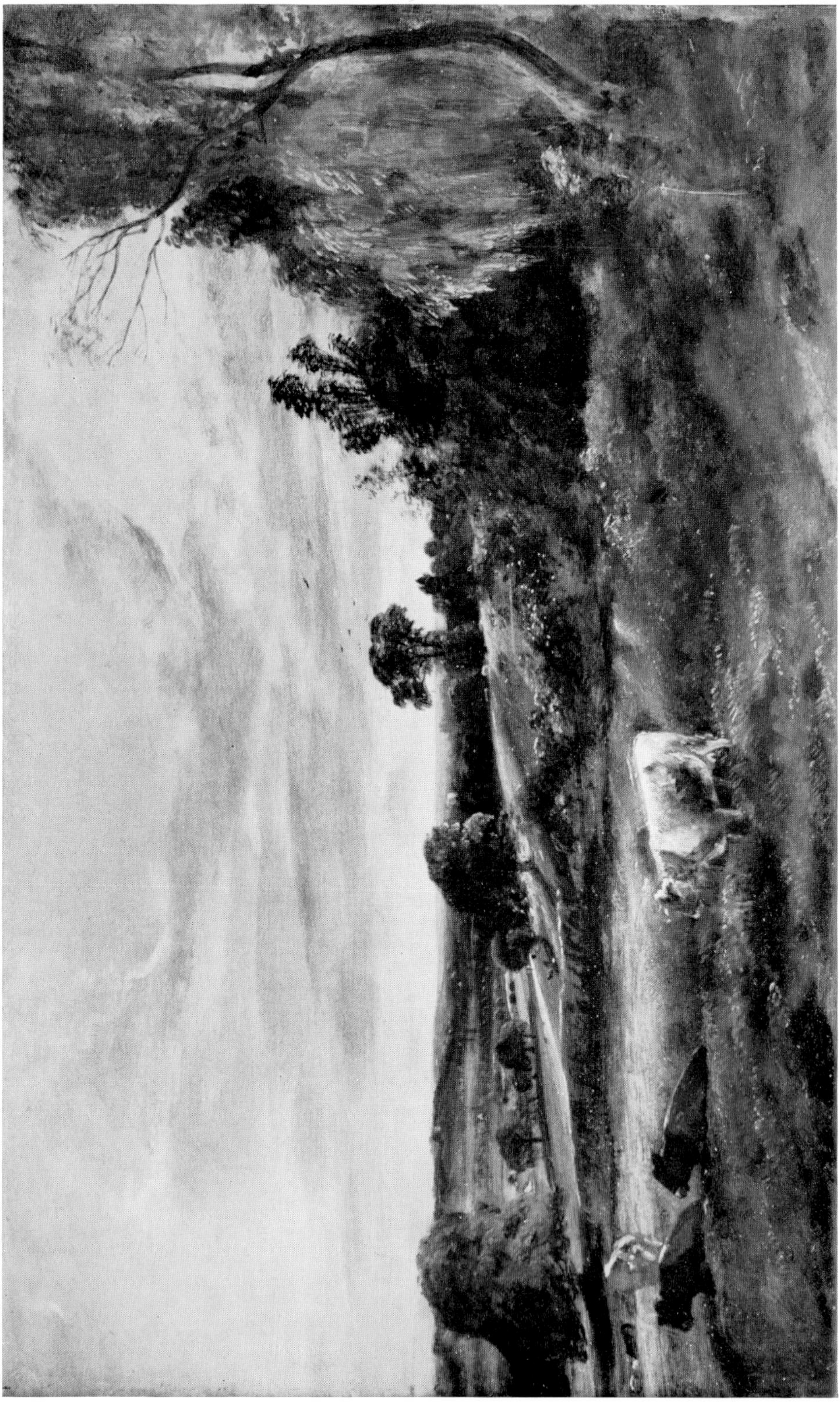

98. Summer Evening.

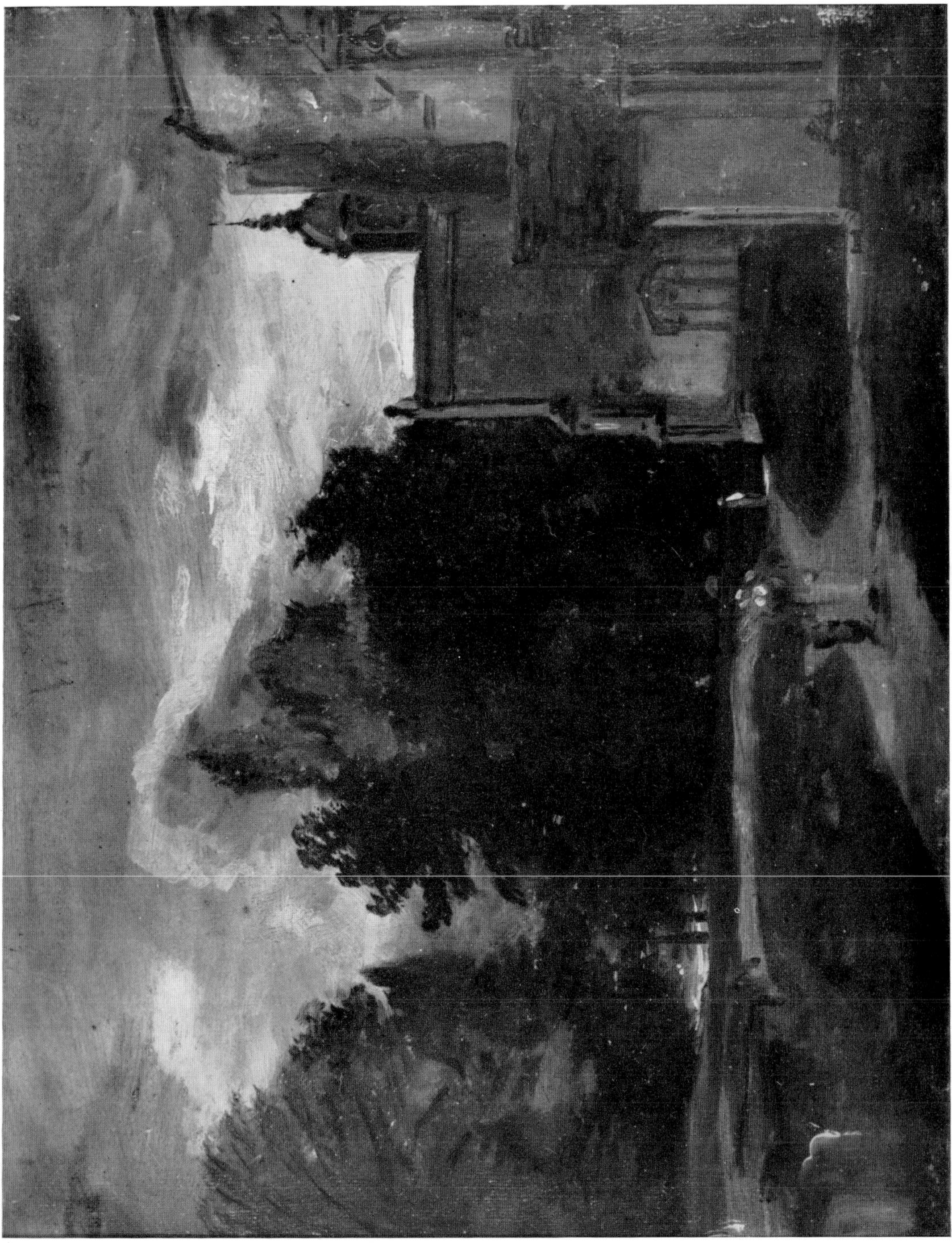

99. Porch of East Bergholt Church.

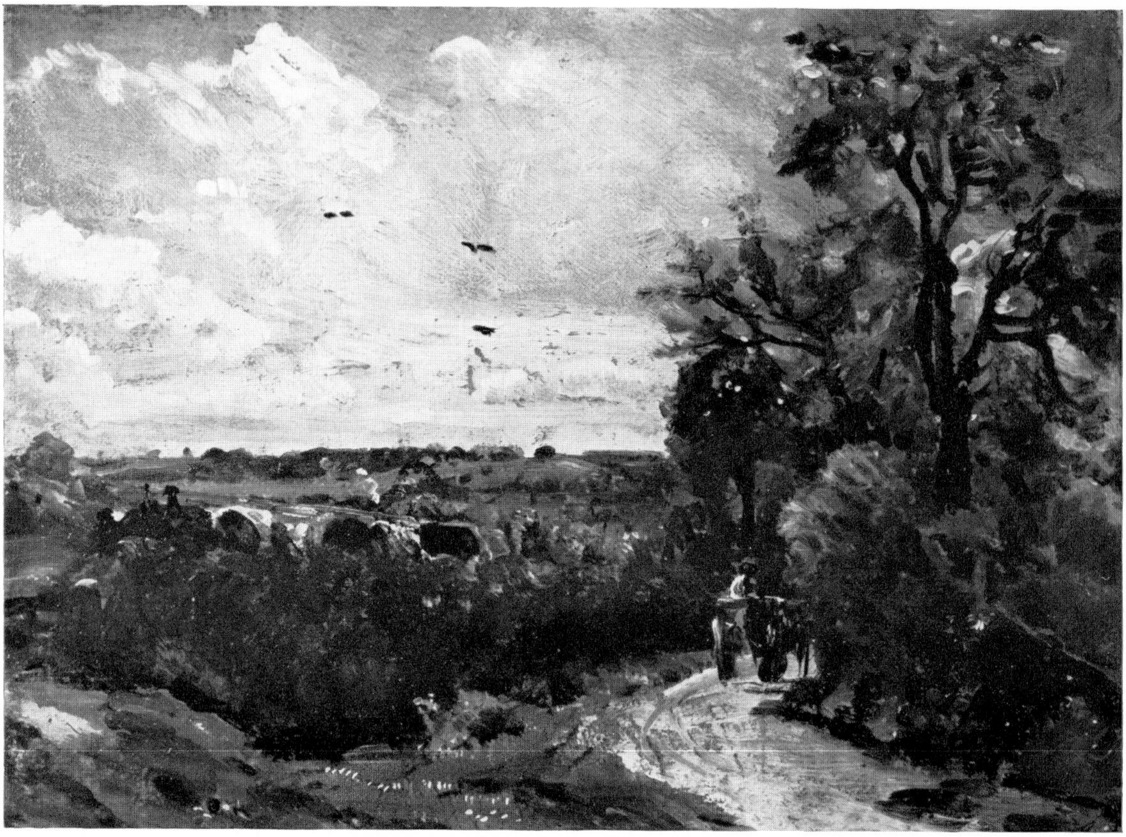

100. A cart on a lane at Flatford.

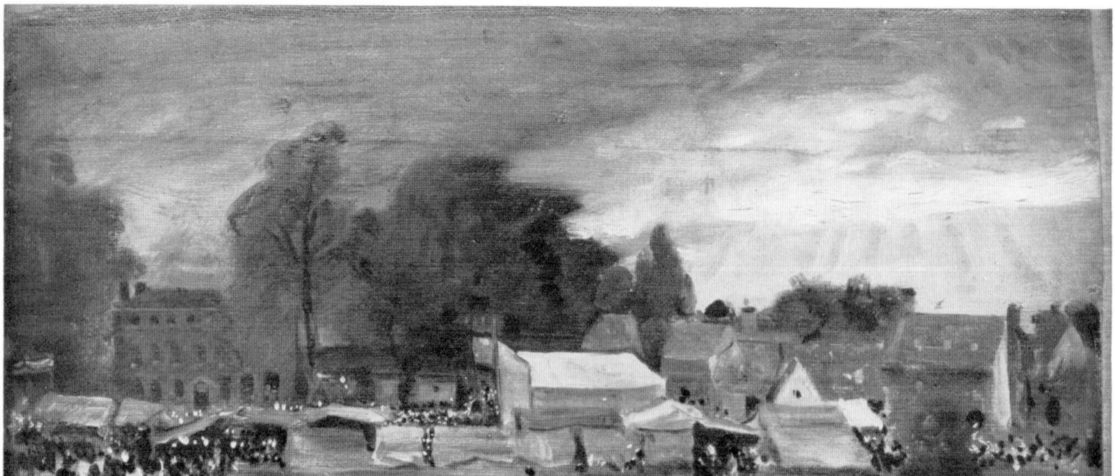

101. A village fair at East Bergholt.

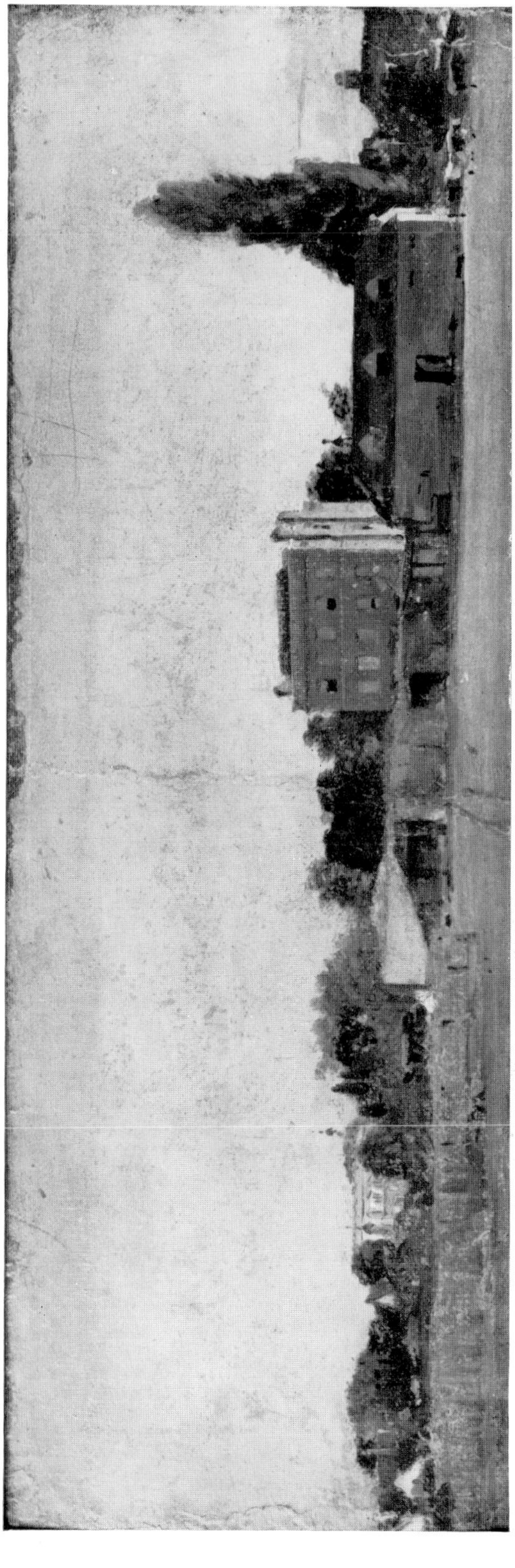

102. Golding Constable's house, East Bergholt.

ccc—x

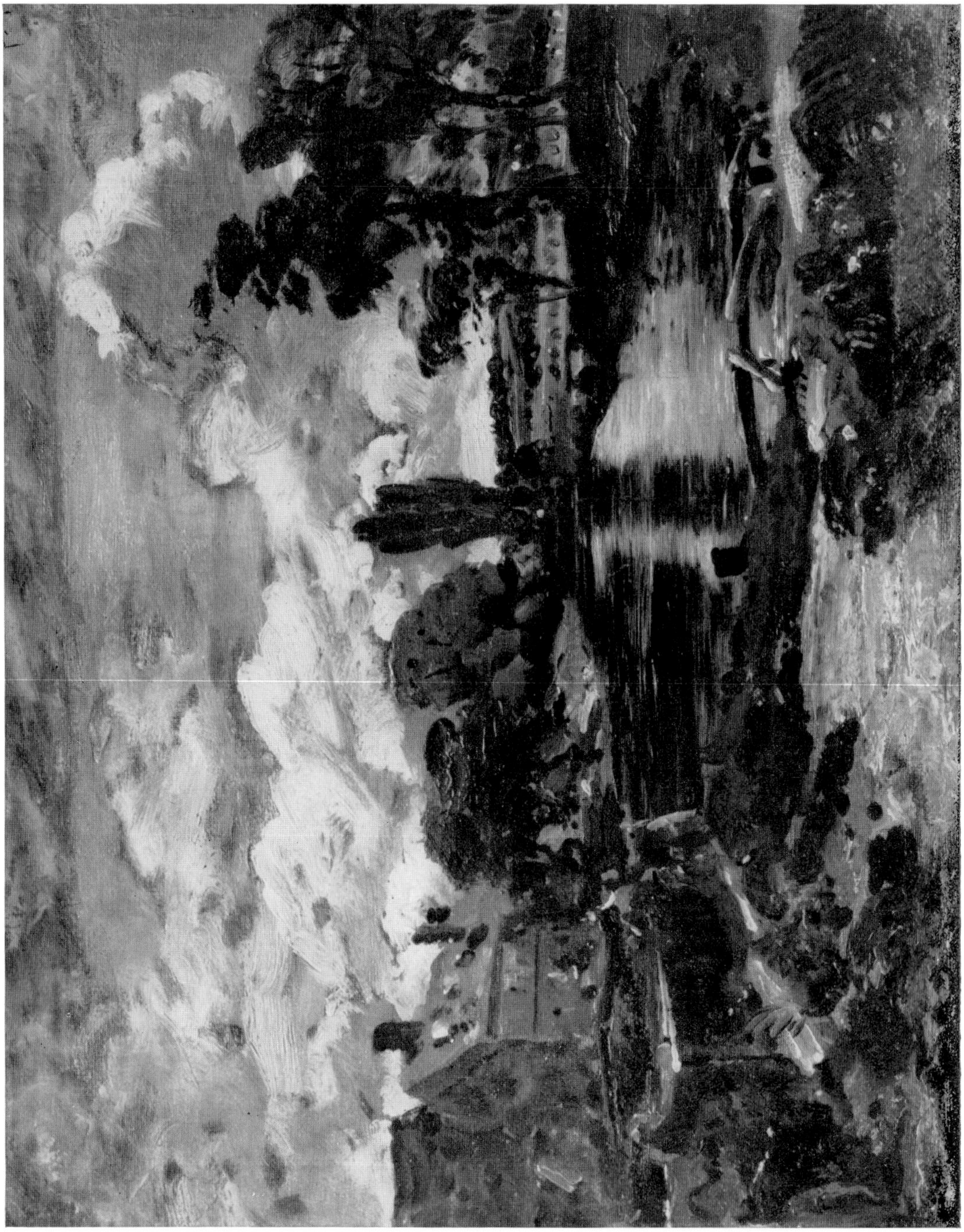

103. Flatford Mill from a lock on the Stour.

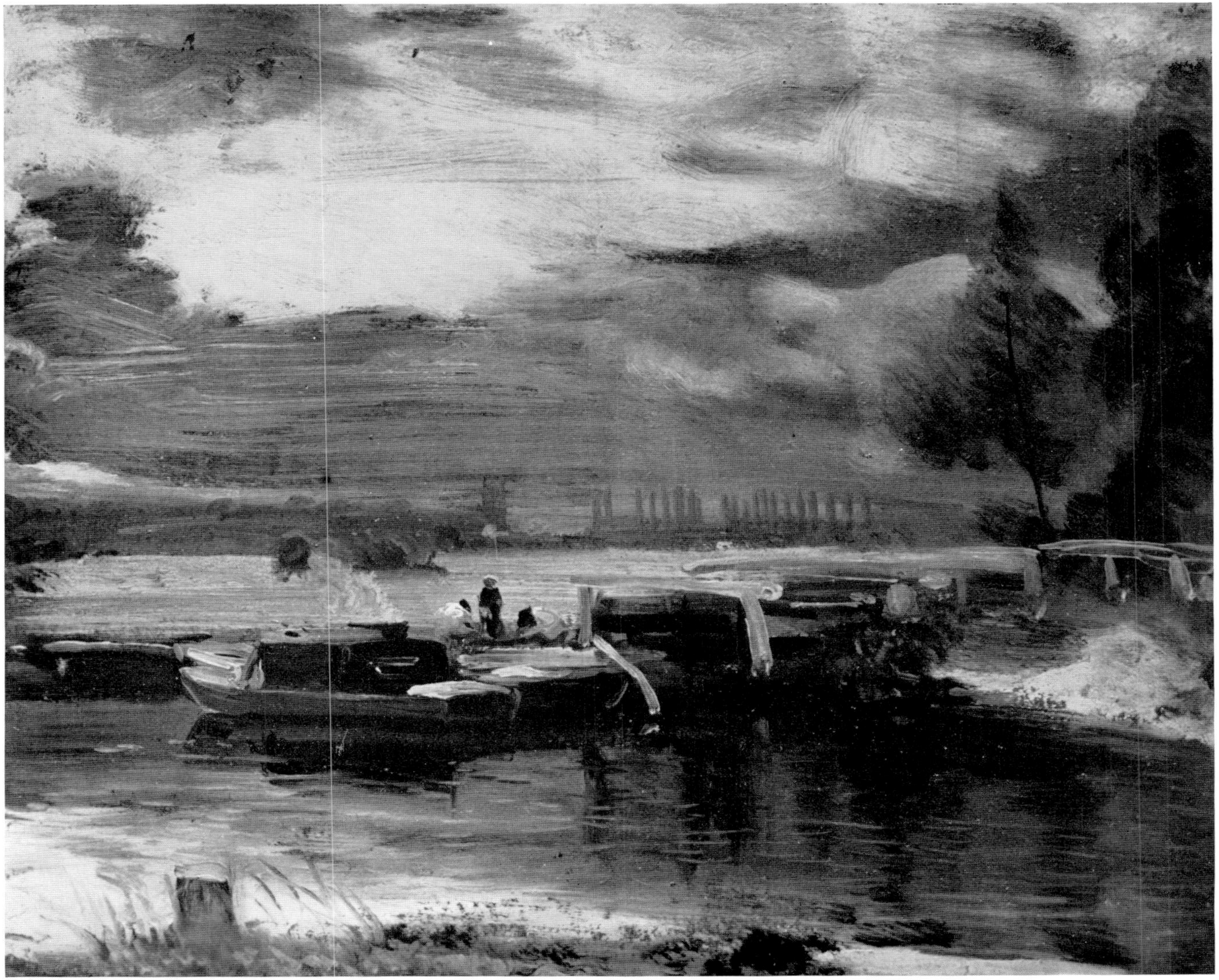

104. Barges on the Stour.

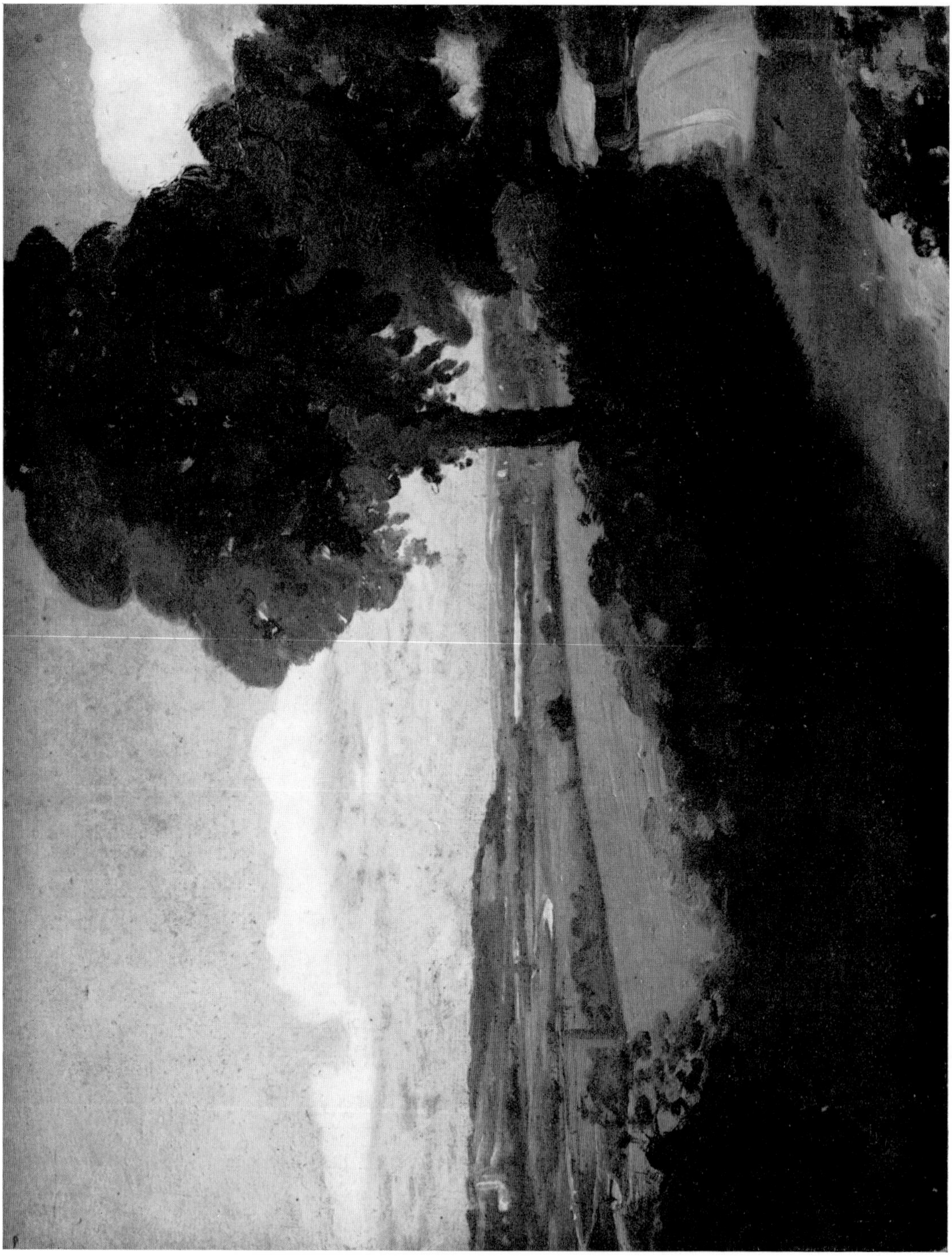

109. View of Dedham from the lane leading from East Bergholt Church to Flatford.

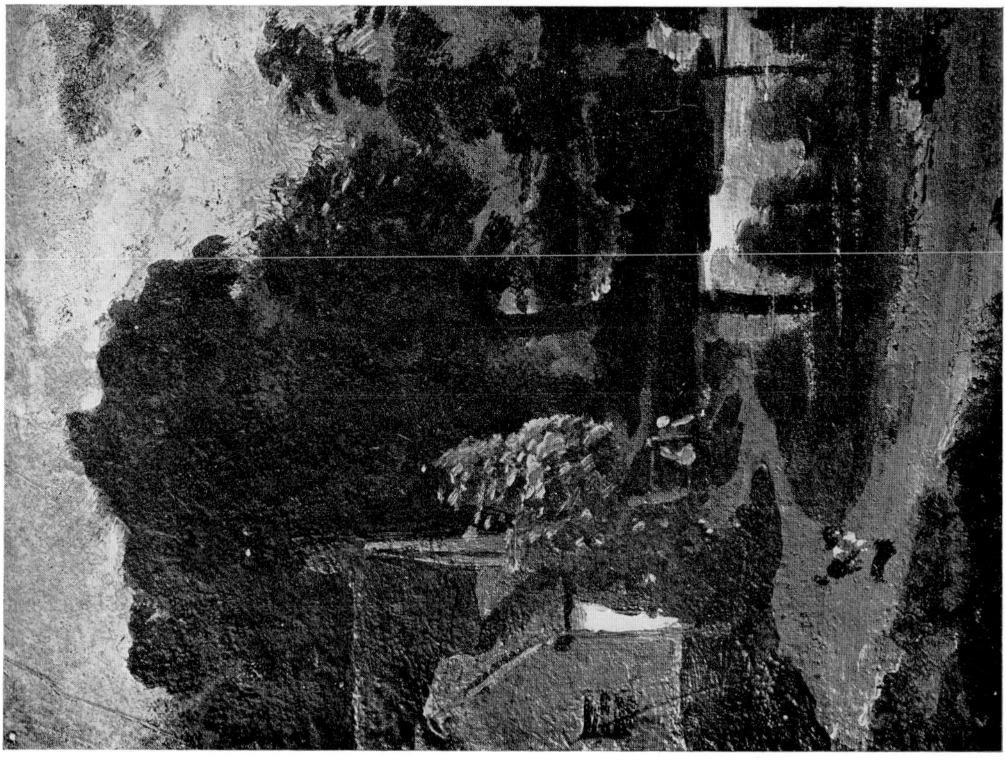

110. Willy Lott's House.

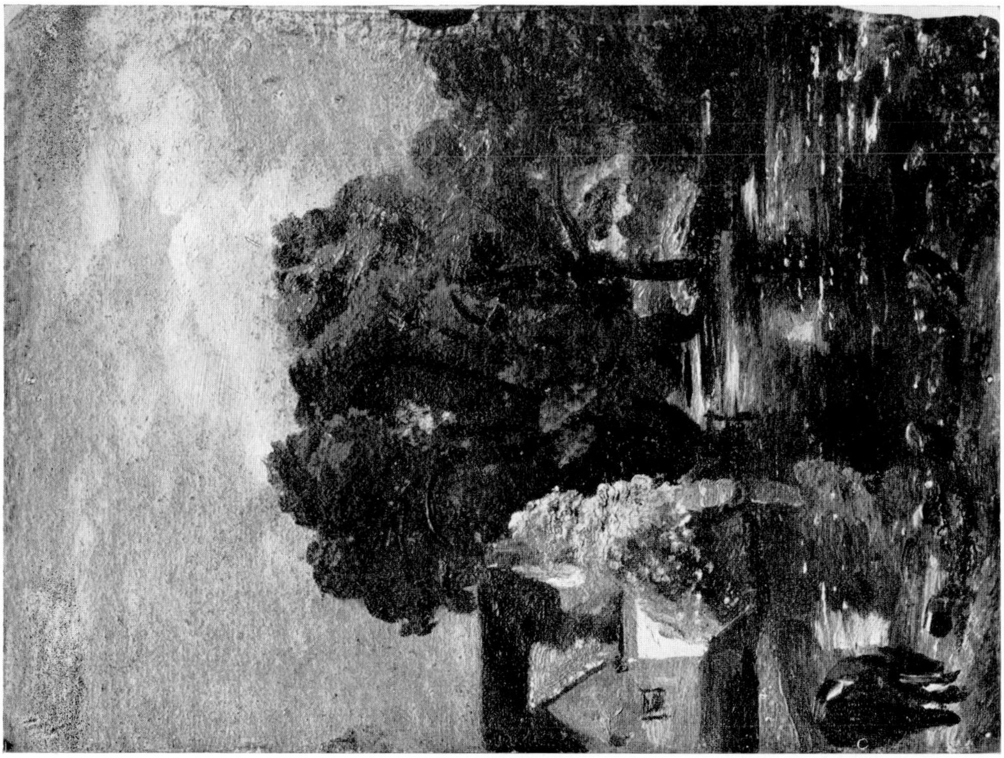

110a. Willy Lott's House.

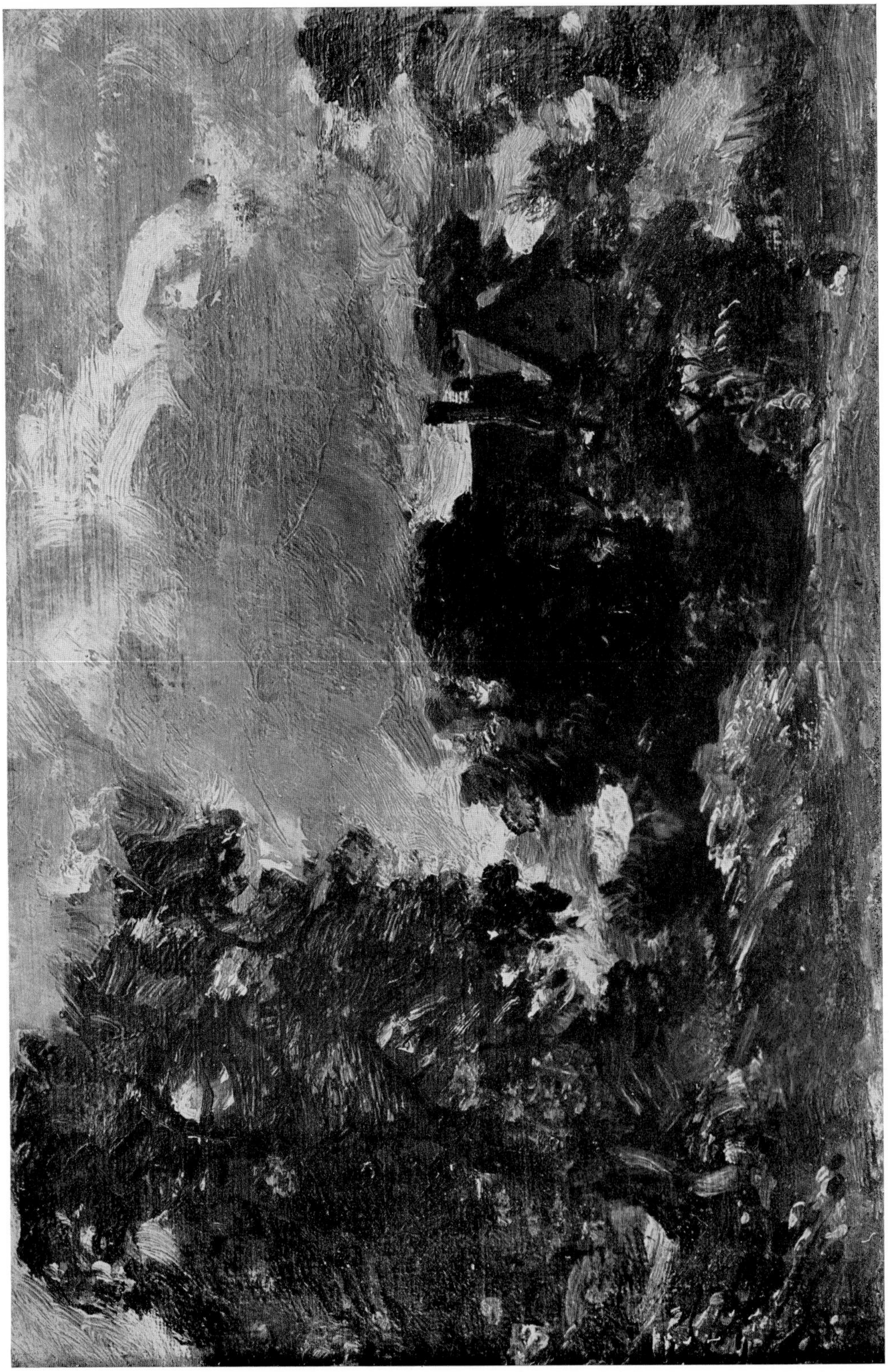

111. A cottage and lane at Langham (sketch for 'The Glebe Farm').

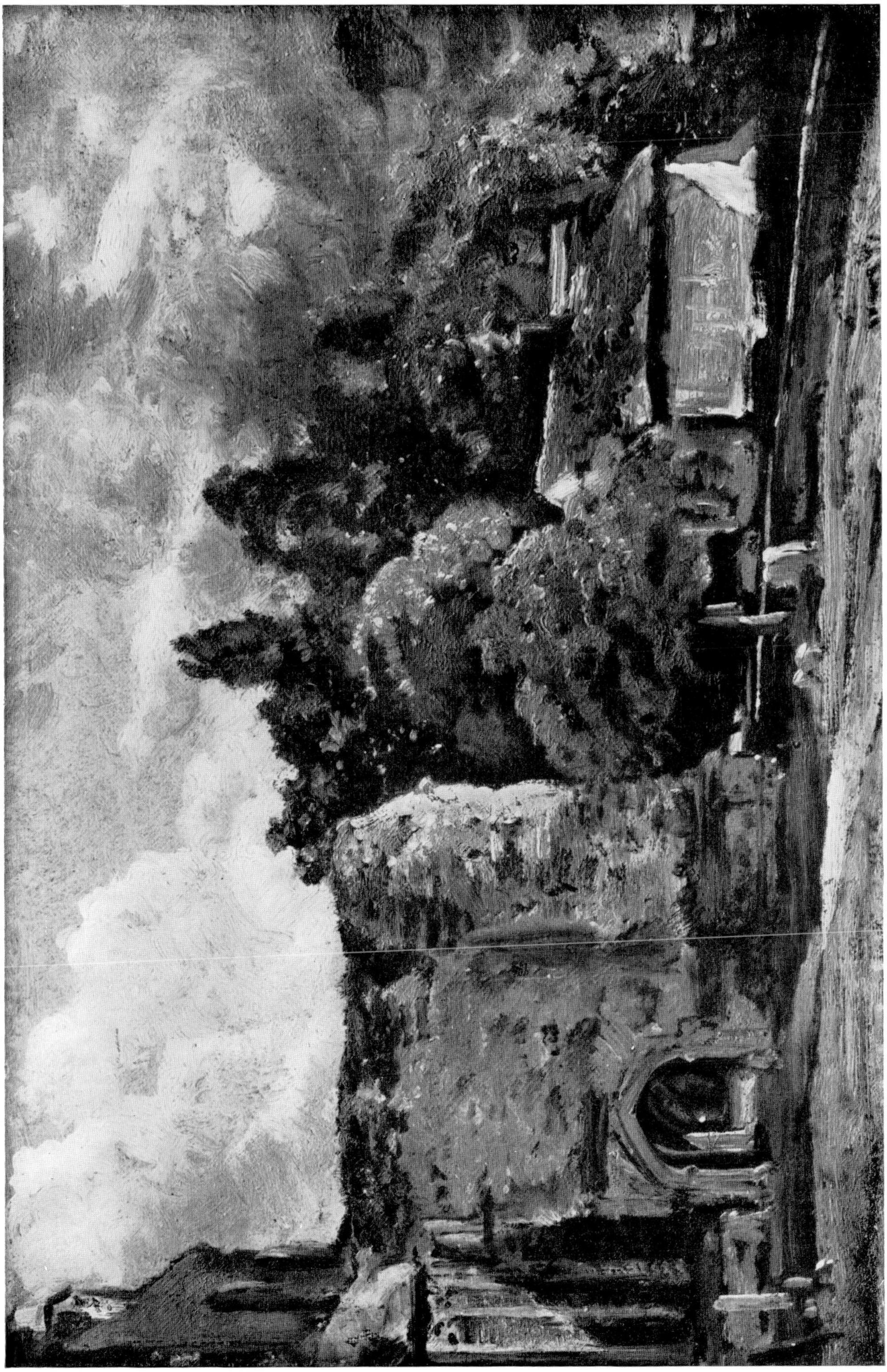

112. East Bergholt Church: ruined tower at W. end.

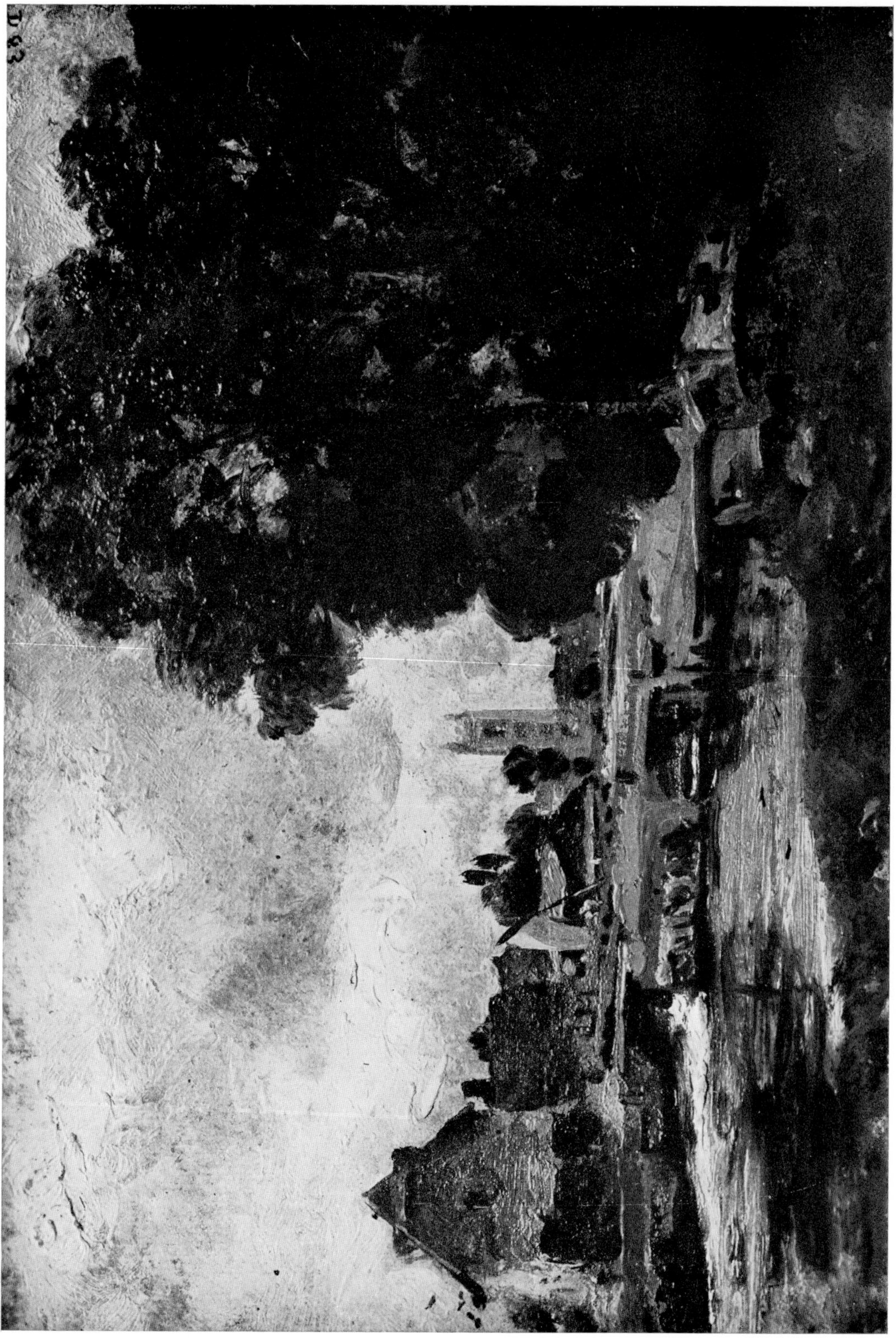

113. Dedham Mill (sketch for No. 184).

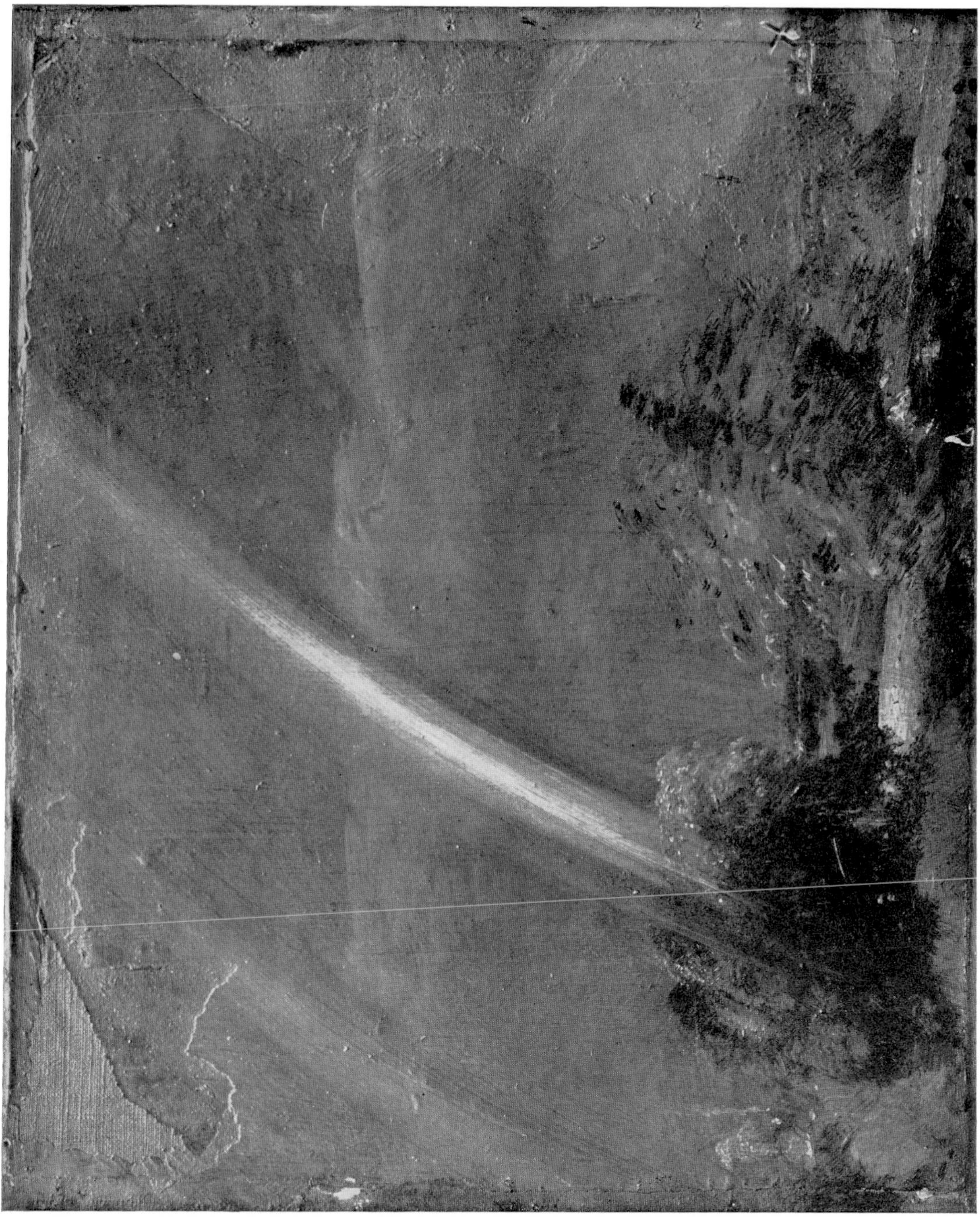

117. Landscape and double rainbow.

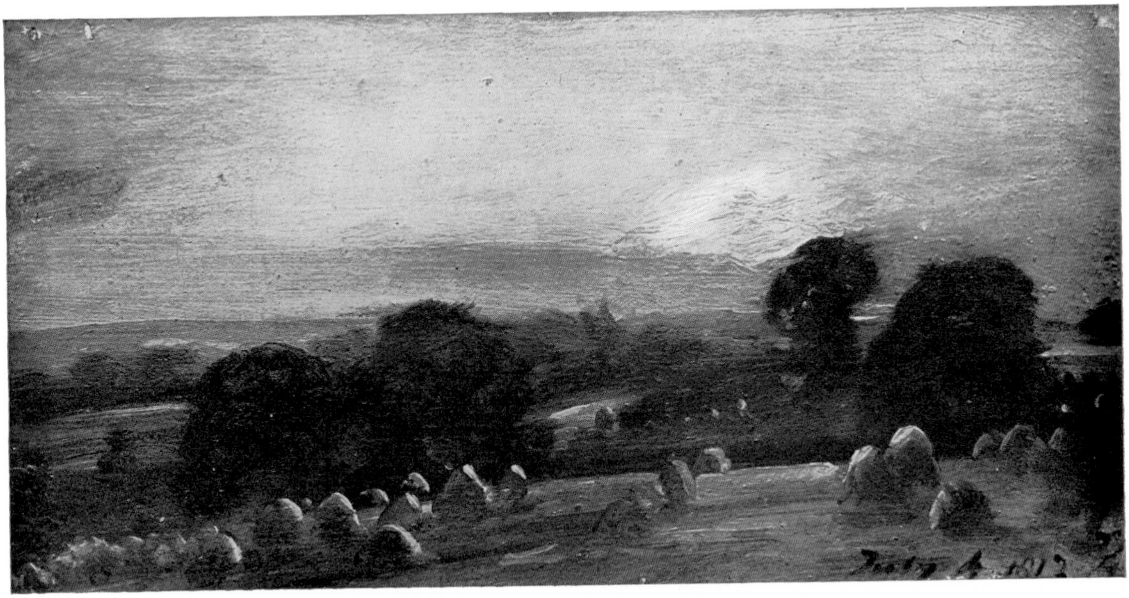

115. A hayfield near East Bergholt at sunset.

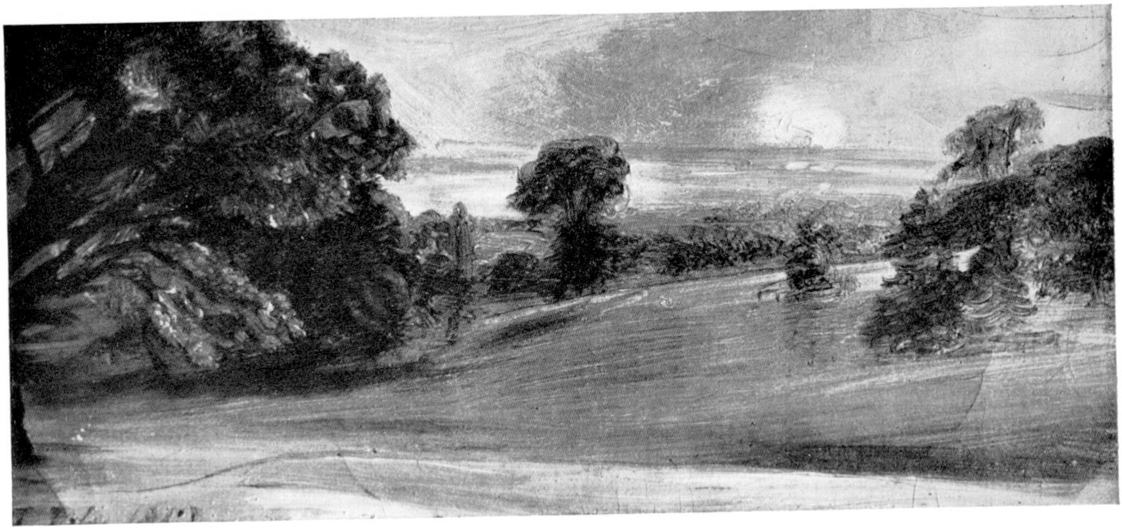

116. A landscape near East Bergholt: evening.

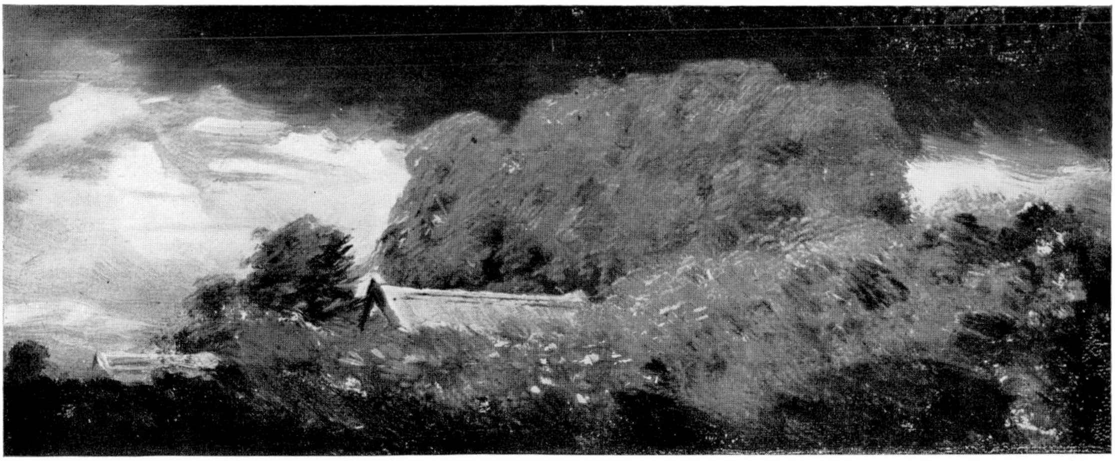

119. Landscape with trees and cottages.

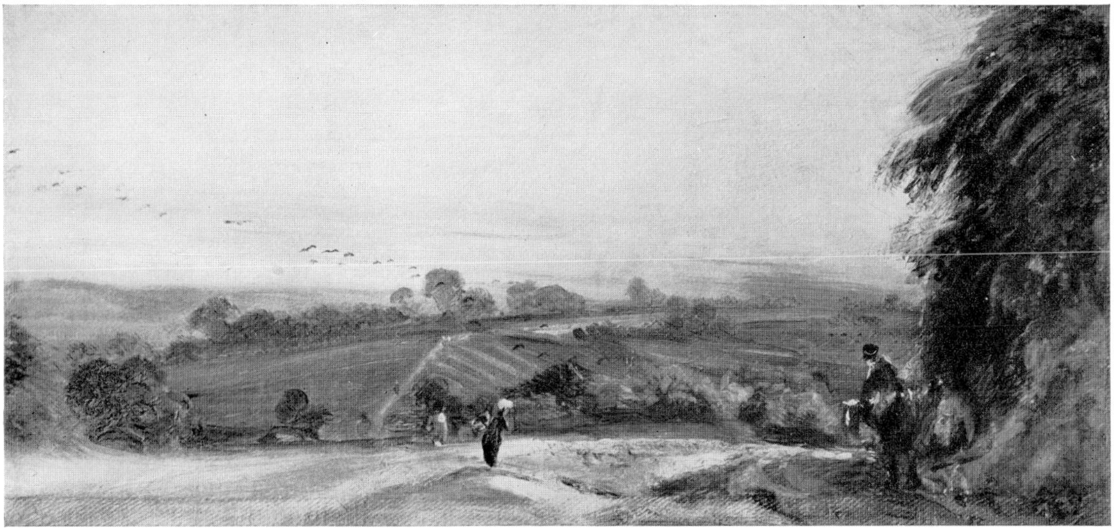

120. Autumnal Sunset.

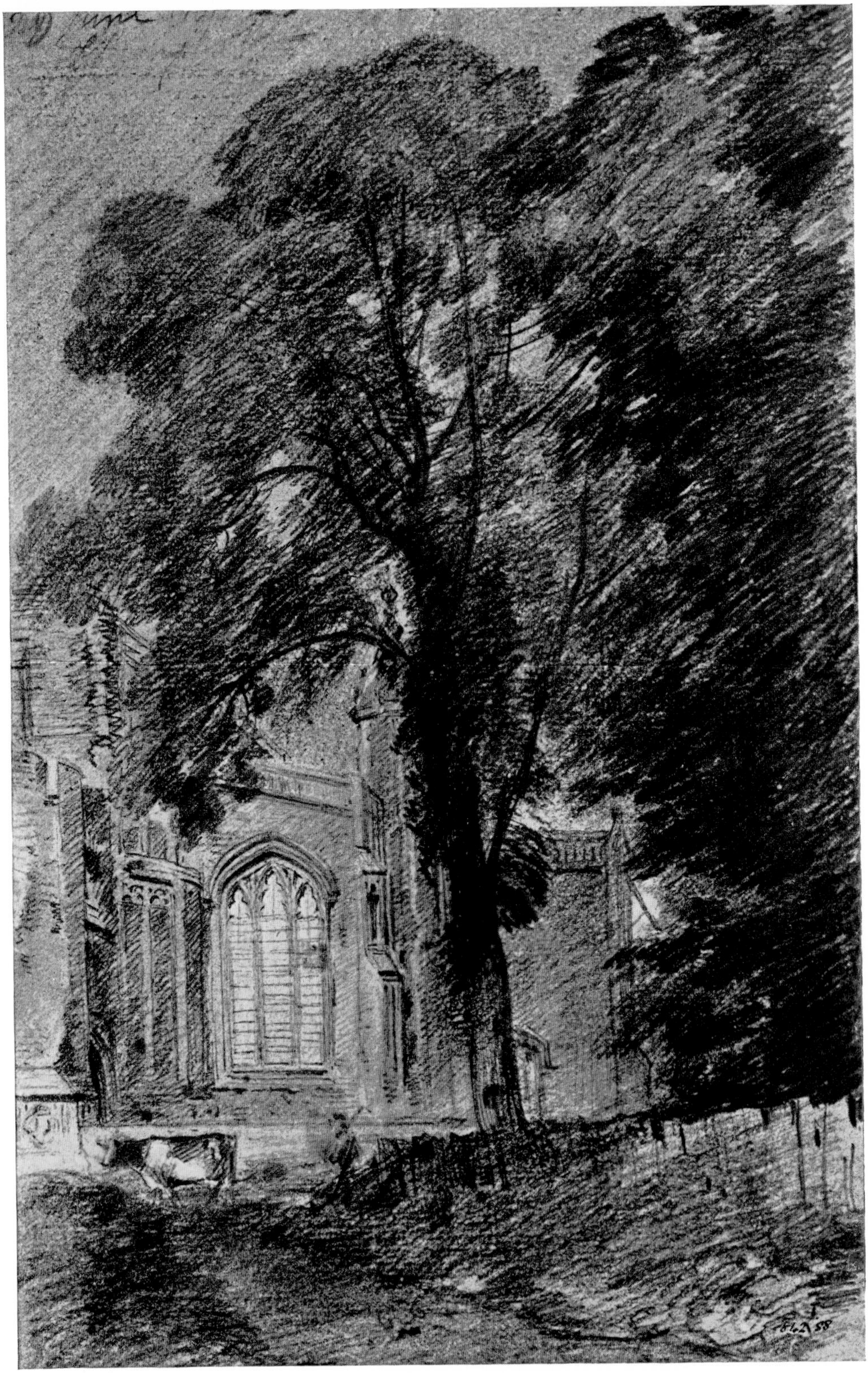

114. East Bergholt Church: W. end.

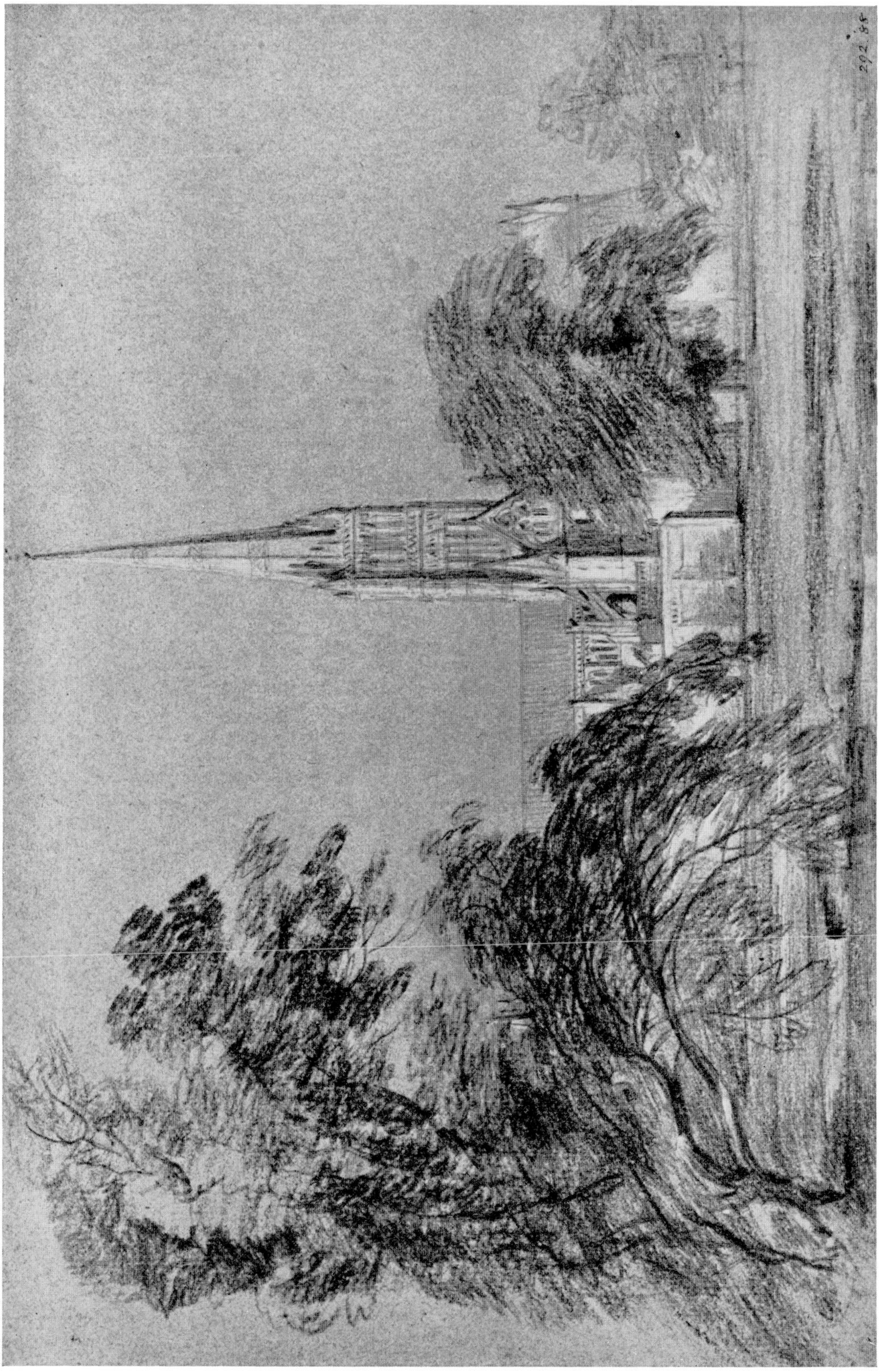

105. Salisbury Cathedral (sketch for No. 254).

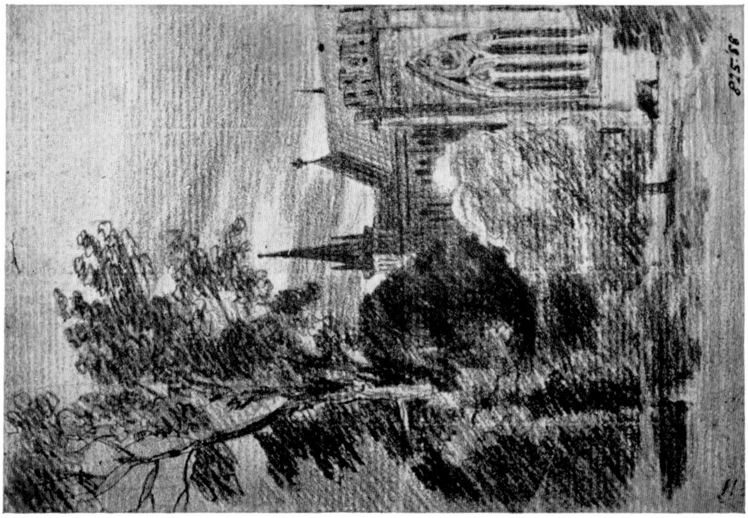

106. Salisbury Cathedral from the S.E.

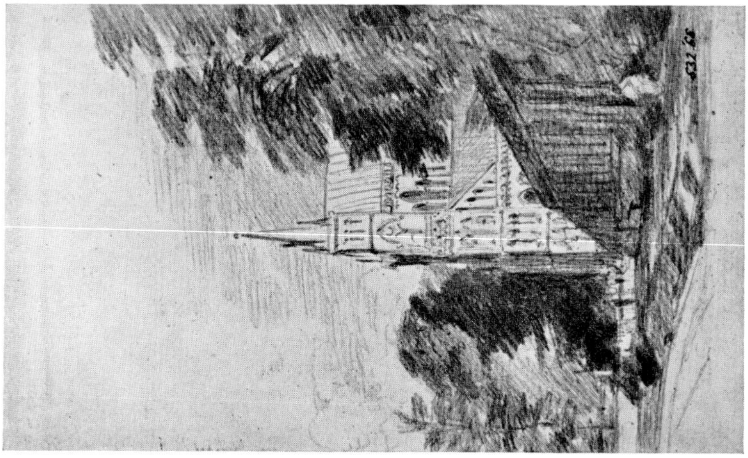

107. Salisbury Cathedral: W. front.

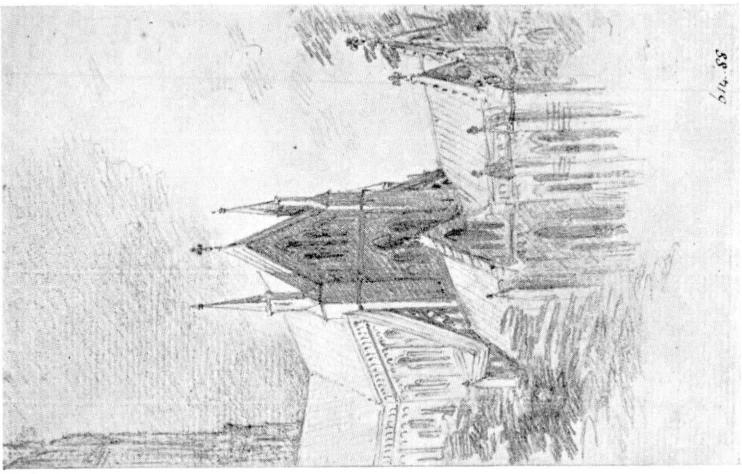

108. Salisbury Cathedral: E. end.

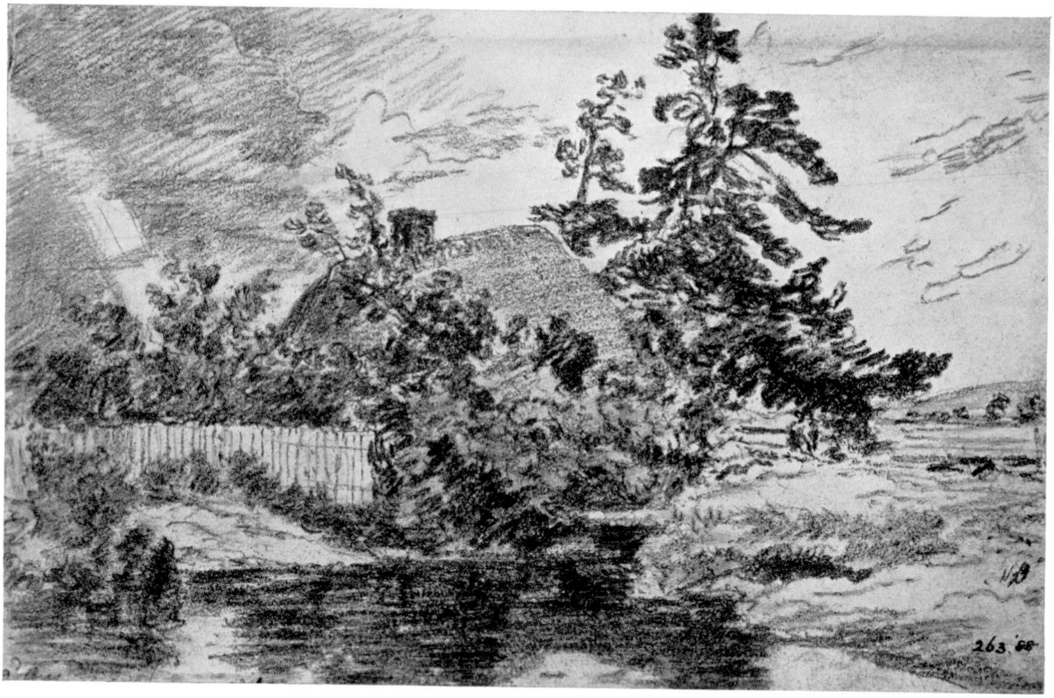

118. Pond and cottage at Salisbury(?).

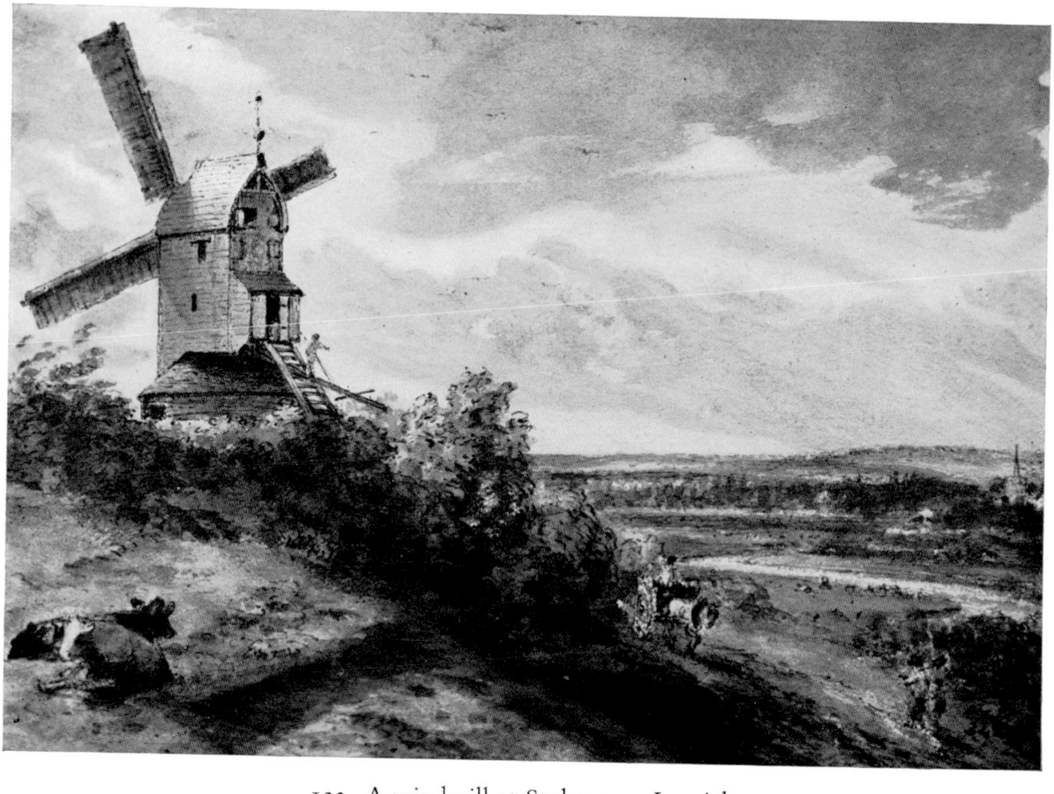

123. A windmill at Stoke, near Ipswich.

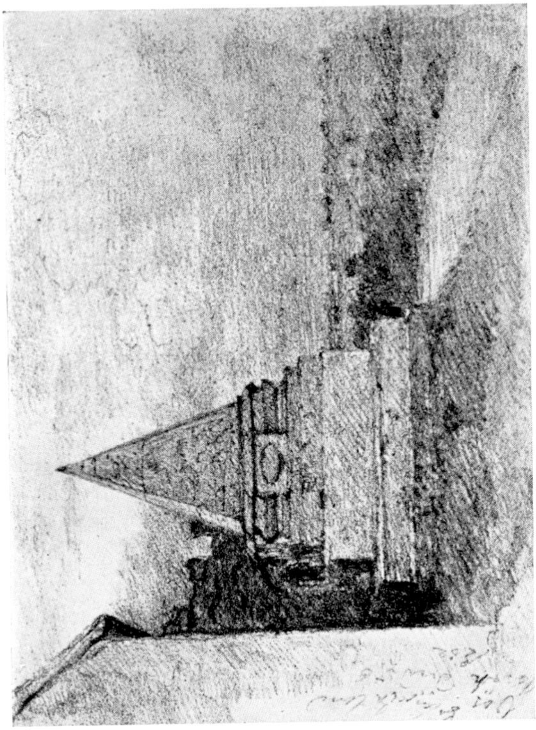

121, p. 3. Tomb at Widford.

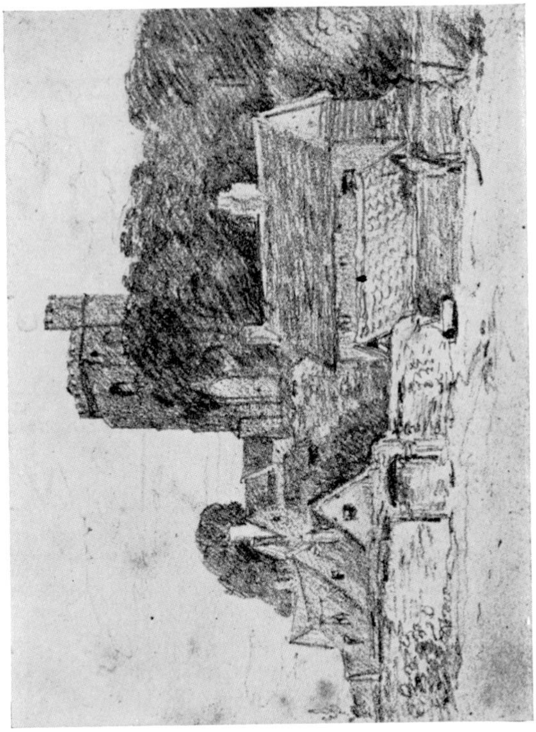

121, p. 5. St. Mary-ad-Murum, Colchester.

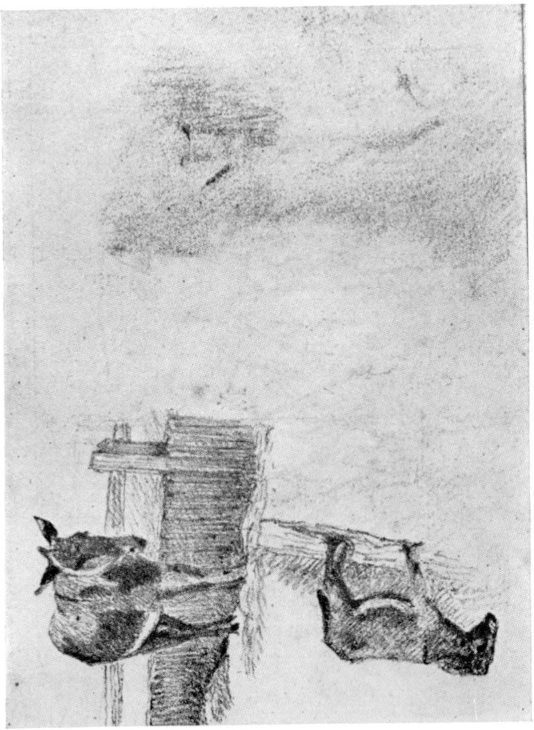

121, p. 7. Donkeys.

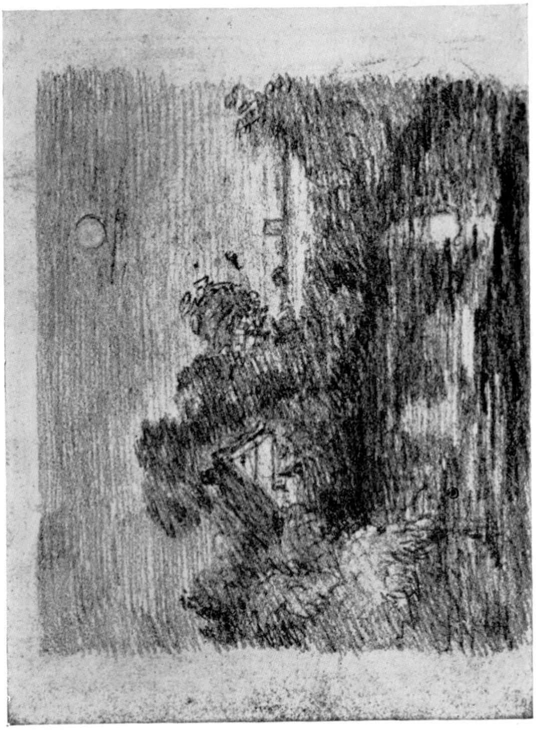

121, p. 8. A pool on the Stour(?).

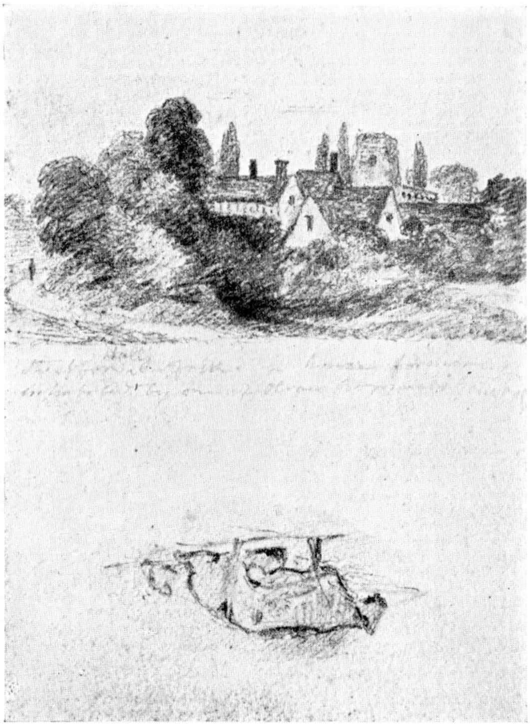

121, p. 9. Stratford Hall.

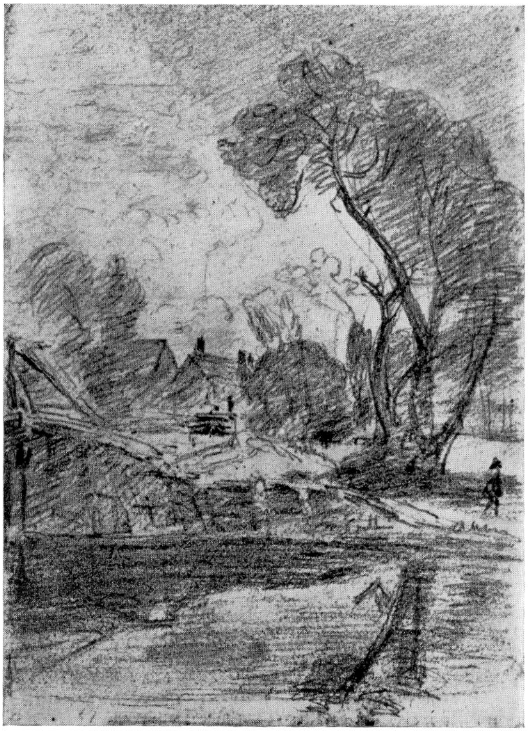

121, p. 10. Flatford Mill.

121, p. 11. Barges.

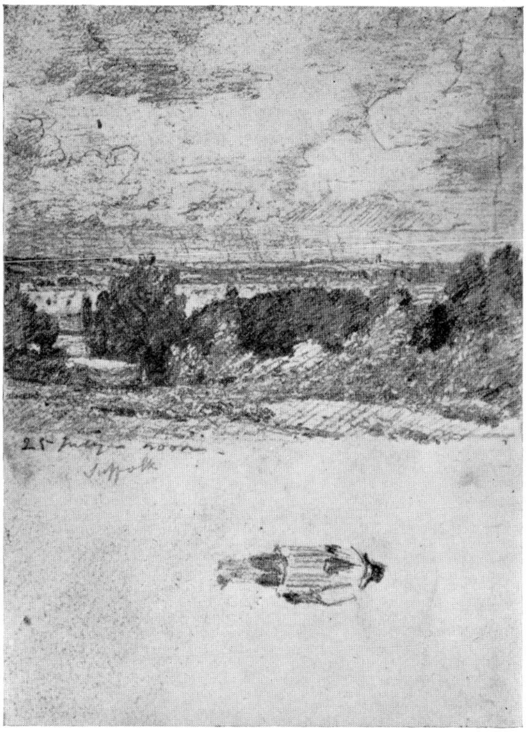

121, p. 12. Dedham Vale.

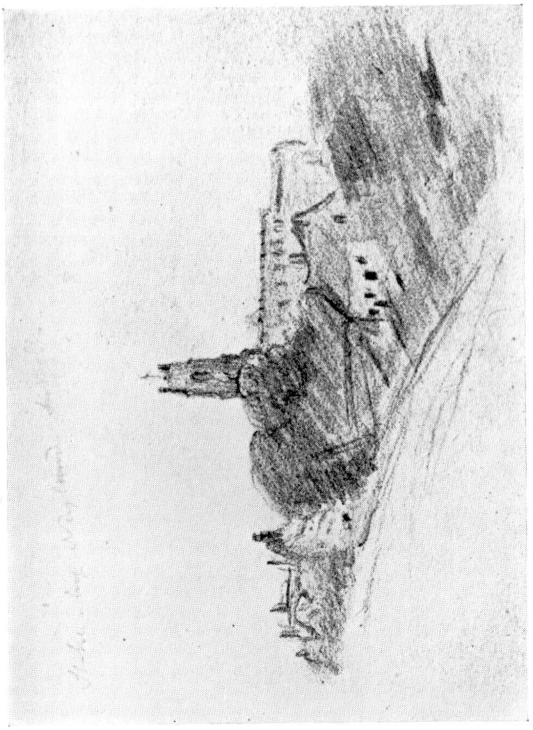

121, p. 13. Stoke-by-Nayland Church.

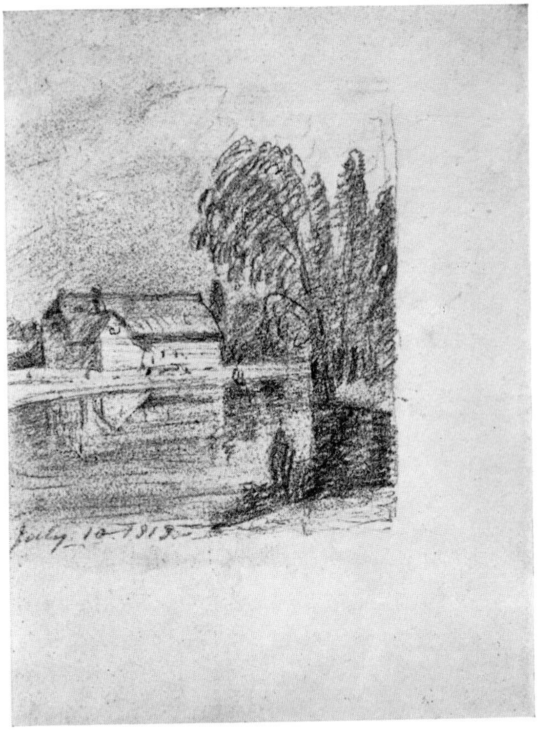

121, p. 14. A mill or barn.

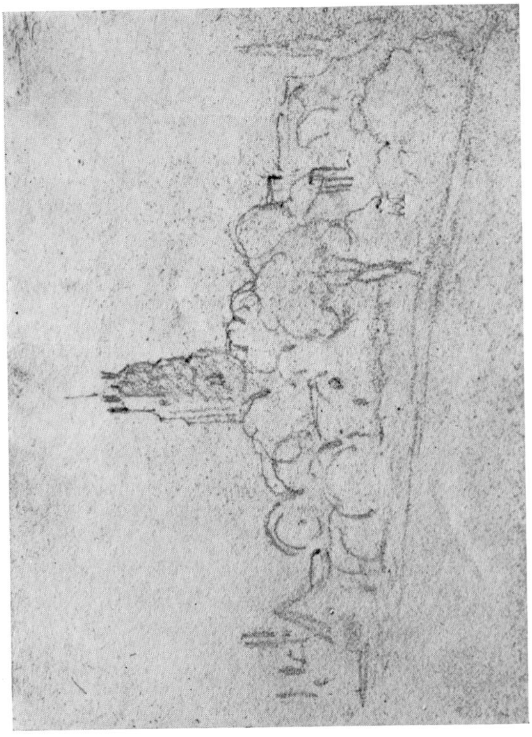

121, p. 15. Stoke-by-Nayland Church.

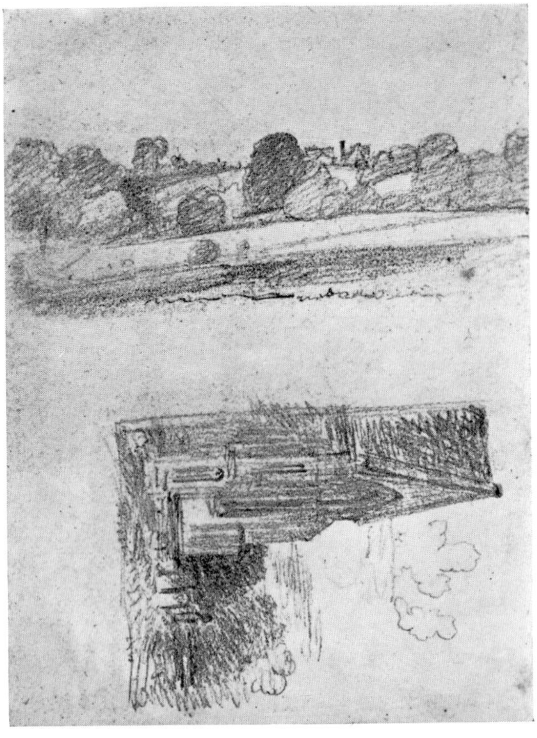

121, p. 16. East Bergholt Church.

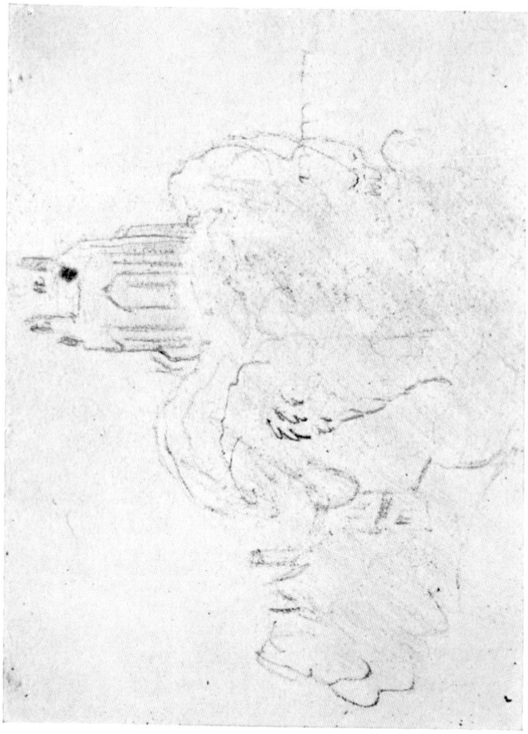

121, p. 17. Stoke-by-Nayland Church.

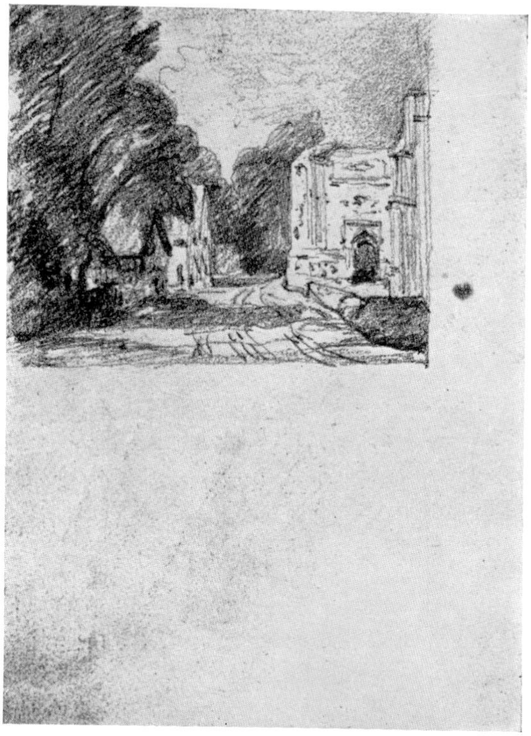

121, p. 18. East Bergholt.

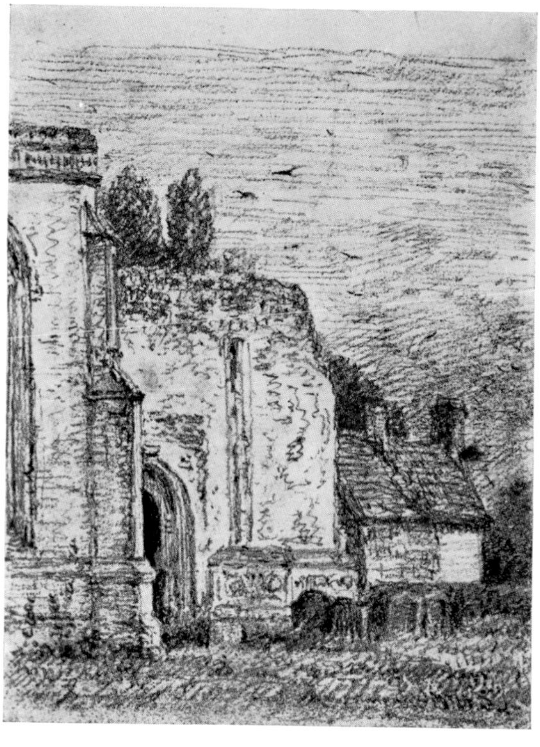

121, p. 19. East Bergholt Church

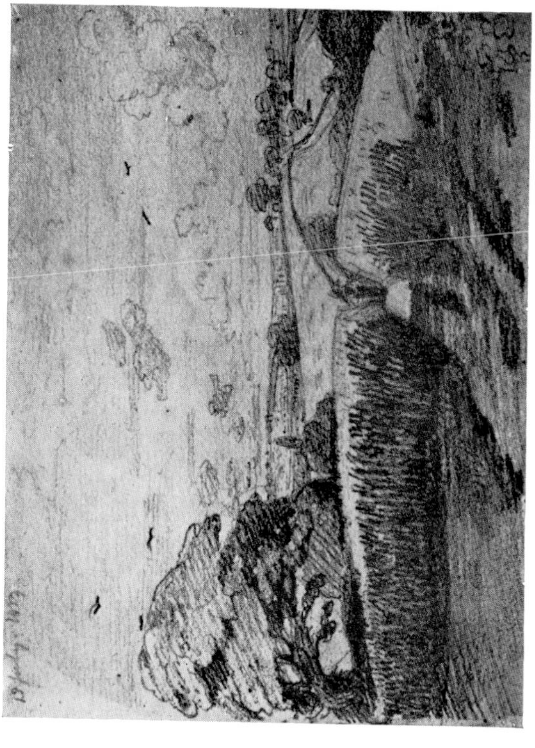

121, p. 21. Cornfield at East Bergholt.

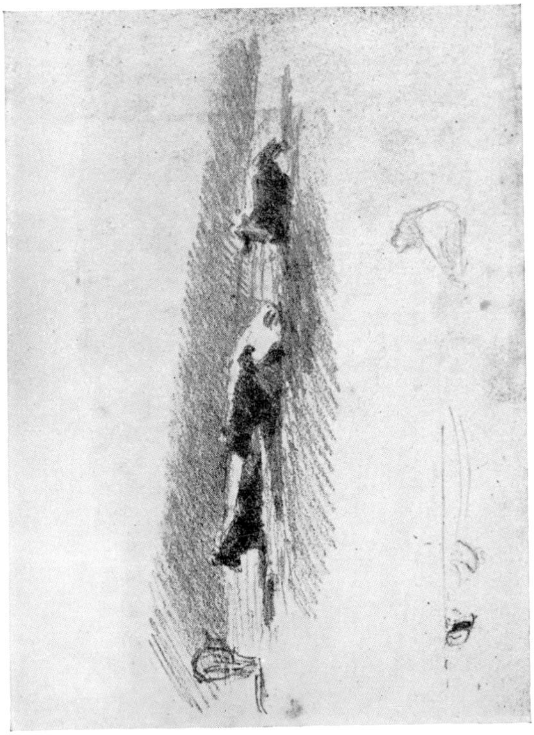

121, p. 23. Cows.

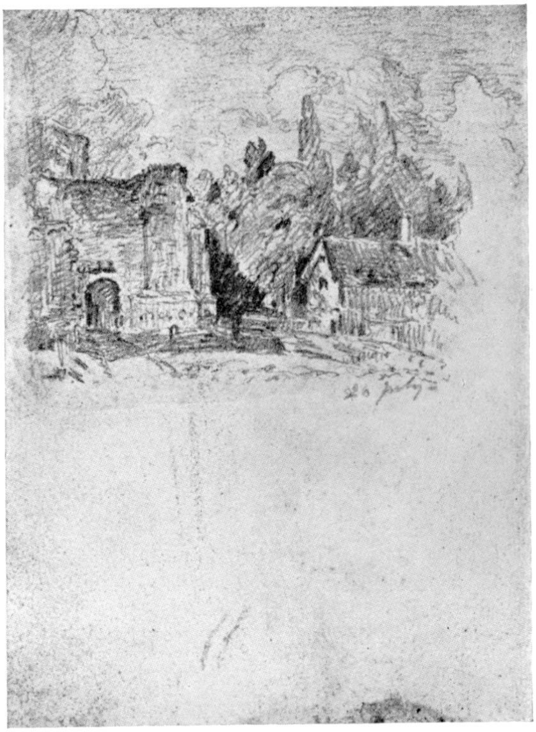

121, p. 24. East Bergholt Church.

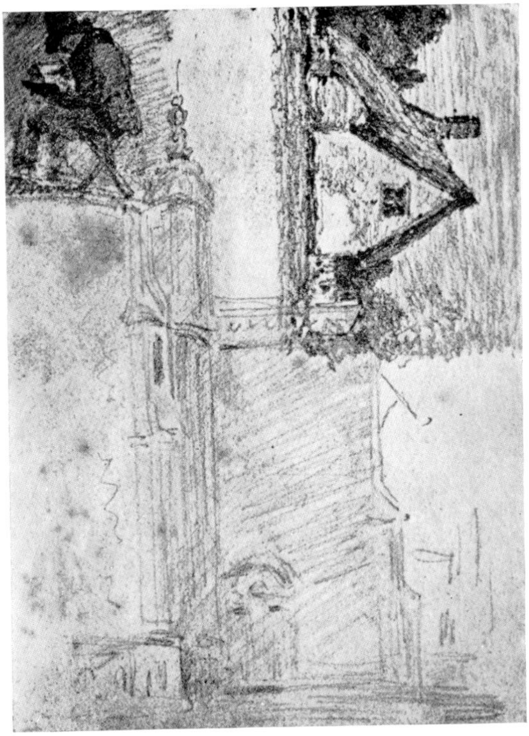

121, p. 25. East Bergholt Church.

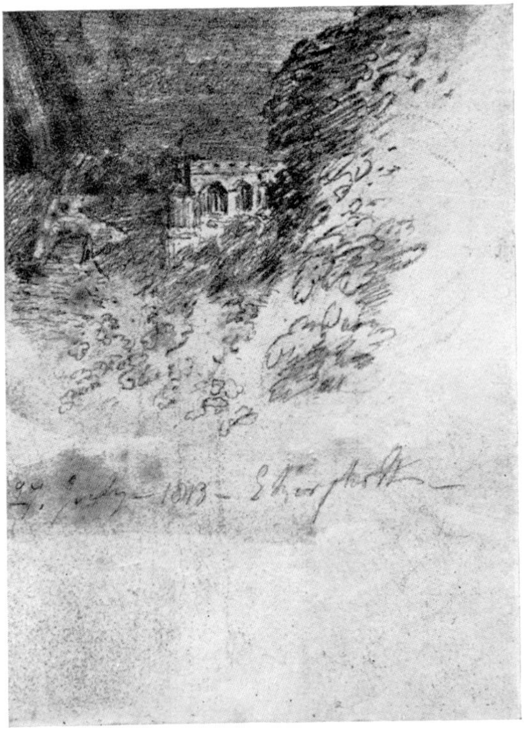

121, p. 26. East Bergholt Church.

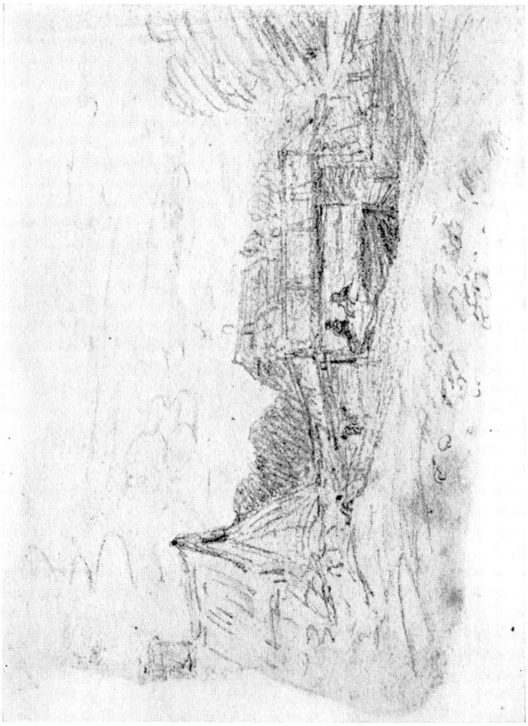

121, p. 27. Flatford Old Bridge.

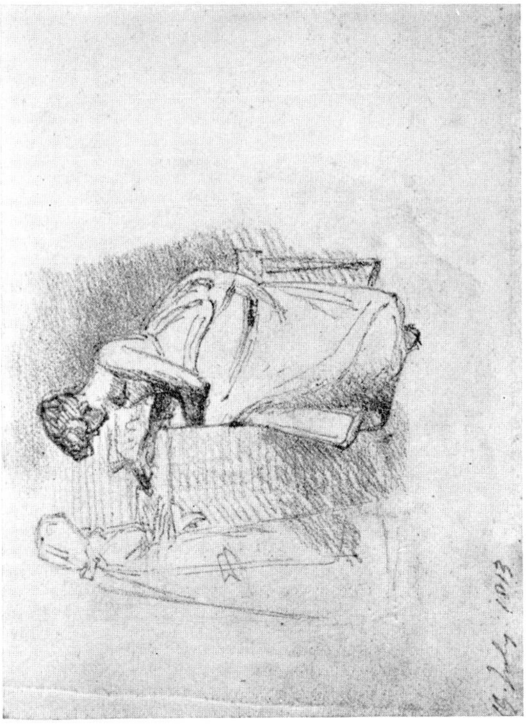

121, p. 28. A woman writing.

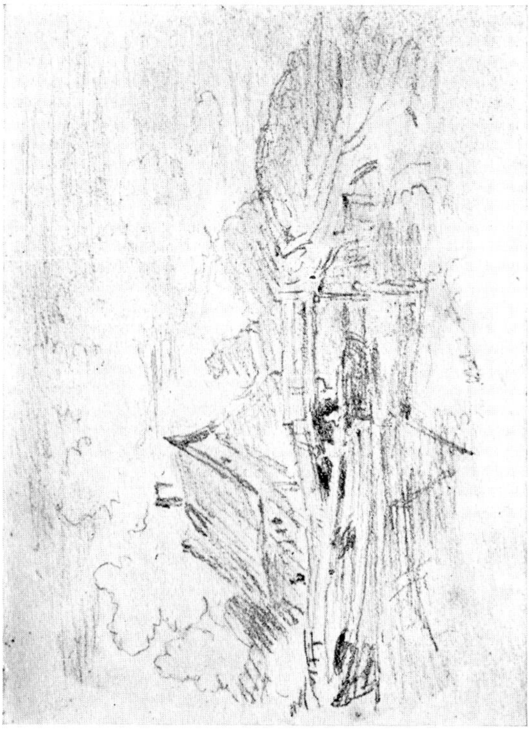

121, p. 29. Flatford Old Bridge.

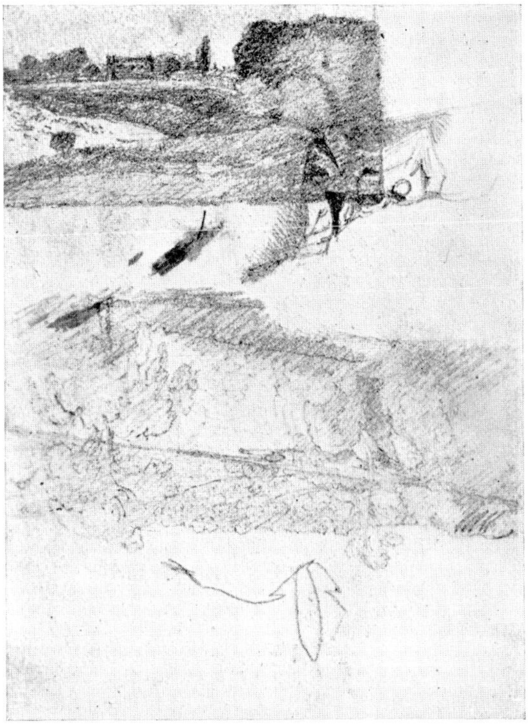

121, p. 30. View at East Bergholt.

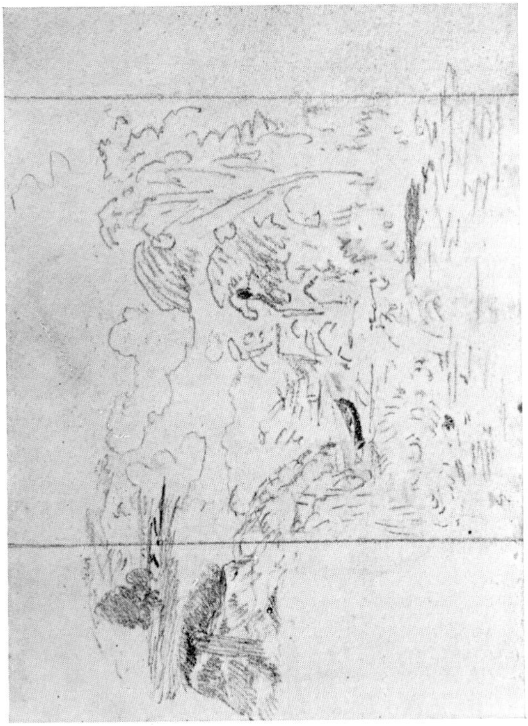

121, p. 31. Sketch for 'The Valley Farm'.

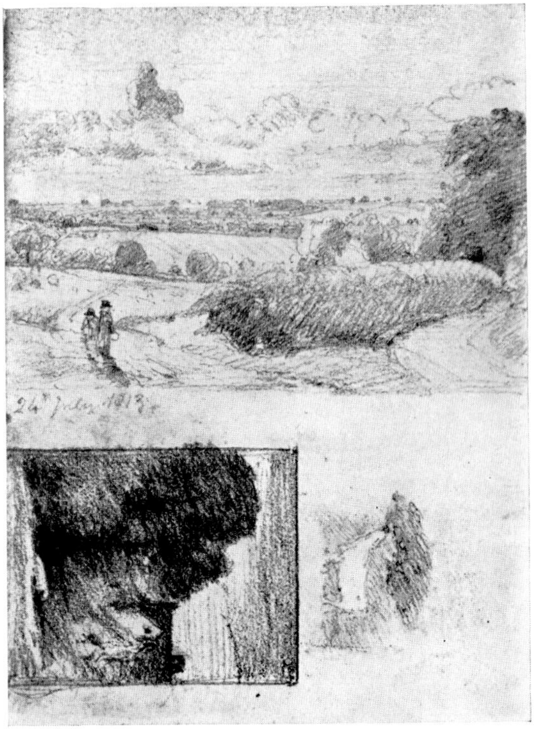

121, p. 32. A valley scene.

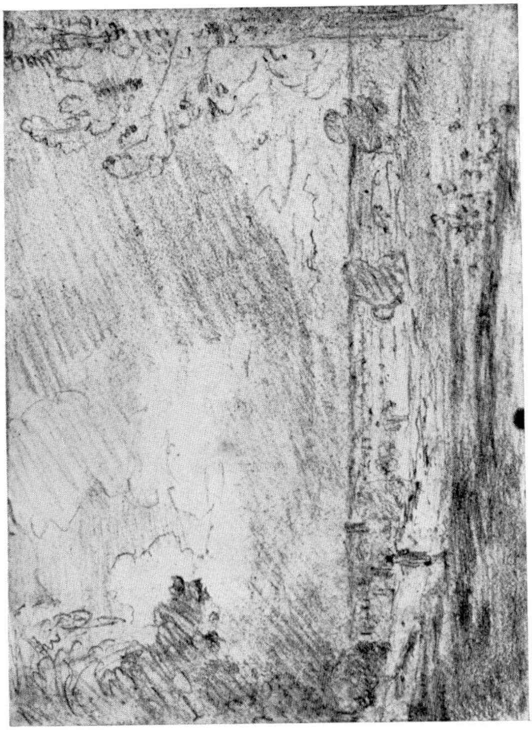

121, p. 33. Dedham Vale.

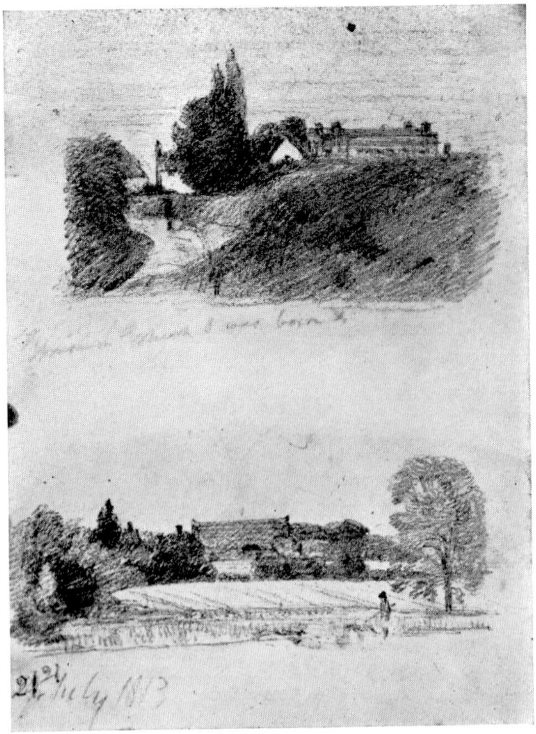

121, p. 34. Golding Constable's house.

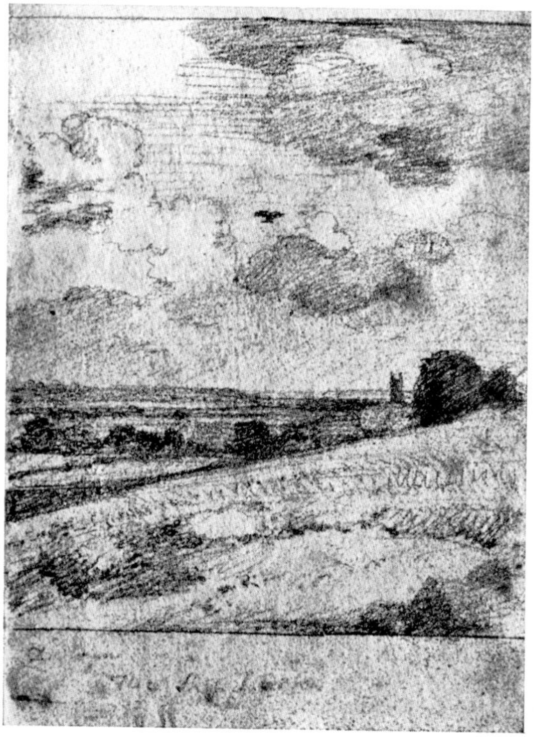

121, p. 36. Dedham. The Sky Lark.

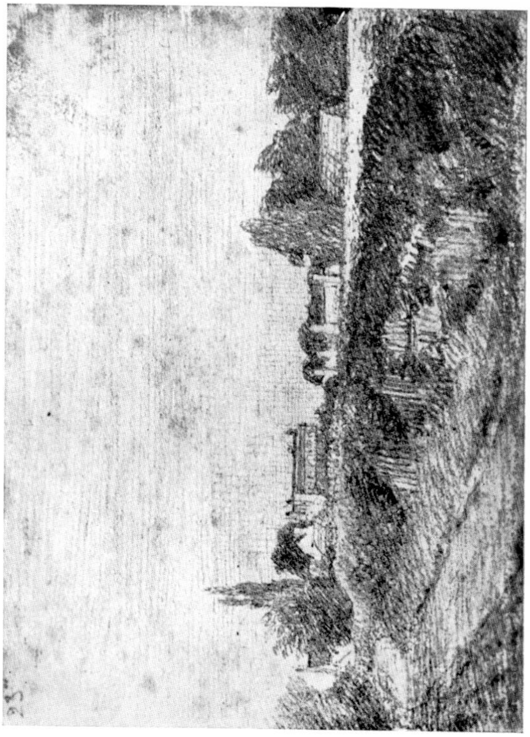

121, p. 37. Golding Constable's house.

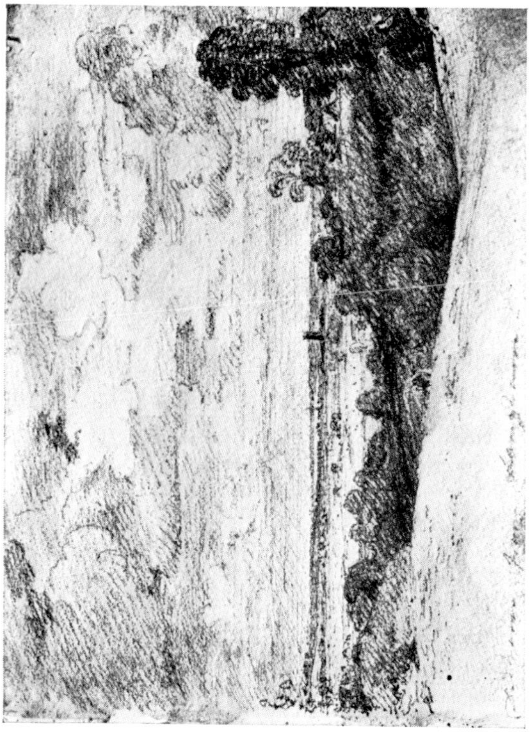

121, p. 39. Dedham from Langham.

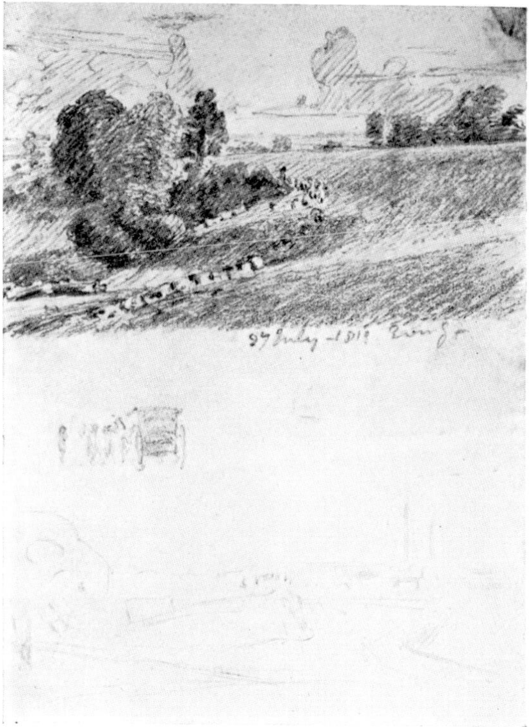

121, p. 41. Landscape with cattle.

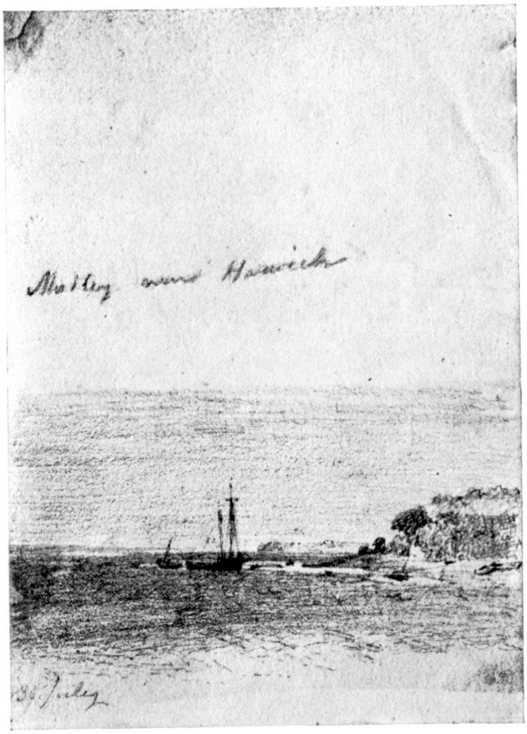

121, p. 42. Mistley.

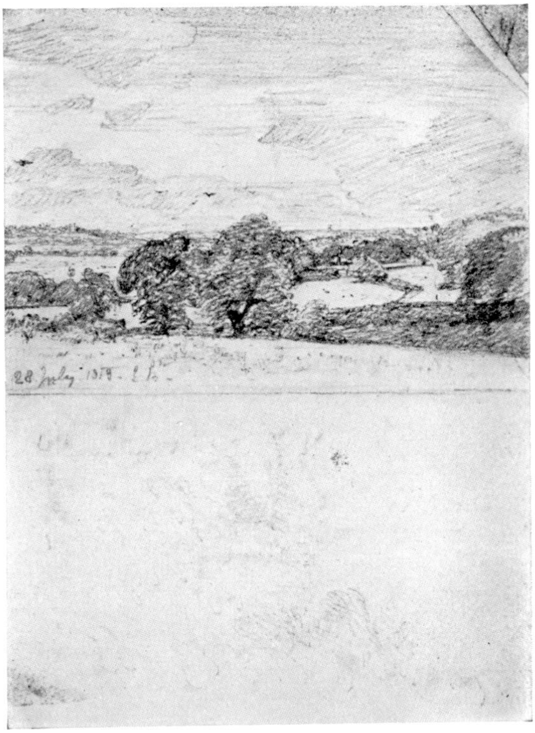

121, p. 43. Dedham Vale.

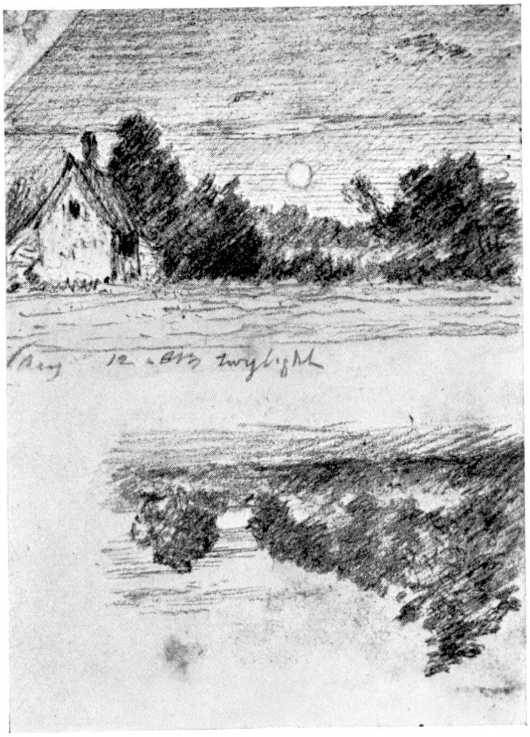

121, p. 44. East Bergholt.

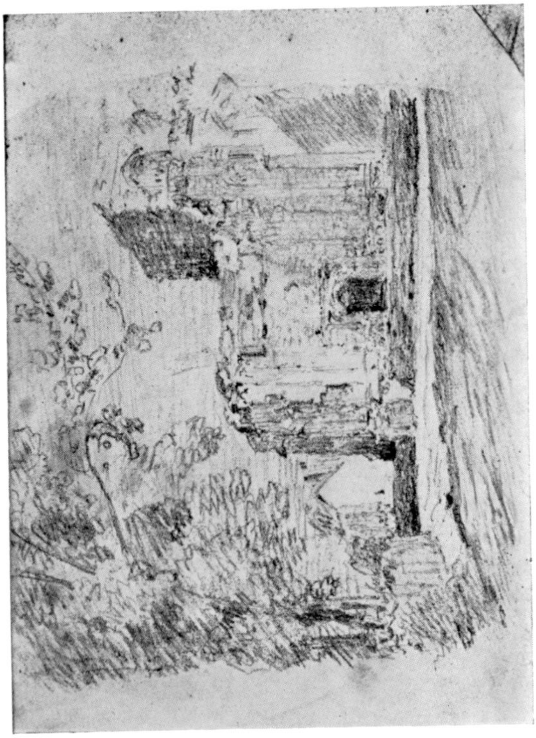

121, p. 45. East Bergholt Church.

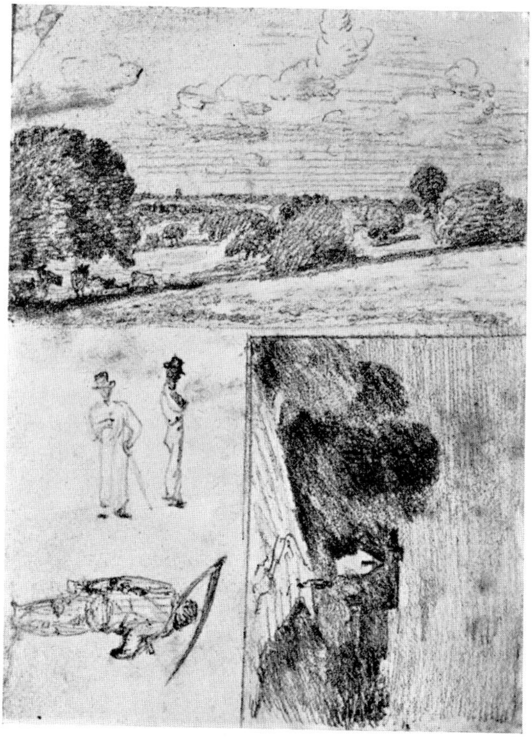

121, p. 46. A wide landscape.

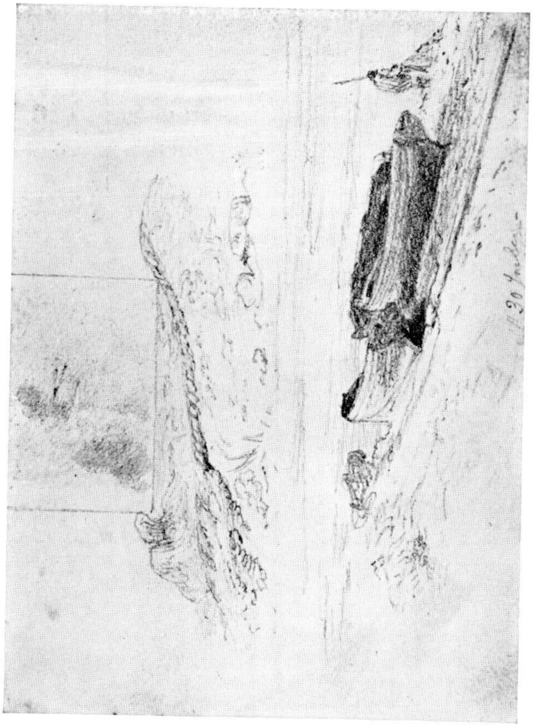

121, p. 47. Coast scenes near Mistley.

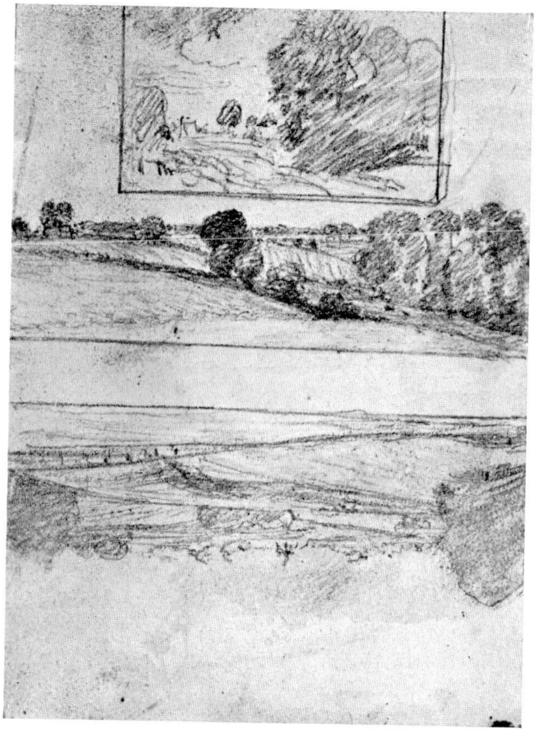

121, p. 48. Landscape studies.

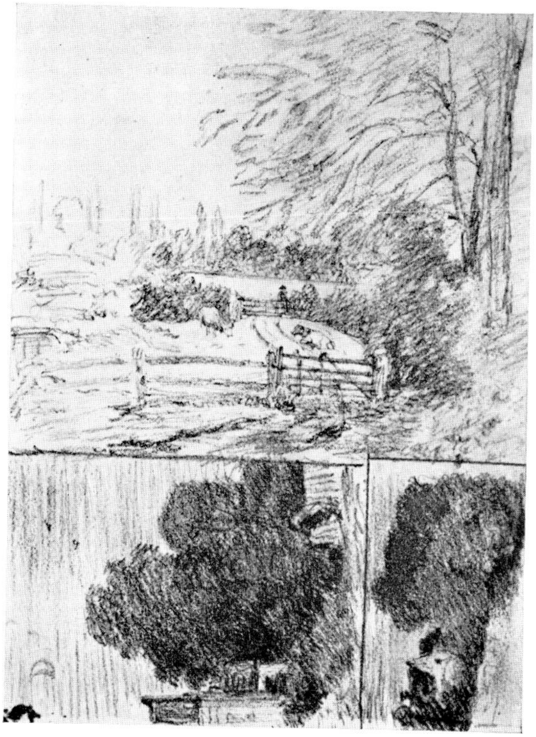

121, p. 49. A path through a field.

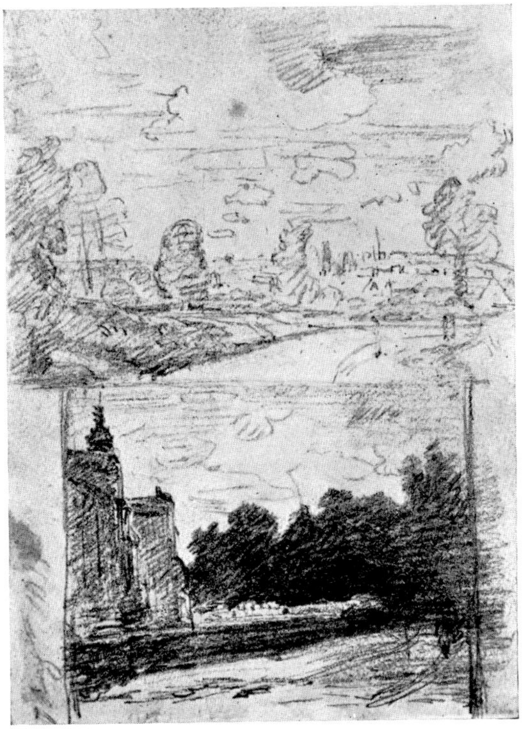

121, p. 50. East Bergholt Church.

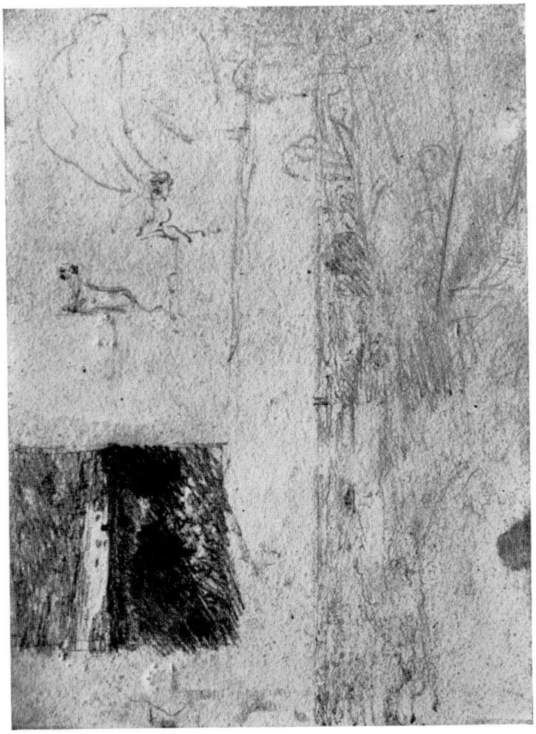

121, p. 51. Dedham from Langham.

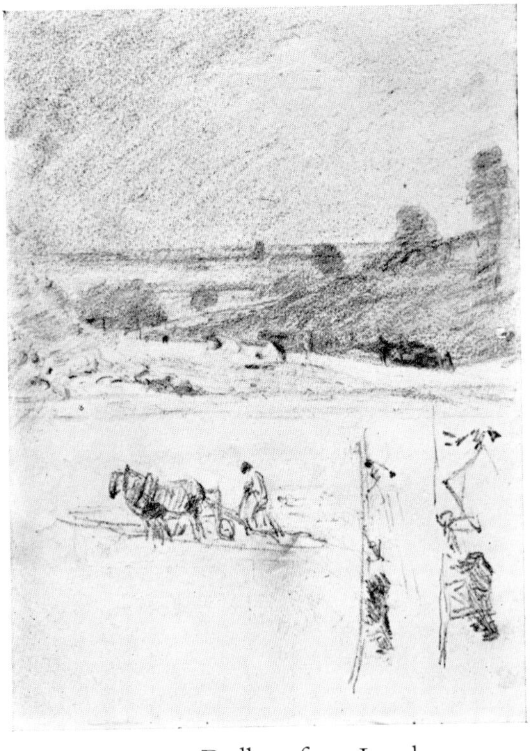

121, p. 52. Dedham from Langham.

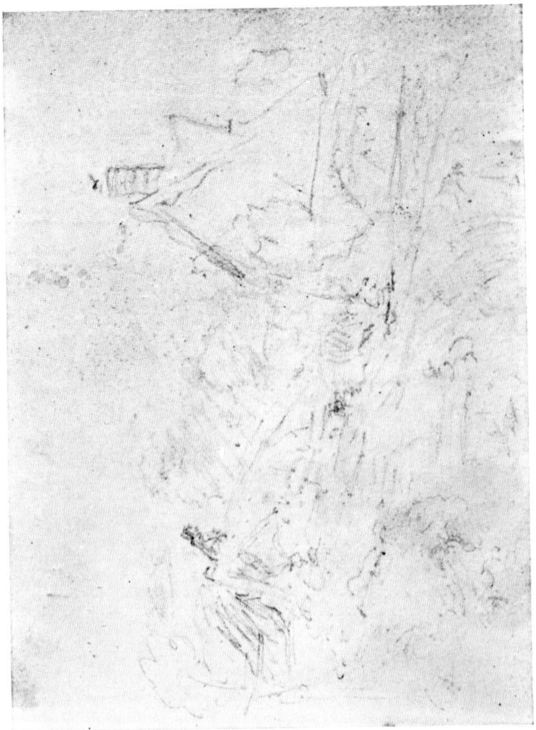

121, p. 53. Flatford Old Bridge.

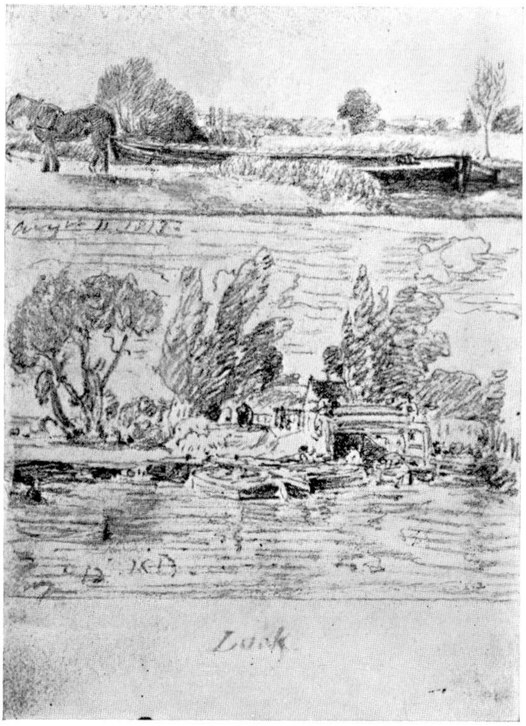

121, p. 54. Scenes on the Stour.

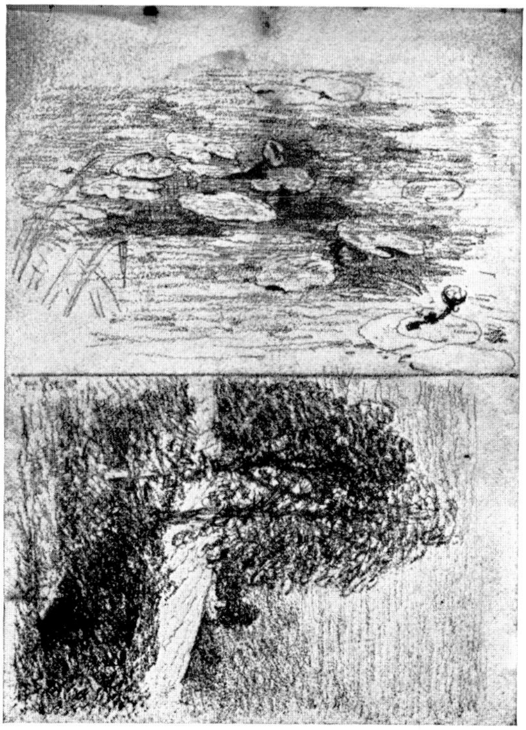

121, p. 55. Water-lilies.

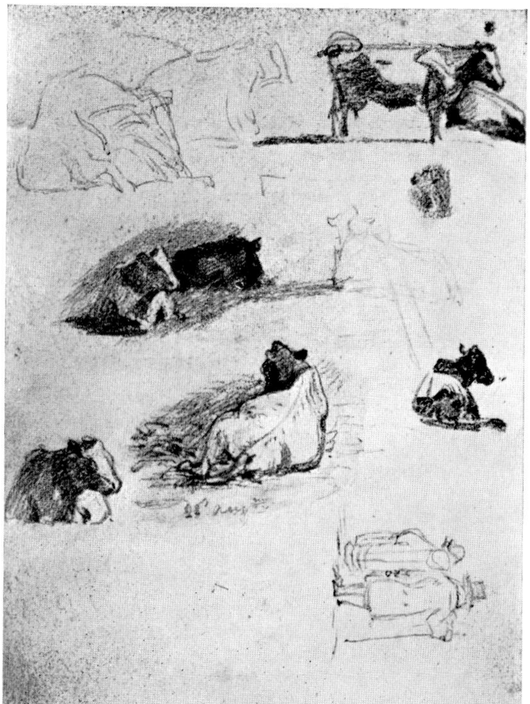

121, p. 56. Cows.

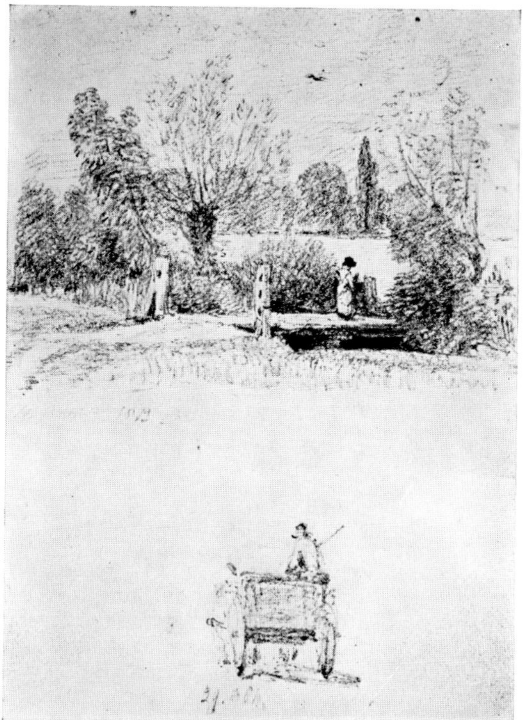

121, p. 57. A woman crossing a footbridge.

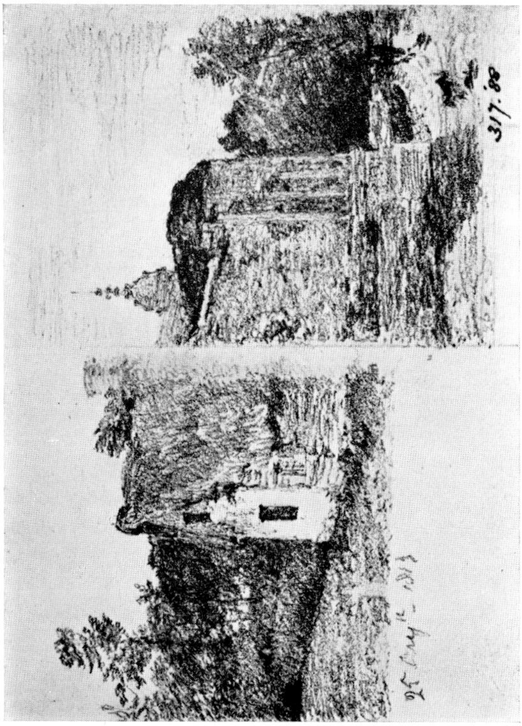

121, p. 59. East Bergholt Church.

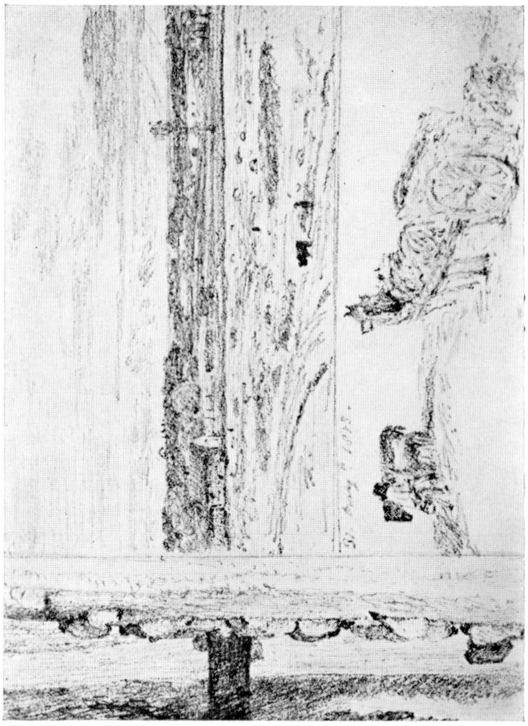

121, p. 61. A landscape with a cottage.

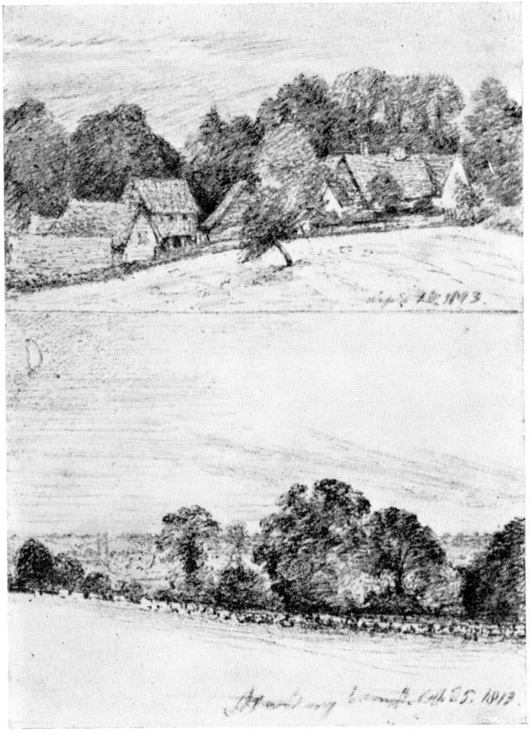

121, p. 63. View towards Dedham(?).

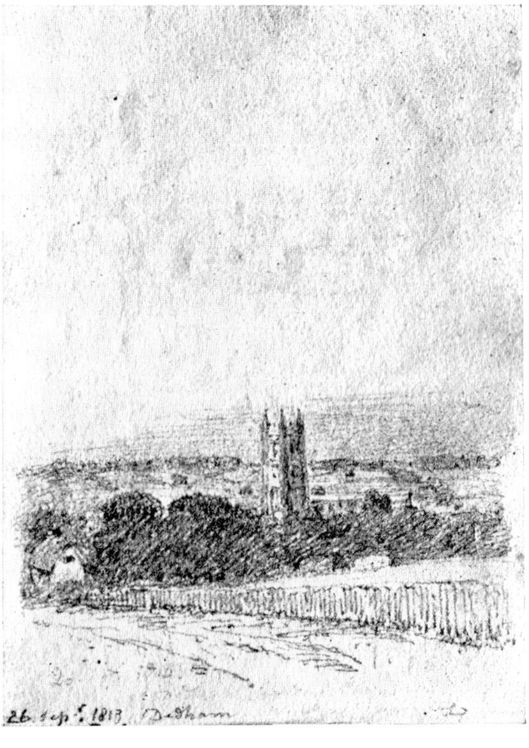

121, p. 65. Dedham Church.

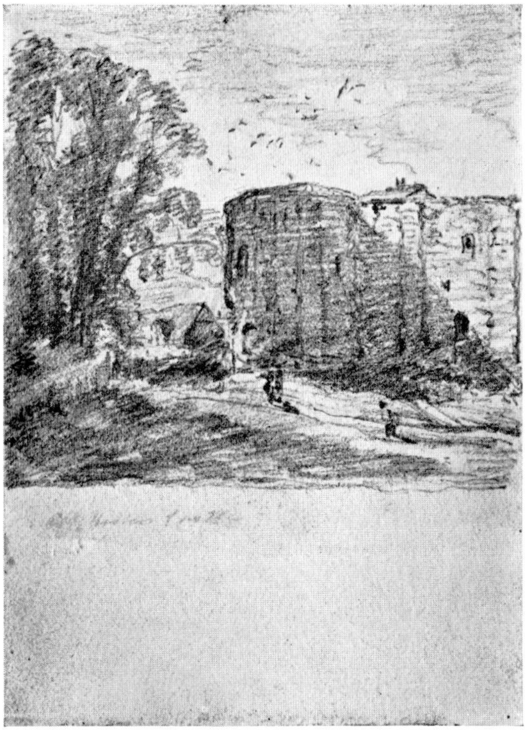

121, p. 66. Colchester Castle.

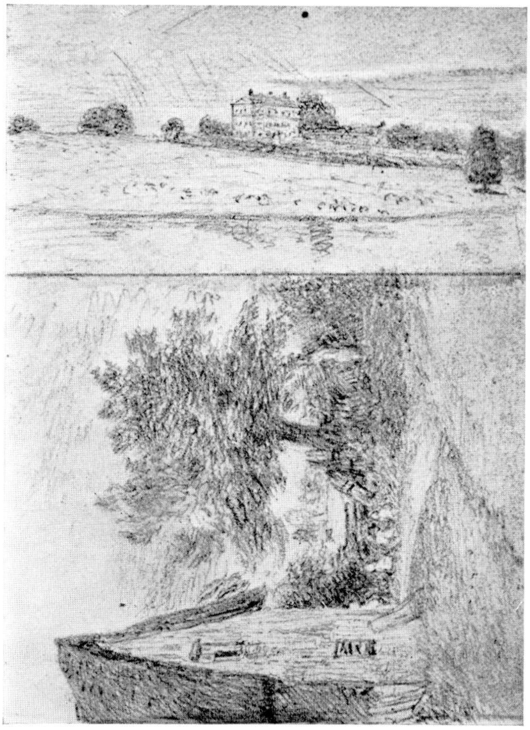

121, p. 67. View towards a mansion.

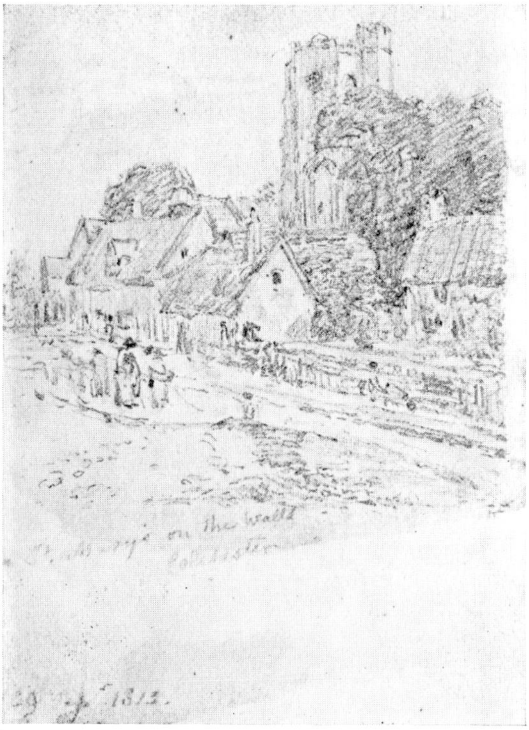

121, p. 68. St. Mary-ad-Murum, Colchester.

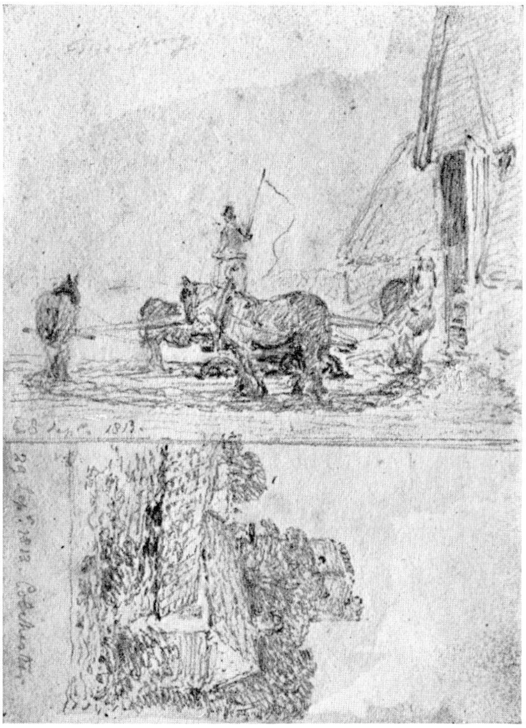

121, p. 69. St. Mary-ad-Murum, Colchester.

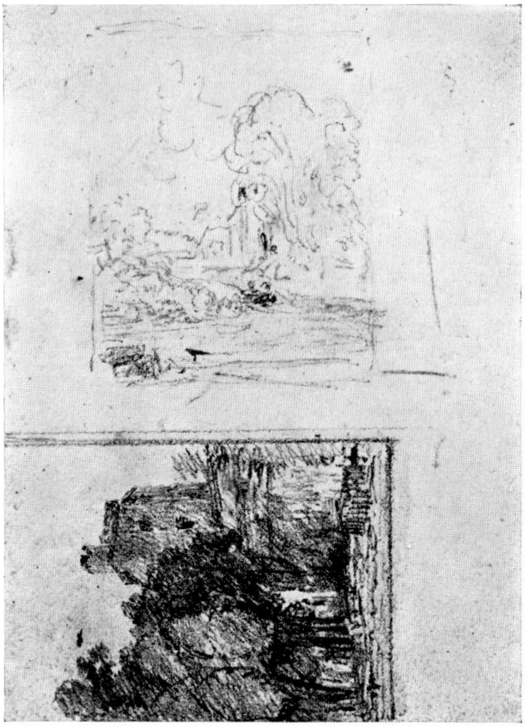

121, p. 70. Sketch for 'The Valley Farm'.

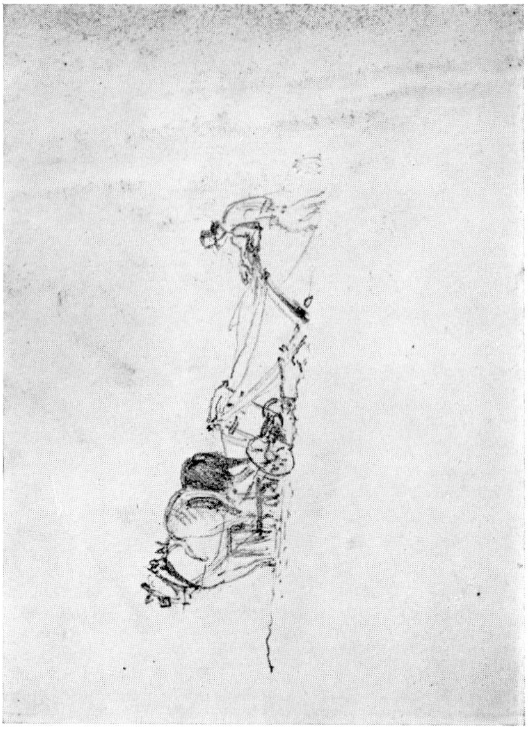

121, p. 71. Sketch for 'A Summerland'.

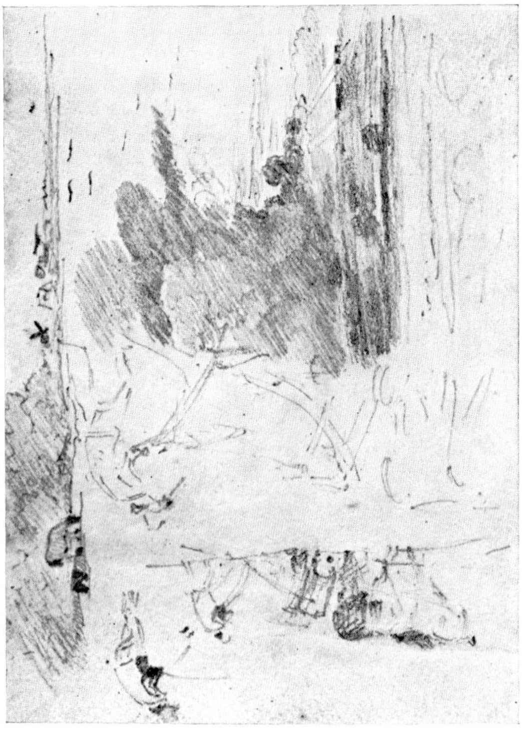

121, p. 72. Cloud study.

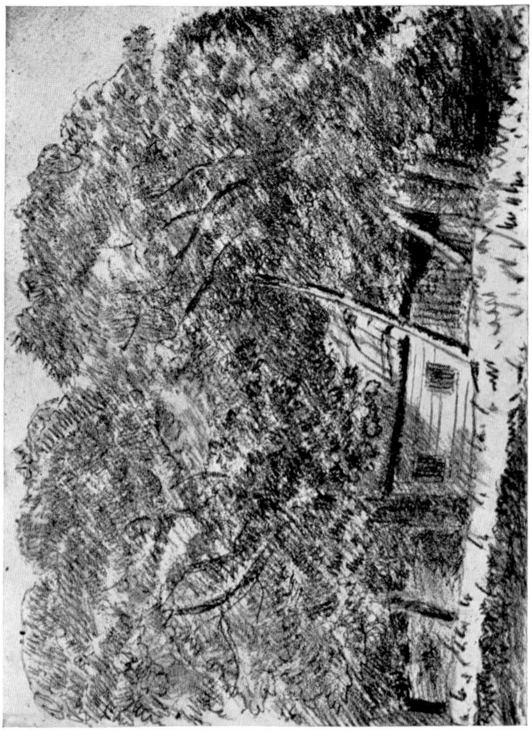

121, p. 75. A cottage amid trees.

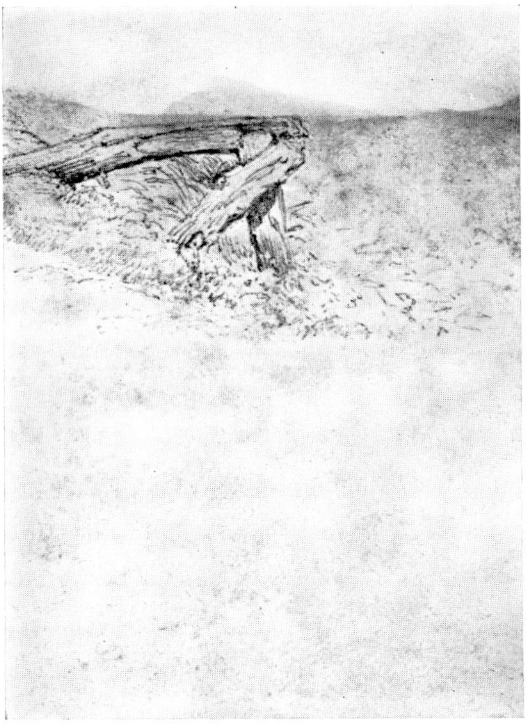

121, p. 76. A mooring post.

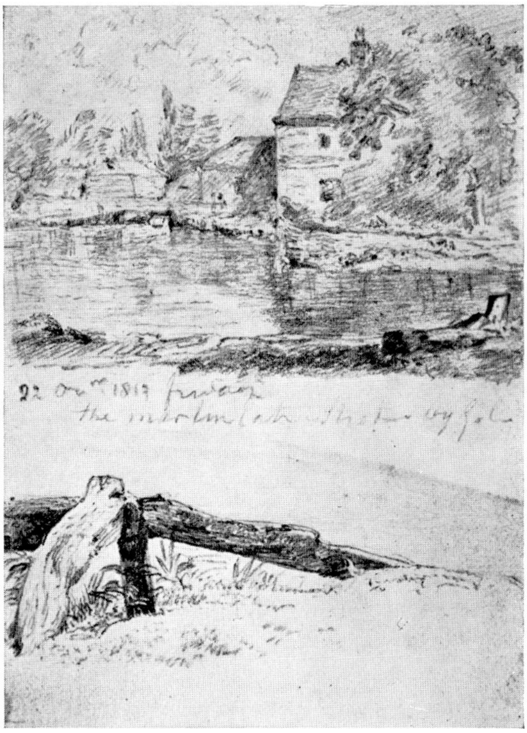

121, p. 77. A mill.

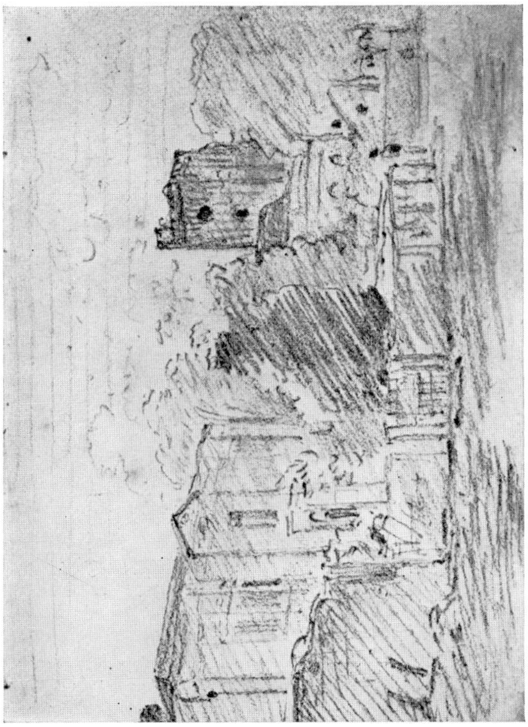

121, p. 78. St. Mary's, Colchester.

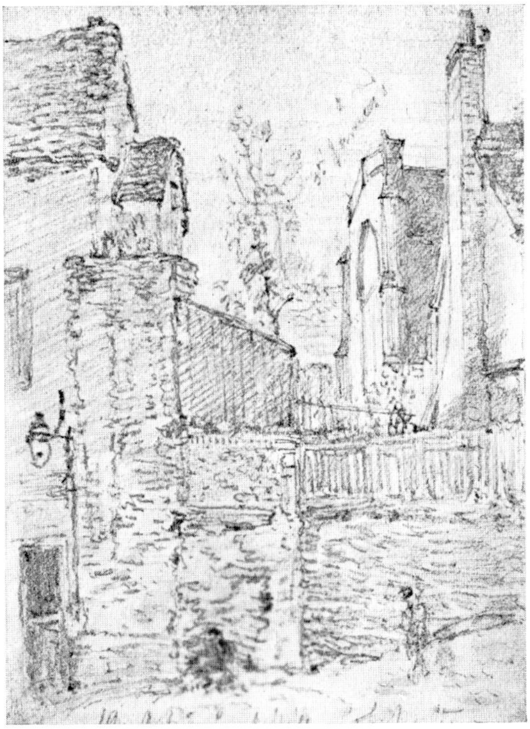

121, p. 80. The Roman wall, Colchester.

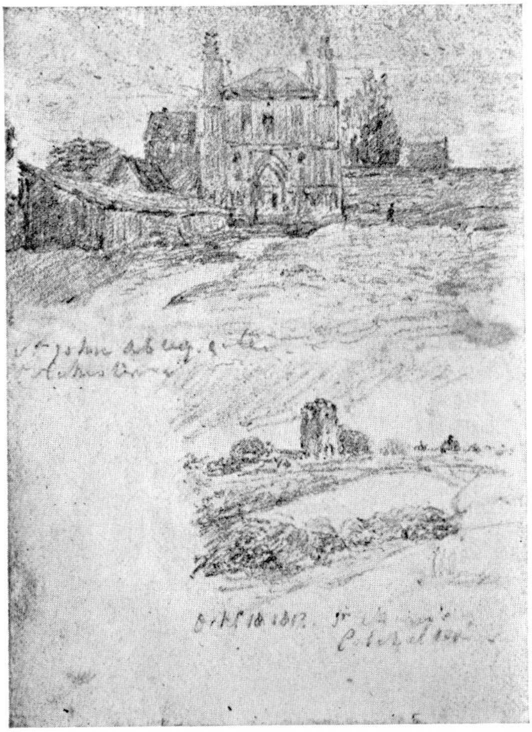

121, p. 81. St. John's Abbey, Colchester.

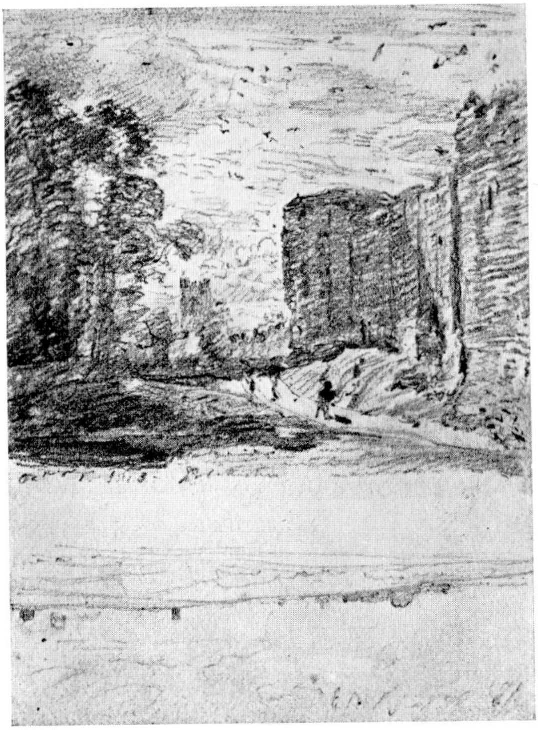

121, p. 82. Colchester Castle.

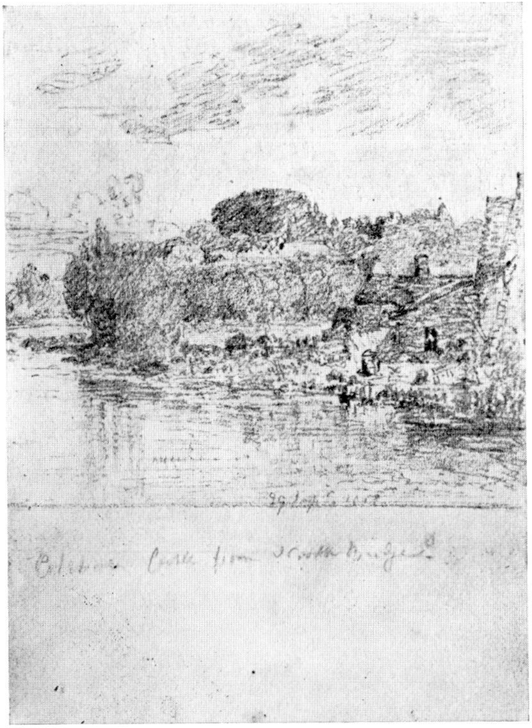

121, p. 83. Colchester.

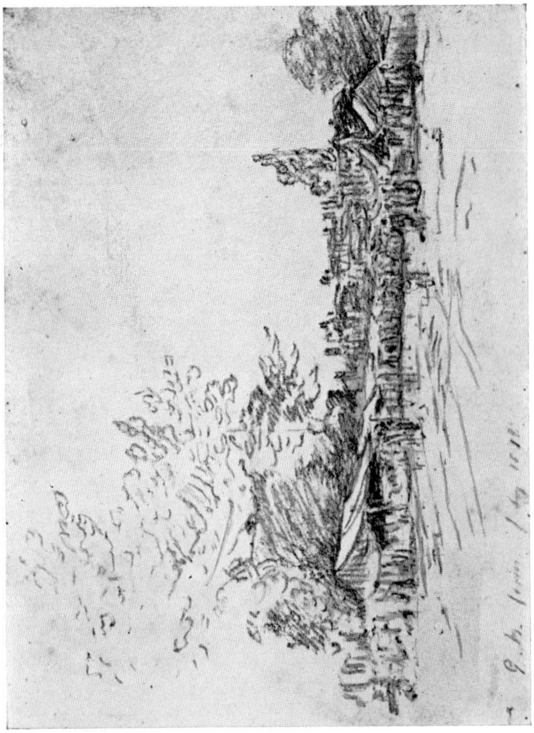

121, p. 85. A fair at East Bergholt.

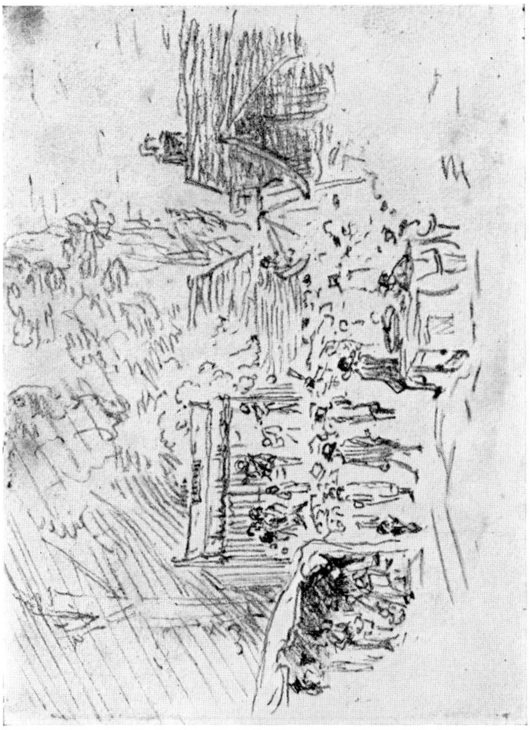

121, p. 87. A village fair.

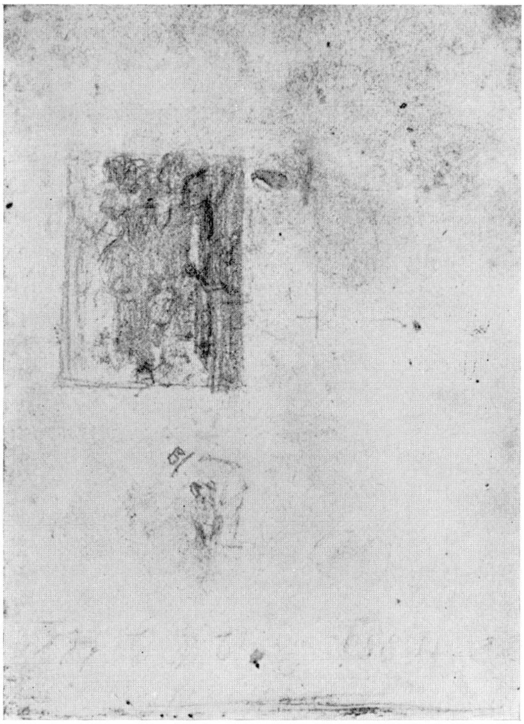

121, p. 88. Barges on a river.

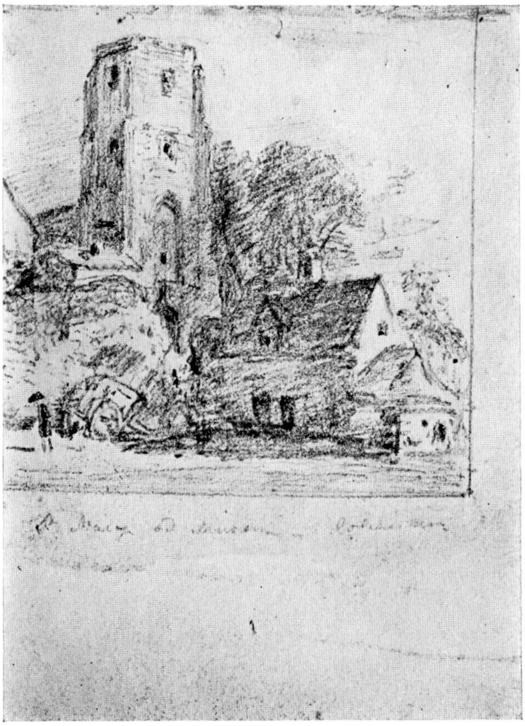

121, p. 89. St. Mary-ad-Murum, Colchester.

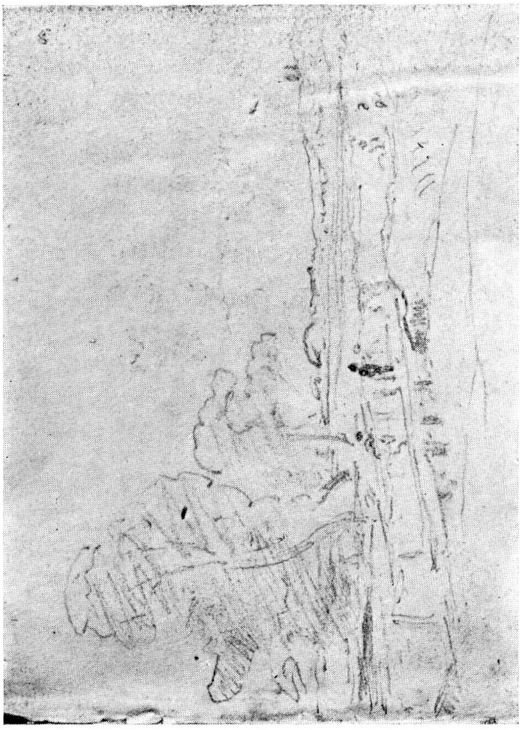

121, p. 90. A bridge over a stream.

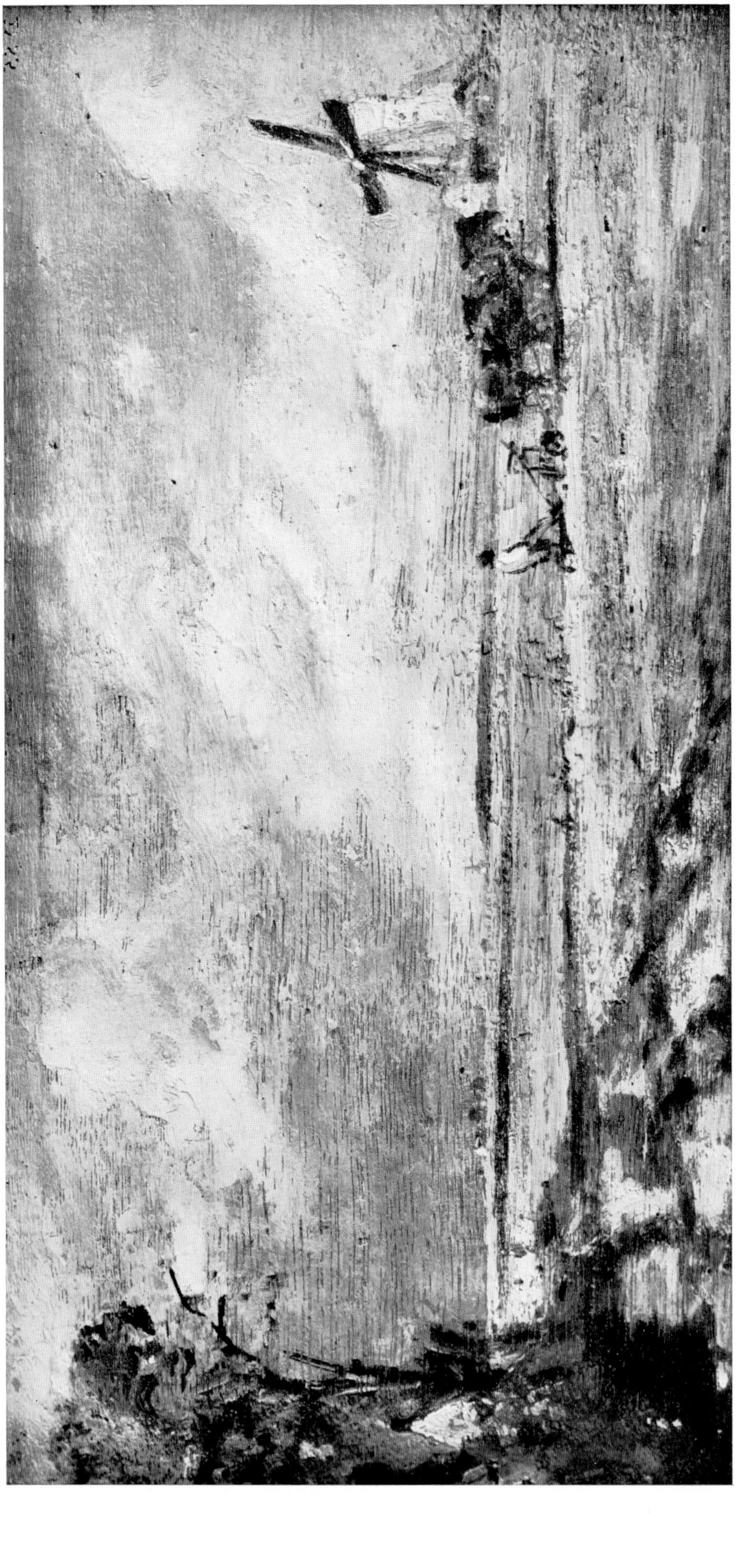

122. Spring. East Bergholt Common.

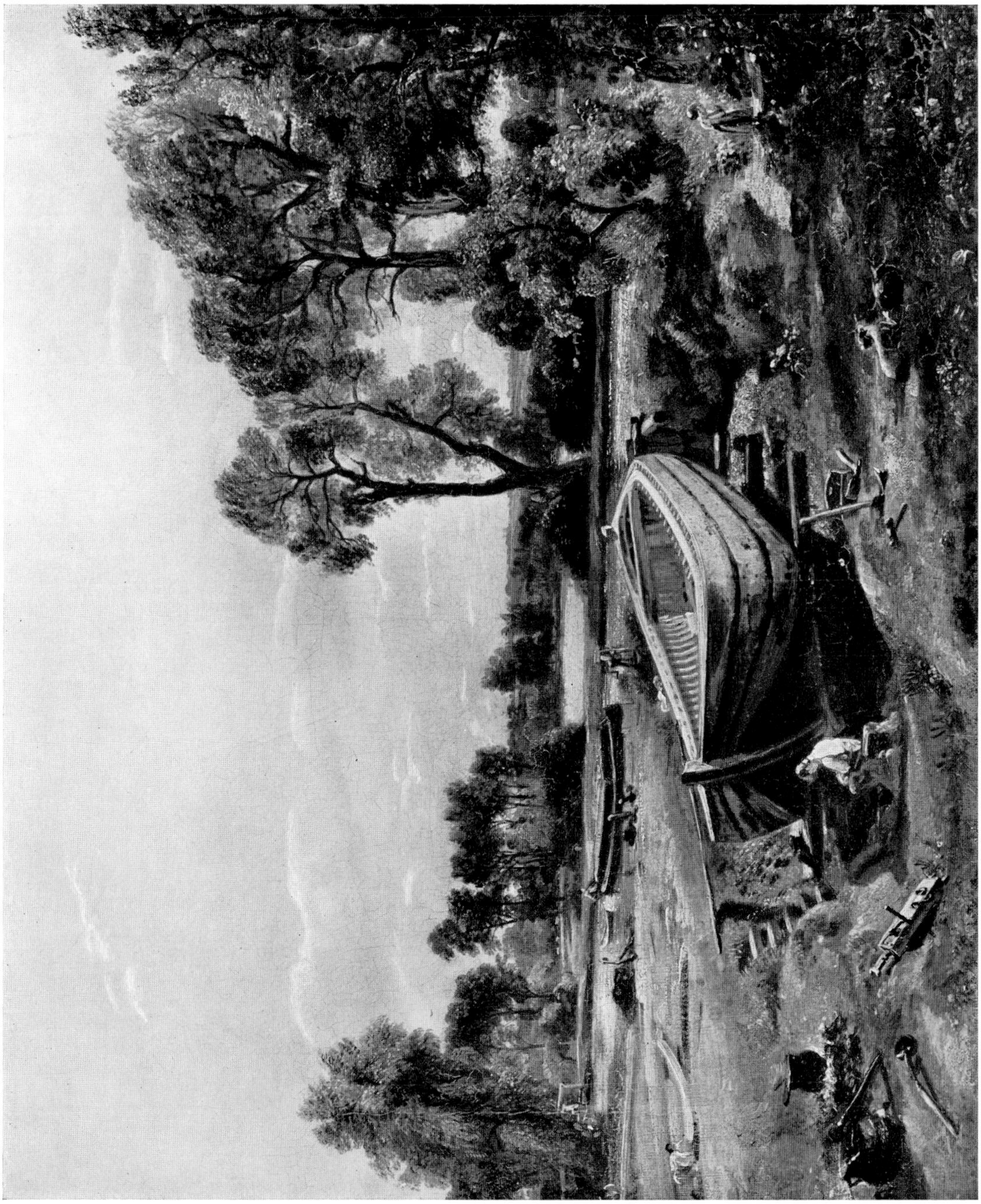

137. Boat-building near Flatford Mill.

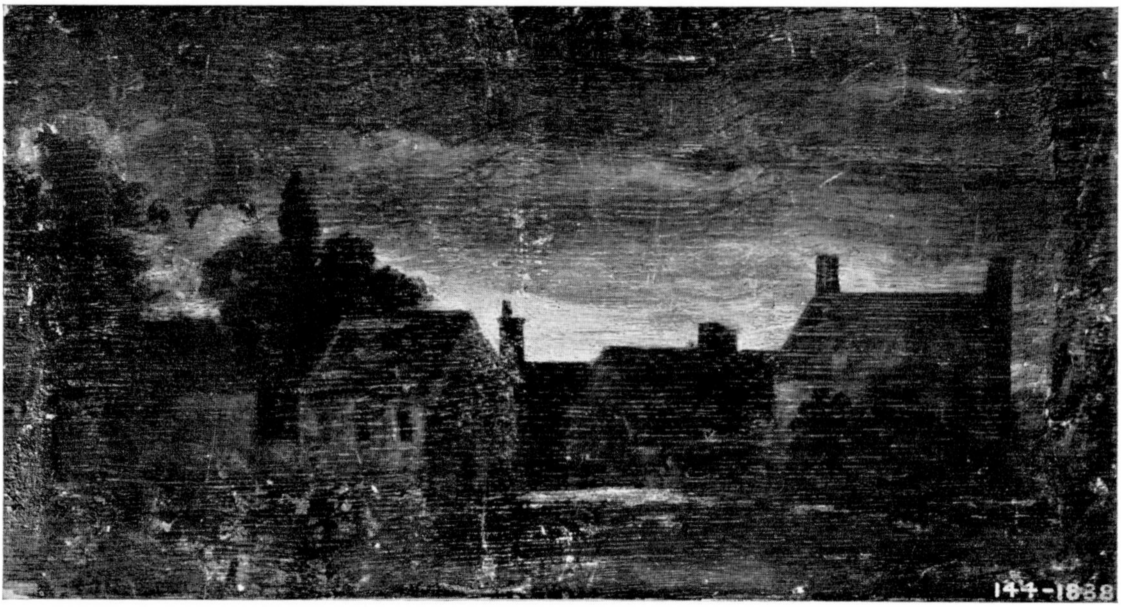

122a. A village street.

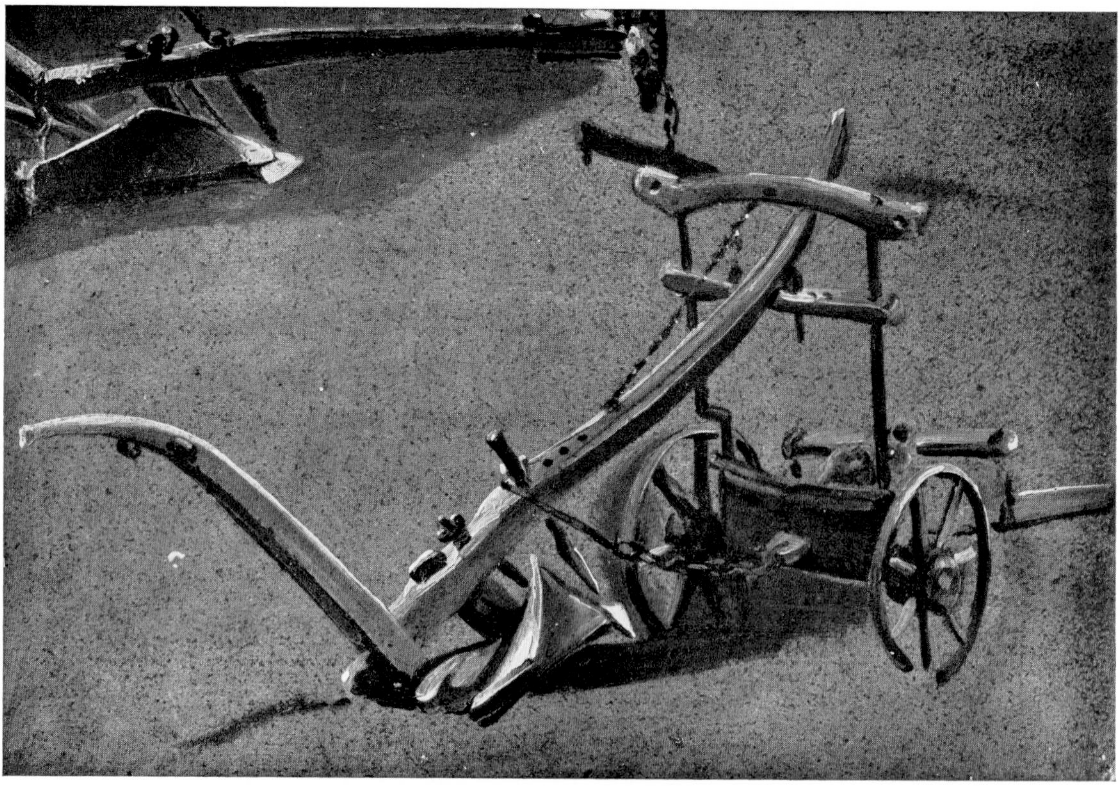

136. Studies of two ploughs.

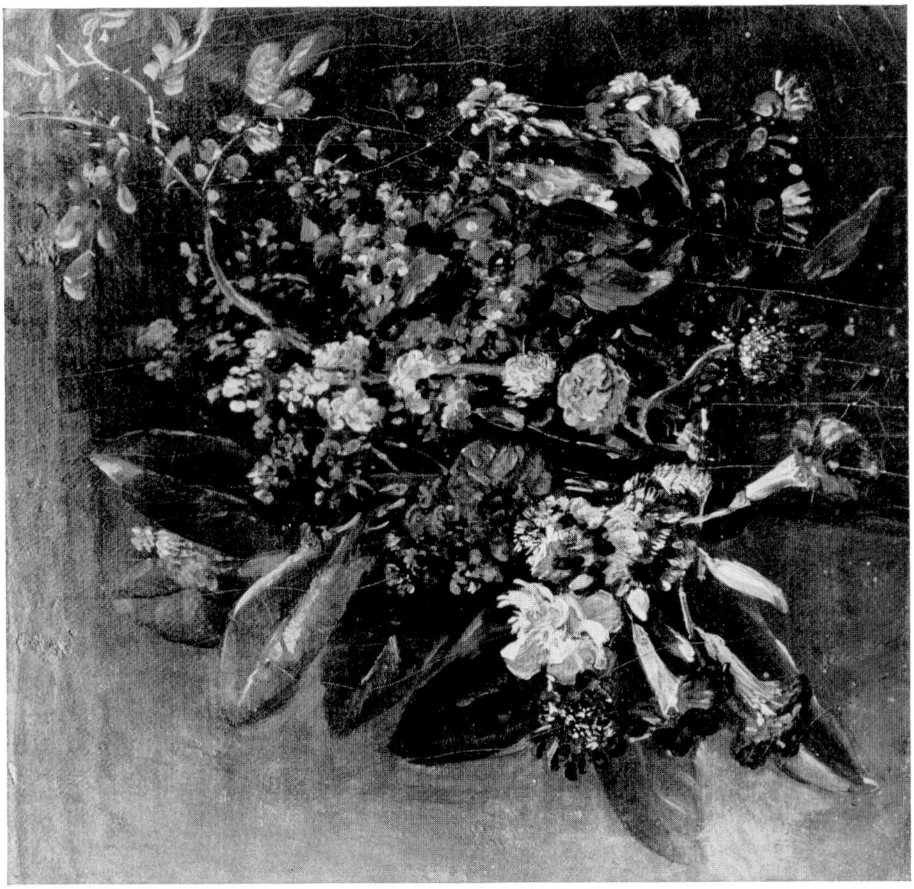

131. Study of flowers.

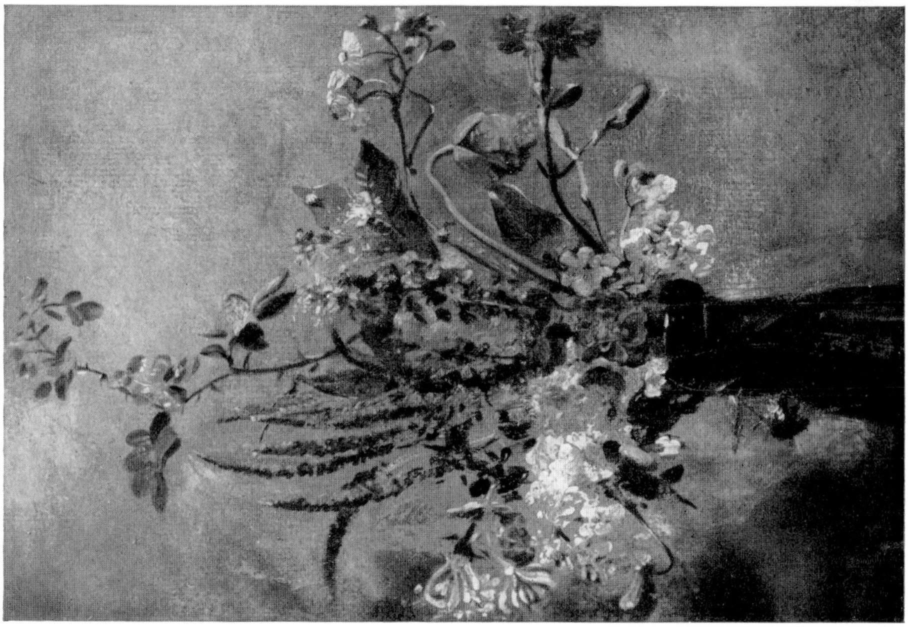

129. Study of flowers.

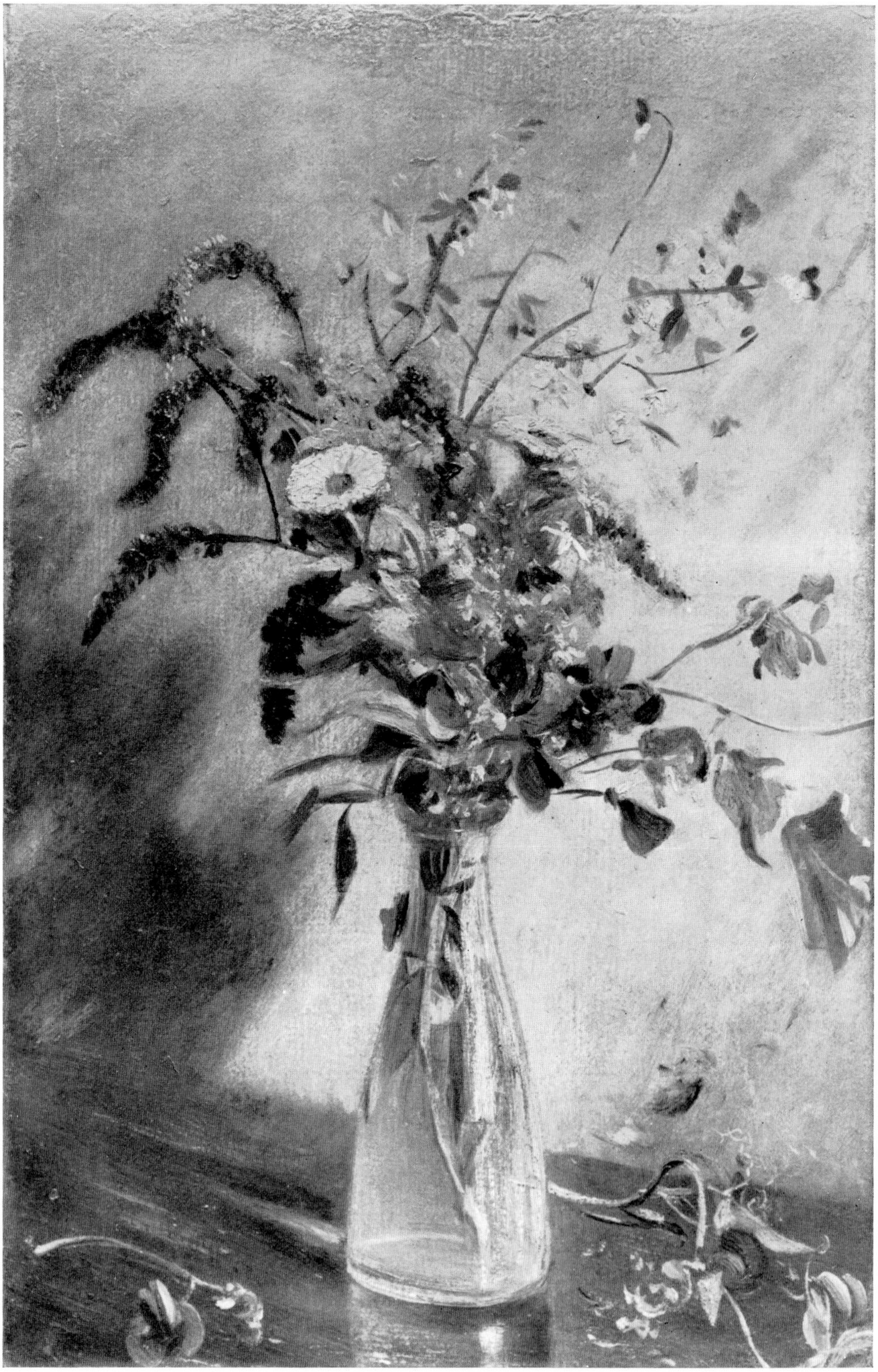

130. Study of flowers.

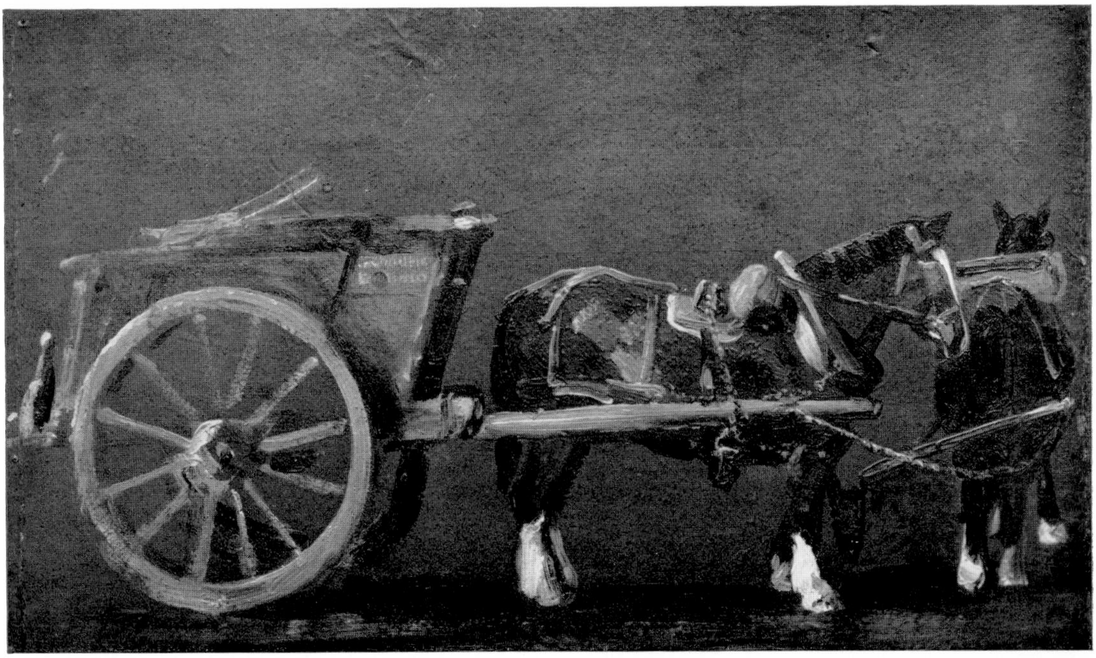

134. A cart and two horses.

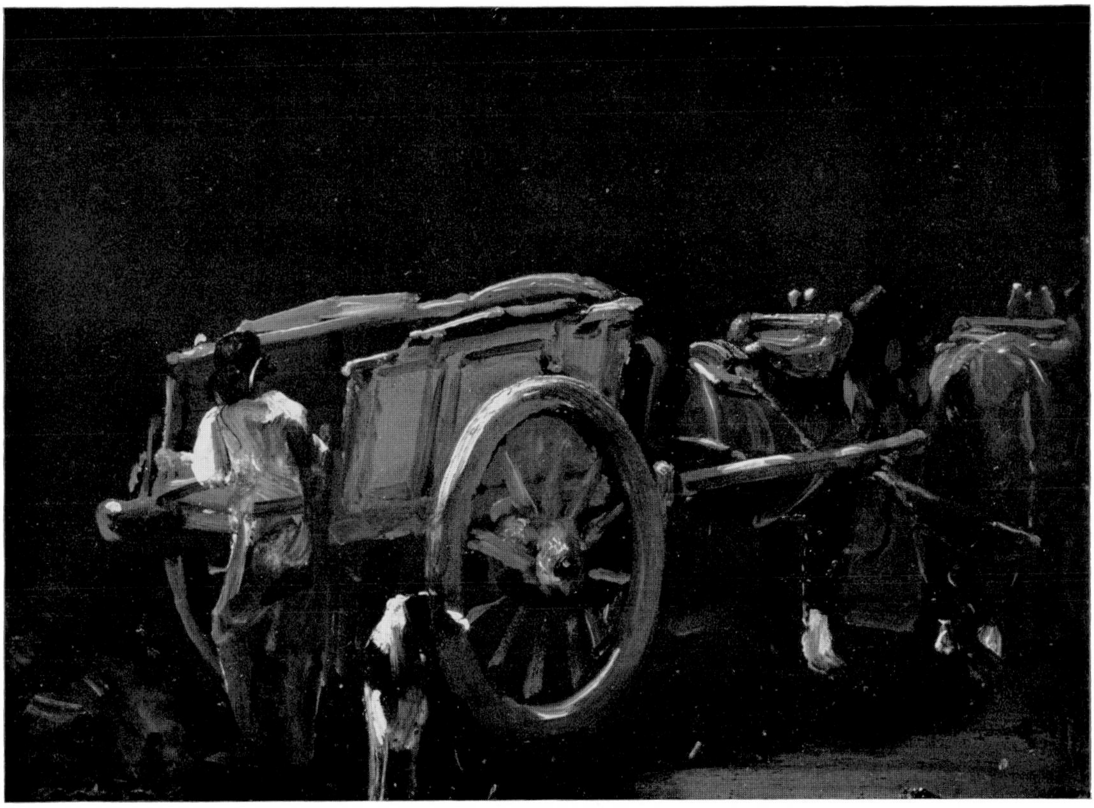

135. A cart and horses (sketch for 'Stour Valley and Dedham Village').

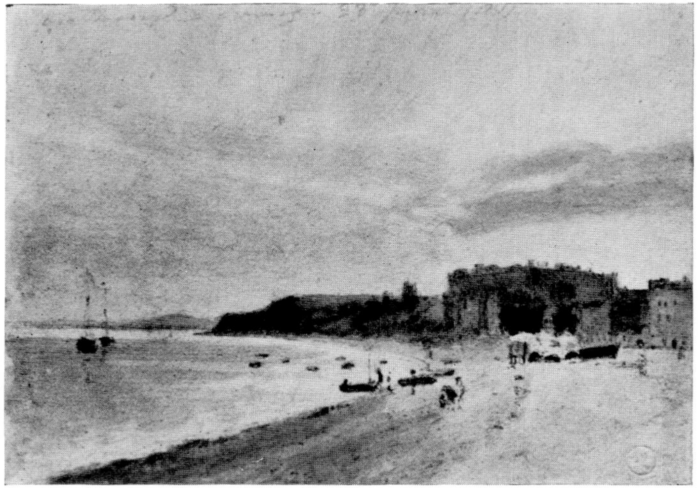

124. Southend.

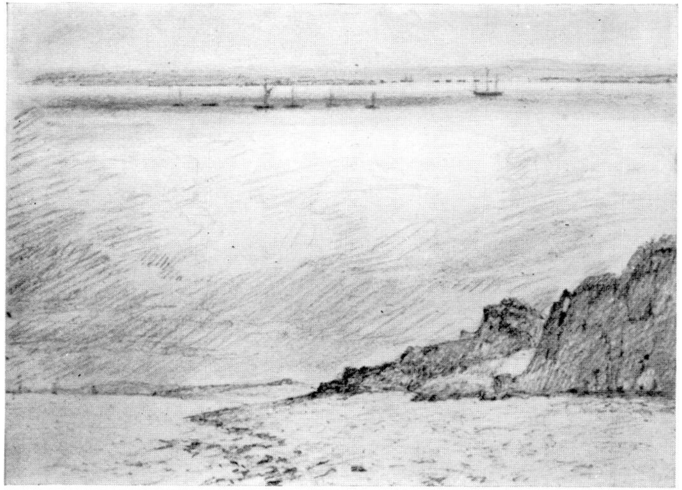

126. Sheerness, and the coast near Southend.

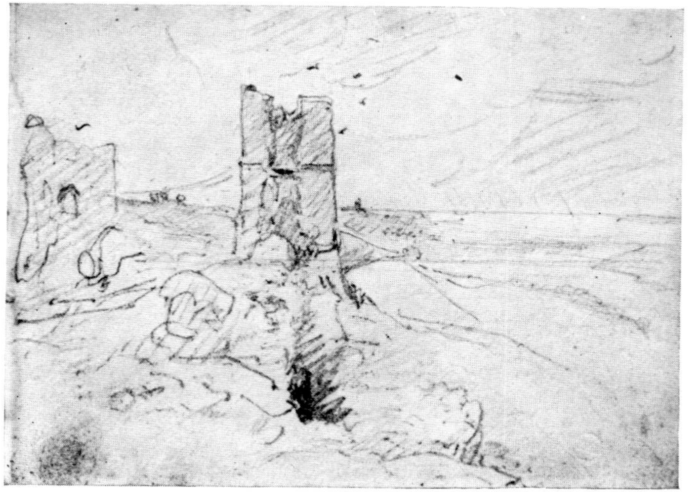

127. Hadleigh Castle.

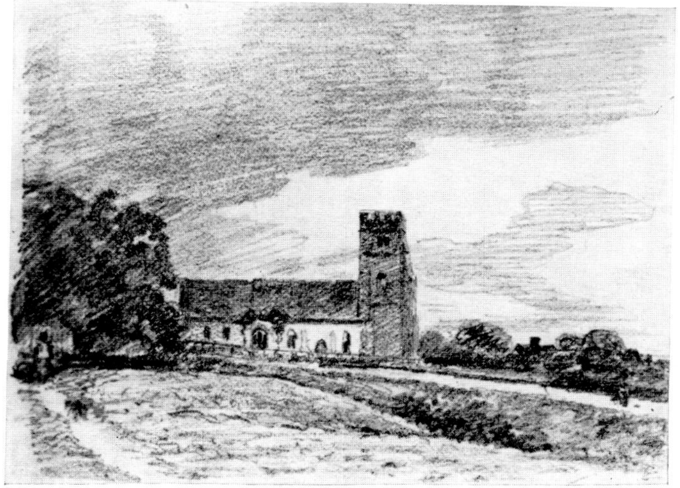

128. Feering Church.

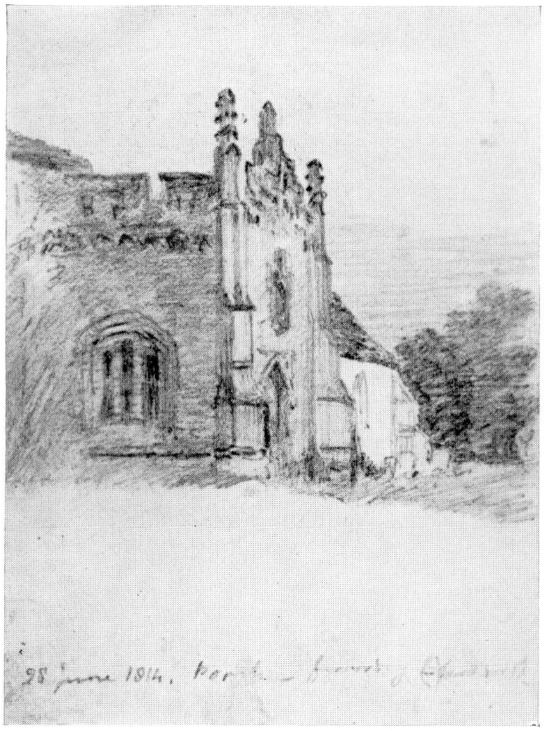

125. Porch of Feering Church.

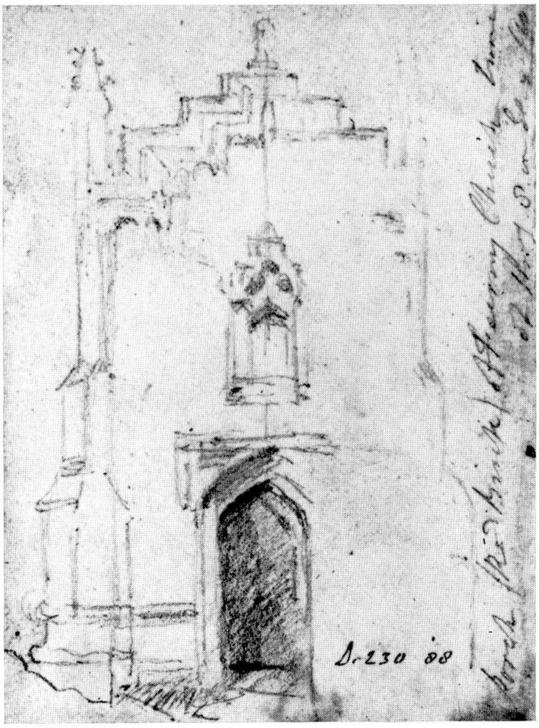

125a. Porch of Feering Church.

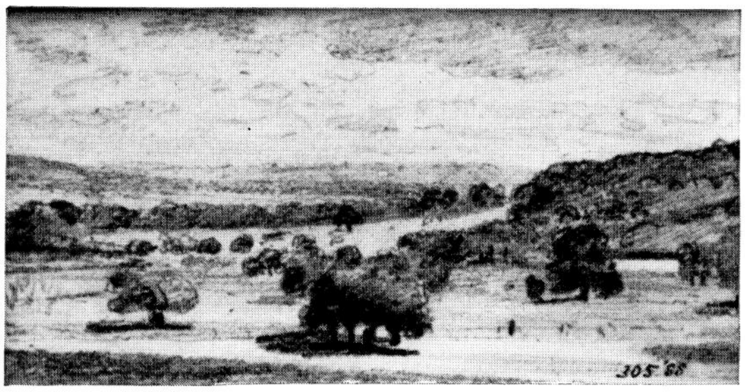

138. Wimbledon Park.

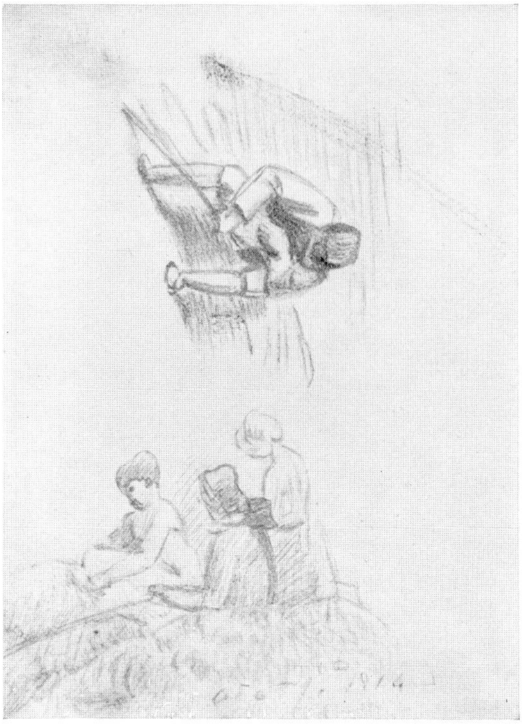

132, p. 3. Studies of figures.

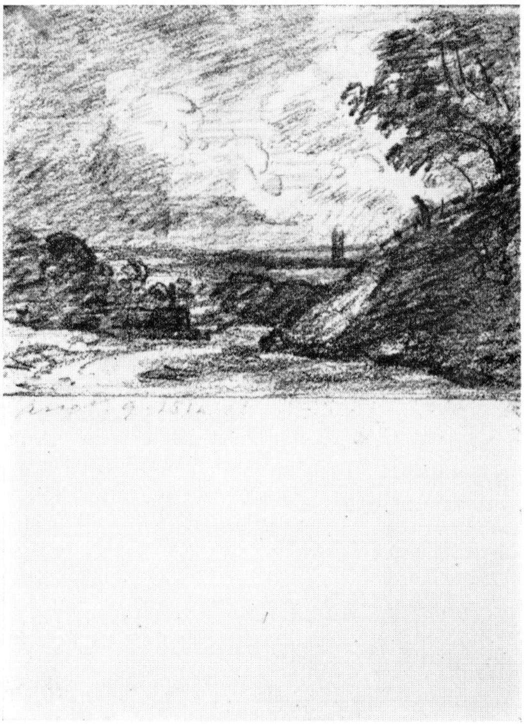

132, p. 6. Dedham.

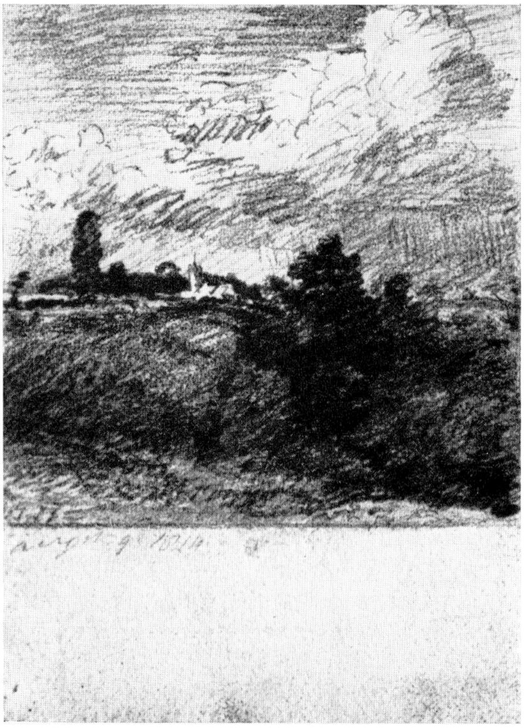

132, p. 7. Landscape with a church.

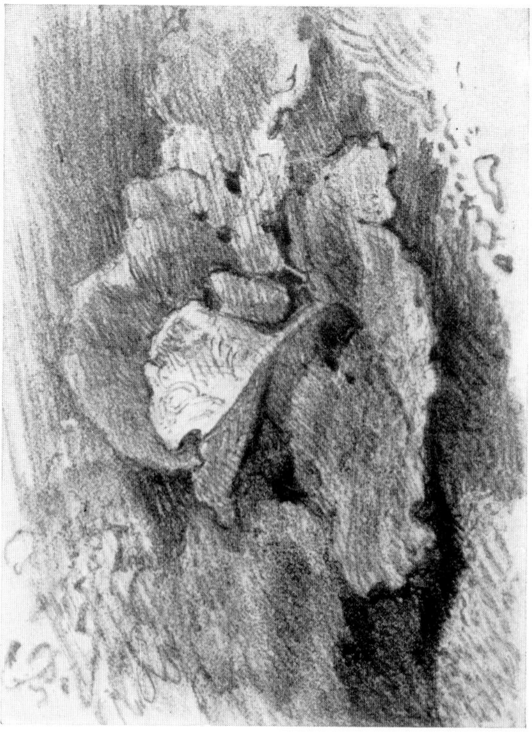

132, p. 9. Dock leaves.

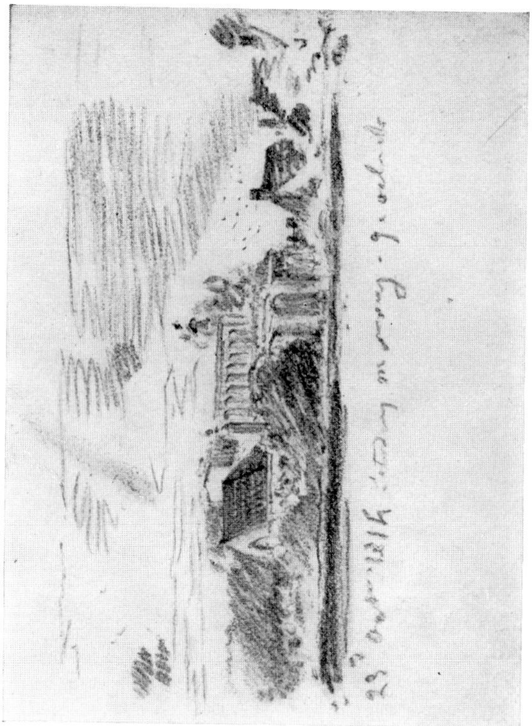

132 p. 11. East Bergholt Church.

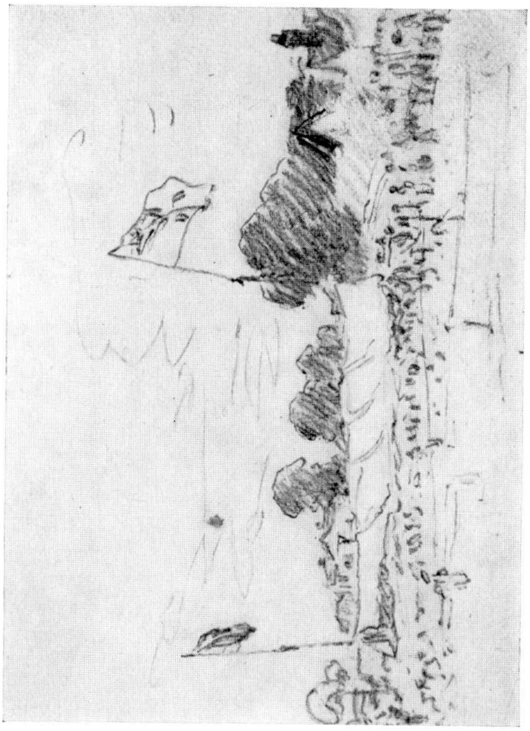

132, p. 13. Fair at East Bergholt.

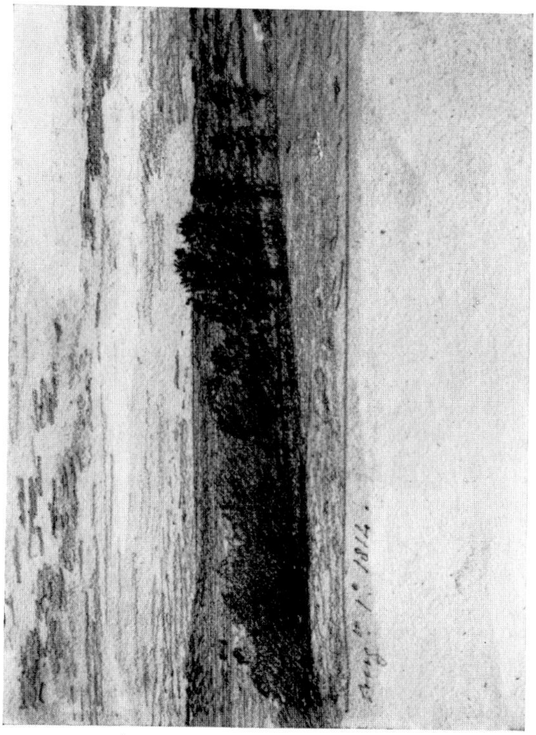

132, p. 15. Dedham Vale(?).

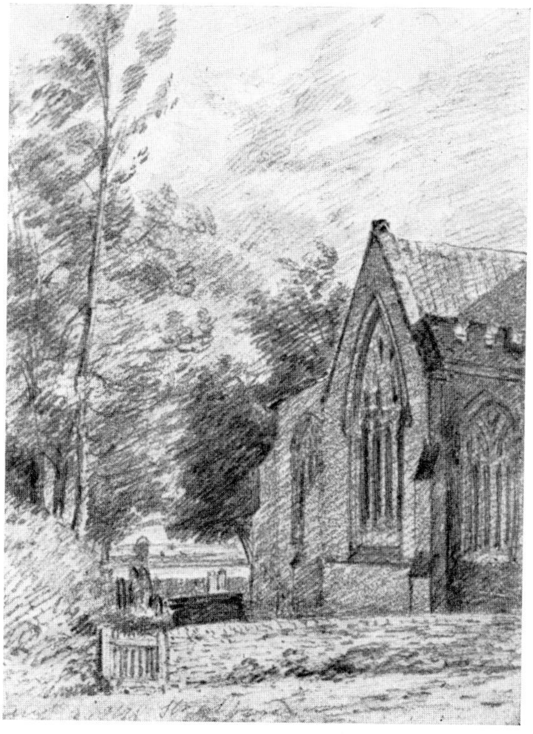

132, p. 19. Stratford Church.

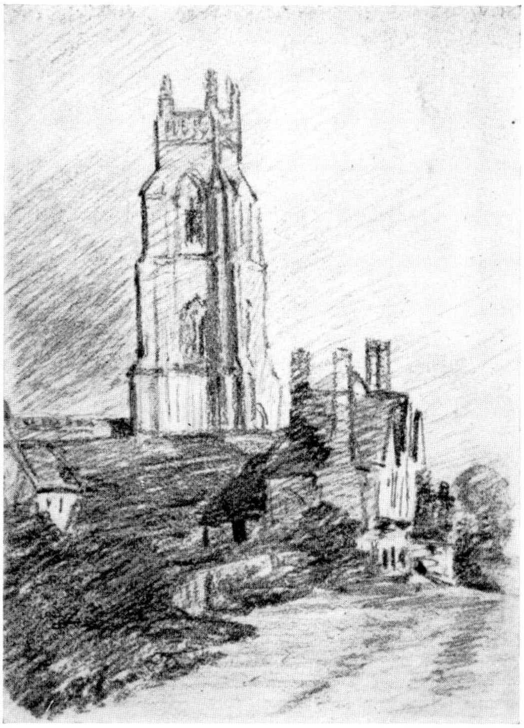

132, p. 21. Stoke-by-Nayland.

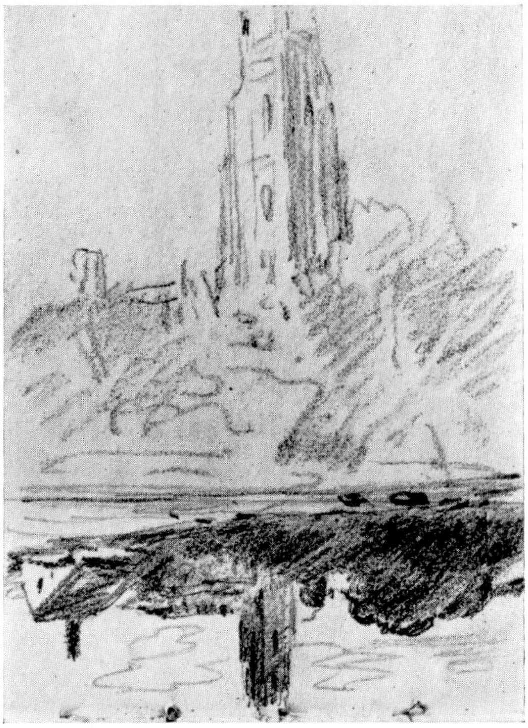

132, p. 23. Stoke-by-Nayland Church.

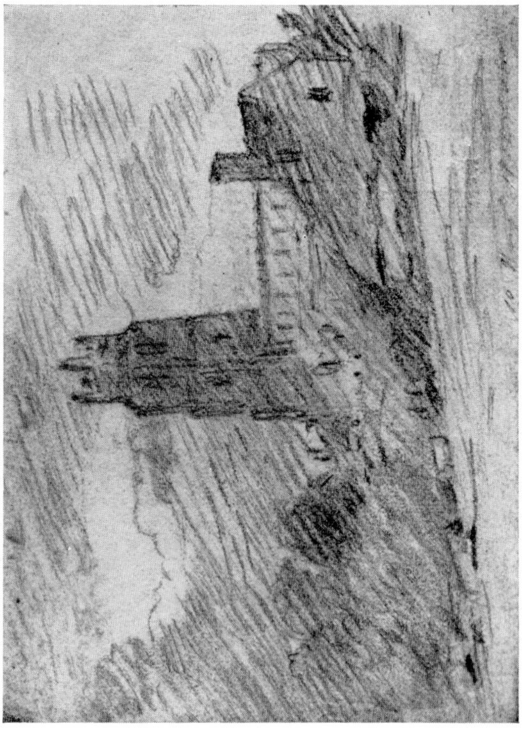

132, p. 24. Stoke-by-Nayland Church.

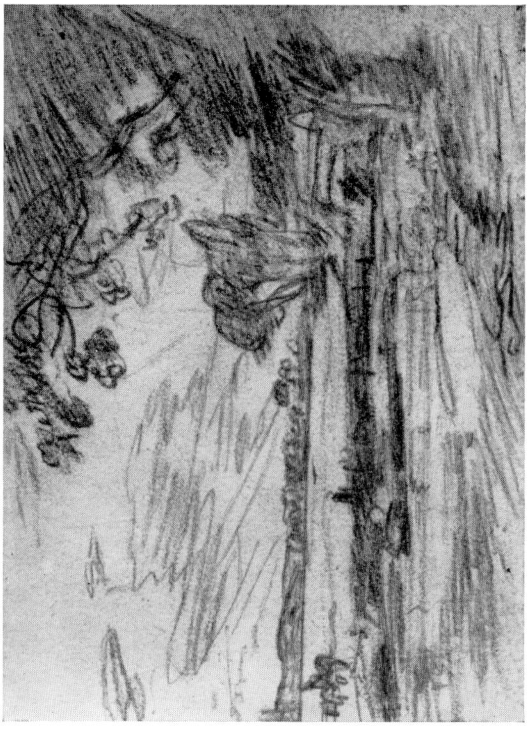

132, p. 25. View on the Stour(?).

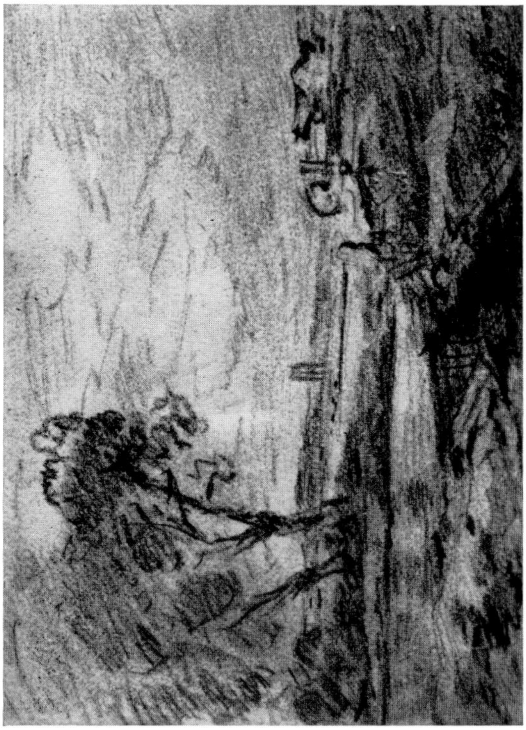

132, p. 27. View on the Stour.

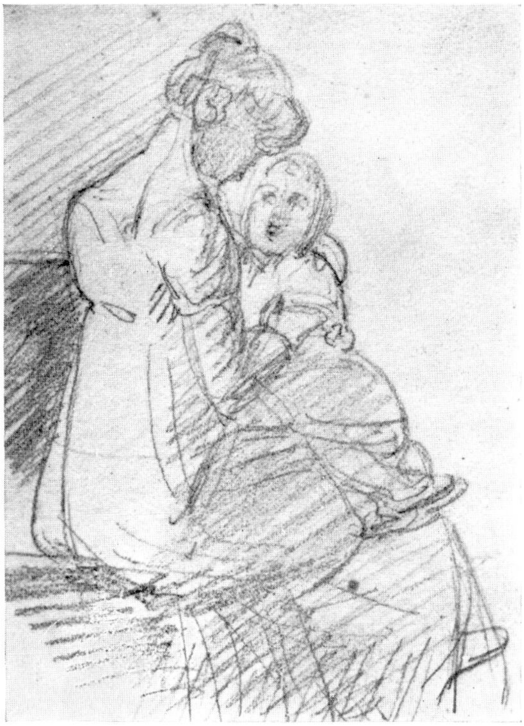

132, p. 31. A woman with a child.

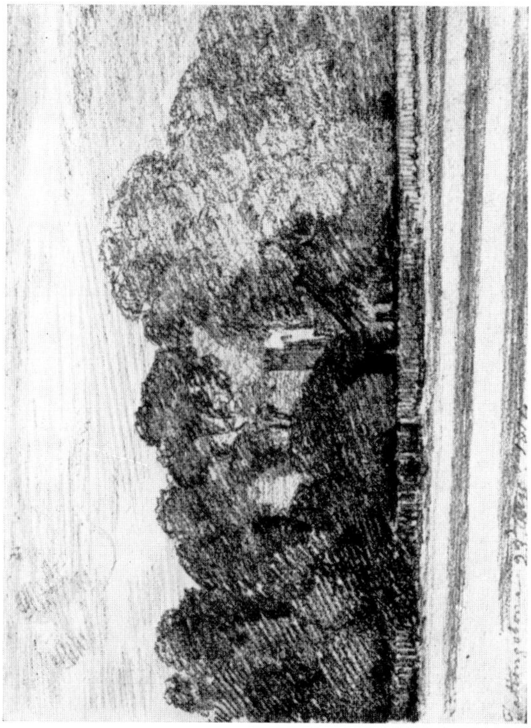

132, p. 33. Tattingstone Church.

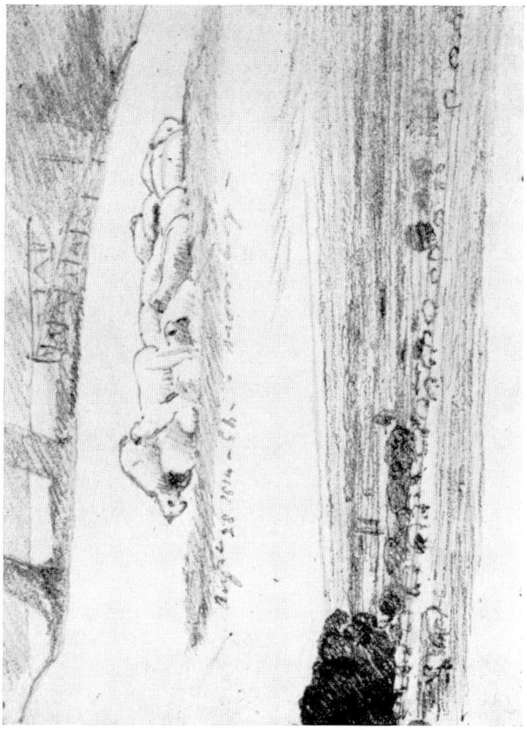

132, p. 35. Dedham Vale.

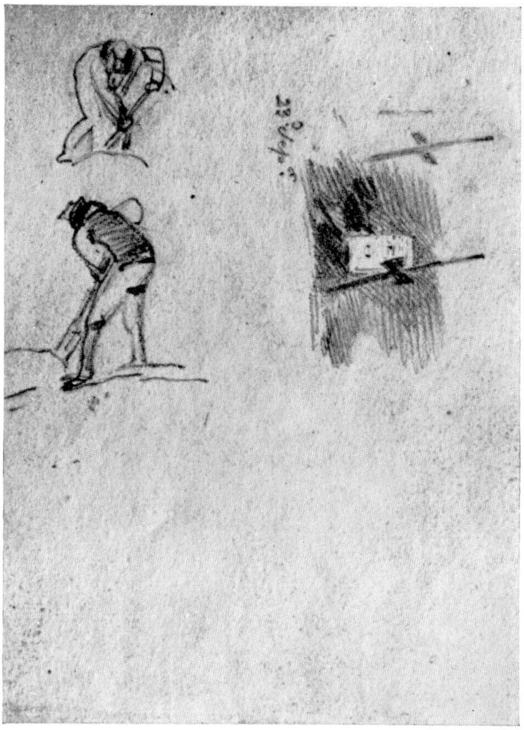

132, p. 36. Men digging.

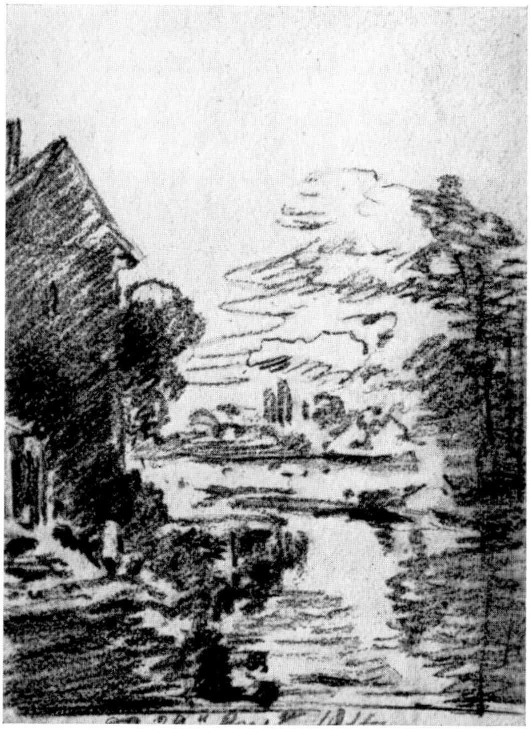

132, p. 37. A building beside water.

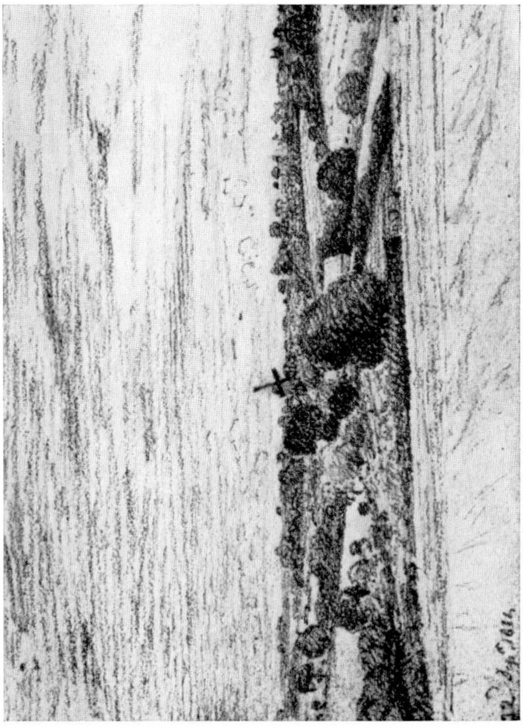

132, p. 38. View from Golding Constable's house.

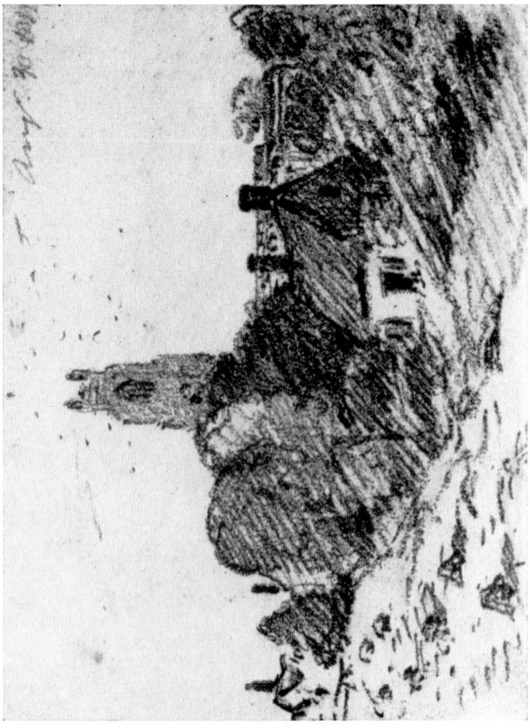

132, p. 39. Stoke-by-Nayland.

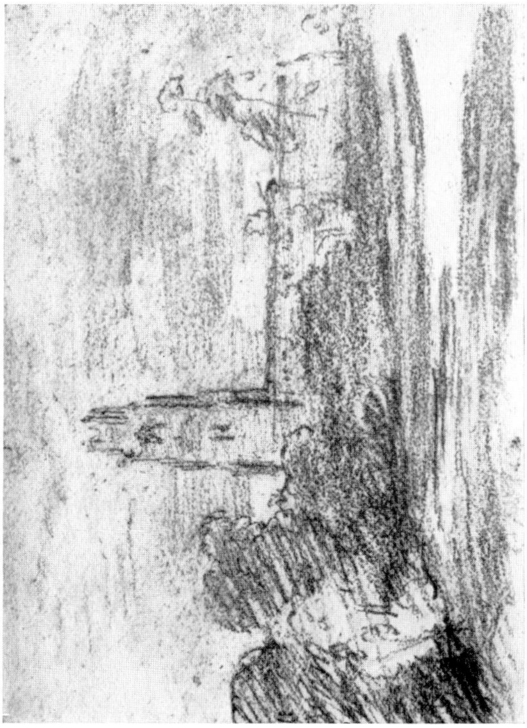

132, p. 40. Stoke-by-Nayland Church.

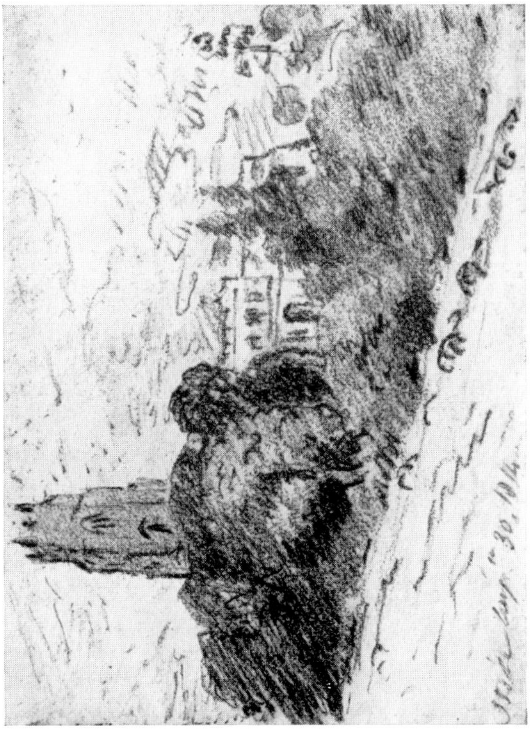

132, p. 41. Stoke-by-Nayland Church.

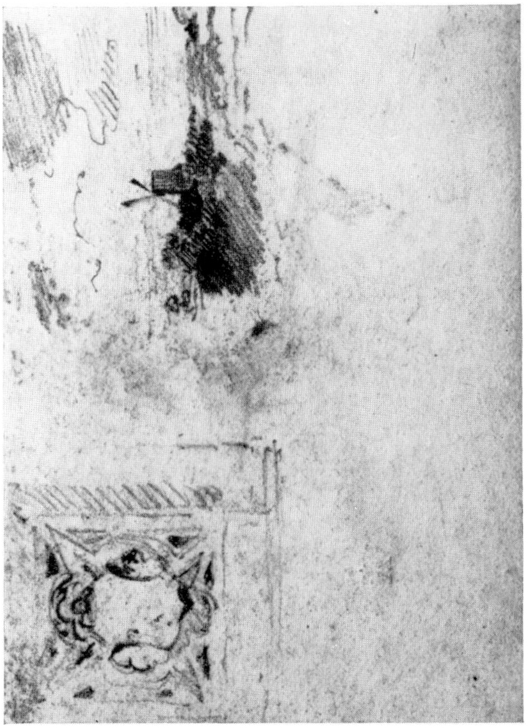

132, p. 42. Landscape with a windmill.

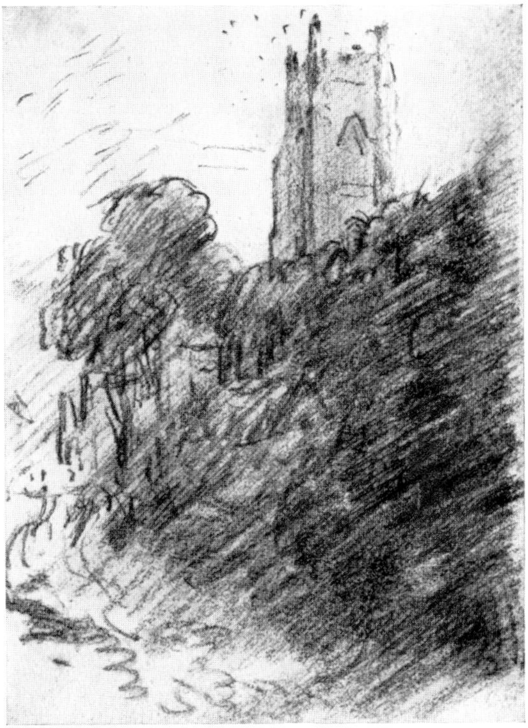

132, p. 43. Stoke-by-Nayland Church.

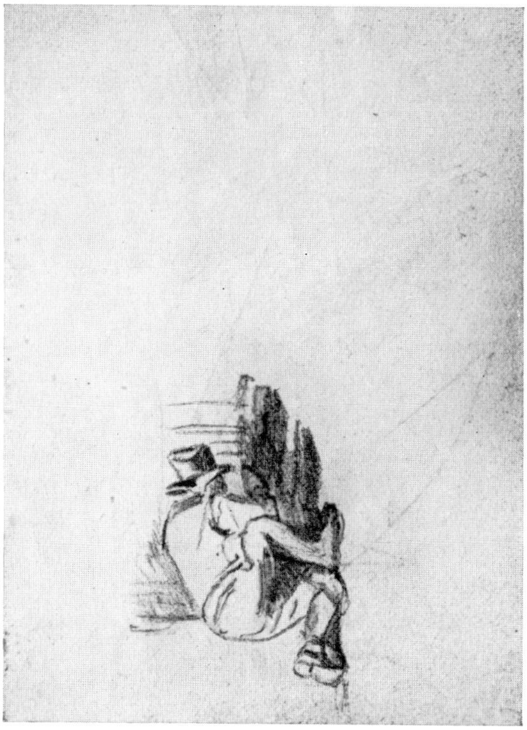

132, p. 46. A workman.

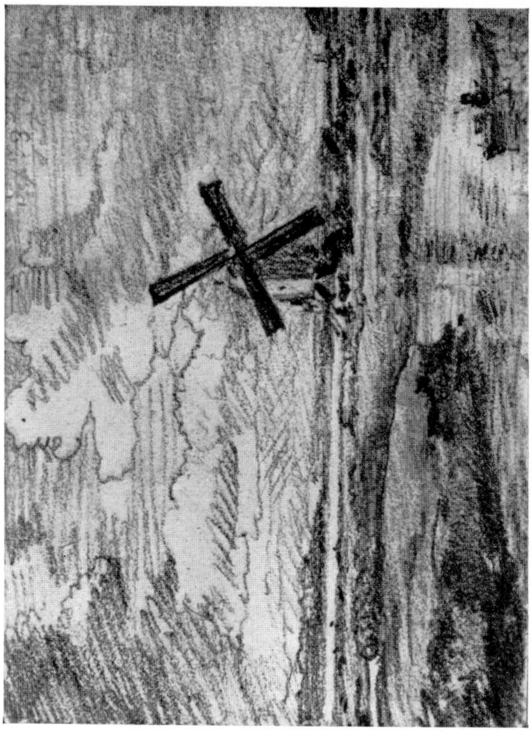

132, p. 47. A windmill by a river.

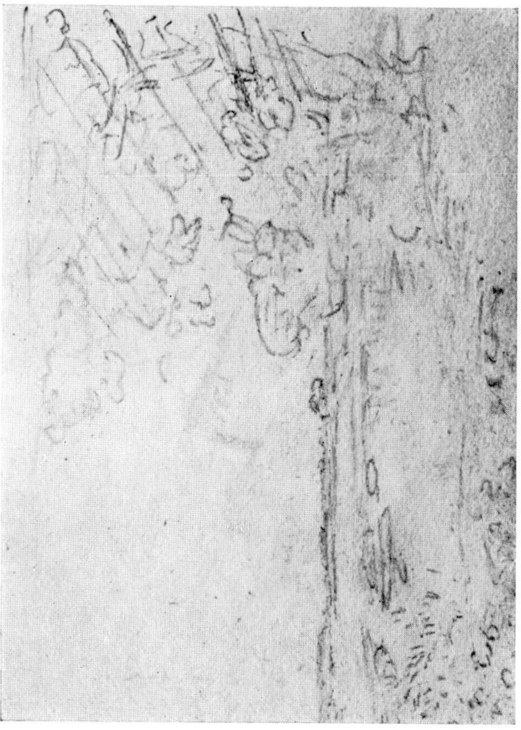

132, p. 48. Water-meadows.

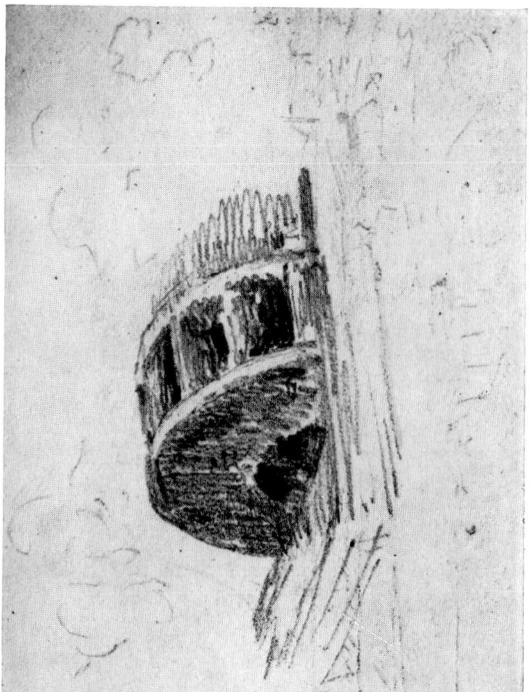

132, p. 49. A water-wheel.

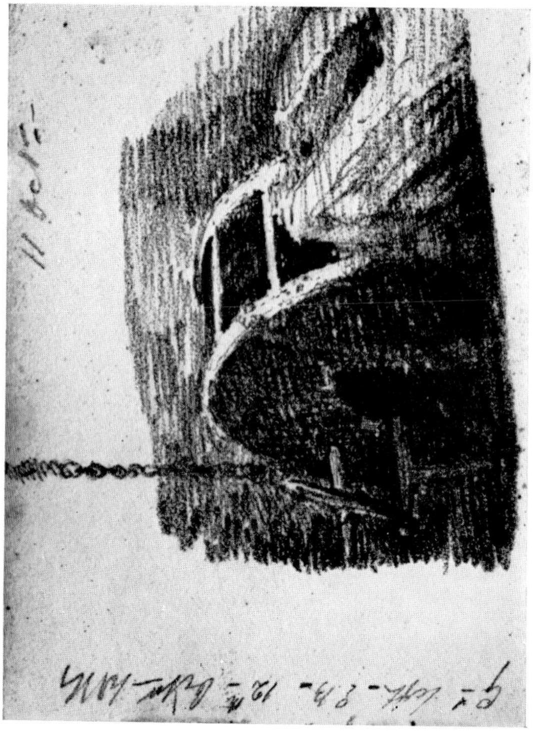

132, p. 50. A water-wheel.

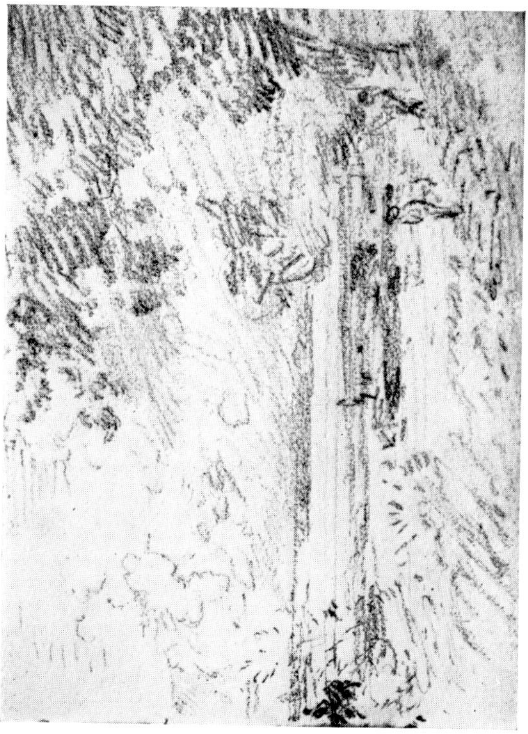

132, p. 51. View on the Stour(?).

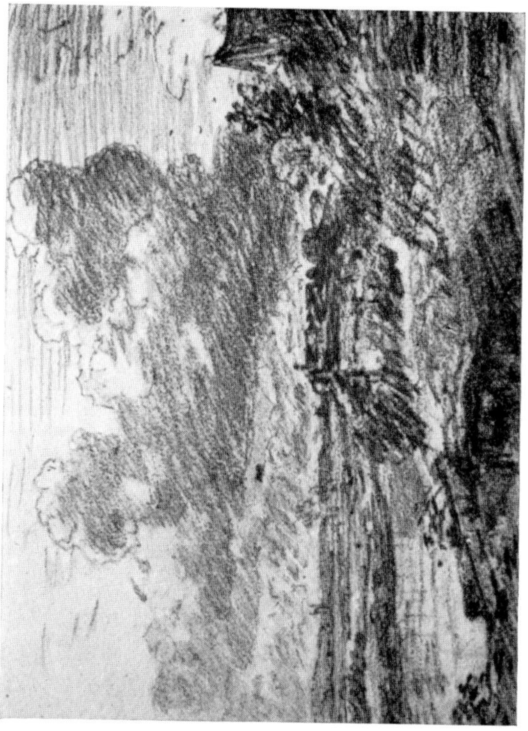

132, p. 52. View on the Stour near Dedham.

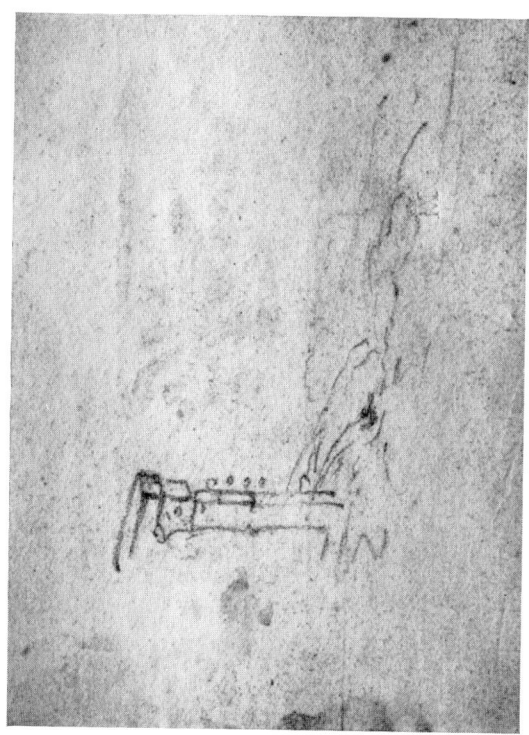

132, p. 53. A post in water.

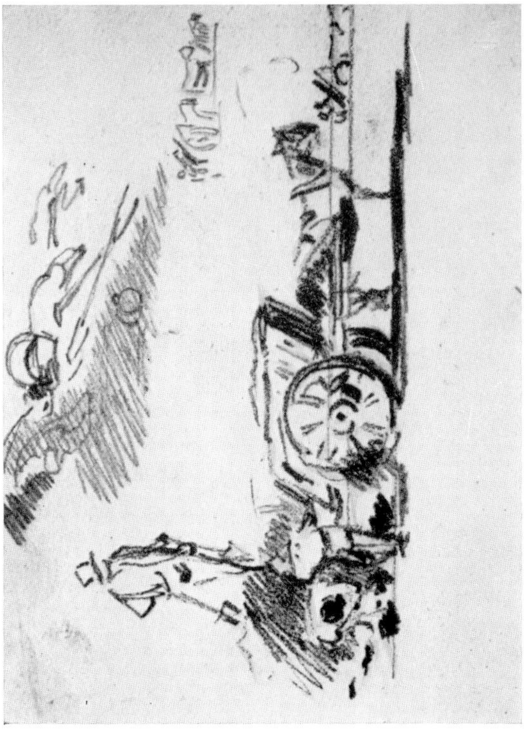

132, p. 54. Men loading a cart.

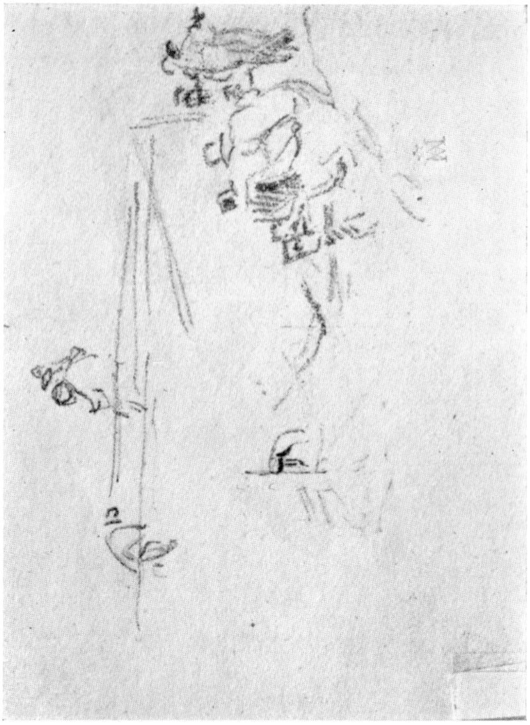

132, p. 55. Men building a boat.

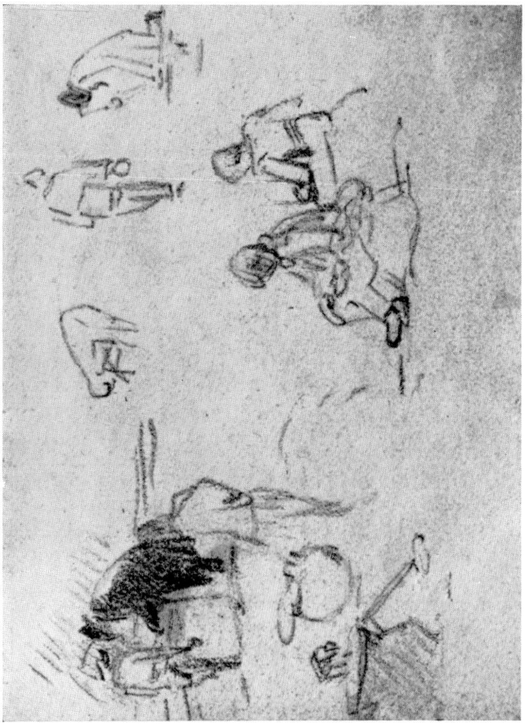

132, p. 56. Sketches for 'Boat-building' (No. 137).

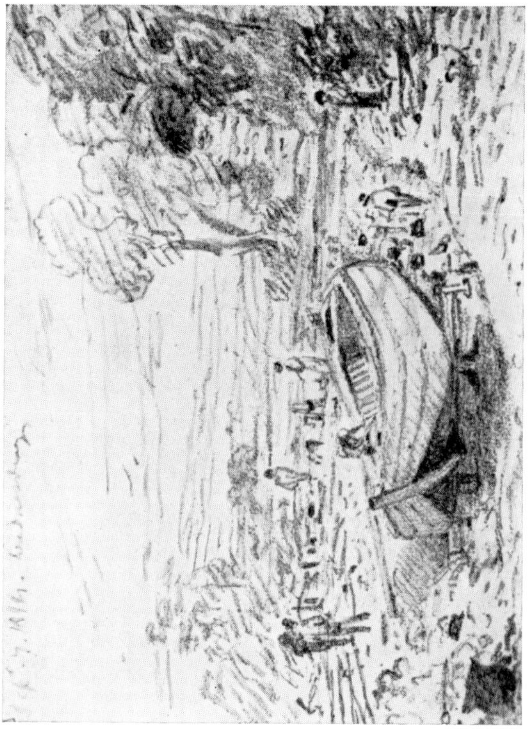

132, p. 57. Study for 'Boat-building' (No. 137).

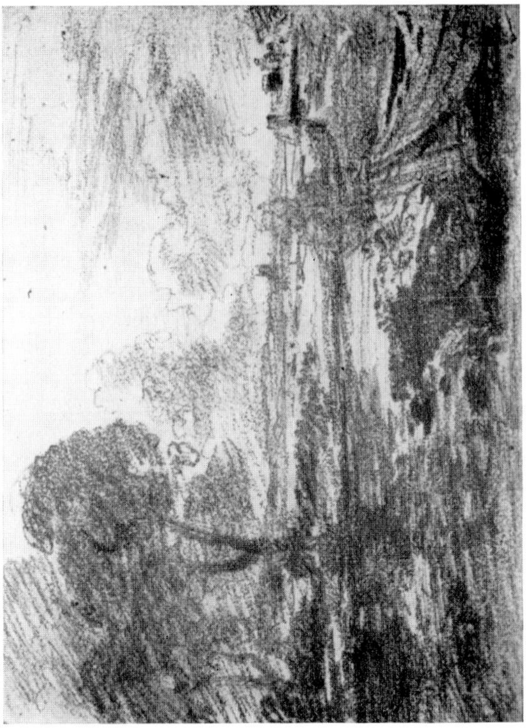

132, p. 59. View on the Stour.

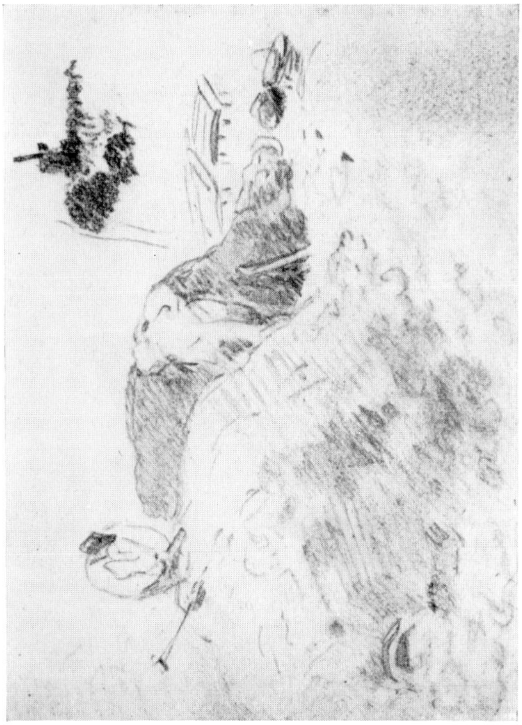

132, p. 60. Men digging gravel.

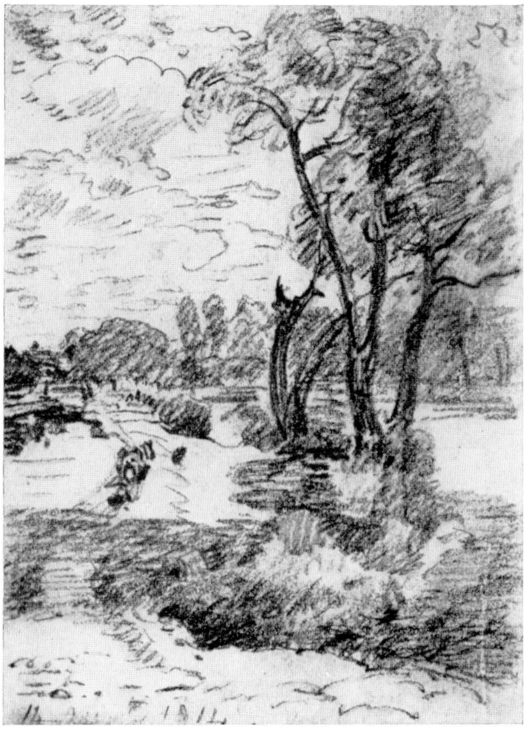

132, p. 61. Towpath near Flatford Mill.

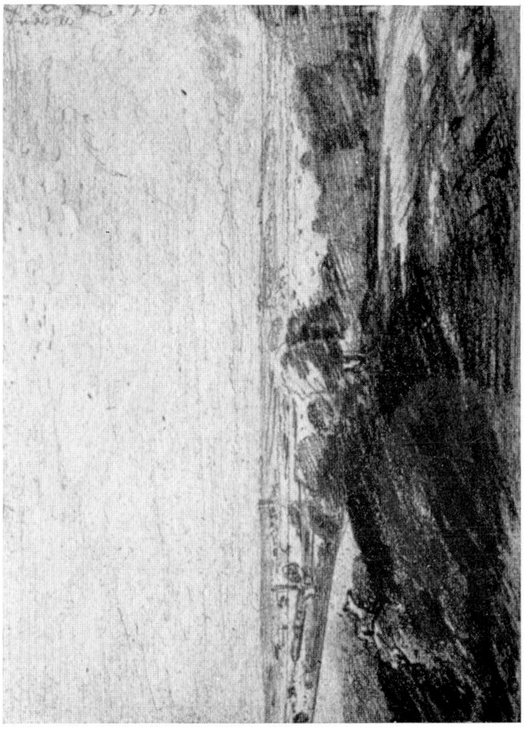

132, p. 62. Dedham Vale.

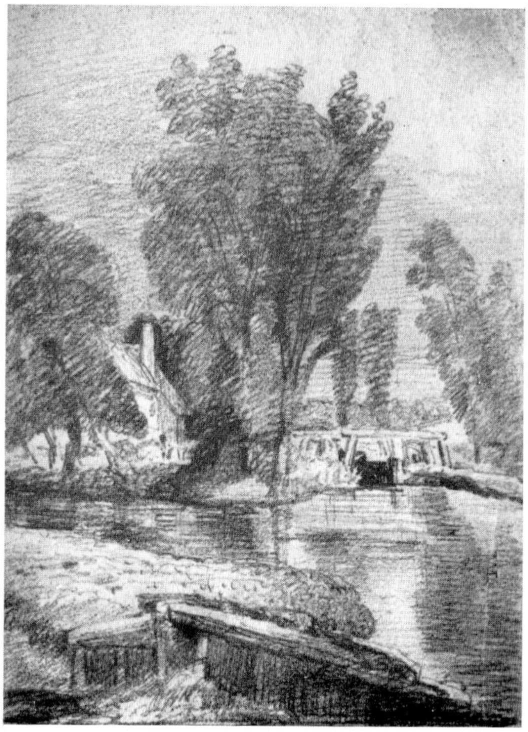

132, p. 63. Flatford Mill.

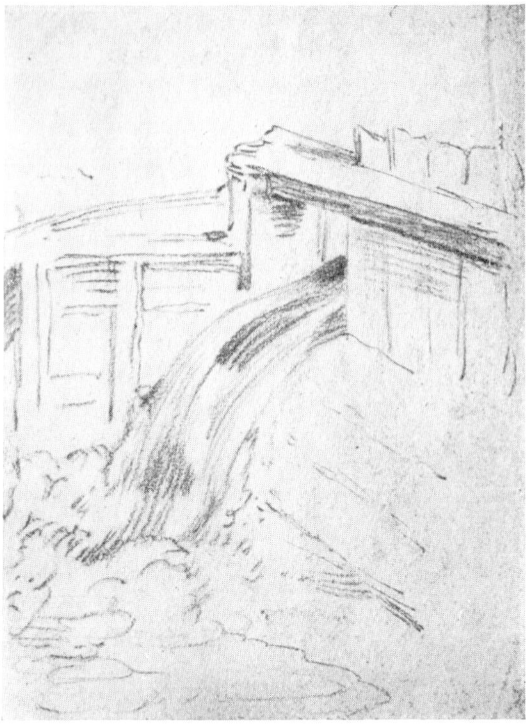

132, p. 64. A sluice.

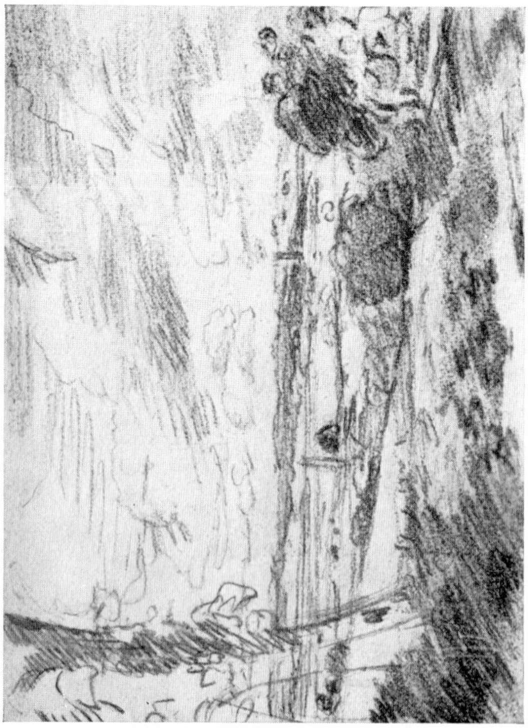

132, p. 65. Dedham Vale.

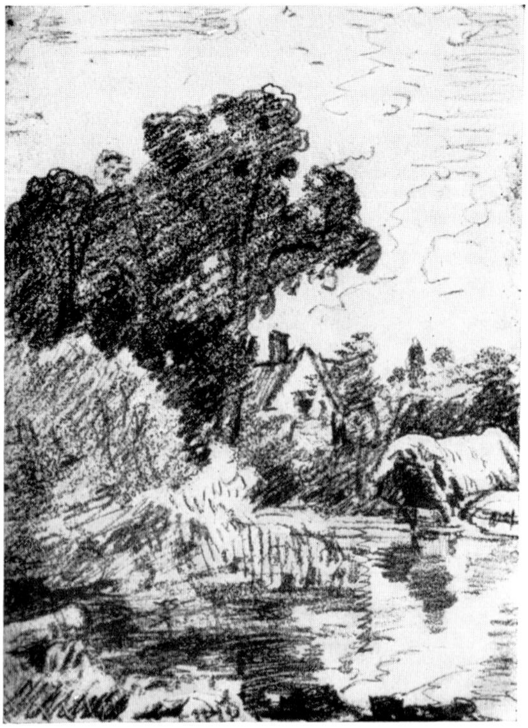

132, p. 66. Sketch for 'The White Horse'.

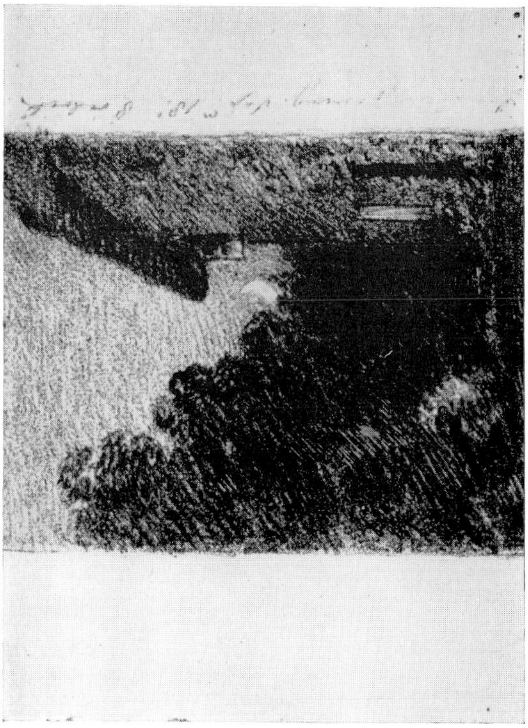

132, p. 67. A cottage by moonlight.

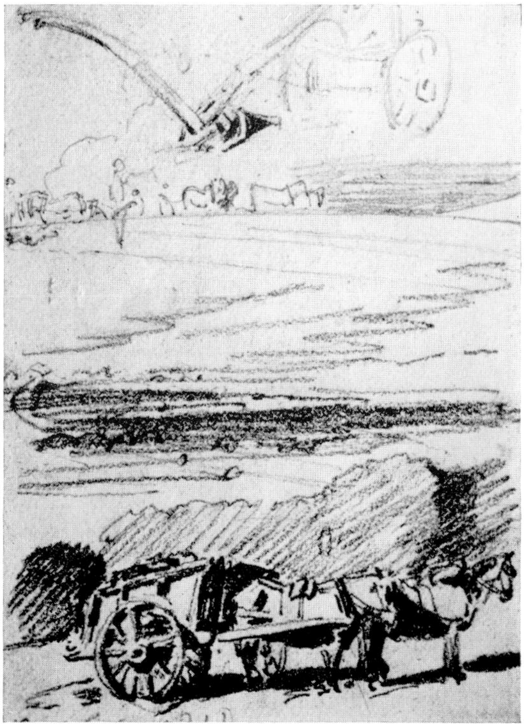

132, p. 68. Cart and horses.

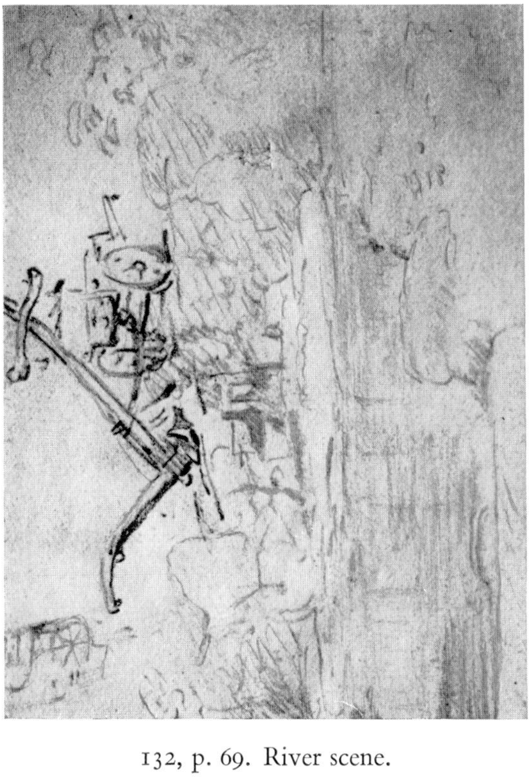

132, p. 69. River scene.

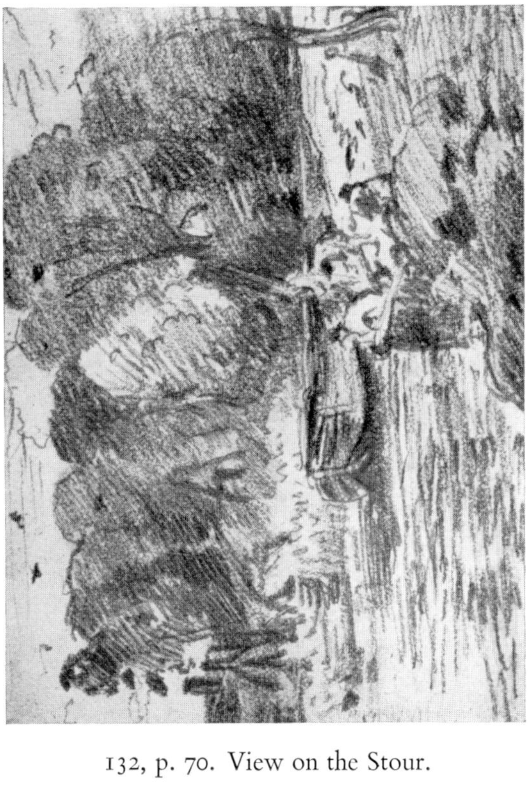

132, p. 70. View on the Stour.

132, p. 72. East Bergholt Church.

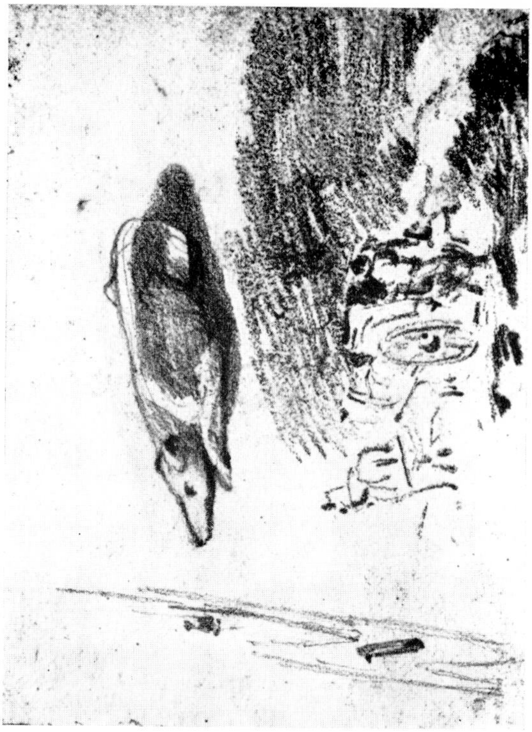

132, p. 73. Study of a dog.

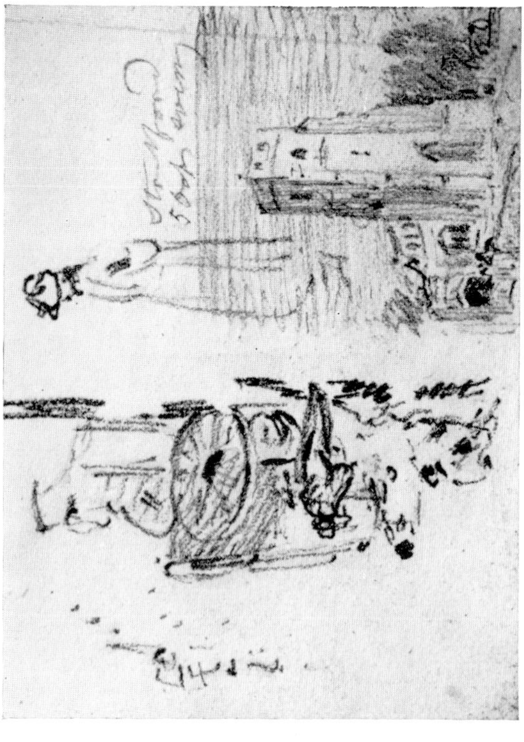

132, p. 74. Stratford St. Mary Church.

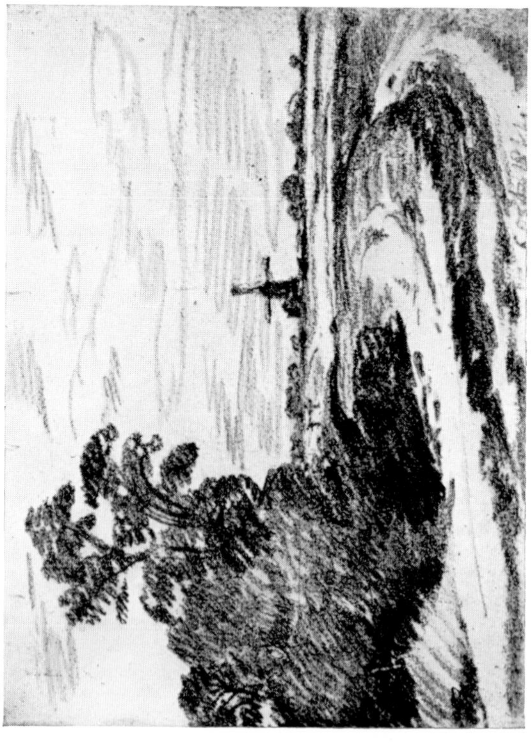

132, p. 75. Landscape with windmill.

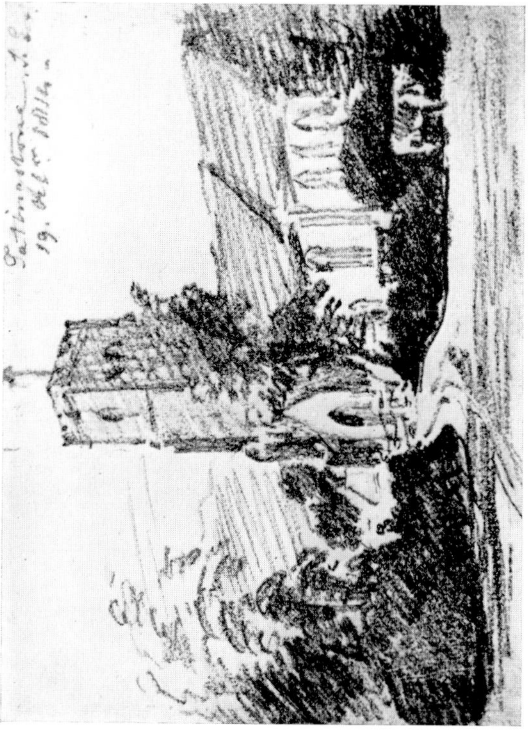

132, p. 77. Tattingstone Church.

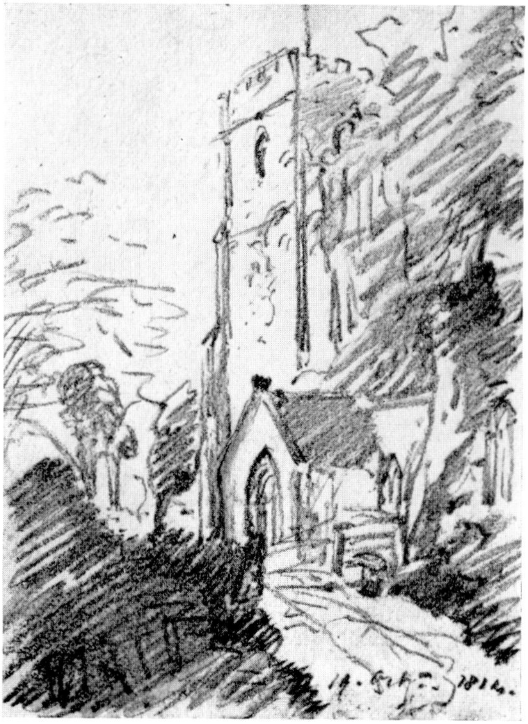

132, p. 78. Tattingstone Church.

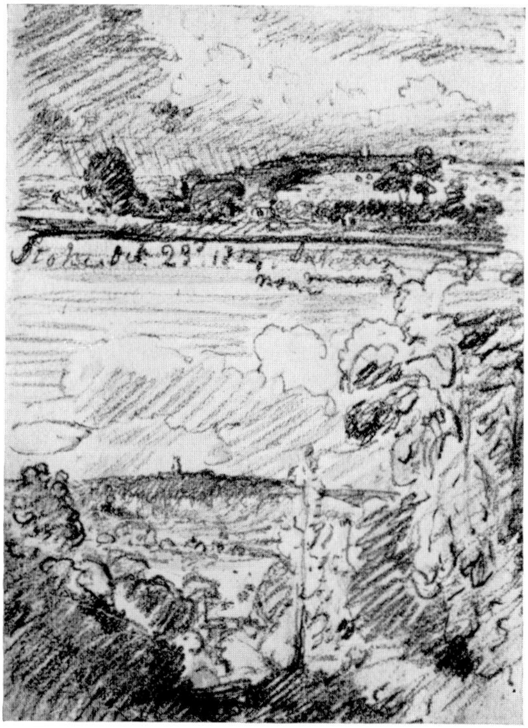

132, p. 79. Stoke-by-Nayland.

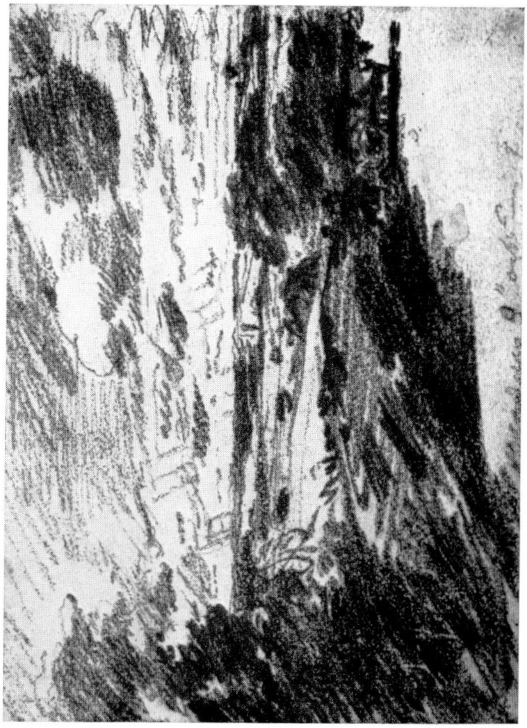

132, p. 81. Dedham Vale.

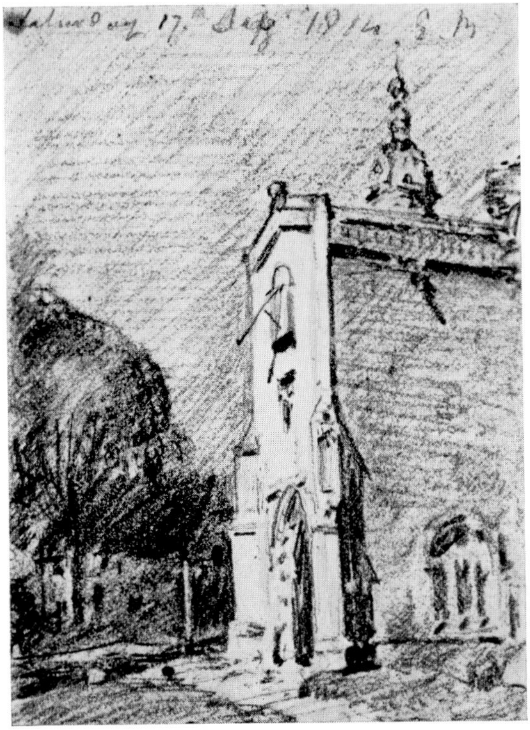

132, p. 82. East Bergholt Church.

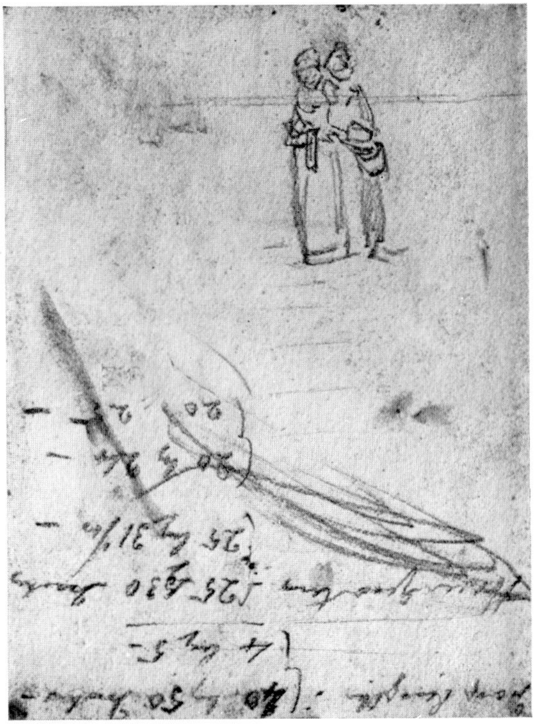

132, p. 83. A woman and child.

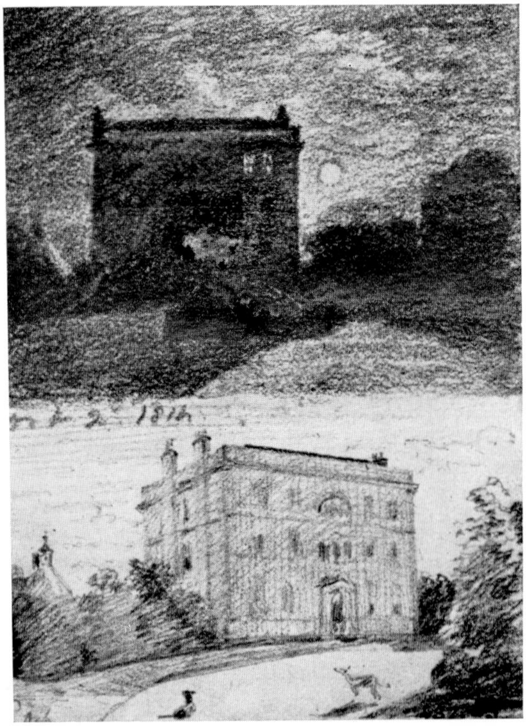

133. Golding Constable's house, East Bergholt.

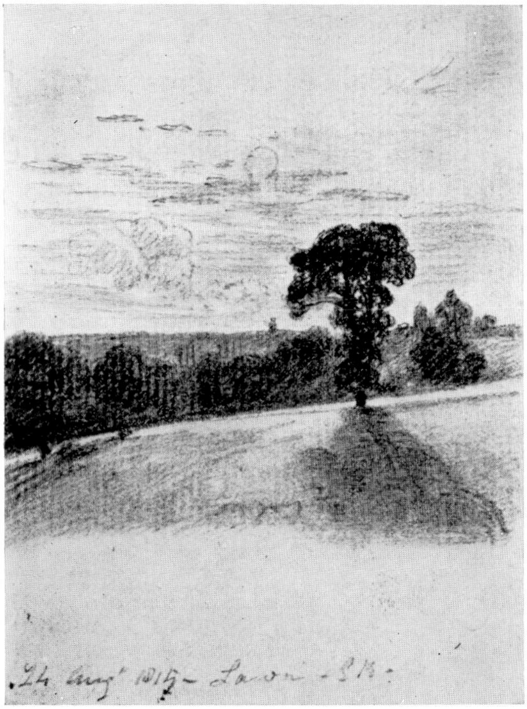

143. A lawn at East Bergholt.

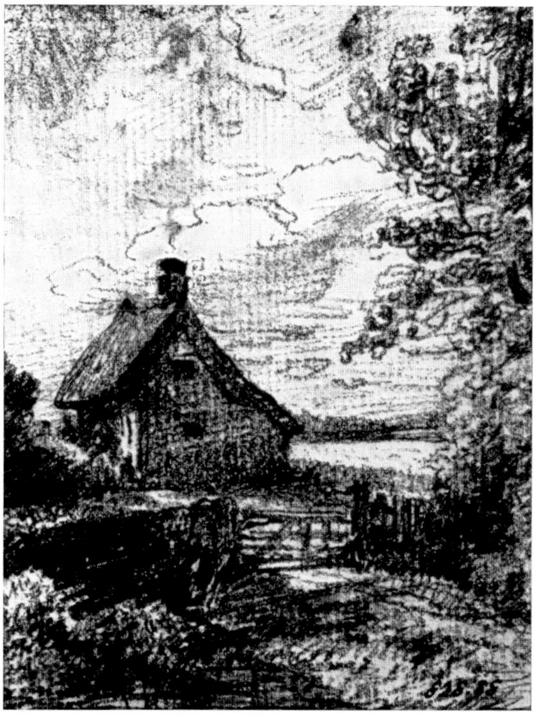

145. Sketch for 'The Cottage in a Cornfield' (No. 352).

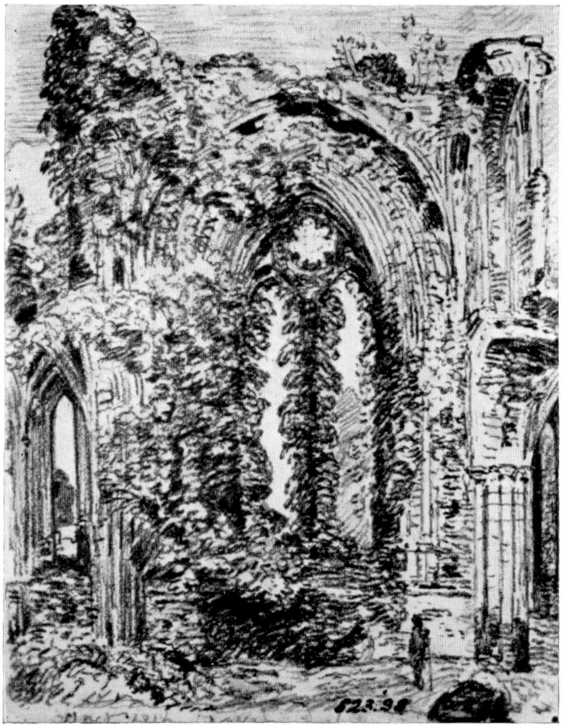

147. Netley Abbey: E. window.

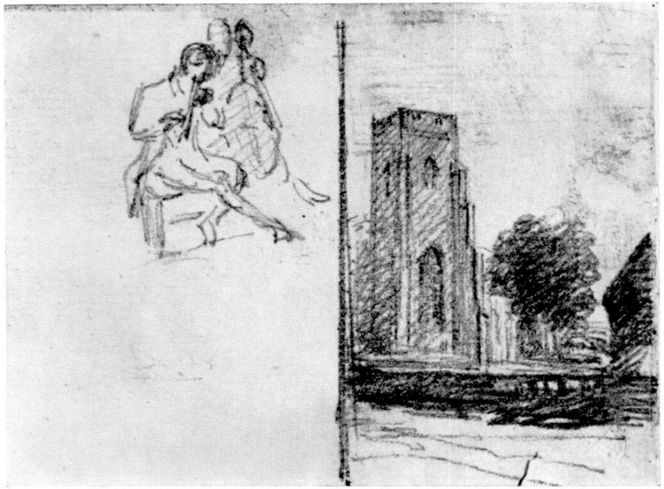

121, p. 91. Stratford St. Mary Church.

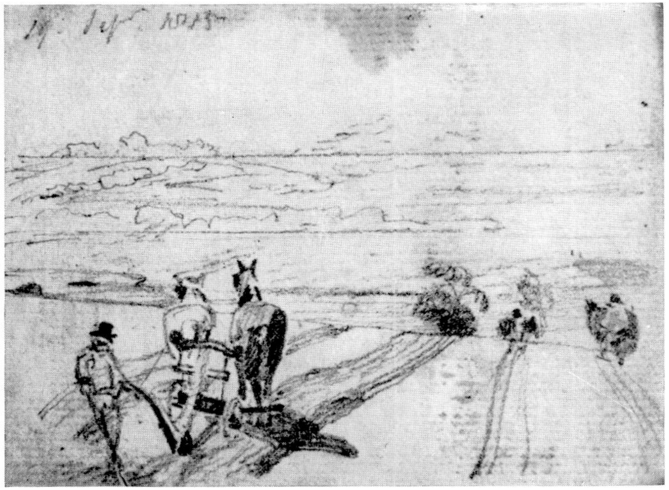

121, p. 92. Landscape with man ploughing.

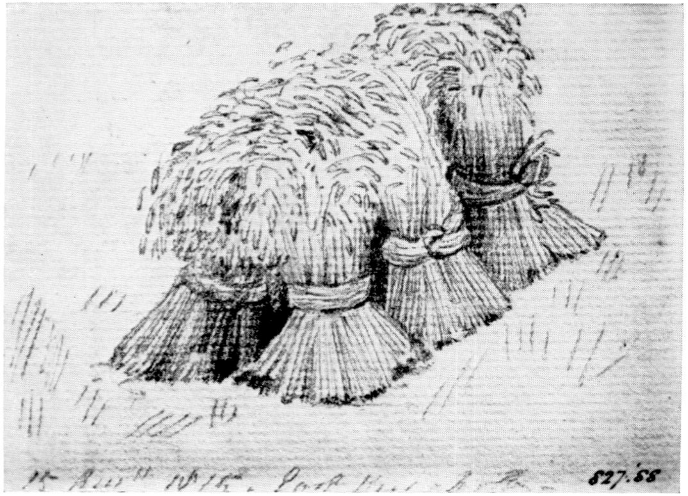

140. Wheatsheaves at East Bergholt.

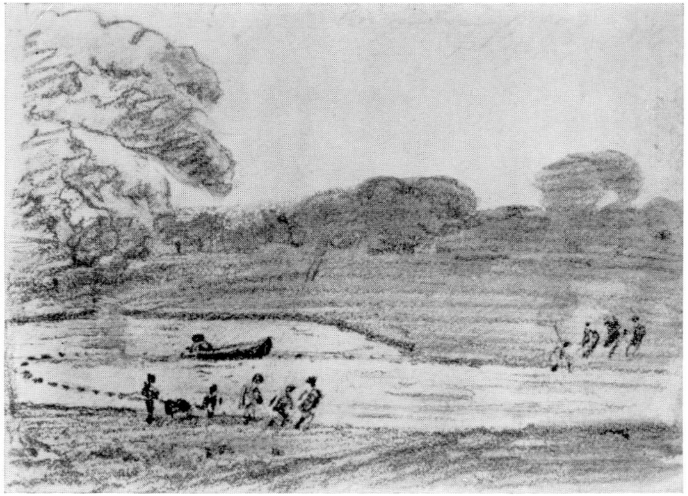

146. Fishing in Wivenhoe Park.

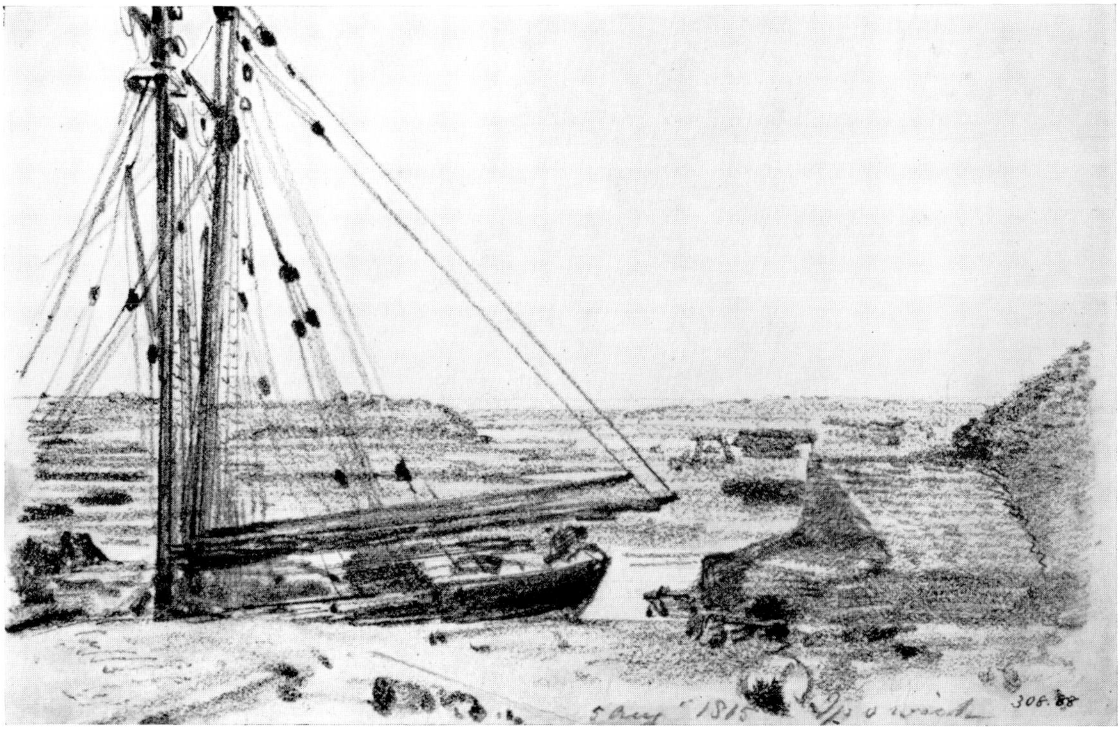

139. Shipping near Ipswich.

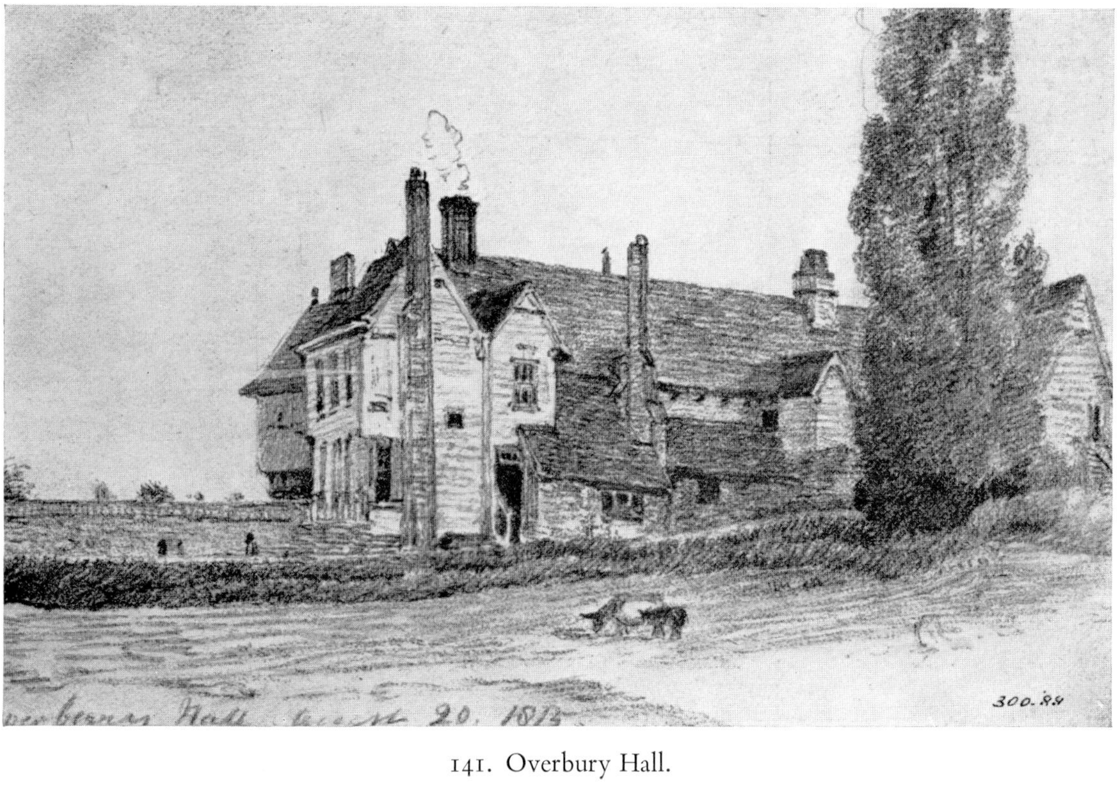

141. Overbury Hall.

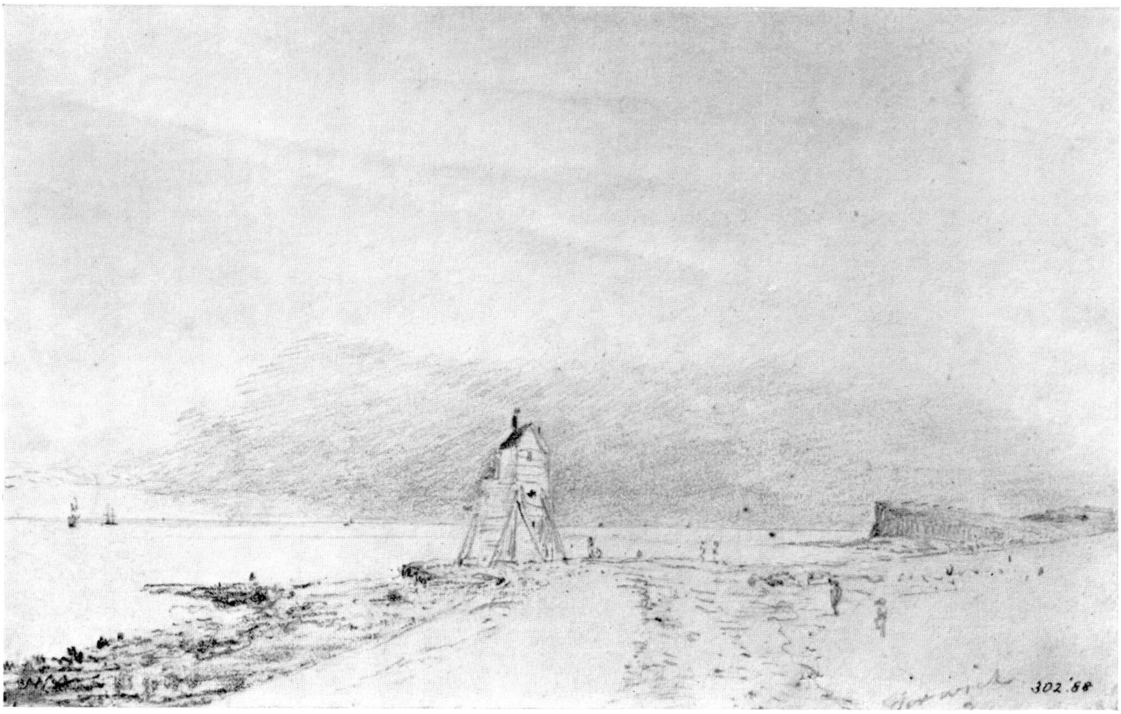

142. Harwich: the seashore and lighthouse.

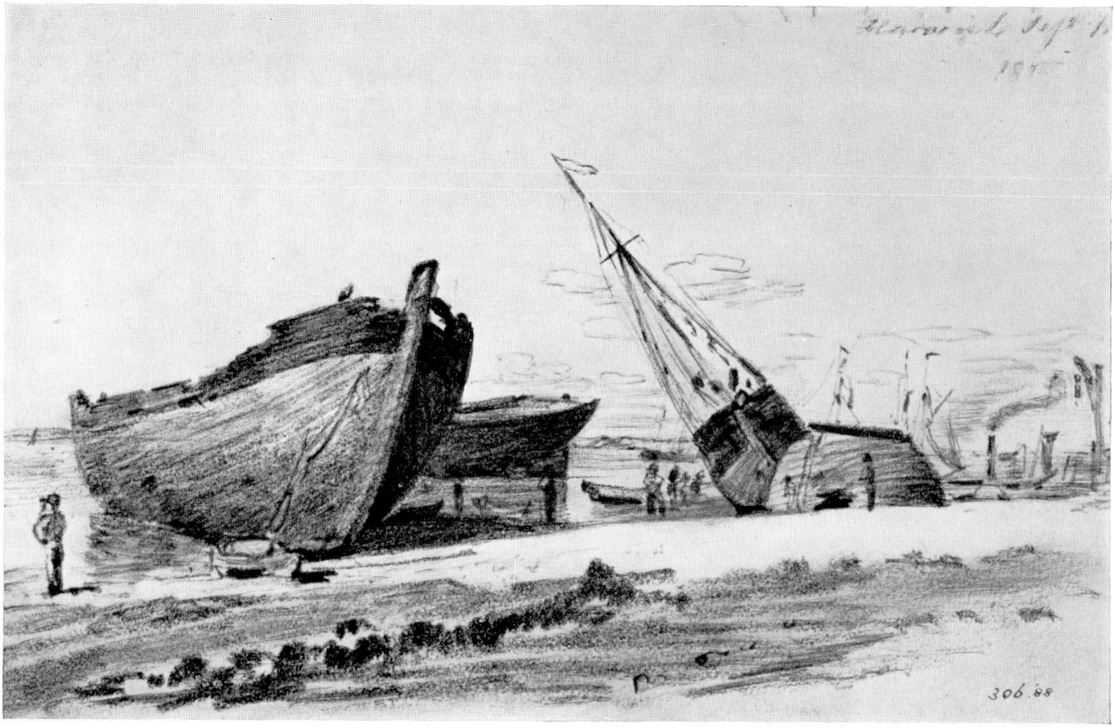

144. Ships on the beach at Harwich.

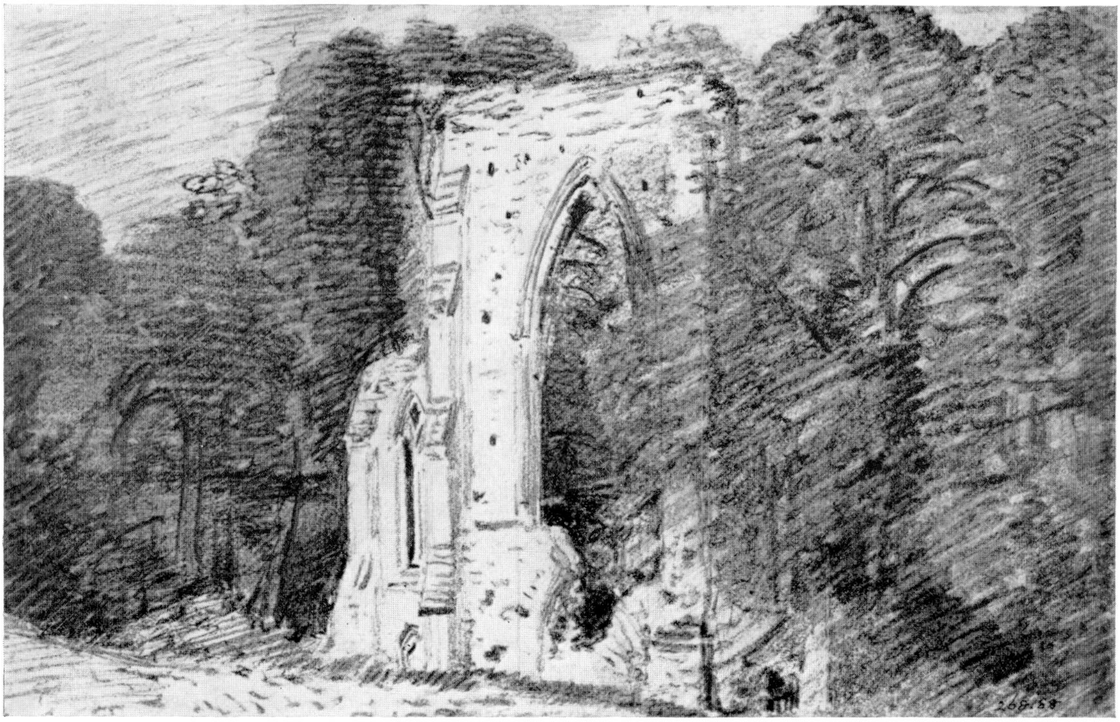

148. Netley Abbey.

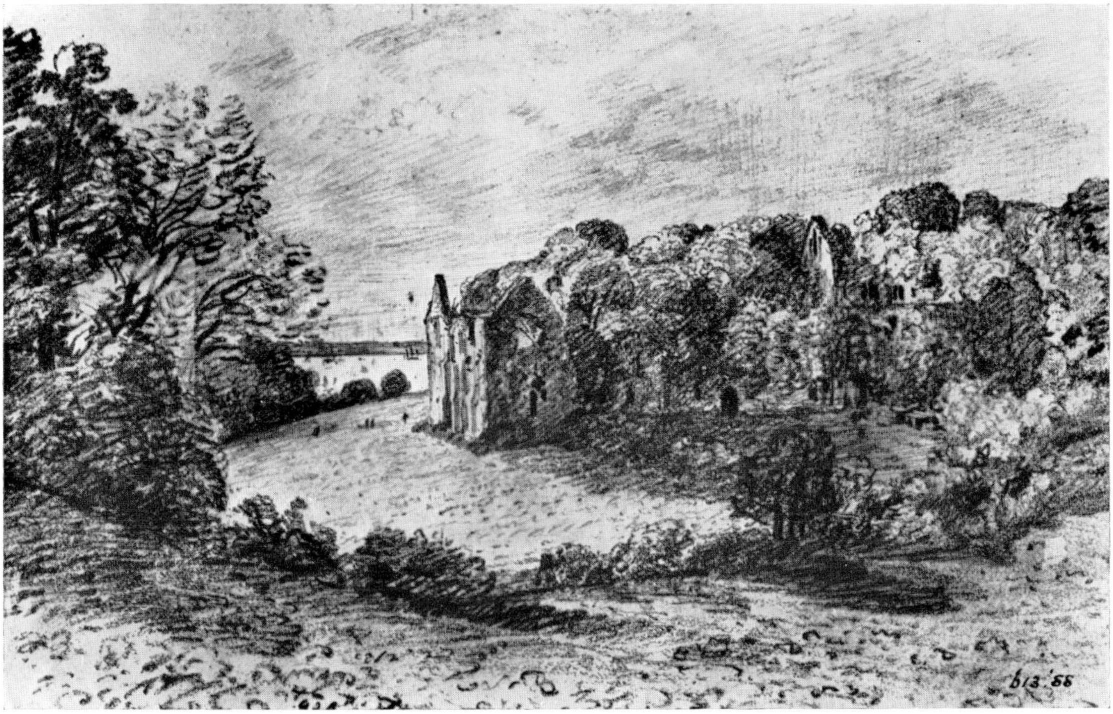

150. Netley Abbey and Southampton Water.

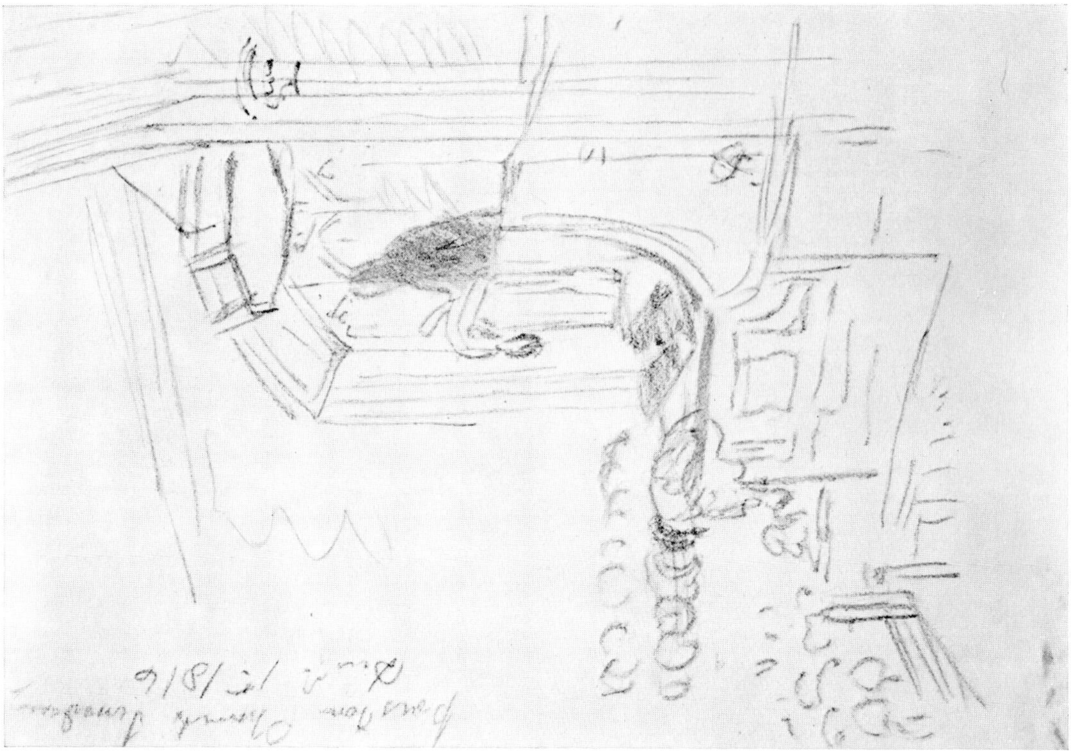

153a. Preston Church: the interior.

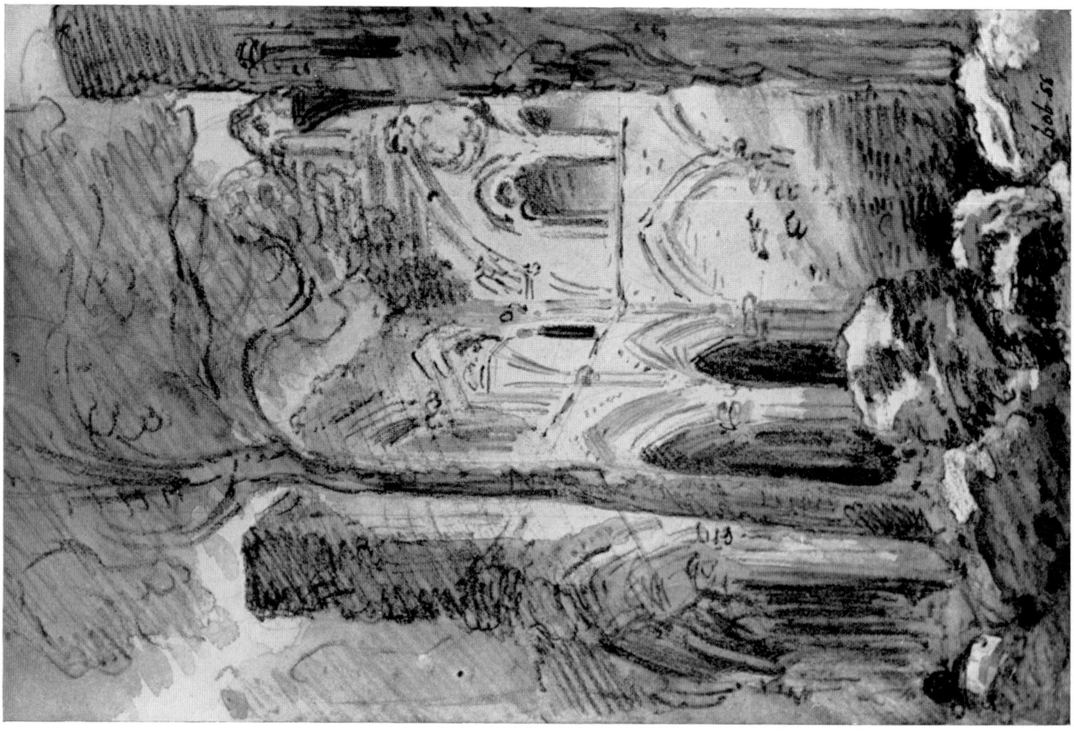

149. Netley Abbey: the interior.

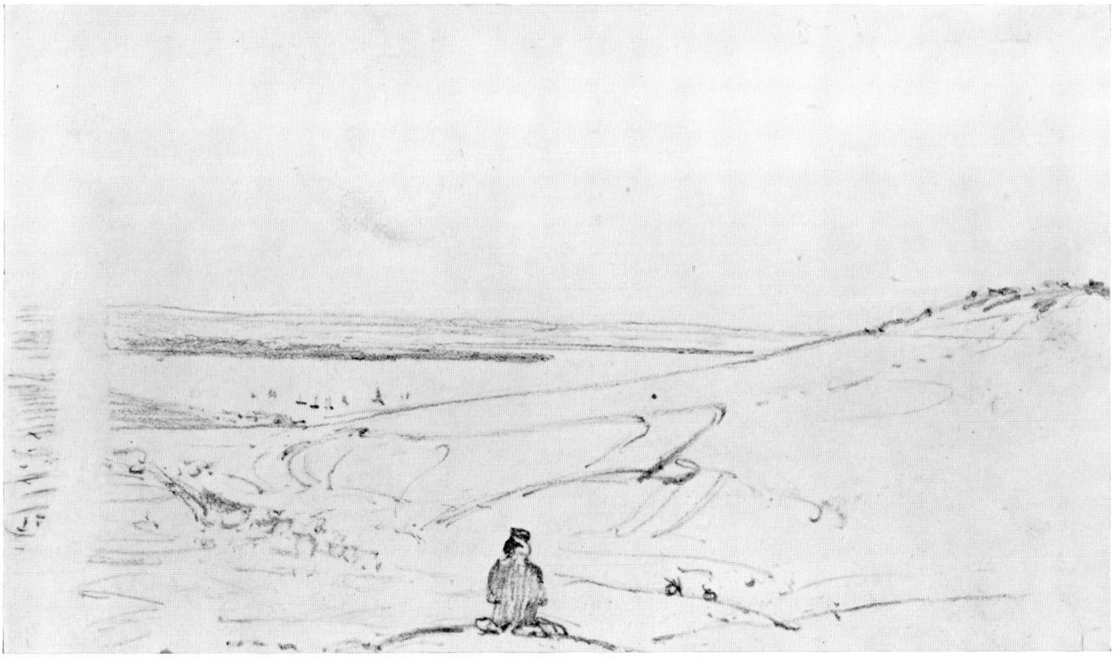

151a. View of Weymouth Bay.

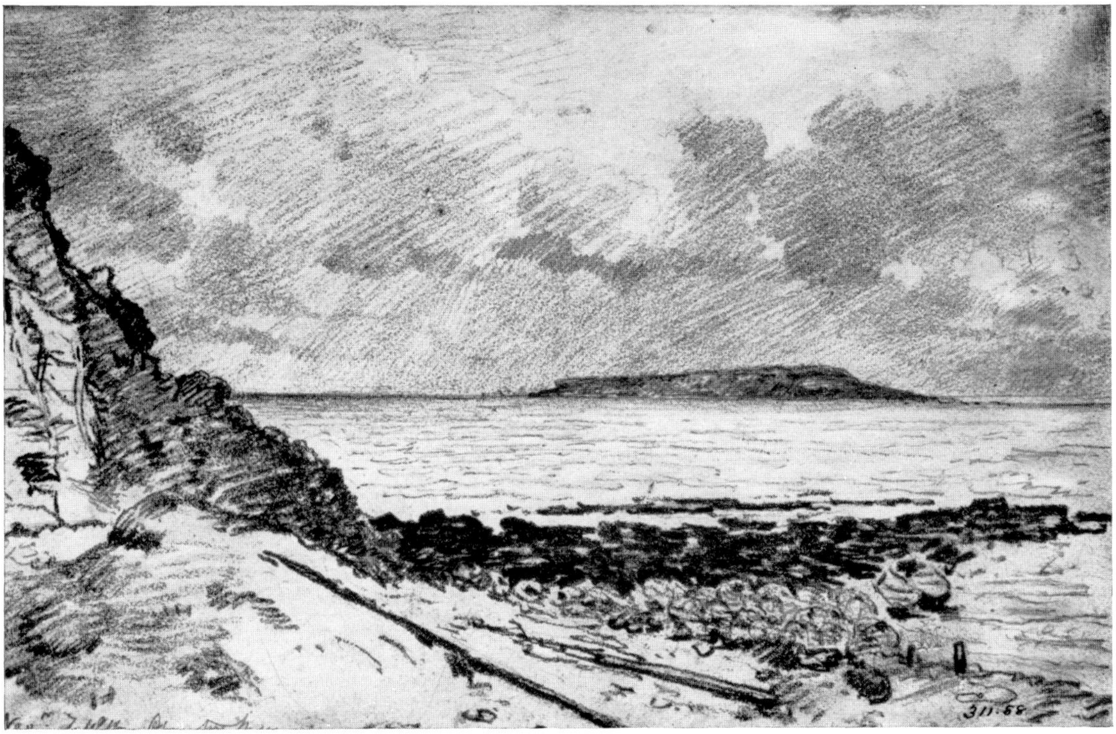

151. Osmington Bay and Portland Island.

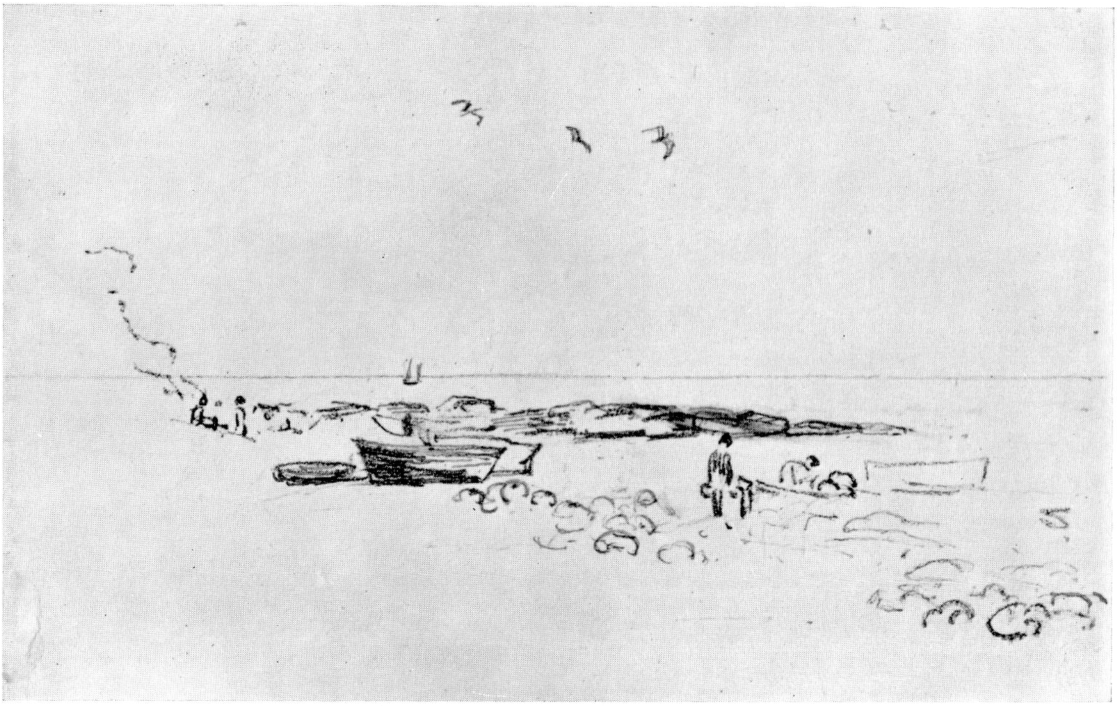

152a. Osmington Bay.

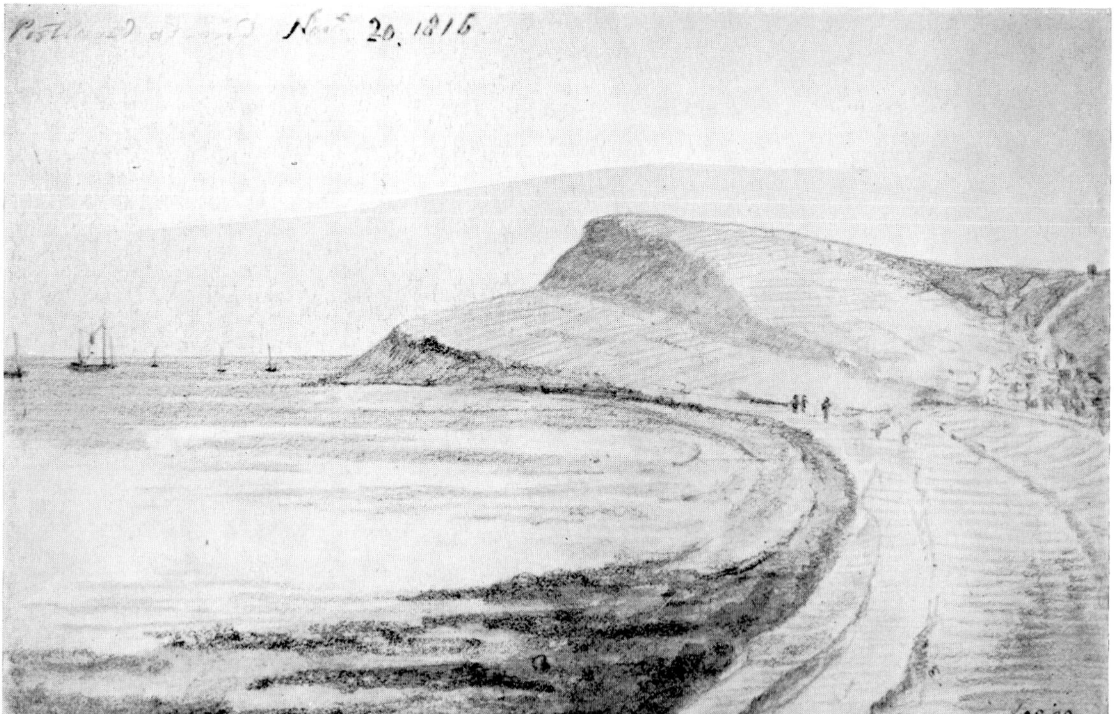

152. Portland Island from Chesil Bank.

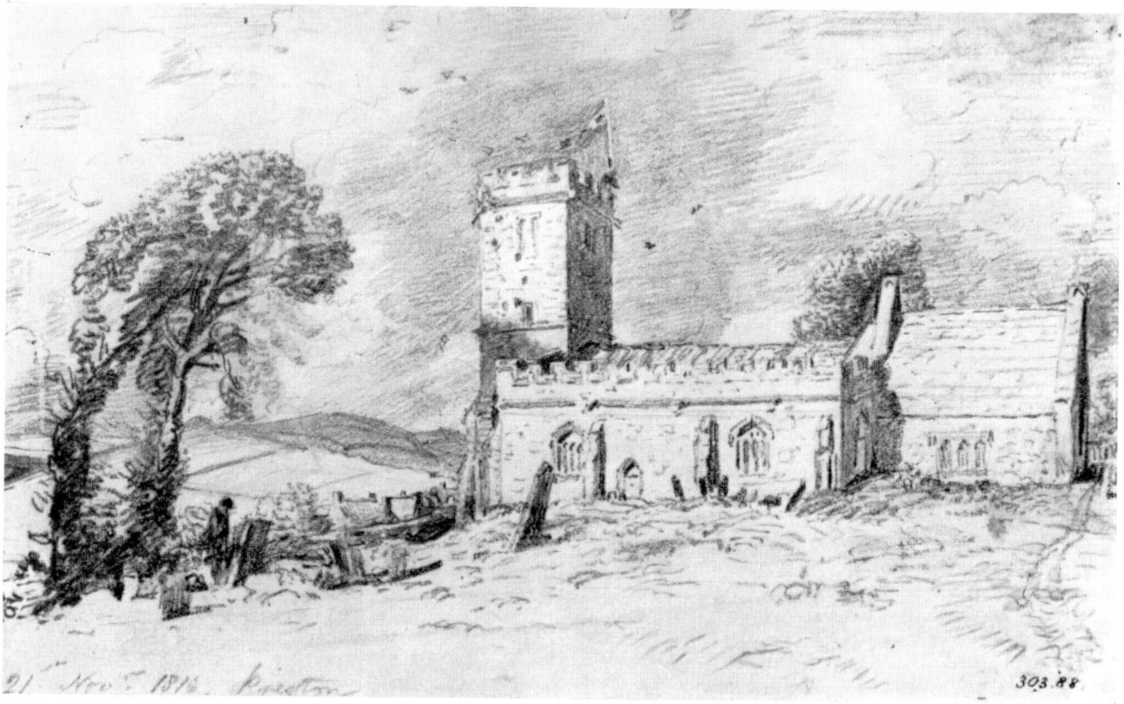

153. Preston Church.

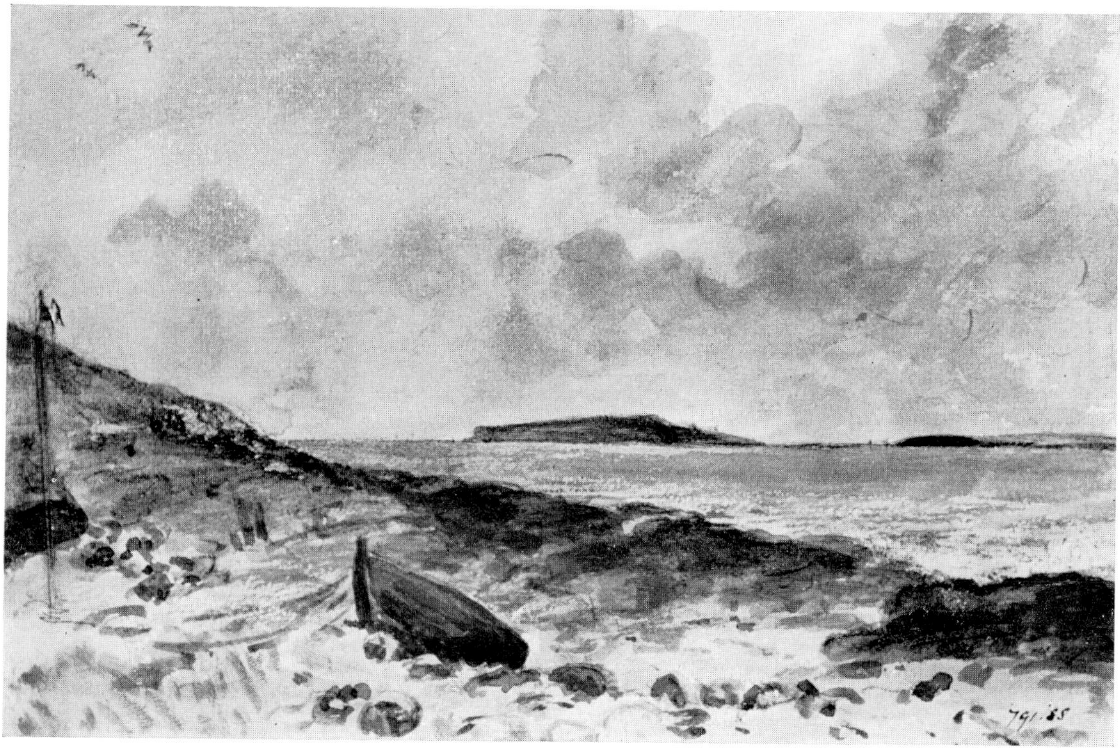

154. Osmington Bay and Portland Island.

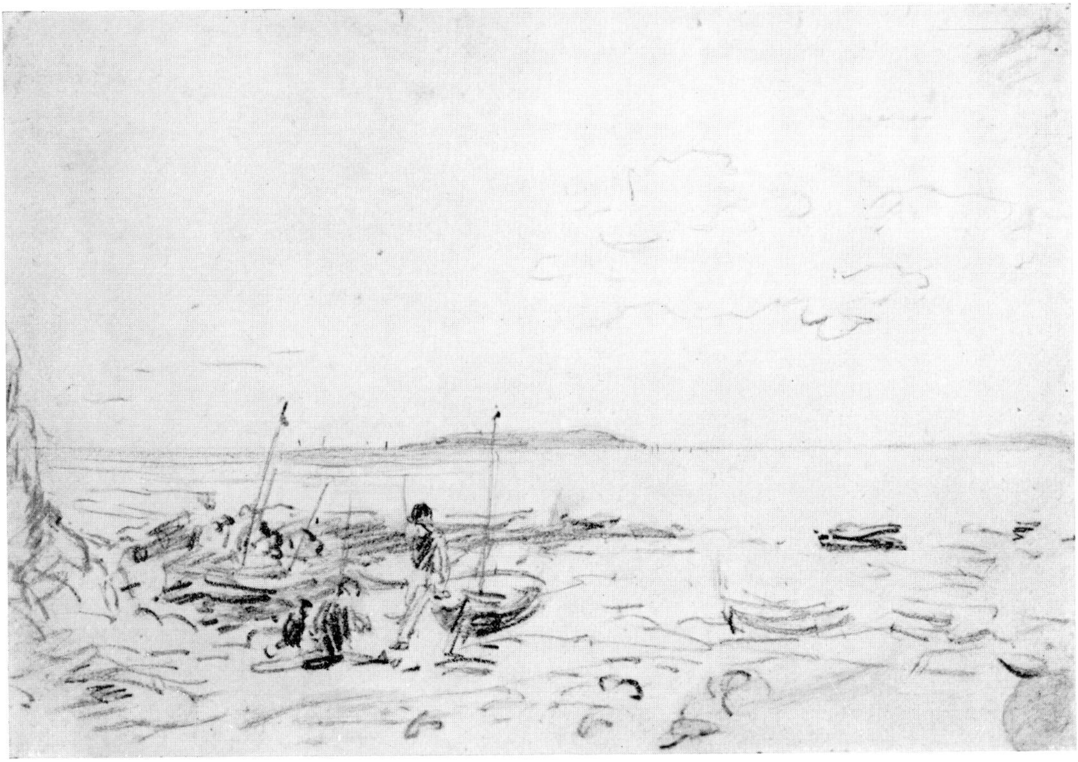

154a. Coast scene with Portland Island.

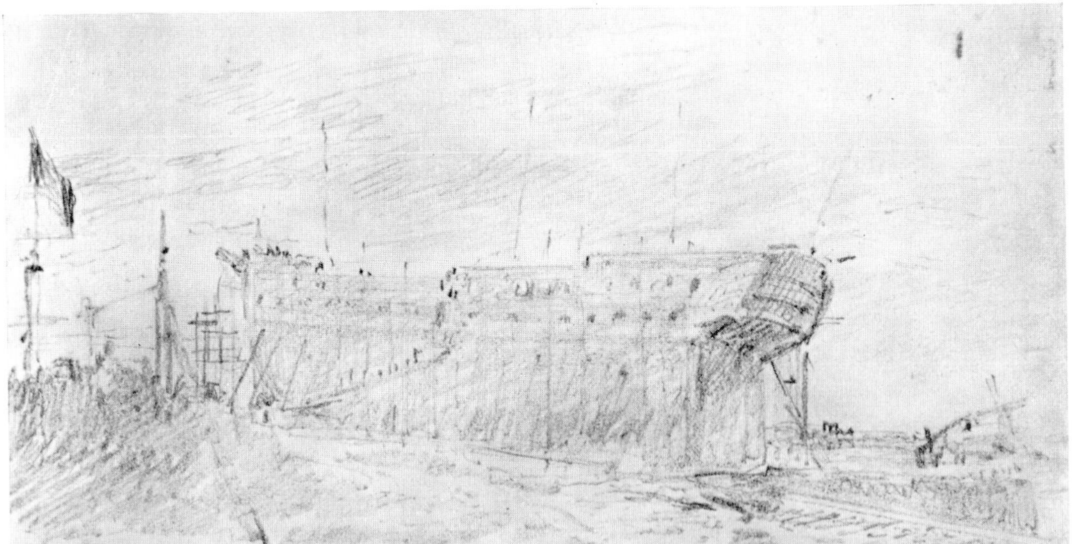

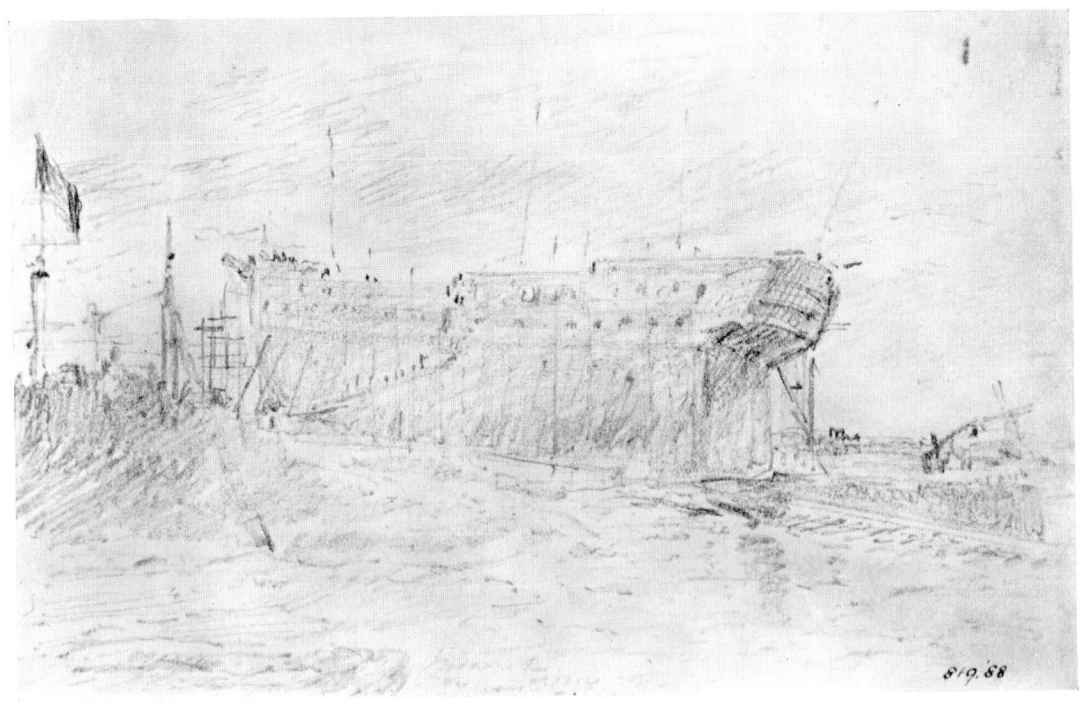

158. Ship on the stocks at Ipswich.

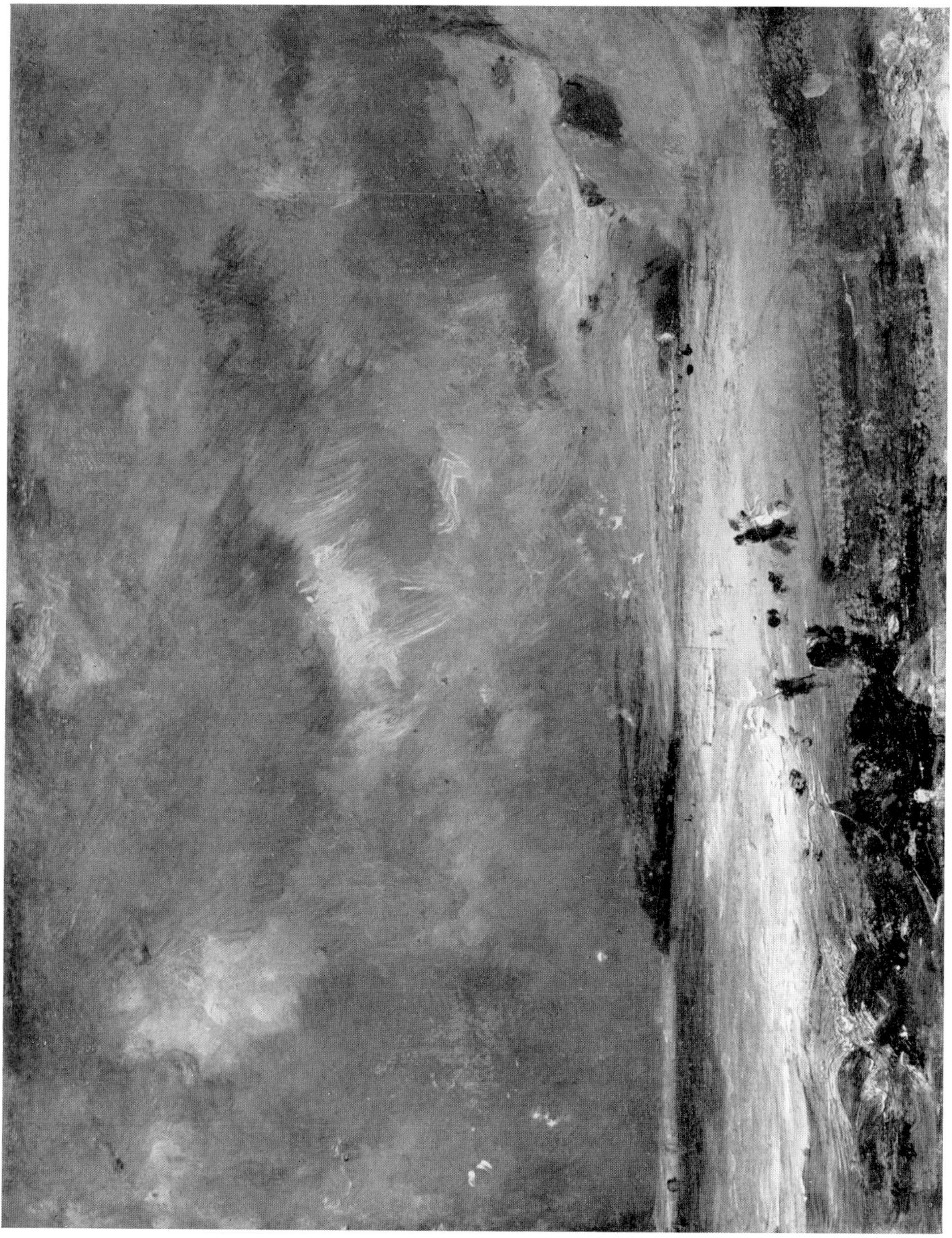

155. Weymouth Bay.

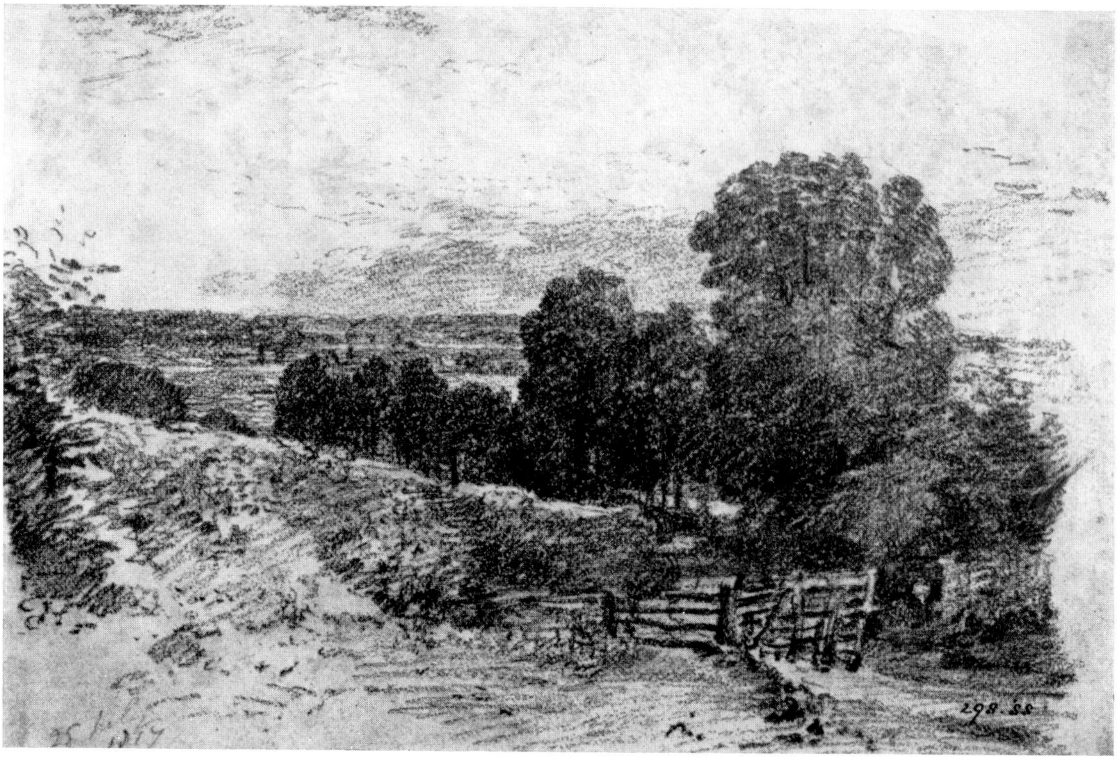

156. A lane near East Bergholt.

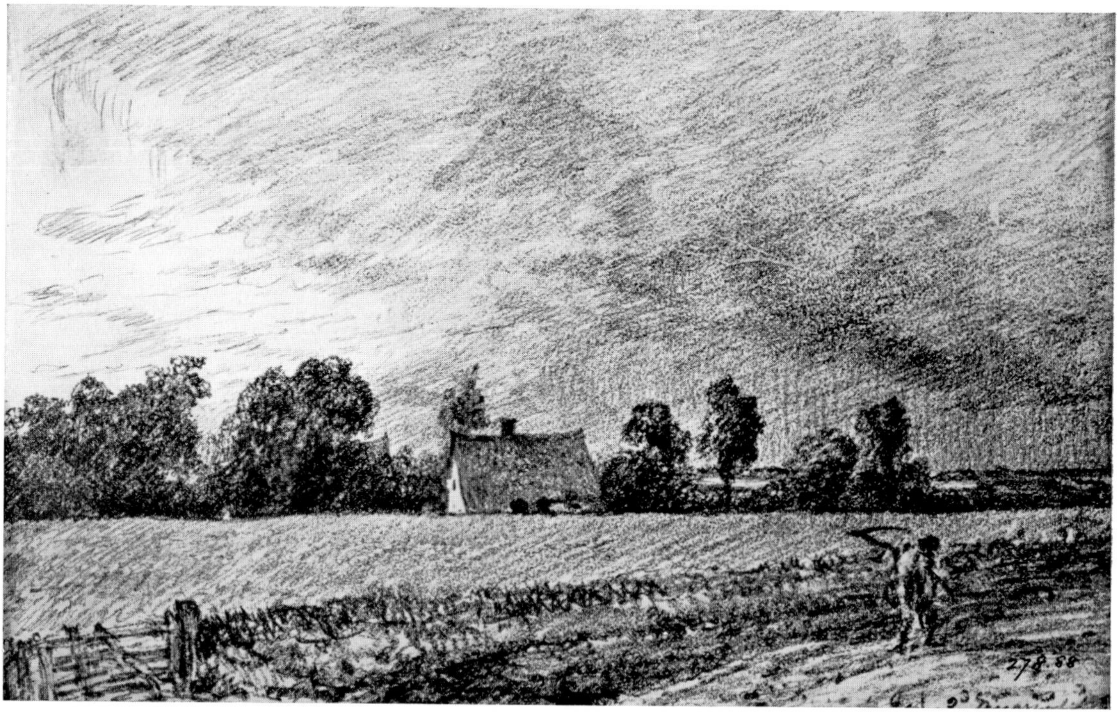

157. Cottage and road at East Bergholt.

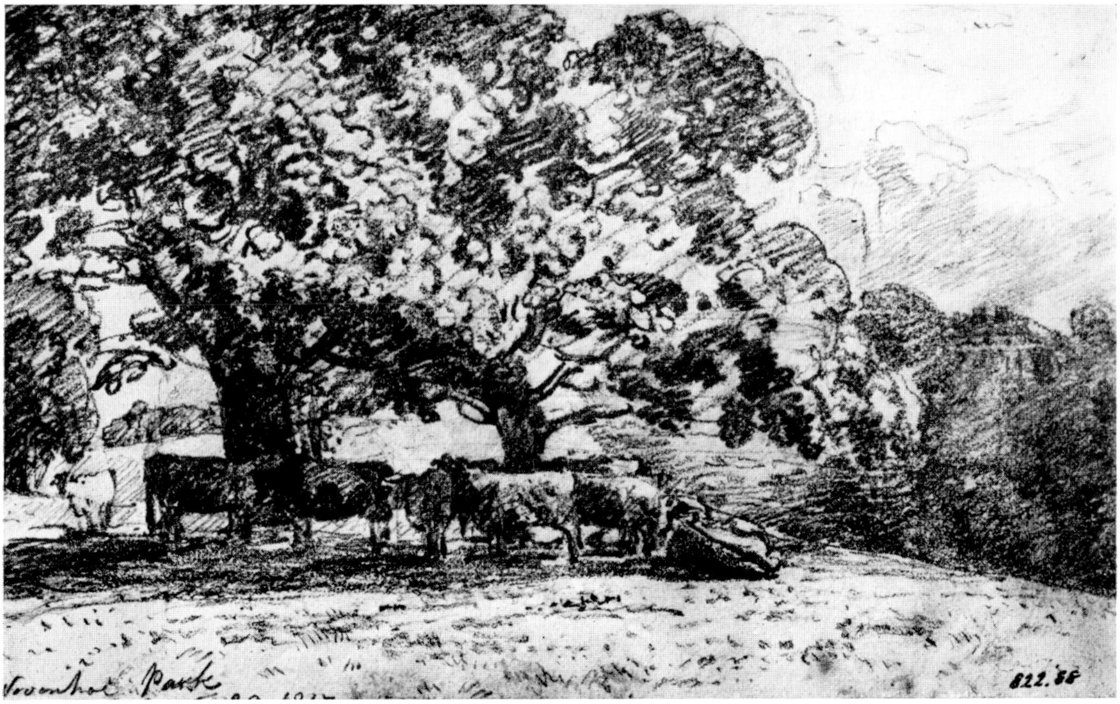

159. Wivenhoe Park.

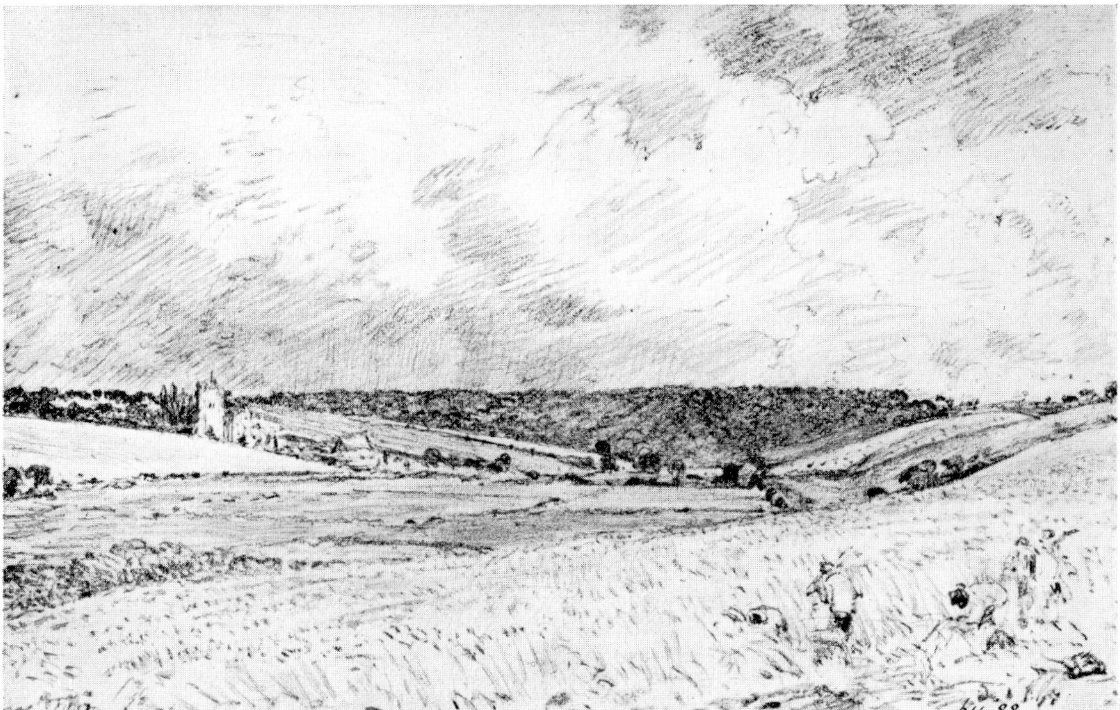

160. Churn Wood and Greenstead Church.

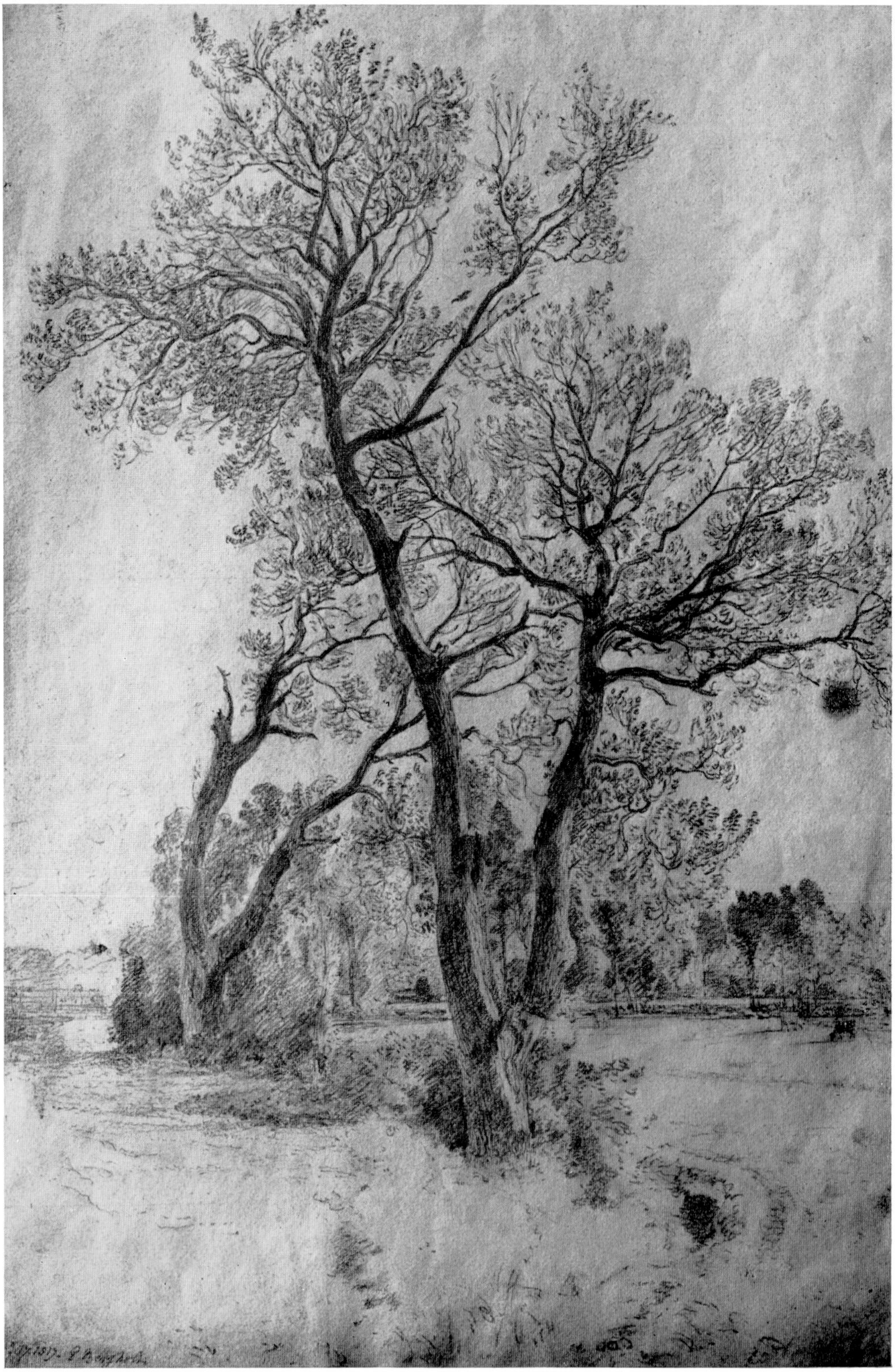

161. Trees at East Bergholt.

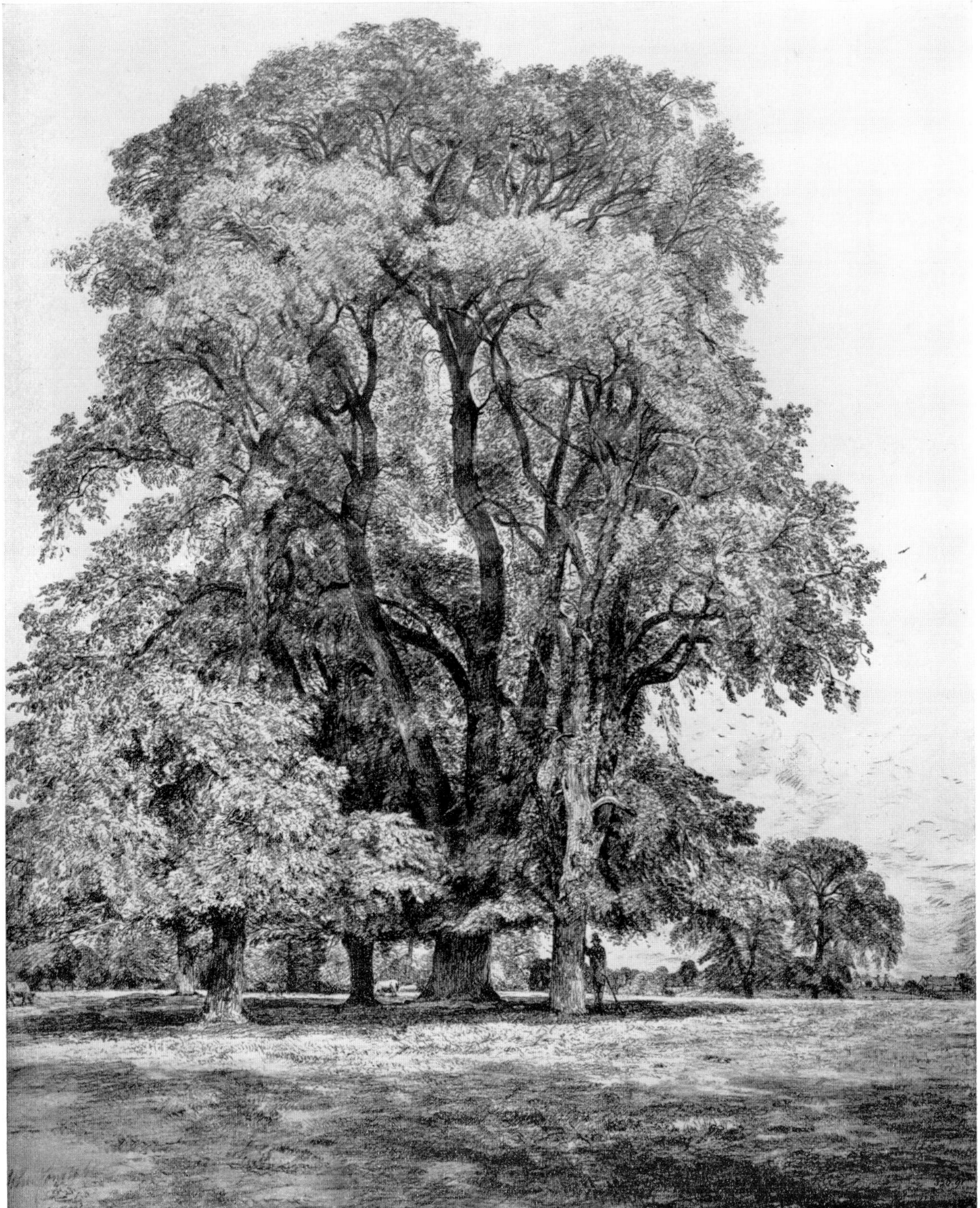

162. Elm trees in Old Hall Park, East Bergholt.

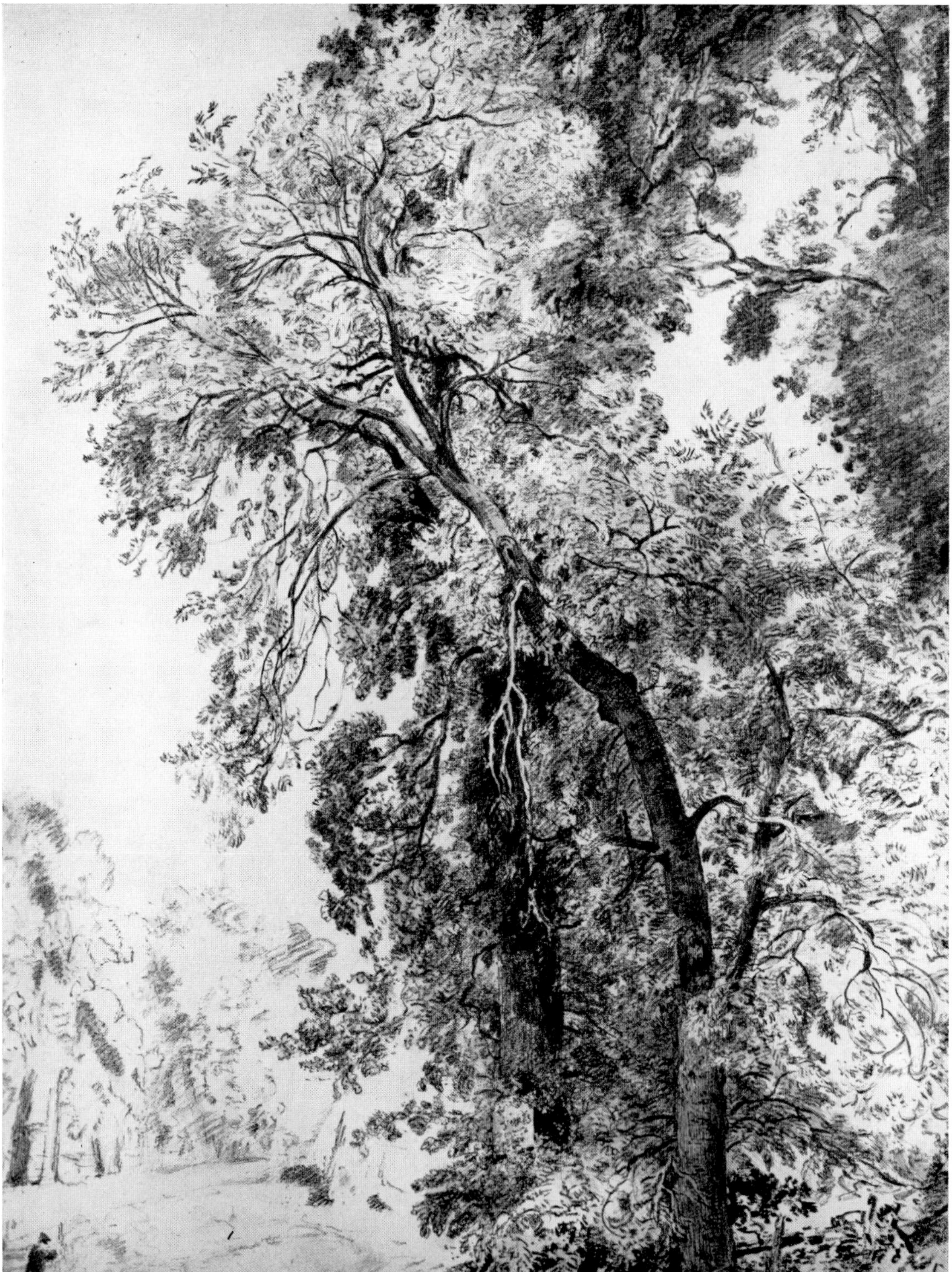

163. Study of ash trees.

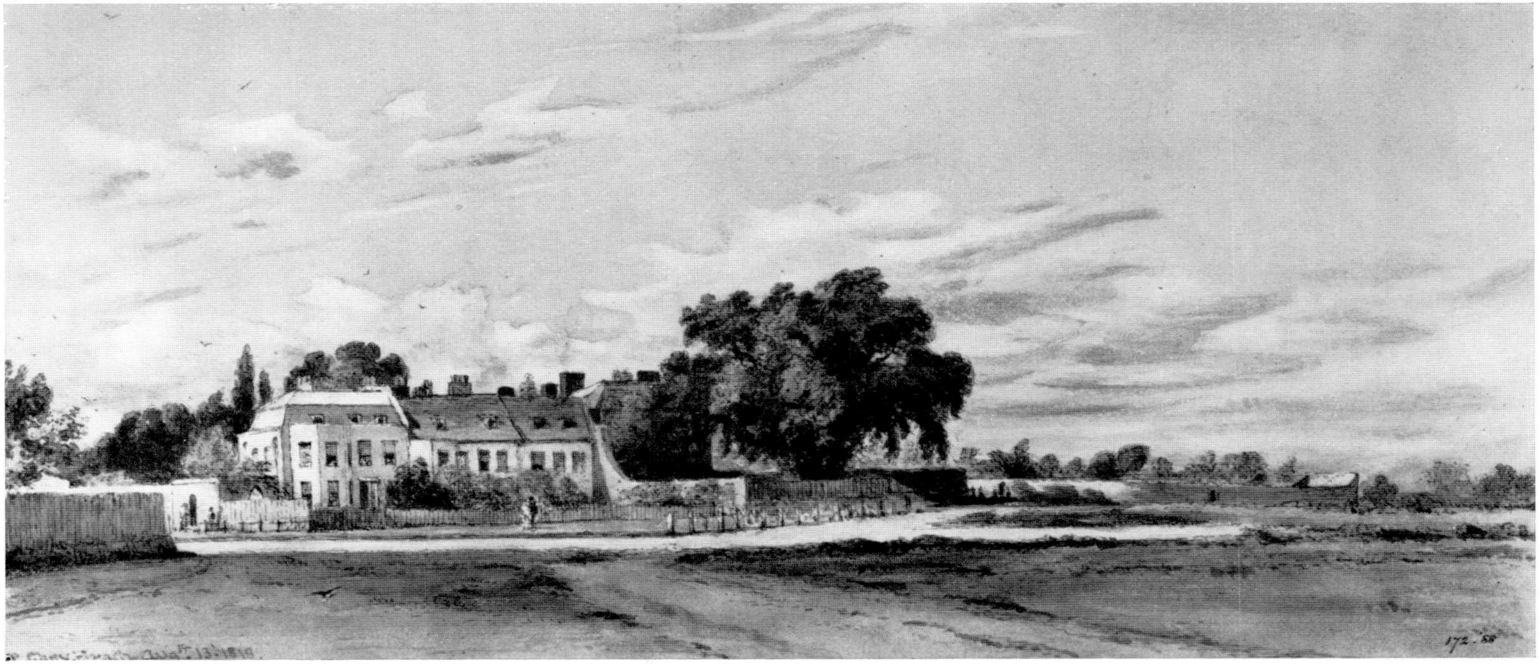

165. Houses at Putney Heath.

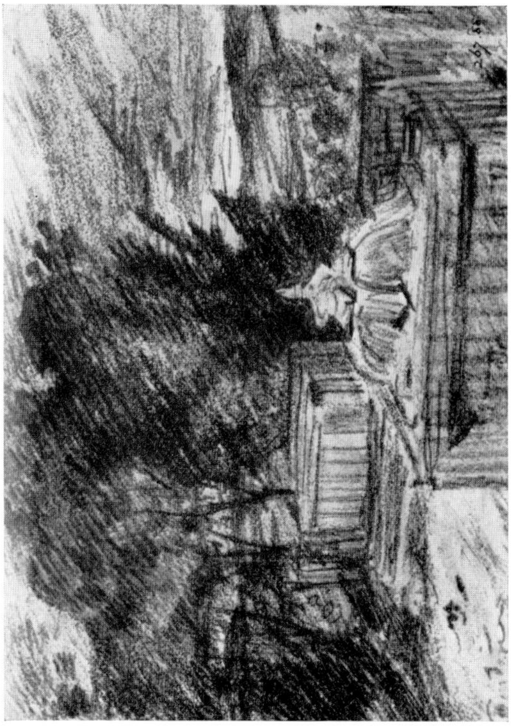

164. St. Mary's churchyard, Hendon.

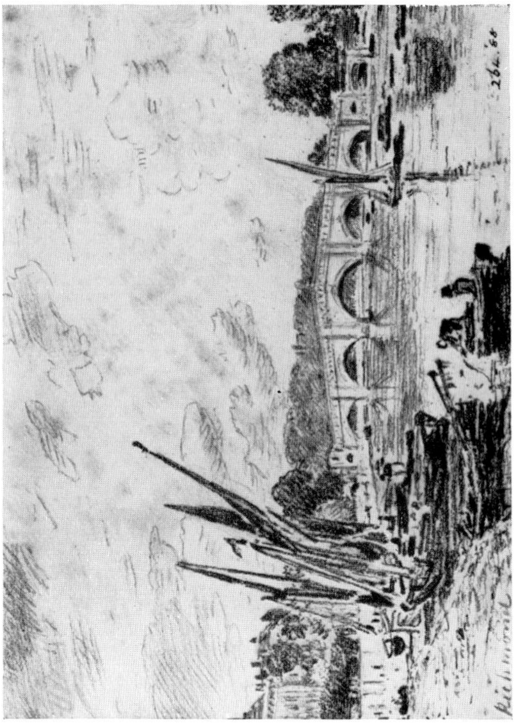

166. Richmond Bridge.

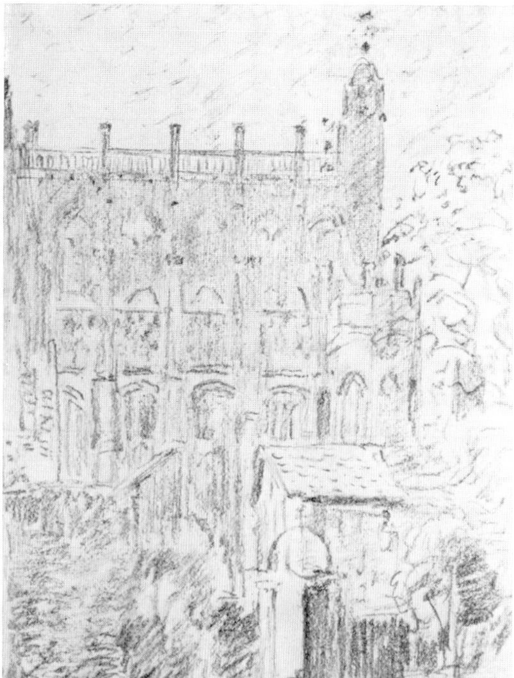

167. St. George's Chapel, Windsor.

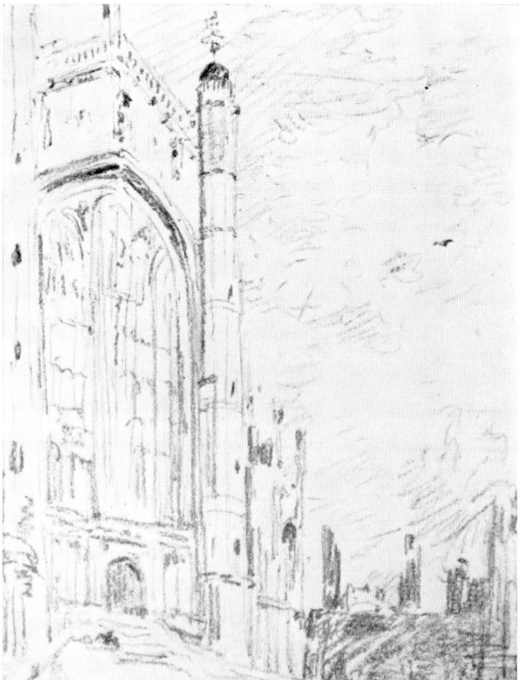

168. St. George's Chapel: W. end.

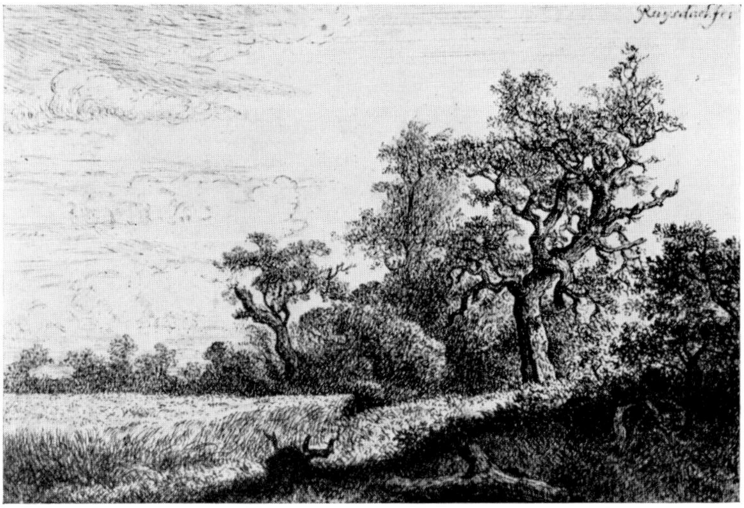

169. The Wheatfield. After Jacob Ruysdael.

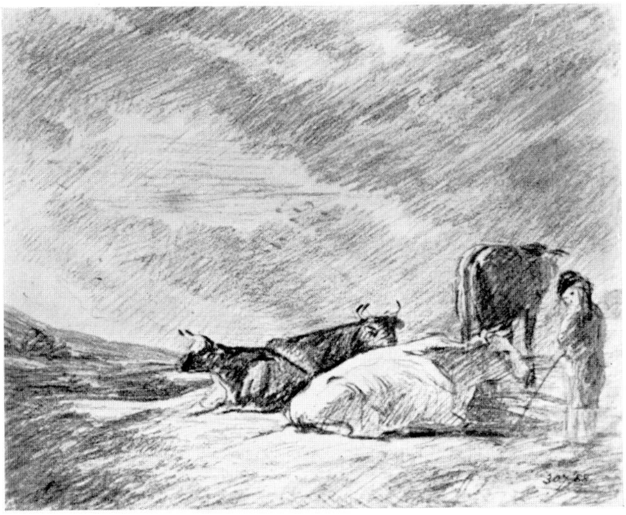

170. Cows and herdboy. After Aelbert Cuyp.

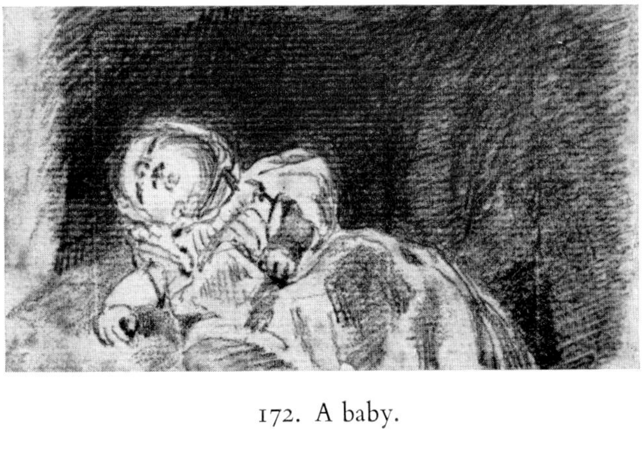

172. A baby.

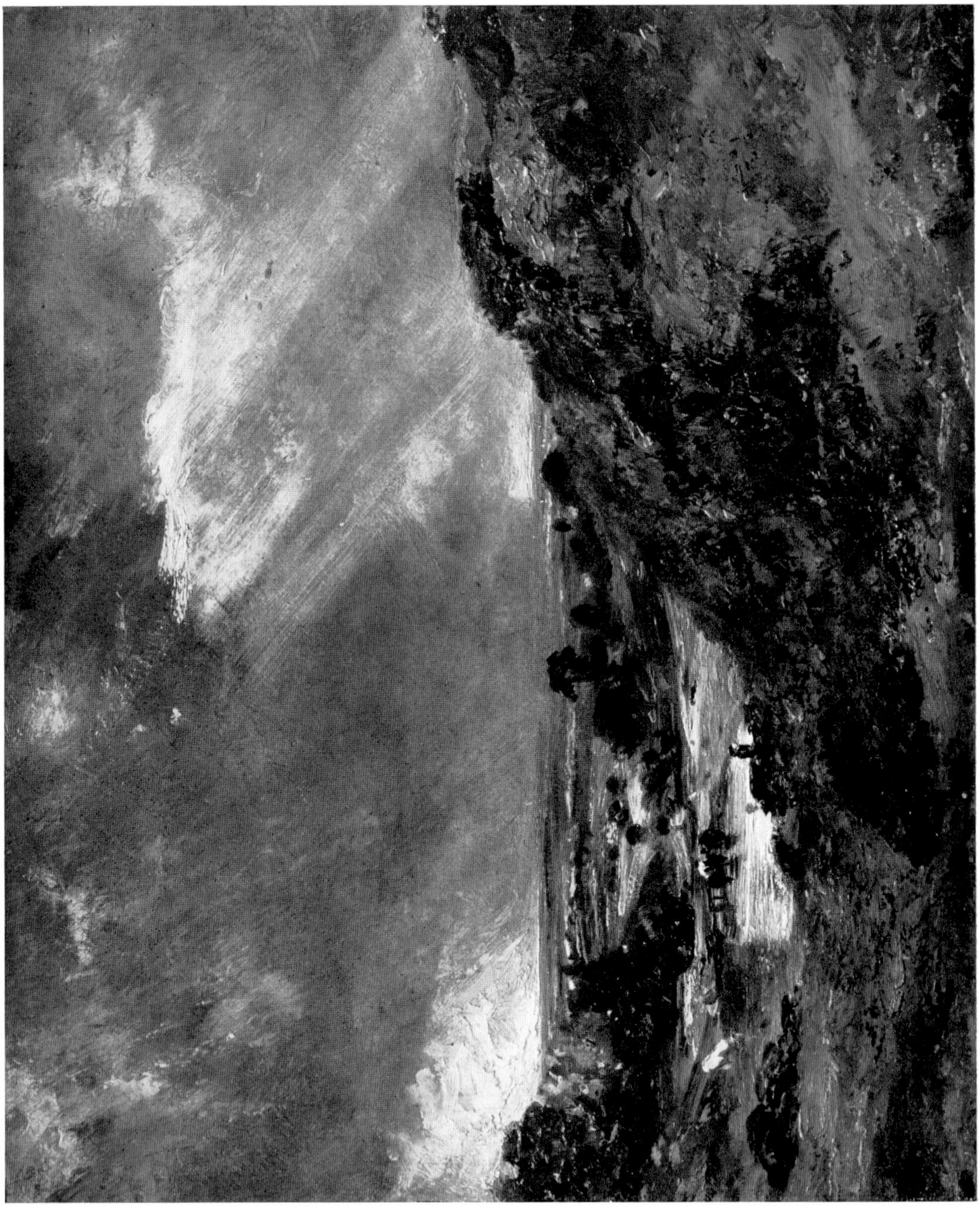

171. Branch Hill Pond, Hampstead.

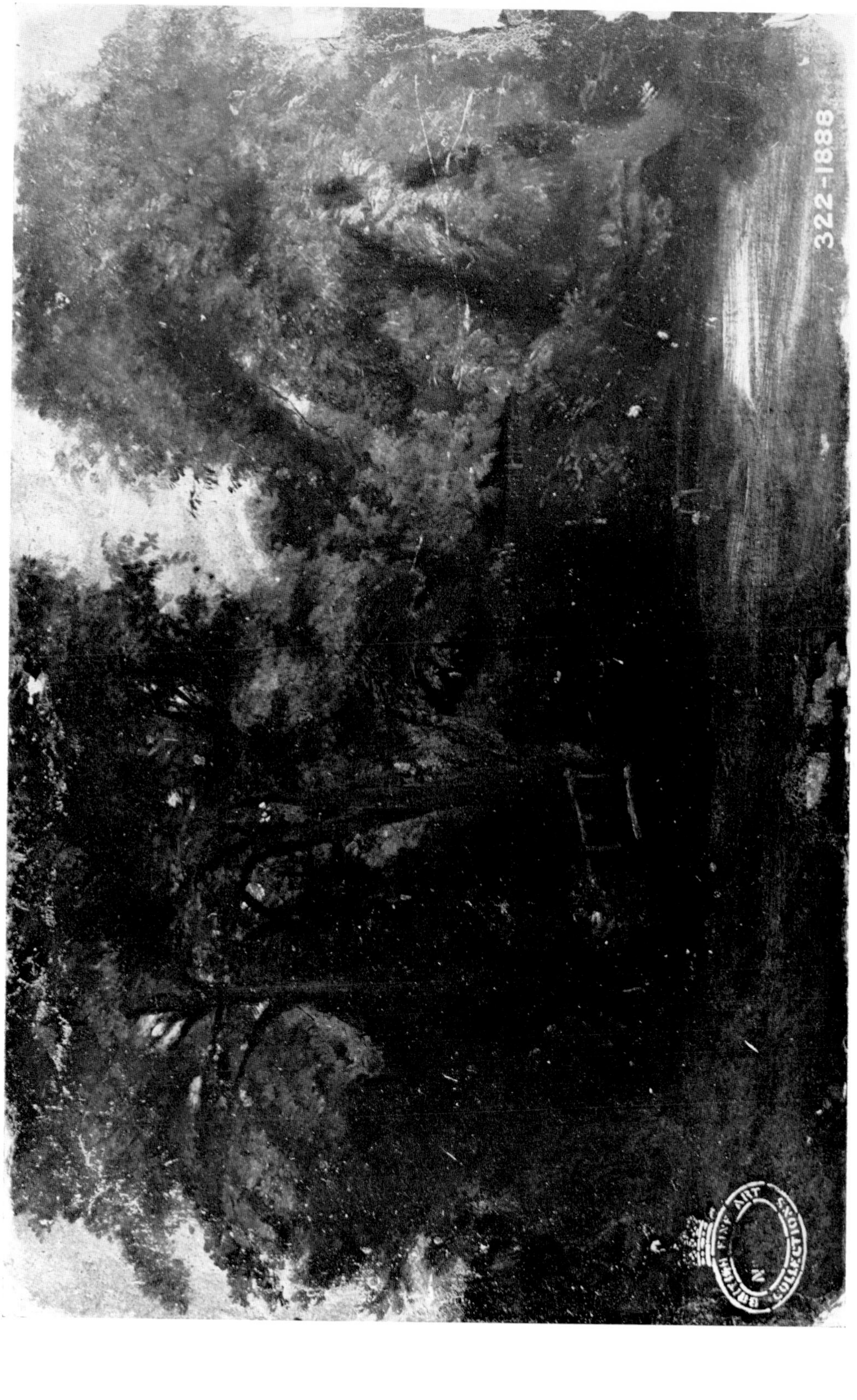

174a. A woodland scene.

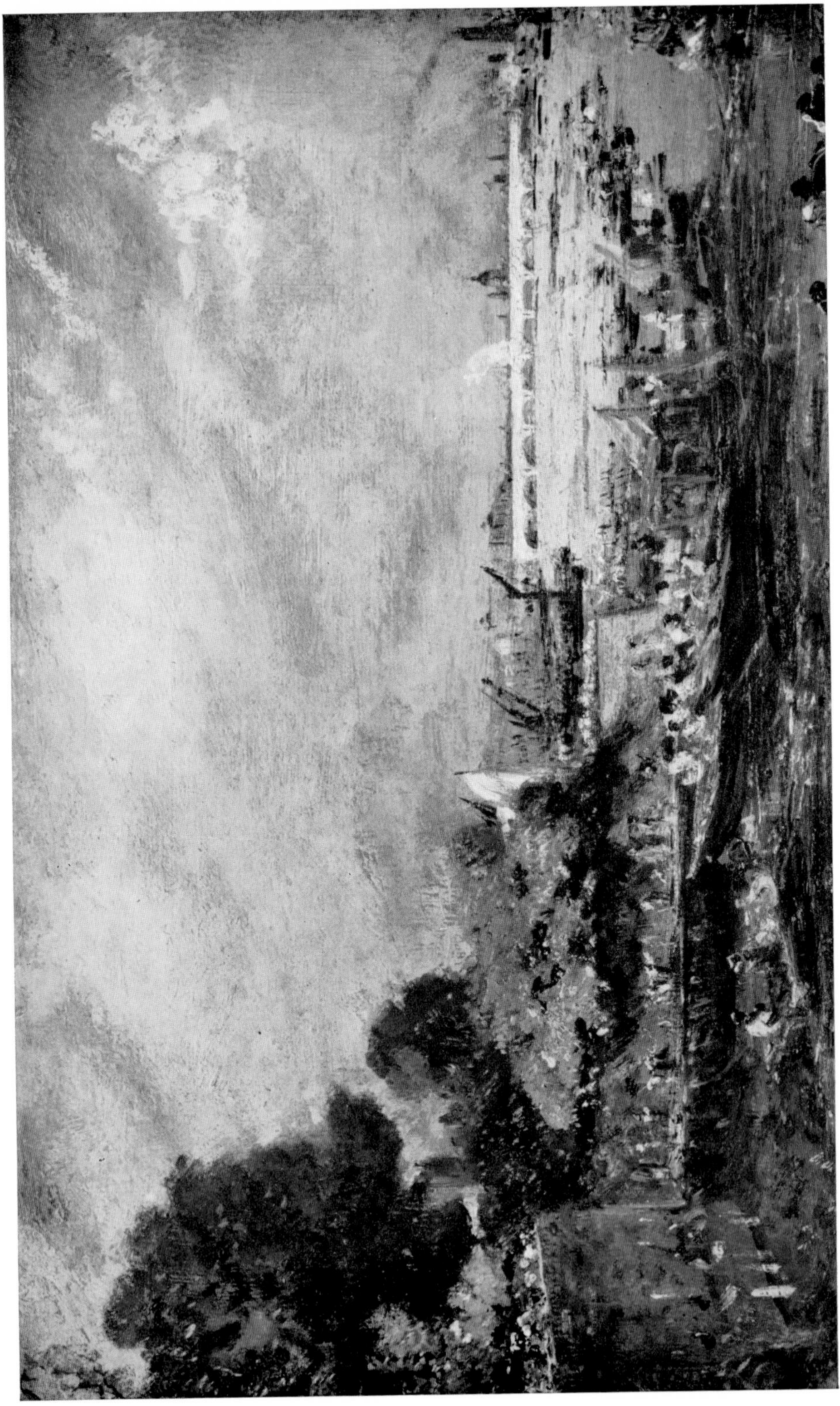

174. Waterloo Bridge from Whitehall Stairs.

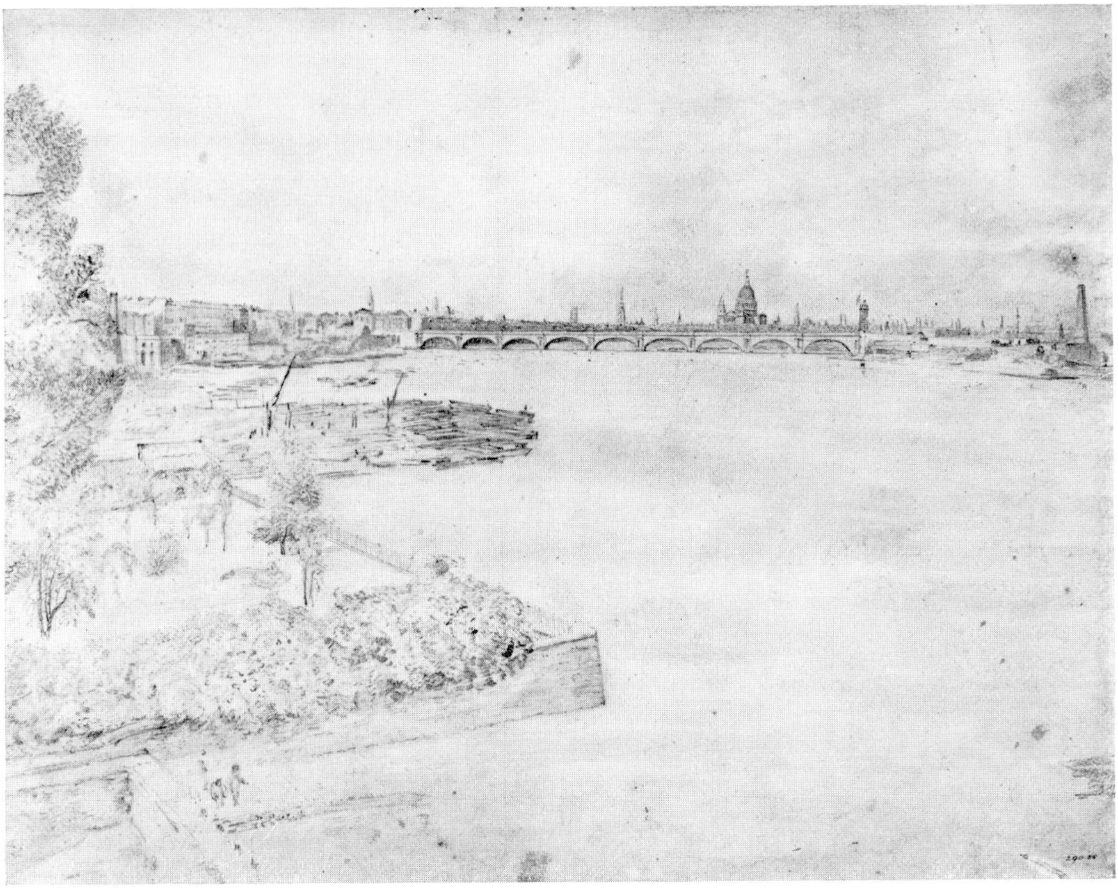

173. Waterloo Bridge.

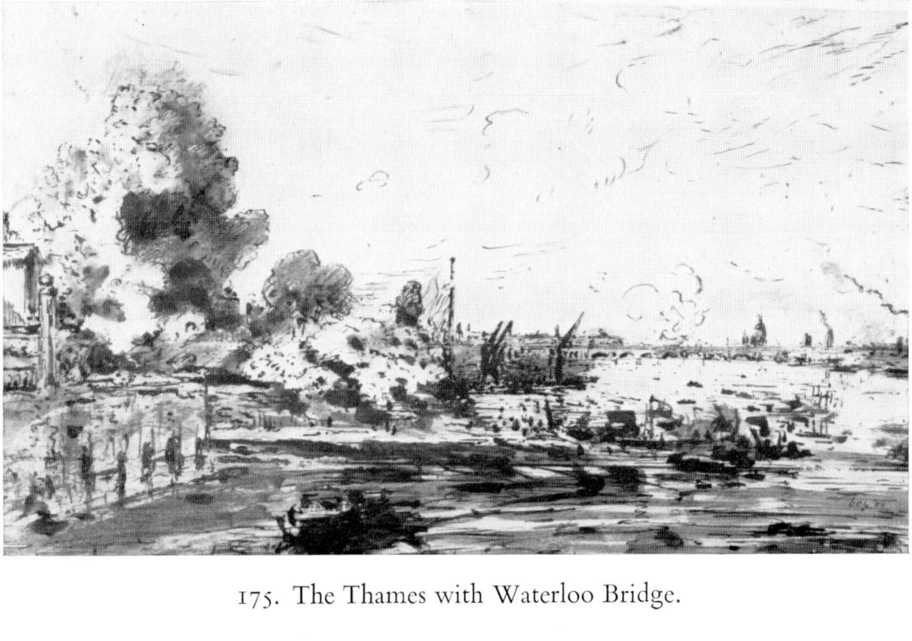

175. The Thames with Waterloo Bridge.

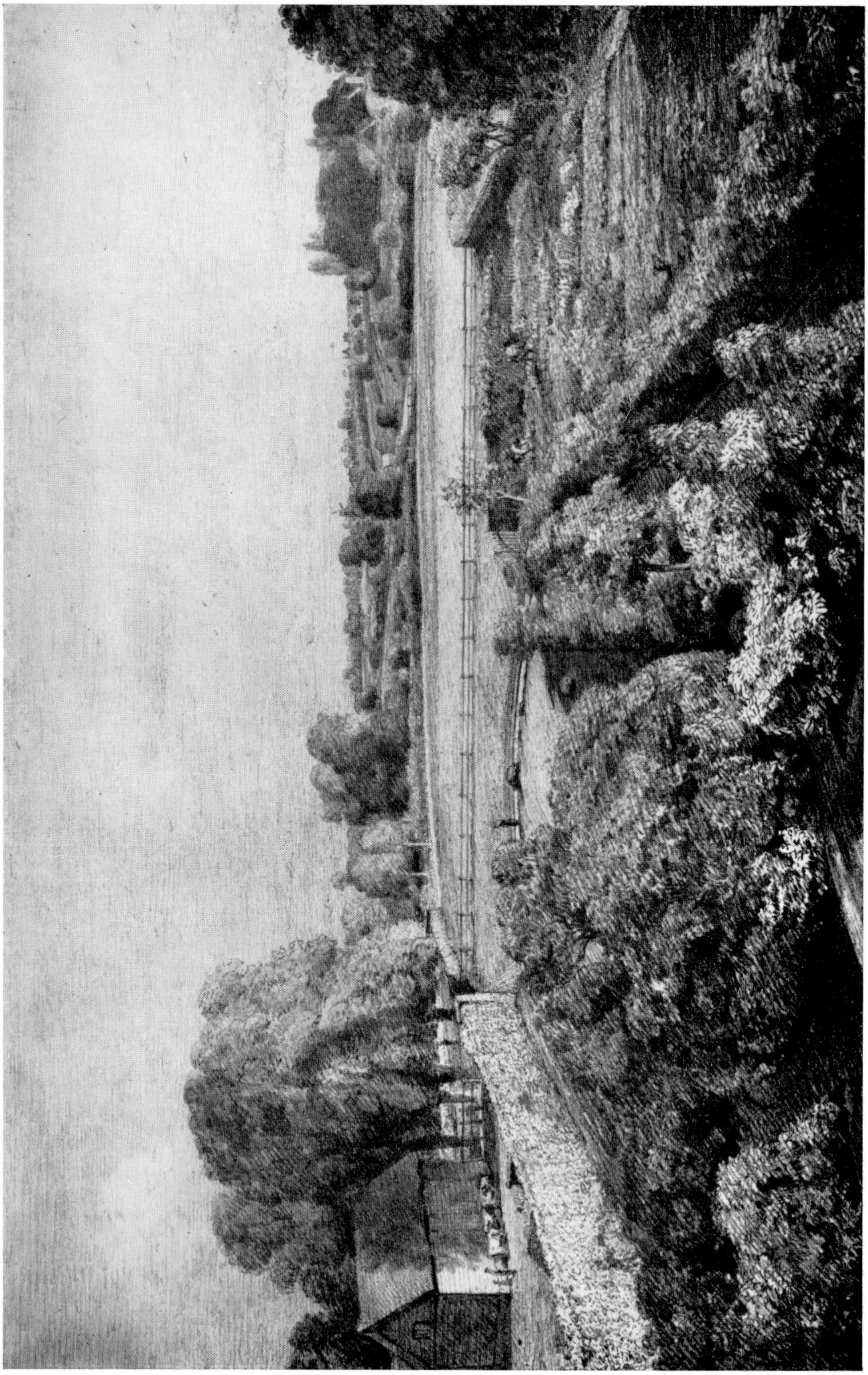

176. The kitchen garden of Golding Constable's house, East Bergholt.

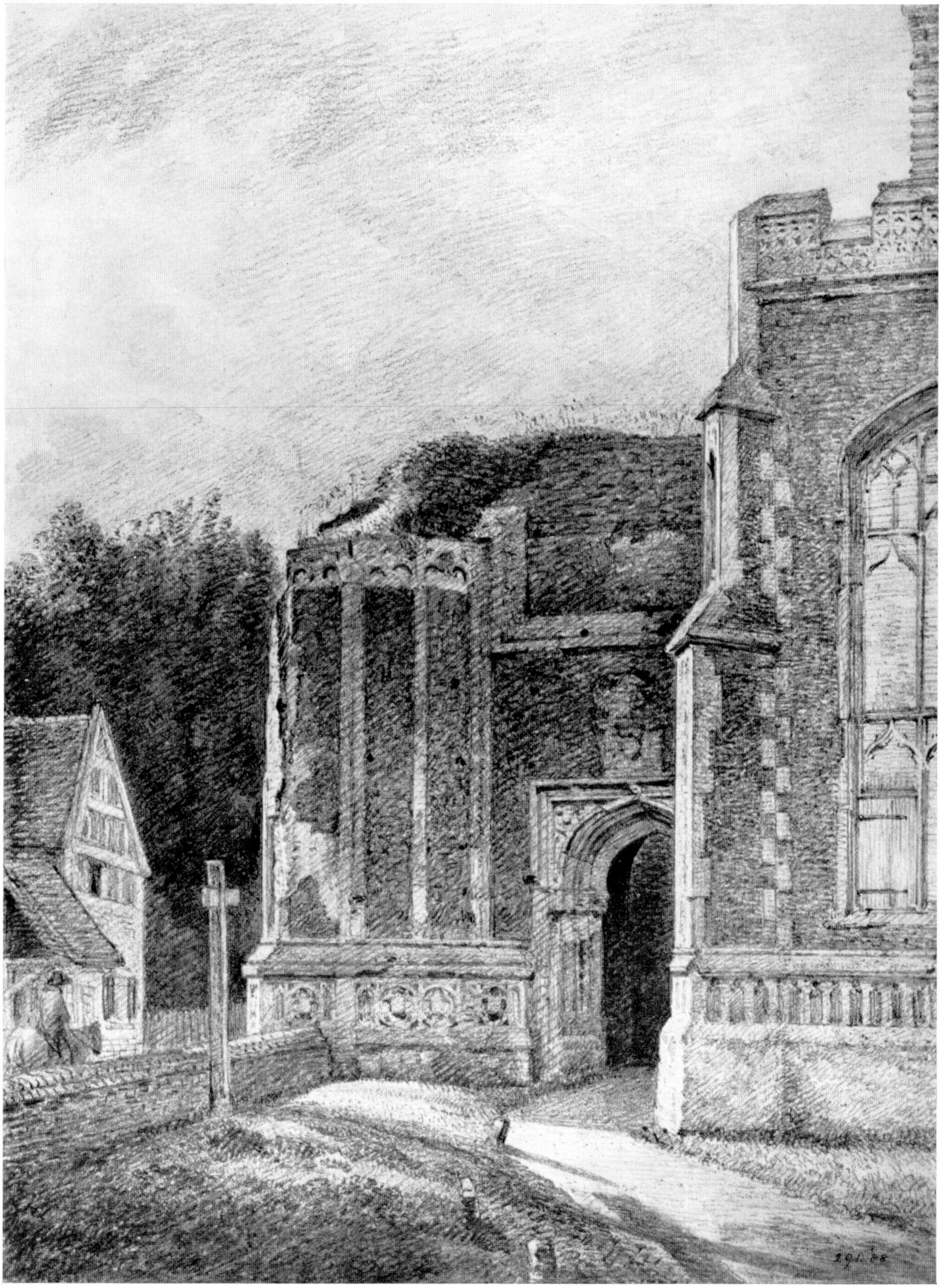

177. East Bergholt Church: S. archway of ruined tower.

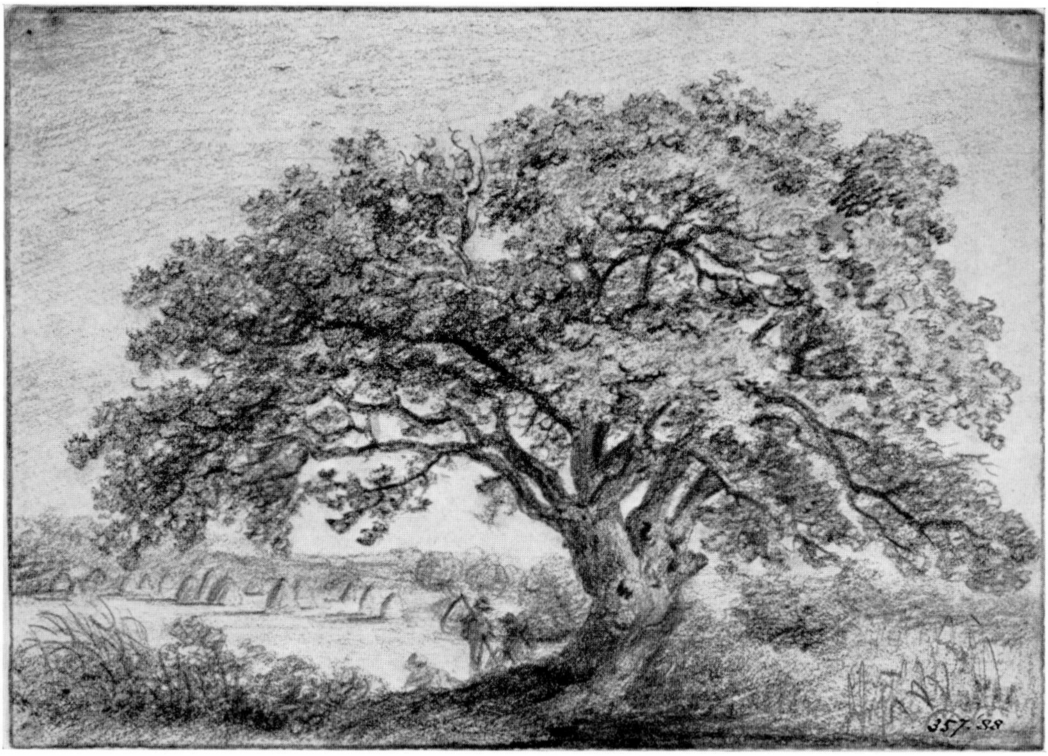

178. An oak tree in a hayfield.

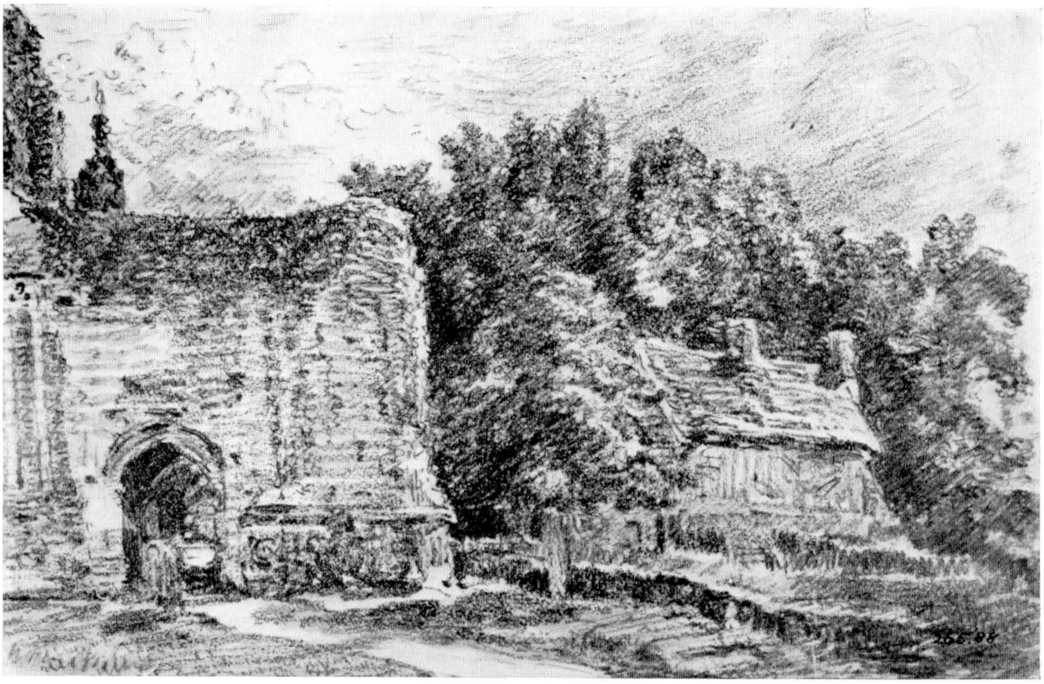

179. East Bergholt Church: ruined tower from the N.

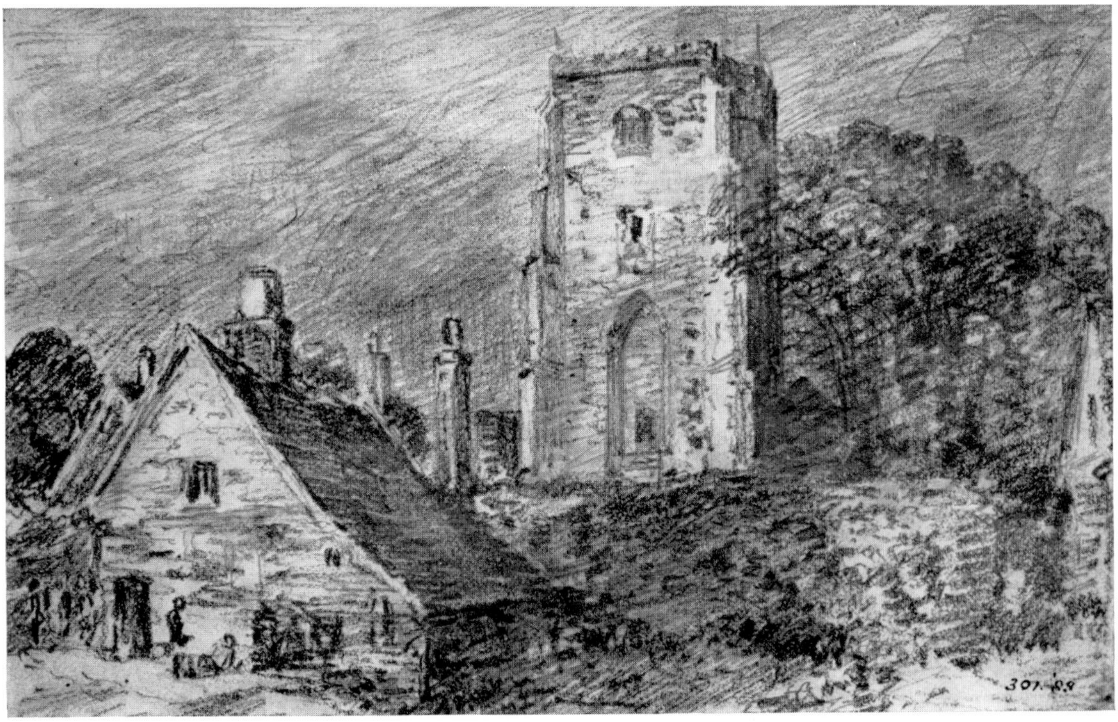

180. St. Mary-ad-Murum, Colchester.

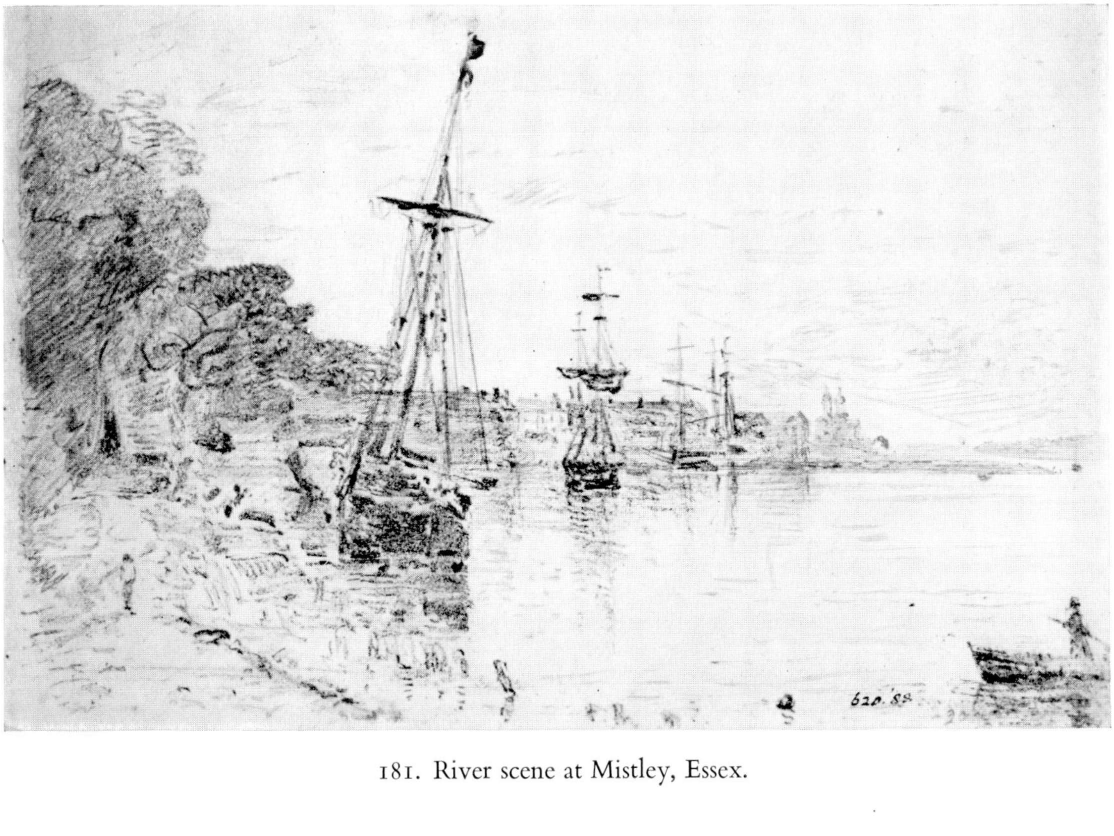

181. River scene at Mistley, Essex.

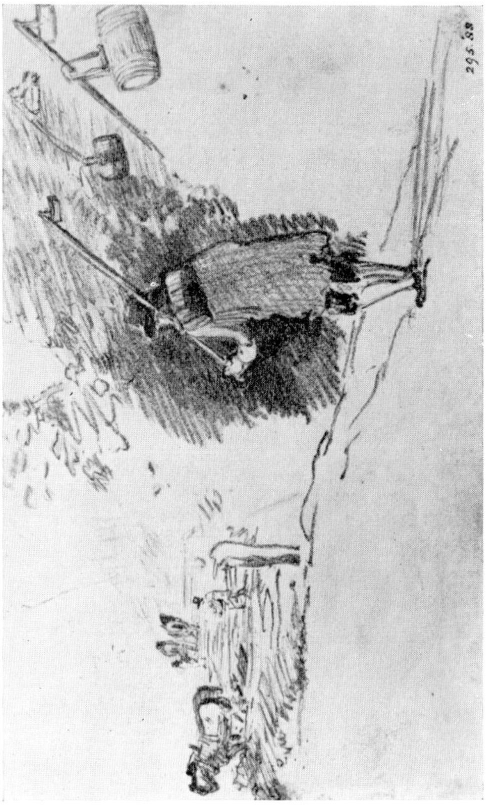

182. A countryman.

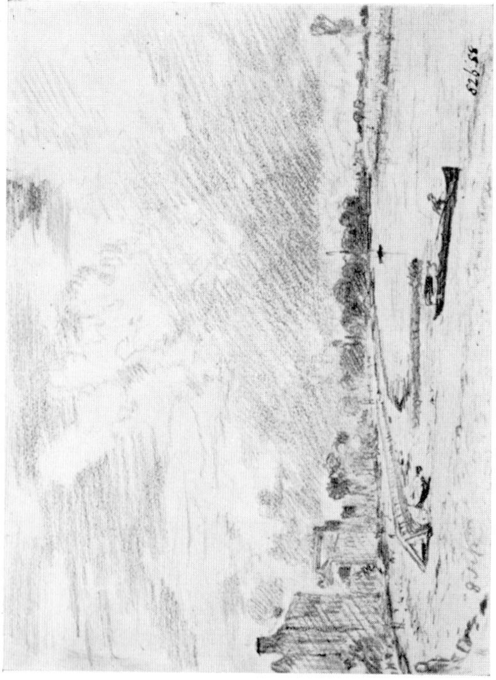

183. River scene with houses.

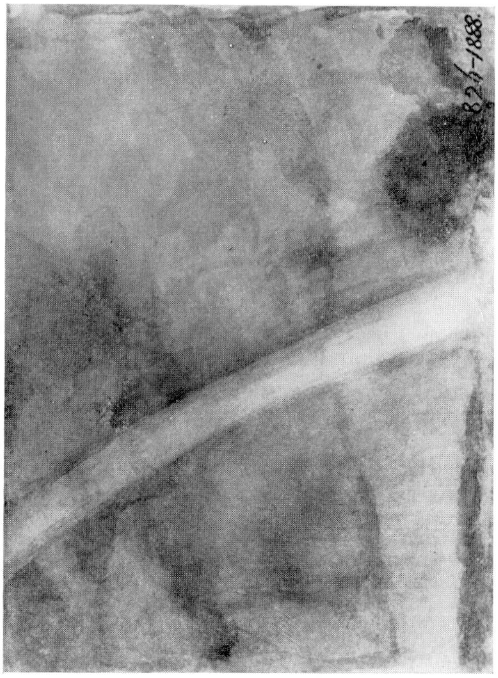

183a. A rainbow.

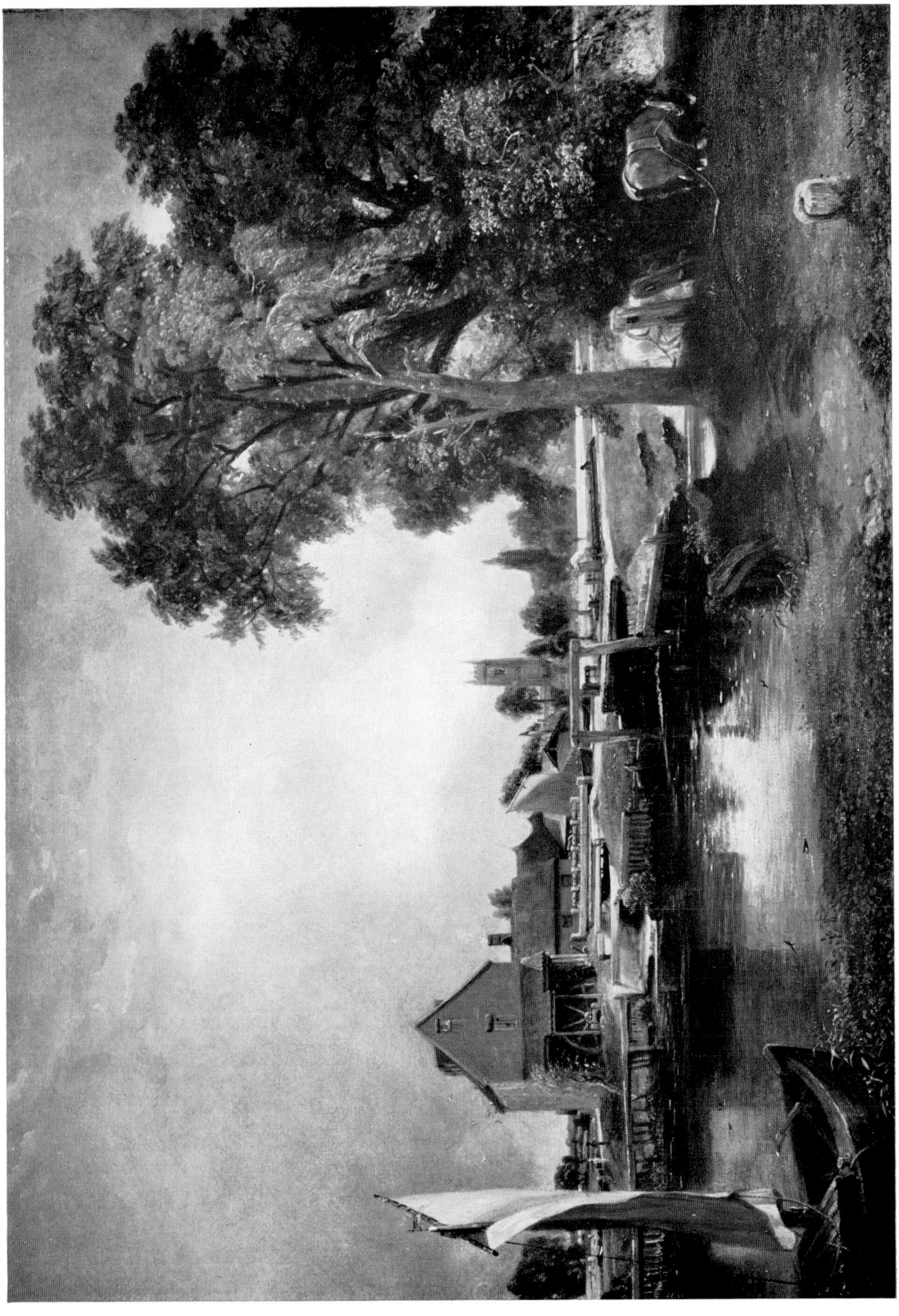

184. Dedham Lock and Mill.

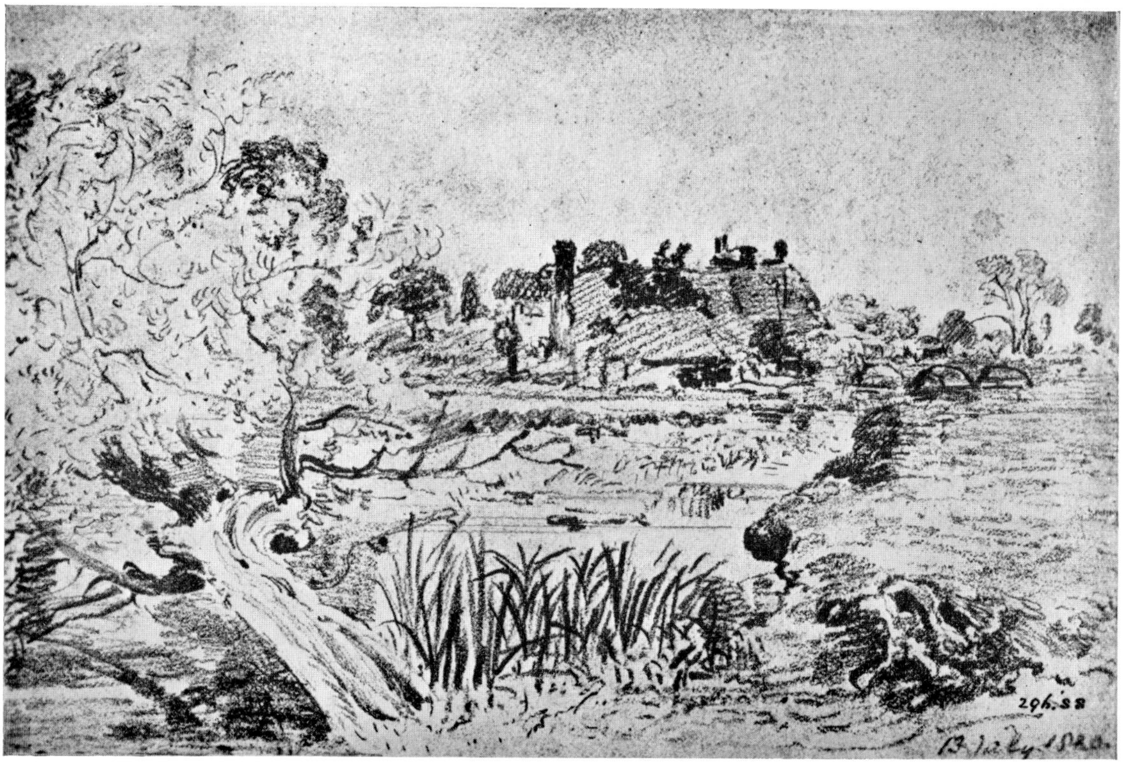

185. Farm buildings and bridge near Salisbury.

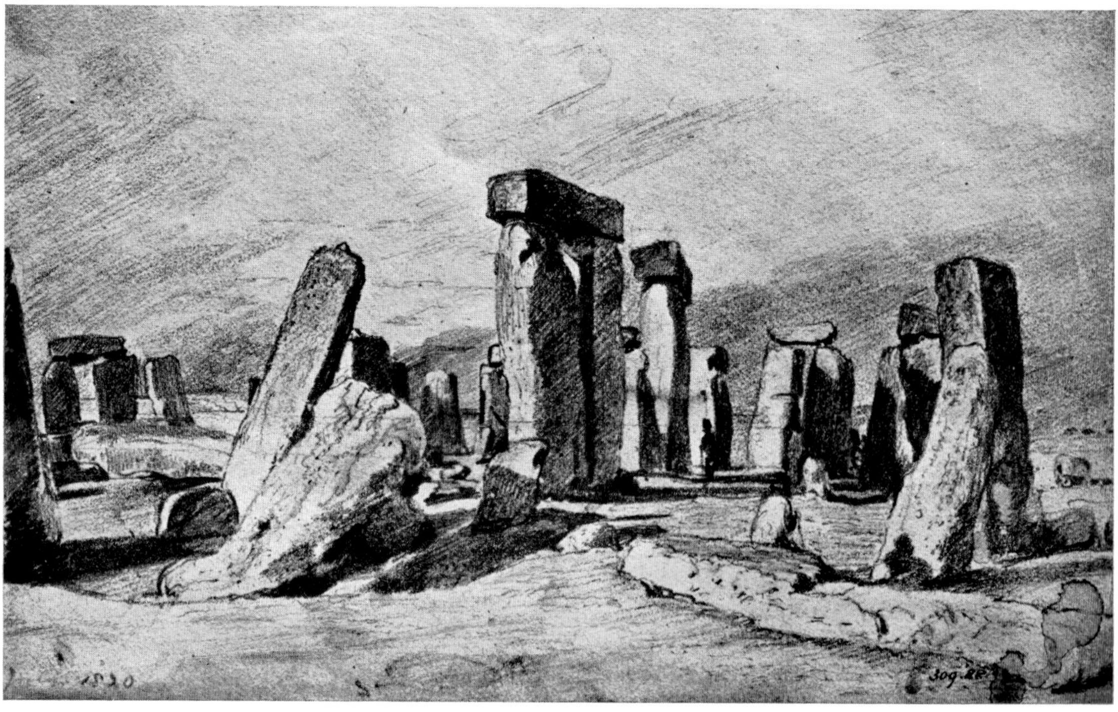

186. Stonehenge.

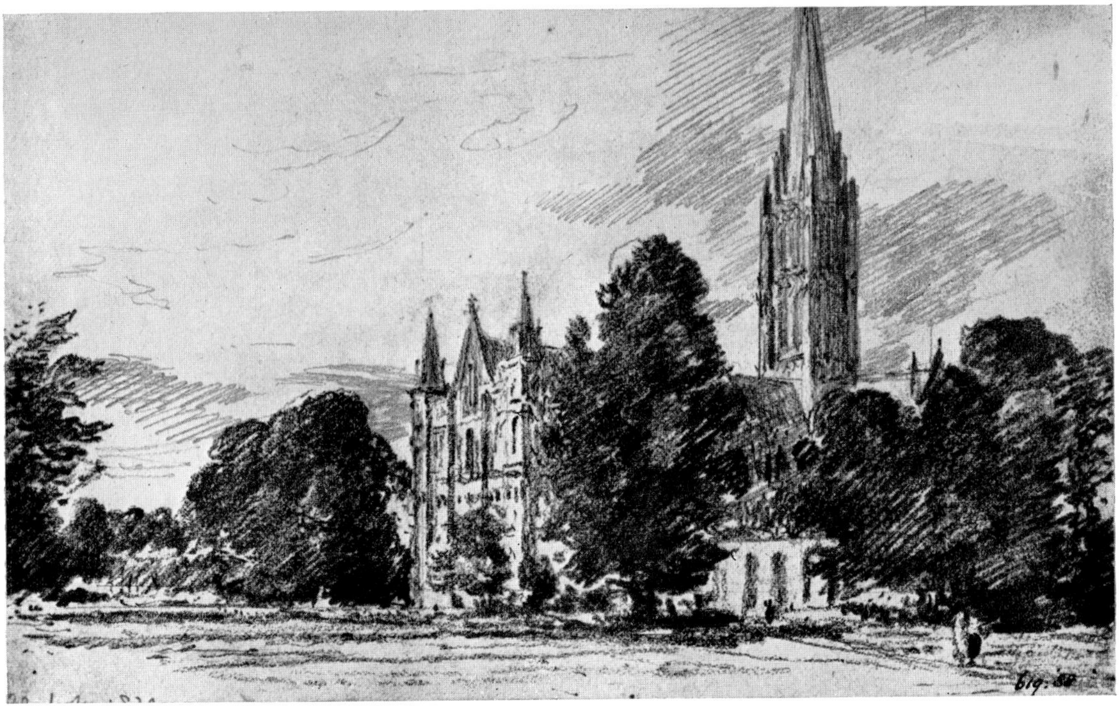

187. Salisbury Cathedral from the S.W.

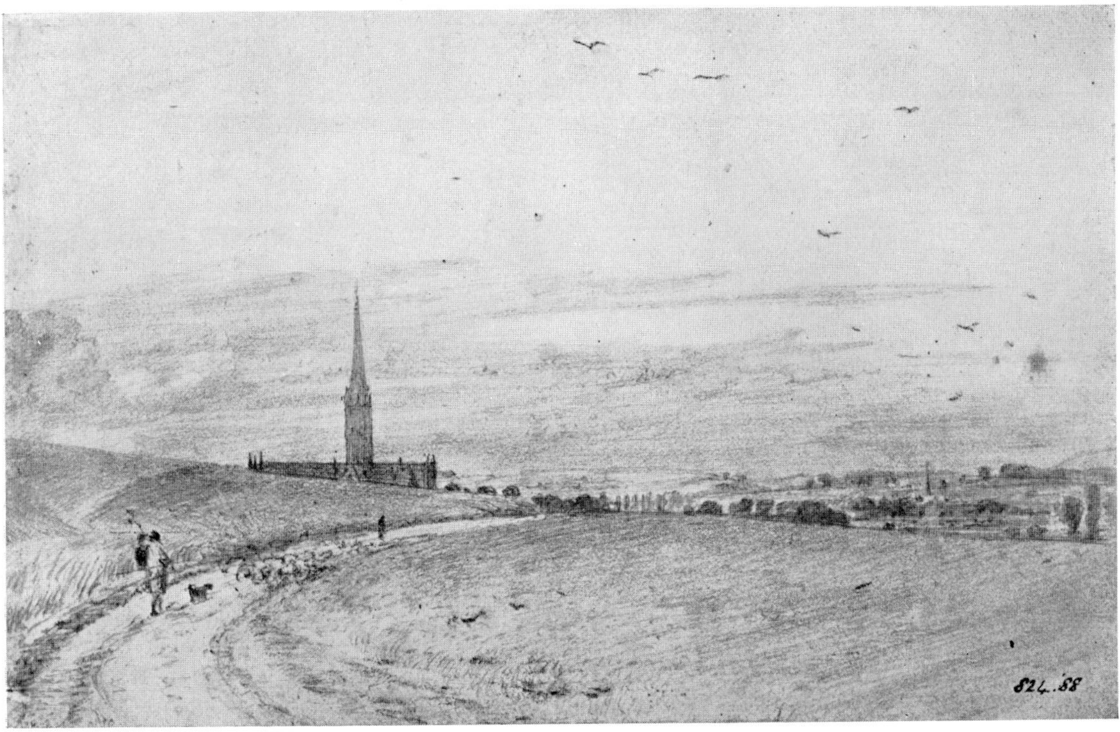

188. View near Salisbury.

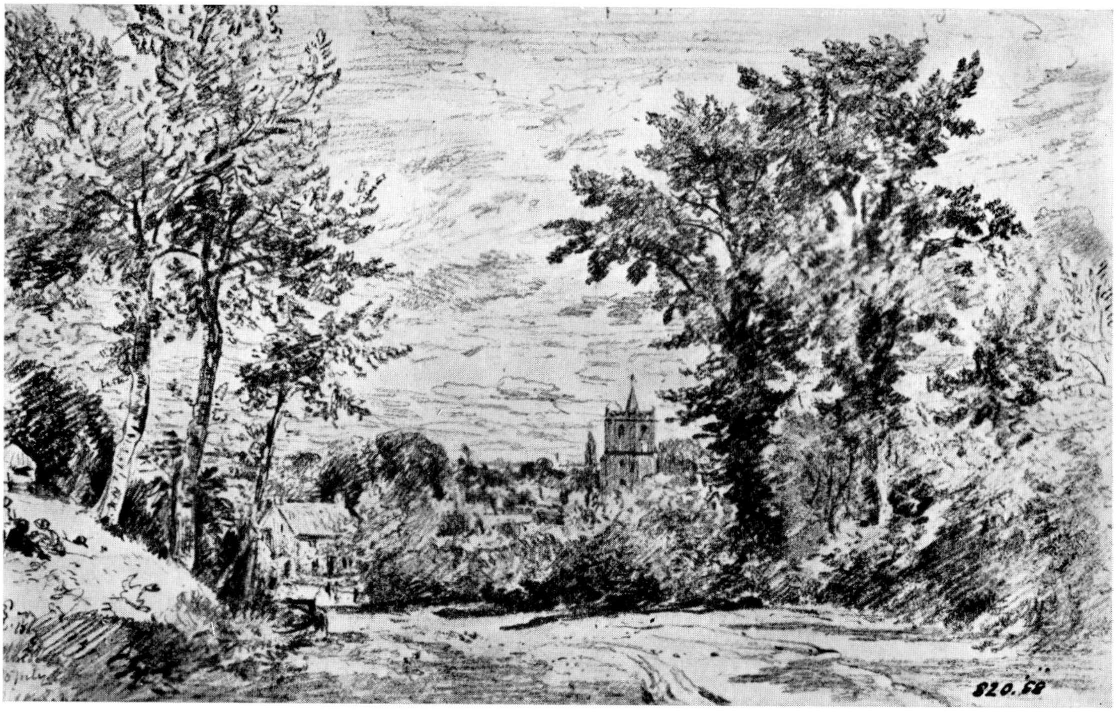

189. Entrance into Gillingham.

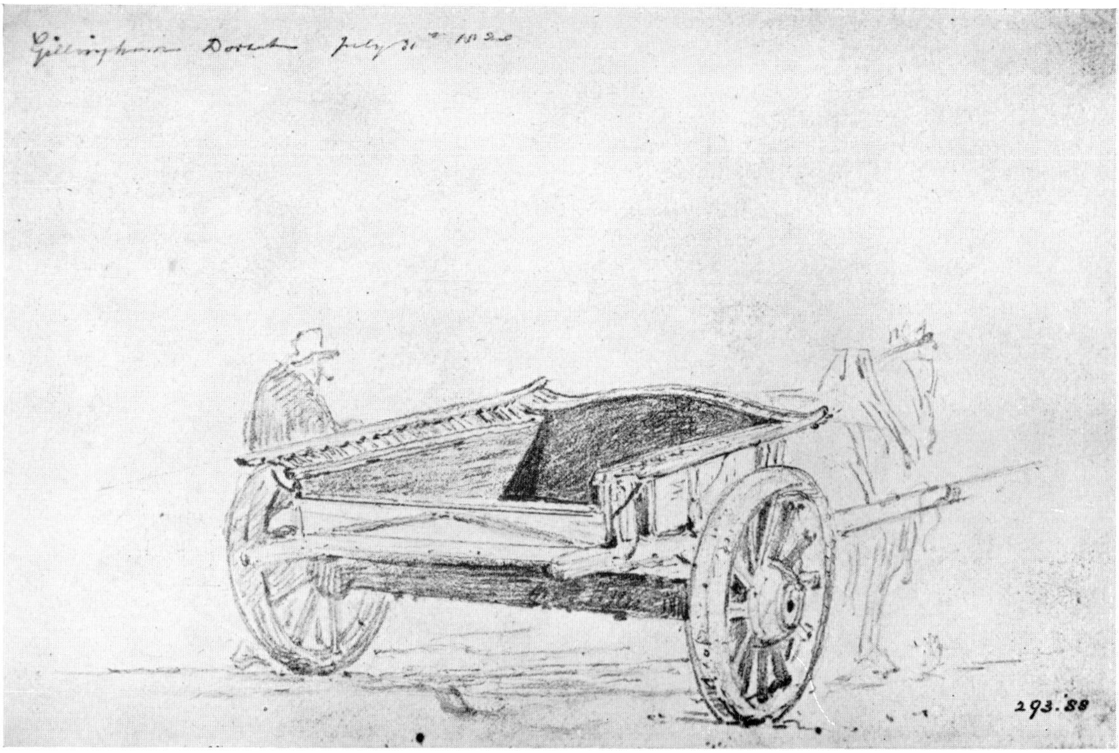

190. A cart at Gillingham.

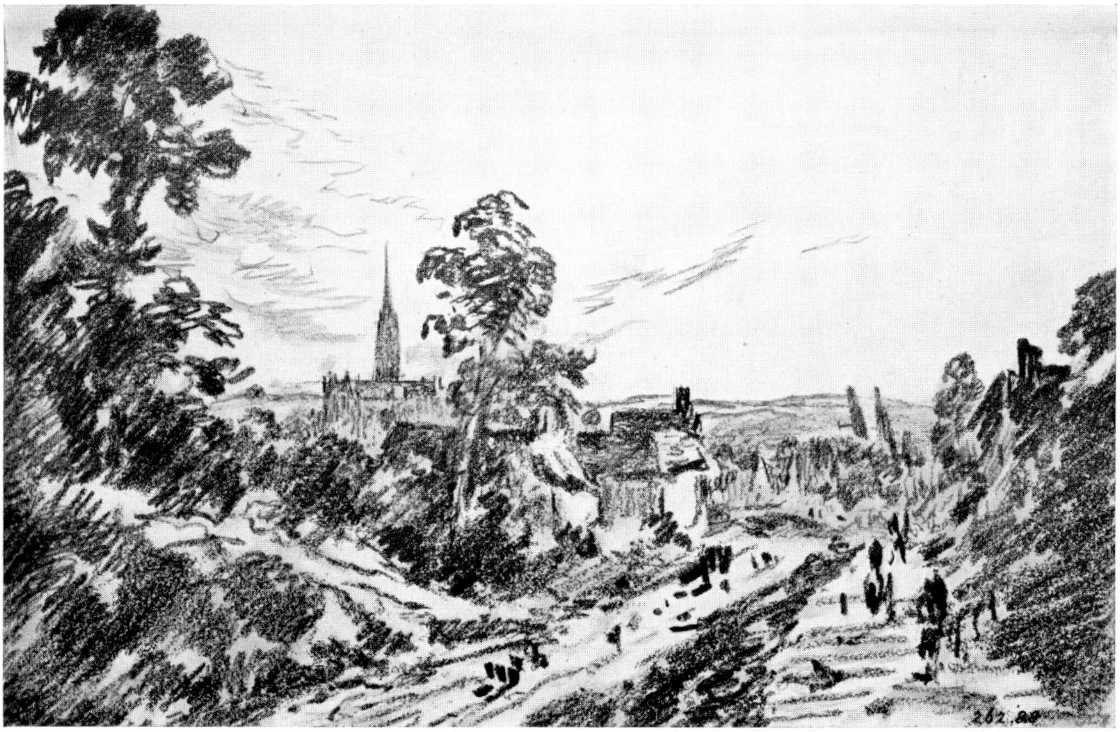

193. A road leading into Salisbury.

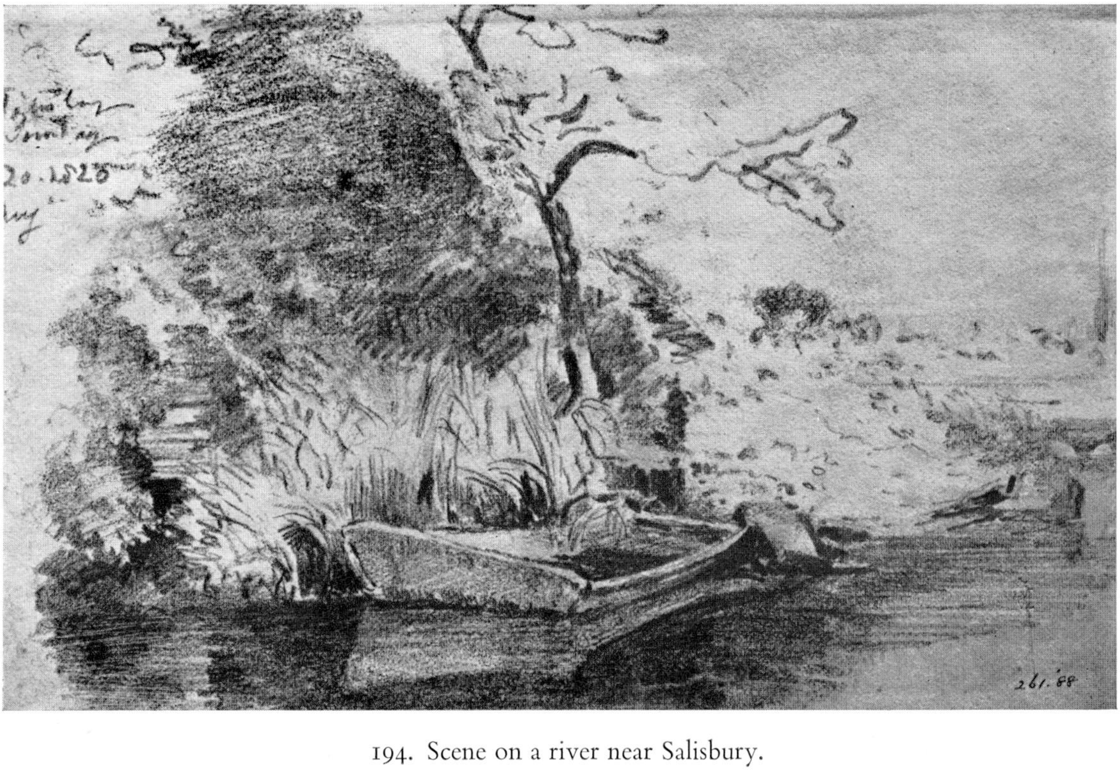

194. Scene on a river near Salisbury.

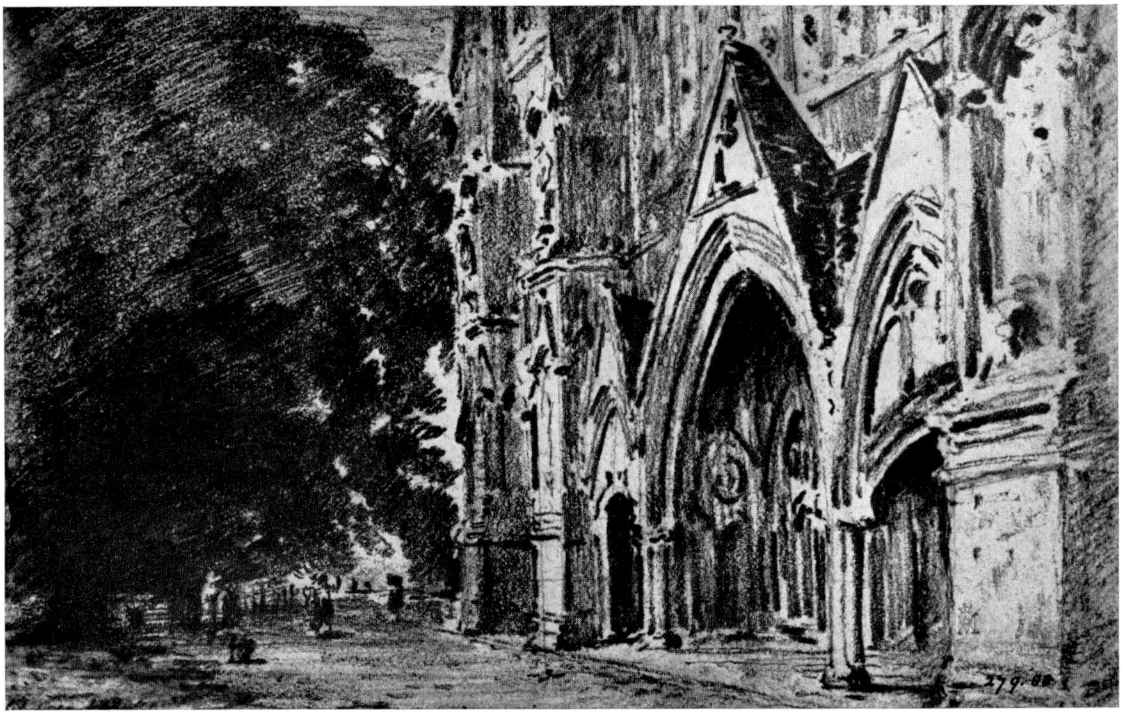

195. Salisbury Cathedral: W. door.

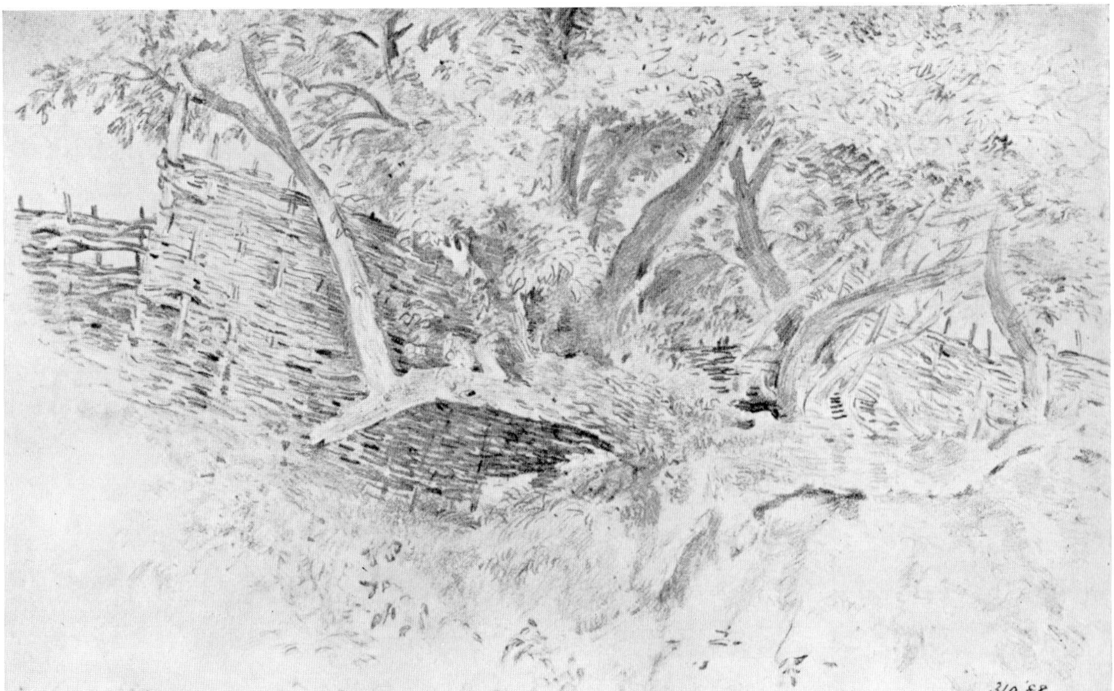

198. Trees and wattle hurdles at Hampstead.

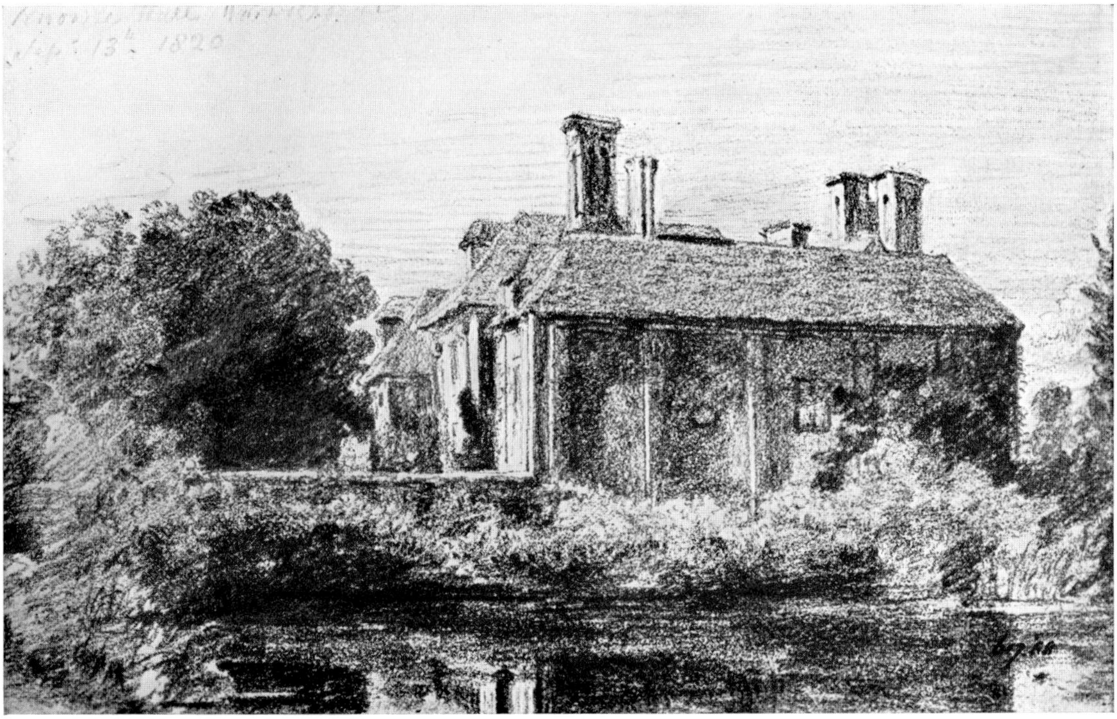

199. Knowle Hall.

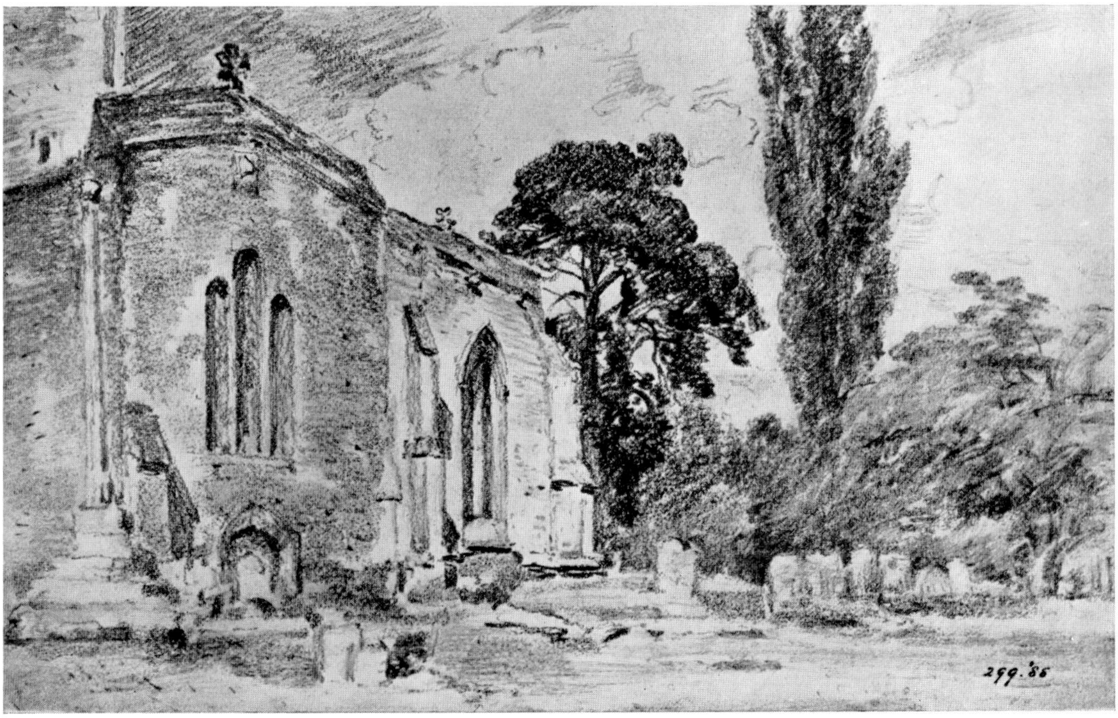

201. A church and graveyard.

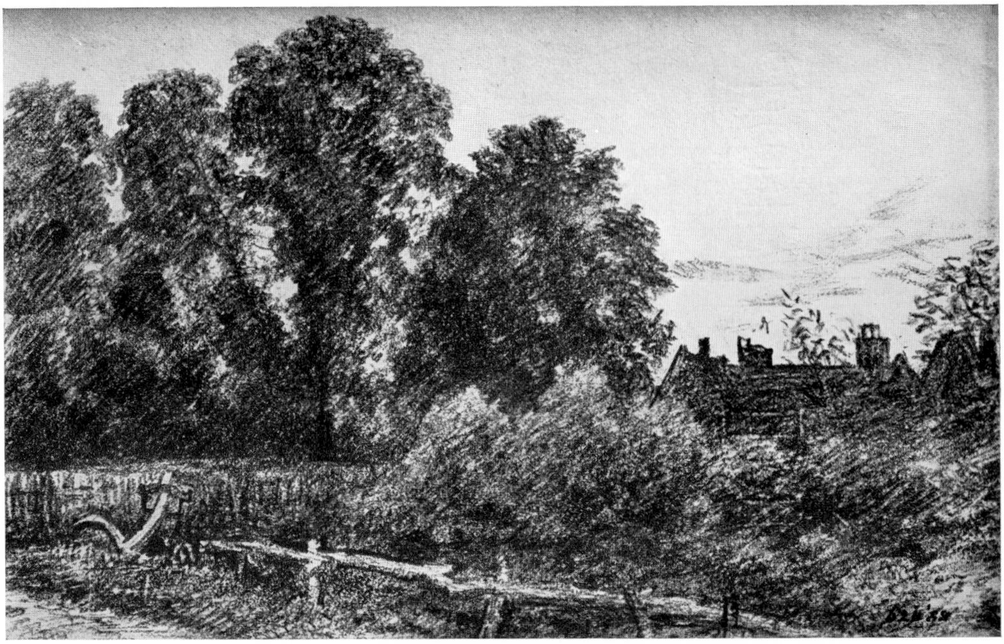

202. Landscape with elm trees and a house.

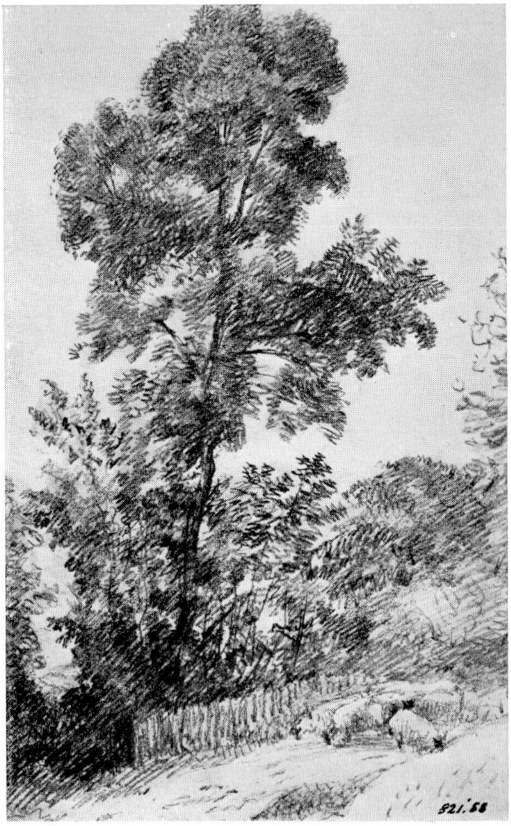

205. Trees at Hampstead.

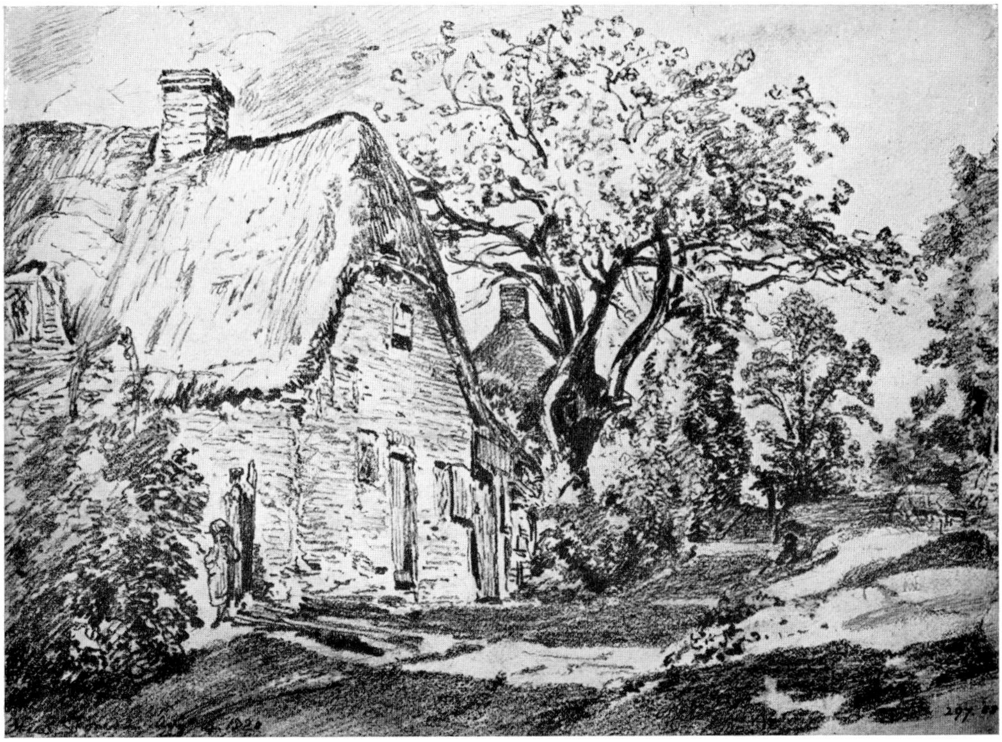

191. Cottages and trees in the New Forest.

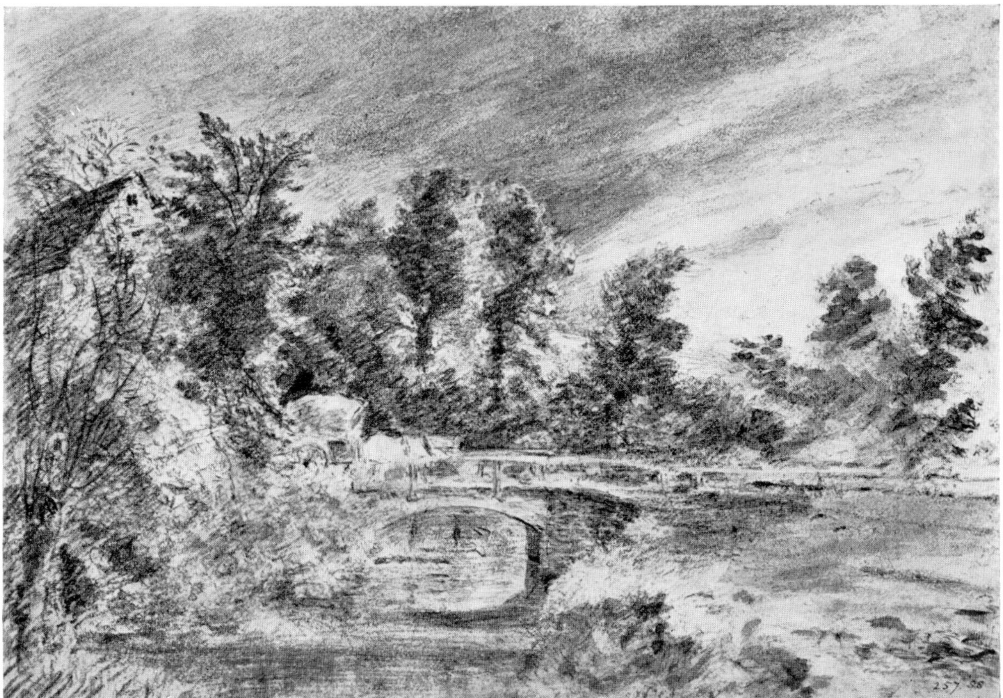

192. A bridge and cart at Gillingham.

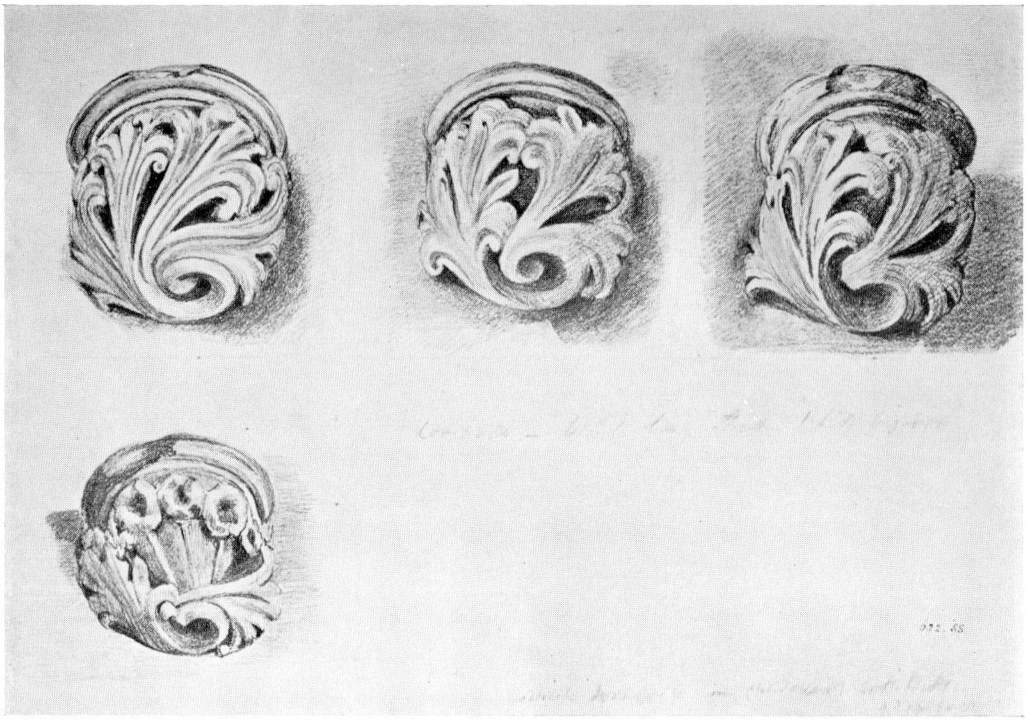

200. Corbels in Solihull Church.

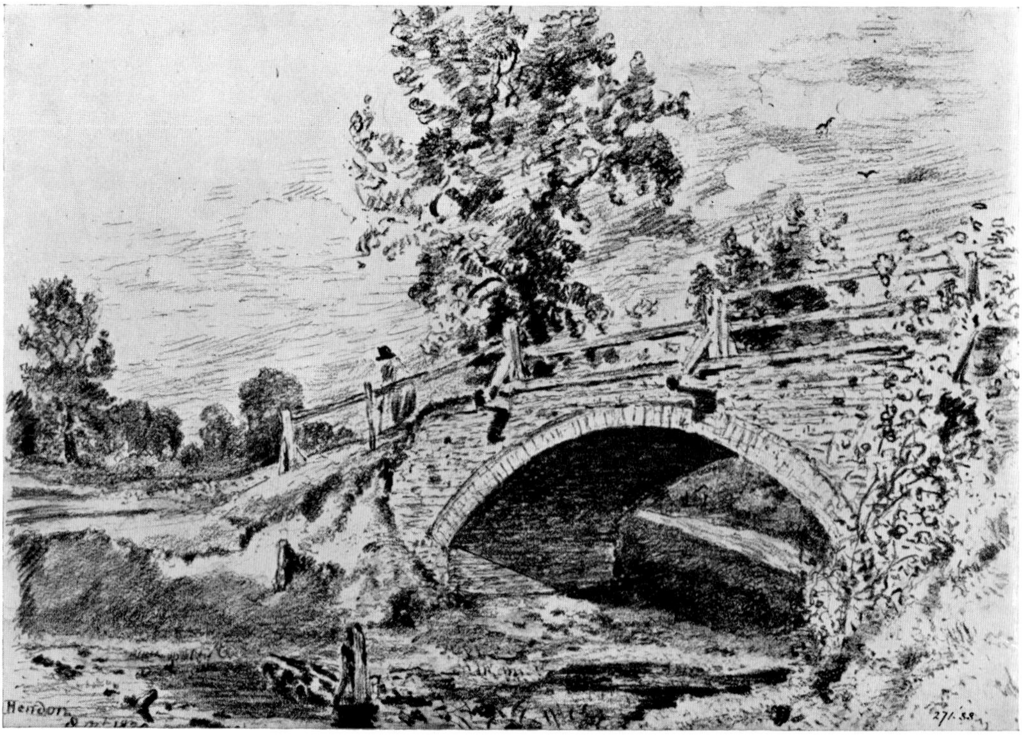

206. Bridge at Hendon.

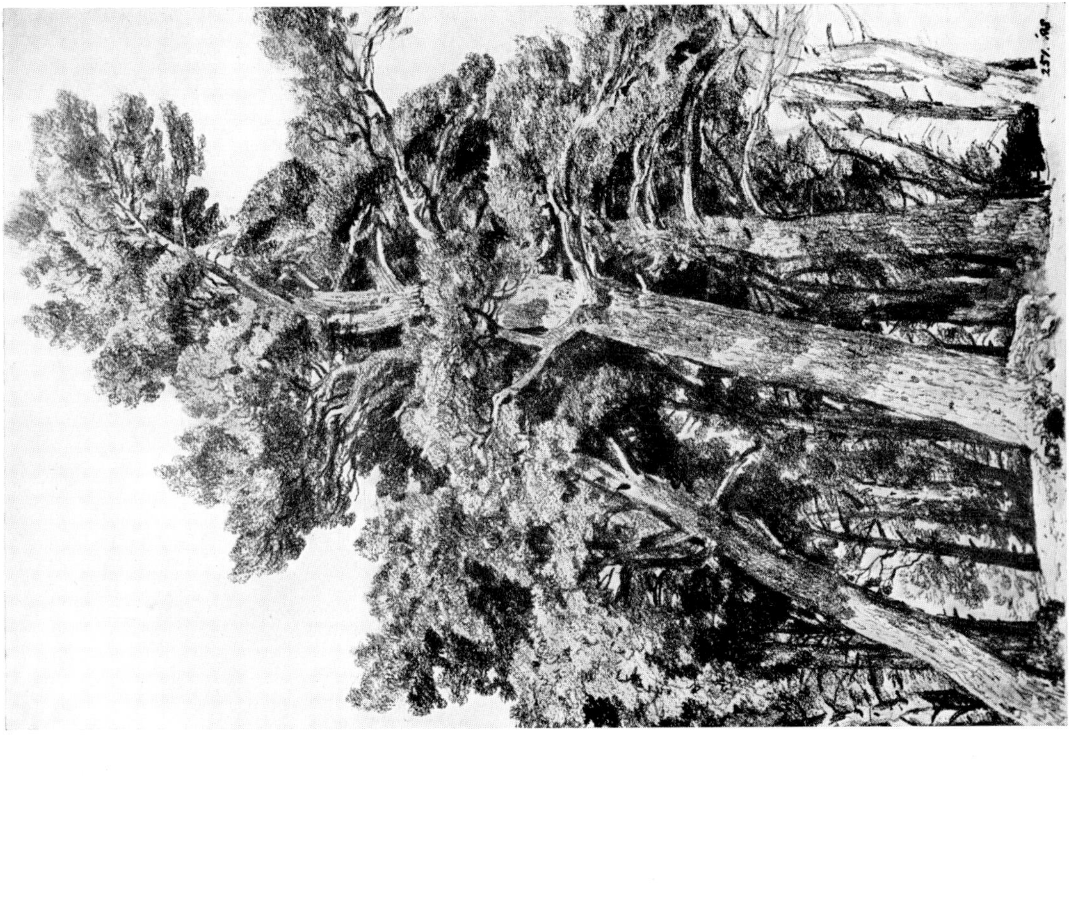

203. Fir trees at Hampstead.

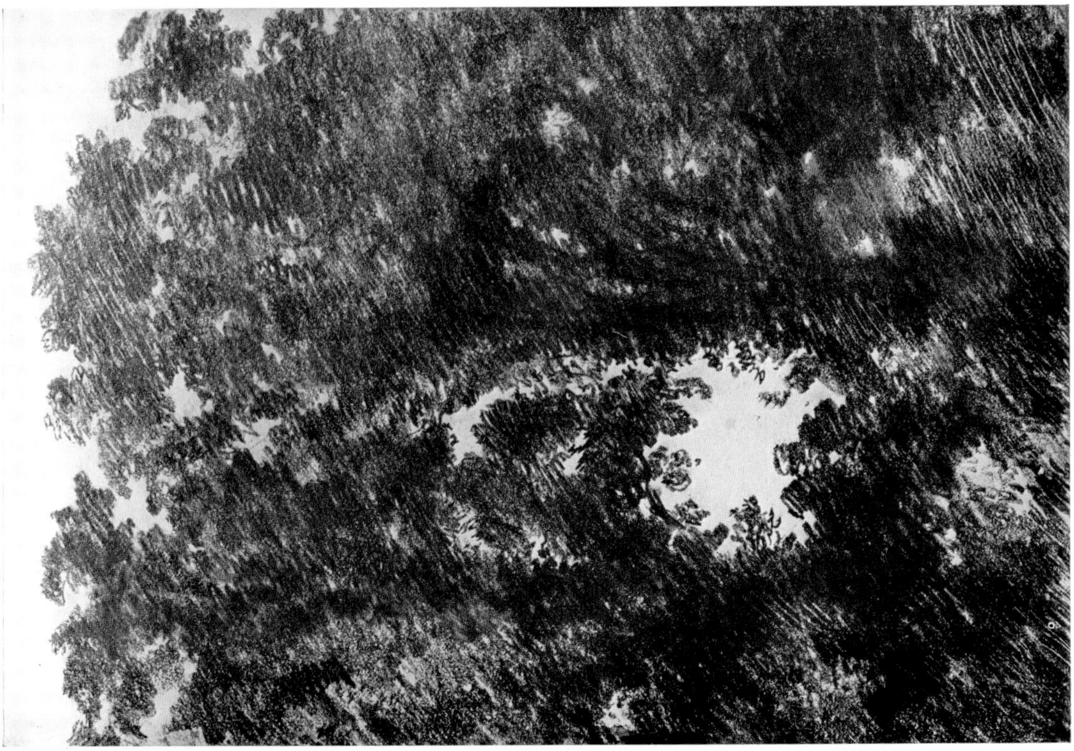

204. Elm trees.

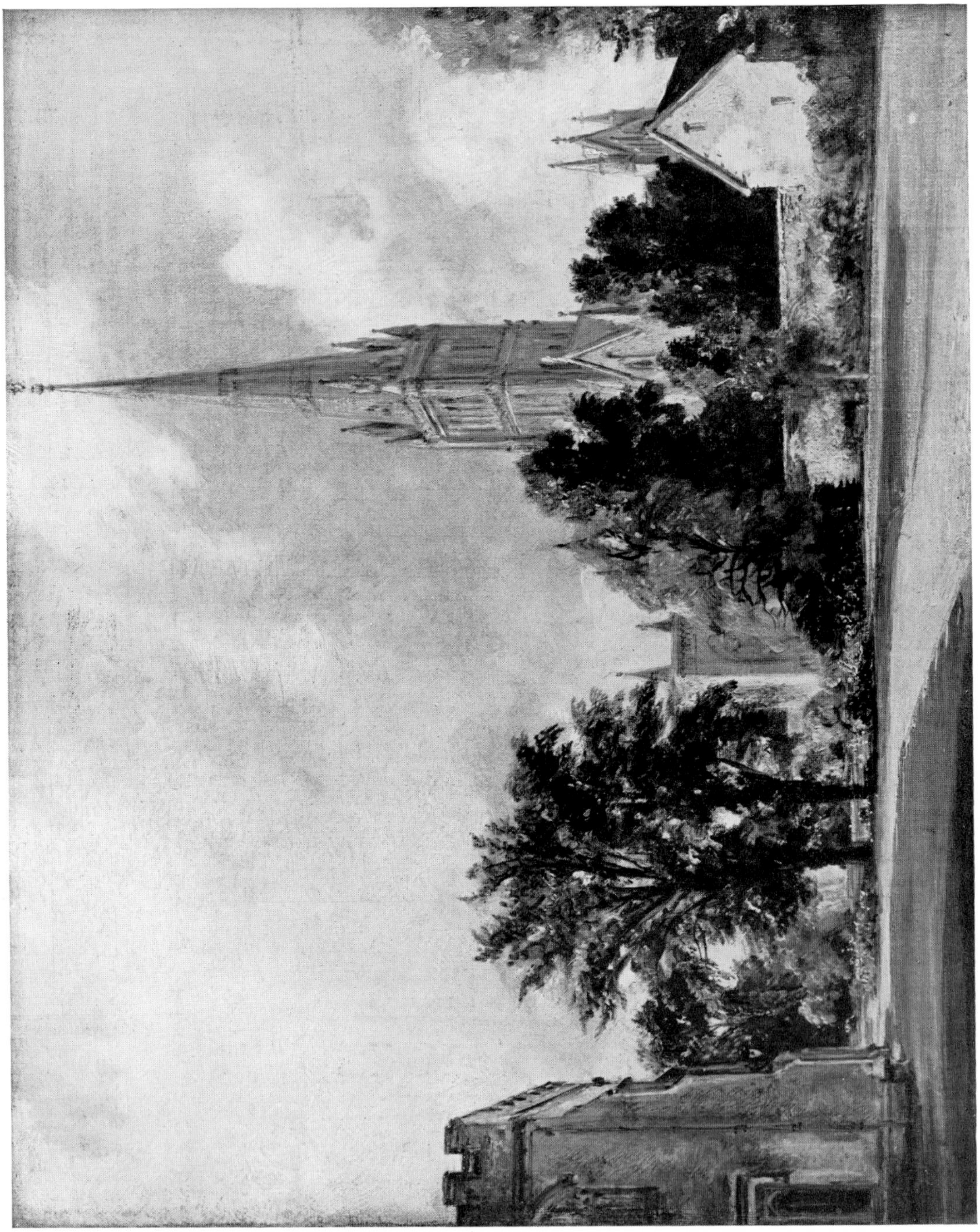

196. Salisbury Cathedral and the Close.

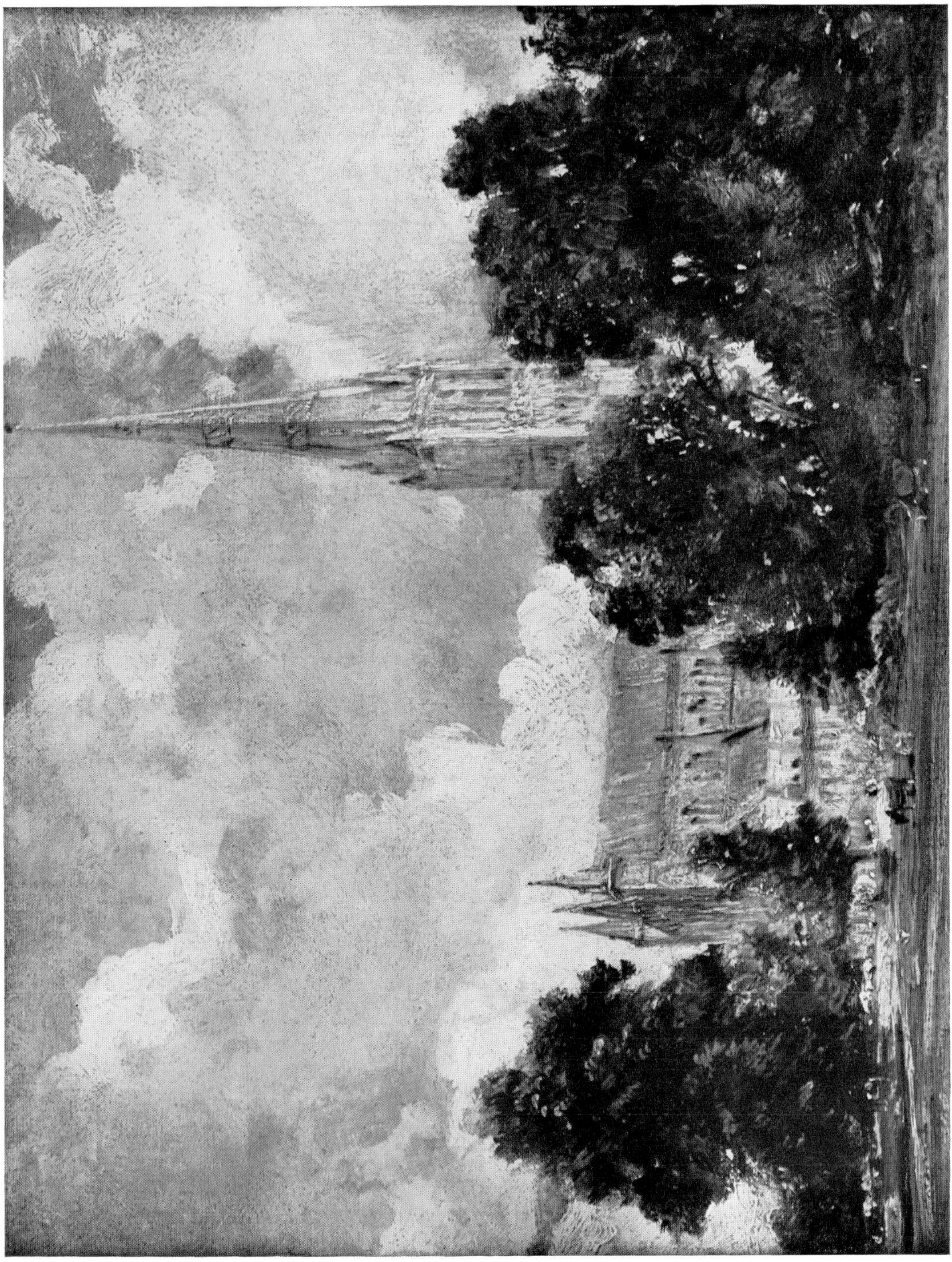

197. Salisbury Cathedral from the S.W.

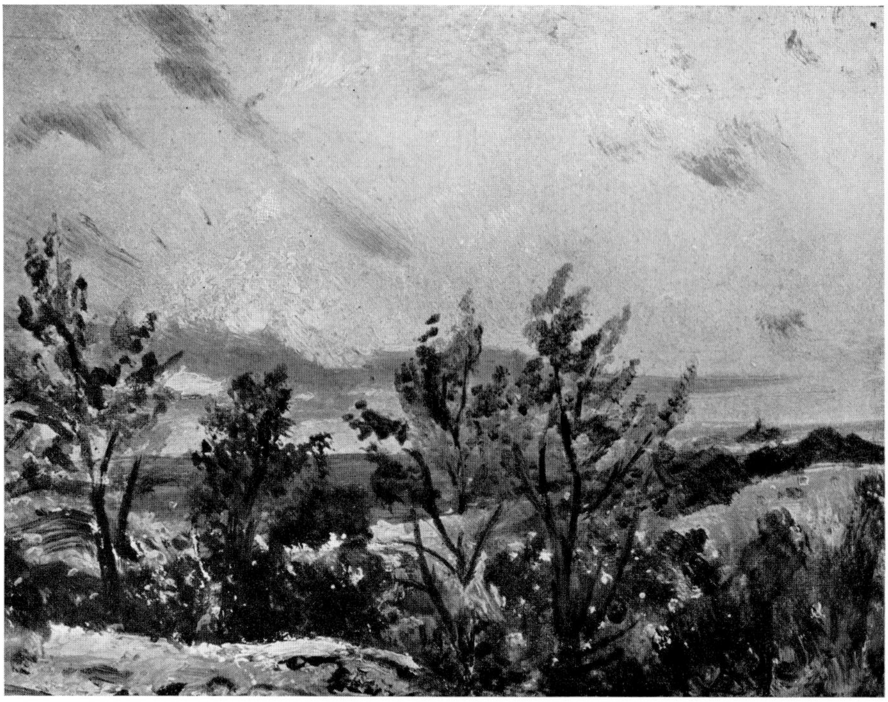

207. Sketch at Hampstead: stormy sunset.

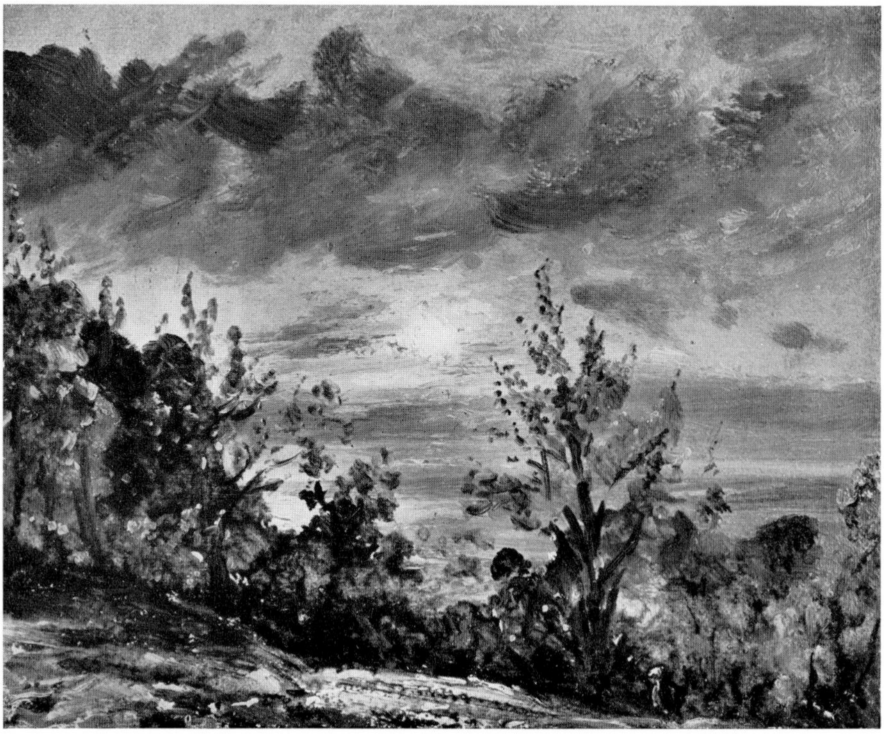

208. Sketch at Hampstead: evening.

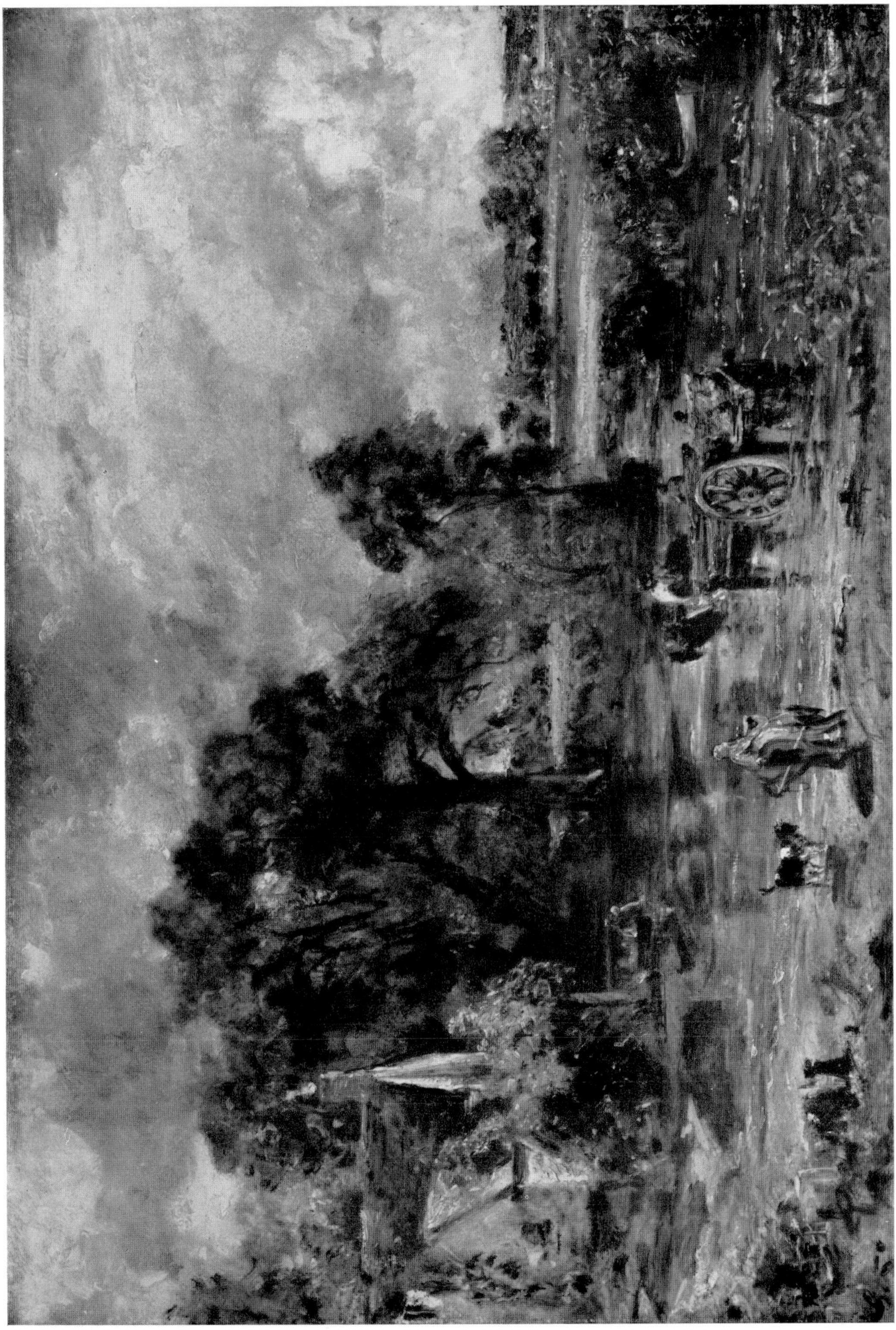

209. Study for 'The Hay Wain'.

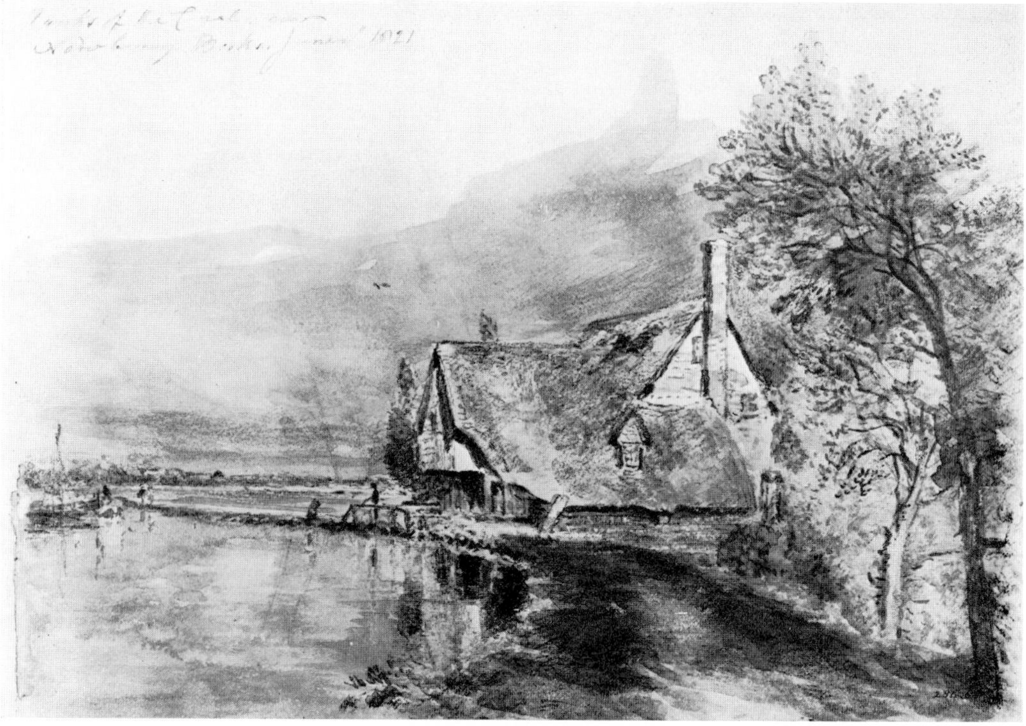

210. Banks of the canal near Newbury.

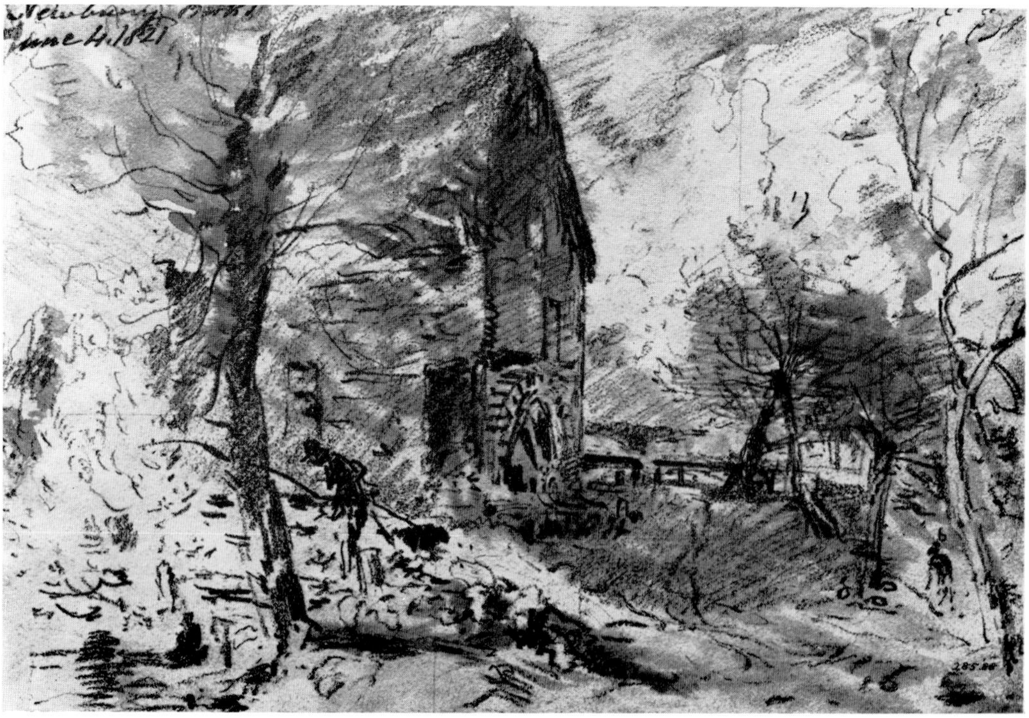

211. A water-mill at Newbury.

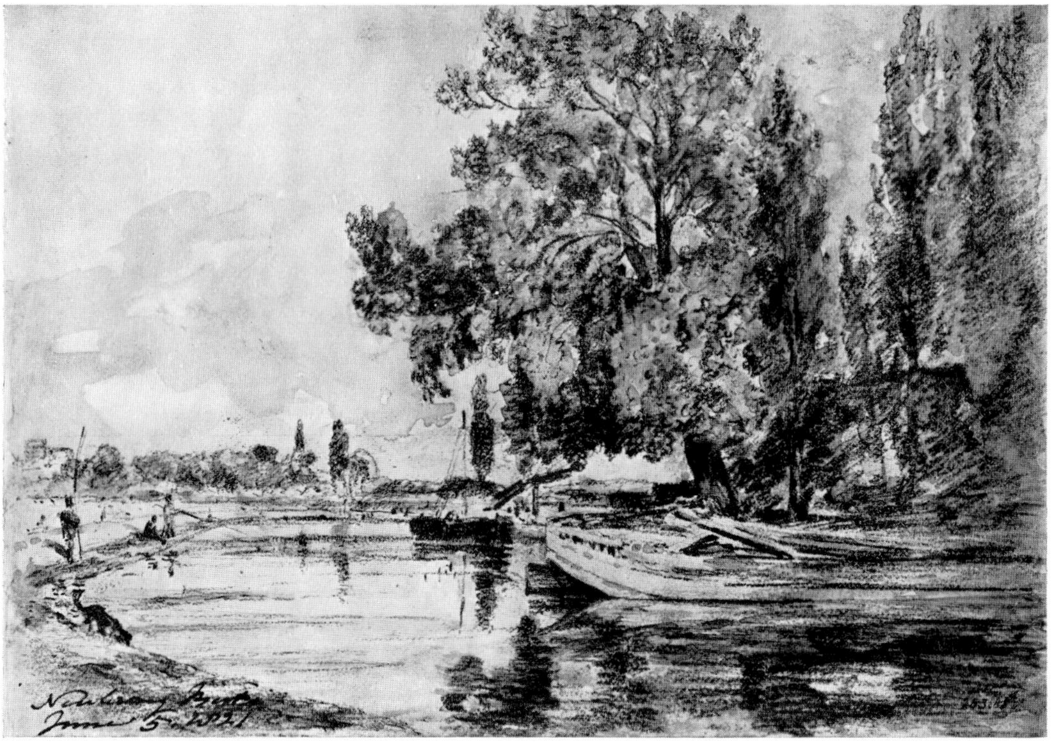

212. A view of the canal, Newbury.

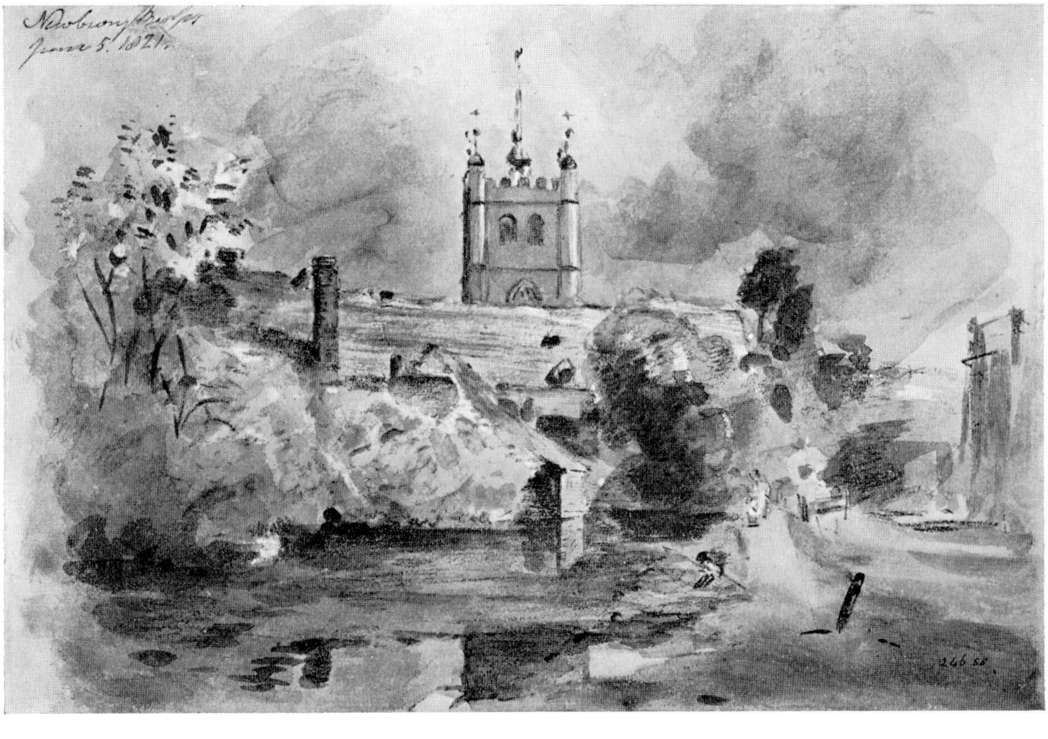

213. A view of Newbury.

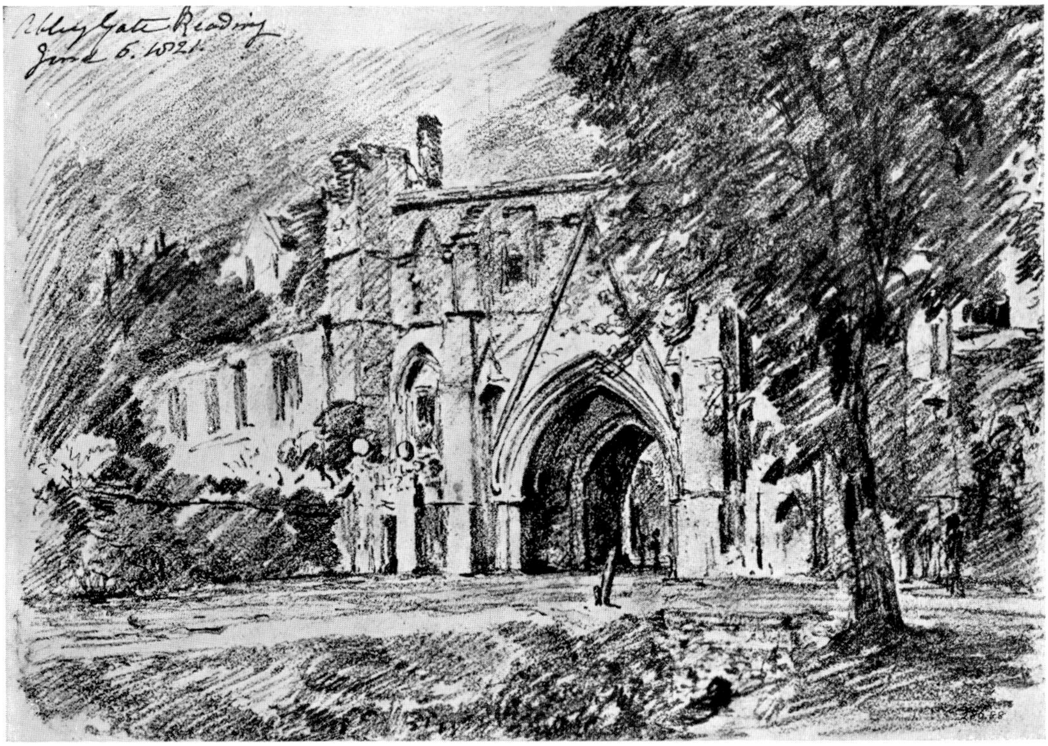

214. The Abbey Gate, Reading.

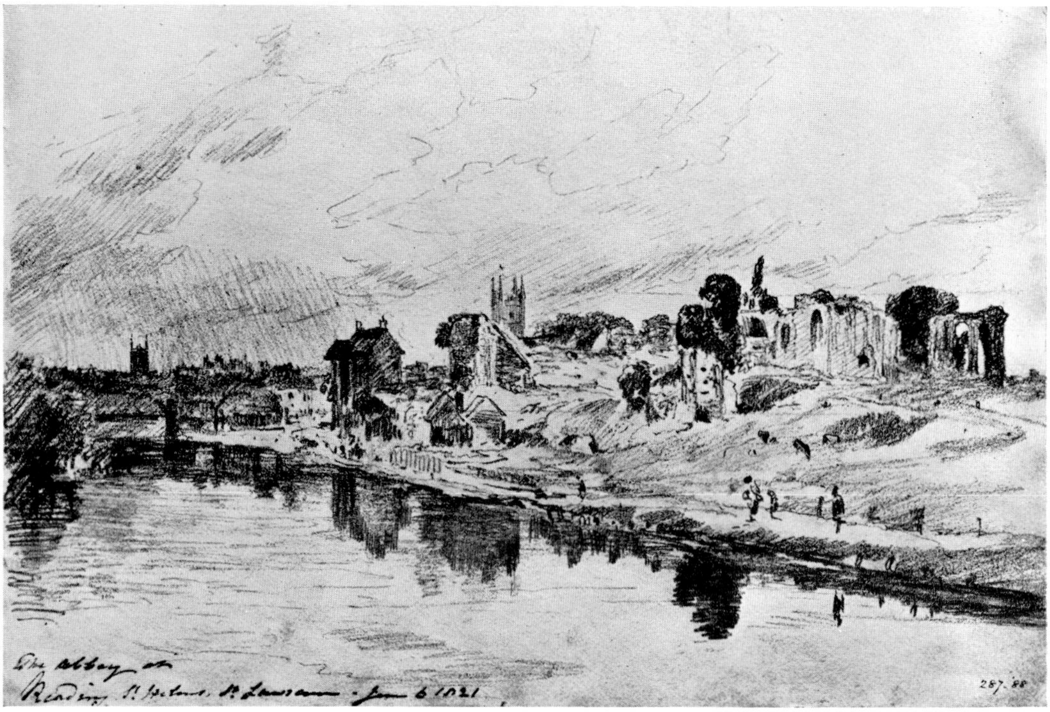

215. A view of Reading from the river.

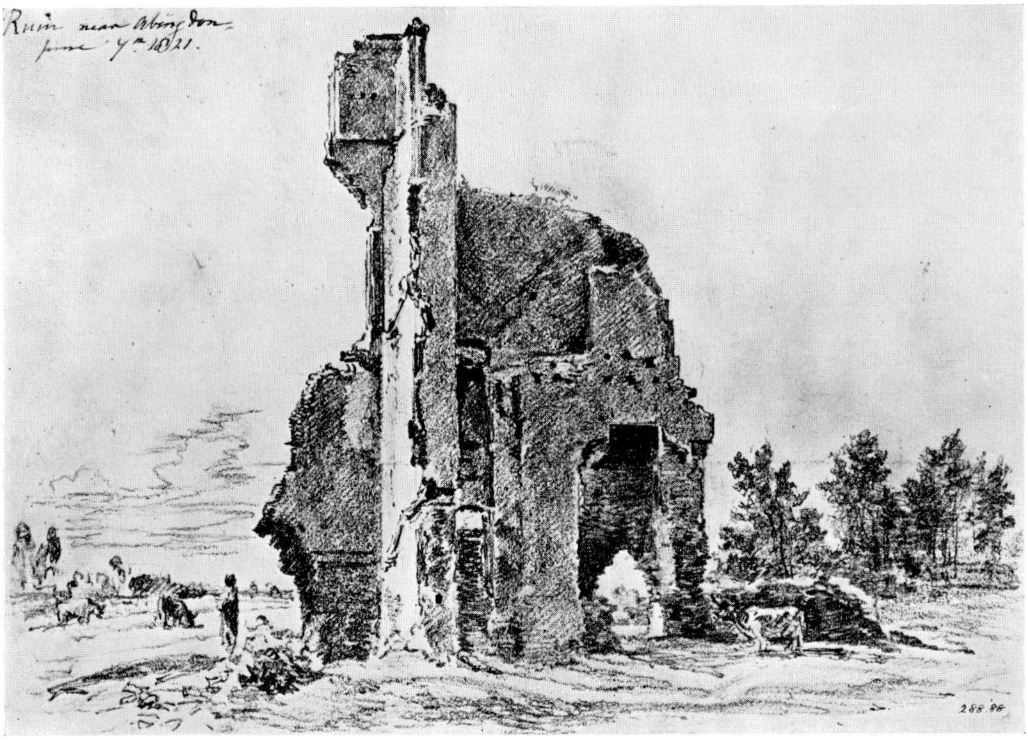

216. A ruin near Abingdon.

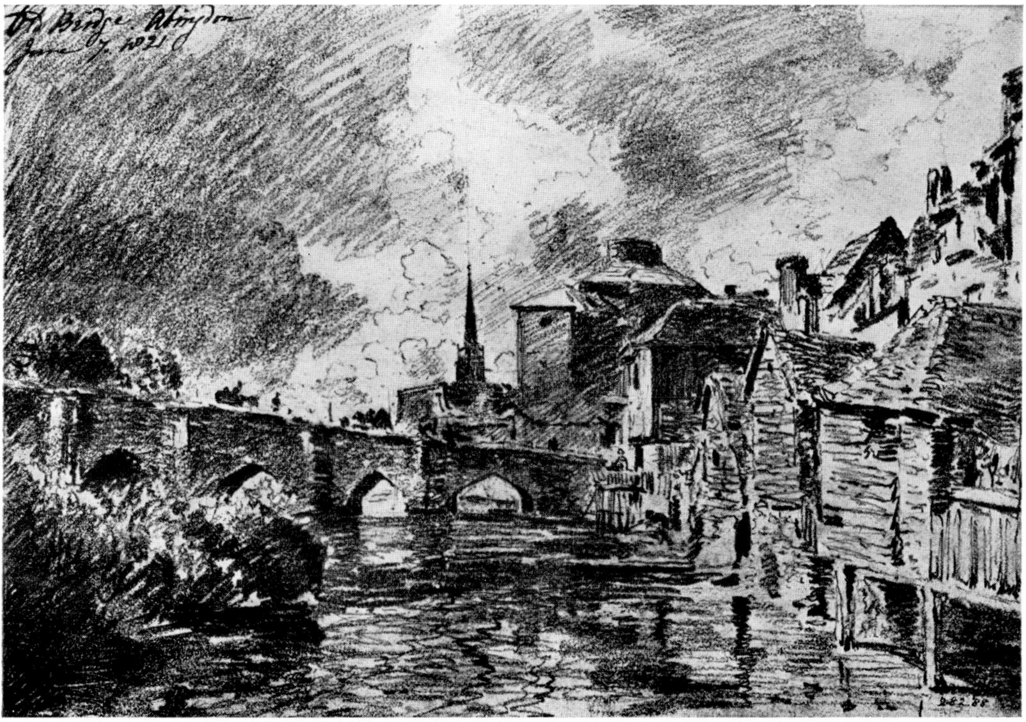

217. The old bridge at Abingdon.

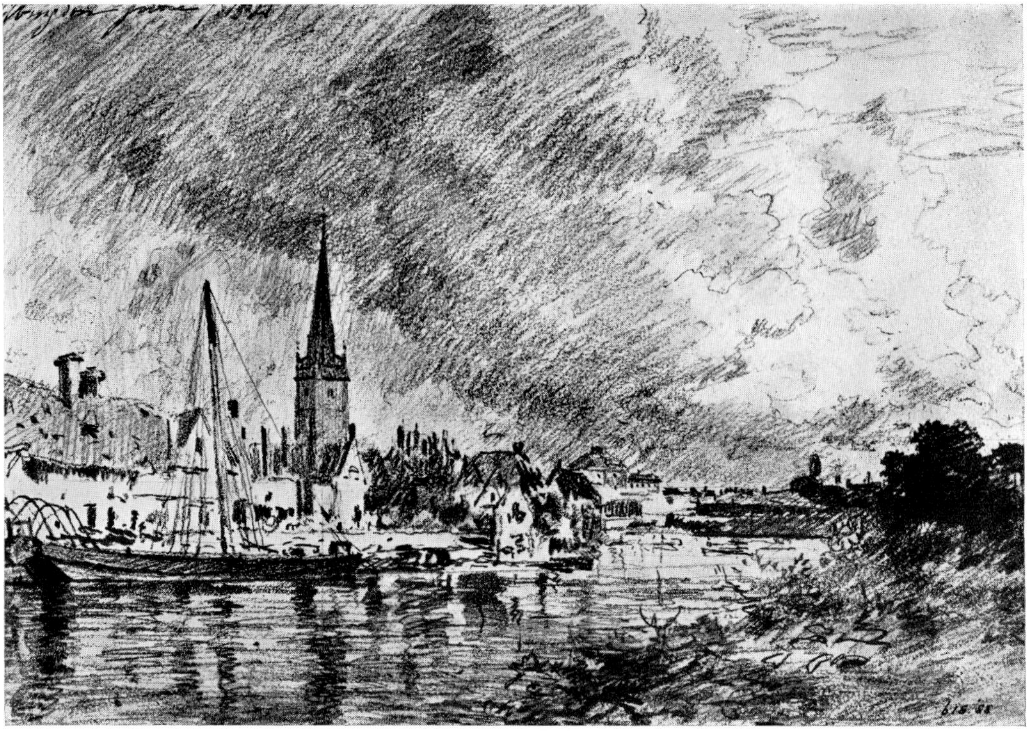

218. A view of Abingdon from the river.

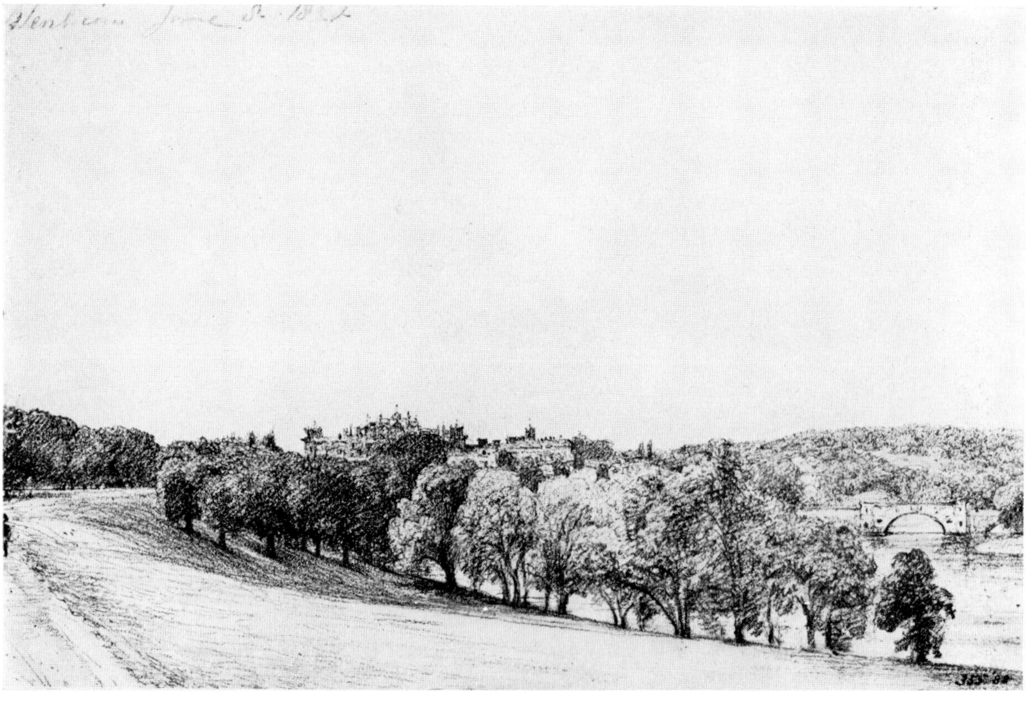

219. Blenheim Palace and Park.

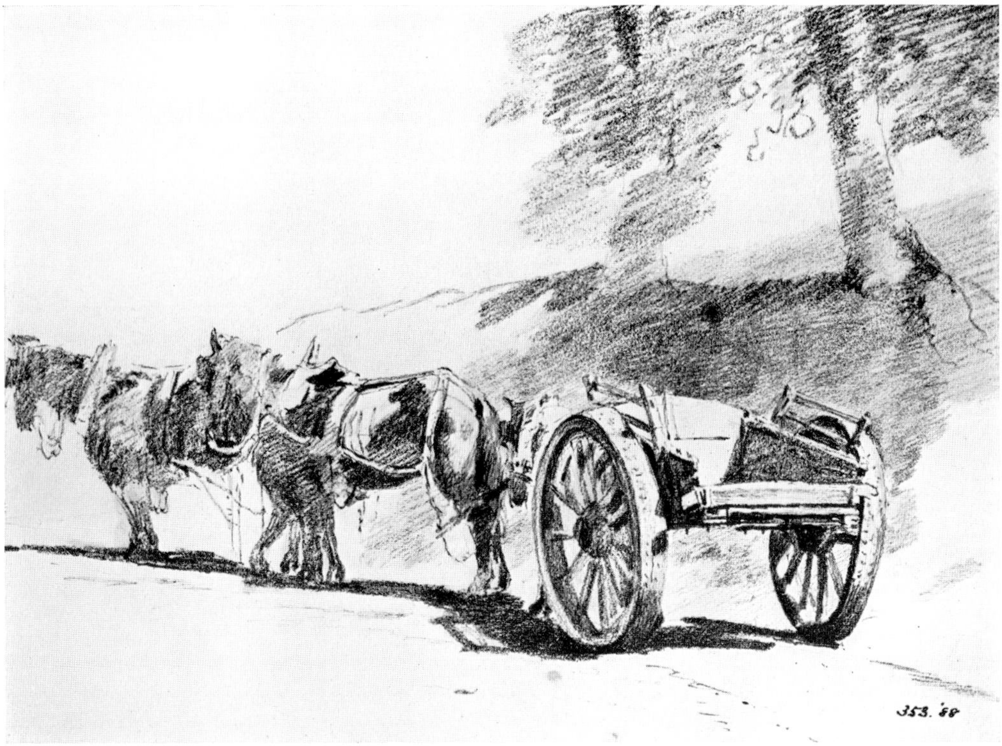

220. A cart and horses.

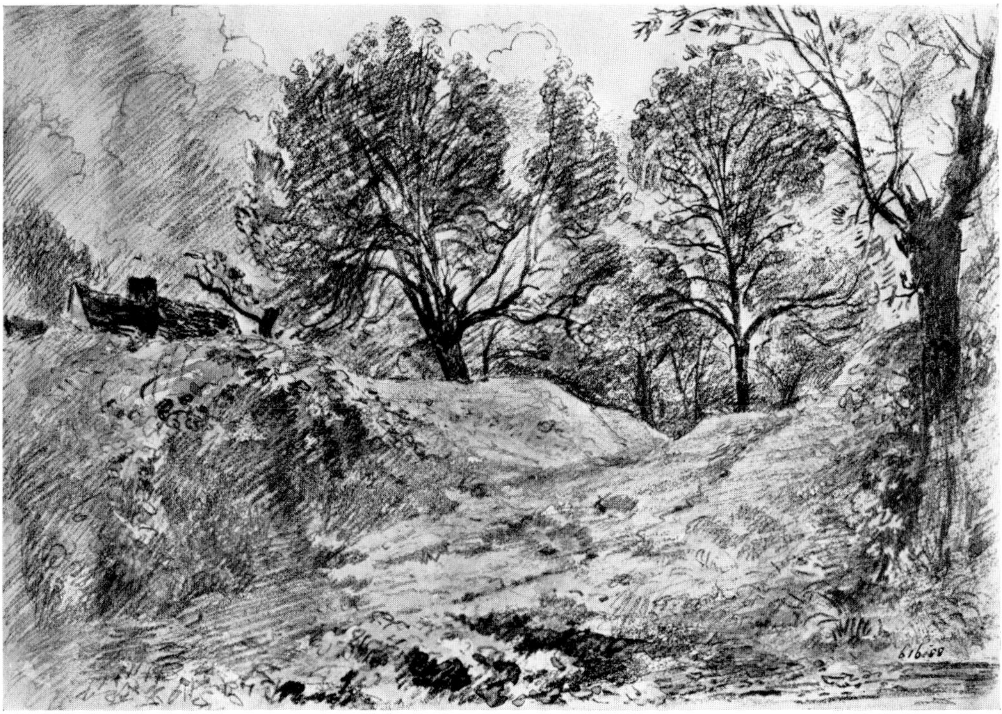

241. A group of trees on broken ground.

221. Study of sky and trees.

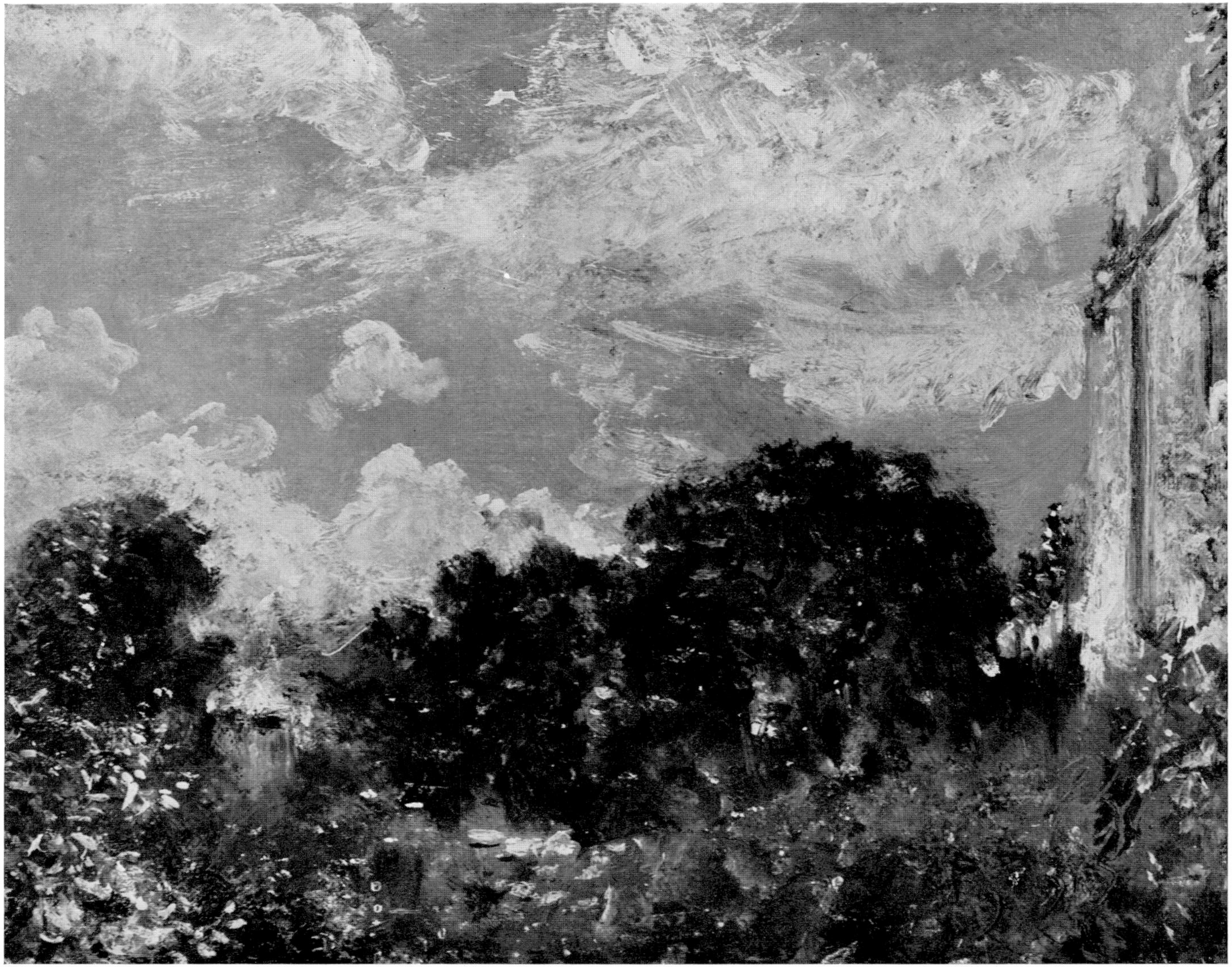

222. Study of sky and trees, with a red house, at Hampstead.

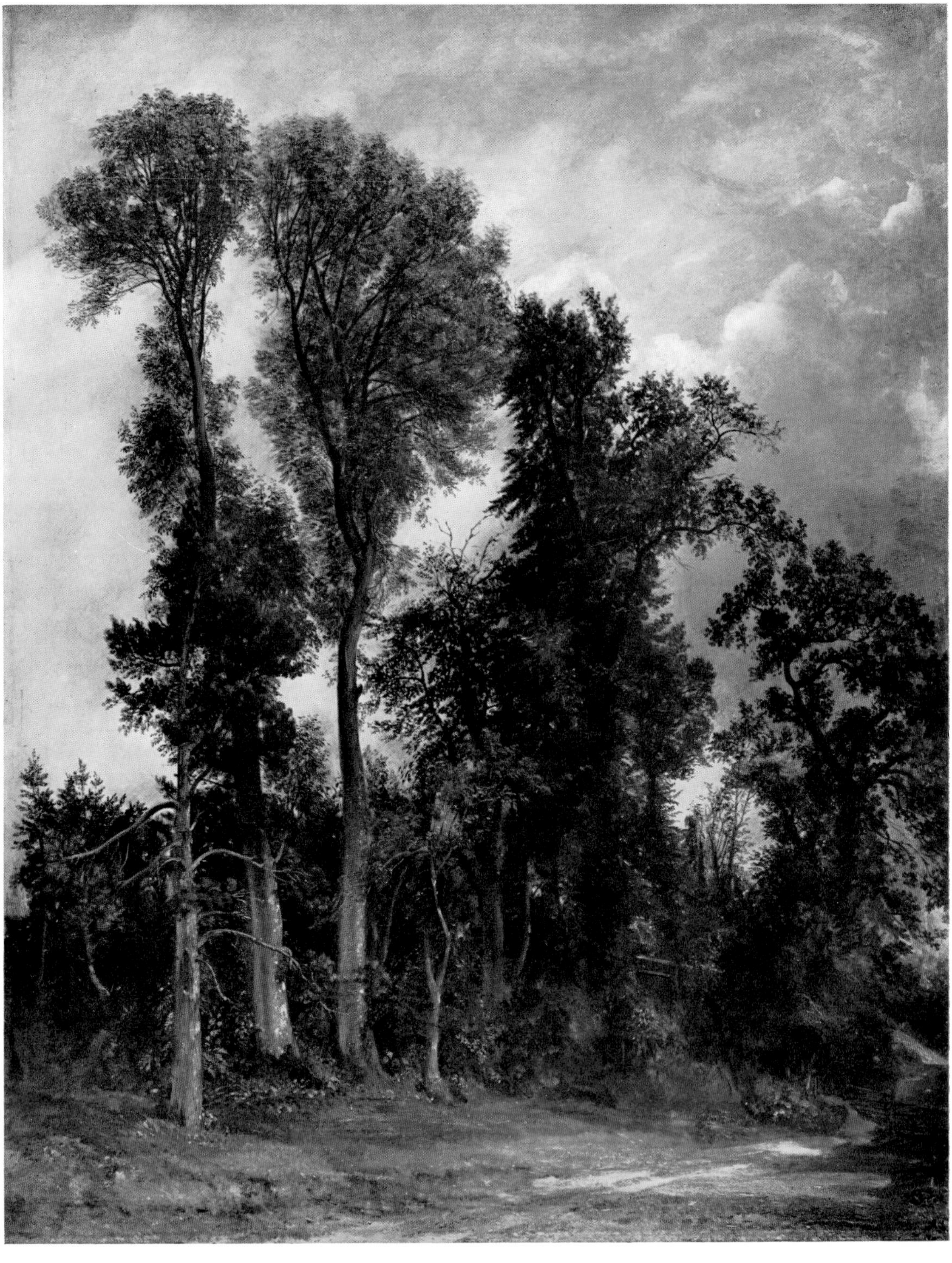

223. Trees at Hampstead: The path to Church.

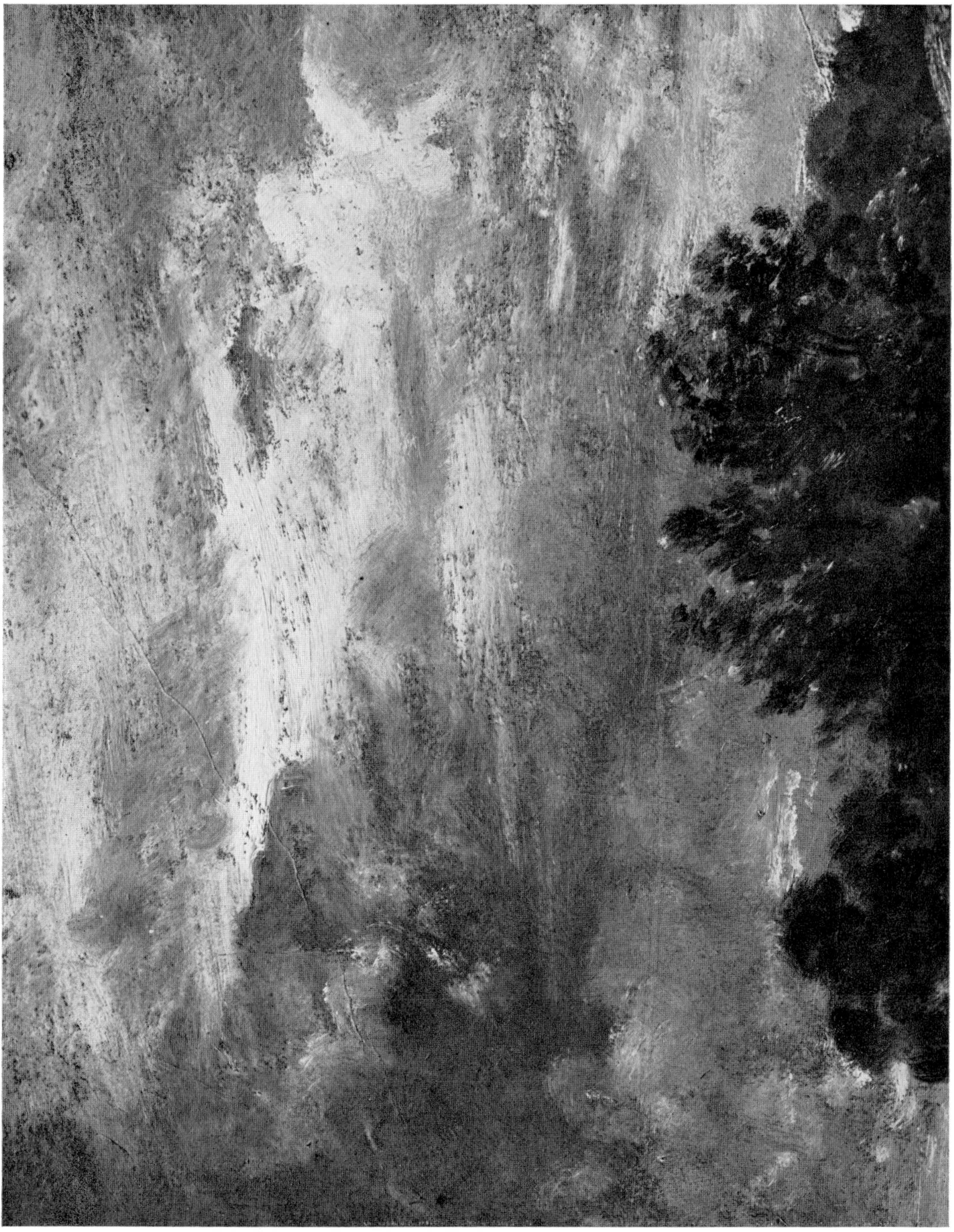

224. Study of sky and trees.

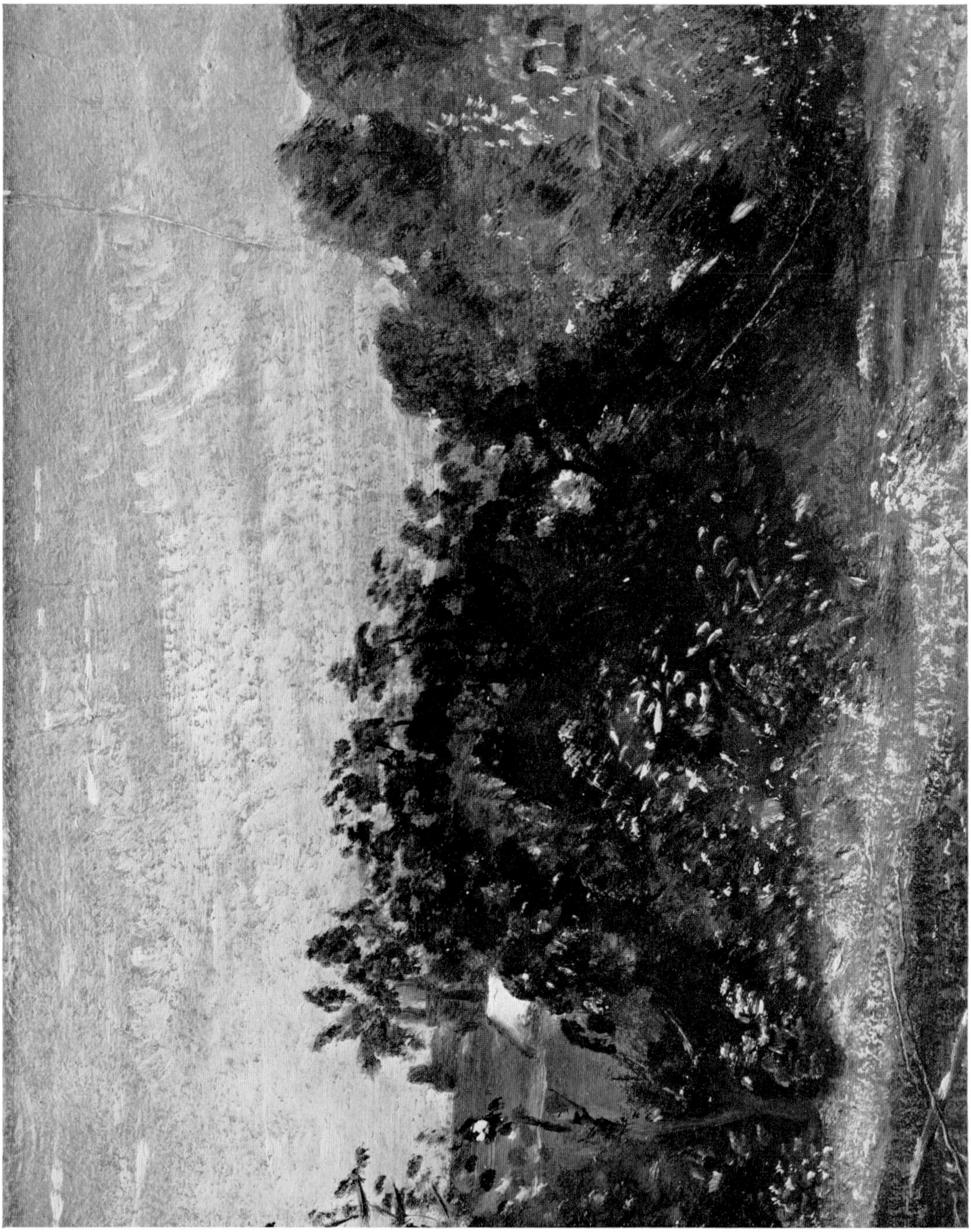

226. Study of sky and trees at Hampstead.

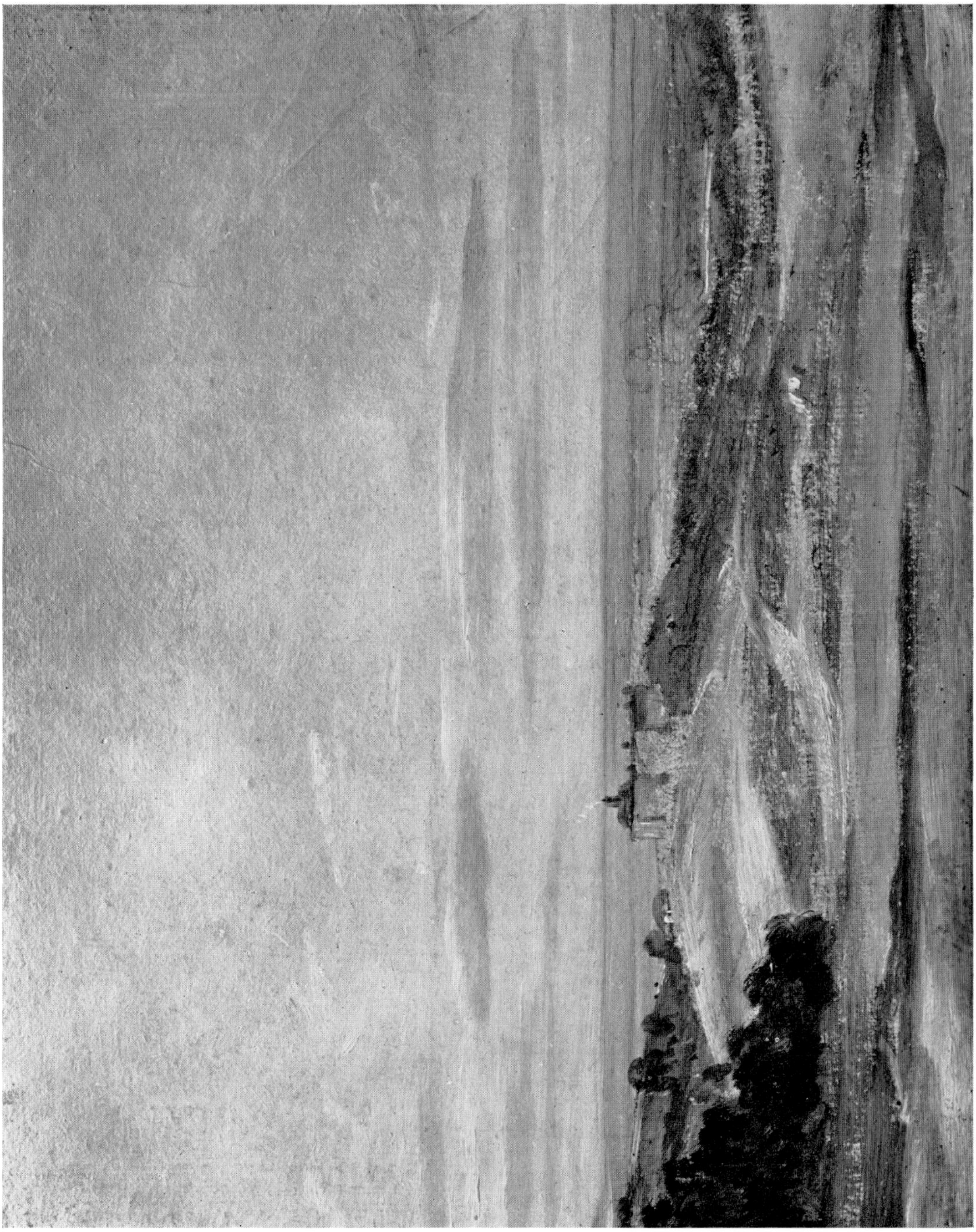

227. Buildings on rising ground near Hampstead.

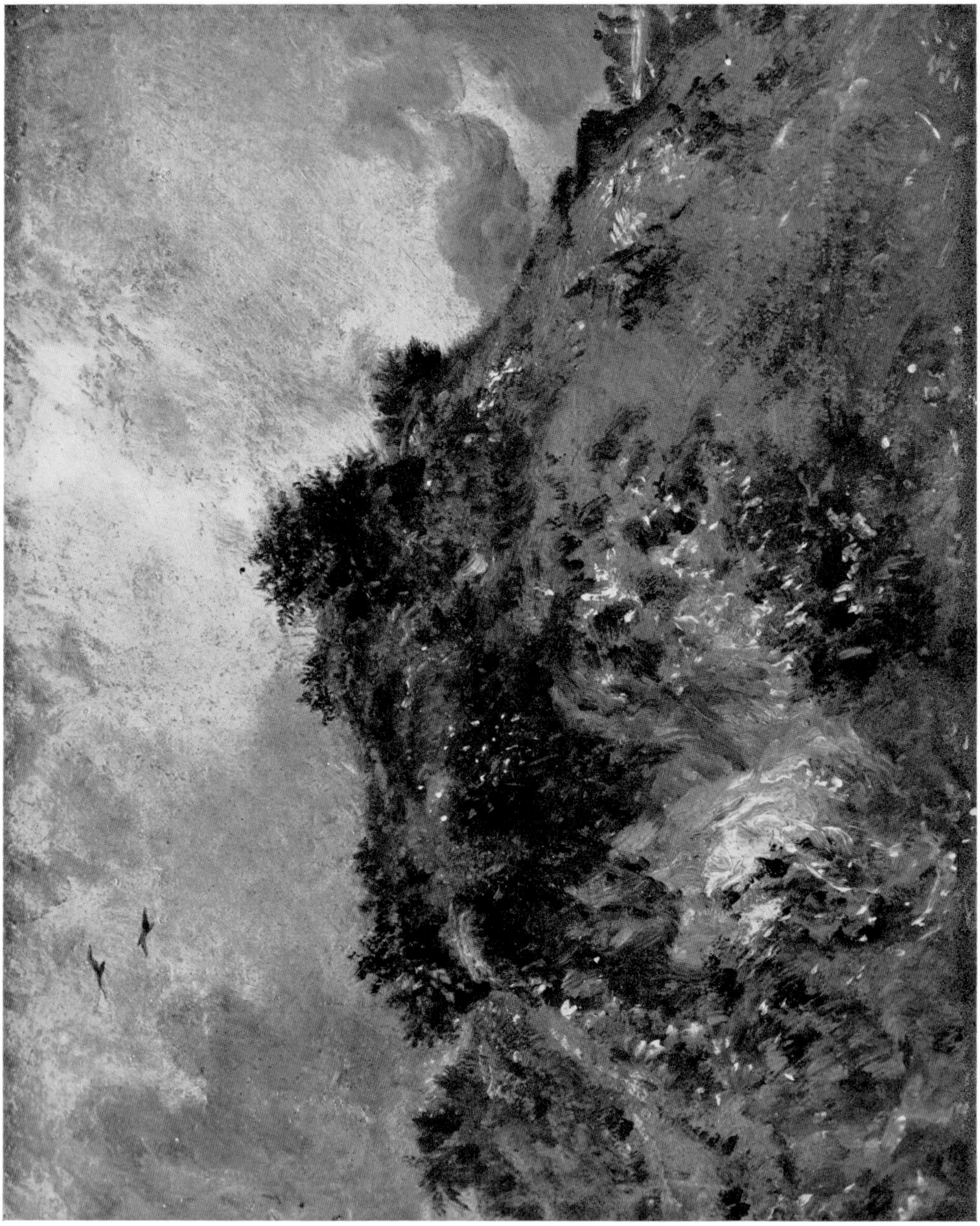

228. A sandbank at Hampstead Heath.

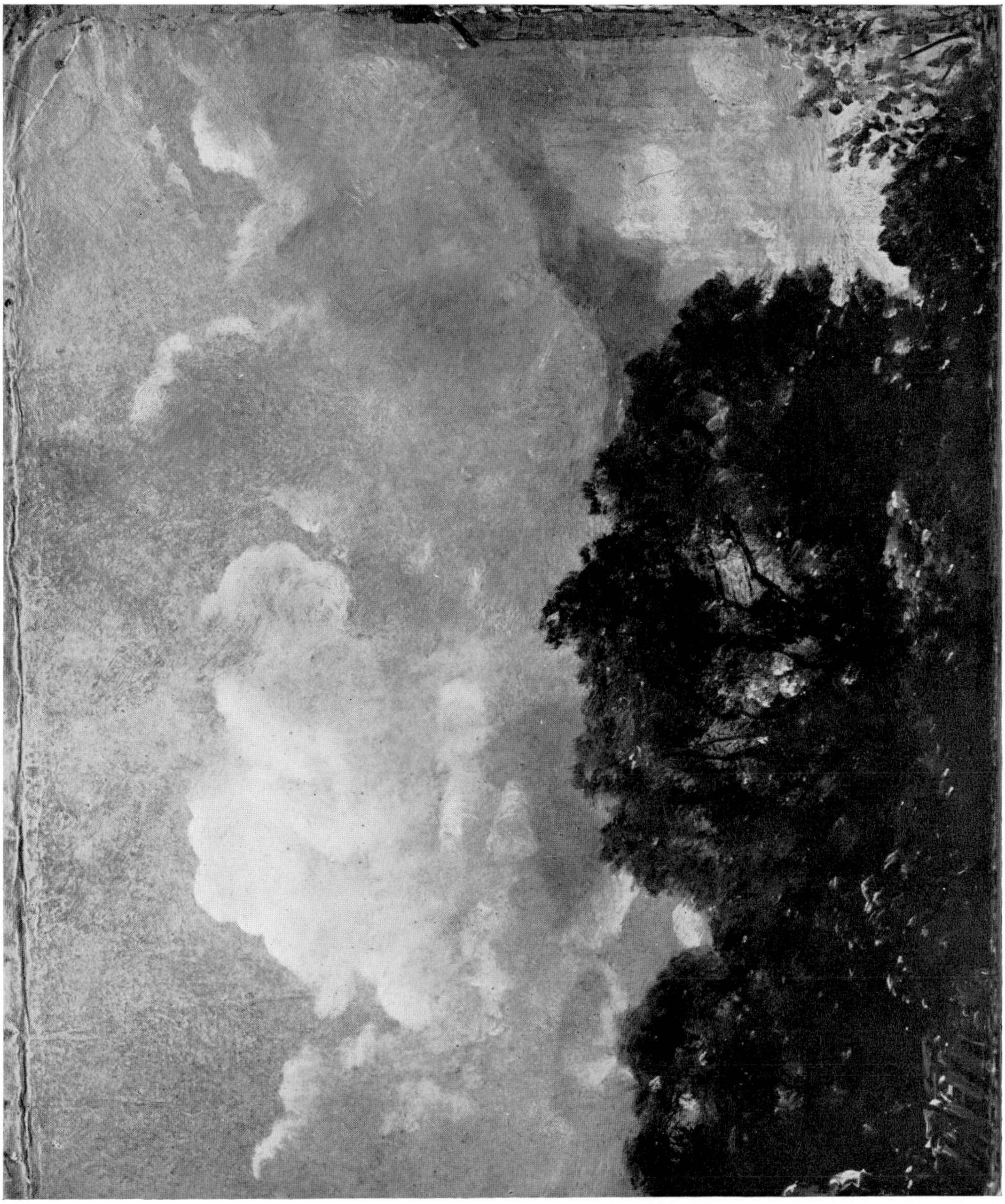

229. Study of sky and trees.

230. Study of sky and trees.

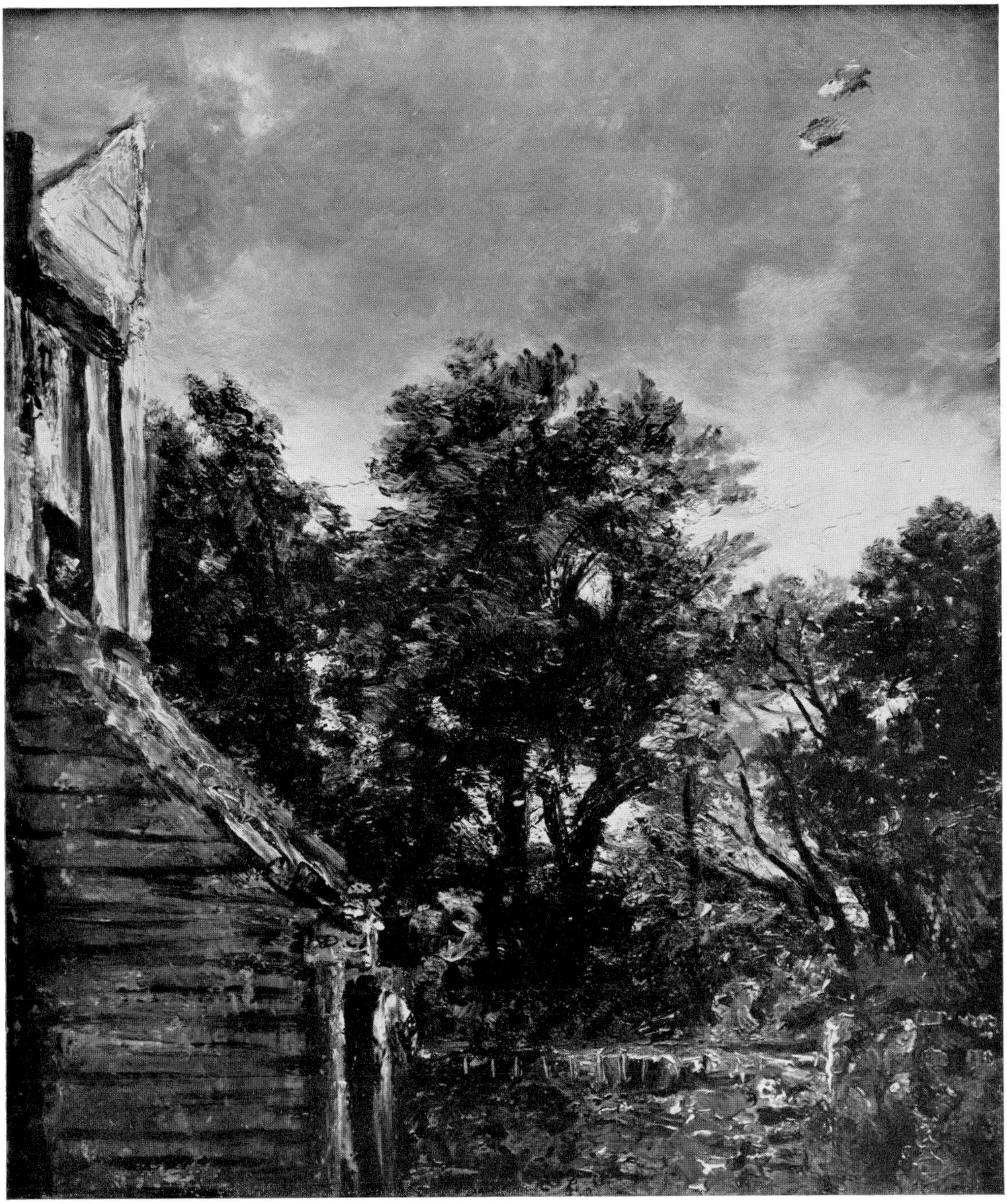

231. View in a garden, with a shed.

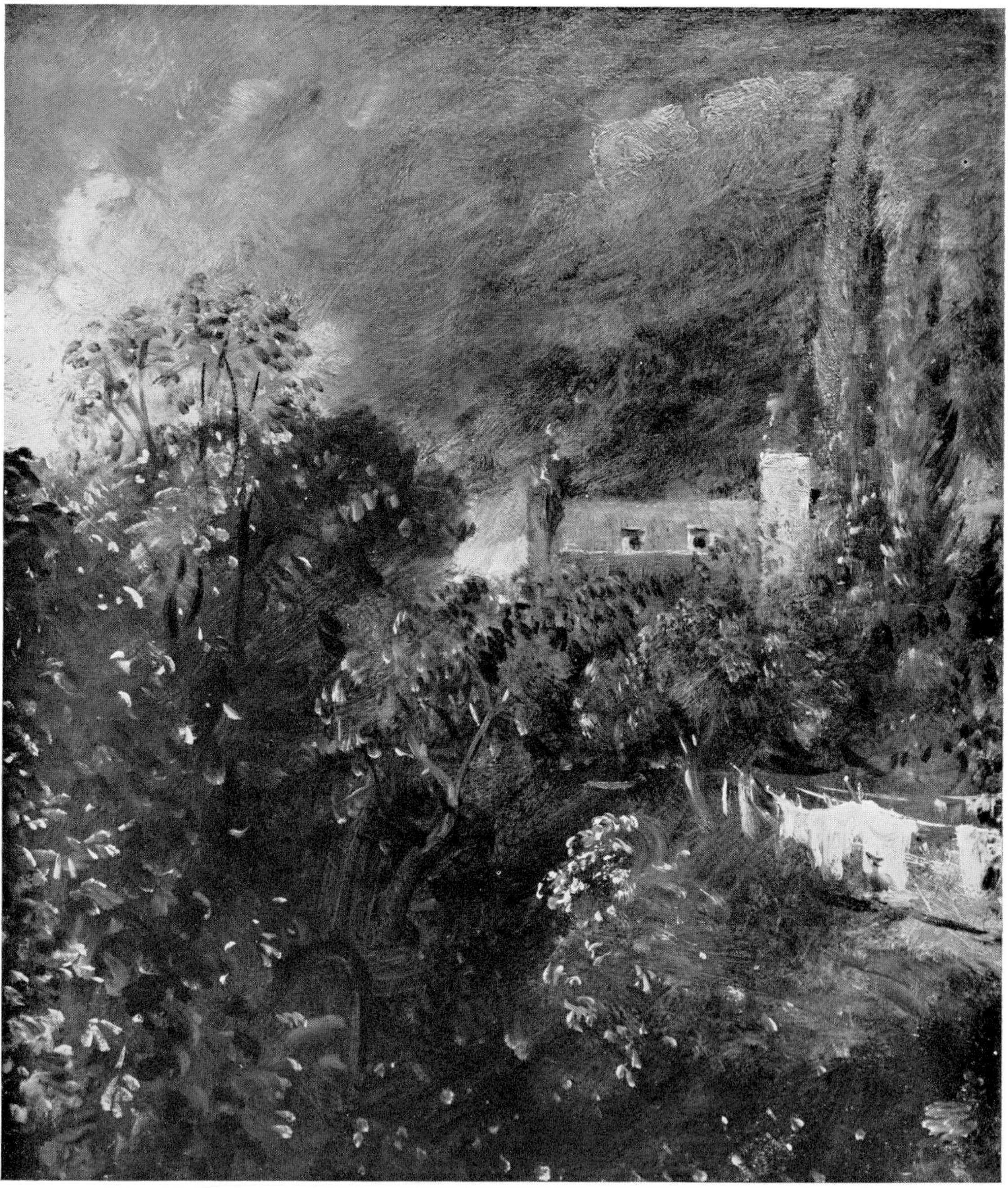

232. View in a garden with a red house beyond.

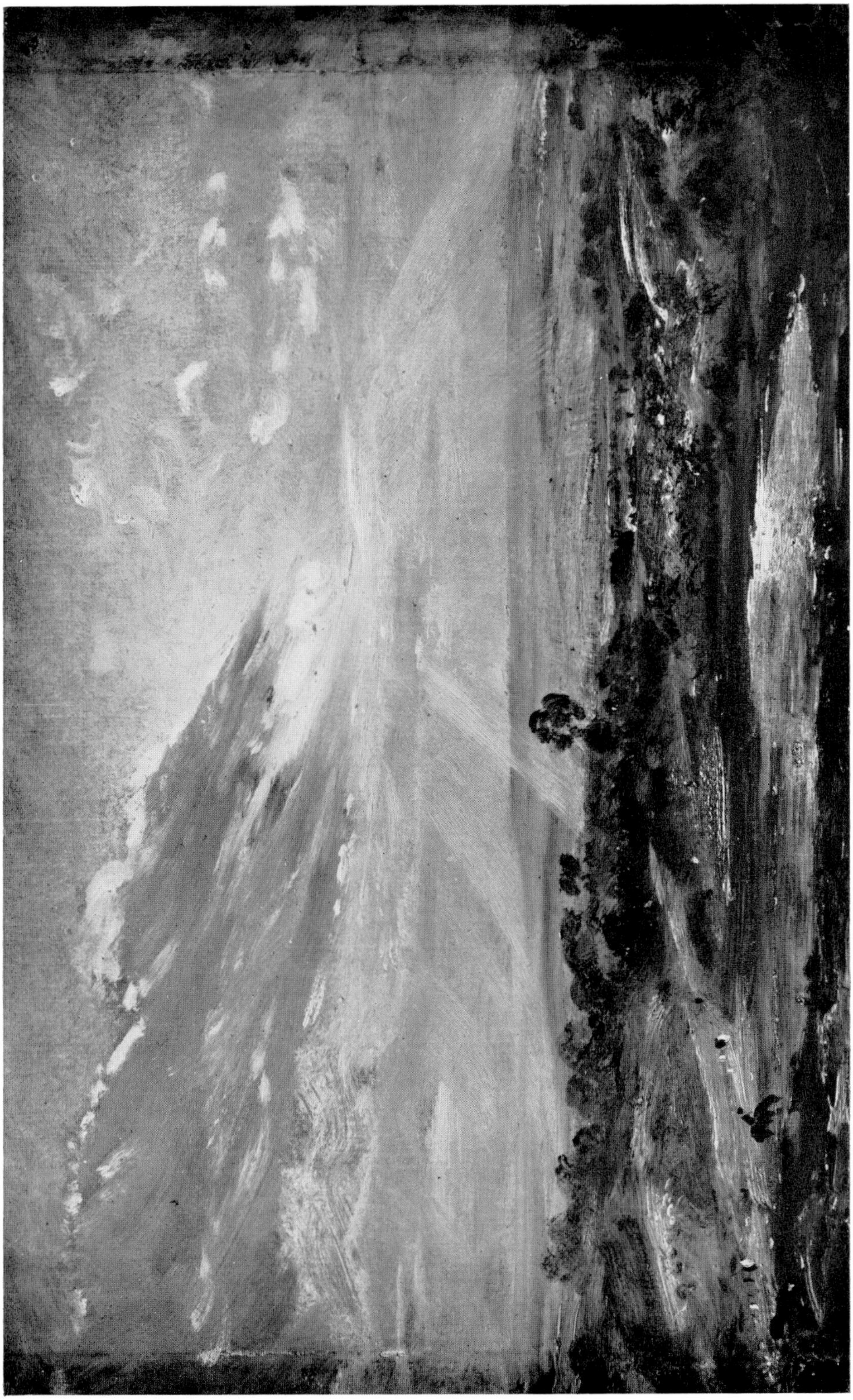

233. Branch Hill Pond, Hampstead(?).

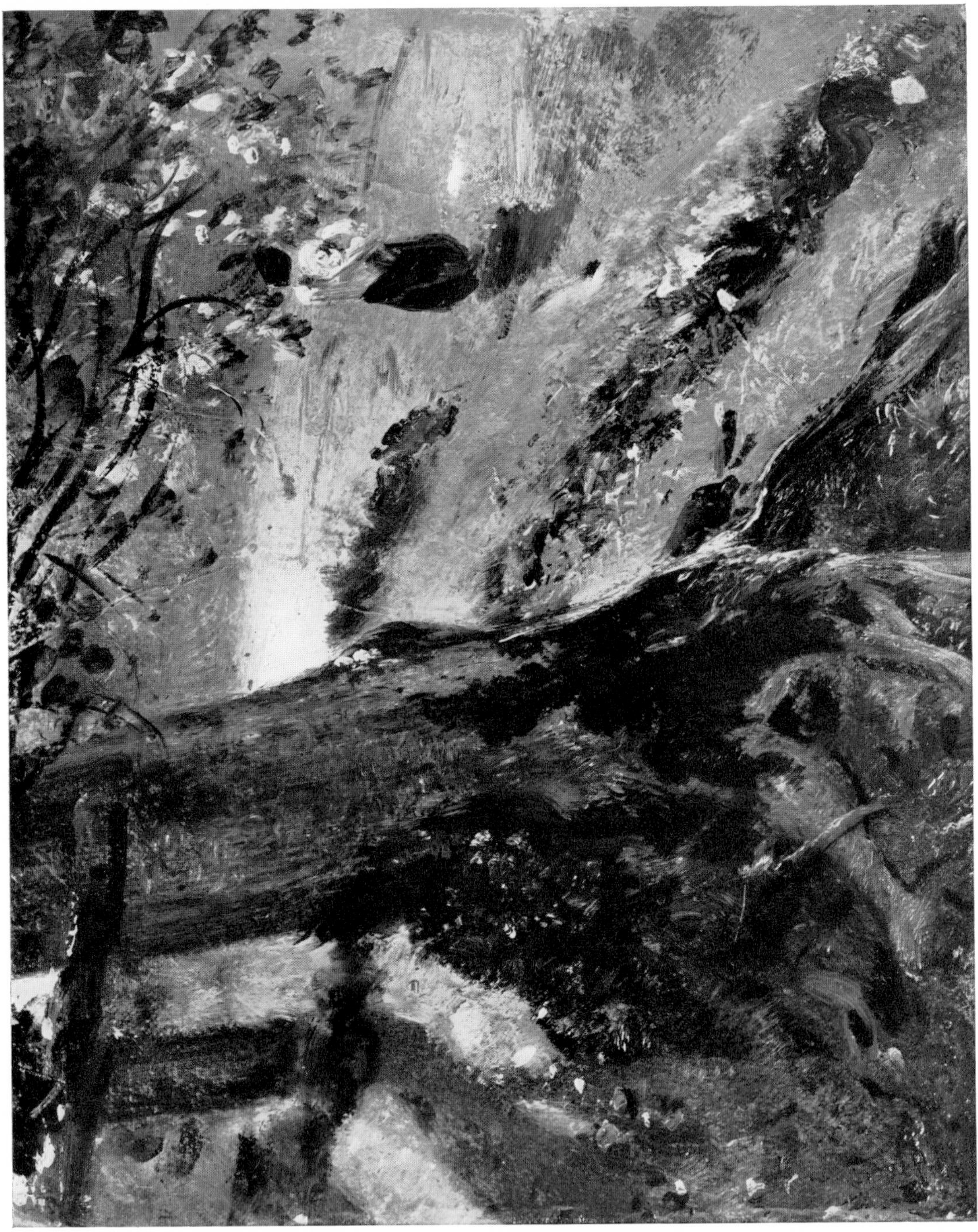

234. Study of tree trunks.

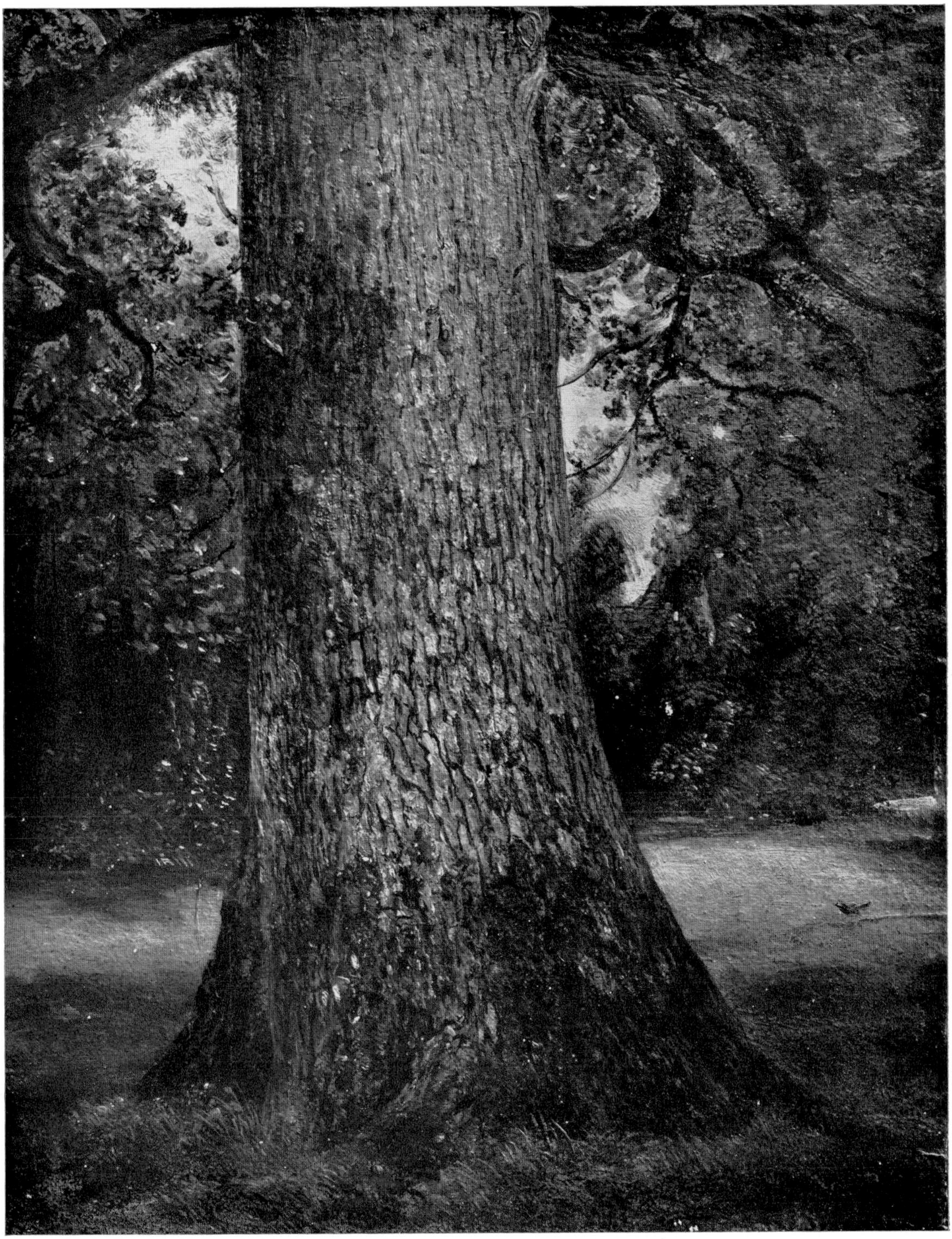

235. Study of the trunk of an elm tree.

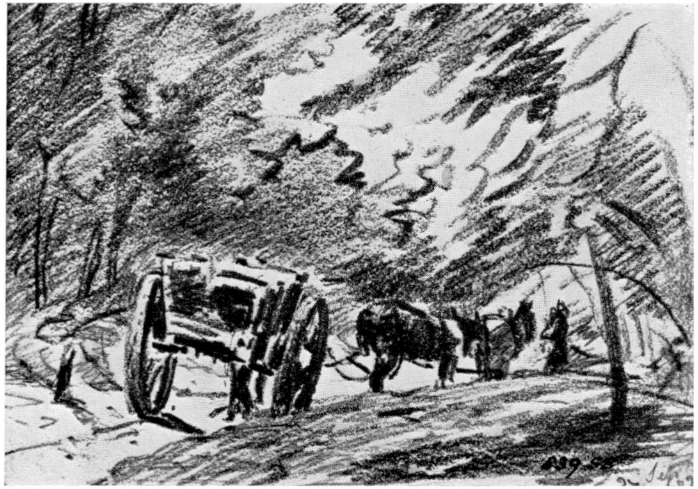

225. A cart and team.

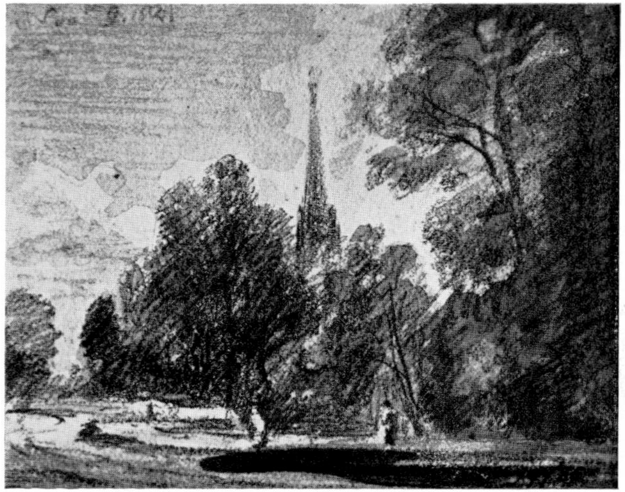

236. Salisbury Cathedral with trees.

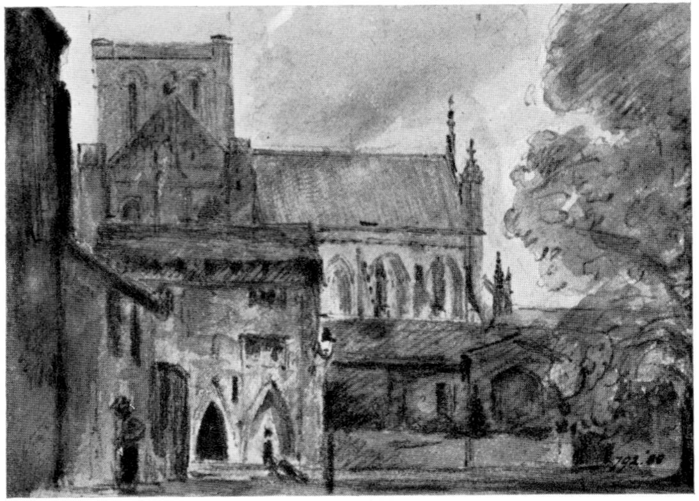

237. Winchester Cathedral.

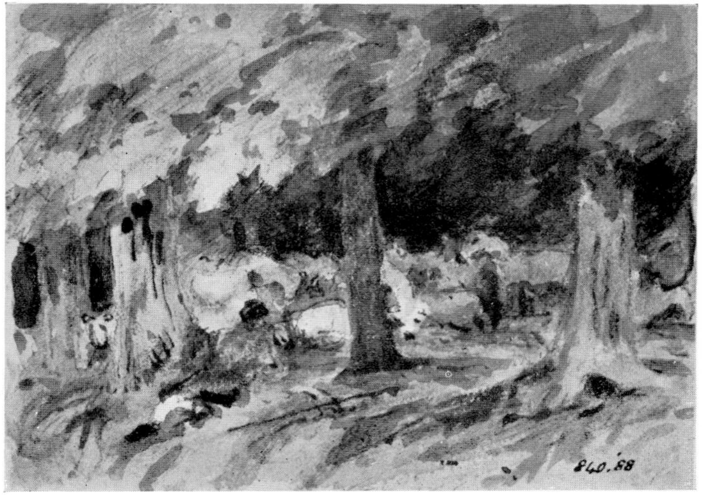

244. Scene in a wood.

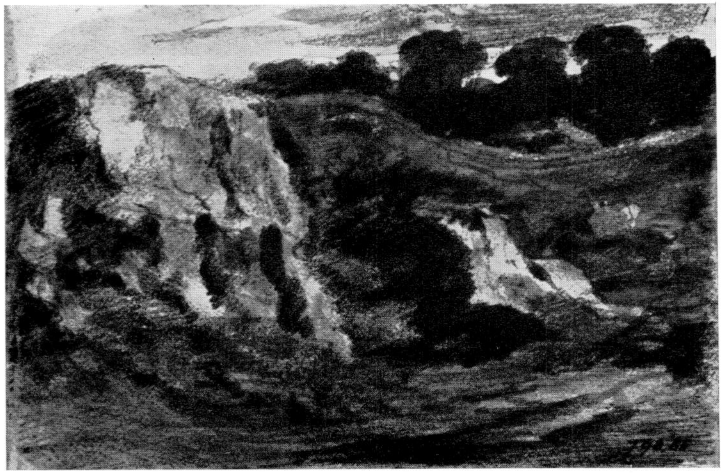

243. Sandbank with trees beyond.

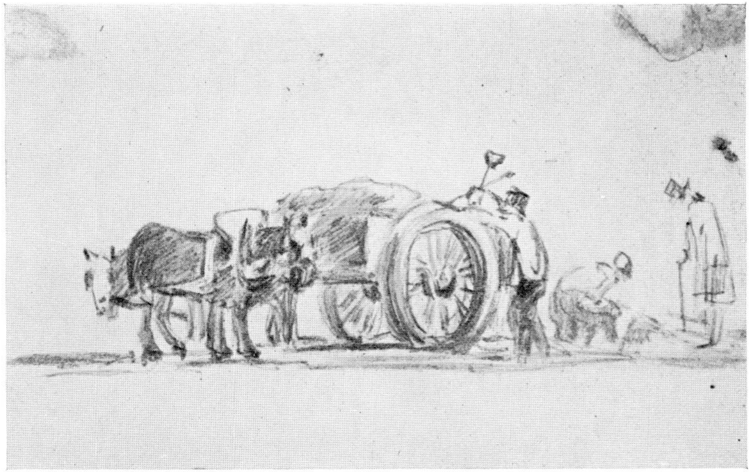

243a. A cart and horses.

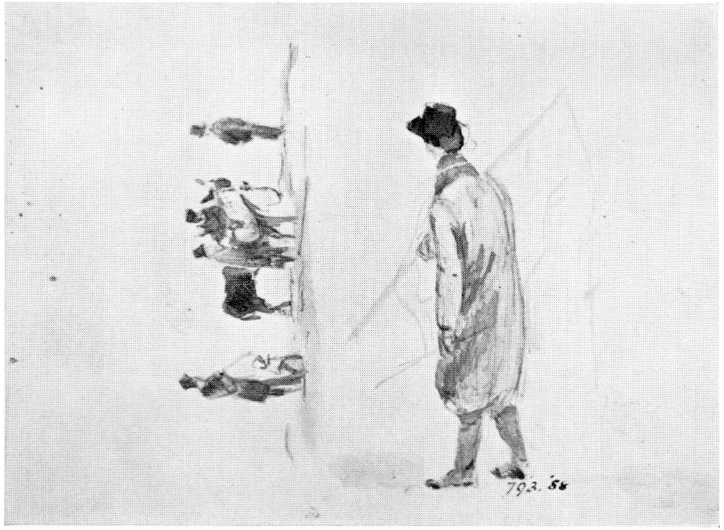

245. A countryman walking.

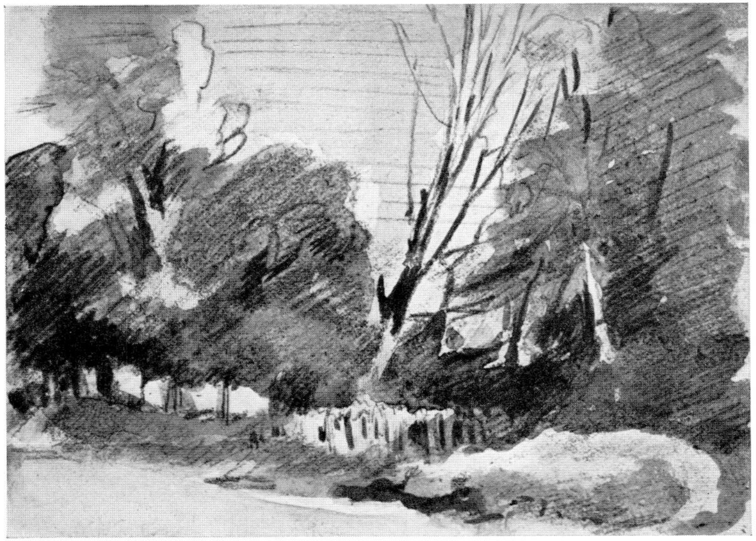

245a. Scene in a wood or park.

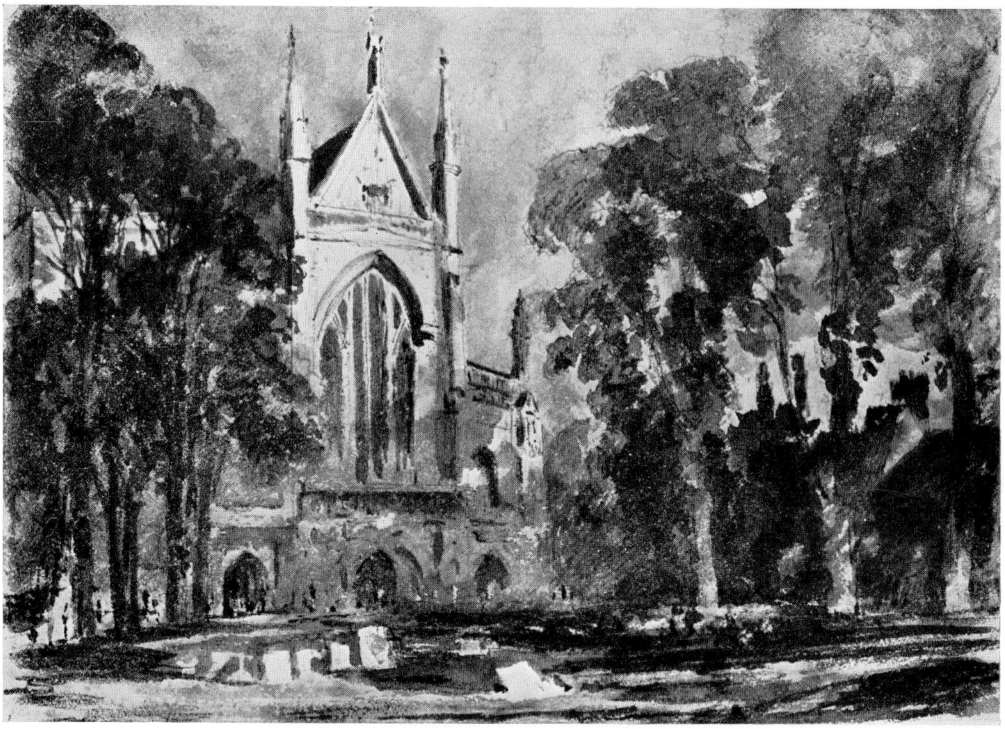

238. Winchester Cathedral: W. front.

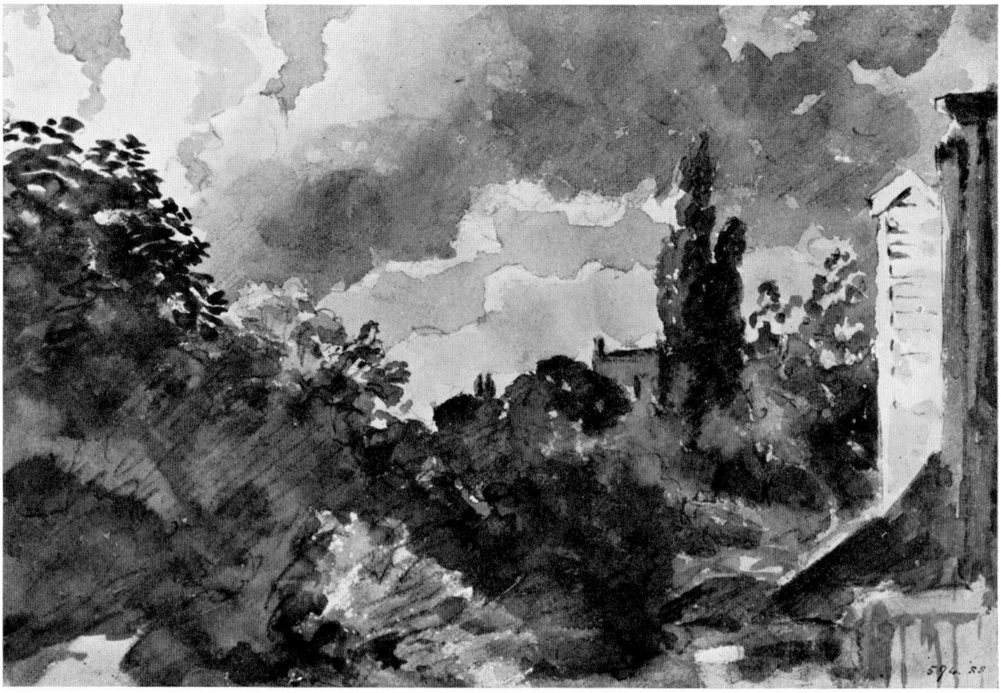

242. Trees, sky and a red house.

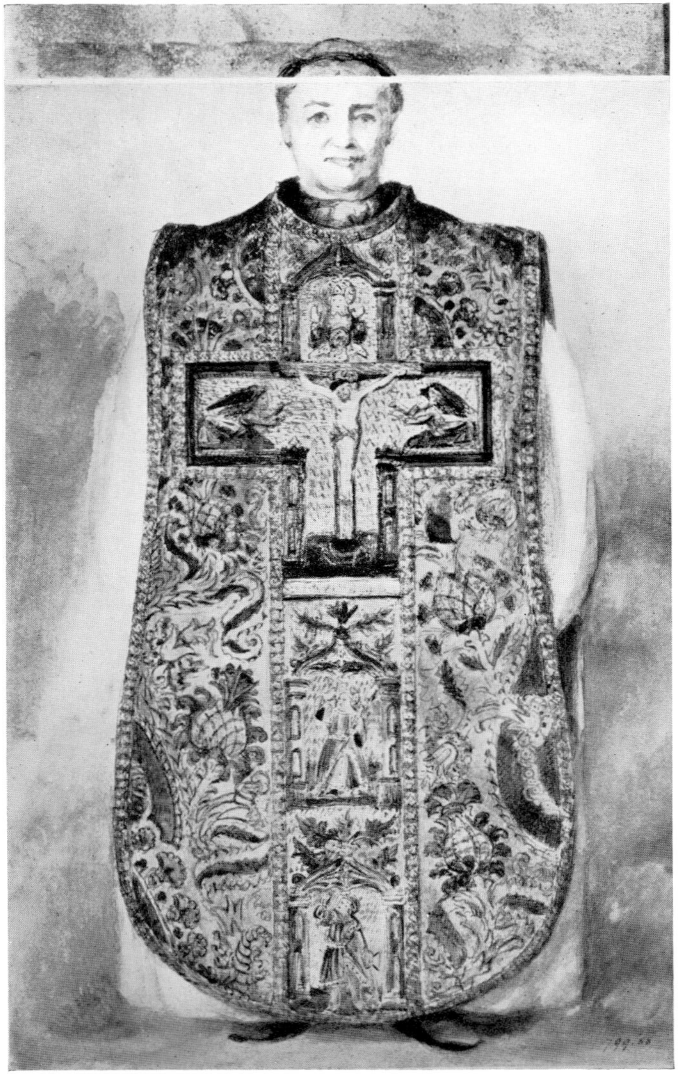

239 and 238a. Rev. E. Benson wearing a medieval chasuble.

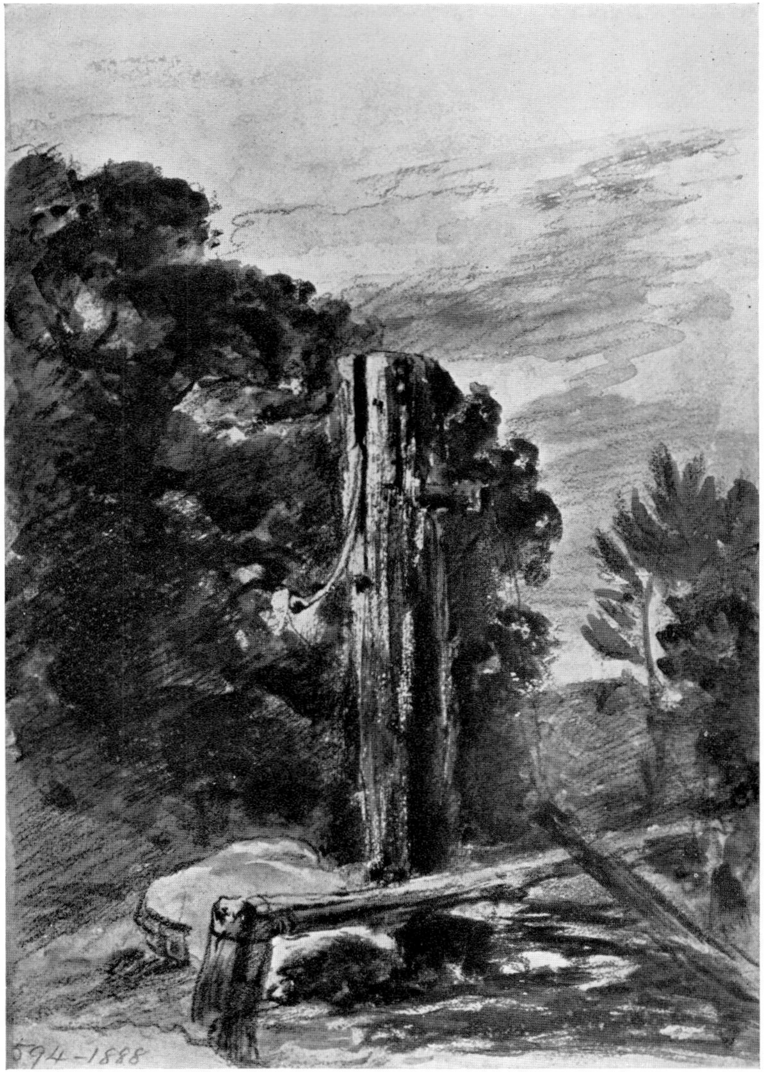

242a. A pump.

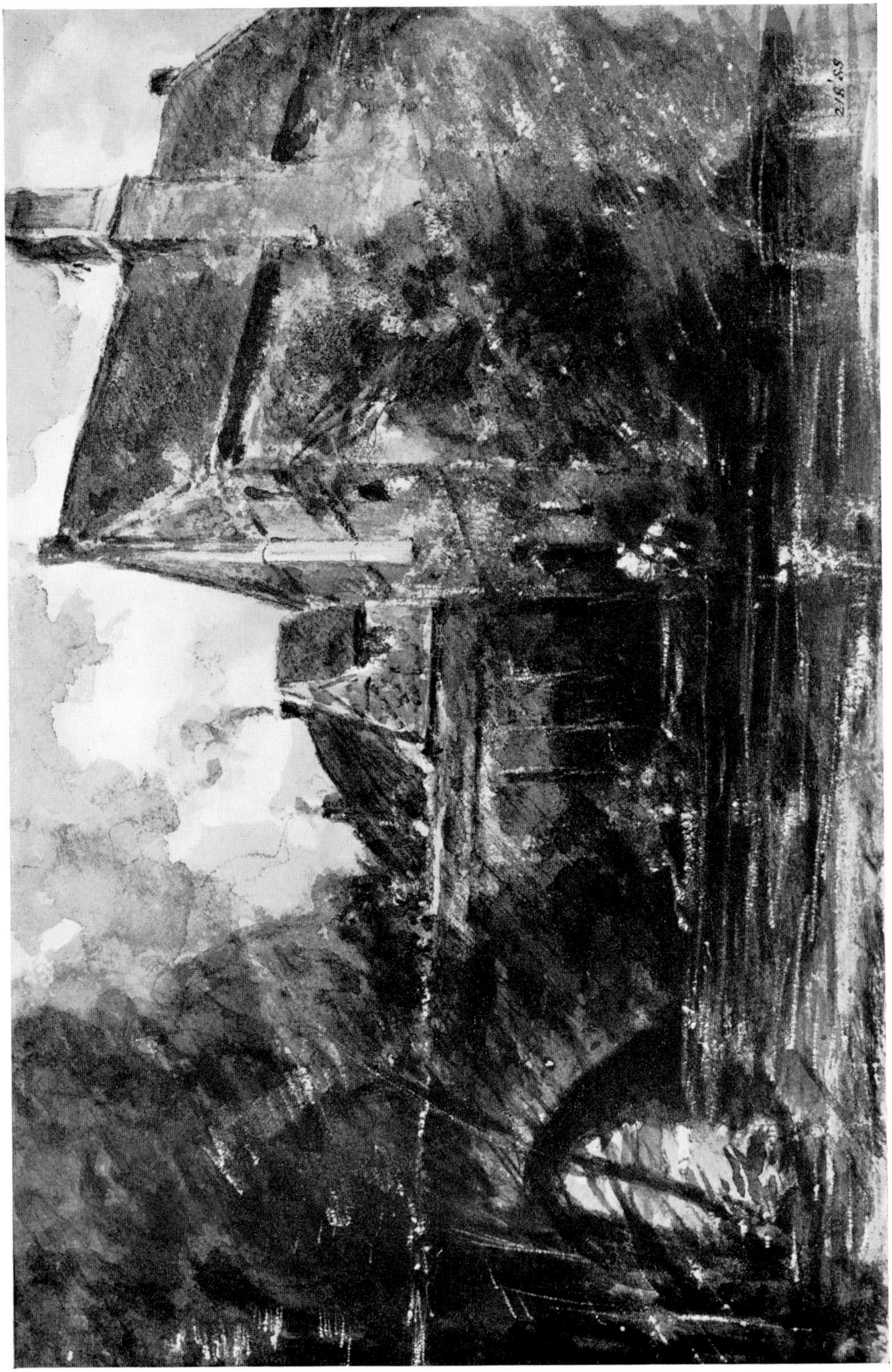

240. Old houses on Harnham Bridge, Salisbury.

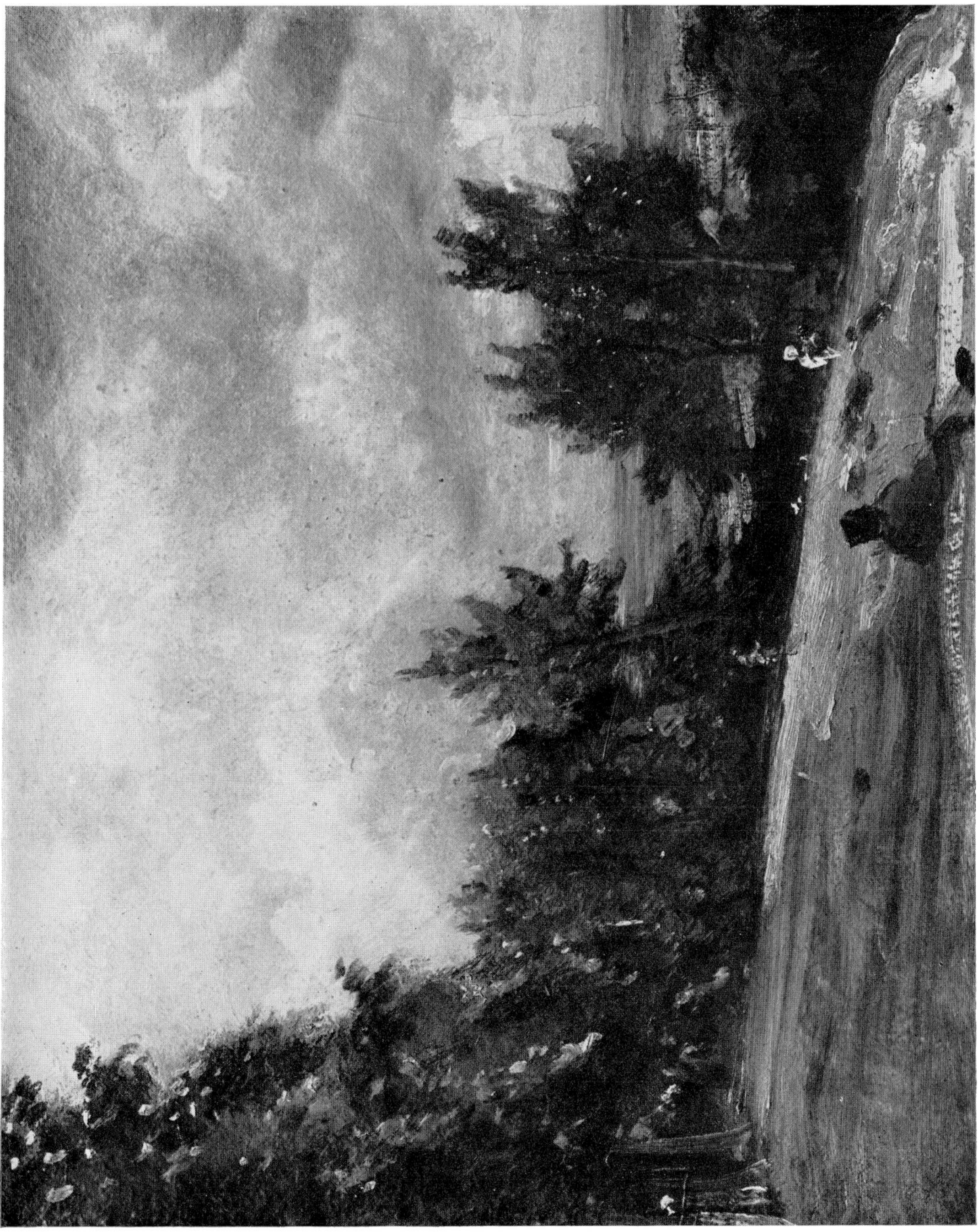

246. A view at Hampstead with trees and figures.

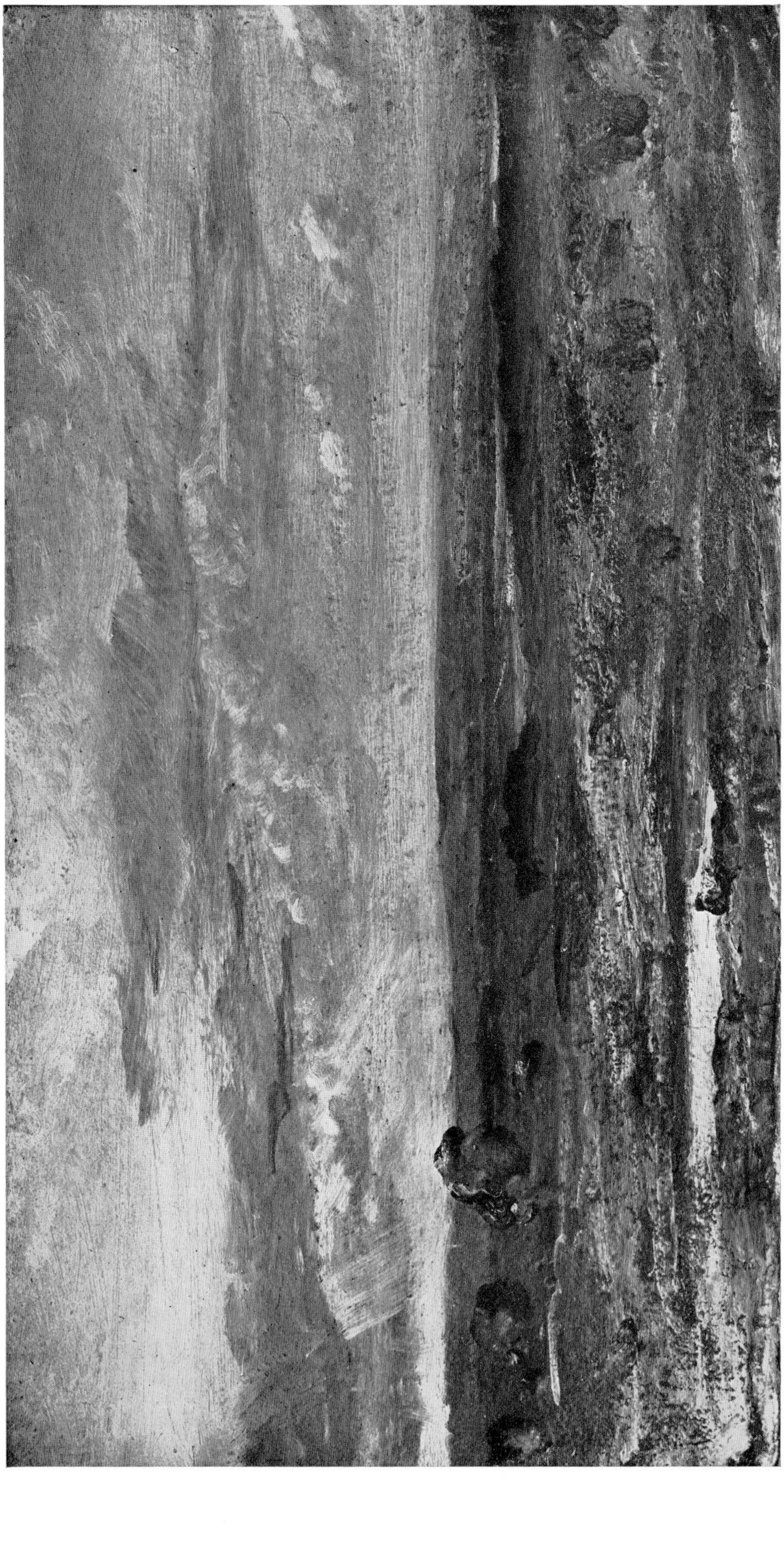

247. A view at Hampstead: evening.

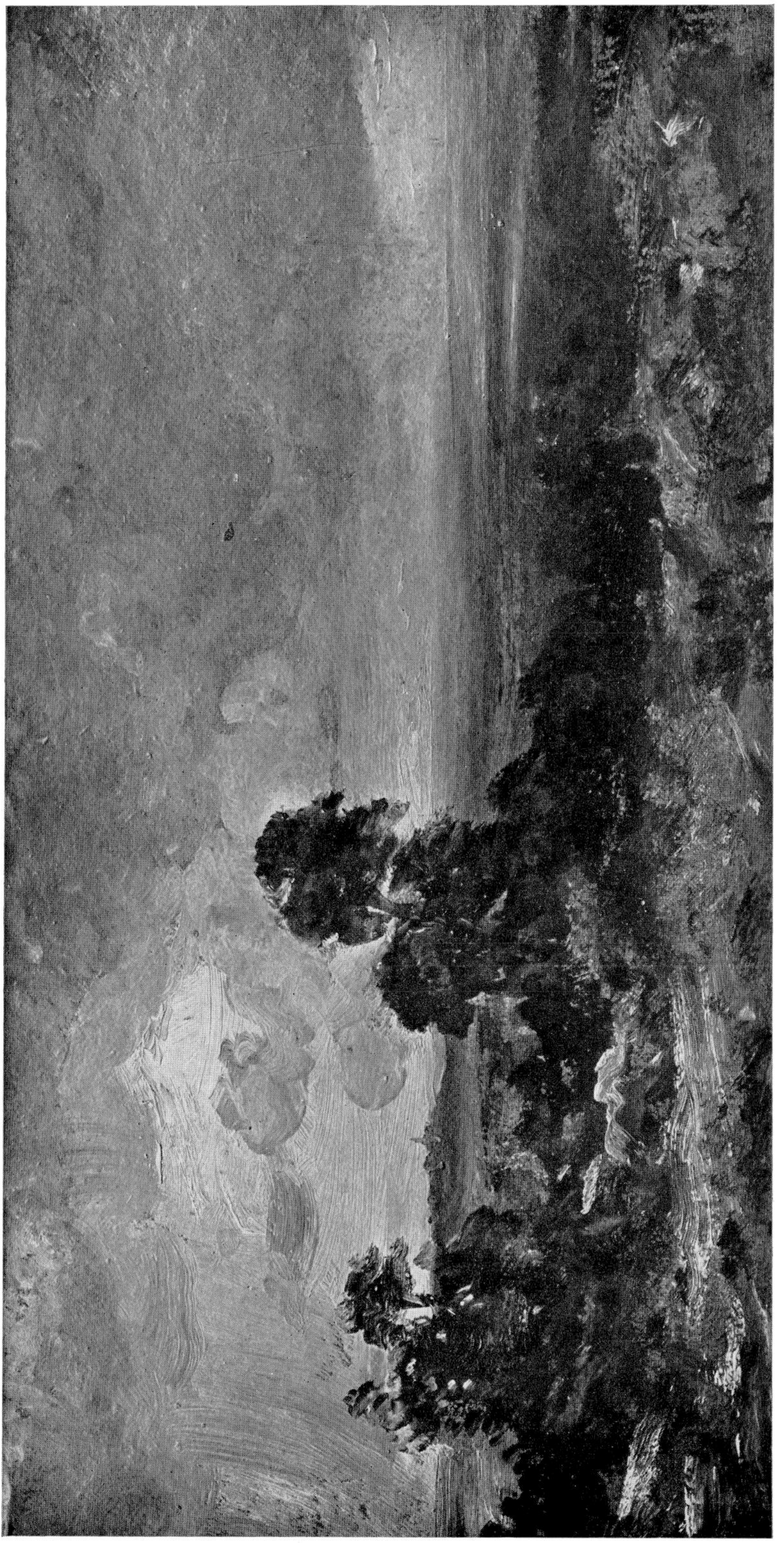

248. Hampstead: stormy sunset.

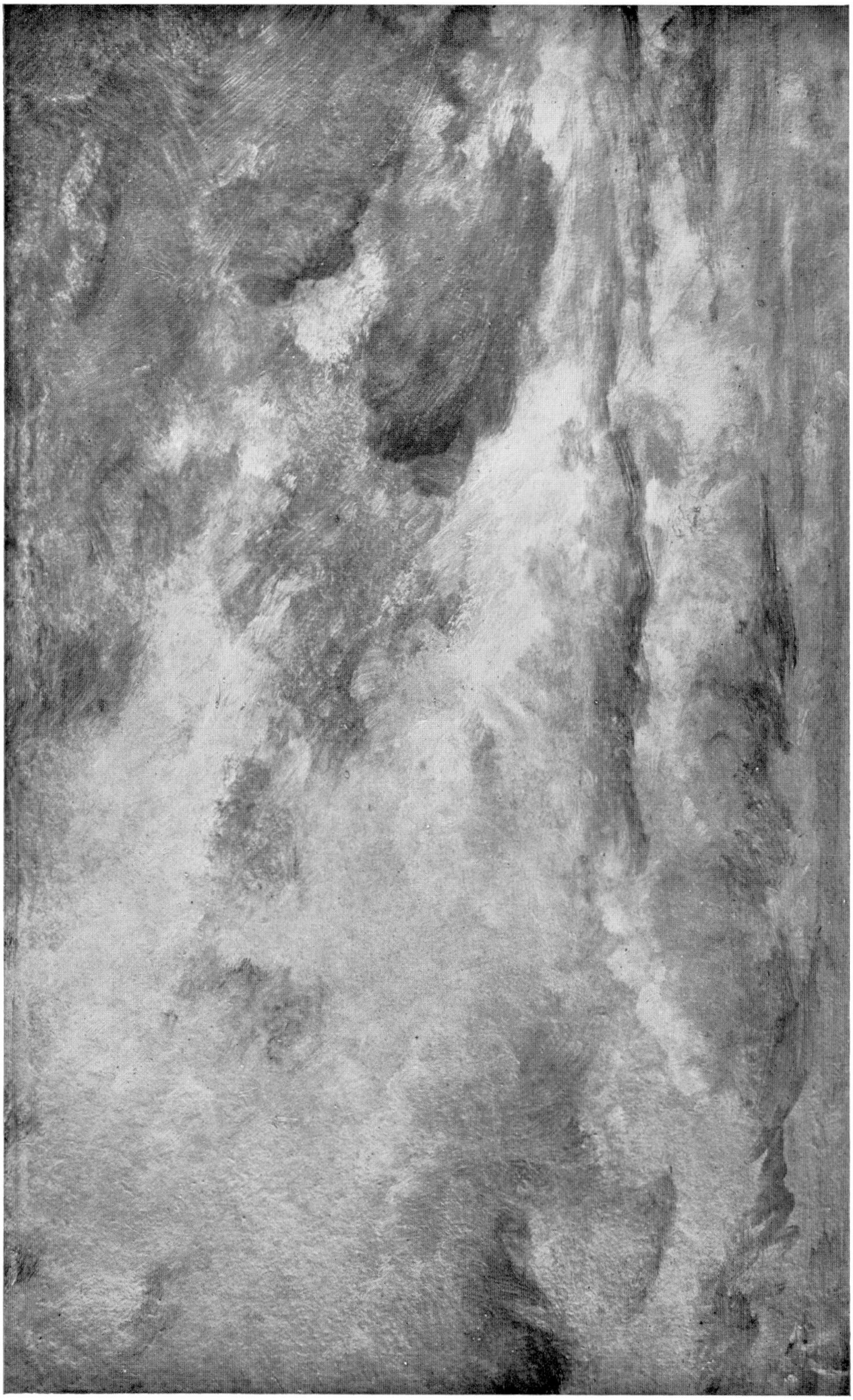

249. Study of clouds.

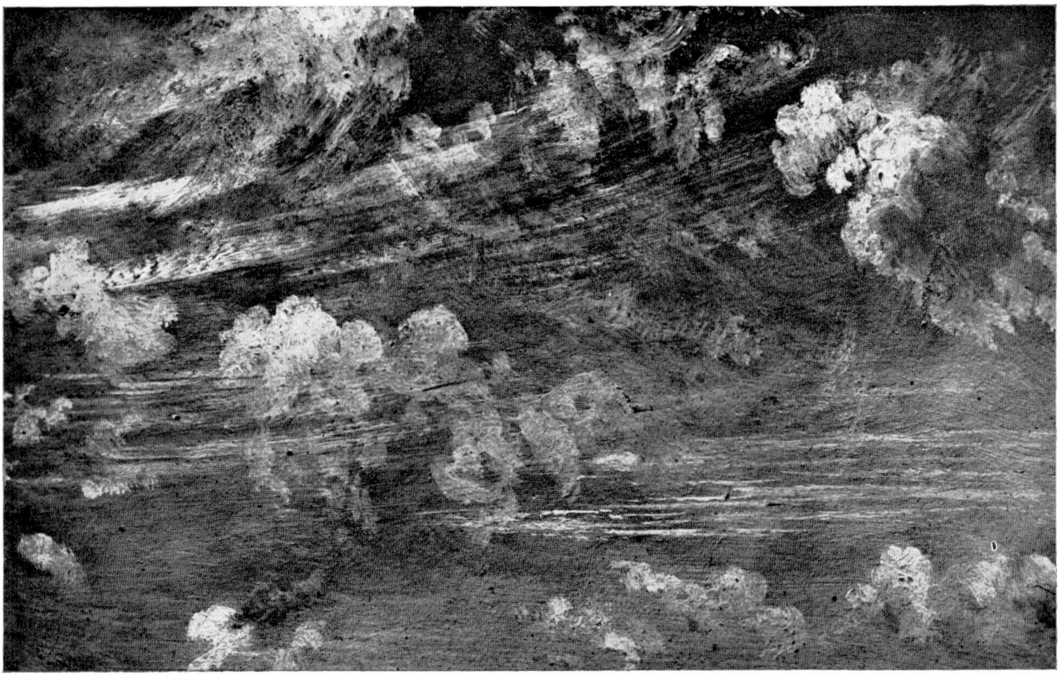

250. Study of cirrus clouds.

251a. Study of clouds.

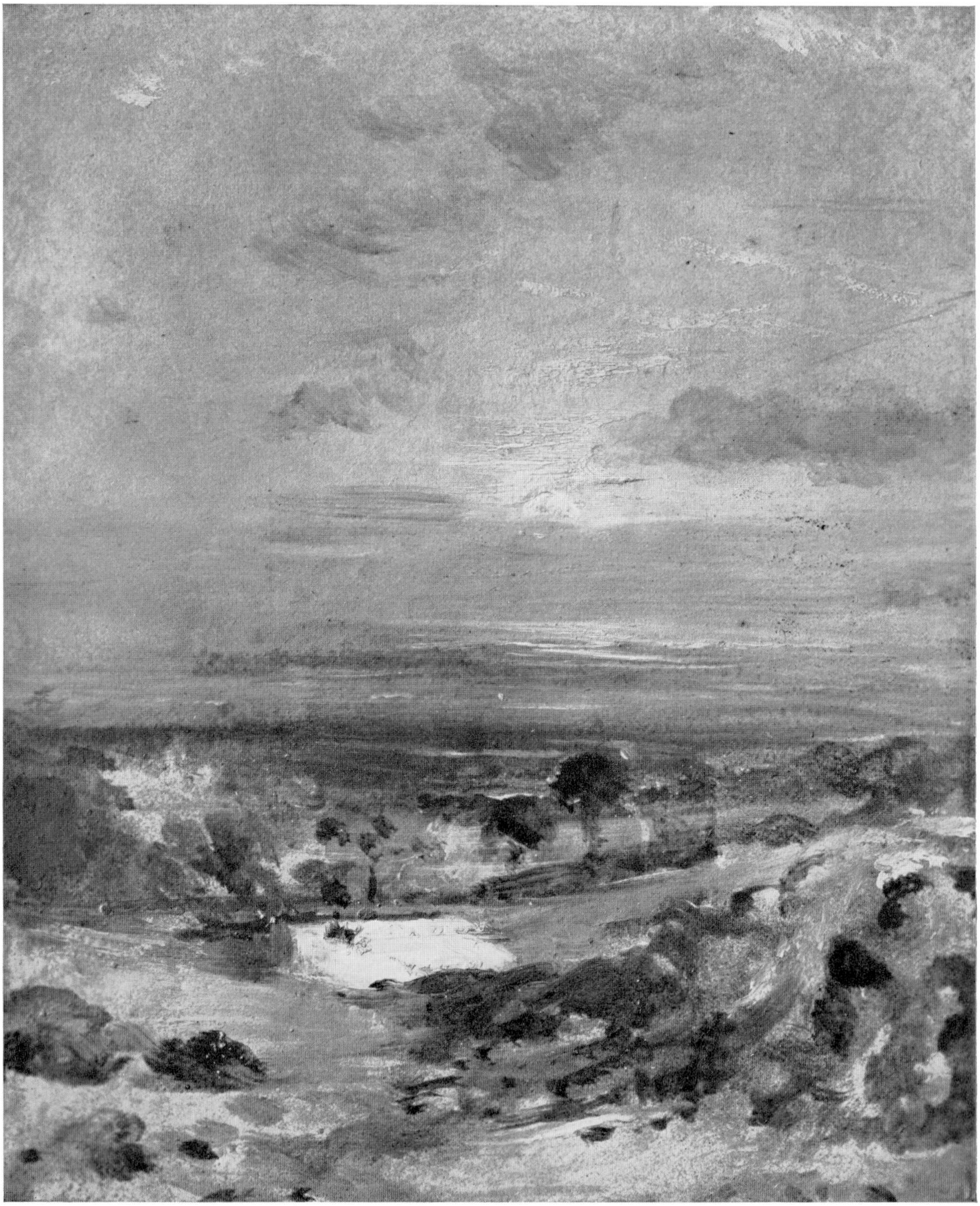

251. Branch Hill Pond: evening.

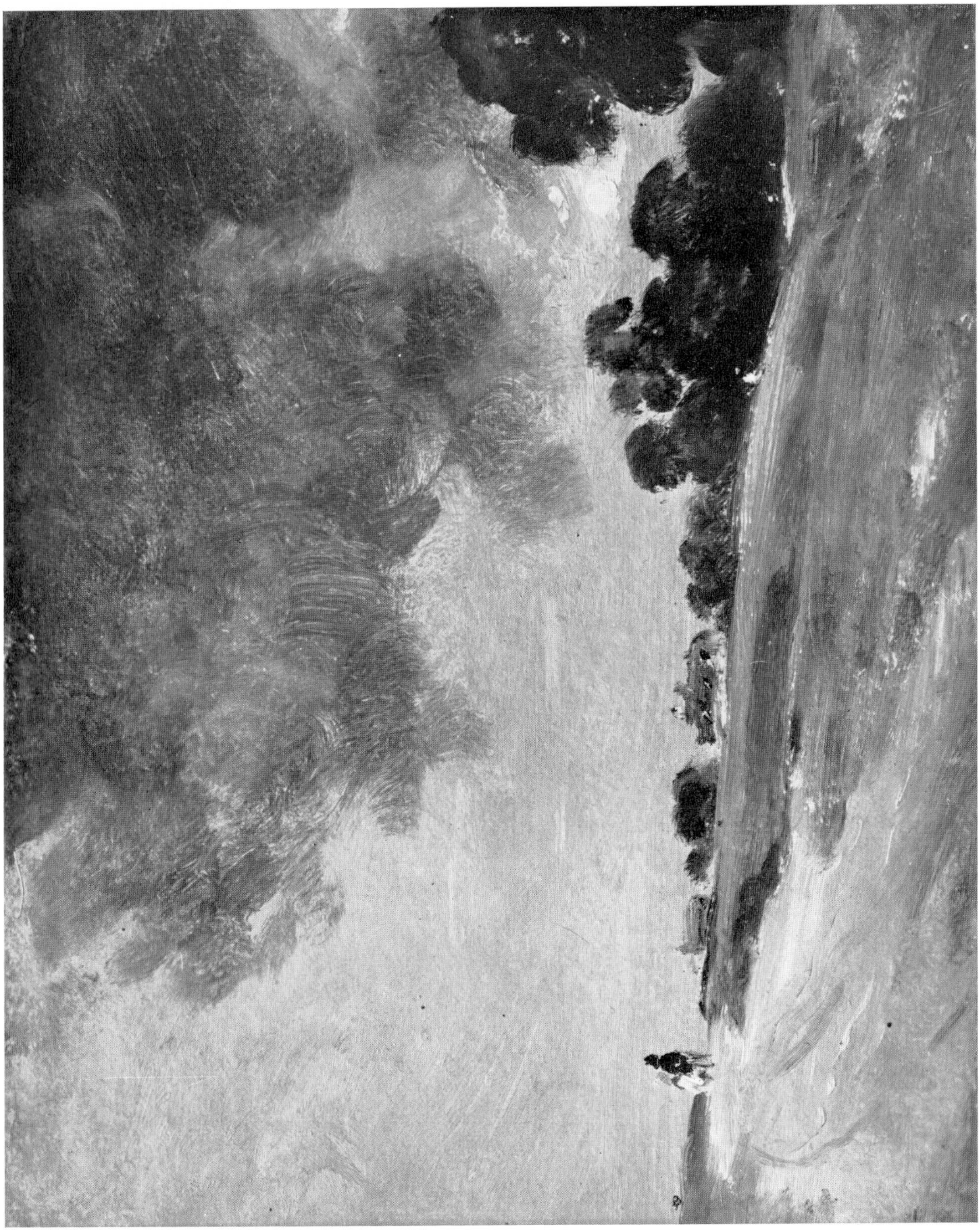

255. View at Hampstead, looking due east.

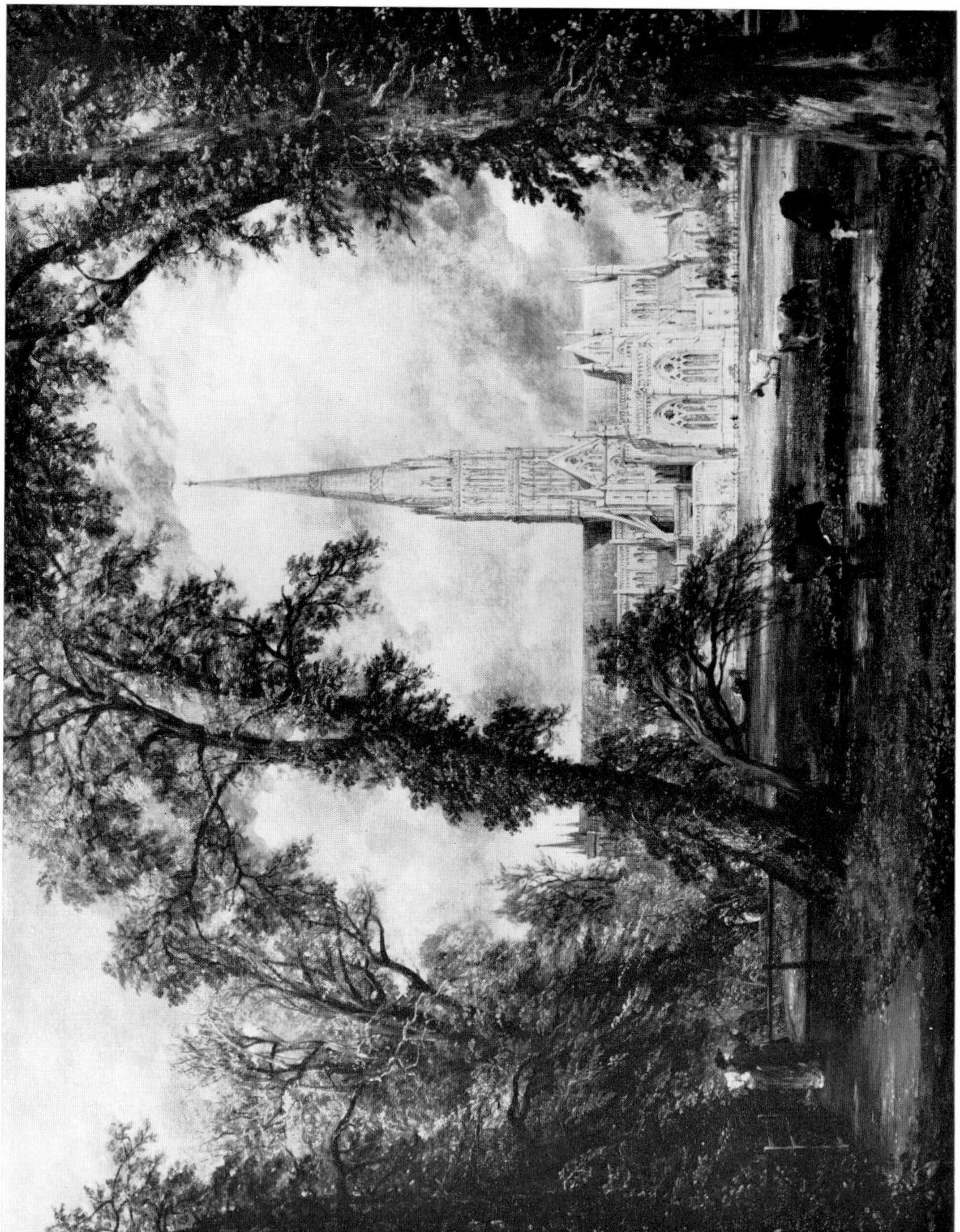

254. Salisbury Cathedral from the Bishop's Grounds.

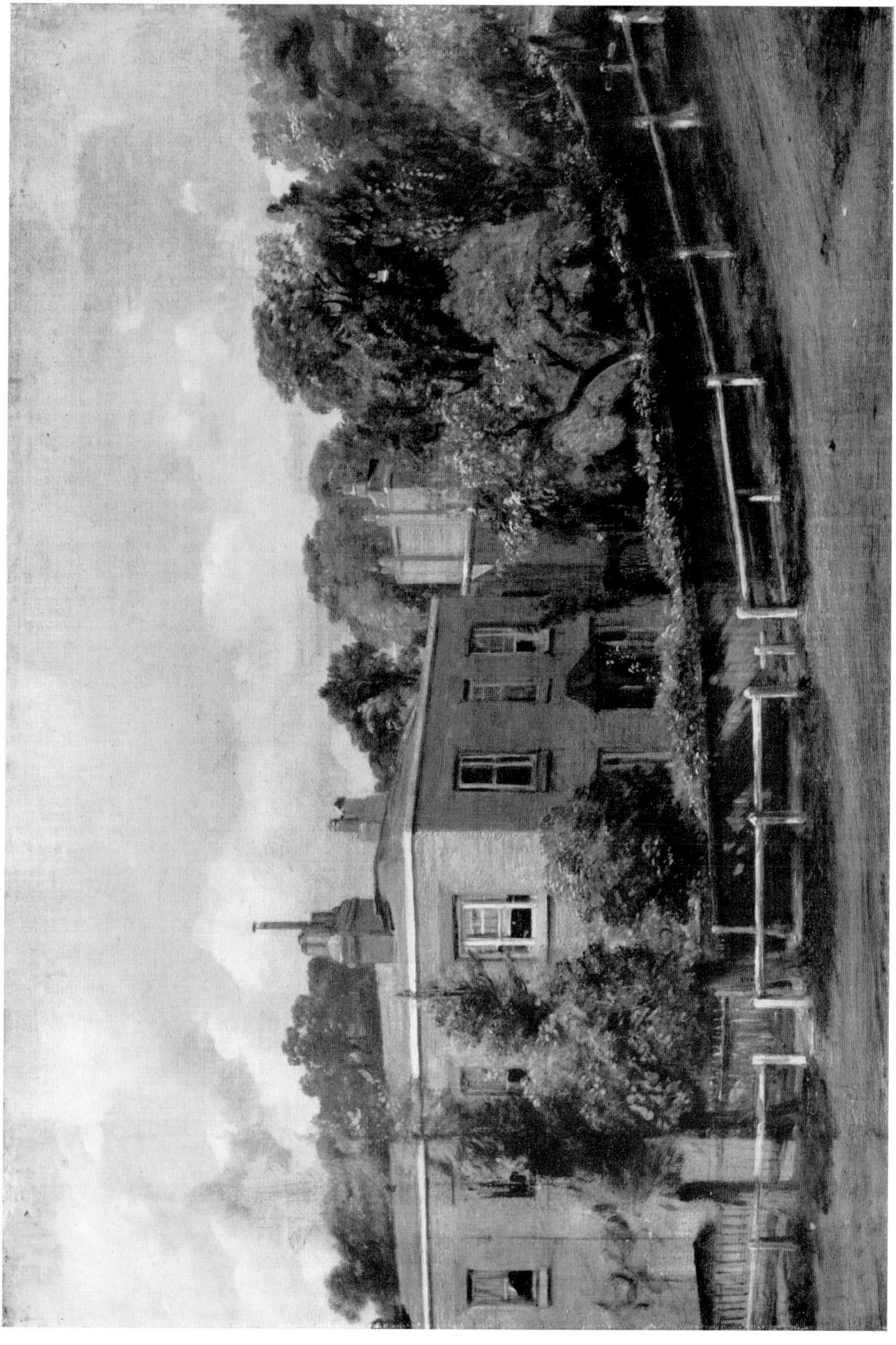

252. View of Lower Terrace, Hampstead.

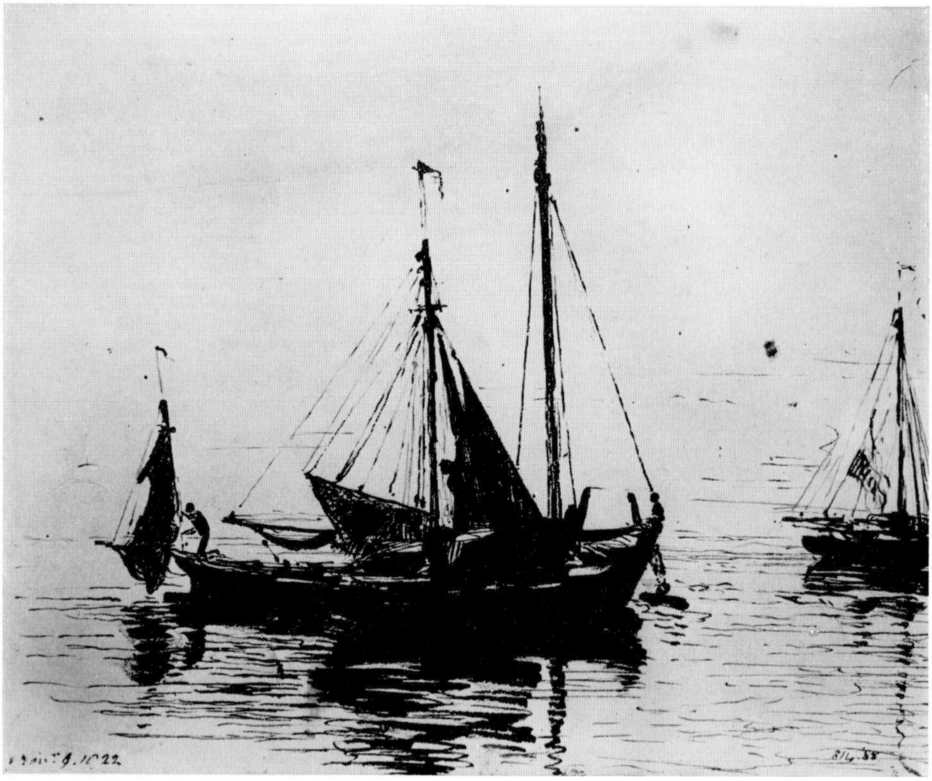

253. Fishing boats at anchor.

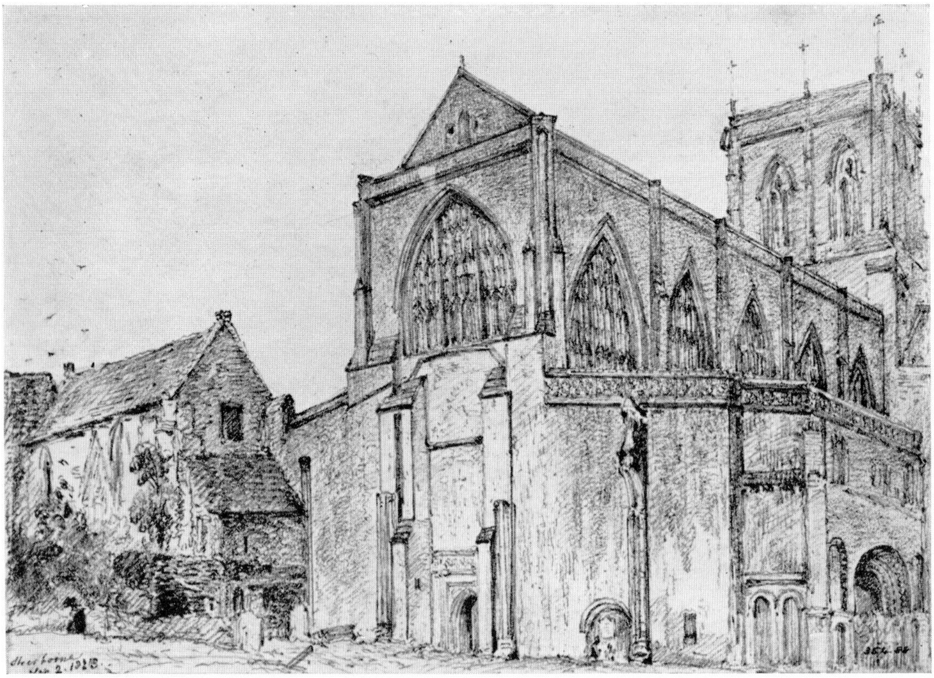

257. The Abbey Church, Sherborne.

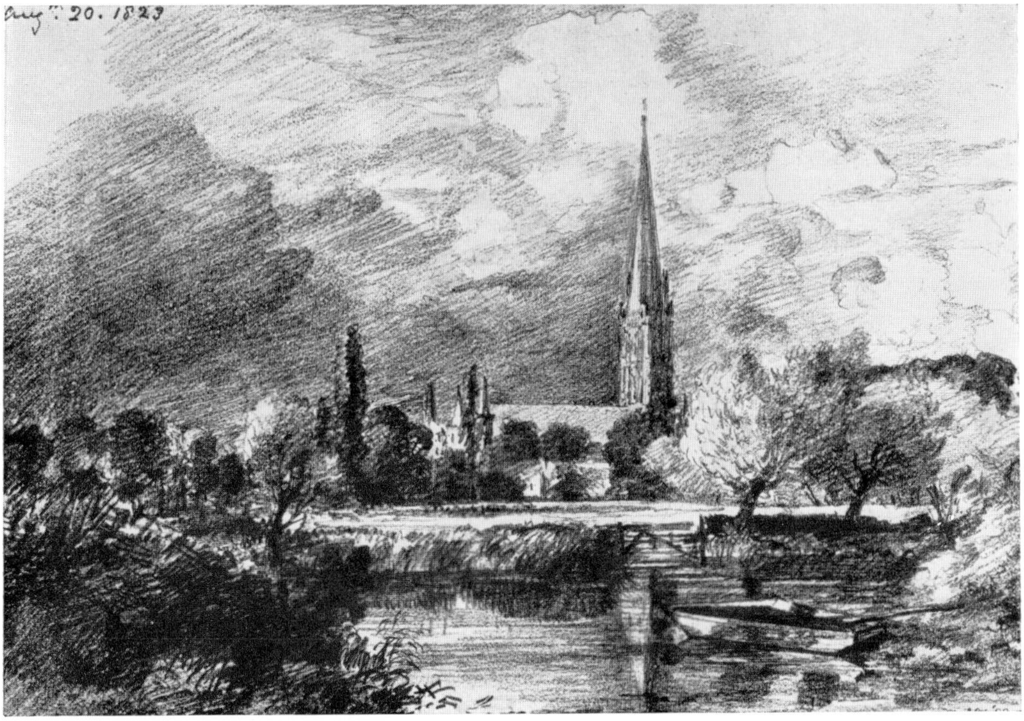

256. Salisbury Cathedral from the river.

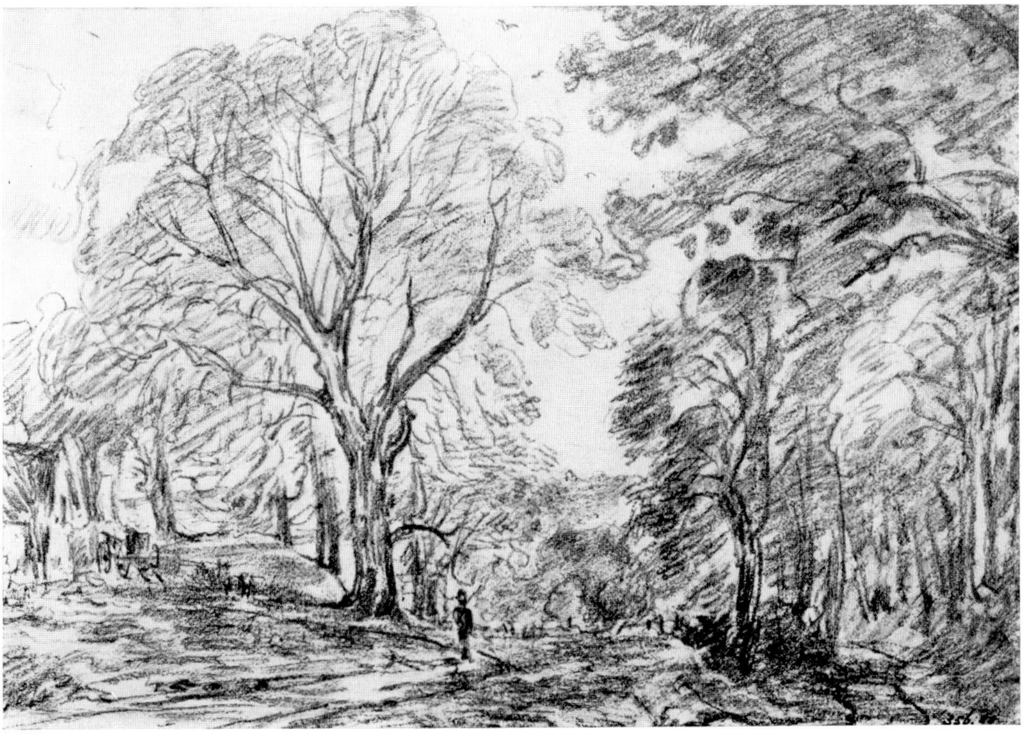

262. Trees at Staunton Harold.

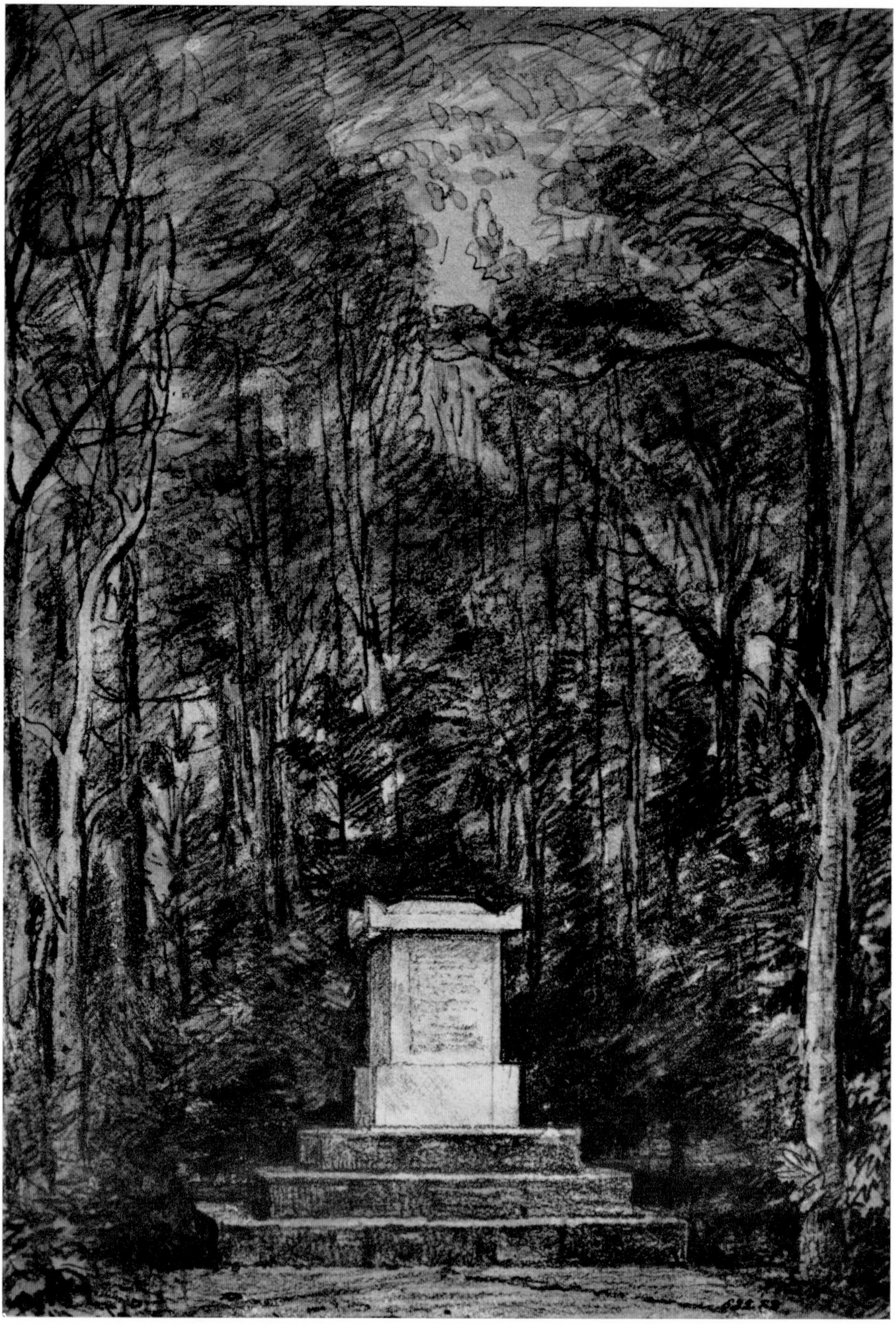

259. Cenotaph to Sir Joshua Reynolds at Coleorton.

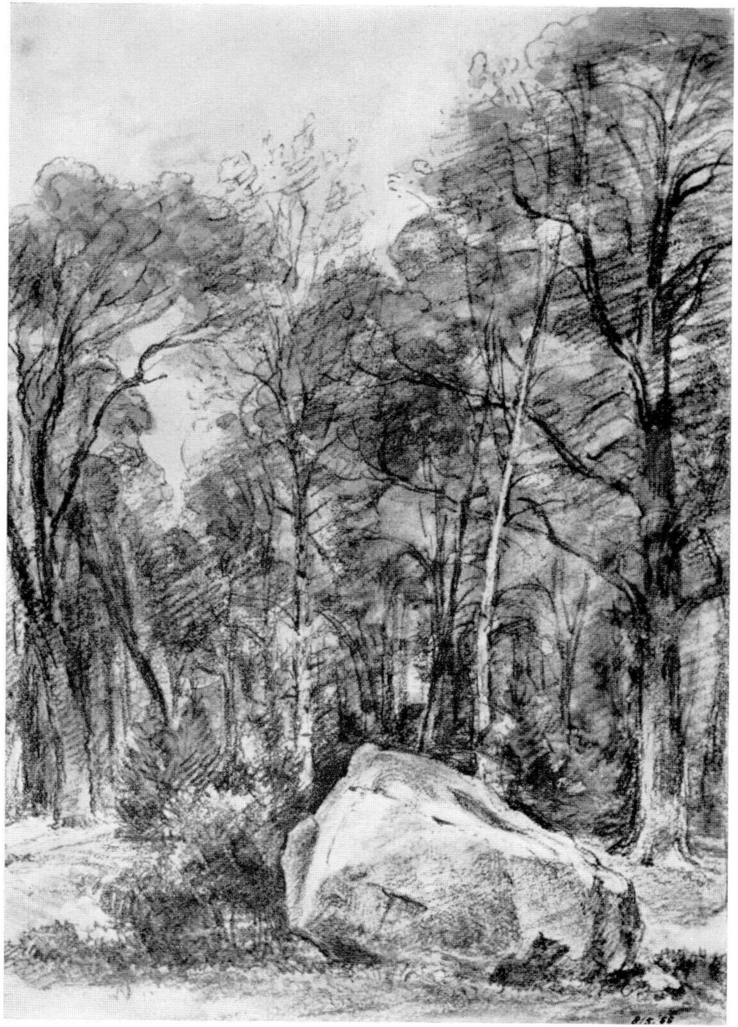

260. A stone dedicated to Richard Wilson at Coleorton.

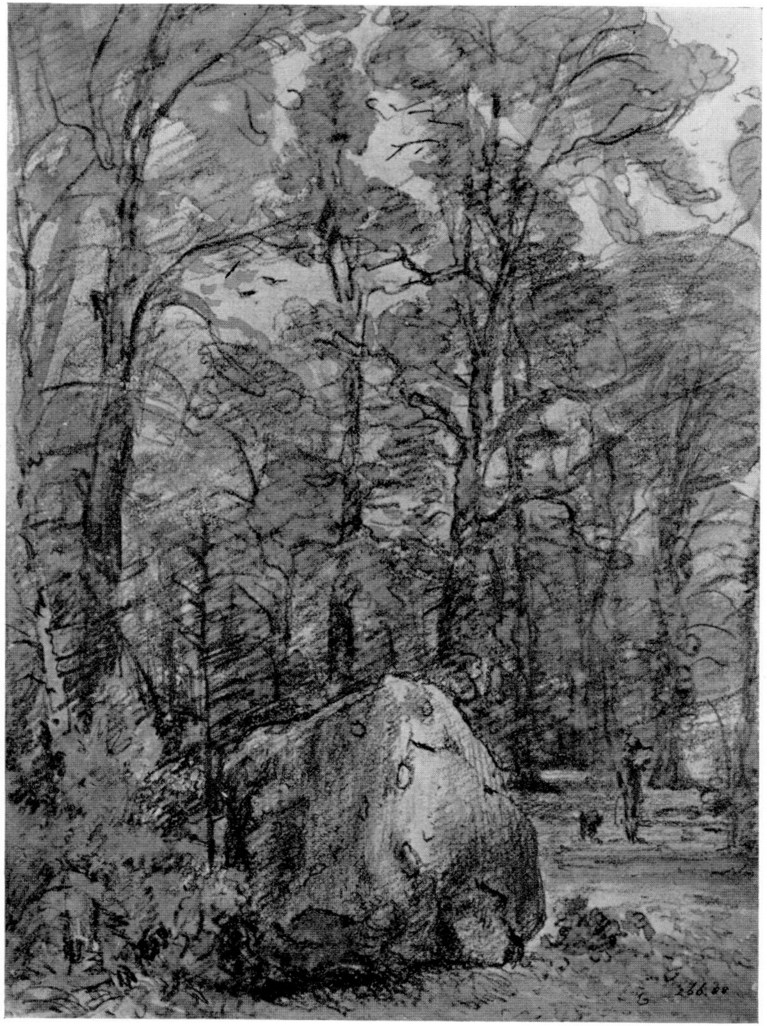

261. A stone in the garden at Coleorton.

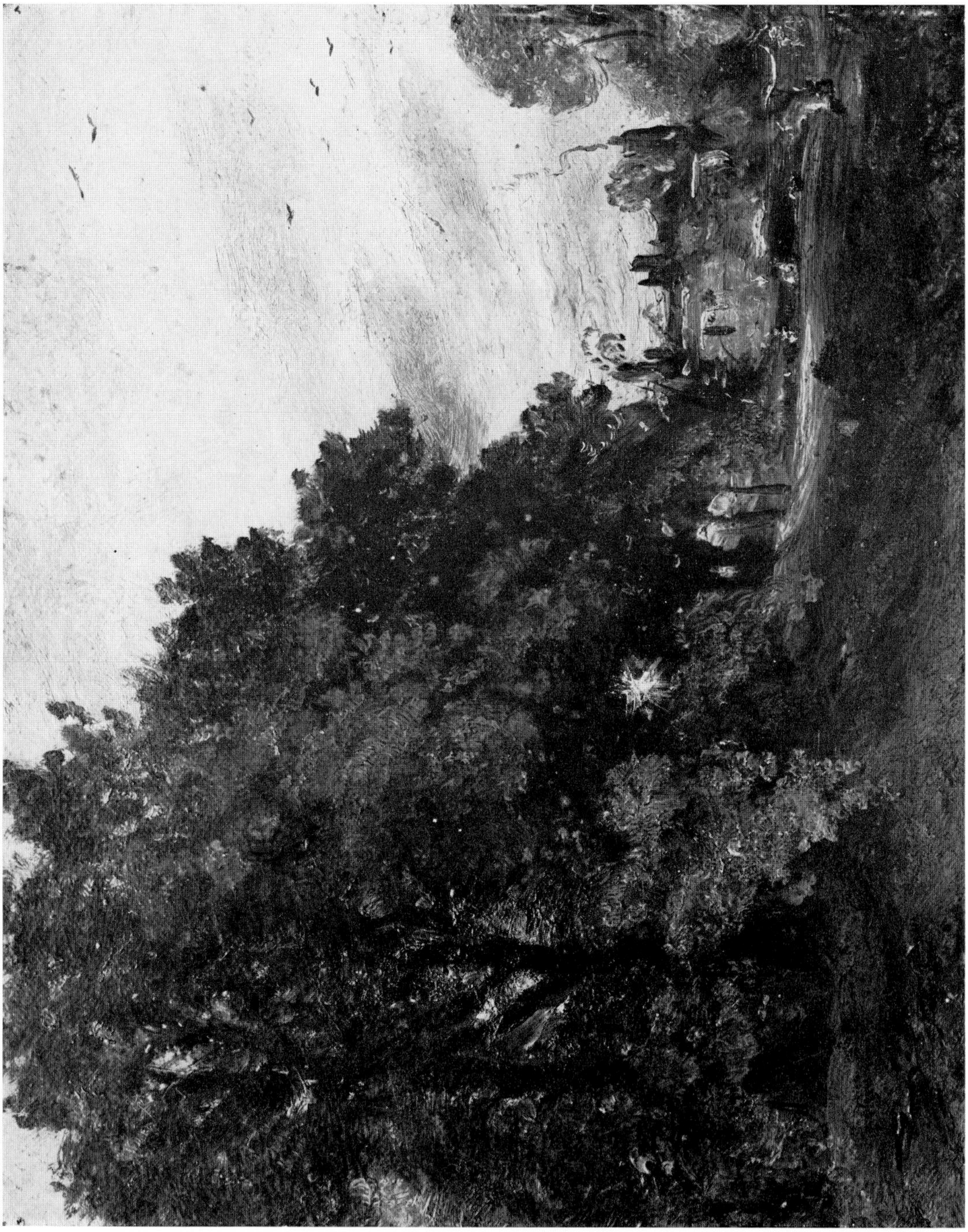

258. Study of a house amidst trees: evening.

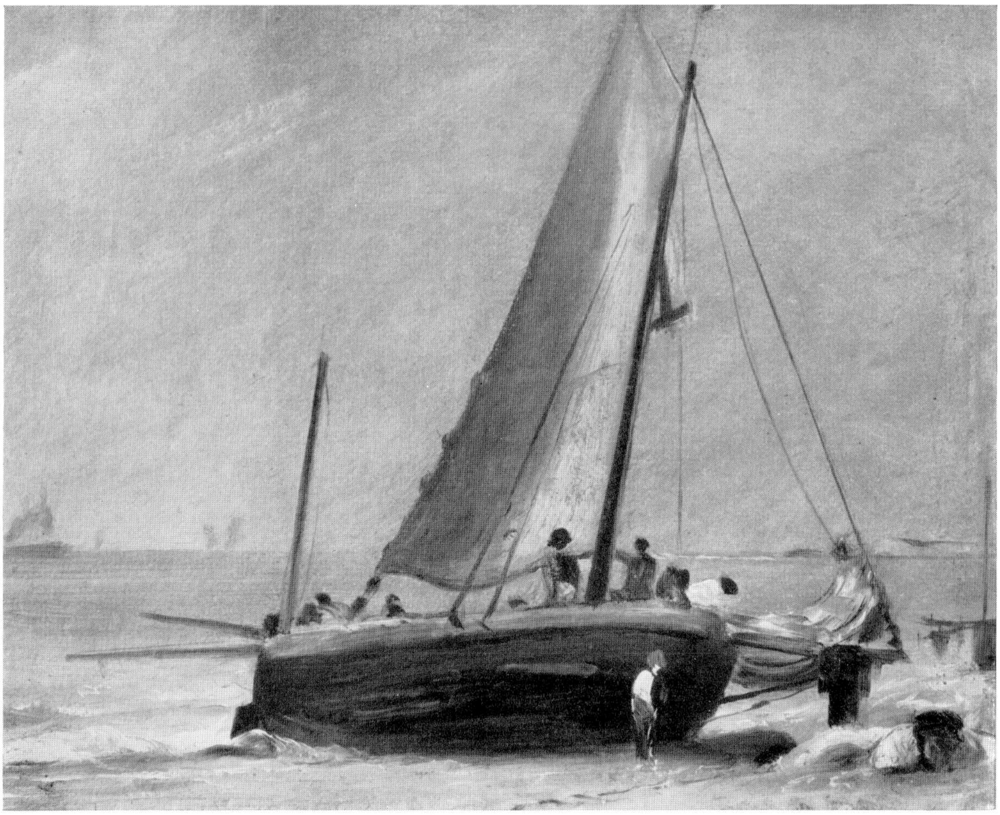

263. Brighton Beach, with fishing boat and crew.

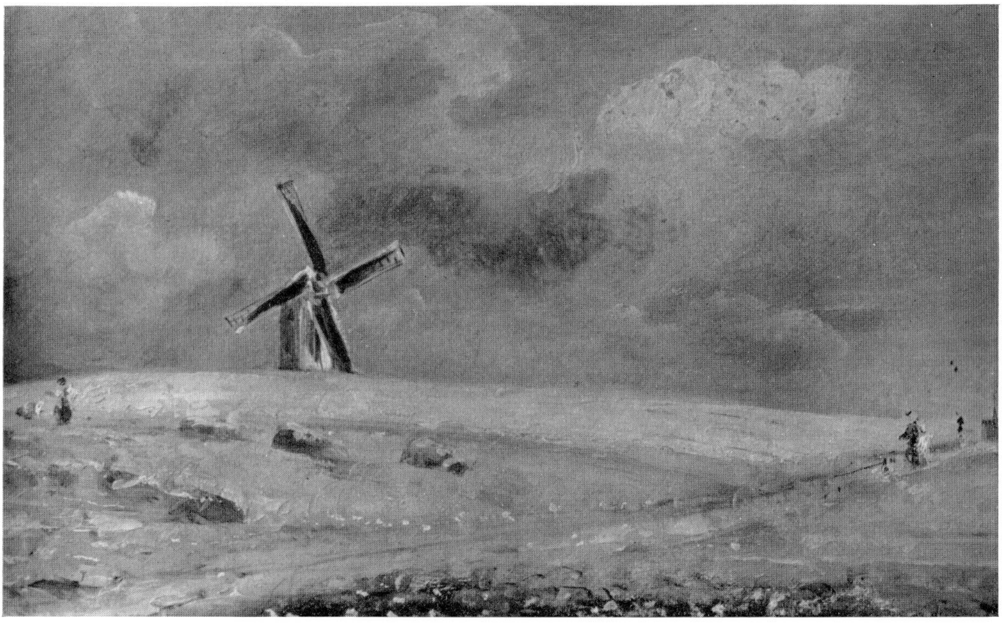

269. A windmill near Brighton.

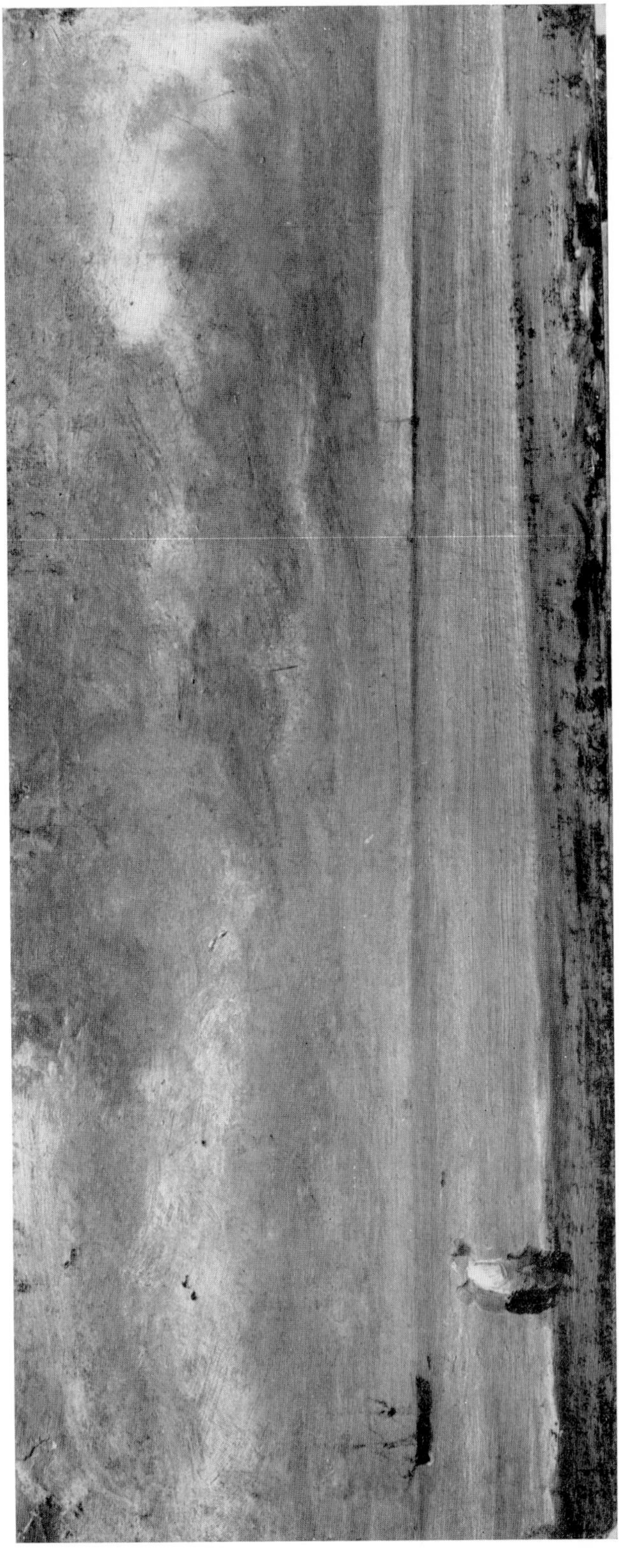

264. Brighton Beach.

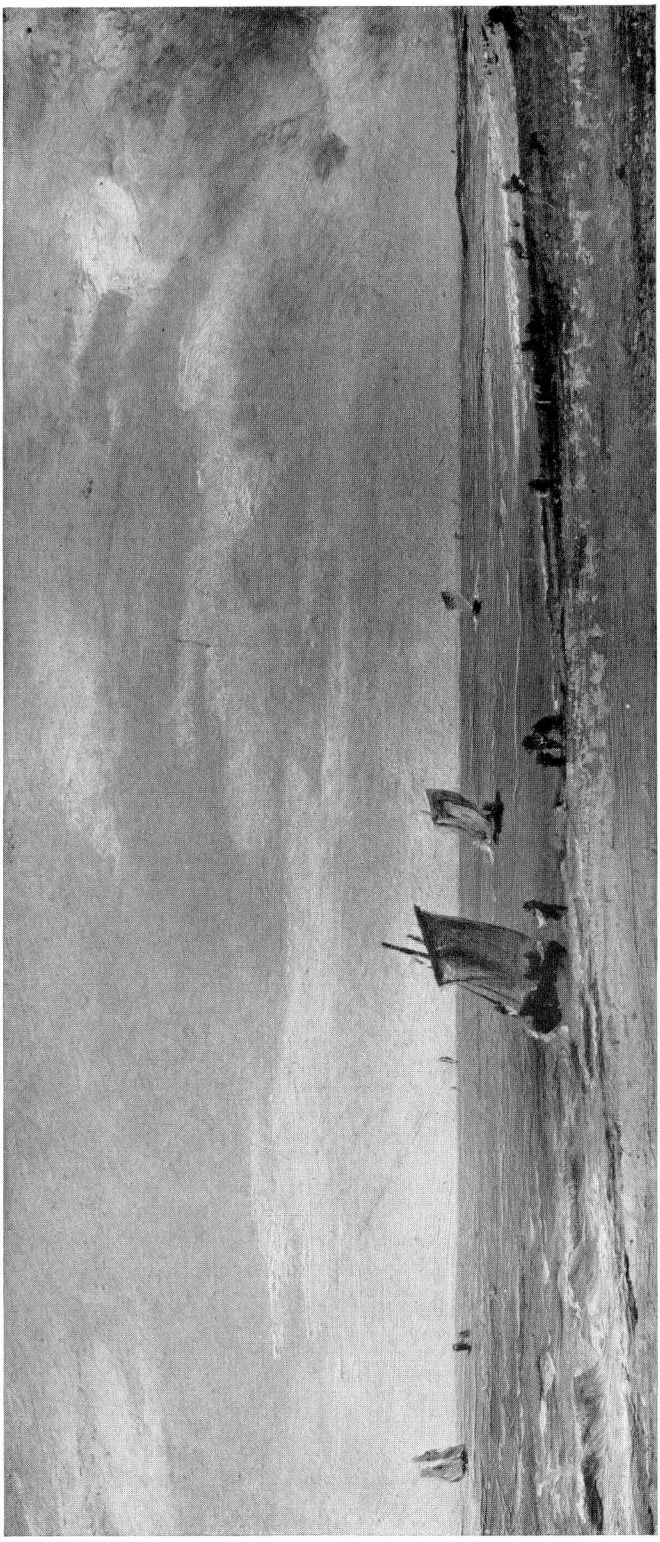

265. Brighton Beach.

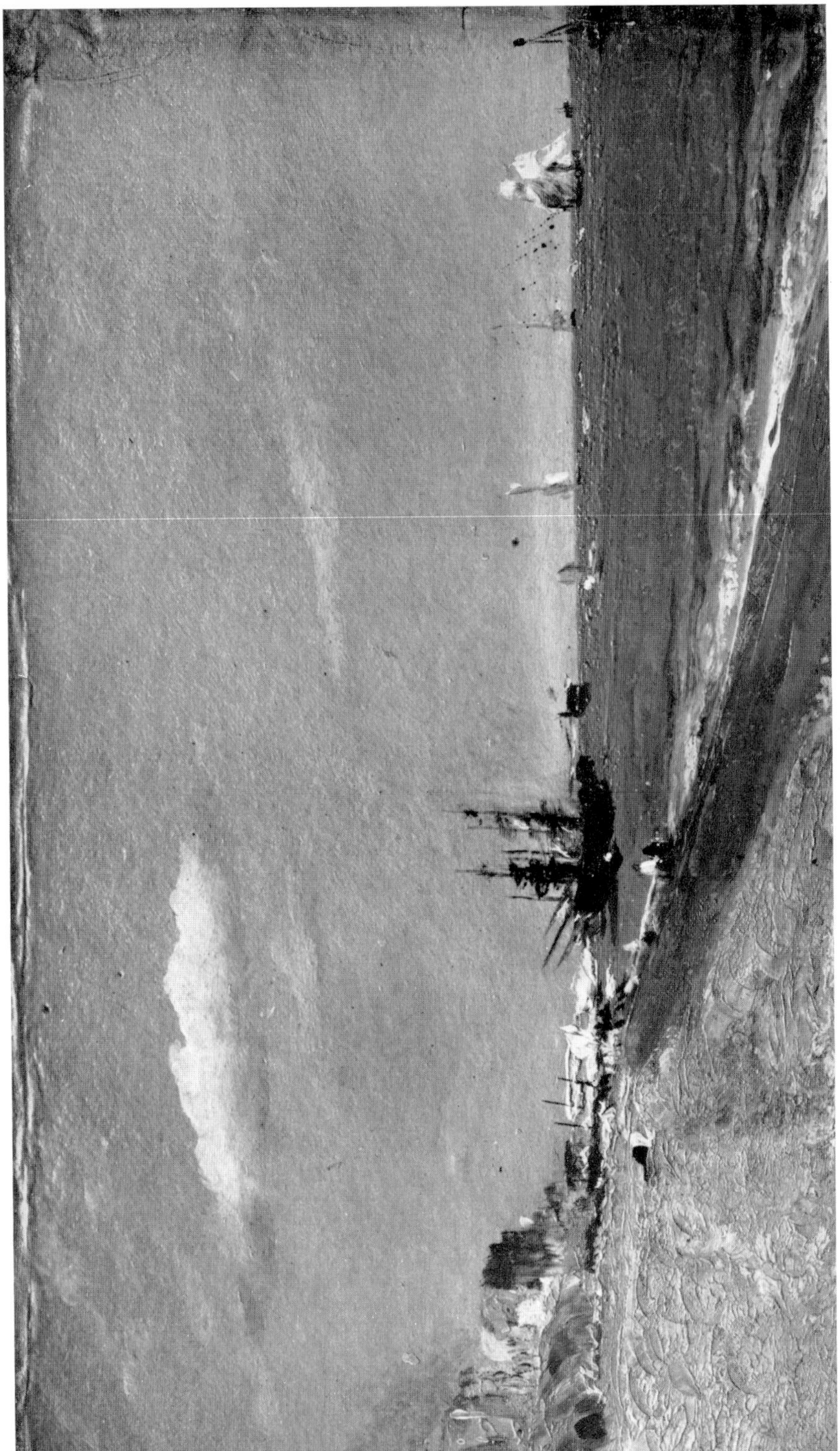

266. Brighton Beach, with colliers.

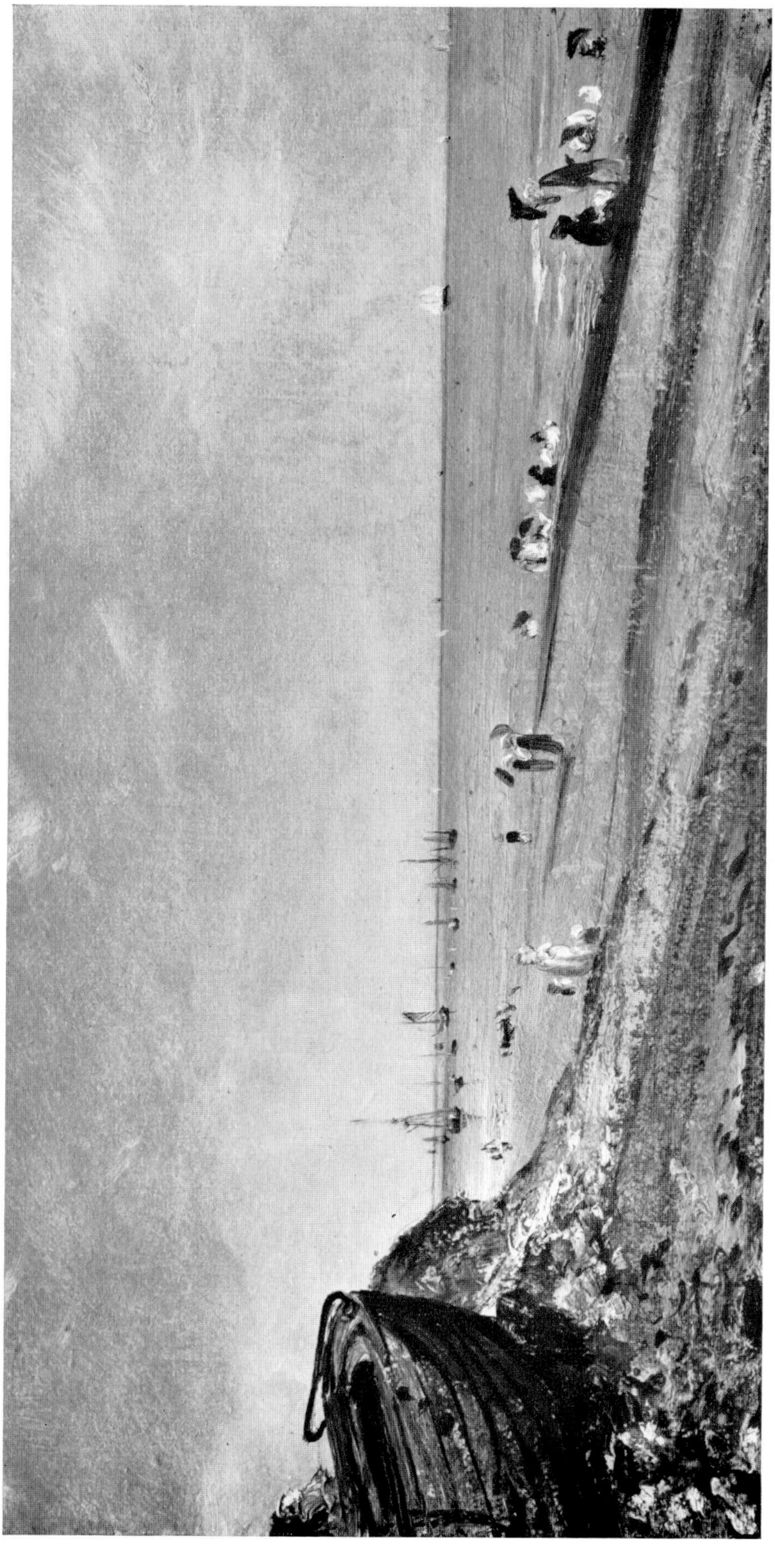

267. Brighton Beach.

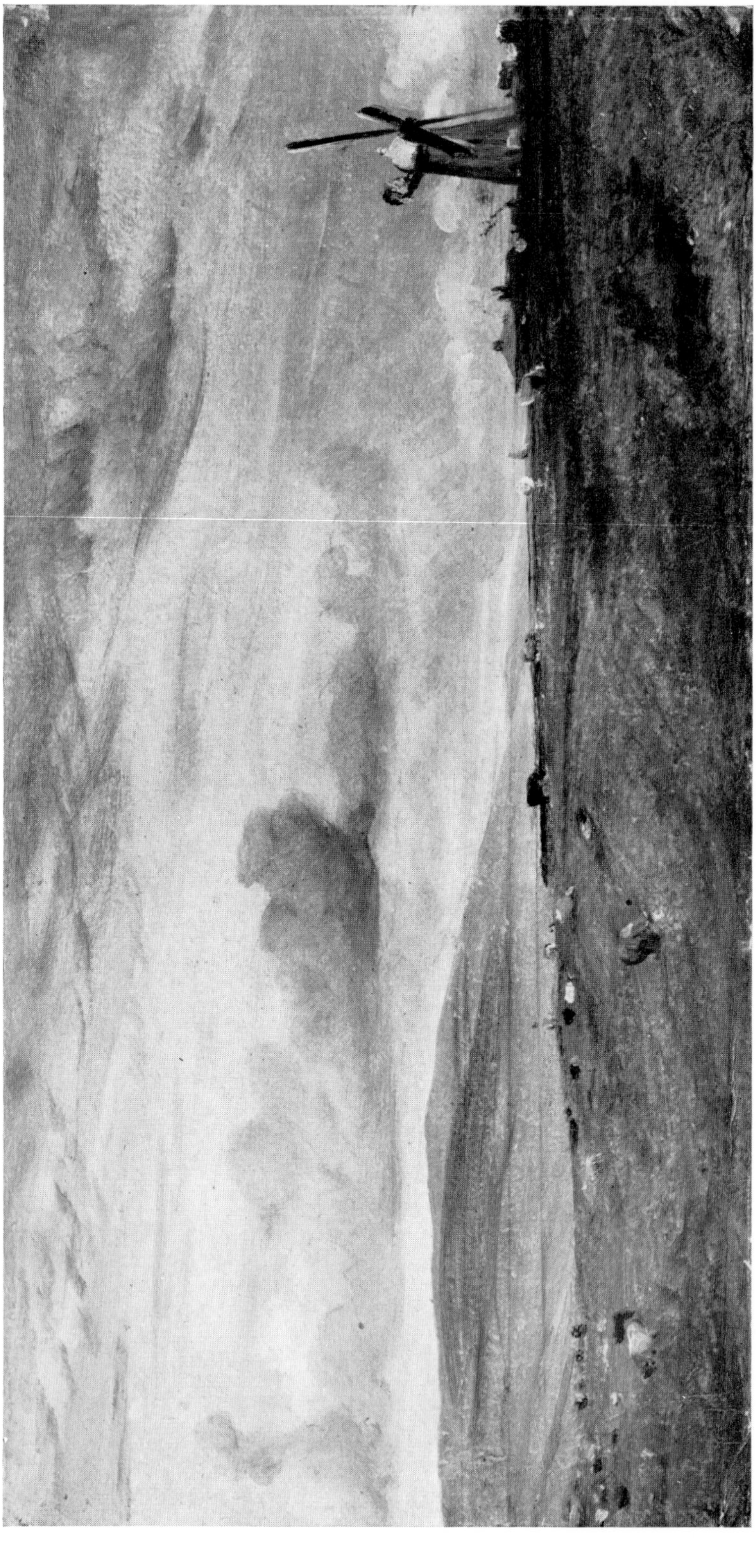

268. A windmill near Brighton.

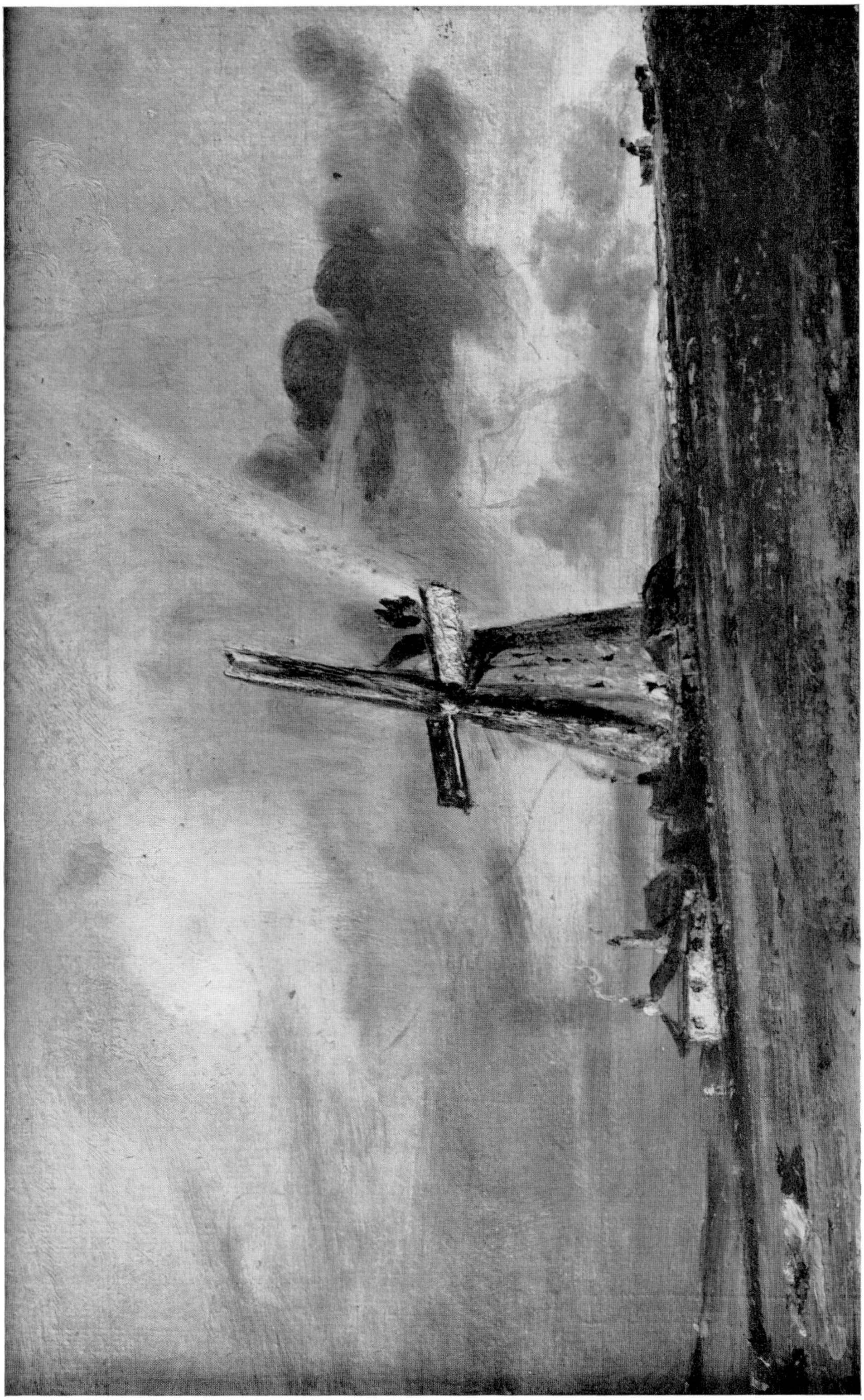

272. A windmill among houses, with a rainbow.

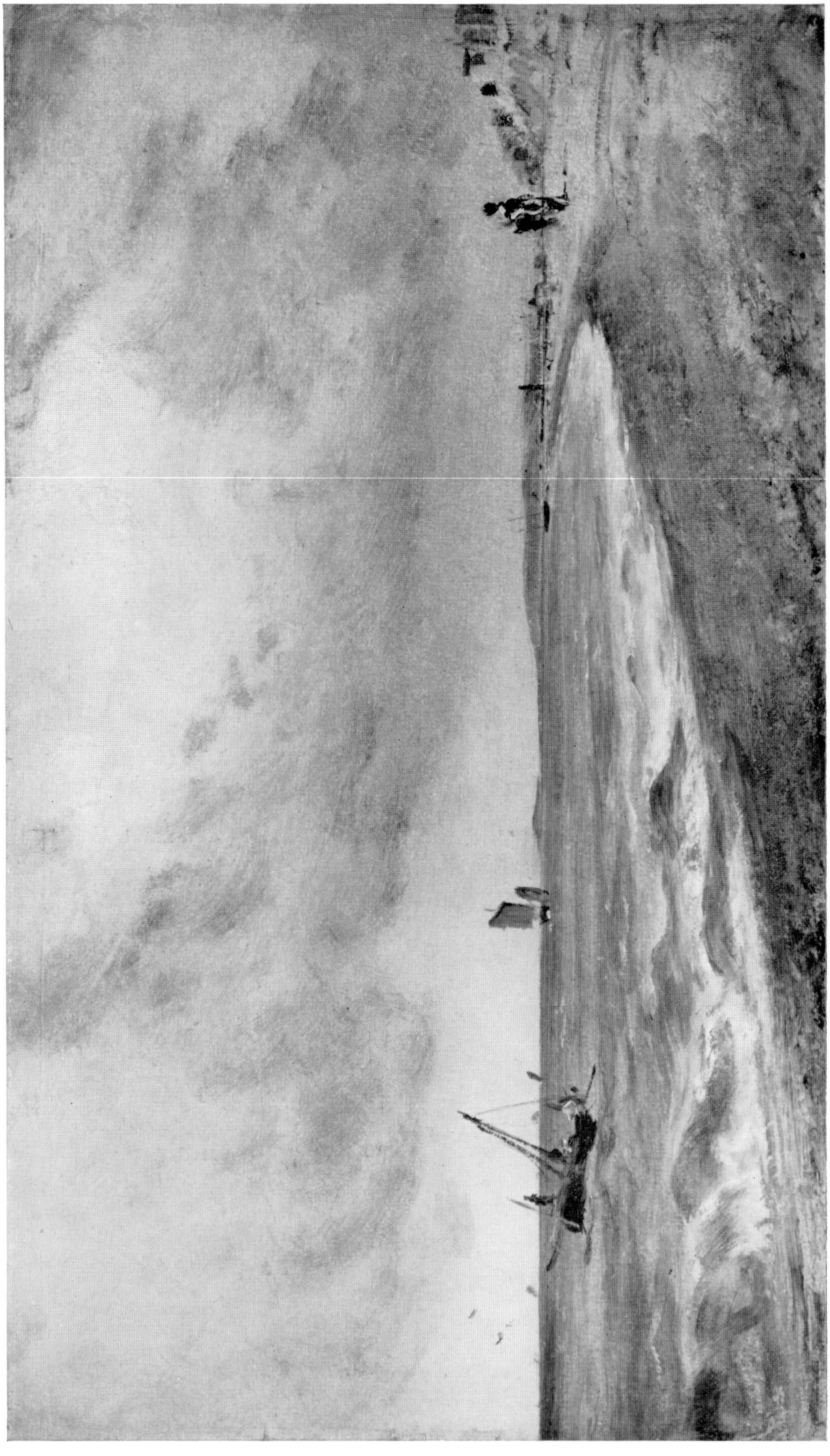

270. Hove Beach, with fishing boats.

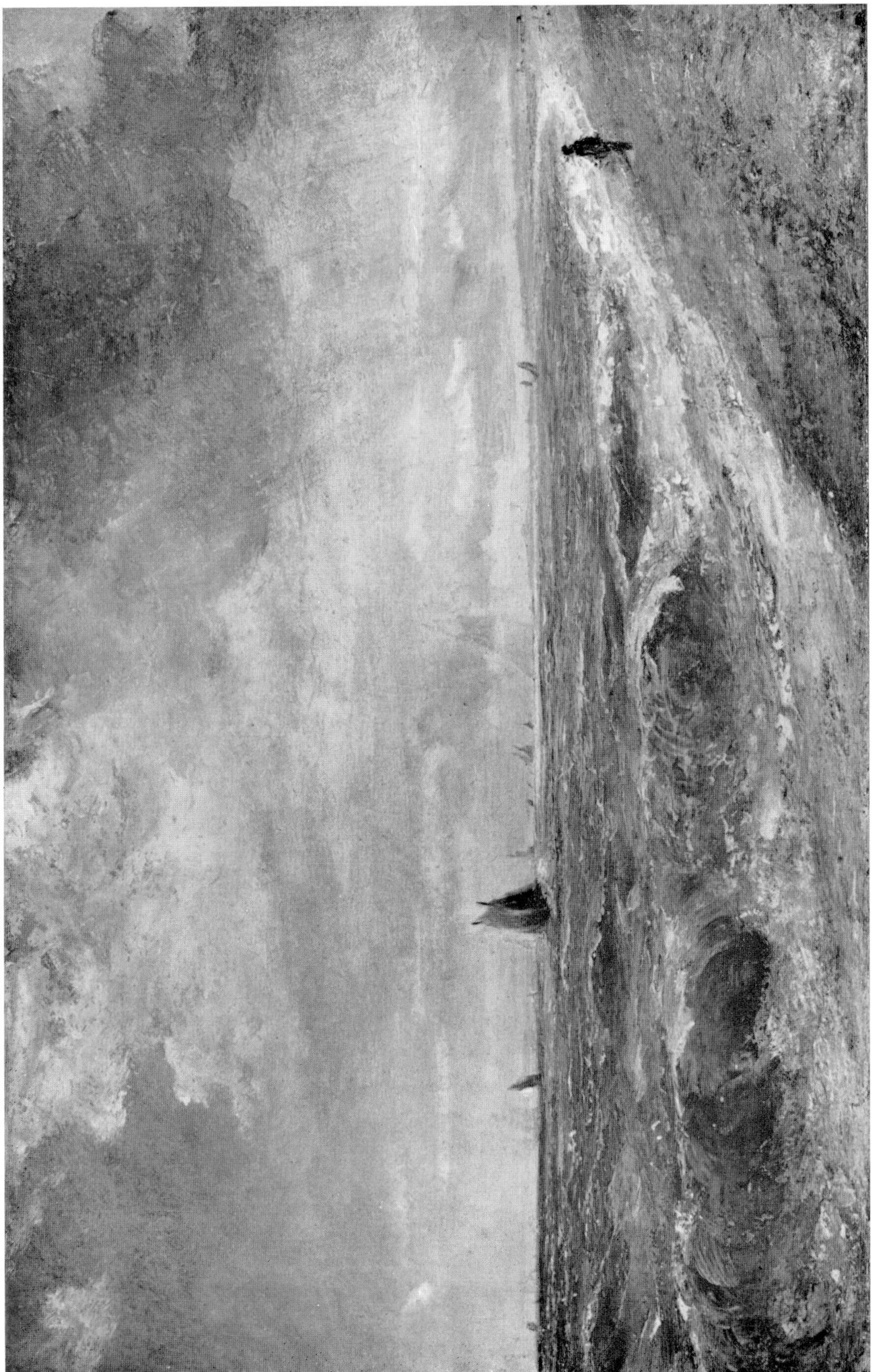

271. Hove Beach.

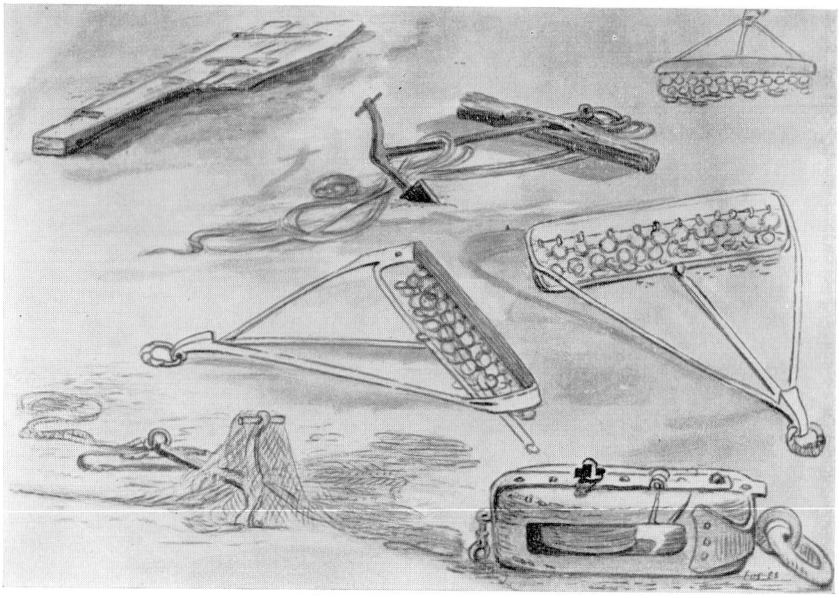

273. Studies of fishing gear at Brighton.

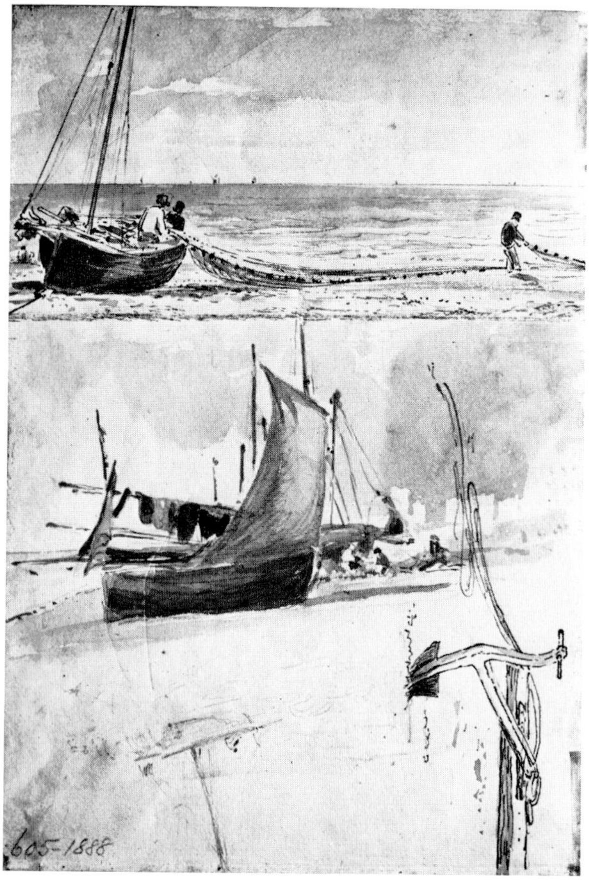

273a. Studies of the beach at Brighton.

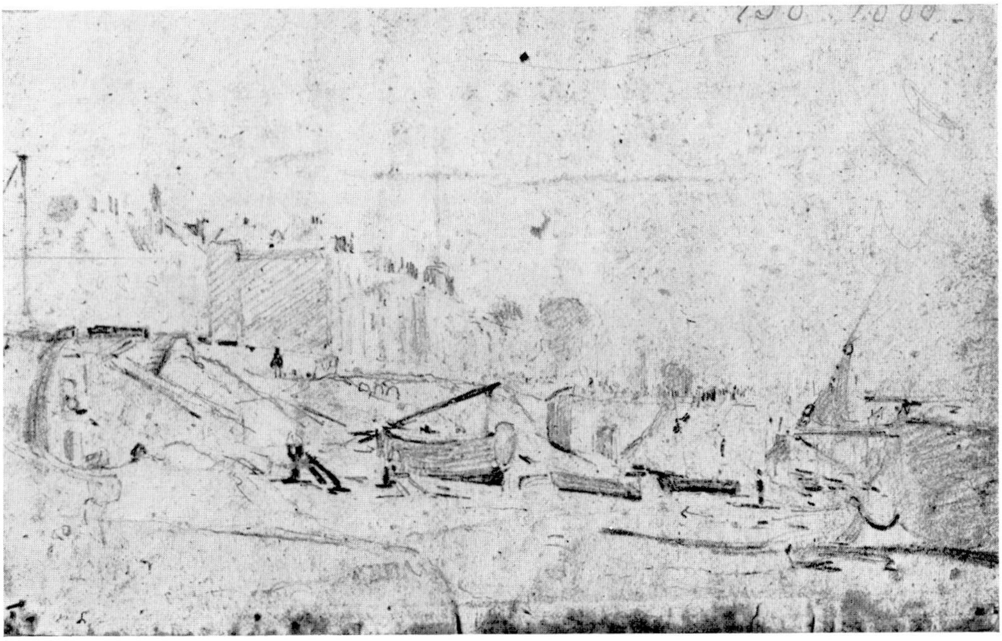

269a. Brighton Beach.

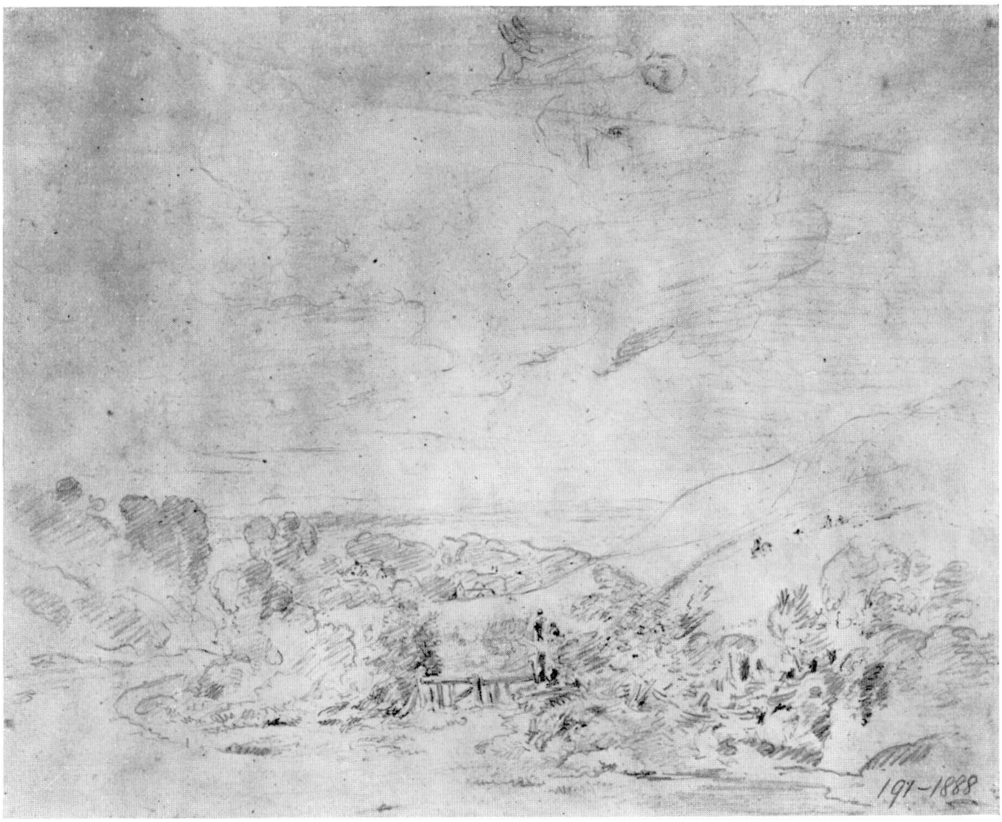

279a. The Devil's Dyke.

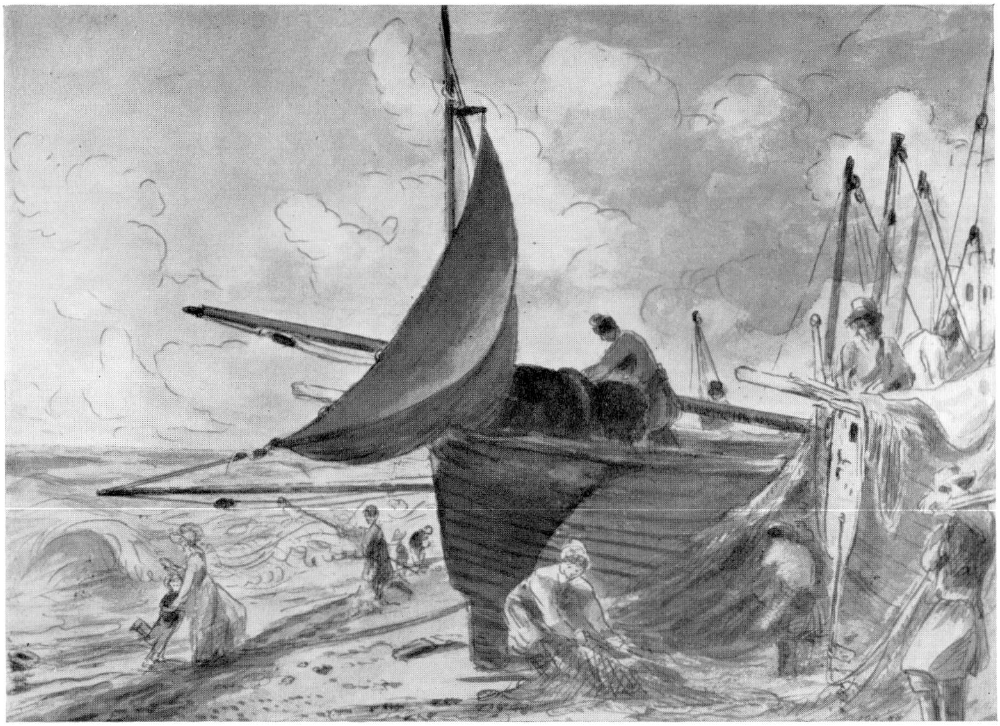

274. Scene on the beach at Brighton.

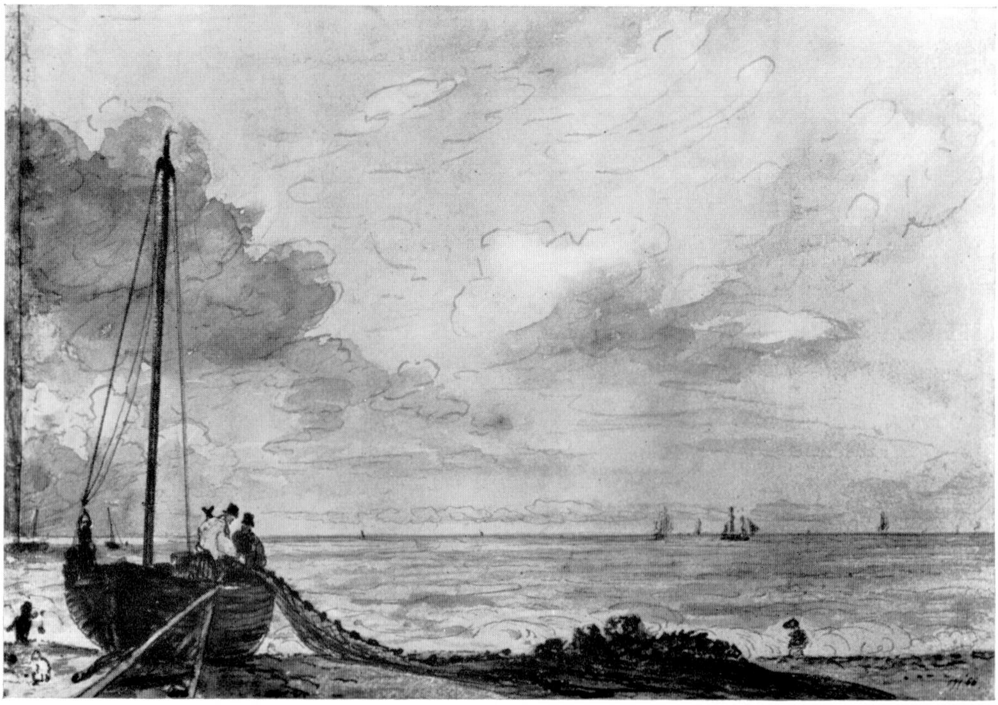

275. Brighton Beach: fishing boat with net.

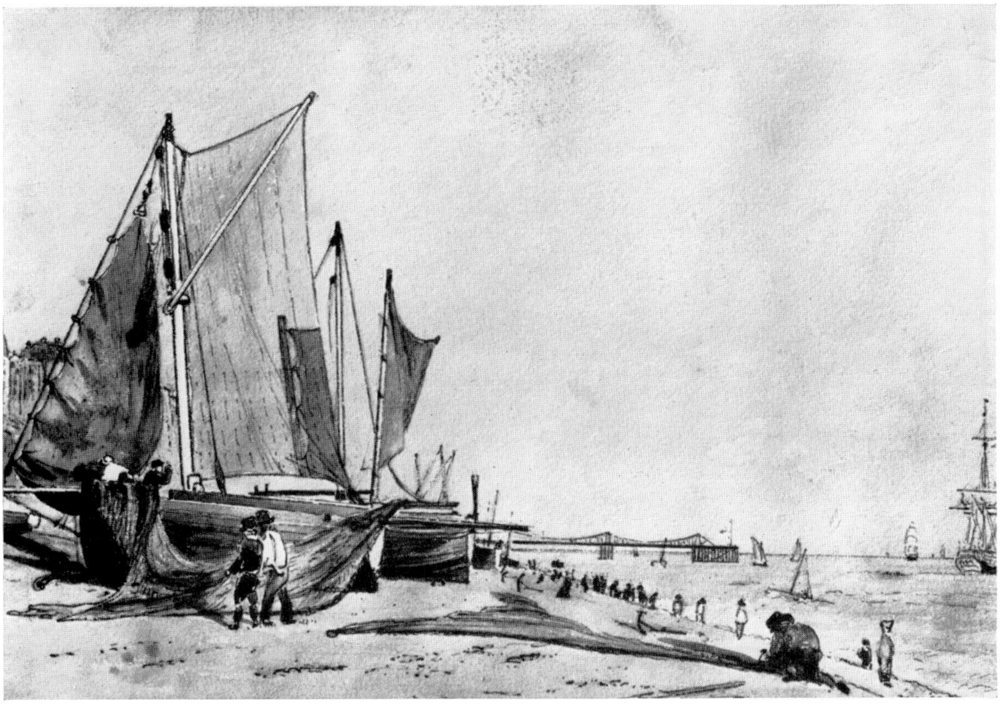

276. Brighton Beach, with fishing boats and the Chain Pier.

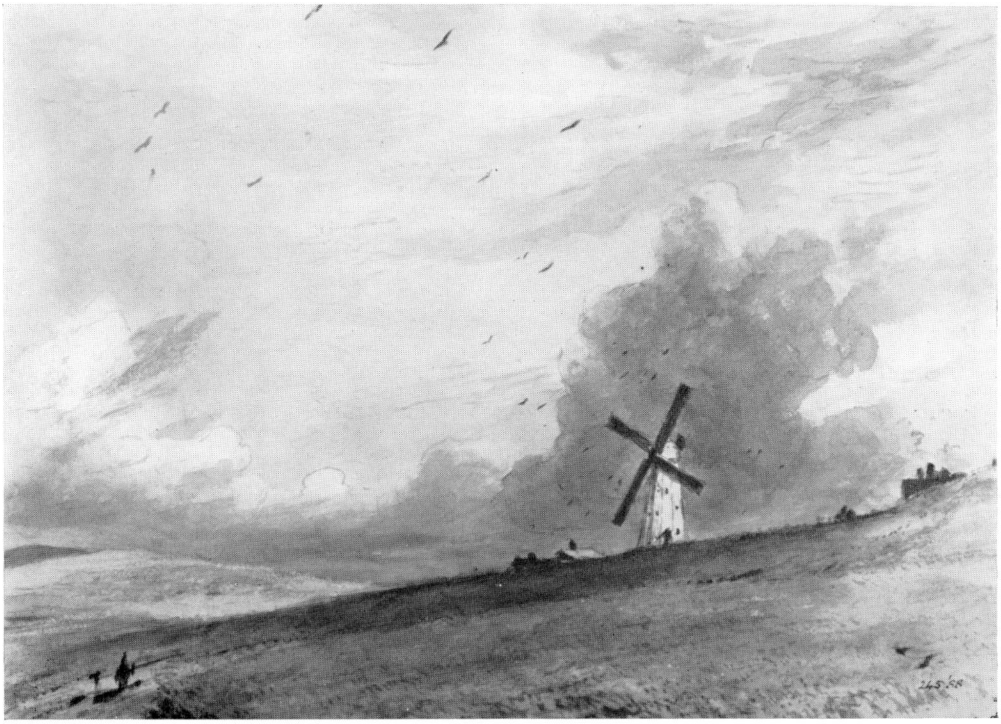

277. A windmill, probably on the Downs near Brighton.

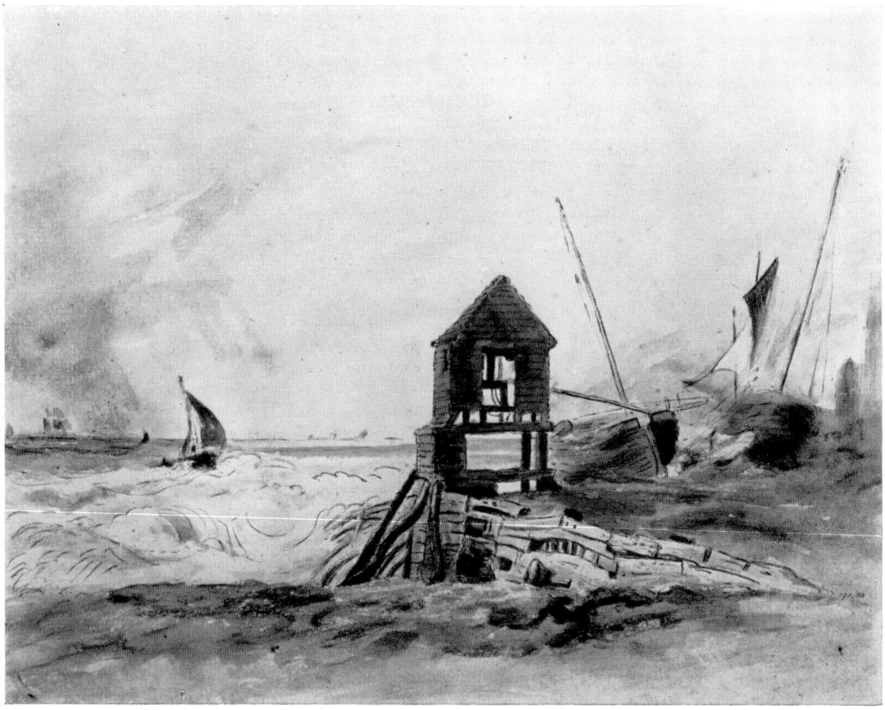

279. Coast scene, Brighton.

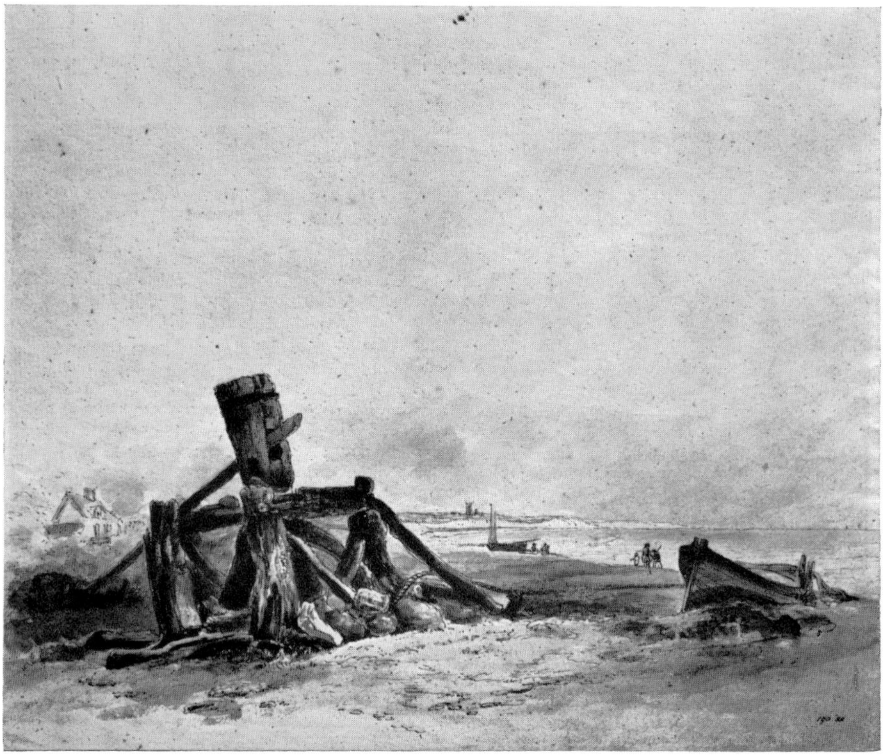

280. Coast scene, probably near Brighton.

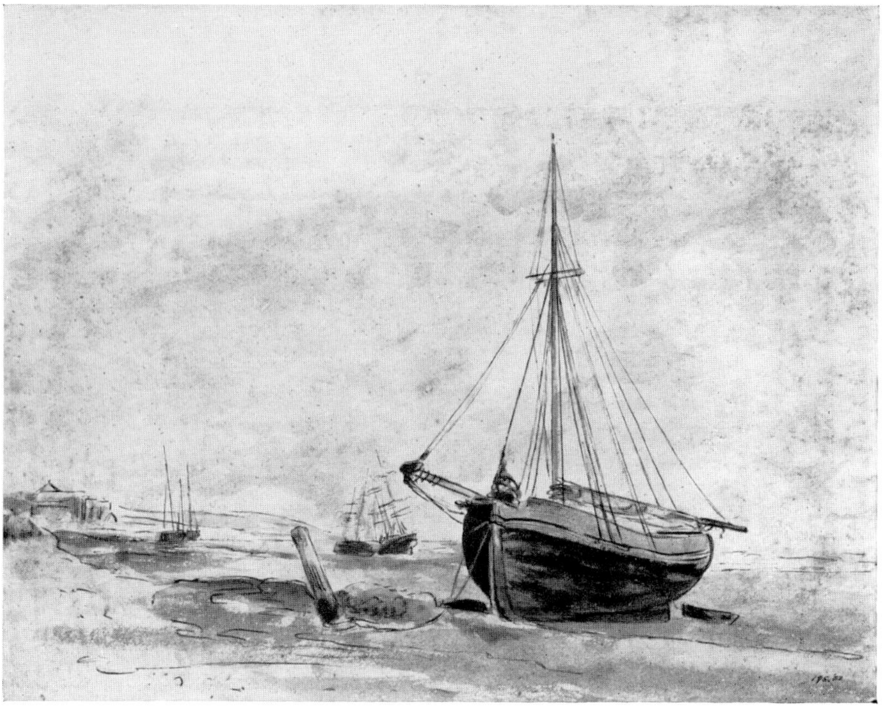

281. Coast scene with shipping, probably near Brighton.

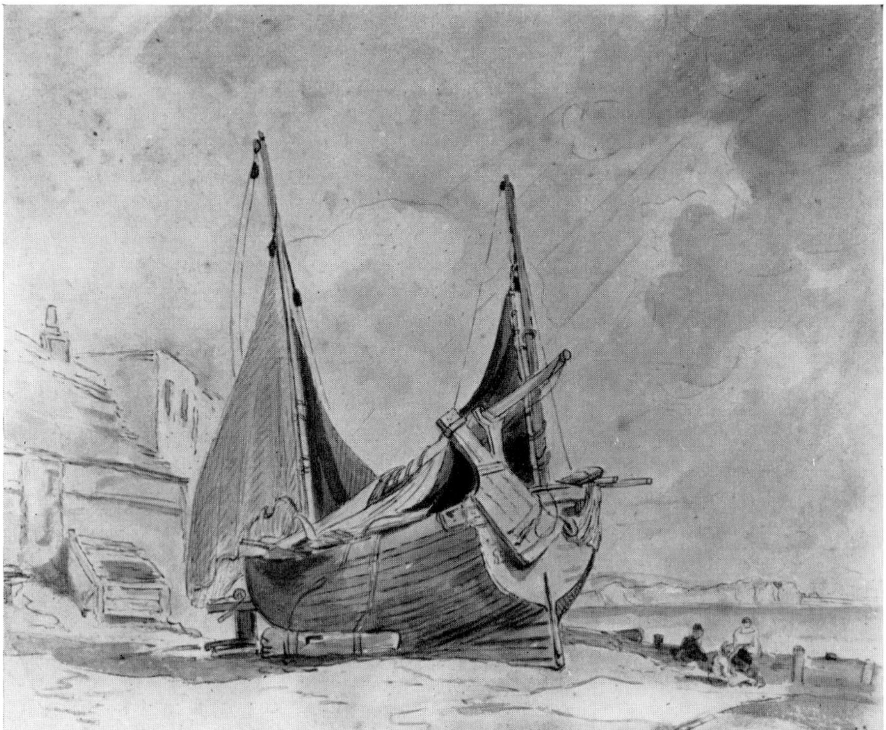

282. Coast scene, probably near Brighton.

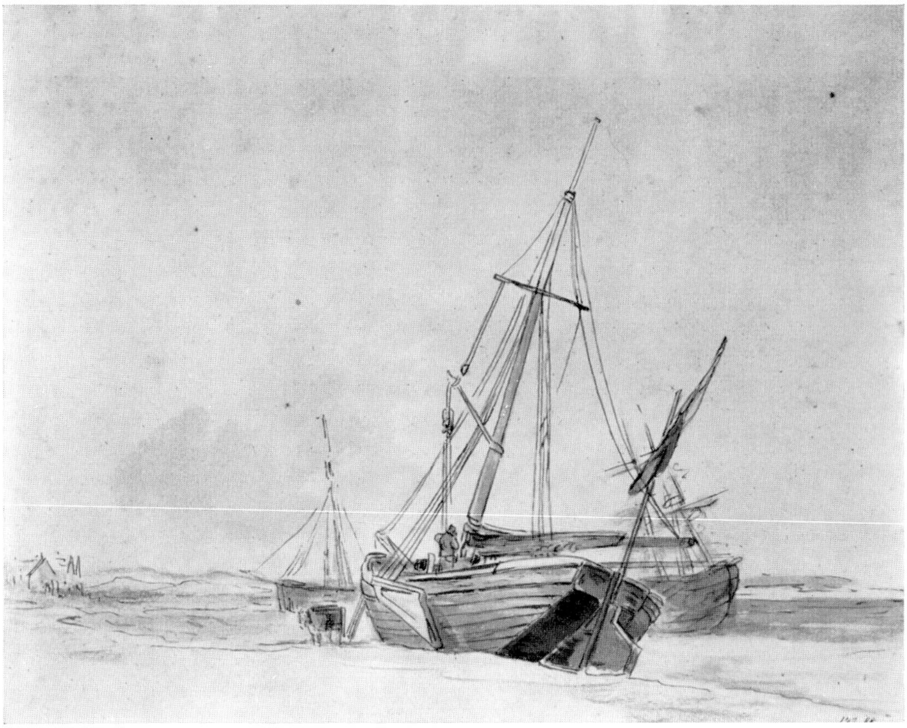

283. Coast scene, probably near Brighton.

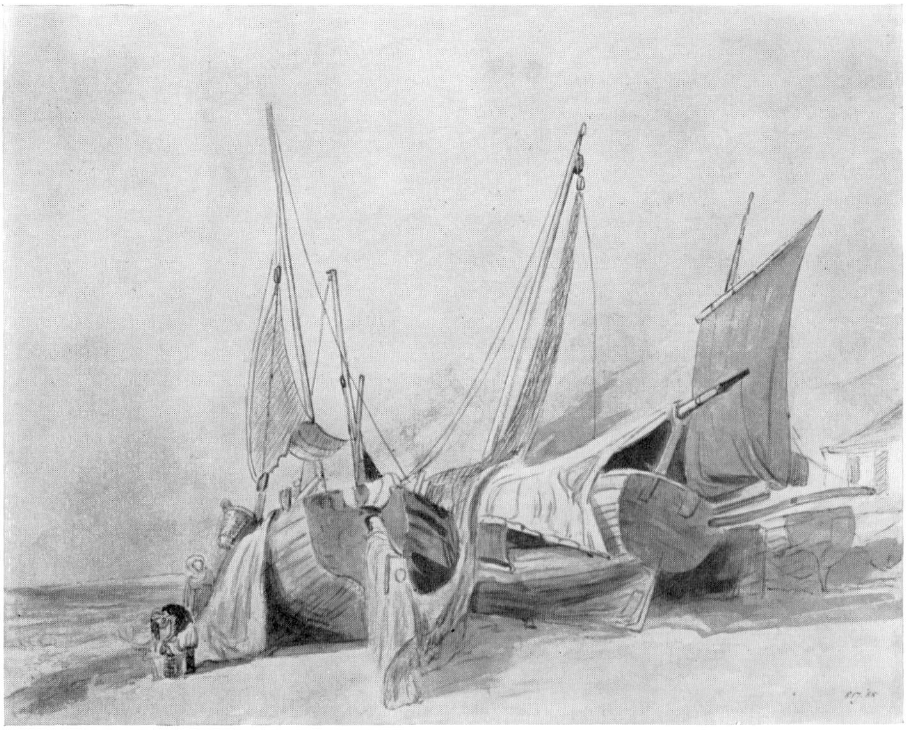

284. Fishing boats, probably at Brighton.

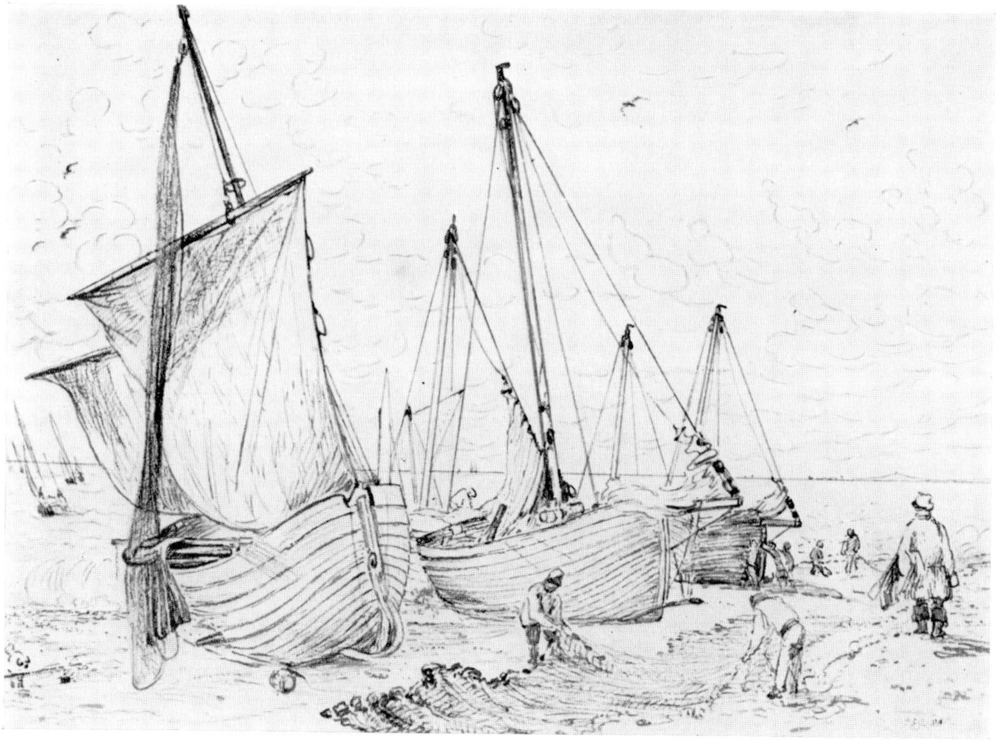

278. Beach scene, with boats and fishermen.

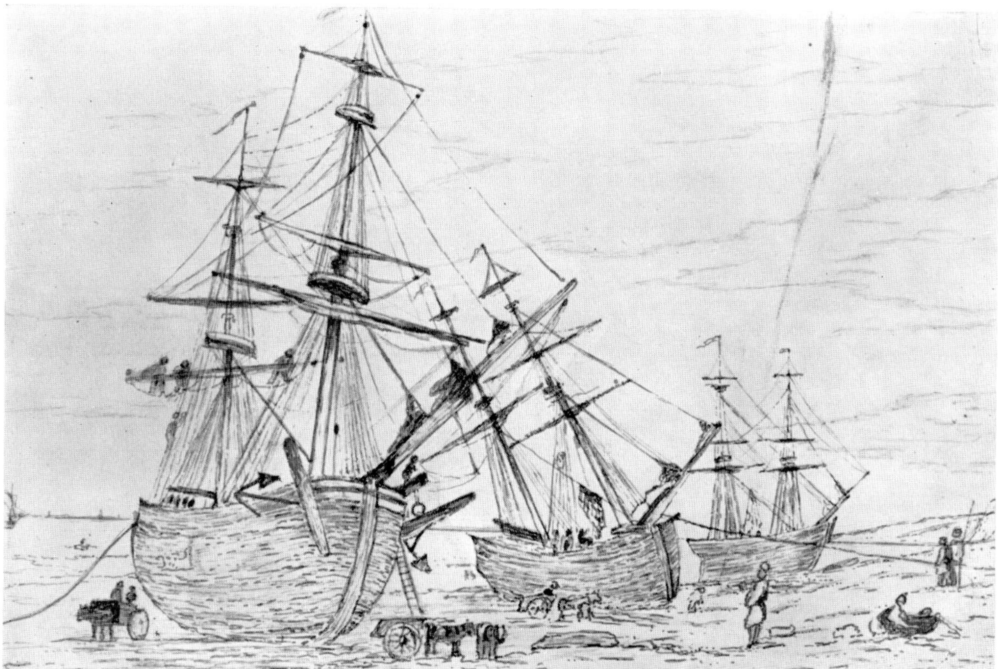

285. Coast scene, perhaps near Brighton.

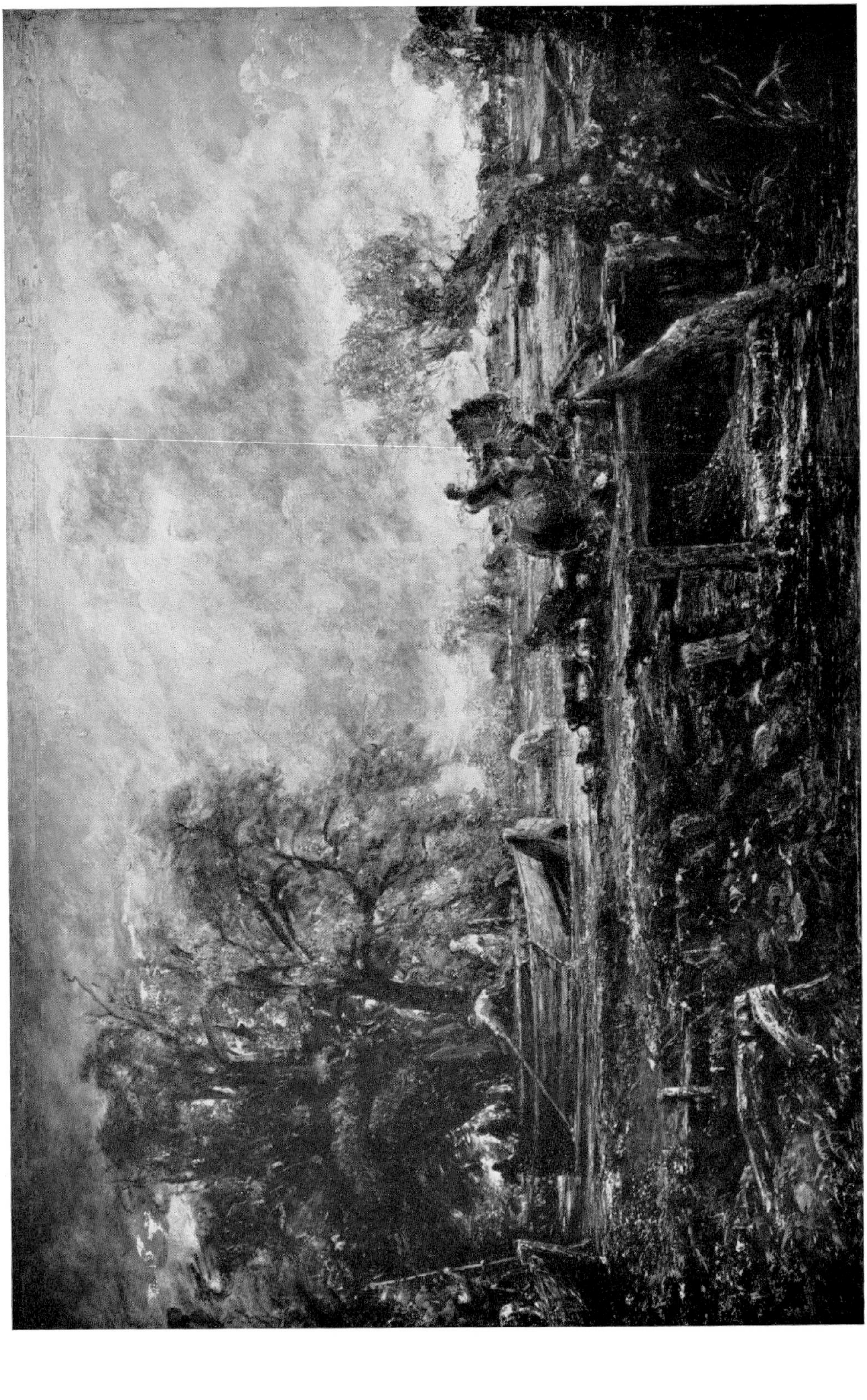

286. Study for 'The Leaping Horse'.

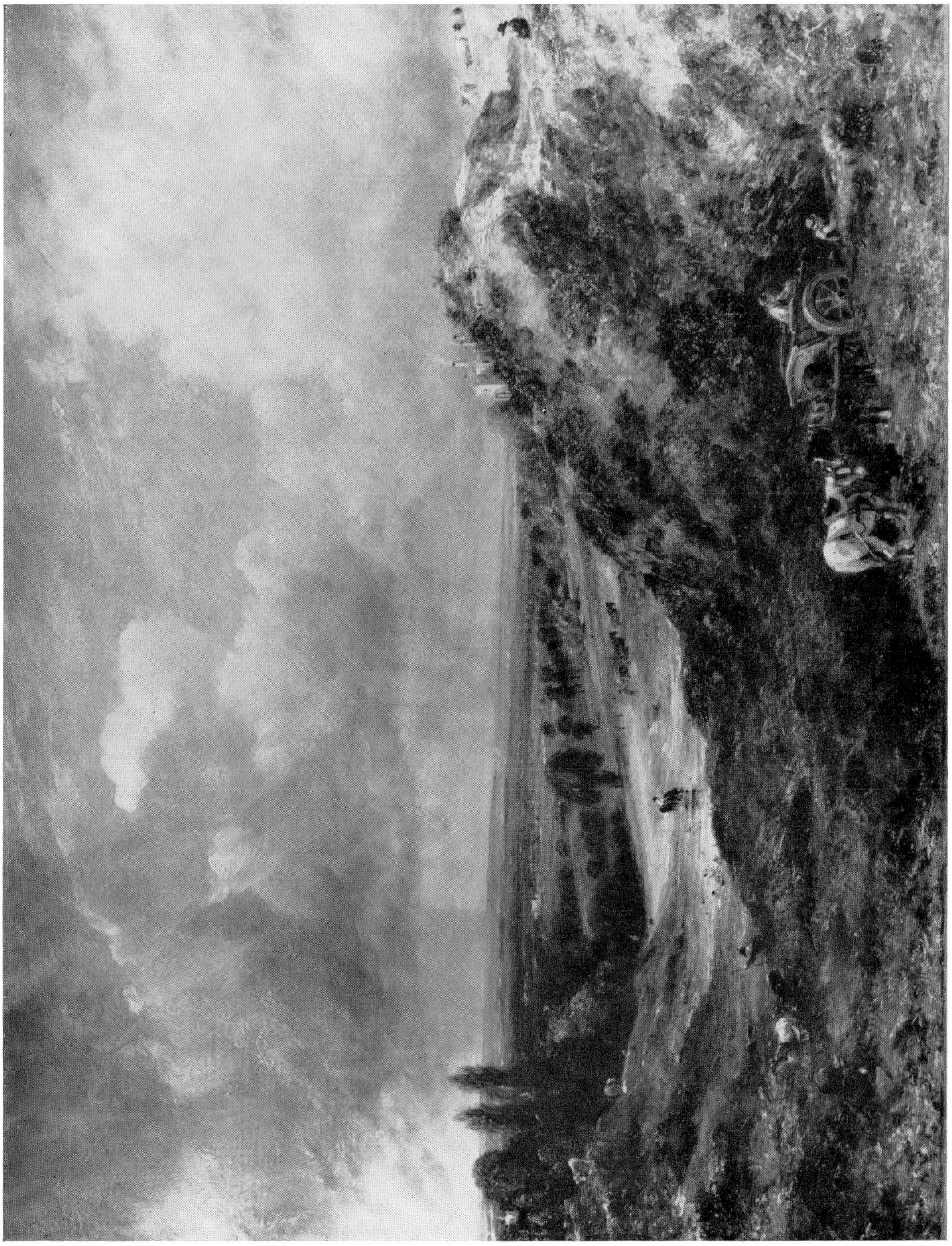

301. Hampstead Heath: Branch Hill Pond.

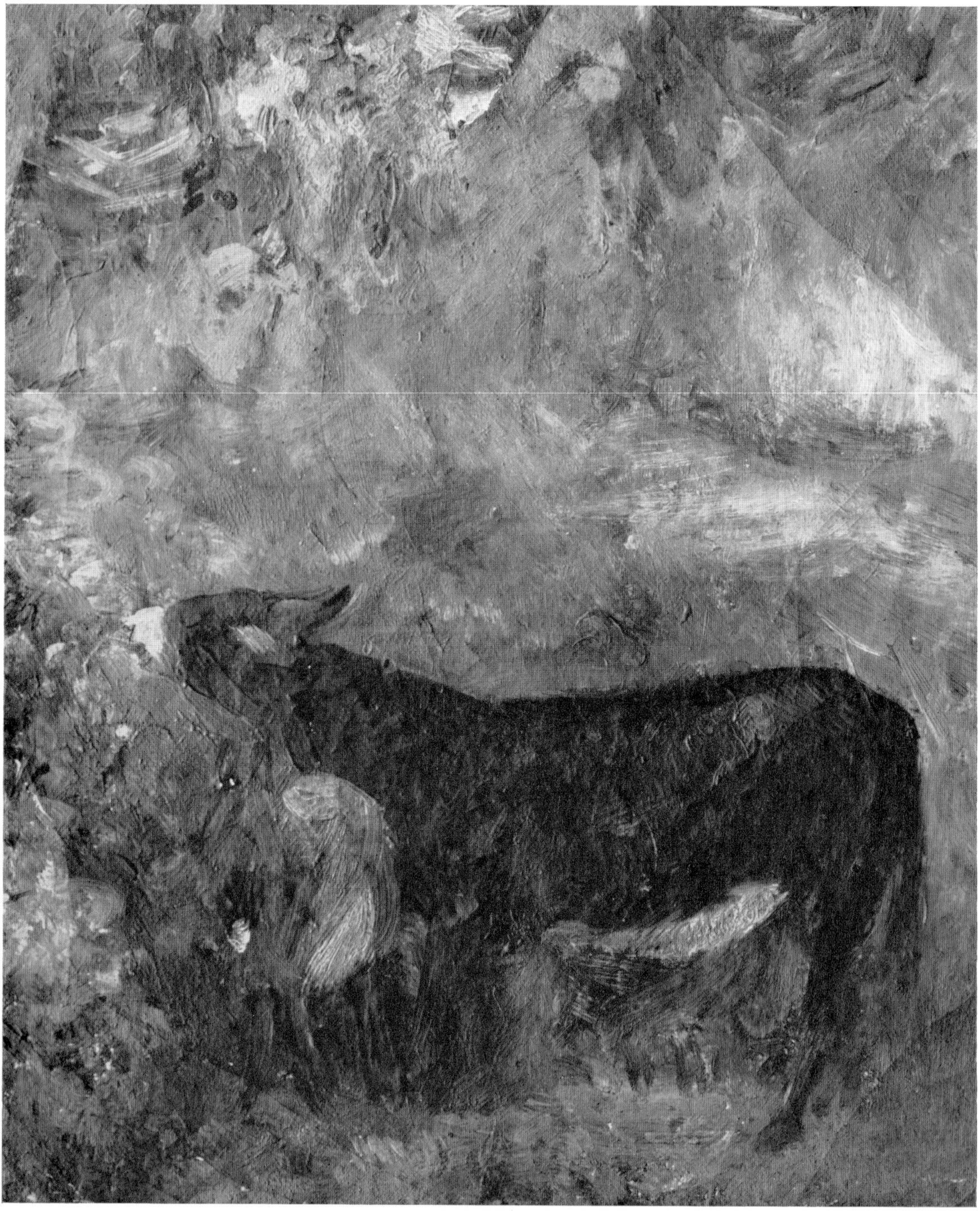

287. A donkey with a foal: study for 'The Cornfield'.

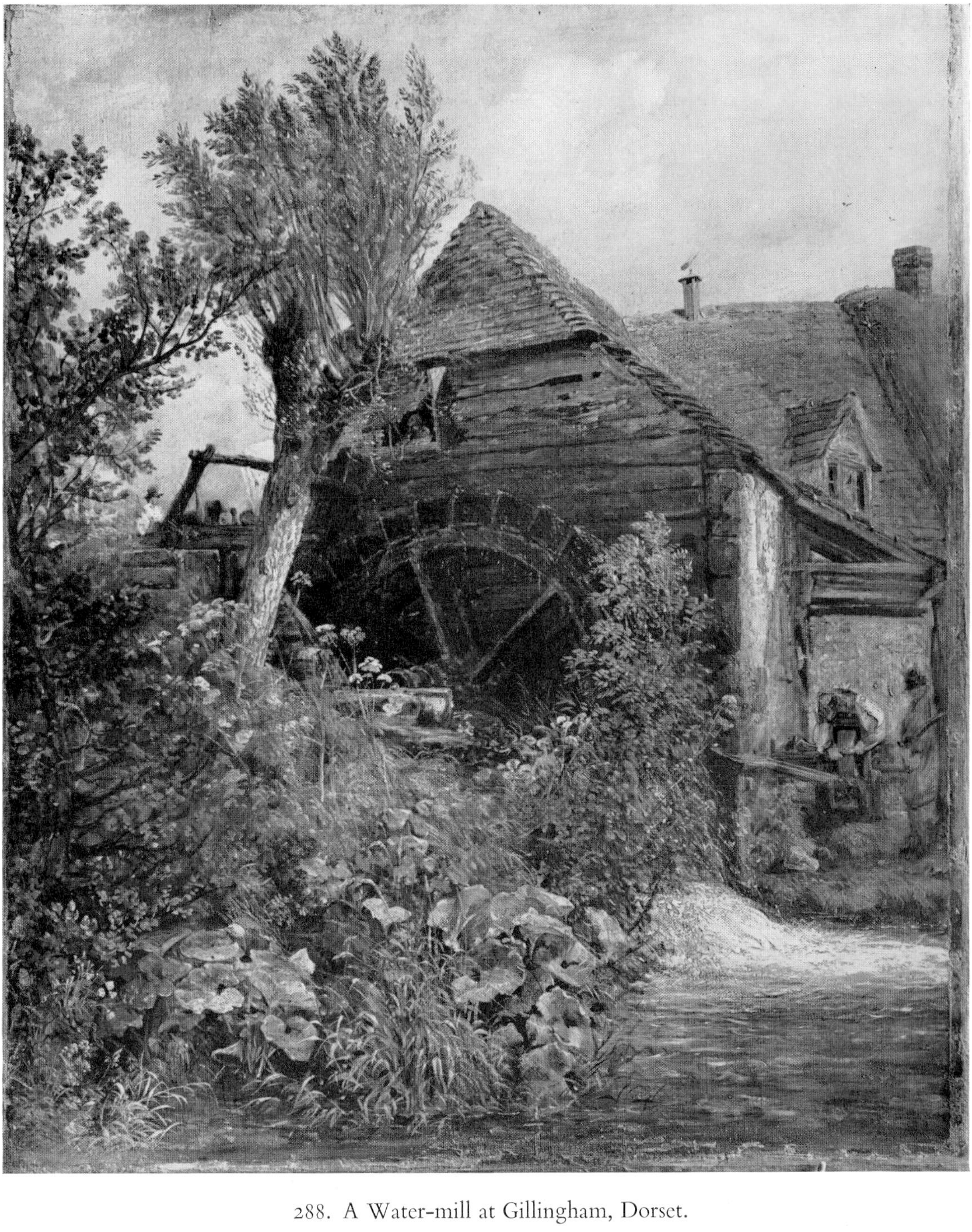

288. A Water-mill at Gillingham, Dorset.

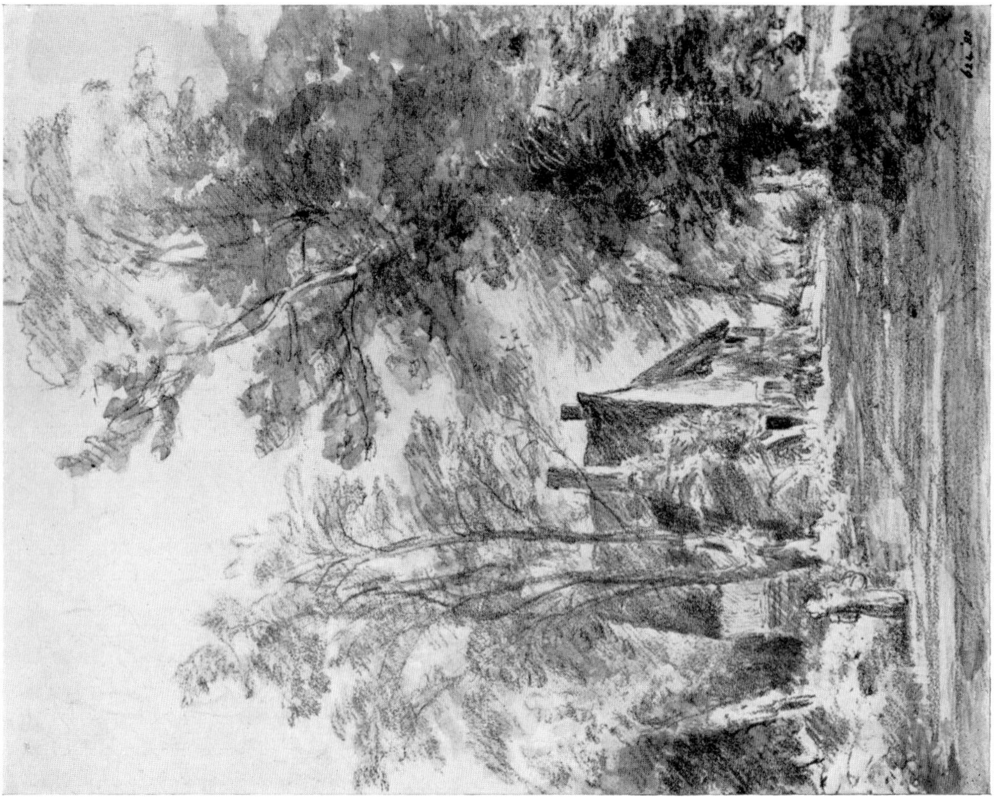

291. Water Lane, Stratford St. Mary.

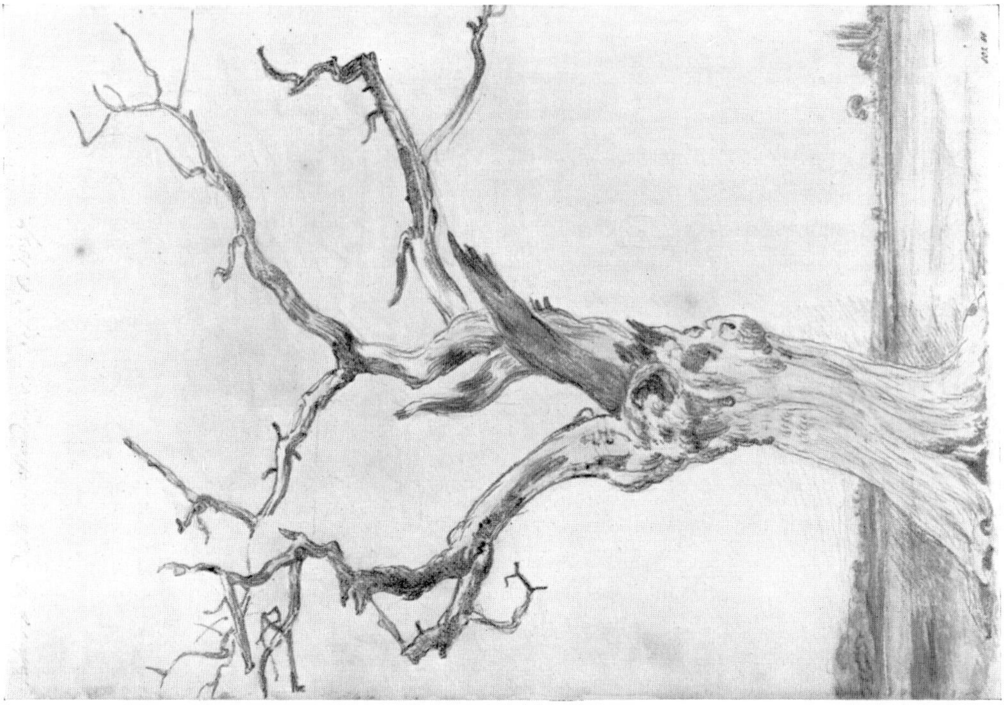

292. An oak in Dedham Meadows.

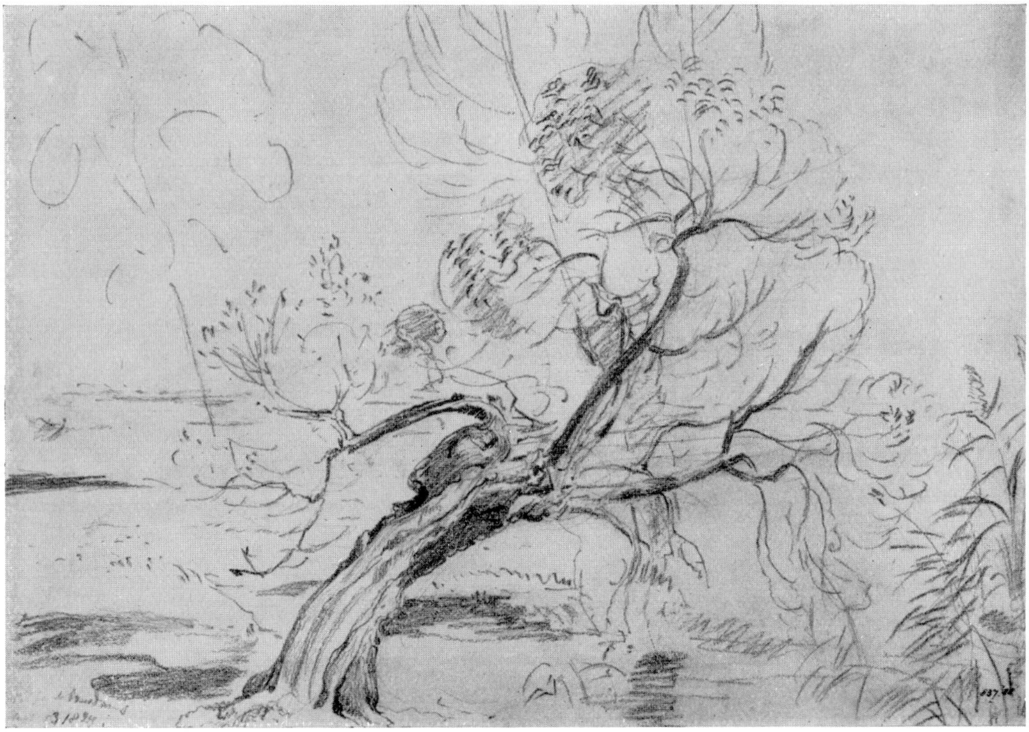

294. A willow tree in Flatford Meadows.

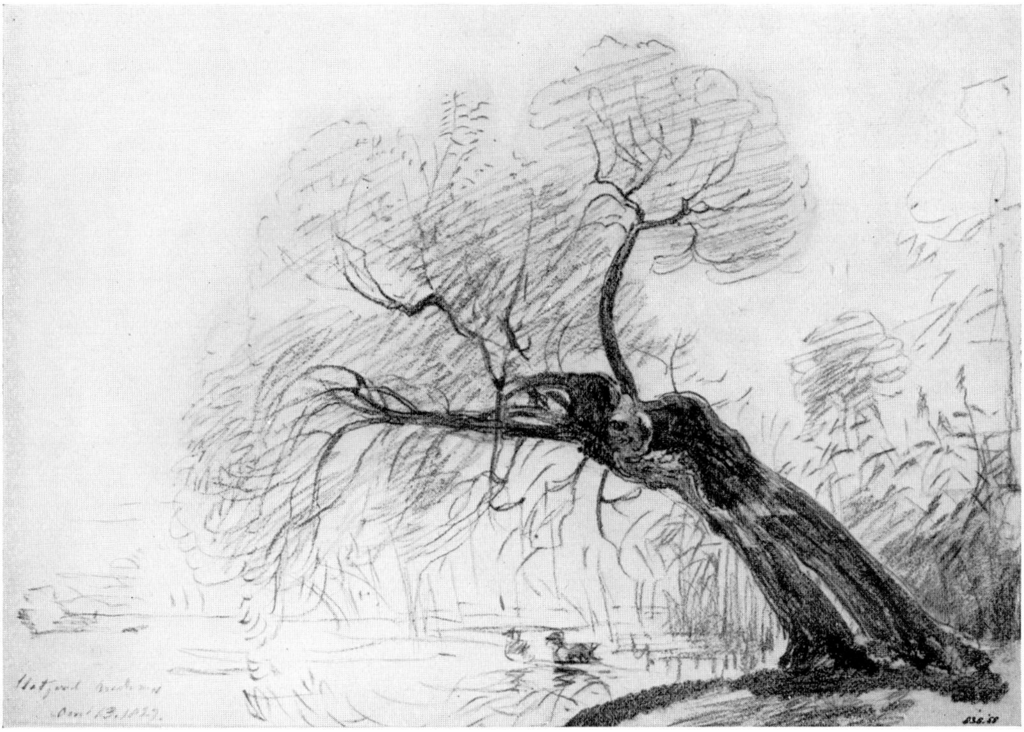

295. A willow tree in Flatford Meadows.

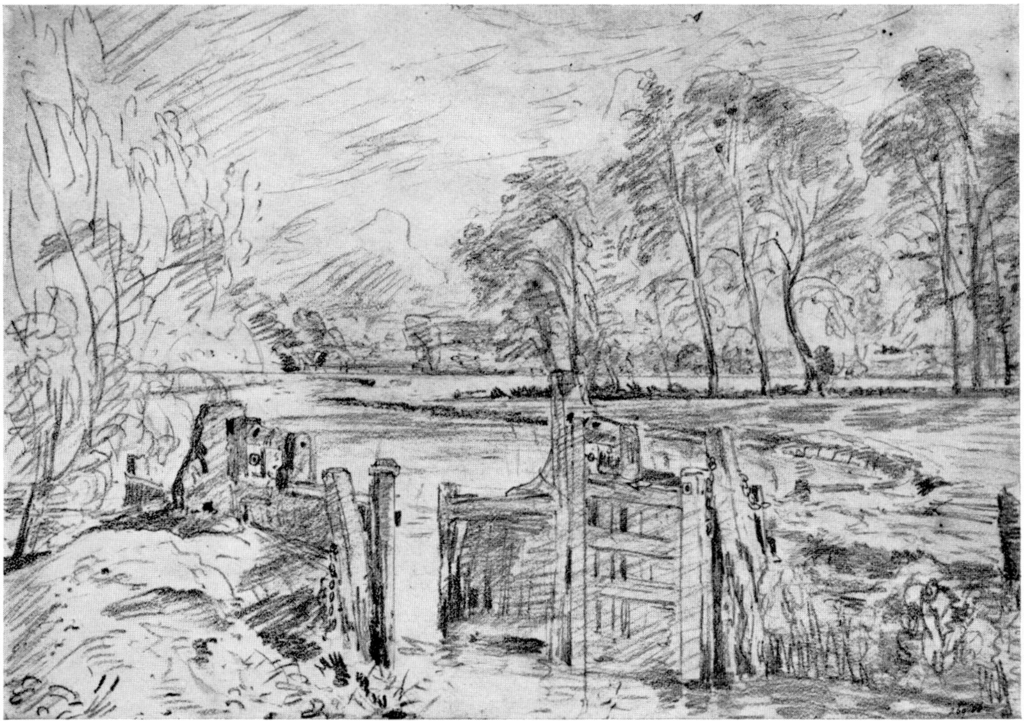

293. A lock on the Stour.

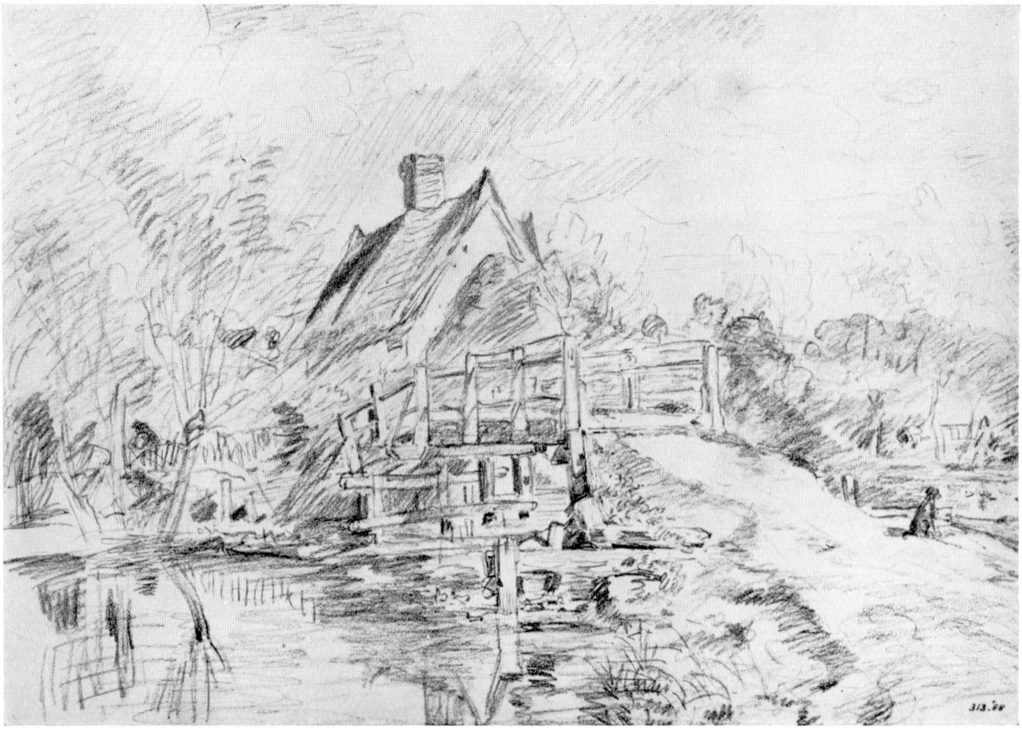

297. Flatford Old Bridge and Bridge Cottage.

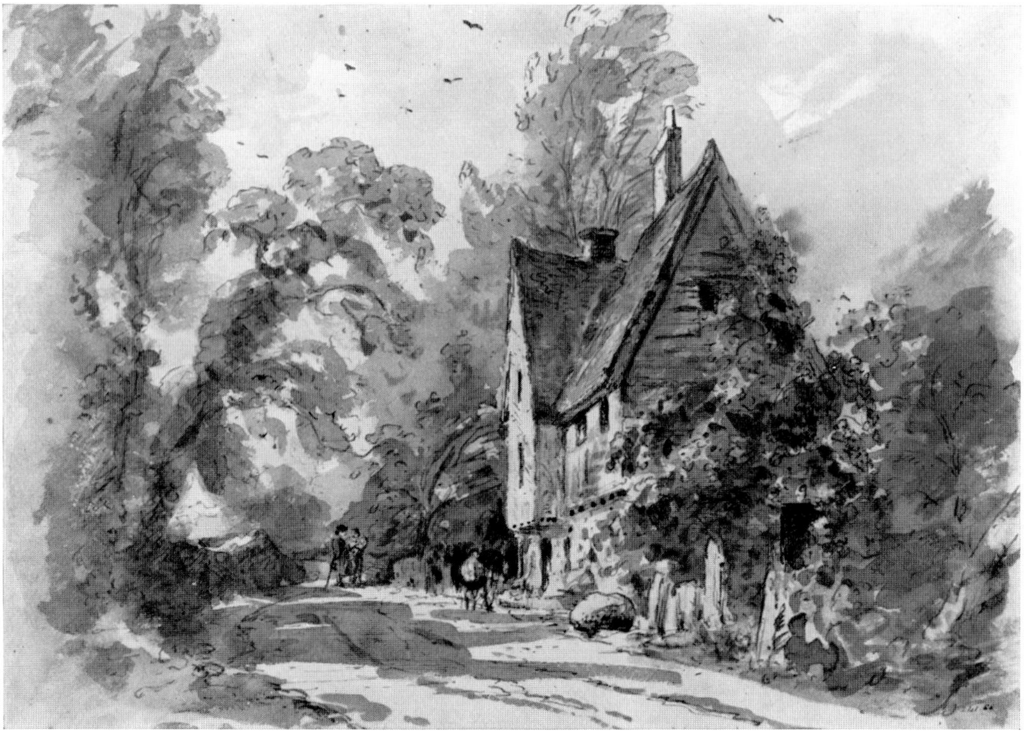

296. Water Lane, Stratford St. Mary.

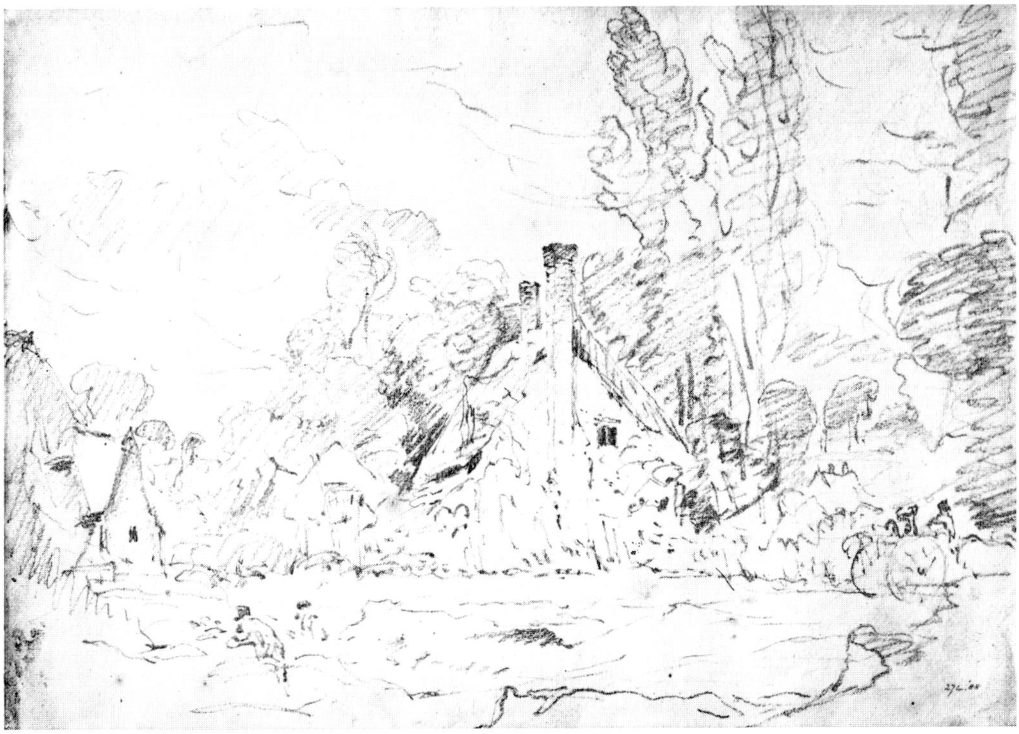

299. A village street.

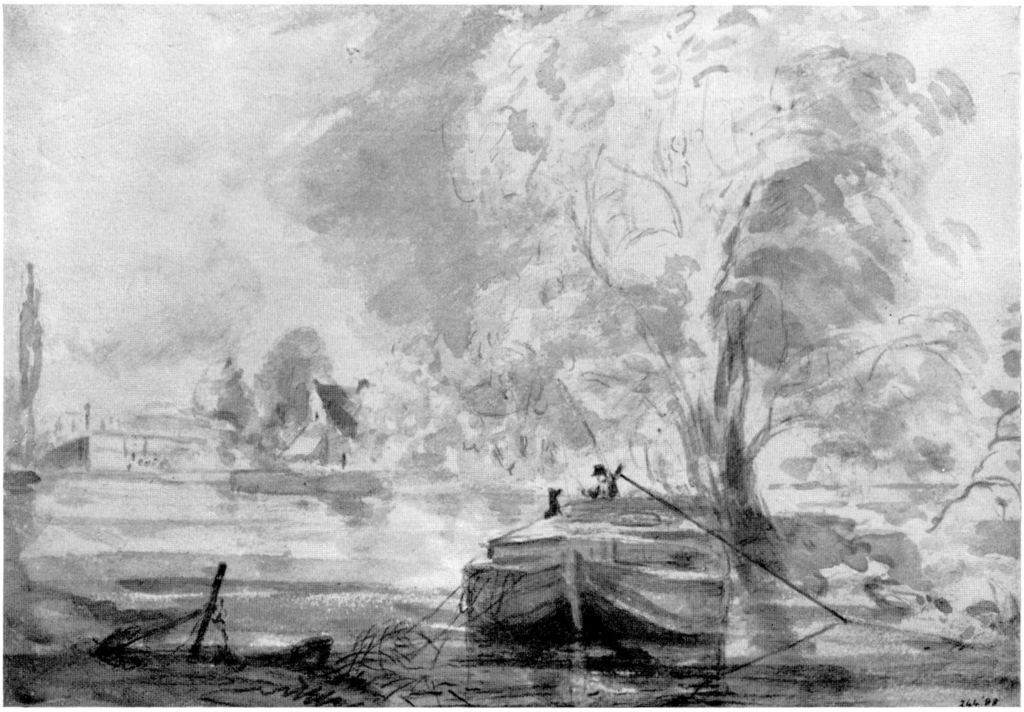

298. A barge on the Stour.

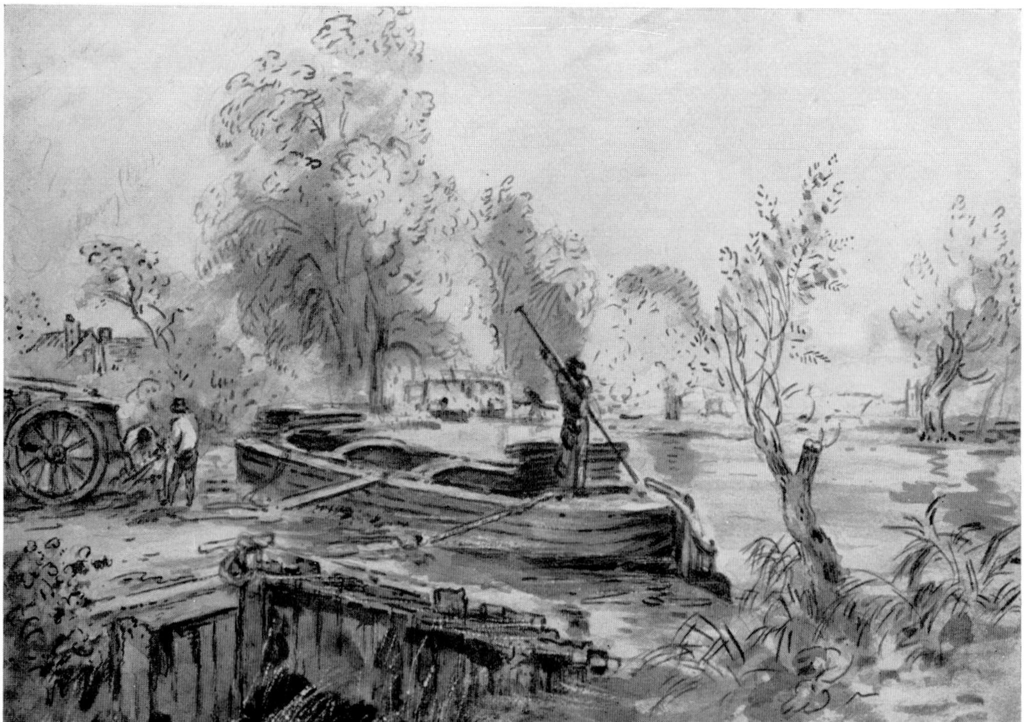

300. Men loading a barge on the Stour.

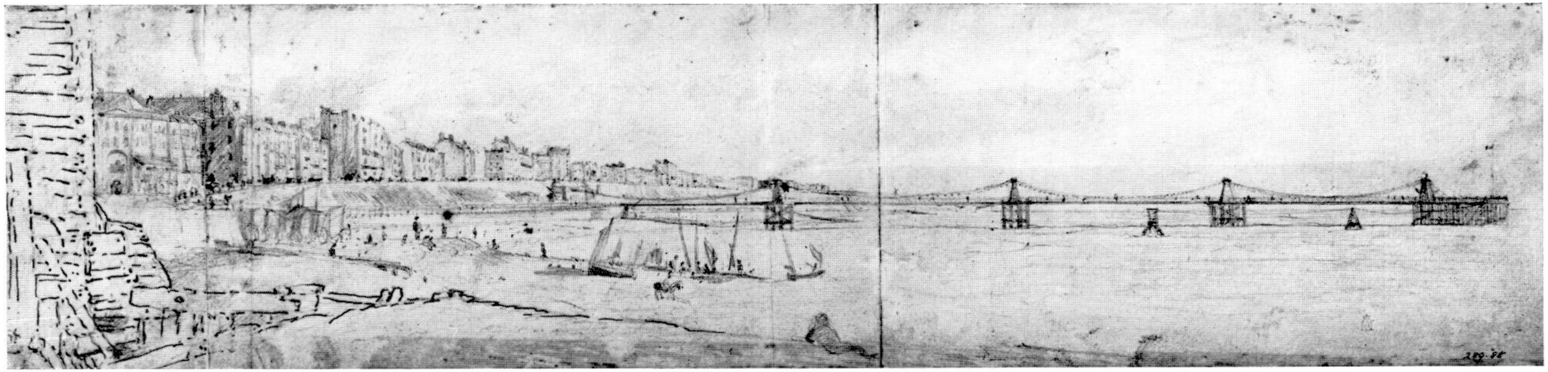

289. The Marine Parade and Chain Pier, Brighton.

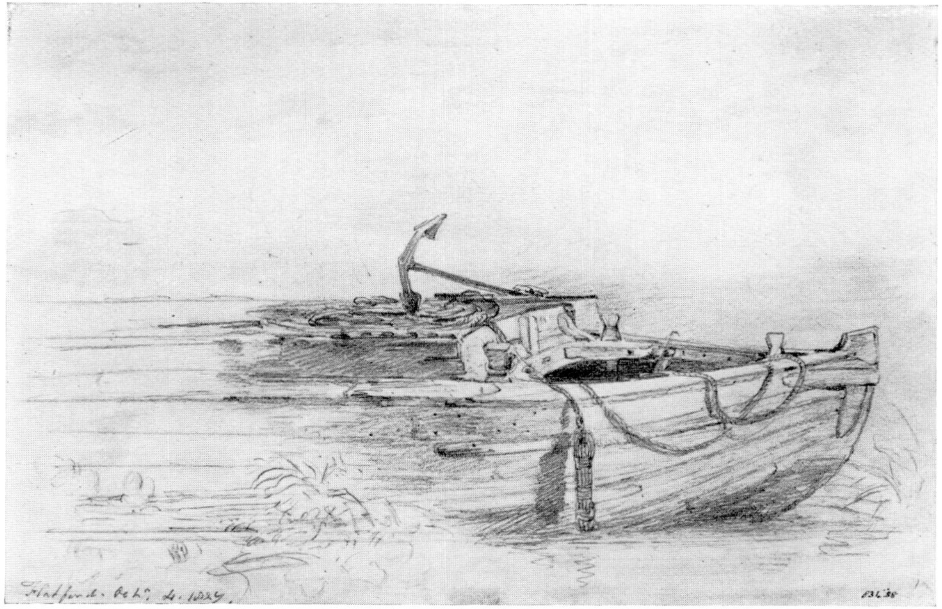

290. The fore-part of a barge at Flatford.

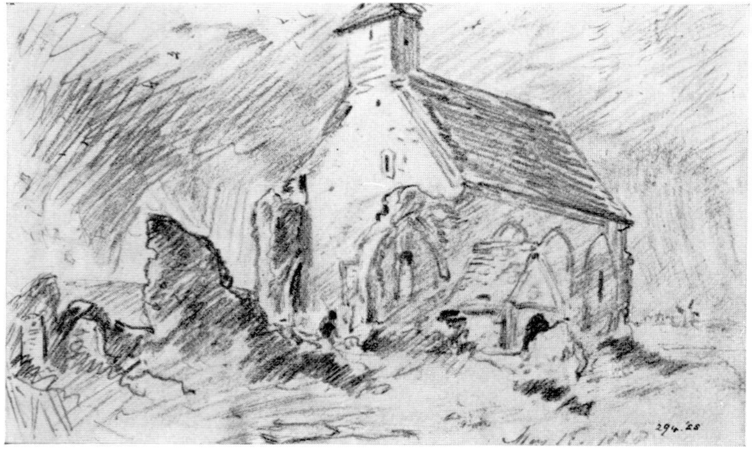

302. The Old Parish Church at Hove.

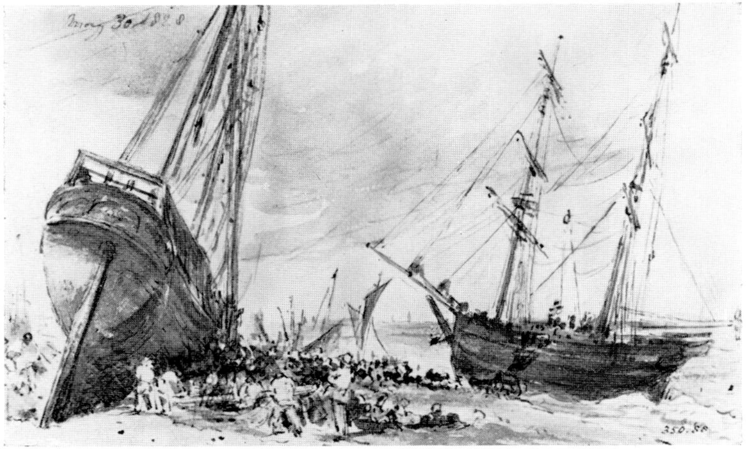

304. Coast scene at Brighton.

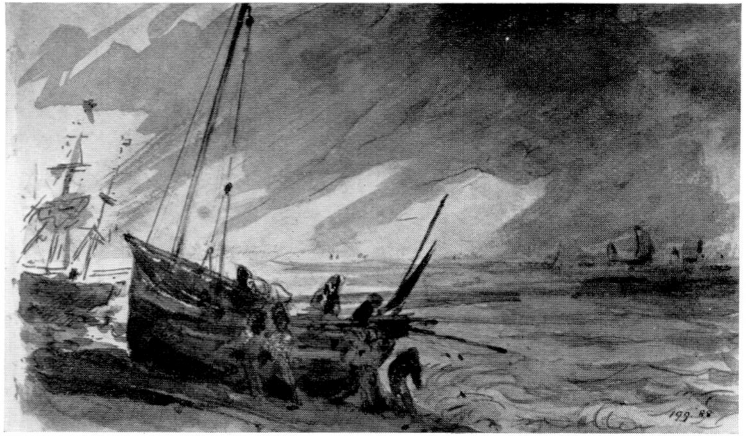

306. Coast scene at Brighton.

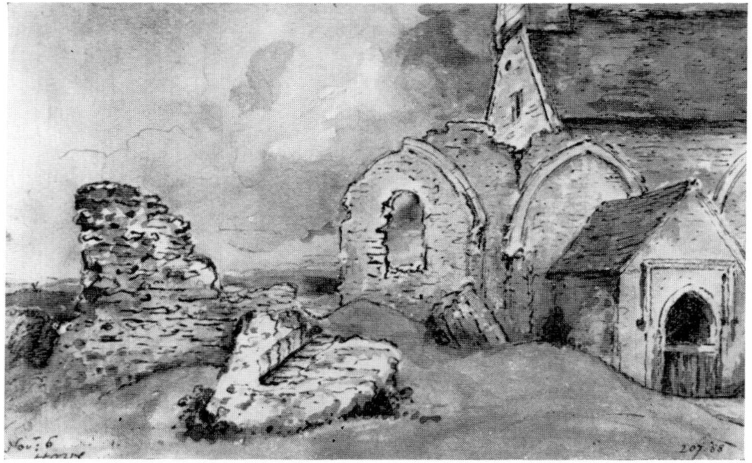

309. The Old Parish Church at Hove.

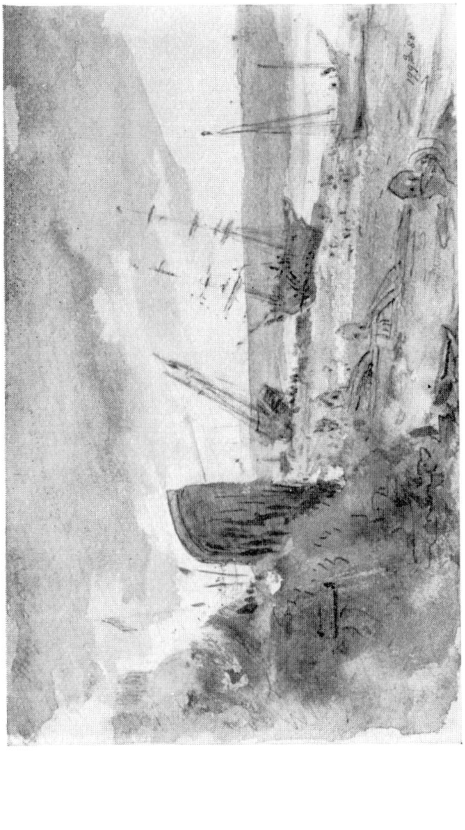

305. Coast scene at Brighton.

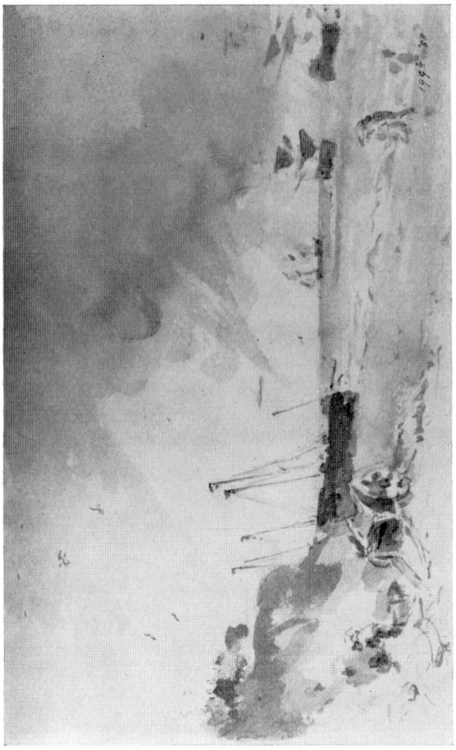

307. Coast scene at Brighton.

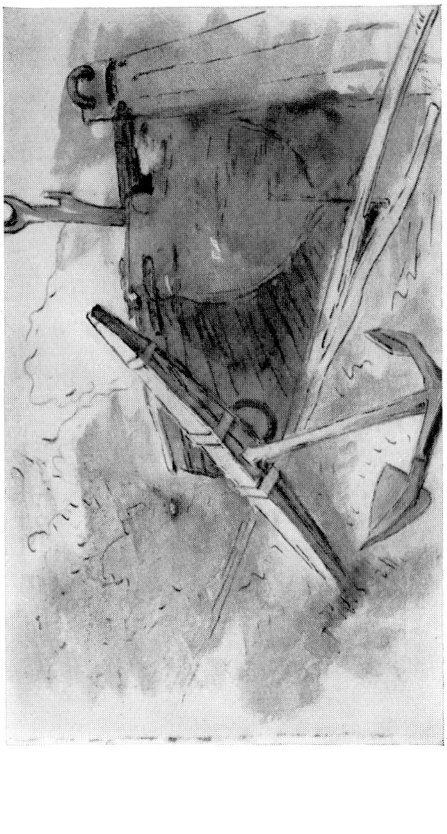

308. A boat and an anchor, Brighton.

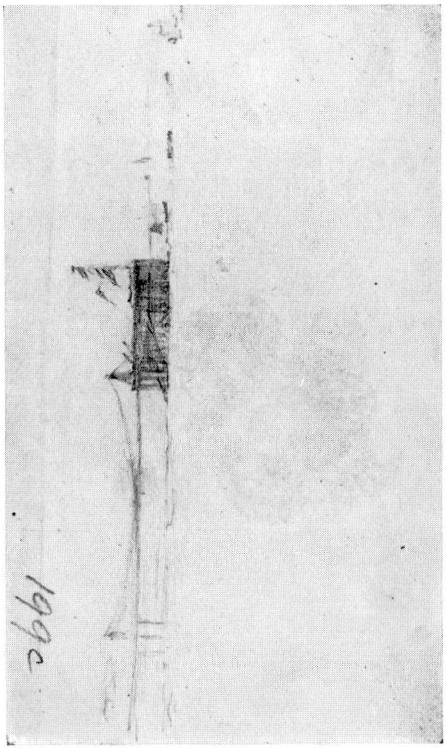

308a. The Chain Pier, Brighton.

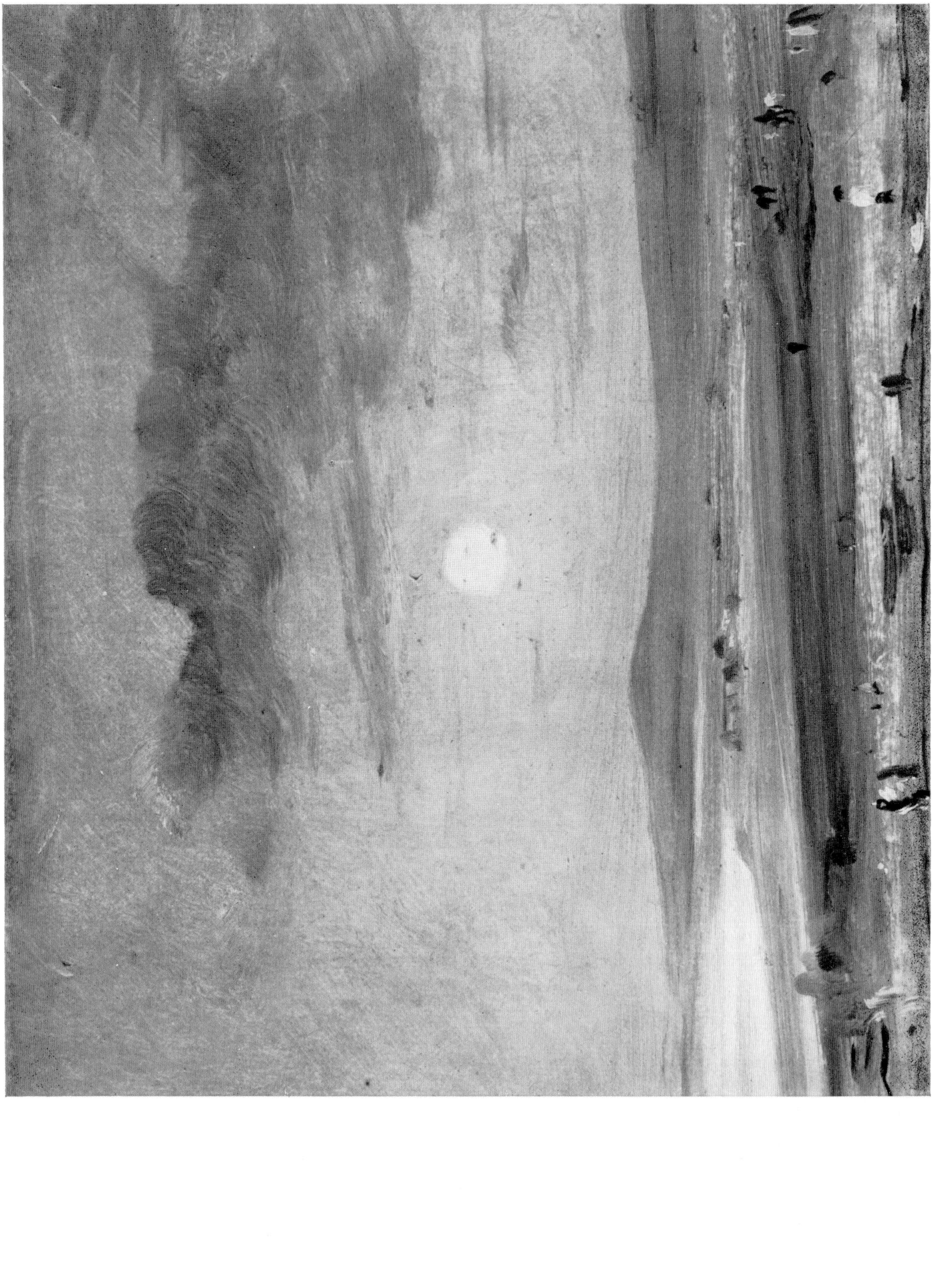

303. Coast scene at Brighton: evening.

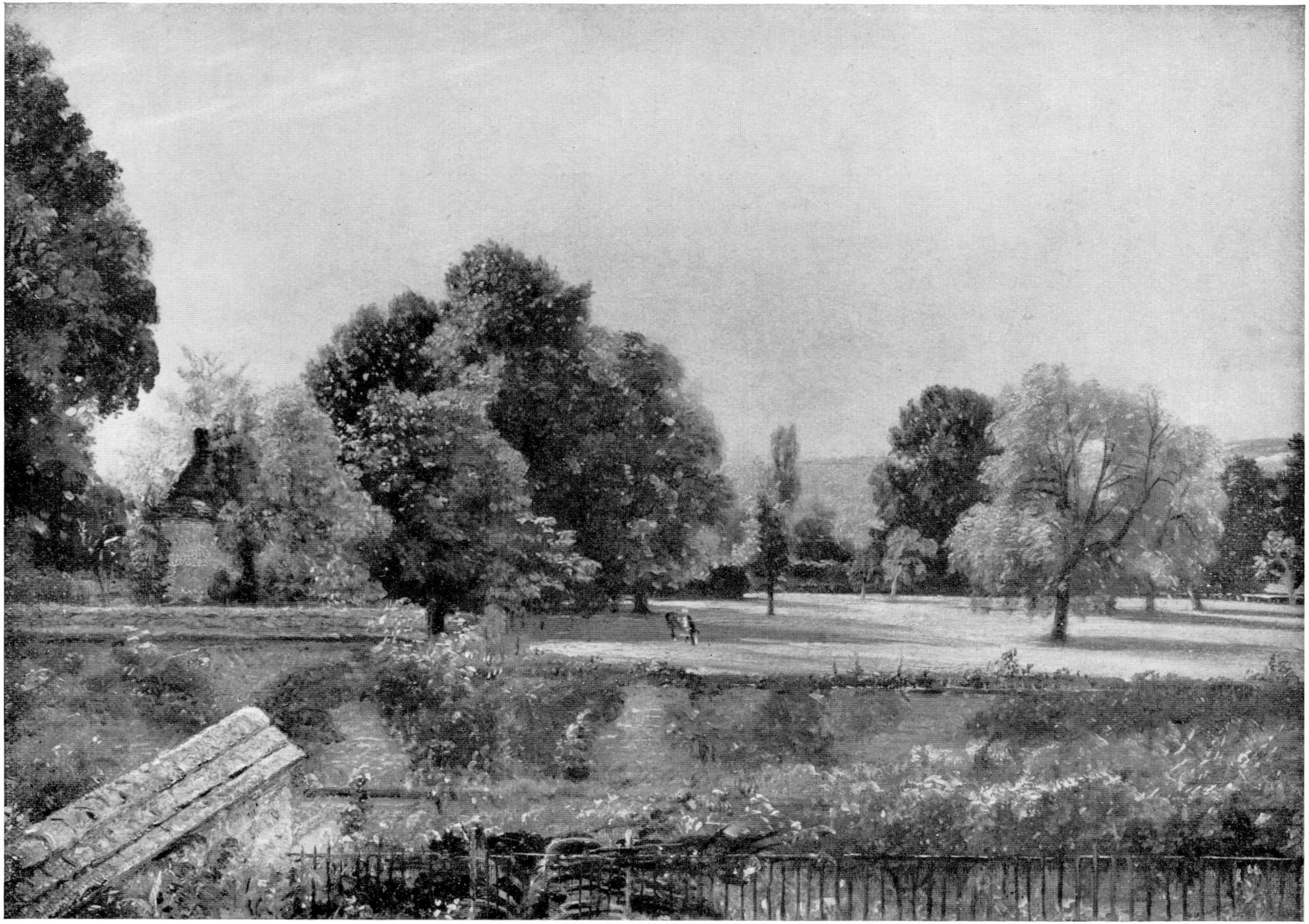

320. A view at Salisbury from Archdeacon Fisher's house.

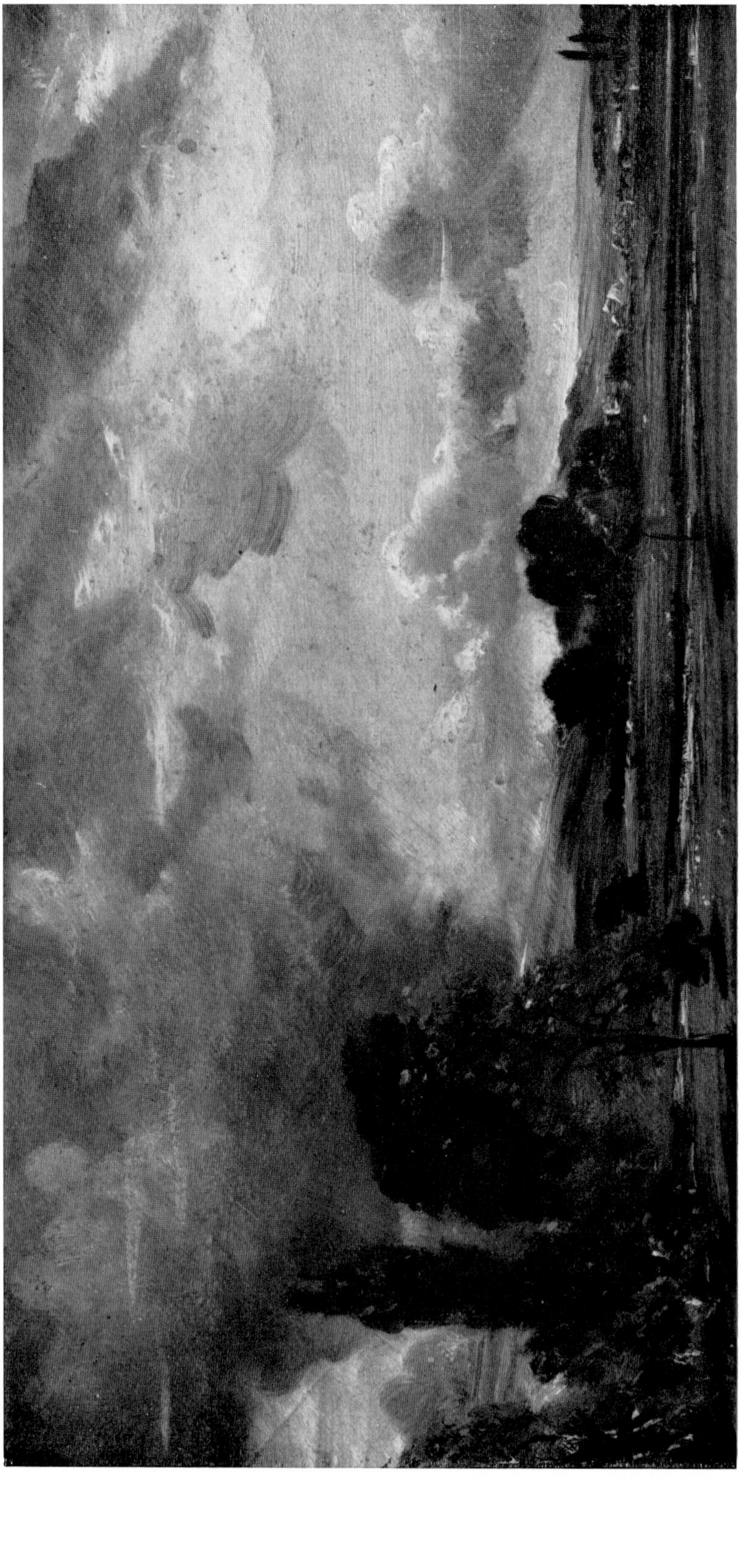

311. A view at Salisbury, from Archdeacon Fisher's library.

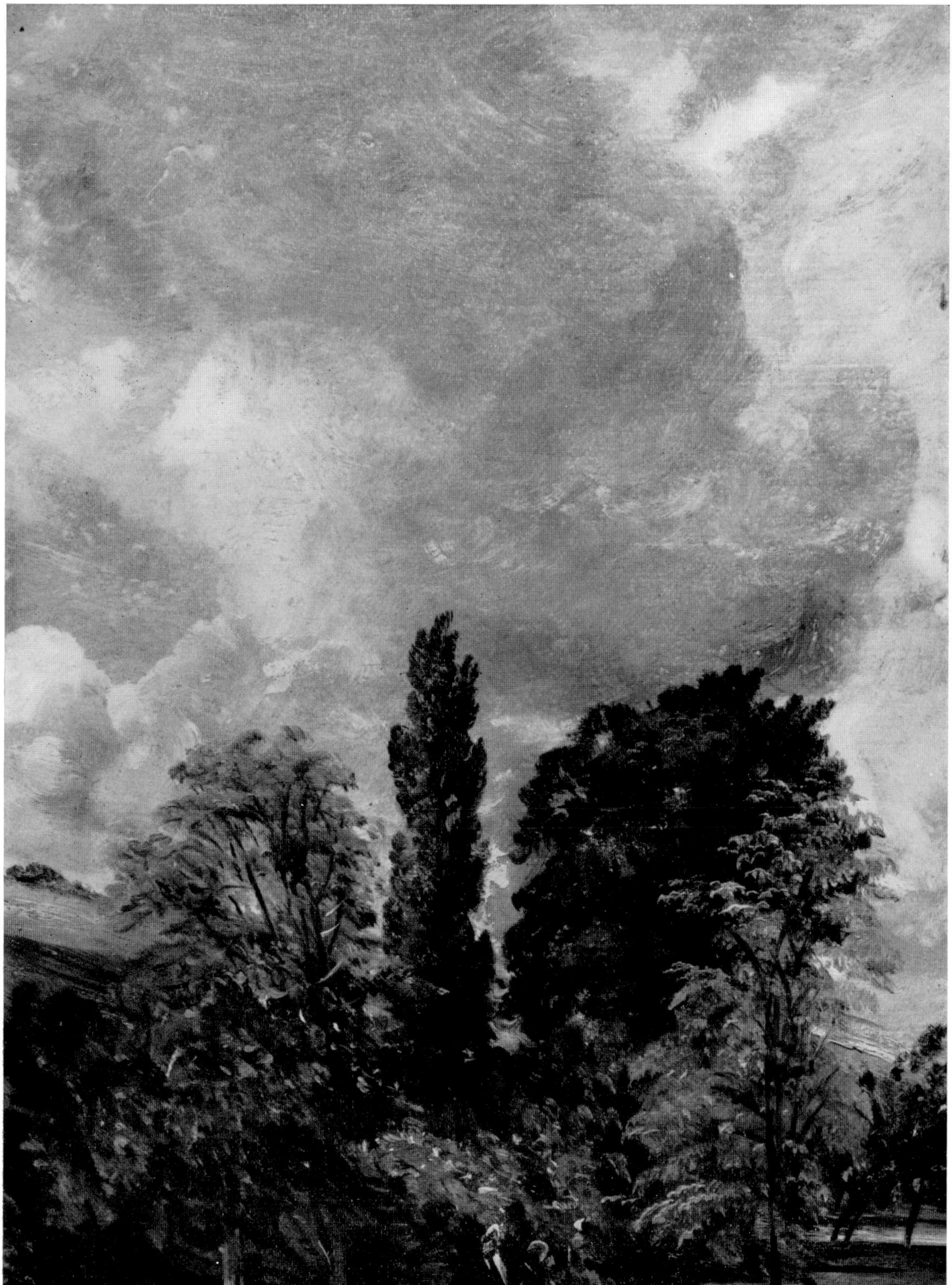

312. The Close, Salisbury.

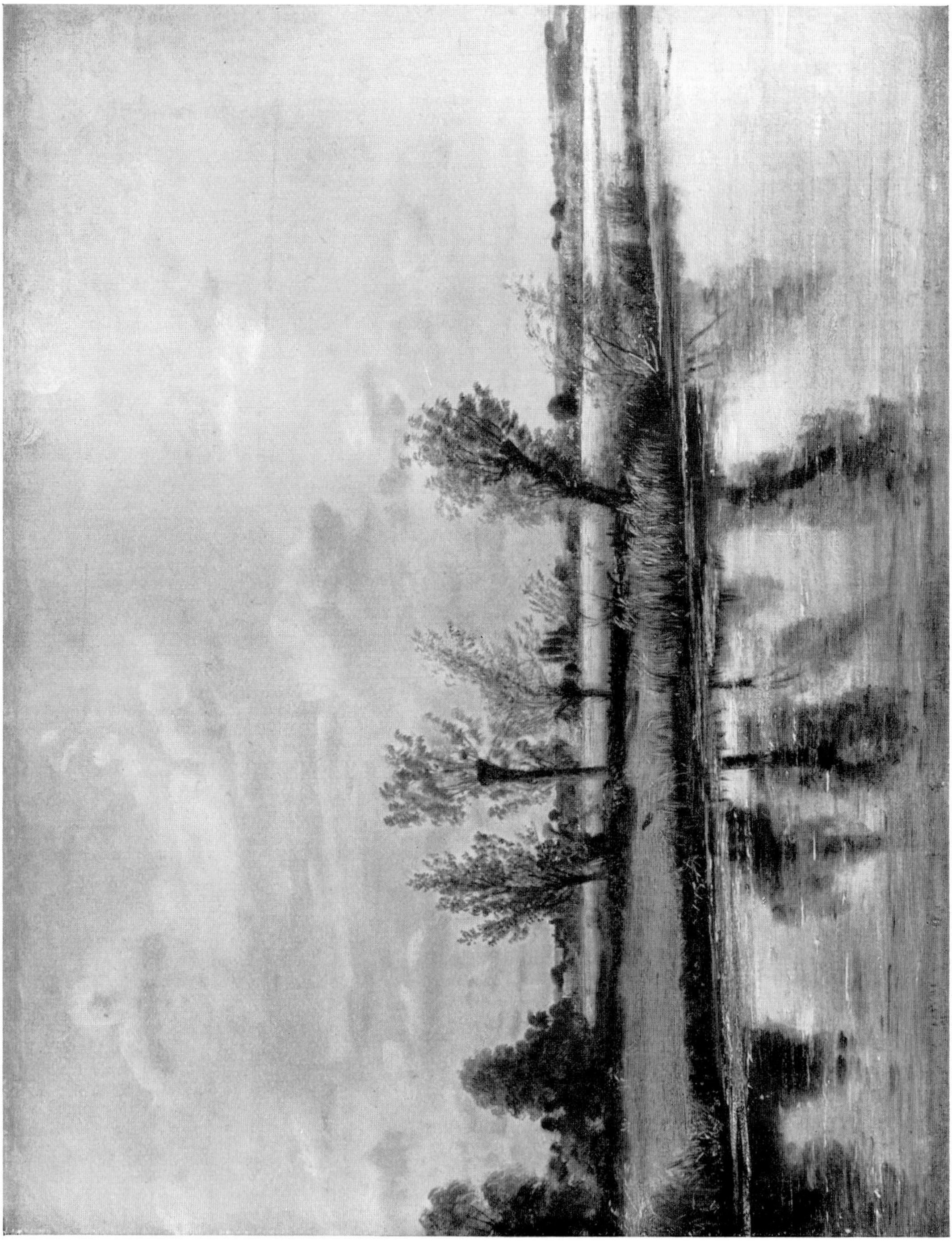

321. Water-meadows near Salisbury.

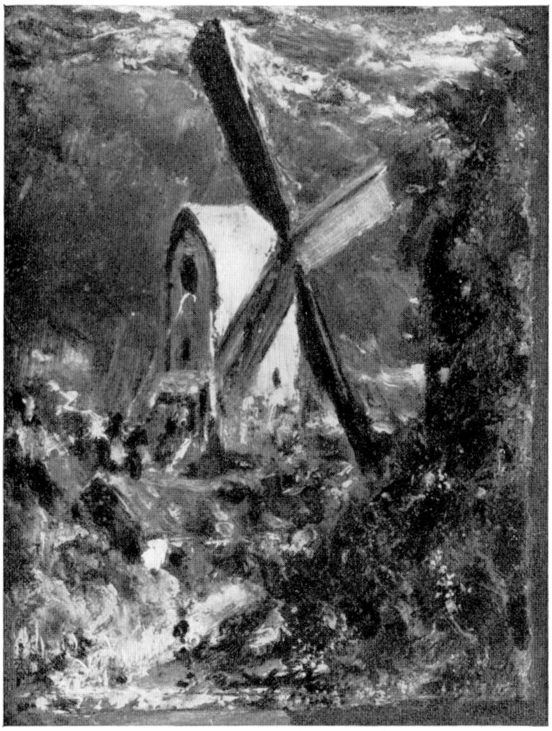

310. A windmill near Brighton.

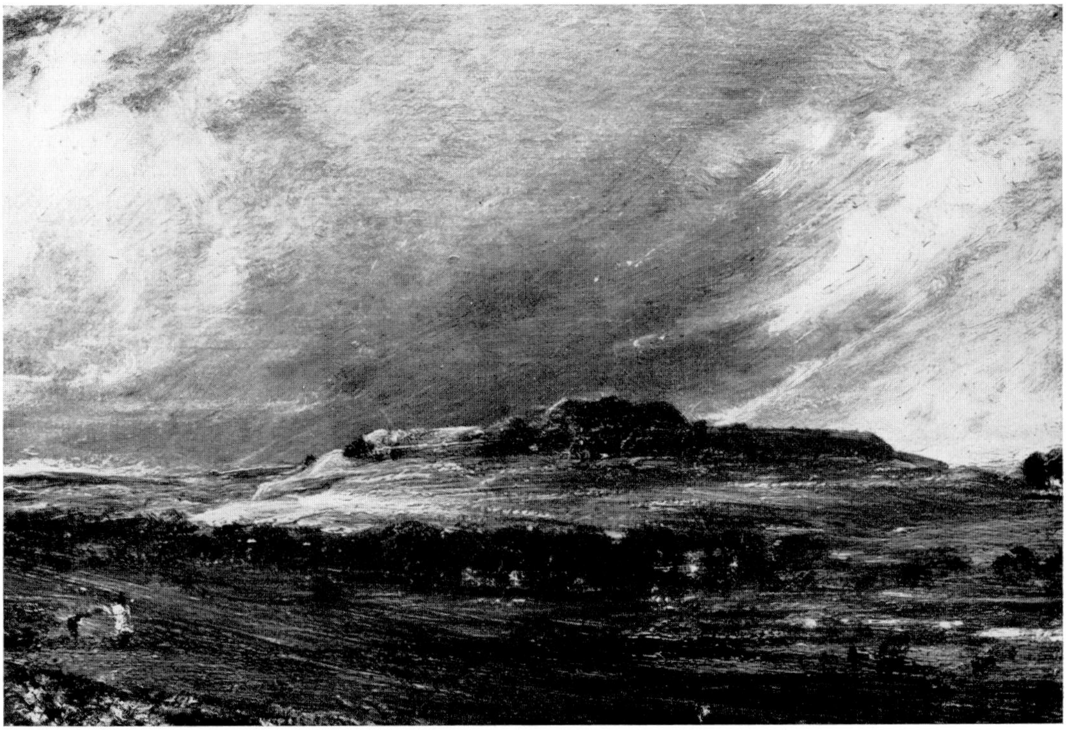

322. Old Sarum.

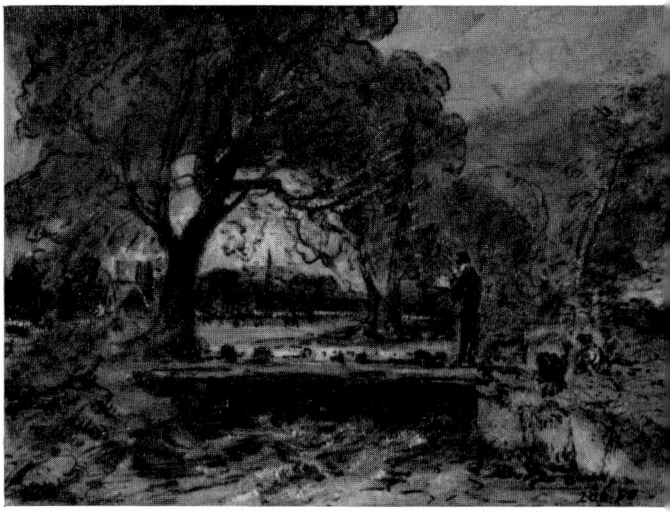

313. Archdeacon Fisher with his dogs.

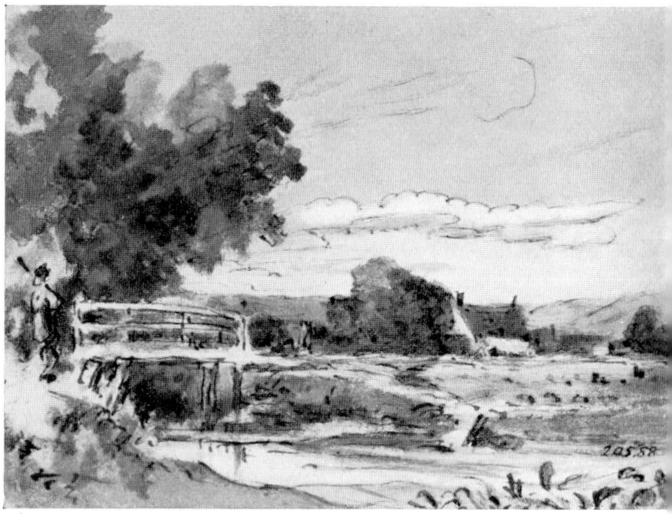

318. A bridge over a stream.

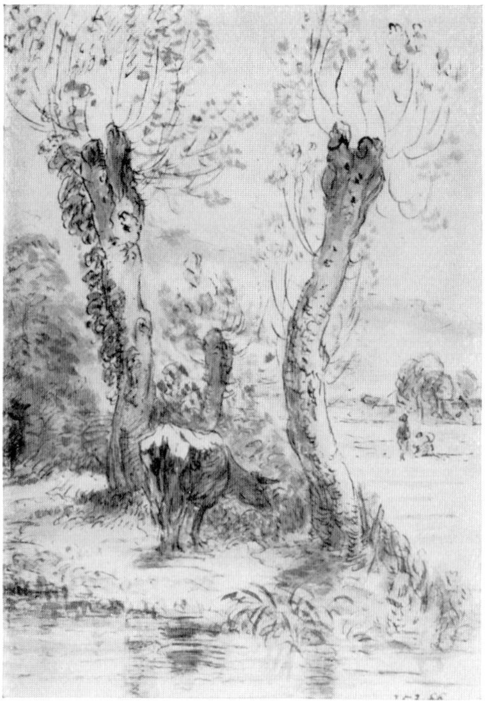

316. Cows grazing, Salisbury.

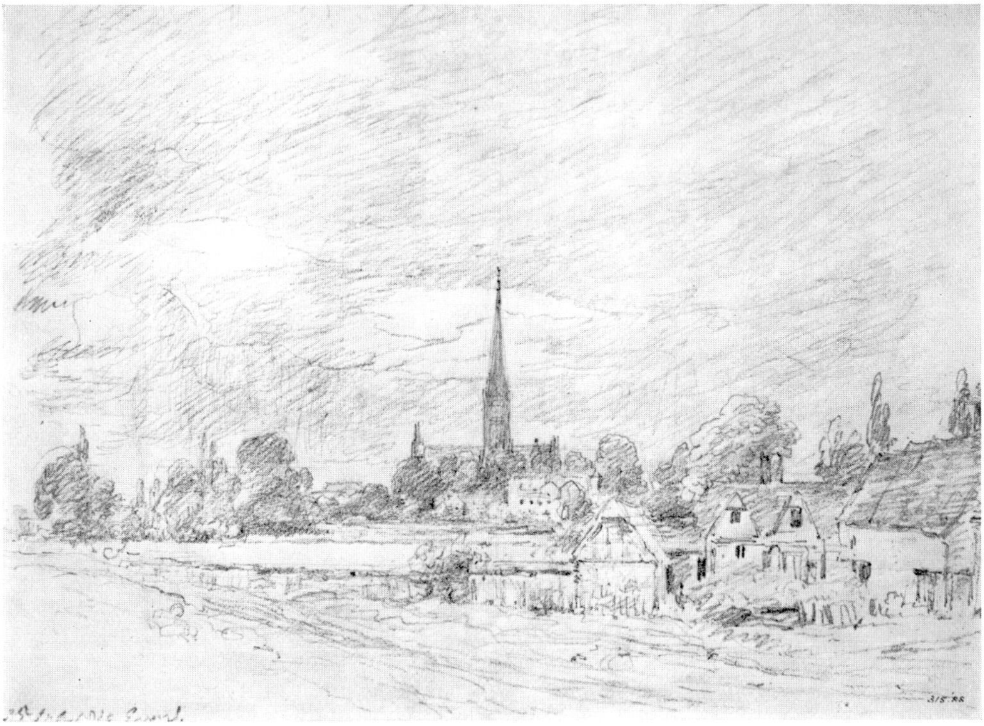

314. Salisbury Cathedral seen from over the river.

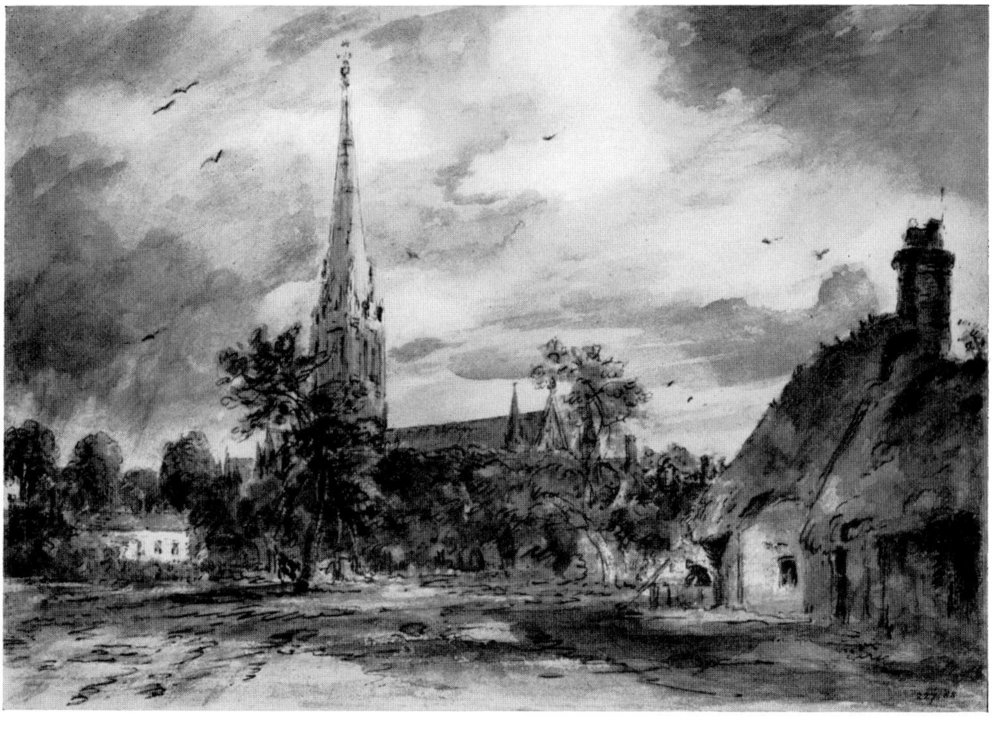

319. Salisbury Cathedral, with cottages.

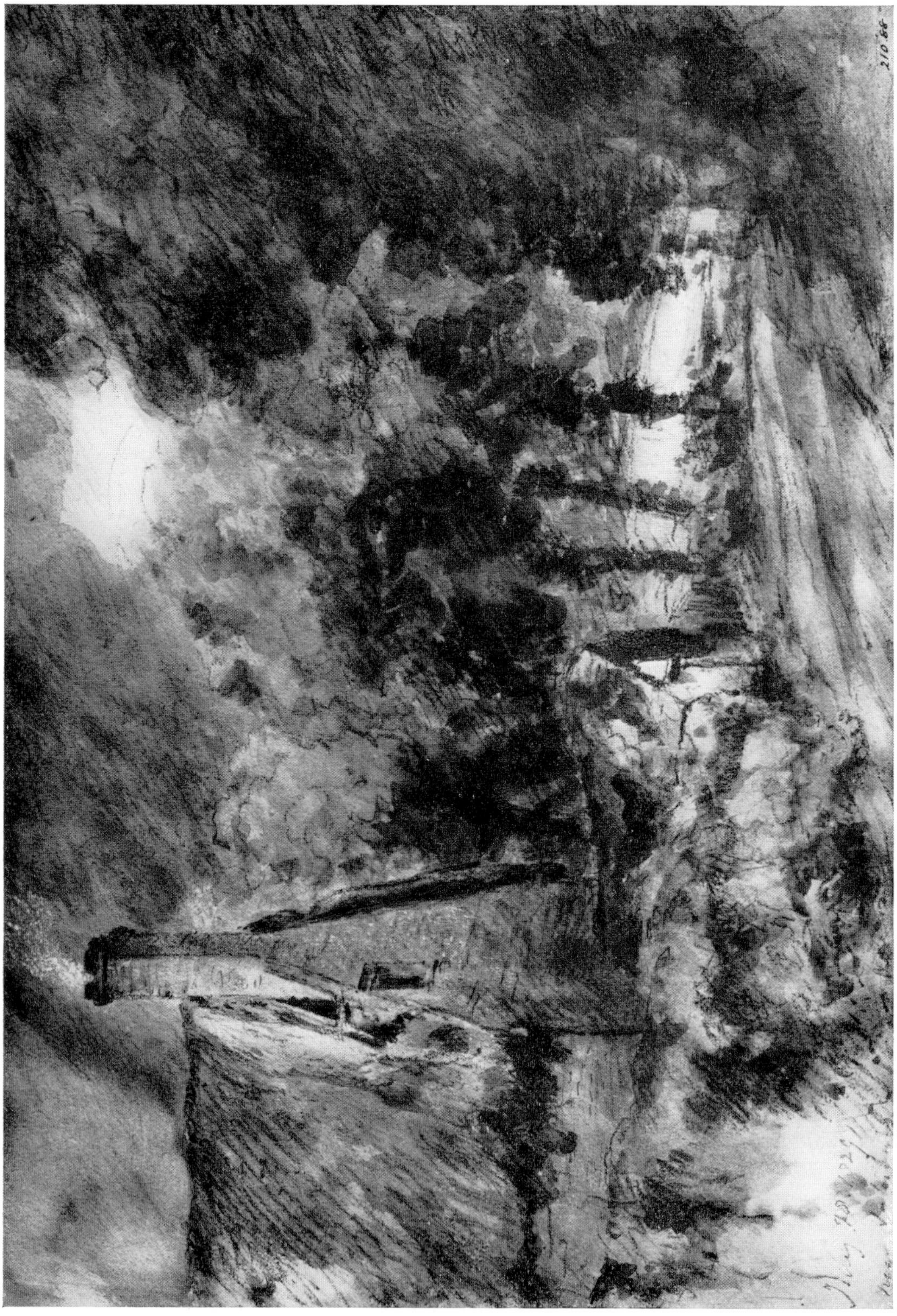

315. A cottage and trees near Salisbury.

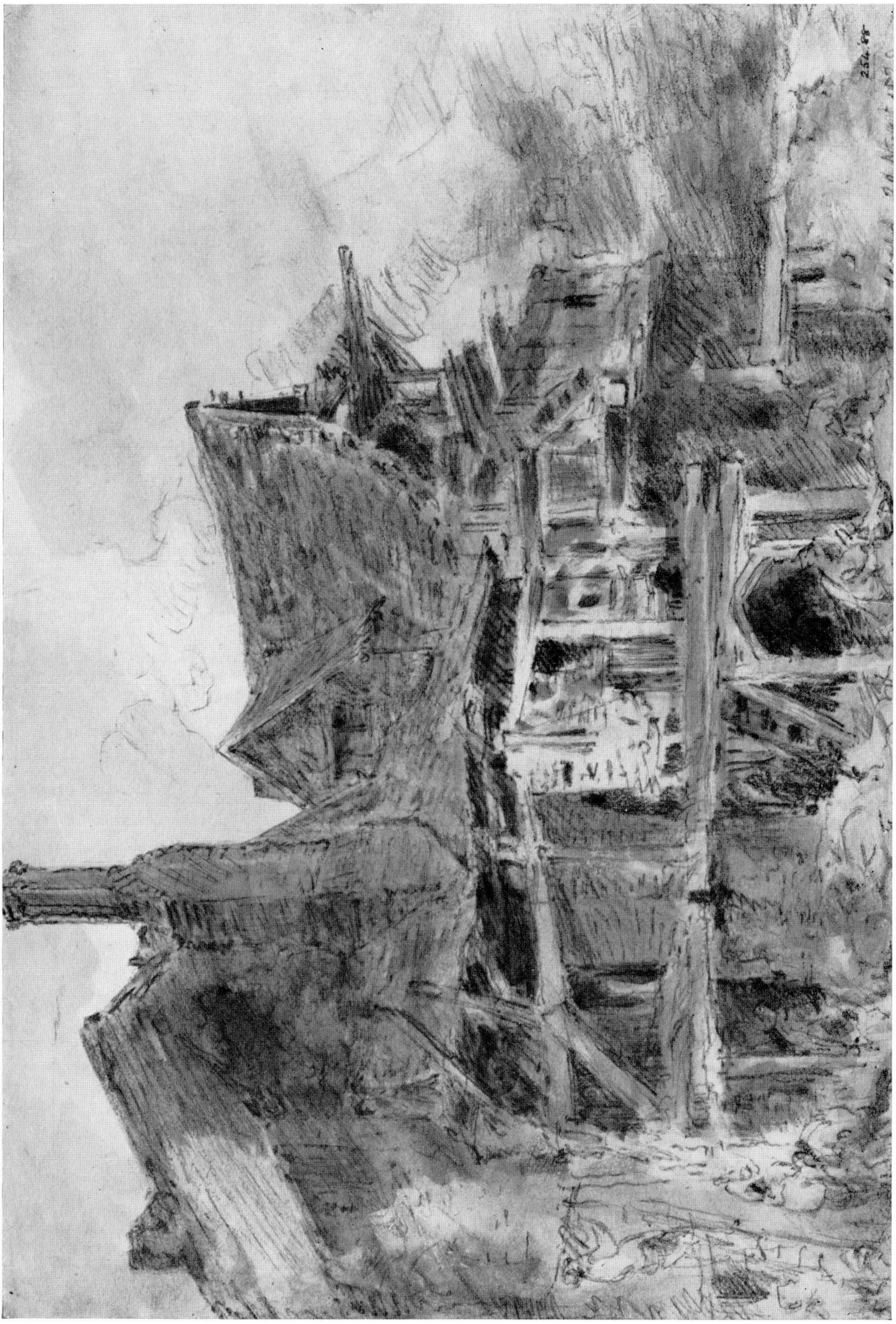

317. The demolition or repair of old houses at Salisbury.

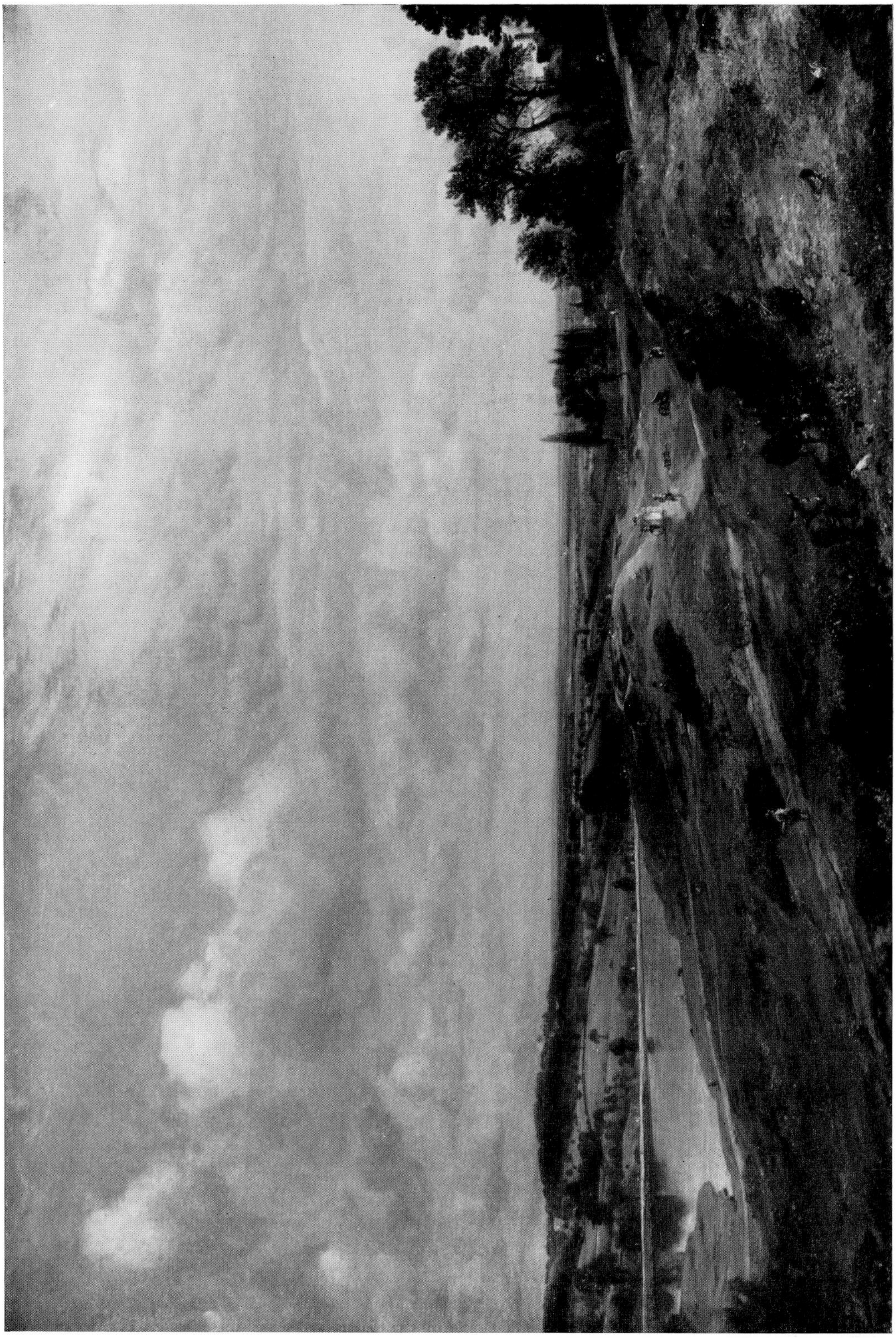

323. Hampstead Heath.

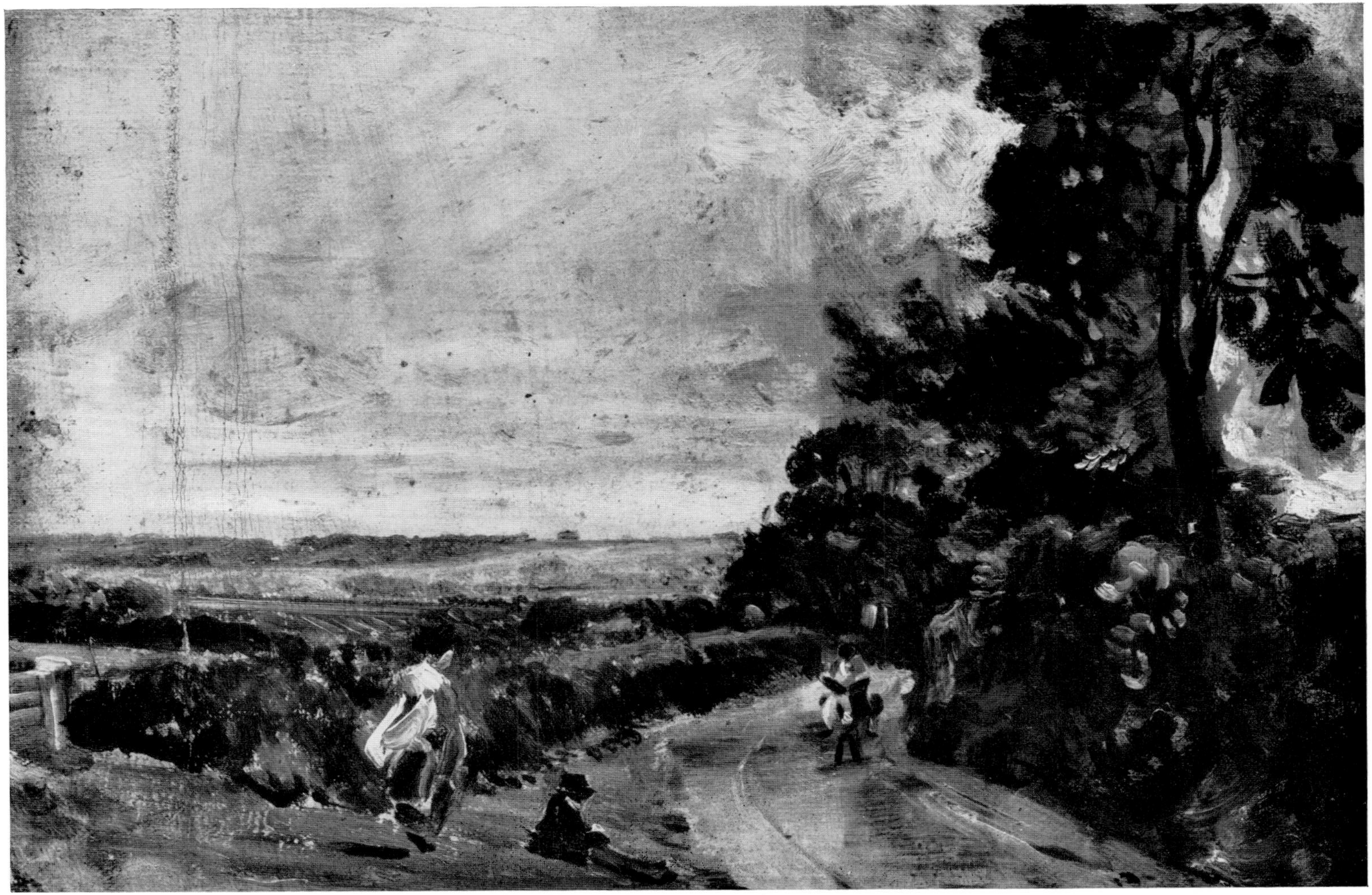

329. A country road with trees and figures.

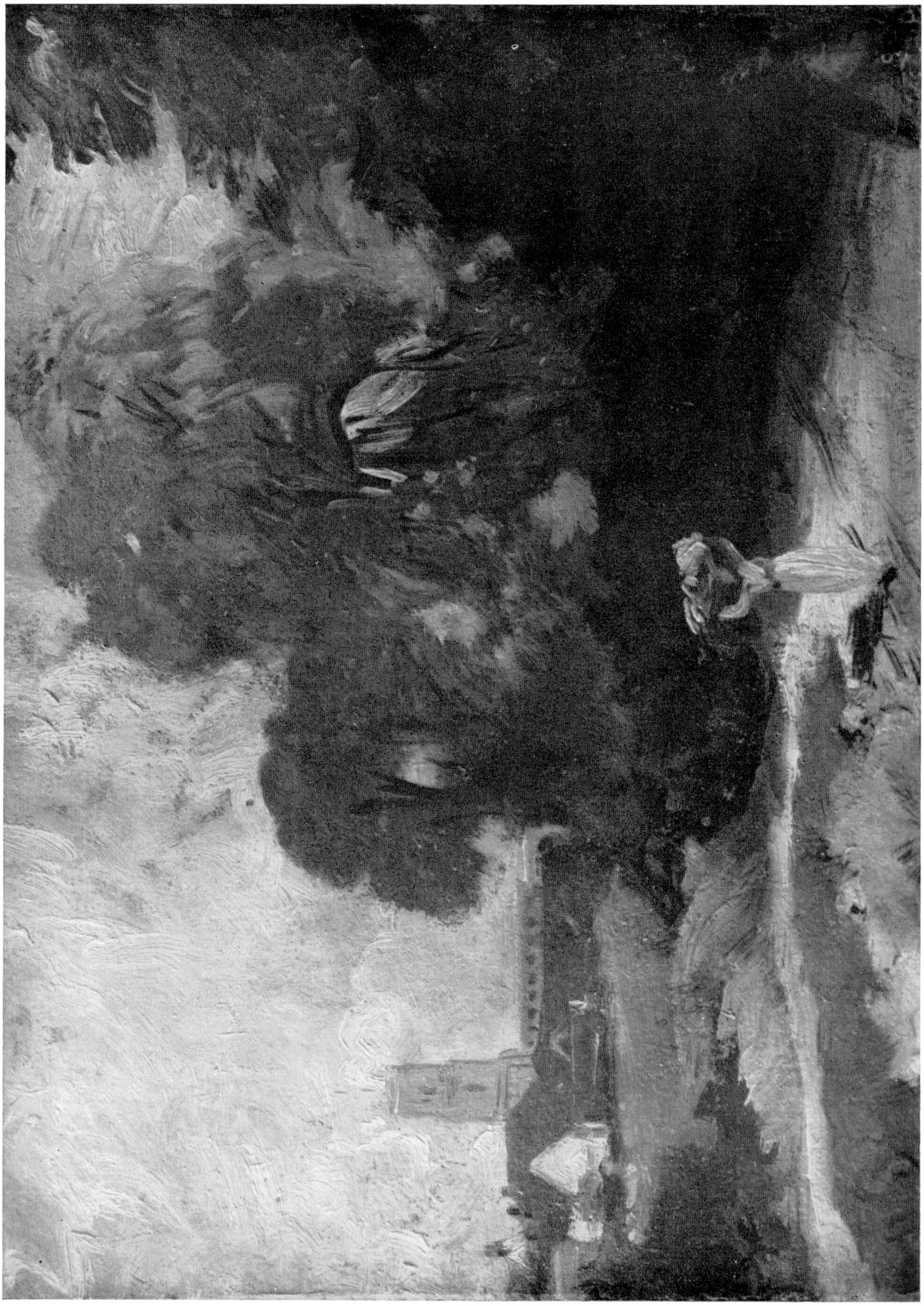

330. Stoke-by-Nayland.

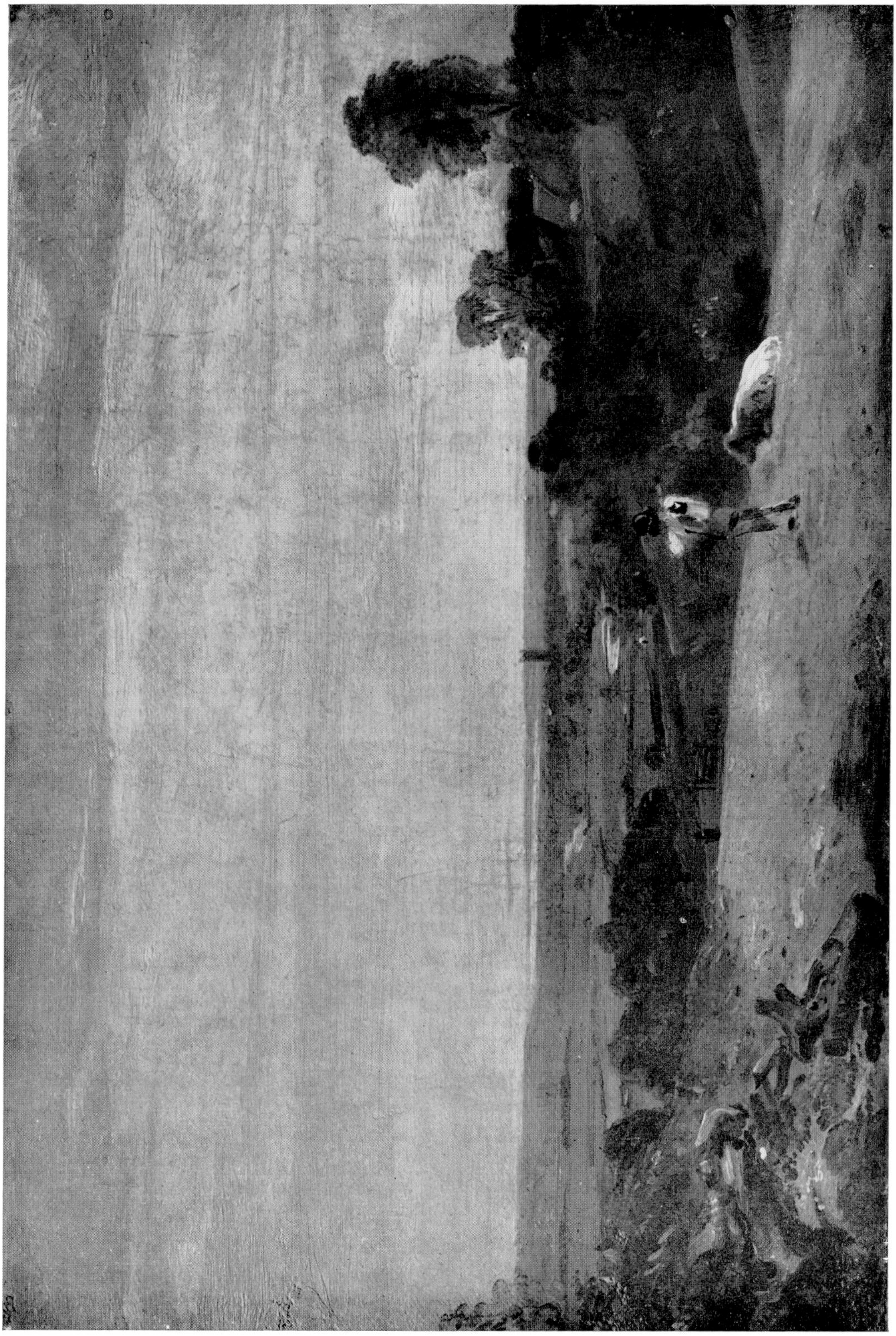

332. Summer Morning: Dedham from Langham.

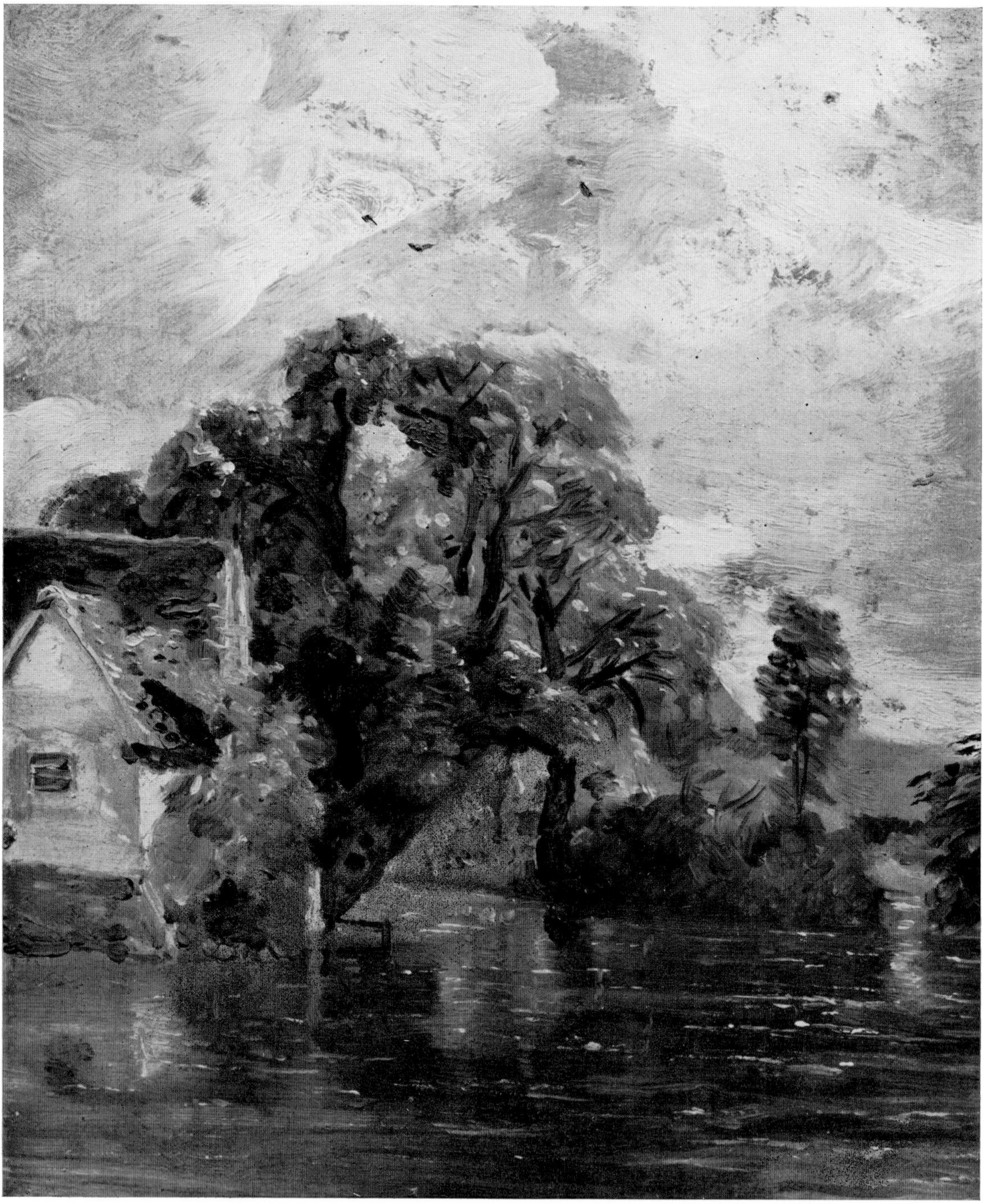

329a. Willy Lott's House.

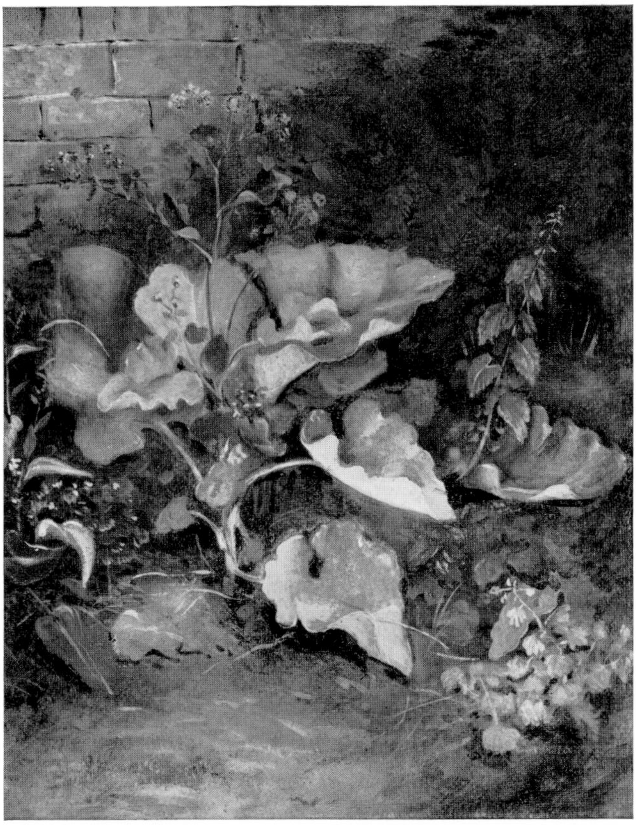

325. Plants growing near a wall.

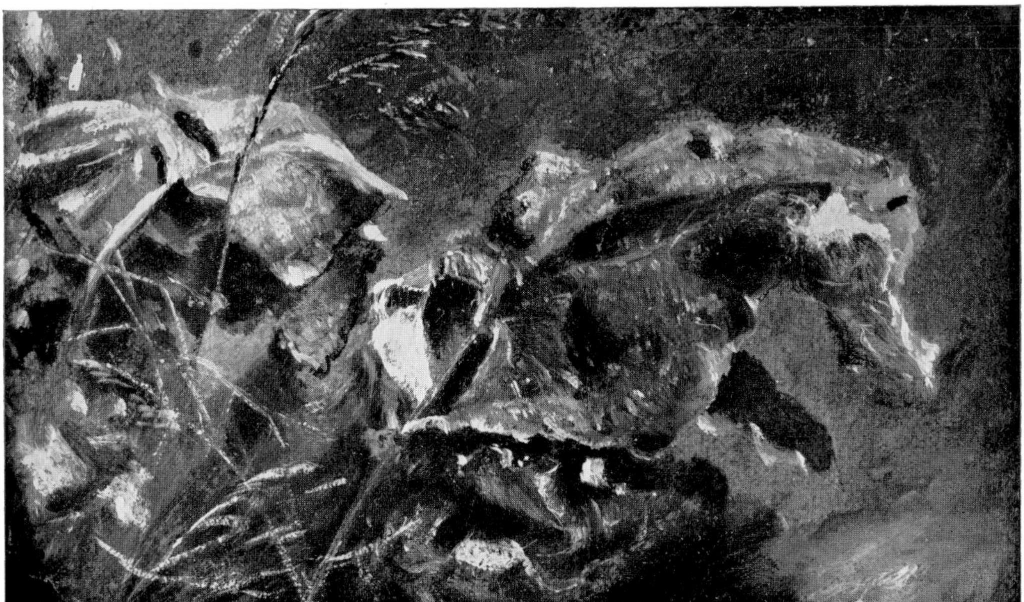

326. Study of foliage.

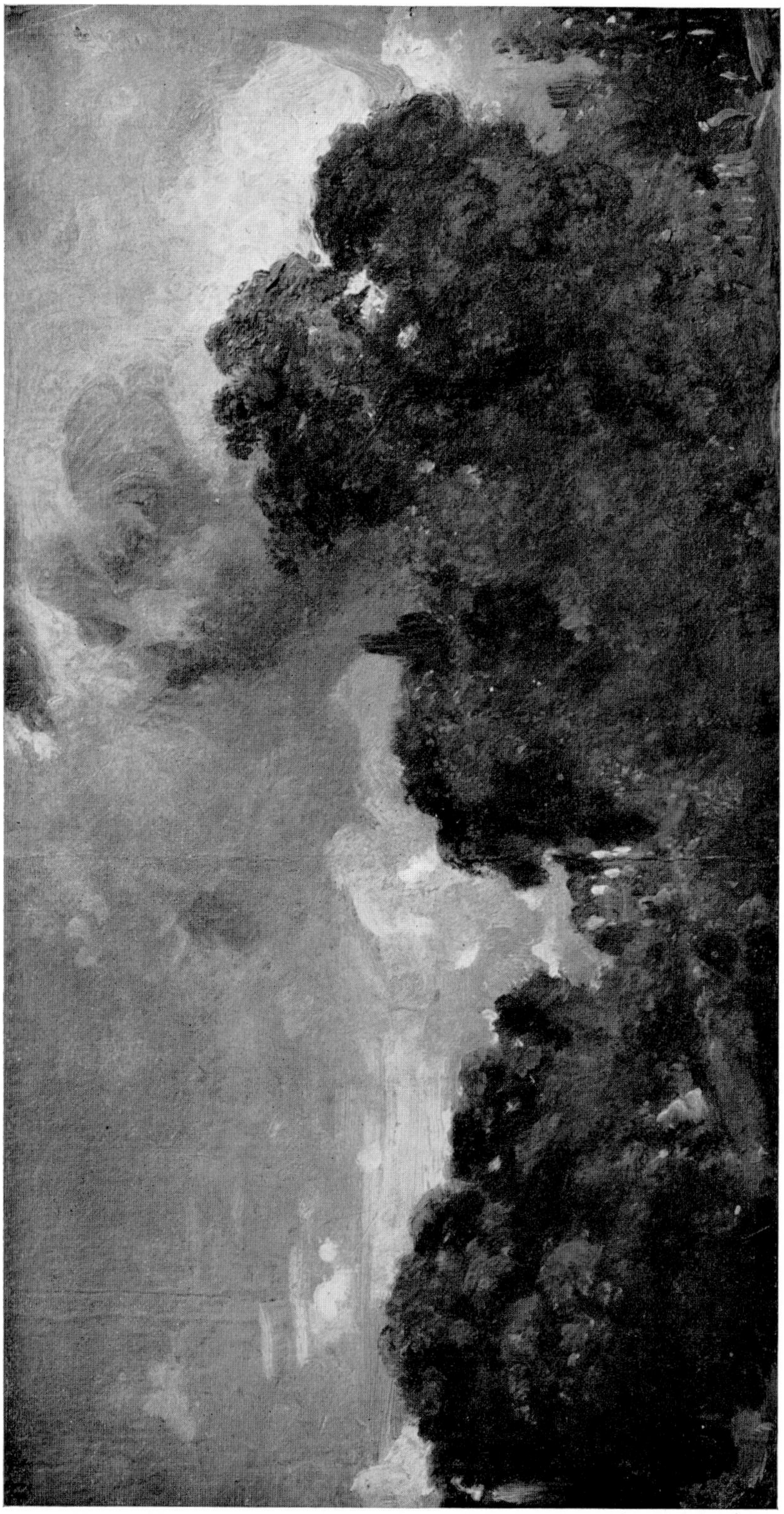

327. On the edge of a wood.

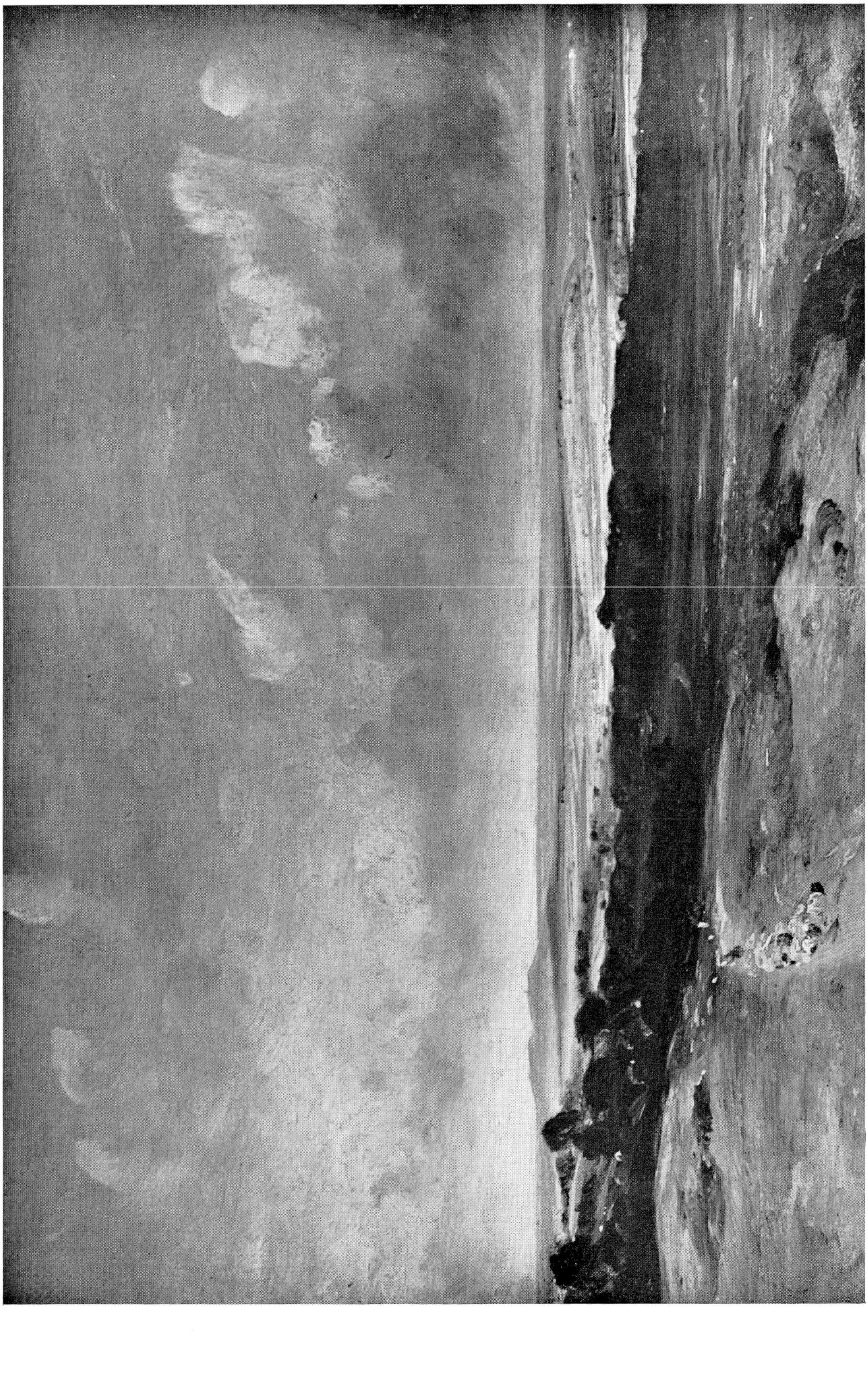

333. Hampstead Heath, Harrow in the distance.

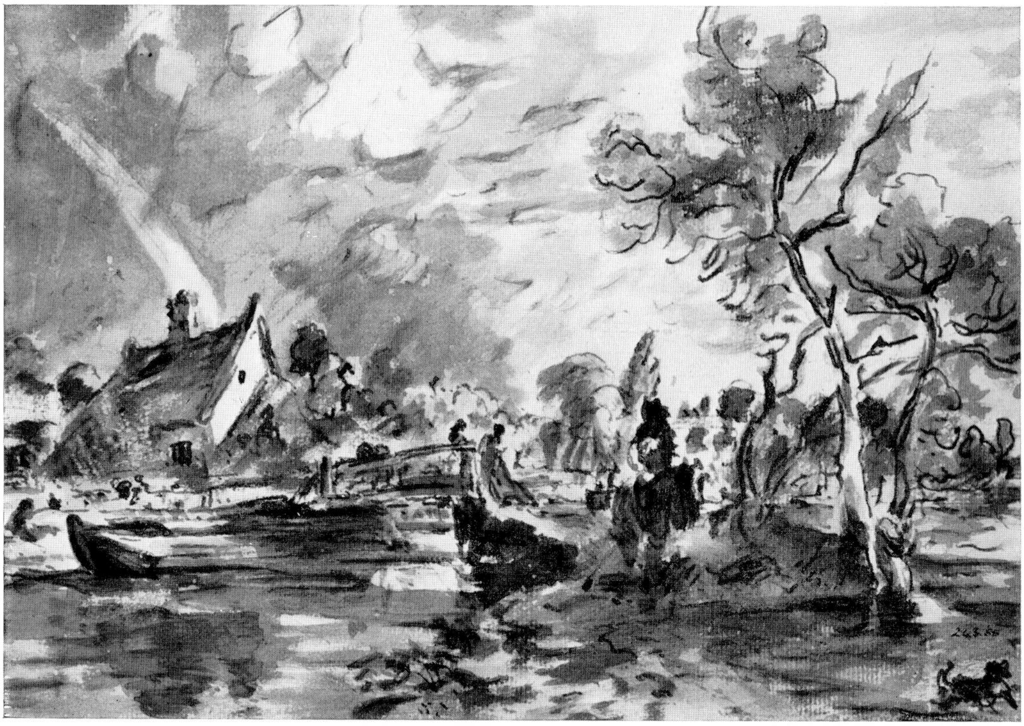

324. Flatford Old Bridge and Bridge Cottage.

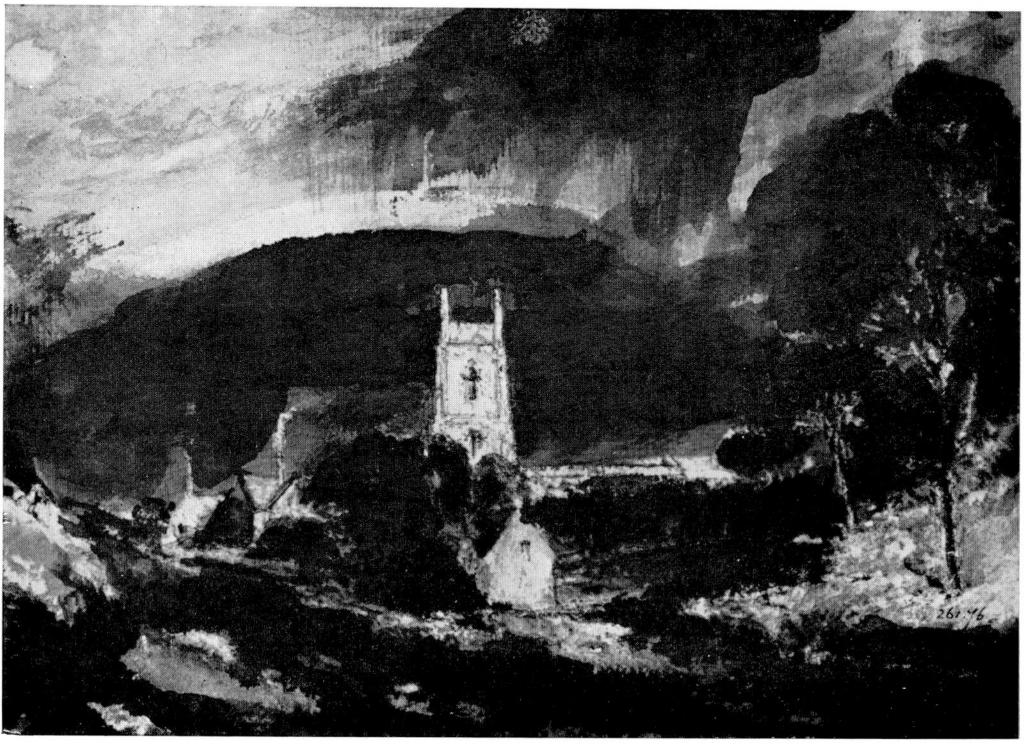

331. Stoke-by-Nayland.

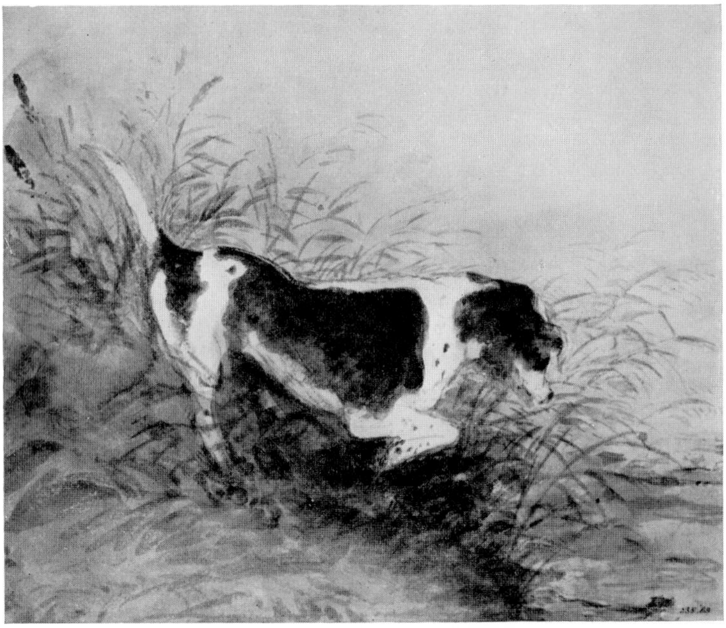

334. A dog watching a rat in the water, Dedham.

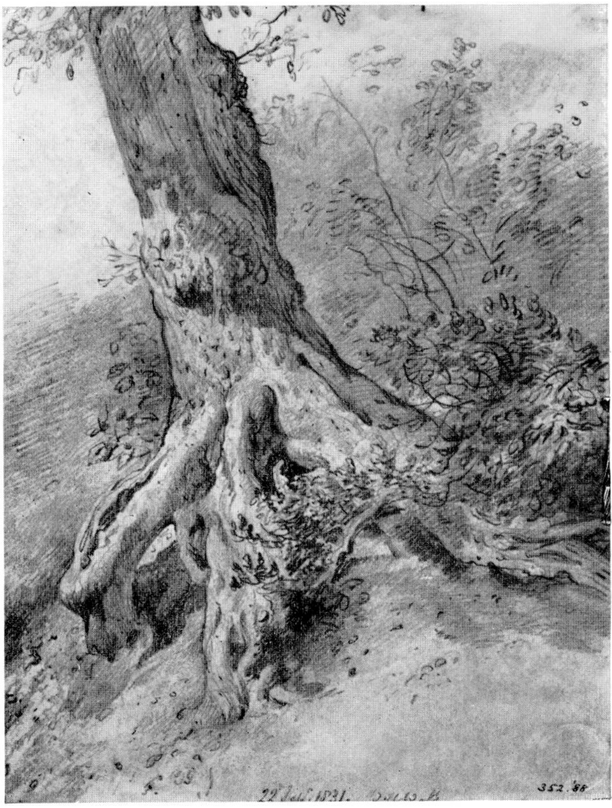

335. The root of a tree, Hampstead.

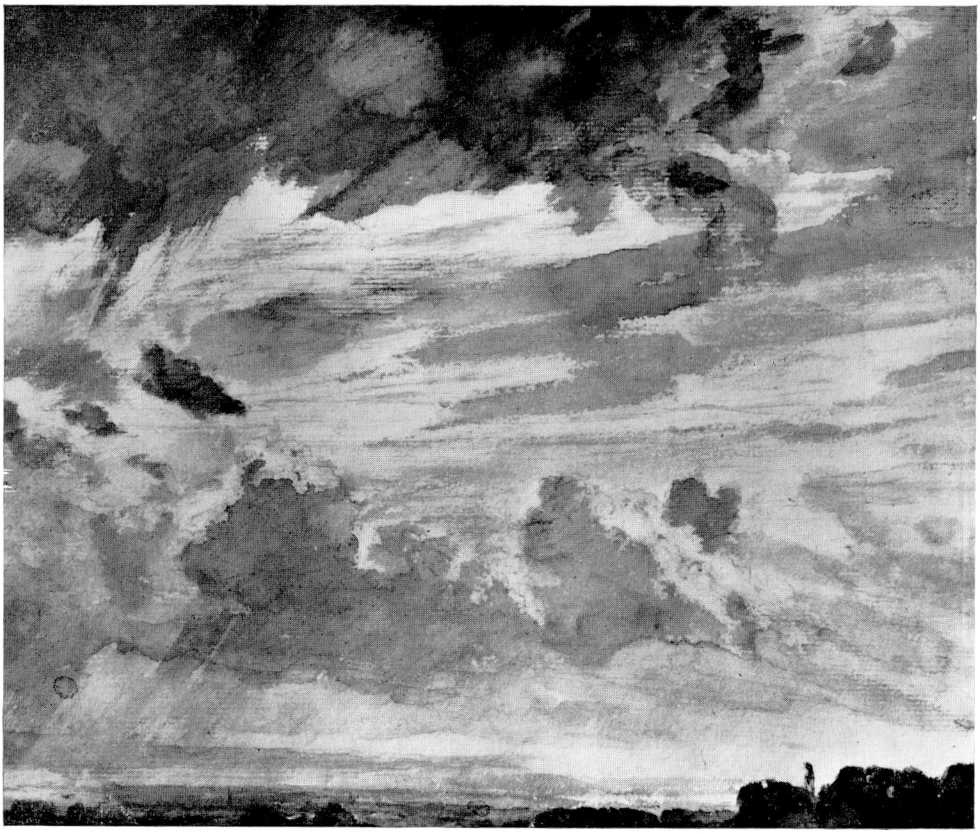

328. Study of clouds above a wide landscape.

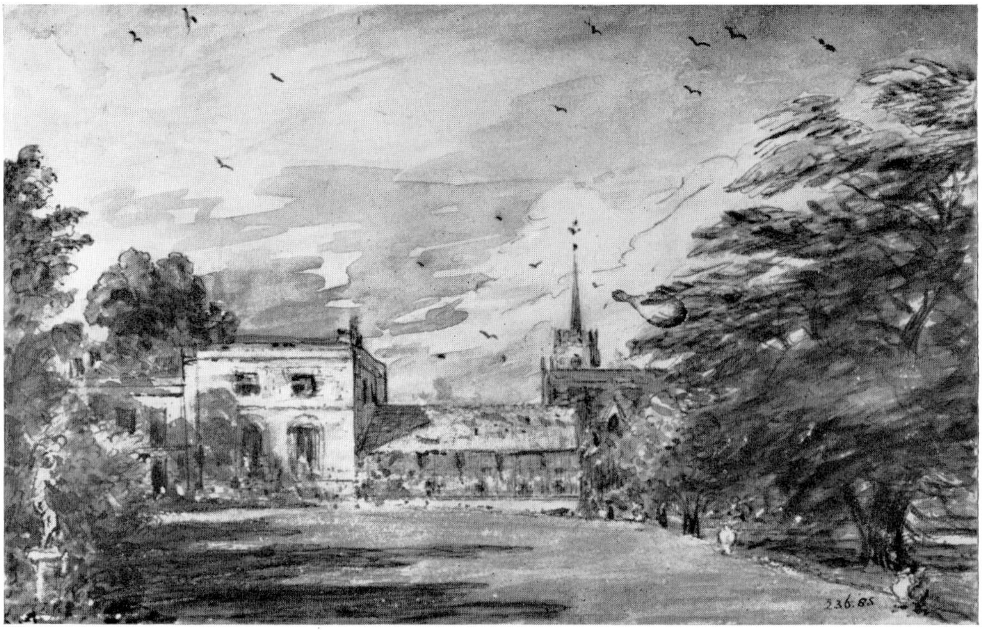

337. Pitt Place, Epsom.

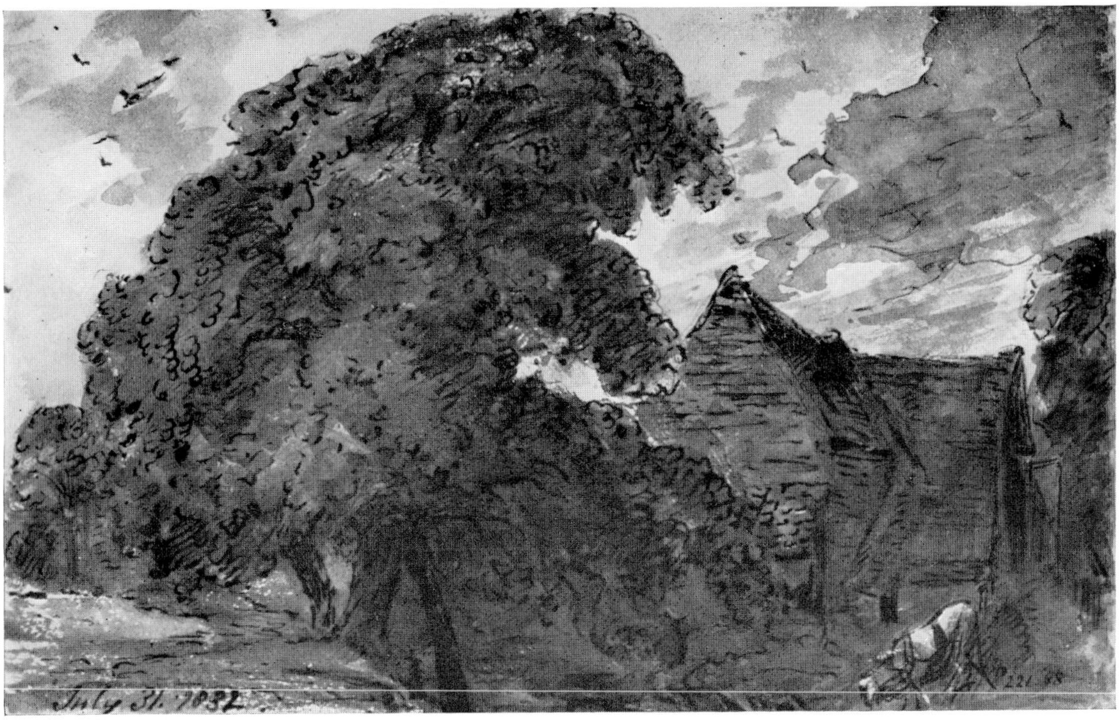

338. A barn, trees and a grey horse, near East Bergholt.

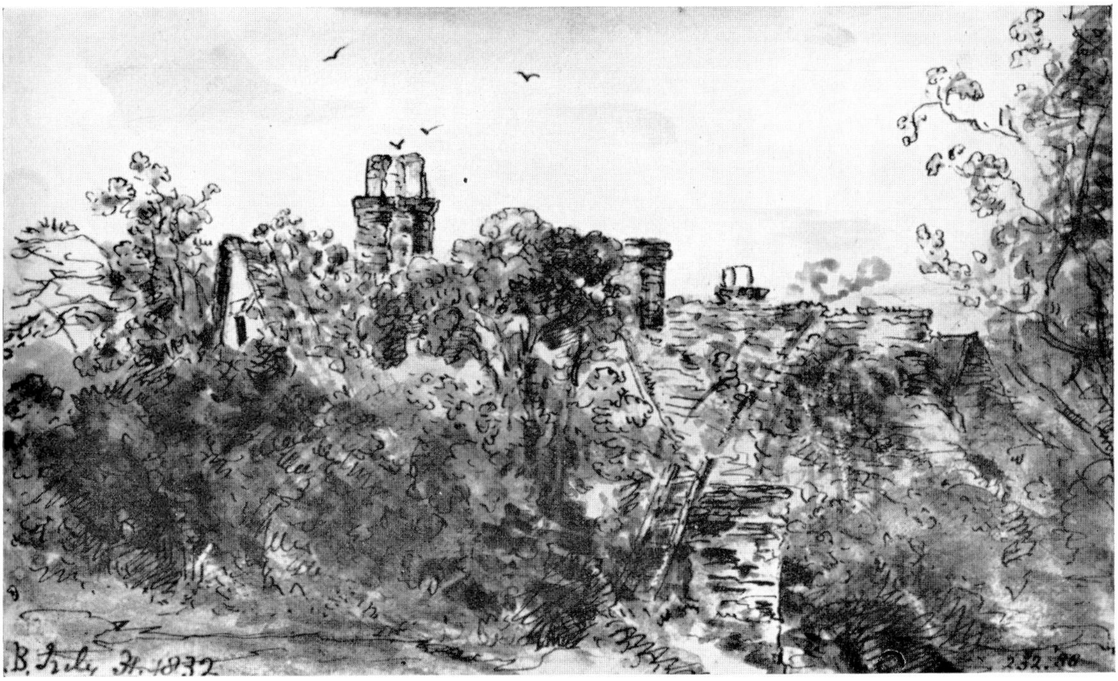

339. Cottages at East Bergholt.

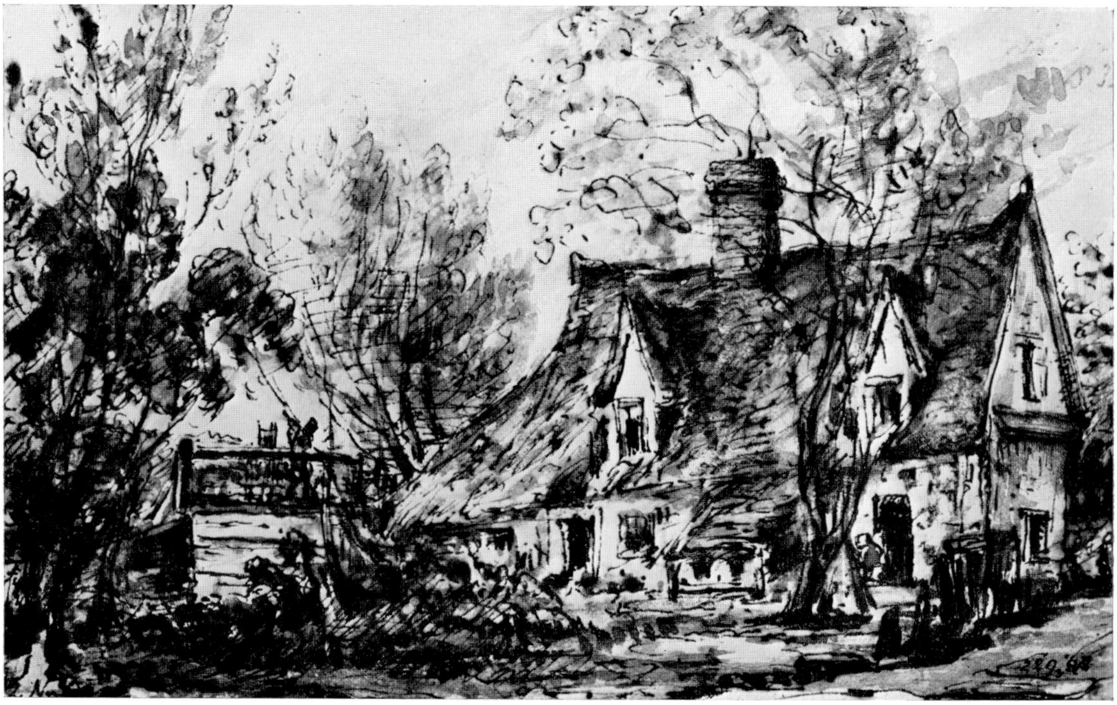

346. Bridge Cottage, Flatford.

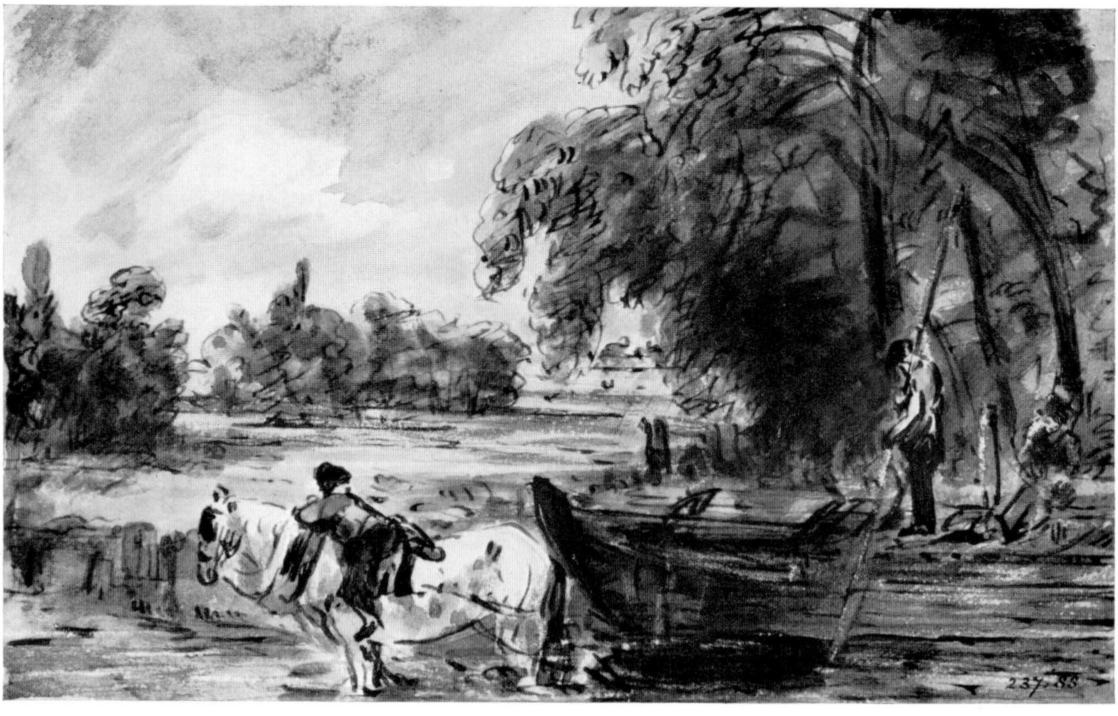

347. A barge on the Stour.

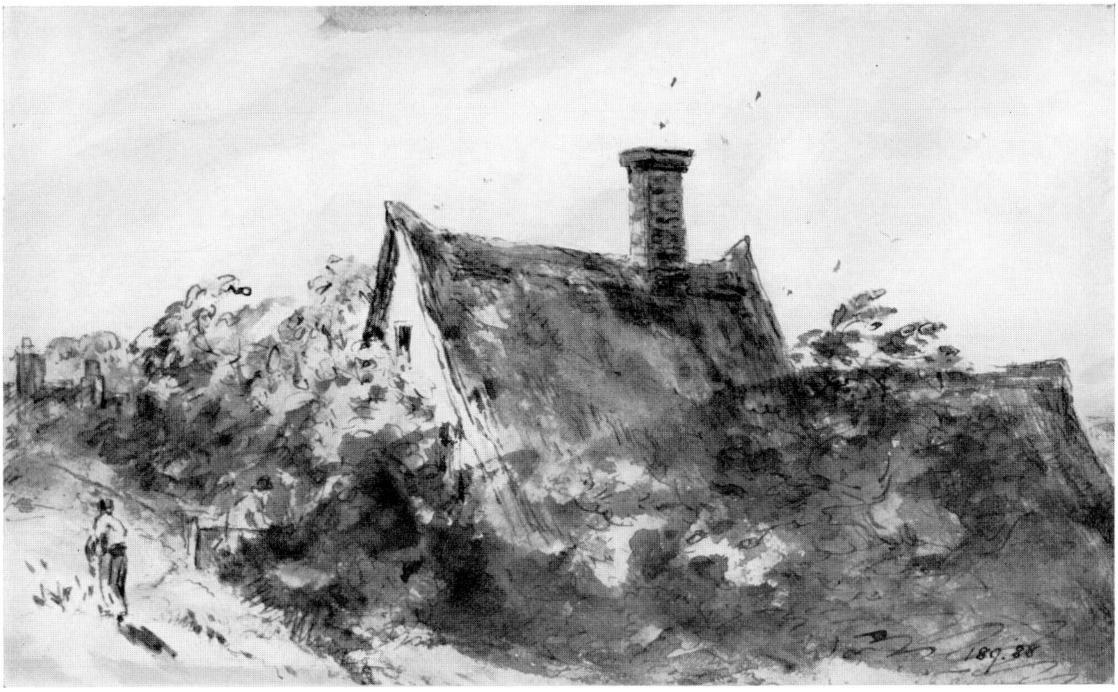

348. A thatched cottage and two figures.

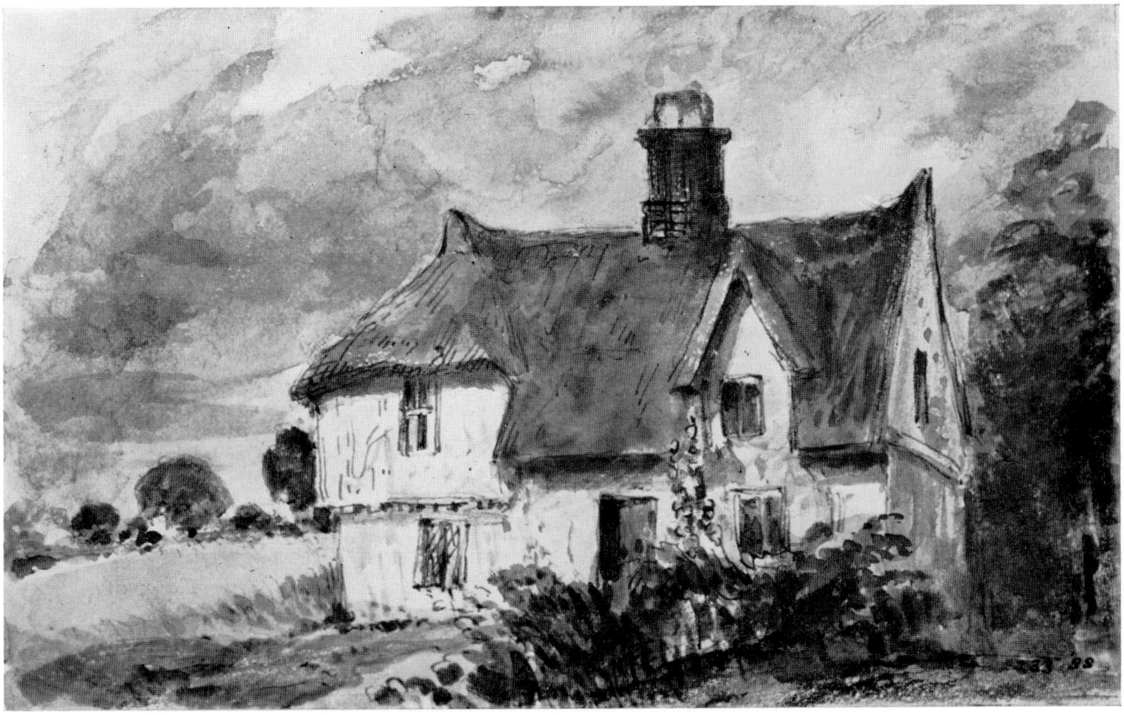

349. A cottage near a cornfield.

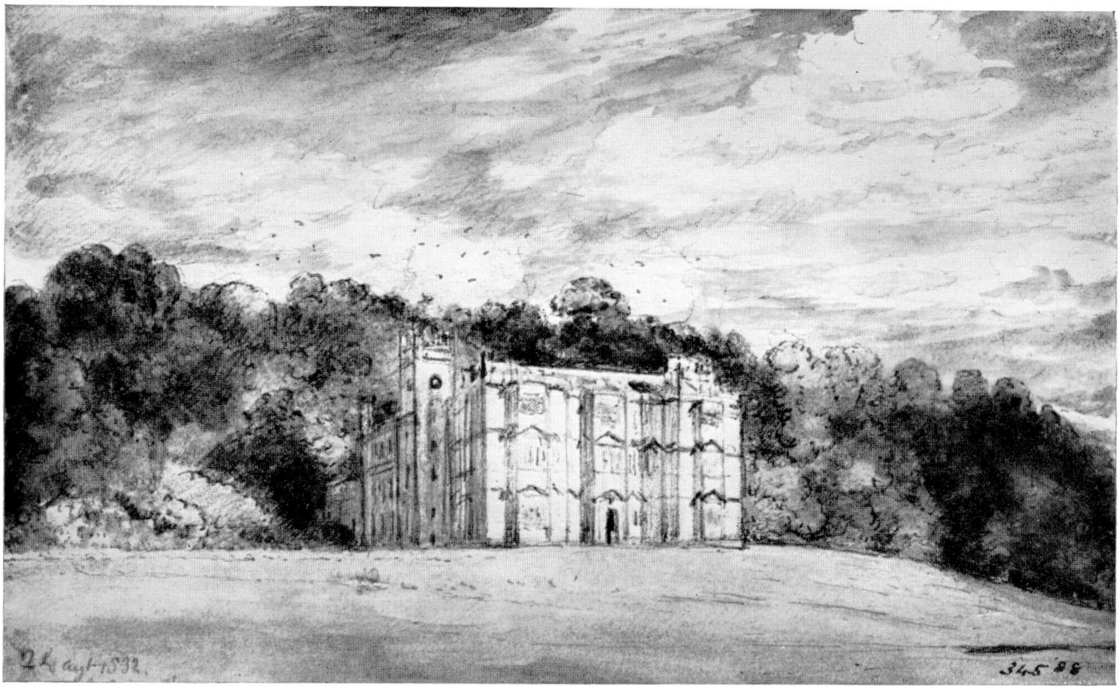

340. Englefield House, Berkshire.

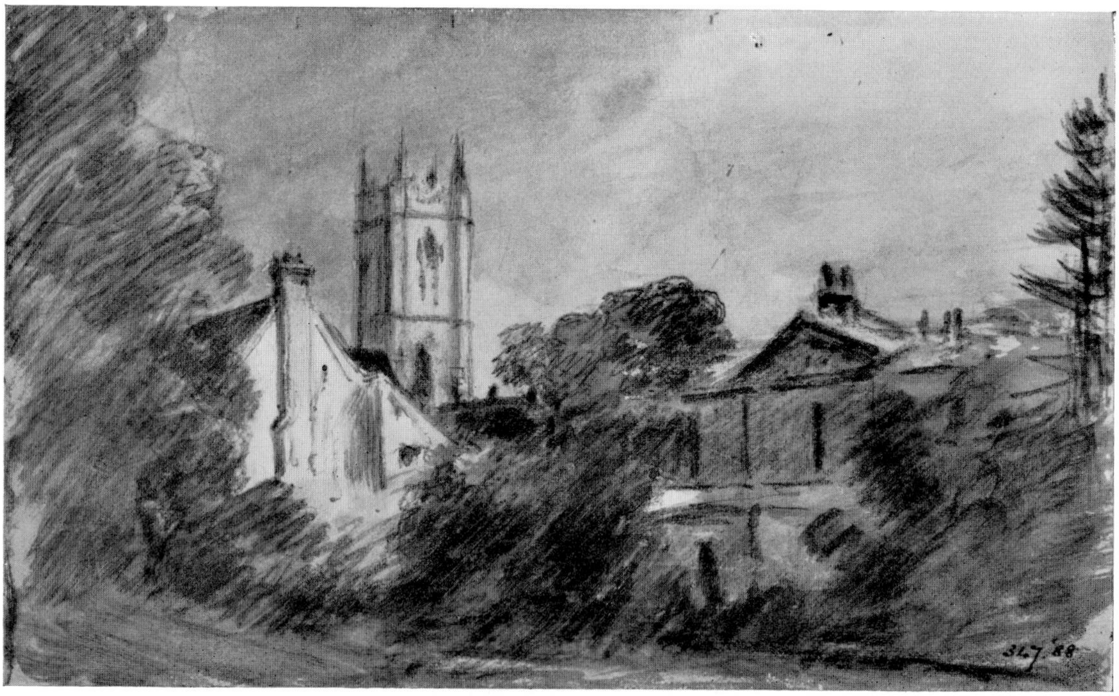

350. Houses in Dedham, with the church tower.

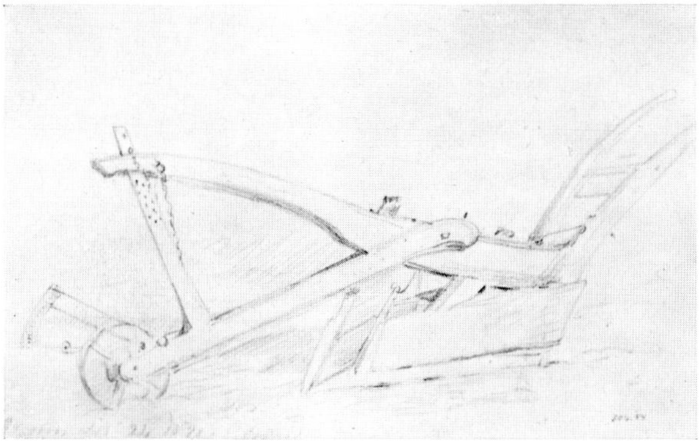

336. Sketch of a plough, Epsom.

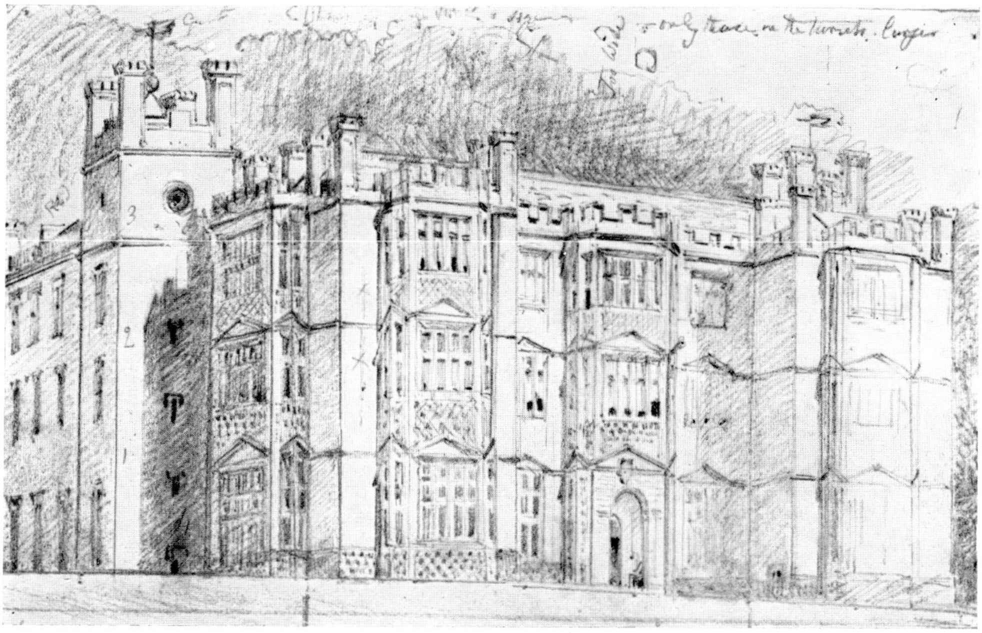

343. Englefield House, Berkshire.

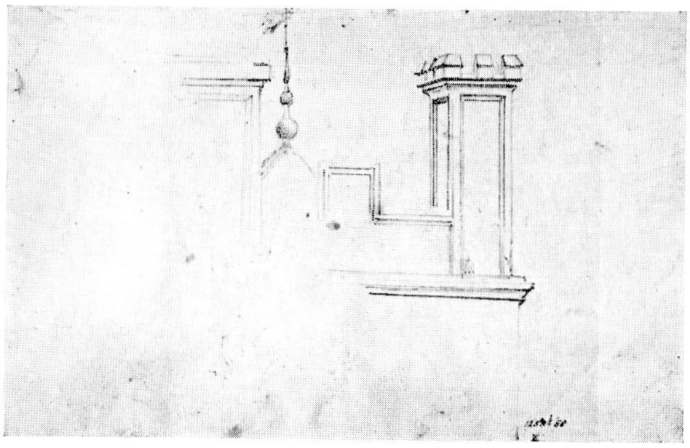

344. Englefield House: detail of turret.

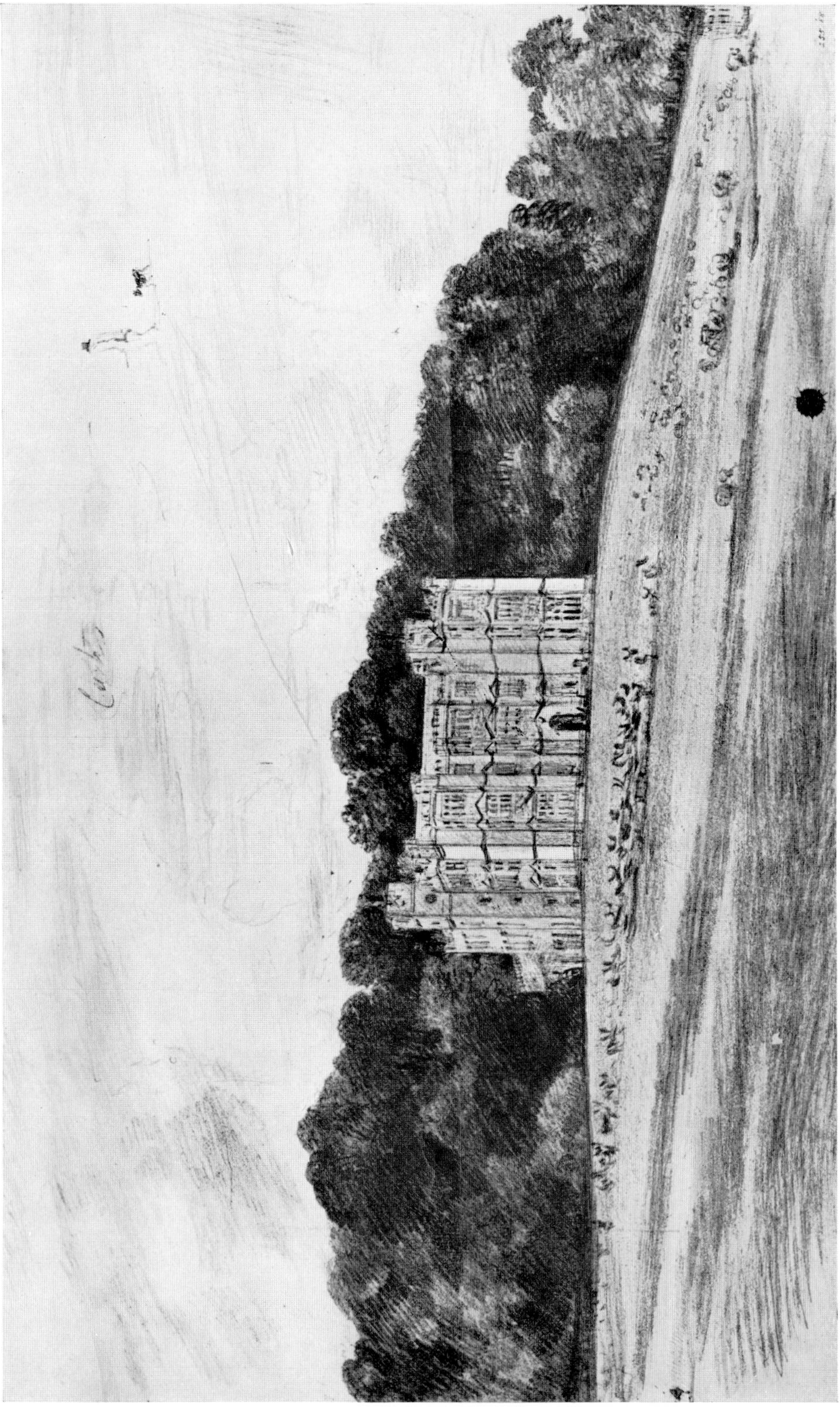

341. Englefield House, Berkshire.

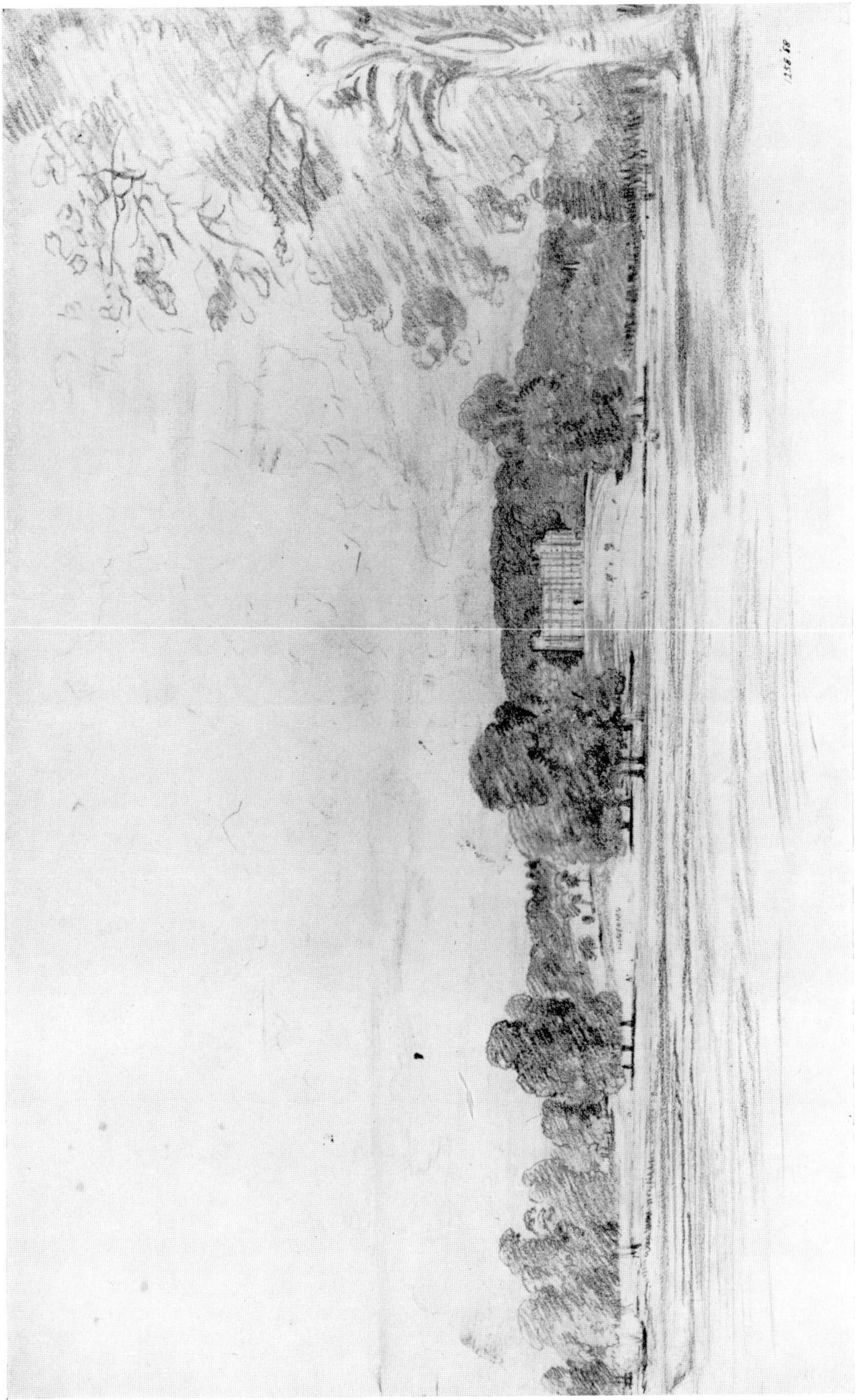

342. Englefield House, Berkshire.

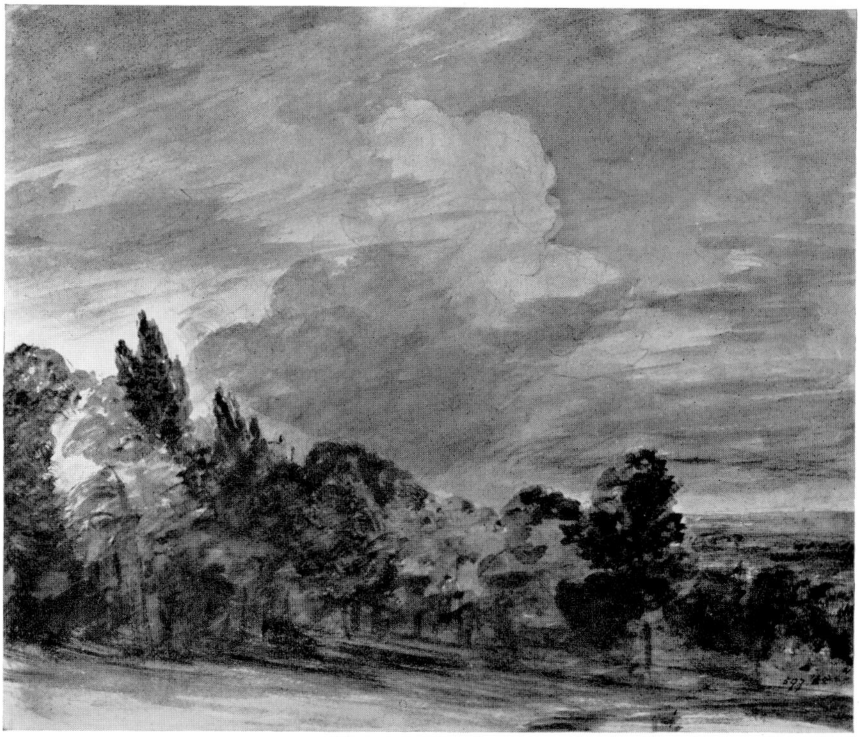

345. View over a wide landscape.

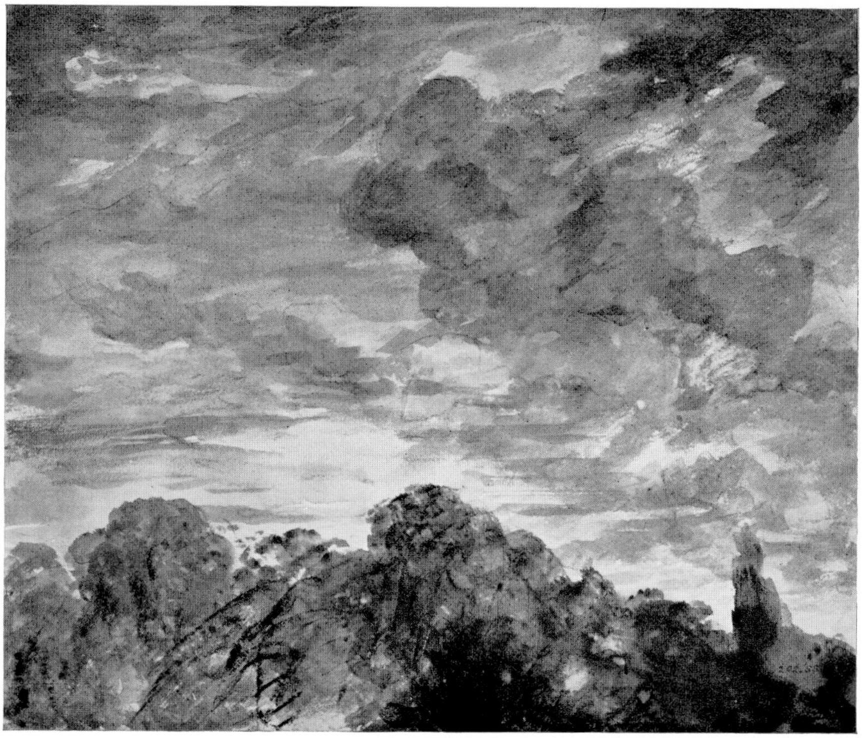

356. Study of sky effect.

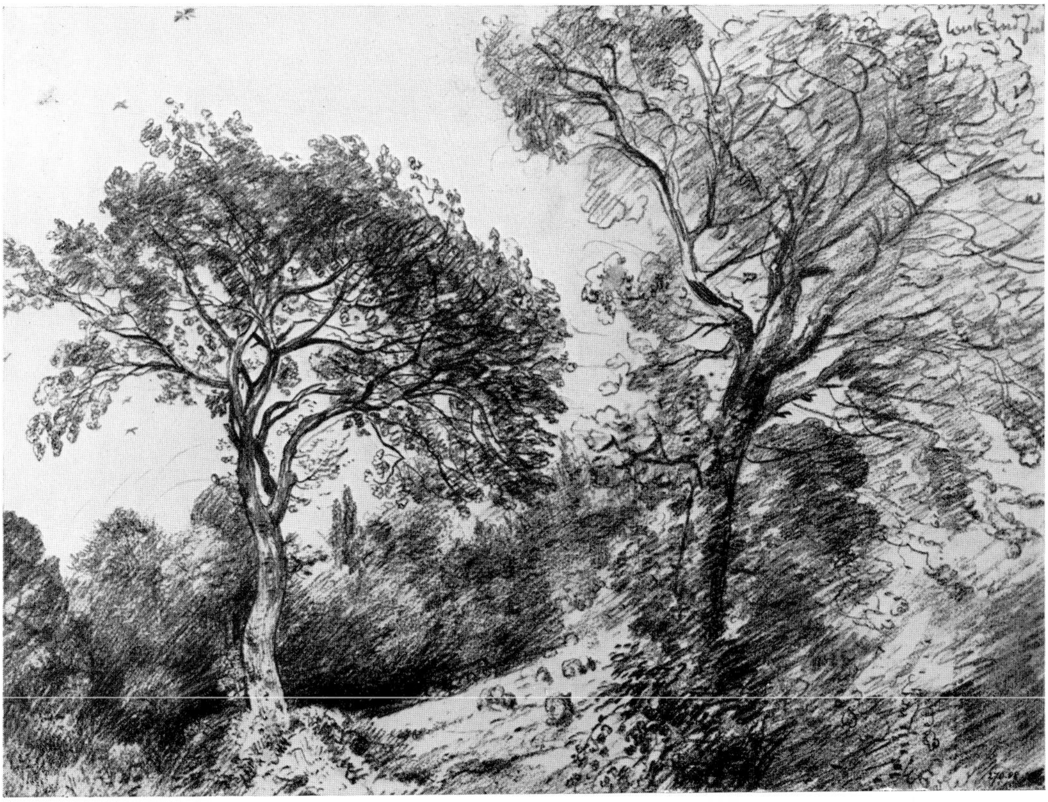

353. Trees in West End Fields, Hampstead.

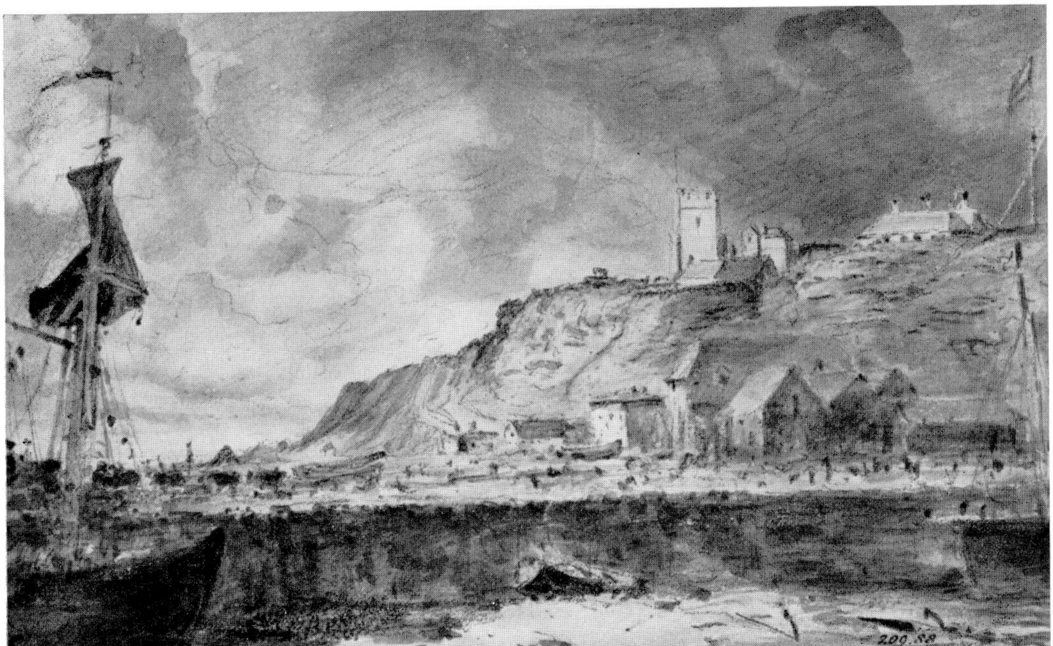

357. Folkestone Harbour.

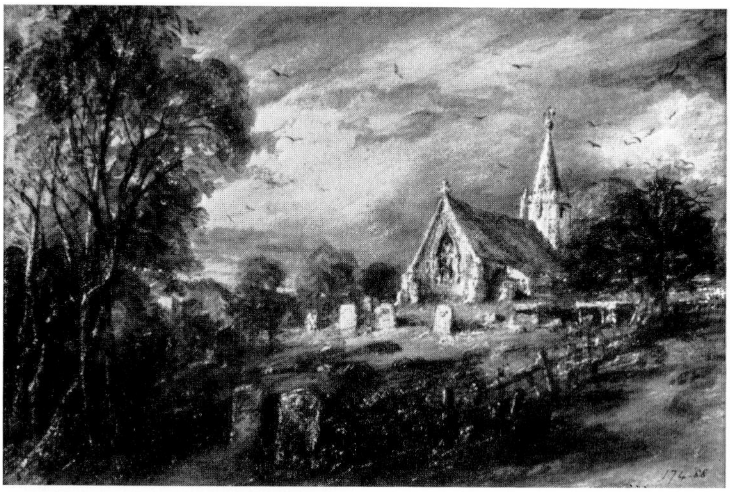

354. Stoke Poges Church.

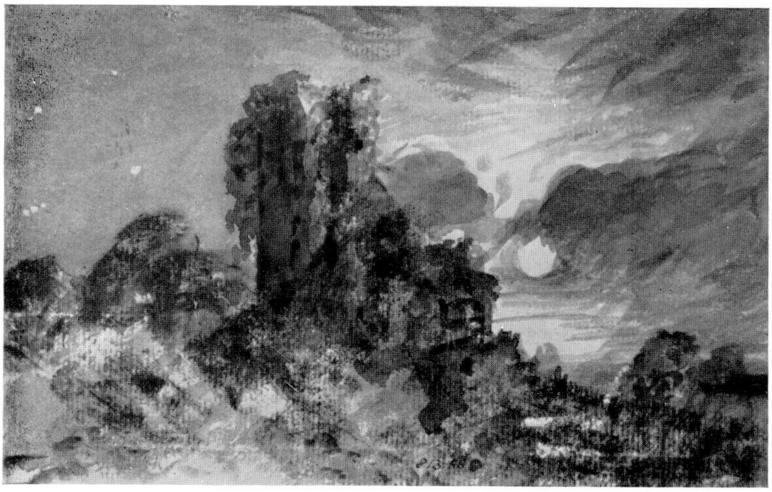

355. Illustration to Gray's *Elegy*.

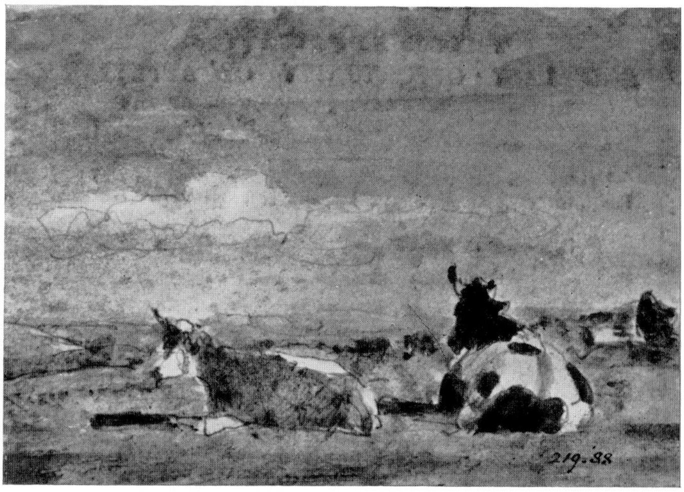

361. Study of cows at Hampstead.

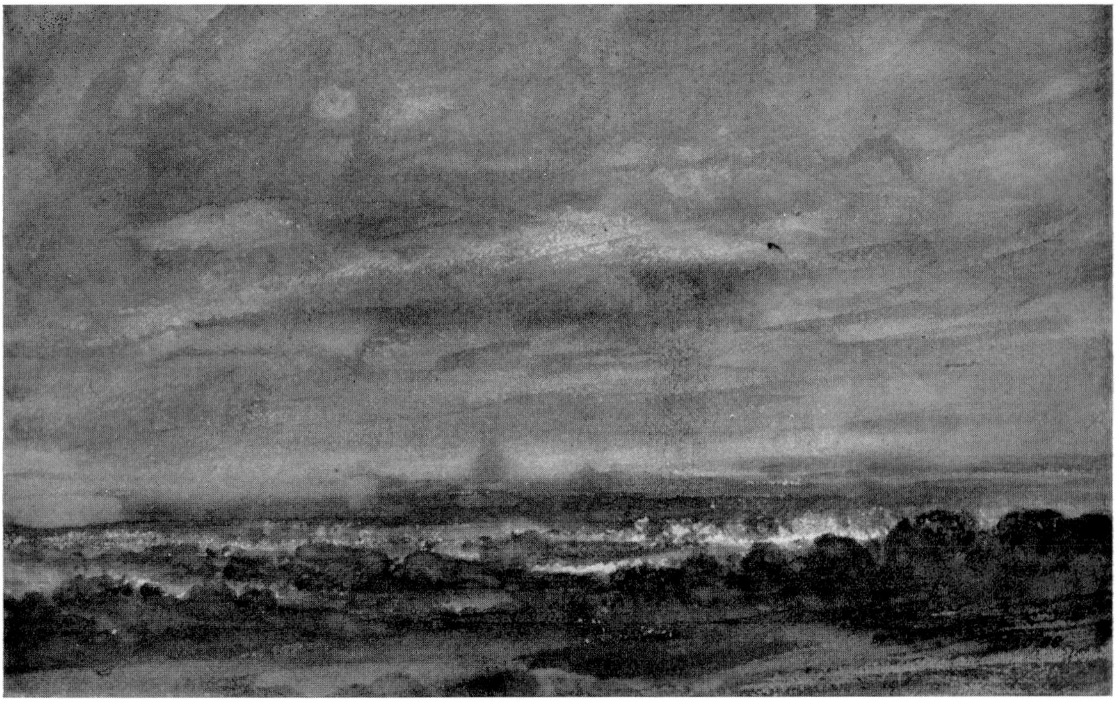

358. View at Hampstead.

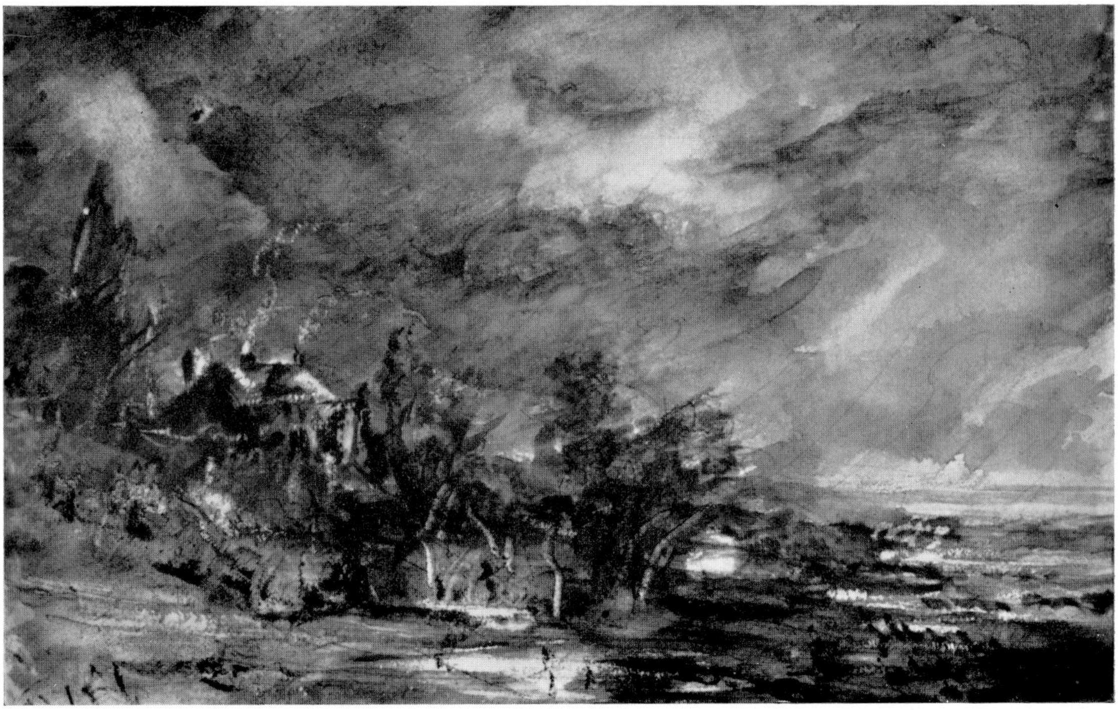

360. Hampstead Heath, from near Well Walk.

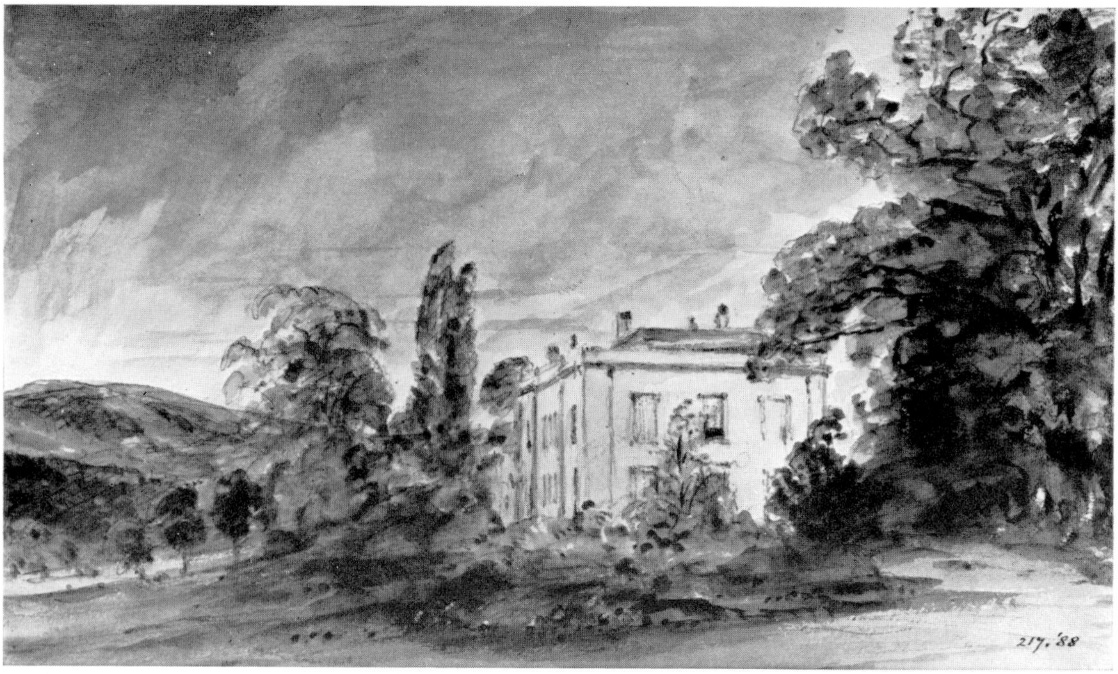

362. Bignor Park, Sussex.

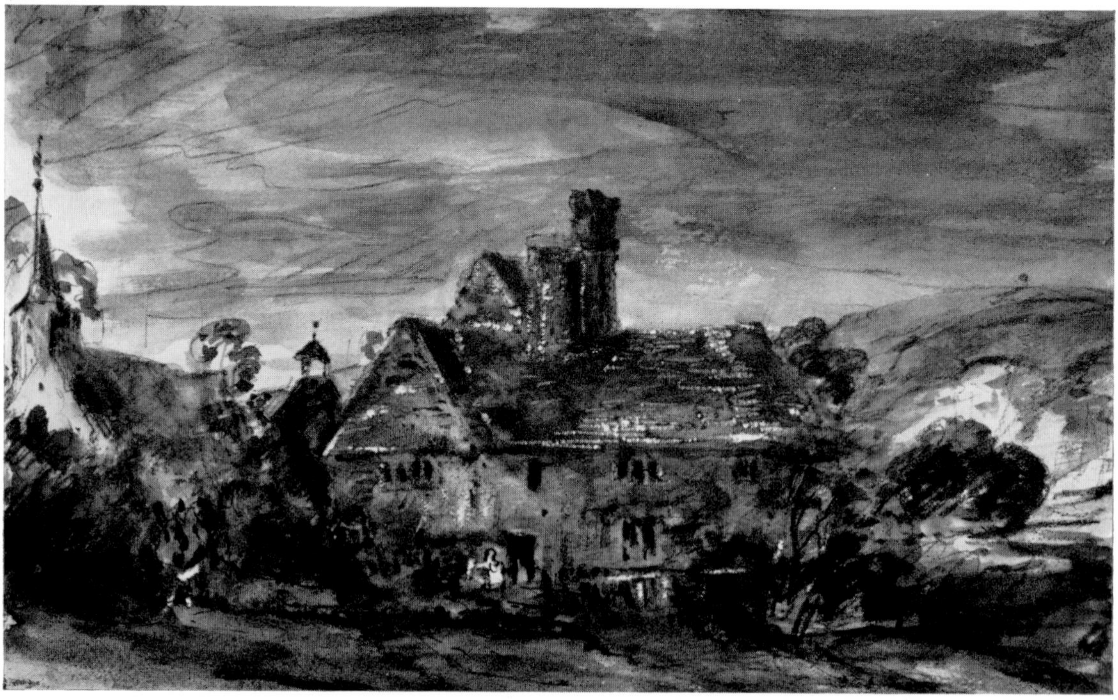

363. A farmhouse at Houghton.

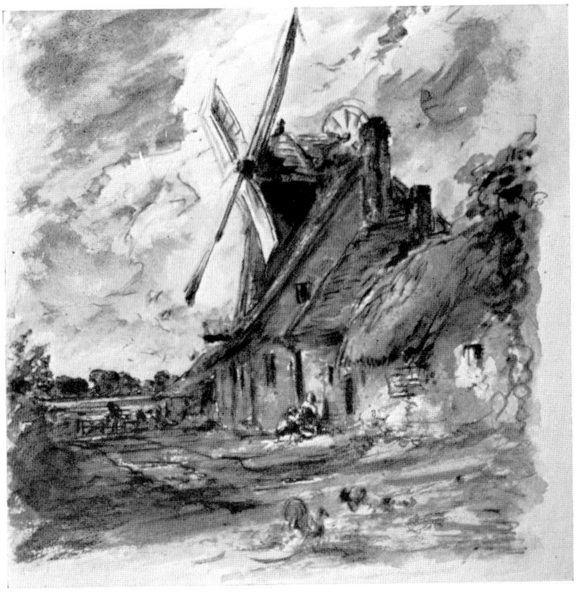

364. A windmill and cottages.

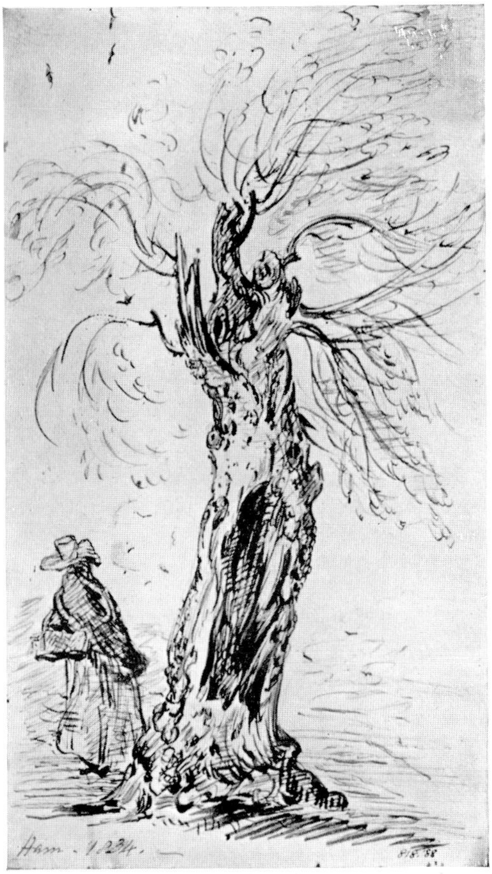

368. A woman by a willow tree at Ham.

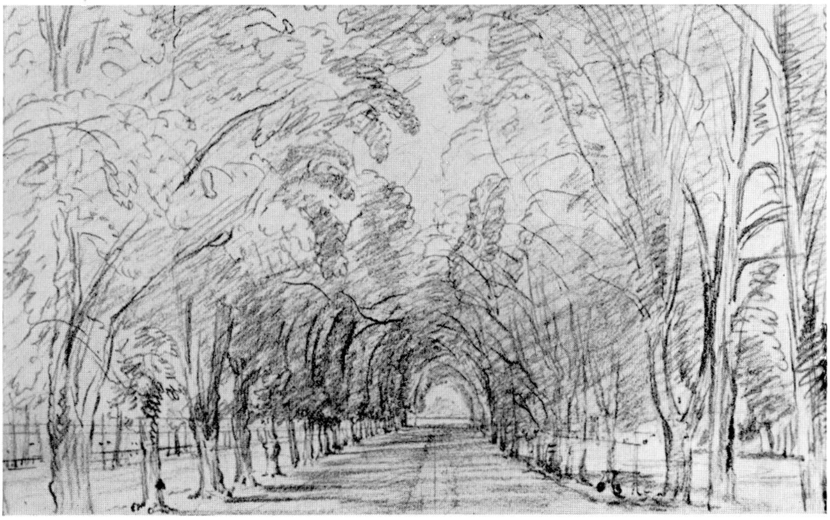

368a. The avenue, Ham.

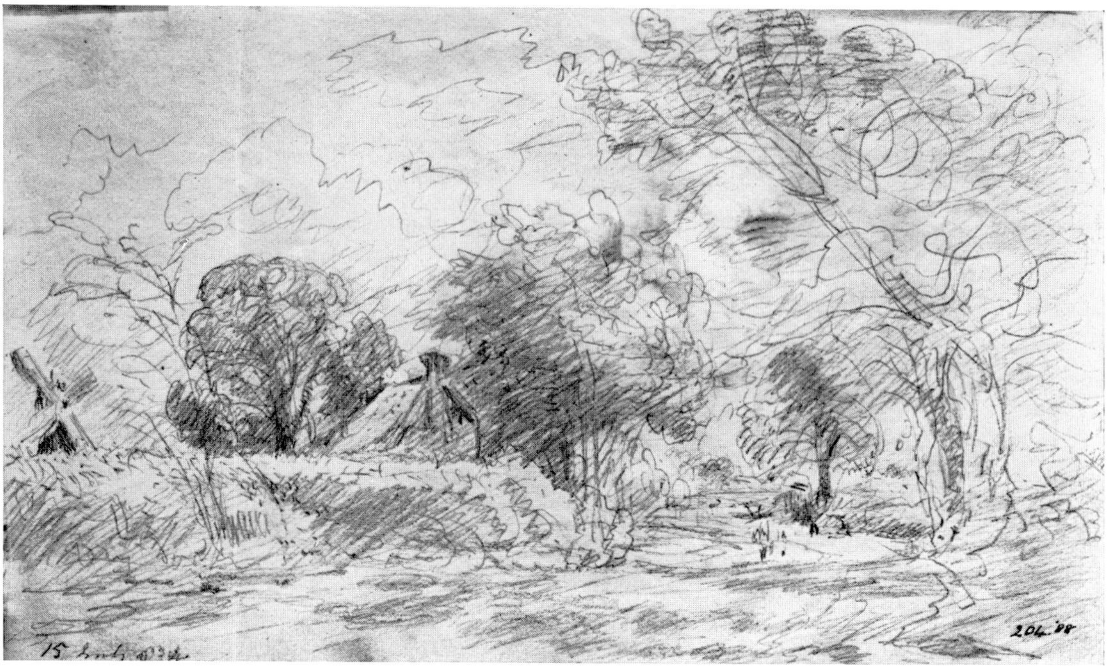

364a. A road, with cottage and windmill.

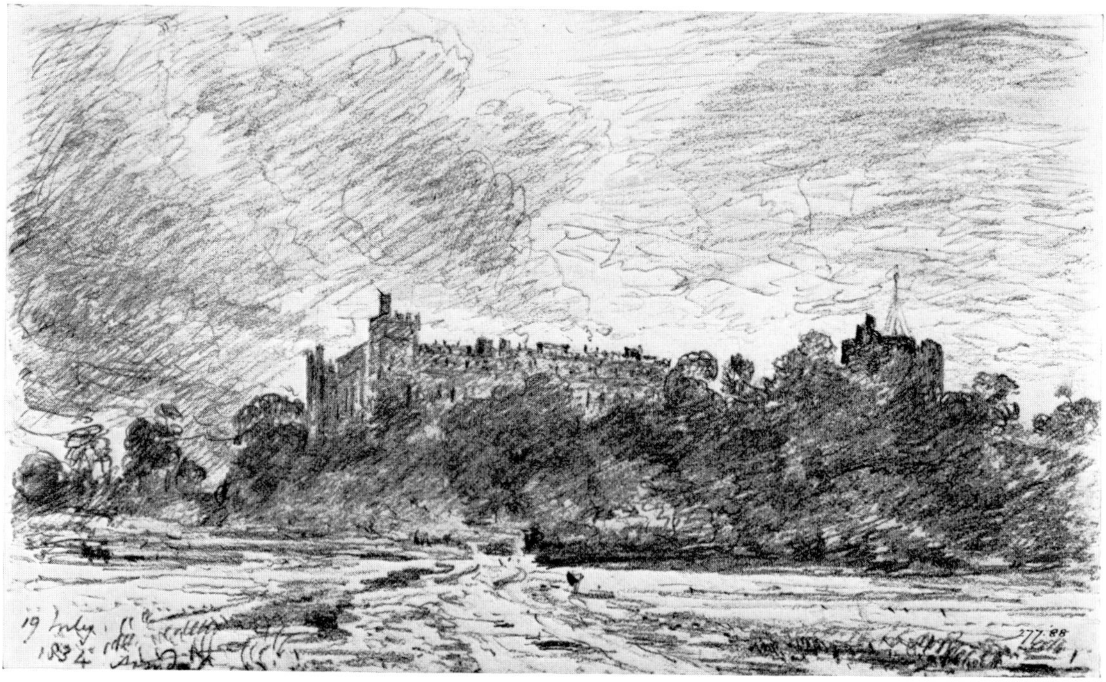

365. Arundel Castle.

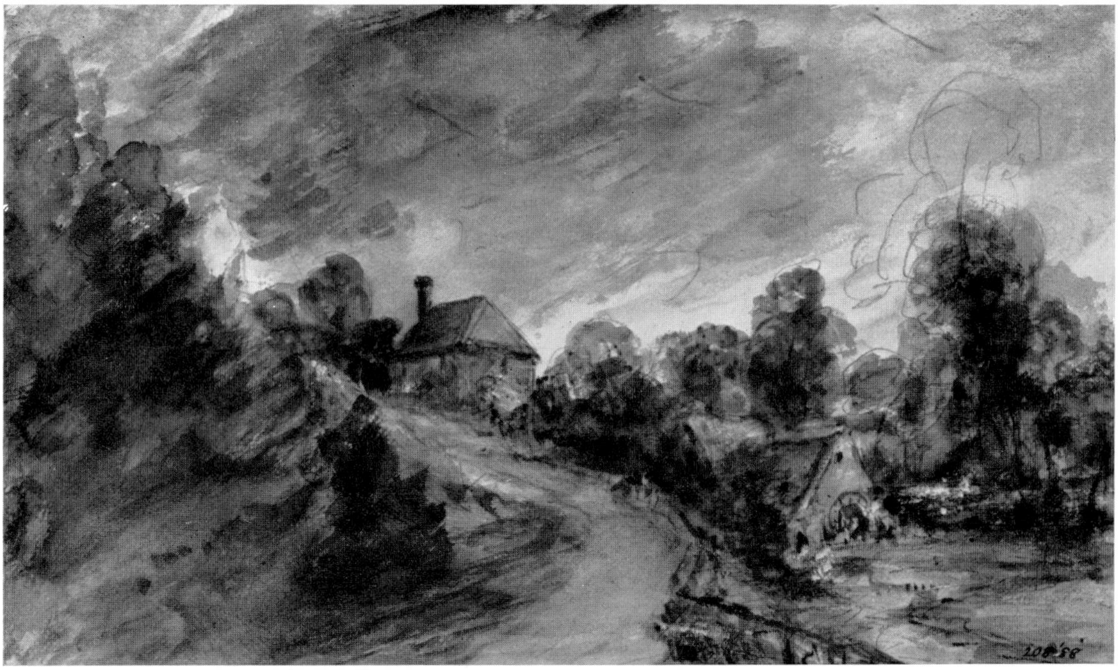

366. A cottage and watermill at Bignor.

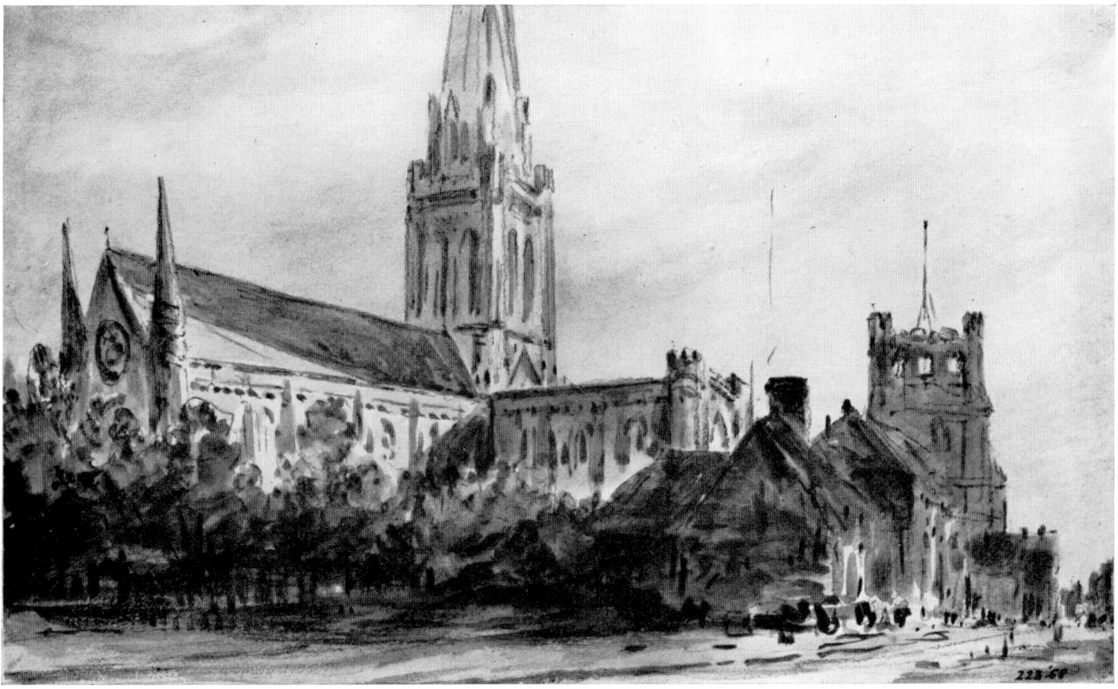

367. Chichester Cathedral.

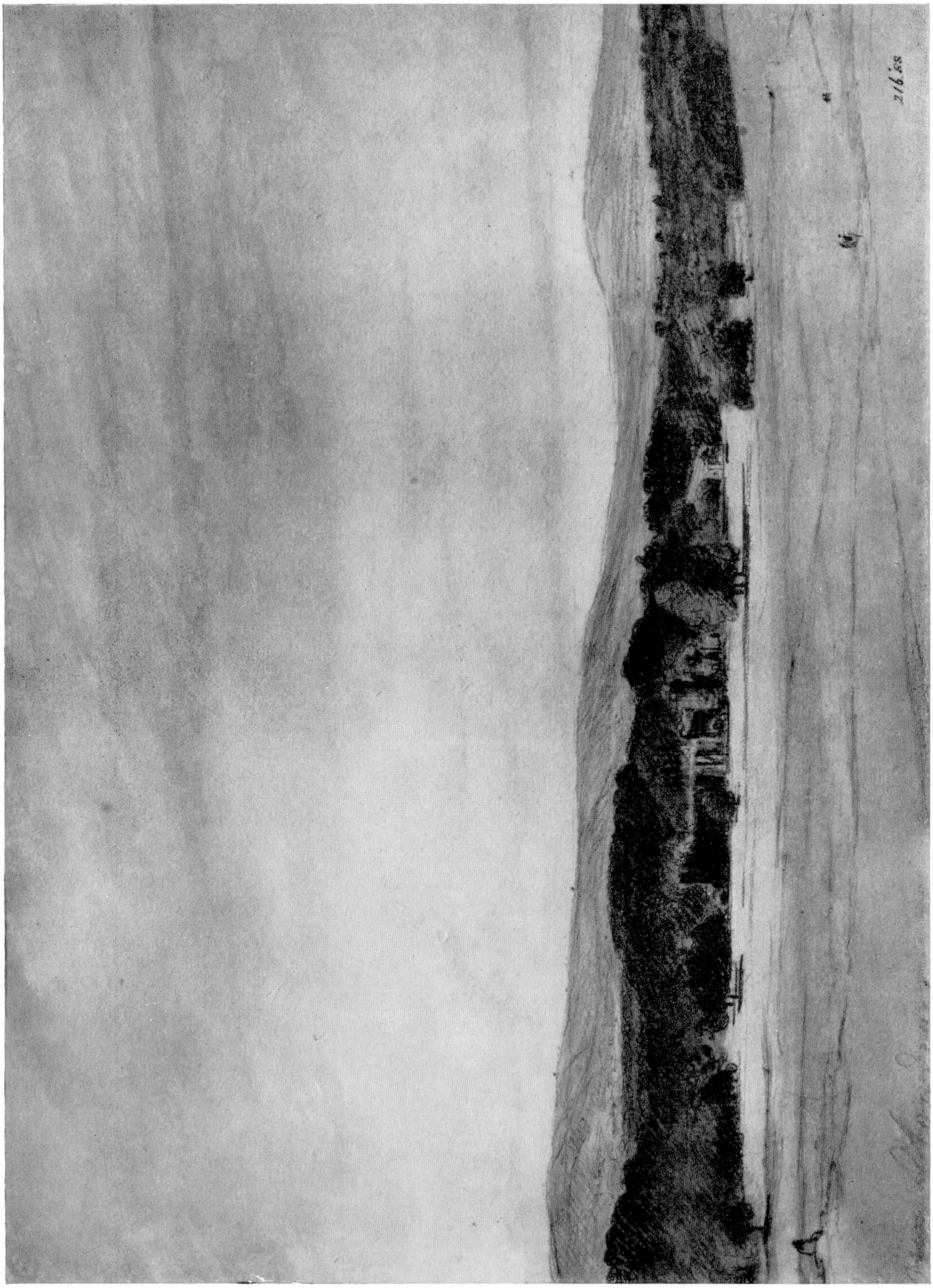

369. The ruins of Cowdray House.

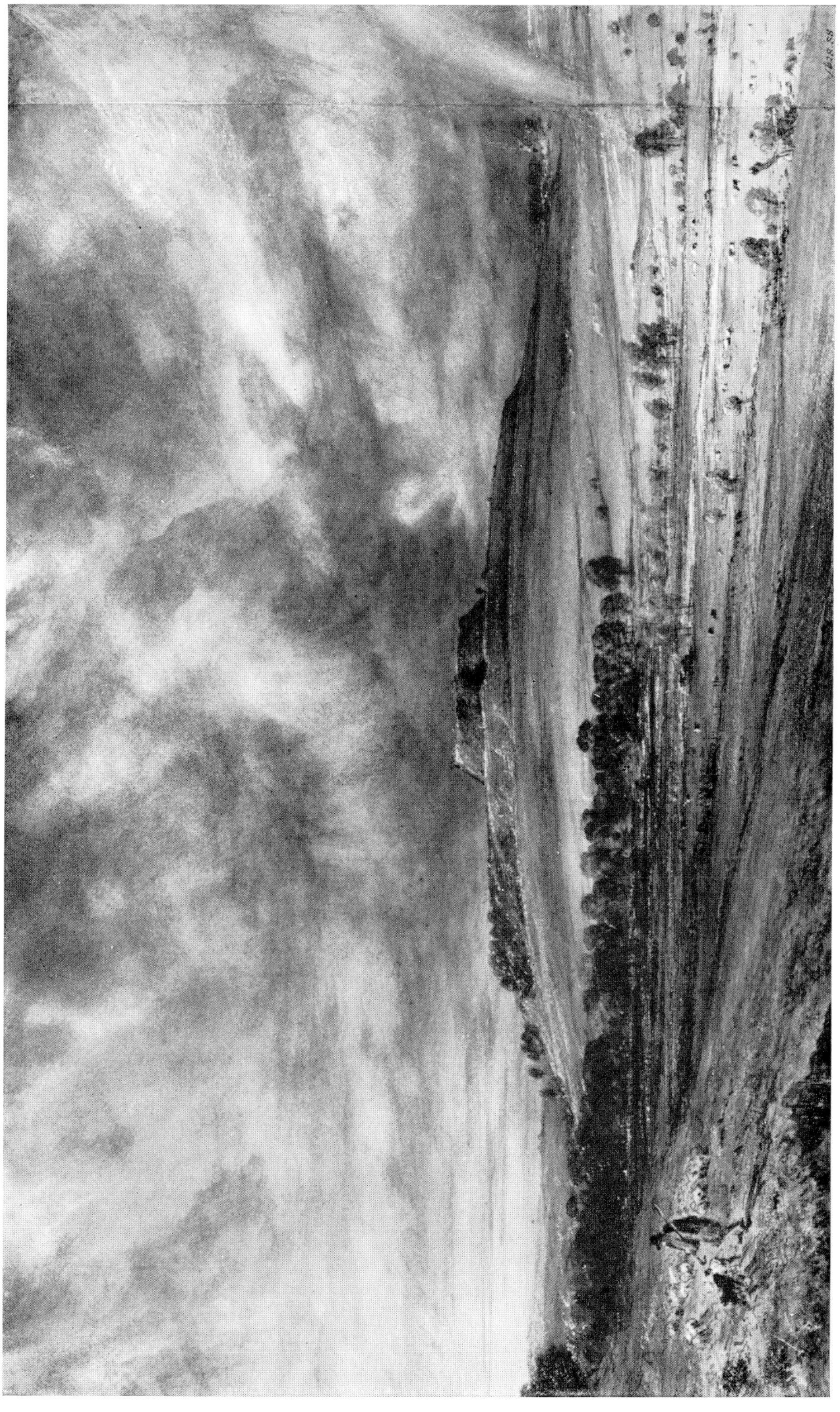

359. Old Sarum.

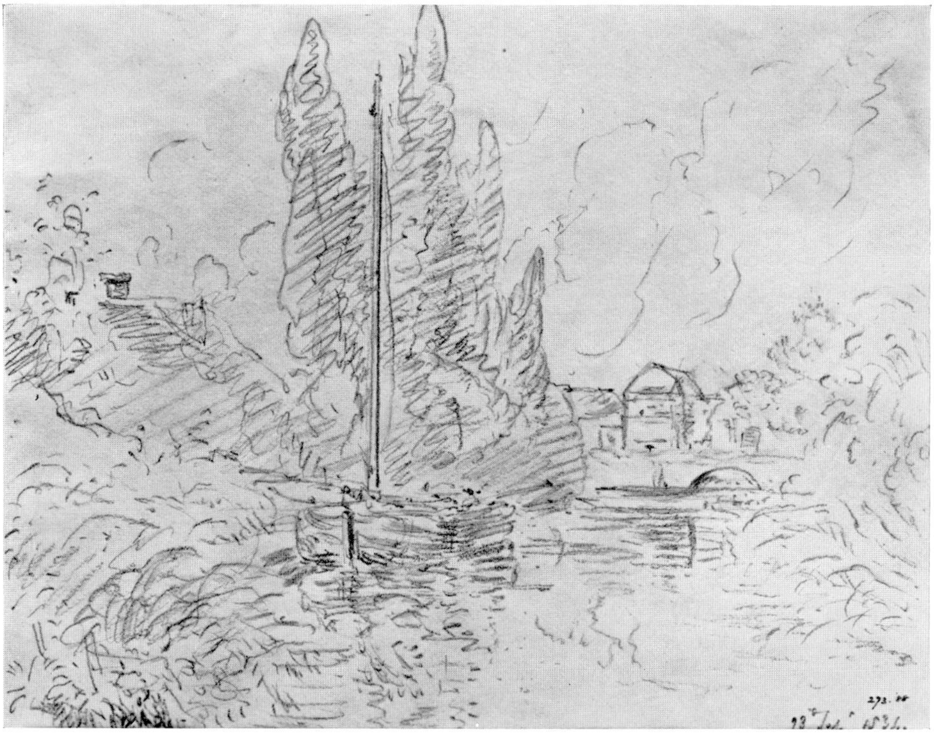

371. Fittleworth Mill and Bridge.

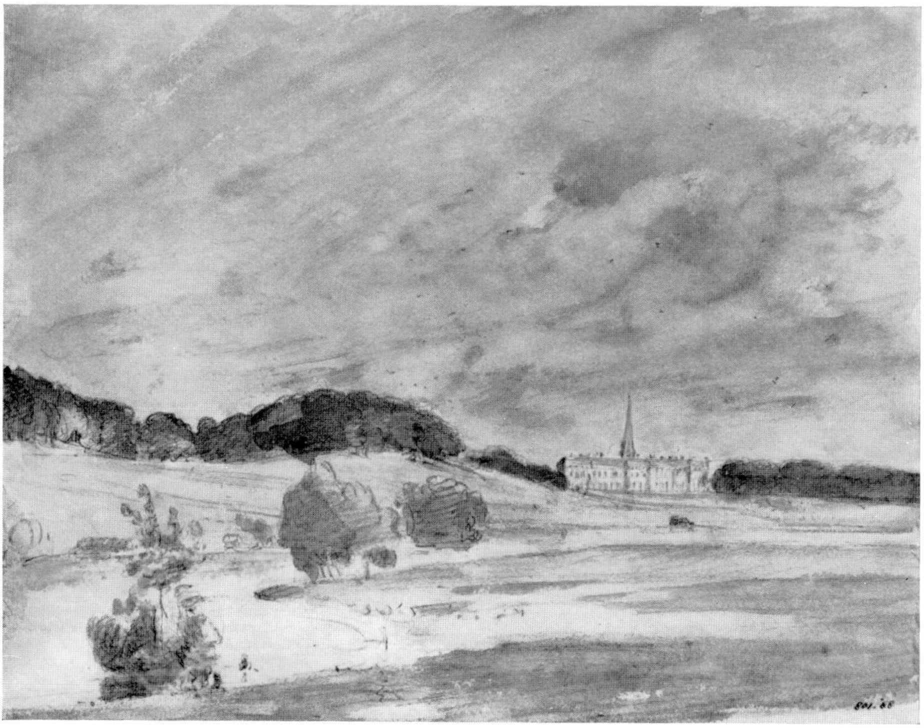

372. Petworth House from the Park.

370. Fittleworth Mill.

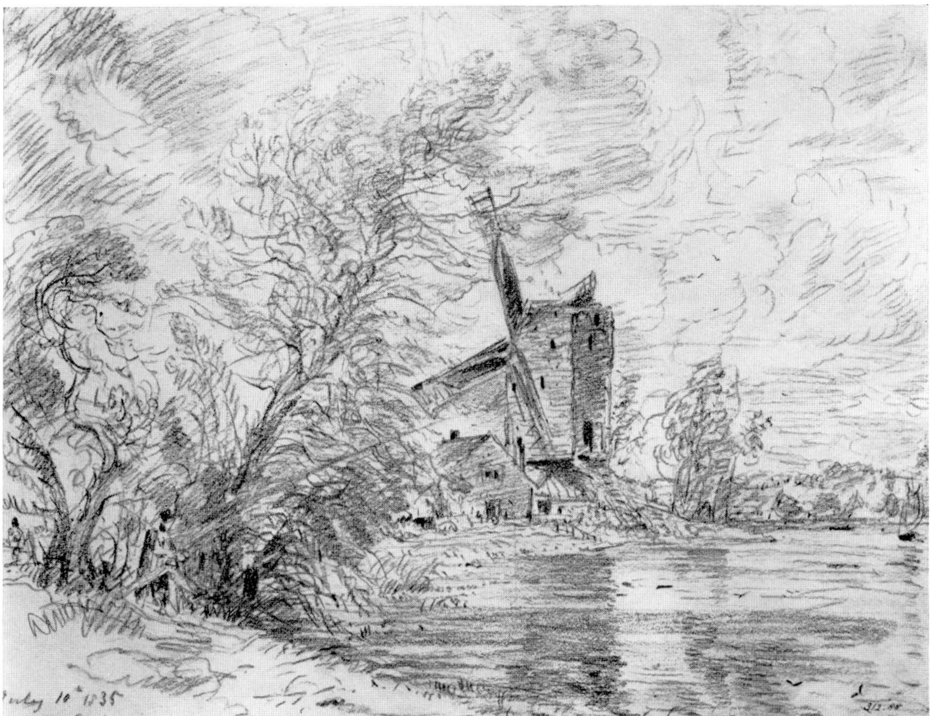

380. A windmill at Arundel.

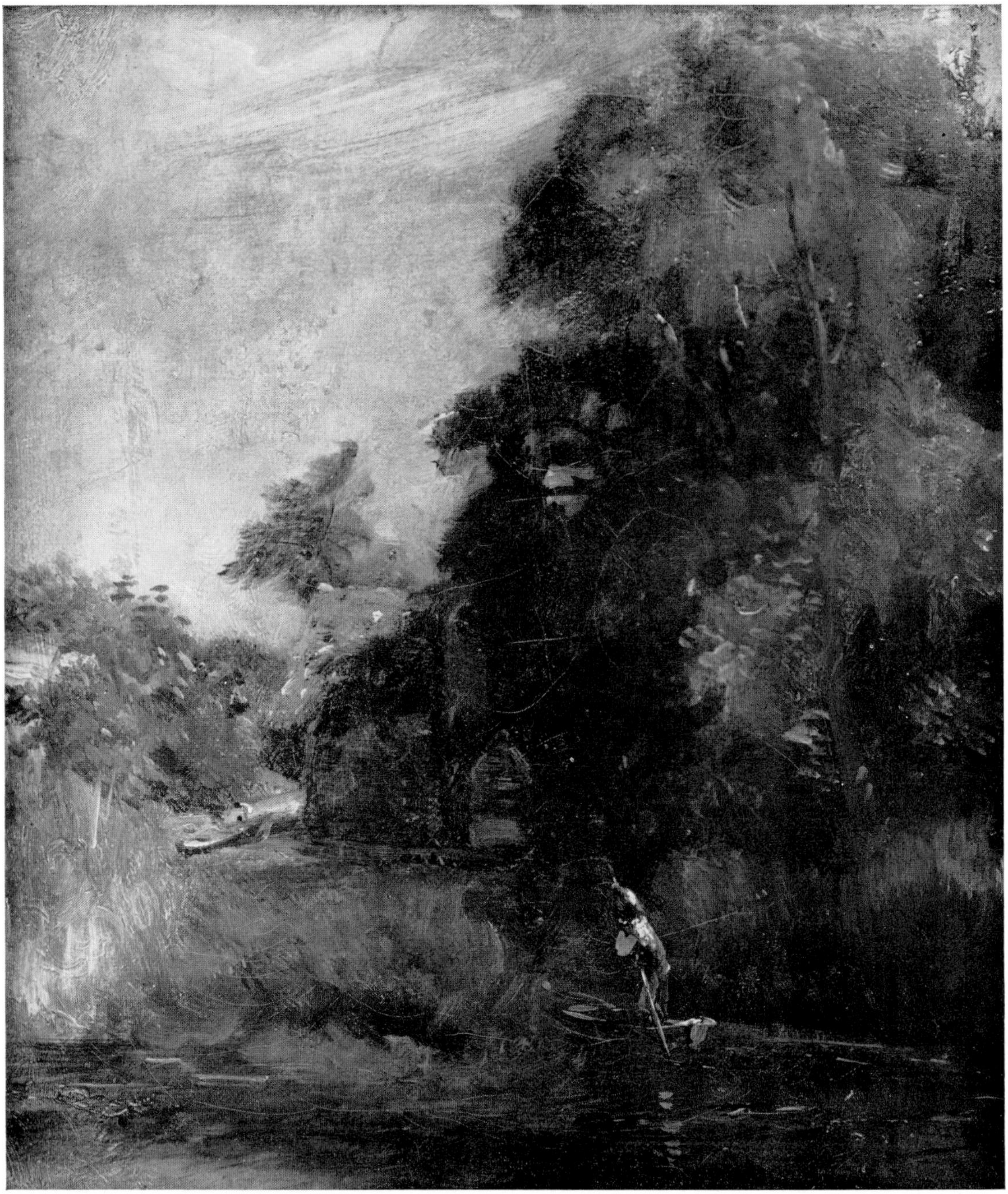

373. Sketch for 'The Valley Farm'.

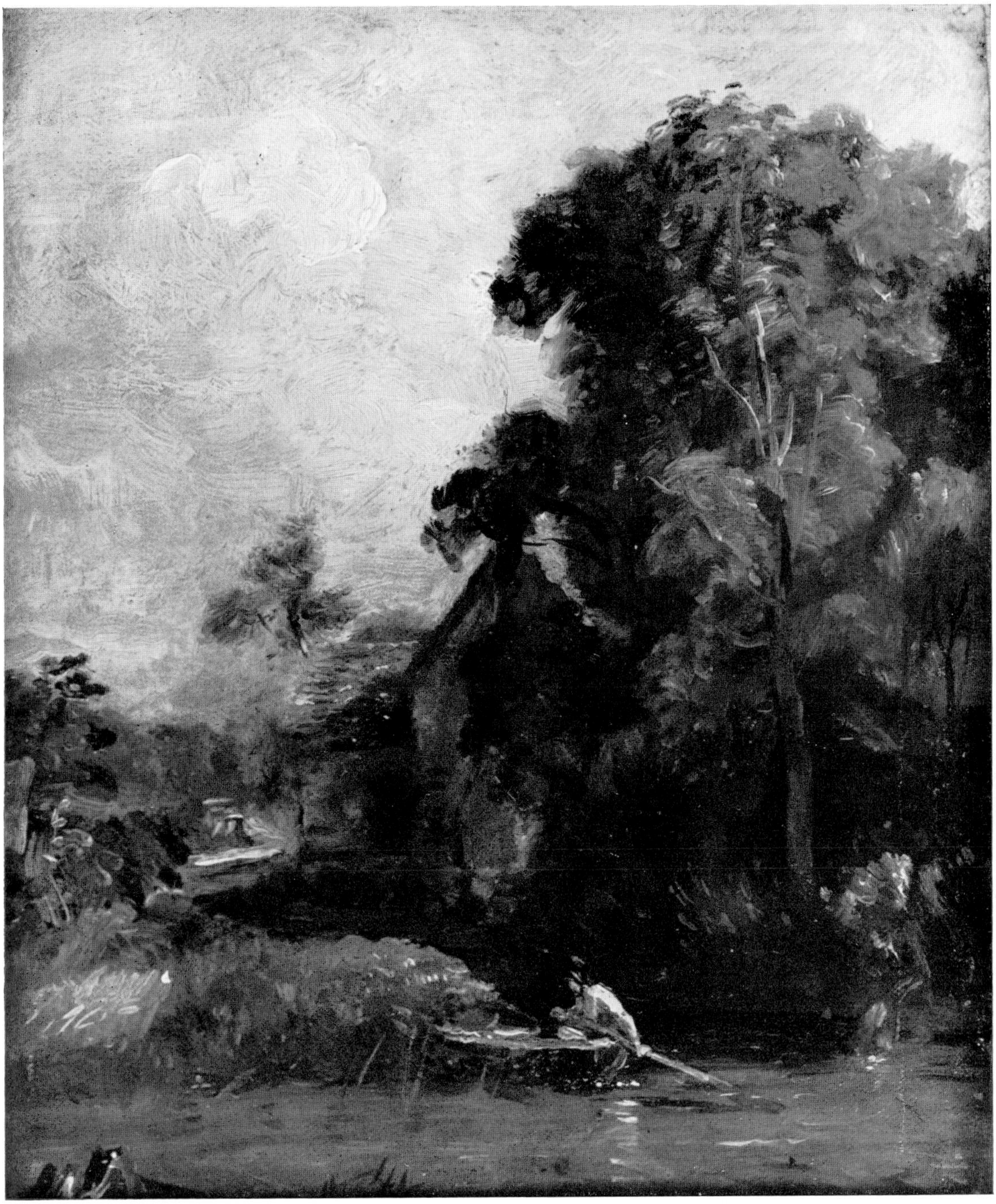

374. Sketch for 'The Valley Farm'.

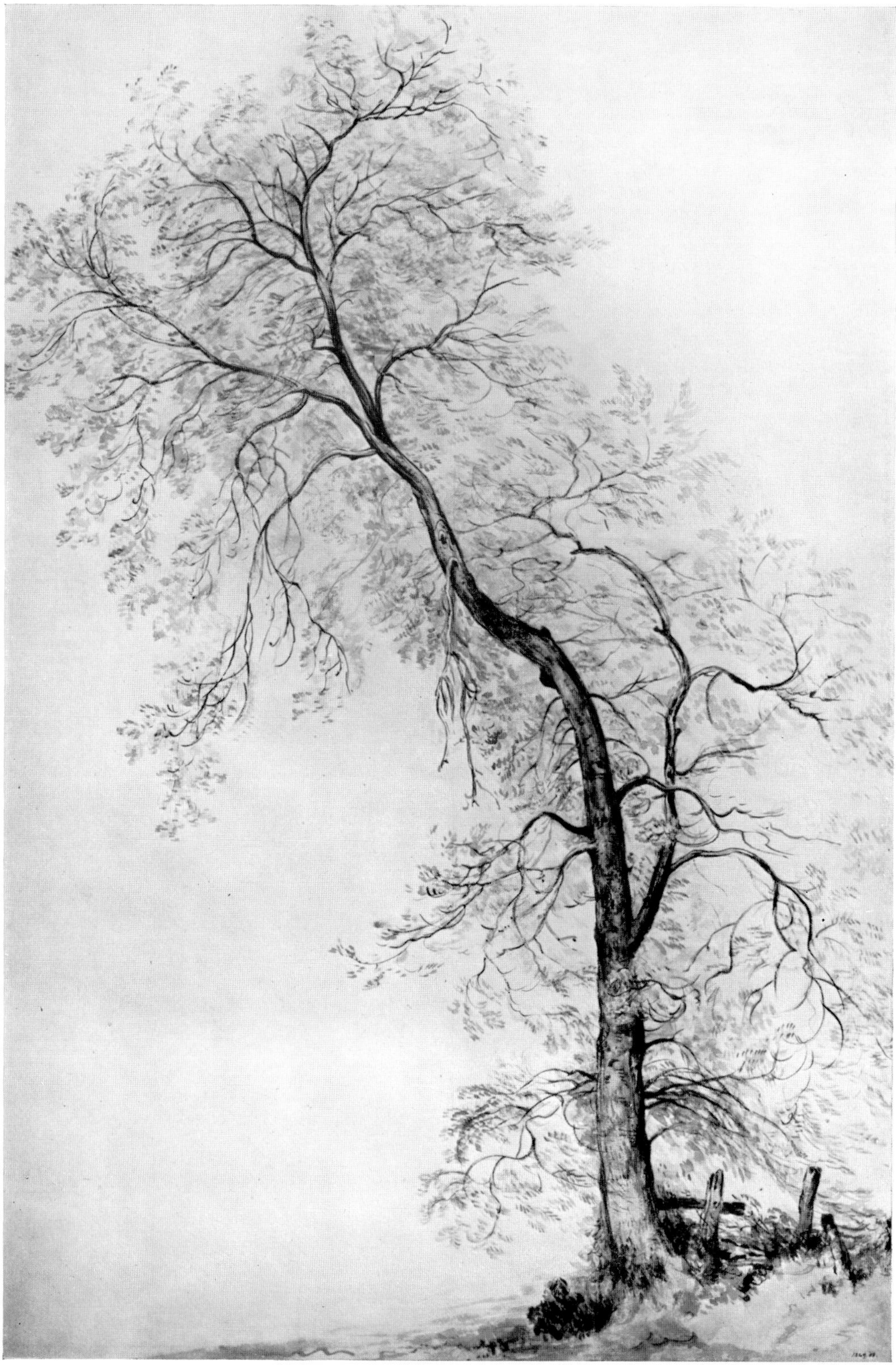

375. An ash tree.

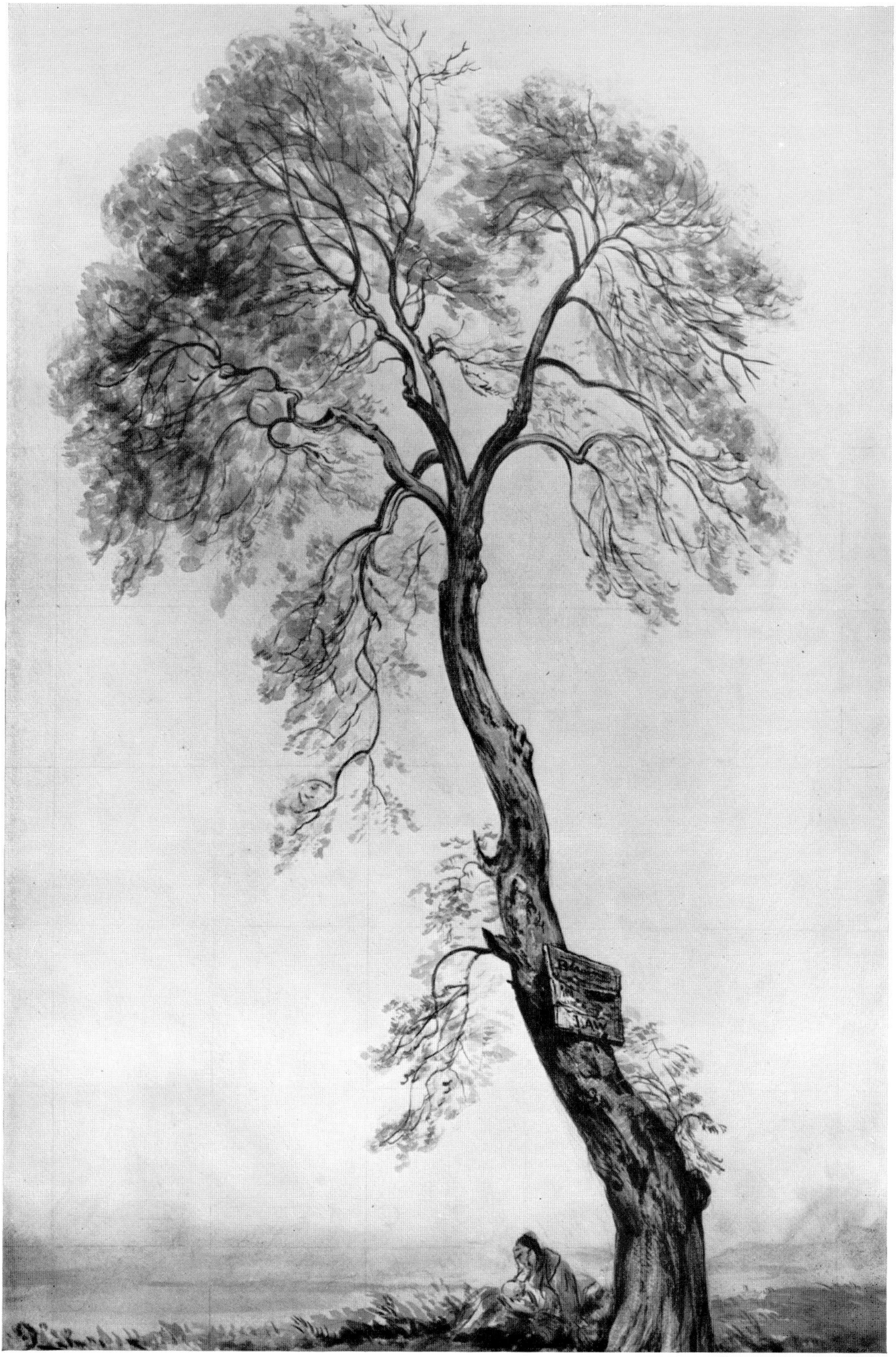

376. An ash tree.

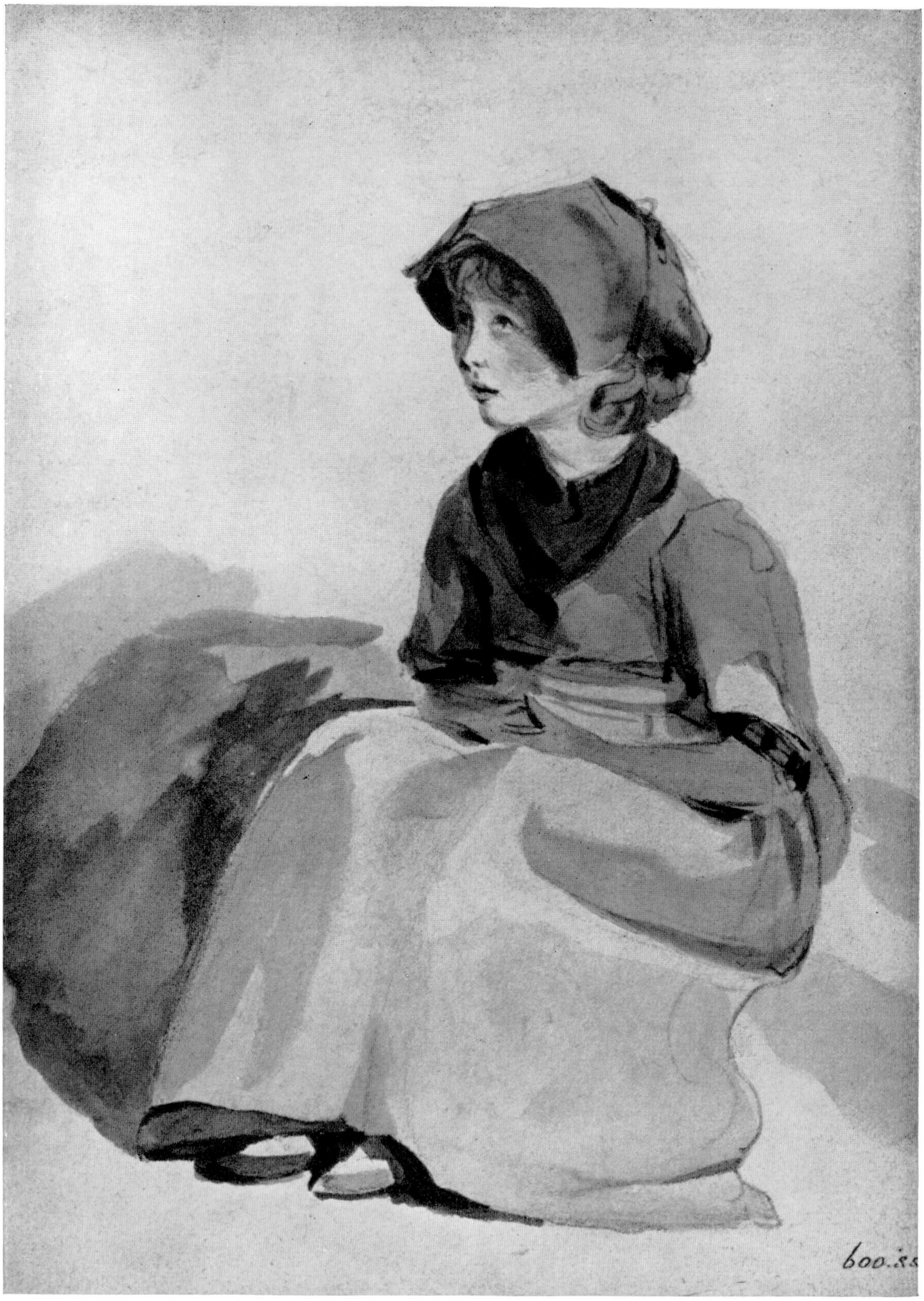

377. A Suffolk Child: sketch for 'The Valley Farm'.

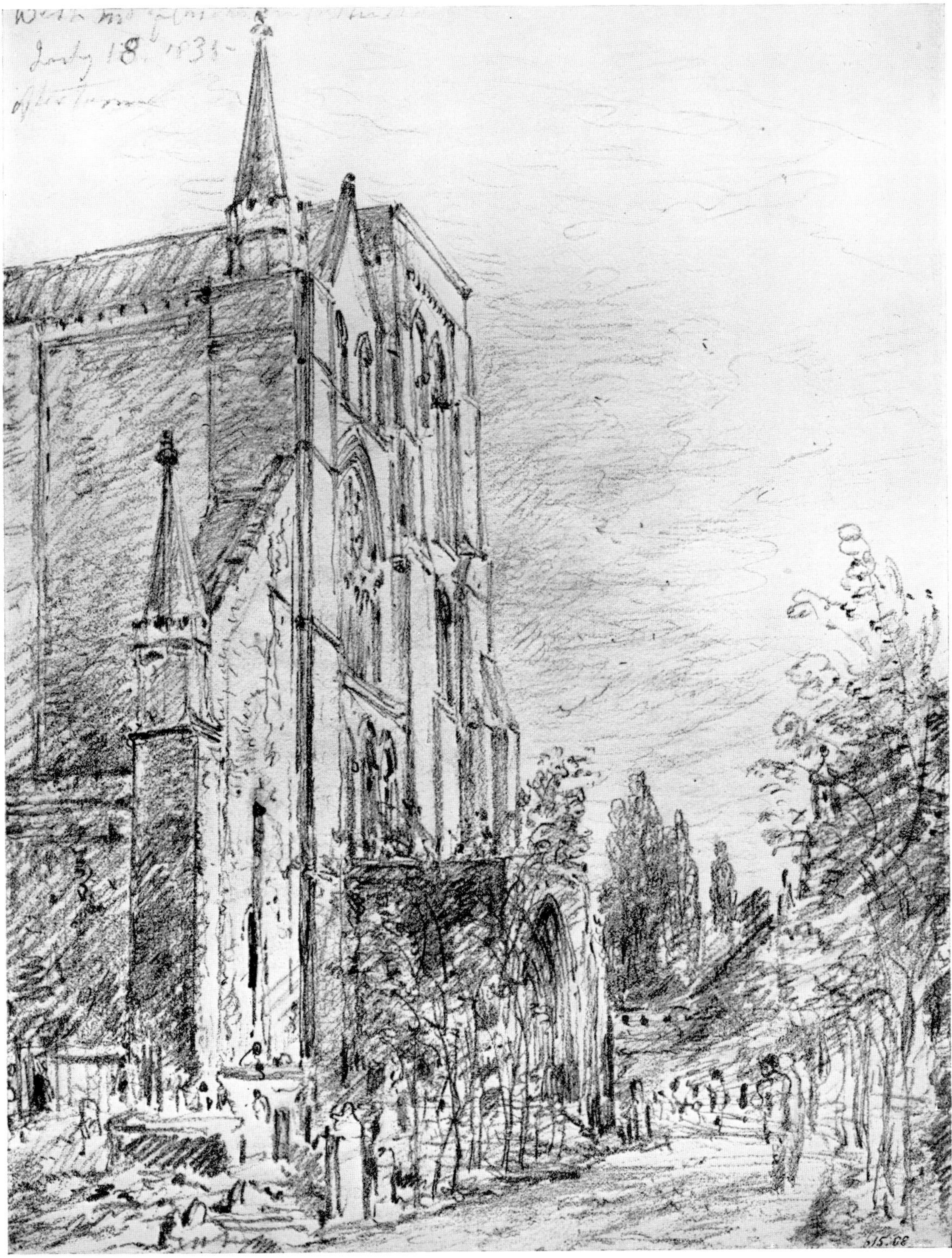

381. Chichester Cathedral: W. end.

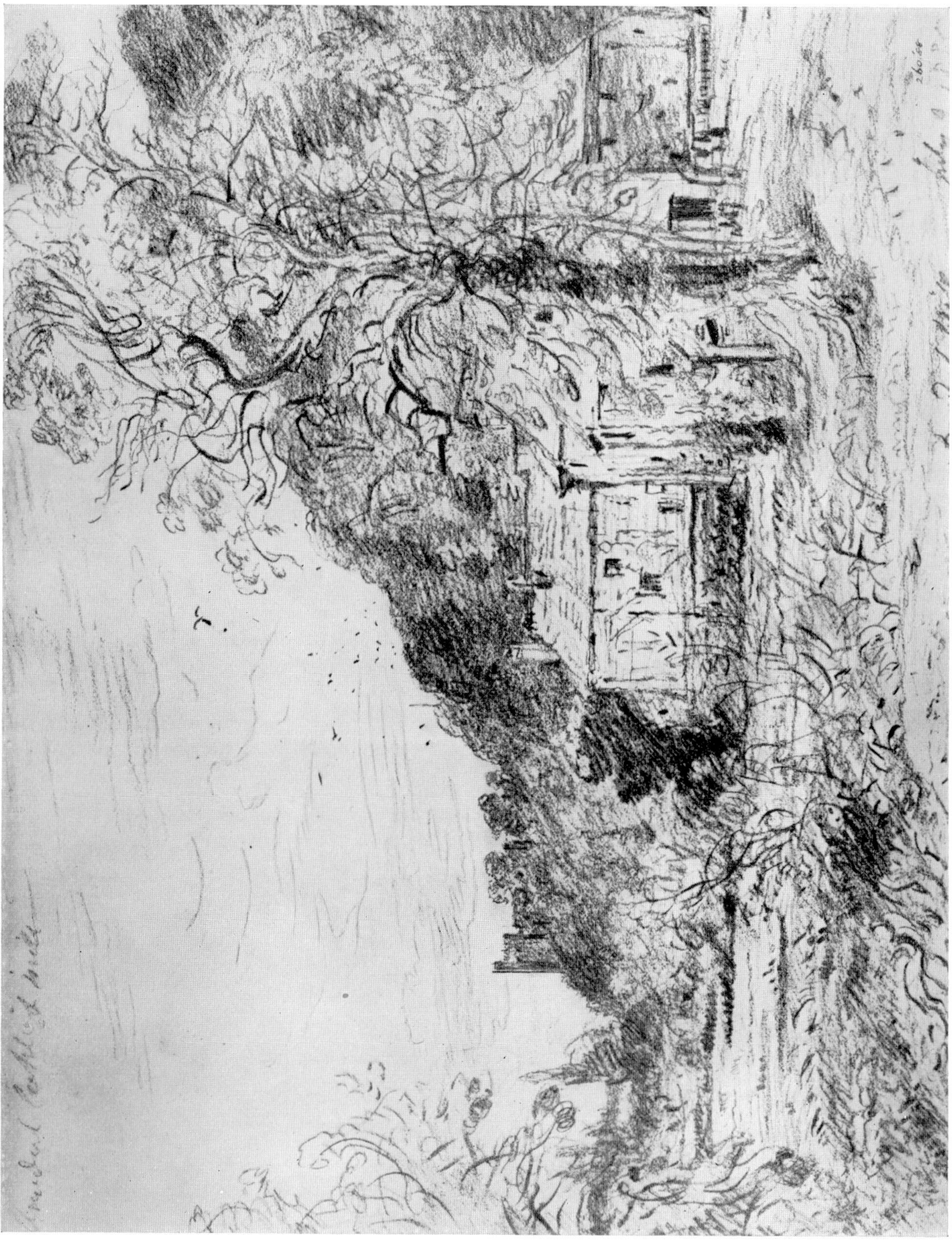

379. Arundel Mill and Castle.

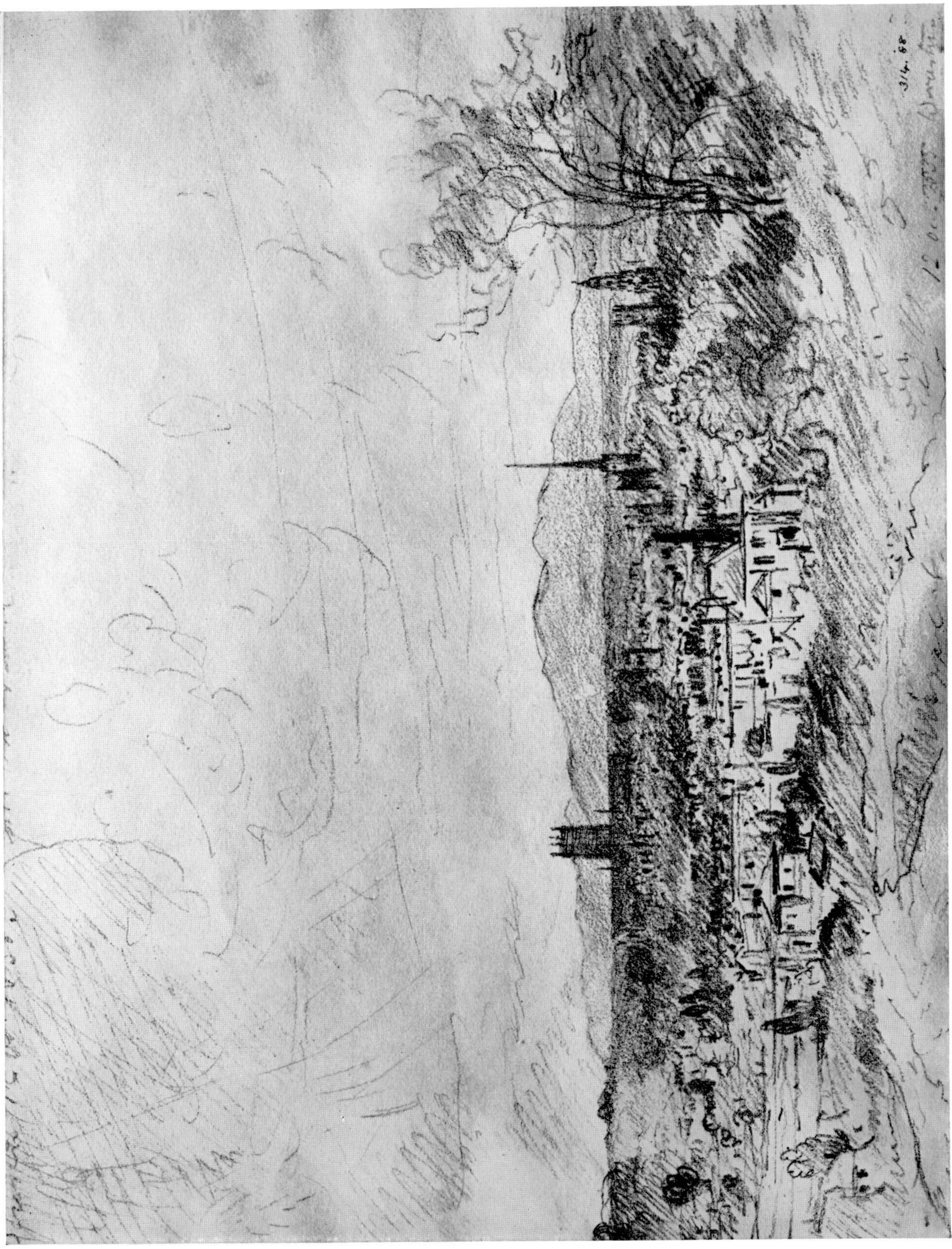

383. A view of Worcester from the N.

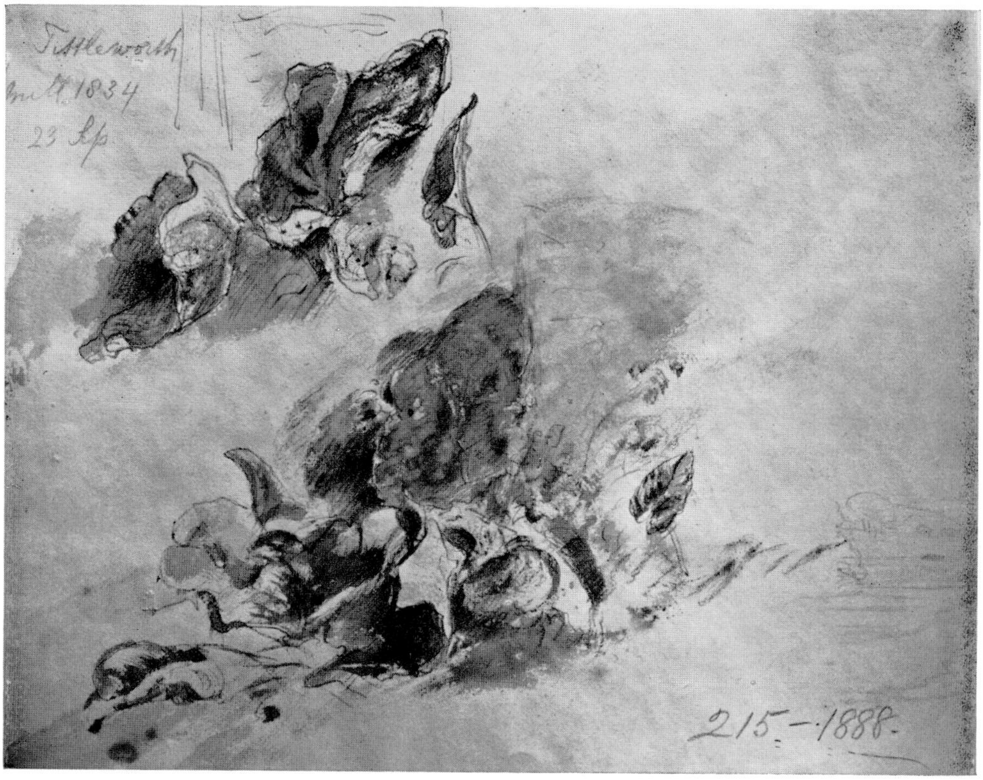

370a. Studies of plants.

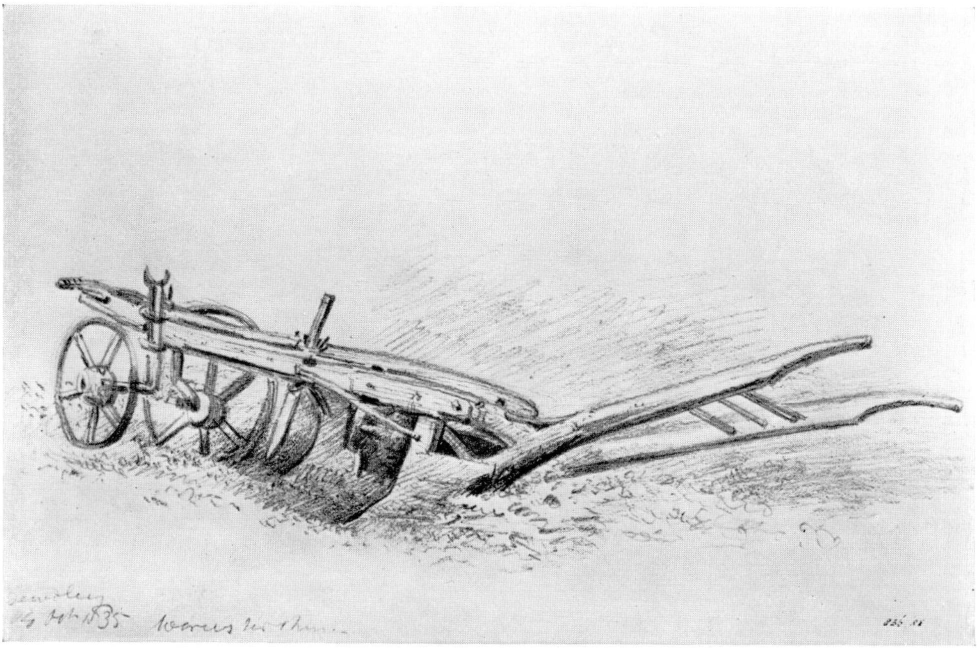

384. A plough at Bewdley.

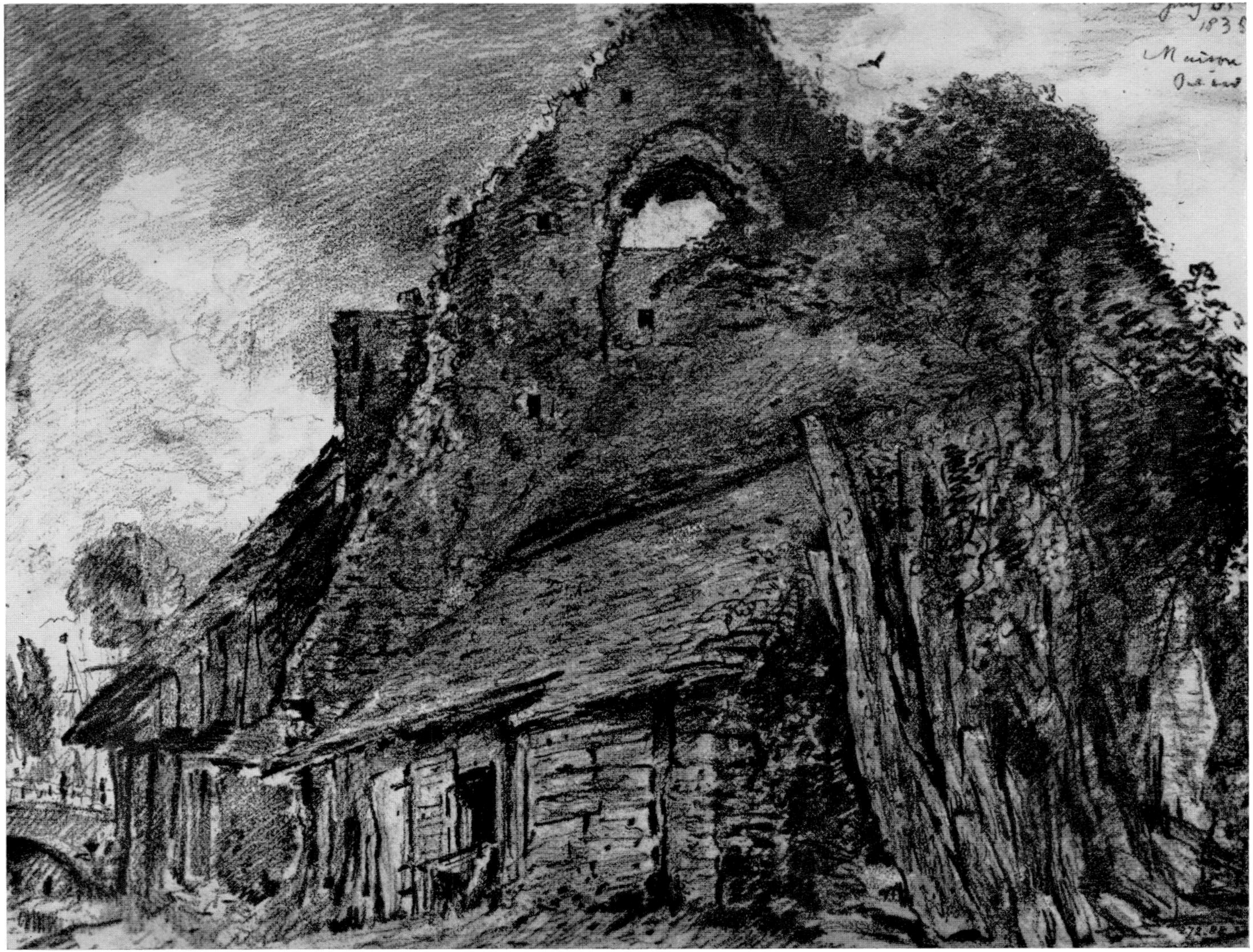

378. The ruins of the Maison Dieu, Arundel.

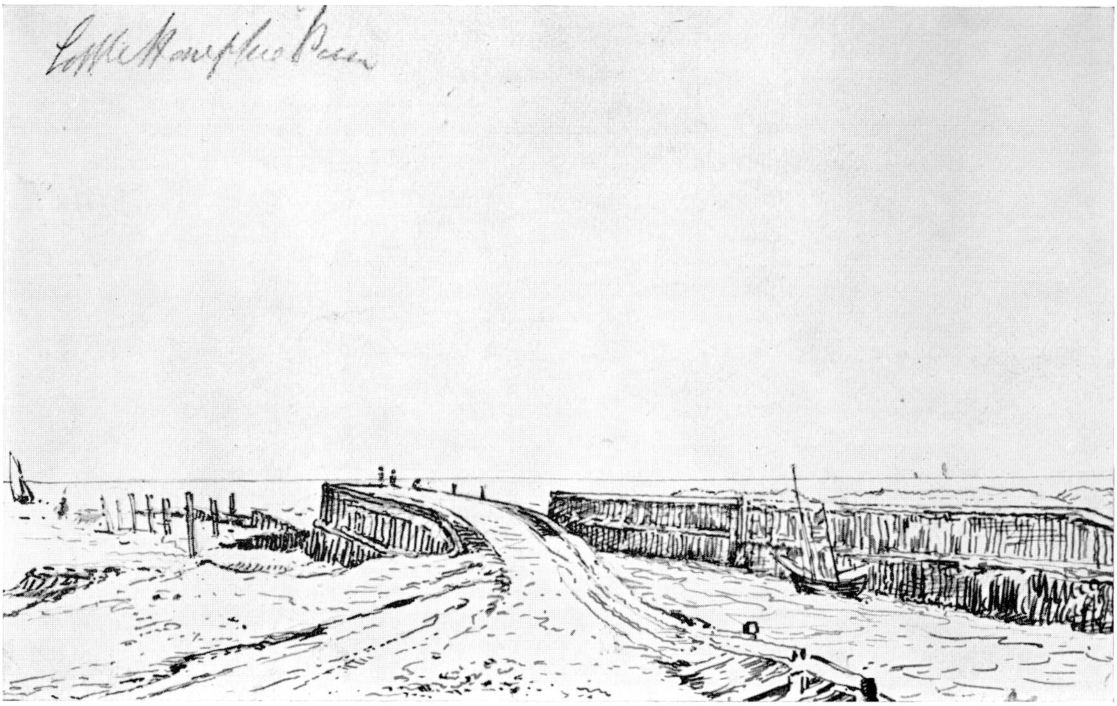

382, p. 1. Littlehampton Pier.

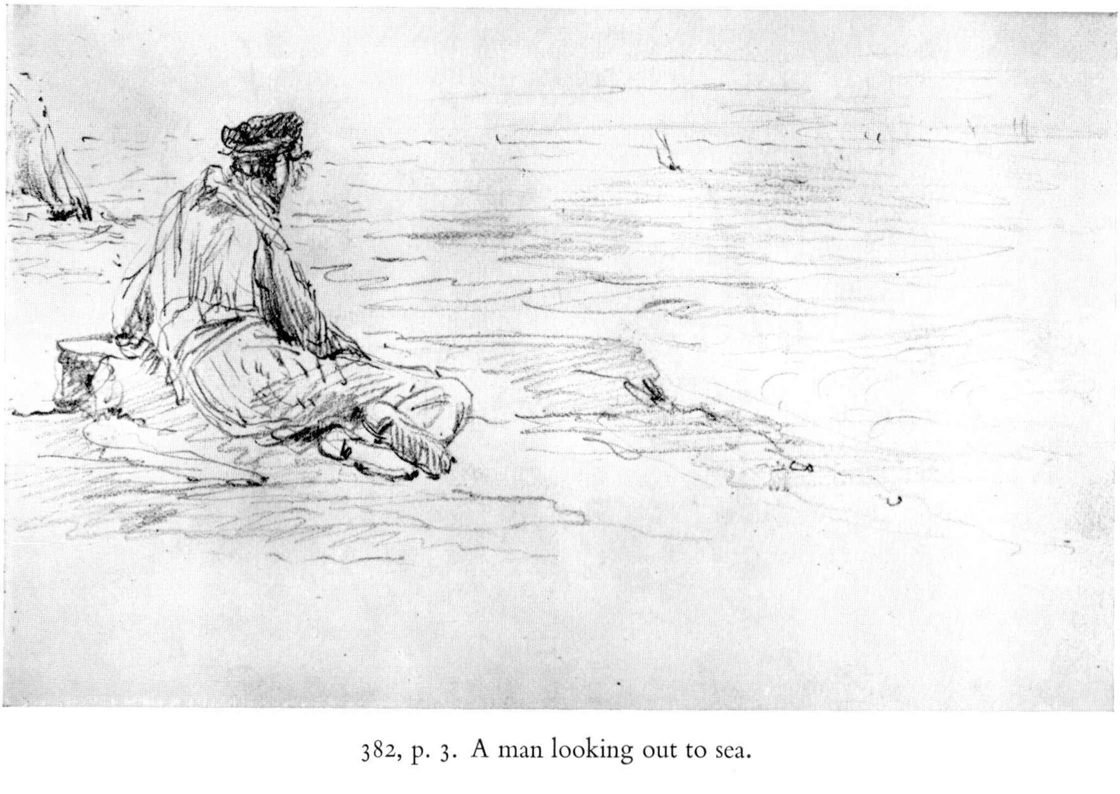

382, p. 3. A man looking out to sea.

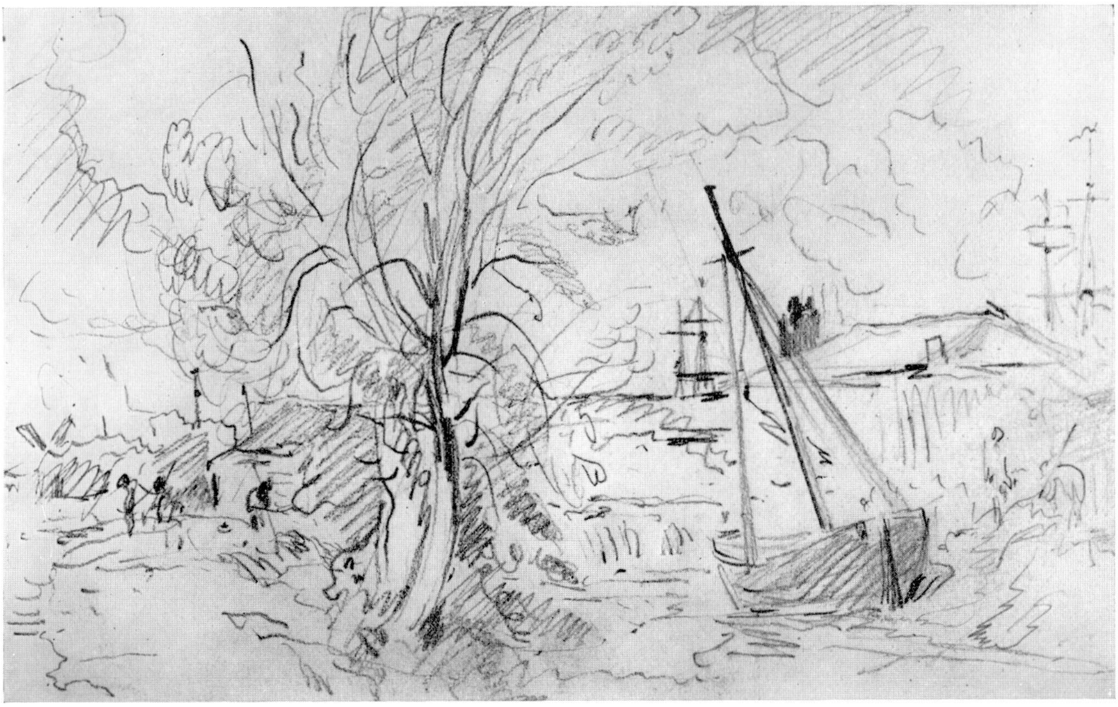

382, p. 5. A seaside village.

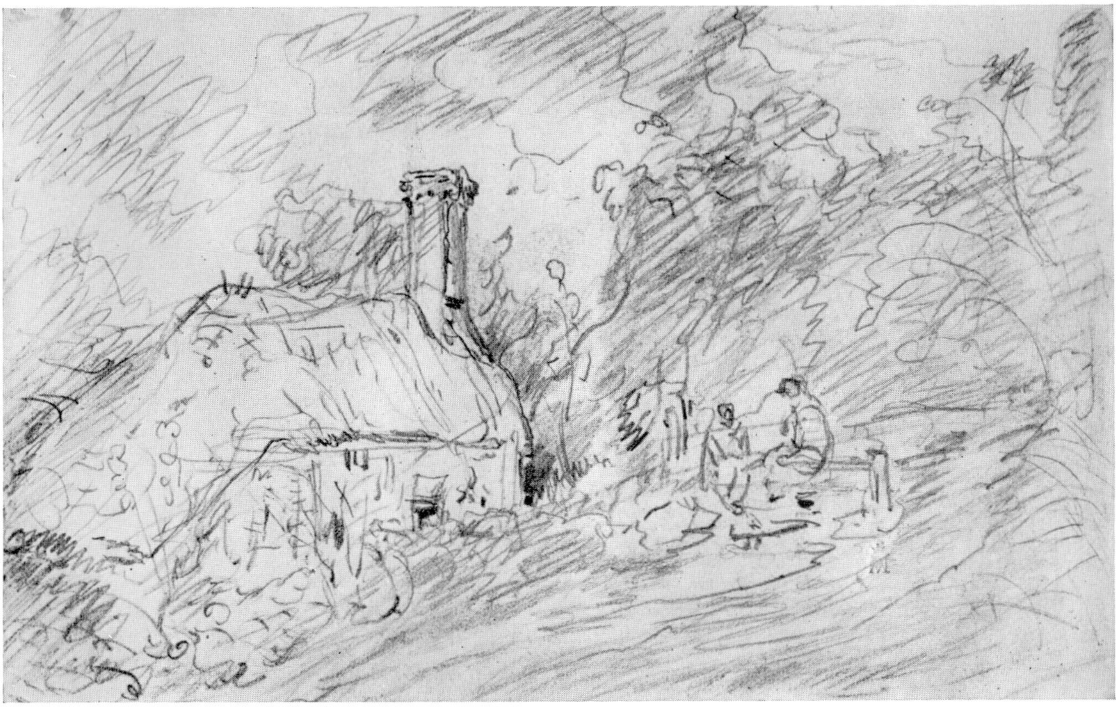

382, p. 7. A thatched cottage.

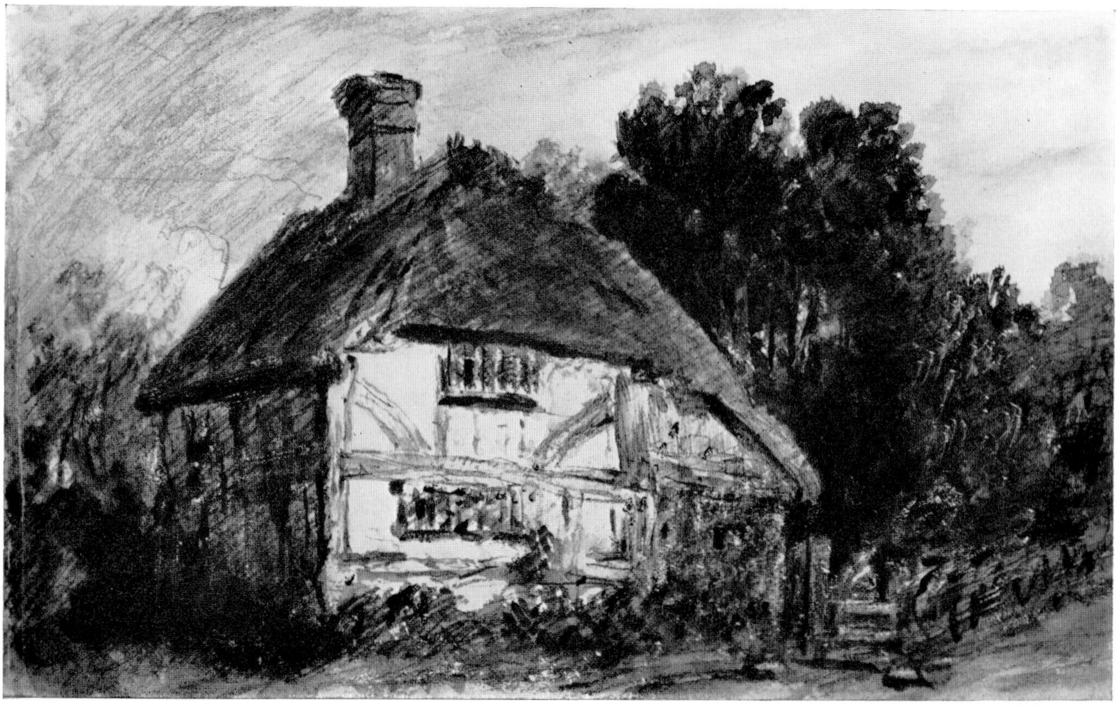

382, p. 9. A cottage in Sussex.

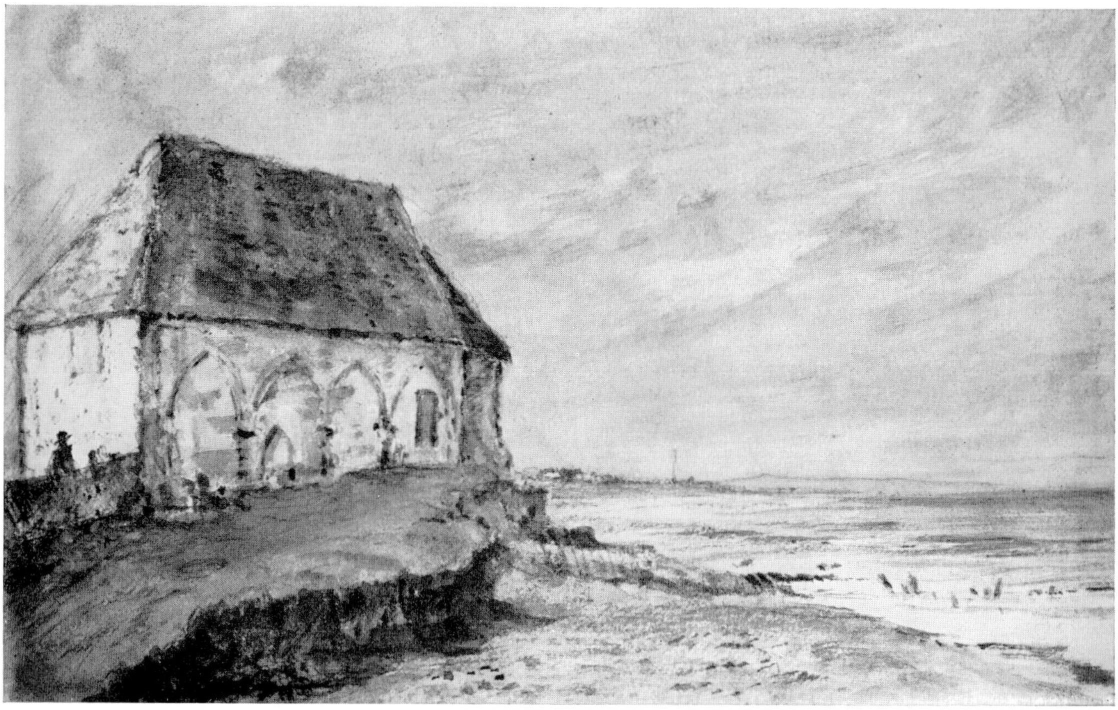

382, p. 11. Middleton Church.

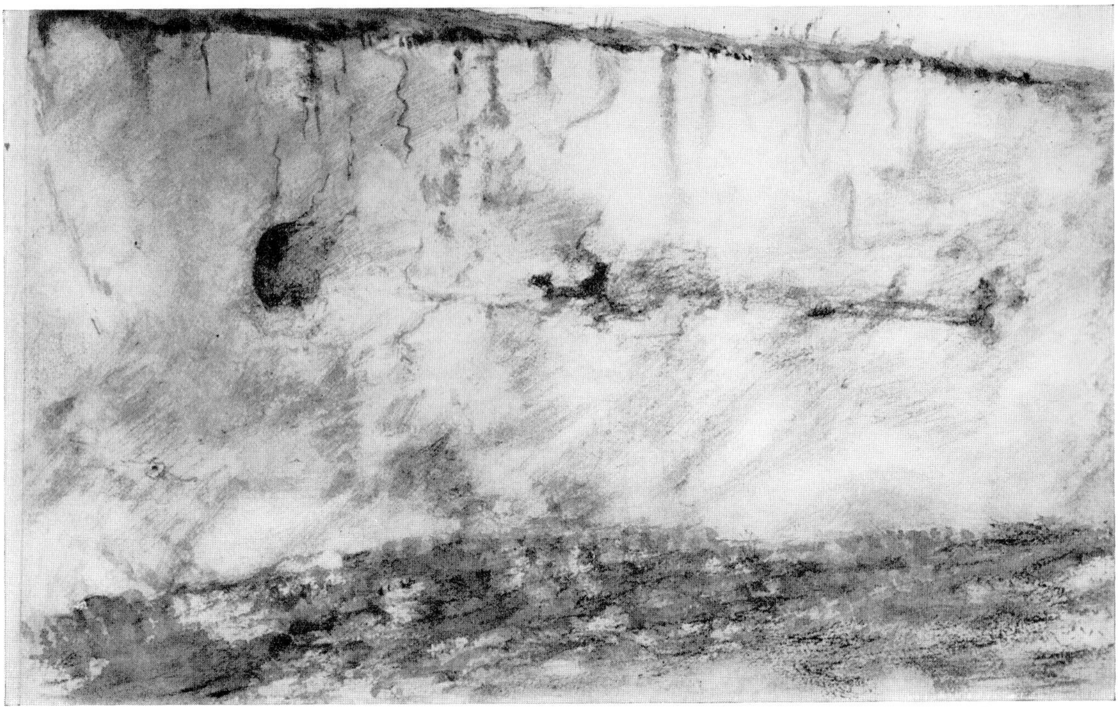

382, p. 13. A skeleton in Middleton churchyard.

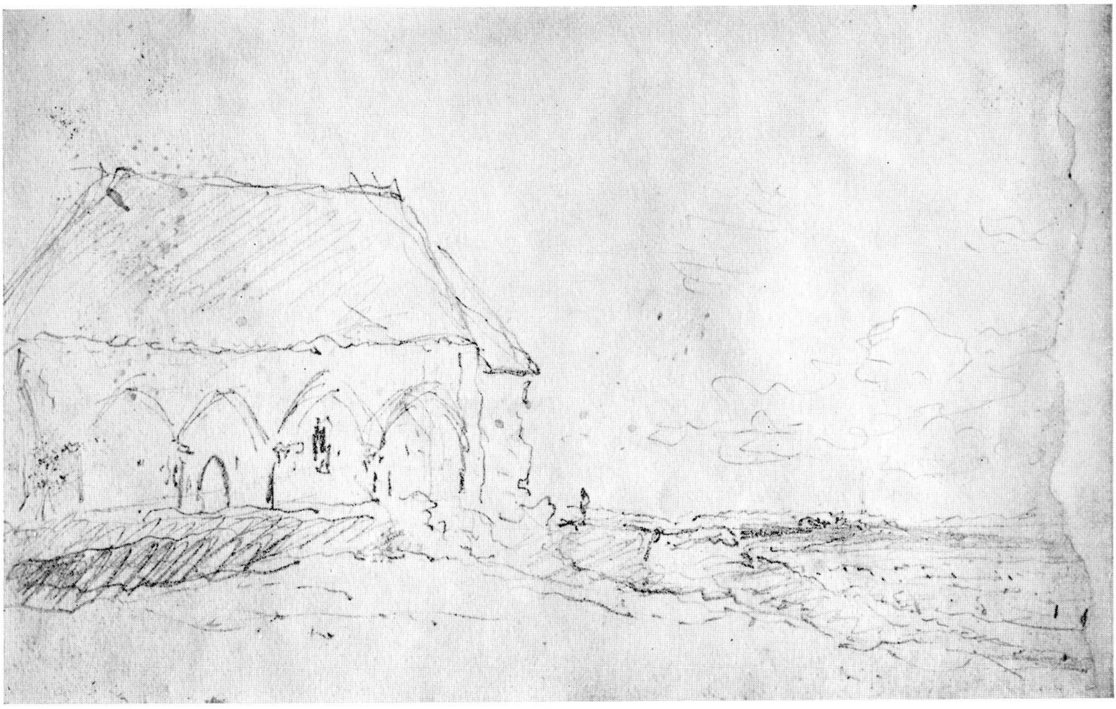

382, p. 14. Middleton Church.

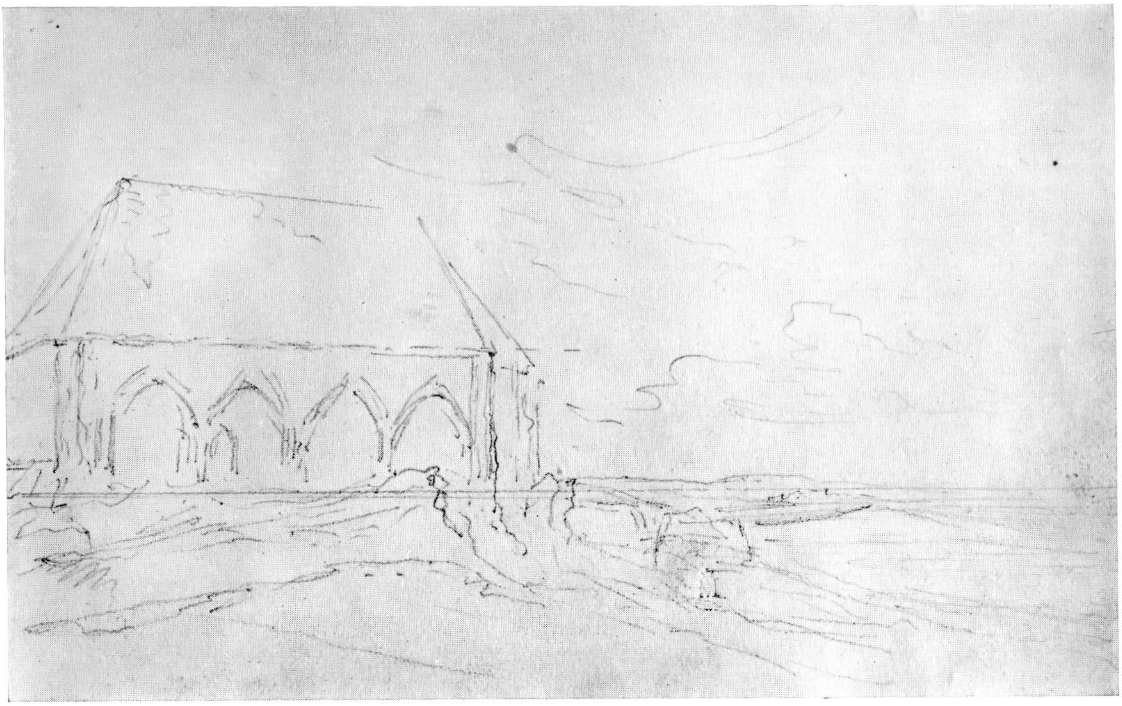

382, p. 15. Middleton Church.

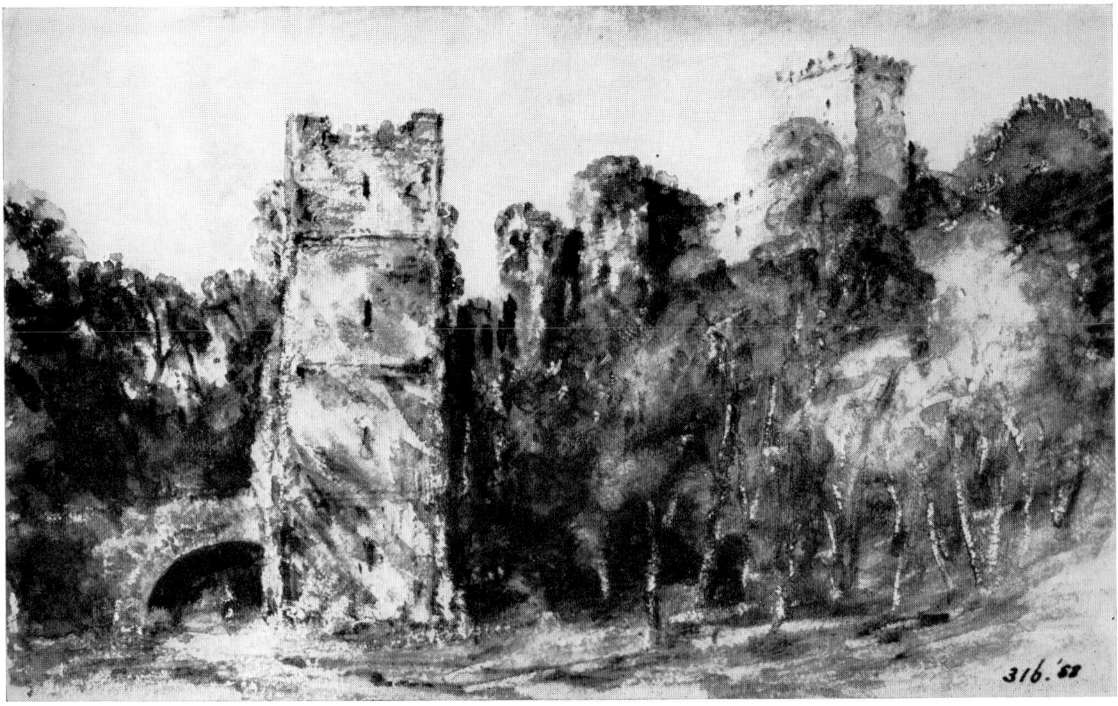

382, p. 17. The grounds of Arundel Castle.

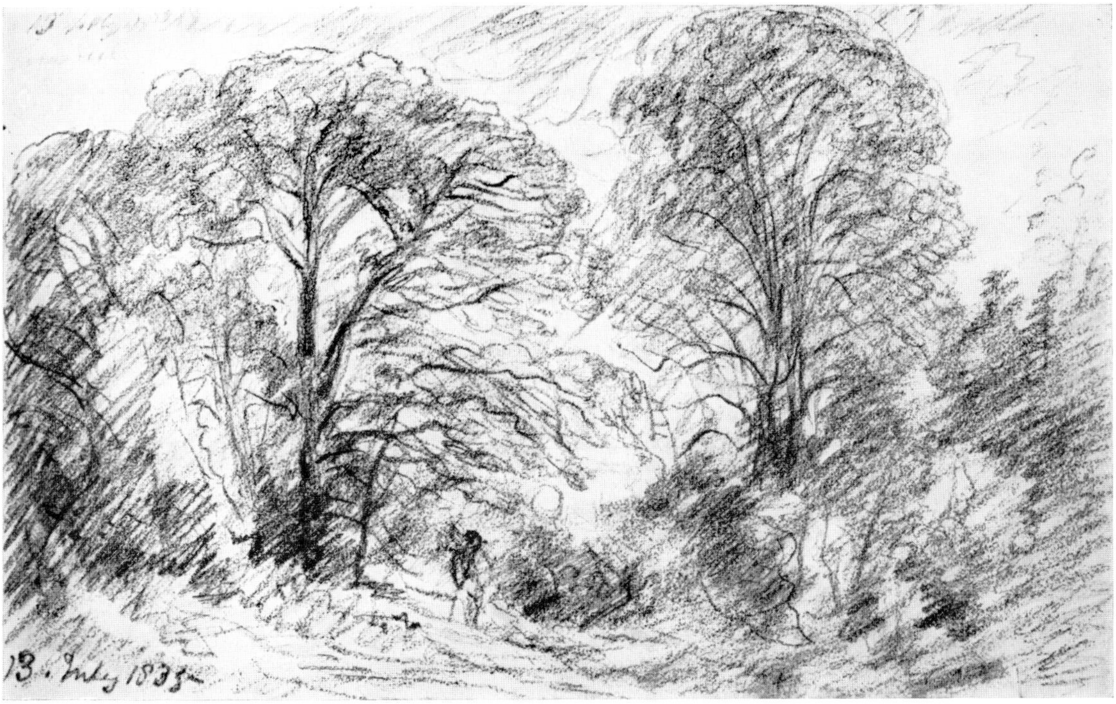

382, p. 19. View at Arundel.

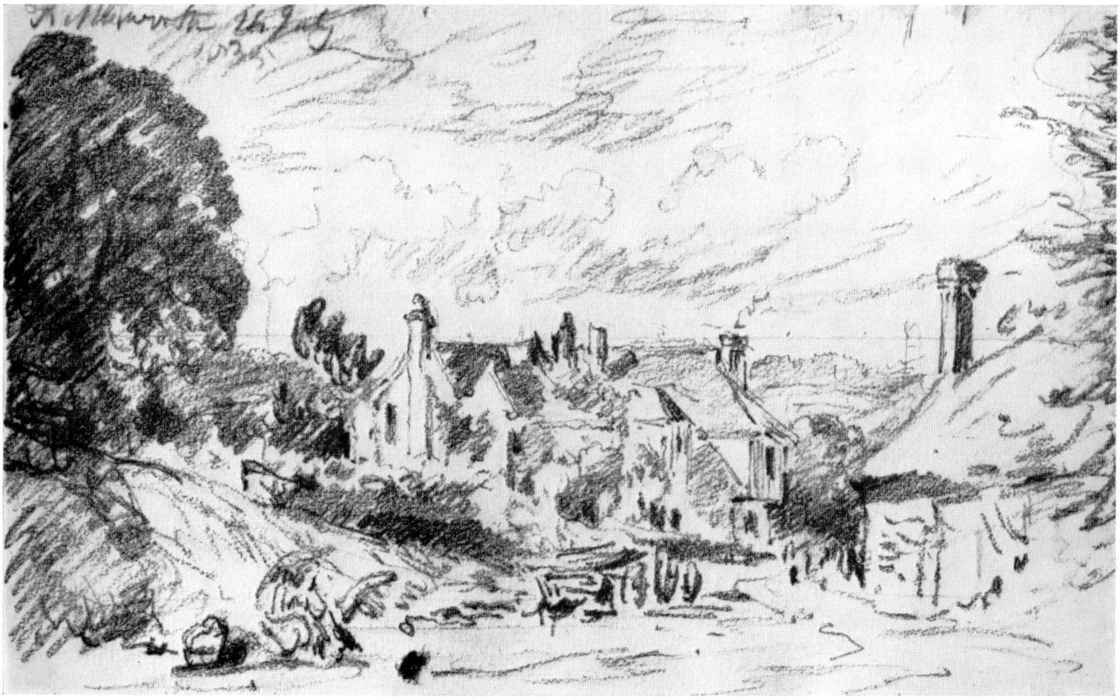

382, p. 21. Fittleworth.

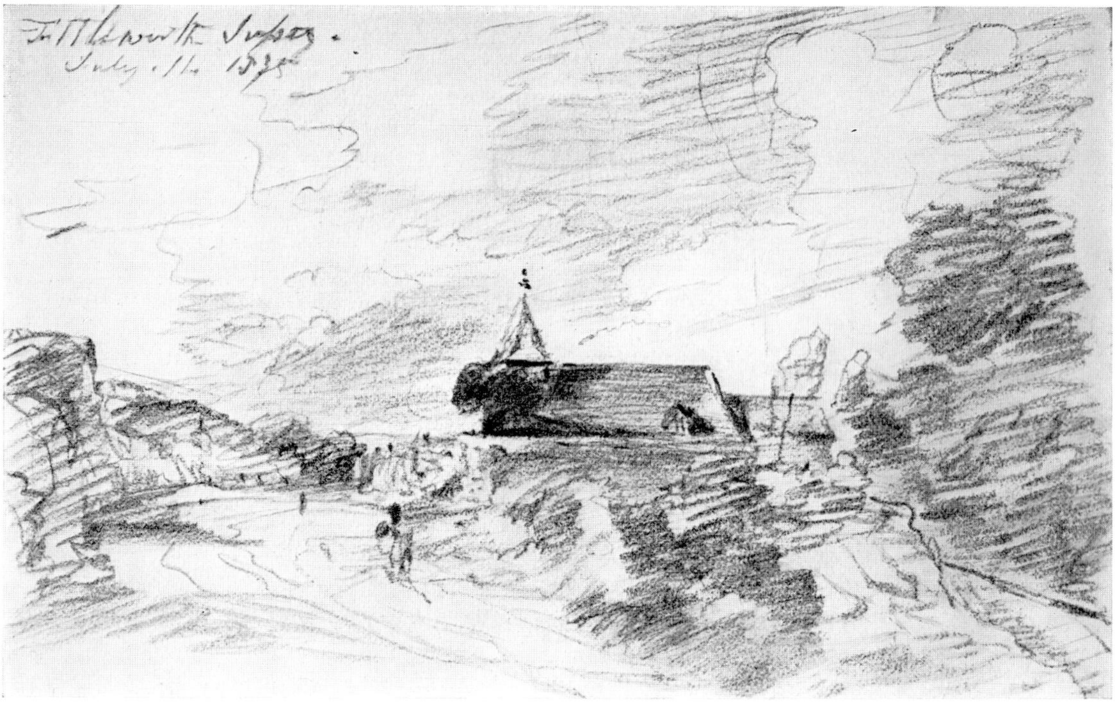

382, p. 23. Fittleworth.

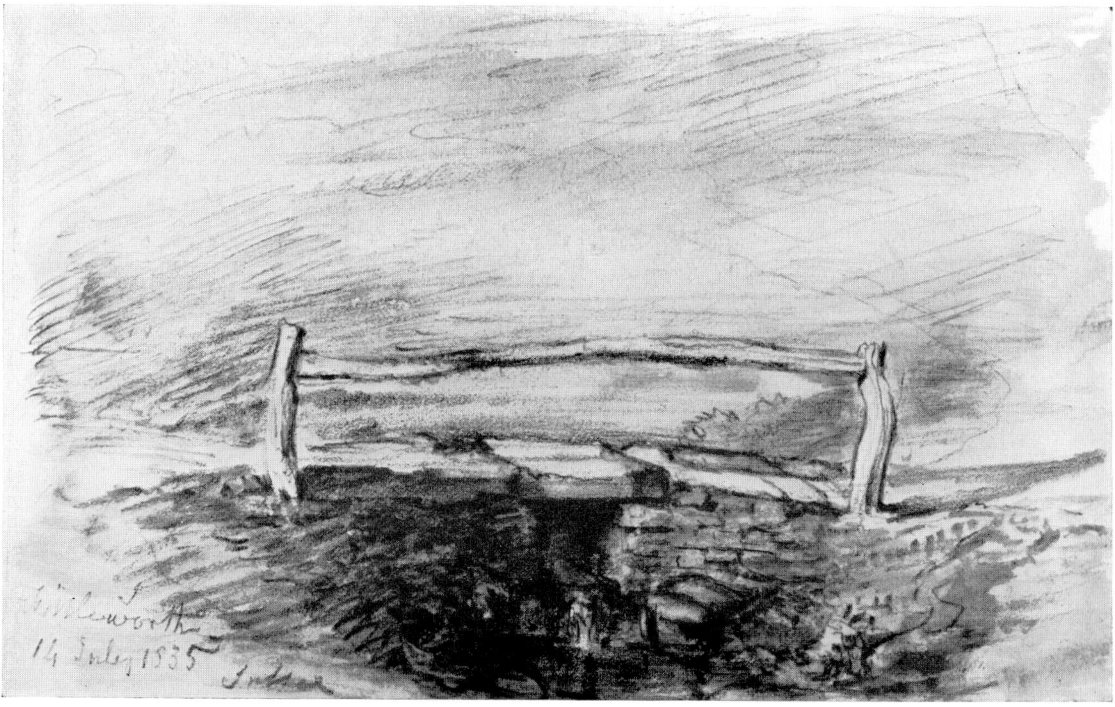

382, p. 25. A bridge over a stream at Fittleworth.

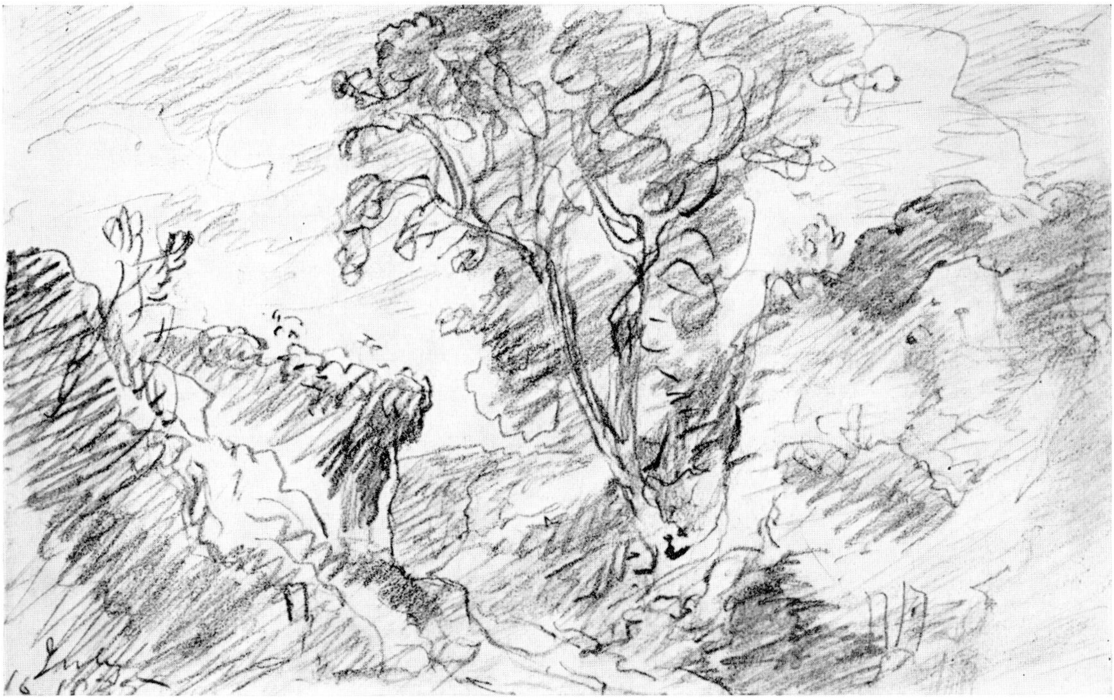

382, p. 27. A lane between steep banks.

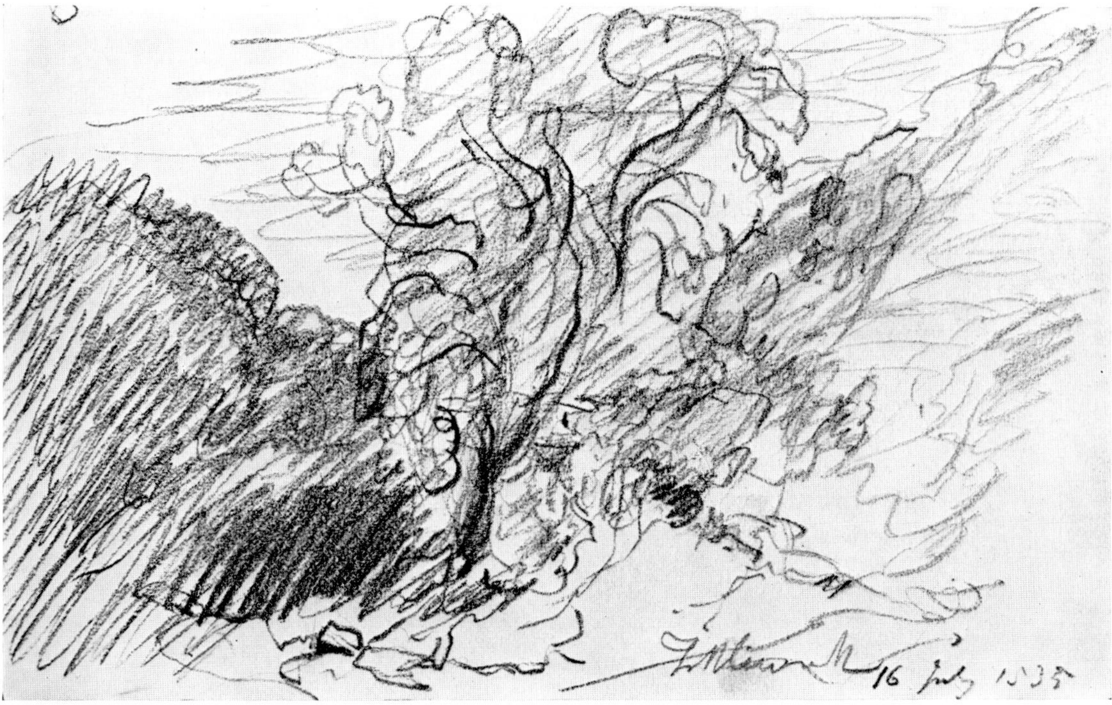

382, p. 29. A tree in a hollow, Fittleworth.

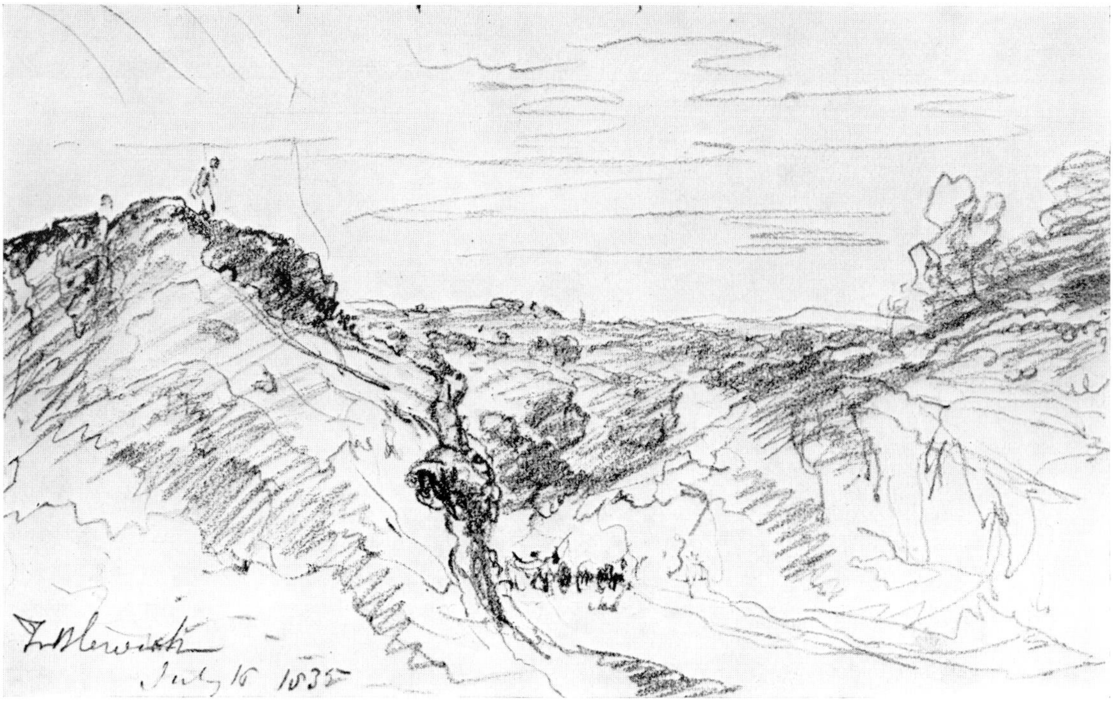

382, p. 31. A sunken road at Fittleworth.

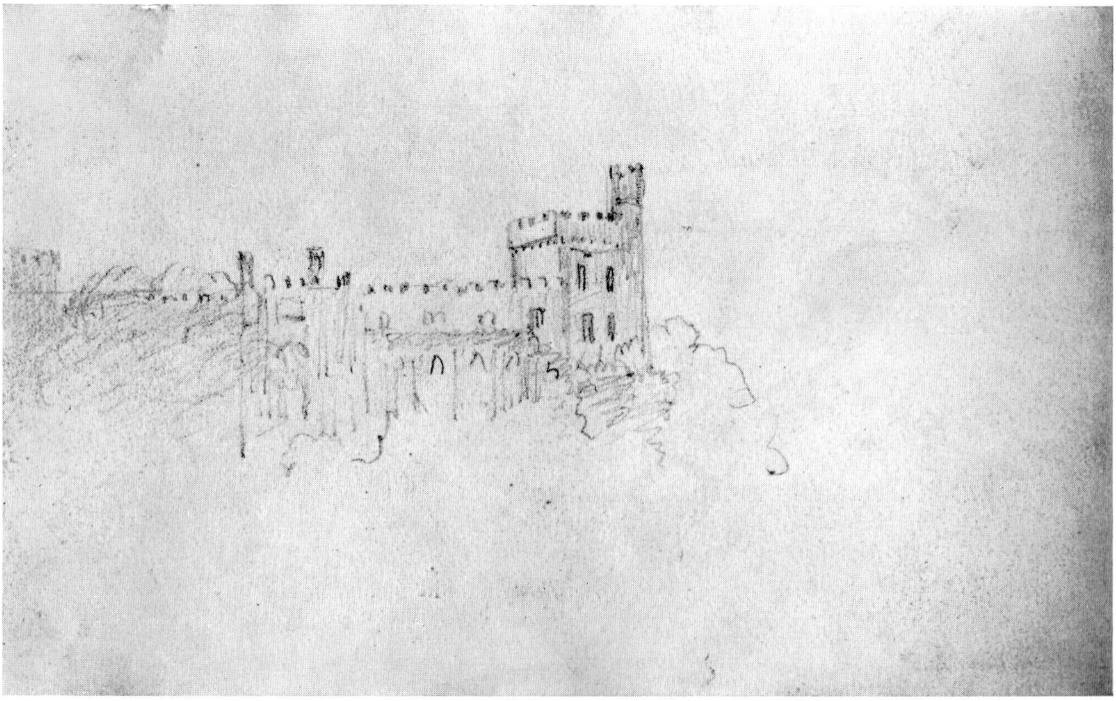

382, p. 32. Arundel Castle.

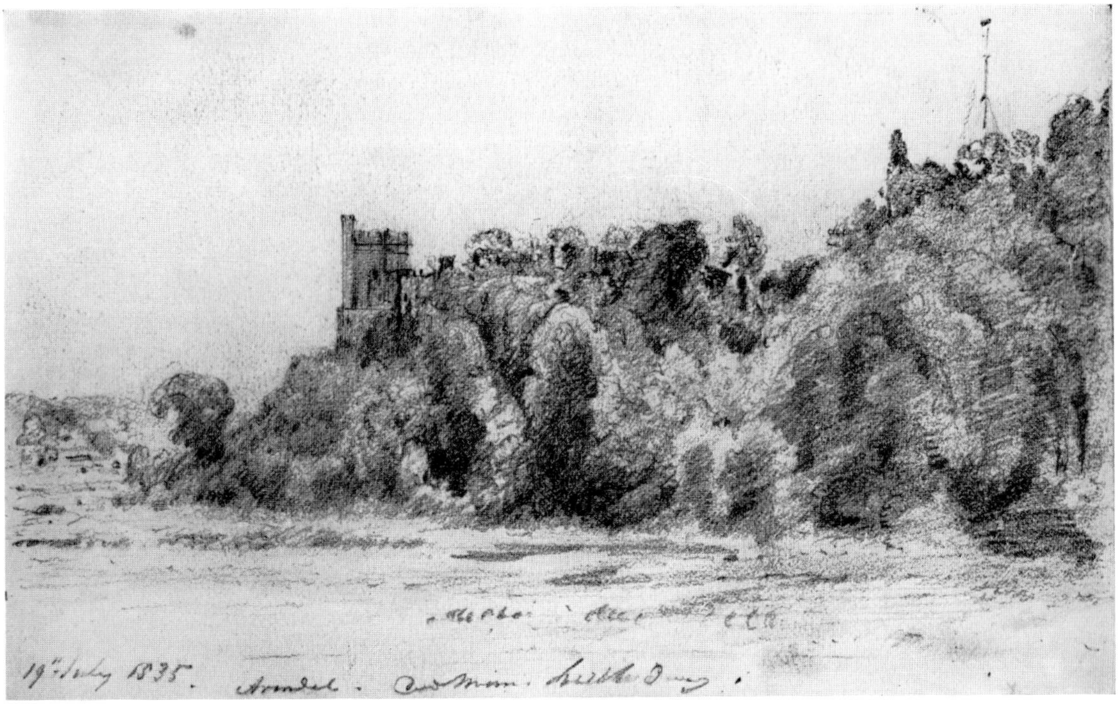

382, p. 33. Arundel Castle.

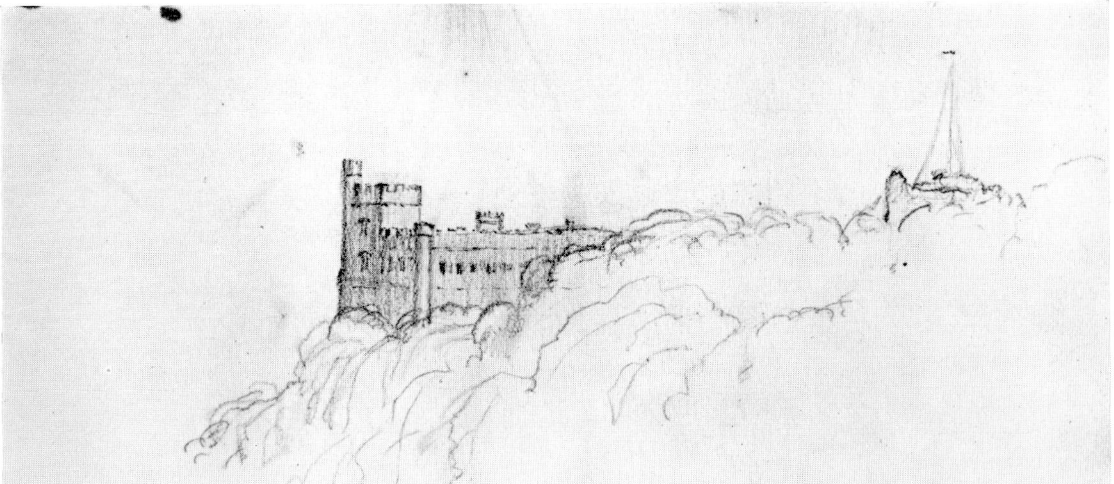

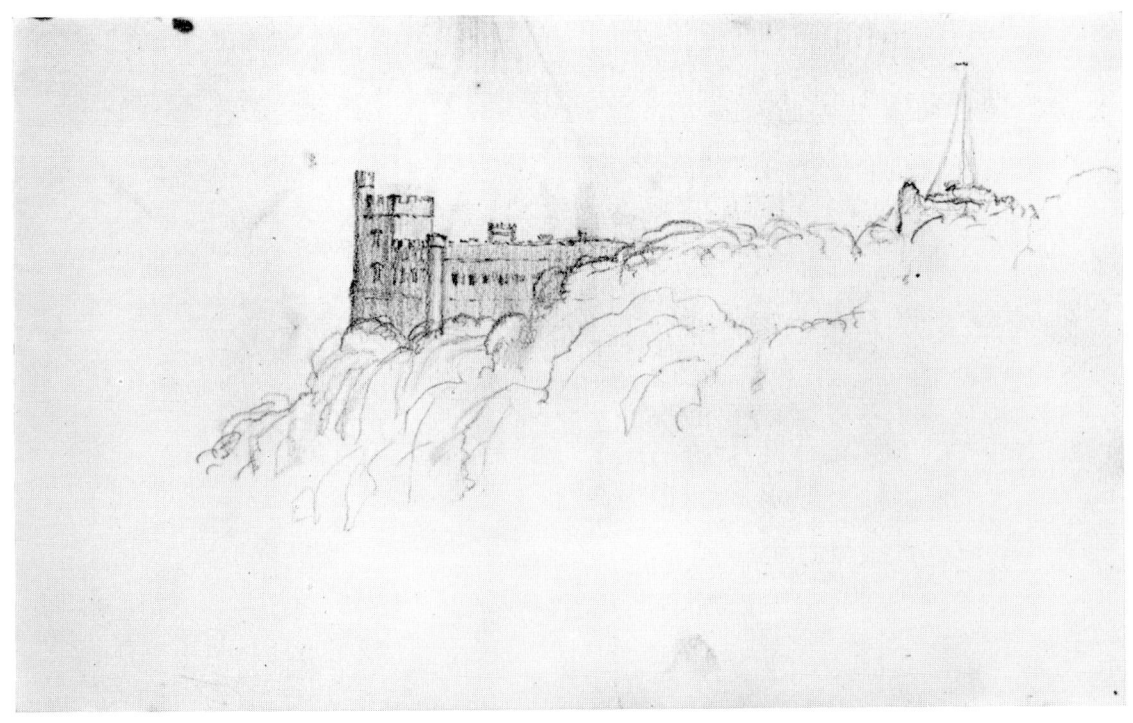

382, p. 35. Arundel Castle.

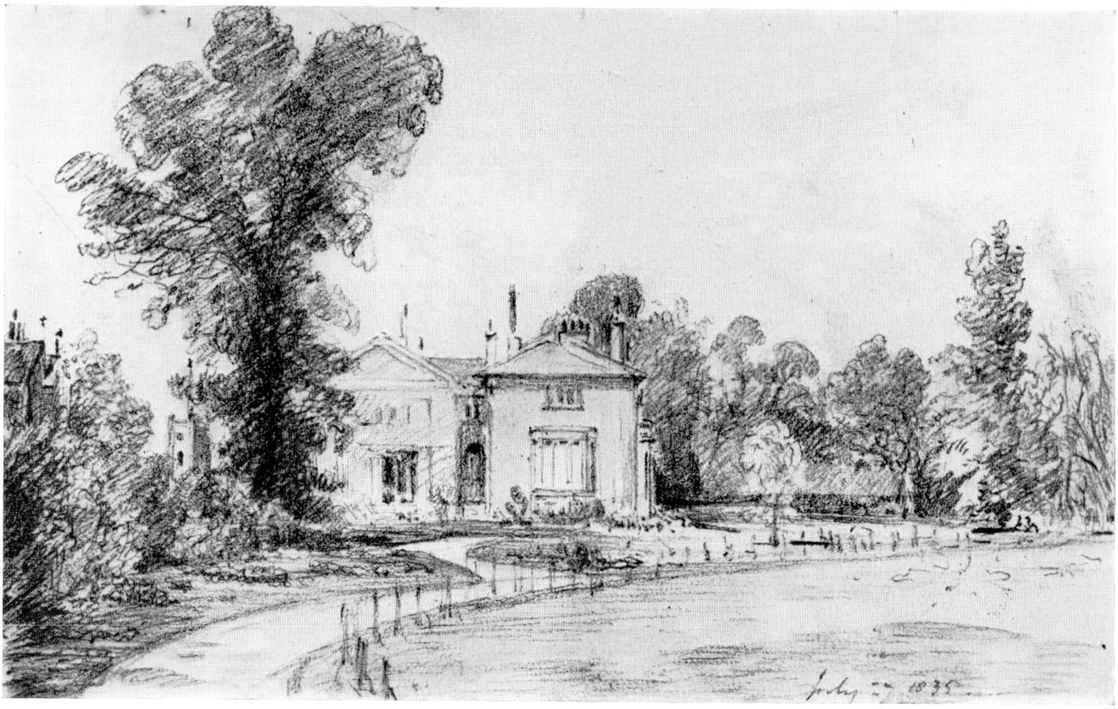

382, p. 37. Canbury House, Kingston-on-Thames.

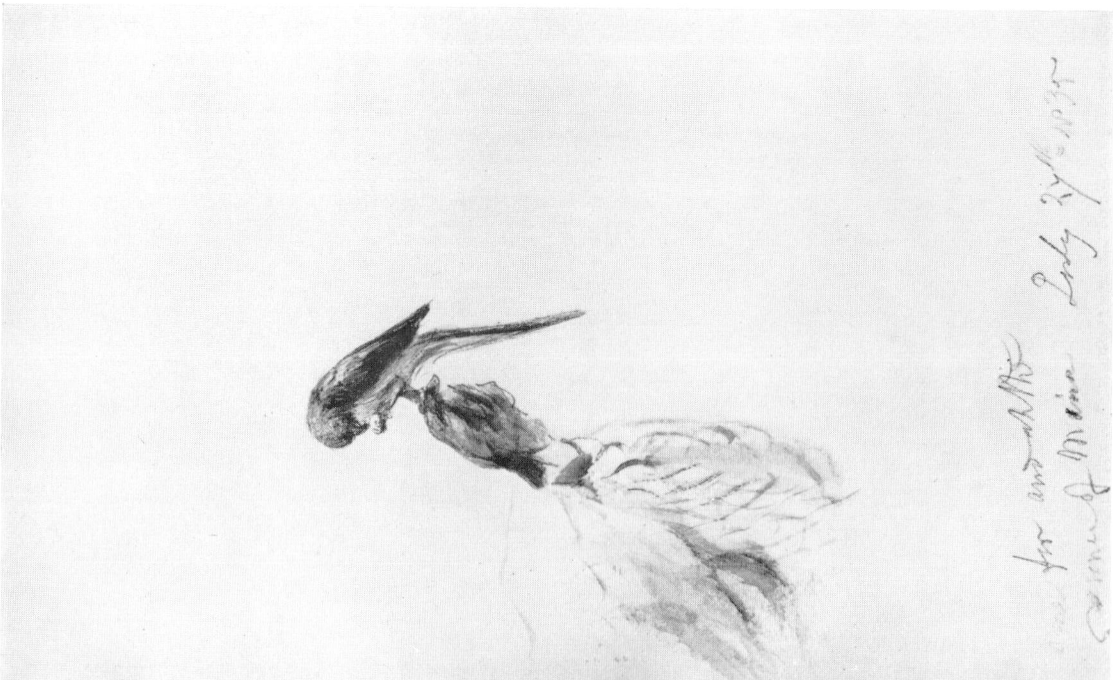

382, p. 46. Study of a parrot.

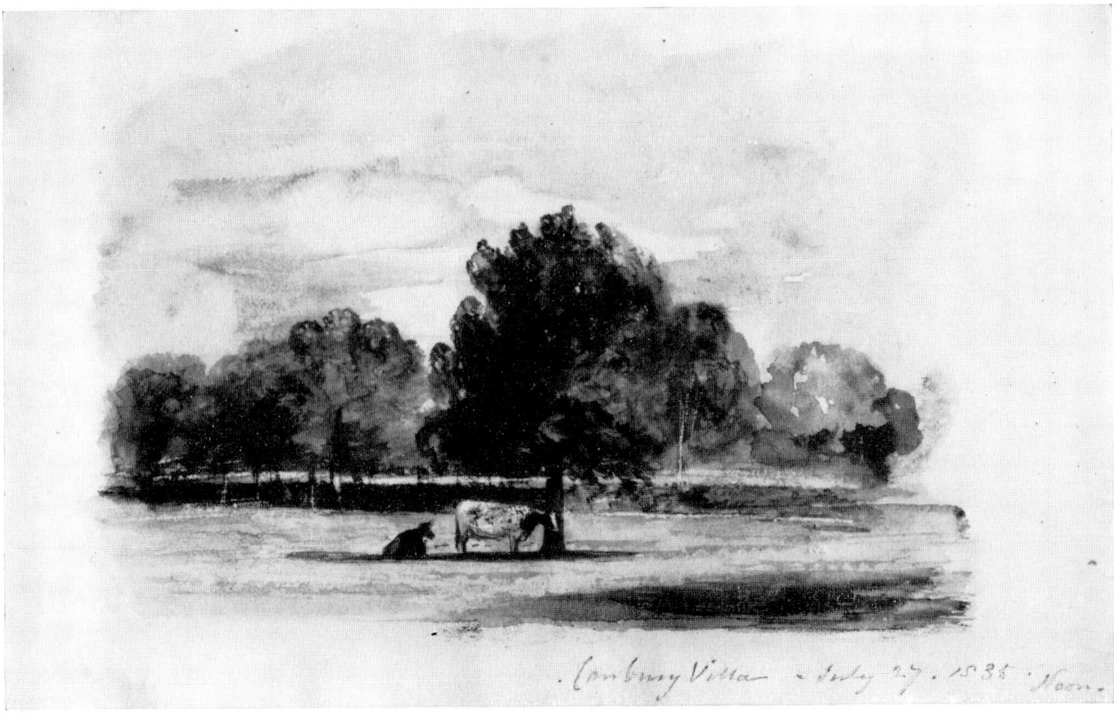

382, p. 48. View in the park, Canbury House.

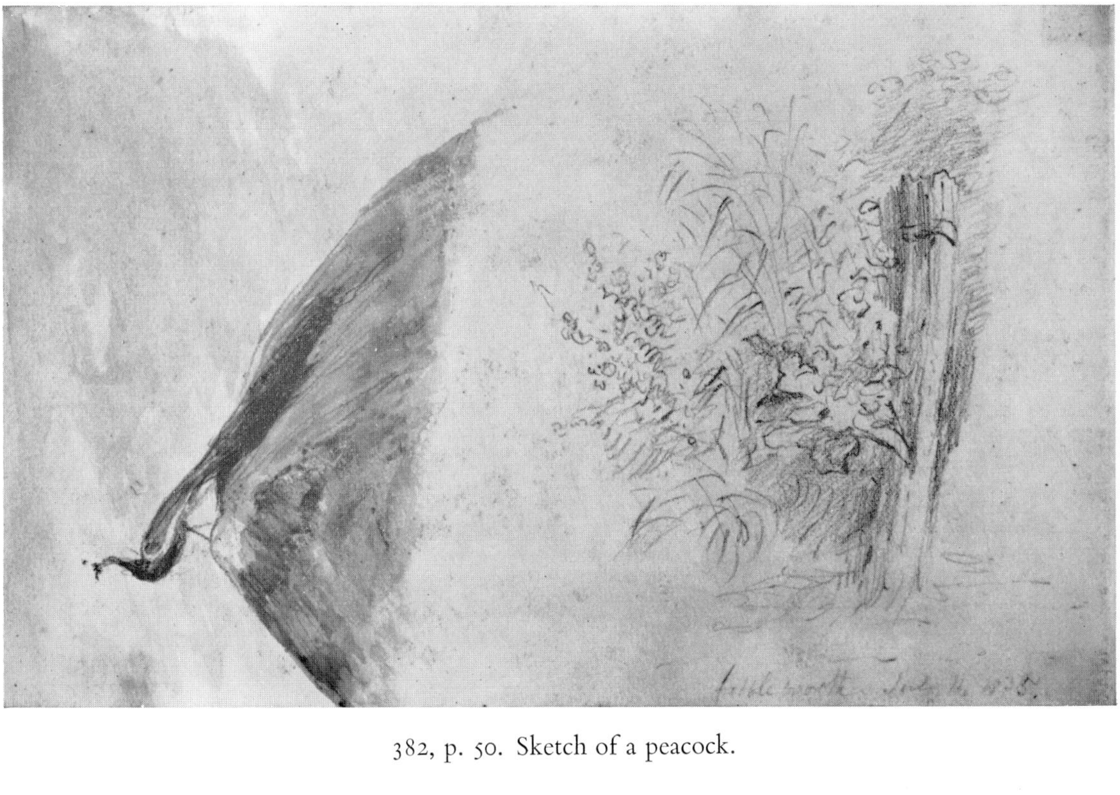

382, p. 50. Sketch of a peacock.

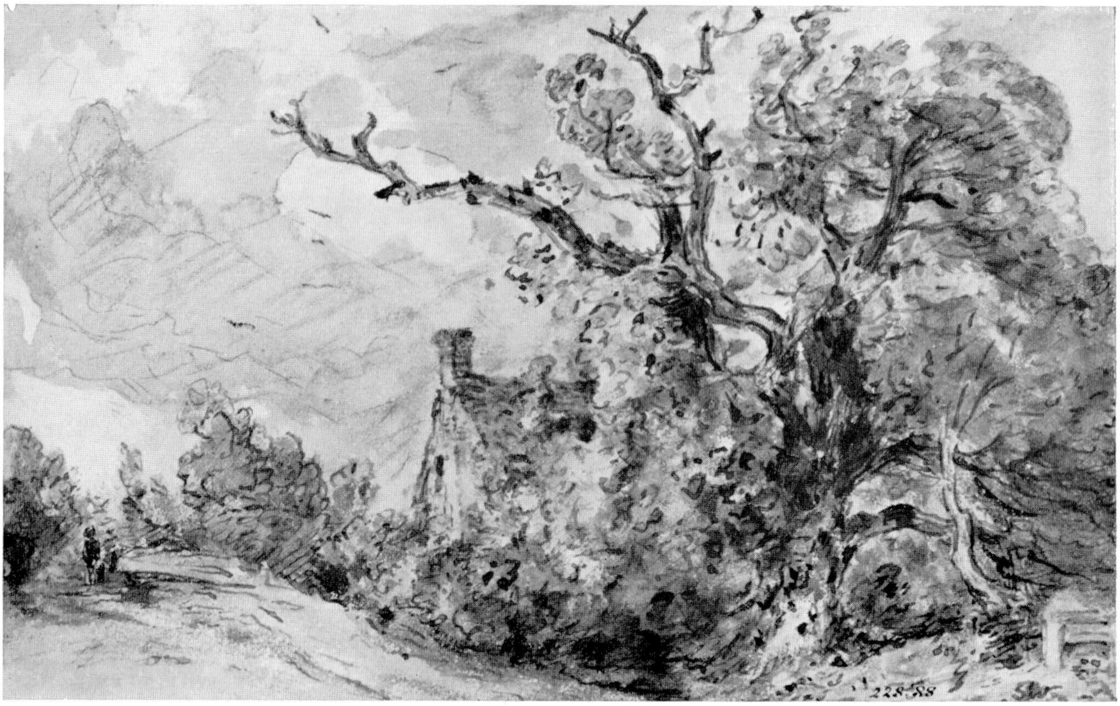

385. A cottage by a wood, Findon.

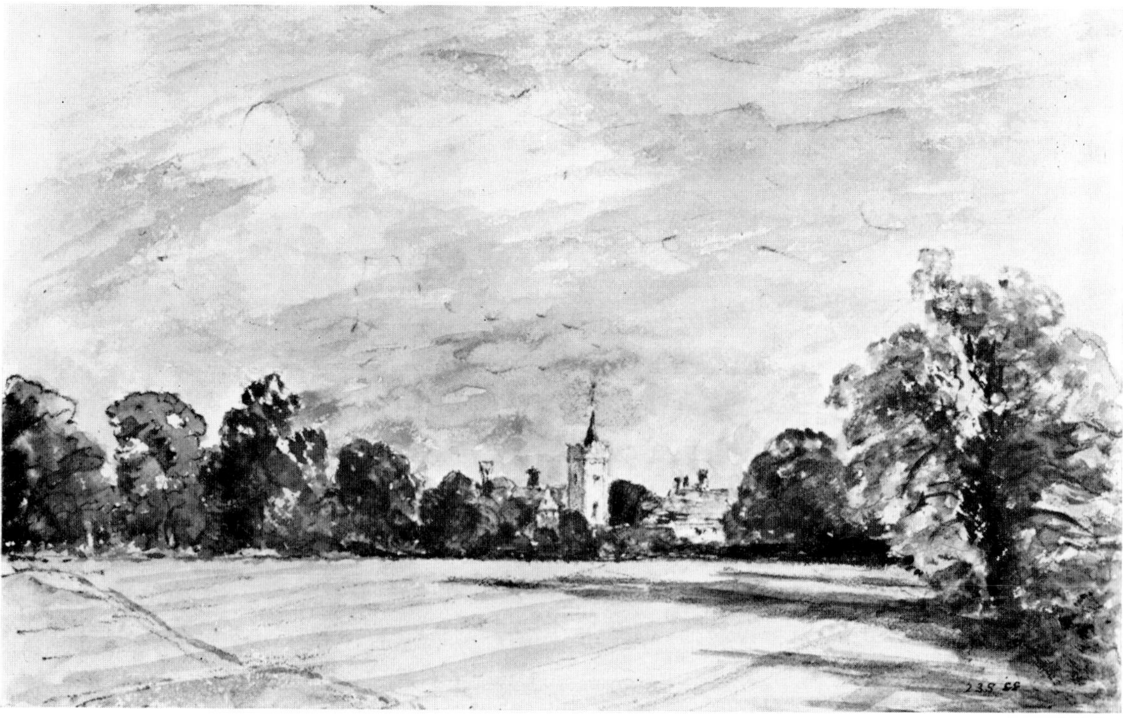

386. A village seen over a ploughed field.

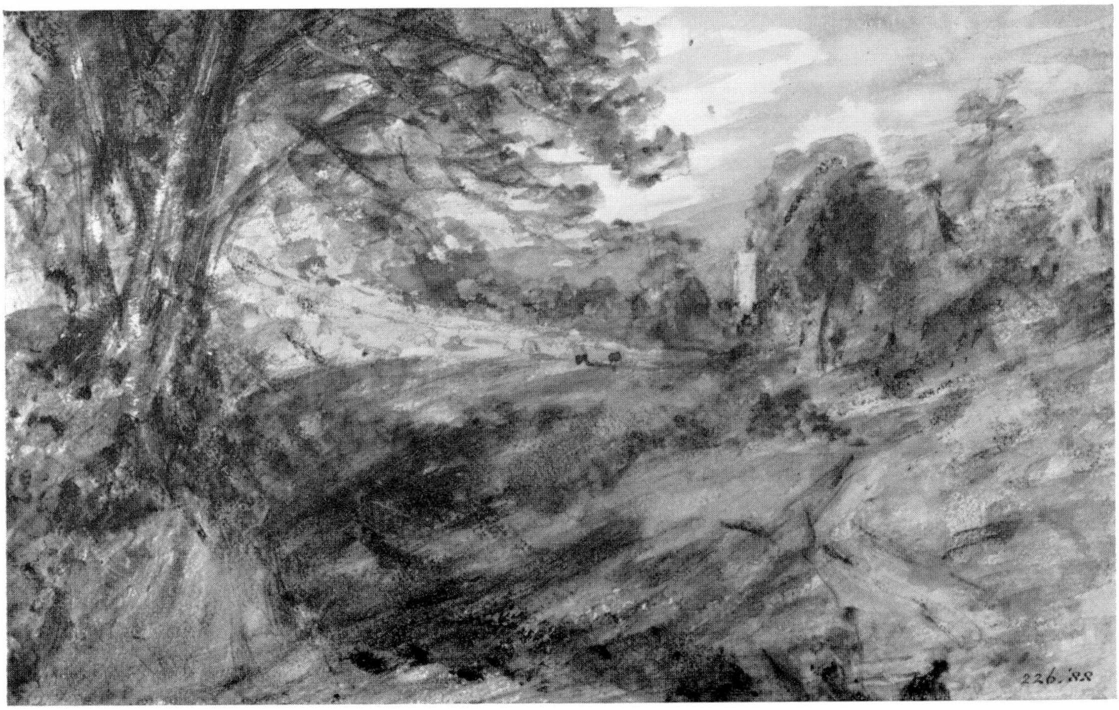

387. Cottages on high ground.

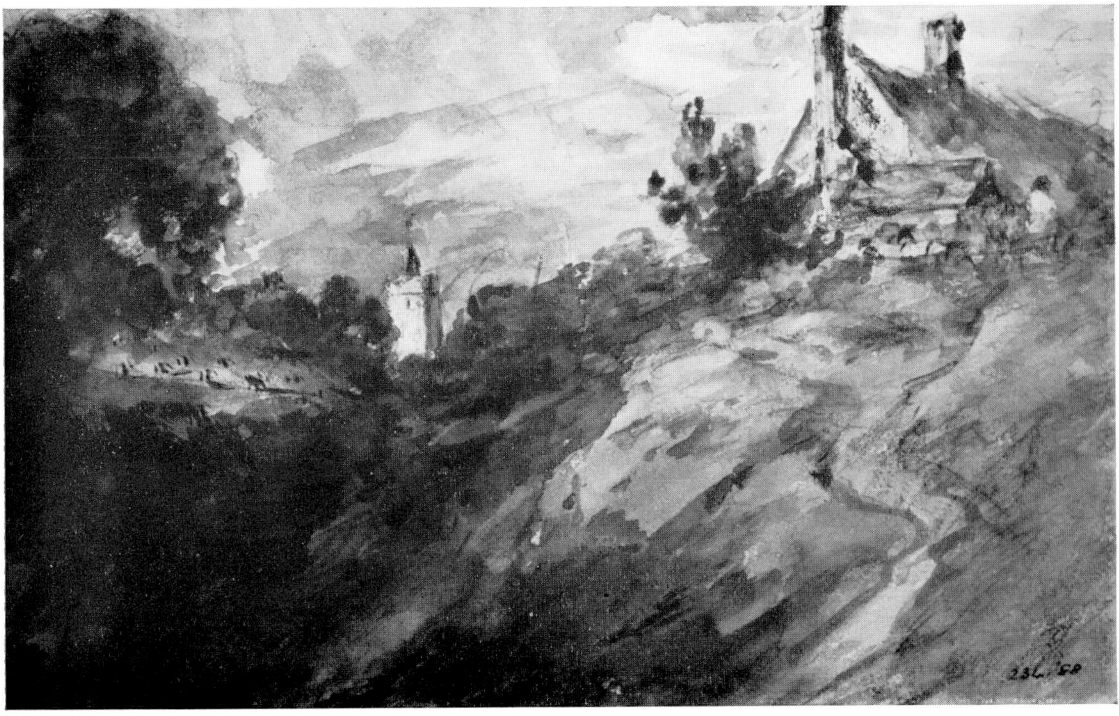

388. Cottages on a high bank.

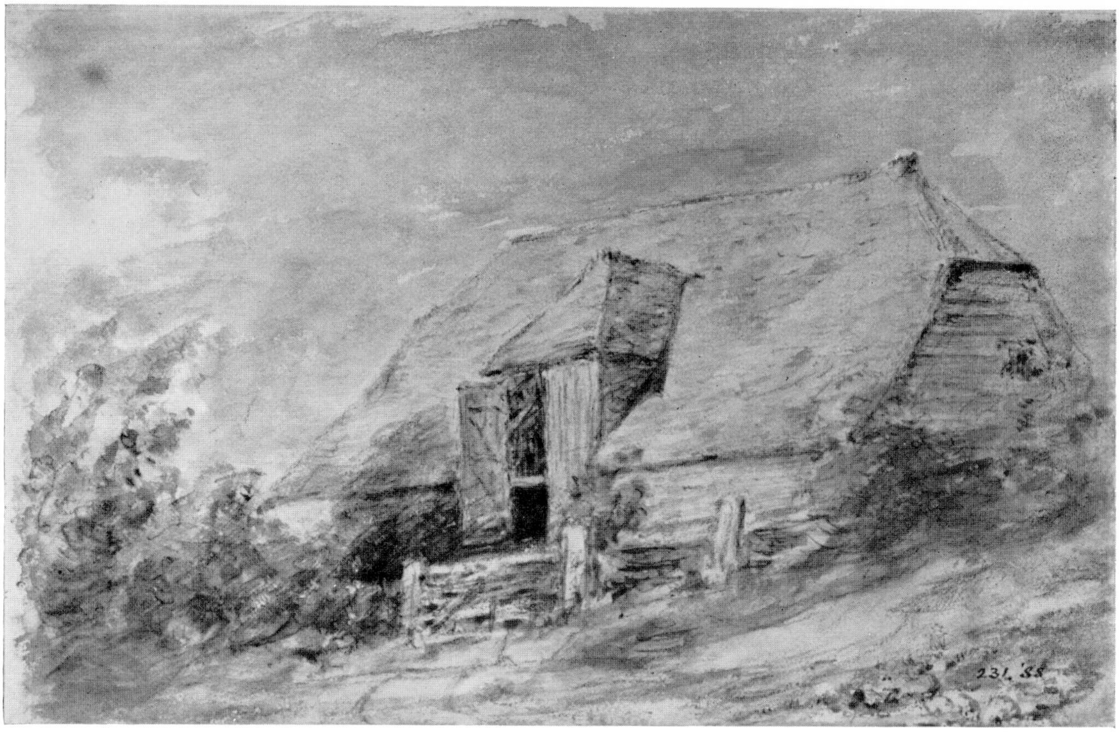

389. A barn.

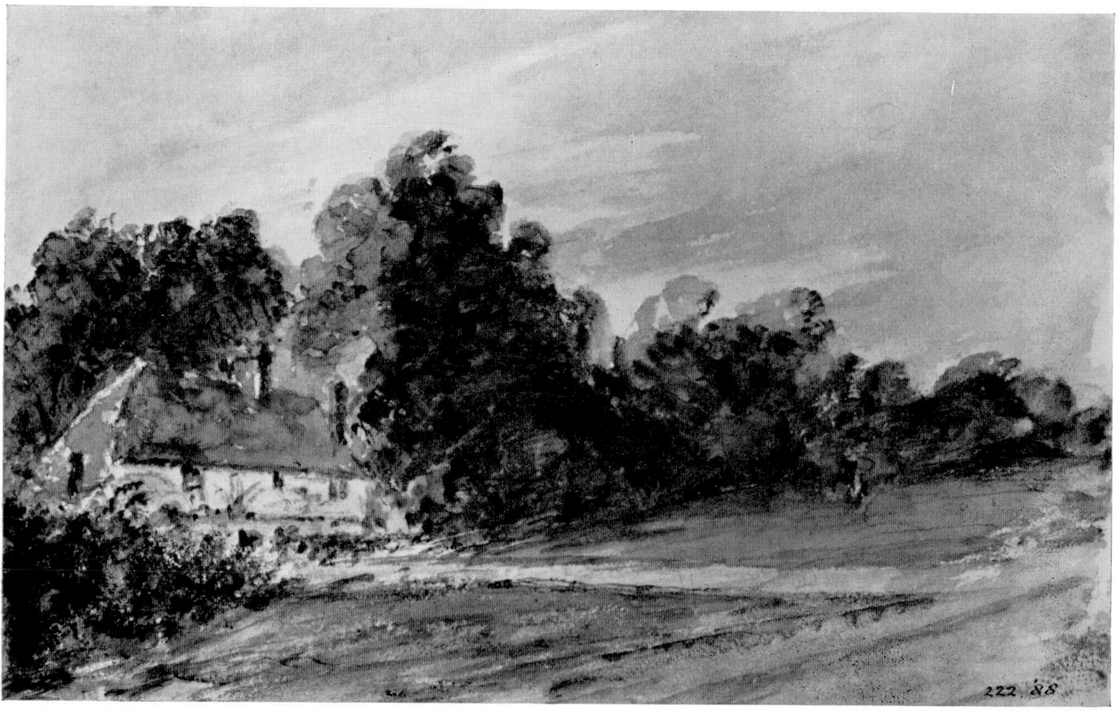

390. A cottage with a red-tiled roof.

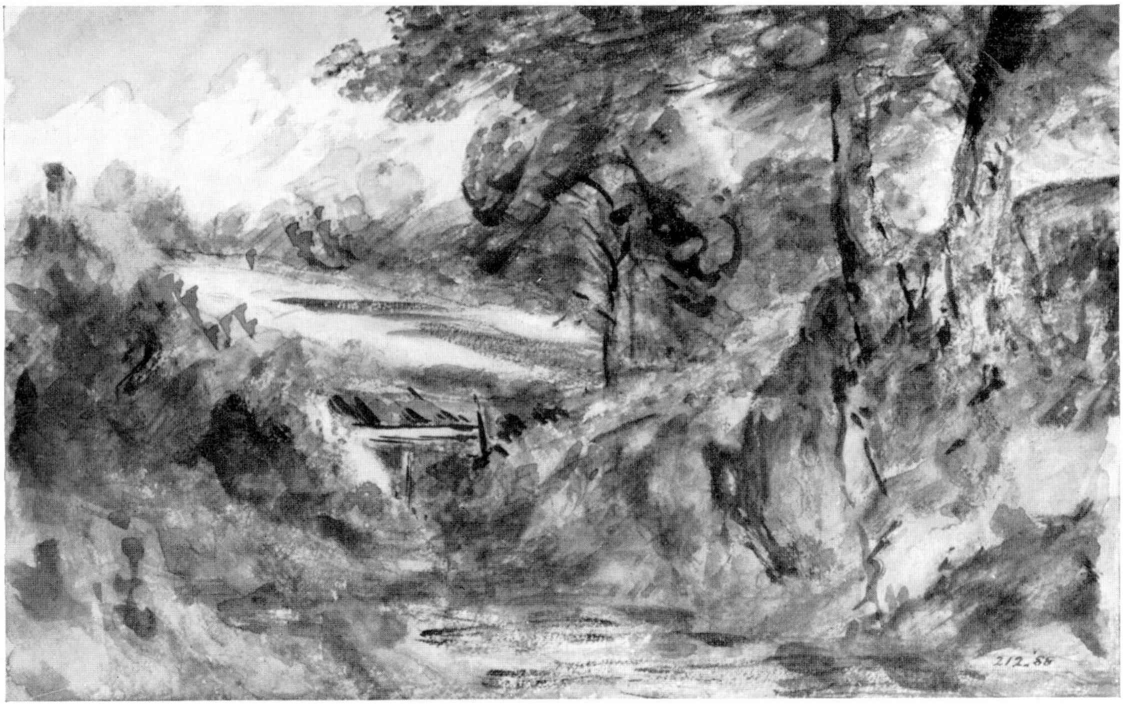

391. A brook with a high bank.

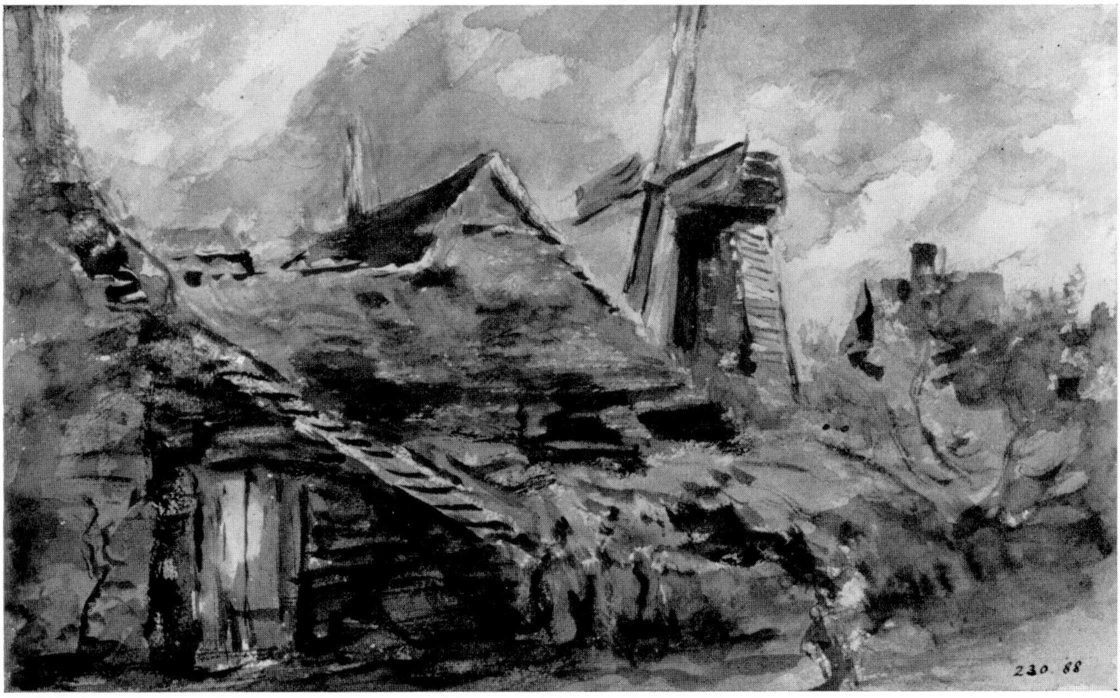

392. A village street, with windmill.

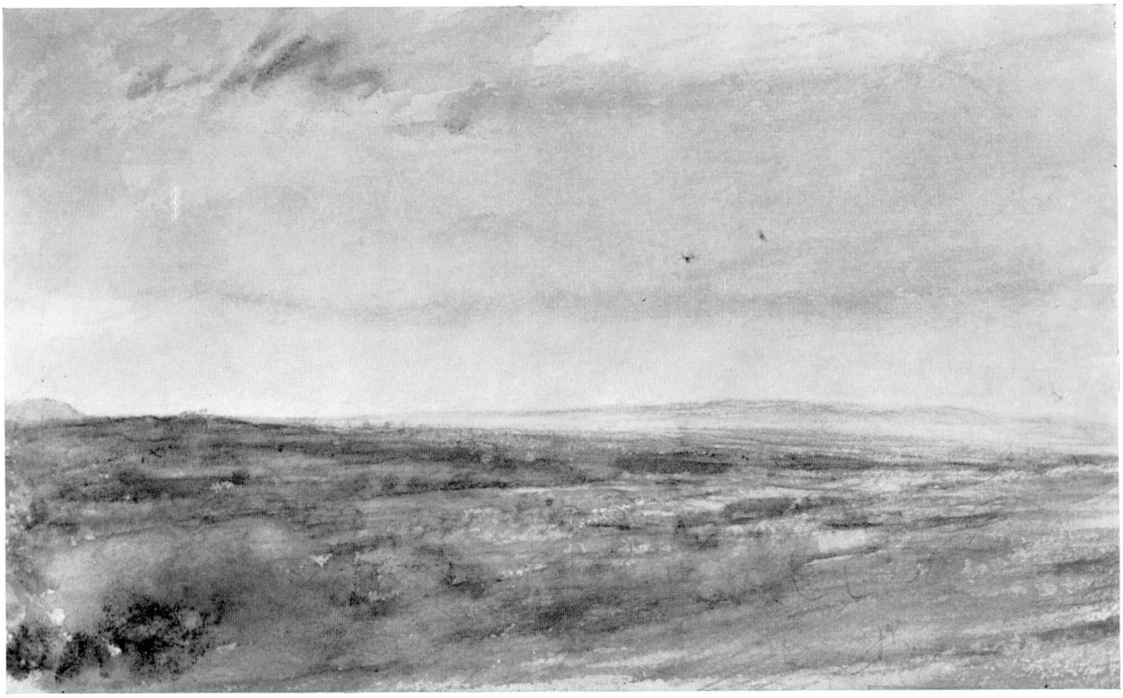

393. A view of downland country.

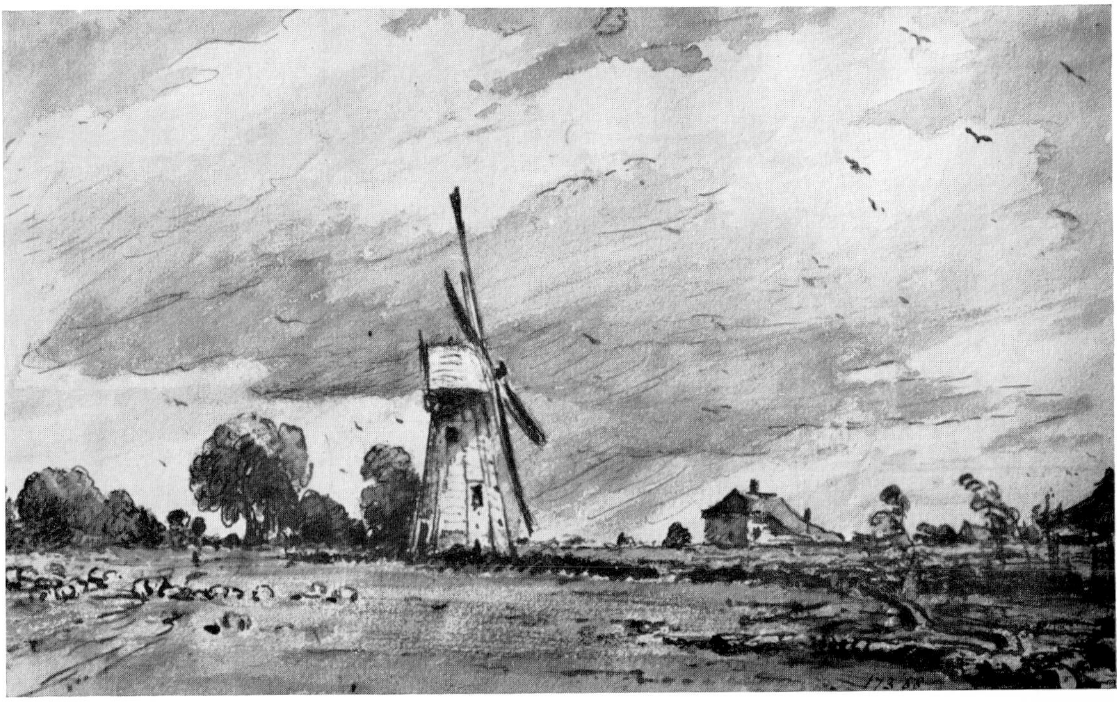

394. A windmill and a flock of sheep.

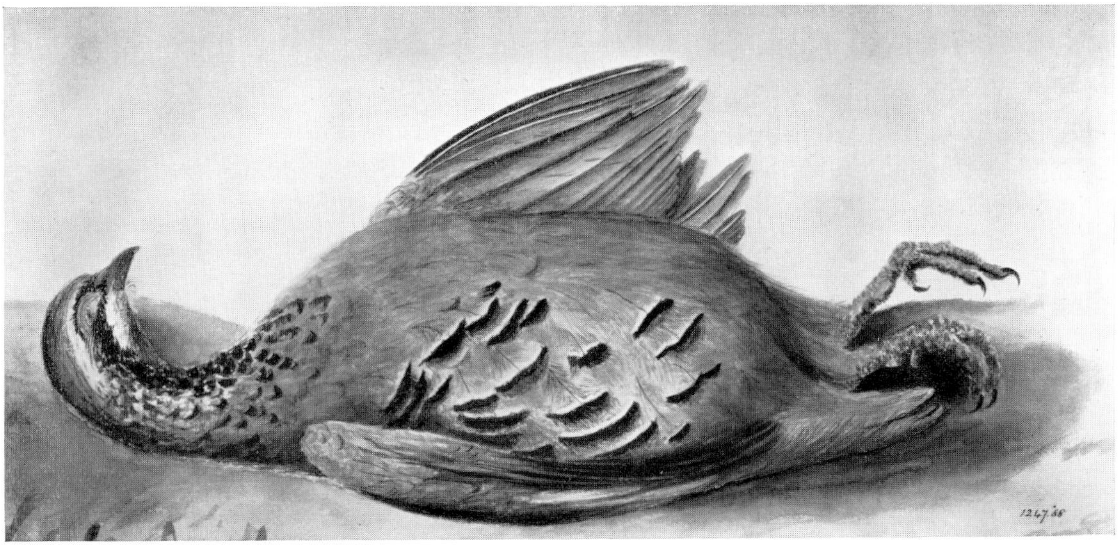

408. Study of a dead French partridge.

408a. Study of clouds.

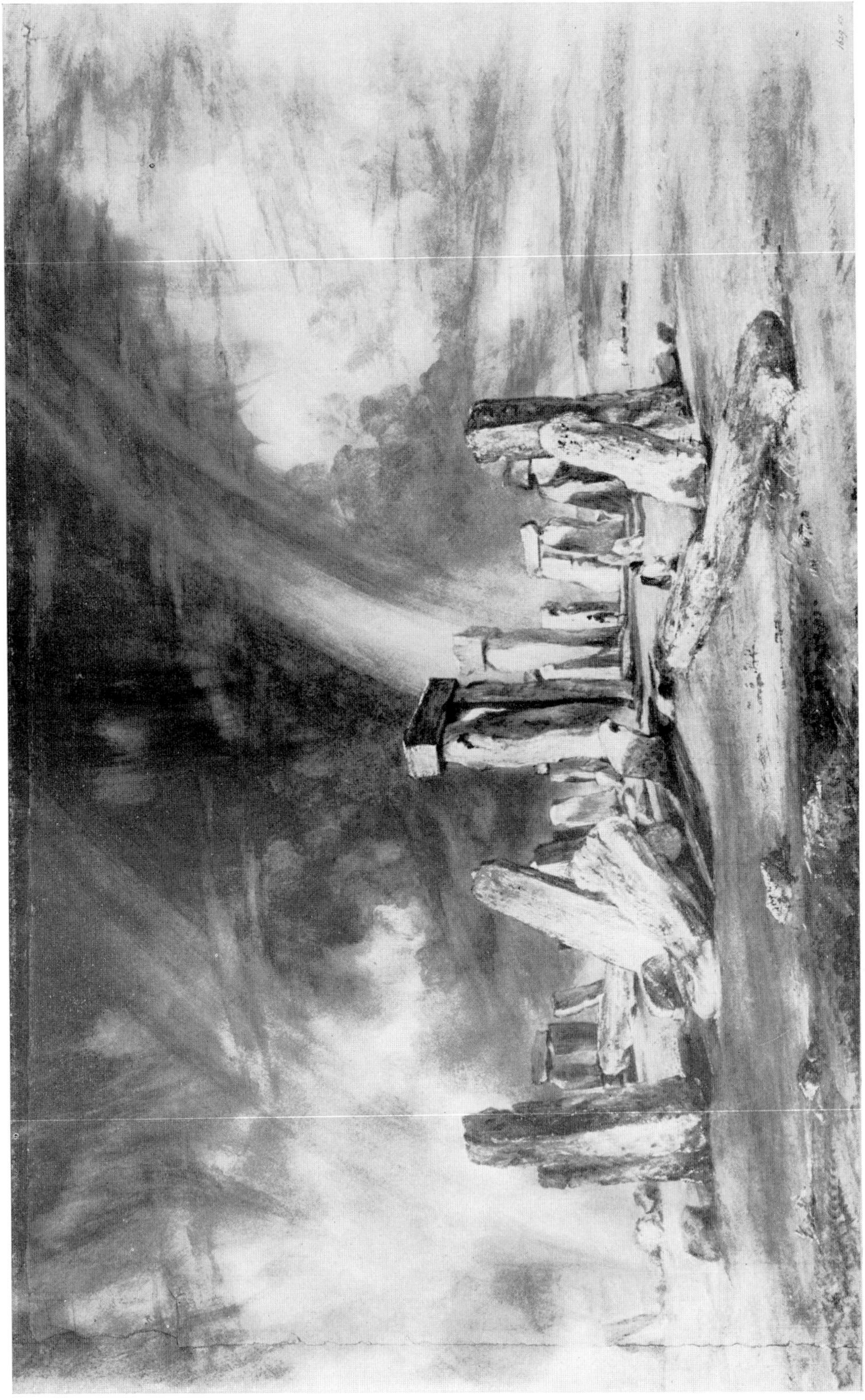

395. Stonehenge.

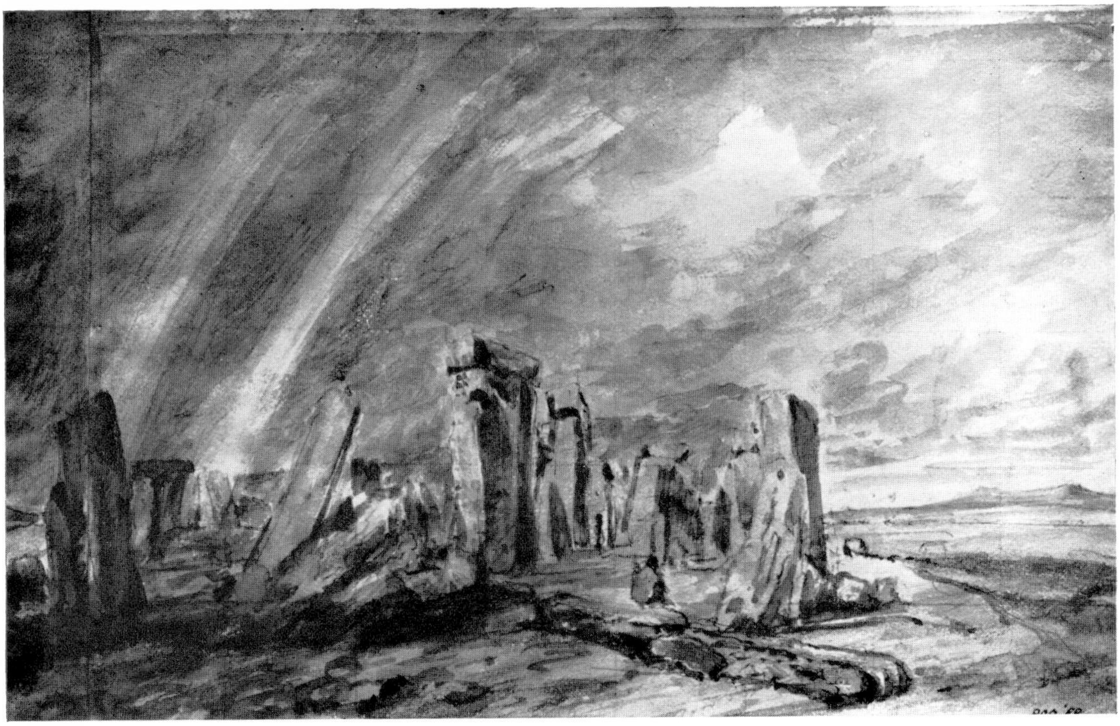

396. Stonehenge (study for No. 395).

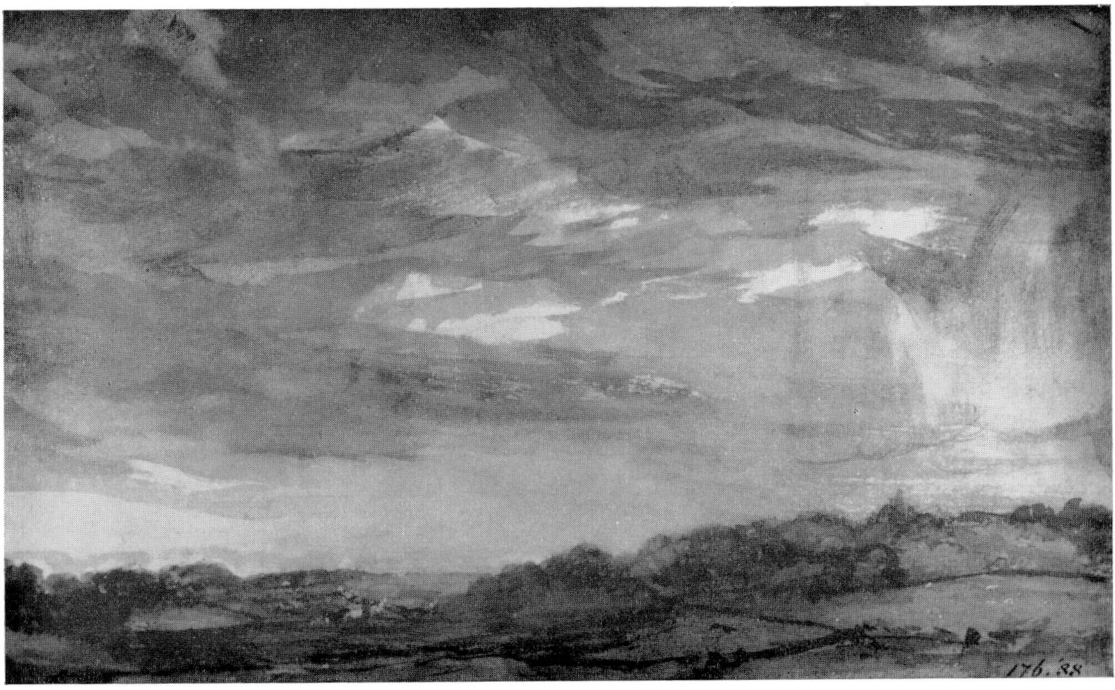

409. View over hilly country.

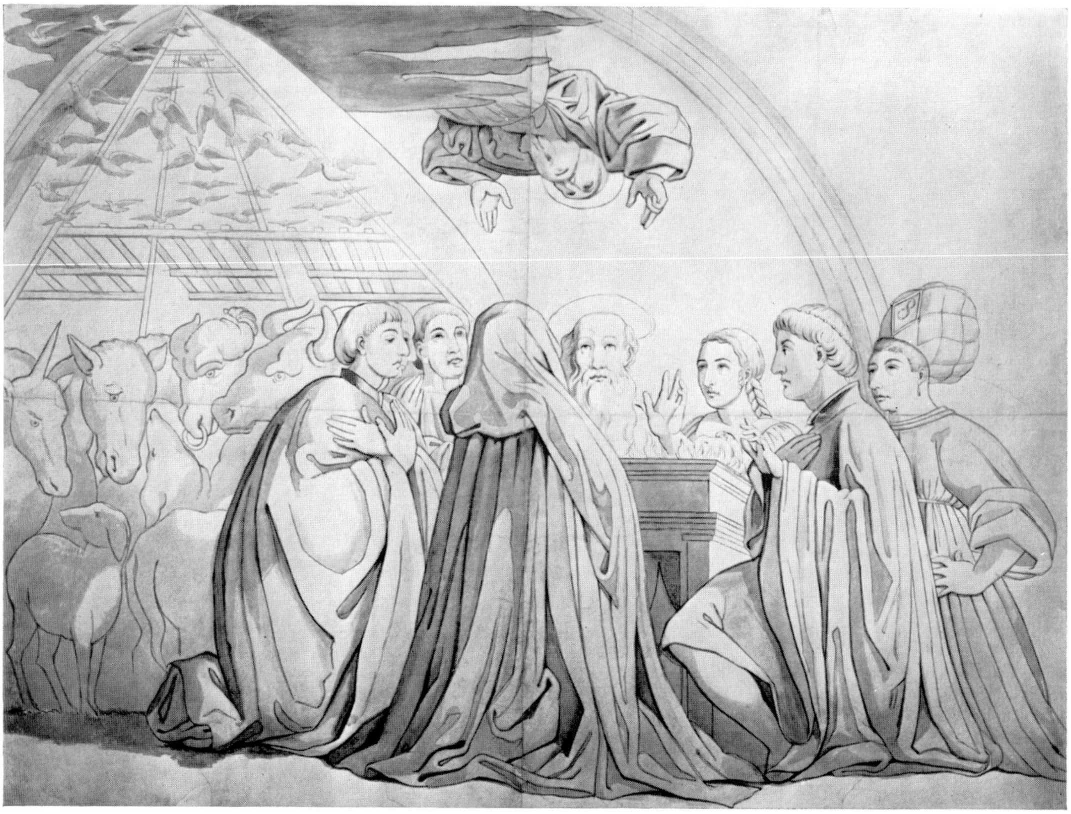

397. The sacrifice of Noah, after Uccello.

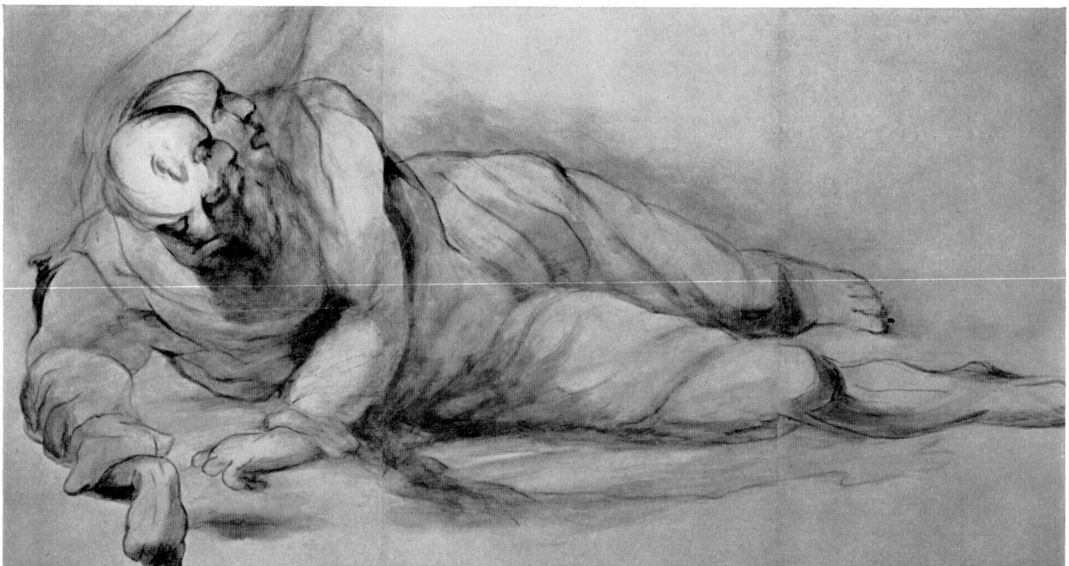

398. Study of the fallen figure of the saint in Titian's 'St. Peter Martyr'.

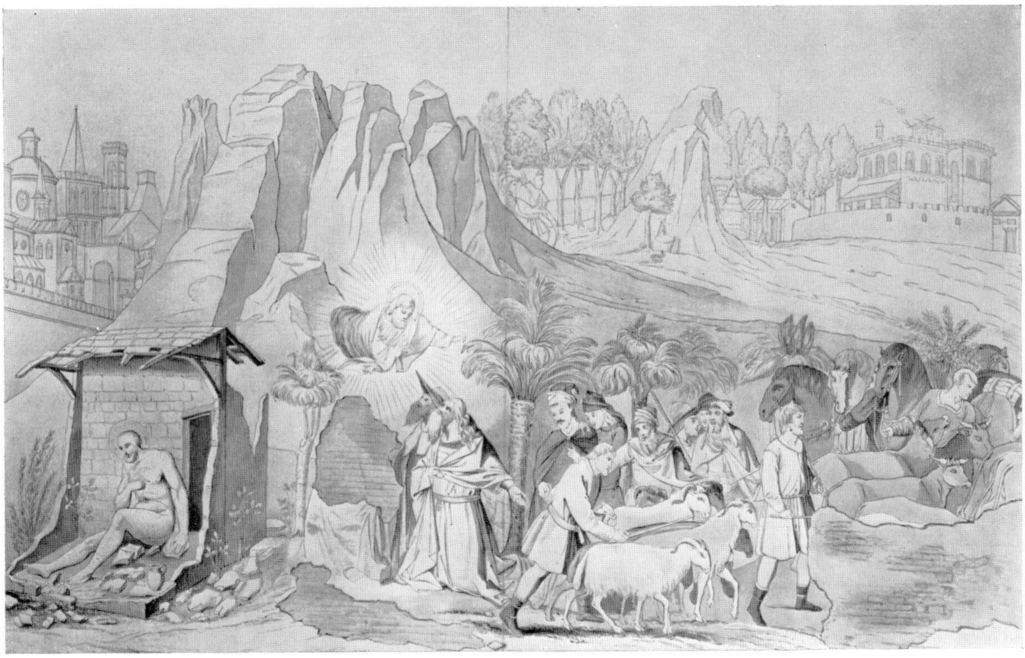

399. Job and his friends, from the fresco at Pisa.

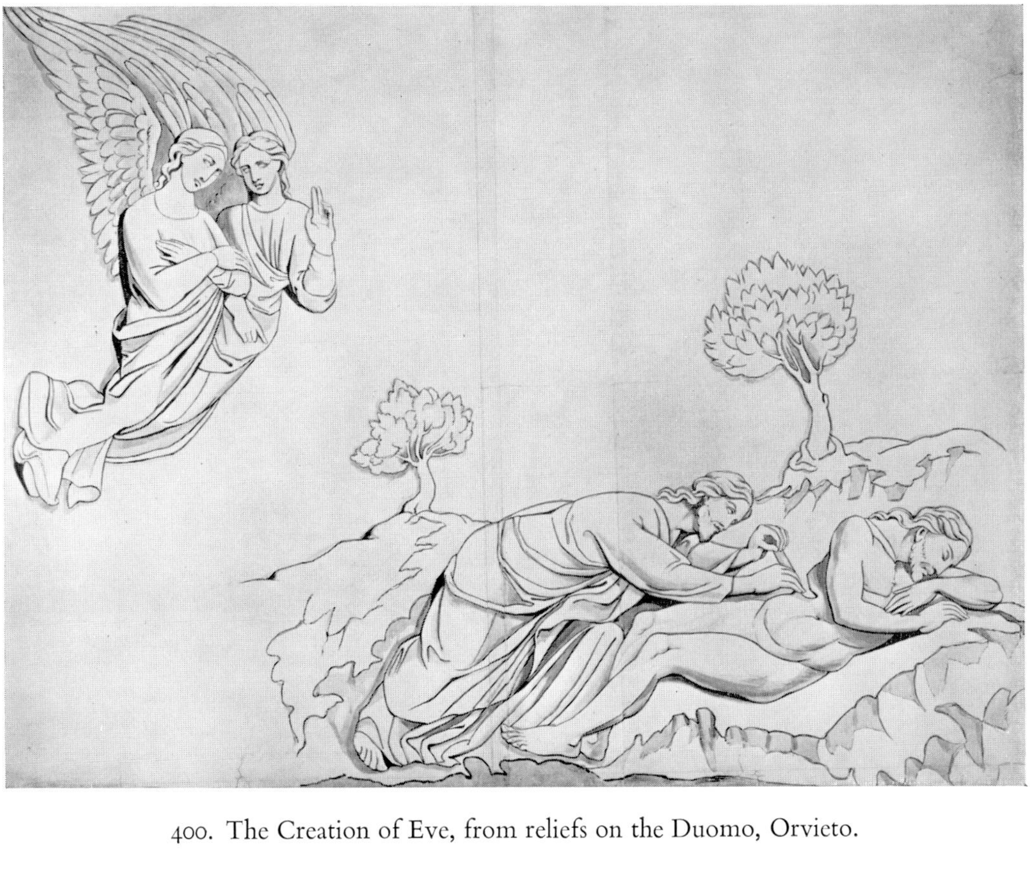

400. The Creation of Eve, from reliefs on the Duomo, Orvieto.

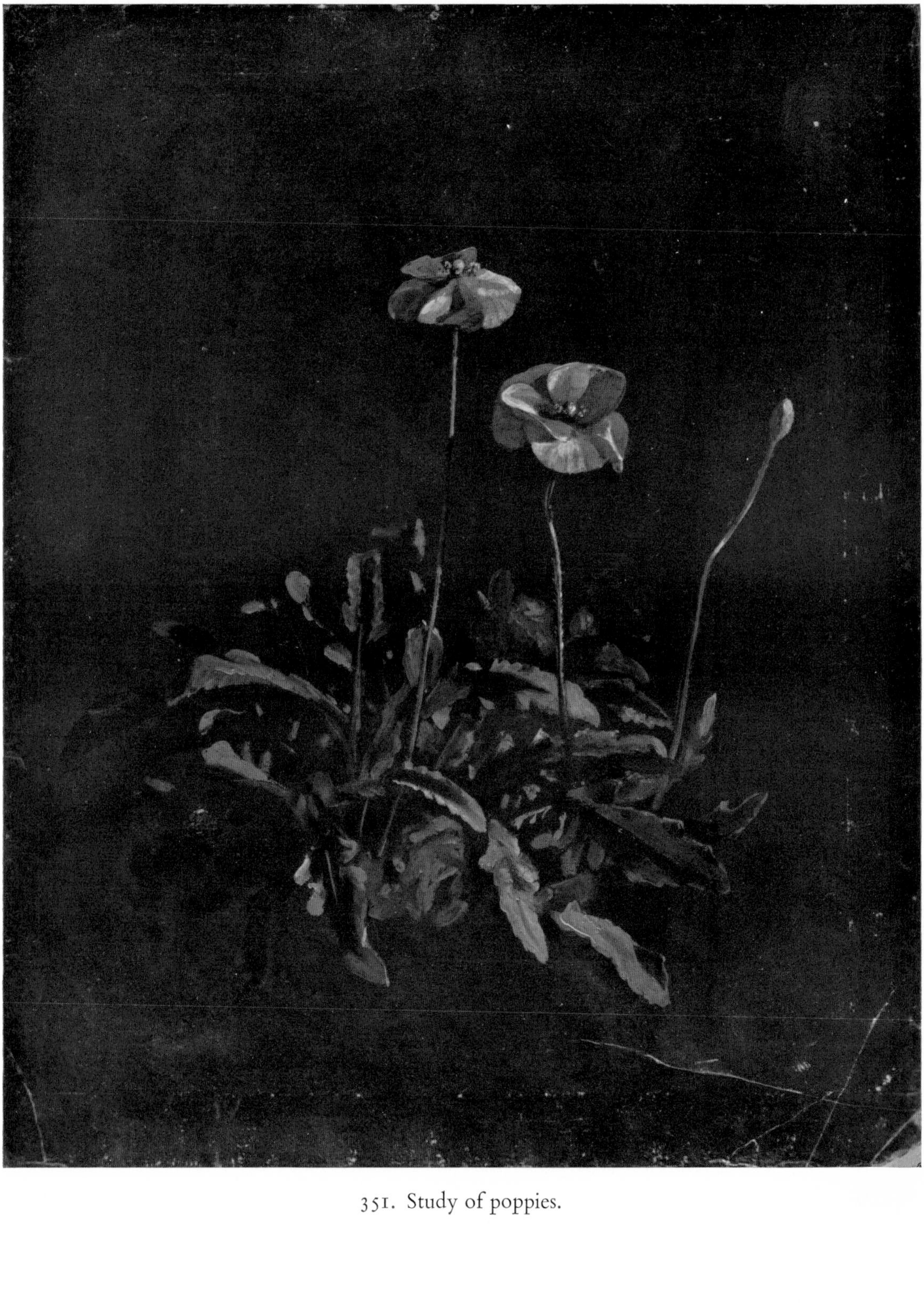

351. Study of poppies.

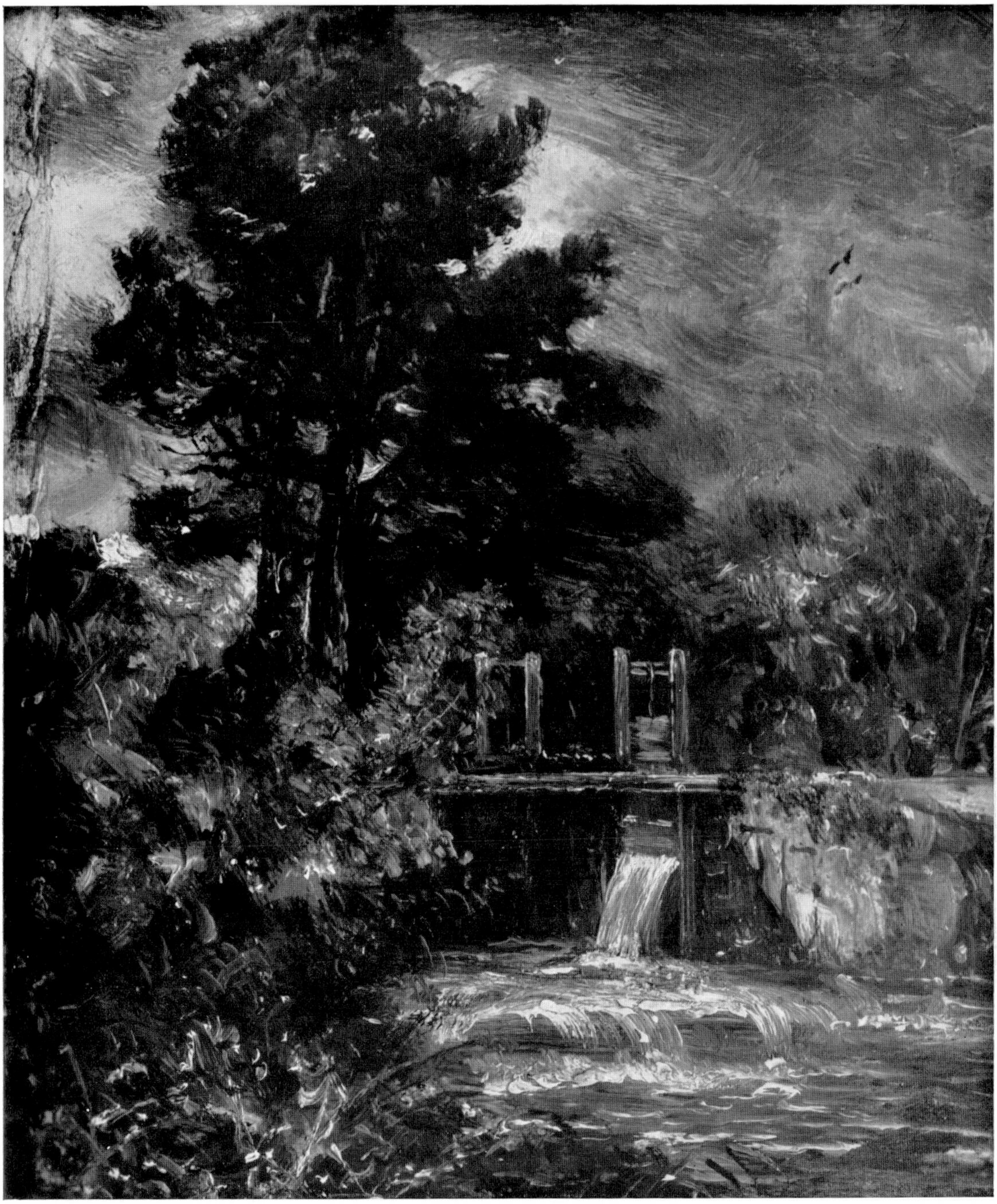

404. A sluice, perhaps on the Stour.

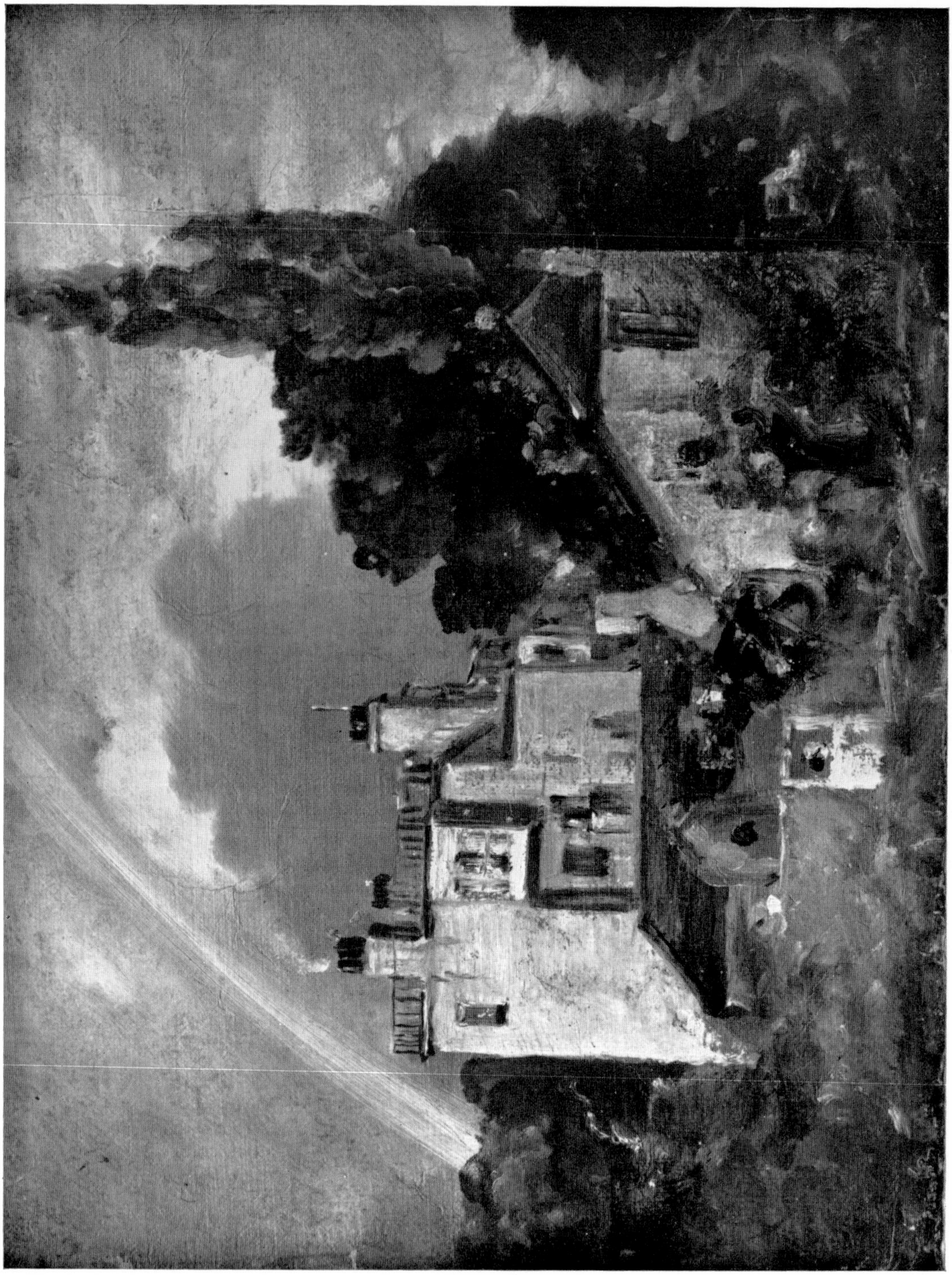

402. The Grove, or Admiral's House, Hampstead.

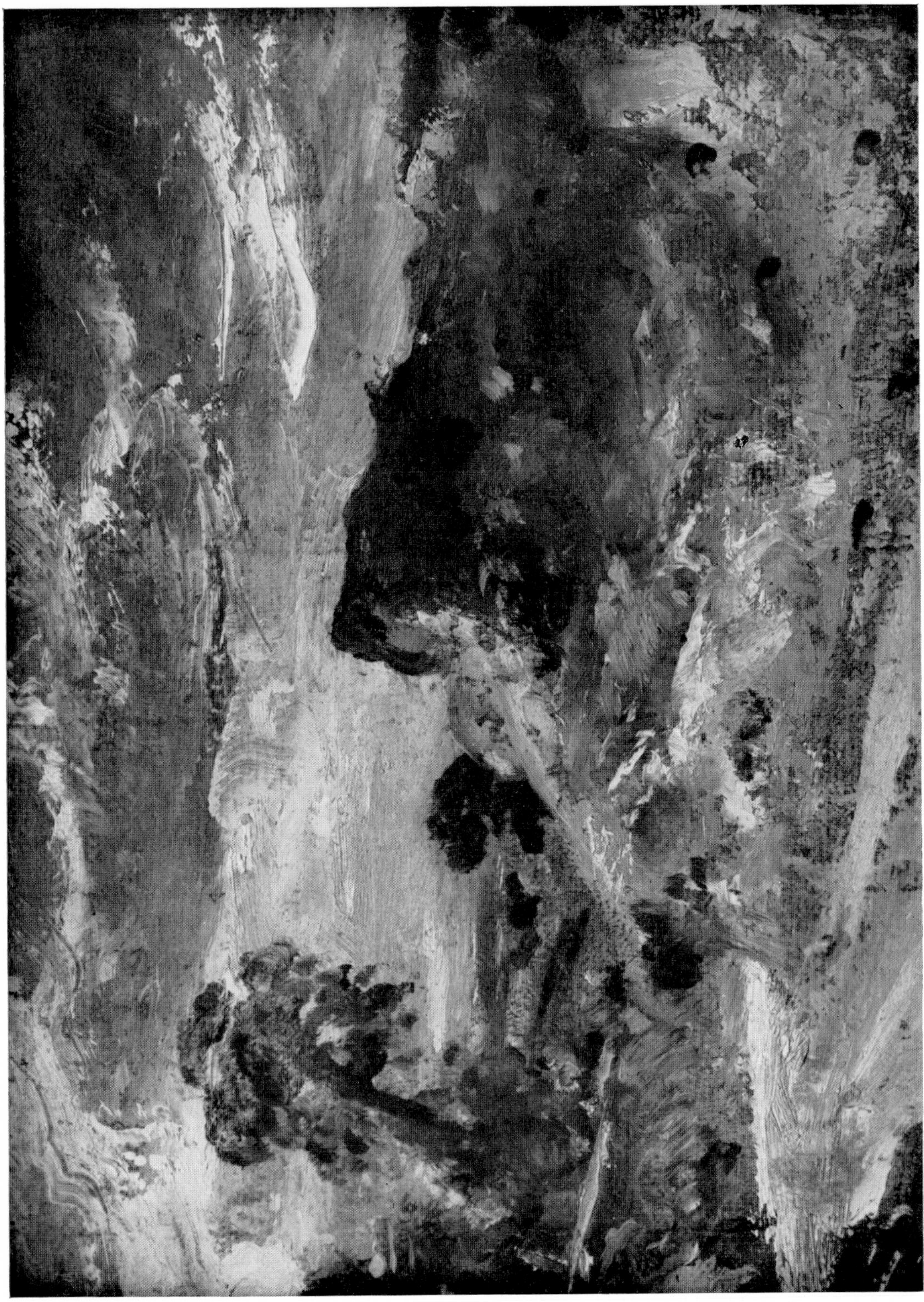

405. A country road and sandbank.

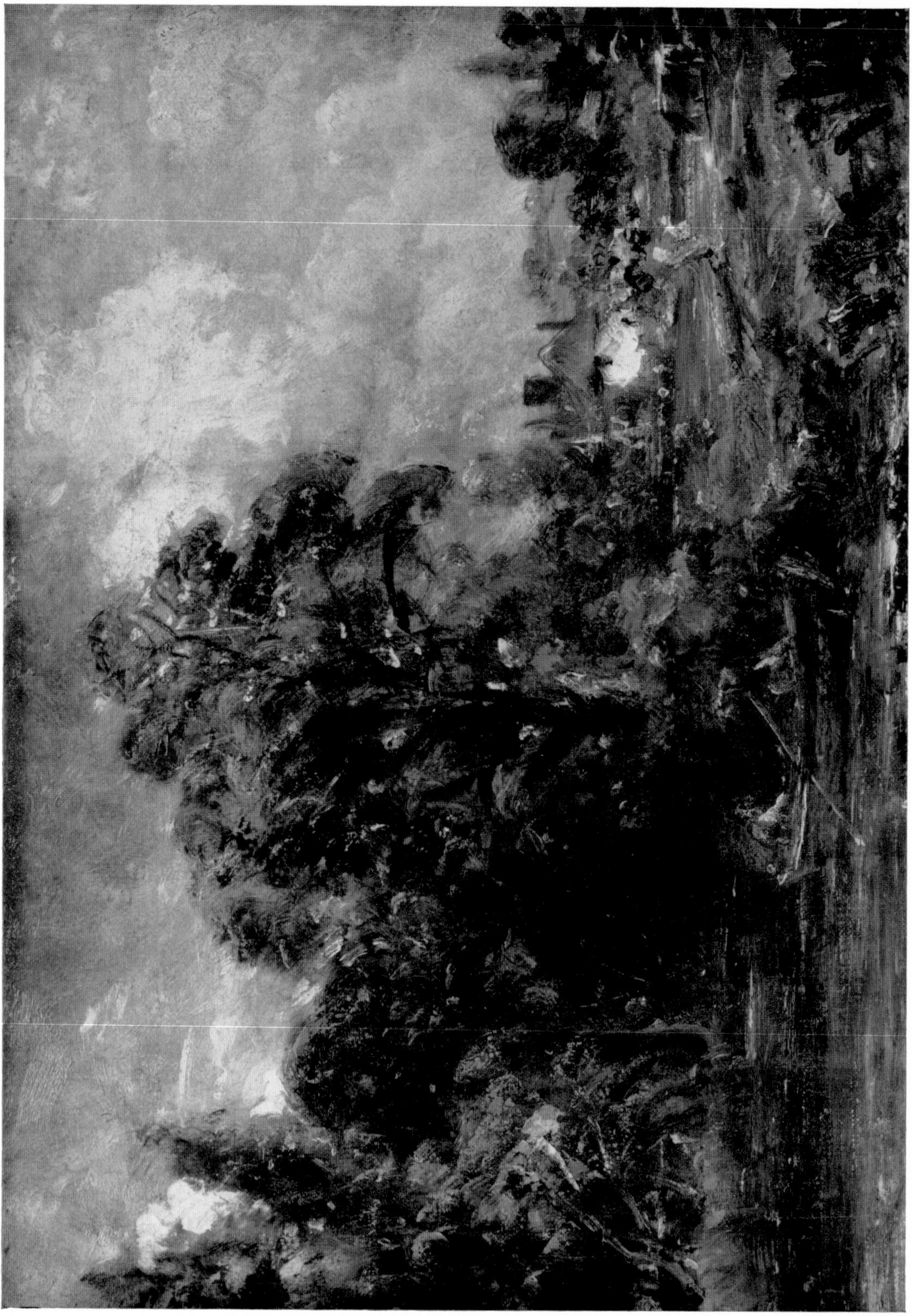

403. A river scene, with a farmhouse near the water's edge.

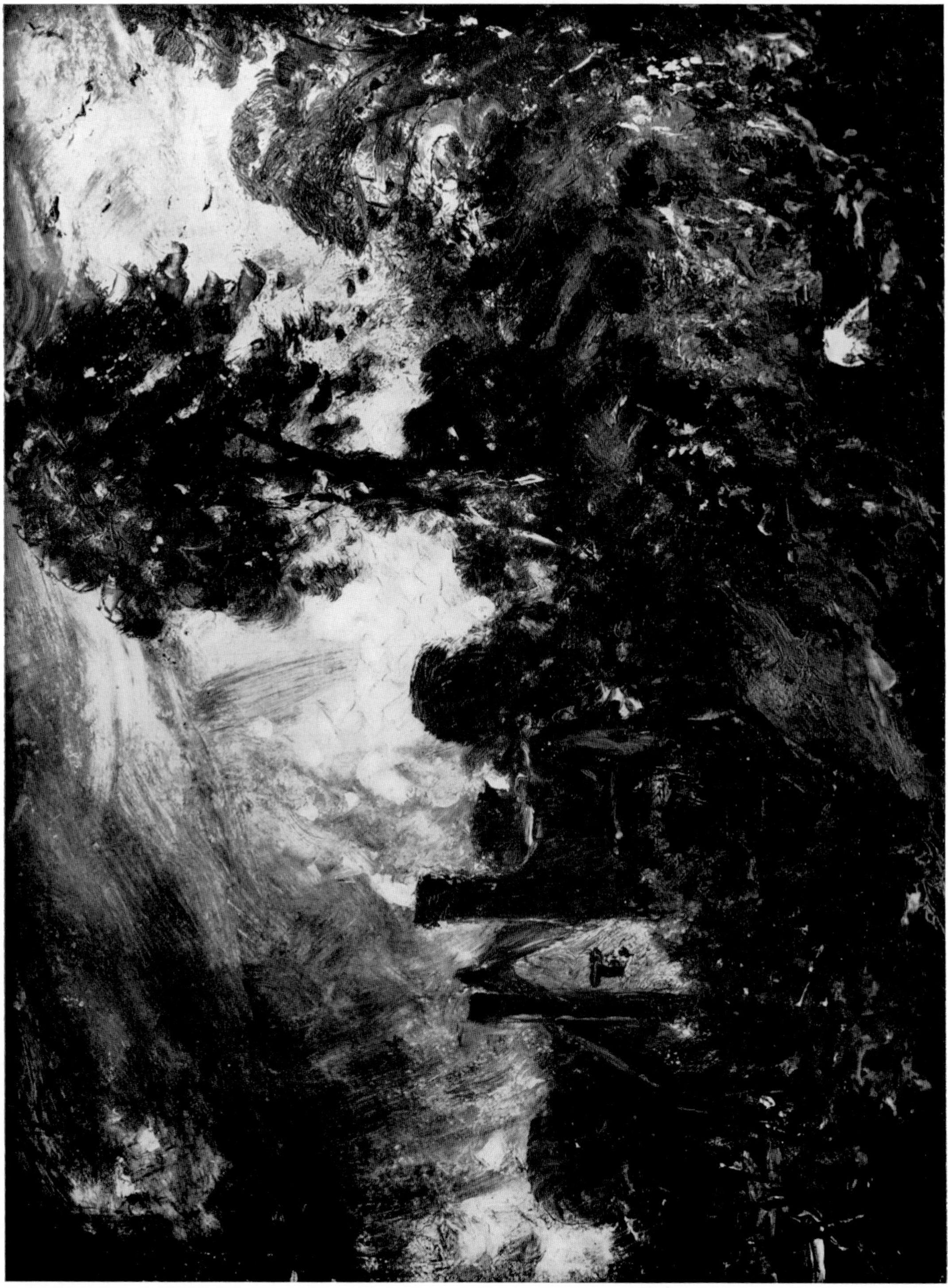

406. A cottage among trees, with a sandbank.

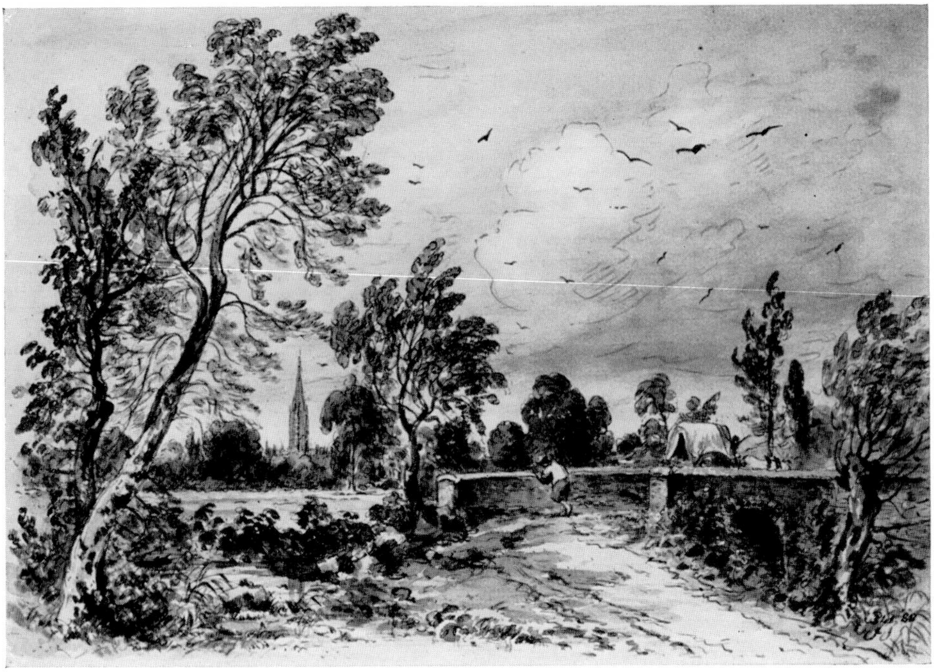

401. Milford Bridge.

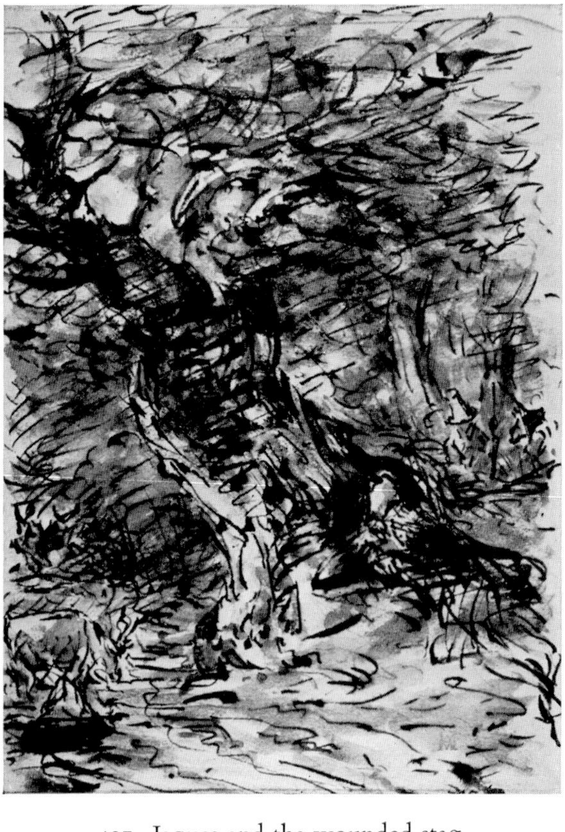

407. Jaques and the wounded stag.

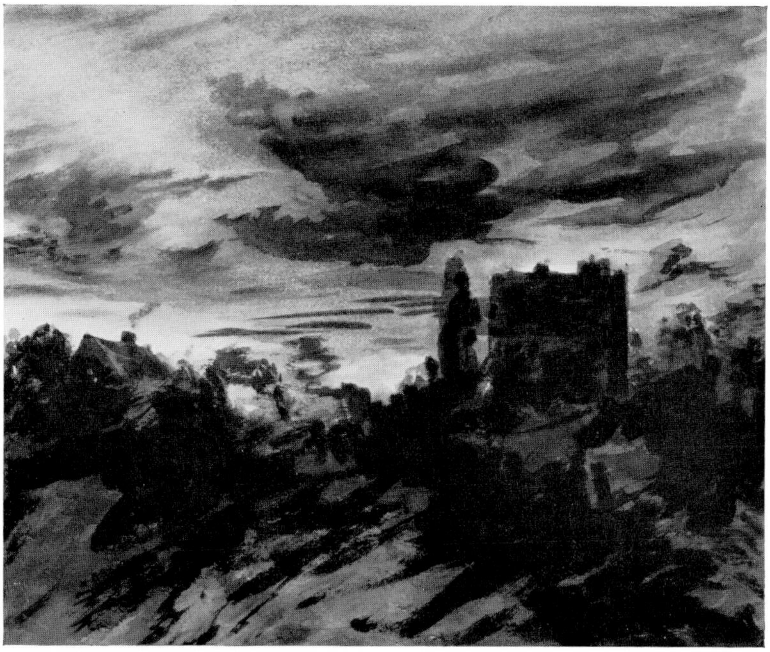

412. A house, cottage and trees by moonlight.

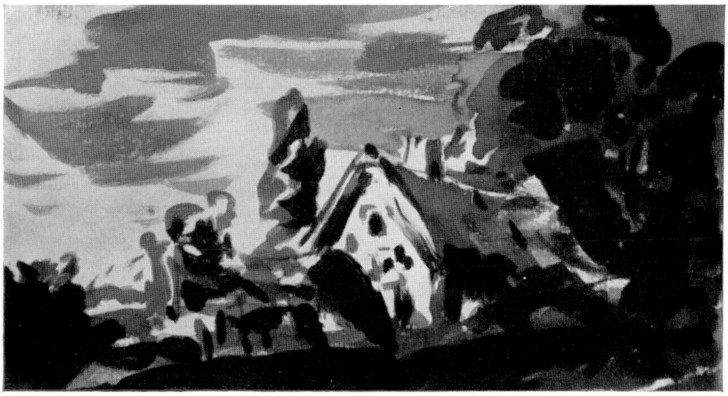

413. A country cottage amid trees.

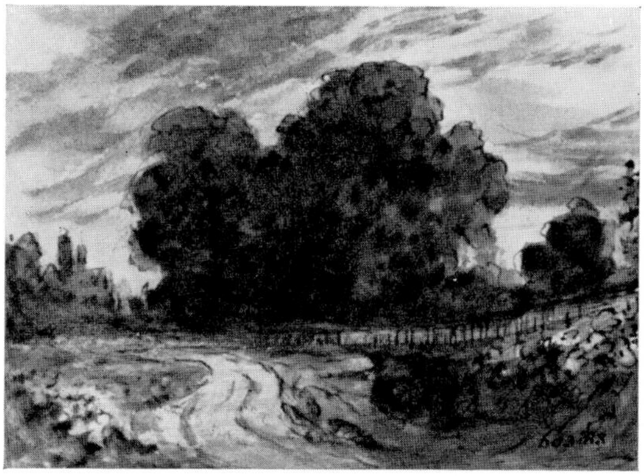

414. A country road with elm trees.

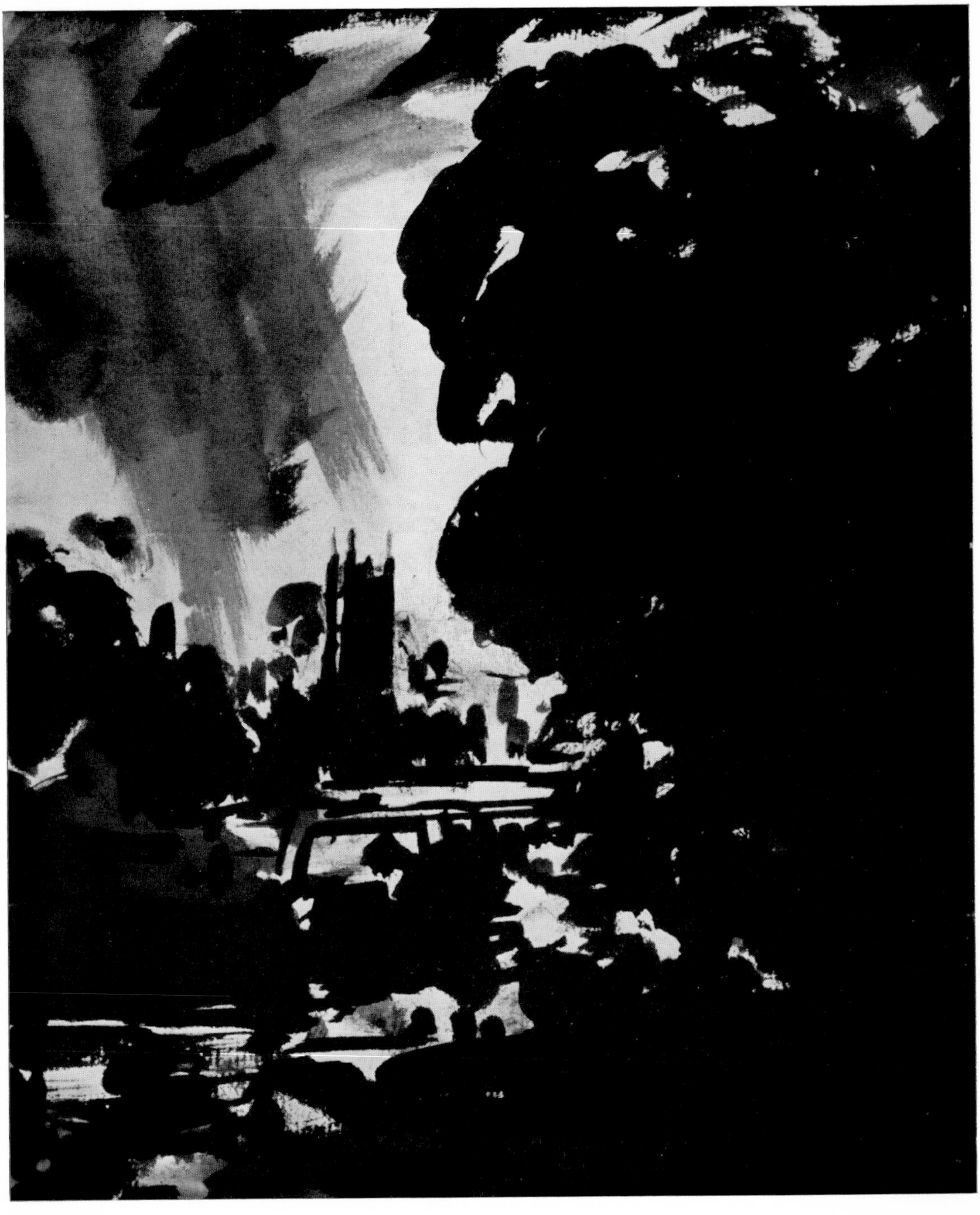

410. View on the Stour: Dedham Church in the distance.

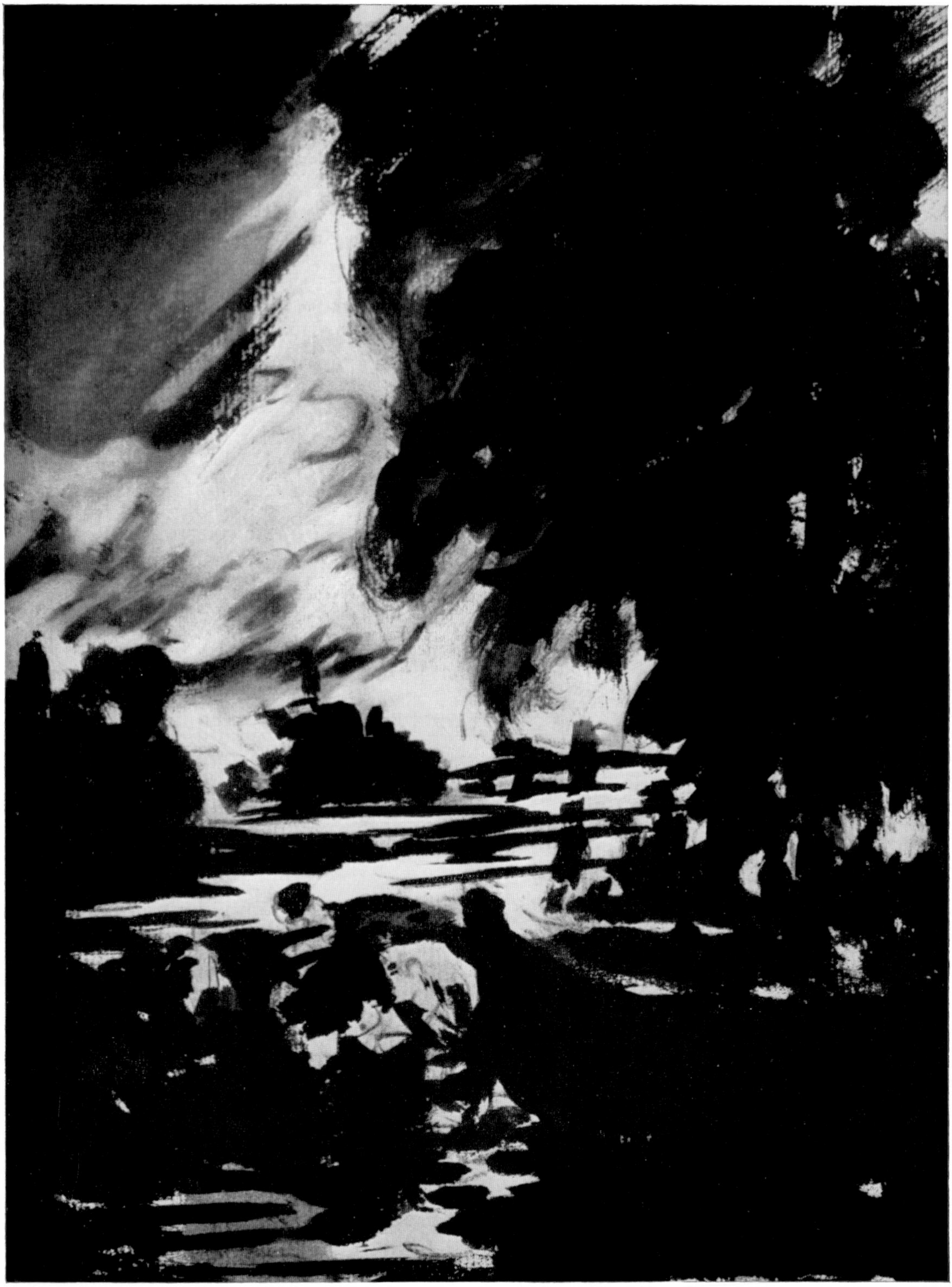

411. Trees and a stretch of water on the Stour.

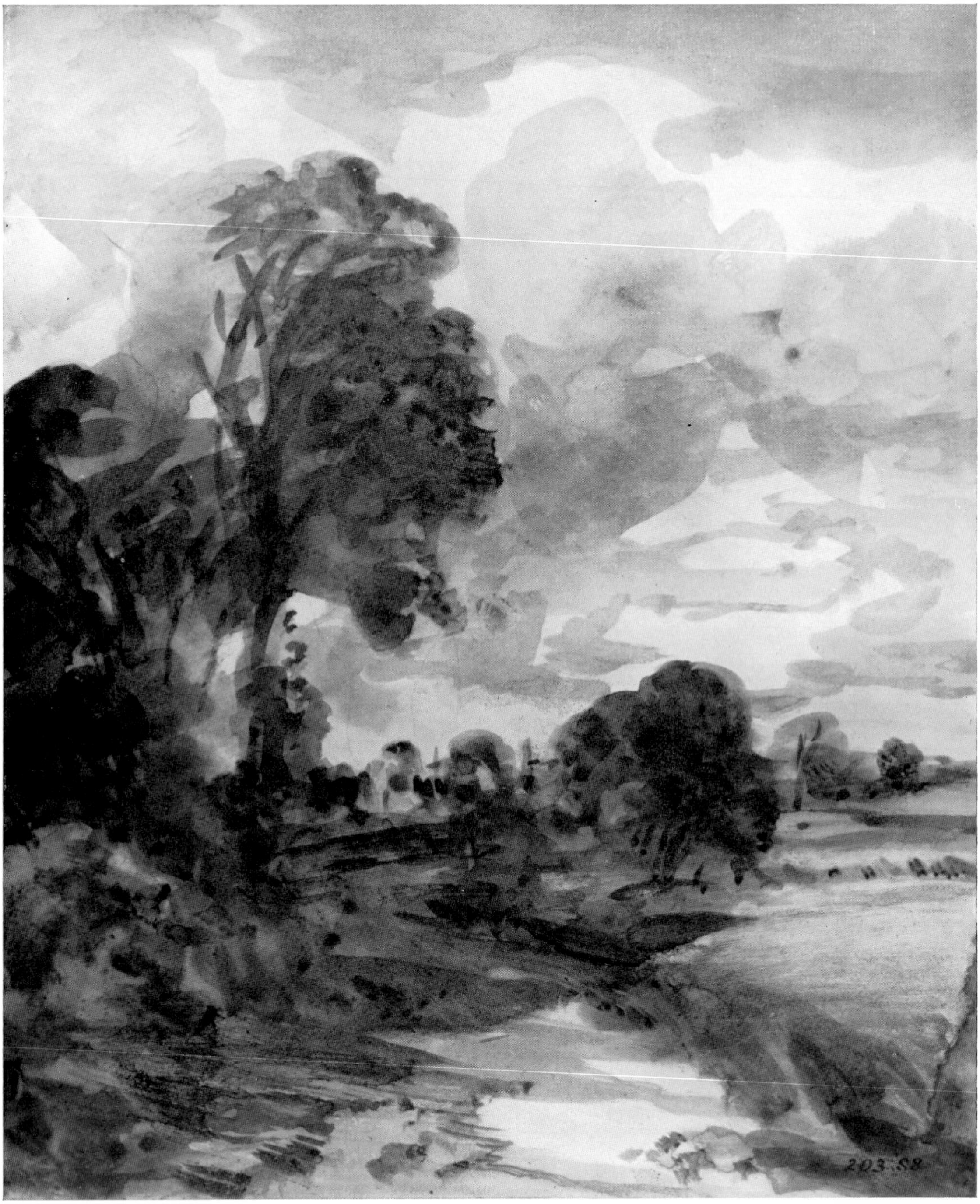

415. Landscape study.

INDEX

NOTES ON THE ARRANGEMENT OF THE INDEX

References to the catalogue numbers are in light-faced numerals thus: 209.

References to the pages of the Introduction are in bold numerals thus: **15**

References to the biographical notes at the beginning of each year are in italic figures thus: *1804*, *1807–1809*.

References to a note following a group of entries thus: 40*n*.

References to the numbered pages of intact sketch-books are in italic figures thus: 121 *pp. 29, 31*.

In general, references in the Introduction and Catalogue to John Constable and the members of his family and to C. R. Leslie (apart from some points of special interest) have been omitted, since they occur *passim*.

The topography of places represented in paintings and drawings alone is indexed, and not of the routes traversed by Constable.

The allocation of paintings between the National Gallery and Tate Gallery, London, refers to their position in 1970; further changes may take place.

Museums and Art Galleries are listed under the towns in which they are situated: *e.g.*, London, British Museum. The abbreviation VAM stands for the Victoria and Albert Museum.

D

E

I

J

K

L

M

N

Printed in England for Her Majesty's Stationery Office
by Butler & Tanner Ltd Frome and London Dd 502033 K 16

B3

THE
UNIVERSITY OF WINNIPEG
PORTAGE & BALMORAL
WINNIPEG 2, MAN. CANADA